THE
YOUNG ADULT
READER'S ADVISER™

VOLUME 2

THE BEST IN
SOCIAL SCIENCES AND HISTORY,
SCIENCE AND HEALTH

THE YOUNG ADULT READER'S ADVISER™

VOLUME 1

The Best in Literature and Language Arts, Mathematics and Computer Science

British Literature • Commonwealth Literature • American Literature • World Literature • Language • Human Communication • Mass Communication • Writing • General Mathematics • Algebra • Geometry • Calculus, Trigonometry, and Analysis • Probability and Statistics • Recreational Mathematics, Puzzles, and Games • History of Computers • Social Impact of Computers • Computer Literacy • Computer Systems and Hardware • Peripherals/Input-Output Devices • Operating Systems • Computer Languages • Software Applications • Computers in Education • Computers in Business • Computers in the Arts • Artificial Intelligence • Advanced Topics in Computer Science

VOLUME 2

The Best in Social Sciences and History, Science and Health

American Government/Civics • Anthropology • Economics • Geography • Psychology • Sociology • United States History • World History • General Science • Biology • Earth Science • Chemistry • Physics • Mental and Emotional Health • Growth and Development • Body Systems • Nutrition, Diet, and Weight Control • Exercise and Fitness • Personal Care • Drugs • Communicable Diseases • Noncommunicable Diseases • Physical Disabilities • Consumer Health • Personal Safety and First Aid • Community Health • The Environment and Health

REVIEWERS AND CONSULTANTS

Kay Alexander
Art Education Consultant
Los Altos, CA

Professor Patricia Burt
School of Library Service
Columbia University
New York, NY

Kate Clarke
Librarian
Sandia Preparatory School
Albuquerque, NM

Dr. Mounir A. Farah
Chairman, Department of Social
    Studies
Monroe Public Schools
Monroe, CT

Marilee Foglesong
YA Coordinator for Manhattan
    Libraries
Office of YA Services
New York, NY

Professor Ellen C. K. Johnson
Department of Social and
    Behavioral Sciences
College of DuPage
Glen Ellyn, IL

Dr. Margaret A. Laughlin
Department of Education
University of Wisconsin at Green
    Bay
Green Bay, WI

Rebecca Leavy
Director, Educational Resources
    Center
Western Kentucky University
Bowling Green, KY

Carolyn Markuson
Supervisor of Libraries and
    Instructional Materials
Brookline Public Schools
Brookline, MA

Philip Meyler
Computer Coordinator
Collegiate School
New York, NY

David E. O'Connor
Department of Social Studies
E. O. Smith High School
Storrs, CT

Allen Stockett
Chairman, Department of English
Dundalk High School
Baltimore, MD

Dr. David A. Thomas
Department of Mathematical
    Science
Montana State University
Bozeman, MT
*Journal of Computers in Mathematics
and Science Teaching*

Dr. Robert Wandberg
Director of Health Education
Minnesota Department of Education
St. Paul, MN

Dr. Richard H. Wilson
Coordinator for Secondary Social
    Studies
Montgomery County Public Schools
Montgomery County, MD

Professor Clarence Wolff
Department of Physics and
    Astronomy
Western Kentucky University
Bowling Green, KY

Dr. Warren Yasso
Chairman, Mathematics and Science
    Education
Teachers College
Columbia University
New York, NY

THE
YOUNG ADULT
READER'S ADVISER™

❧

VOLUME 2

THE BEST IN
SOCIAL SCIENCES AND HISTORY,
SCIENCE AND HEALTH

GENERAL EDITOR

Myra Immell
Education Consultant

CONSULTING EDITOR

Marion Sader

CONTRIBUTORS

Marcia Earnest
Kenneth E. Rogers
Maurice Sabean
Marcia Schneider

R. R. Bowker

NEW PROVIDENCE, NEW JERSEY

Published by R. R. Bowker, a division of Reed Publishing (USA) Inc.
Copyright © 1992 by Reed Publishing (USA) Inc.
All rights reserved
Printed and bound in the United States of America

Library of Congress Cataloging-in-Publication Data
The Young adult reader's adviser / general editor, Myra Immell :
  contributing editor, Marion Sader.
      p.   cm.
  Includes bibliographical references and indexes.
  Contents: v. 1. The best in literature and language arts,
mathematics and computer science — v. 2. The best in social
sciences and history, science and health.
    ISBN 0-8352-3068-6 (set). — ISBN 0-8352-3069-4 (vol. 1). — ISBN
0-8352-3070-8 (vol. 2)
    1. Bibliography—Best books—Young adult literature.   2. Young
adult literature—Bibliography.   3. Young adults—Books and reading.
I. Immell, Myra.   II. Sader, Marion.
Z1037.Y674   1992
[PN1009.A1]
011.62—dc20   92–3232
                                                                        CIP

Editorial Development, Design, and Production
by Book Builders Incorporated, New York, NY

ISBN 0-8352-3068-6

9 780835 230681

CONTENTS

For the convenience of the user, the contents of both volumes are listed beginning on this page.

VOLUME 1

VOLUME 2

Appendix

Indexes

ILLUSTRATIONS

VOLUME 1

ILLUSTRATIONS

VOLUME 2

CHRONOLOGY

Volume 1   Literature and Language Arts
Mathematics and Computer Science

Volume 2   Social Sciences and History
Science and Health

All persons profiled in each of the eight sections of *The Young Adult Reader's Adviser* appear here chronologically according to their birth year. Within each section of the text, profiled persons are arranged alphabetically by surname. For an alphabetical listing of all profiled persons, see the Profile Index.

VOLUME 1   LITERATURE

Homer
  c.700 BC
Aesop
  c.620–c.560 BC
Aeschylus
  524–456 BC
Sophocles
  c.496–c.406 BC
Euripides
  c.485–c.406 BC
Aristophanes
  c.448–c.388 BC
Plautus, Titus Maccius
  c.250–184 BC
Terence
  c.190–159 BC
Virgil
  70–19 BC
Horace
  65–8 BC
Ovid
  43 BC–AD 17
Seneca, Lucius Annaeus
  c.5 BC–AD 65
Dante Alighieri
  1265–1321
Petrarch (Francesco
  Petrarca)
  1304–1374

Boccaccio, Giovanni
  1313–1375
Chaucer, Geoffrey
  c.1340–1400
The Pearl Poet
  c.1390
Malory, Sir Thomas
  c.1405–1471
More, Sir Thomas
  1478–1535
Wyatt, Sir Thomas
  1503–1542
Cervantes Saavedra,
  Miguel de
  1547–1616
Spenser, Edmund
  1552–1599
Sidney, Sir Philip
  1554–1586
Bacon, Sir Francis
  1561–1626
Lope de Vega Carpio, Félix
  1562–1635
Marlowe, Christopher
  1564–1593
Shakespeare, William
  1564–1616
Jonson, Ben
  1572–1637

Donne, John
1573–1631

Webster, John
c.1580–c.1634

Bradford, William
1590–1657

Herrick, Robert
1591–1674

Herbert, George
1593–1633

Calderón de la Barca, Pedro
1600–1681

Milton, John
1608–1674

Bradstreet, Anne
c.1612–1672

Marvell, Andrew
1621–1678

Molière
1622–1673

Vaughan, Henry
1622–1695

Bunyan, John
1628–1688

Dryden, John
1631–1700

Pepys, Samuel
1633–1703

Racine, Jean
1639–1699

Taylor, Edward
c.1642–1729

Defoe, Daniel
1661–1731

Swift, Jonathan
1667–1745

Congreve, William
1670–1729

Pope, Alexander
1688–1744

Richardson, Samuel
1689–1781

Voltaire
1694–1778

Edwards, Jonathan
1703–1758

Fielding, Henry
1707–1754

Johnson, Samuel
1709–1784

Gray, Thomas
1716–1761

Goldsmith, Oliver
1728–1774

Cowper, William
1731–1800

Crèvecoeur, Michel-Guillaume Jean
de
1735–1813

Boswell, James
1740–1795

Goethe, Johann Wolfgang von
1749–1832

Sheridan, Richard Brinsley
1751–1816

Wheatley, Phillis
c.1753–1784

Blake, William
1757–1827

Burns, Robert
1759–1796

Schiller, (Johann Christoph)
Friedrich von
1759–1805

Radcliffe, Anne
1764–1823

Wordsworth, William
1770–1850

Brown, Charles Brockden
1771–1810

Scott, Sir Walter
1771–1832

Coleridge, Samuel Taylor
1772–1834

Austen, Jane
1775–1817

Lamb, Charles
1775–1834

Irving, Washington
1783–1859

Stendhal
1783–1842

Byron, Lord, George Gordon
1788–1824

Marryat, Captain Frederick
1792–1848

Shelley, Percy Bysshe
1792–1822

Bryant, William Cullen
1794–1878

Keats, John
1795–1821

Shelley, Mary Wollstonecraft
1797–1851

Balzac, Honoré de
1799–1850

Pushkin, Aleksandr
1799–1837

Dumas, Alexandre (père)
1802–1870
Hugo, Victor Marie
1802–1885
Emerson, Ralph Waldo
1803–1882
Hawthorne, Nathaniel
1804–1864
Andersen, Hans Christian
1805–1875
Browning, Elizabeth Barrett
1806–1861
Longfellow, Henry Wadsworth
1807–1882
Whittier, John Greenleaf
1807–1892
Gogol, Nikolai
1809–1852
Holmes, Oliver Wendell
1809–1894
Poe, Edgar Allan
1809–1849
Tennyson, Lord, Alfred
1809–1892
Thackeray, William Makepeace
1811–1863
Browning, Robert
1812–1889
Dickens, Charles
1812–1870
Brontë, Charlotte
1816–1855
Brown, William Wells
c.1816–1884
Thoreau, Henry David
1817–1862
Brontë, Emily
1818–1848
Eliot, George
1819–1880
Lowell, James Russell
1819–1891
Melville, Herman
1819–1891
Whitman, Walt
1819–1892
Baudelaire, Charles
1821–1867
Dostoevsky, Fyodor
1821–1881
Flaubert, Gustave
1821–1880
Arnold, Matthew
1822–1888

Collins, Wilkie
1824–1889
Ibsen, Henrik
1828–1906
Rossetti, Dante Gabriel
1828–1882
Tolstoy, Leo
1828–1910
Verne, Jules
1828–1905
Dickinson, Emily
1830–1886
Rossetti, Christina
1830–1894
Alcott, Louisa May
1832–1888
Carroll, Lewis
1832–1898
Alger, Horatio, Jr.
1834–1899
Carducci, Giosue
1835–1907
Twain, Mark
1835–1910
Gilbert, Sir William Schwenk
1836–1911
Harte, Bret (Francis Brett)
1836–1902
Swinburne, Algernon Charles
1837–1909
Hardy, Thomas
1840–1928
Zola, Emile
1840–1902
Bierce, Ambrose Gwinnett
1842–1914?
Lanier, Sidney
1842–1881
James, Henry
1843–1916
Cable, George Washington
1844–1924
France, Anatole
1844–1924
Hopkins, Gerard Manley
1844–1889
Sienkiewicz, Henryk
1846–1916
Stoker, Bram (Abraham)
1847–1912
Jewett, Sarah Orne
1849–1909
Strindberg, August
1849–1912

Maupassant, Guy de
1850–1893
Stevenson, Robert Louis
1850–1894
Chopin, Kate
1851–1904
Wilde, Oscar
1854–1900
Baum, L. (Lyman) Frank
1856–1919
Haggard, Sir Henry Rider
1856–1925
Shaw, George Bernard
1856–1950
Conrad, Joseph
1857–1924
Chesnutt, Charles W. (Waddell)
1858–1932
Aleichem, Sholem
1859–1916
Doyle, Sir Arthur Conan
1859–1930
Hamsun, Knut
1859–1952
Housman, A. E. (Alfred Edward)
1859–1936
Barrie, J. M. (Sir James Matthew)
1860–1937
Chekhov, Anton
1860–1904
Henry, O. (William Sydney Porter)
1862–1910
Wharton, Edith
1862–1937
Jacobs, W. W. (William Wymark)
1863–1943
Unamuno y Jugo, Miguel de
1864–1936
Kipling, Rudyard
1865–1936
Yeats, William Butler
1865–1939
Wells, H. G. (Herbert George)
1866–1946
Darío, Rubén
1867–1916
Galsworthy, John
1867–1933
Pirandello, Luigi
1867–1936
Gide, André
1869–1951
Leacock, Stephen
1869–1944

Masters, Edgar Lee
1869–1950
Robinson, Edwin Arlington
1869–1935
Bunin, Ivan
1870–1953
Norris, Frank (Benjamin Franklin
Norris, Jr.)
1870–1902
Saki
1870–1916
Crane, Stephen
1871–1900
Dreiser, Theodore
1871–1945
Johnson, James Weldon
1871–1938
Synge, John Millington
1871–1909
Dunbar, Paul Laurence
1872–1906
Cather, Willa
1873–1947
Chesterton, G. K. (Gilbert Keith)
1874–1936
Frost, Robert
1874–1963
Glasgow, Ellen
1874–1945
Lowell, Amy
1874–1925
Maugham, W. (William)
Somerset
1874–1965
Montgomery, L. M. (Lucy Maud)
1874–1942
Service, Robert W. (William)
1874–1958
Burroughs, Edgar Rice
1875–1950
Mann, Thomas
1875–1955
Rilke, Rainer Maria
1875–1926
Anderson, Sherwood
1876–1941
London, Jack
1876–1916
Rølvaag, Ole Edvart
1876–1931
Hesse, Hermann
1877–1962
Sandburg, Carl
1878–1967

Sinclair, Upton
1878–1968
Forster, E. M. (Edward Morgan)
1879–1970
Lindsay, Norman
1879–1969
Christie, Dame Agatha
1880–1976
O'Casey, Sean
1880–1964
Colum, Padraic
1881–1972
Wodehouse, P. G. (Pelham
Grenville)
1881–1975
Joyce, James
1882–1941
Undset, Sigrid
1882–1949
Woolf, Virginia
1882–1941
Kafka, Franz
1883–1924
Williams, William Carlos
1883–1963
Dinesen, Isak
1885–1962
Lawrence, D. H. (David
Herbert)
1885–1930
Lewis, Sinclair
1885–1951
Sassoon, Siegfried
1886–1967
Brooke, Rupert
1887–1915
Ferber, Edna
1887–1968
Jeffers, (John) Robinson
1887–1962
Moore, Marianne
1887–1972
Cary, Joyce
1888–1957
Chandler, Raymond
1888–1959
Eliot, T. S. (Thomas Stearns)
1888–1965
Mansfield, Katherine
1888–1923
O'Neill, Eugene
1888–1953
McKay, Claude
1889–1948

Mistral, Gabriela (Lucila Godoy de
Alcayaga)
1889–1957
Capek, Karel
1890–1938
Pasternak, Boris
1890–1960
Porter, Katherine Ann
1890–1980
Lagervist, Pär
1891–1974
Andric, Ivo
1892–1975
Buck, Pearl
1892–1973
MacLeish, Archibald
1892–1982
Millay, Edna St. Vincent
1892–1950
Tolkien, J. R. R. (John Ronald
Reuel)
1892–1973
Owen, Wilfred
1893–1918
Parker, Dorothy
1893–1967
Sayers, Dorothy L. (Leigh)
1893–1957
Cummings, E. E. (Edward Estlin)
1894–1962
Hammett, Dashiell
1894–1961
Huxley, Aldous
1894–1963
Priestley, J. B. (John Boynton)
1894–1984
Thurber, James
1894–1961
Graves, Robert
1895–1985
Cronin, A. J. (Archibald Joseph)
1896–1981
Fitzgerald, F. (Francis) Scott (Key)
1896–1940
Faulkner, William
1897–1962
Mitchinson, Naomi
1897–
Wilder, Thornton
1897–1975
Benét, Stephen Vincent
1898–1943
Brecht, Bertolt
1898–1956

Lewis, C. S. (Clive Staples)
1898–1963
Borges, Jorge Luis
1899–1986
Bowen, Elizabeth
1899–1973
Coward, Sir Noel
1899–1973
Forester, C. S. (Cecil Scott)
1899–1966
García Lorca, Federico
1899–1936
Hemingway, Ernest
1899–1961
Shute, Nevil
1899–1960
Hilton, James
1900–1954
O'Faolain, Sean
1900–
Wolfe, Thomas
1900–1938
Brown, Sterling
1901–1989
Hughes, Langston
1902–1967
Steinbeck, John
1902–1968
Waugh, Evelyn
1902–1966
Callaghan, Morley
1903–
Cullen, Countee
1903–1946
Hurston, Zora Neale
1903–1960
O'Connor, Frank
1903–1966
O'Dell, Scott
1903–1990
Orwell, George
1903–1950
Paton, Alan
1903–1988
Carpentier, Alejo
1904–1980
Greene, Graham
1904–1991
Isherwood, Christopher
1904–1986
Neruda, Pablo
1904–1973
Singer, Isaac Bashevis
1904–1991

West, Nathanael
1904–1940
Hellman, Lillian
1905–1984
Sartre, Jean-Paul
1905–1980
Warren, Robert Penn
1905–1989
Armour, Richard
1906–
Beckett, Samuel
1906–1989
Odets, Clifford
1906–1963
Senghor, Leopold Sedar
1906–
White, T. H. (Terence Hanbury)
1906–1964
Auden, W. H. (Wystan Hugh)
1907–1973
Du Maurier, Daphne
1907–1989
Fry, Christopher
1907–
Godden, (Margaret) Rumer
1907–
Heinlein, Robert
1907–1988
MacNeice, Louis
1907–1963
Michener, James
c.1907–
Moravia, Alberto
1907–1990
Fleming, Ian
1908–1964
L'Amour, Louis
1908–1988
Wright, Richard
1908–1960
Welty, Eudora
1909–
Anouilh, Jean
1910–1987
Golding, William
1911–
Milosz, Czeslaw
1911–
Williams, Tennessee
1911–1983
Boulle, Pierre
1912–
Cheever, John
1912–1982

Durrell, Lawrence
1912–1990
White, Patrick
1912–
Camus, Albert
1913–1960
Davies, Robertson
1913–
Hayden, Robert
1913–
Ellison, Ralph
1914–
Fast, Howard
1914–
Jarrell, Randall
1914–1965
Malamud, Bernard
1914–1986
Paz, Octavio
1914–
Thomas, Dylan
1914–1953
Bellow, Saul
1915–
Miller, Arthur
1915–
Walker, Margaret
1915–
Dahl, Roald
1916–1990
Herriot, James
1916–
Weiss, Peter
1916–1982
Böll, Heinrich
1917–1985
Brooks, Gwendolyn
1917–
Burgess, Anthony (John
Anthony Burgess
Wilson)
1917–
Clarke, Arthur C. (Charles)
1917–
Lowell, Robert
1917–1977
Burnford, Sheila
1918–1984
Solzhenitsyn, Alexandr,
1918–
Spark, Muriel
1918–
Ferlinghetti, Lawrence
1919–

Jackson, Shirley
1919–1965
Lessing, Doris (May)
1919–
Murdoch, Dame Iris
1919–
Pohl, Frederik
1919–
Salinger, J. D. (Jerome David)
1919–
Asimov, Isaac
1920–
Bradbury, Ray
1920–
Childress, Alice
1920–
Herbert, Frank
1920–1986
James, P. D. (Phyllis Dorothy)
1920–
Scott, Paul
1920–1978
Harris, Wilson
1921–
Lem, Stanislaw
1921–
Mowat, Farley
1921–
Amis, Kingsley
1922–
Gallant, Mavis
1922–
Kerouac, Jack
1922–1969
Larkin, Philip
1922–1985
Vonnegut, Kurt, Jr.
1922–
Behan, Brendan
1923–1964
Dickey, James
1923–
Gordimer, Nadine
1923–
Alexander, Lloyd
1924–
Baldwin, James
1924–1987
Bolt, Robert
1924–
Frame, Janet
1924–
Laurence, Margaret
1924–

Uris, Leon
1924–

Cardenal, Father Ernesto
1925–

Cormier, Robert
1925–

Hentoff, Nat (Nathan Irving)
1925–

O'Connor, Flannery
1925–1964

Fowles, John
1926–

Ginsberg, Allen
1926–

Knowles, John
1926–

Lee, Harper (Nelle Harper Lee)
1926–

Shaffer, Peter
1926–

Grass, Günter
1927–

Kerr, M. E.
1927–

Simon, Neil
1927–

Albee, Edward
1928–

Angelou, Maya
1928–

García Márquez, Gabriel
1928–

Guy, Rosa
1928–

Laye, Camara
1928–1980

Sillitoe, Alan
1928–

Wiesel, Elie (Eliezer)
1928–

Fuentes, Carlos
1929–

Kundera, Milan
1929–

Le Guin, Ursula K.
1929–

Osborne, John
1929–

Potok, Chaim
1929–

Rich, Adrienne
1929–

Achebe, Chinua
1930–

Ballard, J. G. (James Graham)
1930–

Hansberry, Lorraine
1930–1965

Hughes, Ted (Edward James)
1930–

Pinter, Harold
1930–

Barthelme, Donald
1931–1989

Goldman, William
1931–

Le Carré, John
1931–

Morrison, Toni
1931–

Munro, Alice
1931–

Richler, Mordecai
1931–

Beti, Mongo
1932–

Heller, Joseph
1932–

Naipaul, V. S. (Vidiadhar Surajprasad)
1932–

Plath, Sylvia
1932–1963

Puig, Manuel
1932–1990

Updike, John
1932–

Gaines, Ernest J.
1933–

Weldon, Fay
1933–

Baraka, Amiri
1934–

Cohen, Leonard
1934–

Greene, Bette
1934–

Peck, Richard
1934–

Soyinka, Wole
1934–

Allen, Woody
1935–

Brautigan, Richard
1935–1984

Gilchrist, Ellen
1935–

Mohr, Nicholasa
1935–
Silverberg, Robert
1935–
Hamilton, Virginia
1936–
Zindel, Paul
1936–
Myers, Walter Dean
1937–
Stoppard, Tom
1937–
Walsh, Gillian Paton
1937–
Blume, Judy
1938–
Klein, Norma
1938–1989
Ngugi Wa Thiong'o
1938–
Atwood, Margaret
1939–
Bambara, Toni
Cade
1939–
Drabble, Margaret
1939–
Hanrahan, Barbara
1939–
Heaney, Seamus
1939–

Lester, Julius
1939–
Coetzee, J. M. (John
Michael)
1940–
Mason, Bobbie Ann
1940–
Tyler, Anne
1941–
Bridgers, Sue Ellen
1942–
Highwater, Jamake
1942–
Voight, Cynthia
1942–
Giovanni, Nikki
1943–
Shepard, Sam
1943–
Taylor, Mildred
1943–
Emecheta, Buchi
1944–
Walker, Alice
1944–
King, Stephen
1947–
Hinton, S. E. (Susan Eloise)
1950–
Adams, Douglas
1952–

VOLUME 1   LANGUAGE ARTS

Webster, Noah
1758–1843
Nast, Thomas
1840–1902
Rogers, Will (William Penn Adair)
1879–1935
Keller, Helen
1880–1968
Mencken, H. L. (Henry Louis)
1880–1956
Thomas, Lowell
1892–1981
Pearson, Drew (Andrew Russell)
1897–1969
Winchell, Walter (Walter Winchel)
1897–1972
White, E. B. (Elwyn Brooks)
1899–1985

Disney, Walt (Walter Elias)
1901–1966
Hayakawa, S. I. (Samuel Ichiye)
1906–
Huston, John
1906–1987
Murrow, Edward R.
1908–1965
McDavid, Raven I., Jr.
1911–
McLuhan, (Herbert) Marshall
1911–1980
Terkel, Studs (Louis)
1912–
Wallace, Mike (Myron Leon)
1918–
Newman, Edwin (Harold)
1919–

Allen, Steve (Stephen
  Valentine Patrick William)
  1921–
Jaffee, Al (Allan)
  1921–
Serling, Rod (Edward
  Rodman)
  1924–1975
Baker, Russell
  1925–
Buchwald, Art (Arthur)
  1925–
Malcolm X (Malcolm Little; El-Hajj
  Malik El-Shabazz)
  1925–1965
Bombeck, Erma
  1927–
Chomsky, Noam
  1928–
Safire, William
  1929–

Wolfe, Tom (Thomas
  Kennerly)
  1931–
Paterson, Katherine
  (Womeldorf)
  1932–
Rank, Hugh (Duke)
  1932–
Moyers, Bill
  1934–
Allen, Woody (Allen
  Stewart Konigsberg)
  1935–
Dillard, Annie
  1945–
Spielberg, Steven
  1947–
Trudeau, Gary
  1948–
Lee, Spike (Shelton Jackson)
  1957–

VOLUME 1   MATHEMATICS

Pythagoras
  c.580–c.500 BC
Euclid
  fl. c.300 BC
Archimedes
  c.287–212 BC
Apollonius of Perga
  fl. 247–205 BC
Diophantus
  c. AD 250
Descartes, René
  1596–1650
Fermat, Pierre de
  1601–1665
Pascal, Blaise
  1623–1662
Leibniz, Gottfried
  Wilhelm
  1646–1716
Bernoulli, Jakob
  1654–1705
Euler, Leonhard
  1707–1783
Gauss, Carl Friedrich
  1777–1855
Cauchy, Augustin
  Louis
  1789–1857

Lobachevsky, Nikolai Ivanovitch
  1793–1856
Galois, Evariste
  1811–1832
Boole, George
  1815–1864
Weierstrass, Karl
  1815–1897
Cantor, Georg
  1845–1918
Klein, Felix
  1849–1925
Poincaré, Henri
  1854–1912
Hilbert, David
  1862–1943
Russell, Bertrand
  1872–1970
Noether, Emmy
  1882–1935
Ramanujan, Srinivara
  1887–1920
Fuller, R. Buckminster (Richard)
  1895–1983
Gödel, Kurt
  1906–1978
Gardner, Martin
  1914–

VOLUME 1 COMPUTER SCIENCE

Babbage, Charles
1791–1871

Lovelace, Countess of, Ada Augusta
1815–1852

Hollerith, Herman
1860–1929

Von Neumann, John
1903–1957

Hopper, Grace Murray
1906–

Mauchly, John
1907–1980

Turing, Alan
1912–1954

Shannon, Claude
1916–

Gates, William
1955–

Jobs, Steven
1955–

VOLUME 2 SOCIAL SCIENCES

Machiavelli, Niccolò
1469–1527

Hobbes, Thomas
1588–1679

Locke, John
1632–1704

Montesquieu, Charles Louis de
Secondat, Baron de la Brède et de
1689–1755

Rousseau, Jean Jacques
1712–1778

Smith, Adam
1723–1790

Burke, Edmund
1729–1797

Bentham, Jeremy
1748–1832

Marshall, John
1755–1835

Malthus, Thomas Robert
1766–1834

Humboldt, Friedrich Heinrich
Alexander von
1769–1859

Ricardo, David
1772–1823

Stevens, Thaddeus
1792–1868

Comte, Auguste
1798–1857

Mill, John Stuart
1806–1873

Guyot, Arnold
1807–1884

Marx, Karl
1818–1883

Engels, Friedrich
1820–1895

Wundt, Wilhelm
1832–1920

Holmes, Oliver Wendell, Jr.
1841–1935

James, William
1842–1910

Marshall, Alfred
1842–1924

Pavlov, Ivan Petrovich
1849–1936

Freud, Sigmund
1856–1939

Binet, Alfred
1857–1911

Veblen, Thorstein
1857–1929

Boas, Franz
1858–1942

Durkheim, Emile
1858–1917

Mackinder, Halford John, Sir
1861–1947

Mead, George Herbert
1863–1931

Weber, Max
1864–1920

Bethune, Mary McLeod
1875–1955

Jung, Carl Gustav
1875–1961

Kroeber, Alfred Louis
1876–1960

Bowman, Isaiah
1878–1950

Watson, John B. (Broadus)
1878–1958
Radcliffe-Brown, A. R. (Alfred
Reginald)
1881–1955
Frankfurter, Felix
1882–1965
Perkins, Frances
1882–1965
Rayburn, Sam (Samuel Taliaferro)
1882–1961
Keynes, John Maynard
1883–1946
Malinowski, Bronislaw
1884–1942
Sapir, Edward
1884–1939
Horney, Karen
1885–1952
Benedict, Ruth
1887–1948
Dulles, John Foster
1888–1959
Sauer, Carl Ortwin
1889–1975
Lewin, Kurt
1890–1947
Warren, Earl
1891–1974
Lynd, Robert Staughton
1892–1970
Lynd, Helen Merrel
1894–1982
Piaget, Jean
1896–1980
Allport, Gordon W. (Willard)
1897–1967
Murdock, George Peter
1897–1985
Redfield, Robert
1897–1958
Myrdal, Gunnar
1898–1987
James, Preston E.
1899–1986
Dollard, John
1900–1980
Stouffer, Samuel A.
1900–1960
Mead, Margaret
1901–1978
Erikson, Erik H.
(Homburger)
1902–

Lasswell, Harold D.
1902–1978
Parsons, Talcott
1902–1979
Leakey, Louis S. B.
1903–1972
Lorenz, Konrad
1903–1989
Robinson, Joan
1903–1983
Skinner, B. F. (Burrhus Frederic)
1904–1990
Galbraith, John Kenneth
1908–
Lévi-Strauss, Claude
1908–
Riesman, David
1909–
Rusk, Dean (David)
1909–
Merton, Robert King
1910–
Friedman, Milton
1912–
Ullman, Edward
1912–1976
Leakey, Mary D.
1913–
Ward, Barbara (Lady Jackson)
1914–1981
Whyte, William Foote
1914–
Bell, Daniel
1919–
Arrow, Kenneth J.
1921–
Kissinger, Henry Alfred
1923–
Chisholm, Shirley Anita St. Hill
1924–
Harris, Marvin
1927–
Kohlberg, Lawrence
1927–1987
Coles, Robert
1929–
O'Connor, Sandra Day
1930–
Rivlin, Alice Mitchell
1931–
Jordan, Barbara Charline
1936–
Leakey, Richard E. F.
1944–

VOLUME 2   HISTORY

Lao-Tzu
c.604–531 BC
Confucius
c.551–479 BC
Herodotus
c.484–425 BC
Thucydides
c.460–400 BC
Aristotle
384–322 BC
Cicero, Marcus Tullius
106–43 BC
Caesar, Julius
c.100–44 BC
Virgil
70–19 BC
Horace
65–8 BC
Livy
59 BC–AD 17
Plutarch
c. AD 46–c.125
Tacitus, Cornelius
c. AD 56–c.117
Pliny the Younger
c. AD 61–c.112
Suetonius
c. AD 69–c.140
St. Augustine
AD 354–430
Saint Bede, the
Venerable
AD 673–735
Averroës
1126–1198
Maimonides, Moses
1135–1204
St. Thomas Aquinas
1225–1274
Polo, Marco
c.1254–c.1324
Ibn Batuta
c.1304–c.1378
Columbus, Christopher
1451–1506
Leonardo da Vinci
1452–1519
Vespucci, Amerigo
1454–1512
Erasmus, Desiderius
c.1466–1536

Dürer, Albrecht
1471–1528
Michelangelo (Buonarroti)
1475–1564
Luther, Martin
1483–1546
Raphael (Raphaello Santi)
c.1483–1520
Cortés, Hernán
1485–1547
Cellini, Benvenuto
1500–1571
Calvin, John
1509–1564
Palestrina (Giovanni
Pierluigi)
c.1525–1594
Drake, Sir Francis
c.1540–1596
Hakluyt, Richard
c.1552–1616
Purcell, Henry
c.1659–1695
Bach, Johann Sebastian
1685–1750
Handel, George Frederick
1685–1759
Franklin, Benjamin
1706–1790
Paine, Thomas
1713–1809
Reynolds, Sir Joshua
1723–1792
Gainsborough, Thomas
1727–1788
Cook, Captain James
1728–1779
Burke, Sir Edmund
1729–1797
Haydn, Franz Joseph
1732–1809
Washington, George
1732–1799
Adams, John
1735–1826
Jefferson, Thomas
1743–1826
Adams, Abigail
1744–1818
Madison, James
1751–1836

Hamilton, Alexander
1757–1804

Monroe, James
1758–1831

Robespierre, Maximilien
1758–1794

Adams, John Quincy
1767–1848

Jackson, Andrew
1767–1845

Bonaparte, Napoleon
1769–1821

Clark, William
1770–1838

Park, Mungo
1771–1806

Metternich, Prince Klemens von
1773–1859

Lewis, Meriwether
1774–1809

Turner, Joseph Mallord William
1775–1851

Constable, John
1776–1837

Clay, Henry
1777–1852

Calhoun, John Caldwell
1782–1850

Webster, Daniel
1782–1852

Audubon, John James
1785–1851

Houston, Samuel
1793–1863

Catlin, George
1796–1872

Mann, Horace
1796–1859

Berlioz, Hector
1803–1869

Disraeli, Benjamin
1804–1881

Garrison, William Lloyd
1805–1879

Garibaldi, Giuseppi
1807–1882

Lee, Robert Edward
1807–1870

Gladstone, William Ewart
1809–1898

Lincoln, Abraham
1809–1865

Chopin, Frédéric
1810–1849

Liszt, Franz
1811–1886

Livingstone, David
1813–1873

Verdi, Giuseppe
1813–1901

Wagner, Richard
1813–1883

Bismarck, Otto von
1815–1898

Douglass, Frederick
1817?–1895

Victoria, Queen of Great Britain
1819–1901

Barton, Clara Harlowe
1821–1912

Burton, Sir Richard Francis
1821–1890

Grant, Ulysses S. (Simpson)
1822–1885

Garfield, James Abram
1831–1881

Brahms, Johannes
1833–1897

Degas, Edgar
1834–1917

Carnegie, Andrew
1835–1919

Homer, Winslow
1836–1910

Adams, Henry
1838–1918

Muir, John
1838–1914

Cézanne, Paul
1839–1906

Custer, George Armstrong
1839–1876

Chief Joseph
1840?–1904

Rodin, Auguste
1840–1917

Tchaikovsky, Peter Ilyich
1840–1893

Cassat, Mary
1845–1926

Gauguin, Paul
1848–1903

Riis, Jacob August
1849–1914

Martí, José
1853–1895

Van Gogh, Vincent
1853–1890

Sousa, John Philip
1854–1932
La Follette, Robert Marion
1855–1925
Sullivan, Louis Henry
1856–1924
Washington, Booker T. (Tallaferro)
1856–1915
Wilson, Woodrow
1856–1924
Taft, William Howard
1857–1930
Roosevelt, Theodore
1858–1919
Dewey, John
1859–1952
Addams, Jane
1860–1935
Bryan, William Jennings
1860–1925
Mahler, Gustav
1860–1911
Debussy, Achille Claude
1862–1918
Lloyd George, David
1863–1945
Strauss, Richard
1864–1949
Wright, Frank Lloyd
1867–1959
Du Bois, W. E. B. (William Edward
Burghardt)
1868–1963
Gandhi, Mohandas
Karamchand
1869–1948
Lenin, Vladimir Ilyich
1870–1924
Coolidge, Calvin
1872–1933
Churchill, Winston S.
1874–1965
Hoover, Herbert Clark
1874–1964
Ravel, Maurice
1875–1937
Duncan, Isadora
1878–1927
Stalin, Joseph
1879–1953
Steichen, Edward
1879–1973
Trotsky, Leon
1879–1940

Marshall, George Catlett
1880–1959
Antin, Mary
1881–1949
Bartók, Béla
1881–1945
Picasso, Pablo (Pablo Ruiz y
Picasso)
1881–1973
Roosevelt, Franklin Delano
1882–1945
Stravinsky, Igor
1882–1971
Gropius, Walter
1883–1969
Roosevelt, Anna Eleanor
1884–1962
Truman, Harry S.
1884–1972
Ben-Gurion, David
1886–1973
Chagall, Marc
1887–1985
Le Corbusier
1887–1965
O'Keeffe, Georgia
1887–1986
Berlin, Irving
1888–1989
Lawrence, T. E. (Thomas Edward)
1888–1935
Hitler, Adolf
1889–1945
Nehru, Jawaharlal
1889–1964
de Gaulle, Charles
1890–1970
Eisenhower, Dwight David
1890–1969
Prokofiev, Sergei
1891–1953
Kenyatta, Jomo
c.1893–1978
Mao Zedong
1893–1976
Khrushchev, Nikita
1894–1971
Lange, Dorothea
1895–1965
Meir, Golda
1898–1978
Ellington, Edward Kennedy
(Duke)
1899–1974

Armstrong, Louis
1900–1971

Adams, Ansel
1902–1984

Kennan, George
1904–

Hammarskjold, Dag (Hjalmar Agne
Carl)
1905–1961

Brezhnev, Leonid
1906–1982

Shostakovich, Dmitri
1906–1975

Carson, Rachel Louise
1907–1964

Johnson, Lyndon Baines
1908–1973

Goldwater, Barry Morris
1909–

Nkrumah, Kwame
1909–1972

Humphrey, Hubert
Horatio
1911–1978

Reagan, Ronald Wilson
1911–

Britten, Benjamin
1913–1976

Ford, Gerald R.
(Rudolph)
1913–

Nixon, Richard Milhous
1913–

Heyerdahl, Thor
1914–

Gandhi, Indira
1917–1984

Kennedy, John Fitzgerald
1917–1963

Wyeth, Andrew
1917–

Bernstein, Leonard
1918–1990

Mandela, Nelson
1918–

Sadat, Anwar
1918–1981

Cunningham, Merce
1919–

Friedan, Betty
1921–

Nyerere, Julius
1921–

McGovern, George Stanley
1922–

Bush, George Herbert Walker
1924–

Carter, James Earl (Jimmy) Jr.
1924–

Kennedy, Robert Francis
1925–1968

Malcolm X (Malcolm Little; El-Hajj
Malik El-Shabazz)
1925–1965

Thatcher, Margaret
1925–

Castro, Fidel
1927–

King, Martin Luther, Jr.
1929–1968

Gorbachev, Mikhail Sergeyevich
1931–

Tutu, Desmond
1931–

VOLUME 2   SCIENCE

Aristotle
384–322 BC

Archimedes
c.287–212 BC

Copernicus, Nicolaus
1473–1543

Brahe, Tycho
1546–1601

Bacon, Francis
1561–1626

Galileo
1564–1642

Kepler, Johannes
1571–1630

Boyle, Robert
1627–1691

Newton, Isaac
1642–1727

Halley, Edmond
1656–1742

Franklin, Benjamin
1706–1790

Linnaeus, Carolus
1707–1778

Hutton, James
1726–1797

Herschel, William
1738–1822

Lavoisier, Antoine Laurent
1743–1794
Lamarck, Jean Baptiste de
Monet de
1744–1829
Dalton, John
1766–1844
Faraday, Michael
1791–1867
Henry, Joseph
1797–1878
Lyell, Charles
1797–1875
Darwin, Charles Robert
1809–1882
Mendel, Gregor Johann
1822–1884
Pasteur, Louis
1822–1895
Wallace, Alfred Russel
1823–1913
Maxwell, James Clerk
1831–1879
Mendeleev, Dimitri Ivanovich
1834–1907
Koch, Robert
1843–1910
Edison, Thomas Alva
1847–1931
Pavlov, Ivan Petrovich
1849–1936
Shaw, William Napier
1854–1945
Planck, Max Karl Ernst
Ludwig
1858–1947
Morgan, Thomas Hunt
1866–1945
Curie, Marie
1867–1934
Rutherford, Ernest
1871–1937
Einstein, Albert
1879–1955
Wegener, Alfred Lothar
1880–1930

Bohr, Niels Henrik David
1885–1962
Frisch, Karl von
1886–1982
Hubble, Edwin Powell
1889–1953
Muller, Hermann Joseph
1890–1967
Oparin, Alexander Ivanovich
1894–1980
Krebs, Hans Adolf
1900–1981
Pauli, Wolfgang
1900–1958
Fermi, Enrico
1901–1954
Pauling, Linus Carl
1901–
McClintock, Barbara
1902–
Lorenz, Konrad Zacharias
1903–1989
Carson, Rachel Louise
1907–1964
Tinbergen, Nikolaas
1907–1988
Cousteau, Jacques–Yves
1910–
von Braun, Wernher
1912–1977
Crick, Francis Harry Compton
1916–
Wilkins, Maurice Hugh Frederick
1916–
Asimov, Isaac
1920–
Watson, James Dewey
1928–
Goodall, Jane
1934–
Sagan, Carl
1934–
Gould, Stephen Jay
1941–
Johanson, Donald Carl
1943–

VOLUME 2   HEALTH

Hippocrates
c.460–377 BC
Galen
c. AD 129–200

Vesalius, Andreas
1514–1546
Harvey, William
1578–1657

Nightingale, Florence
1820–1910
Barton, Clara Harlowe
1821–1912
Osler, William
1849–1919
Cushing, Harvey
1869–1939
Schweitzer, Albert
1875–1965

Fleming, Alexander
1881–1955
White, Paul Dudley
1886–1973
Rusk, Howard
Archibald
1901–
Spock, Benjamin
McLane
1903–

PREFACE

The notion of a reference work that, for younger readers, would serve a function similar to that of Bowker's classic *The Reader's Adviser* became the propelling force in the development of this book.

Considered by many as the ultimate booklover's book, *The Reader's Adviser* is intended to be, as its subtitle states, "A Layman's Guide to Literature." From scholarly examinations of the classics to in-depth looks at new authors, new works, and new disciplines, *The Reader's Adviser,* through 13 editions and for more than 70 years, has been providing broad-based yet detailed book information for the general adult reading public as well as for professional librarians and educators.

By 1988, when *The Reader's Adviser* had grown to a set of six hefty volumes (from the original 1921 pamphlet), it became quite clear that such a set had become too unwieldy, complex, and scholarly for use by most young adult readers. This was coupled with the fact that there were new directions being taken in school curricula (the addition of elective courses, advanced placement courses, modern fiction units, and computer science studies). Also, there began a new type of literature, the growing body of "young adult literature," a publishing category that was virtually nonexistent before the 1960s. Add to these new directions the changing makeup of the school population and various current social and political trends (emphases on the women's movement, the need for multicultural readings, and a growing insistence on non-Western studies), and one is readily able to see the need for a young reader's edition of *The Reader's Adviser.*

Like its parent, *The Young Adult Reader's Adviser* is partly a work of reference and partly a book for browsing; so, one can utilize it to locate specific information and one is also able to read it for pleasure. Each broad discipline, whether it be American literature or world history, geography or computer science, physics or psychology (or any other area), opens with a brief introduction followed by general reading lists (where necessary) and then by profiles (biographical sketches) of individuals noteworthy in each field and subfield. The 851 profiles are followed by lists of selected "books by" and "books about" the individual. The more than 17,000 bibliographic entries are designed so that the user will be able both to locate a book in a library and to know where it is available for purchase and at what price. It is our hope that the young adult users will be so enticed by such a variety of subjects and fascinating personalities that a lifetime reading habit will be established.

The Young Adult Reader's Adviser is Bowker's newest offering in a long tradition of providing valuable reference materials to the school, library, and home. This tradition, now 120 years old, includes such well-known works as *Children's Books in Print, Reference Books for Young Readers, A to Zoo, Books Kids Will Sit Still For,* and the volumes in the *Best Books* series. This title, joining the others in the children's and young adult line of products, makes a vital contribution to our commitment to develop new tools for students and professionals.

Many people were helpful in preparing this premier edition of *The Young Adult Reader's Adviser.* To Myra Immell, general editor of the project, goes credit and our thanks for successfully translating a concept into a book; her editorial and organizational skills are supreme. We are especially grateful also to Lauren Fedorko, who bravely answered our summons to devise a concept and to coordinate all tasks involved in editorial development and production; she has been, throughout the entire process, a most patient and gracious leader and problem solver. Jill Wood, book designer, has proved with these pages that a reference book can also look attractive and be user-friendly. Our thanks also to Diane Schadoff, who, as project coordinator, successfully kept the balls in the air and maintained quality control with the "cast of thousands" involved in production. At Bowker, Julia Raymunt and Roy Crego, editorial production managers, efficiently supervised and reviewed the many production stages of the manuscript; Debbi Dalton, art director, produced the lively and attractive covers; and Angela Szablewski, editorial assistant, cheerfully supported everyone along the way.

MARION SADER
Publisher, R. R. Bowker
January 1992

HOW TO USE THIS BOOK

The Young Adult Reader's Adviser is a two-volume reference tool that encompasses the major areas of study, or the core curriculum, targeted by school systems across the United States—literature, language arts, mathematics, computer science, social sciences, history, science, and health. Easy-to-read and informative, these volumes were developed and designed to achieve two major purposes: (1) to provide students, teachers, and librarians with biographical and other interesting and relevant information about selected individuals of merit in each of the subject areas currently included in the middle school, junior high school, or high school curricula; and (2) to alert students, teachers, and librarians to the great wealth of core and supplementary works they may personally consult or recommend to others gaining insight into a given discipline, individual, topic, or theme.

SCOPE AND SEQUENCE

The Young Adult Reader's Adviser consists of bibliographies arranged by subject matter or by author as well as profiles of hundreds of literary figures, scientists, mathematicians, social scientists, and other notable individuals, both past and present. Great care has been taken in the categorizing of this content to remain within established educational frameworks and to maintain the integrity of each area of study. In each section and subsection, bibliographies and profiles are categorized under topics or themes that correspond to those in the standard curricula as well as to the units and chapters found in most current textbooks. Thus, the wide range of subjects will be familiar to librarians, teachers, and students who wish to locate a particular topic or do research on an individual associated with a given discipline or unit of study in which the researcher is immediately involved.

Each area of study naturally possesses unique characteristics. One of these is vocabulary. For example, in biology, the reader will encounter the subsection "Protists." Like other discipline-specific terms, this one is not defined because it is a term commonly used in biology classes and in textbooks and will be familiar to teachers and students of biology, as well as librarians.

Another characteristic unique to a given discipline is the grade level or levels at which it is taught. In the social sciences, for example, geography may be taught at the middle school, junior high school, and the high school levels, while other disciplines tend to be offered at only one level. An example of the latter case is American government, which is generally taught in grade twelve. For disciplines taught only at the higher grade levels, the bibliographies by necessity reflect a higher concept and reading level.

Still another feature of each discipline is the manner or order in which material is presented during the course of study. For example, in most United States and world history courses, events generally are presented chronologically. Some topics and themes, however, overlap and are intentionally introduced and studied separately. It is not uncommon in a United States history course, for example, to study Reconstruction separately from the settling of the last frontier even though the events of each topic cover much of the same time period. To maintain a parallelism with the existing curricula, as well as to help ensure the comfort level of student users, subsection titles in the history sections of *The Young Adult Reader's Adviser* approximate those of current history textbooks and courses of study.

As in the compilation of almost all reference books, *The Young Adult Reader's Adviser* required selectivity—focusing on some topics, themes, and individuals to the exclusion of others. As explained in greater detail in the introduction to each of the volumes' parts and subsections, determinations generally were made on the basis of: state curriculum guidelines and frameworks; current middle school, junior high school, and high school courses of study; and input by librarians and educators. The sections of the work devoted to history, however, presented a particular dilemma to the editors—having to choose among an overwhelming number of individuals, both past and present, who merit inclusion. With the interests and concerns of their young adult audience in mind, the editorial staff elected to profile primarily those individuals who wrote and published books and whose works are still in print and available for use. As a result of this focus, some highly recognizable figures—such as Marie Antoinette, Elizabeth I, and Hirohito—are not profiled.

ORGANIZATION

In *The Young Adult Reader's Adviser,* information is divided among the four major areas of study, with each volume housing two main sections, or Parts. In Volume 1, Part One is devoted to Literature and Language Arts, while Part Two focuses on Mathematics and Computer Science. In Volume 2, Part One is dedicated to the Social Sciences and History, while Part Two encompasses Science and Health.

For ease of use, each Part is divided further into sections and subsections that parallel commonly accepted courses of study in American schools. Volume 1, Part One (Literature and Language Arts) consists of two primary sections: (a) a literature section divided into subsections devoted to British literature, Commonwealth literature, American literature, and world literature; and (b) a language arts section consisting of subsections dedicated to language, human communication, mass communication, and writing. Part Two (Mathematics and Computer Science) also consists of two main sections: (a) a mathematics section composed of subsections dealing with references and histories as well as with general mathematics, algebra, geometry, calculus and precalculus, trigonometry, analysis, probability and statistics, and recreational math; and (b) a computer science section divided into more than a dozen subsections, each of which focuses on one aspect—software applications, for example—of computer science.

Volume 2, Part One (Social Sciences and History) is also divided into two sections: (a) a social sciences section made up of subsections devoted to the disciplines of American government, anthropology, economics, geography, psychology, and sociology; and (b) a section dedicated to history that is divided into two subsections—United States history and world history. Part Two (Science and Health) consists of: (a) a science section divided into subsections covering the disciplines of general science, biology, earth science, chemistry, and physics; and (b) a health section divided by topic into more than a dozen subsections dealing with such diverse health-related subjects as body systems, mental and emotional health, personal care, drugs, and physical disabilities.

Where appropriate, subsections are broken down still further to focus on specific topics, themes, or periods of time. For example, the reader interested in researching the life and works of the twentieth-century American author Ernest Hemingway would turn first to Volume 1, Part One (Literature and Language Arts); then, more specifically, to the Literature section within Part One; then to the subsection American Literature; and last to the section titled The Twentieth Century, under which Ernest Hemingway and other twentieth-century American authors are chronicled alphabetically.

The organization of each volume and each part is designed to move the reader from the general to the specific. Each part opens with a theme-related piece of art and an introduction that discusses briefly the organization of and the rationale for that part. Immediately following is a specific section with its various subsections. Each subsection opens with a brief introduction that provides a framework for the area of study, the period, or the genre. With the exception of the literature and the science sections, the introduction is followed by listings of surveys, histories, and other reference books. Immediately following the general listings are the divisions devoted to specific themes or topics, each with its own listings of bibliographic entries and biographical profiles.

THE PROFILES

Organized alphabetically by surname, each of the profiles contains biographical information about an individual or group of individuals. The great majority also contain information about the individual's or group's works, achievements, theories, contributions, and role in society at the time. Following each profile are bibliographies of books by and about the person or group. In the "Books By . . ." sections, books are listed alphabetically, with a few clearly marked exceptions—such as the chronological listing of titles within a series. These are intended to provide an overview of the titles and types of books written by a given individual. The "Books About . . ." sections, which are organized alphabetically according to the surname of the author or editor, are intended to suggest where to look for much more extensive information than that provided in a profile.

THE BIBLIOGRAPHIC ENTRIES

The bibliographic entries are designed to help the reader locate a book in the library and, in the case of the librarian, tell him or her if it is available for purchase and at what price. For each title, when applicable, this vital information is provided: the author; title; series title; editor, translator, or compiler; number of volumes; publisher; date of publication; price; and ISBN. Here, for example, is a typical entry.

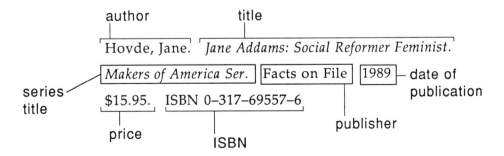

If a title consists of more than one volume and is listed with only one price and ISBN number, this is the price and ISBN number for the entire set. Although prices may change, they are listed primarily to alert the reader to the general price category into which a title falls and to assist the librarian in acquisition.

The titles of some books give an immediate and clear indication of their content or general topics. Others, however, do not. Therefore, to aid in selecting the most appropriate book, many of the bibliographic entries include brief, descriptive annotations. All of the entries in the "Books About . . ." sections, for example, are annotated with one-line descriptions. Also, all of the asterisked (*) or bulleted (■) entries in the "Books by . . ." sections are annotated. For instance, *The Autobiography of Miss Jane Pittman* is followed by this annotation: "Tale of black history in the South as seen through the eyes of a fictional 110-year-old black woman born a slave on a Louisiana plantation."

history of the United States since the Civil War. It is a testimony to Gaines's skill as a writer and storyteller that many people believe Jane Pittman was a real person. Indeed, the novel is frequently misshelved in the biography section of bookstores.

Of Gaines's other works, *Bloodline* (1976), a collection of five short stories, stands out for its powerful portrayals of young men in search of self-respect and dignity.

NOVELS BY GAINES

***The Autobiography of Miss Jane Pittman* (1971). Bantam 1982 $3.95. ISBN 0-553-26357-9
Tale of black history in the South as seen through the eyes of a fictional 110-year-old black woman born a slave on a Louisiana plantation.
Catherine Cormier (1964). North Point 1981 $9.95. ISBN 0-86547-022-7
A Gathering of Old Men (1983). Random 1984 $4.95. ISBN 0-394-72591-3
In My Father's House (1978). Norton 1983 $6.70. ISBN 0-393-30124-9
Of Love and Dust (1967). Norton 1979 $8.95. ISBN 0-393-00914-9

SHORT STORY COLLECTION BY GAINES

**Bloodline (1976). Norton 1976 $7.95. ISBN 0-393-00798-7 Five short stories that portray young men in search of dignity and depict adult life as viewed by children.

BOOK ABOUT GAINES

Stanford, Barbara Dodd, and Karmina Amin. *Black Literature for High School Students.* NCTE 1978. (o.p.) $6.00. ISBN 0-8141-0330-8 A resource book on teaching black

FEATURES

To provide additional information to librarians, teachers, and the younger readers in grades 6 through 8, the following features were made an integral part of *The Young Adult Reader's Adviser.*

(1) Book entries considered to be particularly appropriate for readers in grades 6 through 8 are marked with an asterisk (*) and are always annotated. (An example is the above annotation for *The Autobiography of Miss Jane Pittman.*)

(2) Entries that are marked with a square bullet (■) indicate a title that is appropriate only for very advanced high school students. These entries,

which are also annotated, tend to be found in bibliographies throughout the social sciences section—primarily anthropology, economics, psychology, and sociology. These disciplines are generally classified as one-semester elective courses in the high-school curriculum; in many instances they are offered only in grade 12. Occasionally, the bullet is used also with entries in the history section.

(3) For books written by profiled individuals, the date of the publication of the first edition, regardless of whether that edition is still in print, appears in parentheses after the title. Here is an example:

> **Jane Eyre* (1847). Bantam 1991 $2.50. ISBN 0-553-21140-4 The life and adventures of a young woman who comes to Thornfield Hall as a governess and falls in love with the Hall's mysterious owner, Mr. Rochester.

This book was originally published in 1847; this edition, currently in print, was published in 1991.

(4) Books that are no longer in print are clearly identified by the abbreviation *o.p.,* which appears in parentheses immediately following the publication date. (This out-of-print notice will save the reader time searching in publishers' catalogs and many bookstores for books that are difficult to locate and instead will send the reader to the library, which, fortunately, stocks many books that are no longer in print.)

CROSS-REFERENCES

Cross-references enable the reader to gain from the two volumes of *The Young Adult Reader's Adviser* the maximum amount of information relevant to the person or subject of interest. The reference *See* leads the reader to additional information on *another* person or subject relevant to the one being researched. The reference *See also* leads the reader to additional information on the *same* person or subject being researched.

Cross-references generally provide the name of the individual being referenced, the number of the volume in which the additional information appears, and the subsection name or names. For example, in reading the profile about the mathematician Fermat, the reader would see the statement that Fermat was also influenced by Diophantus. This statement is therefore followed by a cross-reference:

(*See* Diophantus, Vol. 1, Algebra.)

The reference tells the reader that in the Algebra section of Volume 1, he or she will find information about one of the people who influenced the life and thought of Fermat.

APPENDIX AND INDEXES

Each volume of *The Young Adult Reader's Adviser* includes a List of Publishers that lists alphabetically the abbreviations used for the publishers cited throughout the two volumes. Next to each abbreviation is the publisher's full name.

The three indexes appear last. They too appear in each of the two volumes. The first is the Profile Index, which includes, in alphabetical sequence, all authors who are profiled in the two volumes. The second index is the Author

Index, also in alphabetical sequence, which presents the authors of all books listed in the bibliographies of each volume. In addition, this listing includes editors, compilers, and translators. Finally, the alphabetical Title Index presents all books cited in the bibliographies of the two volumes.

The Young Adult Reader's Adviser is designed to provide a wealth of information with a minimum of confusion. As it is used in the library, classroom, or at home, for school reports or for browsing, we hope it will serve as a lively and informative guide to which a reader will turn again and again.

THE
YOUNG ADULT
READER'S ADVISER™

❦

VOLUME 2

THE BEST IN
SOCIAL SCIENCES AND HISTORY,
SCIENCE AND HEALTH

Hémisphère Centrale
Map by Gérard Walk and Pierre Schenk (1600s)
Courtesy of Giraudon/Art Resource

SOCIAL SCIENCES
AND
HISTORY

T he material in Part One has been assembled to provide students, teachers, librarians, and others with a selection of resources that offers information on topics, themes, and individuals normally introduced in the wide variety of social studies courses offered in upper middle school, in junior high school, and in senior high school. These listings of sources will be useful in a number of ways. Readers can scan them when searching for a book on a particular subject, person, area of study, or time period. The profiles of the various individuals and the listings of their major works will be of special help to students gathering sources for a research report.

Teachers can develop or extend supplementary reading lists for units in the social sciences and history by checking to see which works are suitable for their students and what is currently available. Teachers and librarians also will find this part useful for a quick review of a topic, trend, or period or for further developing a primary and secondary source collection.

Of course, a reference book must be selective, focusing on some individuals or topics to the exclusion of others. Some key individuals, regions, or topics will inevitably be left out or treated more briefly than others. The problem of choosing what is to be included and what must be left out of a reference book is always a difficult one. Given the broad spectrum of topics, themes, and individuals inherent in any social science or history curricula, it was an especially challenging task to make choices.

As in the first volume of the *Young Adult Reader's Adviser,* the books that are marked with an asterisk (*) are especially appropriate for younger readers, ages 12–14, in both reading level and content. Many of these books can be read with enjoyment and profit by older readers as well. Although many of the remaining books listed are within the reading range of senior high school students, some are beyond the range of all but the most able readers. Many of the classics, which cannot be overlooked or ignored, were written in the language and tone of a given historical period, which may tend to make them more difficult for some contemporary readers. These have been included primarily for the benefit of the teacher or librarian or because they are considered definitive titles in a specific discipline. In some of the social science disciplines, such as government, economics, psychology, sociology, and anthropology, the basic content tends to be more complex, and fewer books for young adult readers are available. As courses of study, these disciplines tend to be offered as electives at the high-school level, at grade 12 in particular. As a result, in these disciplines, those books most appropriate for the more advanced high school student are marked with a square bullet (•).

The Social Sciences and History part of *The Young Adult Reader's Adviser* is intended as a tool for students of those disciplines. Like any tool, its effectiveness can be determined only by those who use it. The publisher eagerly welcomes suggestions for improvement from the first readers of *The Young Adult Reader's Adviser* so that the next edition can be made even more useful.

SOCIAL SCIENCES

The term *social sciences* as it is used here includes American government/civics, anthropology, economics, geography, psychology, and sociology. Obviously, there is an enormous overlap among these disciplines; for example, it is almost impossible to consider government without taking into consideration certain facets of economics and the economy. Therefore, students and teachers in search of a particular topic are encouraged to begin with the section that seems most applicable and then to skim through other sections, including those devoted to United States and world history, to check for related materials.

To make the selections for the social sciences sections, the editors of *The Young Adult Reader's Adviser* began by studying the National Council of Social Studies guidelines and individual state education frameworks to determine the most prevalent trends in and course requirements for each of the social science disciplines. The editors also studied a number of texts currently in use in grades 6 through 12 to determine focus and relative depth of concentration on specific topics, themes, and individuals. Also taken into consideration were relevant publications by such organizations as the National Council of Economic Education and the Geographic Education National Implementation Project (GENIP).

The profile of each individual presents basic information about that person's life, education, career, achievements, and/or philosophies. The profiles are intended to give students a general idea of the role each individual has played in the development and growth of the discipline and the contributions he or she has made. However, the profiles are by no means complete accounts of any individual's life or achievements.

For the most part, all the works by a given individual that are currently in print are included in the Books By category following each profile. The works included in each Books About category have been selected to give additional information about an individual's life, role in the discipline, and/or achievements. On occasion, more specialized and narrowly focused books have also been included either because they are the only works currently in print or because they have something special to offer. Although due to the nature of *The Young Adult Reader's Adviser* each list has been limited in most instances to three or four titles, the serious student will find additional works about many of the individuals listed in Bowker's *Books in Print.* Every effort has been made to list books that are currently in print and easily available from major publishers, but this was not always possible. In a few instances, despite the importance of the individual profiled, no Books About were available.

HISTORY

To make the selections for the history sections, the editors of *The Young Adult Reader's Adviser* once again began by studying the National Council of Social Studies guidelines and individual state education frameworks to determine the most prevalent trends in and course requirements for United States history and world history. The editors also studied a number of texts currently in use in grades 6 through 12 to determine chronology, focus, and relative depth of concentration on specific topics, themes, and individuals. Also taken into consideration were relevant publications by such organizations as the Bradley Commission on History in Schools.

During the course of their research, the editors became increasingly aware of the need to develop specific criteria for determining which individuals to profile. The decision was made to include primarily those persons who wrote books and whose books were still in print. This decision was reached in part in an effort to enhance this volume's usefulness as a research tool for primary sources.

Another decision reached by the editors was to include novels, many of the historical fiction genre. Works of this nature often have stronger student appeal and effectively present the feeling and attitudes of particular periods of history in an interesting, compelling, and readable manner. In addition, the inclusion of such works is in accordance with the current trend in the social studies to enliven history through the use of literature and the other arts.

The profile of each notable individual presents basic information about his or her personal life, background, and place in history. The profiles are intended to give students a general idea of the role each individual has played and the contributions he or she has made. However, the profiles are by no means complete accounts of any individual's life or achievements.

As with the social sciences, there is an overlap in many areas of United States and world history, not only with each other but with the social sciences as well. For example, a student preparing a paper on the Vietnam War for a United States history class should be encouraged to check the appropriate sections under Geography and World History in addition to the corresponding listings under United States history.

❧❧ SOCIAL SCIENCES ❧❧

AMERICAN GOVERNMENT/CIVICS

The study of government/civics is the major focus of the social science known as political science. This section is devoted to American government. For ease of use it is divided into 13 subsections, the first two of which are General References and Surveys and Theories. The remaining 11 subsections are organized alphabetically. They are Citizenship and Civil Liberties and Rights; Comparative Political Systems; The Constitution; Ethics in Politics; The Federal Executive Branch; The Federal Judicial System; The Federal Legislative System; Federalism and States' Rights; International Relations; Political Behavior, Political Parties, Public Interest Groups; and State and Local Government.

Within a number of the subsections, key individuals associated with the topic are listed alphabetically, their last names appearing first. For each, there is a book or a list of books by that individual. In addition, there is for each a profile that provides personal background and/or information about the individual's role and achievements. Further, the profile may refer the reader to other related individuals and their works, which also can be found in *The Young Adult Reader's Adviser.*

Last, for most profiled individuals, there is a Books About section that, among other types of publications, lists notable biographies for further reading and research. Whenever possible, very recent titles have also been included.

While works relevant to the history of government are included in the American government section, the major focus is on the institutions, principles, and practices. For a comprehensive listing of works on the history of American government and the consequences domestically and internationally of American government policies and actions over time, see the readings under United States history, found in the history section of *The Young Adult Reader's Adviser.*

GENERAL REFERENCES

Barone, Michael. *Almanac of American Politics: 1990 Edition.* Grant Ujifusa (ed). National Journal 1989 $44.95. ISBN 0-89234-044-4

■Baum, Lawrence. *The Supreme Court.* Congressional Quarterly 1988 $17.95. ISBN 0-87187-495-4 Basic, understandable text that explains the Supreme Court in all aspects; includes tables, indexes, bibliography, and more.

Bowman, James S., and Frederick A. Elliston (eds). *Ethics, Government, and Public Policy: A Reference Guide.* Greenwood 1988 $55.00. ISBN 0-313-25912-4

■Bureau of the Census, U.S. Department of Commerce. *Statistical Abstract of the United States.* USGPO 1988 $25.00. Government and private data on population, industry, education, and so on; some international statistics. Published annually, from 1879 to the present.

Commager, Henry S. *Documents of American History. Vol. 2: Since 1898.* Prentice 1974 $36.00. ISBN 0-13-217000-0

Commager, Henry S., and Milton Cantor. *Documents of American History. Vol. 1: To 1898.* Prentice 1988 $36.00. ISBN 0-13-217274-7

*Congressional Quarterly. *American Leaders, 1789–1987: A Biographical Summary.* Congressional Quarterly 1987 $19.95. ISBN 0-87187-413-X Biographical information on government officials from governors to presidents and other facts on all branches of government since 1789.

*Congressional Quarterly. *Congress A to Z: Congressional Quarterly's Ready Reference Encyclopedia.* Congressional Quarterly 1988 $75.00. ISBN 0-87187-447-4 Encyclopedic reference on Congress, with explanations of terms, major functions, directory of members, a bibliography, and more.

*Congressional Quarterly. *Current American Government.* Congressional Quarterly 1989 $10.95. ISBN 0-87187-439-X Current issues; covers AIDS testing, nuclear energy lobby, government budget, and many more legislative and judicial topics. Published every spring and fall.

*Congressional Quarterly. *Guide to U.S. Elections.* Congressional Quarterly 1985 $110.00. ISBN 0-87187-339-7 The most detailed and reliable volume of U.S. election statistics.

Congressional Quarterly. *Guide to U.S. Supreme Court.* Congressional Quarterly 1979 $95.00. ISBN 0-87187-184-X

*Congressional Quarterly. *Washington Information Directory, 1989–1990.* Congressional Quarterly 1989 $59.95. ISBN 0-87187-505-5 Annual reference; names, addresses, and telephone numbers of key figures in the federal government, as well as other types of government information.

*Council of State Governments. *The Book of the States.* Council of State Governments 1988 $42.50. ISBN 0-87292-076-3 State government developments, facts, and trends; published every two years.

*Davidson, Roger H., and Walter J. Oleszek (eds). *Governing: Readings and Cases in American Politics.* Congressional Quarterly 1987 $15.95. ISBN 0-87187-427-X Excellent teaching source for high school and beyond.

*DeGregorio, William A. *The Complete Book of United States Presidents.* Dembner 1989 $29.95. ISBN 0-942637-17-8 Factual information on U.S. presidents.

*Ebenstein, William, and Edwin Fogelman. *Today's Isms: Communism, Fascism, Capitalism, and Socialism.* Prentice 1985 $29.00. ISBN 0-13-924473-5 Clear and easy to understand; widely used in high schools.

*Ehrenhalt, Alan (ed). *Politics in America: The 100th Congress.* Congressional Quarterly 1987 $39.95. ISBN 0-87187-430-X In-depth information on congressional members.

Elliot, Jeffrey M., and Sheikh R. Ali. *The Presidential–Congressional Political Dictionary.* Clio Dictionaries in Political Science Ser. ABC–Clio 1984 $17.00. ISBN 0-87436-358-6

Fenton, S. Martin, and Robert U. Goehlert. *The American Presidency: A Bibliography.* Congressional Quarterly 1987 $85.00. ISBN 0-87187-415-6

Fenton, S. Martin, and Robert U. Goehlert. *American Presidents: A Bibliography.* Congressional Quarterly 1984 $135.00. ISBN 0-87187-416-4

*Foundation for Public Affairs. *Public Interest Profiles, 1988–1989.* Congressional Quarterly 1988 $137.50. ISBN 0-87187-461-X Background and access information on 250 public interest groups.

*Friedman, Leon, and Fred L. Israel (eds). *The Justices of the United States Supreme Court, 1789–1978.* 5 vols. Chelsea 1980 $100.00. ISBN 0-87754-130-2 Profiles each justice, including major decisions and contributions to the Court.

Goehlert, Robert. *Basic Research Resources in Political Science.* Public Administration Ser. Vance Biblios 1986 $6.25. ISBN 1-55590-045-3

Goehlert, Robert. *The Executive Branch of the United States Government: A Bibliography.* Bibliographies and Indexes in Law and Political Science Ser. Greenwood 1988 $49.95. ISBN 0-313-26568-2

Goehlert, Robert. *U.S. Constitutional History: A Selected Bibliography of Books.* Public Administration Ser. Vance Biblios 1988 $3.00. ISBN 1-55590-700-8

Goehlert, Robert, and Martin S. Fenton. *The Presidency: A Research Guide.* ABC–Clio 1985 $35.00. ISBN 0-87436-373-X

Goehlert, Robert, and Frederick W. Musto. *State Legislatures: A Bibliography.* ABC–Clio 1985 $45.00. ISBN 0-87436-422-1

Goehlert, Robert, and John R. Sayre. *The United States Congress: A Bibliography.* Free Pr 1981 $50.00. ISBN 0-02-911900-6

Graff, Henry F. (ed). *The Presidents: A Reference.* Scribner's 1984 $65.00. ISBN 0-684-17607-6

Holler, Frederick L. *Information Sources of Political Science.* ABC–Clio 1986 $75.00. ISBN 0-87436-375-6

King, Gary. *The Elusive Executive: Discovering Statistical Patterns of the Presidency.* Congressional Quarterly 1988 $20.95. ISBN 0-87187-432-6

Laqueur, Walter. *Dictionary of Politics.* Free Pr 1974 $17.95. ISBN 0-02-917950-5

Lockard, Duane, and Walter F. Murphy (eds). *Basic Cases in Constitutional Law.* Congressional Quarterly 1987 $12.95. ISBN 0-87187-428-8

Martis, Kenneth C. *The Historical Atlas of United States Congressional Districts, 1789–1983.* Scribner's 1982 $190.00. ISBN 0-029-20150-0

■ Morehead, Joe. *Introduction to United States Public Documents.* Library Science Text Ser. Libraries Unlimited 1983 $19.50. ISBN 0-87287-362-5 Best introduction to the use of federal government documents; describes the distribution of documents and the tools needed for accessing information.

* Oleszek, Walter J. *Congressional Procedures and the Policy Process.* Congressional Quarterly 1989 $21.95. ISBN 0-87187-487-3 A comprehensive volume that gives details on how Congress works.

■ Plano, Jack C., and Milton Greenberg. *The American Political Dictionary.* Holt 1989. (o.p.) $20.75. ISBN 0-03-022932-4 Clear and concise definitions of U.S. political terms and jargon.

Salomon, Samuel R. *The Governors of the American States, Commonwealths, and Territories: 1900–1980.* Council of State Governments 1980 $4.00. ISBN 0-317-45928-7

Smith, Edward C., and Arnold Zurcher. *Dictionary of American Politics.* Barnes 1968 $26.50. ISBN 0-06-480803-3

■ Sobel, Robert (ed). *Biographical Directory of the United States Executive Branch, 1774–1989.* Greenwood 1990 $56.95. ISBN 0-313-26593-3 Brief sketches of the Presidents, Vice Presidents, and Cabinet officers to 1989.

■ Stanley, Harold, and Richard G. Niemi. *Vital Statistics on American Politics.* Congressional Quarterly 1988 $13.95. ISBN 0-87187-471-7 Helpful resource for recent and past political statistics.

■ United Nations. *Everyone's United Nations.* UN 1986 $9.95. ISBN 92-1-100274-5 Explains how the United Nations was organized and what duties it performs.

United States Government Manual, 1989–1990. USGPO 1989 $21.00. ISBN 0-16-006877-0

■ Van Horn, Carl E. (ed). *The State of the States.* Congressional Quarterly 1989 $18.95. ISBN 0-87187-503-9 Essays by notable authorities on states' efforts to adjust to their added role in American federalism.

■ Weissberg, Robert. *Politics: A Handbook for Students.* Harcourt 1985 $12.00. ISBN 0-15-570740-X Good basic source on politics for young people.

Weissberg, Robert. *Understanding American Government.* McGraw 1985 $29.95. ISBN 0-07-554904-2

■ *Who's Who in American Politics.* Bowker 1991. ISBN 0-8352-2219-5 Brief biographies of prominent people in U.S. politics.

■ Witt, Elder. *The Supreme Court and Individual Rights.* Congressional Quarterly 1988 $17.95. ISBN 0-87187-465-2 Explains case decisions and how they apply to citizens' rights.

■ Zerman, Melvyn B. *Beyond a Reasonable Doubt: Inside the American Jury System.* Harper 1981 $12.89. ISBN 0-690-04095-4 Tells how the jury system works.

See also Vol. 2, Economics: Government and Economics.

SURVEYS AND THEORIES

Congressional Quarterly. *Social Security and Retirement: Private Goals and Public Policy.* Congressional Quarterly 1983 $10.95. ISBN 0-87187-274-9

Easton, David. *The Political System: An Inquiry into the State of Political Science.* Univ of Chicago Pr 1981 $12.50. ISBN 0-226-18017-4

Harrigan, John J. *Political Change in the Metropolis.* Scott 1989 $32.50. ISBN 0-673-39848-X

Harrigan, John J. *Politics and Policy in States and Communities.* Scott 1988 $32.50. ISBN 0-673-39725-4

Harrigan, John J. *Politics and the American Future.* Random 1987 $20.95. ISBN 0-394-36148-2

Jacob, Herbert. *Law and Politics in the United States: An Introduction.* Scott 1986 $26.50. ISBN 0-673-39448-4

Kettner, James H. *The Development of American Citizenship, 1608–1870. Institute of Early American History and Culture Ser.* Univ of North Carolina Pr 1984 $10.95. ISBN 0-8078-4122-6

Lopez, George A., and Michael S. Stohl (eds). *International Relations: Contemporary Theory and Practice.* Congressional Quarterly 1988 $20.95. ISBN 0-87187-476-8

∎ Orwell, George. *Nineteen Eighty-Four: Commemorative Edition.* NAL 1950 $3.95. ISBN 0-451-52123-4 Chilling story of one man's fight to free himself from the control of "Big Brother."

∎ Patterson, James T. *America in the Twentieth Century.* Harcourt 1988 $20.00. ISBN 0-15-502264-4 Clear and vivid history of the modern United States, emphasizing political developments.

Phillips, Kevin. *The Politics of Rich and Poor: Wealth and the American Electorate in the Reagan Aftermath.* Random 1990 $19.95. ISBN 0-394-55954-1

∎ Schlesinger, Arthur M., Jr. (ed). *The Federal Government: How It Works. Know Your Government Ser.* Chelsea 1989 $14.95. ISBN 0-87754-859-5 Good explanation of the workings of the federal government.

∎ *Social Contract: Essays by Locke, Hume, and Rousseau.* Oxford Univ Pr 1980 $9.95. ISBN 0-19-500309-8 Contains three basic writings of the social contract theory of government.

Wood, Gordon S. *The Creation of the American Republic, 1776–1787.* Norton 1972 $10.95. ISBN 0-393-00644-1

BENTHAM, JEREMY   1748–1832

Jeremy Bentham was an English philosopher, economist, political theorist, and jurist who spent his life working for social and political reforms. He expounded the philosophy of utilitarianism, which is based on the principle of "the greatest happiness of the greatest number." In Bentham's view, this was the fundamental principle of morality, one that should govern all judgments about institutions and actions.

Educated as a lawyer at Oxford University, Bentham never practiced law. Instead, he spent much of his life attempting to analyze morals and the law scientifically in an attempt to develop a science of human behavior. His work in reforming English legislation greatly influenced nineteenth-century reforms in prisons, criminal law, judicial organizations, and the parliamentary electorate. He argued for democracy but not economic equality for all people.

Bentham's major work was *An Introduction to the Principles of Morals and Legislation* (1789), which won him recognition throughout the Western world. His philosophy of utilitarianism greatly influenced a number of other thinkers, including British philosopher and economist John Stuart Mill and British economist David Ricardo. (*See* Mill *and* Ricardo, Vol. 2, Economics: World Economy.)

BOOKS BY BENTHAM

A Fragment on Government. Cambridge Texts in the History of Political Thought Ser (1776). J. H.
   Burns and H. L. Hart (eds). Cambridge Univ Pr 1988 $6.95. ISBN 0-521-35929-5
The Principles of Morals and Legislation. Great Books in Philosophy Ser (1789). Prometheus Bks
   1988 $5.95. ISBN 0-87975-434-6
The Theory of Legislation. Rothman 1987 $47.50. ISBN 0-8377-1947-X

BOOKS ABOUT BENTHAM

Atkinson, Charles Milner. *Jeremy Bentham: His Life and Work.* AMS (repr of 1905 ed)
   $8.50. ISBN 0-404-00416-4 Complete portrait of Bentham's life, family, work,
   influences, creeds and aims, and politics.
Dinwiddy, John. *Bentham. Past Masters Ser.* Oxford Univ Pr 1989 $5.95. ISBN 0-19-
   287622-8 Examination of the various components of Bentham's philosophy,
   showing how each was shaped by a radical rethinking entailed by the utilitarian
   approach.
Harrison, Ross. *Bentham. Arguments of the Philosophers Ser.* Routledge 1985 $14.95. ISBN
   0-7102-0742-5 Study of Bentham's philosophical thought and theory of meaning
   drawing on previously unpublished as well as published works, accessible to
   students of history or political theory.
Lyons, David. *In the Interest of the Governed: A Study in Bentham's Philosophy of Utility and Law.*
   Oxford Univ Pr 1973. ISBN 0-19-824503-3 Study of Bentham's important works
   and reinterpretation of his main philosophical doctrines.
Rosenblum, Nancy L. *Bentham's Theory of the Modern State. Harvard Political Studies.* Harvard
   Univ Pr 1978 $18.50. ISBN 0-674-06665-0 Focuses on Bentham's theory of the
   state rather than his historical activism as the real measure of his importance,
   while covering the full range of his writing.

BURKE, EDMUND   1729–1797

See also Burke, Vol. 2, World History: Revolution and Change in England and
America.

Edmund Burke, Irish-born British statesman, political writer, and orator,
is renowned for his theory of social order, his advocacy of conservative politics,
and his sustained hostility to the French Revolution. The son of a Roman
Catholic mother and a Protestant father, he spent the better part of his life
criticizing the English administration in Ireland and the discrimination against
Catholics. Educated at Trinity College in Dublin, he studied law for a short
time in London. He left his studies behind, however, to write and eventually
founded a periodical called *Annual Register.*

In 1765 Burke turned to politics, becoming private secretary to the marquis
of Rockingham, who was prime minister of England. That same year he entered
the English Parliament. As a Whig spokesperson, he criticized the actions of
King George III that increased the power of the monarchy and he sympathized
with American and Irish grievances. He called for conciliation with the American colonies and, urging repeal of the Stamp Act, argued against many of the
Crown's taxation policies. His 1770 work, *Thoughts on the Cause of the Present
Discontents,* made him the first political philosopher to argue the value of political parties. In the 1780s, while serving as postmaster general, he became interested in the East India Company and eventually was instrumental in reforming
it.

Burke is best remembered for his adamant condemnation of the French
Revolution. His essay, *Reflections on the Revolution in France* (1790), is the bible of
political conservatism. He contrasted the French Revolution with social and

political change in Great Britain, where he believed the existing order was peacefully altered when it conflicted with the extension of human freedom. "All government—indeed, every human benefit and enjoyment, every virtue, and every prudent act," he said, "is founded on compromise and barter." Burke's writings greatly influenced conservative political theorists in England, North America, and France into the nineteenth century.

BOOKS BY BURKE

Burke's Politics: Selected Writings and Speeches on Reform, Revolution, and War (1949). Ross J. Hoffman and Paul Levack (eds). Knopf 1949. (o.p.) $3.50.

Selected Letters of Edmund Burke (1984). Harvey C. Mansfield, Jr. (ed). Univ of Chicago Pr 1984 $32.50. ISBN 0-226-08068-4

The Writings and Speeches of Edmund Burke: Party, Parliament, and the American Crisis, 1766–1774. Paul Langford (ed). Vol. 2 Oxford Univ Pr 1981 $120.00. ISBN 0-19-822416-8

BOOKS ABOUT BURKE

Ayling, Stanley. *Edmund Burke: His Life and Opinions.* St. Martin's 1988 $19.95. ISBN 0-312-02686-2 First biography of Burke to be based on his full extant correspondence.

Chapman, Gerald W. *Edmund Burke: The Practical Imagination.* Harvard Univ Pr 1967 $22.00. ISBN 0-674-23750-1 Study of Burke that provides an interpretive summary and analysis of Burke's actual thinking on the great controversies of his time.

Fasel, George. *Edmund Burke. Twayne's English Authors Ser.* G. K. Hall 1983. (o.p.) $15.50. ISBN 0-805-76861-0 Introduction to Burke's life and work.

Kramnick, Isaac (ed). *Edmund Burke.* Prentice 1974. ISBN 0-13-090597-6 Part 1 includes Burke's own words, while Part 2 includes essays showing Burke viewed by his contemporaries and in history.

MacPherson, C. B. *Burke. Past Masters Ser.* Oxford Univ Pr 1980 $4.95. ISBN 0-19-287518-3 New appreciation of Burke introducing the range of his thought and a solution to the main problems it poses.

HOBBES, THOMAS   1588–1679

Thomas Hobbes was an English philosopher and the first of the great English political theorists. Educated at Magdalen College, Oxford, he was interested in physics, mathematics, and rationalism. In his works, he attempted to apply rational thought to the study of human behavior. His view of humans was both materialistic and pessimistic.

His best known-work is *Leviathan* (1651). In it, he states that people are motivated by self-interest and are constantly at war with one another. In his words life is "nasty, brutish, and short." To escape from this anarchy, people agree to establish a state under the authority of a sovereign who, in turn, must protect the people and promote truth. Unlike other theorists of his day, Hobbes rejected the theory of the divine right of kings. According to Hobbes, the authority of the sovereign flows not from God, but from the people. Hobbes did imply, however, that if the sovereign failed in his duties, the citizens did have the right to revolt. Hobbes's theory is known as the social contract.

Although Hobbes was denounced by contemporaries and by later critics as well for his materialistic, antispiritual view of humans, his thought has nevertheless influenced Western thinkers. His theory of the social contract is considered a major contribution to the theory of the state.

BOOKS BY HOBBES

De Cive: The English Version. The Clarendon Edition of the Philosophical Works of Thomas Hobbes (1642). Howard Warrender (ed). Oxford Univ Pr 1983 $85.00. ISBN 0-19-824623-4

The Elements of Law: Natural and Politic (1640). Ferdinand Tonnies (ed). Biblio Dist 1969 $35.00. ISBN 0-7146-2540-X

▪ *Leviathan* (1651). *Great Books in Philosophy.* Prometheus Bks 1988 $4.95. ISBN 0-87975-445-1 Philosophical tract that discusses the origins and uses of government.

BOOKS ABOUT HOBBES

Dietz, Mary G. (ed). *Thomas Hobbes and Political Theory.* Univ Pr of Kansas 1990 $25.00. ISBN 0-7006-0420-0 Discusses the historical credibility of this great figure.

Goldsmith, Maurice. *Hobbes's Science of Politics.* Columbia Univ Pr 1978 $17.50. ISBN 0-231-02804-0 Argues that Hobbes's political philosophy can best be understood as part of his scientific system; analyzes Hobbes's views on the laws of nature, the social contract and the sovereign state, and on morality and religion.

Tuck, Richard. *Hobbes. Past Masters Ser.* Oxford Univ Pr 1989 $5.95. ISBN 0-19-287668-6 Broad introduction to the life and work of Hobbes.

LASSWELL, HAROLD D.   1902–1978

Harold D. Lasswell was a driving force in the development of American political science. He introduced a psychoanalytical perspective into the study of politics.

Beginning in his twenties, Lasswell attempted through his writings to develop a theory about humans and society that draws on and illuminates all the social sciences. When he enrolled in the University of Chicago at age 16, he had already read widely the works of such writers as the German philosopher Immanuel Kant and the Viennese psychoanalyst Sigmund Freud. (*See* Freud, Vol. 2, Psychology: Personality.)

Lasswell's doctoral dissertation, *Propaganda Techniques in the World War,* was published in 1927, and was a major work in the development of communications research. He created a phrase—"Who says what to whom with what effect?"—that set the agenda for communications research for a generation.

After World War I, Lasswell moved to Yale Law School, where he virtually created the field of law, science, and public policy, introducing a generation of law students to the social sciences. He believed that the creation of what he called the "policy sciences" was his greatest achievement.

BOOKS BY LASSWELL

Handbook of Political and Social Indicators. (coauthored with Bruce M. Russell, *et al*) Yale Univ Pr 1964. (o.p.)

Politics: Who Gets What, When, and How (1936). Peter Smith 1950 $21.75. ISBN 0-8446-1277-4

Psychopathology and Politics (1930). Univ of Chicago Pr 1986 $18.95. ISBN 0-226-46919-0

World Politics and Personal Insecurity (1935). Macmillan 1965. (o.p.) $2.45. ISBN 0-029-18050-3

BOOKS ABOUT LASSWELL

McDougall, Derek. *Harold D. Lasswell and the Study of International Relations.* Univ Pr of America 1985 $32.75. ISBN 0-8191-4296-4 Analyzes Lasswell's work, focusing on his contribution to international relations.

Rogow, Arnold A. (ed). *Politics, Personality and Social Science in the Twentieth Century: Essays in Honor of Harold D. Lasswell.* Univ of Chicago Pr 1969 $27.50. ISBN 0-226-72399-2 First full-scale effort to deal fully with the unusual scope of Lasswell's work.

ROUSSEAU, JEAN JACQUES   1712–1778

Jean Jacques Rousseau was a French writer, philosopher, and political theorist. Although he lived much of his life in France, he had been born in Switzerland and generally added "Citizen of Geneva" whenever he signed his name.

In *Discourse on the Inequalities of Men* (1754) and *The Social Contract* (1762), Rousseau elaborated on his theory of the "natural man." He believed that in the state of nature humans were good and equal. It was only when they were faced with the corrupting influences of property, farming, science, and commerce that they became evil and greedy.

Rousseau wrote, "The greatest good is not authority, but liberty." In *The Social Contract,* Rousseau moved from a study of the individual to an analysis of the relationship of the individual to the state. He wrote, "The art of politics consists of making each citizen extremely dependent upon the polis in order to free him from dependence upon other citizens."

This doctrine of sovereignty, the absolute supremacy of the state over its members, has led many to accuse Rousseau of opening doors to despotism, collectivism, and totalitarianism. Others contend that Rousseau meant that the surrender of rights is only apparent, and that in the end individuals retain the rights that they appear to have given up. In effect, these Rousseau supporters say, the social contract is designed to secure or to restore to individuals in the state of civilization the equivalent of the rights they enjoyed in the state of nature. When necessary, the people can rise up in revolt and withdraw the sovereignty they bestowed on an appointed person or persons.

Rousseau's writings had a great influence on the French Revolution and on such philosophers as Immanuel Kant and such writers as Johann Wolfgang von Goethe and Leo Tolstoy. (*See* Goethe, Vol. 1, World Literature: German Language and Literature, *and* Tolstoy, Vol. 1, World Literature: Russian Literature.)

BOOKS BY ROUSSEAU

- *The Confessions of Jean Jacques Rousseau. Penguin Classics Ser.* John M. Cohen (tr.) Penguin 1953 $5.95. ISBN 0-140-44033-X A new personal style of autobiography.
Emile (1762). Alan Bloom (tr). Basic 1979 $14.95. ISBN 0-465-01931-5
The Social Contract (1762). *Great Books in Philosophy.* Prometheus Bks 1988 $3.95. ISBN 0-87975-444-3
The Theory of Inequality Among Men and the Collision of the Cultures (1754). American Classical Coll Pr 1987 $149.75. ISBN 0-89266-606-4

BOOKS ABOUT ROUSSEAU

Bloom, Harold (ed). *Jean-Jacques Rousseau.* Chelsea 1987 $27.50. ISBN 1-55546-296-0 Biography with criticism and interpretation.
Miller, James. *Rousseau: Dreamer of Democracy.* Yale Univ Pr 1986 $10.95. ISBN 0-300-03518-7 Blend of biography, philosophy, and history showing the paradoxes of Rousseau's political thought and how he inspired a generation of radicals.
Shklar, Judith N. *Men and Citizens: A Study of Rousseau's Social Theory.* Cambridge Univ Pr 1985 $16.95. ISBN 0-521-31640-5 Analytical study examining all of Rousseau's writings and thought.
Viroli, Maurizio. *Rousseau and the "Well-Ordered Society."* Derek Hanson (tr). Cambridge Univ Pr 1988 $42.50. ISBN 0-521-33342-3 Study of Rousseau's concept of social order and its implications for the ideal society he envisions.

CITIZENSHIP AND CIVIL LIBERTIES AND RIGHTS

Abraham, Henry J. *Freedom and the Court: Civil Rights and Liberties and Rights in the United States.* Oxford Univ Pr 1988 $16.95. ISBN 0-19-505516-0

■ Bach, Julie. *Civil Liberties. Opposing Viewpoints Ser.* Greenhaven 1988 $7.95. ISBN 0-89908-409-5 Debates on separation of church and state, freedom of speech, right to privacy, government responsibility to minority rights, and other civil liberty issues.

Barber, Benjamin. *Strong Democracy: Participatory Politics for a New Age.* Univ of California Pr 1984 $10.95. ISBN 0-520-05616-7

Bookchin, Murray. *The Rise of Urbanization and the Decline of Citizenship.* Sierra 1987 $22.95. ISBN 0-87156-706-7

■ Branch, Taylor. *Parting the Waters: America in the King Years, 1954–1963.* Simon 1988 $24.45. ISBN 0-671-46097-8 Stresses African-American civil rights, historical events, and the impact of Martin Luther King, Jr., on the nation.

Butts, R. Freeman. *The Revival of Civic Learning: A Rationale for Citizenship Education in American Schools.* Phi Delta Kappa 1980 $6.00. ISBN 0-76367-423-5

■ *Citizenship in the Nation.* BSA 1984 $1.39. ISBN 0-8395-3252-0 Illustrated guide about responsible citizenship.

■ Conta, Marcia Maher. *Women for Human Rights. Movers and Shapers Ser.* Raintree 1979 $13.31. ISBN 0-8172-1378-3 Lives, special goals, and successes of such outstanding women as Rosa Parks, Margaret Kuhn, and Dorothy Day.

Cushman, Robert F. *Cases in Civil Liberties.* Prentice 1989 $33.40. ISBN 0-13-115395-1

Dunbar, Leslie H. *Minority Report: What's Happened to Blacks, Hispanics, American Indians and Other American Minorities in the 1980s?* Pantheon 1984 $7.16. ISBN 0-394-72513-1

Flexner, Eleanor. *Century of Struggle: The Woman's Rights Movement in the United States.* Harvard Univ Pr 1975 $9.95. ISBN 0-674-10652-0

Gastil, Raymond D. *Freedom in the World: Political Rights and Civil Liberties. The Freedom House Annual Ser.* Greenwood 1986 $35.00. ISBN 0-313-25398-6

Haiman, Franklyn S. *Speech and Law in a Free Society.* Univ of Chicago Pr 1984 $15.00. ISBN 0-226-31214-3

* Hentoff, Nat. *The First Freedom: The Tumultuous History of Free Speech in America.* Delacorte 1988 $16.95. ISBN 0-385-29643-6 Historical discussion of how the First Amendment has been interpreted in the past and the status of freedom of speech in this country.

■ King, Martin Luther, Jr. *Stride Toward Freedom: The Montgomery Story.* Harper 1987 $8.95. ISBN 0-06-250490-8 Details the 1955 bus boycott in Montgomery, Alabama, and King's ideas on nonviolence.

■ King, Martin Luther, Jr. *Why We Can't Wait.* NAL 1988 $3.50. ISBN 0-451-62675-3 Describes the Birmingham campaign plan and the origins of the civil rights movement.

Kohn, Rita, *et al. My Country 'Tis of Me: Helping Children Discover Citizenship Through Cultural Heritage.* McFarland 1988 $14.95. ISBN 0-89950-323-3

Laqueur, Walter, and Barry Rubin (eds). *The Human Rights Reader.* NAL 1979 $9.95. ISBN 0-452-00853-0

■ Levinson, Nancy Snider. *First Women Who Spoke Out.* Dillon 1983 $8.95. ISBN 0-87518-235-6 Childhood experiences and adult achievements of women who spoke out for civil rights of women and slaves.

■ Lewis, Anthony. *Gideon's Trumpet.* Random 1989 $6.96. ISBN 0-679-72312-9 Historical account of the court case of Clarence Earl Gideon, whose right to legal counsel had been denied.

McCloskey, Herbert, and Alida Brill. *Dimensions of Tolerance: What Americans Believe About Civil Liberties.* Russell Sage 1986 $17.95. ISBN 0-87154-592-6

Murphy, Paul L. *World War I and the Origin of Civil Liberties in the United States. Essays in American History Ser.* Norton 1980 $7.95. ISBN 0-393-95012-3

■ Ortiz, Victoria. *Sojourner Truth.* Harper 1979 $11.89. ISBN 0-397-31504-X Biography of a woman who achieved national prominence as a fighter for rights of African Americans and women.

■Price, Janet R., and Alan H. Levine. *The Rights of Students: The Basic ACLU Guide to a Student's Rights. American Civil Liberties Union Handbook Ser.* Southern Illinois Univ Pr 1987 $6.95. ISBN 0-8093-1423-1 Presents current laws governing student rights and tells how to protect those rights.

Remy, Richard C. *Handbook of Basic Citizenship Competencies.* Assn Supervision 1980 $4.75. ISBN 0-87120-098-8

■Samuels, Cynthia K. *It's a Free Country! A Young Person's Guide to Politics and Elections.* Macmillan 1988 $12.95. ISBN 0-689-31416-7 Basic guide for young readers.

■Schlesinger, Arthur M., Jr. (ed). *The Commission on Civil Rights. Know Your Government Ser.* Chelsea 1989 $14.95. ISBN 1-55546-127-1 Easy-to-understand description of the workings of the Commission on Civil Rights.

Thoreau, Henry David. *Walden* and *Civil Disobedience.* Penguin 1983 $2.95. ISBN 0-14-039044-8

*Walker, Samuel. *In Defense of American Liberties: A History of the ACLU.* Oxford Univ Pr 1990 $24.95. ISBN 0-19-504539-4 An excellent history of the American Civil Liberties Union, the causes they have defended, and their current struggles.

Williams, Jerr S., *et al. Our Freedoms: Rights and Responsibilities.* Taitte W. Laeson (ed). Univ of Texas Pr 1985 $16.50. ISBN 0-292-76030-2

■Witt, Elder. *The Supreme Court and Individual Rights.* Congressional Quarterly 1988 $17.95. ISBN 0-87187-465-2 Explains case decisions and how they apply to citizens' rights.

BETHUNE, MARY McLEOD   1875–1955

Mary McLeod was born in South Carolina, the youngest of 17 children of former slaves. Like most African Americans at the time, she had little chance to obtain an education. Finally, when she 11 years old, the first free school was opened in her community. Every day McLeod walked five miles each way to go to class. Then, in the evenings, she taught her family everything she had learned. By the time she was 15, she had taken every course the small school had to offer.

In the early 1890s McLeod was given a scholarship to the Moody Bible Institute in Chicago. When she graduated, she decided to "dedicate herself to the education of her own people in the United States." After teaching in a series of southern mission schools, she finally settled in Florida to set up the Daytona Normal and Industrial School for young black women. With the help of her husband, Albert Bethune, who was also a teacher, she eventually transformed the tiny, four-room school into an outstanding educational institution. Over the years hundreds of black girls were given the chance to develop their abilities there. In 1923 the school merged with a men's college in Daytona and became known as Bethune-Cookman College.

While a teacher, Bethune continued to work for the African-American community at large. In 1936, in recognition of her outstanding leadership, she was appointed director of the National Youth Administration's Division of Negro Affairs. At the same time, she founded the National Council of Negro Women. Throughout the 1930s and the early 1940s, she served as official adviser to both President and Mrs. Franklin Delano Roosevelt (*see* F. Roosevelt *and* E. Roosevelt, Vol. 2, United States History: The Great Depression and the New Deal) on minority affairs.

For over 40 years Mary McLeod Bethune devoted herself to the education of others. "The drums of Africa still beat in my heart," she said near the end of her life. "They will not let me rest while there is a single Negro boy or girl without a chance to prove his worth."

BOOKS ABOUT BETHUNE

* Anderson, LaVere. *Mary McLeod Bethune: Teacher with a Dream.* Garrard 1976 $6.69. ISBN 0-8116-321-3 Illustrated biography of Bethune geared to younger readers.
* Carruth, Ella K. *She Wanted to Read: The Story of Mary McLeod Bethune.* Abingdon 1966 $6.75. ISBN 0-687-38353-6 Illustrated biography of Bethune for younger readers.

Hicks, Florence. *Mary McLeod Bethune.* Gaus 1975 $4.95. ISBN 0-14-032219-1 Discussion of Bethune's life and writings.

Meltzer, Milton. *Mary McLeod Bethune.* Penguin 1988 $3.95. ISBN 0-14-032219-1 Discussion of the life and times of Bethune.

STEVENS, THADDEUS   1792–1868

Thaddeus Stevens was the youngest son of a New England shoemaker who disappeared or died, leaving his wife to raise their four young boys. Thaddeus was born in Danville, Vermont. Lame and sickly, he had to have special care early in life. His disabilities, however, did not stop him from becoming a famous horseman and swimmer in later life.

Sally Stevens trained her sons to work hard, to think for themselves, and to be independent. Determined that they be educated, she moved the family to the village of Peacham, Vermont, because there was an academy there. In 1811, Thaddeus Stevens graduated from Peacham and entered Dartmouth College as a sophomore. Following his graduation from Dartmouth three years later, he spent one term and part of another at the University of Vermont. Having decided to practice law, Stevens began reading the law while at Vermont and then studied it under a local lawyer in Pennsylvania while teaching at an academy in York.

In 1816, Stevens passed his bar examinations in Maryland and returned to Pennsylvania, where he practiced law in Gettysburg and then in Lancaster. At first, he had to struggle to survive. Then, using a plea of insanity, he defended a man accused of murder. At that time, such a plea was almost unheard of. Stevens was eloquent, fiery, and aggressive, and the case made his reputation. From then until 1830, he appeared in almost every important case brought before the county bar. He also won almost every appeal he brought before the state supreme court. Additionally during this period, he became a partner in an iron business and became interested in protective tariffs.

Next Stevens turned to politics. In 1833, he was elected to the Pennsylvania House of Representatives as an Anti-Mason. With his strong convictions, talent for speaking, and unwillingness to compromise, he quickly made a name for himself. One piece of legislation he strongly advocated was an act that extended Philadelphia's free school system throughout the state. The act became law, but a year later, in 1835, an attempt was made to repeal the law. Determined to fight the appeal, Stevens presented a defense of free education that, according to some, "produced an effect second to no speech ever uttered in an American legislative assembly." Not only did Stevens's defense win over the House but it also led the Senate to reverse its position. Thanks to Stevens, Pennsylvania could boast free public education. By the time Stevens retired from the legislature in 1841, he had gained recognition as one of the strongest men in the state.

When he left the legislature, Stevens said he was quitting politics. Before long, however, the slavery issue drew him back into the political arena. He had always abhorred slavery. As a young lawyer he had had a practice of defending without fee runaway slaves, gaining freedom for many of them. As far as he was concerned, slavery was "a curse, a shame, and a crime." In 1848, he entered the Thirty-First Congress on the Whig ticket. But in 1853, after two terms, he quit the party and Congress, because they would not take a stronger stand on slavery. He stayed in politics, however, becoming a leading organizer of the Republican party in Pennsylvania.

In 1859, at the age of 67, Stevens was reelected to Congress, where he fought against the South's push to secede from the Union with unparalleled passion. As Chairman of the Ways and Means Committee, he had a great deal of power. During the Civil War, he secured huge appropriations for the Union forces. He also had paper money authorized as legal tender. His antagonism for biased white Southerners deepened even further in 1863 when, during an attack in Pennsylvania, Confederates burned down his ironworks. He made no effort to hide his hatred, proclaiming, "I look upon every man who would permit slavery . . . as a traitor to liberty and disloyal to God."

As a Radical Republican, Stevens opposed President Abraham Lincoln's (*see* Lincoln, Vol. 2, United States History: The Civil War) plan of Reconstruction as too moderate. As far as Stevens was concerned, the Southern states defeated in the Civil War were "conquered provinces" and should be treated as such. Nor was he pleased with President Andrew Johnson's plan for Reconstruction. Johnson further angered him when he refused to accept the Fourteenth Amendment, which Stevens had proposed. Stevens played a major role in the committee that drew up impeachment charges against Johnson. When the Senate voted against impeachment, a furious Stevens loudly proclaimed for all to hear that "the country is going to the devil."

Before Stevens died, he requested that he be buried in a cemetery for black people rather than in a burial ground closed to blacks. It was his way of showing in death "the principles which I advocated throughout a long life: equality of man before his Creator."

BOOKS ABOUT STEVENS

Callender, Edward B. *Thaddeus Stevens, Commoner.* AMS (repr of 1882 ed) $18.00. ISBN 0-404-00011-8
Kongold, Ralph. *Thaddeus Stevens.* Greenwood 1974 $35.00. ISBN 0-8371-7733-2
McCall, Samuel W. *Thaddeus Stevens. American Statesmen Ser: No. 31.* AMS (repr of 1899 ed) $32.50. ISBN 0-404-50881-2 In-depth study of the life, character, and politics of Stevens.

COMPARATIVE POLITICAL SYSTEMS

Brumberg, Abraham (ed). *Chronicle of a Revolution: A Western–Soviet Inquiry into Perestroika.* Pantheon 1990 $14.95. ISBN 0-678-72956-9
Dahl, Robert A. *Democracy and Its Critics.* Yale Univ Pr 1990 $29.95. ISBN 0-300-04409-7
Deutsch, Karl W., *et al. Comparative Government: Politics of Industrialized and Developing Nations.* Houghton 1981 $39.96. ISBN 0-395-29759-1
▪Ebenstein, William, and Edwin Fogelman. *Today's Isms: Communism, Fascism, Capitalism, and Socialism.* Prentice 1985 $29.00. ISBN 0-13-924473-5 Clear and easy to understand; widely used in high schools.
▪Leone, Bruno (ed). *Capitalism: Opposing Viewpoints. ISMS Book Ser.* Greenhaven 1986 $7.95. ISBN 0-89908-359-5 Collection of opposing views on capitalism.
▪Leone, Bruno (ed). *Communism: Opposing Viewpoints. ISMS Book Ser.* Greenhaven 1986 $7.95. ISBN 0-89908-360-9 Anthology of opinions on life and personal freedom under Communist rule and peaceful coexistence with the West.
▪Leone, Bruno (ed). *Socialism: Opposing Viewpoints. ISMS Book Ser.* Greenhaven 1986 $7.95. ISBN 0-89908-361-7 Anthology of viewpoints on Socialist thought and practice.
▪Medvedev, Roy, and Giulietto Chiesa. *Time of Change: An Inside View of Russia's Transforma-*

tion. Pantheon 1990 $24.95. ISBN 0-394-58151-2 Discussion of the progress and problems of perestroika.

■ Minzhu, Han (ed). *Cries for Democracy.* Princeton Univ Pr 1989 $12.95. ISBN 0-691-00857-4 Letters and other communications from those who took part in the democracy movement in China in 1989; intertwined with the social and political history of China.

■ Raynor, Thomas. *Politics, Power and People: Four Governments in Action. Single Title Ser.* Watts 1983 $12.90. ISBN 0-531-04662-1 Discusses the governments of Argentina, the Soviet Union, the United Kingdom, and the United States.

Sargent, Lyman T. *Contemporary Political Ideologies: A Comparative Analysis.* Brooks 1987 $23.75. ISBN 0-534-10822-9

Tocqueville, Alexis de. *Democracy in America* (1840). J. P. Mayer (ed). George Lawrence (tr). Harper 1988 $14.95. ISBN 0-06-091522-6

THE CONSTITUTION

* Adler, Mortimer J. *We Hold These Truths: Understanding the Ideas and Ideals of the Constitution.* Macmillan 1988 $6.95. ISBN 0-02-064130-3 A discussion of the ideas behind the U.S. Constitution and how these have been interpreted.

Agresto, John. *The Supreme Court and Constitutional Democracy.* Cornell Univ Pr 1984 $8.95. ISBN 0-8014-9277-7

■ American Political Science Association, American Historical Association, and Congressional Quarterly. *This Constitution: From Ratification to the Bill of Rights.* Congressional Quarterly 1988 $24.95. ISBN 0-87187-464-4 Explains the origins of the Bill of Rights and the legislation that has been enacted since to ensure those freedoms.

■ American Political Science Association, American Historical Association, and Congressional Quarterly. *This Constitution: Our Enduring Legacy.* Congressional Quarterly 1986 $24.95. ISBN 0-87187-396-6 Unique qualities of the Constitution detailed through relevant documents, ideas, and illustrations.

Beard, Charles A. *An Economic Interpretation of the Constitution of the United States.* Free Pr 1986 $10.95. ISBN 0-02-902480-3

■ Bowen, Catherine Drinker. *Miracle at Philadelphia: The Story of the Constitutional Convention, May to September 1787.* Little 1986 $8.95. ISBN 0-316-10378-0 Tells how delegates viewed the events of the convention; based on James Madison's records.

Cohen, Jeremy. *Congress Shall Make No Law: Oliver Wendell Holmes, the First Amendment and Judicial Decision-Making.* Iowa State Univ Pr 1989 $21.95. ISBN 0-8138-0022-6

Corwin, Edward S. *Edward S. Corwin's Constitution and What It Means Today.* Harold W. Chase and Craig R. Ducat (eds). Princeton Univ Pr 1979 $16.95. ISBN 0-691-02758-7

Elazar, Daniel J. *The American Constitutional Tradition.* Univ of Nebraska Pr 1988 $32.50. ISBN 0-8032-1813-3

Farrand, Max. *The Framing of the Constitution of the United States.* Yale Univ Pr 1962 $11.95. ISBN 0-300-00079-0

Friendly, Fred W., and Martha H. Elliott. *The Constitution: That Delicate Balance.* McGraw 1984 $14.50. ISBN 0-07-554612-4

■ Garraty, John (ed). *Quarrels That Have Shaped the Constitution.* Harper 1987 $22.95. ISBN 0-06-055062-7 Describes historic Supreme Court cases.

Grodzins, Morton. *The American System: A New View of Government in the United States. Political Theory Ser.* Daniel J. Elazar (ed). Transaction 1983 $24.95. ISBN 0-87855-916-7

Hamilton, Alexander, *et al. The Federalist Papers.* Bantam 1982 $3.50. ISBN 0-553-21072-6

Hentoff, Nat. *The First Freedom: The Tumultuous History of Free Speech in America.* Delacorte 1988 $16.95. ISBN 0-385-29643-6

Jensen, Merrill. *Articles of Confederation: An Interpretation of the Social Constitutional History of the American Revolution, 1774–1781.* Univ of Wisconsin Pr 1939 $13.50. ISBN 0-299-00204-7

Jensen, Merrill. *The Making of the American Constitution.* Krieger 1979 $7.50. ISBN 0-88275-904-3

Lieberman, Jethro Koller. *The Enduring Constitution: An Exploration of the First Two Hundred Years.* Harper 1987 $27.95. ISBN 0-06-015700-3

Lockard, Duane, and Walter F. Murphy. *Basic Cases in Constitutional Law.* Congressional Quarterly 1987 $12.95. ISBN 0-87187-428-8

* Morris, Richard B. *Witnesses at the Creation: Hamilton, Madison, Jay and the Constitution.* NAL 1989 $4.50. ISBN 0-451-62686-9 Discusses the role of these three men in the formulation of the Constitution.

Murphy, Walter F., *et al. American Constitutional Interpretation.* Foundation Pr 1986 $34.95. ISBN 0-88277-321-6

■ Preiss, Byron (ed). *Constitution: Keepsake Edition.* Bantam 1987 $9.95. ISBN 0-553-05202-0 Interpretation of the text of the Constitution by noted scholars.

Rembar, Charles. *The Laws of the Land: The Evolution of Our Legal System.* Harper 1989 $9.95. ISBN 0-06-097219-X

Rossiter, Clinton. *Seventeen Eighty-Seven: The Grand Convention.* Norton 1987 $9.70. ISBN 0-393-30404-3

■ Schwartz, Bernard (ed). *The Roots of the Bill of Rights: An Illustrated Source Book of American Freedom.* 5 vols. Chelsea 1981 $85.00. ISBN 0-87754-207-4 Examines the origin of the Bill of Rights.

■ Smith, Edward C., and Harold J. Spaeth (eds). *The Constitution of the United States: Bicentennial Edition.* Harper 1987 $5.95. ISBN 0-06-460209-5 Special edition of the Constitution.

Smith, Page. *The Constitution: A Documentary and Narrative History.* Morrow 1978 $15.95. ISBN 0-688-08349-8

Tribe, Laurence H. *Constitutional Choices.* Harvard Univ Pr 1986 $10.95. ISBN 0-674-16539-X

■ Van Doren, Carl. *The Great Rehearsal: The Story of the Making and Ratifying of the Constitution of the United States.* Penguin 1986 $6.95. ISBN 0-14-008965-9 Classic description of the history of the Constitution; well worth reading.

Wood, Gordon S. *The Creation of the American Republic, 1776–1787.* Norton 1972 $10.95. ISBN 0-393-00644-1

Wood, Gordon S. *The Making of the Constitution.* Baylor Univ Pr 1987 $4.50. ISBN 0-918954-49-5

LOCKE, JOHN 1632–1704

John Locke was an English philosopher who was educated at Christ Church College, Oxford, where he later lectured in Greek, rhetoric, and philosophy. He also studied medicine, which strongly influenced his philosophical thought. In the realm of philosophy, Locke founded the school of British empiricism, which held that the mind is a *tabula rasa,* a blank slate, upon which all knowledge is written through experience. This was in direct contrast to the belief of rationalists, who held that humans were born with certain ideas such as Truth, Beauty, and Justice already in their minds. Locke's empiricist theories were published in 1690 in a work entitled *An Essay Concerning Human Understanding.*

Locke is best known for his political theory. He disputed the doctrine of the divine right of kings, which holds that kings and queens are given the right to rule by God and that to rebel against them is to sin. In his view, governments depend on the consent of the governed. In this realm, his major contribution is *Two Treatises on Civil Government* (1690), which contains a loosely presented theory of government and an analysis of the relationship of the individual to the state. Locke stressed the origin of the state as a mutual contract among people. A sovereign people, he said, may alter the terms of this social contract to meet changing conditions.

Locke also believed that the natural state of humans was one of happiness and that reason and tolerance were primary human characteristics. He saw people as equal and free to pursue the inalienable rights of "life, health, liberty, and possessions." Believing in this form of social contract, Locke believed that the state was guided by natural law and that the natural law guaranteed these rights.

In his writings, Locke described a set of checks and balances on government that were eventually incorporated into the U.S. Constitution. Among Locke's other positions was a belief that revolution under some circumstances is just and that everyone should be guaranteed religious freedom.

Locke's influence on philosophy and political theory can hardly be overestimated. He influenced much of the social, economic, and political thought of the eighteenth century, including that of the founders of the new nation of the United States. With their belief in the middle class and human goodness and their reliance on the new science, Locke's theories are integral to the intellectual movement of the seventeenth and eighteenth centuries known as the Enlightenment.

BOOKS BY LOCKE

An Essay Concerning Human Understanding (1690). Alexander C. Fraser (ed). 2 vols. Peter Smith $37.50. ISBN 0-8446-2478-0

Two Treatises on Civil Government (1690). Peter Laslett (ed). *Cambridge Texts in the History of Political Thought Ser.* Cambridge Univ Pr 1988 $7.95. ISBN 0-521-35730-6

The Works of John Locke. Select Bibliographic Reprint Ser. 2 vols. Ayer 1977 $56.00. ISBNs 0-8369-9980-0, 0-8369-9981-9

BOOKS ABOUT LOCKE

Cranston, Maurice. *John Locke: A Biography.* Oxford Univ Pr 1985 $12.95. ISBN 0-19-283044-9 Complete biography beginning with his childhood and education and covering his works and later years.

Dunn, John. *Locke. Past Masters Ser.* Oxford Univ Pr 1984 $5.95. ISBN 0-19-287560-4 Restoration of Locke's theory of knowledge to its proper context, showing why he reached his conclusions and had such a profound impact on later thinkers.

Grant, Ruth W. *John Locke's Liberalism.* Univ of Chicago Pr 1987 $24.95. ISBN 0-226-30607-0 Study challenging prevailing contemporary interpretations of Locke's political thought.

Squadrito, Kathleen M. *John Locke.* Twayne 1979. ISBN 0-8057-6772-X Clear introduction to Locke's life and writings as well as his thought on religion, ethics, education, and political and social philosophy.

MONTESQUIEU, CHARLES LOUIS DE SECONDAT, BARON DE LA BREDE ET DE   1689–1755

Charles Louis de Secondat, Baron de la Brède et de Montesquieu, was a French philosopher, jurist, and political theorist. He is considered the most important precursor of sociology, the founder of modern historical research, and the first modern political scientist.

The Spirit of the Laws (1748), in which he defended the principle of separation of powers, is considered Montesquieu's masterpiece. On the surface, the work is a treatise on law, but it also describes every domain affecting human behavior and raises questions of philosophical judgment about the merits of various kinds of legislation. Montesquieu believed that government should be separated into legislative, executive, and judicial branches to safeguard the freedom of the individual. This separation and balance of powers was later written into the U.S. Constitution.

The Spirit of the Laws also describes three types of government—republic, monarchy, and despotism—and their principles. According to Montesquieu, virtue is the principle of republics, honor is the principle of monarchies, and fear is the principle of despotism. With these "ideal types" as starting points, Montesquieu goes on to analyze legislation and the state in great detail.

Montesquieu made comparative studies the central method of his political science, and thus, he directed the focus of inquiry from Europe to all societies of the world. His direct influence on the social sciences has been enormous.

BOOK BY MONTESQUIEU

The Spirit of the Laws (1748). Anne M. Cohler, *et al* (eds). *Cambridge Texts in the History of Political Thought Ser.* Cambridge Univ Pr 1989 $16.95. ISBN 0-521-36974-6

BOOKS ABOUT MONTESQUIEU

Cohler, Anne M. *Montesquieu's Comparative Politics and the Spirit of American Constitutionalism.* Univ Pr of Kansas 1988 $22.50. ISBN 0-7006-0376-X Study showing the importance of Montesquieu's teaching for modern legislation and modern political prudence, with specific reference to his impact on *The Federalist* and Tocqueville, suggesting new ways to think about the formation of the constitution.

Hulliung, Mark. *Montesquieu and the Old Regime.* Univ of California Pr 1977 $42.50. ISBN 0-520-03108-3 Argues that Montesquieu vigorously attacked the old social order, drawing on all Montesquieu's writings and his relationship to other thinkers.

Pangle, Thomas L. *Montesquieu's Philosophy of Liberalism: A Commentary on the Spirit of the Laws.* Univ of Chicago Pr 1989 $14.95. ISBN 0-226-64545-2 First comprehensive commentary on *The Spirit of the Laws,* with an attempt to uncover and explicate the plan and reasons for the obscurity of Montesquieu's famous but baffling treatise.

See also Vol. 2, United States History: The United States Constitution.

ETHICS IN POLITICS

Benjamin, Martin. *Splitting the Difference: Compromise and Integrity in Ethics and Politics.* Univ Pr of Kansas 1990 $12.95. ISBN 0-7006-0455-3

Bowman, James S., and Frederick A. Elliston (eds). *Ethics, Government, and Public Policy: A Reference Guide.* Greenwood 1988 $55.00. ISBN 0-313-25912-4

Gutmann, Amy, and Dennis Thompson (eds). *Ethics and Politics: Cases and Comments.* Nelson 1984 $14.95. ISBN 0-8304-1115-1

Johnson, Peter. *Politics, Innocence and the Limits of Goodness.* Routledge 1989 $35.00. ISBN 0-415-01046-2

Lappe, Frances M. *Rediscovering America's Values.* Ballantine 1989 $22.50. ISBN 0-345-32040-9

*Matthews, Christopher. *Hardball: How Politics Is Played—Told by One Who Knows the Game.* Summit Bks 1988 $17.95. ISBN 0-671-63160-8 An informal account of the devices used by various politicians to forward their careers.

Perry, Michael J. *Morality, Politics and Law: A Bicentennial Essay.* Oxford Univ Pr 1988 $29.95. ISBN 0-19-505296-X
Regan, Richard J. *The Moral Dimensions of Politics.* Oxford Univ Pr 1986 $13.95. ISBN 0-19-503975-0

MACHIAVELLI, NICCOLO   1469–1527

Niccolò Machiavelli was an Italian political philosopher, military theorist, civil servant, historian, playwright, and poet who lived during the Renaissance and Golden Age of Florence. His major work, *The Prince* (1532), dedicated to Lorenzo de Medici, the ruler of Florence, advises rulers to use cunning and ruthlessness to retain their power.

In *The Prince,* Machiavelli sought to discern an order in the nature of political activity itself, not in some external cause. He examines politics in a modern, detached, and rational manner, analyzing the ways power is gained and held. He demonstrates the soundness of certain political rules and principles by using a kind of calculus to test them.

Precisely because of the objectivity of his descriptions of the political process and of how power is obtained and held, Machiavelli is often thought of as a kind of evil adviser to princes. In fact, the term "Machiavellian," which means shrewd, scheming, and cynical, remains in use today to refer to a leader who puts political goals before moral principle.

These precepts, however, do not describe Machiavelli as a person. Machiavelli believed in the republic, a form of government in which many people have a voice. His love of liberty and his republican values are unquestioned. After entering Florence's political service in 1498, he rose quickly to the position of defense secretary and instituted reform. After the Medici came to power, he was imprisoned and tortured for allegedly conspiring against them. While Machiavelli described the corrupt state of Florence, he was not corrupt himself. He was critical of the popes and their political activities, but he was born and died a Christian. His writings are controversial to this day, but he is viewed by many as a forerunner of the Enlightenment, the intellectual movement of the seventeenth and eighteenth centuries, and as the first modern political scientist.

BOOKS BY MACHIAVELLI

The Art of War (1521). Peter Whitehorne (tr). AMS 1967 repr of 1905 ed $45.00. ISBN 0-404-51951-2
The Discourses (1532). Bernard Crick (ed). Penguin 1984 $4.95. ISBN 0-14-044428-9
The Prince (1532). Leo P. DeAlvarez (tr). Waveland 1989 $5.95. ISBN 0-88133-444-8

BOOKS ABOUT MACHIAVELLI

Ridolfi, Roberto. *The Life of Niccolò Machiavelli.* Univ of Chicago Pr 1963. (o.p.) Sympathetic biography of a real man in a historical environment.
Skinner, Quentin. *Machiavelli. Past Masters Ser.* Oxford Univ Pr 1981 $4.95. ISBN 0-19-287516-7 Focuses on *The Prince, Discourses,* and *The History of Florence,* providing a brief survey of Machiavelli's life and writing and questioning whether his sinister reputation is really deserved.

THE FEDERAL EXECUTIVE BRANCH

Beard, Charles A., and Detlev Vagts. *Presidents in American History.* Jane Steltenpohl (ed). Messner 1989 $5.95. ISBN 0-671-68575-9

Buchan, Bruce. *The Citizen's Presidency: Standards of Choice and Judgment.* Congressional Quarterly 1987 $12.95. ISBN 0-87187-398-2

Corwin, Edward S. *The President: Office and Powers.* New York Univ Pr 1984 $22.50. ISBN 0-8147-1391-2

■DeGregorio, William A. *The Complete Book of United States Presidents.* Dembner 1989 $29.95. ISBN 0-942637-17-8 Facts about U.S. Presidents.

Edwards, George C., III. *The Public Presidency: The Pursuit of Popular Support.* St. Martin's 1983 $17.35. ISBN 0-312-65564-9

Goehlert, Robert (comp). *The Executive Branch of the United States Government: A Bibliography. Bibliographies and Indexes in Law and Political Science Ser.* Greenwood 1988 $49.95. ISBN 0-313-26568-2

Goehlert, Robert, and Fenton S. Martin. *The Presidency: A Research Guide.* ABC–Clio 1985 $35.00. ISBN 0-87436-373-X

Goldstein, Joel K. *The Modern American Vice Presidency: The Transformation of a Political Institution.* Princeton Univ Pr 1981 $12.50. ISBN 0-691-02208-9

■Halberstam, David. *The Best and the Brightest.* Penguin 1983 $9.95. ISBN 0-14-006983-6 Study of the society, political power, and decision-making process that led the United States into the war in Vietnam.

Kessler, Francis P. *The Dilemmas of Presidential Leadership: Of Caretakers and Kings.* Prentice 1982. (o.p.) ISBN 0-13-214593-6

■King, Anthony (ed). *Both Ends of the Avenue: The Presidency, the Executive Branch and Congress in the 1980s.* Am Enterprise Inst 1983 $13.25. ISBN 0-8447-3497-7 Political workings of government in the 1980s.

Lowi, Theodore J. *The Personal President: Power Invested, Promise Unfulfilled.* Cornell Univ Pr 1985 $8.95. ISBN 0-8014-9426-5

Lyons, Thomas T. (ed). *The President: Preacher, Teacher, Salesman: Selected Presidential Speeches, 1933–1983.* World Eagle 1985 $11.95. ISBN 0-9608014-4-8

Roberts, Paul C. *The Supply-Side Revolution: An Insider's Account of Policymaking in Washington.* Harvard Univ Pr 1985 $9.95. ISBN 0-674-85621-X

Schlesinger, Arthur M. *The Imperial Presidency.* Houghton 1989 $12.95. ISBN 0-395-51561-0

Sorensen, Theodore C. *Decision-Making in the White House: The Olive Branch or the Olives.* Columbia Univ Pr 1963 $12.50. ISBN 0-231-08550-8

■Sorensen, Theodore C. *Let the Word Go Forth: The Speeches, Statements, and Writing of John F. Kennedy, 1946–1963.* Delacorte 1988 $25.00. ISBN 0-440-50041-9 Notable words and works of the former President.

Sorensen, Theodore C. *Watchmen in the Night: Presidential Accountability After Watergate.* MIT Pr 1975 $24.00. ISBN 0-262-19133-4

■White, Theodore H. *The Making of the President, Nineteen Sixty: A Narrative History of American Politics in Action.* Macmillan 1988 $8.95. ISBN 0-689-70803-3 Inside account of the 1960 presidential campaign, written by a noted journalist.

■White, Theodore H. *The Making of the President, Nineteen Sixty-Four.* Macmillan 1965 $10.00. ISBN 0-689-10292-5 Inside account of the 1964 presidential campaign written by a noted journalist.

■White, Theodore H. *The Making of the President, Nineteen Sixty-Eight.* Atheneum 1972. (o.p.) $10.00. ISBN 0-689-10293-3 Inside account of the 1968 presidential campaign written by a noted journalist.

■White, Theodore H. *The Making of the President, Nineteen Seventy-Two.* Macmillan 1973 $10.00. ISBN 0-689-10553-3 Inside account of the 1972 presidential campaign written by a noted journalist.

■White, Theodore H. *The Making of the President, Nineteen Seventy-Six.* Atheneum 1977. (o.p.) Inside account of the 1976 presidential campaign.

■Woodward, Bob, and Carl Bernstein. *All the President's Men.* Simon 1987 $6.95. ISBN 0-671-64644-3 Nonfiction account of the 1972 Watergate scandal.

■Woodward, Bob, and Carl Bernstein. *Final Days.* Simon 1989 $8.95. ISBN 0-671-69087-6 Story of the proposed impeachment and eventual resignation of President Richard M. Nixon.

DULLES, JOHN FOSTER 1888–1959

Born in Washington, DC to a family with a strong diplomatic tradition, John Foster Dulles received his early education in the public schools of Watertown, New York. He went on to graduate from Princeton University; attend the Sorbonne in Paris, France; and receive a law degree from George Washington University in Washington, DC. After being admitted to the bar in 1911, he joined a prestigious New York law firm.

In 1917, Dulles was a special agent for the Department of State in Central America. That same year and the next, he also served as an officer in the U.S. Army Intelligence Service and as an assistant to the chairman of the War Trade Board. He was only 30 years old when President Woodrow Wilson (*see* Wilson, Vol. 2, United States History: World War I) sought his services as counsel to the United States delegation to the 1919 Paris Peace Conference at Versailles. There, he was an adviser to the president and the principal U.S. spokesperson on the Reparations Committee.

By the end of the war, Dulles was a highly prominent international lawyer and was invited to take part in a number of the international conferences that marked the period between World War I and World War II. Both during that time and after the Japanese attack on Pearl Harbor, he served on a number of unofficial diplomatic missions. In 1945, Dulles was appointed adviser to the U.S. delegation at the San Francisco Conference on World Organization. After helping to draft the charter for the United Nations, he went on to serve as a delegate to the organization's General Assembly, and, in 1948, he headed the U.S. delegation in Paris.

In 1949, when Senator Robert F. Wagner of New York resigned his Senate seat, Dulles, also a Republican, was appointed to finish Wagner's term of office. The following year he sought to win the Senate seat in a general election. When he failed to do so, he turned again to the international arena as a U.S. representative to the Fifth General Assembly of the United Nations.

In 1951, another U.S. President, Harry S Truman (*see* Truman, Vol. 2, United States History: World War II), sought out Dulles, awarding him sufficient rank to help negotiate the 1951 peace treaty with Japan. Two years later, on January 20, 1953, President Dwight D. Eisenhower (*see* Eisenhower, Vol. 2, United States History: Postwar Foreign and Domestic Policy) appointed Dulles Secretary of State. Several years later, Eisenhower was to proclaim him "one of our greatest secretaries of state."

As Secretary of State, Dulles engaged in a diplomacy of personal conferences with statesmen of other nations. By the time 1954 had drawn to a close, he had traveled close to 180,000 miles, visited more than 40 countries, and signed numerous treaties and agreements. Strongly opposed to communism, Dulles thought it was not enough to just "contain" Soviet aggression. He believed instead in a policy of "brinkmanship" and in the threat of "massive retaliation." As he saw it, "If you are scared to the brink [of war] you are lost." His idea was to seek an advantage by creating the impression that the United States and its allies were willing and able to pass the brink of nuclear war rather than give in to Soviet attack or aggression. This policy led, among other things, to the launching of the concept of the Southeast Treaty Organization (SEATO), to the strengthening of the North Atlantic Treaty Organization (NATO), and to the Eisenhower Doctrine, which afforded economic and military aid to maintain the independence of Middle Eastern countries.

On April 18, 1959, the cancer from which he had been suffering for more than a year finally forced Dulles to resign his position as Secretary of State. He died five weeks later in Washington, DC and was buried in Arlington National Cemetery. Shortly before his death, he was awarded his nation's highest civil decoration—the Medal of Freedom.

BOOK BY DULLES

Collected Articles and Speeches. Richard Challener (ed). 5 vols. Meckler 1990 $650.00. ISBN 0-88736-671-6

BOOKS ABOUT DULLES

*Finke, Blythe F. *John Foster Dulles: Master of Brinkmanship and Diplomacy. Outstanding Personalities Ser.: No. 10.* SamHar 1972 $2.50. ISBN 0-87157-010-6 Concentrated biographical sketch of Dulles with bibliographical references; ideal for high school students.

Immerman, Richard H. (ed). *John Foster Dulles and the Diplomacy of the Cold War.* Princeton Univ Pr 1990 $29.95. ISBN 0-691-04765-0

Prussen, Ronald W. *John Foster Dulles: The Road to Power.* Free Pr 1982 $19.95. ISBN 0-02-925460-4 Definitive biography of the controversial secretary of state that concentrates on Dulles's life before entry into formal diplomacy.

JORDAN, BARBARA CHARLINE   1936–

In 1972 Barbara Jordan became the first African-American woman to be elected to the U.S. Congress from a southern state. Born in Houston, Texas, the daughter of a Baptist minister, as a girl Jordan considered becoming a pharmacist. "But whoever heard of an outstanding pharmacist?" she later asked. One day while at high school, she heard an address by an African-American lawyer from Chicago. From that day on, she knew that she wanted to become a lawyer. After graduating from Texas Southern University, she received a law degree from Boston University in 1959.

In a few years Jordan scraped up enough money to open her own law office. At the same time, she worked as an administrative assistant to a county judge and became active in Democratic party politics. After two unsuccessful bids for a seat in the Texas House of Representatives, Jordan was elected to the state senate in 1966. An effective legislator, she sponsored the state's first minimum wage law to include farmworkers and others not covered by federal wage standards. She also supported legislation to end discrimination and to deal with environmental problems.

After a second term in the state senate, Jordan decided to run for national office. In the 1972 election, she trounced her Republican challenger to win a seat in the U.S. House of Representatives. As a Congresswoman, Jordan backed legislation to raise the standard of living of poor Americans. In other domestic areas, she voted for increased aid to elementary and secondary schools and for the continuation of the national school lunch program. "My approach," she said, "is to respect the humanity of everybody. Their position on anything is not relevant to the way I can relate to them as a human being. *That* we have in common."

As a member of the House Judiciary Committee, Jordan gained national attention in 1974 when she approved articles of impeachment against President Richard M. Nixon. (*See* Nixon, Vol. 2, United States History: The Nixon and

Ford Years.) The Watergate affair, she later said, "was a cleansing experience" for the political process.

Not only was Jordan a brilliant thinker, she also was an eloquent speaker. In 1976 she electrified the Democratic convention with her keynote address. After being reelected twice to Congress, Jordan choose not to run for office in 1976. Instead she accepted a teaching position at the Lyndon B. Johnson School of Public Affairs at the University of Texas.

BOOK BY JORDAN

Local Government Election Systems. (coauthored with Terrell Blodgett) LBJ Sch Pub Aff 1984 $8.95. ISBN 0-89940-664-5

PERKINS, FRANCES 1882–1965

Frances Perkins was born in Boston, the daughter of a classical scholar and businessman. After graduating from Mount Holyoke College in Massachusetts, she was offered a job as an analytical chemist. But Perkins soon decided that her interests lay elsewhere, and she moved to New York City to become a social worker. Her goal, she said, was to improve the working conditions of women and children.

In 1911 Perkins witnessed the Triangle Shirtwaist Company fire in which 146 girls and young women were killed. She never forgot it. For the next six years, as a member of the New York Committee of Safety, she devoted much of her time to safety legislation. There she became an expert on industrial hazards and hygiene. She also began lobbying in Albany for more comprehensive factory laws and for maximum hour laws for women.

In 1919 Perkins was appointed to the New York State Industrial Board, and she later served as its chairman. During those years, she succeeded in getting state laws passed that shortened working hours for women, limited child labor, and improved working conditions in factories. When Franklin Delano Roosevelt (*see* F. Roosevelt, Vol. 2, United States History: The Great Depression and the New Deal) became governor of New York in 1929, he made Perkins Industrial Commissioner of the state. Her job was to direct the enforcement of factory and labor laws.

When Roosevelt was elected President of the United States in 1933, one of his first acts was to appoint Frances Perkins Secretary of Labor, making her the first woman to ever serve in the Cabinet. Although her appointment was bitterly criticized by business and political leaders alike, Perkins accomplished a great deal in her new job. For example, she helped shape key New Deal programs, including the Social Security Act of 1935. She also continued her efforts to help American workers on the national level by advocating higher wages and improved working conditions.

During her busy career, Perkins traveled and lectured in many parts of the country. She also wrote several books, including *The Roosevelt I Knew* (1946). After Roosevelt's death, she served as a member of the Civil Service Commission under President Harry Truman. (*See* Truman, Vol. 2, United States History: World War II.)

BOOK BY PERKINS

The Roosevelt I Knew (1946). Viking 1947. (o.p.)

BOOK ABOUT PERKINS

Mohr, Lillian H. *Frances Perkins: That Woman in FDR's Cabinet!* North River 1979 $18.00. ISBN 0-88427-019-X Illustrated biography of the life of Frances Perkins.

RUSK, DEAN (DAVID)   1909–

Educator, military commander, and statesman, Dean Rusk was born in Cherokee County, Georgia. His father was an ordained Presbyterian minister and his mother a former schoolteacher. According to one of Rusk's siblings, "We were under constant admonition to excel, to go out in the world and do something. . . . We were always striving for excellence."

When the young Rusk entered school in the second grade, he already knew how to read. A student who almost always received A's, he graduated from Boys' High School in Atlanta, Georgia, in 1925. After graduation, he worked for several years in a law office to earn money for college. He continued to work—at a bank for money to support himself and at a boardinghouse for his meals—while he attended Davidson College in North Carolina, where he majored in politics. This heavy load, however, did not stop him from graduating *magna cum laude* or from taking part in extracurricular activities, including managing the student store, serving as president of the YMCA, and playing varsity basketball. Winner of a Rhodes scholarship upon his graduation in 1931, he went to England to study politics, philosophy, and economics at Oxford University. In addition to earning a bachelor of science degree and a masters degree while there, he won the Cecil Peace Prize for an essay he wrote on international relations.

In 1934, Rusk returned to the United States. After teaching political science for four years at Mills College in Oakland, California, he was appointed dean of the faculty. During the time he was at Mills, he also studied law at the University of California at Berkeley.

In 1940, Rusk joined the U.S. Army. For the services he rendered the military at home and overseas, he was awarded the Legion of Merit and the French Legion of Honor. Discharged in 1946, he entered the State Department as assistant chief of the division of international security affairs. Then he was invited to head the office of special political affairs, where he soon found himself confronted with the many problems created by the establishment of the state of Israel in 1948. By 1949, Rusk had a new title—Assistant Secretary of State for United Nations Affairs. He was the first person to hold that office.

By early 1950, Rusk was named Assistant Secretary of State for Far Eastern Affairs. As Assistant Secretary, he played a major role in the shaping of United States policy during the Korean War. Firmly believing that the way to prevent Soviet aggression in the Far East was to intervene in Korea, he helped formulate the policy that led to U.S. military intervention in the Korean War.

In March 1952, Rusk left government office to serve as president of the Rockefeller Foundation in New York City. During the eight years he held that position, the Foundation distributed about $250 million for a number of different projects, including aid to the developing nations of Latin America, Asia, and Africa.

In 1961, Rusk returned to government service as the nation's fifty-fifth Secretary of State. According to President John F. Kennedy (*see* J. F. Kennedy, Vol. 2, United States History: The Turbulent Sixties), Rusk was the ideal person for the Cabinet office because he brought with him "the long view of the student of world affairs, the concern for peace shared by all those who have known war at first hand, and a practical working experience in the conduct of our foreign relations." Rusk remained in office during the presidency of Lyndon B. Johnson. (*See* Johnson, Vol. 2, United States History: The Turbulent Sixties.)

As Secretary of State during a highly critical period for American foreign policy, Rusk found himself faced with crises all over the world, from Southeast

Asia to Africa to Europe. He believed in "quiet diplomacy"—private negotiation by trained diplomats rather than publicized personal contact between heads of state. He pushed for economic aid to developing countries and saw low tariffs as a way to encourage world trade. In 1963, he came out in favor of the nuclear test ban treaty with the Soviet Union. A firm believer in the use of military force to prevent Communist expansion, Rusk was a strong defender of the Vietnam War.

In 1969, Rusk left public office and returned to the academic world as a professor of international law at the University of Georgia.

BOOKS BY RUSK

As I Saw It (1990). Norton 1990 $29.95. ISBN 0-393-02650-7
Dean Rusk: A Seventy-Fifth Birthday Celebration—A Commemorative Record (1984). (coauthored with others) Univ of Georgia School of Foreign Service 1984 $3.00. ISBN 0-934742-29-4

BOOK ABOUT RUSK

Cohen, Warren I. *Dean Rusk. The American Secretaries of State and Their Diplomacy: Vol. XIX.* Cooper Square 1980 $33.50. ISBN 0-8154-0519-7

See also Vol. 2, United States History, *for individual presidents, their policies, and their administrations.*

THE FEDERAL JUDICIAL SYSTEM

Ackerman, Bruce. *Reconstructing American Law.* Harvard Univ Pr 1984 $8.95. ISBN 0-674-75016-0
Agresto, John. *The Supreme Court and Constitutional Democracy.* Cornell Univ Pr 1984 $8.95. ISBN 0-8014-9277-7
▪Baum, Lawrence. *The Supreme Court.* Congressional Quarterly 1988 $17.95. ISBN 0-87187-495-4 Easy-to-understand explanation of all aspects of the Court.
Brandeis, Louis. *Letters of Louis D. Brandeis.* Melvin I. Urofsky and David W. Levy (eds). Vol. 4 *1916–1921: Mr. Justice Brandeis.* SUNY 1975 $49.50. ISBN 0-87395-297-9
*Carp, Robert A., and Ronald Stidham. *The Federal Courts.* Congressional Quarterly 1990 $17.95. ISBN 0-87187-580-2 A clear introduction to the three levels of the federal judiciary.
Cohen, Jeremy. *Congress Shall Make No Law: Oliver Wendell Holmes, the First Amendment and Judicial Decision-Making.* Iowa State Univ Pr 1989 $21.95. ISBN 0-8138-0022-6
▪Congressional Quarterly. *Guide to the U.S. Supreme Court.* Congressional Quarterly 1979 $95.00. ISBN 0-87187-184-X Classic reference work on the Supreme Court.
Cox, Archibald. *Warren Court: Constitutional Decision as an Instrument of Reform.* Harvard Univ Pr 1968 $5.95. ISBN 0-674-94742-8
▪Garraty, John (ed). *Quarrels That Have Shaped the Constitution.* Harper 1987 $22.95. ISBN 0-06-055062-7 Describes historic Supreme Court cases.
Jacob, Herbert. *Justice in America: Courts, Lawyers, and the Judicial Process.* Scott 1984. (o.p.) $14.95. ISBN 0-673-39447-6
▪Joseph, Joel D. *Black Mondays: Worst Decisions of the Supreme Court.* National Pr 1987 $17.95. ISBN 0-915765-44-6 Description of 24 of the worst decisions by the Court, including internment of Japanese Americans during World War II.

* O'Brien, David M. *Storm Center: The Supreme Court in American Politics.* Norton 1986 $18.95. ISBN 0-393-02330-3 An inside look at how the Supreme Court operates and its day-to-day problems.
* Rehnquist, William H. *The Supreme Court: The Way It Was—the Way It Is.* Morrow 1987 $18.95. ISBN 0-688-0571404 The history of the Supreme Court and prominent justices written by a justice.

Simon, James F. *Independent Journey: The Life of William O. Douglas.* Penguin 1981 $6.95. ISBN 0-14-005982-2

Stephens, Otis H., and Gregory Rathjen. *The Supreme Court and the Allocation of Constitutional Powers.* Freeman 1980 $19.95. ISBN 0-7167-1218-0

Taney, Roger B. *Memoir of Roger B. Taney: Chief Justice of the Supreme Court of the United States. Law, Politics, and History Ser.* Samuel Tyler (ed). Da Capo 1970 $65.00. ISBN 0-306-71688-7

Tribe, Laurence H. *God Save This Honorable Court: How the Choice of Supreme Court Justices Shapes Our History.* NAL 1986 $4.50. ISBN 0-451-62527-7

Wilkinson, J. Harvie. *From Brown to Bakke: The Supreme Court and School Integration 1954– 1978.* Oxford Univ Pr 1979 $9.95. ISBN 0-19-502897-X

* Witt, Elder. *The Supreme Court and Individual Rights.* Congressional Quarterly 1988 $17.95. ISBN 0-87187-465-2 Explains case decisions and how they apply to citizens' rights.
* Woodward, Bob, and Scott Armstrong. *The Brethren: Inside the Supreme Court.* Avon 1981 $5.95. ISBN 0-381-52183-0 Describes the workings of the Supreme Court in the early to mid-1970s.

FRANKFURTER, FELIX 1882–1965

American jurist Felix Frankfurter was born into a cultured Jewish family in Vienna, Austria and did not come to the United States until he was 12 years old. Although he did not know one word of English when he arrived in America, eight years later he graduated third in his class from the City College of New York. Just a few years after that—in 1906—Frankfurter graduated from Harvard Law School with highest honors. After graduation, he went to New York, where for four years he served as assistant to Henry L. Stimson, the U.S. attorney for the southern district of New York. He spent the next three years as a legal officer in the Bureau of Insular Affairs.

In 1914, Frankfurter, a strong advocate of social justice and civil rights and liberties, joined the law faculty of Harvard University. During his 25-year tenure at Harvard, he was involved in various activities outside the academic world as well. In 1919, he went to the Paris Peace Conference as legal adviser to President Woodrow Wilson. (*See* Wilson, Vol. 2, United States History: World War I.) Around the same time, he helped found the American Civil Liberties Union (ACLU) and *The New Republic.* He also fought for the rights of Nicola Sacco and Bartolomeo Vanzetti, two Italian immigrants accused of murdering a paymaster during a robbery in Massachusetts. Many people believed that Sacco and Vanzetti had been found guilty and sentenced to be executed only because they were immigrants and anarchists. One of these people was Frankfurter. Protesting the scheduled executions, he argued that the men were being punished not for murder but for their "alien blood and abhorrent philosophy."

Frankfurter held other important posts during this period as well—legal adviser on industrial problems to the Secretary of War, first secretary and then counsel to the President's Mediation Commission, chairman of the War Labor Policies Board, and behind-the-scenes adviser to President Franklin Delano Roosevelt. (*See* F. Roosevelt, Vol. 2, United States History: The Great Depression and the New Deal.) At the same time, Frankfurter became one of

America's leading constitutional scholars and wrote books and articles about the Supreme Court and its work.

On January 30, 1939, President Roosevelt appointed Frankfurter Associate Justice of the U.S. Supreme Court. Roosevelt had hoped that Frankfurter would strengthen the liberal element among the justices of the Court. But while Frankfurter tended to be liberal and cared a great deal about fair legal procedure, he also believed strongly in judicial restraint. In his view, Congress and state legislatures represented the will of the people. He did not think that government by judges was a good substitute for government by the people. He felt that the Court should show self-restraint when exercising its powers to declare laws unconstitutional. He thought the Court must avoid substituting its members' ideas of wise social policy for those of the Congress and state legislatures. As a justice, he tended to rule against the Congress or institutions of the State only when an individual's basic rights were challenged. Because he so often showed great impartiality and took such care not to intrude on the political processes of democratic government, he came to be considered more conservative than liberal. In time, he became known as the leader of the conservative wing of the Court.

Frankfurter remained on the bench until 1962, when ill health forced him to retire. Three years later, he died in Washington, DC.

BOOKS BY FRANKFURTER

The Commerce Clause Under Marshall, Taney, and Waite (1937). Peter Smith $11.25. ISBN 0-8446-2086-6
Felix Frankfurter Reminisces (1960). Greenwood 1978 $35.00. ISBN 0-313-20466-7
Law and Politics (1939). Peter Smith $11.25. ISBN 0-8446-0097-0
The Labor Injunction. (coauthored with Nathan Greene) Peter Smith 1963 $12.75. ISBN 0-8446-1190-5

BOOKS ABOUT FRANKFURTER

Baker, Leonard. *Brandeis and Frankfurter: A Dual Biography.* New York Univ Pr 1986 $15.00. ISBN 0-8147-1086-7 Highly readable account of Frankfurter and Louis Brandeis, close friends and supreme court justices who helped shape American life for nearly half a century.
Simon, James F. *The Antagonists: Hugo Black, Felix Frankfurter and Civil Liberties in Modern America.* Simon 1989 $19.95. ISBN 0-671-47797-8 Examines the relationship between two brilliant supreme court justices—Black and Frankfurter—and their polarization of the Supreme Court.

HOLMES, OLIVER WENDELL, JR.   1841–1935

Oliver Wendell Holmes, Mr. Justice Holmes, the American jurist, was born in Boston, the son of the author Oliver Wendell Holmes. (*See* Holmes, Vol. 1, American Literature: Romanticism and the American Renaissance.) He received his bachelor's degree from Harvard University in 1861 and earned his law degree from Harvard in 1866. He served with distinction in the Union army in the Civil War. He was then in succession professor of law at Harvard Law School, justice and then chief justice of the Massachusetts Supreme Court, and associate justice of the U.S. Supreme Court (1902–1932).

In addition to letters, diaries, speeches, and judicial decisions, Holmes wrote *The Common Law* (1881), which earned him international recognition for his attack on contemporary views of jurisprudence. For Holmes, the law was a social instrument rather than a set of abstract principles. The *Dissenting Opinions of Mr. Justice Holmes* are masterpieces of clear, forceful legal writing. Many of his dissenting opinions earned him the title "the great dissenter." This title was in honor of the significance of his dissenting opinions, rather than the number of dissents. For example, in *Abrams* v. *United States* (1919), Holmes wrote a forceful dissent in defense of free speech. In his view, freedom of speech must be allowed except when it presents a "clear and present danger"—when the public interest is faced with immediate threat.

Holmes often found himself in disagreement with more conservative Court members over upholding social legislation. Despite this, Holmes favored a policy of judicial restraint. He felt that a judge had to loosen the bounds of restraint and keep legislatures from taking on powers of reprimand or fault-finding.

A former law clerk wrote of Holmes: "Those young men who went to Holmes [as law clerks] in the example of their employer, learned that professional capacity achieves the highest fruitfulness only when it is combined with energy of character and breadth of learning."

BOOKS BY HOLMES

The Common Law (1881). Little 1923 $25.00. ISBN 0-316-37131-9
The Complete Works of Oliver W. Holmes. 13 vols. Reprint Services 1987 $795.00. ISBN 0-317-59641-1
The Dissenting Opinions of Mr. Justice Holmes (1929). Alfred Lief (ed). Rothman 1981 $27.50. ISBN 0-8377-0811-7
The Holmes Reader Julius J. Marke (ed). Oceana 1964 $2.50. ISBN 0-379-11301-5
Representative Opinions of Mr. Justice Holmes (1931). Alfred Lief (ed). Greenwood 1971 $35.00. ISBN 0-8371-6143-6

BOOKS ABOUT HOLMES

▪ Aichele, Gary J. *Oliver Wendell Holmes, Jr.* Twayne 1989 $24.95. ISBN 0-8057-7766-0 A well-researched biography of the liberal, progressive Justice of the Supreme Court.
  Bent, Silas. *Justice Oliver Wendell Holmes: A Biography.* AMS 1969 $28.00. ISBN 0-404-00751-1 Biography showing Holmes as "youth and warrior" in Book I, "jurist and thinker" in Book II, and "statesman and philosopher" in Book III.
* Dunham, Montrew. *Oliver Wendell Holmes, Jr. Boy of Justice.* Bobbs Merrill Childhood of Famous Americans Ser. Macmillan 1961 $5.95. ISBN 0-685-07176-6 Illustrated biography of the young Holmes especially suited for younger readers.
  Howe, Mark De Wolfe. *Justice Oliver Wendell Holmes: The Proving Years 1870–1882.* Harvard Univ Pr 1963. The crucial years of Holmes's life, when he established himself in his field.
  Lerner, Max (ed). *The Mind and Faith of Justice Holmes: His Speeches, Essays, Letters, and Judicial Opinions.* Transaction 1989 $21.95. ISBN 0-88738-765-9 A good look at Mr. Justice Holmes through his writings and decisions.
  Novick, Sheldon. *Honorable Justice: The Life of Oliver Wendell Holmes.* Little 1989 $24.95. ISBN 0-316-61325-8 First biography of Holmes, offering a portrait of a paradoxical yet great American legal thinker.

MARSHALL, JOHN   1755–1835

Born and raised near Germantown, Virginia, John Marshall had little formal schooling and, until he joined the Virginia minutemen in 1775, knew little of the world beyond the Virginia frontier. In 1776, Marshall enlisted in the Continental army, where he fought at Brandywine and Monmouth and spent the bitter winter with George Washington at Valley Forge.

When Marshall returned home, he studied law for a short time and then was admitted to the bar in 1780. His law practice grew as did his interest in public service. Marshall, whose father had served in the Virginia House of Burgesses, was elected to the Virginia Assembly in 1782. As time passed, he became increasingly convinced that the United States needed a strong government. In 1787, when Virginia called for a convention to consider ratification of the U.S. Constitution, Marshall participated and helped convince other delegates to vote in favor of ratification.

In 1797, after several offers, Marshall finally accepted a federal position. President John Adams asked him and several others to travel to France to seek improved relations between that country and the United States. During that trip, French officials said that the American commission would not be received until large bribes had been paid. John Marshall refused to pay, and his rebuke of this proposition was rewarded by tremendous popularity among fellow Americans.

In 1799 Marshall was elected to Congress. The following year he became U.S. Secretary of State. This position was soon followed by his appointments to the U.S. Supreme Court. Thus began a 34-year term as chief justice that helped the new nation create a strong central government in which the Supreme Court shared power with the presidency and Congress.

As chief justice, John Marshall wrote Court opinions that clarified the intent of the Constitution of the United States. In *Marbury* v. *Madison* (1803), Marshall identified the Court's function of judicial review by ruling an act of Congress unconstitutional. In the case of *Fletcher* v. *Peck* (1810), the Court for the first time found a state law to be unconstitutional. This helped establish the authority of the national government over the states. This issue also was addressed in the case of *McCulloch* v. *Maryland* (1819), in which Marshall wrote that Congress could use its implied powers—powers not expressly dictated by the Constitution—to create a bank that could not be taxed by the states. In all these decisions, the Supreme Court, with Marshall at its head, clarified the position of the federal government and its relation to the states of the United States. So great were Marshall's southern charm and his absolute integrity that he won respect from adversaries as well as from friends.

BOOKS BY MARSHALL

An Autobiographical Sketch by John Marshall (1969). *American Constitutional Legal History Ser.* John S. Adams (ed). Da Capo 1973 $19.50. ISBN 0-306-70216-9
The Political and Economic Doctrines of John Marshall. (coauthored with John E. Oster) Burt Franklin 1914 $22.50. ISBN 0-8337-2636-6

BOOKS ABOUT MARSHALL

Faulkner, Robert K. *The Jurisprudence of John Marshall.* Greenwood 1980 $35.00. ISBN 0-313-22508-7 Considers the constitutional understanding of Chief Justice John Marshall and explores the political and economic views behind his Supreme Court.
Loth, David G. *Chief Justice: John Marshall and the Growth of the Republic.* Greenwood 1970 repr of 1949 ed $22.50. ISBN 0-8371-2450-6 Accessible portrait of Marshall's life and times and contribution to the Supreme Court.
*Monsell, Helen A. *John Marshall: Boy of Young America. Bobbs Merrill Childhood of Famous Americans Ser.* Macmillan 1949 $3.95. ISBN 0-672-50105-8 Illustrated story of the life of the famous jurist written for younger readers.
▪Stites, Frances N. *John Marshall: Defender of the Constitution.* Scott 1981 $19.95. ISBN 0-673-39353-4 Biography examining Marshall's contribution in the context of his times and his own life.
Thayer, James Bradley, *et al. James Bradley Thayer, Oliver Wendell Holmes, and Felix Frankfurter on John Marshall.* Univ of Chicago Pr 1967 $1.95. ISBN 0-226-79408-3 Accessible portrait of Marshall's life and thought by Thayer, followed by essays by Holmes and Frankfurter.

O'CONNOR, SANDRA DAY   1930–

Sandra Day O'Connor is the first woman ever to serve on the Supreme Court—the highest court of the United States. Yet she grew up on a ranch in Arizona, thousands of miles from the nation's capital. The daughter of a successful rancher, O'Connor finished high school at the age of 16. Five years later she graduated third in her law school class at Stanford University in California. She soon discovered, however, that no law firms were hiring women—except as secretaries.

Fortunately, O'Connor was persistent and confident of her abilities. She soon was hired as deputy county attorney in San Mateo, California. She and her husband John, also a lawyer, next lived and worked in West Germany for three years. In 1959, with her family increasing in size, O'Connor decided to open her own law practice in Phoenix, Arizona. For much of the time, however, she stayed at home caring for her three children.

By 1969 O'Connor was again ready for a full-time position practicing law. With a growing interest in Republican politics, she decided to take a job as an assistant attorney general in Arizona. Four years later, she was appointed to fill a vacancy in the state senate. Beginning in 1970, she was elected to two terms in her own right. O'Connor quickly moved up the ladder of Arizona politics. In 1972 she was elected majority leader—the first woman majority leader of any state legislature. But despite her love of politics, she was eager to return to practicing law. In 1974 she won a seat as a judge on the Maricopa County Superior Court. Five years later, she was appointed to the Arizona Court of Appeals.

In 1981 President Ronald Reagan (*see* Reagan, Vol. 2, United States History: The Reagan and Bush Years) nominated O'Connor to the Supreme Court. He stressed that she was appointed for her ability, not simply because she was a woman. Over 100 years earlier, in 1873, the United States Supreme Court had ruled that a woman named Myra Bradwell be denied a license to practice law. The judge argued that "the . . . destiny of women [is to] fulfill the noble . . . offices of wife and mother." The appointment of Sandra Day O'Connor to the Supreme Court showed just how much times had changed since then.

O'Connor has gained a reputation as a careful legal thinker with a respect for legal precedent. Although she believes in the policy of judicial restraint, she has not favored it in every case. During her early years as a justice, she tended to side with her more conservative peers. More recently, she has taken a more independent role on the bench and has supported some liberal positions, including support of certain affirmative action employment policies.

BOOKS ABOUT O'CONNOR

■Huber, Peter. *Sandra Day O'Connor.* Chelsea 1990 $17.95. ISBN 1-55546-672-9 Illustrated biography intended for junior high and high school students.
*Woods, Harold and Geraldine Woods. *Equal Justice: A Biography of Sandra Day O'Connor.* Dillon 1985 $12.95. ISBN 0-87518-292-5 Illustrated biography written for younger readers.

WARREN, EARL   1891–1974

Born in California, Earl Warren completed his education there and passed the California bar in 1914. After practicing law for several years, Warren began his work in government at the state level, becoming a district attorney and then attorney general. When he ran for governor, California Republicans and Democrats both supported his candidacy. His only political defeat came at the national level, when he ran for Vice President with Thomas Dewey on the Republican ticket in 1948. In 1953, President Dwight D. Eisenhower nominated Earl Warren as chief justice of the U.S. Supreme Court, a post Warren held until his retirement from the bench in 1969.

In 1954, Warren presided over a case that would change the United States forever—*Brown v. Board of Education of Topeka.* The issue was whether the separate educational facilities for blacks in public school systems were equal to those for whites. In the opinion, writing for a unanimous Court, Warren said, "The doctrine of 'separate but equal' has no place. Separate educational facilities are inherently unequal." This was the first in a series of rulings made by the Supreme Court that, under Warren, promoted racial equality, defended the democratic philosophy of "one man, one vote," and upheld suspects' rights upon arrest.

In 1963 President Lyndon B. Johnson called on Warren to perform a sad task: to preside over the commission that investigated President John F. Kennedy's death. The result was a still-contested document called the *Warren Report,* published in 1964.

Book by Warren

The Public Papers of Chief Justice Earl Warren (1959). Henry M. Christman (ed). Greenwood 1973 $22.50. ISBN 0-8371-7654-9

Books about Warren

Pollack, Jack Harrison. *Earl Warren: The Judge Who Changed America.* Prentice 1979. ISBN 0-13-222315-5 Journalist and long-time friend offers a definitive biography and provides background on the Warren Court's landmark decisions.

Schwartz, Bernard. *Super Chief: Earl Warren and His Supreme Court, a Judicial Biography.* New York Univ Pr 1983 $20.00. ISBN 0-8147-7826-7 Comprehensive assessment of Warren and his Supreme Court, tracing his life from his childhood though his years as Chief Justice.

White, G. Edward. *Earl Warren: A Public Life.* Oxford Univ Pr 1987 $9.95. ISBN 0-19-504936-5 Relates Warren's accomplishments as a judge to the themes of his early life and his early roots in Progressivism.

THE FEDERAL LEGISLATIVE SYSTEM

∎ Barone, Michael. *Almanac of American Politics: 1990 Edition.* Grant Ujifusa (ed). National Journal 1989 $44.95. ISBN 0-89234-044-4 U.S. political history, records, and more.

Congressional Quarterly. *Aging in America: The Federal Government's Role.* Congressional Quarterly 1988 $10.95. ISBN 0-87187-501-2

∎ Congressional Quarterly. *Congress A to Z: Congressional Quarterly's Ready Reference Encyclopedia.* Congressional Quarterly 1988 $75.00. ISBN 0-87187-447-4 Encyclopedic reference on Congress, with explanations of terms, major functions of Congress, directory of members, a bibliography, and more.

∎ Congressional Quarterly. *Current American Government.* Congressional Quarterly 1989 $10.95. ISBN 0-87187-489-X Covers AIDS testing, the nuclear energy lobby, the government budget, parliamentary terms, and other legislative and judicial topics; published every spring and fall.

∎ Congressional Quarterly. *How Congress Works.* Congressional Quarterly 1983 $13.95. ISBN 0-87187-254-4 Complete introduction to the real workings of Congress.

∎Congressional Quarterly. *Members of Congress Since Seventeen Eighty-Nine.* Congressional Quarterly 1985 $10.95. ISBN 0-87187-335-4 Historical perspective on members of Congress.

Congressional Quarterly. *Social Security and Retirement: Private Goals and Public Policy.* Congressional Quarterly 1983 $10.95. ISBN 0-87187-274-9

∎Davidson, Roger H. and Walter J. Oleszek (eds). *Congress and Its Members.* Congressional Quarterly 1989 $19.95. ISBN 0-87187-491-1 Insiders' account of the people and situations that affect Congress.

Davies, Jack. *Legislative Law and Process in a Nutshell.* West Pub 1986 $11.95. ISBN 0-314-21437-2

Dodd, Lawrence C., and Bruce J. Oppenheimer. *Congress Reconsidered.* Congressional Quarterly 1989 $19.95. ISBN 0-87187-490-3

∎Drury, Allen. *Advise and Consent.* Doubleday 1959 $16.95. ISBN 0-385-05419-X Novel centering on duties of the Senate.

∎Ehrenhalt, Alan (ed). *Politics in America: The 100th Congress.* Congressional Quarterly 1987 $39.95. ISBN 0-87187-430-X Provides in-depth information on all congressional members.

Elliot, Jeffery M., and Sheikh R. Ali. *The Presidential–Congressional Political Dictionary. Clio Dictionaries in Political Science.* ABC–Clio 1984 $17.00. ISBN 0-87436-358-6

Fox, Harrison W., Jr., and Susan W. Hammond. *Congressional Staffs: The Invisible Force in American Lawmaking.* Free Pr 1979 $12.95. ISBN 0-02-910430-0

Goehlert, Robert, and Fenton S. Martin. *Congress and Law-Making: Researching the Legislative Process.* ABC–Clio 1989 $35.00. ISBN 0-87436-509-0

Goehlert, Robert, and John Sayre. *The United States Congress: A Bibliography.* Free Pr 1981 $50.00. ISBN 0-02-911900-6

Jacob, Herbert. *Law and Politics in the United States: An Introduction.* Scott 1986 $25.50. ISBN 0-673-39448-4

Keefe, William J., and Morris S. Ogul. *The American Legislative Process: Congress and the States.* Prentice 1989 $40.40. ISBN 0-13-028051-8

Keefe, William J., and Morris S. Ogul. *Congress and the American People.* Prentice 1988 $25.00. ISBN 0-12-167651-2

∎King, Anthony (ed). *Both Ends of the Avenue: The Presidency, the Executive Branch and Congress in the 1980s.* Congressional Quarterly 1988 $13.25. ISBN 0-8447-3497-7 Political workings of the federal government in the 1980s.

Malbin, Michael. *Unelected Representatives: Congressional Staff and the Future of Representative Governments.* Basic 1982 $6.95. ISBN 0-465-08867-8

∎Oleszek, Walter J. (ed). *Congressional Procedures and the Policy Process.* Congressional Quarterly 1988 $15.95. ISBN 0-87187-477-6 Tells of changes in congressional procedures, with additional information on amendments and on how bills become law.

Schlesinger, Arthur M., Jr., and Roger Bruns (eds). *Congress Investigates: A Documented History, 1792–1974.* 5 vols. Chelsea 1975. (o.p.) $62.50. ISBN 0-87754-132-9

Vogler, David J. *The Politics of Congress.* Brown 1988 $27.35. ISBN 0-697-06813-7

CHISHOLM, SHIRLEY ANITA ST. HILL   1924–

Although Shirley Chisholm became the first African-American woman to serve in the United States Congress, she began her career in early childhood education. After studying at Brooklyn College and earning a master's degree from Columbia University, she taught nursery school and directed day-care centers in New York City. Between 1959 and 1964 she worked as an educational consultant for the city's Bureau of Child Welfare.

During this period, Chisholm was also actively involved in several community and civic activities. Her desire to help others grew until she finally decided to run for the New York State Assembly in 1964. At the time she was not a favorite with the politicians of the state. She ran for office, she once said, because "the people wanted me." As a legislator, Chisholm worked hard for publicly supported day-care centers and for unemployment insurance for domestic workers. She also was responsible for the passage of a bill that enabled disadvantaged African-American and Puerto Rican students to enter state universities and receive remedial training.

In 1968 Chisholm ran for the U.S. House of Representatives as a Democrat. Much of her support came from women, some of whom carried on a door-to-door campaign on her behalf. After she was elected to office, Chisholm announced to the press that she did not intend to be "a quiet freshman Congressman." And indeed she was not. One battle arose over her assignment to the House Agriculture Committee in 1969. "Apparently all they know here in Washington about Brooklyn is that a tree grew there," Chisholm remarked. "Only nine black people have been elected to Congress," she continued, "and those nine should be used as effectively as possible." As a result of her protest, she was reassigned to the Committee on Veterans Affairs—a committee on which she felt she could be of greater service to the people of her Brooklyn district.

Chisholm quickly gained national attention as an outspoken critic of the Vietnam War and the House seniority system. During her years in office she also worked for the reform of U.S. political parties and legislatures to meet the needs of the urban poor. In 1972 Chisholm campaigned for, but did not win, the Democratic presidential nomination. Since then she has devoted much of her time to writing and teaching.

BOOKS BY CHISHOLM

Unbought and Unbossed: An Autobiography (1970). Houghton 1970. (o.p.) $4.95.
The Good Fight (1973). Harper 1973. (o.p.) $6.95. ISBN 0-06-010764-2

BOOKS ABOUT CHISHOLM

Duffy, Susan (comp). *Shirley Chisholm: A Bibliography of Writings by & about Her.* Scarecrow 1988 $20.00. ISBN 0-8108-2105-2
Scheader, Catherine. *Shirley Chisholm: Teacher and Congresswoman. Contemporary Women Ser.* Enslow 1990 $15.95. ISBN 0-89490-285-7 Illustrated biography of Shirley Chisholm.

RAYBURN, SAM (SAMUEL TALIAFERRO)   1882–1961

American politician and legislator Sam Rayburn was born near Kingston, in Roane County, Tennessee, but his family moved to Texas when he was just five years old. There, the Rayburns settled near the town of Windom, and their son attended the local rural schools. To earn money, the young Rayburn picked cotton. Working his way through school, he graduated from East Texas Normal College (now East Texas State University) in Commerce, Texas, in 1903. From there he went on to study law at the University of Texas in Austin. Upon being admitted to the bar in 1908, he began to practice law in Bonham, Texas.

A lifelong Democrat, Rayburn's political career got underway when he was still in his twenties—with his 1907 election to the Texas House of Representatives. He remained a member of the Texas legislature until 1912, when he was elected to the U.S. House of Representatives. His interest in national politics developed and grew, and before long, he became a well known personality in the national political arena. During the 1930s, he helped draft and sponsor much New Deal legislation, including the Securities Exchange Act of 1934, which established the Securities and Exchange Commission. In some cases, it was strictly due to Rayburn's efforts that the legislation passed in the House.

From 1937 to 1940, Rayburn served as Majority Leader of the House. On September 16, 1940, he was elected Speaker of the House for the first time. He was elected again in 1949 and in 1955. In fact, except for four years when the Republicans were in control, he served as Speaker continuously until his death in November 1961. As Speaker, he excelled in obtaining votes by "quiet, behind-the-scenes persuasion" and was personally responsible for passage of much of the House legislation. One of his greatest victories came shortly before his death when he succeeded in expanding the House Rules Committee and placing liberal Democrats in control.

Rayburn served 25 consecutive terms in Congress. He set a House record for time in office—47 years. He also set a record for length of service as Speaker—17 years. Thus, the parliamentarian known as "Mr. Sam" earned the distinction of having served as Representative and Speaker for more years than anyone else in the history of the nation.

BOOKS ABOUT RAYBURN

Champagne, Anthony. *Congressman Sam Rayburn.* Rutgers Univ Pr 1984 $40.00. ISBN 0-8135-1012-0 Account of the career of Rayburn based on over 60 interviews with his associates as well as his personal papers.

Hardeman, D. B., and Donald Bacon. *Rayburn: A Biography.* Madison Bks UPA 1989 $14.95. ISBN 0-8191-7294-4 Award-winning biography of one of America's greatest political heros; co-authored by his political advisor and personal confidant, D. B. Hardeman.

FEDERALISM AND STATES' RIGHTS

■Batchelor, John E. *States' Rights. Constitution First Books Ser.* Watts 1986 $10.40. ISBN 0-531-10112-6. Introduction to states' rights.

Bavkis, Herman, and William M. Chandler. *Federalism and the Role of the State.* Univ of Toronto Pr 1987 $18.95. ISBN 0-8020-6621-6

Berger, Raoul. *Federalism: The Founders' Design.* Univ of Oklahoma Pr 1987 $16.95. ISBN 0-8061-2059-2

Commager, Henry S. (ed). *The Blue and the Gray.* 2 vols. Outlet 1982 $12.98. ISBN 0-517-38379-9

Dilger, Robert J. *The Sunbelt–Snowbelt Controversy: The War over Federal Funds.* New York Univ Pr 1984. (o.p.) $35.00.

■Elazer, Daniel J. *American Federalism: A View from the States.* Harper 1984 $16.95. ISBN 0-06-041884-2. Looks at federalism from the point of view of the states.

■Goode, Stephen. *The New Federalism. Single Title Ser.* Watts 1983 $13.90. ISBN 0-531-04501-3 Introduces the reader to policies of the new federalism under the administration of Ronald Reagan.

Hall, Kermit L. (ed). *Federalism: A Nation of States. United States Constitutional and Legal History Ser.* Garland 1987 $70.00. ISBN 0-8240-0131-1

Hamilton, Alexander, *et al. Federalist Papers.* Bantam 1982 $3.50. ISBN 0-553-21072-6

Hawkins, Robert B., Jr. (ed). *American Federalism: A New Partnership for the Republic.* ICS Pr 1982 $7.95. ISBN 0-917616-50-2

Henig, Jeffrey R. *Public Policy and Federalism: Issues in State and Local Politics.* St. Martin's 1985 $19.35. ISBN 0-312-65560-6

Nice, David C. *Federalism: The Politics of Intergovernmental Relations.* St. Martin's 1986 $35.00. ISBN 0-312-28550-7

Patterson, James T. *The New Deal and the States: Federalism in Transition.* Greenwood 1981 $35.00. ISBN 0-313-22841-8

Reagan, Michael D., and John G. Sanzone. *The New Federalism.* Oxford Univ Pr 1981 $9.95. ISBN 0-19-502772-8

Walker, David B. *Toward a Functioning Federalism.* Scott 1981 $16.50. ISBN 0-673-39487-5

Wright, Deil S., and Harvey L. White (eds). *Federalism and Intergovernmental Relations. PAR Classics V.* Am Soc Pub Admin 1984 $14.95. ISBN 0-936678-06-2

INTERNATIONAL RELATIONS

Ambrose, Stephen E. *Rise to Globalism: American Foreign Policy Since 1938.* Penguin 1988 $8.95. ISBN 0-14-022826-8

Aron, Raymond. *Peace and War: A Theory of International Relations.* Krieger 1981 $52.50. ISBN 0-89874-391-5

■Bialer, Seweryn, and Michael Mandelbaum. *Global Rivals.* Knopf 1988 $18.95. ISBN 0-394-57194-0 A history of the U.S. and Russia relationship since World War II.

Bishop, William W., Jr. *International Law: Cases and Materials.* Little 1971 $38.00. ISBN 0-316-09664-4

Brown, Lester R., *et al. State of the World, 1989: A Worldwatch Institute Report on Progress Toward a Sustainable Society.* Norton 1989 $9.95. ISBN 0-393-30567-8

Calvocoressi, Peter. *World Politics Since Nineteen Forty-Five.* Longman 1987.

Chaliand, Gerard. *Revolution in the Third World: Currents and Conflicts in Asia, Africa, and Latin America.* Penguin 1989 $8.95. ISBN 0-14-011845-4

Clark, Grenville, and Louis Sohn. *Introduction to World Peace Through World Law. Modern Classics of Peace Ser.* World Without War 1984 $4.95. ISBN 0-912018-18-6

■Congressional Quarterly. *The Middle East.* Congressional Quarterly 1986 $17.95. ISBN 0-87187-361-1 Explores the conflict between the Arabs and Israelis, Islam, and the value of oil to the region, and describes the major states; provides a chronology, bibliography, and index.

■Congressional Quarterly. *The Soviet Union.* Congressional Quarterly 1986 $17.95. ISBN 0-87187-383-4 Good high school reference; discusses the relationship between the Soviet Union and the United States and includes information on leaders and other aspects of the nation.

Deutsch, Karl W. *The Analysis of International Relations.* Prentice 1988 $29.20. ISBN 0-13-033010-8

■Fincher, E. B. *Mexico and the United States: Their Linked Destinies.* Harper 1983 $12.89. ISBN 0-690-04311-2. Discusses the relationship between the United States and Mexico and some of the problems that they share.

■Foreign Policy Association. *Cartoon History of United States Foreign Policy, 1776–1976.* Foreign Policy $9.95. ISBN 0-317-43272-9 Annotated cartoons on various aspects of American foreign policy over the years.

■Franck, Thomas M. *Nation Against Nation: What Happened to the U.N. Dream and What the U.S. Can Do About It.* Oxford Univ Pr 1985 $22.95. ISBN 0-19-503587-9 Looks at the United Nations' strengths and weaknesses.

Halperin, Morton H. *Limited War in the Nuclear Age.* Greenwood 1978 $22.50. ISBN 0-313-20116-1

Hawkins, Robert G. (ed). *The Economic Effects of Multinational Corporations.* Vol. 1 *Research in International Business and Finance Ser.* JAI 1979 $56.50. ISBN 0-89232-031-1

Laqueur, Walter, and Brad Roberts (eds). *America in the World, 1962–1987: A Strategic and Political Reader.* St. Martin's 1987 $35.00. ISBN 0-312-01318-3

■Leone, Bruno, *et al* (eds). *Internationalism: Opposing Viewpoints Ser.* Greenhaven 1989 $9.95. ISBN 0-89908-547-4 Annual; updates and debates important international issues.

■Lopez, George A., and Michael S. Stohl. *International Relations: Contemporary Theory and Practice.* Congressional Quarterly 1988 $20.95. ISBN 0-87187-476-8 Discussion of the basic concepts of international relations.

Morgenthau, Hans J. *Politics Among Nations.* Kenneth W. Thompson (ed). McGraw 1985 $34.95. ISBN 0-07-554469-5

Oye, Kenneth A., *et al. Eagle Resurgent: The Reagan Era in American Foreign Policy.* Scott 1987 $17.95. ISBN 0-673-39469-7

Power, Thomas. *The Men Who Kept the Secrets: Richard Helms and the C.I.A.* Simon 1983 $4.95. ISBN 0-671-47712-9

•Rohr, Janelle (ed). *The Third World: Opposing Viewpoints.* Greenhaven 1989 $7.95. ISBN 0-89908-422-2 Looks at major issues that the developing nations must face in economics, politics, and society.

Schelling, Thomas C. *Strategy and Arms Control.* Pergamon 1985 $11.95. ISBN 0-08-032390-1

Sick, Gary. *All Fall Down: America's Tragic Encounter with Iran.* Penguin 1986 $8.95. ISBN 0-14-008837-7

Sweet, William. *The Nuclear Age: Atomic Energy, Proliferation, and the Arms Race.* Congressional Quarterly 1988 $14.95. ISBN 0-87187-466-0

Taylor, Charles L., *et al. World Handbook of Political and Social Indicators.* 2 vols. Yale Univ Pr 1983. Vol. 1 $30.00. ISBN 0-300-03027-4. Vol. 2 $24.50. ISBN 0-300-03028-2

Thornton, Richard C. *The Nixon–Kissinger Years: The Reshaping of American Foreign Policy.* Paragon Hse 1989 $24.95. ISBN 0-88702-051-8

•Trager, Oliver (ed). *The Iran-Contra Arms Scandal.* Facts on File 1988 $24.95. ISBN 0-8160-1859-6 Explores various angles of the Iran-Contra scandal.

*United Nations. *Everyone's United Nations.* UN 1986 $9.95. ISBN 92-1-100274-5 Explains how the United Nations was organized and what functions it performs.

Ziegler, David W. *War, Peace, and International Politics.* Scott 1987. (o.p.) $20.50. ISBN 0-673-39501-4

KISSINGER, HENRY ALFRED   1923–

Henry Kissinger was born in Fürth, Germany. However, he lived there only 15 years before his parents, fleeing Nazi persecution, brought him to the United States. Kissinger, who became a naturalized citizen in 1943, served in the United States Army during World War II.

Although as a boy Kissinger thought of becoming an accountant, the government classes he took as a student at Harvard University fascinated him, and he quickly found his calling. He graduated with honors and then joined Harvard's faculty as a lecturer. Starting in the 1950s, Kissinger served as a consultant in international affairs for various government agencies. In this role, he promoted the idea that, with regard to nuclear weapons, sufficiency—not superiority—should be the nation's goal. In 1969 Richard Nixon brought Kissinger to the White House, first as presidential assistant for national security affairs and then as director of the National Security Council. In 1973 Kissinger became secretary of state.

During his government service, Kissinger was instrumental in making several major changes in U.S. foreign policy. Kissinger's meetings with officials of the People's Republic of China led to the opening of trade between the two countries and ultimately to Nixon's historic seven-day visit to the nation with whom the United States had broken relations during the Korean War. In 1972 Kissinger helped orchestrate talks with the Soviet Union that led to agreements limiting each nation's defensive missiles. Kissinger also participated in the negotiations that eventually ended the Vietnam War. For this, he, together with North Vietnamese negotiator Le Duc Tho, received the 1973 Nobel Peace Prize.

Kissinger officially left government service in 1977. He went on to found and become chairman of Kissinger Associates Inc., an international consulting

Varoom!   Roy Lichtenstein (c. 1963).   Courtesy of The
Bettmann Archive.

company based in New York City. In 1983 President Ronald Reagan appointed
him a member of the National Bipartisan Committee on Central America. In
addition, Kissinger has served as a member of the International Advisory
Committee for Chase banks.

BOOKS BY KISSINGER

▪ *American Foreign Policy* (1977). Norton 1977 $9.95. ISBN 0-393-05641-4 Insightful view
of U.S. foreign policy; especially interesting for its analysis of nuclear policy.
American Foreign Policy: A Global View (1982). Gower 1982 $16.95. ISBN 9971-902-54-0
Observations: Selected Speeches and Essays, 1982–1984 (1985). Little 1985 $17.95. ISBN 0-316-
49664-2
▪ *The White House Years* (1979) Little 1979 $29.95. ISBN 0-316-49661-8 Memoir that
provides superb insight into the processes of foreign policy making and the
politics within the White House during the Nixon years.

BOOKS ABOUT KISSINGER

Caldwell, Dan (ed). *Henry Kissinger: His Personality and Policies.* Duke Univ Pr 1983 $27.00.
ISBN 0-8223-0485-6 Assesses the far-reaching effect of Kissinger on U.S. foreign
policy by examining his personality and its influence on his policies.
Ghanayem, Ishaqi, and Alden H. Voth. *The Kissinger Legacy: American Middle East Policy.*
Praeger 1984 $35.00. ISBN 0-275-91168-3 Assessment focusing on U.S. Middle
East policy divided into time periods.
Hersh, Seymour M. *The Price of Power: Kissinger in the Nixon White House.* Summit Bks 1984
$9.70. ISBN 0-671-50688-9 Journalistic portrait from 1968 to 1973 that offers a
fresh account of the crises then hidden.
Israel, Fred L. *Henry Kissinger. World Leaders Past and Present Ser.* Chelsea 1986 $17.95. ISBN

0-87754-588-X Brief introduction to Kissinger as a leading force in U.S. foreign policy.

Kalb, Marvin, and Bernard Kalb. *Kissinger.* Little 1974. Vivid account of Kissinger's past: his emmigration, family, education, and progression to the center of power.

POLITICAL BEHAVIOR, POLITICAL PARTIES, PUBLIC INTEREST GROUPS

Abramson, Paul R. *Political Attitudes in America.* Freeman 1983 $17.95. ISBN 0-7167-1420-5

Asher, Herbert B. *Presidential Elections and American Politics: Voters, Candidates, and Campaigns Since 1952.* Brooks 1988 $18.25. ISBN 0-534-10461-4

Berelson, Bernard R. *Voting: A Study of Opinion Formation in a Presidential Campaign.* Univ of Chicago Pr 1986 $20.00. ISBN 0-226-04350-9

Berry, Jeffrey M. *The Interest Group Society.* Scott 1989 $40.50. ISBN 0-673-39889-7

Berry, Jeffrey M. *Lobbying for the People: The Political Behavior of Public Interest Groups.* Princeton Univ Pr 1977 $12.95. ISBN 0-691-02178-3

Black, Duncan. *The Theory of Committees and Elections.* Kluwer Academic 1987 $29.95. ISBN 0-89838-189-4

Blumenthal, Sidney. *The Rise of the Counter-Establishment: From Conservative Ideology to Political Power.* Harper 1988 $9.95. ISBN 0-06-09714-1

Bogart, Leo. *Polls and the Awareness of Public Opinion.* Transaction 1985 $16.95. ISBN 0-88738-620-2

■ Boller, Paul F. *Presidential Campaigns.* Oxford Univ Pr 1985 $8.95. ISBN 0-19-503722-7 Follows presidential campaigns through U.S. history.

Crotty, William, and John S. Jackson, III. *Presidential Primaries and Nominations.* Congressional Quarterly 1985 $9.95. ISBN 0-87187-260-9

Crotty, William, and Gary C. Jacobson. *American Parties in Decline.* Scott 1984 $15.95. ISBN 0-673-39430-1

Diamond, Edwin. *The Spot: The Rise of Political Advertising on Television.* MIT Pr 1988 $10.95. ISBN 0-262-54049-5

Ferguson, Thomas, and Joel Rogers. *Right Turn: The Decline of the Democrats and the Future of American Politics.* Hill & Wang 1987 $8.95. ISBN 0-8090-0170-5

■ Foundation for Public Affairs. *Public Interest Profiles, 1988–1989.* Congressional Quarterly 1988 $137.50. ISBN 0-87187-461-X Background and access information on 250 public interest groups.

■ Graber, Doris. *Mass Media and American Politics.* Congressional Quarterly 1988 $16.95. ISBN 0-87187-475-X Clearly written source on the role of media in politics.

Graber, Doris. *Media Power in Politics.* Congressional Quarterly 1989 $18.95. ISBN 0-87187-515-2

Harrington, Michael. *The Next Left: The History of a Future.* H. Holt 1988 $8.95. ISBN 0-8050-0792-X

Hill, David B., and Norman R. Luttbeg. *Trends in American Electoral Behavior.* Peacock 1983 $11.50. ISBN 0-87581-296-1

■ Keefe, William J. *Parties, Politics and Public Policy in America.* Congressional Quarterly 1987 $16.95. ISBN 0-87187-424-5 Close look at how political parties develop public policy.

■ Lazarsfeld, Paul F., *et al. The People's Choice: How the Voter Makes Up His Mind in a Presidential Campaign.* Columbia Univ Pr 1968. (o.p.) $14.00. ISBN 0-231-08583-4 One of the classics of American political science: a report on the 1940 presidential election in Sandusky, Ohio.

■ Lindop, Edmund. *By a Single Vote! One-Vote Decisions That Changed American History.* Stackpole 1987 $9.95. ISBN 0-8117-2090-X Delivers the message that everyone's vote counts.

Lippman, Walter. *Public Opinion.* Free Pr 1965 $12.95. ISBN 0-02-919130-0

Lipset, Seymour M., and William Schneider. *The Confidence Gap: Business, Labor and Government in the Public Mind.* Johns Hopkins Univ Pr 1987 $14.95. ISBN 0-8018-3044-3

■McGinniss, Joe. *The Selling of the President.* Penguin 1988 $7.95. ISBN 0-14-011240-5 Campaign tactics used to package 1984 presidential candidates for the electorate.

Navarro, Peter. *The Policy Game: How Special Interests and Ideologies Are Stealing America.* Lexington Bks 1986 $12.95. ISBN 0-669-14112-7

■O'Connor, Edwin. *The Last Hurrah.* Little 1985 $8.95. ISBN 0-316-62659-7 Fictional account of a Boston politician's last election campaign.

Patterson, Thomas E. *The Mass Media Elections: How Americans Choose Their Presidents.* Praeger 1980 $15.95. ISBN 0-275-91502-6

■Piven, Frances F., and Richard A. Cloward. *Why Americans Don't Vote.* Pantheon 1988 $19.95. ISBN 0-317-67577-X Reasons and national conditions that keep people from the polls.

Ranney, Austin. *Channels of Power: The Impact of Television on American Politics.* Basic 1983 $9.95. ISBN 0-465-00935-2

Sabato, Larry J. *PAC Power: Inside the World of Political Action Committees.* Norton 1985 $7.70. ISBN 0-393-30257-1

Sabato, Larry J. *The Party's Just Begun: Shaping Political Parties for America's Future.* Scott 1988 $17.50. ISBN 0-673-39746-7

Sabato, Larry J. *The Rise of Political Consultants: New Ways of Winning Elections.* Basic 1983 $11.95. ISBN 0-465-07039-6

■Salmore, Stephen A., and Barbara G. Salmore. *Candidates, Parties, and Campaigns: Electoral Politics in America.* Congressional Quarterly 1989 $14.95. ISBN 0-87187-484-9 Explains the changes taking place in U.S. political campaigns.

*Samuels, Cynthia K. *It's a Free Country! A Young Person's Guide to Politics and Elections.* Macmillan 1988 $12.95. ISBN 0-689-31416-7 Basic guide for younger readers.

Schlesinger, Arthur M. *History of American Presidential Elections, 1972–1984.* Chelsea 1986 $55.00. ISBN 0-87754-492-1

Wayne, Stephen J. *The Road to the White House: The Politics of Presidential Elections.* St. Martin's 1987 $14.70. ISBN 0-312-00319-6

STATE AND LOCAL GOVERNMENT

Adrian, Charles R. *A History of American City Government: The Emergence of the Metropolis, 1920–1945.* Univ Pr of America 1987 $36.25. ISBN 0-8191-6649-9

Berman, David R. *State and Local Politics.* Brown 1991 $20.95. ISBN 0-697-11130-X

■Beyle, Thad L. (ed). *State Government: C.Q.'s Guide to Current Issues and Activities, 1988–1989.* Congressional Quarterly 1988 $15.95. ISBN 0-87187-467-9 Collection of articles pertaining to state government issues.

Beyle, Thad L., and Lynn R. Muchmore (eds). *Being Governor: The View from the Office.* Duke Univ Pr 1983 $32.50. ISBN 0-8223-0506-2

Bingham, Richard D. *State and Local Government in an Urban Society.* McGraw 1986 $29.95. ISBN 0-07-554395-8

Burns, James MacGregor. *Government by the People: National, State and Local Politics.* Prentice 1987 $43.00. ISBN 0-13-361700-9

Crenson, Matthew A. *Neighborhood Politics.* Harvard Univ Pr 1983 $27.50. ISBN 0-674-60785-6

Dahl, Robert A. *Who Governs: Democracy and Power in an American City. Studies in Political Science.* Yale Univ Pr 1961 $12.95. ISBN 0-300-00051-0

Dye, Thomas R. *Politics in States and Communities.* Prentice 1991 $36.00. ISBN 0-13-682444-7

■Eichner, James A. *The First Book of Local Government.* Watts 1983 $10.40. ISBN 0-531-04642-7 Explains local government and what it does.

Elliot, Jeffrey M., and Sheikh R. Ali. *The State and Local Government Political Dictionary.* ABC-Clio 1988 $17.00. ISBN 0-87436-358-6

Ferman, Barbara. *Governing the Ungovernable City: Political Skill, Leadership and the Modern Mayor.* Temple Univ Pr 1985 $34.95. ISBN 0-87722-376-9

*Gay, Kathlyn. *Cities Under Stress: Can Today's City Systems Be Made to Work? Impact Ser.* Watts 1985 $12.90. ISBN 0-531-04926-4 Discusses the problems within cities that local leaders must try to solve.

Goehlert, Robert, and Frederick W. Musto. *State Legislatures: A Bibliography.* ABC–Clio 1985 $45.00. ISBN 0-87436-422-1

Grant, Daniel, and Lloyd Omdahl. *State and Local Government in America.* Brown 1984 $40.47. ISBN 0-697-06802-1

*Hanmer, Trudy. *The Growth of Cities.* Issues in American History. Watts 1985 $12.90. ISBN 0-531-10056-1 Tells how cities have grown since colonial times.

Henry, Nicholas. *Governing at the Grassroots: State and Local Politics.* Prentice 1987 $37.60. ISBN 0-13-360678-3

*Hyman, Dick. *The Trenton Pickle Ordinance and Other Bonehead Legislation.* Greene 1984 $4.95. ISBN 0-8289-0537-1 Collection of some unusual state and local laws.

Jewell, Malcolm E., and Samuel C. Patterson. *The Legislative Process.* Random 1985 $18.50. ISBN 0-07-554400-8

*Judd, Dennis R. *The Politics of American Cities: Private Power and Public Policy.* Scott 1988 $19.95. ISBN 0-673-39730-0 Looks at how local leaders and private citizens must work together.

Kane, Joseph N. *The American Counties.* Scarecrow 1983 $49.50. ISBN 0-8108-1558-3

Keefe, William J., and Morris S. Ogul. *The American Legislative Process: Congress and the States.* Prentice 1989 $40.40. ISBN 0-13-028051-8

Leach, Richard H., and Timothy G. O'Rourke. *State and Local Government: The Third Century of Federalism.* Prentice 1988. ISBN 0-13-843251-1

Lorch, Robert S. *State and Local Politics: The Great Entanglement.* Prentice 1989. ISBN 0-13-844010-7

Martin, David L. *Capital, Courthouse, and City Hall.* Longman 1988 $16.95. ISBN 0-582-28686-7

Martin, David L. *Running City Hall: Municipal Administration in America.* Univ of Alabama Pr 1982 $7.95. ISBN 0-8173-0155-0

McCarthy, David J., Jr. *Local Government Law in a Nutshell.* West Pub 1983 $10.95. ISBN 0-314-75415-6

Municipal Yearbook. Intl City Management 1989 $75.00. ISBN 0-873326-964-0

*Ransone, Coleman B., Jr. *The American Governorship.* Contributions in Political Science Ser. Greenwood 1982 $35.00. ISBN 0-313-22977-5 A study of the role of governors over the past 20 years.

Salomon, Samuel R. *The Governors of the American States, Commonwealths and Territories: 1900–1980.* Council of State Governments 1980 $4.00. ISBN 0-317-45928-7

Straayer, John. *American State and Local Government.* Merrill 1983 $21.95. ISBN 0-675-20068-7

*Van Horn, Carl E. (ed). *The State of the States.* Congressional Quarterly 1989 $18.95. ISBN 0-87187-503-9 Study of the changes and pressures in state governments brought on by the state government assuming responsibilities formerly assumed by the federal government.

Wright, Deil S. *Understanding Intergovernmental Relations.* Political Science Ser. Brooks 1982 $16.50. ISBN 0-8185-0503-6

Zimmerman, Joseph F. *State-Local Relations: A Partnership Approach.* Praeger 1983 $35.00. ISBN 0-275-91107-1

ANTHROPOLOGY

This section is devoted to anthropology, the study of human beings. The most comprehensive of the social sciences in what it sets out to study, anthropology is concerned with people anywhere in the world and throughout time—with their cultures and their daily lives. Traditionally, anthropologists have studied non-western peoples, especially those of the prehistory period. Today the field of anthropology is far more diverse. For example, physical anthropologists study the development of the human body over time, applied anthropologists concentrate on such problems as the design of seats for automobiles, and urban anthropologists study residents of inner cities. The unifying themes of anthropology are a concern for culture and how it is transmitted and a firm belief in fieldwork as a primary source of data.

For ease of use, in addition to a listing of general surveys and books on anthropological theory, the anthropology section is divided into seven subsections organized alphabetically—Culture, Economy, Evolution, Language and Communication, Modern Societies and Ethnographies, Religion, and Social Structure.

Within a number of the subsections, key individuals or groups of individuals associated with the topic are listed alphabetically. For each, there is a book or a list of books by that individual. In addition, there is for each a profile that provides personal background and/or information about the individual's role and achievements. Further, the profile may refer the reader to other related individuals and their works, which also can be found in *The Young Adult Reader's Adviser.*

Last, for most profiled individuals, there is a Books About section that, among other types of publications, lists notable biographies for further reading and research. Whenever possible, very recent titles have been included.

SURVEYS AND REFERENCES

Agar, Michael H. *The Professional Stranger: An Informal Introduction to Ethnography. Studies in Anthropology Ser.* Academic Pr 1980 $24.95. ISBN 0-12-043850-X

Bernard, H. Russell (ed). *Research Methods in Cultural Anthropology.* Sage 1988 $19.95. ISBN 0-8039-2978-1

Bohannan, Paul, and Mark Glazer. *High Points in Anthropology.* Knopf 1988.

Crane, Julia, and Michael Angrosino. *Field Projects in Anthropology: A Student Handbook.* Waveland 1984 $9.95. ISBN 0-88133-078-7

Diamond, Stanley. *In Search of the Primitive: A Critique of Civilization.* Transaction 1987 $19.95. ISBN 0-87855-582-X

Ember, Carol R., and Melvin Ember. *Anthropology.* Prentice 1989 $40.00. ISBN 0-13-038381-3

Ember, Carol R., and Melvin Ember. *Cultural Anthropology.* Prentice 1989 $36.00. ISBN 0-13-195330-3

Fetterman, David M. *Ethnography: Step by Step.* Sage 1989 $9.95. ISBN 0-8039-2891-2

∎Fisher, Maxine P. *Recent Revolutions in Anthropology. A Science Impact Book.* Watts 1986 $12.90. ISBN 0-531-10240-8 Easy-to-read discussion of what anthropology is and what anthropologists do; surveys recent theories on such topics as communication with primates, sex roles, and cultural change.

Haviland, William A. *Cultural Anthropology.* Holt 1990 $36.00. ISBN 0-03-030213-7

Jorgensen, Danny L. *Participant Observation: A Methodology for Human Studies.* Sage $9.95. ISBN 0-8039-2877-7

Kluckhohn, Clyde. *Mirror for Man: The Relation of Anthropology to Modern Life. Classics of Anthropology Ser.* Univ of Arizona Pr 1985 $10.95. ISBN 0-8165-0919-0

Langness, L. L., and Frank F. Gelya. *Lives: An Anthropological Approach to Biography.* Chandler & Sharp 1981 $10.95. ISBN 0-88316-542-2

Nash, Dennison. *A Little Anthropology.* Prentice 1989 $24.00. ISBN 0-13-537689-0

Peacock, James L. *The Anthropological Lens: Harsh Light, Soft Focus.* Cambridge Univ Pr 1987 $8.95. ISBN 0-521-33748-8

Pelto, Pertti J., and Gretel H. Pelto. *Anthropological Research: The Structure of Inquiry.* Cambridge Univ Pr 1978 $16.95. ISBN 0-521-29228-X

Service, Elman R. *A Century of Controversy. Studies in Anthropology.* Academic Pr 1985 $19.95. ISBN 0-12-637382-5

Spindler, George D. *Being an Anthropologist: Fieldwork in Eleven Cultures.* Waveland 1986 $9.95. ISBN 0-88133-253-4

Spradley, James P. *The Ethnographic Interview.* Holt 1979 $16.95. ISBN 0-03-044496-9

Spradley, James P., and David W. McCurdy. *The Cultural Experience: Ethnography in Complex Society.* Waveland 1988 $13.95. ISBN 0-88133-349-2

Tylor, Edward Burnett. *Researches into the Early History of Mankind and the Development of Civilization. Classics of Anthropology Ser.* Univ of Chicago Pr 1964 $2.95. ISBN 0-226-82122-6

Whitehead, Tony L., and Mary E. Conaway. *Self, Sex, and Gender in Cross-Cultural Fieldwork.* Univ of Illinois Pr 1986 $14.95. ISBN 0-252-01324-7

Winick, Charles. *Dictionary of Anthropology.* Littlefield 1977 $10.50. ISBN 0-8226-0131-1

CULTURE

Douglas, Mary. *Implicit Meanings: Essays in Anthropology.* Routledge 1978 $13.95. ISBN 0-7100-0047-2

Dundes, Alan. *The Study of Folklore.* Prentice 1965 $37.33. ISBN 0-138-58945-5

Geertz, Clifford. *The Interpretation of Cultures.* Basic 1973 $12.95. ISBN 0-465-09719-7

Hall, Edward T. *Beyond Culture.* Doubleday 1977 $7.95. ISBN 0-385-12474-0

Hall, Edward T. *The Dance of Life: The Other Dimension of Time.* Doubleday 1984 $8.95. ISBN 0-385-19248-7

Hallowell, A. Irving. *Culture and Experience.* Waveland 1988 $11.95. ISBN 0-88133-368-9

Hsu, Francis. *Culture and Self: Asian and Western Perspectives.* Tavistock 1985.

Huizinga, Johan. *Homo Ludens: A Study of the Play Element in Culture.* Beacon 1955 $11.95. ISBN 0-8070-4681-7

Levine, Robert A. (ed). *Culture, Behavior and Personality.* Aldine 1982 $39.95. ISBN 0-202-01167-4

Linton, Ralph. *Acculturation in Seven Indian Tribes.* Peter Smith $13.25. ISBN 0-8446-1283-9

Linton, Ralph. *The Cultural Background of Personality.* Greenwood 1981 $25.00. ISBN 0-313-22783-7

Steward, Julian H. *Theory of Culture Change.* Univ of Illinois Pr 1972 $8.95. ISBN 0-252-00295-4

White, Leslie A. *The Concept of Cultural Systems: A Key to Understanding Tribes and Nations.* Columbia Univ Pr 1975 $26.00. ISBN 0-231-03961-1

White, Leslie A. *The Science of Culture: A Study of Man and Civilization.* Farrar 1969. (o.p.)

BENEDICT, RUTH 1887–1948

Ruth Benedict, an American anthropologist and poet, was born in New York City. A graduate student of American anthropologist Franz Boas (*see* Boas, Vol. 2, Anthropology: Culture) at Columbia University, where she later taught for many years, Benedict did extensive fieldwork among Native Americans. The two books that brought her the most fame are *Patterns of Culture* (1934) and *The Chrysanthemum and the Sword* (1946). The latter is a brilliant reconstruction of patterns in traditional Japanese culture on the basis of wartime interviews with Japanese people who had been living in the United States for several decades. It has been criticized, however, for not dealing with changing patterns of Japanese social behavior.

Benedict is credited with helping to illustrate the theory of cultural relativism—what is considered deviant in one culture may be seen as normal in another—and with contributing to the idea that every culture is an integrated whole, with its own pattern.

BOOKS BY BENEDICT

■ *The Chrysanthemum and the Sword: Patterns of Japanese Culture* (1946). Houghton 1989 $9.95. ISBN 0-395-50075-3 Study of the Japanese people, their ways of thinking, and their behavior patterns.

■ *Patterns of Culture* (1934). Houghton 1989 $9.95. ISBN 0-395-50088-5 Description of Benedict's studies of three sharply contrasting cultures—the Pueblo of New Mexico, the natives of Dobu, and the Indians of the Northwest Coast of America.

Race: Science and Politics (1940). Greenwood 1982 $35.00. ISBN 0-313-23597-X

Zuni Mythology (1935). 2 vols. AMS 1969 $70.00. ISBN 0-404-50571-6

BOOKS ABOUT BENEDICT

■ Mead, Margaret. *An Anthropologist at Work.* Avon 1973. (o.p.) $3.95. ISBN 0-380-01022-4 Part biography of Benedict, part autobiography of a longtime friend of Benedict.

■ Mead, Margaret. *Ruth Benedict.* Columbia Univ Pr 1974 $14.00. ISBN 0-231-03520-9 An account of a leader in anthropology; some illustrations; bibliography.

■ Modell, Judith. *Ruth Benedict: Patterns of a Life.* Univ of Penn Pr 1984 $14.95. ISBN 0-8122-1175-8 Relatively objective interpretation of the life and work of Benedict.

BOAS, FRANZ 1858–1942

Franz Boas, a German-born American, became the most influential anthropologist of his time. Educated in Germany, Boas secured his first academic position in America in 1889. The first professor of anthropology at Columbia University (a post he held for 37 years) and curator at the American Museum of Natural History in New York, he founded the field of anthropology in the United States. He also established careful fieldwork as crucial to the study of cultures. Both directly through his own 30 books, which include classic works on Eskimos and Northwest Coast Indians, and indirectly through the influence of such students as Ruth Benedict, Alfred L. Kroeber, and Margaret Mead (*see* Benedict, Kroeber, *and* Mead, Vol. 2, Anthropology: Culture), he set the agenda for much subsequent American study of cultural anthropology. He also established in the English-speaking world the idea of cultural relativity—all cultures are equal and comparable, and no culture is better than any other.

BOOKS BY BOAS

Anthropology and Modern Life (1928). Dover 1986 $5.95. ISBN 0-486-25245-0

The Eskimo of Baffin Land and Hudson Bay (1907). AMS (repr of 1907 ed) $64.50. ISBN 0-404-11631-0

The Mind of Primitive Man (1911). Greenwood 1983 $35.00. ISBN 0-313-24004-3

Primitive Art (1927). Peter Smith 1955 $17.50. ISBN 0-8446-1695-8

Race, Language, and Culture (1940). Univ of Chicago Pr 1988 $23.95. ISBN 0-226-06242-2

BOOKS ABOUT BOAS

Hershovits, Melville. *Franz Boas.* Kelley 1973 repr of 1953 ed $22.50. ISBN 0-678-02761 Brief overview of Boas's contributions to the field of anthropology.

Kroeber, Alfred L. *Franz Boas: Eighteen Fifty-Eight to Nineteen Fourty-Two.* Kraus 1943 $12.00. ISBN 0-527-00560-6 Biography of Boas written by his former student.

Stocking, George W., Jr. *A Franz Boas Reader: Shaping of American Anthropology, 1883–1911.* Univ of Chicago Pr 1989 $17.95. ISBN 0-226-06243-0 Selected addresses, essays, and lectures by Boas.

KROEBER, ALFRED LOUIS   1876–1960

A leading American anthropologist, Alfred L. Kroeber received the first doctorate in anthropology granted by Columbia University. That was in 1902. In 1923 he published *Anthropology*. It was the only textbook at the time and was enormously influential among students, scholars, and the general public. The 1948 edition of the work was subtitled *Race, Language, Culture, Psychology, Prehistory,* indicating the range of Kroeber's interests and contributions.

Much of Kroeber's research was carried out in California, and he taught at the University of California at Berkeley for most of his professional life. A recognized authority on Native Americans, he became a friend to Ishi, the last Yana Indian, about whom his wife Theodora wrote a book—*Ishi, Last of His Tribe.* Kroeber's concept of "cultural configuration" was influential, while his notion of culture as "superorganic"—put together in patterns or configurations—was controversial as well. He used these ideas in discussing the history of civilizations and the distribution of cultures throughout the world. The approach to studying cultures by area can be largely credited to Kroeber.

BOOKS BY KROEBER

Anthropology: Culture, Patterns, and Processes (1923). Harcourt 1963 $9.95. ISBN 0-15-607805-8
Configurations of Culture Growth (1944). Univ of California Pr 1944 $35.00. ISBN 0-520-00669-0
The Nature of Culture (1952). Univ of Chicago Pr 1987 $30.00. ISBN 0-226-45425-8
A Roster of Civilizations and Culture (1962). Greenwood 1985 $35.00. ISBN 0-313-24838-9

BOOKS ABOUT KROEBER

Kroeber, Theodora. *Alfred Kroeber: A Personal Configuration.* Univ of California Pr 1970 $7.95. ISBN 0-520-03720-0 A first-hand account of Kroeber's life by his wife, including background to his books, teaching, and other interests.
Steward, Julian. *Alfred Kroeber.* Columbia Univ Pr 1973 $34.00. ISBN 0-231-03489-X A study that assesses those qualities that make Kroeber one of the major figures of anthropology, characterizes his scholarly point of view, and identifies the influences that brought about this view and Kroeber's achievements.

MALINOWSKI, BRONISLAW   1884–1942

Bronislaw Malinowski, a Polish-born anthropologist who taught in London, was a major contributor to the transformation of nineteenth-century speculative anthropology into an observation-based science. His major interest was in the study of culture as a universal phenomenon and in the development of fieldwork techniques that would describe one culture adequately and at the same time make possible systematic cross-cultural comparisons.

Along with British anthropologist A. R. Radcliffe-Brown (*see* Radcliffe-Brown, Vol. 2, Anthropology: Social Structure) Malinowski is considered a founder of the functional approach in the social sciences. In Malinowski's view, societies function to satisfy the biological and social-psychological needs of individuals. Societies do this, he held, through institutions, groups of people organized for a purpose. Although Malinowski carried out extensive fieldwork in a number of cultures, he is most famous for his research among the Trobrianders, a people who live on a small island off the coast of New Guinea.

BOOKS BY MALINOWSKI

Argonauts of the Western Pacific. Waveland 1984 $12.50. ISBN 0-88133-084-1
A Diary in the Strict Sense of the Term (1967). Stanford Univ Pr 1989 $14.95. ISBN 0-8047-
  1707-9
The Dynamics of Culture Change (1945). Greenwood 1976 $22.50. ISBN 0-8371-8216-6
Freedom and Civilization (1944). Greenwood 1977 $22.50. ISBN 0-8371-9277
Magic, Science and Religion and Other Essays (1948). Greenwood 1984 $45.00. ISBN 0-313-
  24687-4

BOOK ABOUT MALINOWSKI

Ellen, Roy, *et al* (eds). *Malinowski Between Two Worlds: The Polish Roots of an Anthropological
  Tradition.* Cambridge Univ Pr 1989 $39.50. ISBN 0-521-34566-9 Discussion of the
  influence of Malinowski's background on the development of his theories.

MEAD, MARGARET 1901–1978

Margaret Mead, an American anthropologist, was for most of her life a curator
at the American Museum of Natural History in New York. She was famed not
only as an anthropologist but as a public figure, a popularizer of the social
sciences, a spokeswoman for American science, and an analyst of American
society.

While at Columbia University she was a student of anthropologist Franz
Boas (*see* Boas, Vol. 2, Anthropology: Culture), whose teaching assistant, Ruth
Benedict (*see* Benedict, Vol. 2, Anthropology: Culture), became one of Mead's
closest colleagues and friends. After Benedict's death, Mead became her first
biographer and the custodian of her field notes and papers.

Mead, whose main areas of interest were the problems involved in the
rearing of children, personality, and culture, did most of her field work in
Oceania. Her early research in Samoa led to her bestselling *Coming of Age in Samoa*
(1928). It also led, after her death, to a well-publicized attack on her work by
Australian anthropologist Derek Freeman. Mead's importance was not damaged by his book. In fact, there is probably greater awareness today than ever
before of the important role she played in twentieth-century intellectual history as an advocate of tolerance, education, civil liberties, world peace, and the
worldwide ecumenical movement within Christianity. On January 6, 1979,
Mead was posthumously awarded the Presidential Medal of Freedom, America's highest civilian honor.

BOOKS BY MEAD

• *An Anthropologist at Work* (1959). Avon 1973. (o.p.) $3.95. ISBN 0-380-01022-4 Part
  biography of Ruth Benedict, part autobiography.
And Keep Your Powder Dry: An Anthropologist Looks at America. Essay Index Reprint Ser (1942).
  Ayer 1977 $18.00. ISBN 0-369-2416-9
• *Blackberry Winter: My Earlier Years* (1972). Washington Square Pr 1985 $5.95. ISBN
  0-671-54307-5 Mead's personal account of the early life experiences and relation-
  ships that molded her into the person she became.
The Changing Culture of an Indian Tribe. Contributions to Anthropology Ser. AMS $32.50. ISBN
  0-404-5565-1
Coming of Age in Samoa (1928). Morrow 1971 $9.95. ISBN 0-688-30974-7
Cooperation and Competition Among Primitive Peoples (1937). Peter Smith 1976 $13.25. ISBN
  0-8446-2570-1
Cultural Patterns and Technical Change (1955). Greenwood 1985 $52.50. ISBN 0-313-
  24839-7
Sex and Temperament in Three Primitive Societies (1935). Morrow 1971 $9.95. ISBN 0-688-
  06016-1

BOOKS ABOUT MEAD

∎ Bateson, Mary C. *With a Daughter's Eye: A Memoir of Margaret Mead and Gregory Bateson.* Pocket 1985 $4.95. ISBN 0-671-55424-7 The daughter of two well-known anthropologists tells of her life with them as a family and later as a colleague.

Freeman, Derek. *Margaret Mead and Samoa: The Making and Unmaking of an Anthropological Myth.* Penguin 1986 $6.95. ISBN 0-14-022555-2 Detailed empirical evidence used to demonstrate that Mead's account of Samoan culture and character is fundamentally in error.

∎ Howard, Jane. *Margaret Mead: A Life.* Fawcett 1985 $4.95. ISBN 0-449-20836-2 Objective account of the famous anthropologist who touched and was touched by many lives.

∎ Rice, Edward. *Margaret Mead: A Portrait.* Harper 1979 $13.85. ISBN 0-06-025002-X A personalized biography written by a friend.

See also Vol. 2, Sociology: Culture.

ECONOMY

Cohen, Mark Nathan. *The Food Crisis in Prehistory: Overpopulation and Origins of Agriculture.* Yale Univ Pr 1979 $13.95. ISBN 0-300-02351-0

Dalton, George. *Economic Systems and Society.* Education Ser. Penguin 1974 $5.95. ISBN 0-14-080912-0

∎ Douglas, Mary (ed). *Food in the Social Order: Studies of Food and Festivities in Three American Communities.* Russell Sage 1984 $27.50. ISBN 0-87154-210-2 Describes certain traits of our American culture.

Mauss, Marcel. *Gift: The Form and Reason for Exchange in Archaic Societies.* Norton 1990 $9.95. ISBN 0-393-30698-4

Parsons, Talcott, and Neil J. Smelser. *Economy and Society: A Study in the Integration of Economic and Social Theory.* Routledge 1984. (o.p.)

Polanyi, Karl, *et al* (eds). *Trade and Market in the Early Empires: Economies in History and Theory.* Free Pr 1957. (o.p.)

Tawney, Richard H. *The Puritanical Society and the Growth of Capitalism.* 2 vols. American Classical Coll Pr 1989 $247.75. ISBN 0-89266-646-3

HARRIS, MARVIN   1927–

Shortly after receiving his doctorate in anthropology from Columbia University, American Marvin Harris was offered a position as technical adviser to Brazil's Ministry of Education. What he learned about Brazil's culture during this time became material for his first book, *Town and Country in Brazil* (1956). It was the first of many of his books to lead to controversy in the world of anthropology.

Harris believes that the customs practiced by the world's cultures were created to help humans deal with their material environment. He discusses this theory in his book *Cultural Materialism: The Struggle for a Science of Culture* (1974). His other books serve to support this theory. Harris maintains that the Hindu ban on killing and eating cattle exists because, to the Indian, a cow is more valuable alive—for milk, labor, and breeding—than dead. Harris also asserts that the Jewish aversion to eating pork stems from economic factors that, in early times, made raising pigs less profitable than raising other kinds of live-stock.

Currently a professor of anthropology at the University of Florida, Harris continues to create controversy in the anthropological community with his theories of cultural materialism. Although some anthropologists believe his ideas to be simplistic, others find his assertions original and thought provoking.

BOOKS BY HARRIS

■ *Cannibals and Kings: The Origins of Cultures* (1977). Random 1978 $5.95. ISBN 0-394-72700-2 A view of various aspects of cultural evolution.

■ *Cows, Pigs, Wars, and Witches: The Riddles of Culture* (1974). Random 1989 $7.95. ISBN 0-679-72468-0 A collection of cultural riddles and aspects of life-styles from early times to today, many of which seem strange to most Americans.

■ *Cultural Anthropology.* Harper 1987 $35.50. ISBN 0-06-042669-1 Introductory cultural anthropology text.

■ *Culture, People, Nature: An Introduction to General Anthropology* (1980). Harper 1988 $37.95. ISBN 0-06-042697-7 Comprehensive introductory anthropology text that focuses on contemporary issues in modern states.

■ *Our Kind: Who We Are, Where We Came From, Where We Are Going.* Harper 1989 $22.45. ISBN 0-06-015776-3 Exploration of many curious questions about the theories of evolution and what it means to be human.

The Sacred Cow and the Abominable Pig: Riddles of Food and Culture (1985). Simon 1987 $7.95.

Why Nothing Works: The Anthropology of Daily Life. Simon 1981 $7.95. ISBN 0-317-55900-1 An interesting look at some changes in American culture and the reasons for the changes.

BOOK ABOUT HARRIS

Taylor, Mark K. *Beyond Expectation: Religious Dimensions in Cultural Anthropology.* Mercer 1985 $26.95. ISBN 0-86554-165-5 Criticism and interpretation of Harris's theories, written from the point of view of religious studies.

EVOLUTION

Alland, Alexander. *Human Nature: Darwin's View.* Columbia Univ Pr 1985 $27.50. ISBN 0-231-05898-5

Childe, V. Gordon. *Man Makes Himself.* NAL 1983 $9.95. ISBN 0-452-00979-0

Clark, Wilfrid E. *Early Forerunners of Man.* AMS 1977 $40.00. ISBN 0-404-15915-X

Clark, Wilfrid E. *The Fossil Evidence for Human Evolution: An Introduction to the Study of Paleoanthropology.* Univ of Chicago Pr 1979 $16.00. ISBN 0-226-10937-2

Darwin, Charles. *On the Origin of Species by Means of Natural Selection* (1859). NAL 1986 $3.95. ISBN 0-451-62558-7

Darwin, Charles. *The Next Million Years.* Greenwood 1973 $35.00. ISBN 0-8371-6876-7

■ Johanson, Donald C., and Maitland A. Edey. *Lucy: The Beginnings of Human Kind.* Warner Bks 1982 $13.95. ISBN 0-446-38625 Exciting account of the discovery of the oldest human ancestor found to date (1974), a female teenager, named by the discoverers after the girl in the Beatles song "Lucy in the Sky with Diamonds."

Johanson, Donald C., Maitland A. Edey, and James Schreeve. *Lucy's Child: The Search for Our Origins.* Morrow 1989 $22.45. ISBN 0-688-06492-2 An on-the-scene account of the 1986 discovery of parts of another hominid (human ancestor).

Steward, Julian. *Evolution and Ecology: Essays on Social Transformation.* Univ of Illinois Pr 1977 $9.95. ISBN 0-252-00709-3

LEAKEY, LOUIS S. B.   1903–1972, LEAKEY, MARY D.   1913–   , AND LEAKEY, RICHARD E. F.   1944–

The Leakey family of Kenyan paleoanthropologists—scientists who study prehistoric and ancient fossils—has done much to further knowledge of the development of primates and human beings. Louis Leakey, who was born to English missionaries in Kenya, studied anthropology, archaeology, and modern languages at Cambridge University in England. His interest, however, lay in East Africa. In 1931–1932 he first visited Olduvai Gorge, where he and his wife Mary and their son Richard would later work intensively. In 1959, while Louis was in bed with the flu, Mary discovered a skull identified as an early ancestor of humans and later named *Zinjanthropus.*

Soon after, and close to the site where the skull had been found, the Leakeys unearthed a fairly complete skeleton that had once walked upright and possessed a larger brain than earlier specimens. The Leakeys dated the remains at 2 million years. Tools for cutting found with the remains indicate a degree of manual dexterity absent in more ancient skeletons. This find, which the Leakeys and other scientists named *Homo habilis* (skilled human), is considered the oldest known ancestor of modern-day humans.

Louis Leakey died in 1972, but Mary and Richard have continued the work. In 1975 Richard made another important find—a fossil of the category *Homo erectus* (upright human), a closer ancestor to modern humans. In 1984 Richard's team uncovered the world's most complete *Homo erectus* skeleton. Richard has also founded the International Louis Leakey Memorial Institute for African Prehistory, at which students from around the world study Africa's fossils.

Books by Louis S. B. Leakey

- *Adam or Ape: A Sourcebook of Discoveries About Early Man* (1971). Schenkman 1986 $15.95. ISBN 0-87073-701-5 Illustrated account of the many discoveries about early humans and evolutionary theory.

  Olduvai Gorge, Nineteen Fifty-One to Nineteen Sixty-One (1965). (coedited with P. V. Tobias) 2 vols. Cambridge Univ Pr 1967. Vol. 1 $80.00. ISBN 0-521-05527-X. Vol. 2 $110.00. ISBN 0-521-06901-7

  Stone Age Africa: An Outline of Prehistory in Africa (1936). Greenwood 1970 $15.25. ISBN 0-8371-2022-5

- *White African: An Early Autobiography.* Schenkman 1966 $18.95. ISBN 0-87073-720-1 First volume of autobiographical accounts of Leaky's life when he was in his early thirties.

Books by Mary D. Leakey

- *Disclosing the Past* (1984). McGraw 1986 $9.95. ISBN 0-07-036837-6 A personal account of Leakey's life as a member of the well-known family whose contributions to paleoanthropology are acknowledged worldwide.

  Olduvai Gorge, Vol 3: Nineteen Sixty to Nineteen Sixty-Three (1972) (ed). Cambridge Univ Pr 1972 $135.00. ISBN 0-521-07723-0

Books by Richard E. F. Leakey

- *One Life: An Autobiography* (1983). Salem Hse 1984 $18.95. ISBN 0-88162-055-6 Story of the famous anthropologist and his many adventures.

- *Origins: What New Discoveries Reveal About the Emergence of Our Species and Its Possible Future* (1977). (coauthored with Roger Lewin) Dutton 1982 $8.95. ISBN 0-525-48246-6 A well-illustrated history of discoveries about the human species and our possible future.

People of the Lake (1978). (coauthored with Roger Lewin) Avon 1979 $4.95. ISBN 0-380-45575-7

See also Vol. 2, Biology: The Evolution of Life.

LANGUAGE AND COMMUNICATION

Bloomfield, Leonard. *Language.* Univ of Chicago Pr 1984 $15.95. ISBN 0-226-06067-5

Cassirer, Ernst. *Language and Myth.* Peter Smith 1953 $13.50. ISBN 0-8446-1820-9

Chomsky, Noam. *Knowledge of Language: Its Nature, Origin, and Use. Convergence Ser.* Praeger 1986 $11.95. ISBN 0-275-91761-4

Goffman, Erving. *Forms of Talk. Conduct and Communications Ser.* Univ of Penn Pr 1981 $13.95. ISBN 0-8122-1112-X

Greenberg, Joseph H., *et al* (eds). *Universals of Human Language.* 4 vols. Stanford Univ Pr 1978 $175.00. ISBN 0-8047-1012-0

Gumperz, John J. (ed). *Language and Social Identity. Studies in Interactional Sociolinguistics Ser.* Cambridge Univ Pr 1983 $15.95. ISBN 0-521-28897-5

Lenneberg, Eric H. *Biological Foundations of Language.* Krieger 1984 $42.50. ISBN 0-89874-700-1

SAPIR, EDWARD   1884–1939

Edward Sapir, an American anthropologist, was one of the founders of both modern linguistics and the field of personality and culture. He wrote poetry, essays, and music, as well as scholarly works.

In the field of linguistics, Sapir developed phonemic theory—the analysis of the sounds of a language according to the pattern of their distribution—and analyzed some 10 Native American languages.

Sapir regarded language as a guide both to understanding a culture and to understanding thinking. One of his students, Benjamin Lee Whorf, carried on this work on the relationships between language, thought, and behavior. In cultural anthropology, Sapir contributed to personality-and-culture studies by insisting that the true foundation of culture is in the interactions of specific individuals and in the meanings the participants take from these interactions.

Books by Sapir

An Introduction to the Study of Speech. Harcourt 1955 $6.95. ISBN 0-15-648233-9

Selected Writings of Edward Sapir in Language, Culture, and Personality. David G. Mandelbaum (ed). Univ of California Pr 1985 $15.95. ISBN 0-520-05594-2

MODERN SOCIETIES AND ETHNOGRAPHIES

▪Arensberg, Conrad M. *The Irish Countryman: An Anthropological Study.* Waveland 1988 $6.95. ISBN 0-88133-401-4 A classic, definitive work on Irish peasant customs, beliefs, and way of life.

Belmont, Thomas. *The Broken Fountain.* Columbia Univ Pr 1989 $13.00. ISBN 0-231-07059-4

Bourguignon, Erika (ed). *A World of Women: Anthropological Studies of Women in the Societies of the World.* Greenwood 1980 $44.95. ISBN 0-275-90456-3

Lowie, Robert H. *The Crow Indians.* Univ of Nebraska Pr 1983 $9.95. ISBN 0-8032-7909-4

Lowie, Robert H. *Indians of the Plains.* Univ of Nebraska Pr 1982 $7.95. ISBN 0-8032-7907-8

∎ Naisbitt, John. *Megatrends: Ten New Directions Transforming Our Lives.* Nightingale 1989 $8.95. ISBN 1-55525-292-3 While concentrating on the 1980s, the author finds new ways of looking at the future of the United States and of sorting out the jumble of its past.

Naisbitt, John, and Patricia Aburdene. *Megatrends 2000: Ten New Directions for the 1990's.* Morrow 1990 $21.95. ISBN 0-688-07224-0 Another set of new directions for the 1990s, designed to carry the United States into the year 2000.

∎ Riesman, David, *et al. The Lonely Crowd: A Study of the Changing American Character. Studies in National Policy Ser.* Yale Univ Pr 1973 $12.95. ISBN 0-300-00193-2 Investigates social character and the influences leading to its change, such that every social character, however prominent, is eventually replaced by a very different one.

Sayres, Sohnya, *et al* (eds). *The Sixties, Without Apology.* Univ of Minnesota Pr 1984 $15.95. ISBN 0-8166-1337-0

Shi, David E. *The Simple Life: Plain Living and High Thinking in American Culture.* Oxford Univ Pr 1985 $9.95. ISBN 0-19-504013-9

Warner, W. Lloyd, and Paul S. Lunt. *The Social Life of a Modern Community.* Greenwood 1973 $35.00. ISBN 0-8371-6958-5

MURDOCK, GEORGE PETER   1897–1985

George Peter Murdock, an American anthropologist, is known for his comparative study of kinship systems and for his contributions to the study of cross-cultural differences among different peoples. He studied both sociology and anthropology at Yale University, where he eventually taught for many years. He then went to the University of Pittsburgh, where he became Mellon Professor of Anthropology in 1960. He taught there until his retirement in 1973.

Murdock was instrumental in preparing Yale's Human Relations Area Files (HRAF). A major database in the field of anthropology, it is, in fact, an index of the known cultures of the world. His interest in cross-cultural analysis led to many books and to the journal *Ethnology,* which he founded in 1962.

BOOKS BY MURDOCK

Africa: Its People and Their Culture History. McGraw 1959. (o.p.)
Atlas of World Cultures. Univ of Pittsburgh Pr 1981 $18.95. ISBN 0-8229-3432-9
Our Primitive Contemporaries. Macmillan 1934. (o.p.)
Outline of Cultural Materials (1938). (coauthored, *et al*) Human Relations 1982 $15.00. ISBN 0-87536-654-6
Outline of World Cultures (1954) Human Relations 1983 $15.00. ISBN 0-87536-6643
Social Structure (1949). Free Pr 1965 $12.95. ISBN 0-02-922290-7

See also Vol. 2, Sociology: Community *and* Urban Life.

RELIGION

Aberle, David F. *The Peyote Religion Among the Navajo.* Univ of Chicago Pr 1982 $35.00. ISBN 0-226-00082-6

Durkheim, Emile. *The Elementary Forms of the Religious Life.* Joseph W. Swain (tr). Free Pr 1965 $16.95. ISBN 0-02-908010-X

Eliade, Mircea. *Patterns in Comparative Religion.* NAL 1974 $10.95. ISBN 0-452-00905-7

Eliade, Mircea, *et al* (eds). *Encyclopedia of Religion.* 16 vols. Macmillan 1986 $1,100.00. ISBN 0-02-909480-1

Frazer, James George. *Folklore in the Old Testament.* Crown 1988 $9.98. ISBN 0-517-67251-0

• Frazer, James George. *The Golden Bough* (1890). Macmillan 1985 $11.95. ISBN 0-02-095570-7 Classic study of folklore and religion, especially in European cultures, that focuses on an early legend about a Golden Bough from a specific tree.

Geertz, Clifford. *The Religion of Java.* Univ of Chicago Pr 1976 $14.00. ISBN 0-226-28510-3

Jules-Rosette, Bennetta (ed). *The New Religions of Africa.* Modern Sociology Ser. Ablex 1979 $39.50. ISBN 0-89391-014-7

Lessa, William A., and Evon Z. Vogt. *Reader in Comparative Religion: An Anthropological Approach.* Harper 1979 $33.50. ISBN 0-06-043991-2

Norbeck, Edward. *Religion in Human Life: Anthropological Views.* Waveland 1988 $5.95. ISBN 0-88133-354-9

Wallace, Anthony F. *Religion: An Anthropological View.* McGraw 1966 $23.95. ISBN 0-07-55358-0

See also Vol. 2, Sociology: Religion.

SOCIAL STRUCTURE

Bott, Elizabeth. *Family and Social Network: Roles, Norms, and External Relationships.* Free Pr 1972 $12.95. ISBN 0-02-904510-X

Campbell, Joseph, and Bill Moyers. *The Power of Myth.* Doubleday 1988 $27.50. ISBN 0-385-24774-5

Firth, Raymond. *Elements of Social Organization.* Greenwood 1981 $28.50. ISBN 0-313-22745-4

Fox, Robin. *Kinship and Marriage: An Anthropological Perspective. Cambridge Studies in Social Anthropology Ser.* Cambridge Univ Pr 1984 $11.95. ISBN 0-521-27823-6

Friedl, Ernestine. *Women and Men: An Anthropologist's View.* Waveland 1984 $8.95. ISBN 0-88133-040-X

Kertzer, David L., and Jennie Keith (eds). *Age and Anthropological Theory.* Cornell Univ Pr 1984 $12.95. ISBN 0-8014-9258-0

Parsons, Talcott. *Social Structure and Personality.* Free Pr 1964 $3.45. ISBN 0-02-924840-X

Schneider, David. *American Kinship: A Cultural Account.* Univ of Chicago Pr 1980 $7.95. ISBN 0-226-73930-9

LEVI-STRAUSS, CLAUDE 1908–

Claude Lévi-Strauss, a Belgian-born philosopher, social theorist, and anthropologist, is considered by many one of the foremost social anthropologists of this century. Lévi-Strauss studied at the Sorbonne in Paris, France. From

1935 to 1939 he taught sociology at the University of São Paulo in Brazil. During this time, he made several expeditions into the jungles of Brazil to study the various Indian cultures living there. In the early 1940s, he went to the United States, where he spent six years working in New York at the New School for Social Research. He later returned to France and served as a professor of social anthropology at the Collège de France in Paris from 1959 until his retirement in 1982.

Lévi-Strauss is known especially for his work on social structure, particularly on marriage and descent. He also made important contributions to the study of human cognition (thinking) and to structural studies of myth. As Lévi-Strauss described structures, they are mental models people use to deal with reality. He believed that all cultural forms have common underlying structures and that by analyzing such cultural products as artifacts, music, rituals, and myths the structure of the human mind could be discovered. In his later years, he published his 4-volume *Mythologiques (Mythologies)* (1964-1971), which realized his career-long studies in the structural study of myth.

Lévi-Strauss's writings have been enormously influential. Other social sciences, especially French sociology, as well as linguistics and literary and art criticism, have been influenced by his ideas about structuralism.

BOOKS BY LEVI-STRAUSS

The Elementary Structures of Kinship (1949). Beacon 1969 $15.95. ISBN 0-8070-4669-8
Structural Anthropology (1958). Vol. 1 Basic 1963 $14.95. ISBN 0-465-09516-X
Structural Anthropology (1958). Monique Layton (tr). Vol. 2 Univ of Chicago Pr 1983 $14.00. ISBN 0-226-4749-7
Tristes Tropiques. Washington Square Pr 1982 $4.95. ISBN 0-671-45850-7
The View from Afar (1985). Joachím Neugroschel and Phoebe Hoss (trs). Basic 1987 $10.95. ISBN 0-465-090265-5

BOOKS ABOUT LEVI-STRAUSS

Hayes, E. Nelson, and Tanya Hayes (eds). *Claude Lévi-Strauss: The Anthropologist as Hero.* MIT Pr 1970. (o.p.) $3.95. ISBN 0-262-568016-0 Collection of articles, long essays, and reviews focusing on the writings of Lévi-Strauss.
Leach, Edmund. *Claude Lévi-Strauss.* Univ of Chicago Pr 1989 $10.95. ISBN 0-226-46968-9 A sharply critical approach to structuralist theory balanced by a generous recognition of Lévi-Strauss's importance.

RADCLIFFE-BROWN, A. R. (ALFRED REGINALD)   1881–1955

A. R. Radcliffe-Brown, a British social anthropologist, was born in Birmingham, England, and educated at Cambridge University, England, but spent most of his life teaching and working abroad—in Africa, Australia, and the United States. From 1906 to 1908 he did extended field research in the Andaman Islands, the result of which was his work *The Andaman Islanders* (1922), which provided the basis for the structural–functional school of anthropology. Along with Bronislaw Malinowski (*see* Malinowski, Vol. 2, Anthropology: Culture) he is considered the principal architect of modern social anthropology.

In 1910 Radcliffe-Brown went to Australia, where he spent two years doing fieldwork, dealing primarily with kinship and social organization among certain primitive tribes. This fieldwork served as the basis for his work *The Social Organization of Australian Tribes* (1930-1931).

In 1920 Radcliffe-Brown moved to South Africa, where he became a professor of anthropology at the University of Cape Town. Six years later he returned to Australia, this time to serve as professor of anthropology at the

University in Sydney. He then went on to teach at the University of Chicago and at Oxford University in England.

Radcliffe-Brown had considerable influence in both anthropology and sociology. His approach to anthropology was very different from that of his contemporaries. He believed that the social system, not the individual, mattered. In his view, behavior patterns and institutions needed to be examined in terms of how they functioned as part of the social system as a whole. Such patterns and institutions, he theorized, served to maintain the total social order of which they are parts in much the same way as the different organs of the body serve to maintain the body as a whole. He had a genius for applying such theoretical ideas about social structure to the interpretation of the social behavior of primitive tribes. By example and by teaching, he helped establish social anthropology as a generalizing theoretical discipline in both the United States and the United Kingdom.

BOOKS BY RADCLIFFE-BROWN

African Systems of Kinship and Marriage. (coedited with Daryll Forde) Routledge 1987 $19.95. ISBN 0-7103-0234-7
Andaman Islanders (1922). Free Pr 1964 $5.95. ISBN 0-02-925580-5
Structure and Function in Primitive Societies (1952). Free Pr 1965 $13.95. ISBN 0-02-925620-8

REDFIELD, ROBERT   1897–1958

Born in Chicago, Illinois, Robert Redfield attended the University of Chicago, from which he received a doctorate in anthropology in 1928. Early in his career he carried out a study of Tepoztlán, an Indian community in Mexico. In 1927 he joined the faculty of the University of Chicago where he was dean of the social sciences division from 1934 to 1946. In 1944 he served as president of the American Anthropological Association. In 1930 his earlier fieldwork in Tepoztlán was published as *Tepoztlán* and became known as a pioneering study of folk society. This led to a 16-year affiliation with the Carnegie Institution in Washington, D.C., during which time Redfield did research in Mexico's Yucatán and in Guatemala.

Redfield gained recognition for broadening the scope of American anthropological study by taking it beyond the traditional study of primitive tribal peoples. His major focus was on the confrontation of primitive societies with the forces of technology. He also developed the theory known as the folk-urban continuum, which contrasts ways of life in traditional peasant communities with those in urban communities. His ideas about folk culture, little communities, and little and great traditions have been very influential. He viewed the villages he studied as places where people all got along well with one another.

BOOKS BY REDFIELD

The Little Community and Peasant Society and Culture (1955–1956). Univ of Chicago Pr 1989 $14.95. ISBN 0-226-70670-2
The Primitive World and Its Transformations (1953). Cornell Univ Pr 1957 $6.95 ISBN 0-8014-9028-6
Tepoztlán, a Mexican Village: A Study of Folk Life (1930). Univ of Chicago Pr 1973. (o.p.)

See also Vol. 2, Sociology: Social Stratification.

ECONOMICS

This section is devoted to economics, the social science that deals with the choices people and organizations make concerning the allocation of the limited and relatively scarce resources required to satisfy their wants and needs. Economics also deals with what is produced, who produces it, and who gets how much of what is produced. It not only describes economic activity but also is concerned with the reasons that people and institutions make the economic decisions they do.

For ease of use, in addition to a listing of general surveys and books on economic theory, the economics section is divided into 12 subsections based on topics generally studied in a high school economics course. These are organized alphabetically and include Business Cycles; Capitalism and Free Enterprise; Comparative Economic Systems; Consumerism; The Economy; Forms of Business Enterprises; Government and Economics; Income, Wealth, and Poverty; Labor and Work; Money, Banking, and Financial Markets; Public Finance and Policy; and World Economy. Although the emphasis is on the free-enterprise economy of the United States and its various aspects, because of the increasing interdependence of the world's economic systems, books are included on comparative economic systems and the global economy.

Within a number of the subsections, key individuals associated with the topic are listed alphabetically. For each, there is a book or a list of books by that individual. In addition, there is for each a profile that provides personal background and/or information about the individual's role and achievements. Further, the profile may refer the reader to other related individuals and their works, which also can be found in *The Young Adult Reader's Adviser.*

Last, for most profiled individuals, there is a Books About section that, among other types of publications, lists notable biographies for further reading and research. Whenever possible, very recent titles have also been included.

SURVEYS AND THEORIES OF THE FIELD

Ammer, Christine, and Dean Ammer. *Dictionary of Business and Economics.* Free Pr 1984 $34.95. ISBN 0-02-900790-9

Arrow, Kenneth J. *Social Choice and Individual Values.* Yale Univ Pr 1970 $7.95. ISBN 0-300-01364-7

Bastiat, Frederic. *Incongruities, Inconsistencies, Absurdities and Outright Stupidities in Scientific Economics.* Twenty-First Pr 1984 $137.45. ISBN 0-89901-191-8

Baumol, William J., and Alan S. Blinder. *Economics: Principles and Policy.* Harcourt 1988 $33.00. ISBN 0-15-518851-8

Blaug, Mark. *Economic History and the History of Economics.* New York Univ Pr 1987 $15.00. ISBN 0-8147-2100-6

Blaug, Mark. *Economic Theory in Retrospect.* Cambridge Univ Pr 1985 $21.95. ISBN 0-521-31644-8

Blaug, Mark. *Great Economists Since Keynes: An Introduction to the Lives and Works of One Hundred Modern Economists.* Cambridge Univ Pr 1989 $14.95. ISBN 0-521-36742-5

Breit, William, and Roger L. Ransom. *The Academic Scribblers: Economists in Collision.* Dryden 1982.

Canterbury, E. Ray. *The Making of Economics.* Wadsworth 1987 $19.25. ISBN 0-534-06786-7

Deane, Phyllis. *The Evolution of Economic Ideas. Modern Cambridge Economics Ser.* Cambridge Univ Pr 1978 $17.95. ISBN 0-521-29315-4

Encyclopedic Dictionary of Economics. Dushkin 1985 $10.95. ISBN 0-87967-606-X

Fusfeld, Daniel R. *The Age of the Economist.* Scott 1986. ISBN 0-673-18211-8

▪Heilbroner, Robert L. *The Worldly Philosophers: The Lives, Times, and Ideas of the Great Economic Thinkers.* Simon 1987 $9.95. ISBN 0-671-63318-X Lives of great economic philosophers show the development of economic thought throughout history.

Klein, Lawrence. *Economic Theory and Econometrics.* Univ of Penn Pr 1985 $42.95. ISBN 0-8122-7937-9

▪Lee, Susan. *Susan Lee's ABZs of Money and Finance.* Poseidon 1988 $16.95. ISBN 0-671-55712-2 In dictionary format (A-Z), such terms as *equity, depreciation,* and *sinking fund* are explained.

Leftwich, Richard H., and David Gay. *A Basic Framework for Economics.* Irwin 1987 $24.95. ISBN 0-256-03702-7

▪Levi, Maurice. *Thinking Economically: How Economic Principles Can Contribute to Clear Thinking.* Basic 1987 $7.95. ISBN 0-465-08554-7 Teaches the principles of economics and how they can help you.

McConnell, Campbell R. *Economics.* McGraw 1989 $42.95. ISBN 0-07-044967-8

▪McConnell, John. *Ideas of the Great Economists.* Barnes 1980. Discusses the beliefs that have helped shape economic structures.

Samuelson, Paul A., and William D. Nordhaus. *Economics.* McGraw 1989 $39.95. ISBN 0-07-054786-6

Schumpeter, Joseph A. *History of Economic Analysis.* Oxford Univ Pr 1954 $24.95. ISBN 0-19-504185-2

▪Silk, Leonard. *Economics in Plain English: Updated and Expanded.* Simon 1986 $8.95. ISBN 0-671-60613-1 Good resource for understanding economics.

Stigler, George. *Memoirs of an Unregulated Economics.* Basic 1988 $17.95. ISBN 0-465-04443-3

Thurow, Lester. *Dangerous Currents: The State of Economics.* Random 1984 $7.95. ISBN 0-394-72368-6

Weber, Max. *General Economic History. Social Science Classics Ser.* Transaction 1981 $16.96. ISBN 0-87855-690-7

Weber, Max. *The Theory of Social and Economic Organization.* Free Pr 1964 $16.95. ISBN 0-02-934930-3

World Bank Staff. *World Development Report, 1989.* Oxford Univ Pr 1989 $12.95. ISBN 0-19-520788-2

World Economics Data, 1989: A Compendium of Current Economic Information for All Countries of the World. World Facts and Figures Ser. ABC–Clio 1989 $29.95. ISBN 0-87436-111-7

MARSHALL, ALFRED   1842–1924

Alfred Marshall, an English economist, philosopher, and mathematician, was a major contributor to the development of modern economic thought. His *Principles of Economics* (1890) is one of the classic works of economics and brought him recognition as the foremost economist of his time. In fact, the first 25 years of twentieth-century economics have been called the Age of Marshall.

One of Marshall's major contributions was to an understanding of supply and demand. In his view, both influence price. In the long run, however, the amount produced can be increased or decreased, so supply, which is based on cost of production, is the more important factor. Marshall also contributed the concept of marginal utility—the extra utility or satisfaction that is gained from the consumption of an additional unit of a product.

Marshall taught at Cambridge University for 23 years, so he and his followers are called the Cambridge School. Also credited as a founder of the neoclassical school of economics, his influence remains strong today, especially in the field of microeconomics—the branch of economics concerned with decision making and other behavior by government, business, and individuals.

BOOKS BY MARSHALL

Money, Credit and Commerce (1923). Kelley 1965 $39.50. ISBN 0-678-00072-7
Principles of Economics (1890). Porcupine 1982 $24.95. ISBN 0-87991-051-8

BOOK ABOUT MARSHALL

Reisman, David. *Alfred Marshall: Progress and Politics.* St. Martin's 1987 $45.00. ISBN 0-312-00773-6 Critical evolution of Marshall's place in the development of economic theory.

BUSINESS CYCLES

Barro, Robert J. (ed). *Modern Business Cycle Theory.* Harvard Univ Pr 1989 $35.00. ISBN 0-674-57860-0
Gabisch, Gunter, and Hans-Walter Lorenz. *Business Cycle Theory: A Survey of Methods and Concepts.* Springer-Verlag 1989 $25.50. ISBN 0-387-51059-1
Hall, Robert E. (ed). *Inflation: Causes and Effects. National Bureau of Economic Research—Project Report Ser.* Univ of Chicago Pr 1984 $10.95. ISBN 0-226-31324-7
Heilbroner, Robert L. *Beyond Boom and Crash.* Norton 1979 $2.95. ISBN 0-393-05707-0
Klein, Burton H. *Prices, Wages, and Business Cycles: A Dynamic Theory.* Pergamon 1984 $50.00. ISBN 0-08-030126-6
∎Lehmann, Michael B. *The Dow Jones-Irwin Guide to Using "The Wall Street Journal."* Dow Jones 1986 $22.50. ISBN 0-87094-923-3 Useful guide to understanding trends in business.
MacEwan, Arthur, and William K. Tabb (eds). *Instability and Change in the World Economy.* Monthly Review 1989 $15.00. ISBN 0-85345-783-2
Mullineaux, A. W. *The Business Cycle After Keynes: A Contempory Analysis.* Barnes 1984 $25.00. ISBN 0-389-20453-6
Schumpeter, Joseph A. *The Theory of Economic Development: An Inquiry into Profits, Capital, Credit, Interest and the Business Cycle. Social Science Classics Ser.* Transaction 1983 $19.95. ISBN 0-87855-698-2
Stewart, Hugh B. *Recollecting the Future: A View of Business, Technology, and Innovation in the Next 30 Years.* Dow Jones 1988 $24.95. ISBN 1-55623-143-1
Valentine, Lloyd M. *Business Cycles and Forecasting.* South-Western 1986. ISBN 0-538-08550-9
Wolfson, Martin H. *Financial Crises: Understanding the Postwar U.S. Experience.* Sharpe 1986 $15.95. ISBN 0-87332-377-7

CAPITALISM AND FREE ENTERPRISE

Adams, Walter. *The Structure of American Industry.* Macmillan 1990 $26.00. ISBN 0-023-00771-0
Carson, Robert B. *Economic Issues Today: Alternative Approaches.* St. Martin's 1986 $16.00. ISBN 0-312-23455-4
Carson, Robert B. *Enterprises: An Introduction to Business.* Harcourt 1985 $27.00. ISBN 0-15-522800-5
Gilbert, Neil. *Capitalism and the Welfare State: Dilemmas of Social Benevolence.* Yale Univ Pr 1985 $7.95. ISBN 0-300-03477-6
Heilbroner, Robert L. *The Nature and Logic of Capitalism.* Norton 1986 $7.70. ISBN 0-393-95529-X
Leftwich, Richard H. *The Price System and Resource Allocation.* Dryden 1982 $15.75. ISBN 0-030-12533-2

• Lekachman, Robert. *Capitalism for Beginners.* Pantheon 1981 $6.95. ISBN 0-394-73863-2 Discussion of capitalism in comic-book format.

* Leone, Bruno (ed). *Capitalism: Opposing Viewpoints.* Greenhaven 1986 $15.95. ISBN 0-89908-384-6 A collection of primary sources examining the history, vices, and virtues of capitalism.

• Lunt, Steven D. *Free Enterprise in America. Economics Impact Books Ser.* Watts 1985 $12.90. ISBN 0-531-10061-8 Examines free-enterprise system in comparison to socialism and communism basic workings, economic terms, and role of government.

COMPARATIVE ECONOMIC SYSTEMS

• Ebenstein, William, and Edwin Fogelman. *Today's Isms: Communism, Fascism, Capitalism and Socialism.* Prentice 1985 $29.00. ISBN 0-13-924473-5 Widely used in high schools because of its clarity and understandable presentation.

Ellman, Michael. *Socialist Planning. Modern Cambridge Economics Ser.* Cambridge Univ Pr 1989 $18.95. ISBN 0-521-35866-3

• Lekachman, Robert. *Capitalism for Beginners.* Pantheon 1981 $6.95. ISBN 0-394-73863-2 Discussion of capitalism in comic-book format.

Lenin, V. I. *Economic Thought and the Problem of the Unity of the World.* 2 vols. Inst Economic Pol 1987 $257.50. ISBN 0-86722-152-6

• Leone, Bruno (ed). *Capitalism: Opposing Viewpoints. ISMS Book Ser.* Greenhaven 1986 $7.95. ISBN 0-89908-359-5 Collection of opposing views on capitalism, yesterday and tomorrow.

• Leone, Bruno (ed). *Communism: Opposing Viewpoints. ISMS Book Ser.* Greenhaven 1986 $7.95. ISBN 0-89908-360-9 A mid-1980s anthology of opinions on life and personal freedom under Communist rule.

• Leone, Bruno (ed). *Socialism: Opposing Viewpoints. ISMS Book Ser.* Greenhaven 1986 $7.95. ISBN 0-89908-361-7 Anthology of viewpoints on Socialist thought and practices.

Prout, Christopher. *Market Socialism in Yugoslavia.* Oxford Univ Pr 1985 $19.95. ISBN 0-19-828287-7

Schumpeter, Joseph A. *Capitalism, Socialism, and Democracy.* Peter Smith 1983 $17.75. ISBN 0-8446-6027-2

ENGELS, FRIEDRICH   1820–1895

Friedrich Engels was a German businessman and sociologist who collaborated extensively with the German philosopher, economist, and historian Karl Marx (*see* Marx, Vol. 2, Economics: Comparative Economic Systems) and at times provided him with money to live on from his family's textile business in Manchester, England. Engels first met Marx in Paris in 1844, just before the publication of Marx's book on the English working class, and he became the coauthor with Marx of a number of important books, including *The Communist Manifesto* (1848). After Marx's death, Engels completed the second and third volumes of Marx's *Das Kapital (Capital).* With Marx, he developed the theory of dialectical materialism—the idea that all change is the product of a constant conflict between opposites—and was the cofounder of communism. He wrote in 1886, "Marx was a genius; we others were at best talented."

BOOKS BY ENGELS

The Communist Manifesto (1848). (coauthored with Karl Marx) Penguin 1985 $2.95. ISBN 0-14-044478-5

The Condition of the Working Class in England (1845). Academy Chi Pubs 1984 $6.95. ISBN 0-89733-1370

The German Ideology, Part 1 and Selections from Parts 2 and 3. (1845–1846). (coauthored with Karl Marx) C. J. Arthur (ed). Intl Pubs 1970 $4.25. ISBN 0-7178-0302-3

The Origin of the Family: Private Property and the State (1884). Penguin 1986 $5.95. ISBN
    0-14-044465-3
Socialism: Utopian and Scientific (1880). Greenwood 1977 $35.00. ISBN 0-8371-96221

BOOKS ABOUT ENGELS

Carver, Terrell. *Friedrich Engels: His Life and Thought.* Macmillan 1989. Biography that
    relates Engels's personal life to his work.
Carver, Terrell. *Marx and Engels: The Intellectual Relationship.* Indiana Univ Pr 1984. Discus-
    sion of the collaboration between these two founders of communism.
Heilbroner, Robert L. *The Worldly Philosophers: The Lives, Times, and Ideas of the Great Economic
    Thinkers.* Simon 1987 $9.95. ISBN 0-671-63318-X Includes a chapter on Engels.
Henderson, W. O. *Marx and Engels and the English Workers and Other Essays.* Biblio Dist
    1989 $32.50. ISBN 0-7146-3334-8 Collection of the writings of the founders of
    communism.

MARX, KARL   1818–1883

German philosopher and revolutionary, Karl Marx is considered an economist,
a sociologist, and a historian. He is often credited with founding economic
history and sociology, and his writings deeply influenced socialism and Soviet
communism.

As an economic thinker, Marx transformed British economist David
Ricardo's (*see* Ricardo, Vol. 2, Economics: World Economy) labor theory of
value—the doctrine that the amount of labor required for the production of a
good is the main determinant of the commodity's price—into the demand that
workers receive the whole product of their labor. He argued, in his most
famous work, *Capital* (1867–1894), and elsewhere, that capitalism was headed
for an inevitable breakdown, which would be followed by a Socialist revolution. His sociological concept that people's ideas are rooted in their social and
economic life led to such doctrines as the "false class consciousness" of many
workers and to such fields as the sociology of knowledge, which asserts that
knowledge is not a constant but a product of that society that produces it.
Simply put, in his view political, social, and economic reality were based in the
class struggle, the end result of which would be the destruction of capitalism
and the rise of a new social and economic order.

In 1864 Marx, along with his collaborator Friedrich Engels (*see* Engels, Vol.
2, Economics: Comparative Economic Systems), founded the International
Workingmen's Association, which became the First International of the Communist party. In his inaugural address, Marx used the same words with which
he and Engels ended *The Communist Manifesto* (1848): "Workers of the world,
unite!"

BOOKS BY MARX

Capital (1867–1894). 2 vols. Buccaneer 1988. Vol. 1 *The Process of Capitalist Production.*
    $49.95. ISBN 0-89966-641-8. Vol. 2 *The Process of Circulation of Capital.* $39.95. ISBN
    0-89955-642-6. Vol. 3 *The Process of Capitalist Production As a Whole.* $59.95. ISBN
    0-89966-643-4
The Communist Manifesto (1848). (coauthored with Friedrich Engels) Penguin 1985 $2.95.
    ISBN 0-14-044478-5

BOOKS ABOUT MARX

Berlin, Isaiah. *Karl Marx: His Life and Environment.* Oxford Univ Pr 1978 $9.95. ISBN
    0-19-520052-7 Biography that deals with both Marx's personal and political life.
Elster, John (ed). *Karl Marx: A Reader.* Cambridge Univ Pr 1986 $8.95. ISBN 0-521-
    33832-8 Collection of Marx's most important works.

Elster, John (ed). *Making Sense of Marx.* Cambridge Univ Pr 1985 $17.95. ISBN 0-521-29705-2 Critical analysis emphasizing rational-choice theory and the philosophy of explanation.

Gurley, John C. *Challenges to Capitalism: Marx, Lenin, Stalin, and Mao.* Addison 1988 $8.95. ISBN 0-201-08054-0 Policies and politics of the major proponents of socialism–communism.

Heilbroner, Robert L. *The Worldly Philosophers: The Lives, Times, and Ideas of the Great Economic Thinkers.* Simon 1987 $9.95. ISBN 0-671-63318-X Includes chapter on the life and work of Marx.

ROBINSON, JOAN   1903–1983

British economist Joan Robinson was educated at Cambridge University and became a member of the faculty in 1931. She remained there until 1971, becoming a full professor in 1965.

Robinson's most important contribution to economic thought was her development of the theory of imperfect competition. In *The Economics of Imperfect Competition* (1933; 2nd edition 1969), she analyzed the distribution and allocation of resources by business. She particularly looked at exploitation.

At Cambridge, Robinson worked with British economist John Maynard Keynes (*see* Keynes, Vol. 2, Economics: Government and Economics) in critiquing and refining his theory of government intervention in the economy. She, like Keynes, believed that government spending should be used to control a nation's economy and prevent economic depressions. In *Introduction to the Theory of Employment* (1937), Robinson clearly explained Keynes's theories for a general audience.

Robinson also believed capitalism to be an unstable form of government and wrote articles and books, such as *An Essay on Marxian Economics* (1942), sympathetic to Marxist ideologies. Her pro-Marxist beliefs caused much controversy. In 1979, in recognition of her valuable contributions to economic thought, Robinson became the first woman made an honorary fellow at King's College.

BOOKS BY ROBINSON

The Accumulation of Capital (1956). Porcupine 1986 $17.95. ISBN 0-87991-260-X

Aspects of Development and Underdevelopment. Modern Cambridge Economics Ser. Cambridge Univ Pr 1979 $11.95. ISBN 0-521-29589-0

Essays in the Theory of Employment (1950). Hyperion 1985 $21.00. ISBN 0-88355-812-2

The Rate of Interest and Other Essays (1952). Hyperion 1986 $19.00 ISBN 0-88355-959-5

BOOK ABOUT ROBINSON

Feiwell, George R. (ed). *Joan Robinson and Modern Economic Theory.* New York Univ Pr 1989 $150.00. ISBN 0-8147-2591-0 Discussion of Robinson's place in the development of economic theory.

SMITH, ADAM   1723–1790

Adam Smith, a Scot, was a philosopher and economist. Educated at the universities of Glasgow and Oxford, he served as a professor of philosophy at Glasgow. Although a teacher for much of his life, he also served as commissioner of customs in Scotland. With his work *An Inquiry into the Nature and Causes of the Wealth of Nations* (1776) and his theory of the free-market economy, he is considered the creator of the classic system of economics.

According to Smith, the greatest source of power is an economic system and therefore the base of the wealth of all nations is the division of labor. He believed that the value of goods derives from the labor used to produce the goods. Smith is also responsible for the concept of the "invisible hand" that guides and ensures the general stability of an economy. According to his concept of laissez-faire economics, the self-interest of each person in the marketplace ensures the well-being of all. Producers, to their own advantage, provide goods and services that consumers, in their best interests, purchase as cheaply as possible. The Industrial Revolution proved some of Smith's ideas wrong, but his influence on later economists is undeniable.

BOOKS BY SMITH

An Inquiry into the Nature and Causes of the Wealth of Nations (1776). Arthur H. Jenkins (ed). 2 vols. Liberty Fund 1982 $11.00. ISBN 0-86597-008-4
The Theory of Moral Sentiments (1759). Liberty Fund 1977 $9.95. ISBN 0-913966-12-6

BOOKS ABOUT SMITH

Brown, Maurice. *Adam Smith's Economics: Its Place in the Development of Economic Thought.* Routledge 1988 $55.00. ISBN 0-7099-5079-9 Discussion of dialectical materialism.
Heilbroner, Robert L. (ed). *The Essential Adam Smith.* Norton 1986 $22.00. ISBN 0-393-02291-9 Heilbroner's selection of what he considers basic theory in Smith's works.
Heilbroner, Robert L. *The Worldly Philosophers: The Lives, Times, and Ideas of the Great Economic Thinkers.* Simon 1987 $9.95. ISBN 0-671-63318-X Includes a chapter on Smith.
O'Driscoll, Gerald P., Jr. (ed). *Adam Smith and Modern Political Economy: Bicentennial Essays on the Wealth of Nations.* Iowa State Univ Pr 1979 $15.95. ISBN 0-8138-1900-8 Eleven papers presented by economists discussing Smith's theories.

CONSUMERISM

Caplovitz, David. *The Poor Pay More: Consumer Practices of Low Income Families.* Free Pr 1967 $13.95. ISBN 0-02-905250-5
Dusenberry, James S. *Income, Saving and the Theory of Consumer Behavior.* Harvard Univ Pr 1943. (o.p.)
Hill, Martha, *et al* (eds). *Motivation and Economic Mobility.* Inst for Social Research 1985 $20.00. ISBN 0-87944-304-9
Katona, George. *Consumer Response to Income Increases.* Greenwood 1980 $35.00. ISBN 0-313-22298-3
Katona, George. *Essays on Behavioral Economics.* Inst for Social Research 1980 $10.50. ISBN 0-87944-257-3
Katona, George. *The Powerful Consumer: Psychological Studies of the American Economy.* Greenwood 1977 $35.00. ISBN 0-8371-9812-7
∎Nader, Ralph. *Unsafe at Any Speed.* Bantam 1972. (o.p.) Describes the economic pressure and power that paralyze efforts to manufacture safe automobiles and that cost consumers more than just money.
∎Nader, Ralph, *et al. The Lemon Book.* Caroline 1980. (o.p.) Relates the laws and legislation for consumer protection in purchasing an automobile.
Packard, Vance. *The Ultra Rich: How Much Is Too Much?* Little 1989 $22.95. ISBN 0-316-68752-9
∎Porter, Sylvia. *New Money Book For the 80's.* Avon 1980 $10.95. ISBN 0-380-51060-X Candid discussion about personal finances.
∎Schlink, F. J. *Eat, Drink and Be Wary: Getting and Spending: A Consumer's Dilemma.* Ayer (repr of 1935 ed) $24.50. ISBN 0-405-08045-X Brings to light the operations of the government in behalf of consumers.

■Sinclair, Upton. *The Jungle. Airmont Classics Ser.* Airmont 1965 $1.95. ISBN 0-8049-0086-8 Relates the fictional story of a young Indian boy raised by wolves in the jungle.

■Toffler, Alvin. *Future Shock.* Bantam 1971 $4.95. ISBN 0-553-24649-6 Based on the state of the Western world in 1970, but not out of date. Describes change and the affects it has on communities and people as family members and as individuals.

Veblen, Thorstein. *The Theory of the Leisure Class.* Penguin 1979 $4.95. ISBN 0-14-005363-8

THE ECONOMY

Arndt, H. W. *Economic Development: The History of an Idea.* Univ of Chicago Pr 1989 $9.95. ISBN 0-226-02722-8

Arndt, H. W. *The Rise and Fall of Economic Growth: A Study in Contemporary Thought.* Univ of Chicago Pr 1984 $6.95. ISBN 0-226-02717-1

■Bender, David L. (ed). *America's Economy, 1989 Annual. Opposing Viewpoints Sources Ser.* Greenhaven 1989 $9.95. ISBN 0-89908-550-4 Twenty-five viewpoints that debate many current economic issues including the recent savings-and-loan crisis.

■Bonello, Frank J., and Thomas R. Swartz (eds). *Taking Sides: Clashing Views on Controversial Economic Issues.* Dushkin 1988 $9.95. ISBN 0-87967-740-6 Differing points of view on controversial issues in economics.

■Claypool, Jane. *Unemployment. Impact Ser.* Watts 1983. ISBN 0-531-04586-2 Focuses on the relationship between unemployment and inflation, recession, economic depression, and other economic factors; includes oral histories.

■Cole, Don. *Annual Editions: Economics 90/91.* Dushkin 1990 $9.95. ISBN 0-87967-840-2

Stock Exchange. Drypoint etching by K. Dehmann (c. 1915-1920). From the Boyd Collection. Courtesy of The New-York Historical Society, N.Y.C.

Well-rounded collection of issues for the study of economics that are both current and of enduring interest.

Hall, Robert E. (ed). *Inflation: Causes and Effects.* Univ of Chicago Pr 1984 $10.95. ISBN 0-226-31324-7

Heller, Walter. *New Dimensions of Political Economy.* Godkin Lectures Ser. Harvard Univ Pr 1966 $17.00. ISBN 0-674-61100-4

Kuznets, Simon. *Economic Growth of Nations: Total Output and Production Structure.* Harvard Univ Pr 1971 $27.50. ISBN 0-674-22780-8

Olson, Mancur. *The Rise and Decline of Nations: Economic Growth, Stagflation, and Social Rigidities.* Yale Univ Pr 1984 $10.95. ISBN 0-300-03079-7

∎Schumacher, E. F. *Small Is Beautiful: Economics as if People Mattered.* Harper 1989 $8.95. ISBN 0-06-091630-3 A common-sense approach and feasible solutions to many national economic and human problems.

Schumpeter, Joseph A. *The Theory of Economic Development: An Inquiry into Profits, Capital, Credit, Interest and the Business Cycle.* Social Science Classics Ser. Transaction 1983 $19.95. ISBN 0-87855-698-2

Weitzman, Martin L. *The Share Economy: Conquering Stagflation.* Harvard Univ Pr 1986 $7.95. ISBN 0-674-80583-6

FORMS OF BUSINESS ENTERPRISES

Barnard, Chester I. *The Functions of the Executive.* Harvard Univ Pr 1968 $10.95. ISBN 0-674-32803-5

∎Blanchard, Kenneth. *The One Minute Manager.* Berkley 1987 $7.95. ISBN 0-425-09847-8 Offers methods of handling business functions from problem solving to praising employees in minimum time frame.

Davis, Joseph S. *Essays in the Earlier History of American Corporations.* 2 vols. Russell Sage 1965.

Drucker, Peter F. *The Concept of the Corporation.* NAL 1983 $3.95. ISBN 0-451-62197-2

∎Drucker, Peter F. *The Effective Executive.* Harper 1985 $8.95. ISBN 0-06-091209-X Discusses what makes an executive more efficient and valuable as an employer and as an employee.

Ginzberg, Eli, and George Vojta. *Beyond Human Scale: Large Corporations at Risk.* Basic 1987 $7.95. ISBN 0-465-00659-0

Green, Mark, and John F. Berry. *The Challenge of Hidden Profits: Reducing Corporate Bureaucracy and Waste.* Morrow 1985 $19.45. ISBN 0-688-03986-3

Heilbroner, Robert L., and James K. Galbraith. *The Economic Problem.* Prentice 1987 $50.00. ISBN 0-13-233081-4

∎Iacocca, Lee A. *Iacocca: An Autobiography.* Bantam 1987 $10.95. ISBN 0-8161-4254-8 Chrysler CEO's story of survival and triumph in the business world; includes Iacocca's personal insights on business and management.

∎Iacocca, Lee A. *Talking Straight.* Bantam 1989 $4.95. ISBN 0-553-27805-3 A head-on analysis of some major problems in the United States, with suggestions on where and how to start rebuilding and repairing the American image.

Keating, Barry P., and Maryann O. Keating. *Not-for-Profit.* Horton 1980 $19.95. ISBN 0-913878-18-9

Lacy, Robert. *Ford: The Men and the Machine.* Little 1986.

Love, John F. *McDonald's: Behind the Arches.* Bantam 1986 $21.95. ISBN 0-553-05127-X

∎Peters, Thomas J., and Robert H. Walterman, Jr. *In Search of Excellence: Lessons from America's Best Run Companies.* Warner Bks 1984 $12.95. ISBN 0-446-38507-7 Spotlights several U.S. companies that have achieved excellence in their management systems and sustained it over time.

Simon, Herbert. *Models of Bounded Rationality.* Vol. 2 *Behavioral Economics and Business Organization.* MIT Pr 1982 $15.00. ISBN 0-262-69087-X

∎Trump, Donald. *The Art of the Deal.* Warner Bks 1988 $5.95. ISBN 0-446-35325-6 How Trump built his empire.

Veblen, Thorstein. *The Theory of Business Enterprise.* Transaction 1978 $19.95. ISBN 0-887-38699-0

Veblen, Thorstein. *The Theory of the Leisure Class.* Penguin 1979 $4.95. ISBN 0-14-005363-8

Wolfson, Nicholas. *The Modern Corporation: Free Markets versus Regulation.* Free Pr 1984 $25.00. ISBN 0-02-934700-9

ARROW, KENNETH J. 1921–

Kenneth J. Arrow, an American economist, placed his main focus on abstract notions instead of on the more practical concerns dealt with by most marketplace economists. He is known for his contributions to mathematical economics, his studies of risk taking, and his analysis of the economics of organizations. He is also a specialist in welfare economics and general equilibrium theory. In addition to outlining a coherent understanding of risk taking and evolving a theory of welfare, he was a leader in the development of general approaches to several complex problems. One of these was the possibility of predicting trends from the many options at work in the economy. Among his major contributions to the field of economics is his impossibility theorem. In this theorem he uses a mathematical proof to demonstrate that in principle a perfect system of democratic choice-making is not possible.

After teaching at the University of Chicago for two years and at Stanford University for almost 20 years, Arrow went on to teach at Harvard from 1968 to 1979. He then returned to Stanford as the Joan Kenney professor of economics and operations research. In 1962 Arrow served as a member of the President's Council of Economic Advisers. In 1972, while at Harvard, he shared the Nobel Prize in economics with Sir John Richard Hicks of England. They received the prize for their pioneering efforts in the development of general economic equilibrium theory and welfare theory.

BOOKS BY ARROW

Collected Papers of Kenneth J. Arrow: Applied Economics (1983). 2 vols. Harvard Univ Pr 1985 $27.00. ISBN 0-674-13778-7

Frontiers of Economics. (coedited with Seppo Honkapohja) Basil Blackwell 1987 $22.50. ISBN 0-631-15587-2

The Limits of Organization (1974). Norton 1974 $5.95. ISBN 0-393-09323-9

Public Investment, the Rate of Return, and Optimum Fiscal Policy. (coauthored with Mordecai Kurz) Johns Hopkins Univ Pr 1970 $29.00. ISBN 0-801-81124-4

Social Choice and Individual Values (1951). Yale Univ Pr 1970 $7.95. ISBN 0-300-01364-7

BOOK ABOUT ARROW

Feiwell, George R. (ed). *Arrow and the Foundations of the Theory of Economics Policy.* New York Univ Pr 1987 $75.00. ISBN 0-8147-2583-X Emphasis on social choice.

GOVERNMENT AND ECONOMICS

■Davis, Bertha. *The National Debt. Impact Ser.* Watts 1987 $12.90. ISBN 0-531-10415-X Introduction to the government budget-making process, the national debt, and the Gramm-Rudman Act.

Hall, Robert E. (ed). *Inflation: Causes and Effects. National Bureau of Economic Research-Project Report Ser.* Univ of Chicago Pr 1984 $10.95. ISBN 0-226-31324-7

■Iacocca, Lee A. *Talking Straight.* Bantam 1989 $4.95. ISBN 0-553-27805-3 A head-on analysis of some major problems in the United States and suggestions on where and how to start rebuilding and repairing the American image.

Leftwich, Richard H., and Ansel Sharp. *Economics of Social Issues.* Business Pub 1984.

Lekachman, Robert. *Greed Is Not Enough: Reaganomics.* Pantheon 1982 $3.95. ISBN 0-394-71249-8

Lekachman, Robert. *Vision and Nightmares: America After Reagan.* Macmillan 1988 $10.95. ISBN 0-02-073710-6

McGraw, Thomas K. *Prophets of Regulation.* Harvard Univ Pr 1986 $8.95. ISBN 0-674-71608-6

North, Douglas C., and Roger Leroy Miller. *The Economics of Public Issues.* Harper 1985 $13.50. ISBN 0-06-044832-6

Petersen, H. Craig. *Business and Government.* Harper 1988 $37.95. ISBN 0-06-045157-2

Rees, Albert. *Striking a Balance: Making National Economic Policy.* Univ of Chicago Pr 1986 $6.95. ISBN 0-226-70708-3

Stein, Herbert. *Governing the Five Trillion Dollar Economy: A Twentieth Century Fund Essay.* Oxford Univ Pr 1989 $17.95. ISBN 0-19-506038-5

Stein, Hebert. *Presidential Economics: The Making of Economic Policy from Roosevelt to Reagan and Beyond.* Simon 1988 $12.75. ISBN 0-8447-3656-2

Stein, Herbert. *Washington Bedtime Stories: The Politics of Money and Jobs.* Free Pr 1986 $19.95. ISBN 0-317-53675-3

Stelzer, Irwin M. *Selected Antitrust Cases: Landmark Decisions.* Irwin 1986 $20.95. ISBN 0-256-03222-X

Wilcox, Clair, and William G. Shepherd. *Public Policies Toward Business.* Irwin 1990 $41.95. ISBN 0-256-08464-5

Zysman, John. *Governments, Markets, and Growth: Financial Systems and the Politics of Industrial Change.* Cornell Univ Pr 1983 $14.95. ISBN 0-8014-9252-1

FRIEDMAN, MILTON   1912–

Milton Friedman is an influential, conservative American economist who is a strong believer in a free-enterprise economy. A staff member of the National Bureau of Economic Research for many years, he also taught at the University of Chicago from 1946 to 1977.

Friedman's theories are sometimes called monetarist or Chicago School. He believes that changes in the money supply precede changes in general economic activity. Friedman's primary theory is that the quantity of money in circulation is of prime importance. A proponent of laissez-faire capitalism, an economic system in which the government interferes very little in economic affairs, he favors the abolition of such programs as welfare and social security. In his view, policies such as price ceilings (systems under which the highest price that can be charged for goods is set), fixed interest rates (system under which interest rates are set and do not vary), and minimum wages (the lowest legal wage that can be paid to most workers) serve only to keep prices from fulfilling their role as signals. According to Friedman, one of the most important features of the U.S. economy is the freedom to fail.

Friedman is a prolific writer and has been a contributing editor to *Newsweek* magazine since 1971. Friedman won the Nobel Prize in economics in 1976.

BOOKS BY FRIEDMAN

Capitalism and Freedom: With a New Preface (1962). Univ of Chicago Pr 1963 $7.95. ISBN 0-226-26401-7

Essays in Positive Economics (1953). Univ of Chicago Pr 1966 $9.00. ISBN 0-226-26403-3

∎ *Free to Choose: A Personal Statement* (1980). (coauthored with Rose Friedman) Avon 1981 $4.95. ISBN 0-380-52548-8 Tells how American freedom and prosperity have suffered under government. Offers plans to correct the future economy of the United States before it is too late. Conservative, monetarist view.

Monetary History of the United States, 1867–1960 (1963). *Business Cycles Ser.* (coauthored with Anna J. Schwartz) National Bureau of Economic Research 1963 $40.00.

Monetary Trends in the United States and the United Kingdom: Their Relations to Income, Prices, and Interest Rates, 1867–1975. (coauthored with Anna J. Schwartz) Univ of Chicago Pr 1984 $25.00. ISBN 0-226-26410-6 *Monetary versus Fiscal Policy.* (coauthored with Walter H. Heller) Norton 1969 $3.95. ISBN 0-393-09847-8

Studies in the Quantity Theory of Money (1956) (ed). Univ of Chicago Pr 1973 $4.75. ISBN 0-226-26406-8

Unemployment versus Inflation (1975). Transatlantic 1975 $4.25. ISBN 0-255-36069-X

BOOKS ABOUT FRIEDMAN

Butler, Eamonn. *Milton Friedman: A Guide to His Economic Thought.* Universe 1985 $8.95. ISBN 0-87663-878-7 Discussion of Friedman's monetary policy.

Raynak, Elton. *Not So Free to Choose: The Political Economy of Milton Friedman and Ronald Reagan.* Praeger 1986 $38.95. ISBN 0-275-92363-0 Critique of the economist and the supply-side economic policies of the former president.

GALBRAITH, JOHN KENNETH 1908–

John Kenneth Galbraith is a Canadian-born American economist who is perhaps the most widely read economist in the world. He taught at Harvard from 1934 to 1939 and then again from 1949 to 1975. An adviser to President John F. Kennedy, he served from 1961 to 1963 as U.S. ambassador to India. His style and wit in writing and his frequent media appearances have contributed greatly to his fame as an economist.

Galbraith believes that it is not sufficient for government to manage the level of effective demand; government must manage the market itself. Galbraith stated in *American Capitalism* (1952) that the market is far from competitive, and governments and labor unions must serve as "countervailing power." He believes that ultimately "producer sovereignty" takes the place of consumer sovereignty and the producer—not the consumer—becomes ruler of the marketplace.

BOOKS BY GALBRAITH

■ *The Affluent Society* (1958). Houghton 1984 $18.95. ISBN 0-395-36613-5 Description of conditions in the United States after World War II, focusing on the gap between the affluent and the poor and offering recommendations for change.

Ambassador's Journal: A Personal Account of the Kennedy Years (1969). Paragon Hse 1988 $10.95. ISBN 1-55778-071-4

American Capitalism: The Concept of Countervailing Power (1952). Houghton $3.25. ISBN 0-395-08367-2

Capitalism, Communism and Coexistence: From the Bitter Past to a Better Prospect. (coauthored with Stanislav Menshikov) Houghton 1988 $17.95. ISBN 0-395-47316-0

■ *The Galbraith Reader.* Harvard Common Pr 1977 $12.95. ISBN 0-87645-091-5 An anthology of Galbraith's important works.

■ *A Life in Our Times: Memoirs.* Houghton 1981 $16.96. ISBN 0-395-30509-8 Autobiography of the famous economics writer, statesman, and presidential adviser.

Money, Whence It Came, Where It Went. Houghton 1975 $10.00. ISBN 0-395-19843-7

The New Industrial State. (1967). Houghton 1985 $19.95. ISBN 0-395-38991-7

The Voice of the Poor: Essays in Economic and Political Persuasion. Harvard Univ Pr 1984 $3.95. ISBN 0-674-94296-5

BOOKS ABOUT GALBRAITH

■ Gambs, John S. *John Kenneth Galbraith. Twayne's World Leader Ser.* St. Martin's 1975. (o.p.) $4.95. ISBN 0-312-44380-3 Introduces Galbraith and his philosophies.

Hession, Charles H. *John Kenneth Galbraith and His Critics.* NAL 1972. (o.p.) Provides an intellectual exchange between Galbraith and his critics, focusing on a growing recognition of the significance of his works in understanding contemporary American society.

KEYNES, JOHN MAYNARD   1883–1946

John Maynard Keynes, a British economist who taught at Cambridge University, is considered by many to be the most influential economist of the twentieth century. His most important work is *The General Theory of Employment, Interest, and Money* (1936). His stress on the importance to the economy of consumption (demand) greatly influenced the policies of U.S. President Franklin D. Roosevelt's New Deal during the Great Depression. (*See* F. Roosevelt, Vol. 2, United States History: The Great Depression and the New Deal.) Keynes rejected traditional theories of the free market and championed active government intervention in the marketplace. In times of recession he believed the government should spend heavily and ease monetary policies to stimulate business activity, even at the risk of unbalancing the budget and creating a deficit.

The General Theory of Employment, Interest, and Money was the major text of the Keynesian revolution, which transformed all subsequent economic theory—Keynesian or otherwise. After World War II Keynes advocated the creation of the World Bank.

BOOKS BY KEYNES

The Economic Consequences of the Peace (1919). Penguin 1988 $7.95. ISBN 0-14-011380-0
The General Theory of Employment, Interest, and Money (1936). Harcourt 1965 $7.95. ISBN 0-15-634711-3
A Treatise on Money (1930). 2 vols. AMS 1930 $75.00. ISBN 0-404-15000-4

BOOKS ABOUT KEYNES

Heilbroner, Robert J. *The Worldly Philosophers: The Lives, Times, and Ideas of the Great Economic Thinkers.* Simon 1987 $9.95. ISBN 0-671-63318-X Includes a chapter on Keynes.
Hillard, John (ed). *J. M. Keynes in Retrospect: The Legacy of the Keynesian Revolution.* Gower 1989 $37.50. ISBN 1-85278-012-6 Evaluation of the importance and influence of Keynes.
Keynes, Milo (ed). *Essays on John Maynard Keynes.* Cambridge Univ Pr 1980 $16.95. ISBN 0-521-29696-X Volume intended for the general reader as well as for economists, providing a picture of the life of Keynes and his wide range of interests.

RIVLIN, ALICE MITCHELL   1931–

Although Alice Rivlin was born in Philadelphia, she grew up in Bloomington, Indiana, where her father was a professor of nuclear physics. After graduating at the top of her class in high school, she returned to Pennsylvania to study at Bryn Mawr College. Like many of her fellow students, Rivlin was uncertain about the type of career she wanted to follow. At first, she considered becoming a diplomat. But during a summer course at Indiana University, she became fascinated by the study of economics because it "seemed less fuzzy than history or political science."

After obtaining a Ph.D. in economics from Harvard University, Rivlin moved to Washington, D.C. With a definite flair for economic analysis and the development of public policy, she decided to take a job at the Brookings Institution, the so-called "think tank" devoted to independent research, education, and publications on social issues. Except for one four-year period, when she served as Assistant Secretary at the Department of Health, Education, and Welfare, Rivlin remained on the Brookings staff until 1975. During those years, she also wrote and published several articles on economics and related topics.

In 1974 Congress established the Congressional Budget Office (CBO). The purpose of the new agency was to assist Congress in analyzing and forming policy on federal spending and income. At the time, many people thought that Alice Rivlin would be the best choice for the agency's first director. "When I was first approached about this job," she said, "I asked [a friend] if I'd be crazy to take it. He said, 'Crazy? I think you'd be insane!' "

Despite her friend's advice, Rivlin took the job, and the early years at the CBO were often stormy. Although she viewed the new agency as a neutral organization, she was frequently accused of being partisan. "It was an often hostile environment," she once recalled, "because the budget process threatened existing power relationships." Much of Rivlin's problems stemmed from disagreements in Congress over her goals, and from her publicizing of the CBO in the news. Later she disagreed with Ronald Reagan (*see* Reagan, Vol. 2, United States History: The Reagan and Bush Years), arguing that the President would be unable to balance the budget as he had promised.

Despite these problems, Rivlin helped create a professional and well-run agency. When she left the CBO in 1983, Representative James R. Jones said, "The quality of the work that comes out of the CBO is very, very good. It's more professional and reliable than what comes out of the Administration regardless of who is in office. That has to be because of the standards Alice Rivlin sets for the CBO."

BOOKS BY RIVLIN

Systematic Thinking for Social Action (1971). Brookings 1971 $22.95. ISBN 0-8157-7478-8
Caring for the Disabled Elderly: Who Will Pay? (1988) (coauthored with Joshua M. Wiener) Brookings 1988 $31.95. ISBN 0-8157-7498-2
Economic Choices (1984) (ed). Brookings 1984 $22.95. ISBN 0-8157-7487-7
Ethical and Legal Issues of Social Experimentation (1975) (coedited with Michael P. Timpane) Brookings 1975 $26.95. ISBN 0-8157-7482-6
Planned Variation in Education: Should We Give Up or Try Harder? Brookings $49.50. ISBN 0-317-26352-8

INCOME, WEALTH, AND POVERTY

Anderson, Martin. *Welfare: The Political Economy of Welfare Reform in the United States.* Hoover Inst Pr 1978 $16.95. ISBN 0-8179-6811-3
Bergson, Abram. *Welfare, Planning, and Employment: Selected Essays in Economic Theory.* MIT Pr 1982 $39.50. ISBN 0-262-02175-7
Duncan, Greg J. *Years of Poverty, Years of Plenty: The Changing Economic Fortunes of American Workers and Families.* Inst for Social Research 1984 $14.00. ISBN 0-87944-298-0
Giarini, Orio (ed). *Cycles, Value, and Employment: Responses to the Economic Crisis.* Pergamon 1984 $16.25. ISBN 0-08-031283-7
Hall, Robert E. (ed). *Inflation: Causes and Effects. National Bureau of Economic Research-Project Report Ser.* Univ of Chicago Pr 1984 $10.95. ISBN 0-226-31324-7
Harrington, Michael. *The New American Poverty.* Penguin 1985 $17.95. ISBN 0-14-008112-7
Levitan, Sar A. *Programs in Aid of the Poor.* Johns Hopkins Univ Pr 1985 $6.95. ISBN 0-8018-2760-4

North, Douglas C., and Terry L. Anderson. *Growth and Welfare in the American Past.* Prentice 1983 $25.80. ISBN 0-13-366161-X

Novak, Michael. *New Consensus on Family and Welfare: A Community of Self-Reliance.* Am Enterprise Inst 1987 $9.75. ISBN 8-447-03624-4

Sowell, Thomas. *Markets and Minorities.* Basic 1981 $10.95. ISBN 0-465-04399-2

▪Terkel, Louis (Studs). *Hard Times: An Oral History of the Great Depression in America.* Pantheon 1986 $8.95. ISBN 0-394-74691-0 Interesting account of a major crisis in U.S. economic history.

Veblen, Thorstein. *The Theory of the Leisure Class.* Penguin 1979 $4.95. ISBN 0-14-005363-8

MALTHUS, THOMAS ROBERT   1766–1834

Thomas Robert Malthus, an English clergyman, sociologist, and economist, was especially concerned with overpopulation. He was so moved by the publication of a book by the anarchist and socialist William Godwin that he decided to write his own book setting forth his view that unchecked population growth constitutes an absolute barrier to societal progress. In 1798 he published his theories about population and the food supply in *An Essay on the Principles of Population.* The heart of his argument is that the population of a country tends to grow in geometric progression (2, 4, 8, 16, and so on), while food supplies increase only in arithmetic progression (1, 2, 3, 4, and so on). Population growth could be controlled only by famine, war, diseases, and "moral constraint." Since its publication, Malthus's book has been argued over and found to have many limitations.

Malthus also developed the theory of diminishing returns, which says that as more units of a variable resource are applied to a constant amount of other resources, total output will keep rising but only at a diminishing rate. Malthus applied the theory to agriculture, but later it was applied to industry as well. Today it is considered an important tool of economic analysis.

BOOKS BY MALTHUS

Population: The First Essay (1798). Univ of Michigan Pr 1959 $5.95. ISBN 0-472-06031-7

Principles of Political Economy (1820). Kelley 1986 $45.00. ISBN 0-678-00038-7

BOOKS ABOUT MALTHUS

Blaug, Mark. *Economic Theory in Retrospect.* Cambridge Univ Pr 1985 $21.95. ISBN 0-521-31644-8 Critical evaluation of economic theory.

Turner, Michael (ed). *Malthus and His Time.* St. Martin's 1986 $29.95. ISBN 0-312-50942-1 Influence of his contemporary world on the development of Malthus theory.

LABOR AND WORK

▪Berger, Gilda. *Women, Work and Wages.* Watts 1986 $12.90. ISBN 0-531-10074-X Introductory study of discrimination against women in the workplace.

Bernstein, Irving. *Turbulent Years: A History of the American Worker 1933–1941.* Houghton 1971. (o.p.)

▪Birnbach, Lisa. *Going to Work: A Unique Guided Tour Through Corporate America.* Random 1988 $15.95. ISBN 0-394-75874-9 A look at 50 different American corporations; good for young adults exploring business careers.

Brooks, Thomas R. *Picket Lines and Bargaining Tables: Organized Labor Comes of Age, 1935–1955.* Grosset 1985. (o.p.)

■ Claypool, Jane. *Unemployment. Impact Ser.* Watts 1983 $12.90. ISBN 0-531-04586-2 Relationship between unemployment and inflation, recession, economic depression, and other economic factors; includes oral histories.

Freeman, Richard B., and James L. Medoff. *What Do Unions Do?* Basic 1985 $11.95. ISBN 0-465-09132-6

Freeman, Richard B., and James L. Medoff. *Labor Economics. Foundations of Economics Ser.* Prentice 1979 $26.40. ISBN 0-13-517474-0

Marshall, Roy, and Brian Rungeling. *The Role of Unions in the American Economy.* JCEE 1984. (o.p.) $8.50.

Martin, Donald L. *An Ownership Theory of the Trade Union: A New Approach.* Univ of California Pr 1980 $30.00. ISBN 0-520-03884-3

McNulty, Paul J. *The Origins and Development of Labor Economics.* MIT Pr 1981 $9.95. ISBN 0-262-63097-4

* Meltzer, Milton. *Bread and Roses: The Struggle of American Labor.* NAL 1990 $16.95. ISBN 0-8160-2371-9 Interesting history of how labor was organized in America.

Parnes, Herbert S. *Work and Retirement: A Longitudinal Study of Men.* MIT Pr 1981 $45.00. ISBN 0-262-16079-X

Rees, Albert, and Daniel S. Hamermesh. *The Economics of Work and Pay.* Harper 1987 $48.95. ISBN 0-06-045356-7

Rees, Albert. *The Economics of Trade Unions.* Univ of Chicago Pr 1989 $12.95. ISBN 0-226-70710-5

Reynolds, Lloyd G. *Labor Economics and Labor Relations.* Prentice 1986 $48.67. ISBN 0-13-517699-9

Reynolds, Lloyd G., et al. *Economics of Labor.* Prentice 1987 $48.60. ISBN 0-13-225772-6

■ Terkel, Louis (Studs). *Working.* Ballantine 1985 $5.95. ISBN 0-345-32569-9 Interviews with workers about their feelings about the tasks they perform daily.

MONEY, BANKING, AND FINANCIAL MARKETS

■ Bose, Mihir. *Crash! A New Money Crisis?* Watts 1989 $11.90. ISBN 0-531-17138-8 Introduction to how stock exchanges work.

Campbell, Colin, and Rosemary Campbell. *Introduction to Money and Banking.* Dryden 1984 $32.95. ISBN 0-03-063568-3

■ Egan, James P. *Annual Editions: Money and Banking 90/91.* Dushkin 1990 $9.95. ISBN 0-87967-821-6 Covers a wide range of issues and topics in the study of money and banking.

Fitzgibbon, Dan. *All About Your Money.* Atheneum 1984

Gwynne, S. C. *Selling Money: A Young Banker's Account of the Great International Lending Boom and Bust.* Penguin 1987 $7.95. ISBN 0-14-010282-5

Kidwell, David S., and Richard L. Peterson. *Financial Institutions, Markets, and Money.* Dryden 1989 $30.00. ISBN 0-03-030498-9

■ Klebaner, Benjamin J. *American Commercial Banking: A History.* Twayne 1990 $25.95. ISBN 0-8057-9804-8 History of 200 years of the banking industry.

* Little, Jeffrey B. *Wall Street: How It Works.* Chelsea 1988 $9.95. ISBN 1-55546-621-4 Discusses how stocks are issued and traded and provides a history of the stock exchange.

■ Passell, Peter. *How to Read the Financial Pages.* Warner Bks 1986 $3.50. ISBN 0-446-30066-7 Good explanation for the beginner.

Rogers, Colin. *Money, Interest, and Capital: A Study in the Foundations of Monetary Theory.* Cambridge Univ Pr 1989 $17.95. ISBN 0-521-35956-2

Simpson, Thomas D. *Money, Banking and Economic Analysis.* Prentice 1987 $50.00. ISBN 0-13-600222-6

PUBLIC FINANCE AND POLICY

Buchanan, James M., and Marilyn R. Flowers. *Public Finances.* Irwin 1987 $37.50. ISBN 0-256-03340-4

Buchanan, James M., and Robert D. Tollison. *The Theory of Public Choice, II.* Univ of Michigan Pr 1984 $18.95. ISBN 0-472-08041-5

Davis, Ronnie J., and Charles W. Mayer. *Principles of Public Finance.* Prentice 1983. (o.p.) $40.00. ISBN 0-137-09881-2

Goodman, John C., and Edwin G. Dolan. *Economics of Public Policy: The Micro View.* West Pub 1985 $20.25. ISBN 0-314-85238-7

Musgrave, Richard, and Peggy Musgrave. *Public Finance in Theory and Practice.* McGraw 1988 $39.95. ISBN 0-07-044127-8

Pechman, Joseph A. *Who Paid the Taxes, 1966–1985?* Brookings 1985 $8.95. ISBN 0-8157-6997-0

Pechman, Joseph A. (ed). *Options for Tax Reform. Dialogue on Public Policy Ser.* Brookings 1984 $11.95. ISBN 0-8157-6995-4

Quigley, John M., and Daniel L. Rubinfeld (eds). *American Domestic Priorities.* Univ of California Pr 1985 $17.95. ISBN 0-520-05522-5

∎Sapinsley, Barbara. *Taxes. Issues in American History Ser.* Watts 1986 $12.90. ISBN 0-531-10268-8 Describes income and other taxes and the future of the social security system.

WORLD ECONOMY

Adams, John (ed). *The Contemporary International Economy: A Reader.* St. Martin's 1985 $21.30. ISBN 0-312-16672-9

Adams, John. *International Economics: A Self-Teaching Introduction to the Basic Concepts.* Riverdale 1989 $11.95. ISBN 0-913215-46-5

Agmon, Tamir. *Political Economy and Risk in World Financial Markets.* Lexington Bks 1985 $25.00. ISBN 0-669-08339-9

Agmon, Tamir, and Richard Levich (eds). *The Future of the International Monetary System.* Lexington Bks 1984 $35.00. ISBN 0-669-09783-7

Aliber, Robert Z. *The Handbook of International Financial Management.* Dow Jones 1989 $55.00. ISBN 1-55623-019-02

Aliber, Robert Z. *The International Money Game.* Basic 1987 $10.95. ISBN 0-465-03383-0

Bagchi, Amiya Kumar. *The Political Economy of Underdevelopment. Modern Cambridge Economics Ser.* Cambridge Univ Pr 1982 $17.95. ISBN 0-521-28404-X

Bhagwati, Jagdish. *Essays in International Economic Theory.* 2 vols. MIT Pr 1987. Vol. 1 $14.95. ISBN 0-262-52120-2. Vol. 2 $13.95. ISBN 0-262-52121-0

Boulding, Kenneth. *The World as a Total System.* Sage 1985 $25.00. ISBN 0-8039-2443-7

Corden, W. M. *Inflation, Exchange Rates, and the World Economy: Lectures on International Monetary Economics. Studies in Business and Society Ser.* Univ of Chicago Pr 1986 $12.95. ISBN 0-226-11582-8

Culbertson, John. *The Trade Threat and U.S. Trade Policy.* Twenty-First Pr 1989 $9.95. ISBN 0-918357-08-X

∎Davis, Bertha. *Crisis in Industry: Can America Compete?* Watts 1989 $12.90. ISBN 0-531-10659-4 Introductory look at how industrial competition from other countries can affect U.S. industries and the country as a whole.

Edwards, Chris. *The Fragmented World: Competing Perspectives on Trade, Money and Crisis. Development and Underdevelopment Ser.* Routledge 1985 $15.95. ISBN 0-416-73400-6

Eshag, Eprime. *Fiscal and Monetary Policies and Problems in Developing Countries. Modern Cambridge Economics Ser.* Cambridge Univ Pr 1984 $7.95. ISBN 0-521-27049-9

Goldthorpe, John H. (ed). *Order and Conflict in Contemporary Capitalism. Studies in the Political Economy of West European Nations.* Oxford Univ Pr 1984 $18.95. ISBN 0-19-878007-9

•Hart, William B. *The U.S. and World Trade. Economic Impact Books Ser.* Watts 1985 $12.90. ISBN 0-531-10067-7 Illustrated introductory text that covers U.S. trade deficit, strength of United States, and the role of multinationals.

Kenen, Peter B. *The International Economy.* Prentice 1989 $26.40. ISBN 0-13-472911-0

Kindleberger, Charles Poor. *The International Economic Order: Essays on Financial Crisis and International Public Goods.* MIT Pr 1988. ISBN 0-262-11138-1

McKeown, Kieran. *Marxist Political Economy and Marxist Urban Sociology: A Review and Elaboration of Recent Developments.* St. Martin's 1987 $32.50. ISBN 0-312-51794-7

Modigliani, Franco. *The Collected Papers of Franco Modigliani.* Vol. 4 *Monetary Theory and Stabilization Policies.* Simon Johnson (ed). MIT Pr 1989 $40.00. ISBN 0-262-13244-3

Olnek, Jay I. *The Invisible Hand: How Free Trade Is Choking the Life Out of America.* North Stonington 1982.

Rostow, Walter. *Rich Countries and Poor Countries: Reflections from the Past, Lessons for the Future.* Westview 1987 $34.50. ISBN 0-8133-0497-0

Stewart, Michael. *The Age of Interdependence: Economic Policy in a Shrinking World.* MIT Pr 1986 $8.95. ISBN 0-262-69103-5

Todaro, Michael P. *Economic Development in the Third World.* Longman 1989 $26.36. ISBN 0-8013-0210-2

von Hayek, Friedrich A. *Monetary Nationalism and International Stability.* Kelley 1989 $19.50. ISBN 0-678-00047-6

MILL, JOHN STUART   1806–1873

John Stuart Mill was an English philosopher and economist who made many contributions to political thought. For close to 40 years he worked for the East India company in London. He then served as a member of Parliament.

In his *Principles of Political Economy* (1848), Mill analyzed the economics of growth and development, challenging the traditional view that goods and services were distributed by natural law. He was concerned with production, population growth, distribution, and exchange. A strong advocate of free trade, he believed that the actual terms of international trade depend on the demand for a product in a foreign country. A government based on the will of the people, he thought, can exercise tyranny. In his view, the restrictions placed on individuals, whether by law or by opinion, ought to be based on some recognized principle rather than on the preferences and prejudices of some sections of the public. His ideas form the basis of what is today referred to as liberal democracy.

Mill also advocated socialism, women's rights, and reforms like proportional representation in government and the development of labor unions and farm cooperatives. In philosophy he advocated empiricism, the philosophy that considers experience the sole source of knowledge, as the method by which all knowledge was to be derived.

BOOKS BY MILL

Autobiography of John Stuart Mill (1873). Jack Stillinger (ed). Houghton 1957 $7.16. ISBN 0-395-05120

On Liberty: With the Subjection of Women and Chapters on Socialism. Cambridge Texts in the History of Political Thought Ser (1859). Stefan Collini (ed). Cambridge Univ Pr 1989. ISBN 0-521-37917-2

Principles of Political Economy (1848). William J. Ashley (ed). Kelley 1987 $24.95. ISBN 0-678-01453-1

BOOK ABOUT MILL

Schumpeter, Joseph A. *A History of Economic Analysis.* Oxford Univ Pr 1954 $24.95. ISBN 0-19-5041-85-2 The development through social and political history of scientific analysis in economics since Graeco-Roman times; includes analysis of Mill.

RICARDO, DAVID   1772–1823

David Ricardo, an English economist of Dutch-Jewish background, is considered by many the greatest of the classical economists. He made a fortune as a stockbroker, retired at age 40, purchased an estate, and devoted his life to writing. His major work is *Principles of Political Economy and Taxation* (1817), published three years after his retirement. It contains a classic statement of the principle of comparative advantage as applied to international trade. With a lucid numerical example, he showed why it was to the mutual advantage of both countries for England to export wool to Portugal and to import wine in return, even though both products could be produced at lower cost in Portugal.

The book contains much else, including a theory of rent. As Ricardo saw it, rent is the result of ownership of a scarce natural resource—land. Said Ricardo, "the distribution of the produce of the earth goes to the landlords in the form of rent, to the owners of capital in the form of profit and interest, and to the laborers as wages." Eventually there would be conflict over the distribution of society's income.

For more than 50 years, English economics was said to be a comment or an extension of Ricardian economics. Economic thinker Karl Marx's (*see* Marx, Vol. 2, Economics: Comparative Economic Systems) starting point in his attack on capitalism was Ricardo's labor theory of value—the doctrine that the amount of labor required for its production is the major determinant of a commodity's price—which Marx transformed into a demand that workers should receive the whole product of their labor.

BOOKS BY RICARDO

Principles of Political Economy and Taxation (1817). Biblio Dist 1978 $3.95. ISBN 0-460-01590-7

Works and Correspondence of David Ricardo (1951–1955). Cambridge Univ Pr. Vol. 1 Piero Straffa (ed). 1981 $21.85. ISBN 0-521-28505-4. Vol. 2 Piero Straffa and Maurice Dobb (eds). 1973 $62.50. ISBN 0-521-20039-3

BOOKS ABOUT RICARDO

Caravale, G. A. (ed). *The Legacy of Ricardo.* Basil Blackwell 1985 $65.00. ISBN 0-631-13617-7 Discussion in detail with reference to the analytic framework of Ricardo and subsequent theorists.

Hollander, Jacob H. *David Ricardo: A Centenary Estimate. Johns Hopkins Univ. Studies in the Social Science, Twenty Eighth Ser.* AMS 1982 $24.50. ISBN 0-404-61186-9 Reevaluation and critical analysis of Ricardo's place in economic theory.

Wood, John C. (ed). *David Ricardo: Critical Assessments. Series on Leading Economists.* 4 vols. Routledge 1985 $495.00. ISBN 0-7099-2777-0 Comprehensive selection of critical literature that comments both on the life and the works of this major contemporary economist.

WARD, BARBARA (LADY JACKSON)   1914–1981

An outstanding authority on global political, social, and economic issues, Barbara Ward wrote many books for the general reader. Born in Yorkshire, England, Ward was educated in England, France, and Germany. At Somerville College, Oxford, she took first-class honors in philosophy, politics, and economics. She became staff member of the British journal *Economist* in 1939. A year later she became foreign editor. A governor of the British Broadcasting Corporation from 1946 to 1950, in 1958 she was appointed Carnegie Fellow and

Visiting Scholar in International Economic Development at Harvard University. Ten years later, she became Albert Schweitzer Professor of International Economic Development at Columbia University. In January 1967 Pope Paul VI appointed her to the Pontifical Commission of Justice and Peace.

Ward has written a great many popular and interesting works on international relations, including *The West at Bay* (1948), *The Interplay of East and West* (1962), and *Nationalism and Ideology* (1966). In these and in her other works she has stressed the need in the West for unity, idealism, and understanding of the economic and political needs of developing nations.

BOOKS BY WARD

■ *Five Ideas That Change the World* (1959). Greenwood 1984 $27.50. ISBN 0-313-24525-8
   The five ideas are nationalism, industrialism, colonialism, communism, and internationalism.
■ *The Lopsided World.* Norton 1968. (o.p.) $1.95. The needs of the poor nations and the urgency for rich nations to help meet them.
■ *Only One Earth: The Care and Maintenance of a Small Planet* (1972). (coauthored with Rene Dubos) Norton 1983 $5.70. ISBN 0-393-30129-X International cooperation and economic help are needed for developing nations.
   Progress for a Small Planet (1962). Norton 1962 $5.95. ISBN 0-393-00746-4
■ *The Rich Nations and the Poor Nations* (1962). Norton 1962 $5.95. ISBN 0-393-00746-4
   Well-reasoned plea for help from developed nations for developing nations.
■ *Spaceship Earth* (1966). Columbia Univ Pr 1966 $15.00. ISBN 0-231-08586-9 Stresses need for international cooperation and economic aid.

GEOGRAPHY

This section is devoted to geography, the social science concerned with the study of Earth and the people who live on it. Generally, the study of geography is divided into two categories—physical geography, the study of Earth and those things on Earth not made by people, and human geography, the study of people and their activities within their environment. Thus, the study of geography helps explain not only spatial relationships—the relationships between people and places on Earth and between one place or group of places and another—but historical events, cultural developments, scientific and political processes, and social organization as well.

For ease of use, following subsections on Atlases and Gazetteers and on Surveys, the geography section is divided into subsections based roughly along the lines of the five themes devised by the Association of American Geographers and the National Council for Geographic Education to encompass the concepts that can be acquired from the study of geography—location, place, relationships within places, movement, and regions. The subsections are Climate and Weather; Environmental Issues; Landforms and Bodies of Water; Movement; Population Patterns; Regions—including Africa, Asia, Europe, Latin America, The Middle East, North America, Oceania, and The Soviet Union; Tools of the Geographer; Types of Geography; and Urban Patterns.

Within a number of the subsections, individual geographers associated with the encompassing branch of geography are listed alphabetically. For each, there is a book or a list of books by that geographer. In addition, there is for each a profile that provides personal background and/or information about his or her role and achievements. Further, the profile may refer the reader to other related individuals and their works, which also can be found in *The Young Adult Reader's Adviser.*

Last, for most profiled individuals, there is a Books About section that, among other types of publications, lists notable biographies for further reading and research. Whenever possible, very recent titles have been included.

ATLASES AND GAZETTEERS

Atlas of the Third World. George Kurian (ed). Facts on File 1989 $95.00. ISBN 0-8160-1930-4

Atlas of the World Today. Neil Grant (ed). Harper 1987 $10.95. ISBN 0-06-096144-9 Map and graphs on climate, education, energy, trade, population, and other topics.

Atlas of Today. Jon Snow (ed). Watts 1987 $13.90. ISBN 0-531-19028-5

Chambers World Gazetteer: An A–Z of Geographical Information. David Munro (ed). Cambridge Univ Pr 1988 $34.50. ISBN 1-852-96200-3

Goode's World Atlas. Edward B. Epenshade, Jr. and Joel L. Morrison (eds). Rand 1986 $13.28. ISBN 0-528-63006-7 Standard school atlas.

Hammond Physical World Atlas. Hammond 1988 $5.95. ISBN 0-8437-1269-4

Kurian, George T. *Geo-Data: The World Almanac Gazetteer.* Gale 1983 $60.00. ISBN 0-8103-1605-6

Longman Dictionary of Geography: Human and Physical. Audrey N. Clark (ed). Longman 1986 $36.95. ISBN 0-0582-35261-4

Maps on File. Lester A. Sobel (ed). 2 vols. Facts on File Vol. 1 1986 $35.00. ISBN 0-8160-1373-X. Vol. 2 1987 $35.00. ISBN 0-8160-1684-4 Loose-leaf, black and white maps on various areas of the world.

National Geographic Atlas of the World. National Geographic 1981 $44.95. ISBN 0-87044-347-X

National Geographic Picture Atlas of Our Universe. National Geographic 1980 $18.95. ISBN 0-87044-357-7

New International Atlas. Rand 1990 $125.00. ISBN 0-528-83413-4

The New State of the World Atlas. Michael Kidron and Ronald Segal (eds). Simon 1987 $13.95. ISBN 0-671-64555-2

New York Times Atlas of the World. Harper 1987 $49.95. ISBN 0-8129-1626-3

Rand McNally Atlas of the Oceans. Rand 1987 $24.99. ISBN 0-528-83295-6

Rand McNally World Atlas of Nations. Rand 1988 $34.95. ISBN 0-528-83315-4

Reader's Digest Editors. *Guide to Places of the World: A Geographical Dictionary of Countries, Cities, National and Man-made Wonders.* Reader's Digest 1987 $32.95. ISBN 0-276-39826-2

Statesman's Year-Book and World Gazetteer. John Paxton (ed). Humanities 1988 $35.00. ISBN 0-333-39085-7

Webster's New Geographical Dictionary. Merriam Webster 1984 $19.95. ISBN 0-87779-446-4 Provides basic information on countries, regions, cities, and natural features worldwide.

Women in the World: An International Atlas. Ann Olson and Joni Seager (eds). Simon 1986 $12.95. ISBN 0-671-63070-9 Maps and graphics on 40 topics related to such topics as work, marriage, and health.

**World Factbook.* (Annual) Central Intelligence Agency. USGPO 1989 $23.00. Statistical information on various topics, including the geography of the nations of the world.

World Facts and Maps, 1991. Rand 1990 $9.95. ISBN 0-528-83420-7

See also Vol. 2, Geography: Regions.

SURVEYS

Ahmad, N. *Muslim Contributions to Geography.* Kazi $14.50. ISBN 0-686-18450-5
*Brown, Lester R., *et al. State of the World, 1988.* Norton 1991 $10.95. ISBN 0-393-30733-6
  Anthology of viewpoints on world geography and economic issues.
Cole, J. P. *Geography of World Affairs.* Butterworth 1983 $32.95. ISBN 0-408-10842-8
Encyclopedia of Geographic Information. Jennifer Mossman (ed). Gale 1986 $105.00. ISBN
  0-8103-0410-4
Geography and Cartography: A Reference Handbook. Shoe String 1976. (o.p.)
Guide to Information Sources in the Geographical Sciences. Stephen Goddard (ed). B & N Imports
  1983 $27.50. ISBN 0-389-20403-X
Kish, George (ed). *Source Book in Geography.* Harvard Univ Pr 1978 $38.00. ISBN 0-674-
  82270-6
Knox, Paul L., and John A. Agnew. *The Geography of the World Economy.* Routledge 1989
  $21.95. ISBN 0-7131-6517-0
*Kurian, George. *New Book of World Rankings.* Facts on File 1989 $40.00. ISBN 0-8160-
  1931-2 Reference for contemporary statistics.
McClintock, Jack, and David Helgren. *Everything Is Somewhere: The Geography Quiz Book.*
  Morrow 1986 $10.95. ISBN 0-688-05873-6 A trivial pursuit book on world geog-
  raphy.
*Natoli, Salvatore J. (ed). *Careers in Geography.* Assn Amer Geographers 1984 ISBN
  0-89291-184-0 Interesting sourcebook of careers.
*Paxton, John (ed). *The Statesman's Year-Book, 1989–1990.* St. Martin's 1989 $59.95. ISBN
  0-312-03235-8 Source for contemporary world statistics; published annually.
*Pitzl, Gerald R. (ed). *Geography 89/90.* Dushkin $9.50. ISBN 0-87967-792-9 Anthology
  of geographic and environmental issues.
*Tourtellot, Jonathan B. (ed). *Into the Unknown: The Story of Exploration.* National Geographic 1987 $39.95. ISBN 0-87044-695-9 Story of some of the world's most
  famous explorers.

BOWMAN, ISAIAH   1878–1950

Although Isaiah Bowman was born in Ontario, Canada, his father moved the
family to Michigan when Isaiah was an infant. At the age of 17, he became a
teacher, completing his own education during the summers. After graduating
from the State Normal School at Ypsilanti, he went to Harvard and Yale
universities. He received his doctorate from Yale in 1909 and taught there for
four years. While attending Yale, he led the first South American Yale expedition. It was an adventure that greatly influenced his later contributions to the
field of geography.

In 1911, Bowman served as geographer-geologist on a Yale expedition to
Peru. That same year, he published his book *Forest Physiography,* which offered
the first in-depth study of the relief, climate, vegetation, and soils of the United
States. The geography of the United States continued to interest him throughout his career. He was especially interested in what he called the "Pioneer
fringe," the area between early America's wilderness and civilization. Years
later, in 1931, he published a book called *The Pioneer Fringe.* It was the first of
a series on world frontier areas.

In 1913, Bowman led an American Geographical Society expedition to the
central Andes. Two years later, he became the director of the Society. At that
time, the Society was a small, relatively unknown organization, but under
Bowman's direction, it became a highly respected center for geographic research and scholarship. One of the things Bowman did was to initiate a 25-year
study by the Society to map the region known as Hispanic America.

At the end of World War I, Bowman traveled to the Versailles peace conference as President Woodrow Wilson's territorial adviser to help draw the postwar boundaries of European nations. During World War II, he was once again a territorial adviser, this time for the United States State Department. From 1935 to 1948, he was president of Johns Hopkins University, which renamed its geography department in his honor. A member and officer of many geographic and related clubs, boards, associations, and groups, he was considered one of the greatest modern authorities on political geography.

BOOKS BY BOWMAN

The Andes of Southern Peru (1916). Greenwood 1968 $35.00. ISBN 0-8371-0025-9
Desert Trails of Atacama (1924). Ayer $18.50. ISBN 0-404-00964-6
Limits of Land Settlement: A Report on Present-Day Possibilities (1937). Ayer $24.50. ISBN 0-8369-0233-5
The Pioneer Fringe (1931). Ayer $38.50. ISBN 0-8369-0233-5

BOOK ABOUT BOWMAN

Martin, Geoffrey J. *The Life and Thought of Isaiah Bowman.* Shoe String 1980 $29.50. ISBN 0-208-01844-1 Informative biography of scholar, teacher, and administrator Isaiah Bowman's life, emphasizing his major contribution to the understanding and appreciation of United States geography; includes a bibliography and index.

HUMBOLDT, FRIEDRICH HEINRICH ALEXANDER VON 1769–1859

Baron Alexander von Humboldt was born in Berlin, Germany. Although during his early school years he was not particularly interested in science, because his family valued education he studied such subjects as geology, biology, metallurgy, and mining. His main interest was in nature and other lands.

At the age of 27, Humboldt had his first opportunity to travel. He went to the German Alps, where he measured the atmospheric pressure, humidity, and oxygen content of the air. Shortly after, in 1799, he was granted permission by the Spanish king to explore Spain's mysterious holdings in the Americas. For the next five years, traveling more than 6,000 miles by foot, horse, and canoe, he and his companion, Aimé Bonplaud, explored the region that is now Venezuela, Cuba, Colombia, Peru, Ecuador, and Mexico. While he was in the Andes, he fell prey to mountain sickness, which led him to become the first person to explain that the sickness was caused by a lack of oxygen. During these travels, he and Bonplaud collected 60,000 plant specimens; mapped the area; and studied its climates, bodies of water, wildlife, and minerals. The findings of this exhaustive adventure were published in a 23-volume series, *Voyage de Humboldt et Bonplaud* (1805–1834).

In 1829, at the invitation of the Russian government, Humboldt made an expedition to Russia and Siberia, categorizing, observing, and recording as he went. One of the results of this was a 5-volume work, *Kosmos* (1845–1862), in which he tried to combine the vague ideals of the eighteenth century with the exact scientific requirements of his own.

Considered one of the founders of modern geography, Humboldt showed geographers that there was more to the study of geography than the shape of Earth and its regions. He gave them a system of geographic inquiry. He was the first to draw an isothermal map—a map in which lines connect points of similar temperature. He also studied tropical storms and volcanoes and pioneered the field of terrestrial magnetism—the magnetic pull of Earth. Equally important, he was responsible for one of the first examples of international scientific cooperation, which led to the formation of a system of meteorological stations throughout Russia and Great Britain. During one of his many expeditions, he measured the temperature of the current with which his ship sailed from Lima, Peru, to Acapulco, Mexico. Later this current was named the Humboldt Current in his honor.

BOOKS BY HUMBOLDT

Aspects of Nature in Different Lands and Different Climates (1850). Mrs. Sabine (tr). AMS 1970 $32.00. ISBN 0-404-03385-7

Island of Cuba (1856). J. S. Thrasher (tr). Greenwood 1969 $35.00. ISBN 0-8371-2627-4

Personal Narrative of Travels to Equinoctial Regions of America During the Years 1799–1804 (1851). Thomasina Ross (tr). 3 vols. Ayer 1969 $60.00. ISBN 0-405-08642-3

Political Essay on the Kingdom of New Spain (1811). John Black (tr). 4 vols. Univ of Oklahoma Pr 1988 $9.95. ISBN 0-8061-2131-9

BOOK ABOUT HUMBOLDT

von Hagen, Victor Wolfgang. *South America Called Them; Explorations of the Great Naturalists: La Condamine, Humboldt, Darwin, Spence.* AMS 1949 $49.50. ISBN 0-404-20278-0 Critical interpretation of von Humboldt's explorations in South America.

JAMES, PRESTON E.   1899–1986

After completing his education with a doctorate in geography, Preston James became a geography instructor at several universities in the eastern United States. Included among these were Harvard, Radcliffe, and Syracuse. Beginning with his first book, *An Outline of Geography,* published in 1935, making geography understandable was one of his primary goals. To this end, he authored many books for students, including an elementary-school geography series.

As a recognized authority in his field, James represented the United States as a delegate to many geography conferences worldwide and was a member of many geographic organizations. Included among these was the Association of American Geographers, of which he was president in 1951.

BOOKS BY JAMES

All Possible Worlds: A History of Geographical Ideas. (coauthored with Geoffrey J. Martin) Wiley 1981 $54.40. ISBN 0-471-06121-2

The Association of American Geographers: The First Seventy-Five Years. (coauthored with Geoffrey J. Martin) Assn Amer Geographers 1979 $12.00. ISBN 0-89291-134-4

Latin America. (coauthored with Clarence W. Minkel) Wiley 1986 $51.50. ISBN 0-471-05934-X

One World Divided: A Geographer Looks at the Modern World. (coauthored with Kempton Webb) Wiley 1980 $39.50. ISBN 0-471-02687-5

Geography: Inventory and Prospect. (coedited with Clarence F. Jones) Syracuse Univ Pr 1954 $19.95. ISBN 0-8156-2013-6

On Geography: Selected Writings of Preston E. James. Donald Meinig (ed). Syracuse Univ Pr 1971 $14.00. ISBN 0-8156-0084-4

MACKINDER, HALFORD JOHN, SIR   1861–1947

From an early age, John Mackinder was interested in the history of the countryside where he lived in England. He attended Oxford University, but since geography was not an academic subject, he took classes in the subject closest to it that he could find—natural history. After he finished his education, he began to research and explore his nation. Eventually he published *Britain and the British Seas* (1902), which is still considered a definitive work.

Mackinder's interest and experience led to his nomination as professor of geography at Oxford. While at the university, he led England to a renewed interest in geography. He also was responsible for making geography an academic subject. Also an explorer, on one expedition to Africa he became the first European to climb Mount Kenya, Africa's second highest mountain.

From 1903 to 1908, Mackinder served as director of the London School of Economics. In 1909, he became a member of Parliament. He remained a member until 1922 and then went on to hold other government posts. In 1920, he was knighted.

Mackinder was a supporter of geopolitics—a belief that political developments are directly related to geographic space. Like other geopolitical theorists, he emphasized the role geography played in international relations. Mackinder acknowledged that in the past the sea powers had been dominant in the world. But he believed that with the coming of railroads that power had switched to land and that Eurasia had become the world's "heartland." And, in his view, "Who rules the Heartland . . . commands the world." Those in power in Great Britain and the United States paid little attention to this theory, which he discussed in his work entitled *Democratic Ideals and Reality* (1919). But the theory was very convincing to a German geopolitician named Karl Haushofer, whose writings impressed Germany's ruler, Adolf Hitler. Hitler ultimately made the theory part of his master plan of world domination and used it to justify German expansion.

BOOKS BY MACKINDER

Britain and the British Seas (1902). *British Heritage Ser.* Greenwood 1970 $25.00. ISBN 0-8371-2754-8
Democratic Ideas and Reality (1919). Greenwood 1981 $38.50. ISBN 0-313-23150-8

BOOKS ABOUT MACKINDER

Blouet, Brian. *Halford Mackinder: A Biography.* Texas A & M Univ Pr 1987 $21.50. ISBN 0-89096-292-8 Biographical study of a leading British educator and member of Parliament who established geography as a university discipline.
Parker, W. H. *Mackinder: Geography as an Aid to Statecraft.* Oxford Univ Pr 1982 $39.95. ISBN 0-19-823235-7 Discussion of Mackinder's geopolitical theories.

SAUER, CARL ORTWIN   1889–1975

Born in Missouri and a student at the University of Chicago, Carl Sauer led a varied professional life. Among other things, he was a teacher, did fieldwork, and worked for such corporations as Rand McNally, a company known primarily for its maps.

Sauer believed that because human beings have an enormous and far-reaching impact on Earth, the study of history and other disciplines would serve to enhance people's geographic understanding. For this reason, he studied such diverse subjects as archaeology and sociology. He was especially interested in the origins of agriculture and in whether the earliest crops bred and grown were seed or root crops.

Sauer is credited with the development and modernization of geographical field resource techniques. Together with Wellington Jones, he provided geographers in the midwestern United States with the tools they needed to observe and map the physical and cultural aspects of that region. These techniques came to be used successfully in such projects as the Tennessee Valley Authority. Sauer was also interested in the American Southwest and in Mexico and produced works on those areas. One of these was *Pueblo Sites in Southeastern Arizona* (1930).

BOOKS BY SAUER

Aboriginal Population of Northwestern Mexico (1935). AMS $11.50. ISBN 0-404-15670-3
Geography of the Ozark Highland of Missouri (1920). AMS 1970 $17.50. ISBN 0-404-05562-1
Land and Life: A Selection from the Writings of Carl Ortwin Sauer (1950). John Leighly (ed). Univ of California Pr 1982 $37.50. ISBN 0-520-04762-1
Man in Nature: America Before the Days of the White Man. New World Writing Ser. Turtle Island Foundation 1975 $10.95. ISBN 0-913666-01-7
The Road to Cibola (1932). AMS $14.50. ISBN 0-404-15669-X
Selected Essays: 1963–1975. Bob Callahan (ed). Turtle Island Foundation 1981 $19.95. ISBN 0-913666-45-9
Sixteenth-Century North America: The Land and the People as Seen by Europeans. Univ of California Pr 1971 $8.95. ISBN 0-520-02777-9

CLIMATE AND WEATHER

*Allen, Oliver. *Atmosphere.* Silver 1983 $19.94. ISBN 0-8094-4337-6 Illustrated descriptions of atmosphere, weather, and climate.
Barry, Roger, and R. J. Chorley. *Atmosphere, Weather, and Climate.* Routledge 1988 $27.50. ISBN 0-416-07152-4
*Field, Frank. *Dr. Frank Field's Weather Book.* Putnam 1981. (o.p.) Introductory text by television weatherman.
Gallant, Roy A. *Earth's Changing Climate.* Four Winds 1979 $13.95. ISBN 0-02-736840-8
Gentilli, Joseph. *Geography of Climate* (1952). AMS $20.00. ISBN 0-404-16206-1
Gribbin, John (ed). *The Breathing Planet.* Basil Blackwell 1986 $12.95. ISBN 0-631-14289-4
Herman, John, and Richard A. Goldberg. *Sun, Weather and Climate.* Dover 1985 $7.95. ISBN 0-486-64796-X
Lamb, H. H. *Climate, History, and the Modern World.* Routledge 1982 $25.00. ISBN 0-416-33440-7
Lydolph, Paul E. *The Climate of the Earth.* Rowman 1985 $35.00. ISBN 0-86598-119-1
Lydolph, Paul E. *Weather and Climate.* Rowman 1985 $24.95. ISBN 0-86598-120-5

GUYOT, ARNOLD   1807–1884

Arnold Guyot was born in Switzerland. After completing his doctorate in 1825, he spent six weeks in the Alps observing the ways in which ice moved in the mountains. He was the first to formulate laws regarding the movement of glaciers and other ice structures.

Guyot became a professor of history and physical geography in Germany. In 1848, persuaded by his friend Louis Agassiz, he came to the United States to live and work. He taught at Lowell Technological Institute in Massachusetts and then at Princeton University. Turning his attention to mountain ranges in the United States, he was responsible for the development of topographical maps of the Appalachian and Catskill ranges in eastern North America. It was his research that led to the establishment of the U.S. Weather Bureau, now known as the National Weather Service, which still keeps Americans informed of weather conditions.

Among the books Guyot wrote about his observations was *Earth and Man* (1849), which theorizes about Earth's evolution and the place human beings hold in that evolution. He also wrote many geography textbooks for use at the college level. Today, the term *guyot,* in his honor, is used to refer to sea mountains with flat tops.

BOOKS BY GUYOT

Earth and Man: Lectures on Comparative Physical Geography in Its Relation to the History of Mankind (1849). Ayer 1970 $20.00. ISBN 0-405-02669-2

The Influence of Geography Upon the History of Mankind (1855). C. C. Felton (tr). 2 vols. Found Class Repr 1986 $189.75. ISBN 0-89901-275-2

See also Vol. 2, Earth Science: Meteorology.

ENVIRONMENTAL ISSUES

*Allen, John (ed). *Environment 1989–1990. Annual Editions Ser.* Dushkin 1989 $9.95. ISBN 0-87967-795-3 Issues and state of the environment.

*Bach, Julie S., and Lynn Hall (eds). *The Environmental Crisis: Opposing Viewpoints. Opposing Viewpoints Ser.* Greenhaven 1986 $7.95. ISBN 0-89908-366-8 Considers such topics as whether corporations should be held responsible for environmental disasters and whether nuclear power is an acceptable risk.

Boyle, Robert H., and R. Alexander Boyle. *Acid Rain.* Schocken 1983 $8.95. ISBN 0-8052-0746-5

*Bright, Michael. *The Dying Sea.* Watts 1988 $11.90. ISBN 0-531-17126-4 Timely and well-illustrated introductory work, deals with such topics as overfishing.

Brown, Lester R. *State of the World, 1991.* Norton 1991 $10.95. ISBN 0-393-30733-6

Caldwell, Lynton K., et al. *Citizens and the Environment: Case Studies in Popular Action.* Books Demand $119.80.

Dotto, Lydia. *Planet Earth in Jeopardy: Environmental Consequences of Nuclear War.* Wiley 1986 $15.95. ISBN 0-471-99836-2

*Durrell, Lee. *State of the Ark: An Atlas of Conservation in Action.* Doubleday 1986 $14.95. ISBN 0-385-23668-9 Focuses on the issues of conservation and the work of those dedicated to preserving the ecosystem; includes maps, photos, drawings, and over 100 case studies.

**50 Simple Things You Can Do to Save the Earth.* Earthworks 1989 $4.95. ISBN 0-929634-06-3 Practical guide to conservation of Earth's resources.

*Fogel, Barbara R. *Energy Choices for the Future.* Watts 1985 $12.90. ISBN 0-531-10060-X Discusses alternatives to oil as an energy source.

*Gay, Kathlyn. *The Greenhouse Effect.* Watts 1986 $12.90. ISBN 0-531-10154-1 Introductory but comprehensive account of the greenhouse effect.

*Goldfarb, Theodore D. (ed). *Taking Sides: Clashing Views on Environmental Issues. Controversial Environmental Issues Ser.* Dushkin 1989 $9.95. ISBN 0-87967-757-0 Good anthology of opposing viewpoints on environmental issues.

*Goldin, Augusta. *Water: Too Much, Too Little, Too Polluted?* Harcourt 1983 $12.95. ISBN 0-15-294819-8 Good introductory text on the role of and issues relevant to water.

*Hawkes, Nigel. *Toxic Waste and Recycling.* Watts 1988 $11.90. ISBN 0-531-17080-2 Practical ideas for how to clean up and recycle toxic wastes.

*Hillary, Edmund (ed). *Ecology 2000.* Beaufort 1984 $19.95. ISBN 0-8253-0206-4 Anthology of essays on such topics as desertification, climate changes, and pollution.

Hunger Project, The. *Ending Hunger: An Idea Whose Time Has Come.* Praeger 1985 $19.95. ISBN 0-8160-0095-6

*Jackson, Robert (ed). *Global Issues, 1989–1990.* Dushkin 1989 $9.95. ISBN 0-87967-797-X Discusses various world issues, including those related to the environment.

*MacEachern, Diane. *Save Our Planet: 750 Everyday Ways You Can Help Clean Up the Earth.* Dell 1990 $9.95. ISBN 0-440-50267-5 An excellent resource for practical projects.

Marples, David R. *Chernobyl and the Nuclear Power in the USSR.* St. Martin's 1986 $15.95. ISBN 0-312-00457-5.

*McCormick, John. *Acid Rain.* Watts 1986 $11.90. ISBN 0-531-17016-0 Good introduction to the complex topic of acid rain.

McCuen, Gary E. *Our Endangered Atmosphere: Global Warming and the Ozone Layer.* GEM 1987 $11.95. ISBN 0-86596-063-1

*Pringle, Laurence. *Throwing Things Away.* Crowell 1986 $12.70. ISBN 0-690-04429-8 About garbage and waste problems.

*Schneider, Stephen. *Global Warming.* Sierra 1989 $18.95. ISBN 0-87156-693-1 Up-to-date account of the endangered planet.

*Sedge, Michael H. *The Commercialization of the Oceans.* Watts 1987 $12.90. ISBN 0-531-10326-9 Introduction to an increasing problem on a global scale.

Sullivan, Julie. *The American Environment. Reference Shelf 56, No. 3.* Wilson 1984 $10.50. ISBN 0-8242-0698-3

*Taylor, L. B., Jr. *The Commercialization of Space.* Watts 1987 $12.90. ISBN 0-531-10236-X Very readable account of an important, but little-discussed, topic.

*Thomas, William L. (ed). *Man's Role in Changing the Face of the Earth.* Univ of Chicago Pr 1956 $45.00. ISBN 0-226-79603-5 Classic, but not dated, anthology of writings of geographers.

See also Vol. 2, Biology: Ecology and the Environment; Earth Science: Geology; Earth Science: Oceanography; Health: The Environment and Health.

LANDFORMS AND BODIES OF WATER

*Asimov, Isaac. *How Did We Find Out About Volcanoes?* Walker 1981 $10.85. ISBN 0-8027-6412-6 Traces the history of volcanoes and discusses the cause of eruptions.

*Bailey, Ronald. *Glaciers.* Time-Life 1982 $13.99. ISBN 0-8094-4318-X Discusses the forces that move and shape glaciers.

*Bailey, Ronald. *Rivers and Lakes. Planet Earth Ser.* Time-Life 1984 $20.60. ISBN 0-8074-4508-8 Excellent introduction with good photographs.

*Ballard, Robert D. *Exploring Our Living Planet.* Jonathan B. Tourtellot (ed). National Geographic 1983 $21.95. ISBN 0-87044-397-6 Illustrations of various physical features of the planet.

*Barton, Donald. *The Oceans.* Facts on File 1982. (o.p.) Good sourcebook with maps, diagrams, and photographs.

*Bromwede, Martyn. *Rivers and Lakes. Earth Science Ser.* Watts 1987 $11.40. ISBN 0-531-10262-9 Introduction to the science of the development of lakes and rivers.

*Carson, Rachel. *The Edge of the Sea.* Houghton 1979 $9.95. ISBN 0-395-28519-4 Work by the well-known environmentalist of the 1950s and 1960s.

*Carson, Rachel. *The Sea Around Us.* NAL 1954 $4.95. ISBN 0-457-62483-1 Classic description of the role of the sea in the development of life on Earth.

Condie, Kent (ed). *Plate Tectonics and Crustal Evolution.* Pergamon 1989 $49.50. ISBN 0-08-034873-4

*Crump, Donald J. (ed). *America's Magnificent Mountains.* National Geographic 1979 $9.50.

ISBN 0-87044-276-7 Well-written text complements the beautiful photographs of major mountains in the United States, Mexico, and Canada.

*Crump, Donald J. (ed). *America's Majestic Canyons.* National Geographic 1979 $9.50. ISBN 0-087044-276-7 Well-written and well-illustrated work that focuses on the erosion of the canyons of North America, Mexico, and Hawaii.

*Crump, Donald J. (ed). *America's Seashore Wonderlands.* National Geographic 1985 $9.50. ISBN 0-87044-548-0 Emphasis is on natural beauty of many of the major North American sea coasts, but much can be learned about the action of the forces of nature.

*Crump, Donald J. (ed). *America's Wild and Scenic Rivers.* National Geographic 1983 $9.50. ISBN 0-87044-445-X Breathtaking photos and well-researched text dedicated to more than two dozen of the nation's rivers.

*Crump, Donald J. (ed). *Blue Horizons: Paradise Isles of the Pacific.* National Geographic 1985 $9.50. ISBN 0-87044-549-9 Focuses on the physical and cultural features of the major island groups of Polynesia.

*Crump, Donald J. (ed). *Majestic Island Worlds.* National Geographic 1987 $9.50. ISBN 0-87044-630-4 Island nations such as Japan are featured.

*Crump, Donald J. (ed). *Nature's World of Wonders.* National Geographic 1983 $9.50. ISBN 0-87044-444-1 Heavily illustrated overview of the natural physical wonders of the world.

*Crump, Donald J. (ed). *The Ocean Realm.* National Geographic 1978 $9.50. ISBN 0-87044-256-2 Focuses on the environment and resources of the world's oceans.

*Crump, Donald J. (ed). *Our Awesome Earth.* National Geographic 1986 $9.50. ISBN 0-87044-550-2 Explores the major ecosystems of the world.

*Crump, Donald J. (ed). *The World's Wild Shores.* National Geographic 1990 $9.50. Beautiful photographs and informative text about untouched areas in five major climate zones.

Decker, Robert, and Barbara Decker. *Volcanoes.* Freeman 1989 $14.95. ISBN 0-7167-1851-0

*Editors of Time-Life Books *Volcano.* Planet Earth Ser. Time-Life 1982 $13.99. ISBN 0-8094-4304-X Well illustrated and informative study of volcanoes.

Fisher, Ron, *et al. The Emerald Realm: Earth's Precious Rain Forests.* National Geographic 1990 $11.95. ISBN 0-87044-790-4

*Golden, Frederic. *The Trembling Earth: Probing and Predicting Quakes.* Macmillan 1983 $13.95. ISBN 0-684-17884-2 Good introduction to earthquakes and their effects.

Gross, M. Grant. *Oceanography.* Merrill 1985 $15.95. ISBN 0-675-20415-1

Hunt, Cynthia, and Robert M. Garrels. *Water: The Web of Life.* Norton 1972 $3.95. ISBN 0-393-09407-3

*Lye, Keith. *Coasts.* Nancy Furstinger (ed). Silver 1988 $14.96. ISBN 0-382-09790-4 Invaluable description for the nonspecialist of how coastlines are shaped.

*Lye, Keith. *Deserts.* Silver 1987 $12.96. ISBN 0-382-09501-4 Invaluable description for the nonspecialist of how deserts are formed.

*Lye, Keith. *Mountains.* Silver 1987 $12.96. ISBN 0-382-09498-0 Invaluable description for the nonspecialist of the world's mountain systems.

Mabbutt, J. A. *Desert Landforms.* MIT Pr 1977 $35.00. ISBN 0-262-13131-5

*Mulherin, Jenny. *Rivers and Lakes.* Watts 1984 $12.40. ISBN 0-531-04836-5 Describes how rivers and lakes are formed on different continents.

*O'Neill, Thomas. *Lakes, Peaks, and Prairies.* National Geographic 1984 $9.50. ISBN 0-87044-483-2 Probes life along the international border between the United States and Canada.

Polking, Kirk. *Oceans of the World.* Putnam 1983 $14.95. ISBN 0-399-20919-0

*Pringle, Laurence. *Water: The Next Great Resource Battle.* Science for Survival Ser. Macmillan 1982 $12.95. ISBN 0-02-775400-6 Introductory text on complex topic of water resources.

*Seeden, Margaret. *Great Rivers of the World.* National Geographic 1984 $31.95. ISBN 0-87044-539-1 Overview of the world's most important rivers.

Smith, Peter J. (ed). *The Earth.* Macmillan 1986 $50.00. ISBN 0-02-907441-X

Tuttle, Sherwood. *Landforms and Landscapes.* Brown 1980 $18.85. ISBN 0-697-05020-3

*Watson, Jane W. *Volga. Rivers of the World Ser.* Silver $14.96. ISBN 0-382-06373-2 Well-illustrated text complemented by good photos.
 Watson, Jane W. *Deserts of the World: Future Threat or Promise?* Putnam 1981 $14.95. ISBN 0-399-20785-6
*Weiner, Jonathan. *Planet Earth.* Bantam 1986 $14.95. ISBN 0-553-34358-0 Discussion of geology, climate, and resources based on a PBS series.
* *World Book Encyclopedia of Science: The Planet Earth.* World Book 1989 $15.00. ISBN 0-7166-3212-8 Focuses on physical geography.

MOVEMENT

Altshiller, Donald. *Transportation in America.* Wilson 1982 $10.00. ISBN 0-8242-0667-3
Lowe, John C., and S. Moryadas. *Geography of Movement* (1975). Waveland 1984 $27.95. ISBN 0-88133-100-7
Taaffe, Edward, and Howard L. Gauthier. *Geography of Transportation. Foundation of Economic Geography Ser.* Prentice 1973. (o.p.) ISBN 0-13-351387-4

POPULATION PATTERNS

Commoner, Barry, *et al* (eds). *Energy and Human Welfare: A Critical Analysis.* 3 vols. Macmillan 1975 $40.00. ISBN 0-02-468410-4
Drakakis-Smith, David (ed). *Economic Growth and Urbanization in Developing Areas.* Routledge 1989 $66.50. ISBN 0-415-00442-X

Prince Henry the Navigator. Etching by an unknown artist (Eighteenth Century). Courtesy of Culver Pictures, Inc.

Drakakis-Smith, David. *The Third World City. Introductions to Development Ser.* Routledge 1987 $9.95. ISBN 0-416-91970-7
*Ehrlich, Paul R. *Population Bomb.* Ballantine 1986 $4.50. ISBN 0-345-33834-0 Controversial book updated.
*Haupt, Arthur, and Thomas T. Kane. *The Population Handbook.* Population Reference Bureau 1985 $5.00. ISBN 0-917136-09-8 Introduction to basic measures of population.
*Haupt, Arthur, and Thomas T. Kane. *The Population Reference Bureau's Population Handbook: International Edition.* Population Reference Bureau 1986 $5.00. ISBN 0-917136-10-1 Global population statistics.
*Marlin, John T., *et al. Book of World City Rankings.* Free Pr $14.95. ISBN 0-02-920240-X Reference for contemporary data.
McCuen, Gary E. (ed). *World Hunger and Social Justice.* GEM 1986 $11.95. ISBN 0-86596-055-0
Woube, Mengistu. *Geography of Hunger: Some Aspects of the Causes and Impacts of Hunger.* Coronet 1987 $38.50. ISBN 91-506-0656-5

REGIONS: AFRICA

Africa South of the Sahara. Gale 1987 $160.00. ISBN 0-946653-43-7
African Statistical Yearbook. Part I: North Africa. UN 1987 $18.00. ISBN 92-1-125045-5
African Statistical Yearbook. Part II: West Africa. UN 1987 $30.00. ISBN 92-1-125046-3
Becker, Peter. *The Pathfinders: A Saga of Exploration in Southern Africa.* Penguin 1985 $17.95. ISBN 0-670-80126-7
The Cambridge Encyclopedia of Africa. Roland Oliver and Michael Crowder (eds). Cambridge Univ Pr 1981 $49.50. ISBN 0-521-23096-9 Covers the history and geography of Africa through a series of articles and country profiles.
David, Stephen M. *Apartheid's Rebels: Inside South Africa's Hidden War.* Yale Univ Pr 1987 $9.95. ISBN 0-300-03992-1
Dostert, Pierre E. *Africa. World Today Ser.* Stryker-Post 1988 $6.50. ISBN 0-943448-39-5
*Editors of Time-Life Books. *East Africa. Library of Nations Ser.* Time-Life 1987 $14.95. ISBN 0-8094-5194-8 Colorfully illustrated discussion of the lands, peoples, histories, economics, and governments of the nations of East Africa.
*Hanmer, Trudy J. *Uganda.* Watts 1989 $12.40. ISBN 0-531-10816-3 Good introduction to complex historical and contemporary problems.
Hansen, William A. *Geography of Modern Africa.* Columbia Univ Pr 1975 $40.00. ISBN 0-231-03869-0
Kirchherr, Eugene C. *Place Names of Africa, 1935–1986: A Political Gazetteer.* Scarecrow 1987 $17.50. ISBN 0-8108-2061-7
*Kurian, George T. *Facts on File National Profile: East Africa.* Facts on File 1989 $35.00. ISBN 0-8160-2030-2 Excellent sourcebook for contemporary information on the nations of East Africa.
*Laure, Jason, and Ettagale Laure. *South Africa: Coming of Age Under Apartheid.* Farrar 1980 $15.95. ISBN 0-374-37146-6 First-person accounts of young people in contemporary South Africa.
Lewis, L. A., and L. Berry. *African Environments and Resources.* Unwin 1988 $19.95. ISBN 0-04-916011-7
*Lye, Keith. *Africa.* Watts 1987 $12.40. ISBN 0-531-17065-9 Introduction to the African continent.
*Maren, Michael. *Land and People of Kenya. Portraits of the World Ser.* Harper 1989 $14.89. ISBN 0-397-32335-2 Basic introduction to contemporary Kenya.
*Mathabane, Mark. *Kaffir Boy* (1986). NAL 1989 $4.95. ISBN 0-451-15799-0 Nonfiction account of a boy growing up under apartheid.
Meredith, Martin. *The First Dance of Freedom: Black Africa in Postwar Era.* Harper 1985 $23.45. ISBN 0-06-435658-2

Mountjoy, Alan, and David Hilling. *Africa: Geography and Development.* B & N Imports 1987 $24.95. ISBN 0-389-20723-3

*Murray, Jocelyn (ed). *Cultural Atlas of Africa. Cultural Atlas Ser.* Facts on File 1981 $40.00. ISBN 0-87196-558-5 Thoughtful, interesting presentation of information on the lands and peoples of Africa; with hundreds of maps and illustrations.

Patinkin, Mark. *An African Journey.* Books Demand 1985 $20.00. First-hand account of famine in Africa.

Problems of Africa. Opposing Viewpoints Ser. Janelle Rohr (ed). Greenhaven 1986 $7.95. ISBN 0-89908-365-X Treats such issues as poverty, famine, and apartheid.

*Sullivan, Jo. *Global Studies: Africa.* Dushkin 1989 $10.95. ISBN 0-87967-801-1 Includes country statistics and articles on such topics as the struggle for development and the problems of nation building.

*Timberlake, Lloyd. *Famine in Africa.* Watts 1986 $11.90. ISBN 0-531-17017-9 Good introduction to the complex problem of famine.

Van Der Post, Laurens. *The Lost World of the Kalahari.* Harcourt 1977 $8.95. ISBN 0-15-653706-0

*Ungar, Sanford J. *Africa: The People and Politics of an Emerging Continent.* Simon 1989 $14.95. ISBN 0-671-67565-6 Author looks at Africa below the Sahara.

*Williams, Oliver F. *The Apartheid Crisis: How We Can Do Justice in a Land of Violence.* Harper 1986 $8.95. ISBN 0-06-250951-9 Discusses apartheid and how people have reacted to it.

REGIONS: ASIA

*Blunden, Caroline, and Mark Elvin. *Cultural Atlas of China. Cultural Atlas Ser.* Facts on File 1983 $40.00. ISBN 0-87196-132-6 Maps and other data highlighting geographical, historical, and cultural developments in China.

Bunge, Frederica. *Burma: A Country Study. Area Handbook Ser.* USGPO 1984 $14.00. ISBN 0-318-21932-8

Bunge, Frederica. *Indonesia: A Country Study. Area Handbook Ser.* USGPO 1983 $8.00. ISBN 0-318-21843-7

Bunge, Frederica. *Japan: A Country Study. Area Handbook Ser.* USGPO 1983 $14.00. ISBN 0-318-21867-4

Bunge, Frederica. *Malaysia: A Country Study. Area Handbook Ser.* USGPO 1985 $14.00. ISBN 0-318-21871-2

Bunge, Frederica. *Philippines: A Country Study. Area Handbook Ser.* USGPO 1984 $15.00. ISBN 0-318-21886-0

Burks, Ardath. *Japan: A Postindustrial Power.* Westview 1984 $15.95. ISBN 0-86531-714-3

Cannon, Terry, and Alan Jenkins (eds). *Geography of Contemporary China: The Impact of the Past Mao Decade.* Routledge 1988 $49.95. ISBN 0-415-00102-1

*Cohen, David (ed). *A Day in the Life of China.* Collins 1989 $39.95. ISBN 0-00-215321-1 Photographic essay depicting the many facets of an average day in different locales in China.

Croll, Elisabeth, *et al* (eds). *China's One Child Family Policy.* St. Martin's 1985 $39.95. ISBN 0-312-13356-1

A Day in the Life of Japan. Collins 1985 $45.00. ISBN 0-00-217580-0 Photographic essay depicting the many facets of an average day in different locales in Japan.

*Editors of Time-Life Books. *India.* Silver 1986 $19.45. ISBN 0-8094-5315-0 Lavish illustrations and many maps enhance this introduction to India.

*Editors of Time-Life Books. *Southeast Asia. Library of Nations Ser.* Time-Life 1987 $14.95. ISBN 0-8094-5161-1 Colorfully illustrated discussion of the lands, peoples, histories, economies, and governments of the nations of Southeast Asia.

Gibney, Frank. *Japan: The Fragile Superpower.* NAL 1986 $12.95. ISBN 0-452-00967-7

*Hinton, Harold C. *East Asia and the Western Pacific.* Stryker-Post 1988 $6.50. ISBN 0-943448-41-7 From Australia to China, this annual volume profiles each country in East Asia.

*Hook, Brian (ed). *The Cambridge Encyclopedia of China.* Cambridge Univ Pr 1982 $49.50. ISBN 0-521-23099-3 Historical and contemporary overview; written by a number of specialists.

Insight Guide to Thailand. Prentice 1989 $19.95. ISBN 0-13-466459-0

Kaplan, Frederic M., and Julian M. Sobin. *Encyclopedia of China Today.* Eurasia $29.95. ISBN 0-932030-11-4

Myrdal, Gunnar. *Asian Drama: An Inquiry into the Poverty of Nations.* Random 1972 $4.95. ISBN 0-394-71730-9

Nyrop, Richard F. *India: A Country Study. Area Handbook Ser.* USGPO 1986 $20.00. ISBN 0-318-20118-6

Nyrop, Richard F. *Pakistan: A Country Study. Area Handbook Ser.* USGPO 1984 $14.00 ISBN 0-318-21882-8

Nyrop, Richard F., *et al. Sri Lanka: A Country Study. Area Handbook Series.* USGPO 1985 $16.00. ISBN 0-318-23527-7

O'Donnell, Charles P. *Bangladesh: Biography of a Muslim Nation.* Westview 1984 $52.50. ISBN 0-86531-682-1

*Ogden, Suzanne (ed). *Global Studies: China.* Dushkin 1989 $10.95. ISBN 0-87967-802-X Provides insights on the People's Republic of China, Taiwan, and Hong Kong.

Pye, Lucian. *China: An Introduction.* Scott 1984 $15.00. ISBN 0-673-39470-0

Richie, Donald. *Different People: Pictures of Some Japanese.* Kodansha 1988 $16.95. ISBN 0-87011-820-X

Richie, Donald. *The Inland Sea.* David and Charles 1987 $13.95. ISBN 0-7126-9575-3

Roach, James R. *India Two Thousand: The Next Fifteen Years.* Riverdale 1986 $33.00. ISBN 0-913215-11-2

*Sivin, Nathan (ed). *Contemporary Atlas of China.* Houghton 1988 $39.95. ISBN 0-395-47329-2 Contemporary information about China; broad yet in-depth coverage.

Thubron, Colin. *Behind the Wall: A Journey Through China.* Harper 1989 $9.95. ISBN 0-06-097256-4

Van Slyke, Lyman P. *Yangtze: Nature, History, and the River.* Addison 1988 $14.95. ISBN 0-201-08894-0

Varley, H. Paul. *Japanese Culture.* Univ of Hawaii Pr 1984 $12.95. ISBN 0-8248-0927-0

White, Merry. *The Japanese Educational Challenge: A Commitment to Children.* Free Pr 1988 $9.95. ISBN 0-02-933800-X

Worden, Robert L., *et al* (eds). *China: A Country Study. Area Handbook Ser.* USGPO 1989 $27.00. SN 008-020-01159-2

*Ziring, Lawrence, and C. I. Kim. *The Asian Political Dictionary.* ABC-Clio 1985 $17.00. ISBN 0-87436-369-1 Good contemporary reference.

REGIONS: EUROPE

Barzini, Luigi. *The Europeans.* Penguin 1984 $8.95. ISBN 0-14-007150-4

*Cameron, Robert, and Alistair Cooke. *Above London.* Cameron 1980 $24.95. ISBN 0-918684-10-2 Good example of historical geography that provides views of the same area over time.

*Cameron, Robert, and Pierre Salinger. *Above Paris.* Cameron 1984 $24.95. ISBN 0-918684-19-6 Good example of historical geography that provides views of the same area over time.

Clout, Hough, *et al. Western Europe: Geographical Perspectives.* Wiley 1986 $24.95. ISBN 0-470-20443-5

*Editors of Time-Life Books. *Britain. Library of Nations Ser.* Time-Life 1987 $14.95. ISBN 0-8094-5144-1 Well-illustrated description of the lands, peoples, history, economics, and government of Britain.

*Editors of Time-Life Books. *Eastern Europe.* Time-Life 1987 $14.95. ISBN 0-8094-5152-2 Excellent photography and good background information.

*Harris, Jonathan. *Land and People of France. Portraits of Nations Ser.* Harper 1989 $14.89. ISBN 0-397-32321-2 Introduces the geography, people, and culture of contemporary France.

Hoffman, George, W. *Geography of Europe: Problems and Prospects.* Wiley 1983 $52.50. ISBN 0-471-89708-6

John, Brian. *Scandinavia: A New Geography.* Wiley 1984 $29.95. ISBN 0-582-48950-4

*Kurian, George T. *Facts on File National Profile: Benelux Countries.* Facts on File 1989 $35.00. ISBN 0-8160-2026-4 Basic one-volume reference.

*Kurian, George T. *Facts on File National Profile: Scandinavia.* Facts on File 1989 $35.00. ISBN 0-8160-1998-3 Good reference for statistics.

*Lye, Keith. *Europe.* Watts 1987 $12.40. ISBN 0-531-17068-3 Good introductory work with many graphics.

*McEvedy, Colin. *The Penguin Atlas of Recent History: Europe Since 1815.* Penguin 1982 $6.95. ISBN 0-14-070834-0 A concise collection of maps covering political and social Europe from 1815 to 1980.

*Warmenhoven, Henri J. *Global Studies: Western Europe.* Dushkin 1989 $10.95. ISBN 0-87967-693-0 Contains reports on 26 nations of Western Europe.

Zeldin, Theodore. *The French.* Random 1984 $12.95. ISBN 0-394-724212-6

REGIONS: LATIN AMERICA

*Constable, George (ed). *Mexico.* Time-Life 1985 $13.20. ISBN 0-8094-5307-X A clear, lavishly illustrated geography and survey of Mexico.

Dostert, Pierre E. *Latin America, 1987. World Today Ser.* Stryker-Post 1987 $6.50. ISBN 0-0943-448-42-5

Ducan, Kenneth, *et al* (ed) *Land and Labor in Latin America.* Cambridge Univ Pr 1978 $137.30. ISBN 0-317-20619-2

*Fincher, E. B. *Mexico and the United States: Their Linked Destinies.* Harper 1983 $12.89. ISBN 0-690-04311-2 Discussion of the interdependencies that link Mexico and the United States.

*Gelman, Rita Golden. *Inside Nicaragua: Young People's Dreams and Fears.* Watts 1988 $13.90. ISBN 0-531-15038-5 First-hand accounts by young people of life in contemporary Nicaragua.

*Goodwin, Paul. *Global Studies: Latin America.* Dushkin 1988 $10.95. ISBN 0-87967-743-3 Presents geographical, historical, cultural, sociopolitical, and economic information on Latin America.

Gordon, Burton. *A Panama Forest and Shore.* Boxwood 1983 $15.00. ISBN 0-910286-88-4

Griffiths, John. *Latin America in the Twentieth Century.* David and Charles 1985 $19.95. ISBN 0-7134-3840-1

Hinds, Harold E., Jr., and Charles M. Tatum (eds). *Handbook of Latin American Popular Culture.* Greenwood 1985 $50.95. ISBN 0-313-23293-8

*Kurian, George. *Facts on File National Profile: Mexico and Central America.* Facts on File 1989 $35.00. ISBN 0-8160-1997-5 Excellent compendium of contemporary information.

*Lye, Keith. *The Americas.* Watts 1987 $12.40. ISBN 0-531-17066-7 Interesting comparisons among the regions of the Americas.

Morner, Magnus. *The Andean Past: Land, Societies, and Conflicts.* Columbia Univ Pr 1984 $35.00. ISBN 0-231-04726-6

Morris, Arthur. *Latin America: Economic Development and Regional Differences.* B & N Imports 1981 $27.50. ISBN 0-389-20194-4

Morris, Arthur. *South America.* B & N Imports 1987 $24.95. ISBN 0-389-20744-6

Nyrop, Richard F. (ed). *Guatemala: A Country Study. Area Handbook Ser.* USGPO 1984 $7.50.

Nyrop, Richard F. *Panama: A Country Study. Area Handbook Ser.* USGPO 1981 $11.00. ISBN 0-318-21883-6

*Ortiz, Victoria. *Land and People of Cuba. Portrait of the Nation Ser.* Harper 1973 $11.89. ISBN 0-397-31382-9 A bit dated but still useful.

*Ribaroff, Margaret Flesher. *Mexico and the United States Today: Issues Between Neighbors.* Watts 1985 $12.90. ISBN 0-531-04757-1 Good introduction to some old problems and attitudes.

Rudolph, James (ed). *Honduras: A Country Study.* Area Handbook Ser. USGPO 1984 $13.00. ISBN 0-318-21841-0

Rudolph, James (ed). *Mexico: A Country Study.* Area Handbook Ser. USGPO 1985 $16.00. ISBN 0-318-19934-3

Rudolph, James (ed). *Nicaragua: A Country Study.* Area Handbook Ser. USGPO 1987 $12.00. ISBN 008-020-00932-6

*Strange, Ian J. *The Falklands: South Atlantic Islands.* Putnam 1985 $15.95. ISBN 0-396-08616-0 Discusses the history and geography of these islands.

REGIONS: THE MIDDLE EAST

African Statistical Yearbook. Part I: North Africa. UN 1987 $18.00. ISBN 92-1-125045-5

Anderson, Roy R., *et al. Politics and Change in the Middle East: Sources of Conflict and Accommodation.* Prentice 1987 $27.80. ISBN 0-13-685207-6

Beaumont, Peter, *et al. Middle East Geographical Study.* Wiley 1988 $39.95. ISBN 0-470-21040-0

*Clifford, Mary L. *Land and People of Afghanistan.* Portraits of Nations Ser. Harper 1989 $14.89. ISBN 0-397-32337-9 Up-to-date account of the problems the nation faces.

Congressional Quarterly Staff. *The Middle East.* Congressional Quarterly 1986 $17.95. ISBN 0-87187-361-3

Cottrell, Alvin J. (ed). *The Persian Gulf States: A General Study.* Johns Hopkins Univ Pr 1980 $59.00. ISBN 0-8018-2204-1

*Dempsey, M. W. (ed). *Atlas of the Arab World.* Facts on File 1983 $14.95. ISBN 0-87196-779-0 A collection of maps that highlights history and economic development as well as the geography of 21 Arab countries.

Drysdale, Alasdair, and Gerald H. Blake. *The Middle East and North Africa: A Political Geography.* Oxford Univ Pr 1985 $21.00. ISBN 0-19-503538-0

*Evans, Michael. *The Gulf Crisis.* Watts 1988 $11.90. ISBN 0-531-17110-8 Easy-to-understand explanation of the crisis in the Persian Gulf.

Fernea, Elizabeth Warnock (ed). *Women and Family in the Middle East: New Voices of Change.* Univ of Texas Pr 1985 $11.95. ISBN 0-292-75529-5

Khouri, Fred J. *The Arab-Israeli Dilemma.* Syracuse Univ Pr 1985 $15.95. ISBN 0-8156-2340-2

McCuen, Gary E. (ed). *The Iran-Iraq War.* Ideas in Conflict Ser. GEM 1987 $11.95. ISBN 0-86596-060-7

Nugent, Jeffrey B., and Theodore Thomas (eds). *Bahrain and the Gulf: Past Perspectives and Alternative Futures.* St. Martin's 1985 $25.00. ISBN 0-312-06566-3

Nyrop, Richard F. (ed). *Jordan: A Country Study* (1980) *Area Handbook Series.* USGPO 1987 $11.00.

Nyrop, Richard F. (ed). *Persian Gulf States: Country Studies.* Area Handbook Ser. USGPO, 1985 $17.00. ISBN 0-318-18812-0

Nyrop, Richard F. (ed). *Saudi Arabia: A Country Study.* Area Handbook Ser. USGPO 1984 $15.00. ISBN 0-318-21898-4

Nyrop, Richard F. (ed). *Yemen: Country Studies.* Area Handbook Ser. USGPO 1986 $16.50. ISBN 0-318-22481-X

Oz, Amos. *In the Land of Israel.* Random 1984 $6.95. ISBN 0-394-72728-2

Renda, Gunsel, and C. M. Kortepeter (eds). *The Transformation of Turkish Culture.* Kingston 1986 $25.00. ISBN 0-940670-10

*Robinson, Francis. *Atlas of the Islamic World Since 1500.* Facts on File 1982 $40.00. ISBN 0-87196-629-8 A visual history of the Islamic world that covers economics, culture, demographics, and politics.

Said, Edward W. *After the Last Sky: Palestinian Lives.* Pantheon 1986 $17.95. ISBN 0-394-74469-1

*Shapiro, William E. *Lebanon.* Watts 1984 $12.90. ISBN 0-531-04854-3 Historical overview and discussion of recent events in Lebanon.

Shipler, David. *Arab and Jew: Wounded Spirits in a Promised Land.* Penguin 1987 $8.95. ISBN 0-14-010376-7
*Spencer, William. *Global Studies: Middle East.* Dushkin 1988 $10.95. ISBN 0-87967-745-7 Information on the geography, history, culture, politics, and economics of North Africa and the Middle East.
Thesiger, Wilfred. *Arabian Sands.* Penguin 1985 $7.95. ISBN 0-14-009514-4
Thubron, Colin. *Jerusalem.* David and Charles 1988 $13.95. ISBN 0-7126-1492-3
Trench, Richard. *Forbidden Sands: A Search in the Sahara.* Academy Chi Pubs 1982 $7.95. ISBN 0-89733-027-7
*Ziring, Lawrence. *Middle East Political Dictionary.* ABC-Clio 1984. (o.p.) $41.00. ISBN 0-87436-045-5 Good contemporary source.

REGIONS: NORTH AMERICA

Birdsall, Stephen S., and John W. Florin. *Regional Landscapes of the United States and Canada.* Wiley 1985 $49.95. ISBN 0-471-88490-1
*Caen, Herb, and Robert Cameron. *Above San Francisco.* Cameron 1986 $24.95. ISBN 0-918684-28-5 Good example of historical geography that shows views of the same area over time.
*Cameron, Robert. *Above Hawaii.* Cameron 1977 $24.95. ISBN 0-918684-02-1 Focuses on the geographical changes in Hawaii over time.
*Crump, Donald J. (ed). *America's Hidden Wilderness.* National Geographic 1988 $9.50. ISBN 0-87044-671-1 Adventures in seven varied areas of the United States, Canada, and Mexico.
*Crump, Donald J. (ed). *America's Outdoor Wonders.* National Geographic 1987 $9.50. ISBN 0-87044-629-0 Explores America's state parks and sanctuaries.
*Crump, Donald J. (ed). *Traveling the Trans-Canada from Newfoundland to British Columbia.* National Geographic 1987 $9.50. ISBN 0-87044-631-2 Describes the lands and peoples of Canada.
A Day in the Life of America. Collins 1986 $45.00. ISBN 0-00-217705-6 Photographic essays depicting the many facets of an average day in different locales of the United States.
A Day in the Life of Canada. Collins 1985 $45.95. ISBN 0-00-217380-8 Photographic essay that shows life during an average day in Canada.
*Editors of Time-Life Books. *Canada. Library of Nations Ser.* Time-Life 1988 $14.95. ISBN 0-8094-5149-2 Excellent photos and informative text on the lands, history, and contemporary concerns of Canada and Canadians.
Garreau, Joel. *The Nine Nations of North America.* Avon 1982 $8.95. ISBN 0-380-57885-9
Guinness, Paul, and Michael Bradshaw. *North America: A Human Geography.* B & N Imports 1985 $24.50. ISBN 0-389-20557-5
Gutek, Gerald, and Patricia Gutek. *Exploring America's West.* Hippocrene 1989 $11.95.
*Lye, Keith. *The Americas.* Watts 1987 $12.40. ISBN 0-531-17066-7 Interesting comparisons among the regions of the Americas.
Malcolm, Andrew H. *The Canadians.* Bantam 1986 $9.95. ISBN 0-553-34262-2
Matthews, Rupert O. *American Aerial Close Up.* Crown 1986 $15.95. ISBN 0-517-46013-0
*Meinig, D. W. *The Shaping of America*, Vol. 1 *Atlantic America, 1492–1800.* Yale Univ Pr 1986 $45.00. ISBN 0-300-035480-9 First of a projected three-volume series.
Mitchell, Robert D., and Paul A. Groves (eds). *North America: The Historical Geography of a Changing Continent.* Rowman 1987 $28.50. ISBN 0-8476-7549-1
The National Atlas of the United States of America. U.S. Department of the Interior, Geology Survey 1970. (o.p.) Major atlas of the United States, with 335 pages of maps; page references with latitude and longitude provided in index-gazetteer.
*Pierce, Neal R., and Jerry Hagstrom. *The Book of America: Inside 50 States Today.* Warner Bks 1984 $14.95. ISBN 0-446-38036-9 Geographical and other data on each state of the United States.

*Ramsay, Cynthia, *et al. America's Spectacular Northwest.* National Geographic 1982 $9.50. ISBN 0-87044-368-2 Photos and text with emphasis on the natural beauty of the American Northwest.
*Redfern, Ron. *The Making of a Continent.* Times Bks 1986 $19.95 ISBN 0-8129-1617-4 Good introduction to the forces that shaped North America.
Stegner, Wallace. *Beyond the Hundredth Meridian: John Wesley Powell and the Second Opening of the West.* Univ of Nebraska Pr 1982 $12.50. ISBN 0-8032-9128-0
Thompson, Wayne C. *Canada, 1988. World Today Ser.* Stryker-Post 1987 $6.50. ISBN 0-943448-40-9
*Venino, S., *et al. Exploring America's Scenic Highways.* National Geographic 1985 $9.50. ISBN 0-87044-484-0 Well-illustrated work that offers much on the physical geography of the United States.
Weather Atlas of the United States. Gale 1975 $98.00. ISBN 0-8103-1048-1
White, C. Langdon, *et al. Regional Geography of Anglo-America.* Prentice 1985 $46.80. ISBN 0-13-770892-0
Women's Atlas of the United States. Ann Gibson and Timothy Fast (eds). Facts on File 1987 $35.00. ISBN 0-8160-1170-2 One hundred and forty-five maps from federal and state sources showing women's roles.
Zelinsky, Wilbur. *The Cultural Geography of the United States.* Prentice 1973. (o.p.) ISBN 0-13-195495-4

REGIONS: OCEANIA

*Crump, Donald J. (ed). *Voyages to Paradise.* National Geographic 1981 $9.50. ISBN 0-87044-289-9 Follows the voyages of Captain James Cook.
A Day in the Life of Australia. Collins 1981 $45.00. ISBN 0-9594244-0-7 Series of photographs that show what an average day is like in Australia.
*Editors of Time-Life Books. *Australia. Library of Nations Ser.* Time-Life 1987 $14.95. ISBN 0-8094-5164-6 Well-illustrated general introduction to Australia and its people.
*Evans, Howard E., and Mary A. Evans. *Australia: A Natural History.* Smithsonian 1983 $19.95. ISBN 0-87474-417-2 Physical environment of the continent.
*Harrell, Mary Ann. *Surprising Lands Down Under.* National Geographic 1989 $7.95. Journey through Australia and New Zealand.
Jeans, D. N. (ed). *Australia: A Geography.* St. Martin's 1986. (o.p.) $55.00. ISBN 0-424-00114-4
King, Michael. *New Zealand in Color.* St. Martin's 1982 $19.95. ISBN 0-312-571690-0
*Lye, Keith. *Asia and Australasia.* Watts 1987 $12.40. ISBN 0-531-17067-5 Contains helpful "fact panels."
Stanley, David. *Micronesia Handbook: A Guide to the Caroline, Gilbert, Marianas.* Moon 1989 $9.95. ISBN 0-918373-24-7
Tyler, Charles M. *The Island World of the Pacific Ocean.* Gordon Pr 1977 $75.00. ISBN 0-8490-2081-6

REGIONS: THE SOVIET UNION

Binyon, Michael. *Life in Russia.* Berkley 1985 $4.50. ISBN 0-425-08188-5
*Bradley, John. *The Soviet Union: Will Perestroika Work?* Watts 1989 $11.90. ISBN 0-531-17170-1 Introduction to the challenges Soviet leader Mikhail Gorbachev faces in restructuring the Soviet economy.
Cole, J. P. *Geography of the Soviet Union.* Butterworth 1984 $32.95. ISBN 0-408-49752-1
Cressey, George B. *Soviet Potentials: A Geographic Appraisal.* Syracuse Univ Pr 1962 $5.95. ISBN 0-8156-2034-9
Dewdney, John C. *Geography of the Soviet Union.* Pergamon 1979 $19.25. ISBN 0-08-023738-X

*Editors of Time-Life Books. *Soviet Union. Library of Nations Ser.* Time-Life 1986 $23.93. ISBN 0-8094-5108-5 Well-illustrated discussion of the lands, peoples, economics, government, and history of the Soviet Union.

*Goldman, Minton F. *Global Studies: Soviet Union and Eastern Europe.* Dushkin 1988 $10.95. ISBN 0-87967-744-9 Geographic, historic, political, and economic information.

*Jackson, W. A. *Soviet Union. Global Community Ser.* Gateway 1988 $16.95. ISBN 0-934291-34-7 Textbook especially suited for young readers.

Treadgold, Donald. *Twentieth-Century Russia.* Westview 1988 $24.95. ISBN 0-8133-0507-1

*Willis, David K, *Klass: How Russians Really Live.* Avon 1987 $4.50. ISBN 0-380-70263-0 Focuses on how the Soviet system affects daily life.

See also Vol. 2, World History *for historical background on the various regions and nations of the world.*

TOOLS OF THE GEOGRAPHER

Bagrow, Leo, and R. A. Skelton. *History of Cartography.* Transaction 1985 $71.50.

*Blandford, Percy W. *Maps and Compass: A User's Handbook.* TAB 1984 $12.60. ISBN 0-8306-1644-6 Helps guide people who want to do fieldwork and provides explanation of map orientation.

Brown, Lloyd A. *The Story of Maps.* Dover 1979 $8.95. ISBN 0-486-23873-3

Campbell, John. *Introductory Cartography.* Prentice 1984. ISBN 0-13-501304-6

*Carey, Helen H. *How to Use Maps and Globes.* Watts 1983 $11.90. ISBN 0-531-04673-7 Introduction to map symbols and the different kinds of maps.

Cuff, David J., and Mark T. Mattson. *Thematic Maps: Their Design and Production.* Methuen 1982 $15.95. ISBN 0-416-60221-6

Dickinson, G. C. *Maps and Air Photographs: Images of the Earth.* Wiley 1979. (o.p.)

*Fleming, June. *Staying Found: The Complete Map and Compass Handbook.* Random 1982 $7.95. ISBN 0-394-75152-3 Practical uses of orienting skills.

*Gould, Peter. *The Geographer at Work.* Routledge 1985 $18.95. ISBN 0-7102-0494-9 Overview of what a professional geographer does.

Greenhood, David. *Mapping.* Univ of Chicago Pr 1964 $25.00. ISBN 0-226-30696-8

Lounsbury, John F., and Frank T. Aldrich. *Introduction to Geographic Field Methods and Techniques.* Merrill 1986 $19.95. ISBN 0-675-20509-3

*Madden, James F. *The Wonderful World of Maps.* Hammond 1986 $9.95. ISBN 0-8437-3411-6 Map reading.

*March, Susan. *All About Maps and Mapmaking.* Random 1963. (o.p.) Good reference.

*Makower, Joel (ed). *The Map Catalog: Every Kind of Map and Chart on Earth and Even Some Above It.* Random 1986 $14.95. ISBN 0-394-7414-7 Includes map sources and costs.

McKay, Ian A. *Geography: An Introduction to Concept and Method.* Kendall-Hunt 1986 $12.95. ISBN 0-8403-4063-X

Schwartz, Seymour I., and Ralph E. Ehrenberg. *The Mappings of America.* Abrams 1987 $60.00. ISBN 0-8109-1307-0

*Short, Nicholas M., *et al. Mission to Earth: Landsat Views the World.* NASA 1976. (o.p.) Four hundred Landsat photos showing natural features of the earth.

*Tannenbaum, Beulah, and Myra Stillman. *Understanding Maps.* McGraw 1969. (o.p.) In-depth help for students learning about maps.

Wilford, John N. *The Mapmakers.* Knopf 1981 $20.00. ISBN 0-394-46194-0

TYPES OF GEOGRAPHY

de Blij, Harm. *The Earth: A Topical Geography.* Wiley 1987 $42.95. ISBN 0-471-85496-6
East, W. Gordon. *Geography Behind History.* Norton 1967 $7.95. ISBN 0-393-00419-8
McKnight, Tom L. *Physical Geography: A Landscape Appreciation.* Prentice 1987 $46.00. ISBN 0-13-669151-X
Meinig, D. W. (ed). *Interpretation of Ordinary Landscapes.* Oxford Univ Pr 1979 $18.95. ISBN 0-19-502536-9
Miller, E. Willard. *Physical Geography: Earth Systems and Human Interaction.* Merrill 1985 $37.95. ISBN 0-675-20143-8
Muller, Robert A., and Theodore M. Oberlander. *Physical Geography Today: Portrait of a Planet.* McGraw 1984 $39.50. ISBN 0-07-554435-0
Peters, Gary L., and Robert P. Larkin. *Population Geography.* Kendall-Hunt 1983 $23.95. ISBN 0-8403-2925-3
Strahler, Arthur N., and Alan H. Strahler. *Elements of Physical Geography.* Wiley 1989 $45.95. ISBN 0-471-61647-8
Wheeler, James O., and Peter O. Muller. *Economic Geography.* Wiley 1986 $45.95. ISBN 0-471-87916-9
Whyte, Robert O. *Spatial Geography.* Oxford Univ Pr 1982. (o.p.) $26.00. ISBN 0-19-561163-2

ULLMAN, EDWARD   1912–1976

After graduating with a doctorate from the University of Chicago, Edward Ullman began a teaching career that spanned 30 years and took him from Indiana to Vienna to Moscow. He first lectured on economic geography, which focuses on how the location of natural resources affects humans and their economic activities, such as manufacturing and farming.

It was Ullman who brought to the United States the idea of central place theory—the theory that large cities are used by people from other locations. For example, someone might travel many miles to a large city in order to see a medical specialist. Ullman also was a pioneer of the theory of spatial interaction—the relationship between people and places on Earth and between one place or group of places and another place or group of places.

BOOKS BY ULLMAN

The Economic Base of American Cities. (coauthored with others) Univ of Washington Pr 1971 $12.50. ISBN 0-295-95125-7
Geography as Spatial Interaction. Ronald R. Boyce (ed). Univ of Washington Pr 1922 $22.50. ISBN 0-295-95711-5

URBAN PATTERNS

*Gay, Kathlyn. *Cities Under Stress: Can Today's City Systems Be Made to Work?* Watts 1985 $12.90. ISBN 0-531-04926-4 Good introductory work on urban life.
*Hanmer, Trudy. *The Growth of Cities.* Watts 1985 $12.90. ISBN 0-531-10056-1 Focuses on the development and growth of U.S. cities.
Hartshorn, Truman. *Interpreting the City: An Urban Geography.* Wiley 1980 $49.50. ISBN 0-471-05637-5

*Jacobs, Jane. *The Death and Life of Great American Cities.* Random 1963 $9.00. ISBN 0-394-70241-7 Serious study of urban America and need for renewal of our cities.

Kantor, Paul, and Stephen David. *The Dependent City: The Changing Political Economy of American Urban Politics Since 1789.* Scott 1988 $12.50. ISBN 0-673-39782-3

Lowder, Stella. *Geography of Third World Cities.* B & N Imports 1986 $34.95. ISBN 0-389-20671-7

Lynch, Kevin. *Image of the City.* MIT Pr 1960 $6.95. ISBN 0-262-62001-4

*Marlin, John Tepper, and James S. Avery. *The Book of American City Rankings.* Facts on File 1983 $14.95. ISBN 0-8160-0095-6 Source for contemporary data.

*Mumford, Lewis. *The City in History* (1961). Harcourt 1968 $18.95. ISBN 0-15-618035-9 A study of the origins of the city.

Patten, Robert B., and Timothy Unwin. *Geography of Urban Rural Interaction in Developing Countries.* Routledge 1988 $57.50. ISBN 0-415-00444-6

Perin, Constance. *Belonging in America: Reading Between the Lines.* Univ of Wisconsin Pr 1988 $12.50. ISBN 0-299-11580-1

Perin, Constance. *Everything in Its Place: Social Order and Land Use in America.* Princeton Univ Pr 1977 $12.50. ISBN 0-691-02819-2

Timberlake, Michael. *Urbanization in the World Economy.* Academic Pr 1985 $35.50. ISBN 0-12-691290-4

PSYCHOLOGY

This section is devoted to psychology, the one social science that focuses most of its attention on the individual. Psychology usually studies the person as he or she observes or reacts to others in some way. A diverse field, psychology is divided into a variety of branches of study, including physiological psychology, applied psychology, engineering psychology, clinical psychology, and counseling psychology, each with its own particular focus and subtopics.

For ease of use the psychology section, which begins with listings of works that are general references, surveys, or are concerned with methods or the history of the field, is divided into 15 subsections organized alphabetically. The subsections are Attitudes, Beliefs, and Values; Behavior; Cognition; Emotions; Groups; Heredity and Environment; Human Development; Intelligence and Artificial Intelligence; Learning; Motivation; Perception and Sensation; Personality; Psychological Disorders; Psychological Testing; and Stress.

Within a number of the subsections, individual psychologists associated with the particular topic are listed alphabetically. For each, there is a book or a list of books by that psychologist. In addition, there is for each a profile that provides personal background and/or information about his or her role in the field and his or her contributions to it. Further, the profile may refer the reader to other related individuals and their works, which also can be found in *The Young Adult Reader's Adviser.*

Last, for most profiled individuals, there is a Books About section that, when available, lists notable biographies for further reading and research. Whenever possible, very recent titles have also been included.

There is a strong relationship between many of the topics associated with psychology and sociology. For a more comprehensive listing of works related to those topics, see also the readings under sociology, found in the section immediately following this one.

GENERAL REFERENCES

Bruno, Frank J. *Dictionary of Key Words in Psychology.* Routledge 1986 $13.95. ISBN 0-7102-0190-7

Chaplin, J. P. *Dictionary of Psychology.* Dell 1985 $5.95. ISBN 0-440-31925-0

■ *The Encyclopedic Dictionary of Psychology.* Dushkin 1985 $10.95. ISBN 0-87967-608-6 Easily accessed, cross-referenced information on all pertinent areas in the field of psychology.

■ Fitzgerald, Hiram, and Michael G. Walraven (eds). *Annual Editions: Psychology, 90/91.* Dushkin 1990 $9.95. ISBN 0-87967-853-4 Up-to-date articles on topics in psychology. Useful for classroom studies and of general interest.

Lindzey, Gardner, and Elliot Aronson (eds). *The Handbook of Social Psychology.* 2 vols. Erlbaum 1985 $150.00. ISBN 0-89859-720-X

McInnis, Raymond G. *Research Guide for Psychology. Reference Sources for Social Sciences and Humanities.* Greenwood 1982 $50.95. ISBN 0-313-21399-2

Mussen, Paul, *et al* (eds). *Handbook of Child Psychology.* 4 vols. Wiley 1983 $280.96. ISBN 0-471-05194-2

■ Nordby, Vernon J. and Calvin S. Hall. *A Guide to Psychologists and Their Concepts. Psychology Ser.* Freeman 1974 $13.95. ISBN 0-7167-0759-4 Brief biographies of influential psychologists and definitions of principal concepts of psychology.

Statt, David. *Dictionary of Psychology.* Harper 1982 $6.95. ISBN 0-06-463553-8

■ Stratton, Peter, and Nicky Hayes. *A Student's Dictionary of Psychology.* Routledge 1989 $13.95. ISBN 0-7131-6501-4 Provides helpful definitions for students of key terms associated with the field of psychology.

HISTORY, SURVEYS, AND METHODS

Aronson, Elliot, *et al. Methods of Research in Social Psychology.* McGraw 1988 $30.00. ISBN 0-07-002466-9

Ash, Mitchell G., and William R. Woodward (eds). *Psychology in Twentieth-Century Thought and Society.* Cambridge Univ Pr 1989 $15.95. ISBN 0-521-38920-8

Benjamin, Ludy T. *A History of Psychology: Original Sources and Contemporary Research.* McGraw 1988 $23.95. ISBN 0-07-004561-5

Bornstein, Marc H. (ed). *Comparative Methods in Psychology. Crosscurrents in Contemporary Psychology Ser.* Erlbaum 1980 $34.50. ISBN 0-89859-037-X

■ Fancher, Raymond E. *Pioneers in Psychology.* Norton 1979 $9.95. ISBN 0-393-09082-5 History of psychology and those responsible for its beginnings and development.

Grasha, Anthony F. *Practical Applications of Psychology.* Scott 1987 $22.75. ISBN 0-673-39511-1

Greenwood, John D. (ed). *The Ideas of Psychology: Conceptual and Methodological Issues.* Ohio Univ Pr 1988 $15.95. ISBN 9971-69-110-8

Hampden-Turner, Charles. *Maps of the Mind.* Macmillan 1982 $12.95. ISBN 0-02-076870-2

■ Hilgard, Ernest R. *Psychology in America: A Historical Survey.* Harcourt 1987 $30.00. ISBN 0-15-539202-6 History of psychology and psychologists in the United States.

Kagan, Jerome, and Julius Segal. *Psychology: An Introduction.* Harcourt 1988 $29.00. ISBN 0-15-572639-0

Karier, Clarence J. *Scientists of the Mind: Intellectual Founders of Modern Psychology.* Univ of Illinois Pr 1986 $27.50. ISBN 0-252-01182-1

■ Lawless, Joann A. *Mysteries of the Mind. Great Unsolved Mysteries Ser.* Raintree 1977 $15.33. ISBN 0-8172-1066-0 Unanswered questions about the mind from a psychological viewpoint.

Rausch, Friedrich. *Psychology; or, a View of the Human Soul, Including Anthropology. History of Psychology Ser.* Schol Facsimiles 1975 $60.00. ISBN 0-8201-1142-2

Rieber, R. W., and Kurt Salzinger (eds). *The Roots of American Psychology: Historical Influences and Implications for the Future.* NY Acad Sci 1977 $22.00. ISBN 0-89072-037-1

Shideler, Mary M. *Persons, Behavior, and the World: The Descriptive Psychology Approach.* Univ Pr of America 1988 $18.50. ISBN 0-8191-6787-8

■ Stwertka, Eve. *Psychoanalysis: From Freud to the Age of Therapy.* M. Kline (ed). Watts 1988 $10.40. ISBN 0-531-10481-8 History of the study of unconscious mental processes.

Watson, Robert I. *Basic Writings in the History of Psychology.* Oxford Univ Pr 1979 $17.95. ISBN 0-19-502444-3

■ Watson, Robert I. *The Great Psychologists.* Harper 1978 $23.50. ISBN 0-397-47375-3 Discusses the works of psychologists from Aristotle to Freud.

Wundt, Wilhelm. *An Introduction to Psychology. Classics in Psychology Ser.* Ayer (repr of 1976 ed) $16.00. ISBN 0-405-05173-5

JAMES, WILLIAM   1842–1910

New York-born, William James, an American philosopher and psychologist, was the son of a writer on religious topics and brother of novelist Henry James (*see* James, Vol. 1, American Literature: The Rise of Realism) and a professor at Harvard University for most of his life. Originally he wanted to be a painter. Upon discovering that he really did not have enough talent to succeed in this profession, he turned to medicine, receiving a medical degree from Harvard University in 1869. However, he never practiced medicine. Upon returning from travels in Europe, he was invited to teach at Harvard. He taught psychology, anatomy, physiology, and hygiene, and later philosophy. As a philosopher, he is responsible for the doctrine of pragmatism, the belief that the meaning and truth of a concept or course of action is determined by its practical and observable consequences.

James's *The Principles of Psychology* (1890) took 12 years to write and sums up previous work in psychology on human behavior, motivations, and feelings. James came to believe that people had certain feelings because they had certain physical reactions. They were sad because they cried. Other psychologists claimed that bodily changes such as muscle tension and relaxation and sensations in the pit of one's stomach were triggered by emotions.

But James wrote,

> [T]he bodily changes follow directly the perception of the exciting fact, and that our feeling of the same changes as they occur IS the emotion. Commonsense says, we lose our fortune, are sorry and weep; we meet a bear, are frightened and run. . . . [T]he more rational statement is that we feel sorry because we cry, angry because we strike, afraid because we tremble.

BOOKS BY JAMES

Pragmatism (1907). Bruce Kuklick (ed). *Philosophical Classics Ser.* Hackett 1981 $3.95. ISBN 0-915145-05-7

The Principles of Psychology (1890). 2 vols. Harvard Univ Pr 1983 $18.95. ISBN 0-674-70625-0

The Varieties of Religious Experience (1902). Random 1989 $10.50. ISBN 0-679-72491-5

The Will to Believe (1897). *Works of William James Ser.* Harvard Univ Pr 1979 $32.00. ISBN 0-674-95281-2

Writings Nineteen Two to Nineteen Ten. (Includes *The Varieties of Religious Experience; Pragmatism; A Pluralistic Universe; The Meaning of Truth; Some Problems of Philosophy.*) Bruce Kuklick (ed). Lib of America 1988 $27.50. ISBN 0-940450-38-0

BOOKS ABOUT JAMES

Bjork, Daniel W. *William James: The Center of His Vision.* Columbia Univ Pr 1988 $35.00. ISBN 0-231-05674-5 Imaginative biography that integrates James's life and thought, using previously unpublished diaries, notebooks, letters to his wife, and family correspondence.

Brennan, Bernard P. *William James. Twayne's United States Authors Ser.* New Coll Univ Pr 1968 $10.95. ISBN 0-8084-0005-3 Accessible explanation of James's critical thought, including some biographical material.

Edie, James M. *William James and Phenomenology. Studies in Phenomenology and Existential Philosophy Ser.* Indiana Univ Pr 1987 $9.95. ISBN 0-253-20419-4 Complete analysis of James's influence and involvement in phenomenology, the philosophical study of occurrences and facts directly perceived by the senses.

Myers, Gerald E. *William James: His Life and Thought.* Yale Univ Pr 1986 $19.95. ISBN 0-300-04211-6 Critical analysis of James's writing on consciousness, time, space, perception, memory, thought, morality, and so on, using fresh biographical information to illuminate his ideas.

Suckiel, Ellen Kappy. *The Pragmatic Philosophy of William James.* Univ of Notre Dame Pr 1982 $19.95. ISBN 0-268-01548-1 Analysis of James's pragmatism as a systematic world view.

ATTITUDES, BELIEFS, AND VALUES

*Allport, Gordon W. *The Nature of Prejudice* (1954). Addison 1979 $9.57. ISBN 0-201-00179-9 Classic work on the nature of prejudice.

Bem, Daryl J. *Beliefs, Attitudes, and Human Affairs. Basic Concepts in Psychology Ser.* Brooks-Cole 1970 $9.00. ISBN 0-8185-0295-9

Bettelheim, Bruno. *The Uses of Enchantment: The Meaning and Importance of Fairy Tales.* Knopf 1976 $21.45. ISBN 0-394-49771-6

■Bok, Sissela. *Lying: Moral Choice in Public and Private Life.* Random 1979 $6.95. ISBN 0-394-72804-1 Consideration of the various choices we make and the gradations of truth and lies.

Coles, Robert. *The Moral Life of Children.* Houghton 1987 $10.95. ISBN 0-395-43153-0

■Eagon, Andrea B. *Why Am I So Miserable If These Are the Best Years of My Life?* Harper 1976 $12.70. ISBN 0-397-31655-0 Discusses personal changes during teen years.

Eisner, R. J. *The Expression of Attitude.* Springer-Verlag 1987 $29.00. ISBN 0-387-96562-9

Hans, James S. *The Question of Value: Thinking Through Nietzsche, Heidegger, and Freud.* Southern Illinois Univ Pr 1989 $24.95. ISBN 0-8093-1506-8

Icek, Ajzen. *Attitudes, Personality, and Behavior.* Brooks-Cole 1988 $29.75. ISBN 0-256-06936-0

Jung, Carl G. *Psychology and Religion. Terry Lecture Ser.* Yale Univ Pr 1938 $6.95. ISBN 0-300-00137-1

Kohlberg, Lawrence. *The Philosophy of Moral Development: Essays in Moral Development.* Vol. 1 Harper 1981 $24.95. ISBN 0-06-064760-4

Kohlberg, Lawrence. *The Psychology of Moral Development. Essays on Moral Development Ser.* Harper 1983 $35.95. ISBN 0-06-064751-2

Lewin, Kurt. *Resolving Social Conflicts.* Gertrude W. Lewin (ed). Intl Specialized Bk 1978 $4.50. ISBN 0-285-64718-0

Maslow, Abraham H. *Religions, Values, and Peak Experiences.* Peter Smith 1983 $14.75. ISBN 0-8446-6070-1

Maxwell, John. *Your Attitude: Key to Success.* Here's Life 1984 $7.95. ISBN 0-89840-067-8

Rokeach, Milton. *Belief, Attitudes, and Values: A Theory of Organization and Change. Social and Behavioral Science Ser.* Jossey-Bass 1968 $26.95. ISBN 0-87589-013-X

BEHAVIOR

Aronson, Elliot. *The Social Animal.* Freeman 1988 $14.95. ISBN 0-7167-1955-X

Biddle, Bruce J. *Role Theory: Expectations, Identities, and Behaviors.* Academic Pr 1979 $37.50. ISBN 0-12-095950-X

Doherty, Michael, and Kenneth Shemberg. *Asking Questions About Behavior: An Introduction to What Psychologists Do.* Scott 1978 $11.25. ISBN 0-673-15043-7

Dollard, John, and Robert R. Sears. *Frustration and Aggression.* Greenwood 1980 $27.50. ISBN 0-313-22201-0

∎ Duffy, Karen G. *Annual Editions: Personal Growth and Behavior 89/90.* Dushkin 1989 $9.95. ISBN 0-87967-787-2 Articles on topics of personal interest to students.

Freud, Sigmund. *Character and Culture.* Macmillan 1963 $5.95. ISBN 0-02-076200-3

Horney, Karen. *Neurotic Personality of Our Time.* Norton 1965 $4.95. ISBN 0-393-00742-1

Hyde, Margaret O. *Is This Kid "Crazy"? Understanding Unusual Behavior.* Westminster John Knox 1983 $9.95. ISBN 0-664-32707-9

Merton, Robert. *Factors Determining Human Behavior.* Perspectives in Social Inquiry Ser. Ayer 1974 $10.00. ISBN 0-405-05500-5

Milavsky, J. Ronald. *Television and Aggression: Results of a Panel Study.* Quantitative Studies in Social Relations Ser. Academic Pr 1982 $35.50. ISBN 0-12-495980-6

Milgram, Stanley, and Lance R. Shotland. *Television and Antisocial Behavior: Field Experiments.* Academic Pr 1973 $24.00. ISBN 0-12-496350-1

Montagu, Ashley. *Man and Aggression.* Oxford Univ Pr 1973 $7.95. ISBN 0-19-501680-7

Scott, John P. *Aggression.* Univ of Chicago Pr 1976 $4.95. ISBN 0-226-74294-6

Tinbergen, Nikolaus. *The Study of Instinct.* Oxford Univ Pr 1989 $22.50. ISBN 0-19-857740-0

Wilson, Edward O. *Sociobiology: The New Synthesis.* Harvard Univ Pr 1975 $40.50. ISBN 0-674-81621-8

LEWIN, KURT 1890–1947

Born in a small Prussian village in the province of Posen, Kurt Lewin was the second of four children born to a storekeeper and his wife. He and his family moved to Berlin when he was 15 years old. In 1910, after studying at the universities of Freiburg and Munich, he attended the University of Berlin from which he received his doctorate in psychology in 1914. During World War I he served in the German army, rising in the ranks from private to lieutenant. After the war he became a faculty member at the University of Berlin and a research assistant in the Psychological Institute. He immigrated to the United States in 1933 and taught at Stanford University, Cornell University, and the University of Iowa. In 1945 he organized the Research Center for Group Dynamics at the Massachusetts Institute of Technology and remained there as director until his death. At the same time he was with MIT, he served as director of the Commission of Community Interrelations of the American Jewish Congress, an organization devoted to conducting research on community problems.

Lewin conducted research in such diverse fields as cognition, the full range of mental activities used to represent and process knowledge; motivation, the cause of behavior; and group behavior. An early member of the Gestalt school of psychology, which believes humans tend to organize perceptions into "wholes," Lewis is known for his field theory of behavior, especially the concept of group dynamics.

According to his field theory, Lewin saw human behavior as an outcome of an individual's psychological environment. Any individual variations from what is considered normal is a result of tensions between that person's sense of self and his or her perception of the environment. The whole psychological lifespace of the individual must be considered in order to understand that person's behavior. Lifespace refers to the totality of events or facts that determines the behavior of an individual at a given time. To Lewin human behavior is part of a continuum that extends from the past into the present.

Lewin's professional interest in his later years was the theory of group dynamics. He believed that group dynamics change the individual behavior of the group's members. He researched various kinds of social organizations and came to believe that small groups worked best when democratic rules governed their operations. Lewin's work in group dynamics led to the formation of the National Training Laboratories, whose sessions were first held in Bethel, Maine, the summer after Lewin's death. These training sessions for leadership roles became a major link between the behavioral sciences and the professions and industry.

BOOKS BY LEWIN

Field Theory in Social Science (1975). Dorwin Cartwright (ed). *Research Ctr for Group Dynamics Ser.* Greenwood 1983 $45.00. ISBN 0-8371-7236-5
Frustration and Aggression: An Experiment with Young Children. (coauthored with Robert Barker and Tamara Dembo) Univ of Iowa Pr 1941. (o.p.)
Resolving Social Conflicts. Gertrud Lewin (ed). Intl Specialized Bk 1978. (o.p.) $4.50. ISBN 0-285-54718-0

BOOKS ABOUT LEWIN

Marrow, Alfred J. *The Practical Theorist: The Life and Work of Kurt Lewin.* Books Demand $79.80. ISBN 0-317-28352-9 Biography written by a friend and colleague with an intimate knowledge of Lewin's work.
Schellenberg, James A. *Masters of Social Psychology: Freud, Mead, Lewin, and Skinner.* Oxford Univ Pr 1978 $7.95. ISBN 0-19-502622-5 Short biographies of Freud, Mead, Lewin, and Skinner that show the kind of experiences that led each one to formulate his approach.

LORENZ, KONRAD 1903–1989

Konrad Lorenz, an Austrian zoologist, is included in this psychology section because the biological origins of social behavior are of major interest to psychologists. In recent years, Lorenz's theories have been applied to human behavior with attendant controversy.

Lorenz pioneered in the direct study of animal behavior and is the founder of modern ethology, the study of animal behavior by comparative methods. He is known for his studies of instinctive behavior patterns and of imprinting. The latter is the process by which, during a short, sensitive period, a young bird learns by the appearance of its parents what the appearance of its future sexual mate will be.

Lorenz's 1963 book, *On Aggression,* was attacked by many anthropologists, psychologists, and sociologists, who maintained that Lorenz's claim that aggression is inborn means that it cannot be controlled. His supporters assert that Lorenz never stated that inborn traits could not be changed. The conflict continues, with Lorenz a key figure in the midst of this contemporary version of the nature–nurture (heredity vs. environment) debate.

In 1973 Lorenz shared the Nobel Prize in physiology with Karl von Frisch and Nicolaus Tinbergen for his studies of individual and social behavior patterns.

BOOKS BY LORENZ

Behind the Mirror: A Search for a Natural History of Human Knowledge (1973). Ronald Taylor (tr). Harcourt 1978 $3.95. ISBN 0-15-611776-2

Evolution and Modification of Behavior (1961). Univ of Chicago Pr 1986 $9.95. ISBN 0-226-49334-2

■ *King Solomon's Ring* (1952). Peter Smith 1988 $18.00. ISBN 0-8446-6309-3 This Nobel Prize winner describes his life in animal research.

On Aggression (1963). Marjorie K. Wilson (tr). Harcourt 1974 $9.95. ISBN 0-15-668741-0

BOOK ABOUT LORENZ

Montagu, Ashley. *Man and Aggression.* Oxford Univ Pr 1973 $7.95. ISBN 0-19-501680-7 Collection of essays challenging the belief that ethologists can understand human behavior by observing that of lower mammals.

PAVLOV, IVAN PETROVICH   1849–1936

Ivan Petrovich Pavlov, a Russian physiologist and psychologist, was born in the city of Ryazan, the first of the 10 children of a priest who taught Greek and Latin and his wife, who was the daughter of a priest. Like his father, the young Pavlov attended a theological seminary, studying for the priesthood. But after reading several books on physiology, he left the seminary and went to St. Petersburg to study physiology. In 1875, after graduating from that city's university, he attended the Imperial Medioco Surgical Academy until 1883, when he received his doctorate. In 1890, he was appointed professor of pharmacology at the St. Petersburg Institute of Experimental Medicine.

Pavlov demonstrated, by his 62 years of active research, one model of the research career: making a major discovery by studying more and more about less and less. He first studied the neural mechanisms of blood circulation and digestion, then the mechanisms of digestion, and finally salivation. For his research on the physiology of digestion, Pavlov received the Nobel Prize in Physiology and Medicine in 1904.

Pavlov's studies of salivation led to his discovery of the conditioned reflex. A dog trained to associate feeding with the sounding of a bell would salivate when the bell was sounded even though no food was made available. The concept of the conditioned reflex, known familiarly as "Pavlov's dog," and the thousands of experiments that are based on it, have had an enormous impact on experimental psychology in both the Soviet Union and the United States.

BOOKS BY PAVLOV

Conditioned Reflexes: An Investigation of the Psychological Activity of the Cerebral Cortex (1927). G. V. Anrep (ed). Dover 1960 $9.96. ISBN 0-486-60614-7

Lectures on Conditioned Reflexes (1923). *Classics in Psychology Ser.* St. Martin's. (o.p.) ISBN 0-312-47785-6

BOOKS ABOUT PAVLOV

Gray, Jeffrey A. *Ivan Pavlov. Modern Masters Ser.* Penguin 1981. (o.p.) $4.95. ISBN 0-14-005326-3 Concise account of Pavlov's life and works following the development of Piaget's theories of behavior, personality, and brain function based on the concept of conditioning.

Wells, Harry K. *Ivan P. Pavlov: Toward a Scientific Psychology and Psychiatry.* Intl Pubs 1956. (o.p.) Introduction to the teachings of Pavlov pertinent to the field of psychology and psychiatry.

SKINNER, B. F. (BURRHUS FREDERIC) 1904–1990

B. F. Skinner was born in Susquehanna, Pennsylvania. Although his lawyer-father wanted him to study law, the young Skinner wanted to be a writer and majored in literature at Hamilton College in New York. After graduating in 1926, he spent several years pursuing a writing career. His lack of success finally led him to enter Harvard University to study psychology. Since childhood he had had an interest in animal and human behavior. He received his doctorate in psychology from Harvard in 1931 and for the next five years worked in a laboratory run by an experimental biologist.

Skinner was an ardent proponent of behaviorism and was deeply influenced by the work of Ivan Pavlov and John B. Watson. (*See* Pavlov *and* Watson, Vol. 2, Psychology: Behavior.) Skinner is widely known for his work with training animals through the use of rewards and in his application of this research to human learning. His teaching machines and theories about programmed instruction have deeply influenced educational practices in the United States.

In 1938, while teaching at the University of Minnesota, Skinner published *The Behavior of Organisms,* which reported his experiments in the study of reflexes. Ten years later, while beginning his tenure as a professor at Harvard, he published *Walden Two,* a novel of a Utopian community, based on his ideas of social engineering. It describes a planned community in which positive rather than negative reinforcers serve to maintain appropriate behavior. The novel stimulated the founding of some experimental communities. In *Beyond Freedom and Dignity* (1971), Skinner attempted to show that only a technology of behavior, similar to the technology of the biological and social sciences, can save democracy from the many individual and social problems that plague it.

An early example of his technology of behavior is the Skinner box for observational purposes. Skinner devised a number of similar pieces of equipment that he used in his laboratory experiments with animals to train them to perform complex operations, such as pigeons playing Ping-Pong. His work in training animals in step-by-step procedures led Skinner to his research with programmed learning and teaching machines. The teaching machine allowed the student to learn at his or her own pace and rewarded the student for right answers. As in his training of animals, Skinner built his teaching machines around the theory of reinforcement or reward.

Skinner taught at Harvard from 1948 until his retirement. For some he is considered the model of the objective scientist. To others he is seen as being totally unaware of the role of subjectivity in human experience.

BOOKS BY SKINNER

The Analysis of Behavior: A Program for Self-Instruction (1961). (coauthored with James G. Holland) McGraw 1961 $28.95. ISBN 0-07-029565-4

Particulars of My Life: The Shaping of a Behaviorist—A Matter of Consequences (1981). 3 vols. New York Univ Pr 1984 $29.95. ISBN 0-8147-7846-1

Recent Issues in the Analysis of Behavior (1953). Merrill 1989 $19.95. ISBN 0-675-20674-X

■ *Walden Two* (1949). Macmillan 1976 $3.75. ISBN 0-02-411510-X Describes a planned community in which positive rather than negative reinforcers serve to maintain appropriate behavior.

BOOKS ABOUT SKINNER

Carpenter, Finley. *The Skinner Primer: Behind Freedom and Dignity.* Free Pr 1984 $11.95. ISBN 0-02-905900-3 Objective examination of Skinner's position on freedom in clear, nontechnical language, explaining the relationship between freedom and education.

Sagal, Paul T. *Skinner's Philosophy.* Univ Pr of America 1981 $9.75. ISBN 0-8191-1433-2 Presentation of Skinner's work and thought and an introduction to *Beyond Freedom and Dignity.*

Schellenberg, James A. *Masters of Social Psychology: Freud, Mead, Lewin, and Skinner.* Oxford Univ Pr 1978 $7.95. ISBN 0-19-502622-5 Short biographies of Freud, Mead, Lewin, and Skinner that show the kind of experiences that led each man to formulate his approach.

WATSON, JOHN B. (BROADUS)   1878–1958

John B. Watson, an American psychologist born on a farm in Greenville, South Carolina, was the founder of behaviorism, the school of psychology that considers behavior rather than mental processes the subject matter for psychology. This school of thought had a major impact on sociology and political science as well as on contemporary psychology. Although not an accomplished student during his early years, Watson became a student at Furman University when he was only 16 years old. Several years after earning a master's degree at Furman, he entered the University of Chicago, from which he received a doctorate in psychology in 1903. He stayed on at the university for five more years.

In 1913 Watson published a paper entitled "Psychology as a Behaviorist Views It." The paper enunciated the doctrine that psychology is the science of human behavior and should be studied under laboratory conditions. Mentalistic concepts, images, the study of the unconscious, and introspection must all be abandoned, he claimed. They must be replaced by the objective observation of the organism's response to controlled stimuli.

In 1914 Watson published *Behavior: An Introduction to Comparative Psychology,* in which he called for the use of animals as subjects in psychological studies. He also saw instinct as a series of reflexes that heredity activates. Other studies that Watson conducted included research with infants and conditioning.

Watson taught at the University of Chicago and Johns Hopkins University, but a sensational divorce in 1920 forced him to leave the academic world for a business career in New York in the advertising field. By 1924 he was vice president of J. Walter Thompson, one of the largest advertising agencies in the United States. During this time, he continued to give public lectures on and write about behaviorism. In 1925 he published a book for the general reader called *Behaviorism,* which may have made him the second best known psychologist of his time after Sigmund Freud. (*See* Freud, Vol. 2, Psychology: Personality.) For many people Watson's claims that there are no hereditary traits and that behavior consists of learned habits constituted the core of psychology.

There are no pure behaviorists today in the social sciences, but Watson's behaviorism was the predominant American school of psychology in the 1920s and 1930s. Even today Watson's work survives in direct and indirect ways, such as the use of rooms with one-way mirrors for studying behavior.

BOOKS BY WATSON

Behavior: An Introduction to Comparative Psychology (1914). Holt 1914. (o.p.)
Behaviorism (1925). Norton 1970 $7.95. ISBN 0-393-00524-0

Psychological Care of Infant and Child (1928). *Family in America Ser.* Ayer 1972 $11.00. ISBN 0-405-03876-3
Psychology from the Standpoint of a Behaviorist (1919). *Classics of Psychology and Psychiatry Ser.* Pinter 1983. (o.p.)

See also Vol. 2, Biology: Animal Behavior.

COGNITION

Anderson, J. R., and G. H. Bower. *Human Associative Memory.* Erlbaum 1973 $49.95. ISBN 0-89859-108-2
Bandura, Albert. *The Social Foundations of Thought and Action: A Social Cognitive Theory.* Prentice 1986 $41.00. ISBN 0-13-815614-X
Bever, Thomas, *et al.* (eds). *Talking Minds: The Study of Language in Cognitive Sciences.* MIT Pr 1986 $8.95. ISBN 0-262-52114-8
Cole, Michael, and Barbara Means. *Comparative Studies of How People Think: An Introduction.* Harvard Univ Pr 1986 $8.95. ISBN 0-674-15261-1
■ Gallant, Roy A. *Memory: How It Works and How to Improve It.* Macmillan 1985 $11.95. ISBN 0-02-736850-5 Discusses how memory develops and proposes ways one can improve memory.
Izard, Carroll E. *Emotions, Cognition, and Behavior.* Cambridge Univ Pr 1988 $29.95. ISBN 0-521-31246-9
Kagan, James (ed). *Unstable Ideas: Temperament, Cognition, and Self.* Harvard Univ Pr 1989 $25.00. ISBN 0-674-93038-X
Kohlberg, Lawrence. *Child Psychology and Early Childhood Education: A Cognitive–Developmental View.* Longman 1987 $39.95. ISBN 0-582-28302-7
Lorenz, Konrad. *Behind the Mirror: A Search for a Natural History of Human Knowledge.* Ronald Taylor (tr). Harcourt 1978 $3.95. ISBN 0-15-611776-2
Matlin, Margaret. *Cognition.* Holt 1989 $29.00. ISBN 0-03-021659-1
Mussen, Paul, *et al.* (eds). *Handbook of Child Psychology: Cognitive Development.* Vol. 3 Wiley 1983 $82.95. ISBN 0-471-09064-6
Roloff, Michael E., and Charles R. Berger. *Social Cognition and Communication.* Sage 1982 $16.95. ISBN 0-8039-1899-2
Underwood, Benton J. *Attributes of Memory.* Scott 1983 $24.00. ISBN 0-673-15798-9

EMOTIONS

*Agras, Stewart. *Panic: Facing Fears, Phobias, and Anxiety.* Freeman 1985 $12.95. ISBN 0-7167-1731-X Deals with intense fears, their causes, and treatment.
Dollard, John. *Fear in Battle.* AMS 1966 $19.50. ISBN 0-404-14714-3
Dollard, John, and Robert R. Sears. *Frustration and Aggression.* Greenwood 1980 $27.50. ISBN 0-313-22201-0
Fromm, Erich. *The Art of Loving.* Harper 1974 $4.95. ISBN 0-06-080291-X
Fromm, Erich. *Escape from Freedom.* Avon 1982 $4.95. ISBN 0-380-01167-0
Gaylin, Willard. *Feelings: Our Vital Signs.* Harper 1988 $6.95. ISBN 0-06-091480-7
Gaylin, Willard. *Passionate Attachments.* Macmillan 1989 $8.95. ISBN 0-02-911431-4
Gaylin, Willard. *The Rage Within: Anger in Modern Life.* Penguin 1989 $7.95. ISBN 0-14-012003-3

Gaylin, Willard. *Rediscovering Love.* Penguin 1987 $4.50. ISBN 0-14-010431-3
■Gelinas, Paul J. *Coping with Anger. Coping Ser.* Ruth Rosen (ed). Rosen Group 1988 $12.95. ISBN 0-8239-0780-5 How anger arises and how to manage it.
■Gelinas, Paul J. *Coping with Your Emotions. Coping Ser.* Ruth Rosen (ed). Rosen Group 1989 $12.95. ISBN 0-8239-0970-0 Discusses emotions and how to deal with them successfully.
■Gelinas, Paul J. *Coping with Your Fears. Coping Ser.* Rosen Group 1986 $12.95. ISBN 0-8239-0665-5 Discusses fears and how to deal with them.
Izard, Carroll E., and Peter B. Read (eds). *Face of Emotion. Century Psychology Ser.* Irvington 1989 $39.50. ISBN 0-8290-0059-3
Izard, Carroll E., and Peter B. Read (eds). *Measuring Emotions in Infants and Children.* Vol. 2 *Studies in Social and Emotional Development.* Cambridge Univ Pr 1986 $42.50. ISBN 0-521-32367-3
Izard, Carroll E., and Peter B. Read (eds). *Patterns of Emotions.* Academic Pr 1972 $35.50. ISBN 0-12-377750-X
■Lorenz, Konrad. *On Aggression.* Marjorie K. Wilson (tr). Harcourt 1974 $9.95. ISBN 0-15-668741-0 Author explores aggressive behavior using animals as examples.
Yablonsky, Lewis. *Psychodrama: Resolving Emotional Problems Through Role-Playing.* Gardner 1981 $14.95. ISBN 0-89876-016-X

See also Vol. 2, Health: Mental and Emotional Health.

GROUPS

Allport, Gordon. *The Nature of Prejudice.* Addison 1979 $9.57. ISBN 0-201-00179-9
Argyle, Michael. *The Psychology of Interpersonal Behavior.* Penguin 1985. (o.p.) $6.95. ISBN 0-14-022483-1
Homans, George C. *The Human Group.* Harcourt 1950 $24.00. ISBN 0-15-540375-3
Homans, George C. *Sentiments and Activities: Essays in Social Science.* Transaction 1988 $19.95. ISBN 0-88738-725-X
Lewin, Kurt. *Resolving Social Conflicts.* Gertrud W. Lewin (ed). Intl Specialized Bk 1978 $4.50. ISBN 0-285-64718-0
McDougall William. *The Group Mind. Classics in Psychology Ser.* Ayer $26.50. ISBN 0-405-05148-4
Milgram, Stanley, and Lance R. Shotland. *Television and Antisocial Behavior: Field Experiments.* Academic Pr 1973 $24.00. ISBN 0-12-496350-1
Mills, Theodore M. *The Sociology of Small Groups.* Prentice 1984 $19.60. ISBN 0-13-820902-2
Moscovici, Serge. *The Age of the Crowd: A Historical Treatise on Mass Psychology.* J. C. Whitehouse (tr). Cambridge Univ Pr 1985 $18.95. ISBN 0-521-27705-1
Zander, Alvin. *Making Groups Effective. Management Ser.* Jossey-Bass 1982 $21.95. ISBN 0-87589-522-0
Zander, Alvin. *Motives and Goals in Groups. Social Psychology Ser.* Academic Pr 1971 $24.00. ISBN 0-12-775550-0
Zander, Alvin. *The Purposes of Groups and Organizations. Management Ser.* Jossey-Bass 1985 $24.95. ISBN 0-87589-651-0

See also Vol. 2, Sociology: Interaction and Groups.

HEREDITY AND ENVIRONMENT

Altman, I., and E. H. Zube (eds). *Public Spaces and Places. Human Behavior and Environment Ser.* Plenum 1989 $42.50. ISBN 0-306-43079-7

Bandura, Albert. *The Social Foundations of Thought and Action: A Social Cognitive Theory.* Prentice 1986 $41.00. ISBN 0-13-815614-X

Bandura, Albert. *Social Learning Theory.* Prentice 1977 $31.20. ISBN 0-13-816744-3

Cattell, Raymond B. *Personality and Learning Theory: The Structure of Personality in Its Environment.* Vol. 1 Springer-Verlag 1979 $39.90. ISBN 0-8261-2120-9

Davenport, John. *Environmental Stress and Behavioral Adaptation.* Sheridan Med Bks 1984 $14.50. ISBN 0-7099-0854-7

Dollard, John. *Caste and Class in a Southern Town.* Univ of Wisconsin Pr 1988 $14.50. ISBN 0-299-12134-8

Lebon, Gustave. *The Crowd: A Study of the Popular Mind.* Larlin 1969 $8.95. ISBN 0-89783-020-2

Slater, Keith. *Human Comfort.* Thomas 1985 $30.00. ISBN 0-398-05128-3

Wilson, Edward O. *Sociobiology: The New Synthesis.* Harvard Univ Pr 1975 $40.50. ISBN 0-674-81621-8

COLES, ROBERT   1929–

Robert Coles was born in Boston, Massachusetts. After receiving his medical degree from Harvard University, he practiced at several clinics, gathering information and experience in his field of child psychiatry. He currently teaches at Harvard.

Coles's focus—in his research, his teaching, and his writing—is children and how they react to life's experiences, especially to difficult conditions such as poverty and integration. He has spent much of his time studying the children of the southern United States to learn their reactions to and their coping mechanisms for school integration. His best-known work is the multivolume series called *Children of Crisis* (1967–1980). The individual books in the series explore the ways in which children react to stressful or fearful situations. In fact, the first volume is subtitled *A Study in Courage and Fear* (1967). The second and third books of the series won Coles the 1973 Pulitzer Prize for general nonfiction.

Coles's unending interest in the children of the United States has led to his involvement in many charitable and social awareness organizations, such as Reading Is Fundamental, American Freedom from Hunger Foundation, and the National Rural Housing Coalition. Coles is considered one of the leading authorities on poverty and racial discrimination in the United States. Congressional committees often call on him to testify as an expert witness when they consider legislation in the areas of poverty and discrimination in regard to children.

Coles's writing reveals what children really feel, how they react, what they dream about, and what they dread. His colorful, insightful works continue to influence many who daily deal with children.

BOOKS BY COLES

Children of Crisis (1967). Vol. 1 *A Study of Courage and Fear. Children of Crisis Ser.* Little 1977 $19.95. ISBN 0-316-15154-8

Children of Crisis. (1973). Vol. 2 *Migrants, Sharecroppers, Mountaineers. Children of Crises Ser.* Little 1973 $19.95. ISBN 0-316-15176-9

Children of Crisis (1973). Vol. 3 *The South Goes North. Children of Crisis Ser.* Little 1973 $19.95. ISBN 0-316-15177-7

Children of Crisis. (1980). Vol. 5 *Privileged Ones: The Well-Off and Rich in America. Children of Crisis Ser.* Little 1980 $19.95. ISBN 0-316-15177-7

The Moral Life of Children (1986). Peter Davison (ed). Atlantic Monthly 1986 $19.95. ISBN 0-87113-034-3

The Political Life of Children (1986). Peter Davison (ed). Atlantic Monthly 1986 $19.95. ISBN 0-87113-035-1

Spiritual Life of Children (1990). Houghton 1990. ISBN 0-395-55999-5

Uprooted Children: The Early Life of Migrant Farm Workers (1970). *Horace Mann Lecture Ser.* Univ of Pittsburgh Pr 1970 $17.95. ISBN 0-8229-3192-3

BOOK ABOUT COLES

Ronda, Bruce A. *Intellect and Spirit: The Life and Work of Robert Coles.* Continuum 1989 $18.95. ISBN 0-8264-0436-7 In-depth biocritical study based in part on interviews with Coles himself.

See also Vol. 2, Biology: Genetics and Heredity.

HUMAN DEVELOPMENT

Blau, Zena S. (ed). *Current Perspectives on Aging and the Life Cycles.* Vol. 3 JAI 1988 $52.50. ISBN 0-89232-739-1

Blos, Peter. *The Adolescent Passage: Developmental Issues.* International Univ Pr 1979 $55.00. ISBN 0-8236-0095-5

Bower, T. G. *The Perceptual World of the Child. Developing Child Ser.* Jerome Bruner, *et al* (eds). Harvard Univ Pr 1977 $3.95. ISBN 0-674-66192-3

Bower, T. G. *The Rational Infant: Learning in Infancy. Psychology Ser.* Freeman 1989 $13.95. ISBN 0-7167-2007-8

Brim, Orville G., Jr., and Jerome Kagan (eds). *Constancy and Change in Human Development.* Harvard Univ Pr 1980 $40.50. ISBN 0-674-16625-6

Cole, Michael, and Sheila Cole. *The Development of Children.* Freeman 1989 $36.95. ISBN 0-7167-1864-2

• Gaffron, Norma. *Dealing with Death.* Greenhaven 1989 $10.95. ISBN 0-89908-108-1 Focuses on stages of human reaction to death.

Gould, Roger. *Transformations.* Simon 1979 $12.95. ISBN 0-671-25066-3

Horney, Karen. *Neurosis and Human Growth.* Norton 1970 $4.95. ISBN 0-393-00135-0

Horowitz, Frances D., and Marion O'Brien (eds). *The Gifted and Talented: Developmental Perspectives.* American Psychological Assn 1985 $30.00. ISBN 0-912704-94-2

Kagan, Jerome. *Nature of the Child.* Basic 1986 $11.95. ISBN 0-465-04851-X

• Kagan, Jerome. *The Second Year: The Emergence of Self-Awareness.* Harvard Univ Pr 1986 $8.95. ISBN 0-674-79663-2 Study of children as they become aware of themselves as separate people.

Kagan, Jerome, and Sharon Lamb (eds). *The Emergence of Morality in Young Children.* Univ of Chicago Pr 1988 $24.95. ISBN 0-226-42231-3

• Kagan, Jerome, *et al* (eds). *Twelve to Sixteen: Early Adolescence.* Norton 1973 $11.95. ISBN 0-393-09621-1 Discusses the stages of children growing toward maturity, with the attendant problems.

Kegan, Robert. *The Evolving Self: Problem and Process in Human Development.* Harvard Univ Pr 1983 $9.95. ISBN 0-674-27231-5

Kübler-Ross, Elizabeth. *Death: The Final Stage of Growth.* Simon 1986 $7.95. ISBN 0-671-62238-2

• Kübler-Ross, Elizabeth. *Living with Death and Dying.* Macmillan 1982 $5.95. ISBN 0-02-

Don Manuel Osorio.   Detail of painting by
Francisco de Goya (1788).   Courtesy of The
Metropolitan Museum of Art, The Jules Bache
Collection, 1949. (49.7.41)

086490-6 Discusses caring for the terminally ill, including children, and coping
  with the realization of death.
*Kübler-Ross, Elizabeth. *Questions and Answers on Death and Dying.* Macmillan 1974 $5.95.
  ISBN 0-02-089150-4 Addresses common queries on death and offers information
  on terminal care.
*Kübler-Ross, Elizabeth. *Working It Through.* Macmillan 1987 $5.95. ISBN 0-02-
  022000-6 Provides help to those facing death and the survivors.
Lerner, Richard M. *Concepts and Theories of Human Development.* McGraw 1986 $32.95. ISBN
  0-07-554899-2
Lerner, Richard M. (ed). *Developmental Psychology: Historical and Philosophical Perspectives.*
  Erlbaum 1983 $29.95. ISBN 0-89859-247-X
Lerner, Richard M., and Nancy L. Galambos. *Experiencing Adolescence: A Sourcebook for
  Parents, Teachers, and Teens. Reference Library of Social Sciences.* Teachers College 1987
  $18.95. ISBN 0-8077-2884-5
Lerner, Richard M., *et al. Human Development: A Life-Span Perspective.* McGraw 1983 $27.75.
  ISBN 0-07-037216-0
*Levinson, Daniel J., *et al. The Seasons of a Man's Life.* Ballantine 1986 $10.95. ISBN
  0-345-33901-0 Addresses psychological stages of American men facing middle
  age.
*McCoy, Kathy. *Changes and Choices: A Junior High Survival Guide.* Putnam 1989 $10.95.
  ISBN 0-399-51566-6 Addresses everyday social and psychological concerns of
  young adults.
*McCoy, Kathy. *The Teenage Body Book Guide to Dating.* Simon 1983 $6.95. ISBN 0-671-
  45580-X Gives guidance and information on the whys and wherefores of dating.
* Morris, Desmond. *The Book of Ages.* Penguin 1983 $8.95. ISBN 0-14-007929-0 Chronicle
  of human development from ages 0 to 100.
Mussen, Paul, *et al* (eds). *Handbook of Child Psychology: Infancy and Developmental Psychobiology.*
  Vol. 2 Wiley 1983 $82.95. ISBN 0-471-09055-7
*Sheehy, Gail. *Passages.* Bantam 1977 $4.95. ISBN 0-553-24754-9 Addresses life crises

faced by American adults: the Trying 20s, the Catch 30s, the Forlorn 40s, the Refresher or Resigned 50s.

Vining, Elizabeth Gray. *Being Seventy: The Measure of a Year.* Viking 1978. (o.p.) $12.95. ISBN 0-670-15539-X

White, Burton. *The First Three Years of Life.* Prentice 1987 $8.95. ISBN 0-13-319161-3

ERIKSON, ERIK H. (HOMBURGER)   1902–

Psychologist and psychoanalyst Erik H. Erikson was born to Danish parents near Frankfurt, Germany. After graduating from high school, he traveled around Europe for a year and tried to decide what kind of career he wanted. He decided he wanted to be an artist and to teach art. In 1927 he began to teach art, history, and geography at a private school in Vienna that had been founded by a group that included Anna Freud, the daughter of psychologist Sigmund Freud. (*See* Freud, Vol. 2, Psychology: Personality.) He then entered psychoanalysis with Anna Freud and, on her urging, began training at the Vienna Psychoanalytic Society to become a psychoanalyst himself. He immigrated to the United States in 1933, where he continued his study of children and eventually became the first child psychoanalyst in Boston. After stints at Harvard University, Yale University, the University of California at Berkeley, and positions at private institutes, he returned to Harvard in 1960 as a professor of human development. He remained there until he retired in 1970.

Erikson developed theories concerning the biologically determined stages of human development as shaped by the environment. Erikson's theories have had an impact on clinical psychoanalysis, ethics, history, literature, child care, and the emerging interdisciplinary study of the life course.

According to Erikson's life-cycle theory, first published in *Childhood and Society* (1950) after 10 years of studying children in various settings, the sequence of developmental stages has always been the same for the entire human race over time. According to Erikson, there are eight states: infancy, early childhood, play age, school age, adolescence, young adulthood, mature adulthood, and old age. Each stage of life is associated with a particular crisis. For example, the crisis of adolescence is identity versus confusion. The concept of the identity crisis is now firmly embedded in psychiatric theory.

Erikson also studied the relationship between individual history and the historical period in which one lives. His historical–biographical studies of the German monk who founded Protestantism, Martin Luther (*Young Man Luther* [1958]), and Indian leader Mohandas Gandhi (*Gandhi's Truth* [1969]) are outstanding products of this inquiry.

BOOKS BY ERIKSON

Childhood and Society (1950). Norton 1986 $7.70. ISBN 0-393-39288-1

Identity and the Life Cycle (1959). Norton 1980 $4.95. ISBN 0-393-00949-1

Gandhi's Truth: On the Origins of Militant Nonviolence (1969). Norton 1970 $5.95. ISBN 0-393-00741-3

■ *Life Cycle Completed: A Review* (1982). Norton 1985 $4.70. ISBN 0-393-30229-6 Addresses developmental psychology, psychoanalysis, and personality.

Toys and Reasons: Stages in the Ritualization of Experience. Norton 1977. (o.p.) $12.95. ISBN 0-393-01123-2

Themes of Work and Love in Adulthood. (coedited with Neal E. Miller) Harvard Univ Pr 1981 $10.95. ISBN 0-674-87751-9

Vital Involvement in Old Age (1986). Norton 1989 $10.70. ISBN 0-393-30509-0

Young Man Luther (1958). Norton 1962 $5.95. ISBN 0-393-00170-9

BOOKS ABOUT ERIKSON

Coles, Robert. *Erik H. Erikson: The Growth of Work.* Little 1970. (o.p.) $10.00. ISBN 0-316-15166-1 Intellectual biography that looks at the psychological and historical research and the ethical reflections of Erikson as clinician.

Roazen, Paul. *Erik H. Erikson: The Power and Limits of a Vision.* Free Pr 1986 $9.95 ISBN 0-02-927170-3 Comprehensive examination of all of Erikson's writings, covering recent criticism of Erikson's views of femininity and his responses to this criticism.

Stevens, Richard. *Erik Erikson: An Introduction.* St. Martin's 1985 $10.95. ISBN 0-312-25811-9 Comprehensive introduction to the psychoanalytic thought of Erikson that explains and examines different aspects of Erikson's theories.

KOHLBERG, LAWRENCE   1927–1987

When psychologist Lawrence Kohlberg completed his formal training, he entered the fields of research and education. While teaching at Harvard University, Kohlberg wrote *The Philosophy of Moral Development,* in which he studied the ways in which morality is cultivated.

Kohlberg was interested in how children develop moral reasoning—deciding what is right and what is wrong. According to Kohlberg's research, being able to see another's point of view is pivotal in the social and moral development of humans.

Kohlberg identified six stages in the development of moral reasoning. In stage 1 a child is egocentric—concerned only with self. In stage 2 the "marketplace orientation" takes over, and a child learns how to "work the system" for rewards as well as punishments. A stage 3 child is aware of other people and what they want and think. Law and order rather than the approval of others is the focus of stage 4. In stage 5 a person is concerned with the fairness of a law, and in stage 6 the focus is on certain ethical principles, such as the Golden Rule, as they apply to all people.

Besides his book-length works, Kohlberg wrote many articles for various periodicals, including *Psychology Today* and *Journal of Personality and School Psychology.* In 1969 Kohlberg received the National Institute of Mental Health's Research Scientist Award for his studies in the fields of psychology and education.

BOOKS BY KOHLBERG

Child Psychology and Early Childhood Education: A Cognitive–Developmental View. Longman 1987 $39.95. ISBN 0-582-28302-7

The Philosophy of Moral Development. Essays in Moral Development Ser. Vol. 1 Harper 1981. (o.p.) $24.95. ISBN 0-06-064760-4

The Psychology of Moral Development. Essays in Moral Development Ser. Vol. 2 Harper 1984. (o.p.) $35.95. ISBN 0-06-064751-2

• *The Stages of Ethical Development: From Childhood Through Old Age.* (coauthored with Thomas Lickona) Harper 1986 $19.95. ISBN 0-06-064758-2 Discusses how ethics are developed over a life span.

See also Vol. 2, Biology: Reproduction and Development; Health: Growth and Development.

INTELLIGENCE AND ARTIFICIAL INTELLIGENCE

Baron, Jonathon. *Rationality and Intelligence.* Cambridge Univ Pr 1985 $37.50. ISBN 0-521-26717-X

Baron, Jonathon. *Thinking and Deciding.* Cambridge Univ Pr 1988 $22.95. ISBN 0-521-34800-5

Berlay, Louise. *The Magic of the Mind.* Berle 1986 $14.95. ISBN 0-9617296-0-0

Binet, Alfred. *The Development of Intelligence in Children. Classics in Psychology Ser.* Ayer (repr of 1916 ed) $23.50. ISBN 0-405-05135-2

Boden, Margaret. *Artificial Intelligence and Natural Man.* Basic 1987 $14.95. ISBN 0-465-00456-3

Bohman, S. *What Is Intelligence?* Coronet 1980 $26.50. ISBN 91-22-00404-1

*Cohen, Daniel. *Intelligence—What Is It?* M. Evans 1974 $10.95. ISBN 0-87131-127-5 Easy-to-read book on the nature of intelligence.

■ Eccles, John, and Daniel N. Robinson. *The Wonder of Being Human: Our Brain and Our Mind.* Shambhala 1985 $8.95. ISBN 0-87773-312-0 Discusses the unique human capabilities of the mind and body.

Flach, Frederic (ed). *The Creative Mind.* Bearly 1988 $19.95. ISBN 0-943456-27-4

Gardner, Howard. *Frames of Mind: The Theory of Multiple Intelligences.* Basic 1985 $12.95. ISBN 0-465-02509-9

Hyde, Margaret O. *Artificial Intelligence.* Enslow 1986 $15.95. ISBN 0-89490-124-9

Schank, Roger C., and Peter G. Childers. *The Cognitive Computer: On Language, Learning and Artificial Intelligence.* Addison 1985. (o.p.) $12.45. ISBN 0-201-06446-4

Thorndike, Edward L., *et al. The Measurement of Intelligence. Classics in Psychology Ser.* Ayer (repr of 1976 ed) $35.00. ISBN 0-405-05165-4

See also Vol. 1, Computer Science: Artificial Intelligence.

PIAGET, JEAN   1896–1980

Born in Neuchatel, Switzerland, Jean Piaget spent much of his career studying the psychological development of children, largely at his institute in Geneva. The impact of his research on child psychology has been enormous. His theories caused a major reexamination of older concepts about children, learning, and education. Piaget's work became the starting point for those seeking to learn how children view numbers, how they think of cause-and-effect relationships, and how they make moral judgments.

Piaget published his first scientific paper when he was only 10 years old. Deeply interested in the study of mollusks, at age 21 he received a doctorate from the University of Neuchatel. He then took a job in a psychological laboratory in Zurich. Bored with his work there he traveled to Paris, France and worked at constructing reasoning tests for children. He returned to Switzerland and in 1921 became a director of studies at the Institut J. J. Rousseau in Geneva. In 1940 he took a post as professor of psychology at the university there. In his later years, he returned again to France to teach child psychology at the Sorbonne in Paris.

Piaget described children from the child's perspective rather than through the results of intelligence tests. Piaget reached his conclusions by observations of his own daughter and conversations with children. He found that the reasons children gave for their answers to questions on intelligence tests could be far more revealing than their actual answers.

According to Piaget, a child's intellectual development can be divided into four stages. These stages are determined genetically and always—for all children in all cultures—proceed in the same sequential order. The four stages are sensory-motor from birth to about age two, preoperational from about age two to about age seven, concrete-operational from about age seven to about age eleven, and formal-operational from age eleven into adulthood. The ages that Piaget assigned to each stage are guidelines. The actual age at which any one child reaches a particular stage is determined by environment, abilities, and socioeconomic status.

In the sensory-motor stage, children learn to use their senses and various muscular movements in interacting with the environment. Children also realize that they are separate from other people and from objects and learn that other people and objects have their own separate existence. During the preoperational stage, the child learns to use symbols such as words to represent objects and to manipulate the symbols.

In the concrete-operational stage, children begin to think logically. They understand time and number concepts and such abstract concepts as the fact that quantity remains the same even though shape may change. Children also begin to classify objects by sameness and difference. During the last stage—formal-operational—a person shows mastery of logical thought and exhibits flexible thinking about situations. People at this stage make and test hypotheses to solve problems and are aware of the consequences to themselves and to others of proposed actions. They are less self-centered.

Piaget's work has been invaluable, but it is not without critics. Some researchers have found that formal-operational skills are found in less than 50 percent of the population of the United States. Those people who demonstrate formal-operational thinking are most likely to have taken science courses or learned scientific methods of thought. Critics also claim that people in nonliterate cultures show little evidence of the formal-operational stage of intellectual development. Even Piaget came to admit in time that training can influence intellectual development.

BOOKS BY PIAGET

The Child's Conception of the World (1926). Littlefield 1975 $8.95. ISBN 0-8226-0213-X
Construction of Reality in the Child. Ballantine 1986 $4.95. ISBN 0-345-32803-5
The Essential Piaget. Howard E. Gruber and Jacques J. Voeche (eds). Basic 1982 $23.95. ISBN 0-465-02064-X
The Language and Thought of the Child (1923). NAL 1974 $7.95. ISBN 0-452-00722-4
The Moral Judgment of the Child (1932). Marjorie Gabain (tr). Free Pr 1990 $15.95. ISBN 0-02-925240-7
Play, Dreams, and Imitation in Childhood (1946). Peter Smith 1988 $17.00. ISBN 0-8446-6320-4
Psychology of the Child. (coauthored with Barbel Inhelder) Helen Weaver (tr). Basic 1969 $9.95. ISBN 0-465-09500-3

BOOKS ABOUT PIAGET

Décarie, Thérèse G. *Intelligence and Affectivity in Early Childhood: An Experimental Study of Jean Piaget's Object Concept and Object Relationships.* International Univ Pr 1966 $27.50. ISBN 0-8236-2720-9 Experimental study of children up to two years of age that attempts to derive testable hypotheses from the theories of Piaget and the Freudian ego psychologists.

Evans, Richard I. *Jean Piaget: The Man and His Ideas.* Dutton 1973. (o.p.) ISBN 0-525-13660-6 Dialogue with Piaget plus illuminating articles by David Elkind and others.

Furth, Hans G. *Piaget and Knowledge: Theoretical Foundations. Psychology Ser.* Univ of Chicago Pr 1981 $7.50. ISBN 0-226-27420-9 Analysis of Piaget's basic theoretical positions in order to clarify psychological problems, with an introduction by Piaget.

Ginsburg, Herbert, and Sylvia Opper. *Piaget's Theory of Intellectual Development.* Prentice 1988 $13.50 ISBN 0-13-763001-6 Interprets Piaget's theories and provides a concise introduction to Piaget's basic ideas and findings concerning children's intellectual development.

Inhelder, Barbel (ed). *Piaget and His School: A Reader in Developmental Psychology.* C. Zwingman (ed). Springer-Verlag 1976. (o.p.) $26.40. ISBN 0-387-07248-9 Collection of studies (1960–1970) of the Geneva School of Psychology influenced by Piaget, with an introduction by Piaget.

Pulaski, Mary Ann Spencer. *Understanding Piaget: An Introduction to Children's Cognitive Development.* Harper 1980 $15.45 ISBN 0-06-013454-2 Lucid and thorough introduction to Piaget's studies of cognitive development.

LEARNING

Bandura, Albert. *Social Learning Theory.* Prentice 1977 $31.20. ISBN 0-13-816744-3

Bower, Gordon H. (ed). *The Psychology of Learning and Motivation.* Vol. 24 *Advances in Research and Theory.* Academic Pr 1989 $65.00. ISBN 0-12-543324-7

Bower, Gordon H., and Ernest J. Hilgard. *Theories of Learning.* Prentice 1981 $41.00. ISBN 0-13-914432-3

Bower, T. G. *The Rational Infant: Learning in Infancy. Psychology Ser.* Freeman 1989 $13.95. ISBN 0-7167-2007-8

Bruner, Jerome S. *On Knowing: Essays for the Left Hand.* Harvard Univ Pr 1979 $6.95. ISBN 0-674-63525-6

Bruner, Jerome S., and Helen Haste (eds). *Making Sense.* Routledge 1988 $15.95. ISBN 0-416-92490-5

Bruner, Jerome S., *et al. A Study of Thinking. Social Science Classics Ser.* Transaction 1986 $19.95. ISBN 0-88738-565-3

Miller, Neal E., and John Dollard. *Social Learning and Imitation.* Greenwood 1979 $24.75. ISBN 0-313-20714-3

Piaget, Jean. *Play, Dreams, and Imitation in Childhood.* Peter Smith 1988 $17.00. ISBN 0-8446-6320-4

Sahakian, William S. *An Introduction to the Psychology of Learning.* Peacock 1984 $29.95. ISBN 0-87581-284-8

MOTIVATION

Beck, Robert C. *Motivation: Theories and Principles.* Prentice 1983 $48.00. ISBN 0-13-603910-3

Bower, Gordon H. (ed). *The Psychology of Learning and Motivation.* Vol. 24 *Advances in Research and Theory.* Academic Pr 1989 $65.00. ISBN 0-12-543324-7

Buck, Ross. *Human Motivation and Emotion.* Wiley 1988 $44.95. ISBN 0-471-89705-1

Hartman, Dick. *Motivating the Unmotivated.* Valley Hill 1987 $5.95. ISBN 0-9819238-0-6

Maehr, Martin L., and Larry A. Braskamp. *Motivation Factor: A Theory of Personal Investment.* Lexington Bks 1986 $35.00. ISBN 0-669-11226-7

Mann, Stanley. *Triggers: A New Approach to Self-Motivation.* Prentice 1986 $8.95. ISBN 0-13-930793-1

McClelland, D. C. *Achievement Motive: With New Preface.* Irvington 1989 $39.50. ISBN 0-8290-1167-6

McClelland, D. C. *The Achieving Society: With a New Introduction.* Irvington 1989 $47.50. ISBN 0-8290-0870-5

McClelland, D. C. *Human Motivation.* Cambridge Univ Pr 1988 $25.95. ISBN 0-521-36951-7

McClelland, D. C. *Motives, Personality, and Society.* Centennial Psychology Ser. Praeger 1984 $44.95. ISBN 0-275-91224-8

Nuttin, Joseph R., *et al. Motivation, Planning, and Action.* Erlbaum 1984 $29.95. ISBN 0-89859-332-8

PERCEPTION AND SENSATION

Arnheim, Rudolf. *Art and Visual Perception: A Psychology of the Creative Eye—The New Version.* Univ of California Pr 1974 $12.95. ISBN 0-520-02613-6

Arnheim, Rudolf. *Parables of Sun Light: Observations on Psychology, the Arts, and the Rest.* Univ of California Pr 1989 $24.95. ISBN 0-520-06516-6

Arnheim, Rudolf. *New Essays on the Psychology of Art.* Univ of California Pr 1986 $11.95. ISBN 0-520-05554-3

Arnheim, Rudolf. *Visual Thinking.* Univ of California Pr 1980 $12.95. ISBN 0-520-01871-0

Bower, T. G. *The Perceptual World of the Child.* Developing Child Ser. Jerome Bruner, *et al* (eds). Harvard Univ Pr 1977 $3.95. ISBN 0-674-66192-3

Carterette, Edward C., and Morton P. Friedman (eds). *Handbook of Perception.* Academic Pr Vol. 1 1974 $50.00. ISBN 0-12-161901-X. Vol. 2 1974 $60.00. ISBN 0-12-161902-8. Vol. 4 *Hearing.* 1978 $60.00. ISBN 0-12-161904-4. Vol. 5. 1975 $60.00. ISBN 0-12-161905-2. Vol. 6, Part A 1978 $43.00. ISBN 0-12-161906-0. Vol. 6, Part B 1978 $45.00. ISBN 0-12-161922-2. Vol. 7 1976 $60.00. ISBN 0-12-161907-9. Vol. 8 1978 $50.00. ISBN 0-12-161908-7. Vol. 9 1978 $50.00. ISBN 0-12-161909-5. Vol. 10 1978 $60.00. ISBN 0-12-161910-9

Geldard, Frank A. *The Human Senses.* Wiley 1972 $55.95. ISBN 0-471-29570-1

Gibson, James J. *The Senses Considered as Perceptual Systems.* Greenwood 1983 $59.50. ISBN 0-313-23961-4

Goldstein, E. Bruce. *Sensation and Perception.* Wadsworth 1989 $49.50. ISBN 0-534-09672-7

Hentschel, U., *et al* (eds). *The Roots of Perception: Individual Differences in Information Processing Within and Beyond Awareness.* Elsevier 1986 $108.00. ISBN 0-444-70075-7

Koffka, Kurt. *Principles of Gestalt Psychology.* Harcourt 1967. (o.p.) $6.95. ISBN 0-15-674460-0

Kohler, Wolfgang. *Gestalt Psychology.* NAL 1980. (o.p.) $1.50. ISBN 0-451-61432-1

Marks, Lawrence E. *The Unity of the Senses.* Cognition and Perception Ser. Academic Pr 1978 $56.00. ISBN 0-12-472960-6

Matlin, Margaret. *Sensation and Perception.* Allyn 1988 $43.00. ISBN 0-205-11125-4

McBurney, Donald H., and Virginia B. Collings. *Introduction to Sensation Perception.* Prentice 1984 $48.60. ISBN 0-13-496019-X

Rivlin, Robert, and Karen Gravelle. *Deciphering the Senses: The Expanding World of Human Perception.* Simon 1985 $7.95. ISBN 0-317-31522-6

Rock, Irvin. *The Logic of Perception.* MIT Pr 1983 $12.95. ISBN 0-262-68045-9

WUNDT, WILHELM   1832–1920

Wilhelm Wundt, a German physiologist and psychologist, was the first person to identify himself as a psychologist. In 1879 he established the first psychological laboratory. The founder of the first school of psychology, during his lengthy career he taught close to 25,000 students. He was trained in medicine at Heidelberg University and became a physiologist, but he soon collected data on human behavior as well as structure. In 1873, he published a book of 870 pages on physiological psychology. Eventually it became three volumes totaling 2,317 pages in its sixth edition in 1908–1911. These six editions were in effect the history of experimental psychology's first 40 years. From 1875 until 1910, Wundt taught at Leipzig University.

In Wundt's view, psychology was the study of the mind and its structure. The human mind, he said, was another part of the body. Because of this, he reasoned, the mind could be studied scientifically by analyzing its components, an approach that came to be known as structuralism. Wundt's laboratory research was on two topics: sensation and perception and the measurement of reaction times. Remarkably, little that he did has been totally rejected.

BOOKS BY WUNDT

Ethics: An Investigation of the Facts and Laws of the Moral Life (1886). 3 vols. Macmillan 1908–1911. (o.p.)
An Introduction to Psychology (1912). *Classics in Psychology Ser.* Ayer (repr of 1976 ed) $16.00. ISBN 0-405-05173-5
Lectures on Human and Animal Psychology (1864–1965). J. Creighton (tr). *Contributions to the History of Psychology D, I, Comparative Psychology Ser.* Greenwood 1977 $65.00. ISBN 0-313-26945-9
Principles of Physiological Psychology (1873). Macmillan 1905. (o.p.)

BOOK ABOUT WUNDT

Rieber, Robert W. *Wilhelm Wundt and the Making of a Scientific Psychology.* Plenum 1980. (o.p.) $45.00. ISBN 0-306-40483-4 Volume of essays that examine Wundt from a historical perspective and provide an account of his work as one of the founders of experimental psychology.

PERSONALITY

Adorno, T. W., and Else Frenkel-Brunswik. *The Authoritarian Personality.* Norton 1983 $12.95. ISBN 0-393-30042-0
Hall, Calvin S. *A Primer of Freudian Psychology.* Hippocrene 1978 $18.00. ISBN 0-88254-838-7
Hall, Calvin S., et al. *Introduction to Theories of Personality.* Wiley 1985 $42.95. ISBN 0-471-08906-0
Kelly, George A. *Theory of Personality: The Psychology of Personal Constructs.* Norton 1963 $6.95. ISBN 0-393-00152-0
Laufer, William S., and James M. Day (eds). *Personality Theory, Moral Development, and Criminal Behavior.* Lexington Bks 1983. (o.p.) $39.00. ISBN 0-669-05556-5
Maslow, Abraham H. *Toward a Psychology of Being.* Van Nostrand 1968 $12.95. ISBN 0-442-03805-4
Monte, Christopher F. *Beneath the Mask: An Introduction to Theories of Personality.* Holt 1987 $32.95. ISBN 0-03-071487-7
Mussen, Paul, and E. Morris Hetherington (eds). *Handbook of Child Psychology: Socialization, Personality, and Social Development.* Vol. 4 Wiley 1983 $88.95. ISBN 0-471-09065-4
Rogers, Carl. *A Way of Being.* Houghton 1980 $8.95. ISBN 0-395-30067-3
▪ Rogers, Carl. *On Becoming a Person.* Houghton $8.95. ISBN 0-317-59622-5 Study of personal growth and creativity; outgrowth of Rogers's client-centered therapy.

ALLPORT, GORDON W. (WILLARD)   1897–1967

The son of a physician and a schoolteacher, Gordon W. Allport was born in Montezuma, Indiana. The chief founder of the psychological study of personality, he began his teaching career at Robert College in Istanbul, Turkey. When he was 24 years old, he received a doctorate in psychology from Harvard University and then spent several years studying in England and Germany. Following his return to the United States, he spent a year at Dartmouth College and then took a post as a social science instructor at Harvard University. In 1930 he became a professor of psychology there. He remained at Harvard for the rest of his life. His research on attitudes, values, religion, and prejudice, as well as his extensive writings on personality, are much quoted in the contemporary literature of psychology.

Allport did pioneering work on personality traits. He was one of the first psychologists to conduct a systematic search for a basic core of personality traits. He began his search by looking in an unabridged dictionary of the English language for words that described aspects of human personality. He found 18,000 such words, all of which he analyzed, rejecting those that described temporary personality characteristics such as "annoyed." In the end, Allport identified traits as what allows people to recognize that a similar response will work in many different situations. To Allport, traits underlie every person's behavior and make it relatively consistent. He classified traits as being either common or individual. Common traits are shared by many people and often are specific to a certain environment. An example is the competitiveness shared by most athletes. Individual traits, on the other hand, apply to a specific person. An example is an individual's quick wit.

Allport based his approach to psychotherapy on a study of the problems of the adult personality and not on a study of infantile emotions and experiences. He believed with other theorists that adult motives developed from infantile drives. However, he believed that these motives in time became independent of the drives.

Allport's introductory work on personality was *Personality: A Psychological Interpretation* (1937). In *Becoming* (1955), another major work, Allport emphasized the importance of the self and the adult personality. He wrote that the self is an identifiable organism and that unity of personality, higher motives, and continuity of personal memories come from the self. An analysis of prejudice is the basis of another pioneering work, *The Nature of Prejudice* (1954).

BOOKS BY ALLPORT

Becoming: Basic Considerations for a Psychology of Personality (1955). *Terry Lectures Ser.* Yale Univ Pr 1955 $5.95. ISBN 0-300-00002-2

The Nature of Personality: Selected Papers (1950). Greenwood 1975 $35.00. ISBN 0-8371-7432-5

The Nature of Prejudice (1954). Addison 1979 $9.57. ISBN 0-201-00179-9

Personality: A Psychological Interpretation (1937). Holt 1937. (o.p.)

Personality and Social Encounter: Selected Essays (1960). Univ of Chicago Pr 1981. (o.p.) $17.00. ISBN 0-226-01494-0

BOOKS ABOUT ALLPORT

Evans, Richard I. *Dialogue with Gordon Allport.* Praeger 1981 $35.00. ISBN 0-275-90615-9 Dialogue between Allport and psychologist Evans that serves as an introduction to Allport's ideas.

Ghougassian, Joseph P. *Gordon W. Allport's Ontopsychology of the Person.* Philosophical Lib

1972 $10.00. ISBN 0-8022-2069-X Study showing the relevance of Allport's conception of the person in opposition to Freud and others.

Maddi, Salvatore R., and Paul T. Costa. *Humanism in Personology: Allport, Maslow and Murray.* Aldine 1972. (o.p.) Theoretical summary and analysis of the work and thought of these three psychologists.

DOLLARD, JOHN 1900–1980

The American psychologist John Dollard was trained in anthropology, behavior therapy, psychoanalysis, and sociology. Throughout his career he was an outspoken believer in the wholeness of knowledge.

Along with fellow psychologist Neal Miller, Dollard developed a theory of personality that stressed the importance of learning. They wrote, "[I]n order to learn one must want something, notice something, do something, and get something. Stated more exactly, these factors are drive, cue, response, and reward." The two theorists went on to divide drives into primary drives, such as hunger, and secondary, or learned, drives, such as fear. When a drive is aroused, a person is guided by cues that encourage a response. The cues guide a person as to when and where the response will be made and what kind of response to make, such as the response to a call to dinner.

A response can come either from the initial response hierarchy, those responses with which people are born, such as crying, or from the resultant hierarchy, which people learn, such as asking for what they want. Reward or reinforcement encourages similar responses to similar situations.

Learning is central to Dollard and Miller's theory because a person learns responses and learns what works and what does not work as responses to certain situations. By responding to situations, a person develops his or her personality. According to their learning theory of personality, personality is made up of habits—the learned associations among drives, cues, and responses.

Dollard's *Caste and Class in a Southern Town* (1937) is a sociological study of the system that kept children of a black–white union from claiming legitimacy. This work contributed ultimately to the postwar changes in the legal and social status of southern African Americans.

Frustration and Aggression (1939) remains compulsory reading for all psychologists who study these two topics and their interrelationship. *Fear in Battle* (1944), a study of veterans of the all-American Abraham Lincoln Brigade in the 1937–1939 Spanish Civil War, conducted for the military during World War II, demonstrated that all of these soldiers had been afraid. The differences in their behavior during combat resulted from more or less successful ways of learning to cope with fear.

BOOKS BY DOLLARD

Caste and Class in a Southern Town (1937). Univ of Wisconsin Pr 1988 $14.50. ISBN 0-299-12134-8

Fear in Battle (1944). AMS $9.50. ISBN 0-404-14714-3

Frustration and Aggression (1939). (coauthored with Robert R. Sears). Greenwood 1980 $27.50. ISBN 0-313-22201-0

Social Learning and Imitation (1941). (coauthored with Neal E. Miller) Greenwood 1979 $24.75. ISBN 0-313-20714-3

FREUD, SIGMUND   1856–1939

Born in Moravia not far from the border of Poland, Sigmund Freud was the son of a wool merchant. When he was four years old, he, his parents, and his seven brothers and sisters moved to Vienna, Austria. In 1873 he entered the medical school at the University of Vienna. There he trained as a neurologist, a specialist in the brain, spinal column, and nervous system.

Freud, however, did not really have a desire to be a practicing doctor. He wanted instead to become a scientist and a professor. But because he was a Jew, there was little opportunity for him to advance in the academic world. Inspired by one of his professors, with six children to feed and clothe, he became interested in psychiatry and entered private practice as a psychiatrist. He soon found that existing therapies were not effective for most of his patients. He found that a method used by another Viennese psychiatrist, Joseph Breuer, gave better results. It involved having patients talk to him and make free associations. Freud and Breuer collaborated for several years and in 1895 coauthored a book—*Studies in Hysteria.* The free-association, or talking-out, method of treatment eventually became a theory of personality, a form of treatment, and an intellectual movement that has had a profound impact on the Western world. The impact is comparable in many ways to the impact of the theories of Charles Darwin and Karl Marx. (*See* Darwin, Vol. 2, Biology: The Evolution of Life, *and* Marx, Vol. 2, Economics: Comparative Economic Systems.)

The technique of free association allowed the patient to tap into the unconscious and allow repressed material to come out. According to Freud, sexual impulses were the basis of neuroses, some kinds of mental illness. Because of this belief, few practitioners joined him. In 1900 he published *The Interpretation of Dreams,* in which he argued that dreams provide clues to the nature of psychological problems. Other books and articles followed, and Freud became a university professor and lecturer. By 1905 Alfred Adler and Carl Jung (*see* Jung, Vol. 2, Psychology: Personality) were counted among his colleagues. In 1909 Freud finally received recognition by academic psychology and was invited to lecture at Clark University in Massachusetts. The following year the International Psychoanalytic Association was founded, and training institutes for Freud's theories of psychoanalysis were established in many countries.

Freud, who by now was known all over the world, continued to see patients, write, and involve himself in organizational work. When the Nazis came to power in Germany, however, friends began to fear for his safety. Finally, in 1938 they persuaded him to flee Nazi anti-Semitism. He went to London, where he died of cancer the following year.

Freud's theories introduced such concepts as the Oedipus complex, the id, and the superego into the language of psychiatry. His concepts of the unconscious, of the pervasiveness of sexuality, and of conflict, anxiety, and defense have had enormous impact on psychology, anthropology, education, literature, and art.

BOOKS BY FREUD

The Basic Writings of Sigmund Freud (1938). A. A. Brill (ed). Modern Lib $17.95. ISBN 0-394-60400-8

Civilization and Its Discontents. James Strachey (ed). Norton 1984 $4.70. ISBN 0-393-30158-3

Early Psychoanalytic Writings. Macmillan 1985 $4.95. ISBN 0-02-076300-X

General Selections from the Works of Sigmund Freud. Doubleday 1989 $8.95. ISBN 0-385-09325-X

The Standard Edition of the Complete Psychological Works of Sigmund Freud. James Strachey (ed). Norton 1976 $759.00. ISBN 0-393-01128-3

Three Essays on the Theory of Sexuality (1910). James Strachey (tr). Basic 1982 $9.95. ISBN 0-465-08606-3

BOOKS ABOUT FREUD

Bettelheim, Bruno. *Freud and Man's Soul.* Random 1984 $6.95. ISBN 0-394-71036-3 Demonstration of how English translations of Freud's writings have distorted some of the central concepts of psychoanalysis, making it impossible for readers to recognize that Freud's ultimate concern was man's soul and causing a misunderstanding and misuse of psychoanalysis in America.

Dilman, Ilham. *Freud and the Mind.* Basil Blackwell 1984 $45.00. ISBN 0-631-13529-4 Full-scale philosophical treatment of Freud's conception of the mind and of the limits of the individual's autonomy.

Freeman, Lucy, and Herbert S. Strean. *Freud and Women.* Continuum 1987 $10.95. ISBN 0-8044-5374-8 Exploration of Freud's important relationships with women, how Freud both idealized and feared them, loved and hated them.

Fromm, Erich. *The Greatness and Limitations of Freud's Thought.* NAL 1981 $5.95. ISBN 0-452-00958-8 Stimulating critique of Freud's contributions to modern thought, showing how his greatest discoveries were distorted by public and private premises that made certain thoughts unthinkable to Freud.

Gay, Peter. *Freud: A Life for Our Time.* Norton 1988 $24.50. ISBN 0-393-02517-9 Complete biography of Freud, drawing on a vast store of unpublished documents, with an integration of the case histories, technical papers, etc.

Hale, Nathan G., Jr. *Freud and the Americans: The Origin and Foundation of the Psychoanalytic Movement in America, 1876–1918.* Oxford Univ Pr 1971 $27.50. ISBN 0-19-501427-8 Analysis of why America embraced Freud's psychoanalytic theories and techniques more warmly than any other country.

•Jones, Ernest. *The Life and Work of Sigmund Freud.* 3 vols. Basic 1953–1957 $80.00. ISBN 0-465-04015-2 Famous and standard biography that covers the formative years and the great discoveries in Volume 1, 1856–1900; the years of maturity in Volume 2, 1902–1919; and the last phase in Volume 3, 1919–1939.

Marcus, Steven. *Freud and the Culture of Psychoanalysis: Studies in the Transition from Victorian Humanism to Modernity.* Norton 1987 $7.70. ISBN 0-393-30410-8 Assesses Freud as an exemplary late-Victorian and as a pivotal figure in the creation of modern thought and culture.

Masson, Jeffrey Moussaieff. *The Assault on Truth: Freud's Suppression of the Seduction Theory.* Farrar 1984 $16.95. ISBN 0-374-10642-8 Highly controversial exposé of the origins of psychoanalysis, based on letters and other new information discovered at the Freud Archives and in Europe.

Schellenberg, James A. *Masters of Social Psychology: Freud, Mead, Lewin, and Skinner.* Oxford Univ Pr 1978 $7.95. ISBN 0-19-502622-5 Short biographies of Freud, Mead, Lewin, and Skinner that show the kind of experiences that led each to formulate his approach.

HORNEY, KAREN 1885–1952

Karen Horney, born in Hamburg, Germany to a Norwegian father and a Dutch mother, studied medicine at the University of Berlin and graduated in 1912. She then completed her studies in psychoanalysis with one of Sigmund Freud's (*see* Freud, Vol. 2, Psychology: Personality) associates and practiced in Berlin for the next 12 years.

In 1932, Horney resettled in the United States and went to work as associate director of the Institute of Psychoanalysis in Chicago. Two years later,

Horney moved to New York, where she practiced psychoanalysis and joined the teaching staff at the New York Psychoanalytic Institute. It was during this time that Horney developed the theories for which she gained fame in the psychiatric community. These theories disputed several of Freud's ideas about the relationships between women and men. Freud felt that biological drives outlined the relationships between men and women, Horney believed that behaviors, especially those exhibited by the neurotic personality, were determined by the environment and society rather than by biological factors. These theories, which Horney discusses in *The Neurotic Personality of Our Time* (1937) and other books, opened a new avenue of psychoanalytic treatment.

These same theories also led to her expulsion from the New York Psychoanalytic Institute in 1941. But Horney went on to form a separate organization, the Association for the Advancement of Psychoanalysis. With others who shared her beliefs, she also founded the American Institute of Psychoanalysis, a training institute of which she served as dean until her death.

BOOKS BY HORNEY

Feminine Psychology. Harold Kelman (ed). Norton 1973 $4.95. ISBN 0-393-00686-7
Final Lectures. Douglas Ingram (ed). Norton 1987 $14.45. ISBN 0-393-02485-7
Neurosis and Human Growth. Norton 1970 $4.95. ISBN 0-393-00135-0
The Neurotic Personality of Our Time (1937). Norton 1965 $4.95. ISBN 0-393-00742-1
New Ways in Psychoanalysis. Norton 1964 $3.95. ISBN 0-393-00132-6
Our Inner Conflicts (1945). Norton 1966 $4.95. ISBN 0-393-00133-4
Self-Analysis (1942). Norton 1968 $5.95. ISBN 0-393-00134-2

BOOKS ABOUT HORNEY

*Jones, Constance. *Karen Horney.* Chelsea 1989 $16.95. ISBN 1-55546-659-1 Story of the famous psychoanalyst who adjusted Freud's theories to correct a male bias.
■Kelman, Harold. *Helping People: Karen Horney's Psychoanalytic Approach.* Aronson 1971 $35.00. ISBN 0-87668-039-2 Clear look at all of the practical aspects of Horney's contribution, as well as a sensitive biography; useful for students.
Quinn, Susa. *A Mind of Her Own: The Life of Karen Horney.* The Radcliffe Biography Ser. Addison 1988 $14.95. ISBN 0-201-15573-7 Full-scale biography with photographs, using new material and unpublished diaries.
Rubins, Jack L. *Karen Horney: Gentle Rebel of Psychoanalysis.* Dial 1978. ISBN 0-8037-4425-0 Biography focusing on the disputes that led Horney to break with the establishment.
Westkott, Marcia. *The Feminist Legacy of Karen Horney.* Yale Univ Pr 1986 $9.95. ISBN 0-300-04204-3 Interpretation of Horney's work as a historically based psychoanalysis of women; provides a major contribution to contemporary feminist thought.

JUNG, CARL GUSTAV 1875–1961

Even as a child in Switzerland, where he was born in the village of Kesswil on Lake Constance, Carl Jung studied the people around him. He observed the behavior of his Swiss Reform minister father, his high-strung mother, and his teachers and friends, trying to understand their patterns. Although his interests ranged from religion to mythology to the occult, Jung decided to study medicine. He studied first at Basel University (1895-1900) and then at the University of Zurich, from which he received an M.D. in 1902. It was not until his graduation that he realized that his true calling was in psychiatry.

Jung was a contemporary of Sigmund Freud (*see* Freud, Vol. 2, Psychology: Personality), whom he corresponded with for a time before he went to Vienna

The Psychoanalyst. Lithograph by William Sharp (1930s). Courtesy of Art Resource.

in 1907 to meet him. The two men formed a close personal and professional relationship, and together they explored the human psyche. But Jung eventually challenged some of Freud's theories, especially the placement of so much emphasis on sex, and the two parted, each to continue work that would add new dimensions to the search for understanding of the human mind.

Jung lectured in psychiatry at the University of Zurich and in 1905 became senior physician at the psychiatric clinic, all while conducting his own private practice. It was during this time that he set up the studies that gained him worldwide notice—studies of mental patients using the word-association test. In 1909 he made the first of many visits to the United States.

Through his extensive travels and research, Jung came to believe that all cultures have similar symbols that are manifest in their dreams, religion, and art. These symbols, Jung theorized, are universal, and they indicate that all people have the same memories at some level deep in their brains, like echoes heard from all the people who have lived before them. He called this set of memories the collective unconscious. The collective unconscious was in addition to the personal unconscious of repressed or forgotten material. He believed that the most important job for each person was to achieve balance between the conscious and the unconscious.

Jung made many other contributions to the field of psychiatry. He was the first to recognize two distinct personality types: introvert (inward-looking) and extrovert (outward-looking). Jung also identified four functions of the human brain: thinking, feeling, sensation, and intuition and coined the term *complex* to describe certain sets of behavioral responses. He also wrote many books describing his theories. His last book, *Memories, Dreams, Reflections,* was published the year he died. An autobiography, it opens with this statement: "My life is a story of the self-realization of the unconscious."

BOOKS BY JUNG

C. G. Jung Speaking: Interviews and Encounters. William McGuire and R. F. Hull (eds). Princeton Univ Pr 1986 $14.95. ISBN 0-691-01871-5

The Essential Jung (1983). Anthony Storr (ed). Princeton Univ Pr 1983 $9.95. ISBN 0-691-02455-3

The Four Basic Psychological Functions of Man and the Establishment of Uniformities in Human Structures and Human Behavior. 2 vols. Am Inst Psych 1984 $187.75. ISBN 0-89920-120-2

Memories, Dreams, Reflections. Random 1989 $8.95. ISBN 0-679-72395-1

Psychology and Religion (1938). *Terry Lecture Ser.* Yale Univ Pr 1938 $6.95. ISBN 0-300-00137-1

BOOKS ABOUT JUNG

Brome, Vincent. *Jung: Man and Myth.* Atheneum 1978. (o.p.) ISBN 0-689-10853 Objective biography describing the early days of psychoanalysis and Jung's emotional upheavals as a mature man.

Mattoon, Mary-Ann. *Jungian Psychology in Perspective.* Free Pr 1985 $14.95. ISBN 0-02-920650-2 Distillation of much of Jung's large and complex body of work into a comprehensive, systematic, and empirically based presentation of Jung's major concepts and their application to daily life.

Samuels, Andrew. *Jung and the Post-Jungians.* Routledge 1985 $12.95. ISBN 0-7102-0864-2 First comprehensive survey of the developments in Jungian psychology that have taken place since Jung's death in 1961.

Samuels, Andrew, *et al. A Critical Dictionary of Jungian Analysis.* Routledge 1986 $16.95. ISBN 0-7102-0915-0 Helpful guide in dictionary format to the terms and ideas developed, adapted, or transformed by Jung.

Wehr, Demaris S. *Jung and Feminism: Liberating Archetypes.* Beacon 1989 $8.95. ISBN 0-8070-6735-0 Attempt to reclaim Jungian psychology as a freeing therapy for women by bringing the insights of feminist theology to bear on the gap between analytical theology and feminism.

Wehr, Gerhard. *Jung: A Biography.* David M. Weeks (tr). Shambhala 1988 $14.95. ISBN 0-87773-455-0 Carefully researched biography that looks at Jung as physician, scientist, and man involved in a variety of personal and professional relationships.

PSYCHOLOGICAL DISORDERS

Bradley, Brendan P., and Chris Thompson. *Psychological Perspectives in Psychiatry.* Wiley 1986 $64.95. ISBN 0-471-90790-1

Clynes, M., and J. Panksepp (eds). *Emotions and Psychopathology.* Plenum 1988 $49.50. ISBN 0-306-42916-0

Crabtree, Adam. *Multiple Man: Explanations in Possession and Multiple Personality.* Praeger 1985 $35.00. ISBN 0-275-90079-7

Davis, Derek R. *An Introduction to Psychopathology.* Oxford Univ Pr 1984 $12.95. ISBN 0-19-261488-6

Dawson, Geraldine (ed). *Autism: Nature, Diagnosis and Treatment.* Guilford 1989 $45.00. ISBN 0-89862-724-9

Dunner, David L., *et al* (eds). *Relatives at Risk for Mental Disorders. American Psychopathological Assn Ser.* Raven 1988 $79.00. ISBN 0-88167-381-1

Goldstein, Kurt. *A Kurt Goldstein Reader: The Shaping of Neuropsychology.* R. W. Rieber (ed). AMS 1986 $32.50. ISBN 0-404-60868-X

▪Plath, Sylvia. *The Bell Jar.* Bantam 1975 $4.50. ISBN 0-553-26008-1 Autobiographical novel of a young woman's struggle with depression.

▪Schreiber, Flora R. *Sybil.* Warner Bks 1974 $4.95. ISBN 0-446-34313-7 A study of multiple personalities.

Sue, Stanley, *et al. Understanding Abnormal Behavior.* Houghton 1985 $48.76. ISBN 0-395-36947-9

Thigpen, Corbett, and Hervey M. Cleckley. *Three Faces of Eve.* Cleckley-Thigpen 1985 $20.00. ISBN 0-911238-51-4 Describes multiple personality disorders; bibliography included.

Tinbergen, Niko, and Elizabeth A. Tinbergen. *Autistic Children: New Hope for a Cure.* Unwin 1985 $14.95. ISBN 0-04-157011-1

Wenar, Charles. *Developmental Psychopathology from Infancy Through Adolescence.* McGraw 1989 $35.95. ISBN 0-07-557553-1

■Young, Patrick. *Schizophrenia.* Chelsea 1988 $17.95. ISBN 0-7910-0052-4 A look at the origins and treatment of this mysterious disease.

Zimbardo, Philip G., and Alan Hammond. *Readings on Human Behavior: The Best of Science '80–'86.* Scott 1988 $10.50. ISBN 0-673-18941-4

PSYCHOLOGICAL TESTING

American Psychological Association and American Educational Research Association. *Standards for Educational and Psychological Testing.* American Psychological Assn 1985 $23.00. ISBN 0-912704-95-0

Cohen, Ronald J., *et al. Psychological Testing: An Introduction to Tests and Measurement.* Mayfield 1988 $37.95. ISBN 0-87484-752-4

Cowels, Michael. *Statistics in Psychology: A Historical Perspective.* Erlbaum 1989 $39.95. ISBN 0-8058-0031-X

Garrett, Henry E. *Great Experiments in Psychology.* Century Psychology Ser. Irvington 1981 $39.50. ISBN 0-89197-190-4

Kaplan, Robert M., and Dennis P. Saccuzzo *Psychological Testing: Principles, Applications, and Issues.* Psychology Ser. Brooks-Cole 1982 $28.00. ISBN 0-8185-0494-3

Katz, Lawrence. *A Practical Guide to Psychodiagnostic Testing.* Thomas 1985 $29.75. ISBN 0-398-05118-6

Minium, Edward W. *Statistical Reasoning in Psychology and Education.* Wiley 1982 $37.95. ISBN 0-471-08041-1

Murphy, Kevin R., and Charles O. Davidshofer. *Psychological Testing: Principles and Applications.* Prentice 1988 $45.33. ISBN 0-13-732587-8

Rust, John, and Susan Golombok. *Modern Psychometrics: The Science of Psychological Assessment.* Routledge 1989 $14.95. ISBN 0-415-03059-5

Weiner, Elliott A., and Barbara J. Stewart. *Assessing Individuals: Psychological and Educational Tests and Measurements.* Scott 1984 $14.75. ISBN 0-673-39532-4

BINET, ALFRED   1857–1911

Alfred Binet, a French psychologist, was a founder of scientific psychology in France. Initially he worked on pathological psychology, which was the major psychological subspecialty in France at the time. He wrote on such topics as hysteria. However, in 1891 he turned to experimental psychology and established it as a subdiscipline of psychology.

In 1905, at Binet's suggestion, the Ministry of Education considered setting up special classes for mentally retarded children. In order to determine which children could not profit from regular instruction, Binet and fellow psychologist Théodore Simon proposed a series of 30 intelligence tests. Developed between 1905 and 1911, these tests were immediately successful and assured Binet's reputation. A subsequent refinement of Binet's tests was done by psychologist Lewis M. Terman. Prepared at Stanford University in California and known as the Stanford-Binet Intelligence Scale, these tests are still in use today in the United States in schools, industry, and the army.

Binet was one of the originators of the questionnaire method of testing and a pioneer in the study of small groups. He also studied the psychology of mathematics prodigies and chess players. It is for his applied research on intelligence, however, that he is best known.

BOOKS BY BINET

Alterations of Personality (1890) and *On Double Consciousness* (1899). Helen G. Baldwin (tr). *Contributions to the History of Psychology Ser.* Greenwood 1977 $65.00. ISBN 0-313-26944-0

Modern Ideas about Children. Suzanne Heisler (tr). Heisler 1984 $15.00. ISBN 0-9617054-1-8

The Psychology of Reasoning (1896). Routledge 1901. (o.p.)

BOOK ABOUT BINET

Wolf, Theta H. *Alfred Binet.* Univ of Chicago Pr 1973 $20.00. ISBN 0-226-90498-9 Biography on the founder of scientific psychology in France.

STRESS

Anderson, Mac (ed). *How to Handle Stress.* Great Quotations 1988 $7.50. ISBN 0-931089-45-X

Barnett, Rosalind, *et al* (eds). *Gender and Stress.* Free Pr 1987 $29.95. ISBN 0-02-901380-1

▪ Batson, Horace W., and Gary Batson (eds). *Overcoming Stress: Everything You Ever Need to Know.* Welstar 1987 $9.95. ISBN 0-938503-00-6 A how-to book on managing stress.

Chandler, Louis A. *Assessing Stress in Children.* Praeger 1985 $38.95. ISBN 0-275-90072-X

▪ Cohen, Daniel, and Susan Cohen. *Teenage Stress: Understanding the Tensions You Feel at Home, at School, and Among Your Friends.* M. Evans 1988 $10.95. ISBN 0-87131-423-1 Discusses the causes and effects of stress on teenagers and its management.

Corson, John A. *Individual Differences in Response to Stress. Stress in Modern Society Ser.* James H. Humphrey (ed). AMS 1989 $32.50. ISBN 0-404-63263-7

Festinger, Leon. *Conflict, Decision, and Dissonance.* Stanford Univ Pr 1964 $15.00. ISBN 0-8047-0205-5

Flach, Frederic. *Resilience: Discovering a New Strength at Times of Stress.* Fawcett 1989 $7.95. ISBN 0-449-90408-3

Flach, Frederic (ed). *Stress and Its Management.* Norton 1989 $29.95. ISBN 0-393-70072-0

Hardine, Rosetta R. *Medical and Psychological Stress: Guidebook for Reference and Research.* ABBE 1988 $26.50. ISBN 0-88164-819-1

Humphrey, James H. *Profiles in Stress. Stress in Modern Society Ser.* AMS 1986 $32.50. ISBN 0-404-63252-1

▪ Youngs, Bettie B. *A Stress Management Guide for Young People.* Bilicki 1986 $9.95. ISBN 0-940221-00-4 Practical, helpful guide for adolescents confronting the problems of growing up.

SOCIOLOGY

This section is devoted to sociology, the science of social behavior, or the behavior of humans in groups. In general, sociologists use objective techniques to study the social behavior of their own society or of other modern societies. In actual practice, rather than focus on society in general, most sociologists focus on only one aspect of society, such as the family, religion, or interaction. To conduct their studies, sociologists collect and analyze verifiable data under controlled conditions and then present objective findings based on their data.

For ease of use the sociology section, which begins with listings of works that are general references or that are concerned with the methods or the history of the field, is divided into 18 subsections organized alphabetically. The topics of the subsections, which correlate to the various aspects of social behavior studied by sociologists, are as follows: Age and Aging; Communications; Community; Conflict and Conflict Resolution; Crime; Culture; Ethnic Groups; Family, Marriage, Life-Course Events; Interaction and Groups; Organizations; Population; Religion; Social Change; Social Stratification; Socialization; Urban Life; Women; and Work.

Within a number of the subsections, individual sociologists associated with the particular topic are listed alphabetically. For each, there is a book or a list of books by that sociologist. In addition, there is for each a profile that provides personal background and/or information about his or her role in the field and his or her contributions to it. Further, the profile may refer the reader to other related individuals and their works, which also can be found in *The Young Adult Reader's Adviser.*

Last, for most profiled individuals, there is a Books About section that, when available, lists notable biographies for further reading and research. Whenever possible, very recent titles have also been included.

There is a strong relationship between many of the topics associated with sociology and psychology. For a more comprehensive listing of works related to those topics, see also the readings under psychology, found in the section immediately preceding this one.

GENERAL REFERENCES

■Frank, Arthur W., III, *et al* (eds). *Encyclopedic Dictionary of Sociology.* Dushkin 1985 $10.95. ISBN 0-87967-607-8 Helpful reference; expanded entries.

Fairchild, Henry P. (ed). *Dictionary of Sociology and Related Sciences. Quality Paperback Ser.* Littlefield 1977 $12.95. ISBN 0-8226-0120-6

Petersen, William. *Dictionary of Demography.* 2 vols. Greenwood 1985 $125.00. ISBN 0-313-21419-0

Ross, John A. (ed). *International Encyclopedia of Population.* 2 vols. Macmillan 1982 $145.00. ISBN 0-02-927430-3

Smelser, Neil J. (ed). *Handbook of Sociology.* Sage 1988 $89.95. ISBN 0-8039-2665-0

Theodorson, George A., and Achilles A. Theodorson. *A Modern Dictionary of Sociology.* Harper $8.95. ISBN 0-06-463483-3

■Thernstrom, Stephan, *et al* (eds). *Harvard Encyclopedia of American Ethnic Groups.* Harvard Univ Pr 1980 $90.00. ISBN 0-674-37512-2 Useful summary of the history of ethnic groups in the United States.

■Turner, Jonathan H., *Sociology: A Student Handbook.* McGraw 1984 $8.95. ISBN 0-07-554584-5 Useful explanations of key terms and concepts of sociology.

U.S. Department of Commerce, Bureau of the Census. *Statistical Abstract of the United States, 1988.* USGPO 1988 $25.00.

HISTORY, SURVEYS, AND METHODS

Abrams, Philip. *Historical Sociology.* Cornell Univ Pr 1983 $15.95. ISBN 0-8014-9243-2

Bales, Robert F. *Interaction Process Analysis. Midway Reprint Ser.* Univ of Chicago Pr 1976 $10.00. ISBN 0-226-03618-9

■Barnes, LeRoy W. (ed). *Annual Editions: Social Problems 90/91.* Dushkin 1990 $9.95. ISBN 0-87967-854-2 Current social problems worldwide.

Berger, Peter L. *Invitation to Sociology: A Humanistic Perspective.* Doubleday 1963 $5.95. ISBN 0-385-06529-9

■ Coser, Lewis A. *Masters of Sociological Thought: Ideas in Historical and Social Context.* Harcourt 1977 $28.00. ISBN 0-15-555130-2 Excellent introduction to the creators of sociology.

■ Finsterbusch, Kurt (ed). *Annual Editions: Sociology 90/91.* Dushkin 1990 $9.95. ISBN 0-87967-855-0 Anthology of articles on social problems.

■ Finsterbusch, Kurt, and George McKenna. *Taking Sides: Clashing Views on Controversial Social Issues.* Dushkin 1988 $9.95. ISBN 0-87967-742-2 Pro/con exchanges on several major issues of society today.

Giddens, Anthony. *Central Problems in Social Theory: Action, Structure, and Contradiction in Social Analysis.* Univ of California Pr 1979 $12.95. ISBN 0-520-03975-0

Giddens, Anthony. *Social Theory and Modern Sociology.* Stanford Univ Pr 1987 $12.95. ISBN 0-8047-1356-1

Gordon, Milton M. *The Scope of Sociology.* Oxford Univ Pr 1988 $10.95. ISBN 0-19-505303-6

Gurvich, George, and Wilbert E. Moore (eds). *Twentieth-Century Sociology. Essay Index Reprint Ser.* Ayer 1977 $38.50. ISBN 0-8369-2110-0

■ Krause, Elliott. *Why Study Sociology?* Random 1980. ISBN 0-394-32200-2 Interesting and practical presentation of sociology for beginners.

Lazarsfeld, Paul F., and Wayner Thielens, Jr. *The Academic Mind: Social Scientists in Time of Crises.* Walter P. Metszger (ed). Ayer 1977 $35.50. ISBN 0-405-10006-X

Lazarsfeld, Paul F., *et al* (eds). *The Language of Social Research: A Reader in the Methodology of Social Research.* Free Pr 1965 $7.95. ISBN 0-02-918270-0

■ Madge, John H. *Origins of Scientific Sociology.* Free Pr 1962 $10.95. ISBN 0-02-919710-4 Reviews major developments in social research.

Labovitz, Sanford I., and Robert B. Hagedorn. *Introduction to Social Research.* McGraw 1981 $21.95. ISBN 0-07-035777-3

Short, James F., Jr. (ed). *The State of Sociology: Problems and Prospects.* Sage 1981 $14.00. ISBN 0-8039-1658-2

Singewood, Alan. *A Short History of Sociological Thought.* St. Martin's 1984 $12.95. ISBN 0-312-72151-X

Small, Albion, and George Vincent. *An Introduction to the Study of Society. Reprints in Sociology Ser.* Irvington 1971 $14.00. ISBN 0-697-00212-8

Taylor, James C., and David G. Bowers. *Survey of Organizations.* Inst for Social Research 1972 $16.00. ISBN 0-87944-124-0

Zeitlin, Irving. *Ideology and the Development of Sociology Theory.* Prentice 1987 $38.33. ISBN 0-13-450172-1

COMTE, AUGUSTE   1798–1857

French philosopher and social reformer Auguste Comte was educated in Paris. The first to use the term sociology, he founded the school of philosophy known as positivism, which holds that to be meaningful, something must be logically inferred or based solely on observable, scientific facts and their relation to each other.

Comte's goal was a society in which both individuals and nations could live in harmony and in comfort. He believed that positivism could become the basis for the political organization of modern industrial societies. In his view, intellectual development goes through three stages. One is theological, the stage in which events are believed to be due to supernatural forces. The second is metaphysical, the stage in which natural phenomena are thought to be the result of fundamental energies or ideas. The third, and last stage, is positive, the stage in which people turned to observation, hypotheses, and experimentation to explain phenomena. Sociology, said Comte, was the vehicle through which people could find the way to live in harmony and comfort in the new age.

Comte achieved great fame in France and England in the 1800s. Although his influence is acknowledged worldwide, his many books are not widely read today. His insight about the development of sociology as a science, however, remains uncontested.

BOOKS BY COMTE

Introduction to Positive Philosophy. Frederick Ferre (tr). Hackett 1988 $4.25. ISBN 0-87220-050-7

The Positive History of the New Social Order. American Classical Coll Pr 1982 $154.50. ISBN 0-89266-353-7

The Positive Philosophy (1853). Harriet Martineau (tr). AMS $67.50.

Social Statistics and Social Dynamics: The Theory of Order and the Theory of Progress. The Most Meaningful Classics in World Culture Ser. American Classical Coll Pr 1983 $117.45. ISBN 0-89226-425-8

Systems of Positive Polity (1851–1854; 1875–1877) 4 vols. Burt Franklin 1973 $115.00. ISBN 0-8337-0636-5

BOOKS ABOUT COMTE

Aron, Raymond. *Main Currents in Sociological Thought: Montesquieu, Comte, Marx, Tocqueville, the Sociologist, and the Revolution of 1848.* Doubleday 1968 $7.95. ISBN 0-385-08804-3 Course of lectures given in France; includes an analysis of Comte's thought along with analyses of other major thinkers.

Marvin, Francis S. *Comte: The Founder of Sociology.* Russell 1965. (o.p.) Introduction to Comte's philosophy drawing on his life, his thought, and his legacy.

Thompson, Kenneth. *Auguste Comte: The Foundation of Sociology.* Wiley 1975. (o.p.) ISBN 0-470-85988-1 Important introduction to Comte's work; includes translations of his most important social writings.

DURKHEIM, EMILE   1858–1917

French sociologist Emile Durkheim is considered one of the chief founders of modern sociology. After receiving his education in France and in Germany, he taught political science at the University of Bordeaux in France. He then attained a professorship at the Sorbonne in Paris, where he taught sociology and founded and edited the journal *L'Année Sociologique.*

Greatly influenced by the writings of French philosopher August Comte (*see* Comte, Vol. 2, Sociology: History, Surveys, and Methods), he believed that the methods of natural science could be applied to the study of science. Durkheim is renowned for the breadth of his scholarship, for his studies of primitive religion, for creating the concept of division of labor, and for his insistence that sociologists use sociological rather than psychological data. According to Durkheim, sociologists should rely on observable data collected through the scientific methods of research.

In 1897 Durkheim published his work *Suicide,* which is still read today. Although its data are out-of-date, Durkheim's analysis of suicide rates and other data, originally collected for administrative rather than scientific purposes, is considered brilliant by many.

Durkheim also developed the concept of collective consciousness. He believed that the collective mind of society is the source of religion and morality and that the common values developed in society are what holds society together. When an individual loses these values, the result is suicide. When society loses these values, the result is social instability.

BOOKS BY DURKHEIM

The Division of Labor in Society (1893). W. D. Hall (tr). Free Pr 1985 $10.95. ISBN 0-02-907950-0

The Elementary Forms of the Religious Life (1912). Joseph W. Swain (tr). Free Pr 1965 $16.95.
    ISBN 0-02-908010-X
Primitive Classification (1903). (coauthored with Marcel Mauss) Rodney Needham (tr).
    Univ of Chicago Pr 1967 $8.95. ISBN 0-226-17334-8
Professional Ethics and Civic Morals. Cornelia Brookfield (tr). Greenwood 1983 $39.75.
    ISBN 0-313-24114-7
The Rules of Sociological Method (1895). Free Pr 1982 $13.95. ISBN 0-02-908500-4
Suicide (1897). Free Pr 1966 $11.95. ISBN 0-02-908660-4

BOOKS ABOUT DURKHEIM

Alexander, Jeffrey C. (ed). *Durkheimian Sociology: Cultural Studies.* Cambridge Univ Pr 1988
    $39.50. ISBN 0-0521-34622-3 Group of essays that draws on Durkheim's later
    work and provides new interpretations of Durkheim.
Fenton, Steve. *Durkheim and Modern Sociology.* Cambridge Univ Pr 1984 $11.95. ISBN
    0-521-27763-9 Introduction to Durkheim's major works that examines his con-
    tinued inspiration in sociology as well as recent interpretations of his thought.
Giddens, Anthony. *Emile Durkheim. Modern Masters Ser.* Frank Kermode (ed). Viking
    1978. (o.p.) ISBN 0-670-29283-4 Comprehensive account of Durkheim's writings
    with attention to the relevance of his political views for the conception of sociol-
    ogy.
Nisbet, Robert A. *The Sociology of Emile Durkheim.* Oxford Univ Pr 1973 $8.95. ISBN
    0-19-501734-X Complete introduction and analysis of Durkheim's thought in
    such areas of sociology as social structure, social psychology, political sociology,
    social religion, morality, deviance, and social change.
Wolff, Kurt H., *et al* (eds). *Emile Durkheim, 1858–1917: A Collection of Essays, with Translations
    and a Bibliography. Perennial Works in Sociology Ser.* Ayer 1979 $38.00. ISBN 0-405-
    12130-X Collection of essays by major Durkheim scholars covering all areas of
    his thought and contributions to social science.

PARSONS, TALCOTT   1902–1979

Born in Colorado Springs, Colorado, American sociologist Talcott Parsons was
educated at Amherst College in Massachusetts, the London School of Economics in England, and the University of Heidelberg in Germany. After he earned
his Ph.D. at Heidelberg in 1927, he began his teaching career at Harvard
University in the Department of Economics. In 1931 he switched to the teaching of sociology and in 1946 became the chairman of Harvard's new Department of Social Relations. He remained at Harvard until 1974, when he retired.
    The leading theorist of American sociology in the years after World War
II, Parsons gained international recognition for his structural-functional theory, his attempt to construct a single framework in which all of society's
characteristics could be classified. Armed with this theory, he attempted to
study the ways in which the units of a stable social structure work to make
possible the development and maintenance of that system. In other words, he
studied and described a social system in terms of the functions of its parts.
Parsons is also responsible for the fusion of social anthropology and clinical
psychology into the modern discipline of sociology.

BOOKS BY PARSONS

Essays in Sociological Theory (1949). Free Pr 1964 $14.95. ISBN 0-02-924030-1
The Evolution of Societies. Jackson Toby (ed). Prentice 1977. (o.p.) $19.67. ISBN 0-13-
    293639-9
Family, Socialization, and Interaction Process. Macmillan 1955. (o.p.) $8.50. ISBN 0-02-
    924100-6
The Social System (1951). Free Pr 1964 $21.95. ISBN 0-02-924190-1
Sociological Theory and Modern Society (1967). Free Pr 1967 $28.50. ISBN 0-02-924200-2

The Structure of Social Action (1937). 2 vols. Free Pr 1949. Vol. 1 $10.95. ISBN 0-02-924240-1. Vol. 2 $16.95. ISBN 0-02-924250-9

Talcott Parsons on Institutions and Social Evolution: Selected Writings. Heritage of Sociology Ser. Leon H. Mayhew (ed). Univ of Chicago Pr 1985 $14.95. ISBN 0-226-64749-8

Working Papers in the Theory of Action. (coauthored with others) Greenwood 1981. (o.p.) $27.50. ISBN 0-313-22468-4

BOOKS ABOUT PARSONS

Black, Max (ed). *The Social Theories of Talcott Parsons: A Critical Examination.* Southern Illinois Univ Pr 1976 $9.95. ISBN 0-8093-0759-6 Comprehensive survey bringing together a collection of essays on Parsons from various social science departments at Cornell University.

Hamilton, Peter. *Talcott Parsons.* Tavistock 1983 $8.95. ISBN 0-85312-439-6 Introduction to and biography of Parsons and the development of modern sociology.

Rex, John. *Talcott Parsons and the Social Image of Man.* Routledge 1977. (o.p.) ISBN 0-7100-8369-6 Account of Parsons's works that clarifies his basic concepts and shows their interrelation.

Rocher, Guy. *Talcott Parsons and American Sociology.* Barnes. (o.p.) ISBN 0-06-495950-3 Short, authoritative, clear review of Parsons's work; analytical overview of his writings placing them in the context of the development of modern sociology.

STOUFFER, SAMUEL A.   1900–1960

American sociologist Samuel A. Stouffer was a principal founder of large-scale social research. Asked by the Social Science Research Council in 1937 to commission a series of research volumes on the Great Depression, the economic downturn that struck the United States in the 1930s, he not only commissioned 13 volumes but saw them all through to publication that same year.

In 1940, when Swedish economist Gunnar Myrdal (*see* Myrdal, Vol. 2, Sociology: Culture) had to return to Stockholm, Stouffer completed the research for Myrdal's work, *An American Dilemma* (1944), which was the report of a large-scale study of the status of African Americans in American life. Once again, Stouffer did more than complete the research. He did much of the writing as well. Stouffer continued his research efforts during World War II, directing a large staff of social scientists that carried out research for the army. Their research was ultimately published in four volumes. Later, in 1955, Stouffer conducted a major nationwide study of American attitudes toward civil liberties.

A master analyst of survey data, Stouffer created the concept of relative deprivation, a term he used originally in *The American Soldier* (1949). In its broad sense, the term refers to the measurement of deprivation or disadvantage by comparison with the relatively superior advantages of others in a group, rather than by objective standards. In *The American Soldier,* Stouffer uses the term to explain why some soldiers, such as infantrymen, who have poor chances of promotion, did not feel as deprived as far as promotions were concerned as did soldiers in the air force, which had a high promotion rate. His analysis techniques and his writings provide models on which the best in contemporary survey research is based.

BOOKS BY STOUFFER

The American Soldier. Vol. 1 *Adjustment During Army Life.* (coauthored with others) Military Affairs/Aerospace Historian 1949 $30.00. ISBN 0-89126-034-X

The American Soldier. Vol. 2 *Combat and Its Aftermath.* (coauthored with Arthur A. Lumsdaine) Military Affairs/Aerospace Historian 1949 $35.00. ISBN 0-89126-035-8

Communism, Conformity, and Civil Liberties (1955). Peter Smith $11.25. ISBN 0-8446-1426-2
Measurement and Prediction (1950). Peter Smith 1988 $16.50. ISBN 0-8446-3021-7
Social Research to Test Ideas: Selected Writings. Macmillan 1962. (o.p.) $9.50. ISBN 0-02-931710-X

BOOK ABOUT STOUFFER

Merton, Robert K., and Paul F. Lazarsfeld (eds). *Continuities in Social Research: Studies in the Scope and Method of the American Soldier. Perspectives in Social Inquiry Ser.* Ayer 1974 $16.00. ISBN 0-405-05514-5 Demonstrates how the concepts of reference group, primary group, and social prospectivism can be more precisely characterized.

AGE AND AGING

Atchley, Robert C. *Aging: Continuity and Change.* Wadsworth 1987 $23.00. ISBN 0-534-06960-6
Atchley, Robert C. *Social Forces and Aging: An Introduction to Social Gerontology.* Wadsworth 1988 $41.25. ISBN 0-534-08790-6
Binstock, Robert H., and Linda K. George (eds). *Handbook of Aging and the Social Sciences.* Academic Pr 1990 $65.00. ISBN 0-12-099190-X
Brubaker, Timothy H. (ed). *Aging, Health, and Family: Long Term Care. Focus Editions Ser.* Sage 1987 $16.95. ISBN 0-8039-2592-1
Brubaker, Timothy H. (ed). *Family Relationships in Later Life. Sage Focus Editions.* Sage 1983 $16.95. ISBN 0-8039-2105-5
▪Cox, Harold. *Annual Editions: Aging.* Dushkin 1989 $9.95. ISBN 0-87967-764-3 Discusses aging processes from several disciplinary views.
Eisenstadt, Samuel N. *From Generation to Generation: Age Groups and Social Structure.* Free Pr 1964 $7.95. ISBN 0-02-909380-5
Hess, Beth B., and Elizabeth W. Markson. *Aging and Old Age: An Introduction to Social Gerontology.* Macmillan 1980. (o.p.) $23.00. ISBN 0-02-354100-8
Hultsch, David F., and Francine Deutsch. *Adult Development and Aging.* McGraw 1980 $38.95. ISBN 0-07-031156-0
▪Swisher, Karin, and Tara Deal (eds). *The Elderly: Opposing Viewpoints. Opposing Viewpoints Ser.* Greenhaven 1990 $7.95. ISBN 0-89908-450-8 Basic reference; includes discussions of issues of major importance to the aged.
▪Worth, Richard. *You'll Be Old Someday, Too.* Watts 1986 $11.90. ISBN 0-531-10158-4 Good resource on problems and attitudes of the old.

See also Vol. 2, Health: Growth and Development.

COMMUNICATIONS

Ball-Rokeach, Sandra J., and Joel W. Grube. *The Great American Values Test: Influencing Behavior and Belief Through Television.* Free Pr 1984 $27.95. ISBN 0-02-926850-8
▪Bernards, Neal (ed). *Mass Media. Opposing Viewpoints Ser.* Greenhaven 1987 $7.95. ISBN 0-89908-400-1 Discussion of opposing views on media influence in the United States.
Bogart, Leo. *The Press and Public: Who Reads What, Where, and Why in American Newspapers.* Erlbaum 1981 $29.95. ISBN 0-89859-077-9

■Cantril, Hadley. *The Invasion from Mars.* Princeton Univ Pr 1982 $9.95. ISBN 0-691-02827-3 Orson Welles's Halloween prank.

Compaine, Benjamin. *Issues in New Information Technology.* Brenda Dervin (ed). *Communication and Information Science Ser.* Ablex 1988 $24.50. ISBN 0-89391-500-9

DeFleur, Melvin L., and Sandra J. Ball-Rokeach. *Theories of Mass Communication.* Longman 1981 $18.95. ISBN 0-582-28277-2

DeFleur, Melvin L., and Everette E. Dennis. *Understanding Mass Communication.* Houghton 1987 $30.76. ISBN 0-395-36906-1

DeFleur, Melvin L., and Otto N. Larsen. *The Flow of Information: An Experiment in Mass Communication.* Transaction 1986 $16.95. ISBN 0-88738-676-X

Deutsch, Karl W. *The Nerves of Government.* Free Pr 1963 $19.95. ISBN 0-02-907280-8

Katz, Elihu (ed). *Mass Media and Social Change. Sage Studies in International Sociology.* Sage 1981 $26.95. ISBN 0-8039-9807-4

Katz, Elihu, and Paul F. Lazarsfeld. *Personal Influence: The Part Played by People in the Flow of Mass Communications.* Free Pr 1964 $11.95. ISBN 0-02-917150-4

Klapper, Joseph. *The Effects of Mass Communication.* Free Pr 1960 $14.95. ISBN 0-02-917380-9

Lazarsfeld, Paul F. *Radio and the Printed Page: An Introduction to the Study of Radio and Its Role in the Communication of Ideas. History of Broadcasting: Radio to Television Ser.* Ayer 1971 $25.50. ISBN 0-405-03575-6

Lazarsfeld, Paul F., and Patricia L. Kendall. *Radio Listening in America: The People Look at Radio Again. Perennial Works in Sociology Ser.* Lewis A. Coser and Walter W. Powell (eds). Ayer 1979 $15.00. ISBN 0-405-12100-8

McLuhan, Marshall. *Understanding Media: The Extensions of Man.* NAL 1966 $4.95. ISBN 0-451-62496-3

McLuhan, Marshall, and Eric McLuhan. *Laws of Media: The New Science.* Univ of Toronto Pr 1988 $27.50. ISBN 0-8020-5782-9

McLuhan, Marshall, and Bruce R. Powers. *The Global Village: Transformations in World Life and Media in the 21st Century. Communication and Society Ser.* Oxford Univ Pr 1989 $29.95. ISBN 0-19-505444-X

Milavsky, J. Ronald. *Television and Aggression: Results of a Panel Study. Quantitative Studies in Social Relations Ser.* Academic Pr 1982 $35.50. ISBN 0-12-495980-6

Penzias, Arno. *Ideas and Information: Managing in a High Tech World.* Simon 1990 $8.95. ISBN 0-671-69196-1

Schramm, Wilbur. *The Story of Human Communication: Cave Painting to Microchip.* Harper 1987 $20.95. ISBN 0-06-045799-6

Schramm, Wilbur, *et al. Television in the Lives of Our Children.* Stanford Univ Pr 1961 $10.95. ISBN 0-8047-0064-8

Shearer, Benjamin F., and Marilyn Huxford (eds). *Communications and Society: A Bibliography on Communications Technologies and Their Social Impact.* Greenwood 1983 $40.95. ISBN 0-313-23713-1

Steiner, Gray A. *The People Look at Television.* Knopf 1963. (o.p.) $7.95. ISBN 0-394-44022-6

Tannenbaum, Percy H. (ed). *The Entertainment Functions of Television.* Erlbaum 1980 $29.95. ISBN 0-89859-013-2

COMMUNITY

Agger, Robert E., and Bert Swanson. *Rulers and the Ruled.* Irvington 1984. (o.p.) $24.50.

Caplow, Theodore. *Middletown Families: Fifty Years of Change and Continuity.* Univ of Minnesota Pr 1985 $12.95. ISBN 0-8166-1435-0

Coleman, James S. *Community Conflict.* Free Pr 1957. (o.p.) $7.95. ISBN 0-029-06480-5

Coleman, James S., and Thomas Hoffer. *Public and Private High Schools: The Impact of Communities.* Basic 1987 $21.95. ISBN 0-465-06767-0

Dahl, Robert A. *Who Governs: Democracy and Power in an American City.* Yale Univ Pr 1961 $12.95. ISBN 0-300-00051-0

Gans, Herbert J. *The Levittowners: Ways of Life and Politics in a New Suburban Community.* Columbia Univ Pr 1982 $15.00. ISBN 0-231-05571-4

Hunter, Floyd. *Community Power Structure: A Study of Decision Makers.* Univ of North Carolina Pr 1969 $8.95. ISBN 0-8078-4033-5

■Kephart, William M. *Extraordinary Groups: An Examination of Unconventional Life-Styles.* St. Martin's 1986 $11.00. ISBN 0-312-27863-2 Compares community life-styles of the Amish, the Hutterites, and the Mormons.

Lewis, Oscar. *Life in a Mexican Village: Tepoztlàn Restudied.* Univ of Illinois Pr 1963. (o.p.)

Marriott, McKim (ed). *Village India: Studies in the Little Community.* Univ of Chicago Pr 1986 $15.00. ISBN 0-226-50645-2

Nisbet, Robert A. *The Quest for Community: A Study in the Ethics of Order and Freedom.* ICS Pr 1989 $10.95. ISBN 1-55815-058-7

Suttles, Gerald D. *The Social Construction of Communities. Studies of Urban Society Ser.* Univ of Chicago Pr 1972 $8.00. ISBN 0-226-78189-5

Vidich, Arthur J., and Joseph Bensman. *Small Town in Mass Society: Class, Power, and Religion in a Rural Community.* Princeton Univ Pr 1968 $14.95. ISBN 0-691-02807-9

Whyte, William F. *Street Corner Society: The Social Structure of an Italian Slum.* Univ of Chicago Pr 1981 $9.00. ISBN 0-226-89543-2

Wirth, Louis. *The Ghetto. Midway Reprint Ser.* Univ of Chicago Pr 1982 $14.95. ISBN 0-226-90252-8

Zorbaugh, Harvey. *The Gold Coast and the Slum: A Sociological Study of Chicago's Near Northside.* Univ of Chicago Pr 1983 $17.95. ISBN 0-226-98945-3

LYND, ROBERT STAUGHTON   1892–1970, AND LYND, HELEN MERRELL   1894–1982

American sociologists Robert S. Lynd and Helen Merrell Lynd became renowned for their pioneering studies of the small city of Muncie, Indiana, which they called Middletown. Not since French politician and writer Alexis de Tocqueville's four-volume *Democracy in America* (1835–1840), a classic study of America's political philosophies, had there been such a careful analysis of daily life in an American community. The Lynds lived in Muncie for several years just before and during the economic depression of the 1930s. Their goal was to develop an accurate description and understanding of the workings of a small community. To do this, they interviewed many of the people who lived in Muncie. They also carefully studied newspaper files to find out about events that had taken place in the past. They made every attempt to enter fully into small-town life. The Lynds' original work on Middletown, *Middletown* (1929), and its sequel, *Middletown in Transition* (1937), are classics in sociological methodology. These studies were the first to use cultural anthropology in the setting of a modern Western city, and the conclusions they reached about small-town life and change are still important in sociology today.

The research in Middletown won Robert Lynd a professorship at Columbia University in New York City, where he subsequently taught for 30 years, and Helen Lynd one at Sarah Lawrence College in Bronxville, New York.

BOOK BY HELEN MERRELL LYND

England in the Eighteen-Eighties: Toward a Social Basis for Freedom. Transaction 1984 $34.95. ISBN 0-88738-004-2

BOOK BY ROBERT S. LYND

Knowledge for What? The Place of Social Science in American Culture (1939). Wesleyan Univ Pr 1986 $14.95. ISBN 0-8195-6170-3

BOOKS BY ROBERT S. LYND AND HELEN MERRELL LYND

Middletown (1929). Harcourt 1959 $10.95. ISBN 0-15-659550-8
Middletown in Transition: A Study in Cultural Conflicts (1937). Harcourt 1982 $9.95. ISBN
    0-15-659551-6

BOOK ABOUT ROBERT S. LYND AND HELEN MERRELL LYND

Caplow, Theodore, *et al. Middletown Families: Fifty Years of Change and Continuity.* Univ of
    Minnesota Pr 1982 $19.50. ISBN 0-8166-1073-8 Study that returns to the Lynds's
    Middletown 50 years later and shows that continuity, not change, is the dominant
    characteristic of Middletown families.

RIESMAN, DAVID   1909–

American sociologist David Riesman, was trained as a lawyer, but became
interested in the study of contemporary American society. In 1950, his book
The Lonely Crowd became an instant bestseller, as readers saw in it insightful
descriptions of themselves and their neighbors. Since the publication of that
work, Riesman has written extensively on American higher education, a topic
with which he is eminently familiar, having taught first for many years at the
University of Chicago before joining the faculty at Harvard University as
professor of sociology. Within the field of sociology, Riesman is known as a
major exponent of qualitative analysis—of learning about the whole through
careful and detailed interviews with individuals.

BOOKS BY RIESMAN

Abundance for What? And Other Essays. Doubleday 1965. (o.p.)
The Academic Revolution. (coauthored with Christopher Jencks) Univ of Chicago Pr 1977
    $7.95. ISBN 0-226-39628-2
Faces in the Crowd: Individual Studies in Character and Politics. Lewis A. Coser and Walter W.
    Powell (eds). *Perennial Works in Sociology Ser.* Ayer 1979 $54.50. ISBN 0-405-12114-8
Individualism Reconsidered. Macmillan 1954. (o.p.) $2.45. ISBN 0-02-926500-2
The Lonely Crowd: A Study of the Changing American Character. Studies in National Policy Ser
    (1950). (coauthored with others) Yale Univ Pr 1973 $12.95. ISBN 0-300-00193-2
*On Higher Education: The Academic Enterprise in an Era of Rising Student Consumerism. Higher
    Education Ser.* Jossey-Bass 1981 $27.95. ISBN 0-87584-484-4

CONFLICT AND CONFLICT RESOLUTION

Coleman, James S. *Community Conflict.* Free Pr 1957 $3.95. ISBN 0-02-906480-5
Collins, Randall. *Conflict Sociology: Toward an Explanatory Science.* Academic Pr 1975. (o.p.)
    $34.95. ISBN 0-12-181352-X
Coser, Lewis A. *The Functions of Social Conflict.* Free Pr 1964 $14.95. ISBN 0-02-906810-X
Dahrendorf, Ralf. *Class and Class Conflict in Industrial Society.* Stanford Univ Pr 1959 $27.50.
    ISBN 0-8047-0561-5
Dahrendorf, Ralf. *The Modern Social Conflict: An Essay on the Politics of Liberty.* Weidenfeld
    1988 $17.95. ISBN 1-55584-208-9
Deutsch, Morton. *The Resolution of Conflict: Constructive and Destructive Processes.* Yale Univ
    Pr 1973 $14.95. ISBN 0-300-02186-0
Eisenstadt, Samuel N., and E. Ben-Ari (eds). *Japanese Models of Conflict Resolution.* Rout-
    ledge 1990 $78.50. ISBN 0-7103-0342-4
Gluckman, Max. *Custom and Conflict in Africa.* Barnes 1969 $9.95. ISBN 0-480325-2
Lewin, Kurt. *Resolving Social Conflicts.* Gertrud W. Lewin (ed). Intl Specialized Bk 1978
    $4.50. ISBN 0-285-64718-0
Raiffa, Howard. *The Art and Science of Negotiation.* Harvard Univ Pr 1985 $9.95. ISBN
    0-674-04813-X

CRIME

Bedau, Hugo A. (ed). *Capital Punishment in the United States.* Chester M. Pierce (ed). AMS $42.50. ISBN 0-404-10325-1

Bedau, Hugo A. (ed). *The Death Penalty in America.* Oxford Univ Pr 1982 $11.95. ISBN 0-19-502987-9

■Bender, David, and Bruno Leone. *Criminal Justice. Opposing Viewpoints Ser.* Greenhaven 1989 $9.95. ISBN 0-89908-551-2 Basic issues concerning the criminal justice system debated by many contributors.

Clinard, Marshall B. *Black Market: A Study of White Collar Crime. Criminology, Law Enforcement, and Social Problems Ser.* Patterson Smith 1969 $8.00. ISBN 0-87585-912-7

Cohen, A. K. *Delinquent Boys.* Free Pr 1955 $7.95. ISBN 0-02-905770-1

Cressey, Donald R. *Other People's Money: A Study in the Social Psychology of Embezzlement.* Patterson Smith 1973 $15.00. ISBN 0-87585-202-5

■Dudley, William, and David L. Bender (eds). *Crime and Criminals: Opposing Viewpoints. Opposing Viewpoints Ser.* Greenhaven 1989 $7.95. ISBN 0-89908-416-8 Anthology of current topics.

Feeley, Malcolm M. *The Process Is the Punishment: Handling Cases in a Lower Criminal Court.* Russell Sage 1979 $27.50. ISBN 0-87154-253-6

Hirschi, Travis. *Causes of Delinquency.* Univ of California Pr 1969 $11.95. ISBN 0-520-01901-6

*Meltzer, Milton. *Crime in America.* Morrow 1990 $12.95. ISBN 0-688-08513-X Critically looks at poverty and hopelessness in the U.S. and explains that police, courts, and jails are not curing the problems.

Mitford, Jessica. *Kind and Unusual Punishment: The Prison Business.* Random 1974 $9.95. ISBN 0-394-71093-2

Sellin, Thorsten. *Culture, Conflict and Crime.* Kraus. (o.p.) $15.00. ISBN 0-911-40041-9

■Silberman, Charles E. *Criminal Violence, Criminal Justice.* Random 1980 $5.95. ISBN 0-394-74147-1 Gripping report on continuing causes of crime in the United States.

Stinchcombe, Arthur L. *Crime and Punishment: Changing Attitudes in America. Social and Behavioral Sciences Ser.* Jossey-Bass 1980. (o.p.) $29.95. ISBN 0875-89-472-0

Sutherland, Edwain H. (ed). *Professional Thief.* Univ of Chicago Pr 1937 $9.50. ISBN 0-226-78053-8

Sutherland, Edwin H. *White Collar Crime.* Greenwood 1983 $38.50. ISBN 0-313-24227-5

■Szumski, Bonnie (ed). *America's Prisons. Opposing Viewpoints Ser.* Greenhaven 1985 $7.95. ISBN 0-89908-350-1 Discussion and debate about the prison system in the United States.

Taft, Donald R., and R. W. England, Jr. *Criminology.* Macmillan 1964. (o.p.) $18.95. ISBN 0-02-418810-7

Van den Haag, Ernst, and John P. Conrad. *The Death Penalty: A Debate.* Plenum 1983 $19.95. ISBN 0-306-41416-3

Wolfgang, Marvin. *Patterns in Criminal Homicide.* Patterson Smith 1975 $24.00. ISBN 0-87585-211-4

Wolfgang, Marvin E., *et al. From Boy to Man, from Delinquency to Crime. Studies in Crime and Justice Ser.* Univ of Chicago Pr 1987 $29.95. ISBN 0-226-90555-1

CULTURE

Barash, David P. *Hare and the Tortoise: Culture, Biology, and Human Nature.* Penguin 1987 $8.95. ISBN 0-14-008748-6

Barash, David P. *Sociobiology and Behavior.* Elsevier 1982 $21.25. ISBN 0-444-99088-7

Denisoff, R. Serge. *Solid Gold: The Popular Record Industry. Cultural and Society Ser.* Transaction 1981 $14.95. ISBN 0-87855-586-2

Denisoff, R. Serge. *Tarnished Gold: The Record Industry Revisited.* Transaction 1986 $16.95. ISBN 0-88738-618-0

Eastman, Carol M. *Aspects of Language and Culture. Publications in Anthropology Ser.* Chandler 1975 $9.95. ISBN 0-88316-514-7

Fitzpatrick, Joseph P. *One Church, Many Cultures: The Challenge of Diversity.* Sheed & Ward 1987 $8.95. ISBN 0-934134-63-4

Fitzpatrick, Joseph P. *Puerto Rican Americans: The Meaning of Migration to the Mainland.* Prentice 1987 $21.67. ISBN 0-13-740135-3

Freud, Sigmund. *Civilization and Its Discontents.* James Strachey (ed). Norton 1984 $4.70. ISBN 0-393-30158-3

Gans, Herbert J. *Popular Culture and High Culture: An Analysis and Evaluation of Taste.* Basic 1975 $9.95. ISBN 0-465-09717-0

▪Harris, Marvin. *Cows, Pigs, Wars, and Witches: The Riddles of Culture.* Random 1989 $7.95. ISBN 0-679-72468-0 A collection of cultural riddles and aspects of life-styles, many of which seem strange to most Americans.

Slater, Philip. *The Pursuit of Loneliness: American Culture at the Breaking Point.* Beacon 1976 $4.95. ISBN 0-8070-4159-9

Williams, Raymond. *The Sociology of Culture.* Schocken 1982 $7.95. ISBN 0-8052-0696-5

MYRDAL, GUNNAR 1898–1987

Swedish economist, sociologist, and public official, Gunnar Myrdal, graduated from the University of Stockholm in Sweden in 1927. After graduation, he became a lecturer and then a professor of economics there. In 1934, in collaboration with his wife, he wrote *Crisis in the Population Question,* which helped bring about welfare measures in Sweden.

In 1938 Myrdal came to the United States. From then until 1942 he headed a large-scale Carnegie Corporation-supported study of the status of blacks in American life. He was selected by Carnegie to direct the study becuase he was from "a non-imperialist country with no background of discrimination of one race against another." Collaborating on the study with him were nearly all the important people of American social science from Franz Boas (*see* Boas, Vol. 2, Anthropology: Culture) to Samuel Stouffer (*see* Stouffer, Vol. 2, Sociology: History, Surveys, and Methods) to Margaret Mead. (*See* Mead, Vol. 2, Anthropology: Culture.) The result was the 1944 work, *An American Dilemma: The Negro Problem and Modern Democracy,* which won Myrdal fame in American sociology. A classic in its field, cited by the 1954 United States Supreme Court decision on desegregation, its title refers to Myrdal's conclusion that the "black problem" did not concern African Americans only, that the racial problem in the United States was interwoven with the democratic functioning of American society. The problem, as Myrdal saw it, was how to guide individual Americans in reconciling their moral principles with their behavior and attitudes in their dealings with blacks. Myrdal put forth in the work his major theory of cumulative causation: that is, poverty breeds poverty.

After the study was concluded, Myrdal returned to Sweden, where he served as secretary of commerce. In 1947 he became secretary-general of the United Nations Economic Commission for Europe, a position he held for 10 years. In 1957 he published *Rich Lands and Poor,* in which he spoke out for the need to provide more economic help to developing nations. Then, in 1968, he published *Asian Drama: An Inquiry of Nations,* which did much to introduce the rest of the world to the problems of developing countries. In 1974 Myrdal received the Nobel Prize in economics, sharing it with the Austrian economist Friedrich von Hayek.

BOOKS BY MYRDAL

Against the Stream: Critical Essays on Economics (1973). Random 1974. (o.p.)
An American Dilemma (1944). 2 vols. Pantheon 1975. Vol. 1 $5.95. ISBN 0-394-73042-9.
Vol. 2 $5.95. ISBN 0-394-73043-7
Asian Drama: An Inquiry into the Poverty of Nations (1968). Random 1972 $4.95. ISBN
0-394-71730-9
Beyond the Welfare State: Economic Planning and Its International Implications (1960). Greenwood
1982 $38.50. ISBN 0-313-23697-6

BOOKS ABOUT MYRDAL

Carlson, Allan. *The Swedish Experiment in Family Politics: The Myrdals and the Interwar Population
Crisis.* Transaction 1990. ISBN 0-88738-299-1 Critical account of the work of
Gunnar and Alva Myrdal and how they helped engineer a new domestic order
in Sweden.
Southern, David W. *Gunnar Myrdal and Black-White Relations: The Use and Abuse of "An
American Dilemma," 1944–1969.* Louisiana State Univ Pr 1987 $35.00. ISBN 0-8071-
1302-6 Argues that Myrdal's *An American Dilemma* was the *Uncle Tom's Cabin* of the
American civil rights movement.

See also Vol. 2, Anthropology: Culture.

ETHNIC GROUPS

Alford, Harold J. *The Proud Peoples: The Heritage and Culture of Spanish-Speaking Peoples in the
United States.* NAL 1973 $1.75. ISBN 0-451-612434
Allport, Gordon W. *The Nature of Prejudice.* Addison 1979 $9.95. ISBN 0-201-00179-9
Apostle, Richard A., and Marijean Suelzle. *The Anatomy of Racial Attitudes.* Univ of
California Pr 1983 $35.00. ISBN 0-520-04719-2
Blau, Zena S. *Black Children–White Children: Competence, Socialization, and Social Structure.* Free
Pr 1981 $24.95. ISBN 0-02-903640-2
Brown, Dee. *Bury My Heart at Wounded Knee.* Holt 1971 $18.95. ISBN 0-03-085322-2
Campbell, Angus. *White Attitudes Toward Black People.* Inst for Social Research 1971 $8.00.
ISBN 0-87944-006-6
Coleman, James S. *Equality of Educational Opportunity. Perennial Works in Sociology Ser.* Lewis
A. Coser and Walter W. Powell (eds). Ayer 1979. (o.p.) $49.95. ISBN 0-405-
12088-5
Deloria, Vine, Jr., and Clifford Lyttle. *The Nations Within: The Past and Future of American
Indian Sovereignty.* Pantheon 1984 $11.95. ISBN 0-394-72566-2
Du Bois, W. E. B. *W. E. B. Du Bois on Sociology and the Black Community.* Dan S. Green and
Edwin D. Driver (eds). Univ of Chicago Pr 1987 $17.50. ISBN 0-226-16762-3
Farley, Reynolds. *Blacks and Whites: Narrowing the Gap? Social Trends in the United States Ser.*
Harvard Univ Pr 1986 $8.95. ISBN 0-674-07632-X
Gordon, Milton M. *Human Nature, Class, and Ethnicity.* Oxford Univ Pr 1978 $8.95. ISBN
0-19-502237-8
Gordon, Milton M., and Richard D. Lambert (eds). *America As a Multicultural Society.
Annals of the American Academy of Political and Social Science Ser.* Am Acad Pol Soc Sci
1981 $8.95. ISBN 0-87761-261-7
Greeley, Andrew M. *Why Can't They Be Like Us? Facts and Fallacies About Ethnic Differences
and Group Conflicts in America. Institute of Human Relations Press Paperback Ser.* Am Jewish
Comm 1980 $1.50. ISBN 0-87495-009-0
•Leone, Bruno (ed). *Racism: Opposing Viewpoints. Isms Ser.* Greenhaven 1986 $7.95. ISBN

0-89908-357-9 Anthology of essays by writers of opposing views, past and present.

Lincoln, C. Eric. *Race, Religion and the Continuing American Dilemma. American Century Ser.* Hill & Wang 1985 $8.95. ISBN 0-8090-0163-2

Lincoln, C. Eric. *The Black Muslims in America.* Greenwood 1982. (o.p.)

*Martinez, Al (ed). *Rising Voices.* NAL 1974. (o.p.) $1.50. ISBN 0-451-06282-5 Brief biographies of 52 outstanding Spanish-speaking Americans.

Moynihan, Daniel P., and Nathan Glazer. *Beyond the Melting Pot: The Negroes, Puerto Ricans, Jews, Italians, and Irish of New York City.* MIT Pr 1970 $13.95. ISBN 0-262-57022-X

Pettigrew, Thomas F. *The Sociology of Race Relations: Reflection and Reform.* Free Pr 1980 $15.95. ISBN 0-02-925110-9

Portes, Alejandro, and Robert L. Bach. *Latin Journey: Cuban and Mexican Immigrants in the United States.* Univ of California Pr 1984 $12.95. ISBN 0-520-05004-5

Quinley, Harold E., and Charles Y. Glock. *Anti-Semitism in America.* Transaction 1983 $12.95. ISBN 0-87855-940-X

Rose, Peter. *Lives on the Boundary: A Moving Account of the Struggles and Achievements of America's Educational Underclass.* Penguin 1990 $8.95. ISBN 0-14-012403-9

▪Rose, Peter I. *They and We: Racial and Ethnic Relations in the United States.* McGraw 1980 $11.95. ISBN 0-07-554317-6 Clearly written introduction to minority group relations in the United States, focusing on the processes of conflict and accommodation among the groups.

Selznick, Gertrude J., and Stephen Steinberg. *The Tenacity of Prejudice: Anti-Semitism in Contemporary America.* Greenwood 1979 $35.00. ISBN 0-313-209650-0

Simpson, George E., and Milton Yinger. *Racial and Cultural Minorities: An Analysis of Prejudice and Discrimination. Environment, Development, and Public Policy Ser.* Harper 1972 $29.50. ISBN 0-306-41777-4

Steinberg, Stephen. *The Ethnic Myth: Race, Ethnicity and Class in America.* Beacon 1989 $12.95. ISBN 0-8070-4151-3

▪Thernstrom, Stephan, Ann Orlov, and Oscar Handlin (eds). *The Harvard Encyclopedia of American Ethnic Groups.* Harvard Univ Pr 1980 $90.00. ISBN 0-674-37512-2 Useful, informative discussions of the history of the various ethnic groups in the United States.

Van den Berghe, Pierre L. *The Ethnic Phenomenon.* Praeger 1987 $14.95. ISBN 0-275-92709-1

Waddell, Jack O., and O. Michael Watson (eds). *The American Indian in Urban Society.* Univ Pr of America 1984 $17.25. ISBN 0-8191-4038-4

Willie, Charles V. (ed). *Black-Brown-White Relations: Race Relations in the 1970's.* Transaction 1977 $12.95. ISBN 0-87855-596-X

Willie, Charles V. *Caste and Class Controversy.* General Hall 1979 $8.95. ISBN 0-930390-36-9

Wilson, William J. *The Declining Significance of Race: Blacks and Changing American Institutions.* Univ of Chicago Pr 1980 $9.95. ISBN 0-226-90129-7

Wilson, William J. *The Truly Disadvantaged: The Inner City, the Underclass, and Public Policy.* Univ of Chicago Pr 1987 $19.95. ISBN 0-226-90130-0

Wirth, Louis. *The Ghetto. Midway Reprint Ser.* Univ of Chicago Pr 1982 $14.95. ISBN 0-226-90252-8

▪Zangwill, Israel. *The Melting Pot: A Drama in Four Acts. Modern Jewish Experience Ser.* Ayer 1975 $19.00. ISBN 0-405-06756-9 A 1908 play that lent its name to American society.

FAMILY, MARRIAGE, LIFE-COURSE EVENTS

Aries, Philippe. *Centuries of Childhood: A Social History of Family Life.* McGraw 1965 $8.95. ISBN 0-07-553689-7

Becker, Gary S. *A Treatise on the Family.* Harvard Univ Pr 1985 $8.95. ISBN 0-674-90697-7

Reine Lefebvre and Margot.   Pastel by Mary
Cassatt (late 1800s).   Courtesy of UPI/Bettmann.

■Bender, David L., and Bruno Leone. *Death and Dying Annual 1989. Opposing Viewpoints
Sources Ser.* Greenhaven 1989 $9.95. ISBN 0-89908-546-6 Opposing views on such
topics as abortion, AIDS, and euthanasia.
■Bender, David, and Bruno Leone (eds). *Human Sexuality Annual 1989. Opposing Viewpoints
Sources Ser.* Greenhaven 1989 $9.95. ISBN 0-89908-549-0 Opposing views on
major sexual issues of modern society.
■Bender, David, and Bruno Leone (eds). *Male/Female Roles Annual 1989. Opposing Viewpoints
Sources Ser.* Greenhaven 1989 $9.95. ISBN 0-89908-544-X Opposing views on
current issues concerning family roles.
■Bernards, Neal, *et al* (eds). *Teenage Sexuality. Opposing Viewpoints Ser.* Greenhaven 1988
$7.95. ISBN 0-89908-405-2 Debates on attitudes toward sex, sex education, teen-
age pregnancy, and other issues facing American teenagers.
Blau, Zena S., and David I. Kartzer (eds). *Family Relations in the Life Course Perspective.
Current Perspectives on Aging and the Life Cycle Ser.* Vol. 2 JAI 1986 $52.50. ISBN
0-89232-522-4
Cherlin, Andrew. *Marriage, Divorce, Remarriage.* Harvard Univ Pr 1983 $5.95. ISBN
0-674-55081-1
Coles, Robert, and Jane H. Coles. *Sex and the American Teenager.* Harper 1985 $5.95. ISBN
0-06-096002-7
Collins, Randall. *Sociology of Marriage and the Family.* Nelson-Hall 1988 $28.95. ISBN
0-8304-1198-4
D'Antonio, William V., and Joan Aldous (eds). *Families and Religions: Conflict and Change
in Modern Society.* Sage 1983 $16.50. ISBN 0-8039-2468-2
■Finsterbusch, Kurt, and George McKenna. *Taking Sides: Clashing Views on Controversial
Social Issues.* Dushkin 1988 $9.95. ISBN 0-87967-742-2 Opinions of prominent
sociologists on current social issues.
Glaser, Barney G., and Anselm L. Strauss. *Awareness of Dying.* Aldine 1965 $27.95. ISBN
0-202-30001-3

Glenn, Norval D., and Marion T. Coleman. *Family Relations: A Reader.* Wadsworth 1988 $23.50. ISBN 0-534-10545-9

Goode, William J. *The Family.* Prentice 1982 $20.67. ISBN 0-13-301754-0

Goode, William J. *World Revolution and Family Patterns.* Free Pr 1970 $12.95. ISBN 0-02-912460-3

Henslin, James M. (ed). *Marriage and Family in a Changing Society.* Free Pr 1985 $15.95. ISBN 0-02-914870-7

Hinde, Robert A., and Joan Stevenson-Hinde (eds). *Relationships Within Families: Mutual Influences.* Oxford Univ Pr 1988 $45.00. ISBN 0-19-852183-9

Kephart, William M., and Davor Jedlicka. *The Family, Society, and the Individual.* Harper 1987 $35.50. ISBN 0-06-043637-9

∎ Kübler-Ross, Elizabeth. *Living with Death and Dying.* Macmillan 1982 $5.95. ISBN 0-02-086490-6 Discusses caring for the terminally ill, including children, and coping with the reality of death.

∎ Kübler-Ross, Elizabeth. *Questions and Answers on Death and Dying.* Macmillan 1974 $5.95. ISBN 0-02-089159-4 Addresses common queries on death and offers information on care for the terminally ill.

Lasswell, Marcia, and Thomas E. Lasswell. *Marriage and the Family.* Wadsworth 1987 $44.75. ISBN 0-534-07584-3

Melville, Keith. *Marriage and Family Today.* McGraw 1988 $33.95. ISBN 0-07-554748-1

∎ O'Connor, Karen. *Homeless Children.* Overview Ser. Greenhaven 1989 $10.95. ISBN 0-89908-109-X Important introduction to a difficult issue for society.

∎ O'Neill, Terry (ed). *Male/Female Roles: Opposing Viewpoints. Opposing Viewpoints Ser.* Greenhaven 1989 $7.95. ISBN 0-89908-421-4 Debates on changing roles of the sexes and their impact on society.

∎ Park, Angela. *Child Abuse. Understanding Social Issues Ser.* Watts 1988 $11.90. ISBN 0-531-17121-3 Sensitive introduction to a difficult topic; includes helpful resources.

∎ Pocs, Ollie. *Annual Editions: Marriage and Family 89/90.* Dushkin 1989 $9.95. ISBN 0-87967-770-8 Differing views on modern family life.

Rabin, A. I., and Benjamin Beit-Hallahmi. *Twenty Years Later: Kibbutz Children Grown Up.* Springer-Verlag 1982 $27.95. ISBN 0-8261-3310-X

Reiss, Ira. *Journey into Sexuality: An Exploratory Voyage.* Prentice 1986 $38.00. ISBN 0-13-511478-0

Skolnick, Arlene S., and Jerome H. Skolnick. *Family in Transition: Rethinking Marriage, Sexuality, Child Rearing, and Family Organization.* Scott 1989 $20.00. ISBN 0-673-39879-X

Weitman, Lenore J. *The Divorce Revolution: The Unexpected Social and Economic Consequences for Women and Children in America.* Free Pr 1985 $14.95. ISBN 0-02-934710-6

Willie, Charles V. *Five Black Scholars: An Analysis of Family Life, Education, and Career.* Univ Pr of America 1986 $9.75. ISBN 0-8191-5276-5

See also Health: Growth and Development.

INTERACTION AND GROUPS

Conrad, Peter, and Joseph W. Schneider. *Deviance and Medicalization: From Badness to Sickness.* Merrill 1980 $22.95. ISBN 0-675-20608-1

Erasmus, Charles J. *In Search of the Common Good: Utopian Experiments Past and Future.* Free Pr 1977 $12.95. ISBN 0-02-909640-5

Fischer, Claude. *To Dwell Among Friends: Personal Networks in Town and City.* Univ of Chicago Pr 1982 $15.95. ISBN 0-226-25138-1

Frankl, Viktor E. *Man's Search for Meaning.* Pocket 1984 $3.95.
Fromm, Erich. *Escape from Freedom.* Avon 1982 $4.95. ISBN 0-380-01167-0
Gibbons, Don C., and Marvin D. Krohn. *Delinquent Behavior.* Prentice 1986 $42.67. ISBN
   0-13-197989-2
Goffman, Erving. *Interaction Ritual: Essays in Face-to-Face Behavior.* Pantheon 1982 $4.76.
   ISBN 0-394-70631-5
Goffman, Erving. *Presentation of Self in Everyday Life.* Doubleday 1959 $6.95. ISBN 0-385-
   09402-7
Goffman, Erving. *Strategic Interaction.* Univ of Penn Pr 1970 $13.95. ISBN 0-8122-1011-5
Homans, George C. *The Human Group.* Harcourt 1950 $24.00. ISBN 0-15-540375-3
Janis, Irving. *Groupthink: Psychological Studies of Policy Decision.* Houghton 1982 $22.36. ISBN
   0-395-31704-5
Kanter, Rosabeth M. *Commitment and Community: Communes and Utopias in Sociological Perspec-
   tive.* Harvard Univ Pr 1972 $8.95. ISBN 0-674-14576-3
LeBon, Gustave. *Consciousness and Unconsciousness in the Behavior of the Crowds.* 2 vols. Found
   Class Repr 1985 $167.45. ISBN 0-89901-236-1
Slater, Philip. *The Pursuit of Loneliness: American Culture at the Breaking Point.* Beacon 1976
   $4.95. ISBN 0-8070-4159-9
Smelser, Neil, *et al. The Social Importance of Self-Esteem.* Univ of California Pr 1989 $35.00.
   ISBN 0-520-06708-8

MEAD, GEORGE HERBERT   1863–1931

George Herbert Mead was born in South Hadley, Massachusetts and was
educated at Oberlin College in Ohio and at Harvard University. After receiving
his degree from Harvard in 1888, he went on to study in Germany, in Leipzig
and Berlin. In 1894, back in the United States, he joined the faculty of the
University of Chicago, where he was to remain for his entire career. The task
he set for himself was to explain how people learn to think in abstractions,
become self-conscious, and behave purposefully and morally. He contended
that these attributes rest on language and are acquired and maintained through
group life. Social psychology, a field in which Mead was a pioneer, focuses on
the regularities in individual behavior that result from participation in groups.

Mead was something of a cult figure during and after his lifetime. Although he published no books during his lifetime, his works were published
after his death, reconstructed from his notes and from the notes of students.
He was a man far ahead of his time, and many of the concepts he developed
at the turn of the century are widely accepted today. Among these are the
selective nature of perception, cognition through linguistic symbols, role playing, decision processes, reference groups, and socialization through participation in group activities.

Books by Mead

George Herbert Mead on Social Psychology (1964). Anselm Strauss (ed). Univ of Chicago Pr
   1964 $12.00. ISBN 0-226-51665-2
The Individual and the Social Self: Unpublished Work of George Herbert Mead. David L. Miller
   (ed). Univ of Chicago Pr 1982 $12.95. ISBN 0-226-51674-1
Mind, Self, and Society: From the Standpoint of a Social Behaviorist (1934). Charles W. Morris
   (ed). Univ of Chicago Pr 1967 $8.95. ISBN 0-226-51668-7
Selected Writings: George Herbert Mead (1964). Andrew J. Reck (ed). Univ of Chicago Pr
   1981 $10.95. ISBN 0-226-51671-7

Books about Mead

Aboulafia, Mitchell. *The Mediating Self: Mead, Sartre, and Self-Determination.* Yale Univ Pr
   1986 $20.00. ISBN 0-200-03523-3 A comparison of the American pragmatist

Mead with Jean-Paul Sartre, the existentialist; includes a critical analysis of both philosophies and an original analysis of consciousness and self-determination.

Clayton, Alfred Stafford. *Emergent Mind and Education: A Study of George H. Mead's Bio-Social Behaviorism from an Educational Point of View.* AMS 1983 repr of 1943 ed $22.50. ISBN 0-404-55867-4 Complete analysis of Mead's methadology and thinking.

Miller, David L. *George Herbert Mead: Self, Language, and the World.* Univ of Chicago Pr 1980 $7.95. ISBN 0-226-52613-5 Mead's philosophy presented as a system, showing how his social behavioristic theory of mind and self is integrally related to his thought and how his principle of sociality applies to his work.

See also Vol. 2, Psychology: Groups.

ORGANIZATIONS

Barnard, Chester I. *The Functions of the Executive.* Harvard Univ Pr 1968 $10.95. ISBN 0-674-32803-5

Blau, Peter M. *Bureaucracy in Modern Society.* McGraw 1987 $12.95. ISBN 0-07-555033-4

Blau, Peter M. *The Dynamics of Bureaucracy.* Univ of Chicago Pr 1973 $6.95. ISBN 0-226-05726-7

Cyert, Richard M. *The Economic Theory of Organizations and the Firm.* New York Univ Pr 1988 $40.00. ISBN 0-8147-1427-7

Cyert, Richard M., and David C. Mowery (eds). *The Impact of Technological Change on Employment and Economic Growth.* Ballinger 1988 $39.95. ISBN 0-88730-290-4

Festinger, Leon, *et al. When Prophecy Fails: A Social and Psychological Study of a Modern Group That Predicted the Destruction of the World.* Harper 1964 $8.95. ISBN 0-06-131132-4

Kanter, Rosabeth M. *Men and Women of the Corporation.* Basic 1979 $12.95. ISBN 0-465-04453-0

March, James G., and Herbert A. Simon. *Organizations.* Wiley 1958 $59.95. ISBN 0-471-56793-0

Perrow, Charles. *Complex Organizations.* McGraw 1986 $15.50. ISBN 0-07-554799-6

▪Peter, Laurence J., and Raymond Hull. *The Peter Principle: Why Things Always Go Wrong.* Morrow 1971 $3.95. ISBN 0-688-27544-3 Popular study of organizational bureaucracy; originated theory that people rise to their level of incompetence.

Simon, Herbert A. *Administrative Behavior.* Free Pr 1976 $10.95. ISBN 0-02-929000-7

Tannenbaum, Arnold S., and Tamas Rozgonyi (eds). *Authority and Reward in Organizations: An International Research.* Inst of Social Research 1987 $42.00. ISBN 0-87944-309-X

Weber, Max. *The Theory of Social and Economic Organization.* Free Pr 1964 $16.95. ISBN 0-02-934930-3

MERTON, ROBERT KING   1910–

American sociologist Robert King Merton was born in Philadelphia. A graduate of Temple University in Philadelphia and of Harvard University, he has had a major impact not only on almost all branches of sociology but on contemporary intellectual life as well. In 1936, after he received his doctorate from Harvard, he remained there as a member of the faculty until 1939 and then went to Tulane University of Louisiana. In 1941 he moved to Columbia University in New York City, where he was associate director of Columbia's Bureau of Applied Social Research until 1971 and Giddings Professor of Sociology from 1963 until 1974.

Four of Merton's primary interests have been the study of social structure, bureaucracy, mass communications, and the sociology of science. Many of his concepts have become central to sociological research today. The concept of the unanticipated consequences of purposive social action, for example, calls attention to the difference between the intent and the consequences of social behavior. Another concept, the Matthew effect, points out that in science, recognition tends to go to those who already have it. This may not only penalize individuals but also may slow down or even prevent the spread of new ideas. Still another concept—obliteration by incorporation—is a pattern of success in science and scholarship in which a person's work becomes so widely accepted that his or her identity often is not even thought of in connection with the work.

Merton's influence in sociology has been most prominent in his insistence on the scientific method. He is often referred to as the "dean of American sociology."

BOOKS BY MERTON

Continuities in Social Research: Studies in the Scope and Method of the American Soldier (1950). (coedited with Paul Lazarsfeld) *Perspectives in Social Inquiry Ser.* Ayer 1974 $16.00. ISBN 0-405-05514-5

On the Shoulders of Giants: A Shandean Postscript (1965). Harcourt 1985 $14.95. ISBN 0-15-169952-3

Science, Technology and Society in Seventeenth Century England (1938). Fertig 1970 $40.00. ISBN 0-86527-178-X

Social Research and the Practicing Professions. Aaron Rosenblatt and Thomas F. Gieryn (eds). Univ Pr of America 1984 $19.75. ISBN 0-8191-4129-1

Social Theory and Social Structure (1938). Free Pr 1968 $24.95. ISBN 0-02-921130-1

Sociological Traditions from Generation to Generation: Glimpses of the American Experience. Modern Sociology Ser (1980). (coedited with Matilda Riley) Ablex 1980 $22.50. ISBN 0-89391-061-9

The Sociology of Science: Theoretical and Empirical Investigations (1973). Norman W. Storer (ed). Univ of Chicago Pr 1979 $15.95. ISBN 0-226-52092-7 Essays on human and sociological aspects of science.

The Student-Physician: Introductory Studies in the Sociology of Medical Education. (coedited with Patricia Kevall) Harvard Univ Pr 1957. (o.p.) $15.00. ISBN 0-674-84616-8

Toward a Metric of Science: The Advent of Science Indicators. (coauthored with others) Wiley 1978. (o.p.) $44.95. ISBN 0-471-98435-3

BOOKS ABOUT MERTON

Coser, Lewis A. (ed). *The Idea of Social Structure: Papers in Honor of Robert K. Merton.* Harcourt 1975. (o.p.) $20.00. ISBN 0-15-540548-9 Series of varied essays on Merton's work and its influence on current thought.

Sztompka, Piotr. *Robert K. Merton: An Intellectual Profile. Theoretical Traditions in the Social Sciences Ser.* St. Martin's 1986 $11.95. ISBN 0-312-68739-7 Complete intellectual profile of Merton, covering biosocial theory, the method of functional and structural analysis, as well as the sociology of science.

POPULATION

Bean, Frank D., *et al. Mexican and Central American Population and U.S. Immigration Policy.* Univ of Texas Pr 1989 $10.95. ISBN 0-292-75116-8

Bean, Frank D., and Marta Tienda. *The Hispanic Population of the United States. The Population of the United States in the 1980's: A Census Monograph.* Russell Sage 1988 $42.50. ISBN 0-87154-104-1

Bogue, Donald J. *The Population of the United States: Historical Trends and Future Projections.* Free Pr 1985 $100.00. ISBN 0-02-904700-5

Farley, Reynolds, and Walter Allen. *The Color Line and the Quality of Life in America.* Oxford Univ Pr 1989 $14.95. ISBN 0-19-506029-6

Grindstaff, Carl F. *Population and Society: A Sociological Perspective.* Christopher 1981 $8.95. ISBN 0-8158-0397-4

*Jones, Landon. *Great Expectations: America and the Baby Boom Generation.* Ballantine 1986 $3.95. ISBN 0-345-33402-7 Describes effects of one generation on U.S. society.

Keyfitz, Nathan. *Population Change and Social Policy.* Univ Pr of America 1984 $19.75. ISBN 0-8191-4073-2

RELIGION

Arjomand, Said A. (ed). *From Nationalism to Revolutionary Islam: Essays on Social Movements in the Contemporary Near and Middle East.* State Univ of New York Pr 1985 $18.95. ISBN 0-87395-871-3

*Caplow, Theodore, *et al. All Faithful People: Change and Continuity in Middletown's Religion.* Univ of Minnesota Pr 1983 $19.50. ISBN 0-8166-1230-7 Follow-up on the Lynds' classic study of Middletown (Muncie, Indiana).

Fowler, James W. *Stages of Faith: The Psychology of Human Development and the Quest for Meaning.* Harper 1981 $9.95. ISBN 0-06-062840-5

Greeley, Andrew M. *Myths of Religion.* Warner Bks 1989 $16.95. ISBN 0-446-38818-1

Greeley, Andrew M. *Religious Change in America.* Social Trends in the United States Ser. Harvard Univ Pr 1989 $25.00. ISBN 0-674-75840-4

Herberg, Will. *Protestant, Catholic, Jew: An Essay in American Religious Sociology.* Univ of Chicago Pr 1983 $11.95. ISBN 0-226-32734-5

Jules-Rosette, Bennetta (ed). *The New Religions of Africa.* Modern Sociology Ser. Ablex 1979 $39.50. ISBN 0-89391-014-7

McGuire, Meredith B. *Religion: The Social Context.* Wadsworth 1987 $23.75. ISBN 0-534-07242-9

Mead, Sidney E. *Lively Experiment: The Shaping of Christianity in America.* Harper 1963 $9.95. ISBN 0-06-065545-3

Newman, William M., and Peter L. Halvorson. *Patterns in Pluralism: A Portrait of American Religion.* Glenmary Research Center 1980 $6.50. ISBN 0-914422-10-3

*O'Dea, Thomas S., and Janet O. Aviad. *The Sociology of Religion.* Prentice 1983 $26.00. ISBN 0-13-821066-7 General introduction to and overview of the historical and contemporary study of the sociology of religion.

Robbins, Thomas. *In God We Trust: New Patterns of Religious Pluralism in America.* Transaction 1980 $16.95. ISBN 0-87855-746-6

Stark, Rodney, and William S. Bainbridge. *The Future of Religion: Secularization, Revival, and Cult Formation.* Univ of California Pr 1985 $15.95. ISBN 0-520-05731-7

Wuthnow, Robert. *The Struggle for America's Soul: Evangelicals, Liberals, and Secularism.* Eerdmans 1989 $16.95. ISBN 0-8028-0469-1

WEBER, MAX 1864–1920

Max Weber, German political economist, legal historian, and sociologist, has had an impact on the social sciences that is difficult to overestimate. According to a widely held view, he was the founder of the modern way of conceptualizing society and thus the modern social sciences. With his contemporary, French sociologist Emile Durkheim (*see* Durkheim, Vol. 2, Sociology: History, Surveys, and Methods), whom Weber appears not to have known, he created modern sociology.

A major interest of Weber was the process of rationalization, which he believed characterized Western civilization in contrast to cultures with less emphasis on the rational and scientific. This view led Weber to examine three ideal types of domination or authority that characterize hierarchical relationships: charismatic (authority generated by the personality or personal appeal of an individual), traditional (authority conferred by custom and accepted practice), and legal (authority that rests upon rationally established rules). These types were useful to him in comparing societies. Unlike German philosopher and political economist Karl Marx (*see* Marx, Vol. 2, Economics: Comparative Economic Systems), who saw economics as the single force shaping history, Weber saw multiple causes such as politics, law, and religion as determiners of history.

Weber also studied bureaucracy and the world's major religions and examined capitalism. The latter he viewed as a product of the Protestant ethic. To Weber the Protestant emphasis on hard work had became translated into business enterprise. According to his controversial view, Protestantism had given rise to capitalism.

BOOKS BY WEBER

The Agrarian Sociology of Ancient Civilizations. Routledge 1988 $18.95. ISBN 0-86091-938-2
Ancient Judaism (1917–1919). Don Martindale (ed). Hans H. Gerth (tr). Free Pr 1967 $14.95. ISBN 0-02-934130-2
Basic Concepts in Sociology. Carol 1980 $3.95. ISBN 0-8065-0304-1
The Protestant Ethic and the Spirit of Capitalism (1904–1905). Peter Smith 1983 $20.50. ISBN 0-8446-6118-X
The Religion of China (1915). Free Pr 1968 $14.95. ISBN 0-02-934450-6
The Religion of India (1916–1917). Free Pr 1967. (o.p.)
The Sociology of Religion (1922). Ephraim Fischoff (tr). Beacon 1964 $12.95. ISBN 0-8070-4193-9
The Theory of Social and Economic Organization (1922). Free Pr 1964 $16.95. ISBN 0-02-934930-3

BOOKS ABOUT WEBER

Bendix, Reinhard, and Guenther Roth. *Scholarship and Partisanship: Essays on Max Weber.* Univ of California Pr 1980 repr of 1971 ed $35.00. ISBN 0-520-04171-2 Essays covering all aspects of Weber's thought.
Giddens, Anthony. *Capitalism and Modern Social Theory: An Analysis of the Writings of Marx, Durkheim and Max Weber.* Cambridge Univ Pr 1973 $13.95. ISBN 0-521-09785-1 New analysis of Marx, Durkheim, and Weber that clarifies the divergent interpretations of their writings and demonstrates the coherence of their contributions to social theory.
MacRae, Donald S. *Max Weber. Modern Masters Ser.* Frank Kermode (ed). Viking 1974. (o.p.) ISBN 0-670-46327-2 Analysis of Weber's genius: his scholarship; his cultural, legal, and political background; his innovations.
Sica, Alan. *Weber, Irrationality, and Social Order.* Univ of California Pr 1988 $32.50. ISBN 0-520-06149-7 Critical study questioning Weber's theory of rationality.
Wrong, Dennis (ed). *Max Weber. Makers of Modern Social Science Ser.* Prentice 1970 (o.p.) ISBN 0-13-947853-1 Collection of essays by noted authorities on Weber revealing the full impact of his thought on modern social science.

See also Vol. 2, Anthropology: Religion.

SOCIAL CHANGE

Boyer, William H. *America's Future: Transition to the 21st Century.* New Politics 1986 $8.95. ISBN 0-9618153-0-2

Chirot, Daniel, and Robert E. Merton. *Social Change in the Modern Era.* Harper 1986 $16.00. ISBN 0-15-581421-4

Coleman, James S. *Individual Interests and Collective Action: Selected Essays. Studies in Rationality and Social Change.* Cambridge Univ Pr 1986 $57.50. ISBN 0-521-30347-8

Durkheim, Emile. *The Division of Labor in Society.* W. D. Hall (tr). Free Pr 1985 $24.95. ISBN 0-02-907950-0

Eisenstadt, S. N. *Society, Culture and Urbanization.* Sage 1987 $35.00. ISBN 0-8039-2478-X

Inglehart, Ronald. *Culture Shift in Advanced Industrial Society.* Princeton Univ Pr 1989 $14.95. ISBN 0-691-02296-8

• Jones, Landon. *Great Expectations: America and the Baby Boom Generation.* Ballantine 1986 $3.95. ISBN 0-345-33402-7 Describes effects of one generation on U.S. society.

Parsons, Talcott. *Social System.* Free Pr 1964 $21.95. ISBN 0-02-924190-1

Rogers, Everett M. *The Diffusion of Innovations.* Free Pr 1982 $22.95. ISBN 0-02-926650-5

Rogers, Everett M., *et al. Social Change in Rural Societies: An Introduction to Rural Sociology.* Prentice 1988 $41.33. ISBN 0-13-815481-3

Sheldon, Eleanor B., and Wilbert E. Moore (eds). *Indicators of Social Change: Concepts and Measurements.* Russell Sage 1968 $45.00. ISBN 0-87154-771-6

Smelser, Neil J. *Social Change in the Industrial Revolution.* Univ of Chicago Pr 1959 $20.00. ISBN 0-226-76311-0

Sorokin, Pitirim. *Social and Cultural Dynamics: A Study of Changes in Major Systems of Art, Truth, Ethics, and Social Relationships.* Transaction 1981 $26.95. ISBN 0-87855-787-3

Thurow, Lester. *The Zero-Sum Solution.* Simon 1986 $9.95. ISBN 0-671-62814-3

Warner, W. Lloyd, and Paul S. Lunt. *The Social Life of a Modern Community.* Greenwood 1973 $35.00. ISBN 0-8371-6958-5

SOCIAL STRATIFICATION

• Bender, David, and Bruno Leone. *The Homeless. Opposing Viewpoints Ser.* Greenhaven 1990 $7.95. ISBN 0-89908-451-6 Opposing views on a major national problem.

Blau, Peter M. *Inequality and Heterogeneity: A Primitive Theory of Social Structure.* Free Pr 1977 $22.95. ISBN 0-02-903660-7

Blau, Peter M. (ed). *Approaches to the Study of Social Structure.* Free Pr 1975 $19.95. ISBN 0-02-903650-X

Blau, Zena S. *Black Children–White Children: Competence, Socialization, and Social Structure.* Free Pr 1981 $24.95. ISBN 0-02-903640-2

• Cobb, Jonathan, and Richard Sennett. *Hidden Injuries of Class.* Random 1973 $4.96. ISBN 0-394-71940-9 Effects of stratification on individuals and groups.

Cole, Jonathan R., and Stephen Cole. *Social Stratification in Science.* Univ of Chicago Pr 1981 $10.00. ISBN 0-226-11339-6

Duncan, Otis Dudley, *et al. Socioeconomic Background and Achievement.* Academic Pr 1972 $22.00. ISBN 0-12-785174-7

Featherman, David L., and Robert M. Hauser. *Opportunity and Change.* Academic Pr 1978 $41.00. ISBN 0-12-250350-3

• Finsterbusch, Kurt, and George McKenna. *Taking Sides: Clashing Views on Controversial Social Issues.* Dushkin 1988 $9.95. ISBN 0-87967-742-2 Pro/con exchanges on several major current issues of society.

Goode, William J. *The Celebration of Heroes: Prestige As a Social Control System.* Univ of California Pr 1979 $11.95. ISBN 0-520-03811-8

• Harrington, Michael. *The Other America. Pelican Ser.* Penguin 1971 $6.95. ISBN 0-14-021308-2 Landmark study on poverty in the United States.

■Hyde, Margaret O. *Homeless: Profiling the Problem.* Enslow 1989 $15.95. ISBN 0-89490-159-1 Introductory work on the problems of homelessness.

Janowitz, Morris. *The Last Half Century: Societal Change and Politics in America.* Univ of Chicago Pr 1979 $16.00. ISBN 0-226-39207-0

Kohn, Melvin L., and Carmi Schooler. *Work and Personality: An Inquiry into the Impact of Social Stratification.* Ablex 1983 $27.50. ISBN 0-89391-199-2

■Kosof, Anna. *Homeless in America.* Watts 1988 $11.90. ISBN 0-531-10519-9 Introduction to a major social problem.

Lenski, Gerhard E. *Power and Privilege: A Theory of Social Stratification.* Univ of North Carolina Pr 1984 $10.95. ISBN 0-8078-4119-6

Lipset, Seymour M., and Reinhard Bendix. *Revolution and Counterrevolution: Change and Persistence in Social Structure.* Transaction 1987 $19.95. ISBN 0-88738-694-6

Lipset, Seymour M., and Reinhard Bendix. *Social Mobility in Industrial Society.* Transaction 1988 $19.95. ISBN 0-88738-760-8

Merton, Robert K. *Social Theory and Social Structure.* Free Pr 1968 $24.95. ISBN 0-02-921130-1

Mills, C. Wright. *Power Elite.* Oxford Univ Pr 1956 $10.95. ISBN 0-19-500680-1

Momeni, Jamshid A. (ed). *Homeless in the United States.* Vol. 1 *State Surveys.* Contributions in Sociology Ser. Greenwood 1989 $49.95. ISBN 0-313-25566-0

■O'Connor, Karen. *Homeless Children.* Overview Ser. Greenhaven 1989 $10.95. ISBN 0-89908-109-X Important introduction to a difficult issue for society.

Piven, Frances F., and Richard A. Cloward. *Poor People's Movements: Why They Succeed, How They Fail.* Random 1978 $4.76. ISBN 0-394-72697-9

Sewell, William H., and Robert M. Hauser (eds). *Schooling and Achievement in American Society.* Academic Pr 1976 $37.00. ISBN 0-12-637860-6

Tumin, Melvin M. *Social Stratification: The Forms and Functions of Inequality.* Prentice 1985 $20.33. ISBN 0-13-818659-6

Verba, Sidney. *Participation and Political Equality: A Seven-Nation Comparison.* Univ of Chicago Pr 1987 $15.95. ISBN 0-226-85298-9

Verba, Sidney, and Gary Orren. *Equality in America: The View from the Top.* Harvard Univ Pr 1985 $13.50. ISBN 0-674-25961-0

VEBLEN, THORSTEIN 1857–1929

American social scientist and economist Thorstein Veblen was born in Wisconsin and spent his growing-up years in Norwegian-American farm communities. Trained as a philosopher, he studied at Carlton College, Johns Hopkins, Yale University, and Cornell University. He taught at a number of different universities, including the New School for Social Research in New York City, but he was an unorthodox teacher whose ill-health and troubled domestic life kept him from holding an academic position for long. In 1926 he retired to a cabin in California, where he died in poverty three years later.

An original thinker, Veblen challenged the economic theories of his time. He argued that the nature of the economic order changed with society's values, customs, and laws and was influenced by society's institutions. In his many books, written in a dry, satirical style, he criticized the major institutions of American society, in particular American business. He is especially known today for his 1899 work *The Theory of the Leisure Class.* In this work he heaps scorn on the wealthy, who he describes as barbaric and wasteful and accuses of engaging in useless activities and conspicuous consumption—the use of goods or services to impress others with wealth, status, or position.

Veblen's theories did not attract many disciples in his time. Even his supporters criticize as too broad and lacking in a scientific basis his anthropological and historical approach to studying society. Nonetheless, from Veblen's time forward, the influence of social institutions and values on economic behavior is a force with which economists and social scientists have had to reckon.

BOOKS BY VEBLEN

The Engineers and the Price System (1921). *Social Science Classics Ser.* Transaction 1983 $14.95.
  ISBN 0-87855-915-9
The Higher Learning in America (1918). Kelley 1965 $27.50. ISBN 0-678-00055-7
Imperial Germany and the Industrial Revolution (1915). Greenwood 1984 $48.50. ISBN 0-313-
  23495-7
The Portable Veblen (1958). Max Lerner (ed). Penguin 1958. (o.p.)
The Theory of the Leisure Class (1899). Penguin 1979 $4.95. ISBN 0-14-005363-8

BOOKS ABOUT VEBLEN

Dorfman, Joseph. *Thorstein Veblen and His America.* Kelley 1972 $45.00. ISBN 0-678-
  00007-7 Thorough biography that summarizes Veblen's books and illuminated
  his genius.
Dowd, Douglas F. *Thorstein Veblen. The Great American Thinker Ser.* Washington Square
  Pr 1966. (o.p.) Clear portrait of Veblen's life and thought.
Riesman, David. *Thorstein Veblen: A Critical Interpretation.* Continuum 1975. (o.p.) $4.95.
  ISBN 0-8264-0162-7 Critical interpretation of Veblen's system of social science;
  includes a bibliography.

See also Vol. 2, Anthropology: Social Structure.

SOCIALIZATION

Cooley, Charles H. *Human Nature and the Social Order. Social Science Classics Ser.* Transaction
  1983 $21.95. ISBN 0-87855-918-3
Forer, Lucille K. *Birth Order and Life Roles.* Thomas 1969 $19.25. ISBN 0-390-00596-6
Gilligan, Carol. *In a Different Voice: Psychological Theory and Women's Development.* Harvard
  Univ Pr 1983 $6.95. ISBN 0-674-44544-9
Goslin, David A. *Handbook of Socialization Theory and Research.* Houghton 1969. (o.p.)
  $55.00. ISBN 0-395-30611-6
Hess, Beth B., and Elizabeth W. Markson. *Aging and Old Age: An Introduction to Social
  Gerontology.* Macmillan 1980. (o.p.) $23.00. ISBN 0-02-354100-8
Hyman, Herbert H. *Political Socialization: A Study in the Psychology of Political Behavior.* Free
  Pr 1969 $1.95. ISBN 0-02-915680-7
Kohlberg, Lawrence, and Thomas Lickona. *The Stages of Ethical Development: From Childhood
  Through Old Age.* Harper 1986 $19.95. ISBN 0-06-064758-2
Kohn, Melvin L. *Class and Conformity: A Study in Values.* Univ of Chicago Pr 1989 $16.95.
  ISBN 0-226-45026-0
Piaget, Jean. *The Child's Conception of the World.* Littlefield 1975 $8.95. ISBN 0-8226-
  0213-X
Rose, Peter I. (ed). *Socialization and the Life Cycle.* St. Martin's 1979 $15.00. ISBN 0-312-
  73800-5
Rosow, Irving. *Socialization to Old Age.* Univ of California Pr 1975 $10.95. ISBN 0-520-
  03417-1

See also Vol. 2, Psychology: Personality.

URBAN LIFE

Bradbury, Katherine L., and Anthony Downs. *Urban Decline and the Future of American Cities.* Brookings 1982 $12.95. ISBN 0-8157-1053-4

Eisinger, Peter K. *The Politics of Displacement: Racial and Ethnic Transition in Three American Cities. Institute for Research on Poverty Monograph Ser.* Academic Pr 1980 $27.95. ISBN 0-12-235560-1

*Elliot, Jeffrey M. *Annual Editions: Urban Society.* Dushkin 1989 $9.95. ISBN 0-87967-768-6 Anthology of articles on urban society.

Fischer, Claude S. *The Urban Experience.* Harcourt 1984 $13.00. ISBN 0-15-593498-8

Fischer, Claude S., *et al. Networks and Places: Social Relations in the Urban Setting.* Free Pr 1977 $22.95. ISBN 0-02-910240-5

Gans, Herbert J. *The Urban Villagers.* Free Pr 1982 $10.95. ISBN 0-02-911250-8

*Gay, Kathlyn. *Cities Under Stress: Can Today's City Systems Be Made to Work?* Watts 1985 $12.90. ISBN 0-531-04926-4 Good introductory work on urban life.

Gorham, William, and Nathan Glazer (eds). *The Urban Predicament.* Urban Inst 1976 $11.00. ISBN 0-87766-160-X

Hall, Peter. *Cities of Tomorrow: An Intellectual History of Urban Planning and Design in the Twentieth Century.* Basil Blackwell 1988 $34.95. ISBN 0-631-13444-1

Hannerz, Ulf. *Exploring the City: Inquiries Toward an Urban Anthropology.* Columbia Univ Pr 1980 $14.50. ISBN 0-231-08376-9

Laska, Shirley, and Daphne Spain. *Back to the City: The Making of a Movement. Pergamon Policy Studies.* Pergamon 1980 $15.25. ISBN 0-08-024640-0

Lofland, L. *A World of Strangers: Order and Action in Urban Public Space.* Waveland 1985 $9.95. ISBN 0-88133-136-8

Mumford, Lewis. *The City in History: Its Origins, Its Transformations and Its Prospects.* Harcourt 1968 $18.95. ISBN 0-15-618035-9

Park, Robert E. *The City. Heritage of Sociology Ser.* Univ of Chicago Pr 1984 $12.00. ISBN 0-226-64611-4

Sjoberg, Gideon. *The Preindustrial City: Past and Present.* Free Pr 1965 $9.95. ISBN 0-02-928980-7

Stein, Maurice R. *The Eclipse of Community: An Interpretation of American Studies.* Princeton Univ Pr 1971 $13.95. ISBN 0-691-02813-3

Timberlake, Michael. *Urbanization in the World Economy. Studies in Social Discontinuity.* Academic Pr 1985 $46.50. ISBN 0-12-691290-4

Suttle, Gerald. *Social Order of the Slum. Studies of Urban Society Ser.* Univ of Chicago Pr 1970 $9.00. ISBN 0-226-78192-5

Weber, Max. *The City.* Don Martindale and Gertrud Neuwirth (eds). Free Pr 1966 $14.95. ISBN 0-02-934210-4

Wirth, Louis. *Louis Wirth on Cities and Social Life. Heritage of Sociology Ser.* Albert Reiss, Jr. (ed). Univ of Chicago Pr 1982 $15.00. ISBN 0-226-90242-0

See also Vol. 2, Geography: Urban Patterns.

WOMEN

*Berger, Gilda. *Women, Work and Wages.* Watts 1986 $12.90. ISBN 0-531-10074-X Good introduction to the study of discrimination against women in the workplace.

Bernard, Jessie. *The Female World.* Free Pr 1982 $17.95. ISBN 0-02-903060-9

Bernard, Jessie. *Female World from a Global Perspective.* Indiana Univ Pr 1987 $10.95. ISBN 0-253-20431-3

*Cohen, Marcia. *The Sisterhood: The True Story of the Women Who Changed the World.* Simon 1988 $19.95. ISBN 0-671-49553-4 An account of the 1960s feminist movement and the work of Friedan, Steinem, Greer, and Millett.
Cole, Jonathan R. *Fair Science: Women in the Scientific Community.* Columbia Univ Pr 1987 $16.00. ISBN 0-317-59402-8
Coles, Robert, and Jane H. Coles. *Women of Crises.* Dell 1979 $8.95. ISBN 0-385-29169-8
Freeman, Jo (ed). *Women: A Feminist Perspective.* Mayfield 1989 $22.95. ISBN 0-87474-801-6
■Friedan, Betty. *The Feminine Mystique.* Dell 1984 $4.95. ISBN 0-440-32497-1 Classic work; credited with starting the women's movement.
Frieze, Irene, *et al. Women and Sex Roles.* Norton. ISBN 0-393-95382-3
Goode, William J. *Women in Divorce.* Greenwood 1978 $29.75. ISBN 0-313-21026-8
Henning, Margaret, and Ann Jardim. *The Managerial Woman.* Pocket 1983 $3.95. ISBN 0-671-49890-8
Hess, Beth B., and Marvin B. Sussman (eds). *Women and the Family: Two Decades of Change. Marriage and Family Review Ser.* Haworth 1984 $34.95. ISBN 0-86656-291-5
■Hinding, Andrea (ed). *Feminism: Opposing Viewpoints. Isms Ser.* Greenhaven 1986 $7.95. ISBN 0-89908-363-3 Past, present, and future of feminism.
Hourwich, Andrea T., and Gladys L. Palmer (eds). *I Am a Woman Worker: A Scrapbook of Autobiographies. Women in America Ser.* Ayer 1974 $17.00. ISBN 0-405-06102-1
Klein, Ethel. *Gender Politics.* Harvard Univ Pr 1984 $7.95. ISBN 0-674-34197-X
■Lerner, Gerda. *Black Women in White America: A Documentary History.* Random 1973 $9.95. ISBN 0-394-71880-1 Excellent source documents.
Lerner, Gerda. *The Majority Finds Its Past: Placing Women in History.* Oxford Univ Pr 1979 $8.95. ISBN 0-19-502899-6
Lorber, Judith. *Women Physicians: Careers, Status, and Power.* Routledge 1985 $11.95. ISBN 0-422-79050-8
Oakley, Ann. *Sex, Gender, and Society. Towards a New Society Ser.* Gower 1985 $10.95. ISBN 0-85117-020-X
Rosaldo, Michelle Zimbaliste, and Louise Lamphere (eds). *Women, Culture, and Society.* Stanford Univ Pr 1974 $9.95. ISBN 0-8047-0851-7
Rosenberg, Rosalind. *Beyond Separate Spheres: Intellectual Roots of Modern Feminism.* Yale Univ Pr 1983 $11.95. ISBN 0-300-03092-4
Rossi, Alice S. (ed). *Gender and the Life Course.* Aldine 1985 $18.95. ISBN 0-202-30312-8
Rothman, Sheila M. *Woman's Proper Place: A History of Changing Ideals and Practices, 1870 to the Present.* Basic 1980 $12.95. ISBN 0-465-09204-7
Rothschild, Joan (ed). *Machina ex Dea: Feminist Perspectives on Technology.* Pergamon 1983 $16.95. ISBN 0-08-029403-0
Smith, Ralph E. (ed). *The Subtle Revolution: Women at Work.* Urban Inst 1979 $10.00. ISBN 0-87766-260-6
■Wharton, Mandy. *Rights of Women. Understanding Social Issues Ser.* Watts 1989 $11.90. ISBN 0-531-17147-7 Worldwide women's issues; helpful resources included.

WORK

Blau, Peter M., and Otis D. Duncan. *The American Occupational Structure.* Free Pr 1978 $14.95. ISBN 0-02-903670-4
Blau, Zena S. *Work, Retirement, and Social Policy.* Vol. 1 *Current Perspective on Aging and the Life Cycle Ser.* JAI 1985 $52.50. ISBN 0-89232-296-9
Caplow, Theodore. *The Sociology of Work.* Greenwood 1978 $32.00. ISBN 0-313-20111-0
French, John R. P., Jr., *et al. Career Change in Midlife: Stress, Social Support and Adjustment.* Inst for Social Research 1983 $15.00. ISBN 0-87944-290-5
Hourwich, Andrea T., and Gladys L. Palmer (eds). *I Am a Woman Worker: A Scrapbook of Autobiographies. Women in America Ser.* Ayer 1974 $17.00. ISBN 0-405-06102-1
Jackall, Robert, and Henry M. Levin (eds). *Worker Cooperatives in America.* Univ of California Pr 1984 $12.95. ISBN 0-520-05741-4

Nelkin, Dorothy, and Michael S. Brown. *Workers at Risk: Voices from the Workplace.* Univ of Chicago Pr 1986 $9.95. ISBN 0-226-57128-9

Roethlisberger, F. J., and William J. Dickson. *Management and the Worker: An Account of a Research Program Conducted by Western Electric Co.* Harvard Univ Pr 1939 $38.00. ISBN 0-674-54676-8

Smith, Ralph E. (ed). *The Subtle Revolution: Women at Work.* Urban Inst 1979 $10.00. ISBN 0-87766-260-6

▪ Terkel, Louis (Studs). *Working: People Talk About What They Do All Day and How They Feel About What They Do.* Ballantine 1985 $5.95. ISBN 0-345-32569-9 Interviews with workers reveal their feelings about the tasks they perform daily.

Zuboff, Shoshana. *In the Age of the Smart Machine: The Future of Work and Power.* Basic 1988 $19.95. ISBN 0-465-03212-5

BELL, DANIEL 1919–

American sociologist Daniel Bell started his career as a journalist. In the more than 20 years he spent in that profession, he served for four as managing editor of *The New Leader* (1941–1945) and for 10 as labor editor for *Fortune* magazine (1948–1958). In 1959 Bell became professor of sociology at Columbia University, where he also received his doctorate. In 1965, while still at Columbia, he was a cofounder of the quarterly *Public Opinion.* In 1969 he left Columbia to become professor of sociology at Harvard University.

Bell has written extensively on socialism, capitalism, and the meaning of work. His interest is in understanding and describing how political and economic institutions form the individual. Perhaps his best known work is *The Coming of the Post-Industrial Society* (1973), in which he analyzes the role of information in such societies as the United States and Western Europe. He believes that such societies are postindustrial in the sense that the manufacture of industrial products is less important than the production of knowledge and the management of information.

Books by Bell

Bringing Your Employees into the Business: An Employee Ownership Handbook for Small Business. Kent 1988 $9.95. ISBN 0-933522-19-3

The Coming of Post-Industrial Society: A Venture in Social Forecasting (1973). Basic 1976 $14.95. ISBN 0-465-09713-8

The Crisis in Economic Theory. (coedited with Irving Kristol) Basic 1981 $10.95. ISBN 0-465-01477-1

The Cultural Contradiction of Capitalism (1976). Basic 1978 $12.95. ISBN 0-465-09727-8

The Deficits: How Big? How Long? How Dangerous? (coauthored with Lester Thurow) New York Univ Pr 1985 $15.00. ISBN 0-8147-1083-2

The End of Ideology: On the Exhaustion of Political Ideas in the Fifties (1962). Harvard Univ Pr 1988 $12.50. ISBN 0-674-25230-6

The Social Sciences Since the Second World War. Transaction 1981 $10.95. ISBN 0-87855-872-1

Toward the Year 2000. Beacon 1969. (o.p.) $3.95. ISBN 0-807-00259-3

The Winding Passage: Essays and Sociological Journeys, 1960–1980 (1980). Univ Pr of America 1984 $38.00. ISBN 0-8191-4142-9

WHYTE, WILLIAM FOOTE 1914–

Born in Springfield, Massachusetts, William F. Whyte studied sociology at Swarthmore College in Pennsylvania and then at Harvard University. He earned his doctorate from the University of Chicago in 1943. He recently retired from teaching to devote more time to his writing.

Whyte has spent a great deal of time studying the peoples of Venezuela, Peru, Mexico, and Costa Rica. But much of his research centers on the relationship between people and the places in which they work. Several of his books, including *Pattern for Industrial Peace* (1951), focus on humans and their work environment.

Whyte has been writing books on sociology and anthropology for 50 years. One of his early books, *Street Corner Society* (1943), is still used today as a college-level text. Whyte's research for this work made him a pioneer in the use of participant observation, a method in which the investigator takes part in the daily life of the social group he or she is observing. Whyte did his research before World War II by joining and talking informally with members of street-corner groups in run down lower-class neighborhoods. A social worker got him into the first group. He struck up a friendship with that group's leader, who then introduced him to other groups. In time, he became accepted by members of various groups. By "hanging on" the street corner with his new "friends," he was about to learn a great deal about the structure of the groups and the goals and motivations of group members.

BOOKS BY WHYTE

Making Mondragon: The Growth and Dynamics of the Worker Cooperative Complex. International Report Ser. (coauthored with Kathleen K. Whyte) ILR Pr 1988 $16.95. ISBN 0-87546-138-7

Money and Motivation: An Analysis of Incentives in Industry. (coauthored with others) Greenwood 1977 $35.00. ISBN 0-8371-9342-7

Street Corner Society: The Social Structure of an Italian Slum (1943). Univ of Chicago Pr 1981 $9.00. ISBN 0-226-89543-2

Worker Participation and Ownership: Cooperative Strategies for Strengthening Local Economies. ILR Paperback Ser. (coauthored with others) ILR Pr 1983 $10.00. ISBN 0-87546-097-6

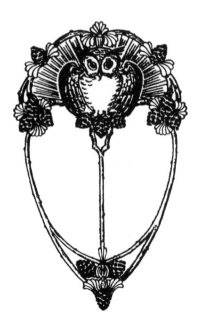

×× HISTORY ××

UNITED STATES HISTORY

The section embracing United States history is organized chronologically. It progresses from the Ice Age, when the ancestors of the first American Indians walked from Asia across a land bridge over the Bering Strait and stepped into the land that is today Alaska, to the present. There are 28 subsections, beginning with a listing of general reference works, surveys, and histories. This is followed by four subsections that deal with the period from America's earliest beginnings—before the arrival of the Europeans—through the Revolutionary War; seven subsections devoted to the beginning of the new nation and its development through the first half of the nineteenth century; five subsections that focus on the themes of the latter half of the nineteenth century; one subsection dealing with the politics, reform, change, and expansion that characterized the Progressive era; five subsections that focus on the years of America's rise to world power from World War I through the cold war; and five subsections that carry the reader from the 1960s to the present. Included are subsections that deal with the arts of the various eras.

Within each subsection, key individuals of the period are listed alphabeti-

Capt. Samuel Chandler. Painting by Winthrop Chandler (1780). Courtesy of The Bettmann Archive.

cally, their last names appearing first. For each, there is a book or a list of books by that individual. In addition, there is for each a profile that provides personal background or information about the individual's place in history and his or her achievements. Further, the profile may refer the reader to other related individuals and their works, which also can be found in *The Young Adult Reader's Adviser.*

Last, for most profiled individuals, there is a Books About section that, among other types of publications, lists notable biographies for further reading and research. Whenever possible, very recent titles have also been included.

While works relevant to all facets of American history are included in the United States history section, additional works on certain topics, such as the Constitution and the workings of the American government, may be found in the social science sections of *The Young Adult Reader's Adviser.* In addition, while works relevant to world history are included in the United States history section, the major focus is on the United States. For a more comprehensive listing of world history, see the readings under World History, found in the section immediately following this one.

HISTORIES, REFERENCES, AND SURVEYS

Arnold, Denis. *The New Oxford Companion to Music.* 2 vols. Oxford Univ Pr 1983 $99.00. ISBN 0-19-311316-3

*Arrington, Karen. *The Commission on Civil Rights. Know Your Government Ser.* Chelsea 1989 $14.95. ISBN 1-55546-127-1 Readable introduction to the Civil Rights Commission.

Bailey, Thomas A., and David M. Kennedy. *The American Pageant: A History of the Republic.* 2 vols. Heath 1988 $27.00. ISBN 0-699-10810-3

*Baron, Robert (ed). *Soul of America.* Fulcrum 1989 $24.95. ISBN 1-55591-047-5 An excellent collection of documents on American history, from 1492 to Nixon's resignation speech of 1974.

Bataille, Gretchen M., and Kathleen N. Sands. *American Indian Women: Telling Their Lives.* Univ of Nebraska Pr 1984 $7.95. ISBN 0-8032-6082-2

*Batterberry, Arianne, and Michael Batterberry. *The Pantheon Story of American Art: For Young People.* Pantheon 1976. (o.p.) History of American art; illustrated.

*Beard, Charles A., and Detlev Vagts. *Presidents in American History.* Jane Steltenpohl (ed). Messner 1989 $5.95. ISBN 0-671-68575-9 Historical account of the American presidents.

*Bennett, Leone, Jr. *Before the Mayflower: A History of Black America.* Penguin 1984 $9.95. ISBN 0-14-007124-4 Excellent, readable source for the history of African Americans.

*Berkin, Carol, and Mary B. Norton. *Women of America: A History.* Houghton 1979 $29.56. ISBN 0-395-27067-7 Good general source for women's history.

*Biracree, Tom, and Nancy Biracree. *Almanac of the American People.* Facts on File 1988 $29.95. ISBN 0-8160-1821-9 Useful, fact-filled volume on the American people.

Boatner, Mark M., III. *The Civil War Dictionary.* Times Bks 1988 $29.45. ISBN 0-8129-1689-1

Boatner, Mark M., III. *Encyclopedia of the American Revolution.* McKay 1974 $9.98. ISBN 0-679-50440-0

Boorstin, Daniel J., and Ruth F. Boorstin. *The Landmark History of the American People. Landmark Giants Ser.* 2 vols. Random 1985. Vol. 1 *From Plymouth to Appomattox.* $11.99. ISBN 0-394-99118-4. Vol. 2 *From Appomattox to the Moon.* $11.99. ISBN 0-394-99119-2

Breckinridge, Sophonisba P. *Women in the Twentieth Century: A Study of Their Political, Social, and Economic Activities. American Women Ser: Images and Realities.* Ayer 1972 $24.50. ISBN 0-405-04450-X

*Burns, James MacGregor. *The Workshop of Democracy: The American Experiment from the*

Emancipation Proclamation to the Eve of the New Deal. Random 1986 $12.95. ISBN 0-394-74320-2 From the Civil War to Roosevelt, by the noted Roosevelt historian.

*Carruth, Gorton (ed). *The Encyclopedia of American Facts and Dates.* Harper 1987 $35.00. Parallel columns show relationships of aspects of American life—politics, art, literature, etc.

*Catton, Bruce. *American Heritage Picture History of the Civil War.* Outlet 1985 $21.95. ISBN 0-517-38556-2 Excellent illustrations and text on the Civil War and its effects by the popular writer/historian.

*Chase, Gilbert. *America's Music: From the Pilgrims to the Present. Music in American Life Ser.* Univ of Illinois Pr 1987 $29.95. ISBN 0-252-00454-X Classic account of music in America that focuses on jazz, folk music, and popular music; includes illustrations of many of the musicians and subjects discussed.

Churchill, Winston S. *A History of the English Speaking Peoples.* Vol. 3 *The Age of Revolution.* Dodd 1983 $9.95. ISBN 0-396-08273-4

Claghorn, Charles E. *Biographical Dictionary of Jazz.* Prentice 1983. (o.p.) $25.00.

*Cook, Fred J. *The Ku Klux Klan: America's Recurring Nightmare.* Jane Steltenpohl (ed). Messner 1989 $12.98. ISBN 0-671-68421-3 Origins and reappearance of the society whose main objective was to maintain "white supremacy."

*Cosner, Sharon. *War Nurses. American History Ser for Young People.* Walker 1988 $16.95. ISBN 0-8027-6826-1 Focuses on the American nurses on the front lines from the Civil War to MASH units in Vietnam.

Craig, Warren. *Sweet and Lowdown: America's Popular Song Writers.* Scarecrow 1978 $40.00. ISBN 0-8108-1089-1

*Daniel, Robert L. *American Women in the Twentieth Century.* Harcourt 1987 $13.00. ISBN 0-15-502950-2 Addresses experiences of working-class minority women, their changing economic roles, treatment under the law, and educational opportunities; highly readable sources.

Davis, Kenneth C. *Don't Know Much About History: Everything You Need to Know About American History But Never Learned.* Crown 1990 $24.95. ISBN 0-517-57706-2

Debo, Angie. *A History of the Indians of the United States. The Civilizations of the American Indian Ser.* Univ of Oklahoma Pr 1984 $13.95. ISBN 0-8061-1888-1

DeConde, Alexander. *A History of American Foreign Policy.* Macmillan. Vol. 1 *Grow to World Power, 1700–1914.* 1978. ISBN 0-02-327970-2. Vol. 2 *Global Power, 1900 to Present.* 1979. ISBN 0-02-327980-X

Dennis, Henry C. *American Indian, 1492–1976: A Chronology and Fact Book. Ethnic Chronology Ser.* Oceana 1977 $8.50. ISBN 0-379-00526-3

Duncan, Greg J. *Years of Poverty, Years of Plenty: The Changing Economic Fortunes of American Workers and Families.* Inst for Social Research 1984 $14.00. ISBN 0-87944-298-0

*Flexner, Eleanor. *Century of Struggle: The Woman's Rights Movement in the United States.* Harvard Univ Pr 1975 $9.95. ISBN 0-674-10652-0 Classic study of women's rights and the suffrage movement; issues, individuals, and organizations since 1608; illustrated.

*Franklin, John Hope, and Alfred Moss. *From Slavery to Freedom: A History of Negro Americans.* Knopf 1987 $19.95. ISBN 0-394-37013-9 Traces black history from early times to the present.

Franklin, John Hope, and August Meier (eds). *Black Leaders in the Twentieth Century. Blacks in the New World Ser.* Univ of Illinois Pr 1982 $9.95. ISBN 0-252-00939-8

Freedman, Milton, and Anna J. Schwartz. *Monetary History of the United States, 1867–1960. Business Cycles Ser.* National Bureau of Economic Research 1963 $40.00.

Friedel, Frank. *Presidents of the United States of America.* White House Hist 1988 $6.95. ISBN 0-912308-25-7

Garraty, John A. *One Thousand and One Things Everyone Should Know About American History.* Doubleday 1989 $19.95. ISBN 0-385-24432-0 Entertaining "fact book" about American history compiled by a noted historian.

*Glackens, Ira. *Did Molly Pitcher Say That?: The Men and Women Who Made American History.* Writers and Readers 1989 $18.95. ISBN 0-86316-097-2 Amusing and fascinating facts in American history.

Graebner, Norman A. *Empire on the Pacific: A Study in American Continental Expansion. Topics in Diplomatic History Ser.* Regina Bks 1983 $8.75. ISBN 0-317-56343-2

Green, Stanley. *Encyclopedia of the Musical Theatre.* Da Capo 1980 $14.95. ISBN 0-306-80113-2

Griffiths, Paul. *The Thames and Hudson Encyclopedia of Twentieth Century Music. World of Art Ser.* Thames Hudson 1989 $11.95. ISBN 0-500-20235-4

*Grout, Donald J. *A History of Western Music.* Norton 1988 $28.95. ISBN 0-393-95627-X Abundantly illustrated history of music with bibliography, chronology, and glossary.

Gwynne, S. C. *Selling Money: A Young Banker's Account of the Great International Lending Boom and Bust.* Penguin 1987 $7.95. ISBN 0-14-010-282-5

Hall, James. *Dictionary of Subjects and Symbols in Art.* Harper 1979. (o.p.) $10.95. ISBN 0-06-430100-1

Hamm, Charles. *Music in the New World.* Norton 1983 $32.50. ISBN 0-393-95193-6

Hamm, Charles. *Yesterdays: Popular Song in America.* Norton 1983 $11.70. ISBN 0-393-30062-5

*Hampton, Henry, and Steve Fayer, with Sarah Flynn. *Voices of Freedom. An Oral History of the Civil Rights Movement from the 1950s Through the 1980s.* Bantam 1990 $25.95. More than 1,000 interviews with the famous and not-so-famous about the civil rights movement; companion volume to the PBS series "Eyes on the Prize."

Highwater, Jamake. *Words in the Blood: Contemporary Indian Writers of North and South America.* NAL 1984 $9.95. ISBN 0-452-00680-5

Hine, Darlene C. *The State of Afro-American History: Past, Present, and Future.* Louisiana State Univ Pr 1986 $27.50. ISBN 0-8071-1254-2

*Hitchcock, H. Wiley. *Music in the United States: A Historical Introduction.* Prentice 1988 $23.00. ISBN 0-13-608407-9 Discusses many styles of American music.

Hitchcock, H. Wiley, and Sadie Stanley (eds). *The New Grove Dictionary of American Music.* 4 vols. Groves Dict Music 1986 $695.00. ISBN 0-943818-36-2

Holbrook, Stewart H. *Story of American Railroads.* Crown 1981 $6.98. ISBN 0-517-00100-4

Honour, Hugh, and John Fleming. *The Visual Arts: A History.* Prentice 1986 $45.00. ISBN 0-13-942533-0

Hosen, Frederick E. *Unfolding Westward in Treaty and Law: Land Documents in United States History from the Appalachians to the Pacific, 1783–1934.* McFarland 1988 $45.00. ISBN 0-89950-308-X

*Hymowitz, Carol, and Michaele Weissman. *History of Women in America.* Bantam 1984 $5.50. ISBN 0-553-26914-3 Focuses on women's contributions to the making of America.

Images of America: A Panorama of History in Photographs. Smithsonian Inst 1989 $39.95. ISBN 0-89599-023-7 Presents history through great photographs.

Inaugural Addresses of the Presidents of the United States from George Washington, 1789, to George Bush, 1989. USGPO 1990 $16.00. ISBN 0-16-006424-4

Inventors and Discoverers: Changing Our World. National Geographic 1988 $19.95. ISBN 0-87044-751-3 Interesting discussions of notable people who have made breakthroughs in technology worldwide.

Jablonski, Edward. *The Encyclopedia of American Music.* Doubleday 1982. (o.p.) $24.95.

*Janson, H. W., and Anthony F. Janson. *History of Art for Young People.* Abrams 1987 $29.95. ISBN 0-8109-1098-5 Art history presented for the appreciation of the younger audience.

Jordan, Winthrop D. *White Over Black: American Attitudes Toward the Negro, 1550–1812.* Norton 1977 $12.95. ISBN 0-393-00841-X

Jordan, Winthrop D. *White Man's Burden: Historical Origins of Racism in the United States.* Oxford Univ Pr 1974 $9.95. ISBN 0-19-501743-9

Kantor, Paul, and Stephen David. *The Dependent City: The Changing Political Economy of American Urban Politics Since 1789.* Scott 1988. ISBN 0-673-39782-3

Klapthor, Margaret Brown. *The First Ladies.* White House Hist 1985 $3.25. ISBN 0-912308-26-5

Lang, Paul H. (ed). *One Hundred Years of Music in America. Music Reprint Ser.* Da Capo 1984 $39.50. ISBN 0-306-76242-0

*Lawson, Don. *The Eagle and the Dragon: The History of U.S.–China Relations.* Harper Jr Bks 1985 $12.89. ISBN 0-690-04486-0 Readable history of relations between two major countries of the world.

Lee, George L. *Interesting People: Black American History Makers.* McFarland 1989 $15.95. ISBN 0-89950-403-5

Link, Arthur S., *et al.* *A Concise History of the American People.* Harlan Davidson 1984 $24.95. ISBN 0-88295-817-8

Link, Arthur S. *The Twentieth Century: An American History.* Harlan Davidson 1983 $18.95. ISBN 0-88295-816-X

*Marlin, John Tepper, and James S. Avery. *The Book of American City Rankings.* Facts on File 1983 $14.95. ISBN 0-8160-0095-6 Source for contemporary data.

*McReynolds, Ginny. *Women in Power.* Movers and Shapers Ser. Raintree 1979 $13.31. ISBN 0-8172-1376-7 Profiles of women in government, some the first women to be elected to a particular office.

*Meier, Matt S., and Feliciana Rivera. *The Chicanos: A History of Mexican Americans.* Hill & Wang 1972 $9.95. ISBN 0-8090-1365-7 Looks at the history of Mexican Americans in the United States.

Mellers, Wilfrid. *Music in a New Found Land: Themes and Developments in the History of American Music.* Oxford Univ Pr 1987 $12.95. ISBN 0-19-520526-X

*Meltzer, Milton. *The Black Americans: A History in Their Own Words, 1619–1983.* Harper Jr Bks 1987 $5.95. ISBN 0-06-446055-X Black Americans give their views in their own words.

*Morison, Samuel Eliot. *The Oxford History of the American People.* Oxford Univ Pr 1965 $39.95. ISBN 0-19-500030-7 Excellent short history.

Morrison, Hugh. *Early American Architecture: From the First Colonial Settlements to the National Period.* Dover 1987 $14.95. ISBN 0-486-25492-5

*Moses, L. G., and Raymond Wilson (eds). *Indian Lives: Essays on Nineteenth and Twentieth Century Native American Leaders.* Univ of New Mexico Pr 1985 $10.95. ISBN 0-8263-0815-5 Illustrated essays on Indian leaders.

*Murphy, Paul C. *What's Happened Since Seventeen Seventy-Six.* Price Stern 1988 $6.95. ISBN 0-8431-2276-5 Year-by-year timeline of American history, covering politics, religion, arts and culture, and science and technology.

*Myers, Bernard S. *McGraw-Hill Dictionary of Art.* McGraw 1969. (o.p.) Comprehensive, well illustrated reference.

*Nabokov, Peter (ed). *Native American Testimony: An Anthology of Indian and White Relations.* Harper Jr Bks 1979 $7.95. ISBN 0-06-131993-7 Native American views on Indian-white relations.

Nevins, Allan. *History of the Bank of New York and Trust Company, 1784–1934.* Companies and Men: Business Enterprises in America. Ayer 1976 $24.50. ISBN 0-405-08088-3

Nevins, Allan, and Henry S. Commager. *A Pocket History of the United States.* Pocket 1983 $4.95.

**Phaidon Encyclopedia of Art and Artists.* Dutton 1978. (o.p.) Comprehensive reference, useful to students.

*Niethammer, Carolyn. *Daughters of the Earth.* Macmillan 1977 $11.95. ISBN 0-02-096150-2 Examines the lives of Native American women from various nations; photos and bibliography.

*Pierce, Neal R., and Jerry Hagstrom. *The Book of America: Inside 50 States Today.* Warner Bks 1984 $14.95. ISBN 0-446-38036-9 Geographical and other data on each state.

*Ravitch, Diane (ed). *The American Reader: Words That Moved a Nation.* Harper 1990 $35.00. ISBN 0-06-016480-8 Speeches, poetry, songs, and more from pre-colonial times to today.

*Riley, Glenda. *Inventing the American Woman: A Perspective on Women's History.* 2 vols. Harlan Davidson 1986. Vol. 1 *1607–1877.* $9.95. ISBN 0-88295-837-2. Vol. 2 *1866 to the Present.* $9.95. ISBN 0-88295-838-0 Very readable presentation of personal data, social narrative, and much more on American women from 1607 to the present.

Roach, Hildreth. *Black American Music Past and Present.* 2 vols. Krieger 1985. Vol. 1 $15.50. ISBN 0-89874-610-8. Vol. 2 $18.50. ISBN 0-89874-775-9

Rubinstein, Charlotte S. *American Women Artists: From Early Indian Times to the Present.* G. K. Hall 1982. (o.p.) $39.95.

*Sandler, Martin. *The Way We Lived: A Photographic Record of Work in a Vanished America.* Little 1977. (o.p.) Photographic essay of life in the United States from the Civil War to World War I.

Schlesinger, Arthur M., Jr. *The Cycles of American History.* Houghton 1987 $11.95. ISBN 0-395-45400-X

Shaw, Arnold. *Black Popular Music in America: From the Spirituals, Minstrels, and Ragtime to Soul, Disco, and Hip-Hop.* Schirmer 1986 $19.95. ISBN 0-02-872310-4

Shaw, Arnold. *A Dictionary of American Pop-Rock.* Schirmer 1983 $12.95. ISBN 0-02-872360-0

Shenkman, Richard. *Legends, Lies, and Cherished Myths of American History.* Morrow 1988 $15.95. ISBN 0-688-06580-5

*Smithsonian Institution Staff. *Every Four Years: The American Presidency.* Norton 1980 $21.95. ISBN 0-393-80005-9 Handsomely illustrated coverage of the office of the presidency and the Americans who filled it from George Washington to contemporary times.

Southern, Eileen. *Biographical Dictionary of Afro-American and African Musicians. Greenwood Encyclopedia of Black Music Ser.* Greenwood 1982 $67.95. ISBN 0-313-21339-9

*Southern, Eileen. *The Music of Black Americans.* Norton 1983 $16.95. ISBN 0-393-95279-7 Introductory history and guide to contributions of African Americans to music.

Stage, John Lewis. *The Birth of America.* Grossett 1975 $35.00. ISBN 0-448-115-45-X

Stambler, Irwin. *The Encyclopedia of Pop, Rock, and Soul.* St. Martin's 1989 $35.00. ISBN 0-312-02573-4

Stambler, Irwin, and Grelun Landon. *The Encyclopedia of Folk, Country, and Western Music.* St. Martin's 1983. (o.p.) $50.00.

Stelzer, Irwin M., and Howard Kitt. *Selected Antitrust Cases: Landmark Decisions.* Irwin 1986 $20.95. ISBN 0-256-03222-X

Turner, Frederick Jackson. *The Frontier in American History.* Univ of Arizona Pr 1985 $10.95. ISBN 0-8165-0946-8

Turner, Frederick Jackson. *Significance of the Frontier in American History. Milestones of Thought Ser.* Harold P. Simonson (ed). Ungar $5.95. ISBN 0-8044-6919-9

Waldrup, Carole C. *Presidents' Wives: The Lives of Forty-Four American Women of Strength.* McFarland 1989 $24.95. ISBN 0-89950-393-4

Wandersee, Winifred D. *Women's Work and Family Values, 1920–1940.* Harvard Univ Pr 1981 $22.00. ISBN 0-674-95535-8

Weatherford, Jack M. *Indian Givers: How the Indians of the Americas Transformed the World.* Crown 1988 $17.95. ISBN 0-517-56969-8

*Weil, Robert (ed). *The Omni Future Almanac.* Newspaper Ent 1983 $8.95. ISBN 0-345-31034-9 Suggests possible advances in technology in the future.

Wertheimer, Barbara M. *We Were There: The Story of Working Women in America.* Pantheon 1977 $9.95. ISBN 0-394-73257-X

*Whitney, Sharon. *The Equal Rights Amendments: The History and the Movements.* Watts 1984 $12.90. ISBN 0-531-04768-7 Identifies the personalities, organizations, and strategies for the Equal Rights Amendments.

Wolfson, Martin H. *Financial Crises: Understanding the Postwar U.S. Experience.* Sharpe 1986 $15.95. ISBN 0-87332-377-7

*Wood, Marian. *Atlas of Ancient America. Cultural Atlas for Young People Ser.* Facts on File 1990 $17.95. ISBN 0-8160-2210-0 Illustrated history of the pre-Columbian Americas.

*Woodward, C. Vann. *The Future of the Past.* Oxford Univ Pr 1989 $24.95. ISBN 0-19-505744-9 Excellent account by a superior historian of how current conditions relate to the past; for very good students.

*Young, Judy. *Chinese Women of America: A Pictorial History.* Univ of Washington Pr 1986 $12.95. ISBN 0-295-96358-1 Interviews and statistics that provide a history of Chinese-American women dating to 1834.

NATIVE AMERICANS AND EARLY EXPLORERS

*Albornoz, Miguel. *Hernando De Soto: Knight of the Americas.* Watts 1986 $22.50. ISBN 0-531-15006-2 Introductory work on a notable Spanish explorer of the 1500s.

American Heritage Illustrated History of the United States, Vol. 1: The New World. Choice Pub 1988 $3.49. ISBN 0-945260-01-6 Well-illustrated presentation of early American history especially suited to younger readers.

Americans Before Columbus: Ice-Age Origins. Ethnology Monographs 1988 $12.00. ISBN 0-945428-01-4

Beazley, Charles R. *Prince Henry the Navigator, the Hero of Portugal and of Modern Discovery, 1394–1460. Research and Source Works Ser.* Burt Franklin 1968 $21.50. ISBN 0-8337-0210-6

*Bitossi, Sergio. *Ferdinand Magellan. Why They Became Famous Ser.* Silver 1985 $6.75. ISBN 0-382-06984-6 Illustrated biography of Spanish explorer of the early 1500s who explored the strait at the tip of South America.

*Blackwood, Alan. *Ferdinand Magellan. Great Lives Ser.* Watts 1986 $11.90. ISBN 0-531-18032-8 Introductory biography of a famous world explorer; illustrated.

Bourne, Edward G. (ed). *Narratives of the Career of Hernando De Soto in the Conquest of Florida As Told by a Knight of Elvas. American Explorers Ser.* Buckingham Smith (tr). 2 vols. AMS (repr of 1922 ed) $60.00. ISBN 0-404-54901-2

Brandon, William. *American Heritage Book of Indians.* Crown 1982 $17.95. ISBN 0-517-39180-5

Brebner, John B. *Explorers of North America, Fourteen Ninety-Two to Eighteen Hundred Six.* AMS (repr of 1933 ed) $67.50. ISBN 0-404-20043-5

British Library Staff. *Sir Francis Drake.* Longwood 1977 $6.00. ISBN 0-7141-0393-4

Day, A. Grove. *Coronado's Quest: Discovery of the American Southwest.* Mutual 1987 $3.95. ISBN 0-935180-37-0

Driver, Harold E. *Indians of North America.* Univ of Chicago Pr 1969 $16.95. ISBN 0-226-16467-5

Eastman, Charles. *From the Deep Woods to Civilization: Chapters in the Autobiography of an Indian.* Univ of Nebraska Pr 1977 $7.95. ISBN 0-8032-5873-9

*Erdoes, Richard, and Alfonso Ortiz. *American Indian Myths and Legends.* Pantheon 1985 $11.95. ISBN 0-394-74018-1 Rich anthology of North American Indian folklore, some never before published, of more than 80 Indian nations.

*Faulk, Odie B., and Laura E. Faulk. *The Modocs. Indians of North America Ser.* Chelsea 1988 $17.95. ISBN 1-55546-716-4 Cultural study of a California group; well-illustrated, with bibliography and maps.

*Gallant, Roy. *Ancient Indians: The First Americans.* Enslow 1989 $15.95. ISBN 0-89490-187-7 Account of the ancestors of the American Indians.

*Haig, Stanley. *The Cheyenne. Indians of North America Ser.* Chelsea 1989 $9.95. ISBN 0-7910-0358-2 Well-researched illustrated study of a Great Plains nation; with bibliography and maps.

Hammond, George P. (ed and tr). *Narratives of the Coronado Expedition, 1540–1542.* AMS (repr of 1940 ed) $30.00. ISBN 0-404-14669-4

Harrisse, Henry. *John Cabot: The Discoverer of North America and Sebastian His Son: A Chapter in Maritime History of England Under the Tudors, 1496–1557.* Argosy 1968 $25.00. ISBN 0-87266-013-3

Henry, Jeannette (ed). *American Indian Reader: Anthology.* Indian Historian Pr 1972 $4.00. ISBN 0-913436-09-7

Hodge, Frederick W., and Theodore H. Lewis (eds). *Spanish Explorers in the Southern United States, 1528–1543.* B & N Imports 1977 $21.50. ISBN 0-06-480372-4

Hoxie, Frederick E. (ed). *Indians in American History.* Harlan Davison 1988 $14.95. ISBN 0-88295-855-0

Indians of North America Ser. 53 vols. Chelsea 1987 $951.35. ISBN 1-55546-685-0

▪Jennings, Jesse D. (ed). *Ancient North Americans.* Freeman 1983 $31.95. ISBN 0-7167-1428-0 A history of the North American Indian prior to the arrival of the white man.

Josephy, Alvin M. *Indian Heritage of America.* Knopf 1968 $24.95. ISBN 0-394-43049-2

*Kehoe, Alice B. *North American Indians: A Comprehensive Account.* Prentice 1981 $38.60. ISBN 0-13-623652-9 Excellent history and analysis of North American Indian civilizations in the United States, from prehistory to the present.

Kelsey, Harry. *Juan Rodriguez Cabrillo.* Huntington Lib 1985 $25.00. ISBN 0-87328-086-5

Las Casas, Bartholomé de. *In Defense of the Indians.* Stafford Poole (tr and ed). Northern Illinois Univ Pr 1974. (o.p.) $30.00. ISBN 0-87580-042-4

*Lehane, Brendan. *Northwest Passage. Seafarers Ser.* Silver $21.27. ISBN 0-8094-2731-1 History of the search for the passage many thought would allow a fast route to Asia.

Ley, Charles D. *Portuguese Voyages, 1498–1663.* Gordon Pr 1977 $59.95. ISBN 0-8490-2459-5

Martin, Paul S., *et al. Indians Before Columbus: Twenty Thousand Years of North American History Revealed by Archaeology.* Univ of Chicago Pr 1975. (o.p.) $6.95. ISBN 0-226-50782-3

Maynarde, Thomas. *Sir Francis Drake, His Voyage, Fifteen Ninety-Five. Hakluyt Society Ser.* Burt Franklin 1971 $22.50. ISBN 0-8337-2308-1

Morison, Samuel Eliot. *European Discovery of America: The Northern Voyages.* Oxford Univ Pr 1971 $35.00. ISBN 0-19-501377-8

Morison, Samuel Eliot. *European Discovery of America: The Southern Voyages.* Oxford Univ Pr 1974 $35.00. ISBN 0-19-501823-0

Morison, Samuel Eliot. *The Great Explorers: The European Discovery of America.* Oxford Univ Pr 1986 $15.95. ISBN 0-19-504222-0

Morison, Samuel Eliot. *Samuel de Champlain: Father of New France.* Atlantic Monthly 1972. (o.p.)

Nebenzahl, Kenneth. *Atlas of Columbus and the Great Discoveries.* Rand 1990 $75.00. ISBN 0-528-283407-X

*O'Dell, Scott. *The King's Fifth.* Houghton 1966 $14.95. ISBN 0-395-06963-7 Fictionalized account of explorers from Spain seeking the Cities of Gold in the American Southwest.

Parkman, Francis. *La Salle and the Discovery of the Great West.* Random 1989 $9.50. ISBN 0-679-72615-2

*Perdue, Theda. *The Cherokee. Indians of North America Ser.* Chelsea 1989 $9.95. ISBN 0-7910-0357-4 Well-illustrated history; cultural study of a southeastern people.

Pohl, Frederick J. *Amerigo Vespucci, Pilot Major.* Hippocrene 1966 $21.50. ISBN 0-374-96499-8

Rawls, James J. *Indians of California: The Changing Image.* Univ of Oklahoma Pr 1986 $9.95. ISBN 0-8061-2020-7

Richman, Irving B. *Spanish Conquerors.* Elliots 1919 $19.50. ISBN 0-686-83782-7

*Ruoff, A. Lavonne. *American Indian Literature. Indians of North America Ser.* Chelsea 1989 $17.95. ISBN 1-55546-688-5 Study of Indian culture—both historical and contemporary—through literature; includes modern and historical illustrations, maps, and more.

Sarabande, William. *Beyond the Sea of Ice: The First Americans.* Book 1 Bantam 1987 $4.50. ISBN 0-553-26889-9

Sarabande, William. *First Americans: Forbidden Land.* Bantam 1989 $4.95. ISBN 0-533-28206-9

Sauts, William. *First Americans.* Mid Atlantic $3.95. ISBN 0-317-66673-8

Steck, Frances B. *The Joliet-Marquette Expedition, 1673.* AMS (repr of 1928 ed) $36.00. ISBN 0-404-57756-3

Thomas, Cyrus. *Cherokees in Pre-Columbian Times.* AMS (repr of 1890 ed) $16.50. ISBN 0-404-15727-0

▪Washburn, Wilcomb E. *The Indian in America. New American Nation Ser.* Harper Jr Bks 1975 $19.45. ISBN 0-06-014534-X A history of the American Indian and his changing role in our modern society.

COLUMBUS, CHRISTOPHER   1451–1506

A man of imagination, dreams, and perseverance, the Italian mariner and navigator Christopher Columbus had tried for almost eight years to persuade different monarchs of Europe to finance his attempt to find a new and faster route to Asia by sailing west. Finally, after spending several years at the Spanish court arguing his case first before Queen Isabella and then before King Ferdinand, they agreed to his plan. In return for their backing, Columbus promised them great wealth for Spain and an opportunity to spread Christianity.

On August 3, 1492, Columbus set sail from Spain with three small ships— the *Niña,* the *Pinta,* and the *Santa María*—and a crew of frightened sailors. Although many learned people in Europe believed the world was round and the seas were not filled with monsters, ordinary people still believed these myths. Entreated many times by his crew to turn back, Columbus insisted they sail on. On October 12 he and his crew reached the shores of an island in what is now the Bahamas that Columbus christened San Salvador. Columbus found people living there, whom he named Indians, but no gold. He believed he had reached the East Indies, islands of the southeast coast of Asia. He returned to Spain, bringing some Indians back with him as proof of his discovery. The grateful Spanish rulers gave him the title of admiral and made him governor of the new lands he had found and any other lands he found on subsequent voyages.

Columbus made three more voyages for Spain between 1492 and 1504. In September 1493 he sailed with 17 ships of colonists to set up trading posts and colonies. They established a colony on Hispaniola, and Columbus sighted Puerto Rico, Jamaica, the Virgin Islands, some of the Lesser Antilles, and the southern coast of Cuba.

On his third voyage, Columbus encountered many troubles. He did explore Trinidad and sighted South America, but the colonists under his authority threatened to revolt because of his supposed repressive methods of governing and favoritism toward his family. An investigator was sent from Spain, and Columbus was sent back in disgrace.

Columbus's fourth voyage lasted from 1502 to 1504. Again he promised to find a route to the east. Instead he found Central America, sailing along what is now the coast of Honduras. He followed the coast south to present-day Panama. After many troubles, once more he returned to Spain in disgrace. He died two years later disappointed, poor, and almost forgotten.

BOOKS BY COLUMBUS

America and Around the World: The First Logs of Columbus and Magellan. (coauthored with Antonio Pigafetta) Branden 1990 $19.95. ISBN 0-8283-1992-8

The Diario of Christopher Columbus' First Voyage to America, 1492–1493. Oliver Dunn and James E. Kelley, Jr. (eds). *The American Exploration and Travel Ser.* Univ of Oklahoma Pr 1989 $57.50. ISBN 0-8061-2101-7

Four Voyages to the New World. R. H. Major (ed and tr). Peter Smith 1978 $16.75. ISBN 0-8446-1883-7

Journal (During His First Voyage, 1492–1493): And Documents Relating to the Voyages of John Cabot and Gaspar Corte Real. Hakluyt Society Ser. Clements R. Markham (ed). Burt Franklin 1972 $29.50. ISBN 0-8337-2230-1

Journal of the First Voyage to America. Select Bibliographies Repr Ser. Ayer 1972 $16.00. ISBN 0-8369-5690-7

Letter to Rafael Sanchez (1493). Johnson Repr (repr of 1493 ed). (o.p.)

BOOKS ABOUT COLUMBUS

Morison, Samuel Eliot. *Admiral of the Ocean Sea: A Life of Christopher Columbus.* Northeastern Univ Pr 1983 $12.95. ISBN 0-930350-37-5 Classic 1942 Pulitzer Prize-winning biography of Columbus; brings the explorer alive as both seaman and navigator through Morison's re-creation of Columbus's journeys.

*Morison, Samuel Eliot. *Christopher Columbus, Mariner.* NAL 1983 $8.95. ISBN 0-452-00992-8 Tells of the life and exploits of Christopher Columbus and his capabilities as a sea captain.

Painter, Desmond. *Columbus. World History Ser.* Malcolm Yapp, *et al* (eds). Greenhaven 1980 $2.95. ISBN 0-89908-017-0 Discusses Columbus's and Vespucci's voyages to the Americas and the search for the United States.

*Provost, Foster. *Columbus Dictionary.* Omnigraphics 1990 $48.00. ISBN 1-55888-151-1 Provides reference to people, places, and events associated with Columbus and his voyages of discovery.

See also Vol. 2, World History: Exploration and Expansion.

SPANISH, FRENCH, AND OTHER EUROPEAN COLONIES

Beck, Warren A. *New Mexico: A History of Four Centuries.* Univ of Oklahoma Pr 1982 $24.95. ISBN 0-8061-0533-X

Blackmar, Frank W. *Spanish Colonization in the Southwest.* AMS (repr of 1890 ed) $11.50. ISBN 0-404-61059-5

Bolton, Herbert E. *Fray Juan Crespi, Missionary Explorer on the Pacific Coast, 1769–1774.* AMS (repr of 1927 ed) $29.50. ISBN 0-404-01838-6

Costo, Rupert, and Jeannette H. Costo. *Missions of California: A Legacy of Genocide.* Indian Historian Pr 1987 $8.50. ISBN 0-317-64539-0

Delanglez, Jean. *French Jesuits in Lower Louisiana (1700–1763).* AMS (repr of 1935 ed) $46.00. ISBN 0-404-57771-7

DeNevi, Don, and Noel Moholy. *Junipero Serra: The Illustrated Story of the Franciscan Founder of California's Missions.* Harper Jr Bks 1985 $14.45. ISBN 0-06-061876-0

*DeVoto, Bernard. *Across the Wide Missouri.* Houghton 1980 $9.95. ISBN 0-385-08374-5 Tells of Indians, mountain men, and the fur trade.

Espinosa, José M. *Spanish Folk-Tales from New Mexico.* Kraus (repr of 1937 ed) $23.00. ISBN 0-527-01082-0

*Finkelstein, Norman. *The Other 1492: Jewish Settlement in the New World.* Scribner's 1989 $12.95. ISBN 0-684-18913-5 Discusses the expulsion of the Jews from Spain in 1492 including their escape to the Americas.

Fogel, Daniel. *Junípero Serra, the Vatican, and Enslavement Theology.* Ism Pr 1988 $9.00. ISBN 0-910383-25-1

Grizzard, Mary. *Spanish Colonial Art and Architecture of Mexico and the U.S. Southwest.* Univ Pr of America 1986 $18.75. ISBN 0-8101-5633-7

*Johnson, W. W. *Spanish West. Old West Ser.* Silver 1976 $19.94. ISBN 0-8094-1535-6 Account of Spanish settlement in the U.S. Southwest.

*Martin, Teri. *Junipero Serra: God's Pioneer.* Paulist 1990 $2.50. ISBN 0-8091-6589-9 Illustrated account of the founder of the California missions.

*Morrice, Polly. *The French Americans.* Chelsea 1988 $16.95. ISBN 0-87754-878-1 Illustrated account of the French who colonized North America; includes history, culture, and a reference section.

Nelson, Helge. *Swedes and the Swedish Settlements in North America.* Franklyn D. Scott (ed). 2 vols. Ayer 1979 $46.00. ISBN 0-405-11654-3

Nutt, Mac. *Bartholomé de Las Casas: His Life, His Apostolate, and His Writings.* AMS (repr of 1909 ed) $32.45. ISBN 0-404-07146-5

Parkman, Francis. *The Jesuits in North America.* Corner 1970 $22.50. ISBN 0-87928-016-6

Pula, James S. *French in America, 1488–1974: A Chronology and Fact Book. Ethnic Chronology Ser.* Oceana 1975 $8.50. ISBN 0-379-00515-8

Rovira, Luis J. *Spanish Proverbs: A Survey of Spanish Culture and Civilization.* Univ Pr of America 1984 $14.25. ISBN 0-8191-3967-X

Schreuder, Yda. *Dutch Catholic Immigrant Settlement in Wisconsin.* Garland 1990 $59.95. ISBN 0-8240-4669-2

Stevenson, Robert. *Spanish Music in the Age of Columbus.* Hyperion 1986 $47.50. ISBN 0-88355-872-6

Wabeke, Bertus H. *Dutch Emigration to North America, 1624–1860.* Ayer 1944 $17.00. ISBN 0-8369-5389-4

THE ENGLISH COLONIES AND COLONIAL LIFE

*Alderman, Clifford Lindsey. *The Story of the Thirteen Colonies. Landmark Ser.* Random 1966 $8.99. ISBN 0-394-90415-X Examines motives of colonists for coming to North America and the circumstances that led to the American Revolution.

**American Heritage Illustrated History of the United States, Vol. 2: Colonial America.* Choice Pub 1988 $3.49. ISBN 0-945260-02-4 Illustrated discussion of the colonies and colonial life especially suited to younger readers.

Bonomi, Patricia. *Under the Cape of Heaven: Religion, Society, and Politics in Colonial America.* Oxford Univ Pr 1988 $9.95. ISBN 0-19-505417-2

*Boorstin, Daniel J. *The Americans.* Vol. 1 *The Colonial Experience.* McGraw 1964 $8.95. ISBN 0-07-553700-1 An account of the 13 colonies from the first days of English settlement to the Revolution. Not easy to read, but good information.

Bridenbaugh, Carl. *Jamestown, Fifteen Forty-Four to Sixteen Ninety-Nine.* Oxford Univ Pr 1980 $35.00. ISBN 0-19-502650-0

Bushman, Richard L. *King and People in Provincial Massachusetts. Institute of Early American History and Culture Ser.* Univ of North Carolina Pr 1985 $14.95. ISBN 0-8078-1624-8

*Clapp, Patricia. *Constance: A Story of Early Plymouth. Puffin Novels Ser.* Penguin 1986 $4.95. ISBN 0-14-032030-X Fictional journal of a young girl's voyage from England to the colonies and her life in Massachusetts.

Cremin, Lawrence. *American Education: The Colonial Experience, 1607–1783.* Harper Jr Bks 1972 $12.95. ISBN 0-06-131670-9

*Daugherty, James. *The Landing of the Pilgrims.* Random 1987 $2.95. ISBN 0-394-84697-4 Examines the first three years of Plymouth Colony, using William Bradford's account; illustrated.

Earle, Alice M. *Child Life in Colonial Days.* Omnigraphics 1989 $50.00. ISBN 1-55888-822-5

Earle, Alice M. *Costume of Colonial Times.* Omnigraphics 1975 $48.00. ISBN 0-8103-3965-X

Earle, Alice M. *Customs and Fashions in Old New England.* Tuttle 1971 $7.50. ISBN 0-8048-0960-7

Earle, Alice M. *Home Life in Colonial Days.* Berkshire Traveller 1974 $10.95. ISBN 0-912944-23-4

Ellis, George W., and John E. Morris. *King Philip's War.* AMS (repr of 1906 ed) $28.50. ISBN 0-404-15529-4

Fiering, Norman. *Jonathan Edwards' Moral Thought and Its British Context. Institute of Early American History and Culture Ser.* Univ of North Carolina Pr 1981 $35.00. ISBN 0-8078-1473-3

Flexner, James T. *History of American Painting.* Vol. 1 *First Flowers of Our Wilderness: American Painting, the Colonial Period. Fine Art Ser.* Dover 1988 $8.95. ISBN 0-486-25707-X

Fradin, Dennis B. *Anne Hutchinson: Fighter for Religious Freedom. Colonial Profiles Ser.* Enslow 1989 $12.95. ISBN 0-89490-229-6

Hoffer, Peter C. (ed). *Africans Become Afro-Americans: Selected Articles on Slavery in the American Colonies. Early American History Ser.* Garland 1988 $60.00. ISBN 0-8240-6237-X

Hoffer, Peter C. (ed). *Colonial Women and Domesticity: Selected Articles on Gender in Early America. Early American History Ser.* Garland 1988 $50.00. ISBN 0-8240-6239-6

Hoffer, Peter C. (ed). *Commerce and Community: Selected Articles on the Middle Atlantic Colonies. Early American History Ser.* Garland 1988 $60.00. ISBN 0-8240-6238-8

Hoffer, Peter C. (ed). *Indians and Europeans: Selected Articles on Indian-White Relations in Colonial North America. Early American History Ser.* Garland 1988 $60.00. ISBN 0-8240-6231-0

Hoffer, Peter C. (ed). *The Marrow of American Divinity: Selected Articles on Colonial Religion. Early American History Ser.* Garland 1988 $70.00. ISBN 0-8240-6241-8

Hoffer, Peter C. (ed). *The Peopling of a World: Selected Articles on Immigration and Settlement Patterns in British North America. Early American History Ser.* Garland 1988 $60.00. ISBN 0-8240-6230-2

Hoffer, Peter C. (ed). *Planters and Yeomen: Selected Articles on the Southern Colonies. Early American History Ser.* Garland 1988 $70.00. ISBN 0-8240-6236-1

Hofstadter, Richard. *America at Seventeen-Fifty: A Social History.* Knopf 1971 $14.45. ISBN 0-394-46589-X

Jacobs, Wilbur R. *Dispossessing the American Indian: Indians and Whites on the Colonial Frontier.* Univ of Oklahoma Pr 1985 $9.95. ISBN 0-8061-1935-7

Leach, Douglas E. *Roots of Conflict: British Armed Forces and Colonial Americans, 1677–1763.* Univ of North Carolina Pr 1989 $10.95. ISBN 0-8078-4258-3

Lockridge, Kenneth A. *A New England Town: The First Hundred Years. Essays in American History Ser.* Norton 1985 $7.95. ISBN 0-393-95459-5

*Madison, Arnold. *How the Colonists Lived.* McKay 1980 $8.95. ISBN 0-679-20685-X Close-up view of life in the early colonies.

Miller, Perry. *The New England Mind: The Seventeenth Century.* Harvard Univ Pr 1983 $12.50. ISBN 0-674-61306-6

Miller, Perry, and T. H. Johnson (eds). *Puritans: A Sourcebook of Their Writings.* 2 vols. Harper Jr Bks 1965 Vol. 1 $9.95. ISBN 0-06-131093-X. 1963 Vol. 2 $10.95. ISBN 0-06-131094-8

Mullins, Lisa C. *Colonial Architecture of the Mid-Atlantic. Architectural Treasures of Early America Ser.* Main Street 1987 $19.95. ISBN 1-55562-041-8

Nash, Gary B. *Race, Class, and Politics: Essays on American Colonial and Revolutionary Society.* Univ of Illinois Pr 1986 $15.95. ISBN 0-252-01313-1

Nash, Gary B. *Red, White, and Black: The Peoples of Early America.* Prentice 1982 $24.00. ISBN 0-13-769786-4

*O'Dell, Scott. *The Serpent Never Sleeps.* Fawcett 1989 $2.95. ISBN 0-449-70328-2 Fictionalized account of a 17-year-old and the hardships she endures as an English colonist in the New World.

*Perkins, Edwin J. *The Economy of Colonial America.* Columbia Univ Pr 1988 $10.00. ISBN 0-231-06339-3 Survey of colonial economy: patterns, problems, and trends.

*Perl, Lila. *Slumps, Grunts, and Snickerdoodles: What Colonial America Ate and Why.* Houghton 1979 $13.95. ISBN 0-395-28923-8 Account of the foods grown and eaten in the colonial period; some recipes included.

Shirley, John W. *Sir Walter Raleigh and the New World. America's Four Hundredth Anniversary Ser.* North Carolina Archives 1985 $5.00. ISBN 0-86526-206-3

Siegel, Beatrice. *Fur Trappers and Traders: The Indians, the Pilgrims, and the Beaver.* Walker 1987 $11.85. ISBN 0-8027-6397-9

*Speare, Elizabeth. *The Witch of Blackbird Pond.* ABC–Clio 1989 $14.95. ISBN 1-55736-138-X Fictional account of a woman accused of being a witch in colonial Connecticut; a Newbery Medal winner.

*Stick, David. *Roanoke Island: The Beginning of English America.* Univ of North Carolina Pr 1983 $7.50. ISBN 0-8078-4110-2 Readable general history of early America with interesting account of England's attempts at settling North America.

*Tunis, Edwin. *Colonial Craftsmen: The Beginnings of American Industry.* Harper Jr Bks 1976 $24.70. ISBN 0-690-01062-1 Discusses skills of early settlers.

Van Dusen, Albert E. (ed). *Adventures for Another World: Jonathan Trumble's Commonplace Book.* Connecticut Historical Soc 1983 $5.95. ISBN 0-940748-87-8

Vaughan, Alden. *American Genesis: Captain John Smith and the Founding of Virginia.* Scott 1975 $8.50. ISBN 0-673-39355-0

Vaughan, Alden. *New England Frontier: Indians and Puritans, 1620–1675.* Norton 1980. (o.p.) $7.95. ISBN 0-393-00950-5

Vaughan, Alden. *Puritans Among the Indians: Accounts of Captivity and Redemptions, 1676–1724.* Harvard Univ Pr 1986 $9.95. ISBN 0-674-73899-3

*Wendell, Barrett. *Cotton Mather. American Men and Women of Letters Ser.* Chelsea 1981 $5.95. ISBN 0-87754-166-3 Biography of the notable Puritan cleric and writer.

Worrell, Arthur J. *Quakers in the Colonial Northeast.* Univ Pr of New England 1980 $30.00. ISBN 0-87451-174-7

*Wright, Louis B. *The Atlantic Frontier: Colonial American Civilization, 1607–1763.* Greenwood 1980 $35.00. ISBN 0-313-22320-3 Historical account of the colonies and the events leading up to the Revolution.

See also Vol. 1, American Literature: The Early Years.

PROTEST, REBELLION, AND REVOLUTION

*American Heritage Illustrated History of the United States, Vol. 3: The Revolution. Choice Pub 1988 $3.49. ISBN 0-945260-03-2 Illustrated history of the period of the Revolution; especially suited to young adults.

■Andrews, Charles M. *The Colonial Background of the American Revolution.* Yale Univ Pr 1961 $9.95. ISBN 0-300-00004-9 Four essays tracing the origins of the Revolutionary War in examinations of colonial life.

Bailyn, Bernard. *Ideological Origins of the American Revolution.* Harvard Univ Pr 1967 $9.95. ISBN 0-674-44301-2

Billias, George A. *The American Revolution: How Revolutionary Was It?* Holt 1980 $13.95. ISBN 0-03-054761-X

Boatner, Mark M., III. *Encyclopedia of the American Revolution.* McKay 1974 $9.95. ISBN 0-679-50440-0

*Brandt, Keith. *John Paul Jones: Hero of the Seas.* Troll 1983 $2.50. ISBN 0-89375-850-7 Biography of the famous colonial naval hero.

*Collier, James L., and Christopher Collier. *My Brother Sam Is Dead.* Scholastic 1985 $2.50. ISBN 0-590-33694-0 Fictional account, based on a true incident, of sons of a New England family who choose opposite sides in the American Revolution.

*Cooper, James Fenimore. *The Last of the Mohicans.* Bantam 1982 $2.95. ISBN 0-553-21329-6 Adventurous fictional account of an Indian scout during the French and Indian War.

*Davis, Burke. *Black Heroes of the American Revolution.* Harcourt 1976 $13.95. ISBN 0-15-208560-2 Stories about the black participants who made a difference in the American Revolution.

*De Pauw, Linda G. *Founding Mothers: Women of America in the Revolutionary Era.* Houghton 1975 $13.95. ISBN 0-395-21896-9 Views the lives and roles of women during the revolutionary period.

Dickinson, John. *Letters from a Farmer in Pennsylvania to the Inhabitants of the British Colonies.* Reprint Services 1988 $59.00.

Eckert, Allan W. *The Conquerors.* Bantam 1984 $4.95. ISBN 0-553-25820-6

Eckert, Allan W. *Wilderness Empire Seventeen Fifty-Five.* Bantam 1985 $4.95. ISBN 0-553-26488-5

Eckert, Allan W. *The Wilderness War.* Bantam 1985 $4.95. ISBN 0-533-26368-4

*Fast, Howard. *The Call of the Fife and Drum: Three Novels of the American Revolution.* Carol 1987 $9.95. ISBN 0-8065-1027-7 Three stories of the Revolutionary War by a popular novelist.

*Forbes, Esther. *Johnny Tremain.* Houghton 1943 $12.95. ISBN 0-395-06766-9 Illustrated story of a young member of the Sons of Liberty before the war for independence.

*Forbes, Esther. *Paul Revere and the World He Lived In.* Houghton 1972 $9.95. ISBN 0-395-08370-2 Biography of the famous night rider who warned that "the British are coming."

Graymont, Barbara. *Iroquois in the American Revolution.* Syracuse Univ Pr $12.95. ISBN 0-8156-0116-6

Hofstadter, Richard. *America at Seventeen-Fifty: A Social History.* Knopf 1971 $14.45. ISBN 0-394-46589-X

Jensen, Merrill. *The New Nation: A History of the United States During the Confederation, 1781–1789.* Univ of Nebraska Pr 1981 $12.95. ISBN 0-930350-14-6

*Knight, James E. *Boston Tea Party: Rebellion in the Colonies.* Troll 1982 $2.50. ISBN 0-89375-735-7 Describes the famous Tea Party and its place in the events leading to war between Great Britain and its colonies.

*Knight, James E. *The Winter at Valley Forge, Survival and Victory.* Troll 1982 $2.50. ISBN 0-89375-739-X Recounts the hardships the American army endured at Valley Forge under George Washington.

*Knollenberg, Bernhard. *Growth of the American Revolution, 1766–1775.* Free Pr 1975 $19.95. ISBN 0-02-917110-5 Detailed description of the events leading to the American Revolution.

*McDowell, Bart. *Revolutionary War: America's Fight for Freedom.* Special Publications Ser. National Geographic 1980 $7.95. ISBN 0-87044-047-0 Illustrated examination of the events surrounding the war for independence.

*Meltzer, Milton. *The American Revolutionaries: A History in Their Own Words.* Harper Jr Bks 1987 $13.89. ISBN 0-690-04643-X Viewpoints of the colonial rebels from diaries, journals, letters, memoirs, and newspapers of the time.

Miller, John C. *Origins of the American Revolution: With a New Introduction and Bibliography.* Stanford Univ Pr 1959 $16.95. ISBN 0-8047-0594-1

*Miller, John C. *Sam Adams: Pioneer in Propaganda.* Stanford Univ Pr 1936 $13.95. ISBN 0-8047-0025-7 Biography of one the most active colonial advocates for independence.

*Morison, Samuel Eliot. *John Paul Jones: A Sailor's Biography.* Northeastern Univ Pr 1985 $11.95. ISBN 0-930350-70-7 Pulitzer Prize-winning biography of the naval hero.

*Morison, Samuel Eliot (ed). *Sources and Documents Illustrating the American Revolution, 1764–1788, and the Formation of the Federal Constitution.* Oxford Univ Pr 1965 $13.95. ISBN 0-19-500262-8 Excellent primary source collection.

*O'Dell, Scott. *Sarah Bishop.* Scholastic 1988 $2.75. ISBN 0-590-42298-7 Story of a young girl orphaned in the Revolutionary War.

*Phelan, Mary K. *The Story of the Boston Massacre.* Harper Jr Bks 1976 $13.70. ISBN 0-690-00716-7 Account of the crowd protest that ended in the death of five people, including Crispus Attucks, and the prosecution of the British soldiers who fired on the crowd.

*Randall, Willard Sterne. *Benedict Arnold: Patriot and Traitor.* Morrow 1990 $25.00. ISBN 1-55710-034-9 Effort to explain the motives of the one-time hero and traitor.

*Rossiter, Clinton. *The First American Revolution: The American Colonies on the Eve of Independence.* Harcourt 1956 $8.95. ISBN 0-15-631121-6 Good introduction to the Revolution by a noted historian.

▪ Smith, Page. *A New Age Now Begins: A People's History of the American Revolution.* Penguin 1989 $31.90. ISBN 0-14-095354-X A two-volume set tracing revolutionary elements in American life during the Colonial period.

Tuchman, Barbara W. *The First Salute: A View of the American Revolution.* Ballantine 1989 $11.95. ISBN 0-345-33667-4

Wills, Garry. *Inventing America: Jefferson's Declaration of Independence.* Random 1979 $8.95. ISBN 0-394-72735-5

▪ Wood, W. J. *Battles of the Revolutionary War, 1775–1781.* Algonquin 1990 $24.95. ISBN 0-945575-03-3 Interesting account of the battles and leaders; includes maps.

PAINE, THOMAS   1713–1809

One of the best known writers of the patriot cause, Thomas Paine was born in Great Britain, the son of Quakers. In 1774 he immigrated to the colonies with letters of introduction from Benjamin Franklin (*see* Franklin, Vol. 2, United States History: The United States Constitution), whom he had met in London. Working in Philadelphia as a journalist, Paine soon became involved in the verbal clashes between the American colonists and England. In early 1776 he published his famous pamphlet *Common Sense,* in which he urged colonists to cut their ties with the British government. The work exerted a powerful influence on the struggle for independence.

During the Revolutionary War, from 1776 to 1783, Paine published a series of 16 pamphlets under the title *The Crisis,* meant to boost the morale of the patriots. In the first of these he spoke of the period as "the times that try men's souls." The phrase "summer soldiers and sunshine patriots" also comes from this series.

In 1787, Paine returned to England. While he was there, he wrote *The Rights of Man* (1791, 1792) as a reply to the British statesman and philosopher Edmund Burke (*see* Burke, Vol. 1, American Government/Civics: Surveys and Theories), who was critical of the French Revolution. Paine believed that only democratic institutions can guarantee an individual's natural rights. Because of his sharp criticism of the British government, he was exiled to France, where he became involved in French politics as a member of the National Convention. His involvement in urging revolt in France led to his imprisonment from 1793 to 1794.

Paine's acceptance of deism, a philosophy that accepted the existence of God but dismissed the need for formal religion and claims of supernatural revelations, resulted in his treatise *The Age of Reason, Being an Investigation of True and Fabulous Theology* (1794, 1795). The work created a furor both abroad and in the United States, and his critical *Letter to Washington* (1796) brought further resentment against him in the United States.

Paine returned to New York in 1802. There the man called an "Englishman by birth, French citizen by decree, and American by adoption" died seven years later, impoverished, embittered, and all but forgotten.

BOOKS BY PAINE

The Age of Reason (1794–1795). Buccaneer 1986 $18.95. ISBN 0-89966-543-8

*Common Sense (1776). Penguin 1982 $2.95. ISBN 0-14-039016-2 The pamphlet that helped convince colonists, including the Continental Congress, to declare independence.

Common Sense, The Rights of Man, and Other Essential Writings of Thomas Paine. NAL 1984 $5.95. ISBN 0-452-00921-9

The Rights of Man (1791–1792). Doubleday 1989. (o.p.)

The Writings of Thomas Paine: The Standard Edition. Moncure D. Conway (ed). 4 vols. AMS (repr of 1896 ed) $130.00. ISBN 0-404-04870-6

BOOKS ABOUT PAINE

Buchanan, John G. *Thomas Paine: American Revolutionary Writer. Outstanding Personalities Ser.* D. Steve Rahmas (ed). SamHar 1976 $3.95. ISBN 0-87157-585-X Straightforward biography; includes important dates.

*Conway, Moncure D. *Thomas Paine. American Men and Women of Letters Ser.* 2 vols. Chelsea

1982 $17.90. ISBN 0-87754-172-8 Good introductory work on the man who coined the phrase "sunshine patriot."
*Vail, John. *Thomas Paine. World Leaders—Past and Present Ser.* Chelsea 1990 $17.95. ISBN 1-55546-819-5 Good introductory evaluation of Paine's place in history.

See also Vol. 2, World History: Revolution and Change in England and America.

THE UNITED STATES CONSTITUTION

Beard, Charles A. *An Economic Interpretation of the Constitution of the United States.* Free Pr 1986 $10.95. ISBN 0-02-902480-3
Bernstein, Richard B., and Kym S. Rice. *Are We to Be a Nation? The Making of the Constitution.* Harvard Univ Pr 1987 $14.95. ISBN 0-674-04476-2
*Bowen, Catherine Drinker. *Miracle at Philadelphia: The Story of the Constitutional Convention, May to September 1787.* Little 1986 $8.95. ISBN 0-316-10378-0 Report of the workings of the convention based largely on Madison's records.
*Collier, Christopher, and James L. Collier. *Decision in Philadelphia: The Constitutional Convention 1787.* Ballantine 1987 $4.95. ISBN 0-345-34652-1 Fictionalized account of the Constitutional Convention.
*Commager, Henry. *Great Constitution.* Macmillan 1961 $7.50. ISBN 0-672-50299-2 Discussion of the importance of the Constitution as the law of the land.
Cooke, Jacob E. (ed). *The Federalist.* Wesleyan Univ Pr 1982 $12.95. ISBN 0-8195-6077-4
Craven, Wesley F. *The Legend of the Founding Fathers.* Greenwood 1983 $35.00. ISBN 0-313-23840-5
Farrand, Max. *Fathers of the Constitution.* Elliots 1921 $8.50. ISBN 0-686-83547-6
Farrand, Max. *The Records of the Federal Convention of Seventeen Eighty-Seven.* 4 vols. Yale Univ Pr 1986. Vol. 1 $15.95. ISBN 0-300-00080-4. Vol. 2 $15.95. ISBN 0-300-00081-2. Vol. 3 $15.95. ISBN 0-300-00082-0. Vol. 4 $14.95. ISBN 0-300-03964-2
*Fritz. Jean. *Shh! We're Writing the Constitution.* Putnam 1987 $5.95. ISBN 0-399-21404-6 Shares differing views of the writers of the Constitution; especially suited to younger readers.
*Gerberg, Mort. *The United States Constitution for Everyone: A Guide to the Most Important Document Written by and for the People of the United States.* Putnam 1987 $4.95. ISBN 0-399-51305-1 Annotated text of the Constitution with illustrations.
*Hauptly, Denis. *A Convention of Delegates: The Creation of the Constitution.* Macmillan 1987 $12.95. ISBN 0-689-31148-6 Focuses on the personalities who took part in the Constitutional Convention of 1787; illustrated.
*Kelly, Alfred H., and Winfred A. Harbison. *American Constitution: Its Origin and Development.* Norton 1982 $27.95. ISBN 0-393-95204-5 Describes how the Constitution came to be.
Kenyon, Cecelia M. (ed). *The Anti-Federalists.* Northeastern Univ Pr 1985 $14.95. ISBN 0-930350-74-X
Levy, Leonard W., and Dennis J. Mahoney. *The Framing and Ratification of the Constitution.* Macmillan 1987 $24.95. ISBN 0-317-62103-3
Lomask, Milton. *The Spirit of Seventeen Eighty-Seven: The Making of Our Constitution.* Farrar 1980 $10.95. ISBN 0-374-37140-0
McDonald, Forrest. *A Constitutional History of the United States.* Krieger 1986 $24.50. ISBN 0-89874-902-6
Main, Jackson T. *The Anti-Federalists: Critics of the Constitution, Seventeen Eighty-One–Seventeen Eighty-Eight.* Norton 1974 $9.95. ISBN 0-393-00760-X

Mee, Charles L., Jr. *The Genius of the People: The Constitutional Convention of 1787.* Harper Jr Bks 1987 $19.95. ISBN 0-06-015702-X

*Morris, Richard B. *Witness at the Creation: Hamilton, Madison, Jay, and the Constitution.* Holt 1985 $16.95. ISBN 0-8050-0469-6 Viewpoints of participants at the creation of the federal Constitution.

Moyers, Bill. *Moyers: Report from Philadelphia: The Constitutional Convention of 1787.* Ballantine 1989 $3.95. ISBN 0-345-36160-1

Van Doren, Carl. *The Great Rehearsal: The Story of the Making and Ratifying of the Constitution of the United States.* Penguin 1986 $6.95. ISBN 0-14-008965-9

FRANKLIN, BENJAMIN   1706–1790

See also Franklin, Vol. 2, Physics: Electricity and Magnetism.

Benjamin Franklin had many careers, but he is perhaps best known as a statesman and as one of the founding fathers of the United States. Born in Boston of a poor family, he moved to Philadelphia in 1723 and began work as a printer. By the age of 42, he had acquired enough money to retire and spend his time writing, experimenting with scientific ideas, and serving the public good.

Franklin had won fame with *Poor Richard's Almanac,* collections of witty proverbs and maxims published between 1732 and 1757. He signed the works "Richard Saunders," and they were undoubtedly derived from the patterns of the English *Poor Robin's Almanac* begun in 1633. Franklin's other well-known work is his *Autobiography* (1791), written in four stages in England, France, and Philadelphia.

As a scientist, Franklin experimented with lightning and proved the existence of electricity in lightning. As a result, he invented the lightning rod. He also invented the Franklin stove and bifocal eyeglasses and developed theories of heat absorption, ocean currents, and meteorology.

As a public servant and statesman, Franklin was responsible for establishing the first lending library in Philadelphia, as well as an insurance company, a hospital, a night watch, a fire company, the first militia, and the academy that became the University of Pennsylvania. From 1753 to 1754 he was deputy postmaster general of the colonies. During the French and Indian War, which began in 1754 and ended in 1763, he helped organize the colonies' defenses. At the same time, at a conference in Albany in 1754, he introduced the Albany Plan of Union, a plan for uniting the colonies.

Stationed in London prior to the Revolutionary War as an agent for Pennsylvania, Franklin worked for conciliation between the colonies and Britain. When he returned home in 1775, he helped the Continental Congress reach the decision to declare independence. The Congress then sent him to France, where he won French support for the colonists. In 1781 he became one of the team to negotiate the treaty ending war with Britain. At the age of 81, Franklin served as a member of the Constitutional Convention in Philadelphia. By the end of the Convention, he was so weak that another delegate had to read his final speech to the others. In the speech Franklin asked the delegates to the Convention to sign the Constitution "because I expect no better, and because I am not sure it is not the best."

BOOKS BY FRANKLIN

An Apology for Printers. Randolph Goodman (ed). Acropolis 1973 $3.95. ISBN 0-87491-146-X

Autobiography and Selected Writings. Modern Lib 1981 $4.00. ISBN 0-07-554271-4

The Autobiography of Benjamin Franklin. Penguin Classics Ser. Kenneth Silverman (ed). Penguin 1986 $3.95. ISBN 0-14-039052-9

The Bagatelles from Passy. Eakins 1967 $20.00. ISBN 0-87130-005-2

**The Sayings of Poor Richard: The Prefaces, Proverbs and Poems of Benjamin Franklin.* Paul Leicester (comp). Burt Franklin 1975 $24.50. ISBN 0-8337-1198-9 Collection of witty adages, sayings, and other writings by Franklin.

BOOKS ABOUT FRANKLIN

*Looby, Christopher. *Benjamin Franklin. World Leaders—Past and Present Ser.* Chelsea 1990 $17.95. ISBN 1-55546-808-X Describes both the personal and historical events that shaped Franklin's life; especially suited to younger readers.

Van Doren, Carl. *Benjamin Franklin.* Crown 1987 $9.98. ISBN 0-517-62532-6 Captures the many faces of this most creative and energetic eighteenth-century figure in his roles as statesman, inventor, and author.

*Weinberg, Lawrence. *Benjamin Franklin.* Childrens 1988 $8.95. ISBN 0-516-09552-8 Presents the life of Franklin as if he were telling the story; especially suited to younger readers.

See also Vol. 2, American Government/Civics: The Constitution.

BEGINNING OF THE NEW NATION—NATIONALISM AND GROWTH

**American Heritage Illustrated History of the United States, Vol. 6: The Frontier.* Choice Pub 1988 $3.49. ISBN 0-945260-06-7 Illustrated description of frontier life, especially suited to younger readers.

**American Heritage Illustrated History of the United States, Vol 4: A New Nation.* Choice Pub 1988 $3.49. ISBN 0-945260-04-0 Illustrated history of the events that took place in the newly formed United States; especially suited to younger readers.

**American Heritage Illustrated History of the United States, Vol. 5: Young America.* Choice Pub 1988 $3.49. ISBN 0-945260-05-9 Illustrated story of the new nation struggling to grow; especially suited to younger readers.

*Baldwin, Leland D. *Whiskey Rebels: The Story of a Frontier Uprising.* Univ of Pittsburgh Pr 1968 $8.95. ISBN 0-8229-5151-7 Illustrated story of the opposition to the whiskey tax.

Clancy, Herbert J. *The Democratic Party: Jefferson to Jackson.* Fordham Univ Pr 1962. (o.p.)

Cooper, James Fenimore. *The Leatherstocking Tales.* Blake Nevius (ed). 2 vols. Lib of America 1985. Vol. 1 *The Pioneers; The Last of the Mohicans; The Prairie.* $27.50. ISBN 0-940450-20-8. Vol. 2 *The Pathfinder; The Deerslayer.* $27.50. ISBN 0-940450-21-6

*Cunliffe, Marcus. *Nation Takes Shape: 1789–1837. Chicago History of American Civilization Ser.* Univ of Chicago Pr 1960 $9.00. ISBN 0-226-12667-6 Standard history of the formation of the new United States.

*Eckert, Allan W. *Blue Jacket: War Chief of the Shawnees.* Landfall 1983 $5.95. ISBN 0-913428-36-1 Story of the white boy who became one of the mightiest Shawnee warriors; especially suited to younger readers.

Eckert, Allan W. *The Frontiersman.* Bantam 1984 $4.95. ISBN 0-553-25799-4

Eckert, Allan W. *Gateway to Empire.* Bantam 1984 $5.95. ISBN 0-553-26010-3

Eckert, Allan W. *Twilight of Empire.* Bantam 1989 $4.95. ISBN 0-553-28059-7

Edmunde, R. David. *Tecumseh and the Quest for Indian Leadership.* Little 1984 $14.95. ISBN 0-316-21151-6

*Fisher, Vardis. *Tale of Valor.* Amereon 1976 $25.95. ISBN 0-89190-834-X Describes the expedition of Lewis and Clark.

*Hale, Edward Everett. *A Man Without a Country.* Lightyear 1976 $25.95. ISBN 0-89968-152-2 Classic novel set in the early 1800s about a young officer and his association with Thomas Jefferson's controversial vice president, Aaron Burr.

*Hickey, Donald R. *The War of Eighteen Twelve: A Forgotten Conflict.* Univ of Illinois Pr 1989 $32.50. ISBN 0-252-01613-0 Illustrated account of the war that nearly caused the demise of the new republic.

*Hilton, Suzanne. *We the People: The Way We Were, 1783–1793.* Westminster John Knox 1981 $12.95. ISBN 0-664-32685-4 Illustrated personal accounts of daily life by those who helped build the new American nation after its independence.

Hofstadter, Richard. *The American Political Tradition.* Random 1989 $7.95. ISBN 0-679-72315-3

Hofstadter, Richard. *The Idea of a Party System: The Rise of Legitimate Opposition in the United States, 1780–1840.* Univ of California Pr 1969 $11.95. ISBN 0-520-01754-4

Jensen, Merrill, and Robert A. Becker (eds). *A Documentary History of the First Federal Elections: 1788–1790.* Vol. 1 Univ of Wisconsin Pr 1976 $50.00. ISBN 0-299-06690-8

*Ketcham, Ralph. *Presidents Above Party: The First American Presidency, 1789–1829. Institute of Early American History and Culture, Williamsburg, Virginia, Ser.* Univ of North Carolina Pr 1987 $9.95. ISBN 0-8078-4179-X Argues that the goal of the early presidents was a political system in which the chief executive was above party politics.

Levy, Leonard W. *Constitutional Opinions: Aspects of the Bill of Rights.* Oxford Univ Pr 1985 $38.00. ISBN 0-19-503641-7

Livermore, Shaw, Jr. *Twilight of Federalism: The Disintegration of the Federalist Party, 1815–1830.* Gordian 1972 $35.00. ISBN 0-87752-137-9

*Marrin, Albert. *Eighteen Twelve: The War Nobody Won.* Macmillan 1985 $12.95. ISBN 0-689-31075-7 Interesting account of the everyday lives of warring Americans, British, and Indians.

Marshall, S. L. *Crimsoned Prairie: The Indian Wars. Quality Paperbacks Ser.* Da Capo 1984 $10.95. ISBN 0-306-80226-0

*O'Dell, Scott. *Streams to the River, River to the Sea: A Novel Of Sacagawea.* G. K. Hall 1989 $14.95. ISBN 0-8161-4811-2 Fictionalized account of the young Indian woman who guided Lewis and Clark on their expedition.

*Phelan, Mary K. *The Story of the Louisiana Purchase.* Harper Jr Bks 1979 $12.89. ISBN 0-690-03956-5 Describes how the United States purchased Louisiana.

Pike, Zebulon Montgomery. *The Expeditions of Zebulon Montgomery Pike.* 2 vols. Dover 1987. Vol. 1 $11.95. ISBN 0-486-25254-X. Vol. 2 $11.95. ISBN 0-486-25255-8

*Schachner, Nathan. *Aaron Burr: A Biography.* AMS (repr of 1937 ed) $57.50. ISBN 0-404-20227-6 Illustrated biography of the controversial figure of the early 1800s.

*Silkett, John T. *Francis Scott Key and the History of the Star Spangled Banner.* Vintage America 1978 $3.25. ISBN 0-932330-50-9 Recounts the circumstances of the writing of what became the national anthem.

*Tunis, Edwin. *Frontier Living.* Harper Jr Bks 1976 $24.70. ISBN 0-690-01064-8 Illustrated description of the lives of settlers moving west.

*Tunis, Edwin. *The Young United States, 1783–1830.* Harper Jr Bks 1976 $24.70. ISBN 0-690-01065-6 Describes the new nation as it matures and grows.

ADAMS, ABIGAIL 1744–1818

A truly liberated woman of high intelligence, great knowledge, and strong opinions, Abigail Adams has served as a model for women everywhere. She was the wife of a President, John Adams (*see* J. Adams, Vol. 2, United States History: Beginning of the New Nation—Nationalism and Growth), the mother of a President, John Quincy Adams (*see* J. Q. Adams, Vol. 2, United States History: Beginning of the New Nation—Nationalism and Growth), and an early advocate of equal rights for women.

Born Abigail Smith, the daughter of a wealthy Congregational minister who was a man of many interests, Adams had no formal schooling. However, she learned to read and write and to express herself clearly by reading the books in her father's large library. She kept up with current events by listening to and participating in the lively conversations carried on in the family home between her father and many influential visitors. In 1764 she became the wife of John Adams, then a young lawyer, and supported his role as a colonial leader in the fight for independence from Great Britain. When her husband was a delegate at the Continental Congress, she pushed for the rights of women in letters to him, urging him to "Remember the ladies, and be more generous and favorable to them than your ancestors." She made it clear that "if particular care and attention" was not paid to them, "we are determined to foment a rebellion, and will not hold ourselves bound by any laws in which we have no voice, or representation."

During her husband's long periods of absence, Adams ran the family farm, raised four children, and became a prolific letter writer to her husband, relatives, and friends. She kept up her correspondence when she followed her husband to Europe during his various political missions and also during her years as First Lady. After her death, her letters were collected and published in several volumes. Today, the letters of Abigail Adams provide historians with an inside look into colonial society and politics.

BOOKS BY ABIGAIL ADAMS

The Book of Abigail and John: Selected Letters of the Adams Family, 1762–1784. (coauthored with John Adams) L. H. Butterfield, *et al* (eds). Harvard Univ Pr 1975 $8.95. ISBN 0-674-07854-3

Familiar Letters of John Adams and His Wife Abigail Adams During the Revolution. Select Bibliographies Repr. Ser. Ayer 1975 $22.00. ISBN 0-8369-5318-5

The Works of Abigail (Smith) Adams, 1744–1818. Reprint Services 1989 $600.00.

BOOKS ABOUT ABIGAIL ADAMS

Fradin, Dennis B. *Abigail Adams: Advisor to a President. Colonial Profiles Ser.* Enslow 1989 $12.95. ISBN 0-89490-228-8 Discusses the role of Abigail Adams as an early supporter of women's rights, First Lady of the United States, and assistant to her husband.

Levin, Phyllis L. *Abigail Adams: A Biography.* Ballantine 1988 $10.95. ISBN 0-345-35473-7 Gives the reader a rare understanding of one of the most fascinating women in the United States.

*Osborne, Angela. *Abigail Adams. American Women of Achievement Ser.* Chelsea 1989 $9.95. ISBN 0-7910-0405-8 Illustrated biography of Adams; especially suitable for young adults.

Witter, Evelyn. *Abigail Adams: First Lady of Faith and Courage. Sower Ser.* Mott Media 1976 $4.95. ISBN 0-915134-94-2 Shows how the second first lady remained strong in a young war-torn country.

ADAMS, JOHN   1735–1826

John Adams was the husband of Abigail Adams and the father of the sixth President of the United States, John Quincy Adams (*see* A. Adams *and* J. Q. Adams, Vol. 2, United States History: Beginning of the New Nation—Nationalism and Growth), as well as a Patriot leader, member of the First and Second Continental Congresses, and the second President of the United States from 1797 to 1801.

Born in Braintree, now Quincy, Massachusetts, Adams graduated from

Harvard University in 1755. He then read for the law and began to practice. Although a moderating voice in the struggles against British oppression before the American Revolution, Adams spoke out strongly against the Stamp Act in 1765. In 1770, he defended the soldiers accused of murder in the Boston Massacre and won their acquittal. Adams said they deserved a fair trial even if the British government did not treat the colonists fairly.

In 1774, Adams was sent by Massachusetts to the First Continental Congress. The following year he returned to Philadelphia as a member of the Second Continental Congress. His arguments on behalf of independence helped sway other members to sign the Declaration of Independence in 1776.

Adams served on the negotiating team that ended the Revolution and acted as envoy to Great Britain from 1785 to 1788. Runner-up to George Washington (*see* Washington, Vol. 2, United States History: Beginning of the New Nation—Nationalism and Growth) in the first two presidential elections, he served as Washington's Vice President. In 1796, after Washington's retirement, Adams, a Federalist, was elected President in the first election that involved political parties.

Adams's term in office was stormy. He was often at odds with the lawyer and statesman Alexander Hamilton (*see* Hamilton, Vol 2, United States History: Beginning of the New Nation—Nationalism and Growth) and other Federalists who wanted the federal government to take more control of the affairs of the new nation. They were especially hostile after Adams, who was pro-British and strongly opposed to France at the time, refused to declare war on France for the French seizure of American ships in the European war against Napoleonic France. His action helped prevent a real war between France and the United States. Adams's refusal to wholeheartedly endorse the Alien and Sedition Acts passed in 1798 by the Federalists in Congress further angered many of his contemporaries. Although the reason given for the passage of the acts was that they were needed to curb possible French intrigues against the new nation, their true purpose was to keep opponents from criticizing the Federalist government and to keep French émigrés from joining the Democratic-Republican party in the near future.

Adams lost the election of 1800 to the Democratic-Republican candidate Thomas Jefferson (*see* Jefferson, Vol. 2, United States History: Beginning of the New Nation—Nationalism and Growth) and retired to Quincy. Although unpopular, Adams had saved the new nation from involvement in a costly European war, which had allowed it to continue to grow and develop.

BOOKS BY JOHN ADAMS

The Book of Abigail and John: Selected Letters of the Adams Family (1762–1784). (coauthored with Abigail Adams) Lyman Butterfield, *et al* (eds). Harvard Univ Pr 1975 $8.95. ISBN 0-674-07854-3

Familiar Letters of John Adams and His Wife Abigail Adams, During the Revolution. Select Bibliographies Repr Ser. (coauthored with Abigail Adams) Ayer (repr of 1875 ed) $22.00. ISBN 0-8369-5318-5

Political Writings of John Adams. Macmillan 1954 $7.87. ISBN 0-672-60010-2

The Works of John Adams, 1704–1740 (1709). 10 vols. Reprint Services 1987 $800.00. ISBN 0-404-00310-9

BOOKS ABOUT JOHN ADAMS

Dwyer, Frank (ed). *John Adams. World Leaders—Past and Present Ser.* Chelsea 1988 $17.95. ISBN 1-55546-801-2 Explains the social, religious, and political climate of Adams's time and describes the personal and historical events that shaped his life.

*Fredman, Lionel E., and Gerald Kurland. *John Adams: American Revolutionary Leader and

President. Outstanding Personalities Ser. SamHar 1973 $3.95. ISBN 0-87157-565-5 Straightforward biography; includes important dates.

Stefoff, Rebecca. *John Adams: Second President of the United States. Presidents of the United States Ser.* Garrett Ed 1988 $12.95. ISBN 0-944483-10-0 Biography that focuses on Adams's childhood, education, employment, and political career.

ADAMS, JOHN QUINCY 1767–1848

John Quincy Adams was the only child of a U.S. President to become President himself. Always a serious and studious child growing up in Braintree, Massachusetts, John Quincy started his public life at a young age. At age 14 he became private secretary to the United States envoy to Russia. After three years, he came home to attend Harvard College and become a lawyer.

Soon, public life pursued him again. He had spent seven years in Europe with his father, John Adams (*see* J. Adams, Vol. 2, United States History: Beginning of the New Nation—Nationalism and Growth) meeting the famous people of the times and recording his reactions in a diary. Then his father, now President Adams, appointed him Minister to Holland and later to Prussia. Upon his return he served in the Massachusetts Senate and then in the United States Senate. As Secretary of State under President James Monroe (*see* Monroe, Vol. 2, United States History: Beginning of the New Nation—Nationalism and Growth), he helped draft the famous Monroe Doctrine of 1823, which stated the U.S. policy of opposition to outside interference in the Americas.

In 1824 the United States had fallen into the rivalry based on local special interests known as sectionalism, and Adams became the presidential candidate popular with people in the North. When no candidate received a majority of

John Quincy Adams. Painting by John Sully (1824).
Courtesy of Culver Pictures, Inc.

the electoral vote, the House of Representatives had to choose the next president. Adams was chosen over Henry Clay of Kentucky (*see* Clay, Vol. 2, United States History: The Age of Jackson) and Andrew Jackson of Tennessee. (*See* Jackson, Vol. 2, United States History: The Age of Jackson.) When Adams named Henry Clay as Secretary of State, Jackson, claiming that a "corrupt bargain" had been made between Adams and Clay, set out to defeat Adams. In the presidential election of 1828, Jackson finally succeeded.

As President, Adams pursued a policy of internal improvements, believing the federal government should support the building of roads and canals to unite the country. He also favored the creation of a national university. When he left the White House, he surprised many people by going back to Congress. Until his death in 1848, he worked in the House of Representatives to uphold free speech and the right of petition and to oppose southern slavery interests.

BOOKS BY JOHN QUINCY ADAMS

The Diary of John Quincy Adams: 1794–1845. Allan Nevins (ed). *American Classics Ser.* Ungar 1969. (o.p.) $30.00.
Memoirs of John Quincy Adams, Comprising Portions of His Diary from 1795–1848. Select Bibliographies Repr Ser. Charles Francis Adams (ed). 12 vols. Ayer $470.00. ISBN 0-8369-5021-6
The Selected Writings of John and John Quincy Adams. Adrienne Koch and William Pedan (eds). AMS (repr of 1946 ed) $40.00. ISBN 0-404-20002-8
The Writings of John Quincy Adams. Worthington C. Ford (ed). 7 vols. Greenwood 1969 $180.00. ISBN 0-8371-9937-9

BOOKS ABOUT JOHN QUINCY ADAMS

*Dwyer, Frank. *John Quincy Adams. World Leaders—Past and Present Ser.* Chelsea 1989 $17.95. ISBN 1-55546-802-0 Explains the social, religious, and political climate of John Quincy Adams's time and describes the personal and historical events that shaped his life.
*Greenblatt, Miriam. *John Quincy Adams: Sixth President of the United States. Presidents of the United States Ser.* Garrett Ed 1990 $17.26. ISBN 0-944483-21-6 Informative biography of Adams written for preteen and teenage readers.

HAMILTON, ALEXANDER   1757–1804

The publication of the papers of Alexander Hamilton focuses attention on this interesting personality and influential founder of the United States. "No one did more for all Americans," wrote Dorothy Bobbe in the *New York Times.* The son of a Scots father and the daughter of a doctor-planter on Nevis in the West Indies, Hamilton came to the colonies in 1772 and studied for two years at King's College, now Columbia University. During the American Revolution, when he was only about 20 years old, he rose to the rank of lieutenant-colonel and became chief aide to the American commander in chief, George Washington. (*See* Washington, Vol. 2, United States History: Beginning of the New Nation—Nationalism and Growth.)

A lawyer in New York City, Hamilton represented New York at the Constitutional Convention, where he advocated setting up a strong central government. He made his greatest service to the new Constitution by contributing to *The Federalist,* the series of articles written during 1787 and 1788 to urge ratification of the Constitution.

Hamilton was appointed first Secretary of the Treasury by President George Washington. In that position he called for full funding of the national debt. This meant that people who had lent money to the country during the Revolutionary War would be repaid in full. He also proposed that the national government take over, or assume, the debts of the states. He suggested further the setting up of a national bank. All of these measures were designed to strengthen the central government. Finally, Hamilton issued a report on manufactures, which gave an early push to economic and industrial development in an economy that was still largely agricultural.

Hamilton was the leader of the Federalist party. The Federalists favored a strong central government, loose interpretation of the Constitution, the creation of a national bank, and supporting Britain over France in international disputes.

In 1804 Hamilton was challenged to a duel by opposing political leader Aaron Burr, who accused Hamilton of slandering him by calling him a "dangerous" man. The two met in Weehawken Heights, New Jersey, and Hamilton was killed in the duel. Because Hamilton was not a native-born American, he could never have been President, but he might have contributed years more of government service had he not been killed.

BOOKS BY HAMILTON

Collection of the Facts and Documents Relative to the Death of Major-General Alexander Hamilton. William Coleman (ed). *Select Bibliographies Reprint Ser.* Ayer (repr of 1904 ed) $27.50. ISBN 0-8369-5025-9

The Federalist Papers. (coauthored with James Madison and John Jay) Bantam 1982 $3.50. ISBN 0-553-21072-6

Industrial and Commercial Correspondence of Alexander Hamilton Anticipating His Report on Manufactures. Arthur H. Cole (ed). Kelly $39.50. ISBN 0-678-00421-8

The Works of Alexander Hamilton. 12 vols. Reprint Services 1987 $795.00. ISBN 0-317-60364-7

BOOKS ABOUT HAMILTON

Kurland, Gerald. *Alexander Hamilton: Architect of American Nationalism. Outstanding Personalities Ser.* SamHar 1972 $3.95. ISBN 0-87157-527-2 Brief, straightforward biographical sketch; includes important dates.

*O'Brien, Steve. *Alexander Hamilton. World Leaders—Past and Present Ser.* Chelsea 1989 $17.95. ISBN 1-55546-810-1 Explains the social, religious, and political climate of Hamilton's time, and describes the personal and historical events that shaped his life.

JEFFERSON, THOMAS   1743–1826

Thomas Jefferson, third President of the United States, was a man of many talents and interests. One of the most important founders of the United States, his service to his nation were enormous and enduring.

A man of outstanding curiosity, versatility, and eloquence, Jefferson was born in Virginia in 1743, his father a surveyor and planter and his mother from an important Virginia family. At a young age, he grew to love learning and began a life-long habit of pursuing avenues opened by his active curiosity. He became expert in the sciences, knew more than six languages, could play the violin, and invented dozens of useful items, including a revolving chair, a portable writing desk, and a clock that told the day of the week.

After graduating from William and Mary College in Williamsburg, Virginia, in 1762, Jefferson practiced law and was elected to the colonial legislature, the House of Burgesses. There he became inspired by the fiery speeches of revolutionary leader and orator Patrick Henry. Jefferson was not himself a powerful speaker, but he could write eloquently. As a member of the Continental Congress, he took up his pen for the cause of independence and drafted the Declaration of Independence, which sets forth the grievances and asserts the natural rights of the revolutionaries in flowing language and a pleasing style.

In the following years, Jefferson served as governor of Virginia, Minister to France, the first Secretary of State, and the second Vice President. He became the head of one of America's first two political parties—the Republicans, the forerunner of today's Democrats. Then, in 1800, he was elected President. During his presidency, Jefferson managed to keep the country out of war, although both France and England were harassing American ships at sea. However, he did send a naval squadron to end the abuse of American shipping in the Mediterranean by the Barbary pirates, adventurers from the Barbary States of North Africa who plundered commercial ships that sailed the Mediterranean.

One of Jefferson's greatest accomplishments was the purchase of Louisiana from France in 1803, thus doubling the size of the nation. He sent an expedition under Meriwether Lewis and William Clark to the new territory to learn about its wildlife, geographic features, and the Native Americans who lived there. (*See* Lewis and Clark, Vol. 2, United States History: Beginning of the New Nation—Nationalism and Growth.)

After completing his term in office, Jefferson returned to his beloved home, Monticello, in Virginia. There he devoted himself to the creation of the University of Virginia, whose buildings he designed. The university opened in 1825, with 40 students.

Throughout his career, Thomas Jefferson worked according to certain principles. He believed in a democracy where voters were educated and farmers played a key role, where states had important rights that superseded those of the nation. He favored strict interpretation of the Constitution and therefore opposed the creation of the Bank of the United States. He also favored religious toleration, an idea he saw embodied in a Virginia law that stated, "no man shall be compelled to frequent or support any religious worship, place, or ministry whatsoever." Jefferson lived into his eighties and died on July 4, 1826—fifty years after the signing of the Declaration of Independence.

BOOKS BY JEFFERSON

Complete Annals of Thomas Jefferson. Franklin R. Sawvel (ed). *American Public Figures Ser.* Da Capo 1970 $37.50. ISBN 0-306-71311-X

Complete Jefferson. Saul K. Padover (ed). *Select Biographies Repr Ser.* Ayer (repr of 1943 ed) $75.00. ISBN 0-8369-5027-5

Democracy. Saul K. Padover (ed). Greenwood 1970 $22.50. ISBN 0-8371-1985-5

Life and Selected Writings. Modern Lib 1978 $10.95. ISBN 0-394-60454-7

The Portable Thomas Jefferson. Merrill D. Peterson (ed). Penguin 1977 $7.95. ISBN 0-14-015080-3

Public and Private Papers. Random 1989 $8.50. ISBN 0-679-72536-9

BOOKS ABOUT JEFFERSON

Bober, Natalie. *Thomas Jefferson: Man on a Mountain.* Macmillan 1988 $14.95. ISBN 0-689-31154-0 Focuses on Jefferson's human side, his years in France, and his personal relationships.

Morgan, Edmund S. *The Meaning of Independence: John Adams, George Washington, Thomas Jefferson.* Univ of Virginia Pr 1979 $10.00. ISBN 0-8139-0694-6 Examines Jefferson's journals and letters in order to find out what independence meant to him and, therefore, what independence meant to original Americans.

*Smith, Kathie. *Thomas Jefferson. Great Americans Ser.* Jane Steltenpohl (ed). Messner 1989

$7.98. ISBN 0-671-67512-5 Follows Jefferson's life from childhood to adulthood; focuses on details interesting to young people and thoroughly examines the impact on today's world.

Stefoff, Rebecca. *Thomas Jefferson: Third President of the United States. Presidents of the United States Ser.* Garrett Ed 1988 $12.95. ISBN 0-944483-07-0 Examines Jefferson's life before politics and the domestic and foreign issues of his career.

LEWIS, MERIWETHER 1774–1809 AND CLARK, WILLIAM 1770–1838

In 1803 U.S. President Thomas Jefferson (*see* Jefferson, Vol. 2, United States History: Beginning of the New Nation—Nationalism and Growth) authorized the purchase of the Louisiana Territory from France for about $15 million. The vast territory west of the Mississippi River more than doubled the size of the United States.

Wanting to learn more about the Louisiana Territory, Jefferson chose Meriwether Lewis, his private secretary, and ex-army officer William Clark to head an expedition into the region. He instructed them to draw maps of the lands they passed, to keep records of plants and animals they saw, to make contact with local groups of Native Americans, and to chart the resources of the area. They were also to learn whether there was a water route to the West—a Northwest Passage.

The Lewis and Clark expedition set out from Missouri in 1804, with about 30 soldiers and 10 civilians. It traveled up the Missouri River and spent the winter in a Mandan village. The following spring the expedition traveled west across the Rocky Mountains, then down the Snake and Columbia rivers to the Pacific Ocean. The expedition was aided by a young Shoshone woman, Sacajawea, who served as interpreter and guide.

Lewis and Clark returned to Missouri in 1806. They had learned that there was no Northwest Passage. Their expedition, however, provided invaluable information about the vast lands west of the Mississippi River.

BOOKS BY LEWIS AND CLARK

Atlas of the Lewis and Clark Expedition. Journals of the Lewis and Clark Expedition Ser. Gary E. Mouton (ed). Univ of Nebraska Pr 1983 $100.00. ISBN 0-8032-2861-9

History of the Expedition Under the Command of Lewis and Clark (1814). Elliott Coues (ed). 3 vols. Peter Smith $46.50. ISBN 0-8446-2468-3

Journals of Lewis and Clark: A New Selection. John Bakeless (ed). NAL 1964 $4.95. ISBN 0-451-62670-2

Letters of the Lewis and Clark Expedition, with Related Documents, 1783–1854. Donald Jackson (ed). 2 vols. Univ of Illinois Pr 1978 $49.95. ISBN 0-252-00697-6

BOOKS ABOUT LEWIS AND CLARK

Bohner, Charles. *Bold Journey: West with Lewis and Clark.* Houghton 1985 $11.95. ISBN 0-395-36691-7 Fictional account of a young man on the famous expedition of Lewis and Clark.

Cutright, Paul R. *Lewis and Clark: Pioneering Naturalists.* Univ of Nebraska Pr 1989 $14.95. ISBN 0-8032-6334-1 Comprehensive account of the scientific studies of Lewis and Clark.

Holloway, David. *Lewis and Clark and the Crossing of North America.* Saturday Review 1974. ISBN 0-8415-0259-5 Readable account of Lewis and Clark's expedition to explore the Louisiana Purchase.

*McGrath, Patrick. *The Lewis and Clark Expedition. Turning Points in American History Ser.* Silver 1989 $7.95. ISBN 0-382-09899-4 Good introduction to the expedition of Lewis and Clark and its importance.

Ronda, James P. *Lewis and Clark Among the Indians.* Univ of Nebraska Pr 1988 $8.95. ISBN 0-8032-8929-4 Focuses on the modern concern of understanding both the Indian's and the white man's points of view; drawn from journals and other narratives.

MADISON, JAMES   1751–1836

The fourth President of the United States, Virginia-born James Madison played a key role in the writing of the Constitution. Known as the "Father of the Constitution," his journals provide the main source of information about the Constitutional Convention of 1787. After the convention he contributed to *The Federalist,* a series of articles written during 1787 and 1788 explaining and supporting ratification of the Constitution. Later, as a member of Congress, he proposed the first ten amendments to the Constitution—the Bill of Rights—which were added to the Constitution on December 15, 1791.

A friend and supporter of Thomas Jefferson (*see* Jefferson, Vol. 2, United States History: Beginning of the Nation—Nationalism and Growth), Jefferson named Madison Secretary of State in 1801. In 1808 he was elected President in his own right, a office he held until 1817. While President, Madison had to settle a conflict that had been brewing between France and Great Britain and had finally come to a head. With the urging of the War Hawks, congressmen mostly from the South and the West who strongly supported nationalism and expansion, Madison finally asked Congress to declare war against Great Britain. One of the main complaints against the British was that they had been seizing American sailors from ships and forcing them to work on British naval ships. However, the French had also been abusing American freedom of the seas. The result was the inconclusive War of 1812, which New Englanders called "Mr. Madison's War." It ended two years later—but not before Washington, D.C., had been burned. The war led to a decline in the Federalist party, which had opposed the war, and to a surge in nationalism.

In 1817 Madison and his wife Dolly retired to Montpelier, their home in Virginia, where Madison served as rector of the University of Virginia. He also worked actively against the forces of states' rights, writing, "The advice nearest to my heart and deepest in my convictions is that the Union of the States be cherished and perpetuated."

BOOKS BY MADISON

Calendar of the Correspondence of James Madison. Bibliography and Reference Ser. Burt Franklin 1970 $51.50. ISBN 0-8337-2179-8

The Complete Madison: His Basic Writings. Saul K. Padover (ed). Kraus (repr of 1953 ed) $48.00. ISBN 0-527-60300-7

Journal of the Federal Convention. E. H. Scott (ed). *Select Bibliography and Reference Ser.* Ayer (repr of 1893 ed) $33.00. ISBN 0-8369-5381-9

Notes of Debates in the Federal Convention of 1787. Norton 1987 $14.70. ISBN 0-393-30405-1

The Virginia Report of 1799–1800, Touching the Alien and Sedition Laws. Civil Liberties in American History Ser. Da Capo 1970 $35.00. ISBN 0-306-71860-X

BOOKS ABOUT MADISON

*Elliot, I. (ed). *James Madison, 1751–1836: Chronology, Documents, Bibliographical Aids. Presidential Chronology Ser.* Oceana 1969 $8.00. ISBN 0-379-12068-2 Presents facts rather than opinions; good starting point for any student researcher.

*Leavell, Perry. *James Madison. World Leaders—Past and Present Ser.* Chelsea 1988 $17.95. ISBN 1-55546-815-2 Illustrated biography of Madison that examines both his personal life and historical events; especially suited to younger readers.

MONROE, JAMES 1758–1831

The fifth President of the United States, James Monroe was born in Westmoreland County, Virginia. He began his long and distinguished career of service to the United States when he was still in his teens. He left the College of William and Mary in 1776 to serve in the Continental Army. Taking part in several battles, he fought in the Battle of Trenton, where he was wounded. In 1780 he began to study law under the patriot Thomas Jefferson. (*See* Jefferson, Vol. 2, United States History: Beginning of the New Nation—Nationalism and Growth.) He studied with Jefferson for several years, during which time they became close friends. The friendship served as a foundation for Madison's eventual career in politics.

Although Monroe served in the Continental Congress, he was not a delegate to the Constitutional Convention, nor did he support ratification of the Constitution. Once it was ratified, however, he served as senator from Virginia and became a strong opponent of the Federalists, including George Washington (*see* Washington, Vol. 2, United States History: Beginning of the New Nation—Nationalism and Growth) and his Secretary of the Treasury Alexander Hamilton (*see* Hamilton, Vol. 2, United States History: Beginning of the New Nation—Nationalism and Growth), and a strong supporter of Jefferson and the Democratic-Republicans, the party that opposed the Federalists. Before Monroe was elected to the presidency (1817–1825), he served as governor of Virginia and held the cabinet posts of secretary of state and secretary of war under James Madison. (*See* Madison, Vol. 2, United States History: Beginning of the New Nation—Nationalism and Growth.)

During Monroe's presidency, which was often called the Era of Good Feelings, the young republic expanded. In 1818 General Andrew Jackson invaded Spanish Florida; in 1819 the cast-iron plow was patented; in 1822, Stephen Austin began his colony in Texas; and in 1823 the United States issued the Monroe Doctrine, warning European nations not to try to colonize any part of North or South America in the future. It was also during Monroe's presidency that slavery and expansion made necessary the Missouri Compromise (1820) and divided the nation into "slave" and "free" states, starting a series of events that eventually led to the Civil War.

When his presidency was over, Monroe retired to his estate in Virginia. In 1829, presiding over the Virginia constitutional convention, he gave his support to the conservatives on the controversial issues of slavery and suffrage. He died in 1831 while visiting New York.

BOOKS BY MONROE

The People, the Sovereigns. James River 1987 $19.95. ISBN 0-940973-02-2
Writings. Stanislaus M. Hamilton (ed). 7 vols. AMS (repr of 1903 ed) $270.00. ISBN 0-404-04400-X

BOOKS ABOUT MONROE

*Stefoff, Rebecca. *James Monroe: Fifth President of the United States. Presidents of the United States Ser.* Garrett Ed 1988 $12.95. ISBN 0-944483-11-9 Looks at Monroe's early life, career, and contributions.
*Wetzel, Charles. *James Monroe. World Leaders—Past and Present Ser.* Chelsea 1989 $17.95. ISBN 1-55546-817-9 Detailed account of Monroe's life complete with illustrations.

WASHINGTON, GEORGE   1732–1799

When George Washington stood on the steps of Federal Hall in New York City in 1787, he took the oath of office to become the first President of the United States. He later observed, "I walk on untrodden ground. There is scarcely any part of my conduct that may not hereafter be drawn into precedent."

Born into a wealthy Virginia family, Washington was made a major in charge of training the militia in his quarter at the age of 20. From there he traveled a long road to the steps of Federal Hall. In his "travels," he had worked as a surveyor, fought in the early battles of the French and Indian War, led the troops of the Continental Army to victory against Great Britain in the Revolutionary War, and been instrumental in the creation of the Constitution of the United States.

The only person ever elected President of the United States unanimously, Washington appointed the first Cabinet and set the style for the relationship between Congress and the President. Although he disapproved of political parties, he was unable to prevent their development. The first two political parties, the Democratic-Republicans and the Federalists, began to form during his presidency.

Washington also believed the United States should avoid long-term alliances with other nations. In this he was more successful, managing to keep the young nation neutral in a growing conflict between France and Great Britain.

Throughout his career, Washington longed for the day when he would be able to return with his wife Martha to their home at Mount Vernon in Virginia. Finally, when he retired from the presidency, they settled in Mount Vernon. Unfortunately, Washington died less than three years later. Americans mourned him, believing that, without George Washington, the American Revolution and the new nation could not have succeeded.

BOOKS BY WASHINGTON

Diaries, 1748–1799. 4 vols. John C. Fitzpatrick (ed). Kraus (repr of 1925 ed) $88.00. ISBN 0-527-94600-1

The Journal of Major George Washington, Sent by the Hon. Robert Dinwiddie to the Commandant of the French Forces, 1754. Territ Pr 1989 $4.50.

Journal of the Proceedings of the President: 1793–1797. Dorothy Twohig (ed). Univ of Virginia Pr 1981 $37.50. ISBN 0-8139-0874-4

Writings from the Original Manuscript Sources, 1754–1799. John C. Fitzpatrick (ed). 39 vols. Greenwood 1968. (o.p.)

BOOKS ABOUT WASHINGTON

Cunliffe, Marcus. *George Washington: Man and Monument.* NAL 1989 $4.95. ISBN 0-451-62461-0 Illuminating biography that skillfully separates myth from reality as it traces the ancestral background, childhood, growth, failures, and achievements of a great American.

*Davidson, Margaret. *The Adventures of George Washington.* Scholastic 1989 $2.50. ISBN 0-590-41814-9 Well-researched introduction to Washington's life.

Flexner, James T. *Washington: The Indispensable Man.* NAL 1984 $4.95. ISBN 0-451-15643-9 Depicts Washington from the rashness of youth to the infirmities of old age.

*Hilton, Suzanne. *The World of Young George Washington.* Walker 1987 $12.95. ISBN 0-8027-6657-9 Account of Washington's early life and career.

*Meltzer, Milton. *George Washington and the Birth of Our Nation.* Watts 1986 $13.90. ISBN

0-531-10253-X Introductory account of Washington's role in the formation of the new nation.

• Nordham, George W. *The Age of Washington: George Washington's Presidency, 1789–1797.* Adams Pr 1989 $24.95. Revealing picture of the first president, with concentration on his two terms in office.

THE AGE OF JACKSON

*Bealer, Alex. *Only the Names Remain: The Cherokees and the Trail of Tears.* Little 1972 $14.95. ISBN 0-316-08520-0 Illustrated account of the forced removal of the Cherokees from Georgia and their 1,000-mile journey west.

Bugg, James L., Jr., and Peter Stewart. *Jacksonian Democracy.* Univ Pr of America 1986 $12.75. ISBN 0-8191-5404-0

Current, Richard N. *Daniel Webster and the Rise of National Conservatism.* Scott 1962. ISBN 0-673-39331-3

Dalzell, Robert F., Jr. *Daniel Webster and the Trial of American Nationalism, 1843–1852.* Norton 1975 $4.95. ISBN 0-393-00782-0

*Fleishman, Glen. *Cherokee Removal, 1838: An Entire Nation Is Forced Out of Its Homeland.* Watts 1971. (o.p.) Deals with the forced removal of the Cherokees from Georgia; good introduction to the topic.

*Remini, Robert V. *The Revolutionary Age of Andrew Jackson.* Harper 1985 $5.95. ISBN 0-06-091290-1 Interesting description of the political changes that took place during the Age of Jackson.

Schlesinger, Arthur M., Jr. *The Age of Jackson.* Little 1988 $10.95. ISBN 0-316-77343-3

Tocqueville, Alexis de. *Democracy in America.* American Past Ser. Phillips Bradley (ed). 2 vols. Random 1990. Vol. 1 $8.95. ISBN 0-679-72825-2. Vol. 2 $8.95. ISBN 0-679-72826-0

Van Deusen, Glyndon G. *Jacksonian Era: Eighteen Twenty-Eight to Eighteen Forty-Eight.* New American Nation Ser. Harper $8.95. ISBN 0-06-133028-0

CALHOUN, JOHN CALDWELL   1782–1850

During the early 1800s new young leaders came to power in national government. Among these was frontier-born, Yale University graduate John C. Calhoun of South Carolina. Entering the House of Representatives in 1811, Calhoun became the principal defender of slavery and the doctrine of states' rights.

Calhoun held numerous posts in public life, including Congressman from 1811 to 1817, Secretary of War under President James Monroe (*see* Monroe, Vol. 2, United States History: Beginning of the New Nation—Nationalism and Growth), Vice President from 1825 to 1832 under John Quincy Adams (*see* J. Q. Adams, Vol. 2, United States History: Beginning of the New Nation—Nationalism and Growth) and Andrew Jackson (*see* Jackson, Vol. 2, United States History: The Age of Jackson), and U.S. Senator from 1832 to 1843 and again from 1845 to 1850. In 1844 and 1845, Calhoun served as Secretary of State under President John Tyler and arranged for the annexation of Texas as a slave state.

Calhoun quarreled with President Jackson over the issue of states' rights. While Jackson held that the national government had to be supreme, Calhoun argued that a state could undo, or nullify, a federal law. In response to the high tariff passed in 1832, Calhoun led South Carolina in its passage of the Ordinance of Nullification. The Ordinance threatened that if the tariff were enforced in South Carolina, the state would leave, or secede, from the Union. The dispute was eventually settled through passage of a compromise tariff, but the issue of states' rights and secession did not go away.

BOOKS BY CALHOUN

Calhoun: Basic Documents. John M. Anderson (ed). Penn State Univ Pr. (o.p) $24.95.
A Disquisition on Government. Peter Smith 1958 $11.25. ISBN 0-8446-1099-2
Works of John C. Calhoun. Richard K. Cralle (ed). 6 vols. Russell 1968. (o.p.)

BOOKS ABOUT CALHOUN

Lindsey, David. *Jackson and Calhoun.* Kenneth Colegrove (ed). *Shapers of History Ser.* Barron 1973 $6.95. ISBN 0-8120-0460-4 Penetrating study of two dynamic but opposing forces in early nineteenth-century American politics.

Peterson, Merril D. *The Great Triumvirate: Webster, Clay, and Calhoun.* Oxford Univ Pr 1988 $12.95. ISBN 0-19-505686-8 Describes the interrelationships among the three most prominent statesmen in the early nineteenth century.

*Von Holst, Hermann E. *John C. Calhoun. American Statesmen Ser.* Chelsea 1980 $5.95. ISBN 0-87754-185-X Introductory biography of a major states' rights advocate.

CLAY, HENRY   1777–1852

Henry Clay, with statesman and orator Daniel Webster and statesman and political philosopher John Calhoun (*see* Webster *and* Calhoun, Vol. 2, United States History: The Age of Jackson), dominated the United States Senate for decades and is generally considered one of the most important people to have served in the Senate in the nation's history. As a speaker of the House of Representatives, as Senator, as Secretary of State under President John Quincy Adams (*see* J. Q. Adams, Vol. 2, United States History: Beginning of the New Nation—Nationalism and Growth), and as three-time candidate for the presidency, Henry Clay was rarely, if ever, far from the center of the stage in U.S. politics.

Born in Vermont, Clay had only three years of formal schooling. In 1792 he obtained a clerk's position in the Virginia court. Seven years later, he moved to Kentucky and became licensed to practice law and quickly earned a reputation as a lawyer and an orator. A Democratic-Republican, he became the spokesman for the western states and an advocate of nationalism. He was one of the leading "War Hawks" who favored war with Great Britain in 1812. The War Hawks saw the war as a way of expanding the United States and driving "the British from our Continent."

Clay promoted the "American system," which would have used federal money to improve a nationwide transportation system, set up a national bank, and establish a high protective tariff. These measures were designed to help the nation as a whole, not just certain regional interests.

Clay became known as the "Great Compromiser" and "Great Pacificator" largely because he designed the Missouri Compromise in 1820, which temporarily saved the Union from splitting over the issue of the extension of slavery into the territories. In 1850, though aged and exhausted, he again helped prevent the Union's collapse by being instrumental in shaping the Compromise of 1850.

BOOKS BY CLAY

The Life and Speeches of the Hon. Henry Clay. (coauthored with Daniel Mallory) Ayer $47.00. ISBN 0-8369-6983-9

Private Correspondence of Henry Clay. Calvin Colton (ed). *Select Bibliographies Repr Ser.* Ayer (repr of 1855 ed) $35.50. ISBN 0-8369-5976-0

BOOKS ABOUT CLAY

Peterson, Merril D. *The Great Triumvirate: Webster, Clay, and Calhoun.* Oxford Univ Pr 1988 $12.95. ISBN 0-19-505686-8 Describes the interrelationships among the three most prominent statesmen in the early nineteenth century.

*Schurz, Carl. *Henry Clay. American Statesmen Ser.* Chelsea 1981 $10.95. ISBN 0-87754-180-9 Introductory biography of a major political figure of the first half of the 1800s.

JACKSON, ANDREW   1767–1845

Lawyer, judge, cotton planter, Indian fighter, senator, general, war hero, and seventh President of the United States, (1829–1837)—these were roles filled by Andrew Jackson during his varied public career.

Jackson, born in a settlement that straddled the border of North and South Carolina, was orphaned at age 14. He was a true southern gentleman, but his personal dignity and courtesy contrasted sharply with the public image manufactured during his political career. In an era when voting privileges were being extended, the common people adopted Jackson as their hero and thought of him as *their* President. They affectionately called him "Old Hickory," like the wood that is strong and unbending. Jackson never backed down from a fight or a cause in which he believed.

The very characteristic that brought Jackson affection, however, also brought him many vocal opponents. When South Carolina, led by the politician John Calhoun (*see* Calhoun, Vol. 2, United States History: The Age of Jackson), threatened nullification of, or refusal to enforce, a tariff law and secession from the Union over high tariffs, Jackson was ready to use force in support of the Union. However, cooler heads worked for a compromise tariff law, and peace prevailed. Jackson also stood firm against the Bank of the United States and vetoed the renewal of the bank's charter. Like many westerners, Jackson did not trust or like the banks and thought that paper money was of no value. When he further insisted that western lands be bought with specie, gold and silver coins, rather than unbacked currency, Jackson's opponents blasted him as a hot-tempered demagogue, dictator, and rabble-rouser.

A former Indian fighter on the frontier, Jackson advocated harsh policies toward the Indians of the Southeast. Under him, the Indian Removal Act of 1830 was passed, which set up Indian resettlement west of the Mississippi River. This affected many Indian nations, including the Cherokee in Georgia. In 1838 they were rounded up and marched to the Indian Territory, in what is now Oklahoma, to free the land for white settlement. Their 1,000 mile trek, on which more than 4,000 died, became known as the "Trail of Tears" because they had to stop every few miles to bury their dead.

After leaving the White House, Jackson retired to the Hermitage, his home near Nashville, Tennessee—now preserved as a national landmark. Jackson was probably the greatest popular hero of his time. He has been viewed by many as the symbol of the democratic feelings of the time—a time of Jacksonian democracy.

BOOK BY JACKSON

Narrative and Writings of Andrew Jackson of Kentucky. Ayer (repr of 1847 ed) $10.75. ISBN 0-8369-8609-1

BOOKS ABOUT JACKSON

Hilton, Suzanne. *The World of Young Andrew Jackson. Young Presidents Ser.* Walker 1988 $12.95. ISBN 0-8027-6814-8 Discusses Jackson's transition from scrappy country boy to the first frontier President, and views the early American colonies and sprawling settlements of his time.

Sabin, Lou. *Andrew Jackson, Frontier Patriot.* Troll 1985 $2.50. ISBN 0-8167-0548-8 Focuses on Jackson's simple background and the courage, devotion, and intelligence that brought greatness to the United States.

*Stefoff, Rebecca. *Andrew Jackson: Seventh President of the United States. Presidents of the United States Ser.* Garrett Ed 1988 $12.95. ISBN 0-944483-08-9 Looks at Jackson's early life, career, and contributions.

*Sumner, William G. *Andrew Jackson. American Statesmen Ser.* Chelsea 1981 $6.95. ISBN 0-87754-176-0 Introductory biography of the seventh President.

WEBSTER, DANIEL   1782–1852

Daniel Webster was born in Franklin, New Hampshire, graduated from Dartmouth College in 1801, and became a lawyer four years later. In 1816 he moved to Boston where he practiced law and represented Massachusetts in the House of Representatives, vigorously championing his state's mercantile and shipping interests.

Elected to the United States Senate in 1828, Webster became the country's best-known orator. He spoke out strongly for the importance of the Union over the rights of individual states. In one of his most famous speeches, he declared that no state had the right to nullify, or put an end to, a law. If they could, he said, the Union would become a mere "rope of sand." Finally, he thundered, "Liberty *and* Union, now and forever, one and inseparable!"

Webster favored the Compromise of 1850 and helped secure its passage. At the time, the danger of civil war seemed very real, with the nation badly split between the states that favored slavery and its extension into the territories and those that opposed it. The Compromise of 1850, a series of laws that tried to appease the two sides, provided for California to enter the Union as a free state, but for other territories in the southwest to allow slavery or not according to the wishes of the people who lived there. It also provided that the slave trade be ended in Washington, D.C., and that new, harsher penalties be given to escaped slaves and people who helped them. Webster favored this compromise, believing that preserving the Union was of higher importance than any other consideration.

BOOKS BY WEBSTER

Webster and Hayne's Speeches in the United States Senate. (coauthored with Robert Y. Hayne) Ayer (repr of 1850 ed) $12.75. ISBN 0-8369-8955-4

The Writings and Speeches of Daniel Webster. J. W. McIntyre (ed). 18 vols. AMS (repr of 1903 ed) $392.00. ISBN 0-404-11950-6

BOOKS ABOUT WEBSTER

Baxter, Maurice G. *Daniel Webster and the Supreme Court.* Univ of Massachusetts Pr 1966 $25.00. ISBN 0-87023-008 Discusses Daniel Webster's cases before the Supreme Court in the early nineteenth century.

Peterson, Merril D. *The Great Triumvirate: Webster, Clay, and Calhoun.* Oxford Univ Pr 1988 $12.95. ISBN 0-19-505686-8 Describes the interrelationships among the three most prominent statesmen in the early nineteenth century.

Sterling, John C. *Daniel Webster and a Small College.* Univ Pr of New England 1965 $15.00. ISBN 0-87451-038-4 Collection of source documents written about Daniel Webster by some of his contemporaries; also includes commentary on each document by modern historians.

REFORM AND EXPANSION

Abernethy, Thomas P. *From Frontier to Plantation in Tennessee: A Study in Frontier Democracy.* Greenwood 1979 $35.00. ISBN 0-313-21124-8

American Heritage Illustrated History of the United States. Vol. 7: The War with Mexico. Choice Pub 1988 $3.49. ISBN 0-945260-07-5 Illustrated account of the troubles with Mexico that led to the forming of the Republic of Texas; especially suited to younger readers.

Bartlett, Richard A. *The New Country: A Social History of the American Frontier, 1776–1890.* Oxford Univ Pr 1976 $12.95. ISBN 0-19-502021-9

Billington, Ray A., and Martin Ridge. *Westward Expansion.* Macmillan 1982. ISBN 0-02-309860-0

*Blos, Joan. *A Gathering of Days: A New England Girl's Journal, 1830–1832.* Macmillan 1982 $3.95. ISBN 0-689-70750-9 Teenage girl's life on a New Hampshire farm.

Blumberg, Rhoda. *The Great American Gold Rush.* Bradbury Pr 1989 $16.59. ISBN 0-02-711681-6

Cochran, Thomas C. *Frontiers of Change: Early Industrialization in America.* Oxford Univ Pr 1981 $10.95. ISBN 0-19-503284-5

*Cremin, Lawrence. *American Education: The National Experience, 1783–1896.* Harper 1980 $34.50. ISBN 0-06-010912-2 Relates the efforts to make education available to the general public.

Crockett, David. *Narrative of the Life of David Crockett of the State of Tennessee.* Univ of Nebraska Pr 1987 $6.95. ISBN 0-8032-6325-2

Cunningham, Hugh. *Leisure in the Industrial Revolution, Seventeen Eighty to Eighteen Eighty.* St. Martin's 1980 $26.00. ISBN 0-312-47894-1

Eckert, Allan W. *The Court Martial of Daniel Boone.* Bantam 1987 $3.50. ISBN 0-553-26283-1

Fehrenbacher, Don E. *Manifest Destiny and the Coming of the Civil War, 1840–1861.* Goldentree Bibliographies in American History Ser. Harlan Davidson 1970 $6.95. ISBN 0-88295-512-8

Fish, Carl R. *The Rise of the Common Man: Eighteen Thirty to Eighteen Fifty.* Greenwood 1983 $48.50. ISBN 0-313-20465-5

Fremont, John Charles. *The Expeditions of John Charles Fremont.* 3 vols. Univ of Illinois Pr Vol. 1 *Travels from 1838 to 1844. Map and Portfolio.* 1970 $49.95. ISBN 0-252-00086-2. Vol. 2 *The Bear Flag Revolt and the Court Martial.* 1973 $32.50. ISBN 0-252-00249-0. Vol. 3 *Travels from 1848–1854.* 1984 $42.50. ISBN 0-252-00416-7

Fremont, John Charles. *The Exploring Expedition to the Rocky Mountains. Exploring the American West Ser.* Smithsonian 1988 $14.95. ISBN 0-87474-439-3

*Garrett, Elisabeth D. *At Home: The American Family.* Abrams 1990 $49.50. ISBN 0-8109-1894-3 Focuses on keeping house and taking care of the family in early America.

*Giblin, James C. *Fireworks, Picnics, and Flags: The Story of the Fourth of July Symbols.* Ticknor 1983 $4.95. ISBN 0-89919-174-6 Events, symbols, and celebrations surrounding the signing of the Declaration of Independence; illustrated.

*Griffith, Elisabeth. *In Her Own Right: The Life of Elizabeth Cady Stanton.* Oxford Univ Pr 1985 $10.95. ISBN 0-19-503729-4 Biography of the famous advocate of women's rights of the 1800s.

*Gúrko, Miriam. *The Ladies of Seneca Falls: The Birth of the Woman's Rights Movement. Studies in the Life of Women.* Schocken 1976 $8.95. ISBN 0-8052-0545-4 History of the early women's rights movement; highlights on notable persons.

*Jensen, Joan M., and Gloria Ricci Lothrop. *California Women: A History. Golden State Ser.* MTL 1987 $7.50. ISBN 0-87835-156-6 Account of the settling of California from the viewpoint of women who were there.

Josephy, Alvin M. *The Nez Percé Indians and the Opening of the Northwest.* Univ of Nebraska Pr 1979 $14.95. ISBN 0-8032-7551-X

Lerner, Gerda. *The Grimké Sisters from South Carolina: Pioneers for Women's Rights and Abolition.* Schocken 1967 $7.95. ISBN 0-8052-0321-4

Lutz, Alma. *Emma Willard: Pioneer Educator of American Women.* Greenwood 1984 $35.00. ISBN 0-313-24254-2

*Magoffin, Susan. *Down the Sante Fe Trail and into Mexico: The Diary of Susan Shelby Magoffin, 1846–1847.* Stella M. Drumm (ed). Univ of Nebraska Pr 1982 $6.95. ISBN 0-8032-8116-1 Diary of a woman settler.

Merk, Frederick, and Lois B. Merk. *Manifest Destiny and Mission in American History: A Reinterpretation.* Greenwood 1983 $38.50. ISBN 0-313-23844-8

*Nevin, David. *Mexican War. Old West Ser.* Silver 1978 $19.94. ISBN 0-8094-2302-2 Details the war for Texas between Mexico and the United States.

North, Douglass C. *Economic Growth of the United States, 1790–1860.* Norton 1966 $8.95. ISBN 0-393-00346-9

*O'Dell, Scott. *Carlotta.* Dell 1989 $2.95. ISBN 0-440-90928-7 The events of the Mexican War, as seen through the eyes of a teenage girl.

*O'Dell, Scott. *Sing Down the Moon.* Dell 1976 $2.95. Story of the 1864 forced migration of the Navajo people as seen through the eyes of a young girl.

*Parkman, Francis. *Oregon Trail. Airmont Classics Ser.* Airmont 1964 $1.50. ISBN 0-8049-0037-X Account of the trip from Missouri to Oregon, 2,000 miles over prairie, rivers, and the Rocky Mountains.

Santos, Richard G. *Santa Anna's Campaign Against Texas, 1835–1836.* Documentary Pubns 1982 $24.95. ISBN 0-89712-107-4

*St. George, Judith. *The Amazing Voyage of the New Orleans.* Betterway Pubs 1989 $6.95. ISBN 1-55870-136-2 Describes a trip down the Ohio and Mississippi rivers by steamboat in 1811.

Trails West. National Geographic 1979 $7.95. ISBN 0-87044-272-4 Discussion of the various overland trails west and the hardships of pioneers traveling them.

Tucker, Barbara M. *Samuel Slater and the Origins of the American Textile Industry, 1790–1860.* Cornell Univ Pr 1984 $29.95. ISBN 0-8014-1594-2

*Twain, Mark. *Life on the Mississippi.* Penguin 1985 $4.95. ISBN 0-14-039050-2 Classic tale of early steamboat days on the Mississippi.

*Tyler, Alice F. *Freedom's Ferment: Phases of American Social History from the Revolution to the Outbreak of the Civil War.* Harper $8.95. ISBN 0-06-131074-3 Summary of major reform efforts from the time of the Revolutionary War to the onset of the Civil War.

*Wallace, Anthony. *The Growth of an American Village in the Early Industrial Revolution.* Knopf 1978. Study of the transformation of Pennsylvania textile towns in the early 1800s.

HOUSTON, SAMUEL   1793–1863

Frontier hero and statesman of Texas, Samuel Houston was born near Lexington, Virginia. Around 1806 he and his family moved to Tennessee. There he spent most of his younger years with the Cherokees, who later adopted him. Seriously wounded in battle against the Creek, he returned to Tennessee and in 1818 began to practice law. He also began his political life with his return to Tennessee, quickly becoming involved in Tennessee politics and holding many state offices.

In 1823 and again in 1825, Houston was elected as a Democrat to the U.S. Congress. In 1827 he became governor of Tennessee. But in 1829 the breakup of his marriage led him to resign from the governorship and rejoin the Cherokee in what is now Oklahoma, serving as a government post trader and as adviser.

In 1833 Houston moved to Texas and in 1836 served as a member of both the convention that set up a provisional government and the constitutional convention that declared Texas a republic. Becoming commander in chief of the Texan revolutionary troops, he played a waiting game until he was able to defeat decisively and capture the Mexican general Santa Anna at the Battle of

San Jacinto in 1836. Later that same year, he was elected the first president of the new republic of Texas, serving two separate terms (1836–1838, 1841–1844).

When Texas was admitted to the Union in 1845, Houston served as one of its first two U. S. senators, holding the post until 1859, when he was elected governor of Texas. He remained governor until 1861, when a Texas vote for secession in face of his staunch refusal to join the confederacy forced him from the governorship and into retirement.

BOOKS BY HOUSTON

The Autobiography of Sam Houston. Donald Day and Harry H. Ullom (eds). Greenwood 1980 $35.00. ISBN 0-313-22704-7
Life of General Sam Houston: A Short Autobiography. Jenkins 1964 $8.50.
The Writings of Sam Houston, 1813–1836. 8 vols. Jenkins $185.00 ISBN 0-685-13280-3

BOOKS ABOUT HOUSTON

Friend, Llerena. *Sam Houston: The Great Designer.* Univ of Texas Pr 1954 $11.95. ISBN 0-292-78422-8 Well-researched biography that traces Houston's life from birth to death; focuses on his years in Texas.
James, Marquis. *The Raven: A Biography of Sam Houston.* Univ of Texas Pr 1988 $10.95. ISBN 0-292-77040-5 Romanticized account of Houston's life; focuses on his early years.

MANN, HORACE   1796–1859

Horace Mann is often thought of as the founder of American public education because of his pioneering educational leadership. In 1837 he became the first Secretary of the Massachusetts State Board of Education.

Born to a poor family in Massachusetts, Mann received little formal education. He taught himself by reading at the town library, and at the age of 20 he gained admission to Brown University in Rhode Island. He graduated from Brown in 1819 with honors and went on to study and then practice law.

When Mann became head of the newly created Massachusetts Board of Education in 1837, he advocated free public education for both boys and girls. As public schools increased in number, there developed a need for more teachers, and Mann was instrumental in helping to organize teacher-education institutions and improving teacher training. He founded the first state normal schools, or teacher-training schools, in the United States.

Mann also worked to organize the local school districts into a statewide educational system and to end the common practice of physical punishment of students by their teachers. He worked tirelessly to get better school buildings and better textbooks. He explained, "If we do not prepare children to become good citizens, then our republic must go down to destruction as others have gone before it." By the 1850s most northern states had compulsory education laws, laws requiring children to attend school until they reached a certain age.

Mann remained as State Board of Education Secretary for 12 years. In 1853 he became the first president of Antioch College in Ohio, where he also taught philosophy and theology. Antioch became one of the first colleges in the nation to allow coeducation of men and women.

BOOKS BY MANN

Lectures on Education. American Education: Its Men, Institutions and Ideas Ser. Ayer 1969 $17.00. ISBN 0-405-01437-6
Slavery, Letters and Speeches. Anti-Slavery Crusade in America Ser. Ayer 1969 $24.50. ISBN 0-405-00643-8

BOOKS ABOUT MANN

Culver, Raymond B. *Horace Mann and Religion in the Massachusetts Public Schools. American Education: Its Men, Institutions and Ideas, Ser.* Ayer 1969 $17.00. ISBN 0-405-01406-6 Detailed account of the bitter conflicts over religious education during Mann's tenure as Secretary of the Massachusetts Board of Education from 1837 to 1848.

Mann, Mary. *Life of Horace Mann.* Ayer (repr of 1865 ed) $20.00. ISBN 0-8369-8624-5 Tribute to Horace Mann by his wife.

THE ARTS FROM 1760 TO 1875

Austin, William W. *Susanna, "Jeanie," and "The Old Folks at Home": The Songs of Stephen C. Foster from His Time to Ours. Music in American Life Ser.* Univ of Illinois Pr 1989 $14.95. ISBN 0-252-06069-5

Baigell, Matthew. *Thomas Cole.* Watson-Guptill 1985 $16.95. ISBN 0-8230-0648-4

Bode, Carl. *The Anatomy of American Popular Culture, 1840–1861.* Greenwood 1983 $38.50. ISBN 0-313-24005-1

Flexner, James T. *History of American Painting.* Vol. 2 *The Light of Distant Skies (1760–1835). Fine Art Ser.* Dover 1988 $8.95. ISBN 0-486-25708-8

Hitchcock, H. Wiley (ed). *The American Music Miscellany. Earlier American Music Ser.* Da Capo 1972 repr of 1798 ed $37.50. ISBN 0-306-77309-0

Sprigg, June. *Shaker: Masterworks of Utilitarian Design Created Between 1800 and 1875 by the Master Craftsmen and Craftswomen of America's Foremost Communal Religious Sect.* Katonah Gallery 1983 $10.00. ISBN 0-915171-00-7

Whitehall, Walter M. *Arts in Early American History. Institute of Early American History and Culture Ser.* Univ of North Carolina Pr 1965 $17.00. ISBN 0-8078-0940-3

AUDUBON, JOHN JAMES   1785–1851

An extraordinary painter of birds and animals of North America, John James Audubon was born in Haiti and spent his boyhood in France, where he developed his interest in birds and painting. At age 18, Audubon came to the United States to manage his father's farm. Throughout his life, however, his business interests suffered because of the time he spent searching out birds and perfecting his technique for drawing them in life-size, lifelike poses in natural habitats. Using a series of wires in his specimens, he shaped each model until he had the most natural of poses. To achieve his goal of drawing an example of every bird in North America, Audubon concentrated on painting just the birds, while other artists painted the plants, flowers, and other parts of the background.

Between 1820 and 1837, Audubon painted 1,065 life-size drawings of birds. For publication, the drawings were engraved on 435 copper plates. Black-and-white prints were then pulled from the plates and hand-colored. The prints were issued to subscribers in 87 sets, or parts, 5 plates, or prints, to a set. The complete work, called *The Birds of America* (1827), formed four volumes and was sold during Audubon's time by subscription for $1,000. While fewer than 200 complete sets were sold, the work firmly established Audubon's reputation as an artist and naturalist. Audubon then turned his attention to four-footed animals, making his last expedition to the upper reaches of the Mississippi River in 1844. After his death in 1851, his sons and friends finished his work.

BOOKS BY AUDUBON

Audubon and His Journals. Select Bibliographies Reprint Ser. Maria R. Audubon (ed). 2 vols. Ayer (repr of 1897 ed) $56.50. ISBN 0-8369-6660-0

The Birds of America (1827). Macmillan 1985 $39.95. ISBN 0-02-504450-8

Delineations of American Scenery and Character. Ayer 1970 $24.50. ISBN 0-405-02655-2

BOOKS ABOUT AUDUBON

Burroughs, John. *John James Audubon.* Overlook Pr 1987 $16.95. ISBN 0-87951-259-8 Classic biography based on Audubon's own journals.

Ford, Alice. *John James Audubon.* Abbeville 1988 $35.00. ISBN 0-89659-744-X Resolves many questions about the great naturalist and portrays his fascinating life in depth.

CATLIN, GEORGE 1796–1872

The first important artist to portray the culture of American Indians, George Catlin trained to be a lawyer. In 1830 he turned his attention to painting in an effort to document what he thought was soon to be a vanishing culture. After first studying Indians on eastern reservations, in 1832 he began studying the Plains Indians. He journeyed by steamer to the headwaters of the upper Missouri River and traveled into Pawnee and Comanche territory with a troop of U.S. soldiers. He also studied the Indians in Wisconsin and Minnesota, where he was the first white to view the quarry from which the Indians took the stone they used to make calumets, or peace pipes. Often called pipestone, the mineral was later called catlinite in honor of the artist.

Catlin used a style that was generally graphic or descriptive. He excelled in watercolor, painted less well in oil, and seldom concerned himself with the techniques of perspective. In all, he painted 470 full-length portraits of Indians and scenes of Indian life.

In 1839 Catlin went to Europe, where he lectured and exhibited his paintings. While there he published several books, among them *Manners, Customs, and Condition of the North American Indians* (1841), a two-volume work with about 300 engravings. After returning to the United States, he traveled extensively through South and Central America and the Far West. In 1868 he recorded his adventures in *Last Rambles Amongst the Indians of the Rocky Mountains and the Andes.*

BOOKS BY CATLIN

Catlin's North American Indian Portfolio: A Reproduction. Ohio Univ Pr 1970 $250.00. ISBN 0-8040-0029-8

George Catlin: Episodes from "Life Among the Indians" and "Last Rambles." Marvin C. Ross (ed). Univ of Oklahoma Pr 1980 $15.95. ISBN 0-8061-1693-5

BOOKS ABOUT CATLIN

Dippie, Brian W. *Catlin and His Contemporaries: The Politics of Patronage.* Univ of Nevada Pr 1990 $50.00. ISBN 0-8032-1683-1 Illustrated examination of the preeminent painter of western Indians.

Millichap, Joseph R. *George Catlin. Western Writers Ser.* Boise State Univ Pr 1977 $2.95. ISBN 0-88430-051-X Provides a brief but authoritative introduction to the life and work of Catlin and the American West.

A DIVIDED NATION—THE COMING OF THE CIVIL WAR

*Blasingame, John W. *The Slave Community: Plantation Life in the Ante-Bellum South.* Oxford Univ Pr 1979 $11.95. ISBN 0-19-502563-6 Account of slave life on plantations in the southern United States.

*Bontemps, Arna. *Great Slave Narratives.* Beacon 1969 $12.95. ISBN 0-8070-5473-9. Stories narrated by slaves recounting memorable times and events in their lives; excellent collection of primary source documents.

*Brandt, Nat. *The Town That Started the Civil War.* Syracuse Univ Pr 1990 $29.95. ISBN 0-8156-0243-X Discusses how the slavery question became centralized when a fugitive slave was saved by the town of Oberlin, Ohio, in 1858.

*Catton, Bruce. *The Coming Fury. The Centennial History of the Civil War Ser.* Washington Square Pr Vol. 1 1972 $5.95. ISBN 0-671-54308-3 Well-executed discussion of the events leading to the Civil War by a Civil War specialist.

Craven, Avery O. *The Coming of the Civil War.* Univ of Chicago Pr 1966 $4.50. ISBN 0-226-11894-0

Curtin, Philip D. *Atlantic Slave Trade: A Census.* Univ of Wisconsin Pr 1972 $12.95. ISBN 0-299-05404-7

Fehrenbacher, Don E. *The Dred Scott Case: Its Significance in American Law and Politics.* Oxford Univ Pr 1978 $39.95. ISBN 0-19-502403-6

Fehrenbacher, Don E. *Slavery, Law, and Politics: The Dred Scott Case in Historical Perspective.* Oxford Univ Pr 1981 $9.95. ISBN 0-19-502883-X

Fogel, Robert W. *Time on the Cross.* Norton 1989 $8.95. ISBN 0-393-30620-8 Addresses the economics of slavery

Foner, Eric. *Free Soil, Free Labor, Free Men: The Ideology of the Republican Party Before the Civil War.* Oxford Univ Pr 1970 $8.95. ISBN 0-19-501352-2

*Freedman, Florence B. *Two Tickets to Freedom: The True Story of Ellen and William Croft, Fugitive Slaves.* Bedrick 1989 $4.95. ISBN 0-87226-221-9 Factual account of an escape from slavery; good introductory work.

Genovese, Eugene D. *Roll, Jordan, Roll: The World the Slaves Made.* Random 1976 $14.95. ISBN 0-394-71652-3

Genovese, Eugene D. *The World the Slaveholders Made: Two Essays in Interpretation.* Wesleyan Univ Pr 1988 $12.95. ISBN 0-8195-6204-1

*Jacobs, Harriet A. *Incidents in the Life of a Slave Girl Written by Herself.* Oxford Univ Pr 1990 $9.95. ISBN 0-19-506670-7 Moving memoir by a slave who describes her life in antebellum North Carolina.

Johannsen, Robert W. *The Frontier, the Union, and Stephen A. Douglas.* Univ of Illinois Pr 1989 $34.95. ISBN 0-252-01577-0

Johannsen, Robert W. *Lincoln-Douglas Debates of Eighteen Fifty-Eight.* Oxford Univ Pr 1965 $11.95. ISBN 0-19-500921-5

*Lester, Julius. *To Be a Slave.* Scholastic 1986 $2.50. ISBN 0-590-40682-5 Describes what it was like to be a slave; good introduction to a sensitive topic.

Oates, Stephen. *The Fires of Jubilee: Nat Turner's Fierce Rebellion.* NAL 1982 $3.95. ISBN 0-451-62308-8

Oates, Stephen. *Our Fiery Trial: Abraham Lincoln, John Brown, and the Civil War Era.* Univ of Massachusetts Pr 1983 $8.95. ISBN 0-87023-397-1

Oates, Stephen. *To Purge This Land with Blood: A Biography of John Brown.* Univ of Massachusetts Pr 1984 $14.95. ISBN 0-87023-458-7

*Ortiz, Victoria. *Sojourner Truth.* Harper 1974 $11.89. ISBN 0-397-31504-X Biography of former slave who struggled for rights of blacks and women.

Parish, Peter J. *Slavery, History, and Historians.* Harper 1989 $16.95. ISBN 0-06-437001-1

Pease, Jane H., and William H. Pease. *Bound with Them in Chains: A Biographical History of the Anti-Slavery Movement. Contributions in American History Ser.* Greenwood 1972 $35.00. ISBN 0-8371-6265-3

*Petry, Ann. *Harriet Tubman: Conductor on the Underground Railway.* Archway 1971 $2.95. ISBN 0-671-50442-8 Biography of former slave who helped others escape north.

Quarles, Benjamin. *Allies for Freedom: Blacks and John Brown.* Oxford Univ Pr 1974. (o.p.)

*Stowe, Harriet Beecher. *Uncle Tom's Cabin.* Bantam 1981 $2.75. ISBN 0-553-21119-6 Classic story about life as a slave; instrumental in encouraging the antislavery movement.

Styron, William. *The Confessions of Nat Turner. Windstone Ser.* Bantam 1981 $4.95. ISBN 0-553-26916-X

Wells, Damon. *Stephen Douglas: The Last Years, 1857–1861.* Univ of Texas Pr 1990 $14.95. ISBN 0-292-77635-7

*Yates, Elizabeth. *Amos Fortune, Free Man.* Penguin 1989 $3.95. ISBN 0-14-034158-7 Story of a black slave who buys his freedom.

DOUGLASS, FREDERICK 1817?–1895

Born a slave in Maryland in about 1817, Frederick Douglass never became accommodated to being held in bondage. He secretly learned to read, although slaves were prohibited from doing so. He fought back against a cruel slave-breaker and finally escaped to New Bedford, Massachusetts, in 1838 at about the age of 21. Despite the danger of being sent back to his owner if discovered, Douglass became an agent and eloquent orator for the Massachusetts Antislavery Society. He lectured extensively in both England and the United States. As an ex-slave, his words had tremendous impact on his listeners.

In 1845 Douglass wrote his autobiography, *Narrative of the Life of Frederick Douglass,* which increased his fame. Concerned that he might be sent back to slavery, he went to Europe. He spent two years in England and Ireland speaking to antislavery groups.

Douglass returned to the United States a free man and settled in Rochester, New York, where he founded a weekly newspaper, *The North Star,* in 1847. In the newspaper he wrote articles supporting the antislavery cause and the cause of human rights. He once wrote, "The lesson which [the American people] must learn, or neglect to do so at their own peril, is that Equal Manhood means Equal Rights, and further, that the American people must stand each for all and all for each without respect to color or race."

During the Civil War, Douglass worked for the Underground Railroad, the secret route of escape for slaves. He also helped recruit African-American soldiers for the Union army. After the war, he continued to write and to speak out against injustice. In addition to advocating education for freed slaves, he served in several government posts, including United States representative to Haiti.

In 1855 a longer version of his autobiography appeared, and in 1895, the year of Douglass's death, a completed version was published. A bestseller in its own time, it has since become available in numerous editions and languages.

BOOKS BY DOUGLASS

Frederick Douglass: The Narrative and Selected Writings. McGraw 1983 $6.95. ISBN 0-07-554375-3

Life and Times of Frederick Douglass. Carol 1984 $8.95. ISBN 0-8065-0865-5

The Life and Writings of Frederick Douglass. Philip S. Foner (ed). 5 vols. Intl Pubs 1975 $35.00. ISBN 0-7178-0118-7

My Bondage and My Freedom. Black Rediscovery Ser. Dover 1969 $6.95. ISBN 0-486-22457-0

Narrative of the Life of Frederick Douglass, an American Slave. Penguin American Lib Ser. Houston A. Baker, Jr. (ed). Penguin 1982 $3.95. ISBN 0-14-039012-X

BOOKS ABOUT DOUGLASS

*Miller, Douglas T. *Frederick Douglass and the Fight for Freedom. Makers of America Ser.* Facts on File 1988 $15.95. ISBN 0-8160-1617-8 Introductory biography of the former slave and abolitionist.

*Myers, Elisabeth P. *Frederick Douglass: Boy Champion of Human Rights. Bobbs Merrill Childhood of Famous Americans Ser.* Macmillan 1970 $5.95. ISBN 0-672-51365-X Account of Douglass's early years; especially suited to younger readers.

*Russell, Sharman. *Frederick Douglass. Black Americans of Achievement Ser.* Chelsea 1989 $9.95.

ISBN 0-7910-0204-7 Biography of Douglass especially suited to younger readers; includes much visual memorabilia of his life and times.

*Washington, Booker T. *Frederick Douglass.* Argosy 1969 $15.00. ISBN 0-87266-035-4 Evaluation of Douglass by the famous, though controversial black leader of the late 1800s and early 1900s.

GARRISON, WILLIAM LLOYD 1805–1879

An outspoken abolitionist from Massachusetts, William Lloyd Garrison was one of the most forceful newspaper editors of his time, giving new focus to the abolitionist movement when he began publishing the *Liberator* on January 1, 1831. Garrison first worked for Benjamin Lundy, another newspaper publisher and abolitionist. Objecting to Lundy's moderate stance toward emancipation, he quit Lundy's paper in 1830, returned to Boston, and began the *Liberator.*

In his paper Garrison asked his readers to think of slavery from the viewpoint of the black slave, not the white slaveholder. He demanded immediate emancipation of all slaves, opposed any compensation to slaveholders, and rejected any efforts at recolonization of freed slaves to Africa. He angered many in the abolitionist movement with his blunt words and intemperate language. At one point he burned a copy of the U.S. Constitution, calling it a "covenant with death and an agreement with Hell" because it permitted slavery.

In 1831 Garrison helped found the New England Antislavery Society. Two years later he established the American Antislavery Society. By 1840 more than 2,000 local offshoots of these societies had approximately 200,000 members, mostly in the North. Garrison, who opposed the Civil War until President Lincoln (*see* Lincoln, Vol. 2, United States History: The Civil War) issued the Emancipation Proclamation, ceased publishing the newspaper in 1865 when the Thirteenth Amendment to the U.S. Constitution abolished slavery. By the time of Garrison's death in 1879, however, efforts to deny African Americans their civil rights had begun.

BOOKS BY GARRISON

Let the Oppressed Go Free, 1861–1867. Letters of William Lloyd Garrison Ser. Harvard Univ Pr 1979 $40.00. ISBN 0-674-52665-1

Letter to Louis Kossuth, Concerning Freedom and Slavery in the United States in Behalf of the American Anti-Slavery Society. Anti-Slavery Crusade in America Ser. (coauthored with others) Ayer 1969 $9.00. ISBN 0-405-00630-6

New Reign of Terror in the Slaveholding States, for 1859–1860. Anti-Slavery Crusade in America Ser. Ayer 1969 $14.00. ISBN 0-405-00631-4

William Lloyd Garrison on Non-Resistance. American History and Americana Ser. Haskell 1973 $75.00. ISBN 0-8383-1717-0

BOOKS ABOUT GARRISON

Chapman, John J. *William Lloyd Garrison. American Newspapermen 1790–1933 Ser.* Beekman 1974 $17.50. ISBN 0-8464-0027-8 Complete biography of William Lloyd Garrison and his impact on the antislavery period.

Garrison, Wendell P., and Francis J. Garrison. *William Lloyd Garrison, 1805–1879.* 4 vols. *Anti-Slavery Crusade in America Ser.* Ayer 1969 repr of 1881 ed $74.00. ISBN 0-405-00629-2 Monumental four-volume biography of Garrison, a champion of human rights, told by his children.

Johnson, Oliver. *W. L. Garrison and His Times. Black Heritage Library Collection Ser.* Ayer (repr of 1881 ed) $19.00. ISBN 0-8369-8613-X Tribute to Garrison by a great American humanitarian who was closely associated with him in antislavery agitation from 1833 on.

THE CIVIL WAR

American Heritage Illustrated History of the United States. Vol. 8: The Civil War. Choice Pub 1988 $3.49. ISBN 0-945260-08-3 Illustrated presentation of the events and leading figures of the Civil War; especially suited to younger readers.

*Beatty, Patricia. *Charley Skedaddle.* Morrow 1987 $12.95. ISBN 0-688-06687-9 Story of a young Union soldier who runs away from the war.

*Beatty, Patricia. *Turn Homeward, Hannalee.* Morrow 1984 $12.95. ISBN 0-688-03871-9 Story of displaced persons in the South during the Civil War.

*Canon, Jill. *Civil War Heroines.* Bellerophon 1989 $3.50. Illustrated look at some of the women who played a part in the war; especially suited to younger readers.

*Catton, Bruce. *American Heritage Picture History of the Civil War.* Outlet 1985 $21.95. ISBN 0-517-38556-2 Excellent pictorial history of the war with easy-to-read text by a noted Civil War writer.

*Catton, Bruce. *Gettysburg: The Final Fury.* Doubleday 1974 $17.95. ISBN 0-385-02060-0. Well-written account of the deadly battle between the North and the South.

*Catton, Bruce. *A Stillness at Appomattox.* Washington Square Pr 1970 $5.95. ISBN 0-671-53143-3 Focuses on the final days of the war and the surrender of the Confederate general Robert E. Lee.

Churchill, Winston S. *American Civil War.* Crown 1985 $4.98. ISBN 0-517-46779-8

*Commager, Henry S. *The Blue and The Gray.* 2 vols. NAL 1973 $4.95 ea. ISBNs 0-451-62536-6, 0-451-62640-0 Accounts of the experiences of Civil War participants, told in their own words.

Commager, Henry S. *Fifty Basic Civil War Documents.* Krieger 1982 $8.50. ISBN 0-89874-497-0

*Crane, Stephen. *Red Badge of Courage.* Puffin Classics Ser. Penguin 1987 $2.25. ISBN 0-14-035055-1 Fictional account of the realities of life and death for a youth fighting on the side of the Union in the Civil War.

Davis, Burke. *Civil War: Strange and Fascinating Facts.* Crown 1982 $5.98. ISBN 0-517-37151-0

Davis, Burke. *Gray Fox: Robert E. Lee and the Civil War.* Crown 1988 $7.98. ISBN 0-517-34772-5

Davis, Burke. *They Called Him Stonewall: A Life of Lt. General T. J. Jackson.* Crown 1988 $7.98. ISBN 0-517-66204-3

*Davis, William C. *Rebels and Yankees: The Fighting Men of the Civil War.* Smith 1989 $24.98. ISBN 0-8317-3264-4 Details the training, camp life, and combat duty of average soldiers on both sides of the Civil War.

Distant Thunder: A Photographic Essay on the American Civil War. Sam Abell (photos by). Thomasson-Grant 1988 $37.50. ISBN 0-934738-35-1 Mixture of modern and archival photographs accompanied by text written by a historian tracing the chronology of the war from beginning to end.

Donald, David H. *Lincoln Reconsidered: Essays on the Civil War Era.* Random 1989 $8.95. ISBN 0-679-72310-2

Eaton, Clement. *Jefferson Davis.* Free Pr 1979 $12.95. ISBN 0-02-908740-6

Foote, Shelby. *The Civil War: Fort Sumter to Perryville.* Random 1986 $15.95. ISBN 0-317-53681-8

Foote, Shelby. *The Civil War: Fredericksburg to Meridian.* Random 1986 $15.95. ISBN 0-317-53679-6

Foote, Shelby. *The Civil War: Red River to Appomattox.* Random 1986 $15.95. ISBN 0-317-53680-X

*Higginson, Thomas W. *Army Life in a Black Regiment.* Norton 1984 $7.70. ISBN 0-393-30157-5 Covers the day-to-day life of black soldiers who fought in the Civil War.

*Hunt, Irene. *Across Five Aprils.* Berkley 1987 $2.75. ISBN 0-425-10241-6 Novel of the Civil War.

*Kantor, MacKinley. *Andersonville.* NAL 1957 $4.95. ISBN 0-451-16021-5 Account of the Confederate prisoner-of-war camp in Georgia where more than 12,000 Union soldiers died.

*Keith, Harold. *Rifles for Watie.* Harper Jr Bks 1987 $2.95. ISBN 0-06-447030-X Chronicles the maturing of a young Union army spy as he learns how deeply others feel about the war.

■Leckie, Robert. *None Died in Vain: The Saga of the American Civil War.* Harper 1990 $29.95. ISBN 0-06-016280-5 Detailed study of the Civil War containing descriptions of the key people.

Leech, Margaret. *Reveille in Washington, 1860–1865.* Carroll & Graf 1986 $11.95. ISBN 0-88184-254-0

McPherson, James M. *Battle Cry of Freedom: The Civil War Era.* History of the United States Ser. Vol. VI Oxford Univ Pr $35.00. ISBN 0-19-503863-0

*Meredith, Roy. *World of Mathew Brady.* Crown 1989 $12.98. ISBN 0-517-21640-X Tribute to the art of the famous Civil War photographer.

*National Geographic Society Staff and Robert P. Jordan. *The Civil War.* National Geographic 1982 $7.95. ISBN 0-87044-077-2 Excellent, well-illustrated portrayal of the causes, battles, and personalities and leaders of the war.

*Newin, D. *Sherman's March.* Civil War Ser. Silver 1986 $19.94. ISBN 0-8094-4813-0 Focuses on the Union march of General Sherman and nearly 100,000 soldiers from Chattanooga to Savannah laying waste to the countryside.

Ransom, Roger L. *Conflicts and Comprise: The Political Economy of Slavery, Emancipation, and the American Civil War.* Cambridge Univ Pr 1989 $12.95. ISBN 0-521-31167-5

Stampp, Kenneth M. *And the War Came: The North and the Secession Crises, 1860–1861.* Greenwood 1980 $35.00. ISBN 0-313-22566-4

Stampp, Kenneth M. *The Imperiled Union: Essays of the Background of the Civil War.* Oxford Univ Pr 1981 $9.95. ISBN 0-19-502991-7

Ward, Geoffrey C., *et al. The Civil War.* Knopf 1990 $49.50. ISBN 0-394-56285-2

*White, Henry. *Robert E. Lee and the Southern Confederacy. American Biography Ser.* Haskell 1969 $59.95. ISBN 0-8383-0259-9 Account of Robert E. Lee's leadership of the Confederate army.

BARTON, CLARA HARLOWE   1821–1912

See also Barton, Vol. 2, Community Health.

Clara Barton was a great American humanitarian and the founder of the American Red Cross. Yet as a young girl growing up in Massachusetts, she was extremely shy. At one point, her mother consulted a doctor who diagnosed his patients by the shape and size of their heads. After feeling the lumps and bumps on young Clara's head, he advised her mother to "throw responsibility on her. As soon as her age will permit, give her a school to teach." So after studying at the Liberal Institute in New York, Barton began teaching at a nearby school in New Jersey. Barton's health, however, was never good. After suffering from a series of nervous collapses, she eventually lost her voice in the classroom. She was forced to resign after nearly 20 years of teaching.

In 1854 Barton moved to Washington, D.C., to become a clerk in the Patent Office. She was still living in the nation's capital when the Civil War broke out in 1861. Like her neighbors, Barton was shocked one summer's day in July to see hundreds of wounded Union soldiers streaming into the capital after their defeat at the battle of Bull Run. Appalled by the lack of medicine and equipment, Barton organized a group of women to obtain needed medical supplies and to nurse the wounded soldiers.

Although women were not allowed on the front lines, Barton frequently delivered many of the supplies by wagon to battlefield hospitals. There she bandaged the wounded and fed and nursed the dying soldiers. Twice she nearly lost her life when fragments of a bomb shell ripped through her clothing. Because of her tremendous efforts, she became known as the "Angel of the Battlefield." When the Civil War was over, President Abraham Lincoln appointed Barton to search for missing prisoners.

Later, while traveling in Europe, Barton became interested in the valuable services performed by the International Red Cross. She tried to introduce the movement into the United States. In spite of continuing nervous collapses, she finally persuaded the Senate to put aside its fear of "foreign entanglements" and ratify a treaty making the United States a member of the International Red Cross. As president of the American Red Cross, she widened the organization's scope to include helping the victims of such natural disasters as floods, epidemics, and famines. Despite her shyness and continuing poor health, Clara Barton was a courageous woman who devoted much of her life to helping those in need.

BOOKS BY BARTON

The Red Cross: A History of This Remarkable International Movement in the Interest of Humanity (1898). (o.p.)
The Red Cross in Peace and War (1899). (o.p.)
The Story of My Childhood (1907). Annette K. Baxter (ed). Ayer 1980 $16.00. ISBN 0-405-12823-1
*A Story of the Red Cross: Glimpses of Field Work (1904). *Airmont Classic Ser.* Airmont 1968 $1.50. ISBN 0-8049-0170-8 Illustrated stories of the work done by the Red Cross, written for younger readers.

BOOKS ABOUT BARTON

*Bains, Rae. *Clara Barton: Angel of the Battlefield.* Troll 1982 $9.79. ISBN 0-89375-752-7 Story of Clara Barton written for grades 4–6.
*Hamilton, Leni. *Clara Barton.* Chelsea 1988 $17.95. ISBN 1-55546-641-9 Focuses on the achievements of Clara Barton; for grades 5 and up.
Pryor, Elizabeth B. *Clara Barton, Professional Angel.* Univ of Penn Pr 1987 $18.95. ISBN 0-8122-1273-8 Discussion of Clara Barton's life.

GARFIELD, JAMES ABRAM   1831–1881

The twentieth President of the United States, James Garfield spent much of his childhood living in poverty on a farm in Ohio. Over the years, he took jobs as a farmer, carpenter, and canal boatman. Somehow he managed to save enough money to obtain an education, graduating first from Hiram College in Ohio and then in 1856 from Williams College in Massachusetts. After graduation, he returned to Hiram to teach ancient languages and literature. From 1857 to 1861 he served as principal there. A brilliant orator, he also was a lay preacher of the Disciples of Christ and in 1859 was admitted to the bar.

During the Civil War, Garfield served in the Union Army and, although he had no previous military experience, soon became a major general of volunteers. He resigned in 1863 to become a member of the House of Representatives. Throughout his political career, Garfield was a loyal Republican, agreeing with most of his party's ideas and principles. By the time he was elected to the United States Senate in 1876, he had become the leader of the Republican party in the House.

Garfield was an ambitious man, and in 1880 he announced his candidacy for the Republican presidential nomination. However, he removed his name to become convention manager for John Sherman, Ohio's leading Republican. In the end, Sherman was opposed by several high-ranking Republicans, and Garfield himself was chosen as a compromise candidate for President.

Garfield's rise from poverty appealed to many voters, which helped him to defeat the Democratic presidential candidate. As President, Garfield showed his distaste for the spoils system, the giving of government jobs to political supporters. When New York Senator Roscoe Conkling sent a request for jobs for some of his loyal party members, Garfield refused. And so a bitter dispute broke out between the President and an important faction of the Republican party.

Then tragedy struck. On July 2, 1881, just four months after he had taken office as President, Garfield was shot in a Washington railroad station by Charles Guiteau, a disappointed office seeker. Although he lived on for three more months, the President never recovered. On September 18, 1881, he informed his doctors, "My work is done." He died the next night.

BOOK BY GARFIELD

Works of James Abram Garfield (1882). Burke A. Hinsdale (ed). 2 vols. Ayer (repr of 1882 ed) $82.50. ISBN 0-8369-5330-4

BOOKS ABOUT GARFIELD

Hendrek, Booraem V. *The Road to Respectability: James A. Garfield & His World, 1844–1852.* Bucknell Univ Pr 1988 $37.50. ISBN 0-8387-5135-0 Discussion of how Garfield rose to become President of the United States.
*Lillegard, Dee. *James A. Garfield.* Childrens 1987 $15.93. ISBN 0-516-01394-7 Life of Garfield written for young readers.
McElroy, Richard L. *James A. Garfield—His Life & Times: A Pictorial History.* Daring 1986 $22.95. ISBN 0-938936-51-4 Primarily photographs of Garfield and his world.

LEE, ROBERT EDWARD   1807–1870

Robert E. Lee is considered by many historians to be the greatest general of the Civil War. Born in Virginia, he was the son of Light-Horse Harry Lee, who had been a hero in the American Revolution. As a young man, Lee was appointed to the United States Military Academy at West Point, where he was the top student in his class. In fact, he received higher grades than any other cadet in the academy's history. Later, as a young officer in the Mexican War, Lee also performed with intelligence and energy.

When the Civil War broke out in 1861, President Abraham Lincoln asked Lee to become commander of the Union army. Although Lee opposed secession, when his home state of Virginia left the Union, he resigned from the Army. "I cannot raise up my hand," he wrote in a letter to his sister, "against my birthplace, my home, my children." After he turned down Lincoln's offer, he took command of the Confederate forces in Virginia. Within a short time he became military adviser to Confederate President Jefferson Davis and was made a Confederate general.

Southern victories at the beginning of the Civil War were due largely to Lee's military genius. With the assistance of General Thomas J. "Stonewall" Jackson, Lee was able to defeat Union armies that were often twice as large as his own. Over and over, he led his army brilliantly. When necessary, he took chances that other generals never would. Always quick to take advantage of his opponents' mistakes, he also was able to inspire his own troops to great effort.

As the leader of the Army of Northern Virginia, Lee scored brilliant successes at the Second Battle of Bull Run in 1862 in Virginia and at Chancellorsville in Virginia in 1863. During this same period, he also made two attempts to invade the North. Both times the Union stopped him. At the Battle of Antietam in Pennsylvania in 1862, he was able to save his army only by retreating. Although the battle lasted just one day, more than 23,000 Union and

Confederate soldiers were killed or wounded. Later, in 1863, in the Battle of Gettysburg in Pennsylvania, Lee's forces again suffered tragically heavy losses.

After Gettysburg, Lee did not take part in any major battles until May 1864, when Union general Ulysses S. Grant moved against him. At the Battle of the Wilderness in Virginia, Lee's forces were able to stop the Union army, although both sides suffered huge casualties. Grant then surprised Lee by stubbornly pressing his troops on toward the city of Richmond in Virginia. The two sides fought bitterly for the next 10 months. Eventually Lee ran out of soldiers as well as supplies. On April 8, he made the painful decision to surrender. Three days later, Lee met Grant at Appomattox Court House in Virginia and presented the Union general with his sword. The Civil War was finally over.

After the war, Lee became president of Washington College in Lexington, Virginia, known today as Washington and Lee University. He remained there until his death in 1870.

BOOKS BY LEE

Lee: In His Own Words and Those of His Contemporaries. Ralston B. Lattimore (ed). Acropolis 1964 $9.50. ISBN 0-87491-111-7 Includes writings of Lee during the Civil War.
The Wartime Papers of Robert E. Lee. Clifford Dowdey and Louis H. Manarin (eds). Da Capo 1987 $18.95. ISBN 0-306-80282-1

BOOKS ABOUT LEE

Anderson, Nancy S., and Dwight Anderson. *The Generals: Ulysses S. Grant and Robert E. Lee.* Random 1989 $12.95. ISBN 0-394-75985-0 Compares the military strategies of Grant and Lee during the Civil War.
Frassanito, William A. *Grant and Lee: The Virginia Campaigns, 1864–1865.* Macmillan 1983 $27.50. ISBN 0-684-17873-7 Discussion of the military efforts of generals Lee and Grant during the Civil War.
Freeman, Douglas S. *Robert E. Lee.* Macmillan 1977 $40.00. ISBN 0-684-15489-7 Abridged edition of Freeman's 4-volume biography of the Confederate general.
Robert E. Lee. World Leaders—Past and Present Ser. Chelsea 1989 $17.95. ISBN 1-55546-814-4 Focuses on Lee's early years, his career, and his contributions.
Tucker, Glenn. *Lee and Longstreet at Gettysburg.* Macmillan 1968 $6.00. ISBN 0-672-50734-X Analyzes Lee's maneuvers at the Battle of Gettysburg.

LINCOLN, ABRAHAM 1809–1865

Abraham Lincoln, sixteenth President of the United States, served during one of the most trying times in American history. In the months between his election and his inauguration, seven southern states seceded from the Union to form the Confederate States of America. A month later the Civil War had begun with the crash of guns at Fort Sumter.

Lincoln was born in a log cabin in Kentucky and grew up very poor on the frontier in Kentucky, Indiana, and Illinois. He helped out his family by splitting rails, cutting wheat, and poling flatboats. But he longed to read. He would walk miles to borrow a book and he went to school whenever there was a teacher in the area. In 1837 he settled in New Salem, Illinois, where he worked in a store and managed a mill. Eventually, in 1836, he became a lawyer.

Lincoln served in the Black Hawk War of 1832, represented his community in the Illinois legislature from 1834 to 1841, and practiced law. In 1842 he married Mary Todd, the daughter of a well-off Kentucky family. In 1846

Lincoln was elected to the House of Representatives, where he spoke out against the Mexican War and the extension of slavery.

After trying in 1855 to become a senator, in 1858 Lincoln ran for the Senate again—this time against Stephen A. Douglas, the United States senator from Illinois and a skilled debater. Once again Lincoln lost the election, but in the famous Lincoln-Douglas debates, he made a nation-wide name for himself. In 1860 the Republicans nominated him for President and he was elected.

In his Inaugural Address, Lincoln made plain his views about the impending civil war between the North and the South. To the South, he said, "In *your* hands, my dissatisfied fellow countrymen, and not in *mine,* is the momentous issue of civil war. The government will not assail *you. . . ."* When war came, he explained that the United States was fighting the war to preserve the Union. Later, in 1863, he issued the Emancipation Proclamation, which freed all the slaves in the Confederacy.

As the end of the war neared, Lincoln began to plan for the future. He hoped to bring the North and South back together in peace. In his second Inaugural Address, he explained, "With malice toward none; with charity for all; with firmness in the right, as God gives us to see the right, let us strive on to finish the work we are in; to bind up the nation's wounds. . . ."

Lincoln was never able to put his rebuilding plans into effect. On April 14, 1865, while attending a performance at Ford's Theater he was shot by John Wilkes Booth, a southern actor. When Lincoln died the next morning, many believed that chances for a smooth reconciliation between North and South died with him.

BOOKS BY LINCOLN

Abraham Lincoln: His Speeches and Writings. Roy P. Basler (ed). Kraus 1968 $73.00. ISBN 0-527-57100-8

Lincoln in Camp.
Illustration by W. R. Leigh (1899).   Courtesy of Culver Pictures, Inc.

Famous Speeches of Abraham Lincoln. Essay Index Repr Ser. Ayer (repr of 1935 ed) $15.00. ISBN 0-8369-1207-1

Selected Writings and Speeches. T. Harry Williams (ed). Hendricks 1980 $5.95. ISBN 0-87532-136-4

Wisdom and Wit. Peter Pauper $5.95. ISBN 0-88088-359-6

BOOKS ABOUT LINCOLN

*Bishop, Jim. *The Day Lincoln Was Shot.* Harper 1964 $4.95. ISBN 0-06-080005-4 Journalist's recreation of the last day in Lincoln's life.

■Handlin, Oscar, and Lilian Handlin. *Abraham Lincoln and the Union.* Scott 1990 $17.95. ISBN 0-673-39340-2 Biography that emphasizes Lincoln's early years.

*Hay, John. *Lincoln and the Civil War in the Diaries and Letters of John Hay. Quality Paperbacks Ser.* Tyler Dennett (ed). Da Capo 1988 $12.95. ISBN 0-306-80340-2 Firsthand account by one of Lincoln's secretaries, later secretary of state under President McKinley.

*Horgan, Paul. *Abraham Lincoln: Citizen of New Salem.* Macmillan 1961 $2.98. ISBN 0-686-74487-X Excellent fictionalized account by a popular author.

*Metzger, Larry. *Abraham Lincoln.* Watts 1987 $10.40. ISBN 0-531-10307-2 Good introductory biography of Lincoln; especially suited to younger readers.

*Sandburg, Carl. *Abe Lincoln Grows Up.* Harcourt 1975 $4.95. ISBN 0-15-602615-5 Classic account by the poet and chronicler of Lincoln.

*Sandburg, Carl. *Abraham Lincoln: The Prairie Years and the War Years.* Harcourt 1974 $14.95. ISBN 0-15-602611-2 Biography of Lincoln by the famous poet and Lincoln enthusiast.

*Vidal, Gore. *Lincoln.* Ballantine 1988 $4.95. ISBN 0-345-00885-5 Fictionalized account of Lincoln as President.

RECONSTRUCTION

Baker, Ray S. *Following the Color Line.* Corner 1973 $18.95. ISBN 0-87928-040-9

Coulter, E. Merton. *The South During the Reconstruction, 1865–1877. History of the South Ser.* Louisiana State Univ Pr 1947 $30.00. ISBN 0-8071-0008-0

*Foner, Eric, and Olivia Mahoney. *A House Divided: America in the Age of Lincoln.* Norton 1990 $35.00. ISBN 0-393-02755-4 Beautifully illustrated account of America following the Civil War.

Foner, Eric. *Reconstruction: America's Unfinished Revolution, 1863–1877.* Harper Jr Bks 1989 $12.95. ISBN 0-06-091453-X

Franklin, John Hope. *Reconstruction After the Civil War. Chicago History of American Civilization Ser.* Univ of Chicago Pr 1962 $10.95. ISBN 0-226-26076-3

*Garland, Hamlin. *Main-Travelled Roads.* Buccaneer 1987 $18.95. ISBN 0-89966-555-1 Addresses post-Civil War problems of Union soldiers returning home.

McFeely, William S. *Yankee Stepfather: General O. O. Howard and the Freedmen.* Norton 1983 $6.25. ISBN 0-393-00537-2

O'Connor, Thomas H. *The Disunited States: The Era of Civil War and Reconstruction.* Harper 1979 $16.95. ISBN 0-06-044878-4

*Sebestyen, Quida. *Words by Heart.* Bantam 1983 $2.95. ISBN 0-553-27179-2 Focuses on the problems of the only black family in an all-white southwestern community.

Sefton, James E. *Andrew Johnson and the Uses of Constitutional Power.* Scott 1980. ISBN 0-673-39351-8

Smith, Gene. *High Crimes and Misdemeanors: The Impeachment and Trial of Andrew Johnson.* McGraw 1985 $7.95. ISBN 0-07-058478-8

Stampp, Kenneth M. *Era of Reconstruction: Eighteen Sixty-Five to Eighteen Seventy-Seven.* Random 1967 $4.95. ISBN 0-394-70388-X

Trefousse, Hans L. *Andrew Johnson: A Biography.* Norton 1989 $24.50. ISBN 0-393-02673-6

GRANT, ULYSSES S. (SIMPSON) 1822–1885

Ulysses S. Grant had tried many ventures before becoming the eighteenth President of the United States in 1869. He had tried unsuccessfully to scratch out a life as a farmer in Ohio and had worked for a time in a real estate office and at a customshouse. But his fame and success came as a Union officer during the Civil War.

Born Hiram Ulysses Grant in Point Pleasant, Ohio, Grant attended West Point. After graduation in 1843, he served in the Mexican War and on an outpost in Oregon. In 1854, however, he was forced to resign from the army because of his excessive use of alcohol. When the Civil War broke out, he was working as a clerk in his family's leather store. Recommissioned in the army, he started out as a driller of volunteer recruits. His success in training raw soldiers led to promotions.

As a brigadier general, Grant set out to capture control of the Mississippi River. He first took Fort Henry on the Tennessee River then Fort Donelson on the Cumberland. Promoted to a major general, he faced the Confederates at Shiloh in Tennessee, one of the bloodiest battles of the Civil War. He went on to take the Mississippi city of Vicksburg after a grueling six-week siege. Having succeeded in splitting the Confederacy in two, Grant was named General-in-Chief by President Abraham Lincoln. (*See* Lincoln, Vol. 2, United States History: The Civil War.) Finally on April 9, 1965, Grant accepted Confederate general Robert E. Lee's surrender at Appomattox Courthouse.

Grant had become a national hero. In 1868 the Republicans drafted him for the presidency and he was elected. Unfortunately, his presidency was not as successful as his military career. Although he was a man of integrity and ethics, many of his appointees were not. Corruption and scandal plagued his years in office.

After leaving Washington, Grant became a partner in a financial firm, but the company went bankrupt. Soon afterwards, he learned he had cancer. Rushing against time, he set out to write his memoirs to pay off his debts and leave some money for his family. Lincoln had once said of Grant, "He has the grip of a bulldog. Once he gets his teeth in, nothing can shake him off." With this same tenacity, he fended off death until he had completed the writing of his memoirs. He died in 1885, soon after finishing the last page.

BOOKS BY GRANT

General Grant's Letters to a Friend, 1861–1880. James G. Wilson (ed). AMS 1973 repr of 1897 ed $14.25. ISBN 0-404-04598-7

Letters of Ulysses S. Grant to His Father and His Youngest Sister. Kraus (repr of 1912 ed) $16.00. ISBN 0-527-35350-7

Personal Memoirs of U. S. Grant. Quality Paperbacks Ser. Da Capo 1982 $13.95. ISBN 0-306-80172-8

BOOKS ABOUT GRANT

Catton, Bruce. *A Stillness at Appomattox.* Washington Square Pr 1970 $5.95. ISBN 0-671-53143-3 The final days of the Civil War and Lee's surrender, written by the popular novelist.

Catton, Bruce. *Grant Moves South.* Little 1960 $25.00. ISBN 0-316-13207-1 Account of Grant's campaigns in Tennessee.

Catton, Bruce. *Grant Takes Command.* Little 1969 $25.00. ISBN 0-316-13210-1 Discusses Grant's assumption of command of the Army of the Potomac.

Catton, Bruce. *U. S. Grant and the American Military Tradition.* Scott 1985. ISBN 0-8488-0279-9 Evaluation of Grant's place in military history.

*Falkof, Lucille. *Ulysses S. Grant: Eighteenth President of the United States. Presidents of the United States Ser.* Garrett Ed 1988 $12.95. ISBN 0-944483-02-X Good introduction to Grant's terms as President; especially suited to younger readers.

McFeely, William S. *Grant: A Biography.* Norton 1982 $14.95. ISBN 0-393-30046-3 Moving and convincing portrait of Grant that shows a deep understanding of the man as well as his period and his country.

Miers, Earl S. *The Web of Victory: Grant at Vicksburg.* Louisiana State Univ Pr 1984 $9.95. ISBN 0-8071-1199-6 Focuses on the siege of Vicksburg, a campaign that might very well have been the turning point of the Civil War as well as the turning point in Grant's military career.

Porter, Horace. *Campaigning with Grant. Collector's Library of the Civil War.* Silver $26.60. ISBN 0-8094-4200-0 Pictorial essay of Grant the soldier.

SETTLING THE LAST FRONTIER

American Heritage Illustrated History of the United State: Vol. 9: Winning the West. Choice Pub 1988 $3.49. Illustrated account of life in the "Wild West"; written especially for younger readers.

*Berger, Thomas. *Little Big Man.* Dell 1985 $5.95. ISBN 0-440-34976-1 Fictional account of the life and adventures of the man who claimed to be a survivor of Custer's Last Stand.

*Brown, Dee. *Bury My Heart at Wounded Knee.* Washington Square Pr $4.95. ISBN 0-671-49412-0 Stirring account of the Indian viewpoint of the "last frontier."

Brown, Dee. *Cavalry Scout.* Dell 1989 $2.95. ISBN 0-440-20227-2

Brown, Dee. *The Gentle Tamers: Women of the Old Wild West.* Univ of Nebraska Pr 1981 $6.50. ISBN 0-8032-5025-8

*Brown, Dee. *Hear That Lonesome Whistle Blow: Railroads in the West.* Holt 1977 $3.95. ISBN 0-03-016936-4 Tells of the westward expansion of railroads.

Brown, Dee. *Showdown at Little Big Horn.* Dell 1988 $2.95. ISBN 0-440-20202-7

*Calvert, Patricia. *The Snowbird.* Macmillan 1989 $12.95. ISBN 0-684-19120-2 Orphaned brother and sister seek their uncle in Dakota Territory; fiction.

*Cather, Willa. *My Antonia.* Houghton 1973 $5.59. ISBN 0-395-08356-7 Fictionalized account of the life of a young woman on the plains.

Cather, Willa. *O Pioneers.* NAL 1989 $3.50. ISBN 0-451-52285-0

*Clarke, Asa Bement. *Travels in Mexico and California.* Texas A & M Univ Pr 1989 $17.50. ISBN 0-89096-354-1 First-hand account of the perils of crossing the continent during pioneer times.

*Conrad, Pam. *Prairie Songs.* Harper Jr Bks 1987 $3.50. ISBN 0-06-440206-1 Novel of a young wife struggling with prairie life.

Dick, Everett. *The Sod-House Frontier, 1854–1890: A Social History of the Northern Plains from the Creation of Kansas and Nebraska to the Admission of the Dakotas.* Univ of Nebraska Pr 1989 $40.00. ISBN 0-8032-1687-4

Durham, Philip, and Everett L. James. *The Negro Cowboys.* Univ of Nebraska Pr 1983 $7.95. ISBN 0-8032-6560-3

Fairbanks, Carol. *Prairie Women: Images in American and Canadian Fiction.* Yale Univ Pr 1986 $22.00. ISBN 0-300-03374-5

Fehrenbach, T. R. *Comanches.* Knopf 1974 $29.95. ISBN 0-394-48856-3

*Freedman, Russell. *Indian Chiefs.* Holiday 1987 $16.95. ISBN 0-8234-0625-3 Discussion of leaders of various Indian nations.

*Freedman, Russell. *Cowboys of the Wild West.* Ticknor 1985 $14.95. ISBN 0-89919-301-3 Interesting descriptions and photographs relating the history of cattle ranching in the Old West.

*Garland, Hamlin. *Boy's Life on the Prairie.* Univ of Nebraska Pr 1961 $9.95. ISBN 0-8032-5070-3. Account of prairie life from a youthful perspective.

*Harte, Bret. *The Luck of Roaring Camp. Classics Ser.* Walter Pauk and Raymond Harris (eds). Jamestown Pubs 1976. ISBN 0-89061-054-1 Classic story of the Wild West mining camp.

*Jackson, Helen Hunt. *Century of Dishonor: A Sketch of the United States Government's Dealings.* Reprint Services 1988 $69.00. ISBN 0-317-90072-2 Classic work that helped persuade Americans to change policies toward Indian nations on the frontier.

*Katz, William L. *Black People Who Made the Old West.* Harper Jr Bks 1977 $12.70. ISBN 0-690-01253-5 Discussion of the contributions of African Americans to the settling of the West.

*Katz, William L. *The Black West.* Open Hand 1987 $14.95. ISBN 0-940880-18-0 Account of African Americans moving west.

*Lasky, Kathryn. *Beyond the Divide.* Dell 1986 $3.25. ISBN 0-440-91021-8 Tells of the adventures of pioneers going over the Rocky Mountains.

Lowrie, Robert H. *Indians of the Plains.* Univ of Nebraska Pr 1982 $7.95. ISBN 0-8032-7907-8

*Luchetti, Cathy, and Carol Olwell. *Women of the West.* Antelope Island 1982 $17.00. ISBN 0-917946-03-0 Focuses on the role of women in settling the West.

Mails, Thomas E. *Mystic Warriors of the Plains.* Doubleday 1972 $50.00. ISBN 0-385-04741-X

Marshall, S. L. *Crimsoned Prairie: The Indian Wars. Quality Paperbacks Ser.* Da Capo 1984 $10.95. ISBN 0-306-80226-0

*Mitchum, Hank. *Cimarron. Stagecoach Station Ser.* Bantam 1984 $2.75. ISBN 0-553-26303-X Novel about the hardships and joys of people in the West.

Prucha, Francis P. (ed). *Americanizing the American Indians: Writings by the "Friends of the Indians," 1880–1990.* Harvard Univ Pr 1973 $25.50. ISBN 0-674-02975-5

Riley, Glenda. *Women and Indians on the Frontier, 1825–1915.* Univ of New Mexico Pr 1984 $13.95. ISBN 0-8263-0780-9

*Rölvaag, O. E. *Giants in the Earth.* Harper Jr Bks 1965 $4.95. ISBN 0-06-083047-6 Novel about Swedish settlers on the North Dakota plains.

*Sandoz, Mari. *Battle of Little Big Horn.* Amereon $15.95. ISBN 0-89190-879-X Chronicles the famous battle between the Indians and pony soldiers commanded by George Custer.

*Sandoz, Mari. *Cheyenne Autumn.* Avon 1976 $4.95. ISBN 0-380-01094-1 A tale of the Cheyennes' waning days on the open plains.

*Schlissel, Lillian, *et al. Far from Home: Families of the Westward Journey.* Schocken 1989 $19.95. ISBN 0-8052-4052-7 The stories of four families, their journeys to the West, and their lives as pioneers; all pieced together from various primary sources.

Stegner, Wallace. *Beyond the Hundredth Meridian: John Wesley Powell and the Second Opening of the West.* Univ of Nebraska Pr 1982 $12.50. ISBN 0-8032-9128-0

*Stone, Irving. *Men to Match My Mountains.* Berkley 1987 $9.95. ISBN 0-425-10544-X Novel about the rugged Americans who opened the West between 1840 and 1900 by a noted author.

*Stratton, Joanna. *Pioneer Women.* Simon 1982 $11.95. ISBN 0-671-44748-3 Collection of letters from women on the plains.

*Turner, Frederick Jackson. *The Frontier in American History.* Univ of Arizona Pr 1985 $10.95. ISBN 0-8165-0946-8 Classic study that signaled the end of the frontier.

Utley, Robert M. *Cavalier in Buckskin: George Armstrong Custer and the Western Military Frontier. The Oklahoma Western Biographies Ser.* Univ of Oklahoma Pr 1988 $19.95. ISBN 0-8061-2150-5

Utley, Robert M. *Custer Battlefield, a History and Guide to the Battle of the Little Bighorn.* USGPO 1988 $4.75.

Utley, Robert M. *The Indian Frontier of the American West, 1846–1890. Histories of the American Frontier Ser.* Univ of New Mexico Pr 1984 $14.95. ISBN 0-8263-0716-7

Utley, Robert M. *Indian, Soldier, and Settler: Experiences in the Struggles for the American West.* Univ of Washington Pr 1977 $6.95. ISBN 0-295-96055-8

Utley, Robert M. *Last Days of the Sioux Nation. Western Americana Ser.* Yale Univ Pr 1963 $12.95. ISBN 0-300-00245-9

Webb, Walter P. *The Great Plains.* Univ of Nebraska Pr 1981 $11.95. ISBN 0-8032-9702-5

Western Writers of America Staff. *Pioneer Trails West: Great Stories of the Westering Americans and the Trails They Followed.* Donald Worcester (ed). Caxton 1985 $24.95. ISBN 0-87004-304-8

*Young, Alida O. *Land of the Iron Dragon.* Doubleday 1978. (o.p.) Fictionalized account of the Chinese workers who helped build the American railroad system.

CHIEF JOSEPH   1840?–1904

The gallant Chief Joseph of the Nez Percé Indians was truly an extraordinary leader. His Indian name, Hinmaton-Yalaktit, meant "thunder coming from the water up over the land." Joseph was born on the Lapwai River in Idaho, although the traditional territory of his people lay in the Wallowa and Imnaha valleys in northeastern Oregon.

In June 1877 the United States government ordered the Nez Percé to move from their homelands to a reservation in Oregon. The Indian lands were to remain open to white settlers. At first the Nez Percé, under the leadership of Chief Joseph, resisted. But soon they were forced to flee. With army troops pursuing them every step of the way, the band of 200 warriors and many women and children headed toward Canada. Over and over they managed to escape from the cavalry.

Then suddenly, after traveling more than 1,000 miles, the Nez Percé were surrounded. For five days Joseph and his warriors fought valiantly. With only 87 remaining men, almost half of them wounded, Chief Joseph saw that he could not win. As he surrendered he spoke the following words: "Hear me, my chiefs. I am tired; my heart is sick and sad. From where the sun now stands, I will fight no more, forever."

After the surrender, Chief Joseph and his people were sent to a reservation in Oklahoma, then part of the Indian Territory. Some years later, Joseph went to Washington, D.C., to plead for the Nez Percé. At last he and some of his followers were moved to a reservation in the state of Washington. Chief Joseph died there in 1904. He had kept his pledge never to fight again.

Today a plaque marks the spot where Chief Joseph surrendered. It reads "The surrender climaxed a 1,000 mile retreat destined to bring Chief Joseph recognition as one of the greatest military strategists who ever lived."

BOOKS ABOUT CHIEF JOSEPH

Beal, Merrill D. *I Will Fight No More Forever.* Ballantine 1985 $4.95. ISBN 0-345-32131-6 Highlights the struggle of Chief Joseph of the Nez Percé.

*Burt, Olive W. *Chief Joseph: Boy of the Nez Percé.* Macmillan 1967 $5.95. ISBN 0-672-50030-2 Life of Chief Joseph intended for grades 3 to 7.

Grant, Matthew G., and Dan Zadra. *Chief Joseph.* Creative Ed 1987 $15.95. ISBN 0-88682-158-4 Discussion of the life and accomplishments of Chief Joseph.

Wood, Erskine. *Days with Chief Joseph: Diary, Recollections & Photos.* Oregon Hist 1970 $2.95. ISBN 0-87595-026-4 Includes writings and pictures of the famous Indian leader.

CUSTER, GEORGE ARMSTRONG   1839–1876

Three days after graduating from the United States Military Academy at West Point, Ohio-born George Armstrong Custer participated in the first battle of Bull Run in Virginia in 1861. A brave fighter and an able strategist, he soon became the youngest brigadier general in the Union army, having jumped in rank over many older men.

Custer continued to distinguish himself during the Civil War. At Gettysburg in Pennsylvania in 1863, he led a cavalry brigade that stopped the South's attempt to cut the Union army's communications. Later, he fought in Virginia at the great cavalry battle at Yellow Tavern. And he was one of the few commanders whose troops were still standing firm when Union General Philip Henry Sheridan made his famous ride from Winchester in 1864. In all the battles fought by the Army of the Potomac, Custer took a leading role. Although some 10 horses were shot out from under him, he received only one minor wound. At the end of the war, he accepted the final Confederate surrender on the battlefield near Appomattox in Virginia.

After the war was over, when the army was reduced in size, Custer became a lieutenant colonel of the 7th Cavalry. However he was court-martialed in 1867 for leaving his command without permission. A year later, he was reinstated when the Cavalry suffered continual Indian defeats without him. During the next several years, Custer's regiment had numerous skirmishes with the Indians in the Black Hills of South Dakota.

In 1876 Custer was ordered to trap hostile groups of Sioux who had left their reservation and had joined other Indian forces near the Bighorn River in Montana. On June 25 he led a troop of 264 men toward what he believed to be a small Sioux camp. Without sending for reinforcements as he had been ordered, Custer rashly decided to attack. Suddenly his tiny force came face to face with between 2,500 and 4,000 Sioux, led by chiefs Sitting Bull and Crazy Horse. The Sioux warriors surrounded Custer's little force. A hail of bullets and arrows poured around them from every direction. One bullet struck Custer in the head, another in the chest. Within half an hour, the entire company, including Custer, was completely wiped out. This was the Battle of the Little Bighorn, or "Custer's Last Stand."

BOOK BY CUSTER

My Life on the Plains (1874). Citadel 1974 $5.95. ISBN 0-8065-0451-X

BOOKS ABOUT CUSTER

Ambrose, Stephen E. *Crazy Horse and Custer: The Parallel Lives of Two American Warriors.* NAL 1986 $12.95. ISBN 0-452-00934-0 Compares and contrasts the lives of Custer and Chief Crazy Horse.

Frost, Lawrence A. *Custer Legends.* Bowling Green Univ Pr 1981 $31.96. ISBN 0-87972-180-4 Discussion of why Custer became a legend.

Rosenberg, Bruce A. *Custer and the Epic of Defeat.* Penn State Univ Pr 1974 $27.50. ISBN 0-271-01172-6 Discussion of how Custer lost the Battle of the Little Bighorn.

*Stevenson, Augusta. *George Custer: Boy of Action.* Macmillan 1963 $5.95. ISBN 0-672-50062-0 Life of Custer written for younger students.

POPULISM AND THE RISE OF INDUSTRY

American Heritage Illustrated History of the United States. Vol. 10: The Age of Steel. Choice Pub 1988 $3.49. Illustrated history of the events and important people of the age of industry; especially suited to younger readers.

American Heritage Illustrated History of the United States. Vol. 11: The Gilded Age. Choice Pub 1988 $3.49. Illustrated history of the events and important people of the Gilded Age; especially suited to younger readers.

Burlingame, Roger. *Machines That Built America.* Harcourt 1953.

■Cashman, Sean Dennis. *America in the Gilded Age.* New York Univ Pr 1988 $16.50. ISBN

0-8147-1418-8 An account of this post Civil War period; contains a number of biographies.

Clemens, John. *Polls, Politics, and Populism.* Gower 1983 $47.95. ISBN 0-566-00602-2

Cochran, Thomas C. *Business in American Life.* McGraw 1974 $6.95. ISBN 0-07-011525-7

De Santis, Vincent. (comp). *Gilded Age, Eighteen Seventy-Five to Eighteen Ninety-Six. Goldentree Bibliographies in American History Ser.* Harlan Davidson 1973 $6.95. ISBN 0-88295-536-5

Dulles, Foster R., and Melvyn Dubofsky. *Labor in America.* Harlan Davidson 1984 $17.95. ISBN 0-88295-825-9

*Fisher, Leonard E. *The Factories. Nineteenth Century America Ser.* Holiday 1979 $9.95. ISBN 0-8234-0367-X Traces industrial development in the United States.

*Ginger, Ray. *Eugene V. Debs: A Biography.* Macmillan 1962 $5.95. ISBN 0-02-003310-9 Life of the labor leader who was jailed in 1918 for opposing U.S. entrance into World War I.

Hicks, John D. *The Populist Revolt: A History of the Farmer's Alliance and the People's Party.* Greenwood 1981 $38.50. ISBN 0-313-22567-2

Hofstadter, Richard. *The American Political Tradition.* Random 1989 $7.95. ISBN 0-679-72315-3

Hofstadter, Richard. *Social Darwinism in American Thought.* Beacon 1955 $10.95. ISBN 0-8070-5461-5

Holbrook, Stewart H. *The Age of the Moguls. Railroads Ser.* Ayer 1981 $35.00. ISBN 0-405-13789-3

Holbrook, Stewart H. *Story of American Railroads.* Crown 1981 $6.98. ISBN 0-517-00100-4

Josephson, Matthew. *Edison.* McGraw 1959 $10.95. ISBN 0-07-033046-8

Josephson, Matthew. *The Robber Barons.* Harcourt 1962 $7.95. ISBN 0-15-676790-2

Lindsey, Almont. *The Pullman Strike.* Univ of Chicago Pr 1964 $12.00. ISBN 0-226-48383-5

*Livesay, Harold. *Samuel Gompers and Organized Labor in America.* Scott 1978. ISBN 0-673-39345-3 Discusses how Samuel Gompers became a prominent figure in unionism.

Nevins, Allan (ed). *Letters of Grover Cleveland, 1850–1908. American Public Figures Ser.* Da Capo 1970 $75.00. ISBN 0-306-71982-7

Orth, Samuel P. *Boss and the Machine.* Elliots 1919 $19.50. ISBN 0-686-83493-3

*Pelta, Kathy. *Alexander Graham Bell. Pioneers in Change Ser.* Silver 1989 $11.98. ISBN 0-382-09529-4 Biography of the inventor of the telephone.

Persico, Joseph. *Imperial Rockefeller.* Washington Square Pr 1983. (o.p.)

Peterson, Florence. *Strikes in the United States.* Reprint Services 1988 repr of 1888 ed $25.00. ISBN 0-8022-2086-X

Porter, Glenn. *Rise of Big Business. American History Ser.* Harlan Davidson 1973 $7.95. ISBN 0-88295-750-3

Rayback, Joseph G. *History of American Labor.* Free Pr 1966 $15.95. ISBN 0-02-925850-2

Seitz, Don C. *Joseph Pulitzer, His Life and Letters.* AMS 1970 $17.50. ISBN 0-404-05699-7

Twain, Mark. *The Gilded Age: A Tale of Today.* NAL 1985 $4.95. ISBN 0-452-00779-8

Walker, Robert H. *Life in the Age of Enterprise.* Krieger 1989. ISBN 0-89464-297-9

BRYAN, WILLIAM JENNINGS 1860–1925

During a long and distinguished career, William Jennings Bryan served as a lawyer, journalist, editor-in-chief of a newspaper, politician, reformer, prohibitionist, and anti-evolutionist. Born in Salem, Illinois, he moved to Lincoln, Nebraska, in 1887, when he was 27 years old. In the presidential election of 1896, at the age of 36, Bryan became the Democratic party's candidate after capturing party members' imaginations at the 1896 convention with his "Cross of Gold" speech in which he advocated the free and unlimited coinage of silver. Bryan saw free silver as the solution to the economic ills that plagued farmers and industrial workers. He lost the election, however, to Republican William McKinley.

In 1900 he was again the Democratic party's presidential candidate, this time opposing McKinley with an anti-imperialism campaign in a losing effort. In 1908, Bryan was nominated a third time by the Democrats. Once again, he lost—this time to Republican William Howard Taft. (*See* Taft, Vol. 2, United States History: The Progressive Era—Politics, Reform, Change, and Expansion.) Despite these losses, he remained active in presidential politics, supporting Woodrow Wilson (*see* Wilson, Vol. 2, United States History: World War I) in the elections of 1912 and 1916, urging the convention to adopt a prohibition plank in 1920, working for William G. McAdoo and prohibition, and against Alfred E. Smith in 1924.

Although Bryan was a three-time loser in his quest for the presidency, he was nonetheless successful in having the nation adopt many of his reforms, including the income tax, popular election of senators, suffrage for women, and prohibition. Under President Woodrow Wilson, he served for a time as Secretary of War. A devout Presbyterian devoted to fundamentalism—a movement based on belief in the Bible as historical fact and unchangeable phophecy—Bryan also opposed attorney Clarence Darrow in the 1925 Scopes trial in Tennessee. Although he won the court trial, he was severely ridiculed for his anti-evolutionist views by Darrow and others. Bryan died in his sleep five days after the trial.

BOOKS BY BRYAN

Bryan on Imperialism. Ayer 1970 $16.00. ISBN 0-405-02005-8
First Battle. 2 vols. *American History and Culture in the Nineteenth Century Ser.* Assoc Faculty Pr 1971 $50.00. ISBN 0-8046-1471-7
Memoirs of William Jennings Bryan. American Biography Ser. (coauthored with M. B. Bryan) Haskell 1970 $75.00. ISBN 0-8383-1165-2

BOOKS ABOUT BRYAN

Ashby, Le Roy. *William Jennings Bryan: Champion of Democracy. Twayne's Twentieth Century American Biography Ser.* G. K. Hall 1987 $10.95. ISBN 0-8057-7776-8 Examination of Bryan's career, private life, political milieu, public image, and impact on modern society.
Glad, Paul W. *The Trumpet Soundeth: William Jennings Bryan and His Democracy, 1896–1912.* Greenwood 1986 $48.50. ISBN 0-313-25049-9 Extensive biography of Bryan; includes an excellent collection of photographs.

CARNEGIE, ANDREW   1835–1919

For many people, Andrew Carnegie personifies the rags-to-riches dream of many immigrants to the United States. His father, who was a weaver in Scotland, brought his family to the United States in 1848 because he could find no work in Scotland. The young Carnegie, only 13 years old at the time, started out by working in a cotton mill as a bobbin boy, changing spools of thread. He quickly advanced himself by reading books and by taking better jobs in the growing railroad industry, first as a telegrapher and then, in 1859, as a superintendent for the Pennsylvania Railroad.

No matter what salary Carnegie earned, he always saved something, investing whenever he could in iron manufactures. In 1865 he resigned his railroad position to devote full time to his growing pool of investments. By 1872 he had begun to concentrate on the production of steel and to acquire small firms, thereby forming the Carnegie Steel Corporation. By 1900 Carnegie controlled the entire steelmaking process, from the gathering of raw materials and their transportation to the coking plants and smelters to the manufacture and sale of the finished products. His mills were producing one-quarter of all the steel in the United States. Carnegie employed 20,000 people, but he strongly opposed unions and resisted all efforts to unionize his plants.

In 1901 Carnegie sold the Carnegie Steel Corporation for $250 million to American financier John Pierpont Morgan, who then established U.S. Steel. On retirement from business, Carnegie put into practice his idea that the rich are trustees of their wealth and should administer it for the good of the public. This idea was expressed in his 1889 essay "The Gospel of Wealth". In all, Carnegie donated about $350 million to institutions, commissions, foundations, and more than 2,500 libraries. Many of those institutions and foundations bear his name today, including Carnegie Hall in New York City and the Carnegie Institute in Washington, D.C.

BOOKS BY CARNEGIE

The Autobiography of Andrew Carnegie. Northeastern Univ Pr 1986 $10.95. ISBN 1-55553-001-X

Empire of Business. Greenwood 1968 $55.00. ISBN 0-8371-0037-2

Miscellaneous Writings. Essay Index Reprint Ser. B. J. Hendrick (ed). Ayer 1933 $40.00. ISBN 0-8369-0105-3

Triumphant Democracy. Johnson Repr 1971 $37.00. ISBN 0-384-07697-1

BOOKS ABOUT CARNEGIE

*Bowman, John. *Andrew Carnegie. The American Dream Ser.* Silver 1989 $11.98. ISBN 0-382-09582-0 Introductory biography of the industrialist.

Hendrick, Burton J. *The Life of Andrew Carnegie.* 2 vols. Transaction 1989 $59.95. ISBN 0-88738-276-2 Extensive biography of the industrialist, written over 50 years ago.

IMMIGRATION, URBANIZATION, AND CIVIL RIGHTS

*Adair, Gene. *George Washington Carver. Black Americans of Achievement Ser.* Chelsea 1989 $17.95. ISBN 1-55546-577-3 Account of how the son of a slave became a world-famous scientist.

*Alger, Horatio. *Making His Way: Frank Courtney's Struggle Upward. Popular Culture in America Ser.* Ayer 1975 $24.50. ISBN 0-405-06361-X One of many books about youthful heroes who achieve wealth and honor in the United States, written by a notable author of the late nineteenth century.

*Bales, Carol. *Tales of the Elders: A Memory Book of Men and Women Who Came to America as Immigrants, 1900–1930.* Follett 1977. (o.p.) Illustrated accounts of immigrants to America.

Barry, Kathleen. *Susan B. Anthony, A Biography: A Singular Feminist.* New York Univ Pr 1988 $27.95. ISBN 0-8147-1105-7

*Beard, Annie E. *Our Foreign-Born Citizens.* Harper Jr Bks 1968 $14.70. ISBN 0-690-60525-0 Story of immigrants to America.

*Beatty, Patricia. *Eight Mules from Monterey.* Morrow 1982 $12.95. ISBN 0-688-01047-4 Story of a librarian who delivers books by mule to California mountain communities.

Bell, James B. *In Search of Liberty: The Story of the Statue of Liberty and Ellis Island.* Doubleday 1984 $10.95. ISBN 0-385-19276-2

Bender, Thomas. *Toward an Urban Vision: Ideas and Institutions in Nineteenth Century America.* Johns Hopkins Univ Pr 1982 $10.95. ISBN 0-8018-2925-9

Brandes, Joseph, and Martin Douglas. *Immigrants to Freedom: Jewish Communities in Rural New Jersey Since 1882.* Univ of Penn Pr 1971 $31.95. ISBN 0-8122-7620-5

*Crane, Stephen. *Maggie: A Girl of the Streets.* Random 1989 $6.50. Fictional account of a girl in New York around 1893.

*Daley, William. *The Chinese Americans. The Peoples of North America Ser.* Chelsea 1987 $17.95. ISBN 0-87754-876-6 Tells the story of the Chinese experience in America with discussion of Chinese culture, history, and traditions.

*Editors of Time-Life Books. *This Fabulous Century.* Vol. 1 *1900–1910.* Time–Life 1969 $17.95. ISBN 0-8094-0121-5. Photographic and interesting brief essay narratives covering all aspects of the era from 1900 to 1910.

*Fisher, Leonard Everett. *Ellis Island: Gateway to the New World.* Holiday 1986 $13.95. ISBN 0-8234-0612-1 Story of Ellis Island and the immigrants who passed through it; includes first-person accounts and photographs.

Green, Constance McLaughlin. *The Rise of Urban America.* Harper 1965. (o.p.).

*Hanmer, Trudy. *The Growth of Cities.* Watts 1985 $12.90. ISBN 0-531-10056-1 Focuses on the development and growth of U.S. cities.

Higham, John. *Send These to Me: Immigrants in Urban America.* Johns Hopkins Univ Pr 1984 $10.95. ISBN 0-8018-2438-9

Higham, John. *Strangers in the Land: Patterns of American Nativism, 1860–1925.* Rutgers Univ Pr 1988 $12.00. ISBN 0-8135-1308-1

*Hoff, Rhoda. *America's Immigrants: Adventures in Eye-Witness History.* Walck 1967. The stories of the immigrants told in their own words.

*Howells, William Dean. *The Rise of Silas Lapham.* Penguin 1983 $5.95. ISBN 0-14-039030-8 Classic title of late 1800s; brought recognition to the author as a writer of realistic fiction.

*Huttenbach, Henry. *The Jewish Americans. The Peoples of North America Ser.* Chelsea 1989 $9.95. ISBN 0-7910-0270-5 Tells the story of Jews in America, why they came to America, and what their life was like after they arrived in the United States.

*Jacobs, William Jay. *Ellis Island: New Hope in a New Land.* Macmillan 1990 $13.95. ISBN 0-684-19171-7 Illustrated description of what it was like to be an immigrant travelling to the United States and arriving at Ellis Island; especially suited to younger readers.

*Katz, William L., and Jacqueline H. Katz. *Making Our Way: America at the Turn of the Century in the Words of the Poor and Powerless.* Dial 1975. (o.p.) American life in early 1900s told by those who were there.

Kolko, Gabriel. *The Triumph of Conservatism: A Reinterpretation of American History, 1900–1916.* Free Pr 1977 $11.95. ISBN 0-02-916650-0

Kraut, Alan M. *The Huddled Masses: The Immigrant in American Society, 1880–1921. The American History Ser.* Harlan Davidson 1982 $9.50. ISBN 0-88295-810-0

*Kurelek, William, and Margaret Englehart. *They Sought A New World.* Tundra 1985 $7.95. ISBN 0-88776-213-1 Colorfully illustrated artwork and highly readable text that describe the immigrant experience in North America.

*Lasky, Kathryn. *The Night Journey. Puffin Novels Ser.* Penguin 1986 $4.95. ISBN 0-14-032048-2 An immigrant relates the story of dangerous escape from Russia to her great-granddaughter.

Lutz, Alma. *Susan B. Anthony: Rebel, Crusader, Humanitarian.* Zenger 1976 $19.95. ISBN 0-89201-017-7

Magnuson, Norris. *Salvation in the Slums: Evangelical Social Welfare Work, 1865–1920.* Scarecrow 1977 $24.00. ISBN 0-8108-1001-8

Mumford, Lewis. *The Culture of Cities.* Greenwood 1981 $48.50. ISBN 0-313-22746-2

*Neidle, Cecyle S. *America's Immigrant Women.* Hippocrene 1976 $4.95. ISBN 0-88254-369-5 Story of women who immigrated to improve their lives.

Pinchot, Gifford. *Breaking New Ground. Conservation Classics Ser.* Island 1987 $19.95. ISBN 0-933280-42-4

Schlesinger, Arthur. *Rise of the City: 1878–1898.* Macmillan 1933. (o.p.)

Takaki, Ronald. *Strangers from a Different Shore: A History of Asian Americans.* Little 1989 $22.95. ISBN 0-316-83109-3

*Weatherford, Doris. *Foreign and Female: Immigrant Women in America, 1840–1930.* Schocken 1987 $18.95. ISBN 0-8052-4017-9 Profiles and excerpts from correspondence of women who were immigrants to the United States.

*Woodward, C. Vann. *The Strange Career of Jim Crow.* Oxford Univ Pr 1974 $7.95. ISBN 0-19-501805-2 Classic, valuable work on American race relations.
*Yep, Laurence. *Dragonwings.* Harper Jr Bks 1977 $3.50. ISBN 0-06-440085-9 Fictionalized account of Chinese boy living in San Francisco.

ADDAMS, JANE   1860–1935

In an age when many immigrants to the United States found themselves involved in the strange urban world of slums and tenements, social worker Jane Addams helped the urban poor cope with the difficulties of life. Born in Cedarville, Illinois, Addams graduated from Rockford College in Illinois in 1881. In 1889, after a visit to England where she learned about the settlement houses built there by Samuel Barnett, Addams, working with Ellen Gates Starr, founded Hull House in Chicago. One of the first settlement houses in the United States, Hull House served as a community, education, and recreation center for the many ethnic groups of the neighborhood. Not only was it important in the civic affairs of Chicago, but it ultimately had a major influence on the settlement movement all across the United States.

Later, Hull House, like other settlement houses in the nation, attracted many young, college-educated women. Trained under Addams, these women—like Addams herself—became ardent reformers, campaigning especially for women's rights and women's suffrage. Politically, Addams opposed entry into World War I and favored ratification of the Versailles Treaty.

For her work with the urban poor, her efforts at reform, and for her stand as an ardent pacifist, Addams received the Nobel Peace Prize in 1931. When she died three weeks after her seventy-fifth birthday, the funeral at Hull House was attended by many of the nation's influential leaders, and the streets overflowed with ordinary people who came to pay their respects.

BOOKS BY ADDAMS

Democracy and Social Ethics. Reprint Services 1988 $75.00. ISBN 0-317-90182-6
Newer Ideals of Peace. Peace Movement in America Ser. Ozer 1972 $21.95. ISBN 0-89198-051-2
Peace and Bread in Time of War (1922). *NASW Classics Ser.* National Assn of Social Workers 1983 $9.95. ISBN 0-87101-110-7
Social Thought of Jane Addams. Christopher Lasch (ed). Irvington 1982 $16.95. ISBN 0-8290-0338-X
The Spirit of Youth and the City Streets (1909). Univ of Illinois Pr 1972 $19.95. ISBN 0-252-00276-8
Twenty Years at Hull-House (1910). Univ of Illinois Pr 1990 $10.95. ISBN 0-252-06107-1

BOOKS ABOUT ADDAMS

Deegan, Mary J. *Jane Addams and the Men of the Chicago School, 1892–1918.* Transaction 1986 $34.95. ISBN 0-88738-077-8 Discusses the development of American social thought and the intellectual contributions of Jane Addams.
Hovde, Jane. *Jane Addams: Social Reformer Feminist. Makers of America Ser.* Facts on File 1989 $15.95. ISBN 0-317-69557-6 Traces the entire career of one of America's greatest social reformers and most ardent feminist crusaders.

ANTIN, MARY   1881–1949

Mary Antin was born in Polotzk, Russia at a time when that country had very strict regulations about where Jews could live and what they could and could not do. Her father was a trader, one of the very few means of livelihood open to Jews. It was in this environment that Antin spent most of her childhood.

UNITED STATES HISTORY **209**

Like other Russian Jews of the time, Antin's father thought he could find a better life in America. So, when Mary was 10 years old, her father emigrated to the United States, promising to bring over his family as soon as he was able. Three years later, Mary's mother, Mary, two of her sisters, and her brother made the long and arduous journey to America.

The family settled in Boston, where Mary's father had opened a refreshment stand. When the refreshment stand failed, the family moved to Chelsea, a town on the outskirts of Boston. But the grocery store the Antins operated there failed as well, and the family was forced to move again—this time to the slums of Boston's South End.

Like most immigrants of the time, Mary Antin did not speak English when she arrived in America. Bright and eager to learn, she quickly mastered the language and became an excellent student. A composition that she wrote so impressed one of her teachers in Chelsea that the teacher had it published in *Primary Education.* This success prompted Antin to write poetry, some of which was printed in the Boston newspapers. Encouraged by her teachers and her family, she entered the Girls' Latin School in Boston and dreamed of going on to higher education at Radcliffe College.

Antin had written a series of letters to her uncle in Russia telling him about her journey to America and about her experiences as an immigrant. The letters were written in Yiddish, the language then commonly spoken by almost all Eastern European Jews. While still in school, Antin translated the letters into English. In 1899, they were published as a book—*From Plotzk* [Polotzk] *to Boston.*

Antin's plan to attend Radcliffe never materialized. While on a field trip with the Boston Society of Natural History, she met a young geologist named Amadeus William Grabau. The son of a German-born Lutheran minister, Grabau was in the process of finishing up his doctorate at Harvard University. In 1901, he and Antin were married. Grabau accepted a professorship at Columbia University, and the couple settled in New York City. For the next three years, Mary took courses at Columbia's Teachers College and at Barnard College.

Meanwhile, Antin continued to write. In 1911, one of her short stories about Polotzk and its people was published in *Atlantic Monthly.* It became the first of a series out of which grew Antin's successful autobiographical work, *The Promised Land.* Published in 1912, *The Promised Land* sold close to 85,000 copies during Antin's lifetime. It tells of her life in Russia and in Boston and inspired many to believe as Antin did that America was truly a land of opportunity. Two years later, *Those Who Knock at Our Gates* was published. Like Antin's other works, it deals with the hopes and experiences of immigrants. At the time the book was published, Americans were having doubts about the desirability of allowing so many immigrants to enter the country, and there was talk of restricting immigration. In her book, Antin justified continued immigration.

Antin fervently believed in America and in its customs and traditions. At the same time, as a strong advocate of immigration, she campaigned against proposals in Congress to adopt legislation that would put restrictions on immigration. Between 1913 and 1918, she gave lectures all over the country on the subject of immigration, discussing such topics as "The Responsibility of American Citizenship," "The Civic Education of the Immigrant," and "The Public School As a Test of American Faith." She also spoke on behalf of the Progressive party and, during World War I, in favor of the Allied cause.

By 1920, Antin's marriage had come to an end. Not fully recovered from an attack of nervous exhaustion she had suffered a few years earlier, she spent most of her time with her family in Winchester, Massachusetts and at a friend's farm in Great Barrington, Massachusetts. Her marriage, among other things, had cut her off from Jewish life and thought. But, in her last essay, "House of the One Father," which appeared in 1941, she writes of her solidarity with her roots.

At the age of 68, Mary Antin died in a nursing home in Suffern, New York from heart complications and cancer.

BOOKS BY ANTIN

From Plotzk to Boston (1899). *Masterworks of Modern Jewish Writing Ser.* Wiener 1986 $6.95. ISBN 0-910129-45-2 Sensitive account of Antin's journey to America.
The Promised Land: The Autobiography of a Russian Immigrant (1912). Princeton Univ Pr 1985 $13.50. ISBN 0-691-80598-2 Antin's recollections of her childhood in Russia and her years in Boston.

DU BOIS, W. E. B. (WILLIAM EDWARD BURGHARDT)   1868–1963

Civil rights leader and author, William Edward Burghart Du Bois was born in Great Barrington, Massachusetts, five years after the Emancipation Proclamation was signed. He earned a B.A. from both Harvard and Fisk universities, an M.A. and Ph.D. from Harvard, and studied at the University of Berlin. He taught briefly at Wilberforce University before he became professor of history and economics at Atlanta University in Ohio (1896–1910). There, he wrote *The Souls of Black Folk* (1903), in which he pointed out that it was up to whites and blacks jointly to solve the problems created by the denial of civil rights to blacks. In 1905 Du Bois became a major figure in the Niagara Movement, a crusading effort to end discrimination. The organization collapsed, but it prepared the way for the founding of the National Association for the Advancement of Colored People (NAACP), in which Du Bois played a major role. In 1910 he became editor of the NAACP magazine, a position he held for more than 20 years.

Du Bois returned to Atlanta University in 1932 and tried to implement a plan to make the Negro Land Grant Colleges centers of black power. Atlanta approved of his idea but later retracted its support. When Du Bois tried to return to the NAACP, it too rejected him.

Active in several Pan-African Congresses, Du Bois came to know Kwame Nkrumah (*see* Nkrumah, Vol. 2, World History: Africa), the first president of Ghana, and Jomo Kenyatta (*see* Kenyatta, Vol. 2, World History: Africa), the president of Kenya. In 1961, the same year Du Bois joined the Communist party, Nkrumah invited him to Ghana as director of an *Encyclopedia Africana* project. He died there two years later, after becoming a citizen of that country.

BOOKS BY DU BOIS

Autobiography of W. E. Burghardt Du Bois: A Soliloquy on Viewing My Life From the Last Decade of Its First Century (1968). Herbert Aptheker (ed). Intl Pubs 1968 $8.95. ISBN 0-7178-0234-5
The Black Folk Then and Now: An Essay in the History and Sociology of The Negro Race. Kraus 1975 $24.00. ISBN 0-527-25275-1
Black North in 1901: A Social Study. American Negro: His History and Literature Ser. Ayer 1970 $9.00. ISBN 0-405-01921-1
Black Reconstruction in America, 1860–1880 (1935). Macmillan 1969 $10.95. ISBN 0-689-70063-6
Color and Democracy: Colonies and Peace. Kraus 1975 $10.00. ISBN 0-527-25290-5
Economic Co-operation Among Negro Americans (1907). *Atlanta Univ Publications Ser.* Kraus $16.00. ISBN 0-527-03113-5
The Education of Black People. 1906–1960: Ten Critiques. Herbert Aptheker (ed). Monthly Review 1975 $8.00. ISBN 0-85345-363-2

Efforts for Social Betterment Among Negro Americans (1909). *Atlanta Univ Publications Ser.* Kraus $15.00. ISBN 0-527-03115-1
The Gift of Black Folk (1924). AMS 1983 $15.00. ISBN 0-404-00152-1
Morals and Manners Among Negro Americans (1914). *Atlanta Univ Publications Ser.* Kraus $15.00. ISBN 0-527-03119-4
The Negro Artisan (1902). *Atlanta Univ Publications Ser.* Kraus $16.00. ISBN 0-527-03110-0
The Negro in Business (1899). AMS 1973 $12.50. ISBN 0-404-00153-X
The Philadelphia Negro: A Social Study (1899). Kraus 1973 $31.00. ISBN 0-527-25320-0
Prayers for Dark People. Herbert Aptheker (ed). Univ of Massachusetts Pr 1980 $7.95. ISBN 0-87023-303-3
The Souls of Black Folk (1903). Bantam 1989 $3.95. ISBN 0-553-21336-9
Suppression of the African Slave Trade, 1638–1870 (1940). Louisiana State Univ Pr 1970 $12.95. ISBN 0-8071-0149-4
The World and Africa: An Inquiry into the Part Which Africa Has Played in World History (1955). Kraus (repr of 1965 ed) $21.00. ISBN 0-527-25340-5

BOOKS ABOUT DU BOIS

De Marco, Joseph P. *The Social Thought of W. E. B. Du Bois.* Univ Pr of America 1983 $14.00. ISBN 0-8191-3236-5 Interprets and surveys the structure, rationale, and development of Du Bois's social philosophy as presented in his non-fiction writing.
*Hamilton, Virginia. *W. E. B. Du Bois: A Biography.* Harper Jr Bks 1972 $13.89. ISBN 0-690-87256-9 Introductory biography of the controversial leader.

RIIS, JACOB AUGUST   1849–1914

Social reformer, journalist, author, and lecturer, Jacob Riis was born in Ribe, Denmark. His concern for reform first came to light when he was only 13 years old. In Ribe there was a rat-infested, filthy tenement built directly over a sewer. Observing the conditions under which the poor people in the tenement lived, the horrified teenager determined to clean up the place. He killed the rats, cleaned out their nests, and scrubbed everywhere. Then, using the money his father had given him for Christmas, he bought whitewash for the walls.

At the age of 14, Riis dropped out of school. For the next four years, he served as an apprentice to a carpenter in Copenhagen. But when the parents of the girl he loved refused to allow their daughter to marry a carpenter, he decided to go to America and make his fortune, hoping eventually to marry his sweetheart.

In 1870, at the age of 21, Riis emigrated to the United States and settled in New York City. When he discovered that he could not find work as a carpenter, he took any job he could find. He mined coal in Pennsylvania and made bricks in New Jersey. He tried farming, peddling, and candlemaking. Meanwhile, he polished his English-language skills.

For three years, he worked on perfecting his English, working at any job he could find. Finally, he got a job at a Long Island weekly newspaper. But, after two weeks, he had received no pay, so he quit. He next secured a job working for a small newspaper in Manhattan, and a few months later, he got a better-paying job with a newspaper in Brooklyn.

In 1876, Riis returned to Ribe and married his boyhood sweetheart. In 1877, shortly after the couple returned to America, Riis managed a job as a police reporter for the New York *Tribune,* a position he held for 11 years. He was assigned to cover the action at police headquarters on Mulberry Street in Mulberry Bend. This was Manhattan's worst slum, with the city's highest rates of murder, robbery, and fire. In 1888, Riis went to work for another New York newspaper—the *Evening Sun*—once again as a police reporter. Later, he supported himself by writing articles and books and by giving lectures.

Determined and committed, Riis waged a literary battle against the injustices suffered by the poor. In his newspaper column, he painted startling personal portraits of the people of Mulberry Street to dramatize the plight of the poor, especially the children, and to organize support for their relief. From the articles he wrote for his column, describing what he had seen on Mulberry Street, came his first book, *How the Other Half Lives.* Published in 1890, the book attracted the attention of many Americans. One of those Americans was Theodore Roosevelt (*see* T. Roosevelt, Vol. 2, United States History: The Progressive Era—Politics, Reform, Change, and Expansion). Roosevelt was to become a lifelong supporter of Riis, whom he called "one of my truest and closest friends," "like my own brother." With Roosevelt's help, Riis was able to set up 16 Good Government Clubs in New York City for members of the middle class who wanted to work for reform. First as governor of New York and then as President of the United States, Roosevelt repeatedly offered Riis political office. Riis refused each and every offer, saying he was too busy to go into politics.

In 1901, Riis published his autobiography, *The Making of an American,* which tells of his life and his many crusades. Three years later, still writing, lecturing, traveling, and working himself to the point of exhaustion, Riis was stricken with heart disease. Illness, however, did not slow him down until 1913 when, on doctor's orders, he entered a sanitarium to rest. He died at home the following year.

Riis believed that the poor needed a chance, not a change, that the solution to their problem was "not charity, but justice." Riis came to be known as the "great emancipator" of the slums. The list of his achievements is a long one. He made the people of New York aware that the site of their water supply—the Hudson River at Croton, New York—was contaminated, leading the city of New York to buy the Croton watershed. He helped push through new laws to improve lighting and ventilation in tenements. He helped win passage of child-labor laws and worked for their enforcement. He exposed the long-hidden dens of vice and crime that existed in the slums and forced the police to close them down. He secured playgrounds for schools and succeeded in having classrooms opened to clubs for boys and girls. In his view, one of his greatest successes was that the tenements of Mulberry Bend were razed and replaced by "a spot of green"—Mulberry Bend Park—and by a Neighborhood House, later named after him.

BOOKS BY RIIS

The Battle with the Slum: A Ten Year War Rewritten (1902). Irvington 1972 $14.00. ISBN 0-8290-0653-2

The Children of the Poor (1892). Ayer 1971 repr of 1892 ed $23.50. ISBN 0-405-03124-6

Children of the Tenements (1903). Irvington (repr of 1903 ed) $19.00. ISBN 0-8398-1757-6

How the Other Half Lives (1890). Dover 1971 $9.95. ISBN 0-486-22012-5

Out of Mulberry Street (1898). Irvington (repr of 1898 ed) $29.75. ISBN 0-8398-1758-4

Theodore Roosevelt, the Citizen (1904). AMS (repr of 1904 ed) $17.50. ISBN 0-404-05335-1

BOOK ABOUT RIIS

Fried, Lewis. *Makers of the City.* Univ of Massachusetts Pr 1990 $30.00. ISBN 0-87023-693-8 Examines the virtues of the American city as portrayed in the writings of Jacob Riis and others.

WASHINGTON, BOOKER T. (TALLAFERRO) 1856–1915

Born into slavery, Booker T. Washington became a leading educator of African Americans. Highly respected both as an educator and as a spokesperson for blacks, he was granted honorary degrees from both Harvard and Dartmouth universities. After graduating from and teaching at Hampton Normal and Industrial Institute in Virginia, he was chosen to found the coeducational Tuskegee Normal and Industrial Institute in Alabama. Between 1880 and 1915, he expanded Tuskegee from two buildings to a higher educational institution of more than 100 buildings, a faculty of 200, and an enrollment exceeding 1,500 students by 1915.

Washington held strong beliefs about the dignity of manual work and the importance of character building, and he promoted these principles in his speeches and writing. In 1895 he gave an address at a large fair in Atlanta. It came to be known as the Atlanta Compromise because in it Washington asserted that blacks should work to gain economic security before seeking equal rights. This belief put him at odds with some members of the African-American community, most notably W. E. B. Du Bois (*see* Du Bois, Vol. 2, United States History: Immigration, Urbanization, and Civil Rights) who maintained that the right to hold a job was not enough, that blacks needed equal rights in all areas to maintain their dignity and self-esteem.

BOOKS BY WASHINGTON

The Booker T. Washington Papers. Louis R. Harlan, *et al* (eds). 14 vols. Univ of Illinois Pr 1972–1989 $35.00. ISBNs 0-252-00242-3, 0-252-00243-1, 0-252-00410-8, 0-252-00529-5, 0-252-00627-5, 0-252-00650-X, 0-252-00666-6, 0-252-00728-X, 0-252-00771-9, 0-252-00800-6, 0-252-00887-1, 0-252-00974-6, 0-252-01125-2, 0-252-01519-3

* Up from Slavery. Carol 1989 $7.95. ISBN 0-8216-0184-9 The story of the slave who later organized the Tuskegee Institute.

The Negro in the South. (coauthored with W. E. B. Du Bois) Carol 1989 $7.95. ISBN 0-8216-0183-0

BOOKS ABOUT WASHINGTON

Hawkins, Hugh. *Booker T. Washington and His Critics. Problems in American Civilization Ser.* Heath 1974 $8.00. ISBN 0-669-87049-8 Biography of Washington that presents conflicting views of this controversial personality.

Smock, Raymond W. (ed). *Booker T. Washington in Perspective: Essays of Louis R. Harlan.* Univ Pr of Mississippi 1988 $25.00. ISBN 0-87805-374-3 Collection of Harlan's essays detailing his experience in writing his acclaimed biography of Washington.

THE ARTS IN THE AGE OF ENTERPRISE

Cahill, Holger. *American Folk Art: The Art of the Common Man in America 1750–1900.* Ayer 1970 repr of 1932 ed $20.00. ISBN 0-405-01530-5

Cahill, Holger. *American Painting and Sculpture: 1862–1932.* Ayer 1970 repr of 1932 ed $18.50. ISBN 0-405-01531-3

Flexner, James T. *History of American Painting.* Vol. 3 *That Wilder Image, the Native School from Thomas Cole to Winslow Homer. Fine Art Ser.* Dover 1988 $8.95. ISBN 0-486-25709-6

Kiehl, David W. (comp). *American Art Posters of the 1890s.* Abrams 1987 $45.00. ISBN 0-8109-1869-2

ADAMS, HENRY 1838–1918

Novelist, essayist, biographer, and historian, Henry Adams was born in Boston, Massachusetts, the son of Charles Francis Adams, the grandson of John Quincy Adams, sixth President of the United States, and the great-grandson of John Adams, second President of the United States. (*See* J. Adams *and* J. Q. Adams, Vol. 2, United States History: Beginning of the New Nation—Nationalism and Growth.) Although he was trained as a lawyer, Adams abandoned law for a career in journalism. He also taught medieval history at Harvard University from 1870 to 1877, serving at the same time as editor of the *North American Review.*

In 1877 Adams moved to Washington, D.C., and turned his attention to writing. As a historian, he published two major works. The first, a nine-volume work titled the *History of the United States During the Administrations of Jefferson and Madison* (1889–1891), considered by historians to be a major achievement in historical writing, is an analysis and interpretation of American history during the administrations of presidents Thomas Jefferson and James Madison. While the work was short on the role that economic forces played in these administrations, it brilliantly summarized the social forces at work in the new republic and also illuminated politics and politicians and the issues with which they struggled. The second major work was *The Education of Henry Adams* (1906), an autobiography written in the third person that described Adams's physical and mental struggles to define a basic philosophy of history and to achieve some degree of mental and intellectual peace, especially after the death of his beloved wife in 1885.

BOOKS BY ADAMS

Democracy, an American Novel. Airmont Classics Ser (1880). Airmont 1968 $82.50. ISBN 0-8049-0164-3

The Education of Henry Adams (1906). Ernest Samuels (ed). Houghton 1973 $8.36. ISBN 0-395-16620-9

History of the United States During the Administrations of Jefferson and Madison (1889–1891). 9 vols. Gordon Pr 1980 $995.00. ISBN 0-8490-3148-6

Letters to a Niece and Prayer to the Virgin of Chartres. Reprint Services 1988 repr of 1920 ed $49.00. ISBN 0-317-90017-X

Mont-Saint-Michel and Chartres (1904). *Classics Ser.* Penguin 1986 $7.95. ISBN 0-14-039054-5

The United States in 1800. Cornell Univ Pr 1955 $6.95. ISBN 0-8014-9014-6

BOOKS ABOUT ADAMS

Blackmur, R. P. *Henry Adams. Quality Paperbacks Ser.* Da Capo 1984 $10.95. ISBN 0-306-80219-8 Critical biography of this exemplary American intellectual.

Rowe, John C. *Henry Adams and Henry James: The Emergence of a Modern Consciousness.* Cornell Univ Pr 1976 $29.95. ISBN 0-8014-0954-3 Illuminates the writings of Adams and James and aids in the understanding of American literary values.

Samuels, Ernest. *Henry Adams.* Harvard Univ Pr 1989 $25.00. ISBN 0-674-38735-X Examines Adams's life and career over 60 years of American political, social, and intellectual life, from the pre-Civil War years to the First World War.

CASSAT, MARY 1845–1926

While other women of the late nineteenth century were making a name for themselves as reformers, educators, and writers, Pittsburgh-born Mary Cassat was becoming an important American painter. Born into a wealthy family,

Cassat went to Paris as a tourist, became interested in art, and stayed to become an important Impressionist painter. Cassat's work, influenced more by the work of her French contemporaries than by the work of those in the United States, was little appreciated in the United States before World War I. Today, however, her work is well represented in the United States in important museums, galleries, and private collections.

Cassat was the only American invited to exhibit her paintings with other outstanding Impressionists such as French painters Edgar Degas and Edouard Manet. Cassat painted vigorously, using bright colors and displaying a charming simplicity, using oils and pastels, and etching dryprints and color prints. Her favorite subject, motherhood, was displayed in several versions of *Mother and Child.* One version hangs in the Metropolitan Museum of Art in New York City and another in the Museum of Fine Arts in Boston. In 1893 she painted a mural, *Modern Woman,* for the women's building at the Chicago World's Fair. Another outstanding example of her work, painted in 1894, is *La Toilette,* which was exhibited in Paris.

BOOK BY CASSATT

The Mary Cassatt Datebook. Hudson Hills 1988 $10.95. ISBN 1-55595-006-X

BOOKS ABOUT CASSATT

Bullard, E. John. *Mary Cassatt, Oils and Pastels.* Watson-Guptill 1984 $16.95. ISBN 0-8230-0570-4 Biography of Mary Cassatt; includes numerous color prints of her work.

Cain, Michael. *Mary Cassatt. American Women of Achievement Ser.* Chelsea 1989 $17.95. ISBN 1-55546-647-8 Illustrated biography of Mary Cassatt that details her contributions to American art.

HOMER, WINSLOW   1836–1910

Landscape and marine artist Winslow Homer was born in Massachusetts. At the age of 25, he was sent to the battlefields of the Civil War as an illustrator and correspondent for *Harper's Weekly.* The series of paintings he produced showing life on the battlefield gained him international fame. After the war he continued his career as a magazine illustrator.

In 1876 Homer abandoned his career as an illustrator and, after a brief period of study in Paris, became a serious painter of landscapes, scenes of American rural life, and seascapes in oils and watercolors. Although he continued to paint for many years, he chose to live the life of a recluse after 1884.

Homer is most famous for scenes of the sea, which he painted at his home in Maine and during his wintertime travels in Florida and the Bahamas. Homer tried to capture reality, using natural light and the colors of his palette to express the intensity of his feelings. Some of his best work was done in watercolors. All of Homer's paintings express the weather-beaten ruggedness of the American landscape and the common people as they plied the sea or farmed the land. *Herring Net,* painted in 1885 and now hanging in the Art Institute of Chicago, is characteristic of the style he used for his watercolors. The painting depicts two fishers—an older man and a young boy—pulling their catch from the rolling sea into their small boat. Characteristic of his oil paintings are *The Gulf Stream,* which he painted in 1899 and which hangs in the Metropolitan Museum of Art in New York City, and *Eight Bells,* which he painted in 1886 and which hangs in the Addison Gallery in Andover, Massachusetts. *The Gulf Stream,* one of Homer's most acclaimed oils, carries as a theme the perils of the sea. In it, a black fisherman lies dazed on the deck of a small boat that has lost its mast, about to be hit by a waterspout, and surrounded by turbulent shark-infested waters. *Eight Bells,* one of the artist's sea epics, depicts two oilskin-clad men on the deck of a big ship taking bearings with octants.

BOOK BY HOMER

Winslow Homer Illustrations: Forty-Four Wood Engravings After Drawings by the Artist (1983). Dover $3.50. ISBN 0-486-24392-3

BOOKS ABOUT HOMER

Cikovsky, Nicolai, Jr. (ed). *Winslow Homer.* National Gallery of Art 1989 $18.00. ISBN 0-89468-132-X Illustrated collection of essays discussing Homer's works.

Wood, Peter H., and Karen C. Dalton. *Winslow Homer's Images of Blacks: The Civil War and Reconstruction Years.* Univ of Texas Pr 1989 $19.95. ISBN 0-292-79047-3 Fully illustrated catalog of a traveling exhibition of Homer's art with an essay analyzing his art's significance.

SOUSA, JOHN PHILIP 1854–1932

Often called the "March King," John Philip Sousa was born in Washington, D.C. Because his father was a member of the United States Marine Band, he grew up in a musical environment and followed in his father's footsteps. Early in his life, he studied violin and harmony. As an apprentice to the U.S. Marine Band, he learned band instruments. As his musical training progressed, Sousa began conducting orchestras for the theater and bands in park concerts, then a popular form of entertainment, and composing his own marches. From 1880 until 1892, he led the U.S. Marine Band. In 1892 he formed his own band and toured the United States, Canada, and Europe as well as other parts of the world. The music of the band and Sousa's original compositions, which number about 100, reflect the self-confident spirit of nationalism that pervaded the United States after the 1898 Spanish-American War.

Sousa's music, with its lively, patriotic spirit and toe-tapping robustness, earned him great wealth and popularity. In explaining the theory behind his compositions, Sousa said, "A march should make a man with a wooden leg step out." The most popular of his marches include "Semper Fidelis," which he composed in 1888; "The Washington Post March," published in 1889; and "The Stars and Stripes Forever," composed in 1897. Sousa also composed comic operas, which were quite popular at the time. Among his peers, he is credited with improving the quality and instrumentation of band music and helping to raise it to its present high level.

BOOKS BY SOUSA

American Phenomenon. Integrity 1986 $9.95. ISBN 0-919048-06-0

The Fifth String. Paganiniana 1981 $11.95. ISBN 0-87666-623-3

Marching Along. Music Reprint Ser. Da Capo 1990 $42.50. ISBN 0-306-79718-6

National Patriotic and Typical Airs of All Lands. Music Reprint Ser. Da Capo 1977 $42.50. ISBN 0-306-70861-2

Sousa's Great Marches in Piano Transcription. Dover 1975 $5.95. ISBN 0-486-23132-1

BOOKS ABOUT SOUSA

Bierly, Philip E. *John Philip Sousa, American Phenomenon.* Integrity 1989 $17.95. ISBN 0-918048-07-9 Biography of America's musical patriot and the story of his legendary band.

Bierly, Paul E. *The Works of John Philip Sousa.* Integrity 1984 $28.50. ISBN 0-918048-04-4 Describes all of Sousa's works, both musical and literary.

SULLIVAN, LOUIS HENRY   1856–1924

Often called the Father of the Skyscraper, American architect Louis Henry Sullivan was a key figure in the development of modern architecture. He was also an eloquent writer on the new style of architecture as he envisioned it.

Sullivan was born in Boston and studied at the Massachusetts Institute of Technology and the École de Beaux Arts in Paris, France. He went to work for the firm of the architect Dankmar Adler, in Chicago, where he rose to chief draftsman and in 1880 to a full member of the firm. The massive Auditorium Building, innovative in the clarity and power of its design, is the chief building of the so-called Chicago school of architecture and a memorial to their noteworthy collaboration, which came to an end in 1894. Sullivan had already designed on his own in 1890 one of the earliest masterpieces of skyscraper architecture in the United States, the Wainwright Building in St. Louis. His next great skyscraper design was the Guaranty Building in Buffalo, New York.

Sullivan was a difficult and lonely man, beset by personal problems. In his later years, his practice dwindled, but he still created some buildings of great beauty—small banks in the Midwest—the Farmer's Bank at Owatonna, Minnesota, being the most famous. He was a master of ornament, although he aimed at clear forms and questioned the role of decoration. Sullivan believed that the purpose of outward form was to faithfully express the function beneath. The famous slogan "form follows function," which he coined, has been interpreted in a variety of different ways. Even so, it has become part of the vocabulary of modern architecture. The master American architect Frank Lloyd Wright (*see* Wright, Vol. 2, United States History: The Arts of the Twentieth Century) was Sullivan's assistant from 1887 to 1893, and Wright considered him his *lieber Meister*, "dear master," and paid him eloquent tribute in his book *Genius and the Mobocracy* (1949). Sullivan himself was a highly poetic and persuasive writer, above all in his *Kindergarten Chats* (1918) and his *Autobiography of an Idea* (1924).

BOOKS BY SULLIVAN

The Autobiography of an Idea (1924). Dover 1924 $7.95. ISBN 0-486-20281-X
Kindergarten Chats and Other Writings (1918). Dover 1980 $5.00. ISBN 0-486-23812-1
The Public Papers. Robert Twombly (ed). Univ of Chicago Pr 1988 $29.95. ISBN 0-226-77996-3

BOOKS ABOUT SULLIVAN

Twombly, Robert. *Louis Sullivan: His Life and Work.* Univ of Chicago Pr 1987 $16.95. ISBN 0-226-82006-8 Illustrative biography of a founding father of American architecture.
Wright, Frank Lloyd. *Genius and the Mobocracy.* Horizon Pr 1971 $25.00. Tribute to Sullivan by his former assistant.

See also Vol. 1, American Literature: The Rise of Realism.

THE PROGRESSIVE ERA—POLITICS, REFORM, CHANGE, AND EXPANSION

American Heritage Illustrated History of the United States. Vol. 12: A World Power. Choice Pub 1988 $3.49. ISBN 0-945260-12-1 Illustrated account of the period of America's history when it started to grow into a global power; especially suited to younger readers.

Beisner, Robert K. *From the Old Diplomacy to the New, 1856–1900. The American History Ser.* Harlan Davidson 1986 $8.95. ISBN 0-88295-833-X

Blum, John M. (ed). *Public Philosopher: Selected Letters of Walter Lippman.* Ticknor 1985 $29.95. ISBN 0-89919-260-2

*Brady, Kathleen. *Ida Tarbell: Portrait of a Muckraker.* Putnam 1984 $17.95. ISBN 0-399-31023-1 Focuses on a notable female voice for reform.

Chambers, John W., II. *The Tyranny of Change: America in the Progressive Era, 1900–1917. Twentieth Century United States History Ser.* St. Martin's 1980. ISBN 0-312-82758-X

Colburn, David R., and George E. Pozzetta. *Reform and Reformers in the Progressive Era.* Greenwood 1982 $35.00. ISBN 0-313-22907-4

Cooper, John M., Jr. *The Warrior and the Priest: Woodrow Wilson and Theodore Roosevelt.* Harvard Univ Pr 1985 $9.95. ISBN 0-674-94751-7

Faulkner, Harold U. *The Decline of Laissez-Faire, 1897–1917. The Economic History of the United States Ser.* Sharpe 1977 $14.95. ISBN 0-87332-102-2

Filler, Louis. *The Muckrakers.* Penn State Univ Pr 1975 $12.50. ISBN 0-271-01213-7

Flink, James J. *America Adopts the Automobile, 1895–1910.* MIT Pr 1970 $30.00. ISBN 0-262-06036-1

Goldman, Eric. *Rendezvous with Destiny: A History of Modern American Reform.* Random 1978 $5.95. ISBN 0-394-72538-7

Gould, Lewis L. *The Progressive Era.* Syracuse Univ Pr 1974 $4.95. ISBN 0-8156-2164-7

Gould, Lewis L. *The Spanish-American War and President McKinley.* Univ of Kansas Pr 1982 $7.95. ISBN 0-7006-0227-5

Hofstadter, Richard. *The Age of Reform: From Bryan to F.D.R.* Random 1960 $6.95. ISBN 0-394-70095-3

Hofstadter, Richard. *The Progressive Movement, Nineteen Hundred to Nineteen Fifteen.* Simon 1986 $7.50. ISBN 0-671-62824-0

*Lawson, Don. *The United States in the Spanish-American War. Young People's History of America's Wars Ser.* Harper Jr Bks 1976 $12.89. ISBN 0-200-00163-9 Illustrated presentation of the role of the United States in the Spanish-American War.

*Liliuokalani. *Hawaii's Story by Hawaii's Queen.* AMS (repr of 1898 ed). ISBN 0-404-14227-3 The story of the island as told by the last reigning Hawaiian queen.

Link, Arthur S., and Richard L. McCormick. *Progressivism. American History Ser.* Harlan Davidson 1983 $8.50. ISBN 0-88295-814-3

*Lord, Walter. *Night to Remember.* Bantam 1983 $3.95. ISBN 0-553-27827-4 Story of the sinking of the luxury liner *Titanic.*

Lundberg, Ferdinand. *Imperial Hearst.* Ayer 1970 $23.00. ISBN 0-045-01685-9

May, Ernest. *Imperial Democracy: The Emergence of America as a Great Power.* Harper 1973. (o.p.)

May, Henry F. *The End of American Innocence: A Study of the First Years of Our Own Time, 1912–1917.* Oxford Univ Pr 1979 $12.95. ISBN 0-19-502528-8

*McCullough, David. *The Path Between the Seas: The Creation of the Panama Canal, 1870–1914.* Simon 1978 $13.95. ISBN 0-671-24409-4 Account of the building of the Panama Canal across Central America.

Merk, Frederick, and Lois B. Merk. *Manifest Destiny and Mission in American History: A Reinterpretation.* Greenwood 1983 $38.50. ISBN 0-313-23844-8

*Norris, Frank. *The Octopus.* Airmont 1968 $1.95. ISBN 0-8049-0179-1 The story of the struggle between wheat farmers and the railroad, written by a noted turn-of-the-century novelist.

*Norris, Frank. *The Pit: A Study of Chicago.* Bentley 1971 $16.00. ISBN 0-8376-0407-9 Story of the speculation that took place on the Chicago grain market, written by a noted turn-of-the-century novelist.

Perkins, Whitney. *Constraint of Empire: The United States and Caribbean Interventions.* Greenwood 1981 $36.95. ISBN 0-313-22266-5

Pratt, Julius. *Expansionists of Eighteen Ninety-Eight: The Acquisition of Hawaii and the Spanish Islands.* Times Bks 1972. (o.p.)

Ruiz, Ramon E. *Cuba: The Making of a Revolution.* Norton 1970 $7.95. ISBN 0-393-00513-5

*Sinclair, Upton. *The Jungle.* Univ of Illinois Pr 1988 $9.95. ISBN 0-252-01480-4 Story of an Indian boy brought up by a pack of wolves.

*Steffens, Lincoln. *The Autobiography of Lincoln Steffens.* Vol. 2 Harcourt 1968 $9.95. ISBN 0-15-609396-0 The story of the famous muckraker in his own words.

Trask, David F. *The War with Spain in Eighteen Ninety-Eight.* *The Macmillan Wars of the United States Ser.* Macmillan 1981 $37.95. ISBN 0-02-932950-7

Vandiver, Frank E. *Black Jack: The Life and Times of John J. Pershing.* 2 vols. Texas A & M Univ Pr 1977 $47.50. ISBN 0-89096-024-0

DEWEY, JOHN   1859–1952

John Dewey came to be known as the foremost authority on progressive education in the United States. A graduate of the University of Vermont and of Johns Hopkins University, in 1899 he published his revolutionary book *The School and Society,* which advocated "progressive schools" that abandoned authoritarian methods and emphasized learning through experimentation and practice. The type of schools he favored flowered in the United States in the 1920s. Taking field trips, making model cities and villages, using dramatization, and freer classrooms with movable furniture are just a few of the elements in which Dewey's view of education as personal inquiry is pursued in education today.

In 1938, when he was nearly 80, Dewey published *Logic: The Theory of Inquiry,* his major philosophical work. He made his field the whole of human experience—including politics and psychology—following eagerly wherever the spirit of inquiry might lead him. He accepted American democracy completely and believed that democracy is a primary ethical value.

Dewey taught at the universities of Michigan and Minnesota before becoming the chairperson of the philosophy and education department at the University of Chicago, a post he held from 1894 to 1904. While at Chicago, he initiated reform movements in educational theory and methods, testing many of them in the university's high school. In 1904 Dewey became professor of philosophy at Columbia University, where he remained until his retirement in 1930.

Dewey was also active in a number of other areas, including the founding of the New School for Social Research and the organization of New York City's first teachers' union. He also was recognized as honorary vice president of the New York State Liberal Party.

BOOKS BY DEWEY

The Child and the Curriculum and *The School and Society.* Univ of Chicago Pr 1956 $6.95. ISBN 0-226-14392-9

Democracy and Education: An Introduction to the Philosophy of Education. Free Pr 1966 $14.95. ISBN 0-02-907370-7

Experience and Education. Peter Smith 1983 $15.00. ISBN 0-8446-5961-4

Experience and Nature. Dover 1929 $8.95. ISBN 0-486-20471-5

How We Think: A Restatement of the Relation of Reflective Thinking to the Educative Process. Heath 1933 $16.00. ISBN 0-669-20024-7

Logic: The Theory of Inquiry (1938). Irvington 1982 $49.50. ISBN 0-89197-836-3

Moral Principles in Education. Southern Illinois Univ Pr 1975 $5.50. ISBN 0-8093-0715-4

School and Society (1899). Southern Illinois Univ Pr 1980 $9.95. ISBN 0-8093-0967-X

BOOKS ABOUT DEWEY

Bernstein, Richard J. *John Dewey*. Ridgeview 1981 $10.00. ISBN 0-917930-15-0 Traces the evolution of Dewey's philosophical theory.

Blewett, John (ed). *John Dewey: His Thought and Influence*. Greenwood 1973 $35.00. ISBN 0-8371-6543-1 Intelligent collection of essays by eight Catholic scholars.

Wirth, Arthur G. *John Dewey as Educator: His Design for Work in Education (1894–1904)*. Univ Pr of America 1989 $17.50. ISBN 0-8191-7329-0 Analyzes Dewey's ideas during his years as a practicing educator.

LA FOLLETTE, ROBERT MARION   1855–1925

Called "Battling Bob" by his friends and opponents alike, Robert La Follette was a lifelong Republican until he broke with the party in 1912. Born in Primrose, Wisconsin, he practiced law in that state and was a district attorney for four years. After two unsuccessful tries for the Wisconsin governorship, first in 1896 and then in 1898, he finally became governor in 1900.

La Follette gained fame as a reform governor. Once in office, he succeeded in winning over the conservatives in the legislature, thus paving the way for a wave of reforms, including a state income tax, a direct primary, civil service, state control of railroads and banks, conservation measures, and higher taxes on corporations. So impressed was President Theodore Roosevelt (*see* T. Roosevelt, Vol. 2, United States History: The Progressive Era—Politics, Reform, Change, and Expansion) that he called Wisconsin "the laboratory of democracy."

In 1906 La Follette entered the United States Senate, where he continued to work for reform. He was an especially strong supporter of direct popular election of senators, and after the 1913 passage of the Seventeenth Amendment, he won election to the Senate from his home state. One of the most powerful men in the Senate from 1919 to 1925, he opposed the Versailles peace treaty and United States membership in the League of Nations and the World Court. In 1924 he ran for the presidency as a Progressive. The campaign, however, proved to be too much for him; he died the following summer.

BOOKS BY LA FOLLETTE

La Follette's Autobiography: A Personal Narrative of Political Experiences (1913). Univ of Wisconsin Pr 1960 $10.50. ISBN 0-299-02194-7

The Making of America: Industry and Finance (1905). (ed). Ayer (repr of 1905 ed) $31.00. ISBN 0-405-05096-8

The Making of America: Labor (1906). (ed). Ayer 1969 repr of 1906 ed $31.00. ISBN 0-405-02132-1

BOOKS ABOUT LA FOLLETTE

Johnson, Robert T. *Robert M. La Follette, Jr. and the Decline of the Progressive Party in Wisconsin*. Shoe String 1970 $29.50. ISBN 0-208-00847-0 Account of the contribution of the highly respected and influential Wisconsin senator.

Thelen, David P. *Robert M. La Follette and the Insurgent Spirit*. Univ of Wisconsin Pr 1986 $9.95. ISBN 0-299-10644-6 Readable biography of the central figure in the American Progressive movement.

MUIR, JOHN   1838–1914

A Scot by birth, John Muir grew up in frontier Wisconsin where he formed a lifelong love of the wilderness. As a young man, he worked in a factory until he almost lost his eyesight in an industrial accident. He then decided to hike the United States to enjoy the wealth of its beauty. His 1,000-mile trek took him to California in 1868, where he explored the Sierra Nevada, calling it "this range of light." Although he also spent some time in Alaska, from that time he made the Sierra Nevada the center of his explorations, writings, and conservation concerns.

To Muir, protecting the wilderness was an act of worship. In 1892 he and a group of San Franciscans founded the Sierra Club, an organization that dedicated itself to "exploring, enjoying, and rendering accessible the mountain regions of the Pacific Coast." Muir served as president of the club for 22 years. Under his direction the club began sponsoring wilderness outings of up to several weeks. The Sierra Club was also instrumental in helping to create the National Park Service, the National Forest Service, and the formation of Olympic National Park, Redwood National Park, and other individual recreation areas.

Representative of Muir's many writings are *Our National Parks* (1901) and *The Yosemite* (1912). The Sierra Club continues the fight begun by John Muir, opposing strip mining, the use of harmful pesticides, and other forms of pollution and human activity that destroy the environment.

BOOKS BY MUIR

Mountains of California. Penguin 1985 $5.95. ISBN 0-14-39038-3
Muir Among the Animals: The Wildlife Writings of John Muir. Lisa Mighetto (ed). Sierra 1986 $17.59. ISBN 0-87156-769-5
My First Summer in the Sierra. Penguin 1987 $7.95. ISBN 0-14-017001-4
Our National Parks (1901). Reprint Services 1988 $49.00.
South of Yosemite: Selected Writings of John Muir. Frederic Gunsky (ed). Wilderness 1988 $11.95. ISBN 0-89997-095-8
Story of My Boyhood and Youth. Sierra 1989 $7.95. ISBN 0-87156-749-0
The Yosemite (1912). Sierra 1988 $9.95. ISBN 0-87156-653-2

BOOKS ABOUT MUIR

Engberg, Robert (ed). *John Muir to Yosemite and Beyond: Writings from the Years 1863–1875.* Univ of Wisconsin Pr 1981. (o.p) $8.95. ISBN 0-299-08274-1 Collection of Muir's journals and manuscripts with biographical material by people who met him.
Turner, Frederick. *Rediscovering America: John Muir in His Time and Ours.* Sierra 1987 $10.95. ISBN 0-87156-704-0 Biography of Muir that reveals the events and ideas that shaped the founder of the Sierra Club and his vision for America.

ROOSEVELT, THEODORE   1858–1919

Vice President of the United States under William McKinley and the nation's twenty-sixth President, Theodore Roosevelt was born in New York City to wealthy socialite parents. After graduating from Harvard College in 1880, Roosevelt studied law at Columbia University, and then entered politics, holding a number of appointive and elective posts—New York assemblyman (1882–1884), member of the United States Civil Service Commission (1889–1895), police commissioner of New York City (1895–1897), Assistant Secretary of the Navy (1897–1898), and governor of New York (1898–1900).

Roosevelt gained national attention when he resigned his post in the Department of the Navy to fight in the Spanish-American War. As a lieutenant-colonel, he headed a cavalry regiment, the "Rough Riders," made up mostly of ranchers, cowhands, and Indians that Roosevelt had personally recruited. He led the charge up San Juan Hill, which enabled the Americans to take the city of Santiago. An aggressive man with strong opinions, Roosevelt became a thorn in the side of Republican leaders who tried to "bury" him politically in the position of vice president under William McKinley. McKinley's assassination in 1901, however, resurrected Roosevelt's political fortunes. As President (1901–1909), Roosevelt made good use of his "bully pulpit." Believing firmly that government should protect the people, he used his powers to that end, advocating reform, breaking up trusts, and calling for the conservation of natural resources in domestic affairs, "dollar diplomacy" in hemispheric affairs, and mediation in foreign affairs. For his efforts, he won the Nobel Peace Prize in 1906.

On leaving the presidency, Roosevelt went to Africa to hunt big game, content that William Howard Taft, his handpicked successor, would continue his policies. (*See* Taft, Vol. 2, United States History: the Progressive Era— Politics, Reform, Change, and Expansion.) But Roosevelt's discontent with Taft's ultraconservative approach led him to split with old guard Republicanism and to run for the presidency on the third-party ticket of the Progressive, or "Bull Moose," party. The three-cornered election of 1912 resulted in a victory for the Democratic party and Woodrow Wilson. (*See* Wilson, Vol. 2, United States History: World War I.)

A prolific writer, Roosevelt was the biographer of Thomas Hart Benton, the artist, and Gouveneur Morris, the financial wizard of the American Revolution. Among his other writings are numerous essays, historical analyses, speeches, and letters.

BOOKS BY ROOSEVELT

American Ideals and Other Essays, Social and Political (1897). AMS 1981 $17.00. ISBN 0-404-05398-X
Autobiography. Quality Paperbacks Ser. Da Capo 1985 $12.95. ISBN 0-306-80232-5
The New Nationalism. Peter Smith $11.25. ISBN 0-8446-0237-X
Presidential Addresses and State Papers. 4 vols. Kraus (repr of 1905 ed) $68.00. ISBN 0-527-76762-X
Ranch Life and the Hunting Trail (1888). Hippocrene 1985 $8.95. ISBN 0-87052-212-4
Rough Riders. Corner 1971 repr of 1899 ed $21.00. ISBN 0-87928-018-2
The Winning of the West. 4 vols. Somerset (repr of 1900 ed) $295.00. ISBN 0-403-04339-5

BOOKS ABOUT ROOSEVELT

*Fritz, Jean. *Bully for You, Teddy Roosevelt!* Putnam 1991 $15.95. ISBN 0-399-21769-X A noted author presents historical details in this upbeat biography.
*Hagedorn, Hermann. *The Rough Riders.* Harper 1927. (o.p.) Account of the Spanish-American War regiment of Teddy Roosevelt that took San Juan Hill.
*Markham, Louis. *Theodore Roosevelt. World Leaders: Past and Present Ser.* Chelsea 1985 $17.95. ISBN 0-87754-553-7 Excellent introductory biography of the Rough Rider and President.
Riis, Jacob A. *Theodore Roosevelt, the Citizen.* AMS 1976 repr of 1904 ed $17.50. ISBN 0-404-05335-1 Famous photographer's view of the President.
Theodore Roosevelt: Twenty-Sixth President of the United States. Presidents of the United States Ser. Garrett Ed 1988 $12.95. ISBN 0-944483-09-7 Looks at Roosevelt's early life, career, and contributions.

TAFT, WILLIAM HOWARD   1857–1930

The nation's twenty-seventh President and tenth Chief Justice, William Howard Taft was born in Cincinnati, Ohio, graduated from Yale University, and got a law degree from Cincinnati law school. His cautious and conservative nature stemmed from his training as a lawyer and his experience as a judge and administrator in Cincinnati. He became prominent in Republican national politics when President Benjamin Harrison chose him to be Solicitor General in 1890. Taft then served as a federal judge and proved himself an able administrator as civil governor of the Philippines.

During the presidency of his friend Theodore Roosevelt (*see* Roosevelt, Vol. 2, United States History: The Progressive Era—Politics, Reform, Change, and Expansion), Taft served as Secretary of War. With Roosevelt's support, he won the Republican nomination in the election of 1908 and easily defeated William Jennings Bryan. (*See* Bryan, Vol. 1, United States History: Populism and the Rise of Industry.) Expected to carry on Roosevelt's policies, Taft angered Roosevelt and his progressive followers by signing into law the high tariff measure, Payne–Aldrich Tariff, and by failing to support efforts to oust dictatorial Speaker of the House of Representatives Joesph Cannon.

When it came time for the election of 1912, the Republicans renominated Taft, but disgruntled progressive Republicans formed the Progressive party and nominated Roosevelt as their candidate. With the Republican vote split, the Democrats easily won the election for their candidate Woodrow Wilson. (*See* Wilson, Vol. 2, United States History: World War I.) Taft then retired from public life and taught law at Yale. In 1921 President Warren G. Harding appointed him Chief Justice of the Supreme Court, making him the only President to have served on the high court. It was a post he held until his death.

BOOKS BY TAFT

Four Aspects of Civic Duty (1906). Kraus (repr of 1906 ed) $18.00. ISBN 0-527-88606-8

The Physical, Political, and International Value of the Panama Canal. 2 vols. Inst of Economics and Finance 1985 $187.45. ISBN 0-86722-107-0

Popular Government: Its Essence, Its Performance, Its Perils (1913). Elliots 1913 $20.00. ISBN 0-686-83709-6

Taft Papers on the League of Nations (1920). T. Marburg and H. Flack (eds). Kraus (repr of 1920 ed) $24.00. ISBN 0-527-88618-1

BOOKS ABOUT TAFT

Burton, David H. *William Howard Taft: In the Public Service.* Krieger 1990 $8.50. ISBN 0-89874-829-1 First biography of Taft in almost 50 years; views Taft's role as a public servant as completely consistent with his ambition and his self-esteem.

*Casey, Jane C. *William Howard Taft.* Encyclopedia of Presidents Ser. Childrens 1989 $15.93. ISBN 0-393-01462-2 Illustrated biography that presents the factual side of Taft's colorful history.

Mason, Alpheus T. *William Howard Taft: Chief Justice.* Univ Pr of America 1983 $22.50. ISBN 0-8191-3091-5 Complete analysis of Taft's career as both President and Chief Justice of the Supreme Court.

WORLD WAR I

American Heritage Illustrated History of the United States. Vol. 13: World War I. Choice Pub 1988 $3.49. ISBN 0-945260-13-X Illustrated history of the events of the Great War; especially suited to younger readers.

Breen, William J. *Uncle Sam at Home: Civilian Mobilization, Wartime Federalism, and the Council of National Defense, 1917–1919.* Greenwood 1984 $35.00. ISBN 0-313-24112-0

Burnett, Constance. *Five for Freedom: Lucretia Mott, Elizabeth Cady Stanton, Lucy Stone, Susan B. Anthony, Carrie Chapman Catt.* Greenwood 1968 $35.00. ISBN 0-8371-0034-8

Dockerill, Michael and J. Douglas Goold. *Peace Without Promise: Britain and the Peace Conferences 1919–1923.* Shoe String 1981 $27.50. ISBN 0-208-01909-X

Freidel, Frank. *Over There: The Story of America's First Great Overseas Crusade.* McGraw 1989 $11.88. ISBN 0-07-557036-X

Gompers, Samuel. *American Labor and the War. The United States in World War I Ser.* Ozer 1974 $29.95. ISBN 0-89198-103-9

Gompers, Samuel. *Labor and the Common Welfare. American Labor, from Conspiracy to Collective Bargaining Ser.* Ayer 1969 $17.00. ISBN 0-405-02124-0

Greenwald, Maurine W. *Women, War, and Work: The Impact of World War I on Women Workers in the United States.* Greenwood 1980 $39.95. ISBN 0-313-21355-0

*Hemingway, Ernest. *A Farewell to Arms.* Macmillan 1987 $4.95. ISBN 0-02-051900-1 Novel set in Europe during World War I.

*Hoehling, Adolph A. *The Great War at Sea: A History of Naval Action, 1914–1918.* Greenwood 1978 $32.00. ISBN 0-313-20468-3 Illustrated history of naval participation in World War I.

*Kennedy, David M. *Over Here: The First World War and American Society.* Oxford Univ Pr 1980 $9.95. ISBN 0-19-503209-8 Discusses life in the United States during World War I.

Kraditor, Aileen S. *The Ideas of the Woman Suffrage Movement, 1880–1920.* Norton 1981 $9.95. ISBN 0-393-00039-7

Marston, Frank S. *Peace Conference of Nineteen Nineteen: Organization and Procedure.* Greenwood 1981 repr of 1944 ed $35.00. ISBN 0-313-22910-4

*McCabe, John. *George M. Cohan: The Man Who Owned Broadway. Quality Paperbacks Ser.* Da Capo 1980 $6.95. ISBN 0-306-80118-3 Biography of the celebrated Broadway playwright, songwriter, producer, and actor who wrote "Over There," which became a popular World War I anthem.

Marshall, Brigadier General S. L. A. *The American Heritage History of World War I.* Crown 1982 $15.98. ISBN 0-517-38555-4

Northedge, F. S. *The League of Nations: Its Life and Times, 1920–1946.* Holmes & Meier 1986 $47.50. ISBN 0-8419-1065-0

*Remarque, Erich M. *All Quiet on the Western Front.* Fawcett 1987 $3.95. ISBN 0-449-21394-3 Novel of World War I from the perspective of a young German soldier.

*Rostkowski, Margaret I. *After the Dancing Days.* Harper Jr Bks 1988 $3.50. ISBN 0-06-440248-7 Story of a young woman helping in a World War I veterans' hospital.

Slosson, Preston W. *The Great Crusade and After, 1914–1928.* AMS 1930 $52.50. ISBN 0-404-20237-3

**This Fabulous Century.* Vol. 2 *1910–1920.* Time–Life 1969 $17.95. ISBN 0-8094-0122-3 Photographic history of the decade 1910–1920.

Tuchman, Barbara W. *The Guns of August.* Bantam 1982 $5.95. ISBN 0-553-25401-4

Tuchman, Barbara W. *Zimmermann Telegram.* Ballantine 1988 $7.95. ISBN 0-345-32425-0

Vaughn, Edwin C. *Some Desperate Glory: The World War I Diary of a British Officer.* Simon 1989 $8.95. ISBN 0-671-67904-X

Walters, Francis P. *A History of the League of Nations.* Greenwood 1986 repr of 1952 ed $115.00. ISBN 0-313-25056-1

*Warren, Mark D. *Lusitania.* Sterling 1987 $39.95. ISBN 0-85059-847-8 Story of the British passenger ship sunk by a German submarine in 1915.

Wiebe, Robert H. *The Search for Order: 1877–1920. Making of America Ser.* Hill & Wang 1966 $7.95. ISBN 0-8090-0104-7

See also Vol. 2, World History: World War I and Its Aftermath.

WILSON, WOODROW   1856–1924

Before becoming the twenty-eighth President of the United States in 1913, Woodrow Wilson was a professor at several universities—Bryn Mawr, 1885–1888; Wesleyan, 1888–1890; and Princeton, 1890–1902. He was also president of Princeton from 1902 to 1910 and governor of New Jersey from 1910 to 1912.

Born in Staunton, Virginia, Wilson first studied law at the University of Virginia. In his view, the study of law was a stepping stone to public office. Finding the practice of law uninteresting, however, he turned to political science, earning recognition as an author, educator, and lecturer. Among his influential books are *Congressional Government* (1885) and *Division and Reunion: 1829–1889* (1893).

Wilson's efforts to make Princeton socially more democratic brought him to the attention of the Democratic party, a move that resulted in his election first as governor of New Jersey (1910–1912) and then as a two-term President of the United States.

As President, he called his domestic program the New Freedom and came out in support of tariff and business reforms, including the establishment of the Federal Trade Commission, new farm and labor laws, and the Federal Reserve System. In foreign affairs, he kept the United States out of World War I until 1918. Once the nation was in the war, however, Wilson attempted to make democratic principles an important part of the peacemaking process through his Fourteen Points, one of which was the establishment of a League of Nations to prevent future wars. Wilson went to the people for support of the Versailles peace treaty and the League of Nations. But his strenuous speaking tour had no effect on the Senate. It rejected both the treaty and United States participation in the league. The speaking tour was such a strain on Wilson that he suffered a stroke. For several months, he could do nothing. Never recovering fully from the stroke or from the disappointment of the Senate's reactions to the League, he kept a very low profile for the remainder of his term as President. Three years after his term of office expired, he died.

BOOKS BY WILSON

Congressional Government: A Study in American Politics. Johns Hopkins Univ Pr 1981 $9.95. ISBN 0-8018-2556-3
Division and Reunion: 1829–1889. Peter Smith $12.00. ISBN 0-8446-3188-4
Mere Literature and Other Essays. Essay Index Repr Ser. Ayer (repr of 1896 ed) $18.00. ISBN 0-8369-2260-3
The Papers of Woodrow Wilson. Arthur S. Link, *et al* (eds). 63 vols. Princeton Univ Pr $30.00–$52.50 each. ISBNs 0-691-04508-9 through 0-691-04775-8
Woodrow Wilson's Case for the League of Nations. Hamilton Foley (ed). Kraus 1969 repr of 1923 ed $20.00. ISBN 0-527-97180-4

BOOKS ABOUT WILSON

*Leavell, Perry. *Woodrow Wilson. World Leaders: Past and Present Ser.* Chelsea 1987 $17.95. ISBN 0-87754-557-X Illustrated biography of Wilson and documentation of the times in which he lived.
Mulder, John M., and Ernest M. White. *Woodrow Wilson. Meckler's Bibliographies of the Presidents of the United States, 1789–1989 Ser.* Carol B. Fitzgerald (ed). 2 vols. Meckler 1989 $110.00. ISBN 0-88736-141-2 Authoritative biography of Wilson; includes primary sources.

THE TWENTIES

*Adams, Samuel Hopkins. *Incredible Era: The Life and Times of Warren Gamaliel Harding.* Hippocrene 1979. (o.p.) Account of the life of the twenty-ninth President.
*Allen, Frederick Lewis. *Only Yesterday.* Harper $5.95. ISBN 0-06-080004-6 Very readable, popular history of the 1920s.
Balliett, Whitney. *Jelly Roll, Jabbo, and Fats: Nineteen Portraits in Jazz.* Oxford Univ Pr 1982 $8.95. ISBN 0-19-503425-2

*Baritz, Loren (ed). *The Culture of the Twenties. American Heritage Ser.* Bobbs 1970 $3.95. ISBN 0-02-306110-3 Documentary history of the 1920s.

Bernstein, Irving. *The Lean Years: A History of the American Worker 1920–1933. Quality Paperbacks Ser.* Da Capo 1983 $11.95. ISBN 0-306-80202-3

Boardman, Tom W. *America and the Jazz Age: A History of the Twenties.* Walck 1968.

*Brandt, Keith. *Babe Ruth, Home Run Hero.* Troll 1985 $2.50. ISBN 0-8167-0554-2 Story of an American baseball hero who made home-run history.

Brownlow, Kevin. *Hollywood: The Pioneers.* Knopf 1980 $20.00. ISBN 0-394-50851-3

*Carter, Paul A. *Twenties in America. American History Ser.* Harlan Davidson 1975 $8.50. ISBN 0-88295-717-1 Depicts the flapper, prohibition, and jazz in the America of the 1920s.

Chalmers, David M. *Hooded Americanism: The History of the Klu Klux Klan.* Duke Univ Pr 1987 $12.95. ISBN 0-8223-0772-3

Dance, Stanley. *The World of Count Basie. Quality Paperbacks Ser.* Da Capo 1985 $10.95. ISBN 0-306-80245-7

Dance, Stanley. *The World of Swing. Quality Paperbacks Ser.* Da Capo 1979 $10.95. ISBN 0-306-80103-5

*Douglas, Emily Taft. *Margaret Sanger: Pioneer of the Future.* Garrett 1975 $9.00. ISBN 0-912048-75-1 Biography of the woman who succeeded in legalizing contraception.

*Editors of Time–Life Books. *This Fabulous Century.* Vol. 3 *1920–1930.* Time–Life 1969 $17.95. ISBN 0-8094-0122-3 Photos and short narrative capturing the mood of the 1920s.

*Edmonds, Walter D. *Bert Breen's Barn.* Little 1975 $14.95. ISBN 0-316-21166-4 Fictionalized account of a boy who wants to help out by raising a barn on family land.

*Evans, Mark. *Scott Joplin and the Ragtime Years.* Dodd 1976. (o.p.) Account of popular jazz composer and musician of the 1920s.

*Fitzgerald, F. Scott. *The Great Gatsby.* Macmillan 1981 $8.95. ISBN 0-684-71760-3 Tells the story of mysterious Jay Gatsby who falls in love with Daisy; perhaps the best novel by this celebrated author of the 1920s and 1930s.

Fitgerald, F. Scott. *This Side of Paradise. Scribner Classics Ser.* Scribner's 1987 $9.95. ISBN 0-317-56224-X

*Galbraith, John Kenneth. *Great Crash of 1929.* Houghton 1988 $8.95. ISBN 0-395-47805-7 Prominent economist gives his view of the 1929 stock-market crash.

*Handlin, Oscar. *Al Smith and His America.* Nebraska Univ Pr 1987 $11.95. ISBN 1-55553-021-4 Story of America's first Catholic presidential candidate.

*Hooks, William H. *Circle of Fire.* Macmillan 1982 $12.95. ISBN 0-689-50241-9 Novel of a young boy who suspects that his father is a Klu Klux Klan member.

Leuchtenburg, William E. *Perils of Prosperity: Nineteen Fourteen to Nineteen Thirty-Two. History of America Civilization Ser.* Univ of Chicago Pr 1958 $8.50. ISBN 0-226-47369-4

Lewis, David L. *When Harlem Was in Vogue.* Knopf 1981 $22.00. ISBN 0-394-49572-1

*Lewis, Sinclair. *Main Street.* NAL 1961 $4.50. ISBN 0-451-52147-1 Satire by one of America's most famous authors of small-town life in the Midwest.

*Lyman, Elizabeth. *Babe Zaharias. American Women of Achievement Ser.* Chelsea 1988 $17.95. ISBN 1-55546-684-2 Introduces Babe Didrikson Zaharias, the female athlete who broke Olympic records and won national golf championships.

Mowry, George E. (ed). *Twenties: Fords, Flappers, and Fanatics.* Prentice 1962 $5.95. ISBN 0-13-934968-5

Murray, Robert K. *Harding Era: Warren G. Harding and His Administration.* Univ of Minnesota Pr 1969 $22.50. ISBN 0-8166-0541-6

Murray, Robert K. *Red Scare: A Study in National Hysteria, 1919–1920.* Greenwood 1980 $32.50. ISBN 0-313-22673-3

*Ross, Walter S. *The Last Hero: Charles A. Lindberg.* Woodhill 1979. Story of the pilot who flew the first solo nonstop flight from New York to Paris in 1927.

*Russell, Francis. *Sacco and Vanzetti: The Case Resolved.* Harper 1986 $16.45. ISBN 0-06-015524-8 Examination of the famous trial of two immigrants accused of robbery and murder in 1921.

Scopes, John. *World's Most Famous Court Trial: State of Tennessee vs. John T. Scopes. Civil Liberties in American History Ser.* Da Capo 1971 $35.00. ISBN 0-306-71975-4

Shaw, Arnold. *The Jazz Age: Popular Music in the 1920s.* Oxford Univ Pr 1989 $9.95. ISBN
0-19-506082-2
Sinclair, Andrew. *Era of Excess: A Social History of the Prohibition Movement.* Harper 1964.
Sobel, Robert. *Great Bull Market: Wall Street in the 1920s.* Norton 1968 $6.95. ISBN
0-393-09817-6
*Williams, Martin. *The Jazz Tradition.* Oxford Univ Pr 1983 $8.95. ISBN 0-19-503291-8
History of jazz music in America.

COOLIDGE, CALVIN   1872–1933

Calvin Coolidge was the thirtieth President of the United States. Born in
Plymouth, Vermont, he was the son of a successful country storekeeper. After
graduating from Amherst College in Massachusetts, he went on to study law.
Coolidge clearly had a love of politics, for after becoming mayor of Northampton, Massachusetts, he was seldom out of public office. From 1912 to 1915 he
served in the state senate. He then spent three terms as lieutenant governor and
in 1919 was elected as the state's governor.

As governor of Massachusetts, Coolidge received national attention when
he called in troops to squelch a strike by the Boston police department. "There
is no right," he said, "to strike against the public safety by anybody, any time,
anywhere!"

In 1920, with the election of Warren G. Harding to the presidency, Coolidge became Vice President of the United States. Three years later Harding was
dead, and Coolidge took over as the nation's highest leader. People came to
know their new President as "Silent Cal" for he was quiet and very reserved.
He also hated to spend money. In fact he was the only modern President who

Grace Goodhue Coolidge.   Detail of painting by Howard
Chandler Christy (1924).   Copyrighted by the White House
Historical Association; Photograph by the National Geographic
Society.

was able to save part of his salary while in office. In 1924 the American public showed that they appreciated Coolidge's virtues. They elected the quiet Vermonter for a term of his own.

Coolidge was also well known for his admiration of American industry and its leaders. He once said that "The business of America is business," and then added that "The man who builds a factory builds a temple." Not surprisingly, Coolidge's policies were designed to help business. He supported tax cuts and opposed any increase in government spending. For example, he vetoed a bill to provide cash payments to war veterans. And he refused to ask Congress to give aid to farmers. "Farmers have never made money," he said. "I don't believe we can do much about it."

In 1927 Coolidge told the nation that he did not want to run for office again. He left the country in a state of general prosperity, with most Americans enjoying the greatest period of economic success in their history. Returning to Northampton, he spent the rest of his life publishing his autobiography and writing articles for newspapers and magazines.

BOOKS BY COOLIDGE

The Autobiography of Calvin Coolidge (1929). C. Coolidge Memorial 1989 $14.95. ISBN 0-944951-03-1
Foundations of the Republic (1926). Ayer 1926 $21.00. ISBN 0-8369-0333-1

BOOKS ABOUT COOLIDGE

Fuess, Claude M. *Calvin Coolidge: The Man from Vermont.* Greenwood 1977 $41.25. ISBN 0-8371-9320-6 Discussion of Coolidge's life and times.
Lathem, Edward C. (ed). *Your Son, Calvin Coolidge.* Academy Bks 1968 $7.50. ISBN 0-914960-35-0 Tells the story of our thirtieth President.
McCoy, Donald R. *Calvin Coolidge: The Quiet President.* Univ Pr of Kansas 1988 $25.00. ISBN 0-7006-0350-6 Focuses on Coolidge's years as President of the United States.
White, William A. *Puritan in Babylon: The Story of Calvin Coolidge.* Peter Smith $13.25. ISBN 0-8446-3173-6 Includes a discussion of Coolidge's New England background.

THE GREAT DEPRESSION AND THE NEW DEAL

Agee, James. *Let Us Now Praise Famous Men.* Houghton 1973 $24.95. ISBN 0-395-07330-8
*Allen, Frederick Lewis. *Since Yesterday: The Nineteen-Thirties in America: Sept. 3, 1929–Sept. 3, 1939.* Harper 1986 $8.95. ISBN 0-06-091322-3 Popular history of the Great Depression years.
American Heritage Illustrated History of the United States. Vol. 14: The Roosevelt Era. Choice Pub 1988 $3.49. ISBN 0-945260-18-0 Illustrated chronicle of the nation under FDR; especially suited to younger readers.
*Armstrong, William. *Sounder.* Harper Jr Bks 1972 $2.95. ISBN 0-06-440020-4 Story of how both a dog and his master become crippled in the South during the Great Depression.
Banks, Ann. *First-Person America.* Random 1981 $4.76. ISBN 0-394-74796-8
Beard, Charles A., and George H. Smith. *The Future Comes: A Study of the New Deal.* Greenwood 1972 $35.00. ISBN 0-8371-5808-7
*Berger, Gilda. *Women, Work and Wages.* Watts 1986 $12.90. ISBN 0-531-10074-X Introductory study of the discrimination of women in the work place.
Bernstein, Irving. *The New Deal Collective Bargaining Policy. FDR and the Era of the New Deal Ser.* Da Capo 1975 $27.50. ISBN 0-306-70703-9

Bernstein, Irving. *Turbulent Years: A History of the American Worker 1933–1941.* Houghton 1971.

Brinkley, Alan. *Voices of Protest: Huey Long, Father Coughlin, and the Great Depression.* Random 1983 $8.95. ISBN 0-394-71628-0

Burner, David. *Herbert Hoover: The Public Life.* Knopf 1978 $17.95. ISBN 0-394-46134-7

*Editors of Time–Life Books. *This Fabulous Century.* Vol. 4 *1930–1940.* Time–Life 1969 $17.95. ISBN 0-8094-0124-X Photos and short narrative capturing the flavor of the 1930s.

*Hearn, Charles R. *The American Dream in the Great Depression. Contributions in American Studies Ser.* Greenwood 1977 $35.00. ISBN 0-8371-9478-4 Discusses the effect of the Great Depression on the American dream.

*Hunt, Irene. *No Promises in the Wind.* Berkley 1987 $2.75. ISBN 0-425-09969-5 Novel in which the Great Depression causes a boy to realize that he must take charge of his own life.

Hurt, R. Douglas. *The Dust Bowl: An Agricultural and Social History.* Nelson-Hall 1981 $13.95. ISBN 0-88229-789-9

*Klingaman, William K. *1929: The Year of the Great Crash.* Harper 1989 $22.50. ISBN 0-06-016081-0 Author describes people's lives, showing effects of the 1929 crash on a variety of Americans.

*Lawson, Don. *FDR's New Deal.* Harper 1979 $12.95. ISBN 0-690-03953-0 Readable and well-illustrated portrayal of America between the wars.

Louchheim, Katie (ed). *The Making of the New Deal: The Insiders Speak.* Harvard Univ Pr 1983 $7.95. ISBN 0-674-54346-7

*McElvaine, Robert S. (ed). *Down and Out in the Great Depression: Letters from the Forgotten Man.* Univ of North Carolina Pr 1983 $9.95. ISBN 0-8078-4099-8 Account of the personal losses suffered because of the Great Depression.

*McKissack, Patricia C. *Mary McLeod Bethune, A Great American Educator. People of Distinction Ser.* Childrens 1985 $15.93. ISBN 0-516-03218-6 Account of the life of a prominent African-American educator and adviser to President Franklin D. Roosevelt.

*Meltzer, Milton. *Brother, Can You Spare a Dime? The Great Depression, 1929–1933.* Facts on File 1990 $16.95. ISBN 0-8160-23172-7 History of the Great Depression; presents material on whether it could be repeated.

Olson, James S. *Herbert Hoover and the Reconstruction Finance Corporation, 1931–1933.* Iowa State Univ Pr 1977 $10.50. ISBN 0-8138-0880-4

*Olson, James S. (ed). *Historical Dictionary of the New Deal: From Inauguration to Preparation for War.* Greenwood 1985 $67.95. ISBN 0-313-23873-1 Reference work with entries about aspects of the New Deal.

*Rogers, Betty. *Will Rogers.* Univ of Oklahoma Pr 1982 $10.95. ISBN 0-8061-1600-5 Account of an outstanding American philosopher and humorist.

Schlesinger, Arthur M., Jr., and D. R. Fox (eds). Vol. 13 *The Age of the Great Depression, 1929–1941. History of American Life Ser.* Macmillan 1948. ISBN 0-02-407380-6

Shannon, David A. *Between the Wars: America, Nineteen Nineteen to Nineteen Forty-One.* Houghton 1979 $25.16. ISBN 0-395-26535-5

*Shore, Nancy. *Amelia Earhart. American Women of Achievement Ser.* Chelsea 1989 $9.95. ISBN 0-7910-0415-5 Story of the first woman to cross the Atlantic in an airplane.

Sitkoff, Harvard. *A New Deal for Blacks: The Emergence of Civil Rights as a National Issue: The Depression Decade.* Oxford Univ Pr 1978 $12.95. ISBN 0-19-502893-7

*Steinbeck, John. *Grapes of Wrath. Fiction Ser.* Penguin 1976 $4.95. ISBN 0-14-004239-3 Classic novel about a family and their struggles during the Great Depression.

Stevens, Irving L. *Fishbones: Hoboing in the 1930s.* Moosehead 1982 $8.95. ISBN 0-9609208-0-3

*Taylor, Mildred D. *Roll of Thunder, Hear My Cry.* Bantam 1984 $2.95. ISBN 0-553-25450-2 Story of the hardships endured by a black family struggling to retain their land and freedom in Mississippi during the Great Depression.

*Terkel, Studs. *Hard Times: An Oral History of the Great Depression in America.* Pantheon 1986 $8.95. ISBN 0-394-74691-0 Personal accounts of the hardships and tragedies caused by the Great Depression.

Warren, Harris G. *Herbert Hoover and the Great Depression.* Greenwood 1980 $32.50. ISBN 0-313-22659-8

Wecter, Dixon. *The Age of the Great Depression, 1929–1941.* AMS 1948 $42.50. ISBN 0-404-20283-7

Will Rogers. *Will Rogers Treasury: Reflections and Observations.* Crown 1986 $6.98. ISBN 0-517-62544-X

*Wilson, Joan H. *Herbert Hoover: The Forgotten Progressive.* Scott 1975. ISBN 0-673-39357-7
    Discusses the thirty-first President of the United States and his accomplishments.

Winslow, Susan. *Brother, Can You Spare a Dime?* Paddington 1976.

Zieger, Robert H. *John L. Lewis: Labor Leader.* Twayne's Twentieth Century American Biography Ser. G. K. Hall 1988 $10.95. ISBN 0-8057-7782-2

HOOVER, HERBERT CLARK   1874–1964

Born in Iowa to a Quaker blacksmith, Herbert Hoover was raised by an uncle in Oregon. After training as a mining engineer at Stanford University in California, Hoover worked for a time in Australia and China. He married his college sweetheart Lou Henry, and together they traveled to many parts of the world. When World War I broke out, they were in England. President Woodrow Wilson (*see* Wilson, Vol. 2, United States History: World War I) appointed Hoover chairman of the American Relief Commission. As chairman, he arranged the return to the United States of more than 150,000 Americans who found themselves stranded in Europe. In 1915 Wilson chose him to head a food relief program for the people of Belgium and northern France. After the United States entered the war in 1917, Hoover became U.S. Food Administrator. His job was to find ways to distribute food efficiently so there would be enough for the Allies and the Americans to continue the war.

After World War I, Hoover headed other relief programs, arranging to send food to millions of starving people in Europe. Then, in 1921, he was appointed Secretary of Commerce, a post he held during the administrations of Presidents Warren G. Harding and Calvin Coolidge. (*See* Coolidge, Vol. 2, United States History: The Twenties.) When he was nominated by the Republicans to run for President in 1928, he said, "We in America today are nearer to the final triumph over poverty than ever before in the history of any land." In the election, he easily defeated Democrat Alfred E. Smith.

Unfortunately for Hoover and for the country, his statement proved untrue. Within a year the stock market had collapsed, many banks and businesses had closed, and the nation had entered the Great Depression, a vast economic downturn. Hoover was a humanitarian, but he believed that most relief from the depression should come from private individuals and agencies, not from the government. He did, however, provide government help to businesses through the Reconstruction Finance Corporation and to farmers. He also expanded public works projects. But these measures did not end the depression nor soften its worst effects. By the time of the election of 1932, many people blamed Hoover for the depression. The nation voted overwhelmingly for his opponent, Franklin D. Roosevelt (*see* F. D. Roosevelt, United States History: The Great Depression and The New Deal), and Hoover retired from public life until World War II, when he was again called on to coordinate relief efforts.

In his later years, Hoover wrote a number of articles and books, including his three-volume *Memoirs* (1951–1952). He also was appointed to presidential commissions in 1947 and 1953 to study and suggest ways to end inefficiency in the federal government. Among the many recommendations made by the commissions that were adopted was the one to establish a Department of Health, Education, and Welfare.

BOOKS BY HOOVER

American Ideals versus the New Deal (1936). Reprint Services 1988 $49.00.
American Individualism (1922) and *The Challenge to Liberty* (1934). Regina Bks 1989 $19.95.
   ISBN 0-938469-05-3
Memoirs (1951–1952). 3 vols. Macmillan. (o.p.)
Problems of Lasting Peace (1942). Kraus 1969 $20.00. ISBN 0-527-42420-X
State Papers and Other Public Writings (1934). W. S. Myers (ed). 2 vols. Kraus (repr of 1934
   ed) $58.00. ISBN 0-527-42430-7

BOOKS ABOUT HOOVER

*Clinton, Susan. *Herbert Hoover. Encyclopedia of Presidents Ser.* Childrens 1988 $6.95. ISBN
   0-516-41355-4 Readable account of the thirty-first President of the United States.
Fausold, Martin L., and George T. Mazuzan (eds). *The Hoover Presidency: A Reappraisal.*
   SUNY 1974 $34.50. ISBN 0-87395-280-4 Interpretations of the Hoover presi-
   dency.
Hilton, Suzanne. *The World of Young Herbert Hoover.* Walker 1987 $12.95. ISBN 0-8027-
   6708-7 Gives insight into the earlier life and times of President Hoover.
Lisio, Donald J. *The President and Protest: Hoover, Conspiracy, and the Bonus Riot.* Univ of
   Missouri Pr 1974 $24.00. ISBN 0-8262-0158-X Presents viewpoints about
   Hoover's actions toward the Bonus Marchers.
Nash, George H. *The Life of Herbert Hoover: The Engineer 1874–1914.* Norton 1983 $25.00.
   ISBN 0-393-01634-X Tells about Hoover's early career.
Nash, George H. *The Life of Herbert Hoover: The Humanitarian, 1914–1917.* Norton 1988
   $25.00. ISBN 0-393-02550-0 Describes Hoover's work with relief agencies.
Nye, Frank T., Jr. *Doors of Opportunity: The Life and Legacy of Herbert Hoover.* Regina Bks 1988
   $14.95. ISBN 0-938469-01-0 Recounts the life of Hoover.
Romasco, Albert U. *Poverty of Abundance: Hoover, the Nation, the Depression.* Oxford Univ
   Pr 1965 $7.95. ISBN 0-19-500760-3 Examines Hoover's response to the Great
   Depression.
Smith, Richard N. *An Uncommon Man: The Triumph of Herbert Hoover.* High Plains 1990
   $14.50. ISBN 0-9623333-1-X Biography of Herbert Hoover.
Warren, Harris G. *Herbert Hoover and the Great Depression.* Greenwood 1980 $35.00. ISBN
   0-313-22659-8 Account of Hoover's presidential actions and attitudes during the
   Great Depression.

LANGE, DOROTHEA   1895–1965

Dorothea Lange, born in New Jersey, was one of America's most famous
journalistic photographers. From 1916 to 1932 she operated a portrait studio.
When the Great Depression devastated the lives of many Americans, she left
the formal atmosphere of her portrait studio and went into the streets to
capture the starkness of the times and the poignant expressions of dignity and
loss in the faces of the people. Representative of the photographs taken during
this time are "White Angel Breadline" (1933) and "Migrant Mother" (1936).
   From 1935 to 1942 Lange documented the poverty of rural places and the
plight of the farmer for the United States Farm Security Administration, helping to create a national awareness of the farm problem. In 1942 she used her
camera to document the forced evacuation of Japanese Americans to relocation
camps, providing a lasting witness of their suffering and humiliation.
   In 1945, while covering the San Francisco Conference that gave birth to the
United Nations, Lange collapsed from overwork. Not until 1951 did she resume
her photographic work, producing photo essays for *Life* magazine. Among them
were "Three Mormon Towns" (1954) and "The Irish Country People" (1955).

Many of her photographs were also included in her books, which include *An American Exodus* (1939), coauthored with her husband Paul Taylor, and *The American Country Women* (1966).

BOOK BY LANGE

An American Exodus: A Record of Human Erosion (1939). (coauthored with Paul S. Taylor)
   Ayer 1975 repr of 1939 ed $20.00. ISBN 0-405-06811-5

BOOKS ABOUT LANGE

Cox, Christopher. *Dorothea Lange. Masters of Photography Ser.* Aperture 1987 $9.95. ISBN
   0-89381-283-8 Features Lange's photographs.
Meltzer, Milton. *Dorothea Lange: Life Through the Camera.* Penguin 1986 $3.95. ISBN
   0-14-032105-5 Includes pictures and narrative about Lange.
Ohrn, Karin B. *Dorothea Lange and the Documentary Tradition.* Louisiana State Univ Pr 1980
   $32.50. ISBN 0-8071-0551-1 Story of Lange's career as a photojournalist.

ROOSEVELT, ANNA ELEANOR   1884–1962

Wife of President Franklin Delano Roosevelt (*see* F. D. Roosevelt, Vol. 2, United States History: The Great Depression and The New Deal), Eleanor Roosevelt became an important public figure in her own right. As the niece of President Theodore Roosevelt, Eleanor had known her distant cousin Franklin as a child. When he was a student at Harvard University, they became better acquainted and finally married in 1905.

At first Eleanor Roosevelt was not much interested or informed about political matters. But when her husband was struck with polio, she helped him reenter public life by keeping him informed on affairs of the day. During his two terms as governor of New York State, she served as his "legs and eyes," traveling around the state at his request, inspecting facilities and reporting back to him.

As First Lady, Roosevelt continued her public activities. She made official visits for the President and took an active part in public policy. For example, she was instrumental in the creation of the National Youth Administration, an agency to help young people during the Great Depression. She lobbied for improvements in housing, education, health, and the status of minorities. During World War II, she visited American military bases in an effort to help raise the spirits of the soldiers. She also became a sought-after public speaker; a columnist writing her daily *My Day* column, which ran in 140 newspapers; and a radio commentator with her own radio show.

When Franklin Roosevelt died in April 1945, Eleanor Roosevelt at first said, "My story is over." Nothing could have been further from the truth, however. That year President Harry S. Truman (*see* Truman, Vol. 2, United States History: World War II) appointed her United States delegate to the United Nations, where she served until 1951 and then again from 1961 to 1962. In 1946 she headed the Human Rights Commission of the United Nations and helped draft the U. N. Declaration of Human Rights. In later years, she campaigned for Democratic candidates for office, taught on the faculty at Brandeis University, and continued her writing and lecturing. She died in 1962, having become one of the most influential American women of the twentieth century, known to many as "First Lady of the World."

BOOKS BY ELEANOR ROOSEVELT

Eleanor Roosevelt's My Day: Her Acclaimed Columns, 1936–1945. Rochelle Chadakoff (ed).
   Pharos 1989 $18.95. ISBN 0-88687-407-6

Mother and Daughter: The Letters of Eleanor and Anna Roosevelt. (coauthored with Anna Roosevelt) Fromm Intl 1988 $9.95. ISBN 0-88064-108-8

This I Remember. Greenwood 1975 repr of 1949 ed $45.00. ISBN 0-8371-7702-2

You Learn by Living. Westminster John Knox 1983 $9.95. ISBN 0-664-24494-7

BOOKS ABOUT ELEANOR ROOSEVELT

Hoff-Wilson, Joan, and Marjorie Lightman (eds). *Without Precedent: The Life and Career of Eleanor Roosevelt.* Indiana Univ Pr 1987 $8.95. ISBN 0-253-20327-9 Recounts Eleanor Roosevelt's remarkable accomplishments.

Lash, Joseph P. *Eleanor and Franklin: The Story of Their Relationship Based on Eleanor Roosevelt's Private Papers.* Norton 1971 $15.95. ISBN 0-393-07459-5 Intimate look at the Roosevelts.

Lash, Joseph P. *Eleanor: The Years Alone.* Walter Pitkin (ed). NAL 1985 $10.95. ISBN 0-452-00771-2 Account of Roosevelt's life after 1945.

*Toor, Rachel. *Eleanor Roosevelt. American Women of Achievement Ser.* Chelsea 1989 $17.95. ISBN 1-55546-674-5 Weaves the tapestry of the historical period from which Eleanor Roosevelt emerged.

Watrous, Hilda. *In League with Eleanor: Eleanor Roosevelt and the League of Women Voters, 1921–1962.* League of Women Voters NYS 1984 $3.00. ISBN 0-938588-05-2 Pamphlet about Roosevelt's work with the League of Women Voters in New York state.

ROOSEVELT, FRANKLIN DELANO   1882–1945

Franklin Delano Roosevelt was born to wealth and social status in Hyde Park, New York, and pampered as a child by a doting mother. Educated at Groton, Harvard, and the Columbia School of Law, he began a career as a lawyer. In 1910, five years after he married Eleanor Roosevelt (*see* E. Roosevelt, Vol. 2, United States History: The Great Depression and The New Deal) he entered the world of politics as a New York state senator.

In 1921, at the age of 39, Roosevelt was afflicted with severe crippling of the legs from polio. This did not affect his ambition to hold high political office as a means of serving his country. He served as governor of New York from 1928 to 1932, having previously served in the New York legislature (1910–1912) and as Assistant Secretary of the Navy under President Woodrow Wilson (1913–1920). (*See* Wilson, Vol. 2, United States History: World War I.) He then secured the democratic nomination for President of the United States in the 1932 election and won, becoming the nation's thirty-second President.

Roosevelt won the presidential election four times, although he died only four months into his fourth term. When he first came to office in the depth of the Great Depression, he galvanized the Congress into passing measures to bring "relief, reform, and recovery" to the nation in a "New Deal." With his informal radio speeches, called "fireside chats," Roosevelt communicated his courage, confidence, and vision as a leader. Many of his New Deal policies had a lasting influence on the social, economic, and political life of the country. Later, when the war clouds of World War II threatened to engulf the United States, Roosevelt mobilized the country and made it "an arsenal for democracy," supplying Great Britain and its allies with weapons to fight the Axis powers. Even today, after numerous analyses and interpretations by both admirers and critics, Roosevelt remains a complex, controversial, and commanding figure.

BOOKS BY FRANKLIN DELANO ROOSEVELT

Franklin D. Roosevelt and Foreign Affairs. Edgar B. Nixon (ed). 3 vols. Harvard Univ Pr 1969 $76.00. ISBN 0-674-31815-3

Franklin D. Roosevelt and Foreign Affairs: Second Series 1937–1939. Donald B. Schewe (ed). 14 vols. N Ross 1979 $450.00. ISBN 0-88354-201-3

Looking Forward. FDR and the Era of the New Deal Ser. Da Capo 1973 repr of 1933 ed $35.00. ISBN 0-306-70477-3

Nothing to Fear. Essay Index Ser. Ayer 1946 $27.50. ISBN 0-8369-1845-2

On Our Way. Da Capo 1973 repr of 1934 ed $39.50. ISBN 0-306-70476-5

BOOKS ABOUT FRANKLIN DELANO ROOSEVELT

Alsop, Joseph. *FDR: A Centenary Remembrance, 1882–1945.* Washington Square Pr 1982 $3.50. ISBN 0-671-45891-4 Illustrated biography; includes history of the period.

Dallek, Robert. *Franklin D. Roosevelt and American Foreign Policy, 1932–1945.* Oxford Univ Pr 1979 $12.95. ISBN 0-19-502894-5 Describes Roosevelt's impact on foreign policy.

Freidel, Frank. *Franklin D. Roosevelt: A Rendezvous with Destiny.* Little 1990 $24.95. ISBN 0-316-29260-5 Complete biography focusing especially on the New Deal and Roosevelt's presidency.

Gallagher, Hugh G. *FDR's Splendid Deception.* Dodd 1985 $16.95. ISBN 0-396-08521-0 Focuses on Roosevelt as a handicapped person, how he was not perceived as being in any major sense disabled, and the careful strategy he used to hide his polio disability.

■Graham, Otis L., Jr., and Meghan Robinson Wander (eds). *Franklin D. Roosevelt, His Life and Times.* G. K. Hall 1985 $42.00. ISBN 0-8161-8667-7 Includes over 300 articles by various authors covering all aspects of Roosevelt.

*Greenblatt, Miriam. *Franklin D. Roosevelt: Thirty-Second President of the United States. Presidents of the United States Ser.* Garrett Ed 1989 $15.95. ISBN 0-944483-06-2 Informative biography of Roosevelt written for preteen and teenage readers.

Hacker, Jeffrey H. *Franklin D. Roosevelt. Impact Biography Ser.* Watts 1983 $12.90. ISBN 0-531-04592-7 Recounts significant events in the life of Roosevelt.

Hearden, Patrick J. *Roosevelt Confronts Hitler: America's Entry into World War II.* Northern Illinois Univ Pr 1987 $9.00. ISBN 0-87580-538-8 Scholarly work about the American road to war.

Morgan, Ted. *FDR: A Biography.* Simon 1986 $12.95. ISBN 0-671-62812-7 Focuses on FDR's private life and offers a new look at his refugee policy toward European Jews and the internment of Japanese Americans during World War II.

Ryan, Halford R. *Franklin D. Roosevelt's Rhetorical Presidency.* Greenwood 1988 $39.95. ISBN 0-313-25567-9 Study of the rhetorical relationship between FDR and the American people, on the way he addressed them between 1933–1945 in order to persuade them to accept his political agenda.

Ward, Geoffrey C. *Before the Trumpet: Young Franklin Roosevelt, 1882–1905.* Harper 1985 $19.45. ISBN 0-06-015451-9 Gives valuable insight into Roosevelt through a look at his early years.

Ward, Geoffrey C. *The First Class Temperament: The Emergence of Franklin Roosevelt.* Harper 1989 $27.95. ISBN 0-06-016066-7 Development of Roosevelt's distinctive temperament and character, beginning with his honeymoon in 1905 and ending twenty-three years later as he returns to public life.

See also Vol. 2, Economics: Income, Wealth, and Poverty.

WORLD WAR II

American Heritage Illustrated History of the United States. Vol 15: World War II. Choice Pub 1988 $3.49. ISBN 0-945260-15-6 Illustrated history of the war years; especially suited to younger readers.

*Blum, John M. *V Was for Victory: Politics and American Culture During World War II.* Harcourt

1977 $9.95. ISBN 0-15-693628-3 Describes the political and cultural environment in the United States during the early 1940s.

Buchanan, Russell. *Black Americans in World War II.* Regina Bks 1977 $7.45. ISBN 0-317-56340-8

Davidowicz, Lucy S. *The War Against the Jews, 1933–1945.* Free Pr 1986 $22.95. ISBN 0-02-908030-4

*Davis, Daniel S. *Behind Barbed Wire: The Imprisonment of Japanese Americans During World War II.* Dutton 1982 $13.95. ISBN 0-525-26320-9 Tells of the confinement of Japanese Americans during the U.S. war with Japan.

*Editors of Time–Life Books. *This Fabulous Century. Vol. 5 1940–1950.* Time–Life 1969 $17.95. ISBN 0-8094-1205-5 Photographs and short narrative of the 1940s.

Freeland, Richard M. *The Truman Doctrine and the Origins of McCarthyism: Foreign Policy, Domestic Policy, and Internal Security, 1946–1948.* New York Univ Pr 1985 $18.50. ISBN 0-8147-2576-7

Greene, Jack. *War at Sea: Pearl Harbor to Midway.* Wieser 1988 $9.98. ISBN 0-914373-11-0

*Harris, Mark Jonathan, *et al.* *The Homefront: America During World War II.* Putnam 1984 $8.95. ISBN 0-399-51124-5 The triumphs and tragedies of the war as voiced by the diverse people who experienced them; written in conjunction with the Public Broadcasting System documentary "The Homefront."

Hartmann, Susan M. *The Home Front and Beyond: American Women in the 1940s. American Women in the Twentieth Century Ser.* G. K. Hall 1983 $8.95. ISBN 0-8057-9903-6

Hastings, Max. *Overlord: D-Day and the Battle of Normandy.* Simon 1985 $8.95. ISBN 0-317-31520-X

Hastings, Max. *Victory over Europe: D-Day to VE Day.* Little 1985 $25.00. ISBN 0-316-81334-6

*Hemingway, Albert. *Ira Hayes: Pima Marine.* Univ Pr of America 1988 $22.50. ISBN 0-8191-7170-0 Story of the noted Native American who became a war hero.

*Hersey, John. *Hiroshima.* Bantam 1986 $2.95. ISBN 0-553-26058-8 Survivors tell of the bombing of Hiroshima and their lives today.

Houston, Jeanne W., and James D. Houston. *Farewell to Manzanar.* Bantam 1983 $2.95. ISBN 0-553-27258-6

*Irons, Peter. *Justice at War: The Inside Story of the Japanese American Internment.* Oxford Univ Pr 1983 $11.95. ISBN 0-19-503497-X Discusses the detainment of Japanese Americans during World War II.

Keegan, John. *Six Armies in Normandy: From D-Day to the Liberation of Paris.* Penguin 1983 $7.95. ISBN 0-14-005293-3

Keegan, John. *The Times Atlas of the Second World War.* Harper 1989 $50.00. ISBN 0-06-016178-7

Kenneth, Lee. *G.I. The American Soldier in World War II.* Warner Bks 1989 $4.50. ISBN 0-446-34895-3

*Larsen, Rachel. *Oppenheimer and The Atomic Bomb.* Watts 1988 $13.90. ISBN 0-531-10607-1 Illustrated presentation of the nuclear physicist who helped develop atomic energy for military purposes; especially suited to younger readers.

Leopard, Donald D. *World War II: A Concise History.* Waveland 1982 $9.50. ISBN 0-917974-89-1

Neu, Charles E. *The Troubled Encounter: The United States and Japan.* Krieger 1979 $11.50. ISBN 0-88275-951-5

*Okubo, Miné. *Citizen 13660.* Univ of Washington Pr 1983 $9.95. ISBN 0-295-95989-4 Recounts the World War II internment of a young Japanese American. Includes well-defined line drawings of the confinement.

Paterson, Katherine. *Jacob Have I Loved.* Avon 1981 $2.95. ISBN 0-380-56499-8

*Purcell, John. *Best-Kept Secret: The Story of the Atomic Bomb.* Vanguard 1963 $14.95. ISBN 0-8149-0378-9 Account of the building and use of the deadly atomic bomb.

Reynolds, David. *The Creation of the Anglo-American Alliance, 1937–1941: A Study in Competitive Cooperation.* Univ of North Carolina Pr 1988 $14.95. ISBN 0-8078-4229-X

Rossiter, Clinton. *Conservatism in America.* Harvard Univ Pr 1982 $8.95. ISBN 0-674-16510-1

*Scherman, David E. *Life Goes to War: A Pictorial History of World War II.* Pocket 1978 $14.95. ISBN 0-671-79077-3 *Life* magazine history of World War II in pictures.

*Shapiro, William E. *Pearl Harbor. Turning Points of World War II Ser.* Watts 1984 $12.90. ISBN 0-531-04865-9 Examines the Japanese attack on United States forces at the Hawaii naval base.

Sherwin, Martin J. *A World Destroyed: Hiroshima and the Origins of the Arms Race.* Random 1977 $9.95. ISBN 0-394-75204-X

*Tavaka, Chester. *Go for Broke: A Pictorial History of the Japanese American 100th Infantry Battalion and the 442nd Regimental Combat Team.* Bess Pr 1988 $34.95. ISBN 0-935-848-71 Story of the much-decorated battalion of Nisei soldiers and their contributions to the fighting war.

Terkel, Studs. *The Good War: An Oral History of World War Two.* Pantheon 1984 $19.45. ISBN 0-394-53103-5

Toland, John. *Rising Sun: The Decline and Fall of the Japanese Empire: 1936–1945.* Random 1970 $25.00. ISBN 0-394-44311-X

*Uchida, Yoshika. *Journey Home.* Macmillan 1982 $2.95. ISBN 0-689-70755-X Story of a Japanese-American girl and her family on their return home from a detention center.

Winkler, Allan M. *Home Front U.S.A. America During World War II. American History Ser.* Harlan Davidson 1986. ISBN 0-88295-835-6

Wohlstetter, Roberta. *Pearl Harbor: Warning and Decision.* Stanford Univ Pr 1962 $11.95. ISBN 0-8047-0598-4

Wright, Gordon. *Ordeal of Total War, 1939–1945. Rise of Modern Europe Ser.* Harper 1968 $8.95. ISBN 0-06-131408-0

See also Vol. 2, World History: World War II and Its Aftermath.

TRUMAN, HARRY S. 1884–1972

Harry S. Truman was born and grew up in Missouri, where he worked on the family farm and at various other jobs. It is believed the middle initial "S." was given to Truman at birth to represent the names of two grandfathers; it is often shown without the period. For a while after his 1919 marriage to Elizabeth Wallace, he was part owner of a haberdashery. In the early 1920s, he turned to politics, becoming first a judge and then a United States Senator. In 1944 he successfully ran for the vice presidency of the United States. He became the nation's thirty-third President on the sudden death of Franklin Delano Roosevelt in 1945. (*See* F. D. Roosevelt, Vol. 2, United States History: The Great Depression and The New Deal.) In 1948 he was elected President in his own right in a surprise victory over his Republican opponent, the New York governor Thomas E. Dewey. Forthright, feisty, and down-to-earth, Truman had worked earnestly while in the Senate to support the New Deal. When Roosevelt died, Truman said that he felt as if "the moon, the stars, and all the planets" had fallen on him.

It is said that as President, Truman grew in office, stepping out from Roosevelt's shadow to become a strong and successful chief executive. He stayed close to his midwestern roots and the feelings of the American people and participated in or approved many of the decisions and policies that shaped the postwar world. For example, he represented the United States at the signing of the United Nations Charter. He also worked to contain the spread of communism in Europe and in developing nations through the Marshall Plan, the Point Four Program, and the North Atlantic Treaty Organization (NATO).

Truman won election in 1948 by waging a relentless whistlestop campaign, traveling almost 32,000 miles in 35 days and making as many as 16 whistle-stop speeches each day. During this time, domestic affairs were influenced by fear of Communist infiltration and by the outbreak of the Korean War. Truman declined to run for reelection in 1952 but remained active in politics, campaigning for Democratic candidates and speaking out on national issues. He also spent time preparing for the 1957 opening of the Harry S. Truman Memorial Library in Independence, Missouri, and writing his memoirs, *Years of Decision* (1955), *Years of Trial and Hope* (1956), and *Mr. Citizen* (1960).

BOOKS BY TRUMAN

The Autobiography of Harry S. Truman. Robert H. Ferrell (ed). Univ of Colorado Pr 1980 $5.95. ISBN 0-87081-091-X

Memoirs of Harry S. Truman: Years of Trial and Hope. Quality Paperbacks Ser. Da Capo 1987 $14.95. ISBN 0-306-80297-X

The Truman Administration, Its Principles and Practice. Louis W. Koenig (ed). Greenwood 1979 repr of 1956 ed $27.50. ISBN 0-313-21186-8

Truman Speaks: On the Presidency, the Constitution, and Statecraft. Columbia Univ Pr 1975 $15.00. ISBN 0-231-08339-4

BOOKS ABOUT TRUMAN

Berman, William C. *The Politics of Civil Rights in the Truman Administration.* Ohio State Univ Pr 1970 $8.00. ISBN 0-8142-0142-3 Study of the internal government debate on civil rights under Truman.

Donovan, Robert. *Conflict and Crisis: The Presidency of Harry S. Truman, 1945–1948.* Norton $9.95. ISBN 0-393-30164-8 A veteran Washington correspondent looks at Truman's first administration.

Ferrell, Robert H. *Harry S. Truman and the Modern American Presidency. Library of American Biographers.* Scott 1983. ISBN 0-673-39337-2 Discusses the Truman administration as an example of the changes that have come to the office of president.

*McCoy, Donald R. *The Presidency of Harry S. Truman.* Univ Pr of Kansas 1984 $25.00. ISBN 0-7006-0252-6 An evaluation of Truman's policies.

Miller, Merle. *Plain Speaking: An Oral Biography of Harry S. Truman.* Berkley 1986 $4.95. ISBN 0-425-09499-5 Popular biography of Truman.

Ross, Irwin. *The Loneliest Campaign: The Truman Victory of 1948.* Greenwood 1977 repr of 1968 ed $22.50. ISBN 0-8371-8353-7 Interesting account of Truman's campaign and surprise victory in 1948.

Truman, Margaret. *Harry S. Truman.* Morrow 1984 $10.95. ISBN 0-688-03924-3 Biography of Truman by his daughter.

POSTWAR FOREIGN AND DOMESTIC POLICY

Alexander, Charles C. *Holding the Line: The Eisenhower Era, 1952–1961.* Indiana Univ Pr 1975 $8.95. ISBN 0-253-20193-4

*Allen, Frederick Lewis. *The Big Change: America Transforms Itself, 1900–1950.* Harper 1986 $7.95. ISBN 0-06-132082-X Popular history recounting changes in America during the first half of the twentieth century.

American Heritage Illustrated History of the United States. Vol. 16: Decades of Cold War 1946–1963. Choice Pub 1988 $3.49. ISBN 0-945260-16-4 Illustrated account of the years of tension between the United States and the Soviet Union; especially suited to younger readers.

Arms, Thomas S., and Eileen Riley. *Encyclopedia of the Cold War.* Facts on File 1991 $45.00. ISBN 0-8160-1975-4

*Bridges, Sue E. *All Together Now.* Knopf 1988 $13.99. ISBN 0-394-94098-9 Story of a young girl who spends a summer with her grandparents while her father serves with the military in Korea.

Brooks, Thomas R. *Picket Lines and Bargaining Tables: Organized Labor Comes of Age, 1935–1955.* Grossett 1986.

Bundy, McGeorge. *Danger and Survival: The Political History of the Nuclear Weapon.* Random 1989 $12.95. ISBN 0-679-72568-7

Chafe, William H., and Harvard Sitkoff (eds). *A History of Our Time: Readings on Postwar America.* Oxford Univ Pr 1987 $13.95. ISBN 0-19-504204-2

*Darby, Jean. *Douglas MacArthur. Biographies Ser.* Lerner 1989 $14.95. ISBN 0-8225-4901-8 Biography of the noted World War II general.

Donovan, Robert J. *The Second Victory: The Marshall Plan and the Postwar Revival of Europe.* Univ Pr of America 1988 $22.95. ISBN 0-8191-6498-4

*Editors of Time–Life Books. *This Fabulous Century. Vol. 6 1950–1960.* Time–Life 1970 $17.95. ISBN 0-8094-0125-8 Photographs and narrative capturing the mood of the 1950s.

*Finke, Blythe F. *George Meany: Modern Leader of the American Federation of Labor. Outstanding Personalities Ser.* SamHar 1972 $2.50. ISBN 0-87157-048-3 Biography of the leader of the AFL in the post-World War II era.

Gaddis, John L. *The United States and the Origins of the Cold War, 1941–1947. Contemporary American History Ser.* Columbia Univ Pr 1972 $14.00. ISBN 0-231-08302-5

*Goldman, Eric. *Crucial Decade and After: America, Nineteen Forty-Five to Nineteen Sixty.* Random 1961 $4.95. ISBN 0-394-70183-6 Discusses the issues facing the country after World War II.

Hart, Jeffrey. *When the Going Was Good: American Life in the Fifties.* Crown 1982.

Hastings, Max. *The Korean War.* Simon 1988 $10.95. ISBN 0-671-66834-X

Hogan, Michael J. *The Marshall Plan: America, Britain, and the Reconstruction of Western Europe, 1947–1952.* Cambridge Univ Pr 1989 $15.95. ISBN 0-521-37840-0

Jackson, Bob. *Berlin Airlift.* Harper 1988 $19.95. ISBN 0-85059-881-8

Jakoubek, Bob. *Ralph Bunche: Diplomat. Black Americans of Achievement Ser.* Chelsea 1989 $17.95. ISBN 1-55546-576-5

*Killian, James R. *Sputnik, Scientists, and Eisenhower: A Memoir of the First Special Assistant to the President for Science and Technology.* MIT Pr 1977 $10.95. ISBN 0-262-61035-3 Describes the founding of NASA.

*King, Martin Luther, Jr. *Stride Toward Freedom: The Montgomery Story.* Harper 1987 $8.95 ISBN 0-06-250490-8 Describes the bus boycott in Montgomery, Alabama, that launched the civil rights movement of the 1950s.

Kurland, Gerald. *Walter Reuther: Modern Leader of the United Automobile Workers Union. Outstanding Personalities Ser.* SamHar 1972 $3.95. ISBN 0-87157-545-0

*Luard, Evan. *A History of the United Nations. Nineteen Forty-Five to Fifty-Five: The Cold War Years.* St. Martin's 1982 $35.00. ISBN 0-312-38654-0 Recounts the United Nations' actions during the cold war era.

*Lukas, J. Anthony. *Common Ground: A Turbulent Decade in the Lives of Three American Families.* Random 1986 $10.95. ISBN 0-394-74616-3 Nonfiction account of school desegregation and its effect on three families.

McKeever, Porter. *Adlai Stevenson: His Life and Legacy.* Morrow 1989 $24.95. ISBN 0-688-06661-5

Marshall, S. L. *Pork Chop Hill: The American Fighting Man in Action: Korea, Spring 1953. Combat Arms Ser.* Battery Pr 1986 $19.95. ISBN 0-89839-090-7

Mee, Charles L., Jr. *The Marshall Plan.* Simon 1985 $8.95.

*Meriwether, Louise. *Don't Ride the Bus on Monday: The Rosa Parks Story.* Prentice 1973. (o.p.) Discusses the bus boycott in Montgomery, Alabama, in 1955.

*Nicholson, Alasdair. *The Cold War. World History Ser.* Malcolm Yapp, *et al* (eds). Greenhaven 1980 $2.95. ISBN 0-89908-211-4 Tells of the conflicts and differences between the United States and other nations.

*Pimlott, John. *The Cold War. Conflict in the Twentieth Century Ser.* Watts 1987 $10.29. ISBN 0-531-10320-X Describes diplomatic relations between the United States and the Soviet Union.

Reeves, Thomas C. *McCarthyism.* Krieger 1989 $8.50. ISBN 0-89464-289-8

Riesman, David, *et al. The Lonely Crowd: A Study of the Changing American Character. Studies in National Policy Ser.* Yale Univ Pr 1973 $12.95. ISBN 0-300-00193-2

*United Nations. *Everyone's United Nations.* UN 1986 $9.95. ISBN 92-1-100274-5 Explains how the United Nations was organized and what duties it performs.

*Walter, Mildred Pitts. *The Girl on the Outside.* Lothrop 1982. A black girl and a white
girl describe their separate viewpoints on the integration of Central High School
in Little Rock, Arkansas.

EISENHOWER, DWIGHT DAVID   1890–1969

Military hero of World War II and the nation's thirty-fourth President, Dwight
David Eisenhower was born in Denison, Texas, and grew up in Abilene, Kansas. A 1915 graduate of West Point, he rose through the ranks to become a
five-star general of the army and commander in chief of Allied forces in
Western Europe during World War II. After resigning as chief of staff in 1948,
he became the president of Columbia University in New York. That same year,
both the Democratic and Republican parties sought him as a presidential candidate. He chose instead, in 1950, to become Supreme Commander of NATO's
Allied Powers in postwar Europe. In 1952 he accepted the Republicans' offer
and ran successfully against Adlai E. Stevenson. The voters responded to Eisenhower's personal warmth and sincerity, his "I Like Ike" slogan, and his promise
to end the Korean War—despite his political inexperience. In 1956 he again ran
against Stevenson for the presidency and again emerged the victor.

During his presidency, Eisenhower relied on the counsel of men of greater
experience, particularly John Foster Dulles, his Secretary of State (*see* Dulles,
Vol. 2, American Government/Civics: The Federal Executive Branch); Sherman
Adams, his personal assistant; and businessmen in his Cabinet. Fiscal restraint
in domestic affairs and containment of communism in foreign affairs were the
primary characteristics of his administration.

For a period after Eisenhower's departure from office, historians viewed his
administration very negatively. More recently, however, scholars have emphasized the positive and peaceful aspects of his presidency, especially his support
for school desegregation and civil rights. Eisenhower chronicled the Allied
defeat of Germany in World War II in his 1948 work *Crusade in Europe* and his
White House years in his 1963 publication *Mandate for Change.*

Books by Eisenhower

At Ease: Stories I Tell to Friends (1967). *Military Classics Ser.* TAB 1988 $14.60. ISBN
0-8306-4003-7
Crusade in Europe (1948). *Politics and Strategy of World War II Ser.* Da Capo 1977 $14.95. ISBN
0-306-80109-4
The Eisenhower Diaries. Robert H. Ferrell (ed). Norton 1981 $19.95. ISBN 0-393-01432-0
Peace with Justice. Columbia Univ Pr $35.00. ISBN 0-231-02472-X

Books about Eisenhower

Ambrose, Stephen E. *Eisenhower.* Simon 1990 $29.95. ISBN 0-671-70107-X Condensed
version of a two-volume biography covering Eisenhower's career as soldier, army
general, president-elect, and President, 1890–1952.
*Beschloss, Michael R. *Eisenhower: A Centennial Life.* Harper 1990 $29.95. ISBN 0-06-
016418-2 To celebrate Eisenhower's one hundredth birthday, this illustrated biography presents a full overview of his life.
Burk, Robert F. *Dwight D. Eisenhower: Hero and Politician. Twayne's Twentieth Century American
Biography Ser.* G. K. Hall 1986 $9.95. ISBN 0-8057-7773-3 Portrait of Eisenhower
as army general and then President.
Divine, Robert A. *Eisenhower and the Cold War.* Oxford Univ Pr 1981 $7.95. ISBN
0-19-502824-4 Examines Eisenhower's foreign policy, with emphasis on relations
with the Communist bloc.

Duram, James C. *A Moderate Among Extremists: Dwight D. Eisenhower and the School Desegregation Crisis.* Nelson-Hall 1981 $24.95. ISBN 0-88229-394-X Discusses Eisenhower's key role in ending the stand-off in Little Rock, Arkansas.

*Sandberg, Peter S. *Dwight D. Eisenhower. World Leaders—Past and Present Ser.* Chelsea 1986 ISBN 0-7910-0566-6 Brief biography of Eisenhower as a military and political leader.

MARSHALL, GEORGE CATLETT   1880–1959

Career soldier, cabinet member, diplomat, statesman, and recipient of the Nobel Peace Prize, George Catlett Marshall was noted for his self-discipline, his excellent study habits, and his ability to motivate his troops. Born in Pennsylvania, he began his military career after graduating from the Virginia Military Institute in 1901. He served in the Philippines and as a staff officer during World War I. From then on he advanced steadily in his military career, seeing service in China from 1924 to 1927, serving as assistant commandant of the Infantry School at Fort Benning, Georgia, from 1927 to 1932, becoming U.S. Army chief of staff in 1939, and reaching the rank of five-star general in 1944. As chief of staff, Marshall directed Allied strategy in World War II.

After resigning from the U.S. Army in 1945, Marshall assisted President Harry S. Truman (*see* Truman, Vol. 2, United States History: World War II) in several diplomatic tasks and cabinet posts. In 1947, in the post of secretary of state, Marshall engineered an aid program for Greece and Turkey. He also carried out the European Recovery Program (ERP), or Marshall Plan, to promote the economic recovery of European nations. It was for his work on the ERP that Marshall received the Nobel Peace Prize in 1953. Marshall resigned his post as secretary of state in 1949 because of ill health. One year later, however, President Truman asked him to take the post of secretary of defense, a post from which he resigned in 1951 at the age of 70.

BOOKS BY MARSHALL

Marshall's Mission to China: December 1945 to January 1947. Lyman P. Van Slyke (ed). 2 vols. Greenwood 1976 $55.00. ISBNs 0-313-26910-6, 0-313-26911-4

The Papers of George Catlett Marshall. Vol. 1 *"The Soldierly Spirit."* Larry I. Bland and Fred L. Hadsel (eds). Johns Hopkins Univ Pr 1981 $39.50. ISBN 0-8018-2552-0

The Papers of George Catlett Marshall. Vol. 2 *"We Cannot Delay": July 1, 1939–December 6, 1941.* Larry I. Bland, *et al* (eds). Johns Hopkins Univ Pr 1986 $39.50. ISBN 0-8018-2553-9

Selected Speeches and Statements of General of the Army George C. Marshall. FDR and the Era of the New Deal Ser. H.A. DeWeerd (ed). Da Capo 1973 repr of 1945 ed $37.50. ISBN 0-306-70556-7

BOOKS ABOUT MARSHALL

*Lubetkin, Wendy. *George Marshall. World Leaders—Past and Present.* Chelsea 1990 $17.95. ISBN 1-55546-843-8 Illustrated biography of the U.S. statesman George Marshall.

Stoler, Mark. *George C. Marshall: Soldier-Statesman of the American Century. Twentieth Century American Biography Ser.* G. K. Hall 1989 $10.95. ISBN 0-8057-7785-7 Interpretive biography of Marshall; examines his career, private life, and political milieu.

See also Vol. 2, World History: World War II and Its Aftermath.

THE TURBULENT SIXTIES

American Heritage Illustrated History of the United States. Vol. 17: The Vietnam Era. Choice Pub 1988 $3.49. ISBN 0-945260-17-2 Illustrated discussion of a turbulent period of time in the United States; especially suited to younger readers.

*Archer, Jules. *The Incredible Sixties: The Stormy Years That Changed America.* Harcourt 1986 $16.95. ISBN 0-15-238298-4 Photographs and narrative about the social conditions and issues of the 1960s.

*Berger, Gilda. *Women, Work, and Wages.* Watts 1986 $12.90. ISBN 0-531-10074-X Introductory study of discrimination against women in the workplace.

Blumberg, Rhoda. *Civil Rights: The Nineteen Sixties Freedom Struggle. Social Movements Past and Present Ser.* G. K. Hall 1984 $9.95. ISBN 0-8057-9708-4

Breakstone, *et al* (eds). *Front Lines: Soldiers' Writings from Vietnam.* Indochina Curriculum Gp 1975 $2.00. ISBN 0-9607794-0-X

Broderick, Francis, *et al* (eds). *Black Protest Thought in the Twentieth Century. American Heritage Ser.* Macmillan 1971. ISBN 0-02-380120-4

Browne, Malcolm. *The New Face of War.* Bantam 1986 $3.95. ISBN 0-553-25894-X

*Burns, Stewart. *Social Movements of the 1960s.* Twayne 1990 $22.95. ISBN 0-8057-9738-8 A history of such movements as civil rights, the Vietnam War protests, and women's rights.

Coles, Robert. *Uprooted Children: The Early Life of Migrant Farm Workers.* Univ of Pittsburgh Pr 1970 $17.95. ISBN 0-8229-3192-3

*Conta, Marcia Maher. *Women for Human Rights. Movers and Shapers Ser.* Raintree 1979 $13.31. ISBN 0-8172-1378-3 Recounts lives, goals, and accomplishments of a few notable women involved in the struggle for human rights.

*Cook, Fred J. *The Cuban Missile Crisis, October 1962: The United States and Russia Face a Nuclear Showdown.* Watts 1972. Describes the events that nearly brought catastrophe during the Cuban Missile Crisis.

*Deloria, Vine, Jr. *Custer Died for Your Sins: An Indian Manifesto.* Univ of Oklahoma Pr 1988 $8.95. ISBN 0-8061-2129-7 Angry but informative account of the mistreatment of Native Americans.

*Editors of Time–Life Books. *This Fabulous Century.* Vol. 7 *1960–1970.* Time–Life 1970 $17.95. ISBN 0-8094-0126-6 Photographs and narrative capturing of the mood of the 1960s.

*Forman, James D. *Freedom's Blood.* Watts 1979. (o.p.) Describes the events surrounding the murders of three civil rights workers in Mississippi.

*Franchere, Ruth. *Cesar Chavez.* Harper Jr Bks 1988 $4.95. ISBN 0-06-4406023-1 Story of a brave farm worker who fought to improve working conditions for all farm workers.

Galbraith, John Kenneth. *The Affluent Society.* Houghton 1984 $18.95. ISBN 0-395-36613-5

*Goode, Stephen. *Assassination! Kennedy, King, Kennedy.* Watts 1979. (o.p.) Looks into the controversies over the assassinations of three American leaders in the 1960s.

*Halberstam, David. *The Best and the Brightest.* Penguin 1983 $9.95. ISBN 0-14-006983-6 Journalist's look at why the United States became involved in Vietnam, despite the fact that the "best and the brightest" people were in government at the time.

*Haskins, James, and Kathleen Benson. *The Sixties Reader. Viking Kestrel Non-Fiction Ser.* Penguin 1988 $13.95. ISBN 0-670-80674-9 Essays, speeches, and writings of the 1960s.

*Hauptly, Denis J. *In Vietnam.* Macmillan 1985 $13.95. ISBN 0-689-31079-X Account of America's involvement in the Vietnam conflict.

Heath, Jim F. *Decade of Disillusionment: The Kennedy–Johnson Years.* Indiana Univ Pr 1975 $9.95. ISBN 0-253-20201-9

*Herring, George C. *America's Longest War: The United States and Vietnam, 1950–1975.* McGraw 1985 $13.50. ISBN 0-07-554795-3 Close look at the Vietnam War.

*Hoobler, Dorothy, and Thomas Hoobler. *Vietnam, Why We Fought: An Illustrated History.* Knopf 1990 $18.99. ISBN 0-394-91943-2 Excellent photos add to the well-written body of this book; a good description of the causes and events in the war we lost.

*Johnson, Jacqueline. *Stokely Carmichael: the Story of Black Power.* Silver 1990 $16.98. Biography of a notable black leader who fought for the rights of black people and popularized the phrase "Black Power".

Larson, David L. *The Cuban Crisis of Nineteen Sixty-Two: Selected Documents, Chronology, and Bibliography.* Univ Pr of America 1986 $25.00. ISBN 0-8191-5299-4

*Lawson, Don. *An Album of the Vietnam War. Picture Albums Ser.* Watts 1986 $13.90. ISBN 0-531-10139-8 Picture history of the war in Vietnam.

*Lawson, Don. *The United States in the Vietnam War.* Harper Jr Bks 1981 $12.89. ISBN 0-690-04105-5 Describes the role of the United States in the Southeast Asian encounter.

MacPherson, Myra. *Long Time Passing.* NAL 1985 $4.95. ISBN 0-451-13607-1

*McGowen, Tom. *Album of Space Flight.* Macmillan 1987 $4.95. ISBN 0-02-688502-6 Illustrated account of the American space program.

Morris, Aldon D. *The Origins of the Civil Rights Movement: Black Communities Organizing for Change.* Free Pr 1986 $9.95. ISBN 0-02-922130-7

Murray, Bruce C. *Journey Into Space: The First Thirty Years of Space Exploration.* Norton 1990 $14.95. ISBN 0-393-30703-4

Murray, Charles, and Catherine Bly Cox. *Apollo: The Ten-Year Race to Put a Man on the Moon.* Simon 1989 $24.95. ISBN 0-671-61101-1

*O'Neill, William L. *Coming Apart: An Informal History of America in the 1960s.* Times Bks 1974 $9.95. ISBN 0-8129-6223-0 View of the struggles of the sixties.

Persons, Albert C. *Bay of Pigs: A Firsthand Account of the Mission by a U. S. Pilot in Support of the Cuban Invasion Force in 1961.* McFarland 1990 $15.95. ISBN 0-89950-483-3

Reed, Adolph, Jr. (ed). *Race, Politics, and Culture: Critical Essays on the Radicalism of the 1960s.* Greenwood 1986 $36.95. ISBN 0-313-24480-4

Rice, Gerard T. *Peace Corps in the Eighties.* USGPO 1986 $6.00. ISBN 0-318-22598-0

Sayres, Sohnya, *et al* (eds). *The Sixties, Without Apology.* Univ of Minnesota Pr 1984 $15.95. ISBN 0-8166-1337-0

*Steinbeck, John. *Travels with Charley in Search of America.* Penguin 1980 $4.95. ISBN 0-14-005320-4 Renowned author describes his travels around America with his poodle, Charley, in a pickup truck.

■Stern, Jane, and Michael Stern. *Sixties People.* Knopf 1990 $24.95. ISBN 0-394-57050-2 Description of various types of people, searching for identity during the sixties.

Viorst, Milton. *Fire in the Streets: America in the Nineteen Sixties.* Simon 1981 $14.95. ISBN 0-671-42814-4

*Weitsman, Madeline. *Peace Corps. Know Your Government Ser.* Chelsea 1989 $14.95. ISBN 0-87754-832-3 Story of the government agency begun by President Kennedy in 1961 to promote world peace and provide skills to the people of other nations.

Westmoreland, William C. *A Soldier Reports. Quality Paperbacks Ser.* Da Capo 1989 $14.95. ISBN 0-306-80376-3

Westmoreland, William C. *The Vietnam War: The Illustrated History of the Conflict in Southeast Asia.* Crown 1987 $14.98. ISBN 0-517-55113-6

*White, Florence M. *Cesar Chavez: Man of Courage. Americans All Ser.* Garrard 1973 $7.12. ISBN 0-8116-4579-7 Describes how this farm worker brought the plight of the migrant workers to the attention of others who could help.

Williams, William A., *et al* (eds). *America in Vietnam: A Documentary History.* Norton 1989 $8.70. ISBN 0-393-30555-4

Williams, William A. *The Tragedy of American Diplomacy.* Norton 1988 $9.70. ISBN 0-393-30493-0

Wolfe, Tom. *The Right Stuff.* Bantam 1984 $4.95. ISBN 0-553-25596-7

Wyden, Peter. *Bay of Pigs.* Simon 1980 $12.95. ISBN 0-671-25413-8

CARSON, RACHEL   1907–1964

See also Carson, Vol. 2, Biology: Ecology and the Environment.

American writer and marine biologist Rachel Carson was born in Springfield, Pennsylvania, where she developed an early love of the outdoors. She received an undergraduate degree from Pennsylvania College for Women (now Chatham College) in 1929, a master's degree from Johns Hopkins in 1932, and did further postgraduate work at Woods Hole Marine Biological Laboratory in Massachusetts. In 1936 Carson became an aquatic biologist with the U.S. Bureau of Fisheries. From 1944 until 1952 she served as editor-in-chief of publications for the U.S. Fish and Wildlife Service.

Carson's first published work was *Under the Sea Wind* (1941). In 1951 she published *The Sea Around Us,* a work that won the National Book Award (1952) for its keen scientific observations and rich poetic description. This work was followed by *The Edge of the Sea* (1954). In 1962 she published her most famous work, *Silent Spring,* a book that alerted the general public to the issue of ecology by describing the delicate relationships that exist between organisms and their environment. Her book explained how pesticides, especially the then popular DDT, passed through the food chain, eventually damaging the birds who ate insects tainted with the pest killer. While the book touched off a controversy between environmentalists and farmers, it resulted in increased awareness of the environment. It also led to more research on the effects of pesticide use and the eventual ban of DDT.

BOOKS BY CARSON

The Edge of the Sea (1954). Houghton 1979 $9.95. ISBN 0-395-28519-4
The Sea Around Us (1951). Oxford Univ Pr 1989 $18.95. ISBN 0-19-506186-1
The Sense of Wonder (1965). Harper Jr Bks 1987 $10.95. ISBN 0-06-091450-5
Silent Spring: Twenty Fifth Anniversary Edition (1962). Houghton 1987 repr of 1962 ed $7.95.
    ISBN 0-395-45390-9

BOOKS ABOUT CARSON

Gartner, Carol B. *Rachel Carson.* Ungar 1983 $16.95. ISBN 0-8044-5425-6 A look at the life of Carson and analyses of her works.
Harlan, Judith. *Sounding the Alarm: A Biography of Rachel Carson. People in Focus Ser.* Dillon 1989 $11.95. ISBN 0-87518-407-3 Life and achievements of a scientist/environmentalist.
*Jezer, Marty. *Rachel Carson. American Women of Achievement Ser.* Chelsea 1988 $17.95. ISBN 1-55546-646-X Biography of a marine biologist who stressed the relationship between humans and natural processes.
*Kudlinski, Kathleen V. *Rachel Carson: Pioneer of Ecology. Women of Our Time Ser.* Penguin 1989 $3.95. ISBN 0-14-032242-6 Brief, illustrated biography of the famous environmentalist.

FRIEDAN, BETTY   1921–

Feminist and founder of the National Organization for Women, or NOW (1966), Betty Friedan was born in Peoria, Illinois, the oldest of three children. Friedan graduated from college with a major in psychology and pursued graduate studies in California before she married in 1947.

As the mother of three children, she stayed at home to care for the needs of her family until the early 1960s, when she began to search for ways to fill her "empty" hours. She turned to writing and became interested in exploring the role of modern women. She researched women's needs and desires through questionnaires and surveys. Then, drawing from her own experiences, her research, and hundreds of interviews with women, Friedan published *The Feminine Mystique* (1963). This book is credited with starting the feminist movement and women's push for equal rights with men. Friedan later published other books, including *It Changed My Life* (1976), a collection of speeches, essays, and interviews, and *The Second Stage* (1981), an assessment of the status of the women's movement as it moved into the 1980s.

In 1966 Friedan became the first president of NOW. Established to achieve "full equality for women in America in a truly equal partnership with men," NOW has continued to champion women's causes throughout the United States and the world. In 1970 Friedan organized and led a nationwide Women's Strike for Equality—the first large-scale protest by women since the suffrage movement. She remains active in the women's movement today.

BOOKS BY FRIEDAN

The Feminine Mystique (1963). Dell 1984 $4.95. ISBN 0-440-32497-1
The Second Stage (1981). Summit Bks 1986 $8.95. ISBN 0-671-63064-4

BOOKS ABOUT FRIEDAN

Blau, Justine. *Betty Friedan. American Women of Achievement Ser.* Chelsea $17.95. ISBN 1-55546-653-2 Discusses the life and career of this important feminist.
Meltzer, Milton. *Betty Friedan: A Voice for Women's Rights. Women of Our Time Ser.* Penguin 1985 $10.95. ISBN 0-670-80786-9 Describes Friedan's struggles and accomplishments in the fight for women's rights.

GOLDWATER, BARRY MORRIS 1909–

Born in Phoenix, Arizona, Barry Goldwater made his mark as a department store entrepreneur; a military reservist, gaining the rank of major general; a Republican member of the U.S. Senate; and an ultraconservative presidential candidate. Goldwater's staunch conservatism ultimately led to his defeat by Lyndon B. Johnson (*see* Johnson, Vol. 2, United States History: The Turbulent Sixties) in the 1964 presidential election. As a conservative, Goldwater advocated right-to-work laws, which outlawed any arrangement requiring a worker to join a labor union. On the federal level he regularly voted against any expansion of federal powers. He worked to decrease appropriations for public welfare and foreign aid and urged total victory over world communism.

Goldwater studied at the University of Arizona until 1929, when he left to work in the family's department-store business. He began his political career as a member of the city council in Phoenix in 1949, a post he held until 1952. After being elected to the U.S. Senate in 1952, he retained his Senate seat until he ran for the presidency in 1964. In 1968, Goldwater again ran for the Senate, winning election and serving until 1980. While Goldwater sponsored no major legislation of his own during his years of service in the Senate, he was well liked, considered sincere and honest, and known as a politician who did not adjust his words to suit the moods of his home-state voters. His views as a conservative are well documented in several of his books, including *The Conscience of a Conservative* (1960) and his autobiography, *With No Apologies* (1979).

BOOKS BY GOLDWATER

The Conscience of a Conservative (1960). Regnery 1990 $17.95. ISBN 0-89526-540-0
Goldwater. (coauthored with Jack Casserly) Doubleday 1988 $21.95. ISBN 0-385-23947-5
Why Not Victory? A Fresh Look at American Foreign Policy. Greenwood 1980 repr of 1962 ed $35.00. ISBN 0-313-22316-5

BOOKS ABOUT GOLDWATER

Bell, Jack. *Mr. Conservative: Barry Goldwater.* Doubleday 1962. Sympathetic account of Goldwater's political career.

Shadegg, Stephen. *Barry Goldwater: Freedom Is His Flight Plan.* Fleet 1962. Discussion of Goldwater's goals and accomplishments by an admirer.

HUMPHREY, HUBERT HORATIO   1911–1978

Although he was born in South Dakota, Hubert Humphrey spent much of his political career representing Minnesota in the United States Senate. Before his attention turned to politics in the early 1940s, however, he first practiced pharmacy and then was a teacher of political science.

A Democrat, Humphrey was a great believer in President Franklin D. Roosevelt's New Deal (*see* F. D. Roosevelt, Vol. 2, United States History: The Great Depression and The New Deal) and played a major role in convincing the Democratic party and the Farmer-Labor party that they should merge. In 1945 Humphrey was elected to the first of his two terms as mayor of the city of Minneapolis. Three years later he became the first Democrat from Minnesota ever to be elected to the U.S. Senate. A staunch and outspoken advocate of civil rights, he was reelected to the Senate again in 1954 and in 1960.

That same year Humphrey campaigned for the office of President. But after a very poor showing in the West Virginia primary, he dropped out of the running. In 1964 Democrat Lyndon Baines Johnson (*see* Johnson, Vol. 2, United States History: The Turbulent Sixties) became the thirty-sixth President of the United States, and Humphrey attained the office of vice president. When Johnson determined not to run for reelection in 1968, Humphrey again campaigned for the Oval Office. Although he was nominated by the Democratic party, he was not successful this time either, largely because the voters associated him with Johnson's Vietnam policies, which had not been popular. In 1972 Humphrey made one more try for the presidency. This time, however, the Democrats chose as their candidate a liberal senator from South Dakota, George McGovern. Six years later Humphrey died of cancer.

BOOKS ABOUT HUMPHREY

Berman, Edgar. *Hubert: The Triumph and Tragedy of the Humphrey I Knew.* Putnam 1979 $10.95. ISBN 0-399-12314-8 Sympathetic look at the last 20 years of Humphrey's life, written by a close friend.

Engelmayer, Sheldon D., and Robert J. Wagman. *Hubert Humphrey: The Man and His Dream, 1911–1978.* Methuen 1978 $12.95. ISBN 0-458-93450-X Biography by two journalists, interspersed with excerpts from Humphrey's speeches.

Solberg, Carl. *Hubert Humphrey: A Political Biography.* Norton 1984 $19.45. ISBN 0-393-01806-7 First full biography of Humphrey, portraying him sympathetically but with recognition of his weaknesses.

JOHNSON, LYNDON BAINES   1908–1973

Becoming the nation's thirty-sixth President in 1963 upon the assassination of President John F. Kennedy (*see* J. F. Kennedy, Vol. 2, United States History: The Turbulent Sixties), Lyndon Baines Johnson proved to be a powerful executive and won election in his own right in 1964. Born near Stonewall, Texas, into a farming family, he graduated from Southwest Texas State Teachers College, now Southwest Texas State University, in 1930. After teaching in a high school for two years, he became secretary to a Texas congressman in Washington, D.C. In 1935 he became director in Texas of the National Youth Administration. Two years later, he was elected to Congress. As a result of his years of service in the Congress, he became well-versed in government and politics and prepared for the presidency. He had served in the House of Representatives from 1937 to 1949 and in the Senate from 1949 to 1961. In the Senate he had held the posts of both minority and majority leader.

As President, Johnson persuaded Congress to pass many of Kennedy's social programs that had been bottlenecked in committees. Johnson went on to promote his own social programs, known as the Great Society. He tried to help America's poor people through his War on Poverty. His efforts led to help for the elderly with the enactment of the Medicare Bill, the expansion of federal aid to education, the creation of the Job Corps, and the passage of the Voting Rights Act of 1965.

Johnson's successes on the domestic front, however, were darkened by his escalation of American involvement in the Vietnam War. In addition, the cost of military escalation ate into the money allotted for Great Society programs. Increasingly, Johnson's popularity declined, as more Americans came to question his policies in Vietnam. By 1968 Johnson had decided not to seek election for a second term.

Johnson's great powers of personal persuasiveness coupled with his use of the awesome powers of the presidency made him a man to be admired as well as feared. His personality could be both charming and overbearing, his actions both cultured and crude. Among historians, evaluations of his presidency remain mixed.

BOOK BY JOHNSON

The Vantage Point: Perspectives on the Presidency, 1963–1969. Holt 1971. (o.p.)

BOOKS ABOUT JOHNSON

■Bornet, Vaughn. *The Presidency of Lyndon B. Johnson.* Univ Pr of Kansas 1984 $14.95. ISBN 0-7006-0242-9 An assessment of Johnson's domestic policy and foreign issues, including the Vietnam War.

Caro, Robert A. *The Years of Lyndon Johnson.* Random 1983 $9.95. ISBN 0-394-71654-X Biography of Johnson and his politics.

Dugger, Ronnie. *The Politician: The Life and Times of Lyndon Johnson.* Norton 1982 $18.95. ISBN 0-393-01598-X Thoroughly researched account of Johnson's career by an investigative reporter and scholar.

*Kaye, Tony. *Lyndon B. Johnson. World Leaders—Past and Present Ser.* Chelsea 1988 $17.95. ISBN 0-87754-536-7 Brief, illustrated biography of Johnson.

Lynch, Dudley. *The President from Texas: Lyndon Baines Johnson.* Harper Jr Bks 1975 $12.70. ISBN 0-690-00627-6 Absorbing and balanced portrayal of this larger-than-life, controversial national figure.

*Middleton, Harry. *LBJ: The White House Years.* Abrams 1990 $45.00. ISBN 0-8109-1191-4 Many photos and brief commentary bring alive Johnson's presidency.

Miller, Merle. *Lyndon: An Oral Biography.* Ballantine 1987 $5.95. ISBN 0-345-34529-0 Fascinating history of Johnson, based on nearly 200 interviews with people who knew him.

KENNEDY, JOHN FITZGERALD   1917–1963

When he was elected the nation's thirty-fifth President, John Fitzgerald Kennedy became the youngest man and the first Roman Catholic elected to the Oval Office. Some Americans had opposed his candidacy because they feared that his religion would influence his decisions as President. Yet fascination with his personality, style, intelligence, wit, and character overshadowed these fears for many people. Articulate and forward looking, but with a great sense of the past, Kennedy was the only U.S. President to be awarded a Pulitzer Prize in biography. He won the prize in 1957 for *Profiles in Courage* (1956), a book about several Americans who had made courageous decisions. Kennedy wrote the book while recuperating from surgery to repair a spinal injury.

Born in Brookline, Massachusetts, to a wealthy and politically ambitious father, Kennedy received a Harvard education. In 1940, while acting as secretary to his ambassador father in London, he wrote *Why England Slept,* an interpretation of England's failure to recognize the danger of the Nazi menace. As a PT-boat commander in World War II, he was seriously injured when his boat was cut in half and sunk. After the war, in 1946, he was elected to the U.S. Congress, where he served three terms in the House of Representatives before election to the Senate in 1952 and again in 1958.

Elected President in 1960 in a close victory over Richard Nixon (*see* Nixon, Vol. 2, United States History: The Nixon and Ford Years), Kennedy hoped to move the nation to a "New Frontier." He urged legislative programs to spur the economy, expand federal aid to education, renew blighted urban areas, eliminate racial segregation in public places, and institute medical care for the aged. But most of Kennedy's programs were stalled in Congress when he was assassinated in November 1963. It was left to Lyndon Johnson (*see* Johnson, Vol. 2, United States History: The Turbulent Sixties)—Kennedy's successor in the presidency—to get Congress to enact the New Frontier legislation.

In foreign affairs, Kennedy did not fare well in the Bay of Pigs invasion of 1961, but he acted strongly in the Cuban Missile Crisis of 1962, averting a military confrontation with the Soviet Union. His call to commitment in his inaugural speech—"Ask not what your country can do for you; ask what you can do for your country"—inspired many young people to enter the Peace Corps, which was formed in 1961 to help people in developing nations, and other areas of government service.

Kennedy's presidency was cut short on November 22, 1963, when he was shot to death while riding in an open car during a political visit to Dallas, Texas. A shocked nation watched as he was buried in Arlington National Cemetery in Virginia.

BOOKS BY JOHN FITZGERALD KENNEDY

A Nation of Immigrants (1964). Harper 1986 $5.95. ISBN 0-06-091367-3
Profiles in Courage (1956). Harper 1988 $4.95. ISBN 0-06-080698-2
The Strategy of Peace (1961). Allan Nevins (ed). Harper 1960. (o.p.) $10.00.
Why England Slept (1940). Greenwood 1981 repr of 1961 ed $29.75. ISBN 0-313-22874-4

BOOKS ABOUT JOHN FITZGERALD KENNEDY

Belin, David W. *Final Disclosure: The Full Truth About the Assassination of President Kennedy.* Scribner's 1988 $19.95. ISBN 0-684-18976-3 Attempt to prove that Oswald was the sole killer and that there was no conspiracy, by the Warren Commission's chief investigator.

Blair, Joan, and Clay Blair, Jr. *The Search for JFK.* Berkley 1976. ISBN 0-399-11418-1 Investigates Kennedy's formative years between prep school and his election to Congress.

Bradlee, Benjamin C. *Conversations with Kennedy.* Norton 1975 $8.95. ISBN 0-393-08722-0 Intimate look at Kennedy's ideas and concerns, as expressed in conversations with a close journalist friend.

Kelly, Regina Z. *John F. Kennedy. Library of American Heroes Ser.* Follett 1969. Interesting retelling of Kennedy's life, including some photographs.

Kurland, Gerald. *Assassination of President John F. Kennedy. Events of Our Times Ser.* SamHar 1973 $3.95. ISBN 0-87157-707-0 Describes the assassination of President Kennedy, the events immediately following it, the funeral, and the conclusion of the Warren Report.
*Langley, Andrew. *John F. Kennedy. Great Lives Ser.* Watts 1986 $11.90. ISBN 0-531-18034-4 Brief, heavily illustrated account of the key events in Kennedy's life.
Manchester, William. *One Brief Shining Moment: Remembering Kennedy.* Little 1988 $16.95. ISBN 0-316-54511-2 Amply illustrated tribute to the life and legacy of John F. Kennedy.
Mills, Judie. *John F. Kennedy.* Watts 1988 $14.90. ISBN 0-531-10520-2 Traces the life and career of a president who helped shape an era.
Schlesinger, Arthur M., Jr. *Thousand Days: John F. Kennedy in the White House.* Houghton 1965. (o.p.) $24.50. Personal memoir of Kennedy's presidency by a member of his inner circle.
Sorensen, Theodore C. *Kennedy.* Harper 1988 $10.95. ISBN 0-06-091530-7 Firsthand account of the Kennedy administration by a close associate.

KENNEDY, ROBERT FRANCIS   1925–1968

Robert "Bobby" Kennedy was the seventh of nine children in the wealthy Kennedy family of Massachusetts. When his elder brother John F. Kennedy (*See* J. F. Kennedy, Vol. 2, United States History: The Turbulent Sixties) became President in 1961, Robert was named Attorney General. The brothers had worked together during the campaign, with Robert serving as his brother's campaign manager.

Robert Kennedy had been educated at Harvard University, served in the Navy during World War II, and received his law degree from Virginia Law School in 1951. Then he worked in the Criminal Division of the Department of Justice in 1951 and 1952, where he helped prosecute corruption and income-tax evasion cases. In the following years he served as congressional investigator for committees on Un-American Activities and on Improper Activities in Labor and Management.

In 1961 Kennedy became Attorney General under President John F. Kennedy, and stayed on under President Lyndon Johnson. (*See* Johnson, Vol. 2, United States History: The Turbulent Sixties.) In that position he actively promoted civil rights by prosecuting people who violated the civil rights of minorities. He continued his pursuit of civil rights when he became Senator from New York in 1964. He also worked for antipoverty programs, medicare, and other social programs, and spoke out strongly against escalating involvement in the war in Vietnam.

Kennedy set out to campaign for the Democratic nomination for President in the 1968 election. He won five of the six primaries he entered and was becoming a formidable challenger, when Sirhan Sirhan, an Arab immigrant, shot him fatally on June 5, 1968.

BOOKS BY ROBERT KENNEDY

The Enemy Within (1960). Greenwood 1982 repr of 1960 ed $35.00. ISBN 0-313-23579-1
Thirteen Days: A Memoir of the Cuban Missile Crisis (1969). Richard Neustadt and Graham Allison (eds). Norton 1971 $5.95. ISBN 0-393-09896-6

BOOKS ABOUT ROBERT KENNEDY

Kurland, Gerald. *Assassination of Robert Kennedy. Events of Our Times Ser.* SamHar 1973 $2.50. ISBN 0-87157-202-8 Describes the assassination of Robert F. Kennedy, the events right before and after it, and the political impact it had.

Schlesinger, Arthur M., Jr. *Robert Kennedy and His Times.* Ballantine 1985 $4.95. ISBN 0-345-32547-8 Discusses the forces, within and without, that shaped the life and career of Robert Kennedy.

Stein, Jean. *American Journey: The Times of Robert Kennedy.* George Plimpton (ed). Harcourt 1970 $8.95. ISBN 0-15-91070-7 Recounts Kennedy's life, with liberal doses of quotations from hundreds of interviews with people who knew him.

Zeiger, Henry A. *Robert F. Kennedy: A Biography.* Meredith Pr 1968. Objective, clear study of Kennedy's career.

KING, MARTIN LUTHER, JR.   1929–1968

Civil rights leader, clergyman, and winner of the 1964 Nobel Peace Prize, Martin Luther King, Jr., was born in Atlanta, Georgia, the son of the pastor of Atlanta's Ebenezer Baptist Church. After graduating from Morehouse College in Georgia in 1948, he went on to obtain degrees from Crozer Theological Seminary and Boston University.

In 1954 King, an ordained minister, became pastor of a Montgomery, Alabama, Baptist church. At about the same time, he became actively involved in the civil rights movement. During the next 20 years or so, he devoted himself to the furthering of the cause of civil rights, becoming the most prominent member of the movement. He achieved his first major victory—and national prominence and recognition—in the mid-1950s when he led a 382-day black boycott of the segregated Montgomery bus system, leading to the 1956 Supreme Court decision holding segregation on buses unconstitutional. The following year he founded and became president of the Southern Christian Leadership Conference, which served as a base for civil rights activities first in the South and eventually across the county.

To fight racial segregation and gain civil rights, King advocated a policy of passive resistance and nonviolence. He saw direct, nonviolent action as a means of forcing people to become aware of injustice. Arrested many times for his part in boycotts, sit-ins, and other nonviolent actions, in 1963 from a Birmingham, Alabama, jail he wrote his "Letter from Birmingham" to his fellow clergy, defending the nonviolent action he advocated. That same year, at a civil rights demonstration in Washington, D.C., in support of black demands for equal rights, more than 200,000 supporters gathered at the Lincoln Memorial to hear his speech stressing the importance of the philosophy of nonviolent protest. An eloquent speaker, King aroused world sentiment with these now-famous words: "I have a dream that this nation will rise up and love out the true meaning of its creed, 'We hold these truths to be self-evident: that all men are created equal.' "

In March of 1965, in support of his ideals, King led more than 3,000 people on a 54-mile march from Selma, Alabama, to Montgomery, Alabama. By then, however, his leadership was being challenged by more militant leaders and groups who wanted more immediate and more encompassing action. Nonetheless, King continued to actively preach and practice his philosophy. At the same time, he began to take a greater interest in and show a greater concern for poverty. In 1968 he planned a Poor People's March to Washington, D.C. He interrupted his plans, however, to go to Memphis, Tennessee, in a show of support for sanitation workers who were striking there. To the horror and grief of the nation, while on his motel balcony in Memphis, he was shot and killed by an escaped convict named James Earl Ray. On January 21, 1986, in memory and honor of King and his many contributions, Martin Luther King Day was officially observed for the first time as a national holiday.

BOOKS BY KING

The Measure of a Man. Augsburg Fortress 1988 $6.95. ISBN 0-8006-0877-1

Strength to Love. Augsburg Fortress 1981 $6.95. ISBN 0-8006-1441-0

Stride Toward Freedom. The Montgomery Story (1958). Harper 1987 $8.95. ISBN 0-06-250490-8

The Trumpet of Conscience. Harper 1989 $7.95. ISBN 0-06-250492-4

Where Do We Go From Here? Chaos or Community (1967). Beacon 1968 $10.95. ISBN 0-8070-057-1

The Words of Martin Luther King, Jr. (selected by Coretta King) Newmarket 1987 $7.95. ISBN 0-937858-79-X

Why We Can't Wait (1964). NAL 1988 $3.95. ISBN 0-451-62754-7

BOOKS ABOUT KING

Garrow, David J. (ed). *Martin Luther King, Jr. Civil Rights Leader, Theologian, Orator.* 3 vols. Carlson 1989 $225.00. ISBN 0-926019-01-5 Three volumes that present the most comprehensive portrait available of the extraordinarily wide-ranging accomplishments and abilities of Martin Luther King, Jr.

*Jakoubek, Robert. *Martin Luther King, Jr. Black Americans of Achievement Ser.* Chelsea 1990 $9.95. ISBN 0-7910-0243-8 Biography of King illustrated with photos, art, and visual memorabilia of King's life and times.

*Shuker, Nancy F. *Martin Luther King Jr. World Leaders—Past and Present Ser.* Chelsea 1985 $17.95. ISBN 0-87754-567-7 Focuses on King's early years, his career, and contributions.

MALCOLM X (MALCOLM LITTLE; EL-HAJJ MALIK EL-SHABAZZ) 1925–1965

See also Malcolm X, Vol. 1, Language Arts: Human Communication.

Malcolm X was an advocate of black pride and black nationalism in the early 1960s. Born Malcolm Little in Omaha, Nebraska, he moved to Michigan, later to Boston, and finally to New York City. There, at the age of 21, he was convicted of stealing a watch and sentenced to 10 years in jail. While in prison, he converted to the Nation of Islam, or Black Muslims, a religious group that was led by Elijah Muhammad. The Black Muslims preached black pride and separation from whites. Calling himself Malcolm X and becoming a Black Muslim minister in 1952 after his release from prison, he eventually attracted a large following of his own.

In 1963 a series of events began that changed Malcolm X's relationship with the Black Muslims. First, Elijah Muhammad ousted him from the Nation of Islam, and Malcolm X formed a rival organization called the Muslim Mosque, Inc. Next, in 1964, he took a trip to Mecca, the holiest city of Islam. As a result of his trip, he converted to traditional Islam and made a startling turnabout in his thinking. Forming the Organization of Afro-American Unity on his return to the United States, he still preached black pride. But his message now rejected violence and urged all blacks and whites to live together peacefully in brotherhood. This contrasted emphatically with the Black Muslim message of hatred for the white race and separation from it. His new attitudes disturbed some Black Muslims so much that, in 1965, he was assassinated by extremists. After his death his life story, *Autobiography* (1965), was published. Eventually, Malcolm X became a hero to many African Americans, who saw his willingness to work for racial harmony, while maintaining black pride, as a worthy model to follow.

BOOKS BY MALCOLM X

The Autobiography of Malcolm X. Ballantine 1977 $3.95. ISBN 0-345-33920-7 Powerful, provocative modern classic among American biographies; details the criminal early years and the later ideological development of the militant orator.

Malcolm X: The End of White World Supremacy: Four Speeches (1971). Arcade 1989 $7.95. ISBN 1-55970-006-8

Malcolm X: The Last Speeches (1989). Pathfinder Pr 1989 $25.00. ISBN 0-87348-544-0

Malcolm X on Afro-American History (1967). Pathfinder Pr 1972 $4.95. ISBN 0-87348-085-6

Malcolm X Speaks: Selected Speeches and Statements (1965). George Breitman (ed). Grove 1988 $8.95. ISBN 0-8021-3051-8

Malcolm X Talks to Young People (1969). Pathfinder Pr 1970 $0.75. ISBN 0-87348-086-4 A good introduction to Malcolm X's thoughts on race, history, and politics.

BOOKS ABOUT MALCOLM X

MacDonald, George. *Malcolm.* Sunrise Bks 1989 $27.50. ISBN 0-940652-53-6 Compassionate, comprehensive biography building on Alex Haley's work of a decade earlier and putting the oratory and assassination of Malcolm X in historical perspective.

*Rummel, Jack. *Malcolm X.* Chelsea 1989 $17.95. ISBN 1-55546-600-1 Anecdotal yet comprehensive biography of the ex-convict who became the "shining prince"; written for young adults.

McGOVERN, GEORGE STANLEY   1922–

A noted liberal Democrat, U.S. Senator, and presidential candidate, George McGovern grew up and attended college in Mitchell, South Dakota, where his father was a Methodist minister. After serving in World War II as a B-24 pilot, McGovern earned a doctorate in history at Northwestern University in Illinois. When he returned to Mitchell, he helped build and revitalize Democratic strength in the state. He then ran for the U.S. House of Representatives, winning election in 1956 and again in 1958. After he lost his 1960 bid for election to the U.S. Senate, President John F. Kennedy (*see* J. F. Kennedy, Vol. 2, United States History: The Turbulent Sixties) appointed him director of the new Food for Peace Program. In this post, McGovern directed efforts to ease world hunger. He discussed these efforts in his book *War Against Want: America's Food for Peace Program* (1964).

As a member of the Senate from 1963 to 1980, McGovern became an outspoken critic of American involvement in Vietnam. As a senator from a farm state, he studied agricultural needs, assessing them in his book *Agricultural Thought in the Twentieth Century* (1966). He also continued his efforts to eliminate hunger and malnutrition. While still a senator, he won the 1972 Democratic nomination for President. He lost the election to Richard Nixon (*see* Nixon, Vol. 2, United States History: The Nixon and Ford Years), mainly because the voters looked on his proposals as too socialistic and perceived him as indecisive.

BOOK BY McGOVERN

Food and Population: The World in Crisis. Ayer 1976 $25.00. ISBN 0-405-06663-5

THE NIXON AND FORD YEARS

Bernstein, Carl, and Bob Woodward. *All the President's Men.* Warner Bks 1976 $4.50. ISBN 0-446-32264-4

Buggey, J. *Energy Crisis: What Are Our Choices?* Prentice 1976 $11.84. ISBN 0-13-277301-5

Dolan, Paul J., and Edward Quinn (eds). *The Sense of the Seventies: A Rhetorical Reader.* Oxford Univ Pr 1978.

*Furniss, Tim. *The First Men on the Moon. Great Journeys Ser.* Watts 1989 $11.90. ISBN 0-531-18240-1 Story of the space missions that carried the man who set foot on the moon for the first time.

Furniss, Tim. *One Small Step: The Apollo Missions, the Astronauts, the Aftermath.* Haynes 1989 $39.96. ISBN 0-85429-586-0

*Greene, Bob. *Homecoming: When the Soldiers Returned from Vietnam.* Putnam 1989 $17.95. ISBN 0-399-13386-0 Focuses on the home-front reception of returning Vietnam veterans.

*Haley, Alex. *Roots.* Dell 1980 $5.95. ISBN 0-440-17464-3 Presents the family history of the author, beginning in Africa and continuing through several generations in America.

*Herring, George. *America's Longest War: The United States and Vietnam, 1950–1975.* McGraw 1985 $13.50. ISBN 0-07-554795-3 Explores America's role in the Vietnam War.

Horne, A.D. (ed). *The Wounded Generation: America After Vietnam.* Prentice 1981.

*Magruder, Jeb. *An American Life: One Man's Road to Watergate.* Atheneum 1974. (o.p.) Personal account of the Watergate scandal.

*Nader, Ralph, and Clarence Ditlow. *The Lemon Book: Auto Rights.* Moyer 1990 $12.95. ISBN 1-55921-020-6 Discusses the laws and legislation protecting consumers in the purchase of an automobile.

*Nader, Ralph. *Unsafe at Any Speed.* Bantam 1972. (o.p.) Describes the economic pressures and power that paralyze the manufacture of safe automobiles and cost consumers more than just money.

Newhouse, John. *War and Peace in the Nuclear Age.* Knopf 1989 $22.95. ISBN 0-394-56217-8

Rustow, Dankwart A. *Oil and Turmoil: America Faces OPEC and the Middle East.* Norton 1982 $5.95. ISBN 0-393-95122-9

Skeet, Ian. *OPEC: Twenty-Five Years of Prices and Politics.* Cambridge Univ Pr 1989 $29.95. ISBN 0-521-33052-1

*Terkel, Studs. *Working.* Ballantine 1985 $5.95. ISBN 0-345-32569-9 Interviews with workers revealing their feelings about the tasks they perform daily.

Thorton, Richard C. *The Nixon-Kissinger Years: The Reshaping of American Foreign Policy.* Paragon Hse 1989 $24.95. ISBN 0-88702-051-8

*Wandersee, Winifred D. *On the Move: American Women in the 1970s. Twayne's American Women in the Twentieth Century Ser.* G. K. Hall 1988 $9.95. ISBN 0-8057-9910-9 Describes the 1970s women's movement and its effect on many areas of everyday life.

White, Theodore H. *The Making of the President, Nineteen Seventy–Two.* Macmillan 1973 $10.00. ISBN 0-689-10553-3

*Woodward, Bob, and Scott Armstrong. *The Brethren.* Avon 1981 $5.95. ISBN 0-380-52183-0 Account of the inner workings of the U.S. Supreme Court.

FORD, GERALD R. (RUDOLPH)   1913–

For 24 years, from 1949 to 1972, Gerald Ford was a loyal, unassuming Republican member of the U.S. House of Representatives, serving as the minority leader from 1965 to 1972. Then in 1973, Ford entered the spotlight when President Richard Nixon (*see* Nixon, Vol. 2, United States History: The Nixon and Ford Years) selected him to replace Spiro Agnew, who had resigned as vice president because of scandal. Within a year, Nixon had resigned to avoid impeachment, and Ford became the nation's thirty-eighth President—the only person in U.S. history to become President without being elected.

Born Leslie Lynch King, Jr., Ford assumed his present name after being adopted by his mother's second husband. Ford graduated from the University of Michigan and the Yale Law School and was admitted to the bar in 1941. As a Republican congressman from Michigan and as minority leader, Ford led the opposition to President Lyndon Johnson's Great Society welfare programs. (*See* Johnson, Vol. 2, United States History: The Turbulent Sixties.) As vice president, he traveled widely to restore the support for Nixon that had been eroded by the Watergate affair. When he became President, he pardoned Nixon, hoping to quiet the storm raised by the Watergate Affair, a scandal that involved the President and members of his staff, and to spare the nation any further anguish. Using his extensive knowledge of how Washington functioned, he worked closely with Congress. In 1976 Ford ran for the presidency in his own right but lost a closely contested election to Jimmy Carter, Democrat from Georgia. (*See* Carter, Vol. 2, United States History: The Carter Years.)

BOOKS BY FORD

Churchill Lecture (1984). Lord John 1984 $100.00. ISBN 0-935716-30-0
Humor and the Presidency. Morrow 1987 $15.95. ISBN 0-87795-918-8
A Vision for America (1981). Lord John 1981 $75.00. ISBN 0-935716-08-4

BOOKS ABOUT FORD

Hersey, John. *The President: A Minute-by-Minute Account of a Week in the Life of Gerald Ford.* Knopf 1975 $2.95. ISBN 0-394-45986-5 Close look at the workings of the Ford White House.
*Sipiera, Paul. *Gerald Ford. Encyclopedia of Presidents Ser.* Childrens 1988 $15.93. ISBN 0-516-01371-8 Brief, illustrated presentation of the life of Ford.

NIXON, RICHARD MILHOUS 1913–

Representative, senator, vice president, and the thirty-seventh President of the United States, Richard Milhous Nixon was born in Yerba Linda, California. After graduating from Whittier College and Duke University Law School, he practiced law for about five years in Whittier, California. He went on to serve in the U.S. Navy in the South Pacific during World War II from 1942 until 1946. In 1946 he won election as a Republican to the U.S. House of Representatives, where he became known for his anti-Communist activities. In 1950 he was elected to the U.S. Senate. Then in 1952 and again in 1956 he was elected vice president under Dwight Eisenhower. (*See* Eisenhower, Vol. 2, United States History: Postwar Foreign and Domestic Policy.) As vice president, he played a visible role in presidential affairs and traveled widely as Eisenhower's representative. Following failed bids for the presidency in 1960 and for the governorship of California in 1962, he ran successfully for the presidency in 1968.

Nixon won the presidential election of 1968 with Spiro Agnew of Maryland as his vice president. During the campaign he promised to bring peace with honor in Vietnam and to unite the American people, who were divided by racial issues and the Vietnam War. Nixon was more successful in foreign affairs than in domestic affairs, visiting China in 1972 and achieving a cease-fire with North Vietnam in 1973. In 1972, however, his administration was rocked by two major scandals. The first was the resignation of Spiro Agnew for improprieties while governor of Maryland. It allowed Nixon to become the first President to appoint a new vice president—Gerald Ford (*see* Ford, Vol. 2, United

Campbell's Soup Can.   Painting by Andy Warhol (1962). Courtesy of UPI/Bettmann.

States History: The Nixon and Ford Years)—under the provisions of the recently ratified Twenty-fifth Amendment to the U.S. Constitution. The second was the Watergate Affair—a break-in of Democratic campaign headquarters ordered by Nixon's campaign staffers. Investigations into a presidential cover-up of the Watergate break-in and other improprieties eventually led to impeachment proceedings against Nixon and Nixon's resignation to avoid impeachment. The only President to have resigned from office because of scandal, he was later pardoned for any and all possible crimes by President Gerald Ford in 1974. After his resignation Nixon returned to his estate in San Clemente, California, and retired from active political life. His most recent book, *In the Arena* (1990), is a candid memoir of his years after the resignation.

BOOKS BY NIXON

Leaders (1982). Touchstone 1990 $12.95. ISBN 0-671-70618-7
Nineteen Ninety-Nine: The Global Challenges We Face in the Next Decade (1988). Simon 1988 $100.00. ISBN 0-671-65992-8
Nineteen Ninety-Nine: Victory Without War (1988). Pocket 1989 $8.95. ISBN 0-671-67834-5
No More Vietnams (1986). Avon 1986 $4.50. ISBN 0-380-70119-7
Real Peace (1984). Little 1984 $16.95. ISBN 0-316-61149-2
The Real War (1980). Warner Bks 1980 $4.50. ISBN 0-446-32280-6

BOOKS ABOUT NIXON

*Larsen, Rebecca. *Richard Nixon: Rise and Fall of a President.* Watts 1991 $14.90. ISBN 0-531-10997-6 For younger readers, this biography attempts to present a more gentle look at this controversial president.
McGinniss, Joe. *The Selling of the President.* Penguin 1988 $7.95. ISBN 0-14-011240-5 Fascinating account of the use of media experts, pollsters, speech writers, and image makers in election politics.

*Ripley, C. Peter. *Nixon. World Leaders—Past and Present Ser.* Chelsea 1987 $17.95. ISBN 0-87754-585-5 Focuses on Nixon's early years, his career, and contributions.

Safire, William. *Before the Fall: An Inside View of the Pre-Watergate White House. Quality Paperbacks Ser.* Da Capo 1988 $15.95. ISBN 0-306-80334-8 Anecdotal history of the Nixon years by a White House insider.

Randolph, Sallie G. *Richard M. Nixon: President. Presidential Biography Ser.* Walker 1990 $12.95. ISBN 0-8027-6848-2 Balanced biography presenting both sides of the major issues and events of Nixon's life.

THE CARTER YEARS

Abramson, Paul R. *Political Attitudes in America.* Freeman 1983 $17.95. ISBN 0-7167-1420-5

Alexander, Yonah, and Allan Nanes. *The United States and Iran: A Documentary History.* Greenwood 1980 $19.95. ISBN 0-313-27054-6

Alexander, Yonah, *et al. Terrorism: What Should Be Our Response?* Am Enterprise Inst 1982 $5.25. ISBN 0-8447-2231-6

*Amdur, Richard. *Menachem Begin. World Leaders—Past and Present Ser.* Chelsea 1988 $17.95. ISBN 0-87754-561-8 Introduction to the prime minister of Israel during the late 1970s and early 1980s.

Carter, Rosalyn. *First Lady from Plains.* Fawcett 1988 $3.95. ISBN 0-449-44529-1

Evans, Christopher. *The Making of the Micro: A History of the Computer.* Van Nostrand 1981 $25.95. ISBN 0-442-22240-8

Friedlander, Melvin A. *Sadat and Begin: The Domestic Politics of Peacemaking.* Westview 1983 $33.00. ISBN 0-86531-949-9

Glazer, Nathan (intro by). *Clamor at the Gates: The New American Immigration.* ICS Pr 1985 $10.95. ISBN 0-917616-69-3

*McCormick, John. *Acid Rain.* Watts 1986 $11.90. ISBN 0-531-17016-0 Good introduction to the complex topic of acid rain.

*Naisbitt, John. *Megatrends: Ten New Directions Transforming Our Lives.* Warner Bks 1989 $8.95. ISBN 1-55525-292-3 Presents new ways of both looking at the future of the United States and sorting out the jumble of its past.

*Perrin, Linda. *Coming to America: Immigrants from the Far East.* Delacorte 1980 $9.95. ISBN 0-440-01072-1 Interesting account of Asian immigration to the United States.

*Pringle, Lawrence. *Restoring Our Earth.* Enslow 1987 $13.95. ISBN 0-89490-143-5 Discusses efforts by organizations and suggested solutions to restore and preserve the earth's resources.

Quandt, William B. *Camp David: Peacemaking and Politics.* Brookings 1986 $12.95. ISBN 0-8157-7289-0

Salinger, Pierre. *America Held Hostage.* Doubleday 1981.

Stephens, Mark. *Three Mile Island.* Random 1981 $11.95. ISBN 0-394-51092-5

*Sullivan, George. *Sadat: The Man Who Changed Mid-East History.* Walker 1981 $9.85. ISBN 0-8027-6435-5 Biography of Anwar Sadat, courageous president of Egypt.

Treaties on the Panama Canal Signed Between the United States of America and the Republic of Panama. (Treaty). OAS 1979 $9.00.

*Whitney, Sharen. *The Equal Rights Amendments: The History and the Movements.* Watts 1984 $12.90. ISBN 0-531-04768-7 Story of the movements to provide equal rights for women.

CARTER, JAMES EARL (JIMMY) JR.   1924–

A 1946 graduate of the U.S. Naval Academy, state senator from 1963 to 1966, governor of Georgia from 1971 to 1975, and thirty-ninth President of the United States, "Jimmy" Carter was born in Plains, Georgia, and grew up on his family's farm. After attending Georgia Tech and graduating from the U.S.

Naval Academy, he served in a nuclear-submarine program and studied nuclear physics at Union College. He left the Navy after his father died in the early 1950s to return home to take care of the family's businesses—warehousing, cotton-ginning, and peanut-farming.

Carter began his political career in 1962 when he was elected to the Georgia Senate. In 1966 he ran unsuccessfully for governor of Georgia. Four years later, he attained that position. Although he was relatively unknown outside Georgia at the start of the 1976 presidential campaign, Carter soon captured the public's attention. He won primary after primary and was nominated by the Democratic Convention on the first ballot. Sensing the anti-Watergate and anti-Vietnam mood of the nation, he promised never to lie to the American people. Winning the electoral votes of every southern state and four northern states, Carter outpolled Republican candidate Gerald Ford (*see* Ford, Vol. 2, United States History: The Nixon and Ford Years) to become the nation's first President from the Deep South since before the Civil War.

A strong supporter of human rights worldwide, Carter's greatest successes as President occurred in the area of foreign affairs. Among these successes were his negotiations leading to the signing and ratification of the Panama Canal treaties in 1977 and his mediation of the Camp David Accords between Egypt and Israel in 1978 to secure Mideast Peace in 1979. His chances for reelection in 1980 were seriously damaged, however, because of his failure to secure the release of the American hostages by Iran during the Iranian Revolution. His chances were also hurt by his struggles with an antagonistic U.S. Congress and his failure to find solutions to high unemployment, inflation, and the energy crisis. In the election Carter faced a popular Republican candidate and was able to secure only 42 percent of the popular vote. Although he lost to conservative Ronald Reagan (*see* Reagan, Vol. 2, United States History: The Reagan and Bush Years), Carter remains a widely respected and important world figure.

BOOKS BY CARTER

Everything to Gain: Making the Most of the Rest of Your Life. (coauthored with Rosalynn Carter) Fawcett 1988 $4.95. ISBN 0-449-14538-7

Negotiation: The Alternative to Hostility. The Carl Vinson Memorial Lecture Ser. Mercer Univ Pr 1984 $12.95. ISBN 0-86554-137-X

BOOKS ABOUT CARTER

Shogan, Robert. *Promises to Keep: Carter's First 100 Days.* Crowell 1977 $8.95. ISBN 0-690-01497-X Assessment of Carter's campaign for office and his administration's early days.

Slavin, Ed. *Jimmy Carter. World Leaders—Past and Present Ser.* Chelsea 1989 $17.95. ISBN 1-55546-828-4 Focuses on Carter's early years, his career, and contributions.

Smith, Betsy C. *Jimmy Carter, President. Presidential Biography Ser.* Walker 1986 $12.09. ISBN 0-8027-6650-1 Readable biography of Carter.

*Wade, Linda R. *James Carter. Encyclopedia of Presidents Ser.* Childrens 1989 $15.93. ISBN 0-516-01372-6 Brief, illustrated discussion of Carter's life.

THE REAGAN AND BUSH YEARS

*Ashabranner, Brent. *Dark Harvest.* Putnam 1986 $14.95. ISBN 0-396-08624-1 Migrant workers' stories told with personal interviews and photographs.

*Barker, Lucius J. *Our Time Has Come: A Delegate's Diary of Jesse Jackson's 1984 Presidential Campaign.* Univ of Illinois Pr 1988 $21.95. ISBN 0-252-01426-X Delegate's view of the 1984 election campaign of Jesse Jackson.

*Bender, David L. (ed). *America's Economy, 1989 Annual. Opposing Viewpoints Sources Ser.* Greenhaven 1989 $9.95. ISBN 0-89908-550-4 Presents 25 views of current economic issues, including the recent savings-and-loan crisis.

Boskin, Michael J. *Reagan and the Economy: The Successes, Failures, and Unfinished Agenda.* ICS Pr 1989 $12.95. ISBN 1-55815-056-0

*Briggs, Carole S. *Women in Space: Reaching the Last Frontier. Space and Aviation Ser.* Lerner 1988 $5.95. ISBN 0-8225-9547-8 Well-illustrated account of women in the NASA space shuttle program.

*Brownstein, Ronald. *Reagan's Ruling Class: Portraits of the President's Top 100 Officials.* Nina Easton (ed). Presidential Acct 1983 $24.50. ISBN 0-936486-03-1 Close-up view of those officials closest to the President.

Burgess, Michael and Alice J. Perez. *Space Log: A Chronological Checklist of Manned Space Flights, 1961–1990.* Borgo Pr $14.95. ISBN 0-89370-919-0

*Cole, Don. *Annual Editions: Economics 89/90.* Dushkin 1989 $9.95. ISBN 0-87967-781-3 Discussions of a well-rounded assortment of issues in the study of economics.

Congressional Quarterly, Inc., and Michael Goldstein. *Guide to the 1988 Presidential Election.* Congressional Quarterly 1988 $10.95. ISBN 0-87187-468-7

Culbertson, John. *The Trade Threat and U.S. Trade Policy.* Twenty-First Pr 1989 $9.95. ISBN 0-918357-08-X

*Davis, Bertha. *Crisis in Industry: Can America Compete?* Watts 1989 $12.90. ISBN 0-531-10659-4 Introductory look at how industrial competition from other countries can affect U.S. industries and the country as a whole.

Davis, Bertha. *The National Debt. Impact Ser.* Watts 1987 $12.90. ISBN 0-531-10415-X

*Dickenson, Mollie. *Thumbs Up: The Jim Brady Story.* Morrow 1987 $19.95. ISBN 0-688-06497-3 Story of President Reagan's press secretary, who was seriously wounded during an assassination attempt on Reagan.

Drew, Elizabeth. *Election Journal: The Political Events of 1987–1988.* Morrow 1989 $19.95. ISBN 0-688-08332-3

Duignan, Peter, and Alvin Rabushka (eds). *The United States in the 1980s.* Hoover Inst Pr 1980 $20.00. ISBN 0-8179-7281-1

Ferraro, Geraldine A., and Linda B. Francke. *Ferraro: My Story.* Bantam 1986 $4.95. ISBN 0-553-25702-1

Feste, Karen (ed). *American and Soviet Intervention: Effects on World Stability.* Taylor & Francis 1990 $22.00. ISBN 0-8448-1632-9

*Fincher, E. B. *Mexico and the United States: Their Linked Destinies.* Harper Jr Bks 1983 $12.89. ISBN 0-690-04311-2 Discussion of the ways in which Mexico and the United States are interdependent.

Findling, John E. *Close Neighbors, Distant Friends: United States-Central American Relations. Contributions in American History Ser.* Greenwood 1987 $39.95. ISBN 0-313-23679-8

Formi, Luigi. *The Dove and the Bear: Did They Avert the Third World War?* Seven Hills 1989 $12.95. ISBN 0-85936-226-4

*Fox, Mary V. *Justice Sandra Day O'Connor.* Enslow 1983 $14.95. ISBN 0-89490-073-0 Examines the life and views of the first woman justice of the U.S. Supreme Court.

*Friedman, Milton, and Rose Friedman. *Free to Choose.* Avon 1981 $4.95. ISBN 0-380-52548-8 Based on a conservative, monetarist view; describes how our freedom and prosperity have suffered under major government control.

Furniss, Tim. *Space Flight: The Records.* Borgo Pr 1989 $28.95. ISBN 0-8095-7522-1

Ginzberg, Eli, and George Vojta. *Beyond Human Scale: Large Corporations at Risk.* Basic 1987 $7.95. ISBN 0-465-00659-0

Graber, Doris. *Mass Media and American Politics.* Congressional Quarterly 1988 $16.95. ISBN 0-87187-475-X

Hamilton, Nora, *et al* (eds). *Crisis in Central America: Regional Dynamics and U. S. Policy in the 1980s.* Westview 1988 $15.95. ISBN 0-8133-7432-4

*Hamilton, Virginia. *Sweet Whispers, Brother Rush.* Putnam 1982 $12.95. ISBN 0-399-20894-1 Story of of the ingenuity of a young girl in a single-parent family.

Harrington, Michael. *The New American Poverty.* Penguin 1985 $7.95. ISBN 0-14-008112-7

*Hart, William B. *The U.S. and World Trade. Economic Impact Books Ser.* Watts 1985 $12.90.

ISBN 0-531-10067-7 Introductory discussion of the U.S. trade deficit, the strength of the United States, and the role of multinational corporations.

Hutcheson, Richard G., Jr. *God in the White House: How Religion Has Changed in Modern Presidency.* Macmillan 1989 $8.95. ISBN 0-02-033661-6

*Iacocca, Lee A. *Talking Straight.* Bantam 1989 $4.95. ISBN 0-553-27805-3 Head-on analysis of some major problems in the United States, with suggestions on how to start rebuilding and repairing our image.

Jakoubek, Robert. *Jesse Jackson. Black Americans of Achievement Ser.* Chelsea 1991 $17.95. ISBN 0-7910-1130-5

Kelley, Donald R., and Hoyt Purvis (eds). *Old Myths and New Realities in United States-Soviet Relations.* Greenwood 1990. ISBN 0-275-93490-5

Kupchan, Charles A. *The Persian Gulf and the West: Dilemmas of Security.* Unwin 1987 $14.95. ISBN 0-04-497058-7

*Lawson, Don. *Geraldine Ferraro: The Woman Who Changed American Politics.* Messner 1985 $9.95. ISBN 0-671-55041-1 Story of the first woman chosen to be the vice-presidential candidate of a major party.

McNaugaher, Thomas L. *Arms and Oil: U. S. Military Strategy and the Persian Gulf.* Brookings 1985 $10.95. ISBN 0-8157-5623-2

Novak, Michael. *New Consensus on Family and Welfare: A Community of Self-Reliance.* Am Enterprise Inst 1987 $9.75. ISBN 0-844-73624-4

Packard, Vance. *The Ultra Rich: How Much Is Too Much?* Little 1989 $22.95. ISBN 0-316-68752-9

Piven, Frances F., and Richard A. Cloward. *Why Americans Don't Vote.* Pantheon 1988 $19.95. ISBN 0-317-67577-X

*Raynor, Thomas P. *Terrorism: Past, Present, Future.* Watts 1987 $13.90. ISBN 0-531-10344-7 Discusses terrorism—inhumane acts for political purposes often directed against innocent bystanders.

Reed, Adolph L., Jr. *The Jesse Jackson Phenomenon: The Crisis of Purpose in Afro-American Politics.* Yale Univ Pr 1986 $8.95. ISBN 0-300-03552-7

*Sewell, John W. and John A. Mathieson. *The Third World: Exploring U. S. Interests. Headline Ser.* Foreign Policy 1982 $4.00. ISBN 0-87124-076-9 Looks at the lure of third world countries for America.

Sobel, Robert. *Panic on Wall Street: A Classic History of America's Financial Disasters—with a Timely Exploration of the Crash of 1987.* Dutton 1988 $12.95. ISBN 0-525-48404-3

Spiegel, Steven L. *The Other Arab-Israeli Conflict: Making America's Middle East Policy, from Truman to Reagan.* Univ of Chicago Pr 1986 $15.95. ISBN 0-226-76962-3

*Weiss, Ann. *Good Neighbors?* Houghton 1985 $12.95. ISBN 0-317-38803-7 Historical background of United States–Latin American relationships and the impact of that history on recent events.

Weiss, Ann E. *The Nuclear Arms Race—Can We Survive It?* Houghton 1983 $10.95. ISBN 0-395-34928-1

Yergin, Daniel. *The Prize: The Epic Quest for Oil, Money, and Power.* Simon 1990 $24.95. ISBN 0-671-50248-4

BUSH, GEORGE HERBERT WALKER 1924–

Phi Beta Kappa, winner of the Distinguished Flying Cross and three Air Medals, Republican National chairman—these were just a few of George Bush's accomplishments before he became the forty-first President of the United States in 1988. The son of a United States senator from Connecticut, Bush attended prestigious Phillips Academy in Andover, Massachusetts. In 1942 he joined the Navy to become, at age 18, its youngest commissioned pilot. After three years in the military, he entered Yale University, graduating less than three years later with a degree in economics.

In 1945 Bush married and moved to Texas, where in the early 1950s he founded an oil company. After an unsuccessful bid for a U.S. Senate seat in Texas in 1964, he moved from one top government position to another—

Congressman (1966–1970); United States delegate to the United Nations with the rank of Ambassador (1971–1973); head of the United States liaison office in Beijing, China (1974–1975); and Director of the Central Intelligence Agency (1976–1977).

Bush then made a bid for the Republican nomination for president. Unsuccessful in his attempt, he became instead Ronald Reagan's (*see* Reagan, Vol. 2, United States History: The Reagan and Bush Years) running mate in the 1980 presidential election. When Reagan won the election, Bush became vice president, an office he held for two terms. At the end of the second term, Bush once again made a bid for the presidency. This time he was victorious.

Bush impressed the American people with his calm and unassuming manner and called on them "to make kinder the face of the nation and gentler the face of the world." As president, domestically he has had to deal with such major issues as the on-going problem of the nation's budget and trade deficits, or shortages; the failures of the Savings and Loans institutions; the Exxon oil spill in Alaska; and the complexities of a war against drugs. On an international scale, although criticized for not supporting strongly enough the efforts being made by the Baltic States for independence or protesting with more vigor the putting-down of the democratic movement in China, he has won approval in other areas. Among these are his confident conduct of various major summit meetings, his support of Soviet reforms and democratization efforts in Eastern Europe, his crackdown on Latin American dictator General Manuel Noriega, and the strong no-compromise position he took toward Iraqi leader Saddam Hussein and the Gulf War.

BOOKS BY BUSH

■*Looking Forward.* Bantam 1988 $4.95. ISBN 0-553-27791-X A candid autobiography dealing with Bush's career into the vice presidency.
National Security Strategy of the United States. Pergamon 1991 $13.95. ISBN 0-08-036732-1
Notes on Genesis. 2 vols. Kregel $32.95. ISBN 0-8254-5050-0
Great Issues 79–80. A Forum on Important Questions Facing the American Public. (coauthored with Philip Crane) Vol. 11 Troy State Univ 1980 $11.95. ISBN 0-916624-32-3

BOOKS ABOUT BUSH

Green, Fitzhugh. *George Bush.* Hippocrene 1989 $17.95. ISBN 0-87052-783-5 Complete colorful picture of Bush's life packed with anecdotes.
*Kent, Zachary. *George Bush. Encyclopedia of Presidents Ser.* Childrens 1989 $6.95. ISBN 0-516-41374-0 Biography of Bush focusing on his political career.
Our Forty-First President: George Bush. Scholastic 1989 $2.50. ISBN 0-590-42644-3 Interesting and informative look at the life of our forty-first President.

REAGAN, RONALD WILSON   1911–

Born in Tampico, Illinois, into a poor family, Ronald Reagan graduated from Eureka College in 1932, when the United States was deep in economic depression. After graduation, he got a job as a sports announcer for a radio station in Des Moines, Iowa. Five years later, he was a successful film actor. During World War II, a captain in the Army Air Force, he continued his film career, after the war serving as president of the screen Actors Guild from 1947 to 1952 and again in 1959.

In 1964, the Democratic actor turned Republican politician, taking an active part in the presidential campaign of conservative Republican Barry Goldwater. (*See* Goldwater, Vol. 2, United States History: The Turbulent Sixties.) Two years later, he was elected governor of California, an office he won again in 1970. Then, in 1980 he secured the Republican nomination for President and began campaigning with an easy, comfortable manner and skillful use of humor that marked his talent for communication with the American public. Reagan won the election. He was reelected for a second term in 1984, making him at age 73, the oldest man ever elected President. Shortly after his first inauguration, he secured the release of the Americans being held hostage in Iran as a result of the revolution there. Under his supply-side economic policies, called "Reaganomics," unemployment fell, and the inflation rate dropped. His policies included a reduction in taxes and an increase in defense spending. These policies, coupled with a tight-money policy, brought on huge budget deficits, or shortages. In foreign affairs, Reagan made his feelings about communism clear by aiding anti-Communist forces in Central America. However, the Iran-Contra affair, basically the revelation that the United States had sold weapons to Iran in exchange for United States hostages being held in Lebanon, marred these efforts.

During his two terms, Reagan appointed four conservatives to the U. S. Supreme Court, including the first woman associate justice and a new Chief Justice. These appointments altered the court's liberal majority. After leaving office, Reagan retired to his ranch in California.

BOOKS BY REAGAN

National Security Strategy of the United States (1988). Pergamon 1988 $10.95. ISBN 0-08-035973-6

Ronald Reagan Talks to America (1983). Devin-Adair 1982 $12.95. ISBN 0-8159-5222-8

Speaking My Mind: Selected Speeches (1989). Simon 1989 $24.95. ISBN 0-671-68857-X

A Time for Choosing: The Speeches of Ronald Reagan (1983). Alfred Balitzer (ed). Regnery 1983 $9.95. ISBN 0-89526-838-8

BOOKS ABOUT REAGAN

Cannon, Lou. *Reagan.* Putnam 1982 $18.95. ISBN 0-399-12756-9 Discusses the years leading to Reagan's successful run for the presidency in 1980.

Carter, Hodding. *The Reagan Years.* Braziller 1988. $17.50. ISBN 0-8076-1209-X Portrait of Reagan's presidency by a well-known journalist and former spokesperson for the Carter administration.

Fox, Mary V. *Mister President: The Story of Ronald Reagan.* Enslow 1986 $16.95. ISBN 0-89490-130-3 Recounts Reagan's life from his boyhood to his college years to his successful careers.

Mandelbaum, Michael, and Strobe Talbott. *Reagan and Gorbachev.* Random $5.95. ISBN 0-394-74721-6 Examines developments in foreign policy under Reagan.

*Schlesinger, Arthur M., Jr. (ed). *Ronald Reagan: U.S. President. World Leaders—Past and Present Ser.* Chelsea 1990 $17.95. ISBN 1-55546-849-7 Brief biography of Reagan.

Speakes, Larry, and Robert Pack. *Speaking Out: The Reagan Presidency from Inside the White House.* Scribner's 1988 $19.95. ISBN 0-684-18929-1 Eyewitness account of the Reagan White House.

Wills, Garry. *Reagan's America: Innocents at Home.* Doubleday 1987 $19.95. ISBN 0-385-18286-4 Study of the connections between Reagan and the places and people he came into contact with and their impact on Reagan and the nation.

THE ARTS OF THE TWENTIETH CENTURY

*Aronson, Joseph. *Encyclopedia of Furniture.* Crown 1965 $19.95. ISBN 0-517-03735-1 Comprehensive furniture guide for young readers.

Baigell, Matthew. *A Concise History of American Painting and Sculpture.* Harper Jr Bks 1984. (o.p.) $16.95. ISBN 0-06-430085-4

Baigell, Matthew. *Dictionary of American Art.* Harper Jr Bks 1979. (o.p.) $10.95. ISBN 0-06-430078-1

Balliett, Whitney. *American Musicians: Fifty-Six Portraits in Jazz.* Oxford Univ Pr 1986 $27.95. ISBN 0-19-503758-8

Balliett, Whitney. *American Singers: Twenty-Seven Portraits in Song.* Oxford Univ Pr 1988 $19.95. ISBN 0-19-504610-2

Barnes, Clive. *Nureyev.* Helene Obolensky 1982 $35.00. ISBN 0-9609736-2-1

Barzun, Jacques (ed). *Pleasures of Music: An Anthology of Writings About Music and Musicians from Cellini to Bernard Shaw.* Univ of Chicago Pr 1977 $10.95. ISBN 0-226-03854-8

Berger, Arthur V. *Aaron Copland. Music Reprint Ser.* Da Capo 1987 repr of 1953 ed $22.50. ISBN 0-306-76266-8

Blesh, Rudi, and Harriet Janis. *They All Played Ragtime.* Music Sales 1966 $9.95. ISBN 0-8256-0091-X

Blumenson, John J. *Identifying American Architecture.* Norton 1990 $10.95. ISBN 0-393-30610-0

Burkholder, J. Peter. *Charles Ives: The Ideas Behind the Music.* Yale Univ Pr 1985 $25.00. ISBN 0-300-03261-7

Butterworth, Neil. *The Music of Aaron Copland.* Universe 1986 $20.00. ISBN 0-87663-495-1

Brown, Milton W., *et al. American Art: Painting, Sculpture, Architecture, Decorative Arts, Photography.* Abrams $49.50. ISBN 0-8109-0658-9

Brown, Peter, and Steven Gaines. *The Love You Make: An Insider's Story of the Beatles.* NAL 1984 $4.95. ISBN 0-451-16067-3

Cage, John. *Silence: Lectures and Writings of John Cage.* Wesleyan Univ Pr 1961 $12.95. ISBN 0-8195-6028-6

Calder, Alexander. *Animal Sketching.* Dover 1973 $2.50. ISBN 0-486-20129-5

Chilton, John. *Who's Who of Jazz. Roots of Jazz Ser.* Da Capo 1985 $11.95. ISBN 0-306-80243-0

Clark, Kenneth. *What Is a Masterpiece?* Peter Smith 1983 $15.50. ISBN 0-8446-5991-6

Collaer, Paul. *Music of the Americas.* Praeger 1971. (o.p.)

Cummings, Paul. *Dictionary of Contemporary American Artists.* St. Martin's 1988. ISBN 0-312-00232-7

Fielding, Mantle. *Dictionary of American Painters, Sculptors, and Engravers.* Editions Publisol 1986 $85.00. ISBN 0-938209-04-5

Gibson, Michael. *Calder. Masters of Modern Art Ser.* Universe 1988 $12.95. ISBN 0-87663-541-9

Green, Stanley. *The Rodgers and Hammerstein Story.* Da Capo 1980 $6.95. ISBN 0-306-80124-8

*Gridley, Mark C. *Jazz Styles: History and Analysis.* Prentice 1987 $30.00. ISBN 0-13-509217-5 Chronological introduction for those unfamiliar with jazz.

Griffiths, Paul. *Modern Music: The Avant Garde Since 1945.* Braziller 1981 $12.95. ISBN 0-8076-1018-6

Grout, Donald J., and Hermine W. Williams. *A Short History of Opera.* Columbia Univ Pr 1987 $39.00. ISBN 0-231-06192-7

Haftmann, Werner. *Painting in the Twentieth Century.* 2 vols. Praeger 1965. (o.p.)

Highwater, Jamake. *The Sweet Grass Lives On: Fifty Contemporary North American Indian Artists.* Harper Jr Bks 1980 $35.00. ISBN 0-690-01925-4

Hamlin, Talbot. *Greek Revival Architecture in America.* Dover 1944 $9.95. ISBN 0-486-21148-7

Hamm, Charles. *Afro-American Music, South Africa, and Apartheid.* Inst for Studies in Am Music 1988 $11.00. ISBN 0-914678-31-0

Harris, Cyril M. *Dictionary of Architecture and Construction.* McGraw 1988 $26.50. ISBN 0-07-026819-3

Hodeir, Andre. *Jazz: Its Evolution and Essence.* David Noakes (tr). *Roots of Jazz Ser.* Da Capo 1975 $35.00. ISBN 0-306-70682-2 Classic work that discusses jazz styles, personalities, and problems.

Igoe, Lynn Moody, and James Igoe (eds). *Two Hundred and Fifty Years of Afro-American Art: An Annotated Bibliography.* Bowker 1981. (o.p.) $149.95. ISBN 0-8352-1376-5

Ives, Charles Edward. *Essays Before a Sonata, the Majority, and Other Writings.* Howard Boatwright (ed). Norton 1970 $7.95. ISBN 0-393-00528-3

Jablonski, Edward. *Gershwin: A Biography.* Doubleday 1987 $21.95. ISBN 0-385-19431-5

Jordy, William H. *American Buildings and Their Architects.* 5 vols. Vols. 1–3 Doubleday 1976. (o.p.) $10.95 ea. Vol. 4-5 Oxford Univ Pr 1986 $15.95 ea. ISBNs 0-19-504218-2, 0-19-504219-0

Kerman, Joseph. *Opera as Drama.* Univ of California Pr 1988 $9.95. ISBN 0-520-06274-4

Kostelanetz, Richard (ed). *John Cage.* R K Edns 1978 $50.00. ISBN 0-932360-09-2

Martin, George W. *The Opera Companion.* Dodd 1979 $13.95. ISBN 0-396-08097-9

Maddow, Ben. *Edward Weston: His Life.* Aperture 1989 $14.95. ISBN 0-89381-369-9

May, Elizabeth (ed). *Musics of Many Cultures: An Introduction.* Univ of California Pr 1982 $19.95. ISBN 0-520-04778-8

Nettl, Bruno. *Folk and Traditional Music of the Western Continents.* Prentice 1973 $28.00. ISBN 0-13-322933-5

Newhall, Beaumont. *The Daguerreotype in America.* Dover 1976 $7.95. ISBN 0-486-23322-7

Newhall, Beaumont. *Supreme Instants: The Photography of Edward Weston.* Little 1986 $50.00. ISBN 0-317-53697-4.

Orrey, Leslie. *Opera: A Concise History. The World of Art Ser.* Thames Hudson 1987 $11.95. ISBN 0-500-20217-6

Osborne, Harold (ed). *The Oxford Companion to Twentieth-Century Art. Oxford Paperback Reference Ser.* Oxford Univ Pr 1988 $21.50. ISBN 0-19-282076-1

Pevsner, Nikolaus, *et al. A Dictionary of Architecture.* Overlook Pr 1976 $32.50. ISBN 0-87951-040-4

Pitts, Terence, *et al. Decade by Decade: Twentieth Century American Photography from the Collection of the Center for Creative Photography.* Little 1989 $40.00. ISBN 0-8212-1721-6

Placksin, Sally. *American Women in Jazz: Nineteen Hundred to the Present: Their Words, Lives, and Music.* Putnam 1982. (o.p.)

Pollock, Bruce. *When Rock Was Young: A Nostalgic Review of the Top Forty Era.* Holt 1981. (o.p.) $6.95.

Quinn, Edward. *Picasso: Photos Nineteen Fifty-One to Nineteen Seventy-Two. Pocket Art Ser.* Barron 1980 $6.95. ISBN 0-8120-2109-6

Rose, Al, and Edmond Souchon. *New Orleans Jazz: A Family Album.* Louisiana State Univ Pr 1984 $19.95. ISBN 0-8071-1173-2

Roth, Leland M. *A Concise History of American Architecture.* Harper 1980 $12.95. ISBN 0-06-430086-2

Sachs, Curt. *The Wellsprings of Music.* Da Capo 1977 $6.95. ISBN 0-306-80073-X

Selz, Peter. *Art in Our Times: A Pictorial History, 1890–1980.* Harcourt 1981 $18.50. ISBN 0-15-503473-1

*Shapiro, Nat, and Nat Hentoff (eds). *Hear Me Talkin' to Ya: The Story of Jazz by the Men Who Made It.* Dover 1966 $7.95. ISBN 0-486-21726-4 Account of jazz by some musicians who helped popularize it.

Shaw, Arnold. *Honkers and Shouters.* Macmillan 1986 $10.95. ISBN 0-02-061740-2

Shaw, Arnold. *The Rockin' Fifties. Quality Paperbacks Ser.* Da Capo 1987 $10.95. ISBN 0-306-80301-1

Shelton, Suzanne. *Divine Dancer: A Biography of Ruth St. Denis.* Doubleday 1981. (o.p.) $15.95.

Simon, George T. *The Big Bands.* Schirmer 1981 $12.95. ISBN 0-02-872430-5

*Smith, G. E. Kidder. *The Architecture of the United States.* 3 vols. Doubleday 1981. (o.p.) $14.95 ea. Comprehensive guide to buildings and other structures across the United States.

Stambler, Irwin. *The Encyclopedia of Pop, Rock, and Soul.* St. Martin's 1989 $35.00. ISBN 0-312-02573-4

*Stearns, Marshall. *Story of Jazz.* Oxford Univ Pr 1956 $11.95. ISBN 0-19-501269-0 Classic history.

Stodelle, Ernestine. *Deep Song: The Dance Story of Martha Graham.* Macmillan 1984 $25.95. ISBN 0-02-872520-4

Taft, Lorado. *History of American Sculpture. Art Histories Collection Ser.* Ayer 1979 repr of 1924 ed $38.50. ISBN 0-405-02228-X

Terkel, Studs. *Giants of Jazz.* Harper Jr Bks 1975 $15.70. ISBN 0-690-00998-4

Thompson, Virgil. *Music with Words: A Composer's View.* Yale Univ Pr 1989 $17.95. ISBN 0-300-04505-0

Traubner, Richard. *Operetta: A Theatrical History.* Oxford Univ Pr 1989 $16.95. ISBN 0-19-520778-5

Who's Who in American Art, 1991–92. Bowker 1991 $159.95. ISBN 0-8352-2897-5

ADAMS, ANSEL   1902–1984

Ansel Adams helped establish photography as an art form, capturing in his photographs the silent and stark beauty of the American landscape, especially that of the American West and Southwest. Adams started out as a professional musician and pursued photography only as a hobby after getting his first camera in 1916. But by 1930, after publishing *Taos Pueblo* (1927), his first portfolio of photographs, he had abandoned music to devote full time to a career in photography.

At the beginning of his career, Adams produced Impressionist photographs with soft, misty effects. In 1930, however, he turned to what he called "straight photography." He began to emphasize the beauty of natural landscapes, especially mountainous panoramas, by capturing tones of light along with sharp detail. Two years later he formed Group f/64, an association of photographers who used large cameras with small apertures to capture the play of light on nature's many textures.

Adams published many books on photographic techniques, beginning with *Making a Photograph* in 1935, which used many of his own photographs as examples. Adams established the first photographic art department at the Museum of Modern Art (1940) and the first college department of photography in 1946 at the California School of Fine Art, later the San Francisco Art Institute. He was also a conservationist and environmentalist, serving many years as a director of the Sierra Club, the national organization dedicated to preserving and expanding parks, wildlife, and wilderness areas. In 1980 President Ronald Reagan awarded Adams the Presidential Medal of Freedom.

BOOKS BY ADAMS

The American Wilderness. Little 1990 $100.00. ISBN 0-8212-1799-2

Ansel Adams: An Autobiography. (coauthored with Mary S. Alinder) Little 1990 $29.95. ISBN 0-8212-1787-9

The Camera. Ansel Adams Photography Ser. Book 1 Bulfinch 1980 $27.50. ISBN 0-8212-1092-0

Examples: The Making of Forty Photographs. Little 1989 $27.50. ISBN 0-8212-1750-X

The Negative. The New Ansel Adams Photography Ser. Book 2 Bulfinch 1981 $27.50. ISBN 0-8212-1131-5

Photographs of the Southwest. Bulfinch 1984 $35.00. ISBN 0-8212-1574-4

The Portfolios of Ansel Adams. Bulfinch 1981 $25.00. ISBN 0-8212-1122-6

The Print. The Ansel Adams Photography Ser. Book 3 Bulfinch 1983 $27.50. ISBN 0-8212-1526-4

BOOK ABOUT ADAMS

Alinder, Mary S., and Andrea G. Stillman (eds). *Ansel Adams: Letters and Images, 1916–1984.* Bulfinch 1988 $50.00. ISBN 0-8212-1691-0 Correspondence of Adams, with pertinent photographs.

ARMSTRONG, LOUIS   1900–1971

"Satchmo" was the nickname for Louis Armstrong, one of the most innovative American jazz trumpeters of his era, and one of the great ambassadors of American jazz. Armstrong began his career in the unsavory districts of New

Orleans, where he was a street singer as a boy and later learned to play the trumpet. In 1922 he moved to Chicago, where he joined the jazz orchestra of Joe "King" Oliver. He quickly became noted for his improvisational style, and by the late 1920s he led his own jazz ensemble called the Louis Armstrong Hot Five, later the Hot Seven.

As Armstrong gained popularity, he made recordings and traveled around the world performing. He had a number of hit records, including "Hello, Dolly" and "Mack the Knife." He also appeared in Broadway shows and in films. His raspy baritone voice and brilliant trumpet playing combined to make an unforgettable musical sound appreciated all over the world.

BOOKS BY ARMSTRONG

Satchmo: My Life in New Orleans. Da Capo 1986 $9.95. ISBN 0-306-80276-7
Swing That Music. Longman 1936. (o.p.).

BOOKS ABOUT ARMSTRONG

Collier, James L. *Louis Armstrong: An American Success Story.* Macmillan 1985 $12.95. ISBN 0-02-722830-4 Absorbing biography of Armstrong by one of America's foremost authorities on jazz.
Jones, Max, and John Chilton. *Louis: The Louis Armstrong Story, 1900–1971.* Quality Paperbacks Ser. Da Capo 1988 $10.95. ISBN 0-306-80324-0 Authorized biography of Armstrong by a friend and writer about jazz and by a fellow musician, a jazz trumpeter.
*Tanenhaus, Sam. *Louis Armstrong. Black Americans of Achievement Ser.* Chelsea 1989 $9.95. ISBN 0-7910-0221-7 Biography of Satchmo for young readers.

BERLIN, IRVING   1888–1989

Composer of popular American music, Irving Berlin came to the United States from Russia when he was five years old. Born Isidore Baline, he began his career in music first as a street musician, singing songs for the pennies and dimes thrown his way, and then as a singing waiter in a Lower East Side restaurant in New York City. In 1909 he began writing lyrics for a music company. On his first published sheet music, the printer made an error, listing his name as Irving Berlin. The fledging lyricist decided to keep the name. Berlin could not read notes and learned music only by ear. Yet in 1911 he began to write music as well as lyrics. "Alexander's Ragtime Band," written in 1911, quickly reached the top of the ragtime hit list. After the tragic death of his first wife in 1913, he wrote his first ballad, "When I Lost You." In 1919 he founded a company to publish his music.

Berlin achieved success writing in many styles and formats—ragtime, jazz, ballads, broadway musicals, and films. Writing his first musical score and lyrics in 1914, he continued with such other successes as *Top Hat,* a 1935 musical; *Holiday Inn,* a 1942 film featuring "White Christmas," the most popular Christmas song ever recorded; *Annie Get Your Gun,* a 1947 musical and a 1950 film; *Easter Parade* written in 1933 and the theme of a 1948 film; and *Call Me Madam,* a 1950s musical and film written with Howard Lindsay and Russel Crouse. In all, Berlin wrote more than 800 songs, many of which have become classics.

BOOKS ABOUT BERLIN

Bergreen, Laurence. *As Thousands Cheer: the Life of Irving Berlin.* Viking 1990 $24.95. ISBN 0-670-81874-7 The most up-to-date and complete biography of Berlin, with emphasis on his personal as well as his professional life.

Whitcomb, Ian. *Irving Berlin and Ragtime America.* Limelight Edns 1988 $18.95. ISBN 0-87910-115-6 Examines the early life and career of Berlin.

Woollcott, Alexander. *The Story of Irving Berlin. Music Ser.* Da Capo 1982 repr of 1925 ed $32.50. ISBN 0-306-76145-9 Entertaining rags to riches story with new index and introduction.

BERNSTEIN, LEONARD   1918–1990

Called by many the greatest figure in American music, Leonard Bernstein was a charismatic and controversial conductor, as well as a gifted teacher, accomplished pianist, and highly admired composer. As a teacher, Bernstein communicated his love for music, whether classical or popular, through his "Young People's Concerts," many of which were televised, and at the Tanglewood Music Center in Lenox, Massachusetts, where he taught many of the present-day conductors of American symphony orchestras. As a composer, he was best known for his popular works, which include the Broadway musicals *West Side Story, Candide,* and *Wonderful Town;* the film score for *On the Waterfront;* and the ballet *Fancy Free*—all of which were published in the 1950s. But it was as a conductor with an exuberant, dynamic, and dramatic style that Bernstein most captured the imagination of the American musical public.

Born to Russian-Jewish immigrants in Lawrence, Massachusetts, Bernstein started taking piano lessons at the age of 10, using his own allowance to pay for the lessons. He attended the Boston Latin School and Harvard University, continuing his musical studies at the Curtis Institute of Music in Philadelphia where he quickly displayed his varied talents as a pupil of the renowned conductor Fritz Reiner. Moving to New York in 1942, Bernstein fell on hard times before he was appointed assistant music director of the New York Philharmonic in 1943. At the age of 25, however, he became an overnight sensation when he substituted for an ailing conductor during a concert. In 1958, when he was named musical director of the Philharmonic, he became the first native-born American to head a top symphony orchestra. His association with the Philharmonic lasted until 1969, when he resigned to concentrate on composing.

BOOKS BY BERNSTEIN

Bernstein on Broadway (1981). Schirmer 1981 $19.95. (o.p.).

The Joy of Music (1963). Simon 1963 $5.95. ISBN 0-671-39721-4

The Unanswered Question: Six Talks at Harvard (1976). Harvard Univ Pr 1976 $14.95. ISBN 0-674-92001-5

West Side Story (1958). (coauthored with others) Random 1958 $13.95. ISBN 0-394-40788-1

BOOKS ABOUT BERNSTEIN

Gradenwitz, Peter. *Leonard Bernstein.* St. Martin's 1987 $21.95. ISBN 0-85496-510-6 Collection of personal contributions about Bernstein by such notables as Yehudi and Diane Menuhin, Isaac Stern, Lukas Foss, Virgil Thomson, and Abba Eban; includes a bibliography, filmography, and discography.

Peyser, Joan. *Bernstein: A Biography.* Ballantine 1988 $5.95. ISBN 0-345-35296-3 Traces both the professional career and personal life of Bernstein.

CUNNINGHAM, MERCE   1919–

As a student of Martha Graham, American dancer, teacher, and choreographer and a celebrated soloist in the Martha Graham Dance Company from 1940 to 1955, Merce Cunningham participated in the third-generation development of modern dance. Born in Centralia, Washington, he began his career in the second-generation period of the American modern-dance theater under the tutelage of Martha Graham. He later became a creator and choreographer of his own dances and in 1950 established his own dance company.

Through the Merce Cunningham Dance Company, Cunningham taught his students to follow new paths of creativity—to choreograph dances to avant-garde musical compositions, to be free of spatial restraints, to replace a strong central focus with a random approach to choreographic patterns, and to devise dances that could be viewed from any angle. Working with American composer John Cage as musical director, Cunningham taught his students to experiment with dances that used electronic and other newly developed forms of music. His best-known works include *Suite by Chance* (1952), a work in which the toss of the dice determined the structure, and *Symphonie pour un homme seul* (1952). Both reveal the spare, expressive style that is the Cunningham hallmark.

Book by Cunningham

The Dancer and the Dance: Merce Cunningham in Conversation with Jacqueline Lesschaeve (1985). (coauthored with Jacqueline Lesschaeve) Henry Nathan (ed). M. Boyars 1985 $27.50. ISBN 0-7145-2809-9

Book about Cunningham

Klosty, James (ed). *Merce Cunningham.* Limelight Edns 1987 $19.95. ISBN 0-87910-055-9 Comprehensive account of Cunningham's life and work.

DUNCAN, ISADORA 1878–1927

A native of San Francisco, Isadora Duncan was known as an innovator and a first-generation pioneer of modern dance. A modernist whose life-style became even more visible and well known than her dancing, she was a feminist and lived her life as the legend it became.

Duncan's dancing was bold and innovative. She danced barefoot, often to music of classical composers Ludwig van Beethoven, Richard Wagner, and Christoph Gluck that was not originally intended as an accompaniment for the dance. Her costume was an adaptation of a Greek tunic, embellished with several colored shoulder scarves. Using natural flowing movements that emanated from her waist, she weaved and whirled to express the emotions prompted by the music. Although Duncan established schools in Berlin, Paris, Moscow, and London, her dance technique was so improvisational, abstract, and personal that her many imitators were largely unsuccessful. They lacked her daring and dynamic personality. Duncan's accidental death in Paris was a tragedy mourned by the whole dance world.

Books by Duncan

Art of the Dance. Sheldon Chevey (ed). Theatre Arts 1969 $19.95. ISBN 0-87830-005-8
Isadora Speaks. City Lights 1981 $5.95. ISBN 0-87286-133-3
My Life. Liveright 1972 $8.95. ISBN 0-87140-274-2

ELLINGTON, EDWARD KENNEDY (DUKE) 1899–1974

Jazz pianist, composer, and popular bandleader, Edward Ellington was known as "Duke" to his contemporaries. His skill as a pianist and his popularity as a bandleader are surpassed only by the impressive depth and quality of his work as a composer. Born in Washington, D.C., Ellington began to study the piano at the age of seven, and he organized his first band at the age of 18, The Duke's Serenaders.

In 1923, Ellington moved to New York, where he and his band, The Washingtonians, performed at nightclubs in Harlem and at the Kentucky Club in downtown Manhattan. Utilizing the popularity of phonographic recordings, Ellington began to record his performances and reorganized the band as Ellington's Kentucky Club Orchestra. From 1927 through 1932, he and his band made frequent radio broadcasts. Soon Ellington and jazz were synonymous, and many other musicians attempted to copy his musical style. These attempts led to many instrumental innovations in the musical language of jazz.

The range of Ellington's musical compositions is impressive. Many of his short compositions, including "Mood Indigo" (1930), "Solitude" (1933), and "Sophisticated Lady" (1933), remain popular staples of jazz instrumentalists everywhere. His longer works, such as *Creole Rhapsody* (1932); *Black, Brown, and Beige* (1943), a 50-minute work that told the story of American blacks; *Liberian Suite* (1947); *Harlem Nights* (1951); and *Night Creatures* (1955), include complex orchestration. These works helped shift jazz from the smoky confines of nightclubs to the sophisticated setting of the concert stage. In addition to jazz festivals and concert tours, both in this country and around the world, Ellington appeared in several films and made many recordings.

BOOKS BY ELLINGTON

Great Music of Duke Ellington. Dover $12.95. ISBN 0-486-20757-9
Music Is My Mistress (1973). Da Capo 1976 $12.95. ISBN 0-306-80033-0

BOOKS ABOUT ELLINGTON

Dance, Stanley. *The World of Duke Ellington.* Da Capo 1980 $10.95. ISBN 0-306-80136-1 Discusses Ellington's music and times.
Frankl, Ron. *Duke Ellington. Black Americans of Achievement Ser.* Chelsea 1989 $9.95. ISBN 0-7910-0208-X Brief, illustrated biography of Ellington.
Ellington, Mercer, and Stanley Dance. *Duke Ellington in Person: An Intimate Memoir.* Houghton 1978 $10.95. ISBN 0-395-27511-5 Account of Ellington's life and music.

GROPIUS, WALTER   1883–1969

As teacher and designer, Walter Gropius was a dominant figure of twentieth-century architecture. Born in Berlin, Germany, he strove in the years after World War I to bring architecture into harmony with the new industrial age. He was one of the first architects to use such modern materials as glass and steel in many of his early buildings.

In 1919 Gropius became director of the Weimar School of Design, which he reorganized and renamed the Bauhaus. Its goal was to educate designers who would create functional and rational architecture and objects of art for daily use. In 1925 the Bauhaus moved to Dessau, where, for its new quarters, Gropius designed buildings in a clean, functional, highly innovative style. The Nazis, who came to power in Germany in 1933, considered the Bauhaus radical and moved to suppress it, leading Gropius to flee to England in 1934.

Three years later, Gropius came to the United States, where he headed the highly influential department of architecture at Harvard University until 1952. A firm believer in teamwork, Gropius founded The Architects Collaborative (TAC). Members of TAC designed, among many other buildings, the United

States Embassy in Athens, Greece, and the Pan American Building in New York City. Working with a team of young architects, Gropius also designed the Harvard University Graduate Center. He also wrote several books, among them *The Scope of Total Architecture* (1952).

BOOKS BY GROPIUS

Four Great Makers of Modern Architecture: Gropius, Le Corbusier, Mies van der Rohe, Wright (1970). (coauthored with others) *Architecture and Decorative Art Ser.* Da Capo 1970 $39.50. ISBN 0-306-70065-4
New Architecture and the Bauhaus (1965). MIT Pr 1965 $6.95. ISBN 0-262-57006-8
The Theater of the Bauhaus (1987). (coedited with Arthur S. Wensinger) Arthur S. Wensinger (tr). Wesleyan Univ Pr 1987 $10.95. ISBN 0-8195-6020-0

BOOKS ABOUT GROPIUS

Vance, Mary. *Walter Gropius: Selected Journal Articles Published 1970–1986. Architecture Ser.* Vance Biblios 1987 $3.00. ISBN 1-55590-340-1 Discussion of Groipius's ideas and work by a leader of the Bauhaus school.
Winger, Hans. *Bauhaus: Weimar, Dessau, Berlin, Chicago.* MIT Pr 1969. (o.p.) Examines works by adherents of the Bauhaus school of art and architecture.

O'KEEFFE, GEORGIA   1887–1986

A truly American artist, Georgia O'Keeffe developed an intensely personal and abstract style of painting. Born in Wisconsin, she was encouraged by her mother, who saw that she had art lessons along with a well-rounded education. While O'Keeffe was always doggedly determined to remain independent, she became famous with the help and patronage of world-renowned photographer and gallery owner Alfred Stieglitz. She eventually married Stieglitz in 1924.

Although her early works depict scenes of New York City, for most of her life, O'Keeffe lived in the Southwest. It was to the Southwest that she looked for the themes and motifs of her work. In her later work, she painted huge canvases—their space beautifully filled with bleached bones, barren rolling hills, desert blooms, adobe churches, and brightly colored close-ups of simple flowers. The work occupied a middle ground between abstraction and realism.

O'Keeffe's paintings are in many museums and private collections. *Cow's Skull, Red, White, and Blue* (1931) and *Sunflower, New Mexico No. 2* (1934) are two of her works that can be seen at the Metropolitan Museum of Art in New York City. Throughout her life, O'Keeffe insisted that her paintings needed no analysis or interpretation to be understood and appreciated. When she died at the age of 98, this self-sufficient woman was already a legend in the art world.

BOOKS BY O'KEEFFE

Poppy, Nineteen Twenty-Seven. Fine Art Jigsaw Puzzles Ser. Battle Rd 1989 $9.95.
A Woman on Paper. Simon 1988 $24.45. ISBN 0-671-66431-X

BOOKS ABOUT O'KEEFFE

Berry, Michael. *Georgia O'Keeffe. American Women of Achievement Ser.* Chelsea 1989 $9.95. ISBN 0-7910-0420-1 Informative, easy-to-read biography of the artist.
Lisle, Laurie. *Portrait of an Artist: A Biography of Georgia O'Keeffe.* Washington Square Pr 1981 $4.95. ISBN 0-671-42182-4 First full-length account of O'Keeffe's personal life as an artist and as the wife of Alfred Stieglitz.
Robinson, Roxana. *Georgia O'Keeffe: A Life.* Harper 1989 $25.00. ISBN 0-06-015965-0 Detailed and moving story of O'Keeffe's life and work.

STEICHEN, EDWARD   1879–1973

Along with other pioneers in photography, Edward Steichen was instrumental in establishing photography as an art form. Born in Luxembourg, Steichen came to the United States as a child and settled in Michigan. At age 16 he became an apprentice lithographer. At the same time he became interested in painting and photography. He went to Paris to study art and became acquainted with the works of French artists Paul Cézanne, Auguste Rodin, Pablo Picasso, and Henri Matisse. Later, when he returned to the United States to open art and photography galleries, he brought the work of these artists to the attention of Americans.

During the 1920s and 1930s, Steichen became a successful portrait and fashion photographer, working out of his own studio as well as for Condé Nast publications. During World War I he helped develop aerial photography, and during World War II he assisted the U.S. Navy with combat photography. From 1947 to 1962, Steichen directed the department of photography at the Museum of Modern Art in New York City. As director, he organized the 1955 Family of Man exhibition. Considered the greatest photographic exhibition ever mounted, it mirrored "the essential oneness" of humanity. Steichen neglected his own work during this time, but when he was able to return to it, it was filled with the same creative imagination and forceful imagery that characterized his earlier works.

BOOKS BY STEICHEN

The Family of Man. Simon 1987 $14.95. ISBN 0-671-55411-5
Steichen: A Life in Photography. Crown 1985 $12.95. ISBN 0-517-55696-0
Steichen at War. Crown 1987 $19.95. ISBN 0-517-63227-6

WRIGHT, FRANK LLOYD   1867–1959

Frank Lloyd Wright is widely considered to be the greatest American architect of all time and certainly the most influential. Throughout a career of nearly 70 years, he produced masterpiece after masterpiece, each different and boldly new and yet each with the unmistakable touch of Wright's genius in both the treatment of detailing and in overall concept.

Born in Richland Center, Wisconsin to a minister and a schoolteacher of Welsh ancestry, deserted by his father, Wright had to go to work on a farm when he was 14 years old to help support his mother and the other children. After graduating from high school, he studied civil engineering at the University of Wisconsin. He left after three years to pursue the career in architecture that his mother had always urged him to pursue. The collapse of a newly built wing of the Wisconsin State Capitol had convinced him that engineering principles should be applied to architecture, and he set out to attain this goal.

Wright began his career in Chicago as chief assistant to Louis Henry Sullivan (*see* Sullivan, Vol. 2, United States History: The Arts in the Age of Enterprise), America's first modern architect. Sullivan believed that in architecture "form must follow function." By this he meant that the design of a building should be based on its use. This idea, new at the time, greatly influenced Wright. It was at this time that he developed the so-called Prairie Style, which featured open interiors and wide, overhung roofs. The Robie House in Chicago and the Avery Coonley House in Riverdale, Illinois, are outstanding examples of this style.

The masterworks of Wright's later years are the Johnson Wax Building in Racine, Wisconsin, and Fallingwater in Bear Run, Pennsylvania. Fallingwater, with its bold cantilevered balconies over a running stream, is probably the most admired and pictured private house in American architecture. Wright also designed the Guggenheim Museum in New York City.

Wright's own houses and studios were also masterpieces. He built Taliesin West, a true paradise in the Arizona desert, as a winter home, away from the severe winters in Wisconsin where he had built his extraordinary Taliesin East.

BOOKS BY WRIGHT

Frank Lloyd Wright: His Living Voice. Bruce B. Pfeiffer (ed). California State Univ Pr 1987 $17.95. ISBN 0-912201-14-2

The Guggenheim Correspondence. Bruce B. Pfeiffer (ed). California State Univ Pr 1986 $17.95.

In the Cause of Architecture. McGraw 1988 $16.95. ISBN 0-07-072031-2

Living City. NAL 1970 $9.95. ISBN 0-452-00842-5

Natural House. NAL 1970 $8.95. ISBN 0-452-00841-7

Treasures of Taliesin: Seventy-Six Unbuilt Designs of Frank Lloyd Wright. Bruce B. Pfeiffer (ed). Southern Illinois Univ Pr 1985 $60.00. ISBN 0-8093-1235-2

BOOKS ABOUT WRIGHT

Meehan, Patrick J. (ed). *The Master Architect: Conversations with Frank Lloyd Wright.* Wiley 1984 $33.50. ISBN 0-471-80025-2 The architect's own words about his work.

*Murphy, Wendy B. *Frank Lloyd Wright.* Silver 1990 $17.98. ISBN 0-382-09905-2 Brief biography that presents a lively picture of the architect's life; includes many illustrations and quotations.

Tafel, Edgar. *Years with Frank Lloyd Wright: Apprentice to Genius. Architecture Ser.* Dover 1985 $9.95. ISBN 0-486-24801-1 Comprehensive look at Wright's life.

Twombly, Robert C. *Frank Lloyd Wright: An Interpretive Biography.* Harper Jr Bks 1973 $10.00. ISBN 0-06-014467-X Interpretation of Wright's style, influence, and accomplishments.

Wright, Olgivanna Lloyd. *Frank Lloyd Wright: His Life, His Work, His Words.* Horizon Pr 1966. Complete Study of Wright's ideas and work.

WYETH, ANDREW   1917–

Ranking among the best known and best beloved of all American artists, Andrew Wyeth was trained by his father, N. C. Wyeth, a noted illustrator, and by Peter Hurd, a student under his father from whom he learned to paint in the medium of tempera. Wyeth always painted far from the urban centers of the art world. He has spent his life painting the people and places of two sites—Chadds Ford, Pennsylvania, where he was born, and Cushing, Maine. His works reflect a somber, rural world of old buildings, rolling hills, and barren fields with simple, spare people. The paintings use earth colors of russets, browns, tans, greens bordering on black, and a spot of enlivening red or blue.

Strongly influenced at age 16 by the works of American painter Winslow Homer (*see* Homer, Vol. 2, United States History: The Arts in the Age of Enterprise), Wyeth had his first one-man show in 1937 at the age of 20. In 1967 the Whitney Museum of Art in New York City held a retrospective show that contained more than 200 of his works. Three years later, the White House honored Wyeth with a one-man show, an event believed to be the first for a living American artist. In 1977 Wyeth was elected to the French Académie des Beaux Arts, only the second American to receive the honor. In 1980 he was

elected to Britain's Royal Academy. His meticulous and naturalistic, yet vision-
ary style is best represented by his most famous work, *Christina's World,* painted
in 1948, and now hanging in the Museum of Modern Art in New York City.

BOOK BY WYETH

Andrew Wyeth: The Helga Pictures. Abrams 1987 $40.00. ISBN 0-8109-1788-2

BOOKS ABOUT WYETH

Duff, James H., *et al. An American Vision: Three Generations of Wyeth Art.* Little 1989 $24.95.
ISBN 0-8212-1652-X Essays on illustrator N. C. Wyeth by Andrew Wyeth, on
Andrew Wyeth by Thomas Hoving, and on James Wyeth by Lincoln Kirstein,
with many colored illustrations.
Logsdon, Gene. *Wyeth People: A Portrait of Andrew Wyeth as Seen by His Friends and Neighbors.*
Taylor 1988 $13.95. ISBN 0-87833-634-6 Intimate look at the artist and his work.

See also Vol. 1, American Literature: The Twentieth Century.

WORLD HISTORY

The section devoted to world history follows the chronology of human history
from its prehistoric roots, when there were no written records, to present times.
There are 33 subsections, beginning with listings of general reference works,
surveys, and histories. This is followed by six subsections that deal with
prehistory and the ancient civilizations of the Middle East, India and China,
Greece, Rome, and Africa and the Americas; three subsections that are devoted
to the medieval period in the Byzantine Empire, Europe, India, China, and
Japan; eight subsections that cover world events from the fourteenth through
the nineteenth centuries, the period of transition from medieval to modern
times; five subsections that encompass the major themes of eighteenth-, nine-
teenth-, and early twentieth-century world history; three subsections that
focus on events during the crisis years of the twentieth century, 1914 through
1945; and seven subsections that deal with the themes of the contemporary
world, from 1945 to the present. Included are subsections that deal with the
arts of the various eras.

Within each subsection, key individuals of the period are listed alphabetically, their last names appearing first. For each, there is a book or a list of books
by that individual. In addition, there is for each a profile that provides personal
background or information about the individual's place in history and his or
her achievements. Further, the profile may refer the reader to other related
individuals and their works, which also can be found in *The Young Adult Reader's
Adviser.*

Last, for most profiled individuals, there is a Books About section that,
among other types of publications, lists notable biographies for further reading
and research. Whenever possible, very recent titles have also been included.

While works relevant to American history are included in the world history section, the major focus is on other parts of the world. For a comprehensive
listing of works on American history, see the readings under United States

Astronomical Globe: Celestial Sphere on the Back of Pegasus. Globe by Gerhardt Emmoser (1579). Courtesy of The Metropolitan Museum of Art, Gift of J. Pierpont Morgan, 1917. (17.190.636)

history, found in the section immediately preceding this one. For a comprehensive listing of works of a regional geographical nature, see the readings under Geography, found in the social sciences section of *The Young Adult Reader's Adviser*.

HISTORIES, REFERENCES, AND SURVEYS

African Statistical Yearbook. Part I *North Africa.* UN 1987 $18.00. ISBN 92-1-125045-5. Part II *West Africa.* UN 1987 $30.00. ISBN 92-1-125046-3

Ajayi, J. F., and Michael Crowder (eds). *Historical Atlas of Africa.* Cambridge Univ Pr 1985 $90.00. ISBN 0-521-25353-5

Al Faruqi, Isma'il, and Lamya Lois. *Cultural Atlas of Islam.* Macmillan 1986 $90.00. ISBN 0-02-910190-5

Asimov, Isaac. *Asimov's Chronology of Science and Discovery: How Science Has Shaped the World and How the World Has Affected Science from 4,000,000 B.C. to the Present.* Harper 1989 $29.95. ISBN 0-06-015612-0

Bailey, Helen M., and Abraham P. Nasatir. *Latin America: The Development of Its Civilization.* Prentice 1973.

Barraclough, Geoffrey (ed). *The Times Atlas of World History.* Hammond 1989 $85.00.

Barzini, Luigi. *The Europeans.* Penguin 1984 $8.95. ISBN 0-14-007150-4

Basham, A. L. (ed). *A Cultural History of India.* Oxford Univ Pr 1984 $29.95. ISBN 0-19-561520-4

Beard, Mary, and John North (eds). *Pagan Priests: Religion and Power in the Ancient World.* Cornell Univ Pr 1989 $39.95. ISBN 0-8014-2401-1

Beard, Mary R. *Woman as Force in History: A Study in Tradition and Realities.* Persea 1987 $12.95. ISBN 0-89255-113-5

Bennett, Norman R. *Africa and Europe from Roman Times to National Independence.* Holmes & Meier 1975 $14.95. ISBN 0-8419-0901-6

*Blunden, Caroline, and Mark Elvin. *Cultural Atlas of China. Cultural Atlas Ser.* Facts on File 1983 $40.00. ISBN 0-87196-132-6 Covers China's culture, geography, history, and more.

Branigan, Keith (ed). *The Atlas of Archaeology.* State Mutual 1982 $60.00. ISBN 0-356-06253-8

Brinton, Crane, *et al. A History of Civilization: 1815 to the Present.* Prentice 1984.

Brinton, Crane, *et al. A History of Civilization: Prehistory to 1300.* Prentice 1976 $18.95.

Brinton, Crane, *et al. A History of Civilization: 1300 to 1815.* Prentice 1976 $16.95.

*Brown, Lester R., *et al. State of the World, 1988.* Norton 1988 $9.20. ISBN 0-393-30440-X Anthology of different viewpoints on world geography issues.

Brownell, David, and Harry Knill (eds). *Kings and Queens of England.* Bellerophon 1978 $3.50. ISBN 0-88388-053-9

*Buchanan, Keith. *China.* Little 1981. Illustrated account of Chinese civilization; with charts, diagrams, maps, and photographs.

*Burne, Jerome (ed). *Chronicle of the World.* ECAM 1990 $49.95. ISBN 0-13-133463-8 Story of people and events from all centuries and continents that have shaped world history.

Cameron, Averil, and Amelie Kuhrt (eds). *Images of Women in Antiquity.* Wayne State Univ Pr 1984 $16.00. ISBN 0-8143-1763-4

Cannon, John, and Ralph Griffiths. *The Oxford Illustrated History of the British Monarchy.* Oxford Univ Pr 1988 $39.95. ISBN 0-19-822786-8

Cantor, Norman F., and Michael S. Werthman. *Ancient Civilizations: Four Thousand B.C. to Four Hundred A.D. Structure of European History Ser.* Harlan Davidson 1972 $7.95. ISBN 0-88295-710-4

Casson, Lionel. *Ships and Seamanship in the Ancient World.* Princeton Univ Pr 1986 $19.50. ISBN 0-691-00215-0

*Chadwick, Henry, and Gillian R. Evans (eds). *Atlas of the Christian Church. Cultural Atlas Ser.* Facts on File 1987 $40.00. ISBN 0-8160-1643-7 Discusses Christian traditions and gives an account of the Christian Church as it affected the development of Western civilization.

Cheilik, Michael. *Ancient History: From Its Beginnings to the Fall of Rome.* Harper 1969 $7.95. ISBN 0-06-460001-7

*Chisholm, J. *World History Dates.* EDC 1987 $9.95. ISBN 0-86020-954-7 Provides dates of notable events from the Stone Age to the present.

Cole, Bruce, and Adelheid Gealt. *Art of the Western World: From Ancient Greece to Post-Modernism.* Summit Bks 1989 $35.00. ISBN 0-671-67007-7

Collcutt, Martin, *et al. Cultural Atlas of Japan.* Facts on File 1988 $40.00. ISBN 0-8160-1927-4

Collier, Simon. *From Cortés to Castro: An Introduction to the History of Latin America.* Macmillan 1974.

Cook, Chris, and John Stevenson. *The Longman Handbook of Modern European History 1763–1985.* Longman 1987 $22.95. ISBN 0-582-48584-3

Cotterell, Arthur, *et al. China's Civilization: A Survey of Its History, Arts, and Technology.* Irvington 1982.

Cotterell, Arthur. *Macmillan Illustrated Encyclopedia of Myths and Legends.* Macmillan 1989 $29.95. ISBN 0-02-580181-3

Cotterell, Arthur (ed). *The Penguin Encyclopedia of Ancient Civilizations.* Penguin 1989 $17.95. ISBN 0-14-011434-3

Cottrell, Alvin J. (ed). *The Persian Gulf States: A General Study.* Johns Hopkins Univ Pr 1980 $59.00. ISBN 0-8018-2204-1

Crummel, Alex. *Africa and America. Black Heritage Library Collection Ser.* Ayer (repr of 1891 ed) $20.25. ISBN 0-8369-8550-8

*Davison, Marshall B. *A History of Art: From Twenty-Five Thousand B.C. to the Present.* Random 1984 $8.95. ISBN 0-394-85181-1 Readable illustrated history of art from ancient times to today.

Drakakis-Smith, David. *The Third World City. Introductions to Development Ser.* Routledge 1987 $9.95. ISBN 0-416-91970-7

Drakakis-Smith, David (ed). *Economic Growth and Urbanization in Developing Areas.* Routledge 1989 $66.50. ISBN 0-415-00442-X

*Earhart, H. Byron. *Japanese Religion: Unity and Diversity. The Religious Life of Man Ser.* Wadsworth 1982. ISBN 0-534-01028-8 Presents various traditions that are part of Japanese religion.

*Ebenstein, William, and Edwin Fogelman. *Today's Isms: Communism, Fascism, Capitalism and Socialism.* Prentice 1985 $29.00. ISBN 0-13-924473-5 Clear, easily understandable examination of communism, fascism, capitalism, and socialism.

Editors of Time–Life Books. *Japan.* Time–Life 1986 $14.95. ISBN 0-8094-5334-7

*Editors of Time–Life Books. *Library of Nations. Time–Life Books Ser.* 18 vols. Silver 1984–1988 $28.60 ea. ISBNs 0-8094-5303-7 through 0-8094-5320-7 Each volume focuses on a specific country and its people.

*Editors of Time–Life Books. *World War II. Time–Life Ser.* 39 vols. Silver 1976–1983 $19.93 ea. ISBNs 0-8094-2452-5 through 0-8094-3435-0 Each volume provides illustrated, historical insight on a specific campaign of or participant in World War II.

*Ehrlich, Paul R. *Population Bomb.* Ballantine 1986 $4.50. ISBN 0-345-33834-0 Controversial book on the effects of population growth.

Esposito, John L. *Islam: The Straight Path.* Oxford Univ Pr 1990 $19.95. ISBN 0-19-506225-6

Galbraith, John Kenneth, and Stanislav Menshikov. *Capitalism, Communism and Coexistence: From the Bitter Past to a Better Prospect.* Houghton 1988 $17.95. ISBN 0-395-47316-0

Grant, Michael. *The Ancient Mediterranean.* NAL 1988 $9.95. ISBN 0-452-00949-9

Grant, Michael, and Rachel Kitzinger (eds). *Civilization of the Ancient Mediterranean.* 3 vols. Scribner's 1988 $195.00.

*Green, Peter. *Ancient Greece: An Illustrated History.* Thames Hudson 1979 $10.95. ISBN 0-500-27161-5 Readable account of ancient Greece.

Greenberg, Stan. *Olympic Games: The Records 776 B.C. to A.D. 1988.* Sterling 1988 $17.95. ISBN 0-85112-897-1

*Gurney, Gene. *Kingdoms of Asia, the Middle East, and Africa: An Illustrated Encyclopedia of Ruling Monarchs from Ancient Times to the Present.* Crown 1985 $24.95. ISBN 0-517-55256-6 Discusses Asian, Middle Eastern, and African rulers and their kingdoms from earliest records to modern times.

*Gurney, Gene. *Kingdoms of Europe: An Illustrated Encyclopedia of Ruling Monarchs from Ancient Times to the Present.* Crown 1982 $24.95. ISBN 0-517-54395-8 Describes European rulers and their kingdoms from earliest records to modern times.

Hagg, Thomas. *Nubian Culture: Past and Present. Kungl Vitterhets Historie Ser.* Coronet Bks 1987 $44.50. ISBN 91-7402-188-5

*Haupt, Arthur, and Thomas T. Kane. *The Population Reference Bureau's Population Handbook: International Edition.* Population Reference Bureau 1986 $5.00. ISBN 0-917136-10-1 Presents contemporary global population statistics.

Hefele, Bernhard. *Jazz Bibliography: An International Literature on Jazz, Blues, Spirituals, Gospel, and Ragtime Music with a Selected List of Works on the Social and Cultural Background from the Beginning to the Present.* K. G. Saur 1981 $36.00. ISBN 3-598-10205-4

Hibbert, Christopher. *The English: A Social History, 1066–1956.* Norton 1987 $39.45. ISBN 0-393-02371-0

*Hinds, Harold E., Jr., and Charles M. Tatum (eds). *Handbook of Latin American Popular Culture.* Greenwood 1985 $50.95. ISBN 0-313-23293-8 Articles on Latin American religion, sports, films, popular music, and more.

Hitti, Philip K. *Islam and the West: A Historical Cultural Survey. Anvil Ser.* Krieger 1979 $7.50. ISBN 0-88275-787-3

*Hook, Brian (ed). *The Cambridge Encyclopedia of China.* Cambridge Univ Pr 1982 $49.50. ISBN 0-521-23099-3 Basic information on traditional and modern China.

*Ikime, Obaro (ed). *African Historical Biographies.* Heinemann. (o.p.) Biographies by African historians of 13 notable African figures of history.

Jansen, Marius B. *Japan and Its World: Two Centuries of Change.* Princeton Univ Pr 1980 $16.50. ISBN 0-691-05310-3

*Kaplan, Frederic M., and Julian M. Sobin. *Encyclopedia of China Today.* Eurasia $29.95.

ISBN 0-932030-11-4 Presents varied reference information on China and includes charts, chronological listings, maps, and more.

Keegan, John (ed). *World Armies.* Gale 1984 $80.00. ISBN 0-8103-1515-7

Keen, Benjamin (ed). *Latin American Civilization: History and Society, 1492 to the Present.* Westview 1986 $19.95. ISBN 0-8133-0319-2

Keen, Benjamin, and Mark Wasserman. *A History of Latin America.* Houghton 1987 $27.96. ISBN 0-395-35942-2

Keene, Donald (ed). *Anthology of Japanese Literature: From the Earliest Era to the Mid-Nineteenth Century.* Grove 1988 $13.95. ISBN 0-8021-5058-6

Keene, Donald. *Travelers of a Hundred Ages: The Japanese as Revealed Through 1,000 Years of Diaries.* H. Holt 1989 $29.95. ISBN 0-8050-0751-2

Kennedy, Paul. *The Rise and Fall of Great Powers: Economic Change and Military Conflict from 1500 to 2000.* Random 1989 $12.95. ISBN 0-679-72019-7

Kirchherr, Eugene C. *Place Names of Africa, 1935–1986: A Political Gazetteer.* Scarecrow 1987 $17.50. ISBN 0-8108-2061-7

*Kodansha Encyclopedia of Japan. 9 vols. Kodansha 1983 $720.00. ISBN 0-87011-620-7 General reference encyclopedia on Japan.

Kohn, Hans. *The Age of Nationalism: The First Era of Global History.* Greenwood 1976 repr of 1962 ed $35.00. ISBN 0-8371-9087-8

Kohn, Hans. *Nationalism and Realism.* Anvil Ser. Krieger 1968 $8.50. ISBN 0-442-00096-0

Kohn, Hans. *Nationalism: Its Meaning and History.* Krieger 1982 $7.50. ISBN 0-89874-479-2

Kurian, George (ed). *Encyclopedia of the Third World.* Facts on File 1990 $195.00. ISBN 0-8160-2261-5

*Kurian, George T. *New Book of World Rankings.* Facts on File 1989 $40.00. ISBN 0-8160-1931-2 Reference book of contemporary statistics.

La Cour, Donna Ward. *Artists in Quotation: A Dictionary of the Creative Thoughts of Painters, Sculptors, Designers, Writers, Educators, and Others.* McFarland 1989 $29.95. ISBN 0-89950-379-9

Langer, William L. (ed). *Encyclopedia of World History.* Houghton 1973 $40.00. ISBN 0-395-13592-3

Levi, Peter. *The Pelican History of Greek Literature.* Penguin 1986 $7.95. ISBN 0-14-022392-4

*Lye, Keith. *Europe.* Watts 1987 $12.40. ISBN 0-531-17068-3 Good introductory work on Europe; with many graphics.

*Marlin, John T., *et al. Book of World City Rankings.* Free Pr $14.95. ISBN 0-02-920240-X Reference book of contemporary data on world cities.

Martin, Michael R., and Gabriel H. Lovett. *Encyclopedia of Latin-American History.* Fritz L. Hoffman and Robert L. Hughes (eds). Greenwood 1981 repr of 1968 ed $35.00. ISBN 0-313-22881-7

McEvedy, Colin. *The Penguin Atlas of North American History to 1870.* Penguin 1988 $6.95. ISBN 0-14-051128-8

McEvedy, Colin. *World History Factfinder.* Smith 1989 $15.98. ISBN 0-8317-9557-3

McKendrick, Melveena. *The Horizon Concise History of Spain.* American Heritage 1973.

Meltzer, Milton. *All Times, All Peoples: A World History of Slavery.* Harper Jr Bks 1980 $13.89. ISBN 0-06-024187-X

*Milner, Gulland R. *Cultural Atlas of Russia and the Soviet Union.* Facts on File 1989 $40.00. ISBN 0-8160-2207-0 Covers Russian and Soviet culture, geography, history, and more.

Morgan, Kenneth O. (ed). *The Oxford Illustrated History of Britain.* Oxford Univ Pr 1986 $18.95. ISBN 0-19-285174-8

*Mundy. *Story of Music. Story of Art Ser.* EDC 1980 $4.95. ISBN 0-86020-443-X Introduction to classical music, life-styles of great composers, and more.

Murphy, E. Jefferson. *History of African Civilization.* Dell 1974 $4.95. ISBN 0-385-28415-2

*Murray, Jocelyn (ed). *Cultural Atlas of Africa. Cultural Atlas Ser.* Facts on File 1981 $40.00. ISBN 0-87196-558-5 Interesting presentation of information on the culture, geography, and history of Africa.

Newhall, Beaumont. *The History of Photography: From 1839 to the Present Day.* Bulfinch 1982 $23.50. ISBN 0-87070-381-1

O'Grada, Cormac. *Ireland Before and After the Famine: Explorations in Economic History, 1800–1925.* St. Martin's 1988 $39.95. ISBN 0-7190-1785-8

Oliver, Roland, and A. Atmore. *Africa Since Eighteen Hundred.* Cambridge Univ Pr 1981 $14.95. ISBN 0-521-29975-6

Oliver, Roland, and A. Atmore. *African Middle Ages, Fourteen Hundred to Eighteen Hundred.* Cambridge Univ Pr 1981 $13.95. ISBN 0-521-29894-6

Oliver, Roland, and Michael Crowder (eds). *The Cambridge Encyclopedia of Africa.* Cambridge Univ Pr 1981 $49.50. ISBN 0-521-23096-9

Oliver, Roland, and J. D. Fage. *A Short History of Africa.* Facts on File 1989 $24.95. ISBN 0-8160-2089-2

Opfell, Olga S. *Queens, Empresses, Grand Duchesses and Regents: Women Rulers of Europe, A.D. 1328–1989.* McFarland 1989 $25.95. ISBN 0-89950-385-3

Palmer, Alan. *The Facts on File Dictionary of Twentieth-Century History.* Facts on File 1981 $24.95.

Parrinder, Geoffrey (ed). *World Religions: From Ancient History to the Present.* Facts on File 1984 $15.95. ISBN 0-8160-1289-X

Parrott, Fred J. *Introduction of African Art of Kenya, Zaire, and Nigeria.* Arco 1972.

Patmore, K. A. *Seven Edwards of England.* Assoc Faculty Pr 1971 repr of 1911 ed $26.00. ISBN 0-8046-1241-2

*Peppin. *Story of Painting. Story of Art Ser.* EDC 1980 $4.95. ISBN 0-86020-441-3 Introduces great paintings and the lives of the old masters.

Pollard, Sidney. *Peaceful Conquest: The Industrialization of Europe, 1760–1970.* Oxford Univ Pr 1981 $14.95. ISBN 0-19-877095-2

Previte-Orton, C. W. (ed). *The Shorter Cambridge Medieval History.* 2 vols. Cambridge Univ Pr 1984 $137.50. ISBN 0-521-05993-3

Radhakrishnan, S. *Indian Religions. Orient Paperbacks Ser.* Ind–US 1981 $3.95. ISBN 0-86578-084-6

Raeburn, Michael, and Alan Kendall (eds). *Heritage of Music.* 4 vols: *Classical Music and Its Origins; The Romantic Era; The 19th Century Legacy; Music in the 20th Century.* Oxford Univ Pr 1989 $195.00. ISBN 0-19-520493-X

*Raghavan, G. N. *Introducing India.* Asia Bk Corp 1983 $10.95. Indian history from the Indus Valley civilization to modern times.

Rand McNally Atlas of World History. Rand 1987 $18.95. ISBN 0-528-83288-3

Rhoodie, Eschel M. *Discrimination Against Women: A Global Survey of the Economic, Educational, Social and Political Status of Women.* McFarland 1989 $39.95. ISBN 0-89950-448-5

Riasanovsky, Nicholas V. *A History of Russia.* Oxford Univ Pr 1984 $32.00. ISBN 0-19-503361-2

Rice, Edward E. *Wars of the Third Kind: Conflict in Underdeveloped Countries.* Univ of California Pr 1988 $18.95. ISBN 0-520-06236-1

Rochelle, Mercedes. *Historical Art Index, A.D. 400–1650: People, Places, and Events Depicted.* McFarland 1989 $39.95. ISBN 0-89950-449-3

Rogerson, John. *Atlas of the Bible. Cultural Atlas Ser.* Facts on File 1984 $40.00. ISBN 0-8160-1207-5

Sachar, Howard M. *A History of Israel: From the Rise of Zionism to Our Time.* Knopf 1979 $19.95. ISBN 0-394-73679-6

Sachar, Howard M. *A History of Israel: From the Aftermath of the Yom Kippur War.* Oxford Univ Pr 1988 $9.95. ISBN 0-19-504623-4

Sagay, J. O., and D. A. Wilson. *Africa, a Modern History: Eighteen Hundred to Nineteen Seventy Five.* Holmes & Meier 1981 $24.50. ISBN 0-8419-0543-6

Seaman, L. C. *From Vienna to Versailles.* Greenwood 1985 repr of 1963 ed $38.50. ISBN 0-313-24841-9

Seaman, L. C. *A New History of England: 410–1975.* B & N Imports 1982 $29.95. ISBN 0-389-20256-8

Serwer-Bernstein, Blanche, and Dov Noy. *Ancient Folktales from Around the World.* Shapolsky 1988 $6.95. ISBN 0-933503-25-3

Seton-Watson, Hugh. *From Lenin to Khrushchev: The History of World Communism. Encore Editions Ser.* Westview 1985 $41.50. ISBN 0-8133-7091-4

*Sivin, Nathan (ed). *Contemporary Atlas of China.* Houghton 1988 $39.95. ISBN 0-395-47329-2 Contemporary information about China; includes broad yet in-depth coverage.

Splendors of the Past: Lost Cities of the Ancient World. National Geographic 1981 $19.95. ISBN 0-87044-358-5 Discusses ancient civilizations.

Starr, Chester G. *The Influence of Sea Power on Ancient History.* Oxford Univ Pr 1988 $8.95. ISBN 0-19-505667-1

Stearns, Peter N., et al (eds). *Documents in World History.* 2 vols. Harper 1987 $15.95 ea. Vol. 1 *The Great Traditions—From Ancient Times to 1500.* ISBN 0-06-046382-1. Vol. 2 *The Modern Centuries—From 1500 to the Present.* ISBN 0-06-046432-1

Stewart, John. *African States and Rulers: An Encyclopedia of Native, Colonial and Independent States and Rulers Past and Present.* McFarland 1989 $45.00. ISBN 0-89950-390-X

Taute, Anne, and John Brook-Little (comps). *Kings and Queens of Great Britain: A Genealogical Chart Showing Their Descent and Relationship.* Crown 1973 $3.95. ISBN 0-517-50344-1

Traynor, John. *International Peacekeeping, 1918–86.* Macmillan 1988 $6.75.

Treadgold, Donald W. *The West in Russia and China. Encore Editions Ser.* Vol. 1 *Russia 1472–1917.* Westview 1985 $30.00. ISBN 0-8133-0254-4

*Van Meter, Vandelia. *World History for Children and Young Adults.* Libraries Unlimited 1990 $29.50. ISBN 0-87287-732-9 Introduction to world history for younger readers.

Varley, H. Paul. *Japanese Culture.* Univ of Hawaii Pr 1984 $12.95. ISBN 0-8248-0927-0

*Waley, Arthur. *The Originality of Japanese Civilization.* Gordon Pr 1980 $60.00. ISBN 0-8490-3199-0 Describes unique aspects of the Japanese way of life.

Ward, Harriet. *World Powers in the Twentieth Century.* Heinemann 1985 $13.00. ISBN 0-435-31911-6

*Wasserman, Burton. *Exploring the Visual Arts.* George F. Horn and Sarita R. Rainey (eds). Davis Pubns 1976 $17.95. ISBN 0-87192-085-9 Illustrated examination of the visual arts.

Wassing, Rene S. *African Art: Its Backgrounds and Tradition.* Crown 1988 $22.95. ISBN 0-517-66271-X

*Williams, E. N. *Facts on File Dictionary of European History: 1485–1789.* Facts on File 1980 $24.95. ISBN 0-87196-327-2 Covers three hundred years of European history, from Tudor England to the French Revolution.

Wright, Arthur F. *Buddhism in Chinese History.* Stanford Univ Pr 1959 $7.95. ISBN 0-8047-0548-8

Wright, Arthur F. (ed). *The Confucian Persuasion.* Stanford Univ Pr 1960 $39.50. ISBN 0-8047-0018-4

Wright, Arthur F. (ed). *Confucianism and Chinese Civilization.* Stanford Univ Pr 1964 $12.95. ISBN 0-8047-0891-6

*Ziring, Lawrence. *Middle East Political Dictionary.* ABC–Clio 1991 $55.00. ISBN 0-87436-612-7 Provides basic information relative to the Middle East.

*Ziring, Lawrence, and C. I. Kim. *The Asian Political Dictionary.* ABC-Clio 1985 $17.00. ISBN 0-87436-369-1 Good contemporary reference on Asia.

PREHISTORY

Asimov, Isaac. *Beginnings: The Story of Origins, of Mankind, Life, the Earth, the Universe.* Berkley 1989 $4.50. ISBN 0-425-11586-0

Auel, Jean M. *The Clan of the Cave Bear. Earth's Children* ™ *Ser.* Bantam 1984 $5.50. ISBN 0-553-25042-6

Auel, Jean M. *The Mammoth Hunters. Earth's Children* ™ *Ser.* Bantam 1986 $4.95. ISBN 0-553-26096-0

Auel, Jean M. *The Plains of Passage. Earth's Children* ™ *Ser.* Crown 1990 $24.95. ISBN 0-517-58049-7

Auel, Jean M. *The Valley of Horses. Earth's Children* ™ *Ser.* Bantam 1984 $5.50. ISBN 0-553-25053-1

*Barry, Iris. *Discovering Archaeology: Stonehenge.* Amer Mus of Nat Hist 1981. Deals with carbon dating, artifact decoding, and the development of writing.

*Baumann, Hans. *The Caves of the Great Hunters.* Pantheon 1962 $3.95. ISBN 0-394-

81006-0 Tells about prehistoric people in Europe living in caves during the Ice Age.

*Branigan, Keith. *Prehistory. History as Evidence Ser.* Watts 1986 $12.40. ISBN 0-531-03745-2 Introduction to prehistory.

Breuil, Henri. *Four Hundred Centuries of Cave Art.* Mary E. Boyle (tr). Hacker 1979 repr of 1952 ed $90.00. ISBN 0-87817-247-5

Breuil, Henri, and M. C. Burkitt. *Rock Paintings of Southern Andalusia: A Description of a Neolithic and Copper Age Art Group.* AMS (repr of 1929 ed) $30.00. ISBN 0-404-15935-4

*Burgess, Robert F. *Man: 12,000 Years Under the Sea.* Dodd 1980. Discussion of underwater archeology and the ability of archeologists to reconstruct past times and events.

*Caselli, Giovanni. *The First Civilizations. History of Everyday Things Ser.* Bedrick 1985 $15.95. ISBN 0-911745-59-9 Examines everyday customs of the earliest societies.

*Ceram, C. W. *Gods, Graves, and Scholars: The Story of Archaeology.* Random 1986 $5.95. ISBN 0-394-74319-9 Discusses archeological contributions of notable persons.

Clark, Wilfrid E. *Early Forerunners of Man.* AMS (repr of 1934 ed) $40.00. ISBN 0-404-15951-X

Clark, Wilfrid E. *The Fossil Evidence for Human Evolution: An Introduction to the Study of Paleoanthropology.* Univ of Chicago Pr 1979 $16.00. ISBN 0-226-10937-2

Cohen, Mark Nathan. *The Food Crisis in Prehistory: Overpopulation and Origins of Agriculture.* Yale Univ Pr 1979 $13.95. ISBN 0-300-02351-0

*Crump, Donald J. (ed). *Mysteries of the Ancient World. Special Publications Ser.* National Geographic 1979 $7.95. ISBN 0-87044-254-6 Probes such mysteries of the distant past as Jericho, the monoliths of Easter Island, and civilizations of the Etruscans, Minoans, and Mycenaeans.

Fagan, Brian M. *Archaeology: A Brief Introduction.* Scott 1988. ISBN 0-673-39719-X

Fagan, Brian M. *People of the Earth: An Introduction to World Prehistory.* Scott 1989. ISBN 0-673-39908-7

Fagan, Brian M. *Quest for the Past: Great Discoveries in Archaeology.* Waveland 1988 $13.95. ISBN 0-88133-344-1

*Gallant, Roy A. *Earth's Changing Climate.* Macmillan 1979 $13.95. ISBN 0-02-736840-8 Examines the effects of changing climate on the earth.

*Gallant, Roy A. *Ice Ages. First Book Ser.* Watts 1985 $10.40. ISBN 0-531-04912-4 Examines time periods when ice sheets covered much of the earth.

Granet, M. *Archaeological Finds from Pre-Qin Sites in Guangdong.* Coronet Bks 1984 $32.50. ISBN 0-317-65567-1

*Johanson, Donald C., and Maitland A. Edey. *Lucy: The Beginnings of Human Kind.* Warner Bks 1982 $13.95. ISBN 0-446-38625 Exciting account of the discovery of "Lucy," the oldest human ancestor yet found.

*Johanson, Donald C., and James Schreeve. *Lucy's Child: The Search for Our Origins.* Morrow 1989 $22.45. ISBN 0-688-06492-2 On-the-scene account of the 1986 discovery of an early hominid, or human ancestor.

Kramer, Samuel Noah (ed). *Mythologies of the Ancient World.* Doubleday 1961 $6.95. ISBN 0-385-09567-8

*McCord, A. *Early Man.* EDC 1977 $5.95. ISBN 0-86020-130-9 Introduction to prehistoric humans.

McEvedy, Colin. *The Penguin Atlas of Ancient History.* Penguin 1986 $6.95. ISBN 0-14-051151-2

*McIntosh, Jane. *The Practical Archaeologist.* Facts on File 1986 $22.95. ISBN 0-8160-1400-0 Describes the work of archeologists and the procedures they use to uncover the past.

*Merriman, Nick. *Early Humans.* Knopf 1989 $12.95. ISBN 0-394-82257-9 Excellent discussion of early humans, with up-to-date findings.

*Millard, A., and J. Chisholm. *First Civilizations.* EDC 1990 $8.95. ISBN 0-7460-0328-5. Illustrated introduction to earliest civilizations.

*Reader, John. *Missing Links: The Hunt for Earliest Man.* Penguin 1989 $7.95. ISBN 0-14-022808-X Illustrated chronological account of human fossil discoveries and the people who found them.

Reader, John. *The Rise of Life: The First 3.5 Billion Years.* Knopf 1986 $15.95. ISBN 0-394-74051-3

*Reynolds, Peter J. *Life in the Iron Age.* Lerner 1979 $8.95. ISBN 0-8225-1214-9 Daily life in an Iron Age civilization.

Ruspoli, Mario. *Cave of Lascaux: The Final Photographs.* Abrams 1987 $49.50. ISBN 0-8109-1267-8

Starr, Chester G. *Early Man: Prehistory and the Civilizations of the Ancient Near East.* Oxford Univ Pr 1973 $14.95. ISBN 0-19-501640-8

*Starr, Chester G. *A History of the Ancient World.* Oxford Univ Pr 1983 $28.00. ISBN 0-19-503144-X Examines social and economic structures of prehistoric societies.

*Whitehouse, Ruth D. (ed). *The Facts on File Dictionary of Archaeology. Facts on File Science Dictionaries Ser.* Facts on File 1988 $12.95. ISBN 0-8160-1893-6 Helpful reference on archeological terms, technology, sites, and more.

*Wolf, Josef. *The Dawn of Man.* Abrams 1978. (o.p.) Interesting illustrated text about prehistoric people.

Wood, Michael. *World Atlas of Archaeology.* Crown 1988 $29.95. ISBN 0-517-66876-9

See also Vol. 2, Anthropology: Evolution.

THE ANCIENT MIDDLE EAST

*Aldred, Cyril. *Akhenaten: King of Egypt.* Thames Hudson 1988 $35.00. ISBN 0-500-05048-1 Discussion of the Egyptian pharaoh who ruled about 1360 BC.

Aldred, Cyril. *Egyptian Art. World of Art Ser.* Thames Hudson 1985 $11.95. ISBN 0-500-20180-3

*Aldred, Cyril. *The Egyptians. Ancient Peoples and Places Ser.* Thames Hudson 1987 $11.95. ISBN 0-500-27345-6 Discusses the earliest people of Egypt and their culture.

*Allan, T. *Pharaohs and Pyramids.* EDC 1977 $5.95. ISBN 0-86020-084-1 Account of life in ancient Egypt during the time of the pharaohs and the building of the pyramids.

*Baines, John, and Jaromir Malek. *Atlas of Ancient Egypt. Cultural Atlas Ser.* Facts on File 1980 $40.00. ISBN 0-87196-334-5 Covers ancient Egypt's culture, geography, history, and more.

*Bowman, Alan K. *Egypt After the Pharaohs.* Univ of California Pr 1989 $12.95. ISBN 0-520-06665-0 History of Egypt from 332 BC to AD 642.

Budge, Ernest A. *Babylonian Life and History.* AMS (repr of 1925 ed) $22.50. ISBN 0-404-11308-7

*Carter, Howard, and A. C. Mace. *The Discovery of the Tomb of Tutankhamen.* Dover 1977 $6.95. ISBN 0-486-23500-9 Describes the discovery of the Egyptian king's tomb, its treasures, and the mysteries surrounding its discovery.

*Carter, Jimmy C., Jr. *The Blood of Abraham: Insights into the Middle East.* Houghton 1985 $15.95. ISBN 0-395-37722-6 Focuses on the biblical and historical background of the present-day Arab-Israeli conflict.

*Caselli, Giovanni. *An Egyptian Craftsman. The Everyday Life of Ser.* Bedrick 1986 $9.95. ISBN 0-87226-100-X Describes the daily duties of a skilled Egyptian.

*Cohen, Daniel. *Ancient Egypt.* Doubleday 1989 $9.95. ISBN 0-385-24586-6 Up-to-date findings on ancient Egypt.

David, A. Rosalie. *Ancient Egyptians: Religious Beliefs and Practices. Religious Beliefs and Practices Ser.* Routledge 1982 $19.95. ISBN 0-7100-0878-3

David, A. Rosalie. *Pyramid Builders of Ancient Egypt: A Modern Investigation of Pharaoh's Workforce.* Routledge 1986 $37.50. ISBN 0-7100-9909-6

■Davidovits, Joseph, and Margie Morris. *The Pyramids: An Enigma Solved.* Hippocrene 1988 $16.95. ISBN 0-87052-559-X Discusses new theories concerning the construction of the pyramids.

*Davies, W. V. *Egyptian Hieroglyphs.* Univ of California Pr 1988 $7.95. ISBN 0-520-06287-6 Examines the writing of ancient Egypt.

*de Lange, Nicholas. *Atlas of the Jewish World. Cultural Atlas Ser.* Facts on File 1984 $40.00. ISBN 0-87196-043-5 Presents the history of the Jewish people in atlas form.

Durant, Will. *Our Oriental Heritage.* Simon 1935 $29.95. ISBN 0-671-54800-X

*Eban, Abba. *Heritage: Civilization and the Jews.* Summit Bks 1986 $16.95. ISBN 0-671-62881-X Account of Jewish civilization from its beginnings to its rebirth in Israel.

*Editors of Time–Life Books. *Age of God–Kings: Time Frame 3000–1500 B.C. Time Frame Ser.* Time–Life 1987 $14.95. ISBN 0-8094-6400-4 Account of ancient civilizations brought to life with illustrations and photographs.

Fischer, Henry G. *Ancient Egyptian Calligraphy: A Beginner's Guide to Writing Hieroglyphs.* Metropolitan Mus of Art 1983 $15.00. ISBN 0-87099-198-1

Gilgamesh. John Gardner and John R. Maier (trs). Random 1985 $12.95. ISBN 0-394-74089-0

*Grant, Michael. *The History of Ancient Israel.* Scribner's 1984 $14.95. ISBN 0-684-18084-7 Illustrated account of the early Hebrews and their kingdoms.

*Harris, Geraldine. *Atlas of Ancient Egypt. Cultural Atlas for Young People Ser.* Facts on File 1990 $17.95. ISBN 0-8160-1971-1 Illustrated introduction to the ancient lands of Egypt.

*Higham, Charles. *The Earliest Farmers and the First Cities.* Lerner 1977 $8.95. ISBN 0-8225-1203-3 History of agriculture and how it affected the people of the ancient Middle East.

Hitti, Philip K. *Arabs: A Short History.* Regnery 1956 $6.95. ISBN 0-89526-982-1

Hurston, Zora Neale. *Moses: Man of the Mountain.* Univ of Illinois Pr 1984 $8.95. ISBN 0-252-01122-8

*Katan, Norma J., and Barbara Mintz. *Hieroglyphs: The Writing of Ancient Egypt.* Macmillan 1981 $12.95. ISBN 0-689-50176-5 Discusses the origins of hieroglyphics and their importance.

*Knapp, Ron. *Tutankhamun and the Mysteries of Ancient Egypt.* Messner 1979 $8.79. ISBN 0-671-33036-5 Story of Egypt's boy-king and the mysteries of that period of Egyptian history.

Kramer, Samuel N. *History Begins at Sumer: Thirty-Nine "Firsts" in Man's Recorded History.* Univ of Penn Pr 1981 $17.95. ISBN 0-8122-1276-2

Kramer, Samuel N. *In the World of Sumer: An Autobiography.* Wayne State Univ Pr 1986 $14.95. ISBN 0-8143-2121-6

Kramer, Samuel N. *Sumerian Mythology: A Study of Spiritual and Literary Achievement in the Third Millennium B.C.* Greenwood 1988 $39.75. ISBN 0-313-26363-9

Kramer, Samuel N. *Sumerians: Their History, Culture, and Character.* Univ of Chicago Pr 1971 $13.95. ISBN 0-226-45238-7

Lepre, J. P. *The Egyptian Pyramids: A Comprehensive, Illustrated Reference.* McFarland 1990 $49.95. ISBN 0-89950-461-2

Lesko, Barbara S. *Remarkable Women of Ancient Egypt.* B. C. Scribe 1987 $8.95. ISBN 0-930548-09-4

Lloyd, Seton, and Hans W. Muller. *Ancient Architecture: Mesopotamia, Egypt, Crete. History of World Architecture Ser.* Rizzoli 1986 $25.00. ISBN 0-8478-0692-8

*Macaulay, David. *Pyramid.* Houghton 1975 $14.95. ISBN 0-395-21407-6 Illustrated account of the construction of the tombs of ancient Egyptian pharaohs.

*Miquel, Pierre. *Ancient Egyptians. Silver Burdett Picture Histories Ser.* Silver 1985 $8.95. ISBN 0-382-06926-9 Illustrated account for younger readers of the earliest people of Egypt.

Oates, Joan. *Babylon. Ancient People and Places Ser.* Thames Hudson 1986 $11.95. ISBN 0-500-27384-7

*Odijk, Pamela. *Phoenicians. Ancient World Ser.* Silver 1989 $14.98. ISBN 0-382-09891-9 Story of the ancient Phoenicians and their culture.

*Pace, Mildred M. *Pyramids: Tombs for Eternity.* McGraw 1981. Discusses how the ancient pyramids were constructed.

*Pace, Mildred M. *Wrapped for Eternity: The Story of the Egyptian Mummies.* McGraw 1974. Discusses the process of mummification.

*Romer, John. *Ancient Lives: Daily Life in Egypt of the Pharaohs.* Holt $18.45. Account of daily customs in early Egypt.

Roux, Georges. *Ancient Iraq.* Penguin 1976 $7.95. ISBN 0-14-020828-3

Samson, Julia. *Nefertiti and Cleopatra—Queen-Monarchs of Ancient Egypt.* Intl Specialized Bk 1987 $19.95. ISBN 0-948695-00-5

Shanks, Hershel. *Ancient Israel.* Prentice 1988 $20.00. ISBN 0-13-036435-5

▪Stead, Miriam. *Egyptian Life.* Harvard Univ Pr 1986 $8.95. ISBN 0-674-24151-7 Discusses everyday life in ancient Egypt, including costume, religion, and social life.

*Unstead, R. J. *Egyptian Town.* *See Inside Ser.* Watts 1986 $11.90. ISBN 0-531-19012-9 Illustrated depiction of a town in ancient Egypt.

West, John A. *Serpent in the Sky: The High Wisdom of Ancient Egypt.* Crown 1987 $12.95. ISBN 0-517-56635-4

*White, J. Manchip. *Ancient Egypt: Its Culture and History.* Dover 1970 $4.95. ISBN 0-486-22548-8 Describes life and events in earliest Egypt.

See also Vol. 1, World Literature: Middle Eastern Literature.

ANCIENT INDIA AND CHINA

Ahir, D. C. *Heritage of Buddhism.* South Asia Bks 1989 $33.50. ISBN 81-7018-552-1

*Barrett, G. W. *Ancient China.* *Then and There Ser.* Longman 1969 $5.25. ISBN 0-582-20453-4 Illustrated account of the earliest times in China.

*Brockington, J. L. *Sacred Thread: Hinduism in Continuity and Diversity.* Columbia Univ Pr 1981 $10.50. ISBN 0-85224-393-6 Presents historical background on the development of Hinduism.

*Buchanan, Keith. *China.* Little 1981. Story of Chinese civilization through photos, maps, charts, and text.

Chang, K. C. *The Archaeology of Ancient China.* Yale Univ Pr 1987 $17.95. ISBN 0-300-03784-8

Chang, K. C. *Art, Myth, and Ritual: The Path to Political Authority in Ancient China.* Harvard Univ Pr 1988 $8.95. ISBN 0-674-04808-3

Chang, K. C. *Food in Chinese Culture: Anthropological and Historical Perspectives.* Yale Univ Pr 1981 $14.95. ISBN 0-300-02759-1

Chou, Hsiang-Kuang. *A History of Chinese Buddhism.* AMS (repr of 1956 ed) $38.00. ISBN 0-404-17255-5

Cotterell, Arthur. *China: A Concise Cultural History.* NAL 1988 $10.95. ISBN 0-452-00950-2

Cotterell, Arthur. *The First Emperor of China.* Penguin 1988 $12.95. ISBN 0-14-011567-6

*Ebrey, Patricia B. (ed). *Chinese Civilization and Society: A Sourcebook.* Free Pr 1981 $16.95. ISBN 0-02-908760-0 Contains sociological and anthropological primary sources.

Ebrey, Patricia B. (tr). *Family and Property in Sung China: Yuan Ts'ai's Precepts for Social Life.* Princeton Univ Pr 1984 $41.50. ISBN 0-691-05426-6

*Goff, Denise. *Early China.* Watts 1986 $11.90. ISBN 0-531-17025-X Introduction to early civilizations in China.

Hirth, Friedrich. *Ancient History of China to the End of the Chou Dynasty.* AMS (repr of 1923 ed) $21.50. ISBN 0-404-03275-3

Kaltenmark, Max. *Lao Tzu and Taoism.* Roger Greaves (tr). Stanford Univ Pr 1969 $7.95. ISBN 0-8047-0689-1

*Kanitkar, Helen, and Hemant Kanitkar. *Asoka and Indian Civilization.* *World History Ser.*

Malcolm Yapp, *et al* (eds). Greenhaven 1980 $2.95. ISBN 0-89908-010-3 Story of the king of Magadha and Indian civilization about 259 BC.

Keightley, David N. (ed). *Early China.* Univ of California Inst of East Asian Studies 1989 $30.00. ISBN 1-55729-011-3

*Keightley, David N. *The Origins of Chinese Civilization.* Univ of California Pr 1983 $18.95. ISBN 0-520-04230-1 Collection of articles on the emergence of China from 5000 to 500 BC.

Keightley, David N. *Sources of Shang History: The Oracle-Bone Inscriptions of Bronze Age China.* Univ of California Pr 1979 $22.50. ISBN 0-520-05455-5

MacKay, Ernest J. *Indus Civilization.* AMS 1983 repr of 1935 ed $27.50. ISBN 0-404-16673-3

*McKillop, Beth. *China.* Great Civilizations Ser. Watts 1988 $11.90. ISBN 0-531-10536-9 Discusses Chinese civilization.

Pande, G. C. *Studies in the Origin of Buddhism.* Orient Bk Dist 1974 $22.50. ISBN 0-8426-0547-9

*Possehl, Gregory L., and M. H. Raval. *Harappan Civilization and Rojdi.* E. J. Brill 1990 $50.00. ISBN 90-04-09157-2 Account of one of the first civilizations of the Indus River valley.

*Radhakrishnan, S. *The Hindu View of Life.* Unwin Paperbacks Ser. Unwin 1988 $9.95. ISBN 0-04-294115-6 Short work on Hindu beliefs and practices.

Rapson, E. J. *Ancient India: From the Earliest Times to the First Century A.D.* Ares 1974 $15.00. ISBN 0-89005-029-5

Rawson, Jessica. *Ancient China: Art and Archaeology.* Harper 1980 $10.95. ISBN 0-06-430109-5

Saha, B. P., and K. S. Bahera. *Ancient History of India.* Advent 1988 $40.00. ISBN 0-7069-3820-8

Sen, Sailendra N. *Ancient Indian History and Civilization.* South Asia Bks 1988 $16.50. ISBN 81-224-0012-4

Twitchett, Denis, and Michael Loewe (eds). *The Cambridge History of China.* Vol. 1 *The Ch'in and Han Empires, 221 BC–AD 220.* Cambridge Univ Pr 1986 $120.00. ISBN 0-521-24327-0

CONFUCIUS *c.* 551–479 BC

Foremost among Chinese philosophers and teachers, Confucius was born to a noble family in northwest China during the Zhou dynasty in a period of great instability caused by constant warfare among rival feudal states. Distressed by the confused state of Zhou society and the poor condition of the Chinese government, Confucius sought to analyze the causes of instability and establish principles by which leaders could govern wisely and people could live together peacefully. Confucius's parents died when he was young, so he had to make his own way in the world. After completing his studies, he entered government service and also served as a teacher. He attracted a great many disciples, some in high government positions who spread his teachings. His views, however, gained him enemies, and eventually he was forced to resign his government post. He spent the final years of his life teaching and studying literary classics. After his teachings became widely known, he was given the title of Supreme Sage and Foremost Teacher.

Confucius's teachings were recorded by his followers in the *Analects,* which later became one of the Chinese classics. A collection of thoughts, dialogues, and sayings, it shows Confucius's concern with proper human behavior, which he spelled out through the "Five Relationships"—the obligations and responsibilities of ruler and the ruled, father and son, husband and wife, brother and brother, and neighbor and neighbor. Confucius's teachings served as a foundation for an education system that provided the country with "gentlemen scholars," or bureaucrats, who became the backbone of Chinese government. Confucius's teachings also became the foundation of a philosophy of life known as Confucianism. Gradually over time, Confucianism became a religion for the Chinese people, the practice of which continued well into the twentieth century.

BOOKS BY CONFUCIUS

The Analects of Confucius. American Classical Coll Pr 1986 $127.75. ISBN 0-89266-538-6
Sayings of Confucius. James R. Ware (tr). NAL 1955 $3.95. ISBN 0-451-62672-9
The Wisdom of Confucius. Lin Yutang (ed and tr). Modern Lib 1938 $6.95. ISBN 0-394-60426-1

BOOKS ABOUT CONFUCIUS

*Johnson, Spencer. *The Value of Honesty: The Story of Confucius. Value Tales Ser.* Oak Tree 1979 $7.95. ISBN 0-916392-36-8 Recounts the life of the renowned Chinese sage whose teachings and sayings have been handed down over the centuries.
*Paley, Alan L. *Confucius: Ancient Chinese Philosopher. Outstanding Personalities Ser.* D. Steve Rahmas (ed). SamHar 1973 $2.50. ISBN 0-87157-059-9 Account of the renowned philosopher of ancient China.
*Rowland-Entwistle, Theodore. *Confucius and Ancient China. Life and Times Ser.* Watts 1987 $12.40. ISBN 0-513-18101-4 Introductory account of the notable Chinese philosopher.

LAO-TZU   *c.* 604–531 BC

The Chinese philosopher known as Lao-Tzu, or "the Master," was born about 604 BC. and served as chief librarian at the royal court. According to legend, in about 531 BC, at the age of 73, Lao-Tzu set off for Tibet on the back of a water buffalo. At the border he was stopped by a guard and asked to write down his beliefs before leaving China. Lao-Tzu agreed, and the result was a small volume, of about 5,000 characters, much of it in rhymed verse, called *Tao Te Ching,* or "The Way and Its Power." This book became the basis for a school of thought called Taoism, and Lao-Tzu riding on a water buffalo became one of the most popular subjects in Chinese painting.

Taoism teaches that people should ignore such values as money and political power. Instead, they should try to live close to nature and concentrate on developing individual talents. In that way, they will be in harmony with *tao,* the force that governs the universe. Taoism offers a mystical view of life that is very different from Confucianism. (*See* Confucius, Vol. 2, World History: Ancient India and China.) It distrusts human institutions, such as government, and also human ambition and striving, which are all important elements of Confucian thought.

Although Lao-Tzu did not establish a religion, Taoism eventually developed a series of gods and goddesses and a hierarchy of priests. For a time it also included a belief in magic, including an elixir of immortality and charms that protected against disease and wild animals. Around the seventh and eighth centuries AD, certain elements of Taoism combined with Buddhism to form Zen Buddhism, which eventually spread to Japan and became one of that country's main religions. In China, Taoism was officially abolished by the Communists in the 1950s.

BOOKS BY LAO-TZU

The Light of China: Selections. Krishna $79.95. ISBN 0-87968-534-4
Way of Life: Tao Te Ching. R. B. Blakney (tr). NAL 1955 $3.95. ISBN 0-451-62563-3

BOOKS ABOUT LAO-TZU

Commentary on the Lao Tzu by Wang Pi. Ariane Rump and Wing-Tsit Chan (trs). Univ of Hawaii Pr 1979 $11.00. ISBN 0-8248-0677-8 Close analysis of the writings of Lao-Tzu.

Man-ch'ing, Cheng. *Lao-Tzu: My Words Are Very Easy to Understand.* Tam Gibbs and Juh-Hua Huang (trs). North Atlantic 1981 $9.95. ISBN 0-913028-91-6 Examination of the meaning of Lao-Tzu's writings.

Welch, Holmes. *Taoism: The Parting of the Way.* Beacon 1966 $9.95. ISBN 0-8070-5973-0 Examines the philosophy of Taoism expounded by the ancient Chinese philosopher Lao-Tzu.

ANCIENT GREECE

*Asimov, Isaac. *Greeks: A Great Adventure.* Houghton 1965 $14.95. ISBN 0-395-06574-7 History of Greece from 2000 BC to about AD 1204.

Biers, William R. *The Archaeology of Greece: An Introduction.* Cornell Univ Pr 1987 $17.95. ISBN 0-8014-9406-0

Bingham, Marjorie W., and Susan H. Gross. *Women in Ancient Greece and Rome.* Glenhurst 1983 $8.95. ISBN 0-914227-00-9

Bloom, Harold (ed). *Sophocles.* Modern Critical Views Ser. Chelsea 1990 $26.50. ISBN 1-55546-323-1

Boardman, John. *The Greeks Overseas: Their Early Colonies and Trade.* Thames Hudson 1982 $12.95. ISBN 0-500-27233-6

Boardman, John (ed). *The Oxford History of the Classical World: Greece and the Hellenistic World.* Oxford Univ Pr 1988 $18.95. ISBN 0-19-282165-2

Bowder, Diana. *Who Was Who in the Greek World.* Washington Square Pr 1984 $8.95. ISBN 0-671-50159-3

Burford, Alison. *Craftsmen in Greek and Roman Society.* Cornell Univ Pr 1972. (o.p.)

*Caselli, Giovanni. *The Greek Potter.* The Everyday Life of Ser. Bedrick 1986 $9.95. ISBN 0-87226-101-8 Account of activities of an early Greek potter.

*Connolly, Peter. *The Greek Armies.* Armies of the Past Ser. Silver 1985 $8.75. ISBN 0-382-06909-9 Account of ancient Greek armies and how they fought.

*Crosher, Judith. *The Greeks.* Peoples of the Past Ser. Silver 1985 $6.75. ISBN 0-382-06913-7 Describes the lives of ancient Greeks.

*Davis, William S. *Day in Old Athens.* Biblo (repr of 1914 ed) $16.00. ISBN 0-8196-0111-X Presents daily life and customs of ancient Athenians.

*Durant, Will. *Life of Greece.* Simon 1939 $29.95. ISBN 0-671-41800-9 History of Greek civilization.

*Evans, C., and A. Millard. *Greek and Norse Legends.* Myths and Legends Ser. EDC 1987 $10.95. ISBN 0-7460-0240-8 Informative reference on Greek mythology.

*Evans, C., and A. Millard. *Greek Myths and Legends.* Myths and Legends Ser. EDC 1986 $6.95. ISBN 0-86020-946-6 Stories of ancient Greek gods, goddesses, and monsters.

*Fine, John V. *The Ancient Greeks: A Critical History.* Harvard Univ Pr 1985 $16.95. ISBN 0-674-03314-0 Examines critically the history of ancient Greece.

Finley, M. I. *Early Greece: The Bronze and Archaic Ages.* Ancient Culture and Society Ser. Norton 1982 $5.95. ISBN 0-393-30051-X

Finley, M. I. *The World of Odysseus.* Peter Smith 1988 $15.75. ISBN 0-8446-6298-4

Fisher, Leonard E. *Olympians: Great Gods and Goddesses of Ancient Greece.* Holiday 1984 $5.95. ISBN 0-8234-0740-3

Fitzhardings, L. F. *The Spartans.* Ancient Peoples and Places Ser. Thames Hudson 1985 $10.95. ISBN 0-500-27364-2

Gardner, Ernest A. *Ancient Athens.* World History Ser. Haskell 1969 repr of 1902 ed $59.95. ISBN 0-8383-0945-3

*Glubok, Shirley, and Alfred Tamarin. *Olympic Games in Ancient Greece.* Harper Jr Bks 1976 $13.89. ISBN 0-06-022048-1 Account of earliest Olympic games.

*Grant, Michael. *The Classical Greeks.* Macmillan 1989 $27.50. ISBN 0-684-19126-1 Profiles 37 notable ancient Greeks and their impact on the past and present Greek world.

*Grant, Michael. *From Alexander to Cleopatra: The Hellenistic World.* Scribner's 1982 $14.95. ISBN 0-684-17819-2 Overview of the Hellenistic period of ancient Greece.

Green, Peter. *The Shadow of the Parthenon: Studies in Ancient History and Literature.* Univ of California Pr 1973 $35.00. ISBN 0-520-02322-6

Harris, H. A. *Sport in Greece and Rome. Aspects of Greek and Roman Life Ser.* Cornell Univ Pr 1972 $27.95. ISBN 0-8014-0718-4

*Ipsen, D. C. *Archimedes.* Enslow 1989 $13.95. ISBN 0-89490-161-3 General biography of the ancient Greek mathematician, physicist, and inventor.

*King, Perry S. *Pericles. World Leaders—Past and Present Ser.* Chelsea 1988 $17.95. ISBN 0-87754-547-2 Introduction to the Greek statesman who improved the Athenian city–state during his years as elected leader, 460–429 BC.

*Kitto, H. D. *The Greeks.* Peter Smith 1988 $15.25. ISBN 0-8446-6303-4 Describes the people of classical Greece and their warfare.

Lacey, W. K. *The Family in Classical Greece. Aspects of Greek and Roman Life Ser.* Cornell Univ Pr 1984 $13.95. ISBN 0-8014-9274-2

Lefkowitz, Mary R., and Maureen B. Fant (eds). *Women's Life in Greece and Rome.* Johns Hopkins Univ Pr 1982 $12.00. ISBN 0-8018-2866-X

*Levi, Peter. *Atlas of the Greek World. Cultural Atlas Ser.* Facts on File 1981 $40.00. ISBN 0-87196-448-1 Cultural study of ancient Greece from the Bronze Age through Pericles and Alexander the Great.

*Ling, Roger. *The Greek World.* Bedrick 1990 $19.95. ISBN 0-87226-301-0 Describes life in ancient Greece through many illustrations as well as text.

MacKendrick, Paul. *The Greek Stones Speak: The Story of Archaeology in Greek Lands.* Norton 1983 $12.95. ISBN 0-393-30111-7

*McLellan, Elizabeth. *Minoan Crete. Aspects of Greek Life Ser.* Longman 1976 $4.95. ISBN 0-582-20671-5 Illustrated account of life in the ancient Minoan civilization.

*Millard, A., and S. Peach. *The Greeks.* EDC 1990 $8.95. ISBN 0-7460-0342-0 Greek history in pictures, charts, maps, and text.

Phillips, E. D. *Aspects of Greek Medicine.* Charles 1987 repr of 1973 ed $23.95. ISBN 0-914783-18-1

*Rutland, Jonathan. *Ancient Greek Town. See Inside Ser.* Watts 1986 $11.90. ISBN 0-531-19010-2 Illustrated description of an ancient Greek town.

*Starr, Chester G. *Ancient Greeks.* Oxford Univ Pr 1971 $14.95. ISBN 0-19-501248-8 Introduces the people of ancient Greece.

Starr, Chester G. *The Economic and Social Growth of Early Greece, 800–500 BC.* Oxford Univ Pr 1977 $7.95. ISBN 0-19-502224-6

*Starr, Chester G. *Individual and Community: The Rise of Polis, 800–500 BC.* Oxford Univ Pr 1986 $24.95. ISBN 0-19-503971-8 Describes the development of city–states in early Greece.

*Stone, I. F. *The Trial of Socrates.* Doubleday 1989 $9.95. ISBN 0-385-26032-6 Account of the great philosopher's trial, conviction, and execution.

*Thubron, Colin. *The Ancient Mariners. Seafarers Ser.* Silver 1981. (o.p.) $21.27. ISBN 0-8094-2739-7 History of naval battles of the ancient Greeks and Romans.

Turner, E. G. *Greek Papyri: An Introduction.* Oxford Univ Pr 1981 $24.00. ISBN 0-19-814841-0

Wallbank, R. W. *The Hellenistic World.* Harvard Univ Pr 1982 $8.95. ISBN 0-674-38725-2

White, K. D. *Greek and Roman Technology. Aspects of Greek and Roman Life Ser.* Cornell Univ Pr 1983 $44.50. ISBN 0-8014-1439-3

*Wood, Michael. *In Search of the Trojan War.* NAL 1987 $12.95. ISBN 0-452-25960-6 Examines archeological evidence for historical facts to support the epic of the Trojan War written by the Greek poet Homer.

Yartz, Frank J. *Ancient Greek Philosophy: Sourcebook and Perspective.* McFarland 1984 $25.95. ISBN 0-89950-111-7

ARISTOTLE 384–322 BC

See also Aristotle, Vol. 2, Biology: The Classification of Organisms.

Aristotle, one of the world's greatest philosophers, was born in northern Greece in the small town of Stagira. His father was the personal physician to Amyntas II, the king of Macedonia and grandfather of Alexander the Great. At age 17, Aristotle went to the city of Athens to attend the Academy, the school of the great philosopher and teacher Plato. At the Academy young men studied a variety of subjects, from medicine and biology to astronomy and mathematics. Each student shared a common commitment to organize human knowledge in a systematic way and expand it in all areas.

Aristotle remained at the Academy for 20 years, first as a student and then as a teacher. After Plato's death in 347 BC, Aristotle left the Academy and went to the court of Hermias of Atarneus, where he became advisor to the ruler and married his daughter. Four years later, in 343 BC, his fame as a teacher led him to the Macedonian court to tutor the young Alexander the Great. When Alexander became king of Macedonia, Aristotle returned to Athens and started his own school, the Lyceum. While Aristotle taught at the Lyceum, Athens lost its independence and became a part of Alexander the Great's empire, causing a great deal of resentment among many of the city's citizens.

Soon after Alexander the Great died in 323 BC, there was an outbreak of anti-Macedonian feeling in Athens. Aristotle had enemies because of his ties to Alexander and the Macedonian court. He was charged with impiety, or failure to honor the gods, and faced prosecution. Rather than stand trial, Aristotle fled to the city of Chalcis; he died the following year.

The Death of Socrates. Engraving after the painting by David (1797). Courtesy of Historical Picture Service.

Aristotle and his teacher Plato are generally considered the two most influential philosophers in the history of Western thought. Aristotle's special contribution was his attempt to systematize all the knowledge of the time. This attempt resulted in his thinking and writing in a number of disciplines, including logic, ethics, and literature. In the area of logic, Aristotle was the first to propose the idea of deductive reasoning, in which a truth may be deduced from other facts. In ethics he held that the ultimate purpose of human life was the quest for the good, which he defined as moderation in all things. In his work, the *Poetics,* Aristotle put forth ideas about tragedy that greatly influenced modern classical drama.

From the third century onward, Aristotle's ideas were eclipsed in Western Europe by those of Plato, which were more compatible with the religious thought of the time. In the Middle Ages, however, Aristotle was reintroduced to the West through the writings of Arab and Jewish scholars. The effects of his thinking continue to be felt today.

BOOKS BY ARISTOTLE

Aristotle's Constitution of Athens. The Philosophy of Plato and Aristotle Ser. Ayer (repr of 1912 ed) $23.00. ISBN 0-405-04857-2
Politics. Ernest Barker (tr). Oxford Univ Pr 1946 $9.95. ISBN 0-19-500306-3

BOOKS ABOUT ARISTOTLE

Adler, Mortimer J. *Aristotle for Everybody.* Bantam 1983 $4.50. ISBN 0-553-26776-0 Introduction to Aristotle and his work.
Jaeger, Werner. *Aristotle.* Oxford Univ Pr 1948. (o.p.) Basic history of Aristotle's development as a philosopher.

HERODOTUS *c.* 484–425 BC

The Greek historian Herodotus, often called the Father of History, was born in Asia Minor in the fifth century BC. Even as a young man Herodotus was curious about the events happening around him. He traveled over much of the known world, visiting Egypt, Mesopotamia, parts of southern Russia, and most of the northern coast of Africa. Everywhere he went, Herodotus wrote lively descriptions of the people he met and the places he visited.

Herodotus spent much of his life writing a detailed account of the Persian Wars, the great conflict between the Greeks and Persians that had taken place before he was born. Although he wrote his *History* over 2,000 years ago, Herodotus' style remains simple and understandable. The book presents a wonderful story—a story full of adventure and tragedy, heroes and villains, glory and sadness.

In his writing, Herodotus tried to be as accurate as possible. While relying partly on ancient stories and legends, he was careful to make his own investigations of recent events. Throughout his *History,* Herodotus distinguishes between the things he had personally seen or researched and those he had simply heard about. If there were conflicting accounts of an event, Herodotus would record them all and indicate to his readers which description was probably the most accurate.

Once dubbed the "Father of Lies," Herodotus has been proven by modern research to be a fairly reliable source of history. His work presents not only a reasonably accurate description of an important period in history but also a brilliant and entertaining story.

BOOKS BY HERODOTUS

Histories. Penguin Classics Ser. Aubrey de Selincourt (tr). Penguin 1954 $5.95. ISBN 0-14-044034-8

The Persian Wars. George R. Rawlinson (tr). McGraw 1964 $6.95. ISBN 0-07-553640-4

BOOKS ABOUT HERODOTUS

Dahlmann, Friedrich C. *The Life of Herodotus.* G. Valentine Cox (tr). Longwood 1979 repr of 1845 ed $20.00. ISBN 0-89341-256-2 Introduction to Herodotus and his work as a historian.

Evans, J. A. *Herodotus. Twayne's World Authors Ser.* G. K. Hall 1982. (o.p.) $16.95. Profile of Herodotus for the general reader.

Immerwahr, Henry R. *Form and Thought in Herodotus.* Scholars Pr 1983 $27.00. ISBN 0-89130-478-9 Scholarly treatment of Herodotus and his work.

Lowe, W. D. *Herodotus: The Wars of Greece and Persia.* Bolchazy–Carducci 1984 $10.00. ISBN 0-86516-054-6 Discusses Herodotus' history of the Persian Wars.

Waters, K. H. *Herodotus the Historian: His Problems, Methods, and Originality.* Univ of Oklahoma Pr 1985 $21.50. ISBN 0-8061-1928-4 Comprehensive introduction to Herodotus' background, aims, and methods.

PLUTARCH *c.* AD 46–*c.* 125

The Greek essayist and biographer Plutarch was born into a well-to-do Greek family. Plutarch studied at Athens and then traveled widely through Greece, Asia Minor, Egypt, and Rome. While living in Rome (*c.* 69–70), he lectured on philosophy. On returning to his home in Chaeronea, near Delphi, Plutarch conducted a private school. He also served as a chief magistrate and a market commissioner and became a priest at Delphi. An exceptionally well-read person, he spent most of his spare time reading, writing, and conversing with people.

Plutarch's masterwork, *Parallel Lives of Greeks and Romans,* consists of 50 biographies of prominent Greeks and Romans. Forty-six of these biographies are arranged in pairs—a biography of a Greek followed by one of a Roman and then a comparison of the two. The emphasis in *Parallel Lives* is on moral character, and the biographies focus on the virtues and vices of the individuals as seen through their actions. Although originally written to inspire young readers, the chief value of Plutarch's biographies today is the historical information they provide. In addition to *Parallel Lives,* Plutarch also wrote numerous essays on a wide range of subjects. The 78 essays that survive today are known collectively as the "Moralia."

The works of Plutarch were not published until the eleventh century, by which time some had already been lost. In 1579 *Parallel Lives* was translated into English for the first time. This translation became an important source used by William Shakespeare for his plays *Julius Caesar, Antony and Cleopatra,* and *Coriolanus.* (*See* Shakespeare, Vol. 1, British Literature: The Renaissance.)

BOOKS BY PLUTARCH

The Age of Alexander. Penguin Classics Ser. Ian Scott-Kilvert (tr). Penguin 1973 $5.95. ISBN 0-14-044286-3

The Fall of the Roman Republic: Six Roman Lives. Penguin Classics Ser. Rex Warner (tr). Penguin 1954 $6.95. ISBN 0-14-044084-4

The Makers of Rome: Nine Lives by Plutarch. Ian Scott-Kilvert (tr). Hippocrene 1985 $16.95. ISBN 0-88029-045-5

Parallel Lives. 11 vols. Harvard Univ Pr. Vol. 1 $14.50. ISBN 0-674-99052-8. Vol. 2 $14.50. ISBN 0-674-99053-6. Vol. 3 $14.50. ISBN 0-674-99072-2. Vol. 6 $14.50.

ISBN 0-674-99109-5. Vol. 7 $14.50. ISBN 0-674-99110-9. Vol. 8 $14.50. ISBN 0-674-99111-7. Vol. 9 $14.50. ISBN 0-674-99112-5. Vol. 10 $14.50. ISBN 0-674-99113-3. Vol. 11 $14.50. ISBN 0-674-99114-1

Plutarch's Lives. John S. White (ed). Biblo (repr of 1900 ed) $18.00. ISBN 0-8196-0174-8

The Rise and Fall of Athens: Nine Greek Lives. Penguin Classics Ser. Ian Scott-Kilvert (tr). Penguin 1960 $5.95. ISBN 0-14-044102-6

BOOKS ABOUT PLUTARCH

Barrow, Reginald H. *Plutarch and His Times.* AMS (repr of 1967 ed) $19.00. ISBN 0-404-15276-7 Biography of the Greek essayist and biographer that focuses on his times.

Jones, C. P. *Plutarch and Rome.* Clarendon 1971. ISBN 0-10-814363-X Part 1 places Plutarch against his background; Part 2 examines his attitude toward Rome.

Stradter, Philip A. *A Commentary on Plutarch's Pericles.* Univ of North Carolina Pr 1989 $45.00. ISBN 0-8078-1861-5 Critical discussion of Plutarch's biography of the great Athenian statesman.

Stradter, Philip A. *Plutarch's Historical Methods: An Analysis of the Mulierum Virtues. Loeb Classic Lib.* Harvard Univ Pr 1965. (o.p.) $12.50. Analysis of one of Plutarch's essays, focusing on his historical method.

THUCYDIDES *c.* 460–400 BC

The Athenian historian Thucydides is considered by many to be the greatest historian of ancient Greece. The first to write about contemporary events in which he himself participated, Thucydides set very high standards for accuracy and criticized other historians for including myths and inaccuracies in their histories and chronologies.

Born in Athens around the year 460 BC, Thucydides was of an aristocratic family from Thrace. He was educated in Athens during the Golden Age of the statesman Pericles. During the early years of the Peloponnesian War between Athens and Sparta, Thucydides served in the Athenian navy and was made a general in 424–423 BC. While stationed in Thrace, he failed to prevent a Spartan general from capturing an Athenian colony there and was exiled from Athens as a result. For the rest of the war he remained in Thrace or traveled around collecting material for a history of the war. Although he returned to Athens in 403 after the city fell to the Spartans, it is believed that he died in Thrace.

Thucydides wrote his *History of the Peloponnesian War* in order to provide an exact account of what happened and to help predict and control future events. His view that future events would resemble those of the past was based on a belief that human nature remains basically unchanged overtime and is the primary cause of events. To depict character and human nature, Thucydides inserted speeches into his narrative. These speeches, some of which, like the funeral oration of Pericles, are quite eloquent, are brilliant portraits of human motivation and psychology.

Unfortunately, Thucydides did not live to complete his history. It ends, virtually in mid-sentence, while discussing the events of the year 404 BC.

BOOK BY THUCYDIDES

The Peloponnesian War. Richard Crawley (tr). Modern Lib 1981 $3.00. ISBN 0-394-30951-0

BOOKS ABOUT THUCYDIDES

Cogan, Marc. *The Human Thing: The Speeches and Principles of Thucydides' History.* Univ of Chicago Pr 1981 $20.00. ISBN 0-226-11194-6 Commentary on the speeches of

Thucydides' history and an analysis of their interpretation of the Peloponnesian War.

Connor, W. Robert. *Thucydides.* Princeton Univ Pr 1984 $34.50. ISBN 0-691-03569-5 Comprehensive account of the Greek historian and his work.

Woodhead, A. Geoffrey. *Thucydides on the Nature of Power.* Harvard Univ Pr 1970. ISBN 0-674-89136-8 Examination of Thucydides' view of power and the implications of his hostility toward democracy.

See also Vol. 1, World Literature: Classical Greek Literature.

ANCIENT ROME

*Amery, H., and P. Vanags. *Rome and Romans.* EDC 1976 $6.95. ISBN 0-86020-070-1 Colorfully illustrated account of life in ancient Rome.

Balsdon, John. *Roman Women, Their History and Habits.* Greenwood 1975 repr of 1962 ed $48.50. ISBN 0-8371-8040-6

Birley, Anthony. *Marcus Aurelius.* Yale Univ Pr 1987 $30.00. ISBN 0-300-03844-5

Boardman, John (ed). *The Oxford History of the Classical World: The Roman World.* Oxford Univ Pr 1988 $18.95. ISBN 0-19-282166-0

Bowder, Diana. *Who Was Who in the Roman World.* Washington Square Pr 1984 $8.95. ISBN 0-671-50160-7

*Carcopino, Jerome. *Daily Life in Ancient Rome: The People and the City at the Height of the Empire.* Henry T. Rowell (ed). E. O. Lorimer (tr). Yale Univ Pr 1940 $11.95. ISBN 0-300-00031-6 Discusses social conditions in ancient Rome.

*Caselli, Giovanni. *The Roman Empire and the Dark Ages. History of Everyday Things Ser.* Bedrick 1985 $15.95. ISBN 0-911745-58-0 Illustrated account of everyday events during the Roman Empire.

*Caselli, Giovanni. *A Roman Soldier. Everyday Life of Ser.* Bedrick 1986 $9.95. ISBN 0-87226-106-9 Account of a Roman soldier performing his scheduled duties.

*Chadwick, Henry, and Gillian R. Evans (eds). *Atlas of the Christian Church. Cultural Atlas Ser.* Facts on File 1987 $40.00. ISBN 0-8160-1643-7 Looks at Christian tradition and its impact on Western civilization.

*Connolly, Peter. *Hannibal and the Enemies of Rome. Armies of the Past Ser.* Silver 1985 $8.75. ISBN 0-382-06911-0 Tells about Rome's enemies and how Romans dealt with them.

*Corbishley, Mike. *Roman World.* Watts 1986 $13.90. ISBN 0-531-19018-8 Account of Rome during its early history.

*Cornell, Tim, and John Matthews. *Atlas of the Roman World. Cultural Atlas Ser.* Facts on File 1982 $40.00. ISBN 0-87196-652-2 Atlas and historical account of Rome from its beginnings in the eighth century BC to the mid-sixth century AD.

*Davis, William S. *Day in Old Rome.* Biblo $16.00. ISBN 0-8196-0106-3 Describes daily life and customs in ancient Rome.

Gibbon, Edward. *The Decline and Fall of the Roman Empire.* Fawcett 1987 $3.95. ISBN 0-449-30056-0

*Grant, Michael. *The Etruscans.* Scribner's 1981 $17.50. ISBN 0-684-16724-7 Account of the first advanced civilization in Italy.

Grant, Michael. *History of Rome.* Macmillan 1978. ISBN 0-02-345610-8

*Grant, Michael. *Nero. Reprints Ser.* Dorset 1989 $15.95. ISBN 0-88029-311-X Story of a cruel Roman emperor who ruled during the first century AD.

Grant, Michael. *The Roman Emperors: A Biographical Guide to the Rulers of Imperial Rome: 31 BC–AD 476* Scribner's 1985 $25.00. ISBN 0-684-18388-9

*Hodge, Peter. *Roman Towns. Aspects of Roman Life Ser.* Longman 1977 $4.95. ISBN 0-582-20301-5 Discusses life and customs in the towns of ancient Rome.

*Hoobler, Dorothy, and Thomas Hoobler. *Cleopatra. World Leaders—Past and Present Ser.* Chelsea 1986 $17.95. ISBN 0-87754-589-8 Story of the queen of Egypt at whose death Egypt became a province of the Roman Empire.

*Kittredge, Mary. *Marc Antony. World Leaders—Past and Present Ser.* Chelsea 1988 $17.95. ISBN 0-87754-505-7 Account of the Roman politician, soldier, and friend of Julius Caesar who ruled the eastern part of the Roman world and fell in love with Cleopatra.

*Macaulay, David. *City: A Story of Roman Planning and Construction.* Houghton 1983 $6.95. ISBN 0-395-34922-2 Planning a make-believe city in the Roman Empire.

MacDonald, William L. *The Architecture of the Roman Empire: An Introductory Study.* Yale Univ Pr 1982 $17.95. ISBN 0-300-02819-9

Mack, Sara. *Ovid.* Yale Univ Pr 1988 $27.50. ISBN 0-300-04294-9

MacKendrick, Paul. *The Mute Stones Speak: The Story of Archaeology in Italy.* Norton 1983 $11.70. ISBN 0-393-30119-2

Millar, Fergus, and Erich Segal (eds). *Caesar Augustus: Seven Aspects.* Oxford Univ Pr 1984 $19.95. ISBN 0-19-814858-5

*Miquel, Pierre. *Life in Ancient Rome. Silver Burdett Picture Histories Ser.* Silver 1984 $8.95. ISBN 0-382-06925-0 Interesting illustrated account for younger people of ancient Roman life.

Scarborough, John. *Roman Medicine. Aspects of Greek and Roman Life Ser.* Cornell Univ Pr 1970. (o.p.) $29.50.

*Schlesinger, Arthur M., Jr. (ed). *Attila: King of the Huns. World Leaders—Past and Present Ser.* Chelsea 1989 $17.95. ISBN 1-55546-803-9 Account of the feared Asian leader who attacked the Roman Empire.

*Starr, Chester G. *Ancient Romans.* Oxford Univ Pr 1971 $14.95. ISBN 0-19-501454-5 Introduction to the people of ancient Rome.

Starr, Chester G. *The Beginnings of Imperial Rome: Rome in the Mid-Republic.* Univ of Michigan Pr 1980 $12.50. ISBN 0-472-09317-7

Starr, Chester G. *The Emergence of Rome: As a Ruler of the Western World. The Development of Western Civilization Ser.* Greenwood 1982 repr of 1953 ed $35.00. ISBN 0-313-23561-9

Starr, Chester G. *The Roman Empire, Twenty-Seven BC to Four Hundred Seventy-Six AD: A Study in Survival.* Oxford Univ Pr 1982 $11.95. ISBN 0-19-503130-X

*Tingay, Graham I. F., and John Badcock. *These Were the Romans.* Dufour 1989 $14.95. ISBN 0-8023-1285-3 An excellent source of all kinds of information about Rome and its empire that contains many photographs and quotes from the original documents.

*Tingay, Graham I. F., and A. Marks. *The Romans.* EDC 1990 $8.95. ISBN 0-7460-0340-4 Illustrated history of the ancient Romans.

*Walworth, Nancy Z. *Constantine the Great: Roman Emperor. World Leaders—Past and Present Ser.* Chelsea 1989 $17.95. ISBN 1-55546-805-5 Account of the first Christian emperor of Rome.

Ware, William. *Zenobia; or, the Fall of Palmyra.* 2 vols. AMS (repr of 1837 ed) $75.00. ISBN 0-404-17430-2

CAESAR, JULIUS   *c.* 100–44 BC

Julius Caesar, the outstanding general and ancient Roman leader, was born into a noble family that had fallen from influence. Early in his life he allied himself with Gaius Marius, a popular general and member of the Roman Senate. To strengthen his ties to Marius, Caesar married Cornelia, the daughter of a powerful friend of Marius. When Lucius Sulla, a powerful senator, defeated Marius and his supporters in a civil war, he ordered Caesar to divorce Cornelia. Caesar refused and fled Rome.

After Sulla's death, Caesar returned to Rome and gained increasing prominance as a result of a series of well-run political and military campaigns. In 60 and 59 BC he and two important senators—Crassus, the richest man in Rome, and Pompey, a prominant general—formed the First Triumvirate and controlled Roman legislation. For the next 10 years Caesar was also governor of three important Roman provinces—Illyricum, Cisalpine Gaul, and Transalpine Gaul. To carry out his responsibilities as governor, he raised and trained a large army, which he led brilliantly in conquests of Gaul (present-day France) and Britain. The wealth and fame gained from these conquests made the victorious general enormously popular with his soldiers and with the Roman people.

In 49 BC, after Caesar's former ally Pompey and others in the Senate tried to prevent Caesar from taking the position of Roman Consul, Caesar brought his army across the Rubicon River dividing Gaul from Italy, an act that began a civil war with Pompey. Caesar's well-trained army quickly routed Pompey, who fled with his troops to Greece. Caesar followed and defeated Pompey, who this time fled to Egypt. Again Caesar followed, but on arriving in Egypt he found that Pompey had been murdered. While there, Caesar met Cleopatra and made her queen of Egypt.

Caesar returned to Rome in 45 BC and was made dictator. As dictator he introduced numerous popular reforms, which helped increase his power. He limited the distribution of free grain, reduced debts, gave land to poor farmers, revised the tax structure, and extended Roman citizenship to many non-Romans. One of his most enduring reforms was the introduction of a new, improved calendar. As Caesar's popularity and power increased, his enemies began to fear that he intended to make himself king, and they plotted his overthrow. On the Ides of March (March 15), 44 BC, Caesar was stabbed to death by a group of conspirators who had once been his friends.

In addition to his remarkable career as a general and political leader, Julius Caesar wrote an account of his military campaigns that is considered a model of Latin style and clear writing.

BOOKS BY CAESAR

The Civil War. Penguin Classics Ser. Jane E. Mitchell (tr). Penguin 1976 $5.95. ISBN 0-14-044187-5
The Conquest of Gaul. Penguin Classics Ser. S. A. Handford (tr). Penguin 1983 $5.95. ISBN 0-14-044433-5

BOOKS ABOUT CAESAR

*Bruns, Roger. *Julius Caesar. World Leaders—Past and Present.* Chelsea 1987 $17.95. ISBN 0-87754-514-6 Account of the life of the prominent Roman leader.
Fowler, William W. *Julius Caesar and the Foundation of the Roman Imperial System. Heroes of the Nations Ser.* AMS (repr of 1892 ed) $30.00. ISBN 0-404-58261-3 Focuses on Caesar's role in establishing the imperial system of ancient Rome.
*Wells, Reuben F. *On Land and Sea with Caesar.* Biblo 1926 $15.00. ISBN 0-8196-0107-1 Story of one of the greatest military commanders in history.

CICERO, MARCUS TULLIUS 106–43 BC

The most famous orator in ancient Rome, Marcus Tullius Cicero was also a noted politician and writer. Born in the town of Arpinum, Cicero moved to Rome with his family when he was a boy. In Rome he received the finest education that money could buy, including studies in law, philosophy, and public speaking. His first major appearance as a public speaker was in 70 BC, when his defense of an accused murderer became a defense of the freedom of the courts against undue influence by corrupt officials.

Cicero's popularity and political career grew steadily, and by 63 BC he had reached the highest office in the Roman Republic—the consulship. As consul, he took a conservative outlook, allying with the upper classes to maintain stability and order and working against a bill to distribute land to the needy, a position that won him enemies. During the election for consul, Cicero defeated Catiline, a revolutionary leader who was popular among the Roman masses. Catiline denounced the election as unfair and organized a conspiracy to murder Cicero and seize power. Cicero discovered the plot and delivered a powerful speech against Catiline in the Roman senate. So effective was Cicero's oratory that Cataline fled and was killed soon after. Some of his coconspirators were also executed.

As a champion of constitutional government, Cicero opposed Julius Caesar (*see* Caesar, Vol. 2, World History: Ancient Rome) when he rose to power, because he believed that Caesar would destroy Rome's republican system of government. He played no part in the assassination of Caesar in 44 BC, but he agreed that the act was in Rome's best interest. When Caesar's chief lieutenant, Mark Antony, gained power, Cicero delivered brilliant and bitter attacks against Antony and his plans for a dictatorship in a series of orations called the *Philippics.* Cicero was then murdered by Antony's followers and his head and hands were hung in the Roman Forum.

Of Cicero's extensive writings, 58 speeches survive, as well as several essays and 925 personal letters. The letters reveal the private side of the man and provide a picture of a prominent Roman that is more complete than that of any other public figure of ancient Rome.

BOOKS BY CICERO

Murder Trials. Michael Grant (tr). Hippocrene 1986 $16.95. ISBN 0-88029-075-7

Selected Letters. Penguin Classics Ser. D. R. Shackleton-Bailey (tr). Penguin 1986 $5.95. ISBN 0-14-044458-0

Selected Political Speeches. Penguin Classics Ser. Michael Grant (tr). Penguin 1977 $5.95. ISBN 0-14-044214-6

Selected Works. Penguin Classics Ser. Michael Grant (tr). Penguin 1960 $5.95. ISBN 0-14-044099-2

BOOKS ABOUT CICERO

Rawson, Elizabeth. *Cicero: A Portrait.* Cornell Univ Pr 1983 $12.95. ISBN 0-8014-9256-4 Life of the great Roman orator and philosopher.

Richards, G. C. *Cicero.* Greenwood 1970 repr of 1935 ed $35.00. ISBN 0-8371-4321-7 Portrait of Cicero that judges him not only as a politician but as an orator and major influence on the civilization of the world.

Strachan-Davidson, James L. *Cicero and the Fall of the Roman Republic. Heroes of the Nations Ser.* AMS (repr of 1894 ed) $30.00. ISBN 0-404-58287-7 Story of Cicero's life in the context of the concluding age of the Roman Empire.

HORACE   65–8 BC

See also Horace, Vol. 1, World Literature: Latin Literature.

The great Roman poet Horace was born in the town of Venusia, in southern Italy, in 65 BC. His father had been a slave but won his freedom and earned enough to send his son to Rome to study. At age 20, Horace went to study in Athens, still a great cultural center. While in Athens, the young Horace joined in the civil war between the statesman Brutus and Octavius Caesar, who were seeking leadership of Rome. However, during the Battle of Philippi (42 BC),

Horace fled. One of the poems Horace wrote about his experience humorously shows that he was meant to be a writer rather than a soldier.

Back in Rome, Horace was introduced to the Roman statesman Maecenas, a patron of the arts, who introduced the young poet to Roman literary and political society. Maecenas also gave Horace a farm in the countryside near Rome, where the poet lived and worked until his death in 8 BC.

Horace's poetry represents the peaceful period in Rome known as the Augustan Age. His poetry had a great influence on late English writers. His early poems show the influence of the witty Greek poet Archilochus. Later he adapted the poems of various Greek poets to the Latin language. As his genius grew, Horace's themes changed. While his early poems often made fun of people who were either dead or insignificant, later poems tended to be more positive, often describing the joys of country life. Looking back at history, he believed that human greed was the root of many problems. He criticized the luxurious lives of many wealthy Romans and concluded that Romans would be better off if they followed the Greek ideal of moderation. For Horace, the simple life of the country was best.

BOOKS BY HORACE

Art of Poetry. Burton Raffel (ed and tr). SUNY 1974 $14.95. ISBN 0-87395-240-5
The Essential Horace: Odes, Epodes, Satires and Epistles. Burton Raffel (tr). North Point 1983 $13.50. ISBN 0-86547-112-6
Horace's Satires and Epistles. Jacob Fuchs (tr). Norton 1977 $3.95. ISBN 0-393-09093-0
Horace Talks: The Satires. Select Bibliographies Repr Ser. Henry H. Chamberlain (tr). Ayer (repr of 1940 ed) $17.00. ISBN 0-8369-6653-8
Poems of Horace. Brome (tr). AMS (repr of 1666 ed) $40.00. ISBN 0-404-54119-4
The Works of Horace. 2 vols. AMS 1976 repr of 1792 ed $87.50. ISBN 0-404-54150-X

BOOKS ABOUT HORACE

Commager, Henry Steele. *The Odes of Horace: A Critical Study.* Yale Univ Pr 1962. (o.p.) Critical analysis of the poet's odes.
Fraenkel, Eduard. *Horace.* Oxford Univ Pr 1957 $29.95. ISBN 0-19-814376-1 Comprehensive look at the life and work of the noted Roman poet.
Perret, Jacques. *Horace.* Bertha Humez (tr). New York Univ Pr 1964. (o.p.) Introduction to the poet, his biography, development of style, and ideas on poetry.
Seller, William Y. *Roman Poets of the Augustan Age: Horace and the Elegiac Poets.* Biblo (repr of 1892 ed) $20.00. ISBN 0-8196-0165-9 Examination of the personal lives and literature of the satirists, the literary critics, and the lyrical poets.
Showerman, Grant. *Horace and His Influence: Our Debt to Greece and Rome.* Cooper Square (repr of 1930 ed) $28.50. ISBN 0-8154-0206-6 Analyzes the influence Horace's work had on later poetry.

LIVY 59 BC–AD 17

Titus Livy, or Livy, as he is known, was one of the greatest Roman historians. Despite his prominence, however, few details are known about his life. He was born in the Italian city of Patavium (modern-day Padua) in 59 BC and lived most of his life in Rome. It is clear from his writings that he had an extensive education, for he was familiar with the ancient Greek and Latin authors.

Although Livy wrote several works on philosophy and literary criticism, his masterpiece and life work was the *History of Rome.* This set of 142 volumes, which he worked on for over 40 years, covers hundreds of years of Roman history, from the founding of Rome in 753 BC to Livy's time. Only 35 volumes of this monumental work have survived to the present day.

The value of history, Livy said, was in its application to life. When he wrote his *History of Rome,* he believed that Rome was in a state of moral decay. He looked back fondly to a simpler and nobler time, and concluded that Rome's greatness was founded on personal and national virtue and discipline. Rome's decline, he felt, was caused by the decay of these virtues. Wealth and luxury, he wrote, led to "the dark dawning of our modern day, when we can neither endure our vices nor face the remedies needed to cure them."

According to modern standards, Livy was not an impressive historian, primarily because his work is not always accurate. Nevertheless, it is still a valuable piece of writing. In addition to the moral lessons he presents, he tells a great story and presents his tales briefly and with powerful dramatic effect. The *History of Rome* is also filled with wonderful, moving portraits, for Livy had a keen eye for character.

BOOKS BY LIVY

The Early History of Rome. Penguin Classics Ser. Aubrey de Selincourt (tr). Penguin 1960 $5.95. ISBN 0-14-044104-2
Rome and Italy. Penguin Classics Ser. Penguin 1982 $5.95. ISBN 0-14-044388-6
Rome and the Mediterranean. Penguin Classics Ser. Henry Bettenson (tr). Penguin 1976 $6.95. ISBN 0-14-044318-5
The War with Hannibal. Penguin Classics Ser. Aubrey de Selincourt (tr). Penguin 1965 $6.95. ISBN 0-14-044145-X

BOOK ABOUT LIVY

Lake, E., and F. Porter. *Livy: Hannibal the Scourge of Rome: Selections from Book XXI.* Focus Information 1984 repr of 1934 ed $14.50. ISBN 0-86292-131-7 Discusses Livy's history of the Carthaginian general who tried to conquer Rome.

PLINY THE YOUNGER *c.* AD 61–*c.* AD 112

Gaius Plinius Caecilius Secundus, known as Pliny the Younger, was a Roman lawyer, orator, and statesman best known for his letters, which are a major source of information about Roman life during his time.

Born in Como in Northern Italy, Pliny was orphaned at an early age and adopted by his uncle, Pliny the Elder. The younger Pliny studied and practiced law, became a Roman senator around the year AD 90, and was elected Roman consul in AD 100. Around the year AD 112, Pliny was named governor of Bithynia in Asia Minor, where he came in contact with Christians, whom he viewed as superstitious but harmless.

Pliny the Younger wrote 370 letters, which were published in 10 books. Because these were written with the intention of being published, they are somewhat affected. Nonetheless, they provide a wealth of information about Roman life during Pliny's lifetime. Books I through IX are made up of letters addressed to friends. Book X contains Pliny's correspondence with the Emperor Trajan and includes letters concerning his responsibilities as governor of Bithynia, among them questions about the treatment of the Christians there. Most interesting of Pliny's letters to his friends is a firsthand account of the eruption of Mount Vesuvius in AD 79, which buried the ancient city of Pompeii. In this letter Pliny describes his uncle's death by asphyxiation during the eruption.

BOOKS BY PLINY THE YOUNGER

The Intimate Life of Ancient Rome from the Personal Letters of the Younger Pliny. Found Class Repr 1982 $127.75. ISBN 0-89901-045-8

Letters. 2 vols. Harvard Univ Pr. Vol. 1 $14.50. ISBN 0-674-99061-7. Vol. 2 $14.50.
   ISBN 0-674-99066-8
The Letters of the Younger Pliny. Penguin Classics Ser. Betty Radice (tr). Penguin 1963 $6.95.
   ISBN 0-14-044127-1

SUETONIUS   *c.* AD 69–*c.* AD 140

The Roman biographer Suetonius (Caius Suetonius Tranquillus) was born
about AD 69 on the north coast of Africa. Although few details are known about
his life, he is famous for a book entitled *The Lives of the Caesars* (*c.* AD 121). This
work is a set of biographies of Julius Caesar and the first 11 emperors of Rome.
In his job as an imperial secretary under the emperor Hadrian, Suetonius was
able to gain access to documents that were of great use to him as a writer.
However, he lost this position in AD 121, apparently for failing to show the
proper respect for Hadrian's wife.

Many scholars have criticized Suetonius's work as an historian. His writing
is filled with anecdotes and superfluous details, he loved to repeat scandalous
stories and racy gossip, and there is little critical historical inquiry. Yet despite
these drawbacks, the biographies are still valuable because they not only provide important records about the times, but also make for lively historical
reading.

In addition to the *Lives of the Caesars,* Suetonius wrote a much larger collection of biographies called the *Lives of Illustrious Men* (*c.* AD 113). Here too, he
gathered together all sorts of lively anecdotes and gossipy stories that make the
biographies popular even today.

BOOKS BY SUETONIUS

Lives of the Caesars. Loeb Class Lib. 2 vols. Harvard Univ Pr. Vol. 1 $14.50. ISBN 0-674-
   99035-8. Vol. 2 $14.50. ISBN 0-674-99042-0

BOOKS ABOUT SUETONIUS

Baldwin, B. *Suetonius: The Biographer of the Caesars.* Coronet Bks 1983 $87.50. ISBN
   0-317-46477-9 Account of the Roman biographer whose work was a model for
   later biographers.
Wallace-Hadrill, Andrew. *Suetonius: The Scholar and His Caesars.* Yale Univ Pr 1984. (o.p.)
   $22.50. Discusses the scholarly aspects of the work of Suetonius.

TACITUS, CORNELIUS   *c.* AD 56–*c.* AD 117

A Roman senator known for his historical writing, Cornelius Tacitus lived
during the Flavian dynasty, including the reign of the emperor Trajan. Although little is known about his life, it is believed that he was a friend of the
ancient Roman lawyer, orator, and statesman Pliny the Younger (*see* Pliny the
Younger, Vol. 2, World History: Ancient Rome) and husband of the daughter
of the Roman general who conquered Britain, Julius Agricola. In AD 97 he was
appointed substitute consul and in time became proconsul of Asia. His first
written work was the *Dialogue on Oratory* (*c.* AD 80), a discussion of the
Ciceronian style of oratory, a topic Tacitus was well qualified to write about
because of his reputation as an excellent speaker. Another noted work is his
biography of his father-in-law, Agricola. The work that established his reputation as a historian is *The Germania,* a record of events concerning the early
Germanic peoples. In *Germania* Tacitus glorified the Germanic people by com-

paring their simple way of life with the corruption, immorality, and decadent life-style of the Romans of his time.

Solidifying Tacitus' reputation as a historian were *The Histories* and *The Annals,* two long works of which only parts survive. Within these books are character sketches of noted Romans, including the emperors Tiberius and Nero; obituary notices; passages containing moral instruction; and sketches of military campaigns. Tacitus' creation of a historical style that reflected the period was an accomplishment that went unmatched for several centuries after his death. Many consider him to be Rome's greatest historian.

BOOKS BY TACITUS

The Agricola and The Germania. Penguin Classics Ser. Hugh Mattingly (tr). Penguin 1971 $4.95. ISBN 0-14-044241-3

The Annals of Imperial Rome. Penguin Classics Ser. Michael Grant (tr). Penguin 1956 $5.95. ISBN 0-14-044060-7

Complete Works. Modern Lib Coll Eds Ser. Moses Hadas (ed). McGraw 1964 $7.50. ISBN 0-07-553639-0

The Histories. Penguin Classics Ser. Kenneth Wellesley (tr). Penguin 1976 $5.95. ISBN 0-14-044150-6

BOOKS ABOUT TACITUS

Schellhase, Kenneth C. *Tacitus in Renaissance Political Thought.* Univ of Chicago Pr 1977 $24.00. ISBN 0-226-73700-4 Discusses the influence of Tacitus on European political thinkers from the fourteenth to the seventeenth centuries.

Syme, Ronald. *Tacitus.* 2 vols. Oxford Univ Pr 1980 $115.00. ISBN 0-19-814327-3 Comprehensive look at the life and work of the renowned Roman historian.

VIRGIL 70–19 BC

One of the greatest of Roman poets, Virgil was born on his father's farm near Mantua during a time of instability in the Roman Empire. As a result of his upbringing and experience, Virgil's poetry often celebrated his rural and pastoral roots and also reflected the instability of a land beset by civil war. Virgil studied in Cremona, Milan, Naples, and Rome, becoming familiar with many of the works of literature that preceded him. When his father's farm was confiscated by the state, Virgil went to Rome where he became a part of a literary circle that was indebted to the patronage of Emperor Augustus.

Virgil's first works include the *Eclogues* (42–37 BC), a collection of 10 pastoral poems that idealize rural life and speak of the necessity of tranquillity and peace for achieving progress. Another collection of poems, *The Georgics* (36–29 BC), describes the practical goals to be obtained in a peaceful setting. Thereafter, Virgil devoted the rest of his life to writing his lofty epic, the *Aeneid.*

The *Aeneid* is one of the greatest long poems in world literature. At one level, the poem is a mythical tale of the distant past—the founding of Rome by Aeneas of Troy. At another level, it is a story of the present and the future—a glorification of the emperor Augustus as the founder of a new Rome. The poem tells the story of Aeneas, whom Virgil makes a paragon of revered Roman virtues—devotion to family, loyalty to the state, and piety based on devotion to the gods. In fact, there are two virtues celebrated by Virgil in the poem: *humanitas,* the feeling for others (humanity), and *pietas,* the faithfulness to one's family and one's social obligations. While the *Aeneid* contains 12 books detailing Aeneas' adventures, it was left incomplete when Virgil died of a fever contracted during a visit to Greece. Virgil's poetry influenced many readers and writers who came after him, including the medieval Italian poet Dante.

BOOKS BY VIRGIL

Aeneid. James H. Mantinband (tr). Ungar 1964 $9.95. ISBN 0-8044-6952-0
The Eclogues. Penguin Classics Ser. Guy Lee (tr). Penguin 1984 $4.95. ISBN 0-14-044419-X
The Georgics. L. P. Wilkinson (tr). Penguin 1983 $5.95. ISBN 0-14-044414-9
Virgil's Aeneid. Airmont Classics Ser. John Dryden (tr). Airmont 1968 $1.95. ISBN 0-8049-0177-5

BOOKS ABOUT VIRGIL

Bloom, Harold (ed). *Virgil. Modern Critical Views Ser.* Chelsea 1986 $24.50. ISBN 0-87754-728-9 Basic introduction to the life and work of the Roman poet.
Loomis, Julia. *Monarch Notes on Virgil's Aeneid and Other Works.* Monarch Pr 1964 $3.95. ISBN 0-671-00509-X Helps students understand Virgil's *Aeneid* and other works through overview, notes, and analyses.

See also Vol. 1, World Literature: Latin Literature.

ANCIENT AFRICA AND THE AMERICAS

Ajayi, J. F., and Michael Crowder. *History of West Africa.* 2 vols. Longman. $29.95 ea. Vol. 1 1985. ISBN 0-582-64683-9. Vol. 2 1987. ISBN 0-582-01604-5
*Barton, I. M. *Africa in the Roman Empire.* Focus Information 1972 $9.95. ISBN 0-87676-144-9 Discusses Africa's role in the Roman Empire.
*Berdan, Frances F. *The Aztecs. The Indians of North America Ser.* Chelsea 1989 $9.95. ISBN 0-7910-0354-X Account of the Indian hunters and gatherers who settled in central Mexico.
Bernal, Ignacio. *A History of Mexican Archaeology: The Vanished Civilizations of Middle America.* Thames Hudson 1983 $9.95. ISBN 0-500-79008-6
Bernal, Ignacio. *The Olmec World.* Doris Heyden and Fernando Horcasitas (trs). Univ of California Pr 1969 $14.95. ISBN 0-520-02891-0
*Bierhorst, John. *Black Rainbow: Legends of the Incas and Myths of Ancient Peru.* Farrar 1976 $9.95. ISBN 0-374-30829-2 Presents myths and legends of ancient civilizations of the Americas.
Bingham, Hiram. *Lost City of the Incas.* Greenwood 1981 repr of 1948 ed $55.00. ISBN 0-313-22950-3
Bingham, Hiram. *Machu Picchu: A Citadel of the Incas.* Hacker 1979 repr of 1930 ed $50.00. ISBN 0-87817-252-1
*Brundage, Burr Cartwright. *Empire of the Inca. The Civilization of the American Indian Ser.* Univ of Oklahoma Pr 1985 $12.95. ISBN 0-8061-1924-1 Political history of Spanish conquistadores according to archeological finds.
Brundage, Burr C. *Fifth Sun: Aztec Gods, Aztec World. Texas Pan American Ser.* Univ of Texas Pr 1979 $9.95. ISBN 0-292-72438-1
Brundage, Burr C. *The Jade Steps: A Ritual Life of the Aztecs.* Univ of Utah Pr 1985 $22.50. ISBN 0-87480-247-4
Brundage, Burr C. *Lords of Cuzco: A History and Description of the Inca People in Their Final Days. The Civilization of the American Indian Ser.* Univ of Oklahoma Pr 1985 $14.95. ISBN 0-8061-1955-1
*Cable, Mary. *The African Kings.* Tree Communications 1983. Story of early African kings through historical writings, artifacts, photographic portfolios, and other sources.
Cantrell, Jacqueline P. *Ancient Mexico: Art, Architecture, and Culture in the Land of the Feathered Serpent.* Kendall-Hunt 1989 $18.95. ISBN 0-8403-5125-9

*Chijioki, F. A. *Ancient Africa.* Holmes & Meier 1969 $5.50. ISBN 0-8419-0013-2 Account of the earliest times in Africa.

*Chu, Daniel, and Elliot Skinner. *A Glorious Age in Africa.* Doubleday 1965. (o.p.) Account of the early African empires of Ghana, Mali, and Songhai.

*Coe, Michael, *et al. Atlas of Ancient America.* Facts on File 1986 $40.00. ISBN 0-8160-1199-0 Covers pre-Columbian history in the Americas.

*Coe, Michael D. *The Maya. Ancient Peoples and Places Ser.* Thames Hudson 1987 $11.95. ISBN 0-500-27455-X Introduction to Indian civilization of southeastern Mexico and northern Central America from around AD 300 to AD 900.

Coe, Michael D. *Mexico. Ancient Peoples and Places Ser.* Thames Hudson 1986 $10.95. ISBN 0-500-27328-6 Illustrated account of the early history of the southwestern neighbor of the United States.

*Coe, Michael D., and Richard A. Diehl. *In the Land of the Olmec.* 2 vols. Univ of Texas Pr 1980 $100.00. ISBN 0-292-77549-0 Account of Indians who ruled an empire stretching from central Mexico to mid-Central America around 1200 BC.

*Connah, Graham. *African Civilizations: Precolonial Cities and States in Tropical Africa—An Archaeological Perspective.* Cambridge Univ Pr 1987 $15.95. ISBN 0-521-31992-7 Illustrated account of the patterns of early African settlement.

Connah, Graham. *Three Thousand Years in Africa: Man and His Environment in the Lake Chad Region of Nigeria.* Cambridge Univ Pr 1981 $75.00. ISBN 0-521-22848-4

*Crosher, Judith. *The Aztecs. Peoples of the Past Ser.* Silver 1985 $6.95. ISBN 0-382-06918-8 Describes the life of the ancient Aztecs.

Davidson, Basil. *A History of West Africa, One Thousand to Eighteen Hundred. The Growth of African Civilisation Ser.* Longman 1978 $13.95. ISBN 0-582-60340-4

Davies, Nigel. *Toltec Heritage: From the Fall of Tula to the Rise of Tenochtitlan.* Univ of Oklahoma Pr 1980 $29.50. ISBN 0-8061-1505-X

Davies, Nigel. *Toltecs: Until the Fall of Tula. Civilization of the American Indian Ser.* Univ of Oklahoma Pr 1987 $16.95. ISBN 0-8061-2071-1

Diop, Cheikh A. (ed). *African Origin of Civilization: Myth or Reality.* Mercer Cook (tr). Chicago Review 1974 $9.95. ISBN 0-88208-022-9

Duggan-Cronin, Alfred M. *Bantu Tribes of South Africa.* 4 vols. AMS (repr of 1935 ed) $450.00. ISBN 0-404-12050-4

Fagan, Brian M. *The Great Journey: The Peopling of Ancient America.* Thames Hudson 1987 $19.95. ISBN 0-500-05045-7

Fage, J. D. *An Atlas of African History.* Holmes & Meier 1978 $29.50. ISBN 0-8419-0430-8

*Fage, J. D. *A History of Africa.* Knopf 1979 $29.45. ISBN 0-394-47490-2 African history from its birth to the modern era.

*Ferguson, William M., *et al. Mesoamerica's Ancient Cities.* Univ of Colorado Pr 1990 $45.00. ISBN 0-87081-173-8 History and culture of ancient Latin American cities and societies; includes aerial photos and timelines.

*Gallant, Roy. *Ancient Indians: The First Americans.* Enslow 1989 $15.95. ISBN 0-89490-187-7 Story of the early ancestors of North and South American Indians.

Gallenkamp, Charles. *Maya. Art and Archaeology Ser.* Penguin 1985 $22.95. ISBN 0-670-80387-1

*Gallenkamp, Charles. *Maya: The Riddle and Rediscovery of a Lost Civilization.* Penguin 1987 $7.95. ISBN 0-14-008831-8 Outlines the Mayan civilization of Central America.

Gallenkamp, Charles, and Regina E. Johnson (eds). *Maya: Treasures of an Ancient Civilization.* Abrams 1985 $39.95. ISBN 0-8109-1826-9

*Gardner, John L. (ed). *Mysteries of the Ancient Americas.* Reader's Digest 1986 $29.45. ISBN 0-895-77183-7 Discloses new facts and information about past civilizations of the Americas.

Gasparini, Graziano, and Luise Margolies. *Inca Architecture.* Patricia J. Lyon (tr). Indiana Univ Pr 1980 $35.00. ISBN 0-253-30443-1

Harris, Joseph. *Africans and Their History.* NAL 1972 $4.95. ISBN 0-451-62556-0

Hewett, Edgar L. *Ancient Life in Mexico and Central America.* Biblo 1968 repr of 1936 ed $20.00. ISBN 0-8196-0205-1

Hobley, C. W. *Bantu Beliefs and Magic.* Biblio Dist 1967 $32.50. ISBN 0-7146-1009-7

*Jackson, John G. *Ethiopia and the Origin of Civilization.* Black Classic 1985 $2.00. ISBN 0-933121-14-8 Story of Ethiopia in ancient times.

Jackson, John G. *Introduction to African Civilization.* Carol 1974 $6.95. ISBN 0-8065-0420-X

Jennings, Gary. *Aztec.* Avon 1981 $4.95. ISBN 0-380-55889-0

MacKendrick, Paul. *The North African Stones Speak.* Univ of North Carolina Pr 1980 $30.00. ISBN 0-8078-1414-8

Morley, Sylvanus G., and George W. Brainerd. *Ancient Maya.* Stanford Univ Pr 1983 $16.95. ISBN 0-8047-1288-3

Murdock, George P. *Africa: Its People and Their Culture History.* McGraw 1959. (o.p.)

*Murphy, E. Jefferson. *History of African Civilization.* Dell 1974 $4.95. ISBN 0-385-28415-2 Anthropological and historical views of early African civilizations.

Oliver, Roland, and B. M. Fagan. *Africa in the Iron Age.* Cambridge Univ Pr 1975 $12.95. ISBN 0-521-09900-5

*Parrinder, Geoffrey. *African Mythology.* Bedrick 1986 $19.95. ISBN 0-87226-042-9 Discusses the mythological beliefs of African people, including those relating to the origins of Africa.

Reader's Digest. *Mysteries of the Ancient Americas.* Reader's Digest 1986 $28.95. ISBN 0-89577-183-7

*Rosenthau, Ricky. *The Splendor That Was Africa.* Oceana 1967. (o.p.) $7.50. Brief history of the Ghana, Mali, and Songhai empires.

*Schele, Linda, and Mary Ellen Miller. *The Blood of Kings: Dynasty and Ritual in Maya Art.* Kimbell Art 1986 $28.00. ISBN 0-912804-22-X History of the Mayan civilization that encompasses art, politics, and religion.

Snowden, Frank M., Jr. *Blacks in Antiquity: Ethiopians in the Greco–Roman Experience.* Harvard Univ Pr 1970 $10.95. ISBN 0-674-07626-5

Stuart, Gene S. *The Mighty Aztecs.* National Geographic 1981 $7.95. ISBN 0-87044-362-3

Stuart, George E., and Gene S. Stuart. *The Mysterious Maya.* National Geographic 1977 $7.95. ISBN 0-87044-233-3

Swanson, Earl H., *et al. Ancient Americas: The Making of the Past.* Bedrick 1989 $16.95. ISBN 0-87226-214-6

*Vlahos, Olivia. *African Beginnings.* Viking 1967. (o.p.) $2.45. ISBN 0-670-00257-7 Account of the kingdoms of ancient Africa.

Whitecotton, Joseph W. *Zapotecs: The Princes, Priests, and Peasants. The Civilization of the American Indian Ser.* Univ of Oklahoma Pr 1984 $9.95. ISBN 0-8061-1914-4

IBN BATUTA   *c.* 1304–*c.* 1378

One of the world's great travelers, Ibn Batuta was born about the year 1304 in the city of Tangier, Morocco, in northwest Africa. A student of Islamic law, he began his travels at the age of 21 with a trip across North Africa as part of a pilgrimage to the Islamic holy city of Mecca in Saudi Arabia. He found this journey so interesting that he determined to visit every Muslim country in the world, never traveling "any road a second time." He spent the next 30 years fulfilling his dream, covering about 75,000 miles in all.

Ibn Batuta began to fulfill his dream by exploring Arabia, Iraq, and Persia. After extensive travels in the Middle East, he went to India by way of the city of Samarkand in Central Asia. He spent almost eight years in India, where he worked for the sultan of Delhi as a judge and as an ambassador to China. While in Asia, he also visited the islands of Sri Lanka and Sumatra. About 1350 Ibn Batuta returned home to Tangier but soon set out again on more travels, including a trip to Spain and a trip across the Sahara Desert to the city of Timbuktu in West Africa. In 1354 he returned to Morocco, where he settled down to write about the people and places he had seen.

Ibn Batuta's work, *Travels of Ibn Batuta* (*c.* 1357), provides an impressive look at the geography and the social and cultural history of the Islamic world in the fourteenth century. His keen eye captured a wide range of subjects, from an account of the intellectual life at a university in Timbuktu to a description of hippopotamuses in the Niger River.

BOOKS BY IBN BATUTA

Travels in Asia and Africa, 1325–1354. Kelley 1969 repr of 1929 ed $45.00. ISBN 0-678-06523-3

The Travels of Ibn Batuta. Burt Franklin (repr of 1829 ed) $18.50. ISBN 0-8337-2051-1

BOOKS ABOUT IBN BATUTA

Dunn, Ross E. *The Adventures of Ibn Batuta: A Muslim Traveler of the Fourteenth Century.* Univ of California Pr 1986 $37.50. ISBN 0-520-05771-6 Entertaining account of this amazing traveler; also provides a portrait of Islam in the fourteenth century.

THE BYZANTINE EMPIRE AND THE EMERGENCE OF ISLAM

*Andrae, Tor. *Mohammed: The Man and His Faith. Select Bibliographies Reprint Ser.* Theophil Menzel (tr). Ayer (repr of 1936 ed) $19.95. ISBN 0-8369-5821-7 Account of the life and religious beliefs of the founder of Islam.

*Bainton, Roland H. *Christianity.* American Heritage 1986 $9.95. ISBN 0-8281-0489-1 General history of Christianity.

Bainton, Roland H. *Early Christianity.* Krieger 1984 $7.50. ISBN 0-89874-735-X

Browning, Robert. *Greek Classical Byzantine.* Crown 1989 $19.95. ISBN 0-517-67418-1

*Browning, Robert. *Justinian and Theodora.* Thames Hudson 1987 repr of 1971 ed $22.50. ISBN 0-500-25099-5 Examines the relationship between the emperor Justinian and the empress Theodora.

Editors of Time–Life Books. *The March of Islam: 600–800. Time Frame Ser.* Time–Life 1988 $22.60. ISBN 0-8094-6420-9

Lewis, Bernard. *Arabs in History.* Harper $6.95. ISBN 0-06-131029-8

*Lyons, Malcolm C., and David E. Jackson. *Saladin: The Politics of the Holy War. Oriental Publications Ser.* Cambridge Univ Pr 1985 $16.95. ISBN 0-521-31739-8 Discusses the role of the famous Islamic leader in the Crusades.

Mango, Cyril. *Byzantine Architecture. History of World Architecture Ser.* Rizzoli 1985 $25.00. ISBN 0-8478-0615-4

*Patai, Raphael. *The Arab Mind.* Scribner's 1976 $9.95. ISBN 0-684-14547-2 Explores Arab and Islamic histories and cultures.

*Pickthal, Marmaduke. *Meaning of the Glorious Koran.* Hippocrene 1988 $18.95. ISBN 0-88029-209-1 Offers an explanation and translation of the Islamic holy book.

Treadgold, Warren. *The Byzantine Revival, 780–842.* Stanford Univ Pr 1988 $49.50. ISBN 0-8047-1462-2

AVERROES   1126–1198

Averroës is the Latin name for Abu-al-Walid ibn Rushd, an Islamic philosopher born in Cordoba, Spain, in 1126. Trained in law and medicine, Averroës served as a judge in the cities of Seville and Cordoba, and as chief physician at the royal court of the caliph. He is best known, however, for his philosophical writings, in which he comments on the scientific teachings of the Greek philosopher Aristotle. (*See* Aristotle, Vol. 2, Biology: Classification of Organisms *and* World History: Ancient Greece.)

Averroës insisted that people have the right to think about and evaluate all knowledge, including religion. He held that faith and reason are not in conflict, and that truth derives from reason rather than faith. As a result, Averroës asserted that the Islamic faith and aristotelian science can coexist, and that observant Muslims can become scientists.

Translated from Arabic into Latin, Averroës' writings were widely read by Christian scholars in Western Europe. Many were disturbed by some of his assertions. For example, Averroës argued that the universe has always existed, whereas Christians believe it has been created by God. Averroës also did not believe in the immortality of the human soul, whereas Christians believe in a life after death. Despite such differences, the writings of Averroës helped bring the scientific ideas of Aristotle to the attention of Western Europe. This greatly influenced both medieval philosophy and the development of a scientific tradition in western civilization.

BOOK BY AVERROES

Averroës on Plato's Republic. Ralph Lerner (tr). Cornell Univ Pr 1974 $8.95. ISBN 0-8014-9145-2

BOOKS ABOUT AVERROES

Butterworth, C. E., and A. Abd Al-Magid Haridi (eds). *Averroës's Middle Commentary on Aristotle's Topic.* Eisenbrauns 1979 $9.50. ISBN 0-686-30893-X Discusses the medieval philosopher's writings on the Greek philosopher Aristotle.

Kogan, Barry S. *Avenues and the Metaphysics of Causation.* SUNY 1985 $19.95. ISBN 0-88706-065-X Examines the controversial causation issue; argues that Averroës' discussion of causation represents a dialogue across the ages.

Mohammed, Ovey N. *Averroes' Doctrine of Immortality: A Matter of Controversy.* Wilfred Laurier Pr 1984. ISBN 0-88920-178-1 Clear and careful analysis of the links between Averroës and Aristotle, and an explication of Averroës' impact on Christian theology and St. Thomas Aquinas.

MAIMONIDES, MOSES 1135–1204

Moses ben Maimon, better known by his Greek name Moses Maimonides, was a great Jewish philosopher, rabbi, and physician. Born in the Spanish city of Cordoba, Maimonides fled from there at age 13 when the city was invaded by a Muslim sect that insisted that all Jews and Christians convert to Islam. After several years of wandering, he settled in Egypt, where Jews were free to practice their religion. In 1174 Maimonides was appointed personal physician to the sultan in Cairo. Although the position was time-consuming, it provided both financial security and the opportunity to write. Among his works are treatises on diet, hygiene, and the treatment of diseases. He is best known, however, for two works on philosophy and religion—the *Mishneh Torah* (1180) and *The Guide for the Perplexed* (1190).

In the *Mishneh Torah,* written in Hebrew, Maimonides codifies the legal interpretations of Jewish rabbis and judges over the previous 1,500 years in a form that lay people can read, comprehend, and refer to easily. *The Guide for the Perplexed,* written in Arabic, is even more ambitious. In this work Maimonides tries to reconcile Judaism with the teachings of the Greek philosopher Aristotle (*see* Aristotle, Vol. 2, Biology: The Classification of Organisms *and* World History: Ancient Greece) and to show that science does not harm religious teachings. Many conservative Jews were shocked by Maimonides' belief that certain stories in the Bible—such as Adam and Eve and the serpent in the

Garden of Eden—should not be taken literally, but are important because of the message they contain. More liberal Jews, however, as well as many Muslim and Christian thinkers, adopted Maimonides's approach that knowledge comes by reason as well as revelation.

BOOKS BY MAIMONIDES

The Book of Women: The Code of Maimonides. Judaica Ser. Isaac Klein (ed). Yale Univ Pr 1972 $50.00. ISBN 0-300-01438-4

Eight Chapters of Maimonides on Ethics. AMS (repr of 1912 ed) $24.50. ISBN 0-404-50497-3

Introduction to the Code of Maimonides (Mishneh Torah). (coauthored with Isadore Twersky) Yale Univ Pr 1980 $15.95. ISBN 0-300-02846-6

Guide for the Perplexed. M. Friedlander (tr). Dover 1904 $7.95. ISBN 0-8446-2512-4

BOOKS ABOUT MAIMONIDES

Burrell, David B. *Knowing the Unknowable God: Ibn-Sina, Maimonides, Aquinas.* Univ of Notre Dame Pr 1986 $8.95. ISBN 0-268-01226-1 Examines the religious thoughts of three prominent theologians including Maimonides.

Dienstag, Jacob I. *Maimonides and St. Thomas Aquinas.* Ktav 1974 $39.50. ISBN 0-87068-249-0 Compares the religious thoughts of the theologians Maimonides and Aquinas.

Hartman, David. *Maimonides-Torah and Philosophic Quest.* JPS 1977 $7.95. ISBN 0-8276-0255-3 Integration of Maimonides' study of the Torah with his philosophy; includes a bibliography.

Leaman, Oliver. *Moses Maimonides.* Routledge 1990 $15.95. ISBN 0-415-03608-9 Comprehensive biography of the notable medieval Jewish scholar and philosopher.

Minkin, Jacob. *The Teachings of Maimonides.* Aronson 1987 repr of 1957 ed $40.00. ISBN 0-87668-953-5 Examines the philosophical and religious works of the medieval Jewish scholar.

Yellin, David, and Israel Abrahams. *Maimonides: His Life and Works.* Hermon 1989 $9.75. ISBN 0-87203-121-7 Standard account of the life and times of the notable Jewish scholar.

ST. AUGUSTINE AD 354–430

A Christian theologian and philosopher, St. Augustine was one of a group of early Christian scholars whose works had a major impact on the development of the Roman Catholic church. His influence on Christian thought was so great that many consider him the founder of theology. St. Augustine was born in 354 in North Africa to a pagan father and a Christian mother. Although taught Christian principles by his mother, he grew up with little piety or devotion to that faith. Educated in the Greek and Roman classics, he lived for a time in Carthage in North Africa and later traveled to Rome and Milan, Italy, where he worked as a teacher of rhetoric. Then in 386, after much soul-searching, he converted to Christianity and returned to North Africa and a monastic life. Four years later he was ordained a priest, and then in 396 he became bishop of the North African city of Hippo, where he remained until his death.

St. Augustine's two major works are *The Confessions* (*c.* 400) and *City of God* (*c.* 412–426). *The Confessions,* written in the form of a prayer, is an autobiography in which St. Augustine describes the struggle between his spiritual dreams and his love of material well-being and explains his religious conversion. A beautifully written book, its style greatly influenced later European writers.

In *City of God,* written while the Roman Empire was crumbling from Germanic invasions, St. Augustine asserts that Rome fell because it had persecuted Christians during the first and second centuries and because its people were more concerned with becoming rich than with saving their souls. Besides, St. Augustine argues, no earthly city lasts forever; only the spiritual City of God is eternal. *City of God* also reflects an important political theory. St. Augustine believed that since the Church is responsible for people's salvation, its political power is superior to that of kings. This theory had a great influence on people in Western Europe from the eleventh to the fourteenth centuries.

BOOKS BY ST. AUGUSTINE

An Augustine Treasury: Selections from the Writings of St. Augustine. Jules Brady (ed). Daughters St. Paul 1981 $4.00. ISBN 0-8198-0707-9

The Catholic and Manichaean Ways of Life. Fathers of the Church Ser. Catholic Univ Pr 1966 $14.95. ISBN 0-8132-0056-3

Christian Instruction, Admonition, and Grace, the Christian Combat, Faith, Hope, and Charity. Fathers of the Church Ser. Catholic Univ Pr 1950 $34.95. ISBN 0-8132-0002-4

Commentary on the Lord's Sermon on the Mount with Seventeen Related Sermons. Fathers of the Church Ser. Catholic Univ Pr 1951 $21.95. ISBN 0-8132-0011-3

The Happy Life and Other Works. Fathers of the Church Ser. Catholic Univ Pr 1948 $22.95. ISBN 0-8132-0005-9

St. Augustine: The Greatness of the Soul. J. Quasten and J. Plumpe (eds). Joseph M. Colleran (tr). Ancient Christian Writers Ser. Paulist 1950 $14.95. ISBN 0-8091-0060-6

The Teacher, the Free Choice of the Will, Grace, and Free Will. Fathers of the Church Ser. Catholic Univ Pr 1968 $17.95. ISBN 0-8132-0059-8

The Trinity. Fathers of the Church Ser. Catholic Univ Pr 1963 $27.95. ISBN 0-8132-0045-8

BOOKS ABOUT ST. AUGUSTINE

Brown, Peter. *Augustine of Hippo.* Hippocrene $22.50. ISBN 0-88029-098-6 Definitive biography of the most influential teacher in the history of Christianity.

Marshall, Michael. *The Restless Heart: The Life and Influence of St. Augustine.* Eerdmans 1987 $19.95. ISBN 0-8028-3632-1 Examines the life, accomplishments, and influence of the notable early Christian bishop and saint.

O'Donnell, James J. *Augustine.* World Authors Ser. G. K. Hall 1985 $21.95. ISBN 0-8057-6609-X Standard biography of the notable Catholic saint.

Possidius. *The Life of Saint Augustine.* The Augustinian Ser. John E. Rotelle (ed). Matthew O'Connell (tr). Augustinian 1988 $7.95. ISBN 0-941491-19-6 Focuses on the life and work of St. Augustine.

Trape, Augustine. *St. Augustine: Man, Pastor, Mystic.* Catholic Bk Pub 1985 $6.95. ISBN 0-89942-172-5 Examines St. Augustine's roles as a religious leader and Christian theologian, as well as his personal life.

See also Vol. 1, World Literature: Middle Eastern Literature.

MEDIEVAL EUROPE

Artz, Frederick B. *The Mind of the Middle Ages: An Historical Survey: AD 200–1500.* Univ of Chicago Pr 1980 $17.95. ISBN 0-226-02840-2

Bainton, Roland H. *The Medieval Church.* Anvil Ser. Krieger 1979 $7.50. ISBN 0-88275-786-5

Barraclough, Geoffrey. *The Crucible of Europe: The Ninth and Tenth Centuries in European History.* Univ of California Pr 1976 $9.95. ISBN 0-520-03118-0

Barraclough, Geoffrey. *The Medieval Papacy.* Norton 1979 $9.95. ISBN 0-393-95100-6

▪ Billings, Malcolm. *The Cross and the Crescent: A History of the Crusades.* Sterling 1988 $19.95.

ISBN 0-8069-6904-0 A well-illustrated history of this 700-year-long war to free the Holy Land.

*Bishop, Morris. *Middle Ages.* American Heritage 1986 $9.95. ISBN 0-8281-0487-5 Tells of European life and culture in the period between ancient and modern times.

Brooks, Polly S. *Queen Eleanor: Independent Spirit of the Medieval World: A Biography of Eleanor of Aquitaine.* Harper Jr Bks 1983 $12.89. ISBN 0-397-31995-9

Brown, R. Allen. *The Architecture of Castles.* Facts on File $16.95. ISBN 0-8160-1146-X

*Brown, R. Allen. *Normans and the Norman Conquest.* Longwood 1985 $36.00. ISBN 0-85115-427-1 Story of the Normans and their encroachment on other lands, including their conquest of England.

*Caselli, Giovanni. *A Medieval Monk. The Everyday Life of Ser.* Bedrick 1986 $9.95. ISBN 0-87226-105-0 Illustrated account of the life of a medieval monk.

*Caselli, Giovanni. *The Middle Ages. The History of Everyday Things Ser.* Bedrick 1988 $15.95. ISBN 0-87226-176-X Presents a picture of life during the Middle Ages.

*Chippindale, Christopher. *Stonehenge Complete.* Cornell Univ Pr 1987 $24.95. ISBN 0-8014-9451-6 Discusses the famous prehistoric stone structure in southwest England, including theories of its construction and purpose.

Cole, Bruce. *Giotto and Florentine Painting, 1280–1375.* Harper 1977 $9.95. ISBN 0-06-430071-4

*Cruise O'Brien, Maire. *The Story of Ireland.* Viking 1972. Describes Ireland's political and religious problems in medieval times.

Cunliffe, Barry B. *Celtic World: An Illustrated History of the Celtic Race, Their Culture, Customs and Legends.* Crown 1986 $14.98. ISBN 0-517-61533-9

Duby, Georges. *The Age of the Cathedrals: Art and Society, 980–1420.* Eleanor Levieux and Barbara Thompson (trs). Univ of Chicago Pr 1983 $11.95. ISBN 0-226-16770-4

*Duby, Georges. *William Marshall: The Flower of Chivalry.* Pantheon 1987 $6.95. ISBN 0-394-75154-X Examines the life of a medieval knight.

*Duke, Dulcie. *The Growth of a Medieval Town.* Cambridge Univ Pr 1988 $5.25. ISBN 0-521-33725-9 Follows the growth of an average town in Europe during the period from 1200 to 1499.

*Durant, Will. *Age of Faith.* Simon 1950 $32.95. ISBN 0-671-01200-2 History of Christian, Islamic, and Judaic civilizations in medieval times.

Editors of Time–Life Books. *The Age of Calamity: 1300–1400. Time Frame Ser.* Time–Life 1989 $22.60. ISBN 0-8094-6441-1

Editors of Time–Life Books. *The Divine Campaigns: 1100–1200. Time Frame Ser.* Time–Life 1989 $22.60. ISBN 0-8094-6433-0

Fine, John V. *The Early Medieval Balkans: A Critical Survey from the Sixth to the Late Twelfth Century.* Univ of Michigan Pr 1983 $34.50. ISBN 0-472-10025-4

*Gies, Frances. *The Knight in History.* Harper 1987 $8.95. ISBN 0-06-091413-0 Discusses chivalry and the role of the knight in history.

*Gies, Frances, and Joseph Gies. *Life in a Medieval Village.* Harper 1990 $22.95. ISBN 0-06-016215-5 A clear and accurate account of everyday life in a typical English village.

*Gies, Frances, and Joseph Gies. *Marriage and the Family in the Middle Ages.* Harper 1989 $8.95. ISBN 0-06-091468-8 Account of family life in medieval times.

*Gies, Joseph, and Frances Gies. *Life in a Medieval Castle.* Harper 1979 $7.95. ISBN 0-06-090674-X Considers the medieval castle as a home, a center of feudal order, and a military target.

*Gies, Joseph, and Frances Gies. *Women in the Middle Ages.* Harper 1980 $6.95. ISBN 0-06-464037-X Examines the lives of women during medieval times.

Hallam, Elizabeth (ed). *The Four Gothic Kings: The Turbulent History of Medieval England and the Plantagenet Kings (1216–1377)—Henry III, Edward I, Edward II, Edward III—Seen Through the Eyes of Their Contemporaries.* Weidenfeld 1987 $35.00. ISBN 1-55584-171-6

*Hallam, Elizabeth (ed). *The Plantagenet Chronicles.* Weidenfeld 1986 $35.00. ISBN 1-55584-018-3 Story of the reigns of King Henry II of England and his sons, the Magna Carta, the Crusades, and more.

Hallam, Elizabeth (ed). *The Wars of the Roses: From Richard II to the Fall of Richard III at Bosworth*

Field Seen Through the Eyes of Their Contemporaries. Weidenfeld 1988 $35.00. ISBN 1-55584-240-2

*Heer, Friedrich. *Medieval World: Europe Eleven Hundred to Thirteen Fifty.* NAL 1964 $5.95. ISBN 0-451-62542-0 Deals with life and historical events in medieval Europe during a period of two and one-half centuries.

*Heller, Julek, and Deirdre Headon. *Knights.* Schocken 1989 $15.95. ISBN 0-8052-0971-9 Stories of famous knights and how they spent their days.

*Hindley. *Knights and Castles.* EDC 1976 $5.95. ISBN 0-86020-068-X Interesting facts about the days of knights and castles.

*Jones, Gwyn. *A History of the Vikings.* Oxford Univ Pr 1984 $12.95. ISBN 0-19-285139-X Account of Viking life in medieval times based on historical data and archeological findings.

*Kelley, Amy. *Eleanor of Aquitaine and the Four Kings.* Harvard Univ Pr 1950 $9.95. ISBN 0-674-24254-8 Interesting biography of the noted English queen and her influence on four kings, including her husband and sons.

Lamb, Harold. *The Crusades: The Flame of Islam.* Third World Bk 1987 $12.95. ISBN 0-9616005-1-9

Levi, Peter. *The Frontiers of Paradise: A Study of Monks and Monasteries.* Weidenfeld 1988 $16.95. ISBN 1-55584-197-X

*Maalouf, Amin. *The Crusades Through Arab Eyes.* Schocken 1989 $12.95. ISBN 0-8052-0898-4 Discusses the Crusades from the Arab perspective.

*Macaulay, David. *Castle.* Houghton 1977 $14.95. ISBN 0-395-25784-0 Illustrated account of the construction of a medieval castle.

*Macaulay, David. *Cathedral.* Houghton 1981 $6.95. ISBN 0-395-31668-5 Detailed drawings and text show how a cathedral is built.

Male, Emile. *Art and Artists of the Middle Ages.* Art of the Middle Ages Ser. Sylvia S. Lowe (tr). Black Swan Bks 1986 $35.00. ISBN 0-933806-06-X

McEvedy, Colin. *The Penguin Atlas of Medieval History.* Penguin 1986 $6.95. ISBN 0-14-051152-0

*Mills, Dorothy. *The Middle Ages.* Putnam's 1935. Interesting and easy-to-read account of the religion, behavior, dwellings, economics, travel, towns, and more for the period AD 300–1500; also tells of Charlemagne and Norsemen.

*Miquel, Pierre. *Castles of the Middle Ages.* Silver Burdett Picture Histories Ser. Silver 1985 $8.95. ISBN 0-382-06927-7 Looks at the homes and fortresses of medieval kings and noblemen; especially suited to younger readers.

*Miquel, Pierre. *Days of Knights and Castles.* Silver Burdett Picture Histories Ser. Silver 1985 $8.95. ISBN 0-382-06921-8 Story of the armored warriors of medieval kings and of fortified medieval dwellings; especially suited to younger readers.

*Miquel, Pierre. *The Days of the Musketeers.* Silver Burdett Picture Histories Ser. Silver 1985 $7.75. ISBN 0-382-06923-4 Heavily illustrated account of medieval times; especially suited to younger readers.

Simon, Edith. *The Anglo–Saxon Manner: The English Contribution to Civilization.* Beekman 1972 $19.95. ISBN 0-8464-0136-3

*Thompson, E. A. *Who Was St. Patrick?* St. Martin's 1986 $24.95. ISBN 0-312-87084-1 Story of the early Christian missionary and patron saint of Ireland.

Tuchman, Barbara. *A Distant Mirror: The Calamitous 14th Century.* Ballantine 1987 $12.95. ISBN 0-345-34957-1

*Wood, Michael. *In Search of the Dark Ages.* In Search of Ser. Facts on File 1987 $22.95. ISBN 0-8160-1686-0 Offers archeological evidence of English kingdoms during the period of the Dark Ages.

ST. THOMAS AQUINAS   1225–1274

St. Thomas Aquinas was one of the leading Christian philosophers and theologians of the Middle Ages. Born into an influential family in 1225 near Monte Cassino, Italy, he became a Dominican friar at age 19 and spent most of his life teaching at the universities of Paris and Naples. In his youth, St. Thomas

Aquinas was known as "the dumb ox" because he was quite stout, moved slowly, and spoke in a soft, deliberate manner. However, as people came to recognize his great intelligence, he became known as "the angelic doctor."

Like many other medieval thinkers, Aquinas tried to combine different approaches to truth, in particular Christianity and the scientific reason of the Greek thinker Aristotle. (*See* Aristotle, Vol. 2, Biology: Classification of Organisms *and* World History: Ancient Greece.) He argued that since God created both faith and reason, both have a place in Christian thinking and they cannot contradict each other. They do, however, serve different purposes. Reason helps explain the physical world in which people live, while religion and faith help explain questions such as "What is the purpose of God's universe?" In his major work, *Summa Theologiae* (1267–1273), Aquinas presents his ideas in the form of questions, with arguments both for and against a particular point of view. He then provides a definite answer for each question. St. Thomas's success in synthesizing the philosophy of Aristotle with Christian belief was one of the greatest achievements of medieval philosophy. This synthesis became a cornerstone in the doctrines of the Roman Catholic church. Aquinas was made a saint in 1323.

BOOKS BY AQUINAS

Selected Writings of St. Thomas Aquinas. Robert P. Goodwin (tr). Macmillan 1965 $4.24. ISBN 0-672-60469-8

Summa Theologiae—A Concise Translation. Timothy McDermott (ed). Christian Classics 1989 $78.00. ISBN 0-87061-170-4

The Three Greatest Prayers: Commentaries on the Lord's Prayer, the Hail Mary, and the Apostles' Creed. Sophia Inst Pr 1990 $16.95. ISBN 0-918477-05-0

BOOKS ABOUT AQUINAS

Burrell, David B. *Knowing the Unknowable God: Ibn-Sina, Maimonides, Aquinas.* Univ of Notre Dame Pr 1986 $8.95. ISBN 0-268-01226-1 Examines the religious thoughts of three prominent theologians, including St. Thomas Aquinas.

Chesterton, G. K. *St. Thomas Aquinas.* Doubleday 1974 $4.95. ISBN 0-385-09002-1 Notable biography of the Italian philosopher and theologian.

Copleston, F. C. *Aquinas.* Penguin 1956 $6.95. ISBN 0-14-020349-4 Sympathetic account of Aquinas' life that stresses the modern implications of his philosophy.

Gilson, Etienne. *The Christian Philosophy of St. Thomas Aquinas.* Hippocrene 1983 repr of 1956 ed $45.00. ISBN 0-88254-874-3 Analyzes the theology of the notable philosopher.

Kenny, Anthony. *Aquinas. Past Masters Ser.* Oxford Univ Pr 1980 $4.95. ISBN 0-19-287500-0 Comprehensive account of the life, times, and thought of the Italian philosopher, theologian, and saint.

SAINT BEDE, THE VENERABLE   AD 673–735

Bede, also called the Venerable Bede, was an English historian and theologian, as well as a Benedictine monk. Probably the most learned man of his time in Western Europe, Bede was canonized a saint of the Roman Catholic church in 1899. Little is known of his parentage, but very early in life Bede was entrusted to the care of a Benedictine abbot. Then, at age seven, Bede was taken to the monastery of St. Peter near Sunderlund, Durham, where he spent the rest of his life.

Ordained a priest at age 30, Bede spent his days reading scripture and writing scriptural commentaries based on his interpretations of the writings of the Church fathers. Bede also researched the conversion to Christianity of the

Anglo-Saxons in England and wrote about it in the *Ecclesiastical History of the English People* (*c.* 731). This work recorded events in England from the raids of the Roman general Julius Caesar in 55 BC to the arrival of St. Augustine in Kent in AD 597. (*See* Caesar, Vol. 2, World History: Ancient Rome and St. Augustine, Vol. 2, World History: The Byzantine Empire and the Emergence of Islam.) In addition to this work, Bede wrote several biographies, the most famous of which is *Lives of the Abbots* (*c.* 725). He also wrote two chronologies concerned with the reckoning of time and with determining the date of Easter; from these came the practice of using BC and AD to place events.

Copies of Bede's works, which were written in Latin, were made for many of Western Europe's monastic libraries. Bede was a discriminating scholar and critical reporter. Like modern scholars, he researched many documents, quoted sources, assessed their accuracy, used only what he considered trustworthy, and stated his own opinions, noting them as such. At the time of his canonization, he was proclaimed a Doctor of the Church, the only person of English birth to receive this distinction.

BOOK BY BEDE

The Ecclesiastical History of England. John A. Giles (ed). *Bohn's Antiquarian Lib.* AMS (repr of 1849 ed) $42.50.

BOOK ABOUT BEDE

*Brown, George H. *Bede the Venerable. Twayne's English Authors Ser.* G. K. Hall 1987 $19.95. ISBN 0-8057-6940-4 Introduction to the life and work of the venerated English saint and historian.

POLO, MARCO   *c.*1254–*c.* 1324

The Venetian traveler Marco Polo was one of the greatest European explorers of the Middle Ages. The record of his journey to Central Asia and China was the main source for European ideas about the Far East until the late nineteenth century.

Marco Polo was born in Venice around the year 1254. Between 1260 and 1269, his father and uncle traveled to China as merchants. When they left Venice in 1271 to return to the Far East, the 17-year-old Marco went with them. In 1275, after years of travel across central Asia, the Polos finally arrived in Shan-tu, the summer capital of Kublai Khan, the Mongol emperor of China. The emperor already knew the elder Polos and he welcomed them all with honor. Although it is not known exactly what the Polos did during their many years in the Far East, it is believed that, during some of that time, Marco Polo served as an envoy for Kublai Khan in distant parts of the empire.

Kublai Khan liked the Polos and was reluctant to have the Venetians leave his court. However, in 1292 he finally agreed that they should accompany a royal mission to the Mongol prince of Persia. From Persia, the Polos finally reached Venice in 1295 after an absence of 24 years. According to legend, the travelers were not recognized on their return.

Sometime after his return, Marco Polo took part in a naval battle between the Italian states of Venice and Genoa and was taken prisoner by the Genoese. While in prison, he dictated the story of his wondrous experiences to a fellow prisoner. This manuscript was the famous travel narrative, *The Travels of Marco Polo.* Released from prison in 1299, Marco Polo returned to his career as a merchant, married, and fathered three daughters. On his death bed, he is reported to have said, "I did not tell half of what I saw, because I knew I would not be believed."

The Travels of Marco Polo (c. 1298) is more a work of science than an autobiography or a travel book. It contains little of Polo's personality (only the prologue tells of Polo's life) or even of his adventures. Instead, it contains descriptions of land forms, animals, plants, customs, governments, and religions. Polo's account of amazing things and a technologically superior culture was met with disbelief by many of his contemporaries. Nonetheless, it stimulated interest in the Far East and trade with the cultures there. The book even inspired the Italian explorer Christopher Columbus, who sailed west in 1492 in search of the riches of the East. (*See* Columbus, Vol. 2, United States History: Native Americans and Early Explorers.) Until the late nineteenth century, Polo's description of parts of Central Asia were the only western descriptions available.

BOOKS BY POLO

The Book of Sir Marco Polo, the Venetian, Concerning the Kingdoms and Marvels of the East. 3 vols. Henry Yule (ed and tr). AMS (repr of 1920 ed) $245.00. ISBN 0-404-11540-3
The Description of the World. 2 vols. AMS (repr of 1938 ed) $225.00. ISBN 0-404-11525-X
The Travels of Marco Polo. Airmont Classics Ser. Airmont 1968 $1.50. ISBN 0-8049-0186-4

BOOKS ABOUT POLO

*Ceserani, Gian P. *Marco Polo.* Putnam 1982 $9.95. ISBN 0-399-20843-7 Story of the noted Italian explorer of central Asia and China.
Hart, Henry H. *Marco Polo: Venetian Adventurer.* Univ of Oklahoma Pr 1967. (o.p.) $17.95. The story of Marco Polo's adventures that expands on an earlier text and uses new editions of Marco Polo's narrative as well as new research and studies.
Marco Polo. MacDonald Educational Ser. Intl Book Ctr $3.50. ISBN 0-86685-207-7 Account of the explorer and his travels.

MEDIEVAL INDIA, CHINA, AND JAPAN

*Birch, Cyril (tr). *Stories from a Ming Collection.* Grove 1968 $9.95. ISBN 0-394-17308-2 Offers stories from the Chinese dynasty that ruled from AD 1368 to 1644.
Dramer, Kim. *Kublai Khan: Mongol Emperor. World Leaders—Past and Present Ser.* Chelsea 1989 $17.95. ISBN 1-55546-812-8
Editors of Time–Life Books. *Light in the East: 1000–1100. Time Frame Ser.* Time–Life 1988 $22.60. ISBN 0-8094-6429-2
Editors of Time–Life Books. *The Mongol Conquests: 1200–1300. Time Frame Ser.* Time–Life 1989 $22.60. ISBN 0-8094-6437-3
*Godden, Jon, and Rumer Godden. *Shiva's Pigeons: An Experience of India.* Penguin 1972 $25.00. ISBN 0-670-64055-7 Interesting portrayal of India in a poetic manner; with illustrations, symbols, and more.
Saunders, Tao I. *Dragons, Gods, and Spirits from Chinese Mythology. World Mythologies Ser.* Schocken 1983 $16.95. ISBN 0-8052-3799-2
Twitchett, Denis. *Printing and Publishing in Medieval China.* Beil 1983 $14.95. ISBN 0-913720-08-9
Twitchett, Denis (ed). *The Cambridge History of China.* Vol. 3 *Sui and Tang China: 589–906 AD, Part 1.* Cambridge Univ Pr 1979 $130.00. ISBN 0-521-21446-7
*Varley, H. Paul. *Japanese Culture.* Univ of Hawaii Pr 1984 $12.95. ISBN 0-8248-0927-0 Presents Japanese art, religion, and culture over a period of 2,000 years.
*Zimmer, Heinrich. *Myths and Symbols in Indian Art and Civilization.* Joseph Campbell (ed). Princeton Univ Pr 1971 $9.95. ISBN 0-691-01778-6 Study of Indian symbolism and basic Hindu beliefs.

THE RENAISSANCE AND REFORMATION

Bainton, Roland H. *Erasmus of Christendom.* Scribner's 1969 $20.00. ISBN 0-684-15380-7

Bainton, Roland H. *Reformation of the Sixteenth Century.* Beacon 1985 $10.95. ISBN 0-8070-1301-3

Bassani, Ezio, and William Fagg. *Africa and the Renaissance: Art in Ivory.* TeNeues 1988 $60.00. ISBN 3-7913-0880-7

*Burckhardt, Jacob. *Civilization of the Renaissance in Italy.* 2 vols. Peter Smith $31.00. ISBN 0-8446-1775-X Offers an overview of life and times during the Italian Renaissance.

Caselli, Giovanni. *The Renaissance and the New World.* The History of Everyday Things Ser. Bedrick 1986 $15.95. ISBN 0-87226-050-X

*Chamberlain, E. R. *Florence in the Time of the Medici.* Then and There Ser. Longman 1982 $5.25. ISBN 0-582-20489-5 Account of Florence, Italy, during the rule of the noted Medici family.

Cole, Bruce. *Italian Art, 1250–1550: The Relation of Art to Life and Society.* Harper Jr Bks 1987 $34.50. ISBN 0-06-430162-1

Cole, Bruce. *Masaccio and the Art of Early Renaissance Florence.* Indiana Univ Pr 1980 $29.95. ISBN 0-253-12298-8

Cole, Bruce. *The Renaissance Artist at Work: From Pisano to Titian.* Harper Jr Bks 1983 $10.95. ISBN 0-06-430129-X

Cole, Bruce. *Sienese Painting in the Age of the Renaissance.* Indiana Univ Pr 1985 $37.50. ISBN 0-253-18130-5

*Durant, Will. *Reformation* Simon 1957 $29.95. ISBN 0-671-61050-3 Deals with the Reformation from the time of the English reformer John Wycliffe to the time of the French Protestant theologian John Calvin.

Durant, Will. *Renaissance.* Simon 1953 $29.95. ISBN 0-671-61600-5

Editors of Time–Life Books. *The European Emergence: 1500–1600.* Time Frame Ser. Time–Life 1989 $22.60. ISBN 0-8094-6450-0

*George, Margaret. *The Autobiography of Henry VIII.* Ballantine 1987 $9.95. ISBN 0-345-34275-5 Novel account of the noted English monarch.

George, Margaret. *Women in the First Capitalist Society: Experiences in Seventeenth-Century England.* Univ of Illinois Pr 1988 $29.95. ISBN 0-252-01534-7

Goldstein, Thomas. *Dawn of Modern Science.* Houghton 1988 $9.95. ISBN 0-395-48924-5

*Grimm, Harold J. *The Reformation Era: 1500–1650.* Macmillan 1973. ISBN 0-02-347270-7 Discusses the era of religious reform that brought about Protestantism.

Hale, J. R. (ed). *Concise Encyclopedia of the Italian Renaissance.* The World of Art Ser. Thames Hudson 1985 $11.95. ISBN 0-500-20191-9

Hale, J. R. *Renaissance Europe: The Individual and Society, 1480–1520.* Univ of California Pr 1978 $10.95.

Hale, J. R. *War and Society in Renaissance Europe, 1450–1620.* Johns Hopkins Univ Pr 1986 $10.95. ISBN 0-8018-3196-2

Hibbert, Christopher. *The House of Medici: Its Rise and Fall.* Morrow 1980 $12.95. ISBN 0-688-05339-4

*Kristeller, Paul O. *Renaissance Thought and Its Sources.* Columbia Univ Pr 1979 $16.50. ISBN 0-231-04513-1 Examines the ideas of the Renaissance era and the people and conditions that originated those ideas.

Labarge, Margaret Wade. *A Small Sound of the Trumpet: Women in the Medieval Life.* Beacon 1988 $12.95. ISBN 0-8070-5627-8

*Mattingly, Garrett. *Catherine of Aragon.* AMS (repr of 1942 ed) $32.50. ISBN 0-404-20169-5 Biographical account of the first wife of King Henry VIII of England.

Mattingly, Garrett. *Renaissance Diplomacy.* Dover 1988 $7.95. ISBN 0-486-25570-0

Scarre, Geoffrey. *Witchcraft and Magic in Sixteenth and Seventeenth Century Europe.* Humanities 1987 $8.50. ISBN 0-391-03505-3

Smith, Lacey B. *Henry VIII: The Mask of Royalty.* Academy Chi Pubs 1987 $7.95. ISBN 0-89733-056-0

Smith, Lacey B. *This Realm of England: 1399 to 1688. A History of England Ser.* Heath 1987 $11.50. ISBN 0-669-13422-8

Treadgold, Warren. *Renaissance Before the Renaissance: Cultural Revivals of Late Antiquity and the Middle Ages.* Stanford Univ Pr 1984 $29.50. ISBN 0-8047-1198-4

Trevelyan, George M. *England in the Age of Wycliffe.* AMS (repr of 1900 ed) $34.50. ISBN 0-404-56677-4

CALVIN, JOHN   1509–1564

John Calvin, one of the most influential Protestant theologians of the Reformation, was born in Picardy in France in 1509. By age 14 he had begun preparing for a career as a priest in the Roman Catholic church. Gradually, however, his thinking on theological matters began to differ from official church teachings, and he turned to a study of the law, Latin, and the classics. In 1533 Calvin experienced a sudden conversion and devoted all his attention to the Protestant Reformation. He began to systematize Protestant thought, completing his *The Institutes of the Christian Religion* in 1536. Considered one of the most influential theological works of all time, this book contains the basic principles of Calvinist theology, including the rejection of papal authority, justification by faith alone, and predestination.

Settling in Geneva, Switzerland, Calvin attempted to put his ideas of a rigorously controlled church state into practice. Ousted from Geneva in 1538, Calvin returned in 1541 and began instituting a government that was subordinate to the church. Calvinist theology differed from Lutheran theology on several matters, including the essence of the Lord's Supper, which Calvin maintained was a spiritual presence rather than a real one. Calvinism offered a counterpoint to Lutheranism, resulting in a split that produced the Reformed churches. In a world changing from a farming-based economy to a manufacturing and industrial one, Calvin's teachings on thrift, hard work, sobriety, and responsibility had a profound influence on the acceptance of capitalism as a driving economic force.

BOOKS BY CALVIN

The Institutes of the Christian Religion (1536). Tony Lane and Hilary Osborne (eds). Baker Bk 1987 $7.95. ISBN 0-8010-2524-9

Letters of John Calvin. Banner of Truth $7.95. ISBN 0-85151-323-9

A Reformation Debate. (coedited with Jacopo Sadoleto) Baker Bk 1976 $4.95. ISBN 0-8010-2390-4

BOOKS ABOUT CALVIN

Bouwsma, William J. *John Calvin: A Sixteenth-Century Portrait.* Oxford Univ Pr 1989 $8.95. ISBN 0-19-505951-4 Comprehensive look at the religious reformer and his theology that places him in the context of the humanist tradition.

Fillingham, Patricia. *John Calvin.* Warthog 1983 $5.00. ISBN 0-942292-04-9 Introduction to Calvin's life and thought.

*Stepanek, Sally. *John Calvin. World Leaders—Past and Present Ser.* Chelsea 1987 $17.95. ISBN 0-87754-515-4 Account of the religious leader of the sixteenth century.

Wallace, Ronald S. *Calvin, Geneva, and the Reformation: A Study of Calvin As Social Reformer, Churchman, Pastor, and Theologian.* Baker Bk 1989 $29.95. ISBN 0-8010-9692-8 Focuses on Calvin's work in Geneva and on his impact on Protestant theology and society.

CELLINI, BENVENUTO   1500–1571

A native of Florence, Italy, Benvenuto Cellini was one of the best-known craftsmen of his time. Cellini's father, an architect and musician, wanted his son to study the flute. But the young Cellini, ever strong-willed, apprenticed himself to a goldsmith instead. Exiled from Florence at age 16 for participating in a duel, Cellini spent many years on the move, practicing his craft in several Italian cities, including Rome, as well as at the French court. Popes and aristocrats were his patrons.

Cellini's most famous work in gold was created for King Francis I of France. An elaborate salt cellar—small dish or shaker that holds and dispenses salt—it depicts Neptune, symbolizing the sea, and a female figure that represents Earth. The salt cellar, which combines grace, complexity of detail, and technical excellence, is typical of Cellini's style.

Though trained as a goldsmith, Cellini also achieved fame as a sculptor. His best known work is a larger-than-life-size sculpture of the Greek hero Perseus holding up the bloody head of hideous-faced, snake-haired mortal Medusa. Its casting was a triumph of technique. Cellini is also well known for his *Autobiography,* written between 1558 and 1566 but first published in 1728. It is an unapologetic tale of bitter rivalry, hatred, theft, murder, and sensuality. Although the story of his many dishonorable adventures reads like a novel, it presents a vivid picture of the Renaissance in sixteenth-century Italy.

Books by Cellini

Autobiography. Penguin Classic Ser. (c. 1558–1562). Penguin 1956 $5.95. ISBN 0-14-044049-6
Treatises of Benvenuto Cellini on Goldsmithing and Sculpture. C. R. Ashbee (tr). Dover 1966 $6.95. ISBN 0-486-21568-7

Book about Cellini

Pope-Hennessey, John. *Cellini.* Abbeville 1985 $85.00. ISBN 0-89659-453-X Well-illustrated look at the works of the noted Italian sculptor and metalsmith.

DURER, ALBRECHT   1471–1528

The German artist Albrecht Dürer was the leading figure of Renaissance art in northern Europe. His art is a blend of Italian Renaissance idealism and northern European attention to detail and mysticism. As a true Renaissance man, Dürer excelled in many fields, including painting, printmaking, and the writing of art theory.

Born in Nuremberg, Germany, in 1471, Dürer was the son of a goldsmith. At an early age, he was apprenticed to his father and gained valuable experience with metalwork and the use of tools. It soon became apparent, however, that the young Dürer was more interested in painting and drawing than in goldsmithing. So at the age of 15 he was apprenticed to a painter and print-maker from whom he learned techniques for doing woodcuts and engravings as well as for painting.

In the fall of 1494, soon after his marriage, Dürer took his first trip to Italy, where he was profoundly affected by the art of the High Renaissance. After returning to Nuremberg, he devoted himself full-time to painting and print-

Nobleman on horseback followed by knight. Woodcut by Albrecht Dürer (1496). Courtesy of The Bettmann Archive.

making and became increasingly interested in the problems of perspective and proportion, probably as a result of his contacts with Italian art. He traveled to Italy again in 1505 and shortly after his return to Germany painted two works, *Adam* and *Eve,* that clearly show the influence of the Italian Renaissance.

During a trip to the Netherlands in 1520, Dürer was received as a master, making him the first German artist to gain major recognition outside his own country. There he also met the Dutch philosopher Erasmus. (*See* Erasmus, Vol. 2, World History: The Renaissance and Reformation.) Dürer's diaries of the trip are among the most interesting documents in art history. On this trip he may have contracted the malaria that caused his death several years later.

A fine painter, Dürer really excelled as a graphic artist, producing more that 350 woodcuts, 100 engravings, and approximately 900 drawings and watercolors. He was also deeply concerned with art theory and wrote treatises on perspective and proportion. In his writings, Dürer argues for an art that is based on scholarly principles. He insisted, for example, that a knowledge of proportion and anatomy is essential to capture the beauty of the human body. His insistence on scientific methods was a result of his contact with the Italian Renaissance and was a break with the mysticism of northern traditions in art. He differed, however, from his Italian mentors in his acceptance of all forms of nature, whether beautiful or monstrous. To Dürer, the genius in art is to represent nature as it is, not as it should be.

BOOKS BY DURER

Albrecht Dürer: Sketchbook of His Journey to the Netherlands, 1520–1521. Praeger 1971. (o.p.)
Complete Engravings, Etchings, and Dry Points of Albrecht Dürer. Walter L. Strauss (ed). Dover 1972 $8.95. ISBN 0-486-22851-7

BOOKS ABOUT DURER

Panofsky, Erwin. *Life and Art of Albrecht Dürer.* Princeton Univ Pr 1955 $22.50. ISBN 0-691-00303-3 Comprehensive, scholarly account of the artist and his work.

*Raboff, Ernest. *Albrecht Dürer. Art for Children Ser.* Harper Jr Bks 1988 repr of 1970 ed $11.70. ISBN 0-397-32216-X Life and works of the celebrated artist; especially suitable for younger readers.

Strauss, Walter L. (ed). *The Complete Engravings, Etchings and Drypoints of Albrecht Dürer.* Dover 1973. ISBN 0-486-22852-7 Includes plates of each engraving, etching, and drypoint, comments on each, and a bibliography.

ERASMUS, DESIDERIUS *c.* 1466–1536

The Dutch scholar Desiderius Erasmus, a leading figure of the Renaissance in northern Europe, is considered the greatest Renaissance humanist. Erasmus studied the classics in his youth and was sent to a monastery in 1487. Ordained a priest in 1492, he obtained a release from his vows three years later in order to study at the University of Paris in France. Erasmus spent the rest of his life doing scholarly research and writing. In addition to producing numerous books, he carried on correspondence with hundreds of scholars throughout Europe.

Some of Erasmus's works are church writings. For example, he prepared a new edition of the New Testament in Latin (1516) based on several versions in the original Greek. He also edited numerous ancient Greek and Roman classics.

Erasmus was concerned about abuses within the Roman Catholic church, particularly the poor training of many church officials and their preoccupation with such worldly matters as wealth and power. Erasmus was also concerned with issues involving learning. For example, he felt that many scholars wasted time on minor problems instead of trying to eliminate ignorance and superstition. Erasmus satirized the life and religious practices of his time in his most famous work, *The Praise of Folly* (1509), and also in *Colloquies* (1518). Many of his criticisms were later echoed by the German monk Martin Luther (*see* Luther, Vol. 2, World History: The Renaissance and Reformation) and other Protestant reformers. Although Erasmus favored church reform, he opposed the Protestant Reformation and remained a loyal Catholic. He wanted the church to be purified rather than divided, and he condemned the religious wars that resulted from Luther's actions.

BOOKS BY ERASMUS

The Critical Writing by Desiderius Erasmus on the Spiritual Conditions of His Times and the Psychological Impulses Motivating the Actions of Men. Am Inst Psych 1984 $100.50. ISBN 0-89920-106-7

The Historical Significance of Desiderius Erasmus in the Light of the Protestant Revolution and the Catholic Church as Revealed by His Most Famous Pronouncements. 2 vols. American Classical Coll Pr 1985 $207.50.

Praise of Folly. Penguin Classics Ser. Betty Radice (tr). Penguin 1971 $5.95. ISBN 0-14-044240-5

Discourse on Free Will. (coauthored with Martin Luther) Ernst F. Winter (tr). Ungar $8.95. ISBN 0-8044-6140-6

BOOKS ABOUT ERASMUS

*Amey, Peter, *et al. Luther, Erasmus, and Loyola.* Malcolm Yapp, *et al* (eds). Greenhaven 1980 $2.95. ISBN 0-89908-018-9 Discusses three prominent religious leaders during the period of the Reformation and Counter Reformation.

Facer, G. S. *Erasmus and His Times: Selections from the Letters of Erasmus and His Circle.* Bolchazy-Carducci 1988 $11.00. ISBN 0-86516-213-1 Looks at Erasmus and the
Reformation through primary sources.

Mangan, John J. *Life, Character, and Influence of Desiderius Erasmus of Rotterdam.* 2 vols. AMS
(repr of 1972 ed) $78.50. ISBN 0-404-04178-7 Comprehensive account of the life
and times of the noted Dutch humanist.

Rummel, Erika. *Erasmus as Translator of the Classics.* Univ of Toronto Pr 1984. ISBN
0-8020-5653-9 Illustrates the importance of Erasmus's Greek studies and translations.

Screech, M. A. *Erasmus: Ecstasy and the Praise of Folly.* Penguin 1989 $7.95. ISBN 0-14-
055235-9 Portrait of Erasmus as humanist, critic, international pacifist, and guide
to the human soul.

LEONARDO DA VINCI   1452–1519

A towering genius in the fields of science, engineering, and technology, Leonardo da Vinci was also one of the world's greatest artists. A leading figure of
the Renaissance, he is the original "Renaissance man"—one who excels in all
areas. Though always recognized for his art, Leonardo da Vinci's scientific
achievements were rediscovered only in the twentieth century as his notebooks
became widely known.

Born illegitimately in the town of Vinci, near Florence, Italy, to a Florentine
notary and a peasant girl, Leonardo da Vinci was apprenticed at an early age
to the Italian artist Andrea del Verrocchio, a well-known Renaissance master.
By 1472, he had become a member of Florence's painters guild and he began
to receive recognition for his work. In 1482 da Vinci went to Milan, Italy, and
worked for the Duke of Milan as a military engineer, a painter, a sculptor, and
an architect. During the next 17 years in Milan, he designed part of the tower
of Milan's cathedral and painted many works including *The Last Supper* (c. 1498),
a mural in the church of Santa Maria delle Grazie. This painting is considered
one of his greatest creations and one of the most important works of Western
art. During these creative years in Milan, Leonardo da Vinci wrote his *Treatise
on Painting* (1489–1518) and began to fill notebooks with ideas about scientific
matters. He also became increasingly interested in a variety of fields, including
anatomy, biology, mathematics, and physics.

When Leonardo's patron, the Duke of Milan, fell from power in 1499, the
artist returned to Florence, where he did theoretical work in mathematics and
studied anatomy at the hospital of Santa Maria Nuova. It was there that he
painted another of his world-famous canvases, the *Mona Lisa* (c. 1503), the
portrait of the wife of a Florentine merchant. After 1506, however, scientific
research began to occupy more and more of his time, and he used his artistic
talents in the service of scientific illustration. His illustrations communicate a
profound understanding of the structure of things.

After a short and unsuccessful time in Rome (1513–1516), Leonardo settled
in France, where he became architectural advisor to King Francis I. He died in
France in 1519 at the age of 67.

BOOKS BY LEONARDO DA VINCI

Leonardo Da Vinci Drawings. Dover 1983 $3.50. ISBN 0-486-23951-9

The Madrid Codices of Leonardo Da Vinci. Ladislao Reti (tr). McGraw 1974 $400.00. ISBN
0-07-037194-6

The Notebooks of Leonardo Da Vinci. 2 vols. Jean-Paul Richter (ed). Peter Smith $40.00.
ISBN 0-8446-4535-4

BOOKS ABOUT LEONARDO DA VINCI

*Amey, Peter, *et al. Leonardo da Vinci. World History Ser.* Malcolm Yapp, *et al* (eds). Greenhaven 1980 $2.95. ISBN 0-89908-016-2 Introduction to the life and work of the world-renowned artist.

Clark, Kenneth. *Leonardo Da Vinci.* Penguin 1989 $14.95. ISBN 0-14-022707-5 Classic study of the painter; recently reissued with an introduction by Martin Kemp.

Freud, Sigmund. *Leonardo Da Vinci and a Memory of His Childhood.* James Strachey (ed). Alan Tyson (tr). Norton 1965 $5.95. ISBN 0-393-00149-0 Reconstructs the emotional life of the artist's early childhood years through psychoanalysis.

Galluzzi, Paolo (ed). *Leonardo da Vinci: Engineer and Architect.* Univ of Nebraska Pr 1988 $65.00. ISBN 2-89192-084-8 Focuses on Leonardo's work in architectural and engineering design.

Gibbs-Smith, Charles. *The Inventions of Leonardo da Vinci.* Scribner's 1978 $2.95. ISBN 0-684-15746-2 Looks at some of Leonardo's many inventions.

Goldscheider, Ludwig. *Leonardo da Vinci: Life and Work, Paintings and Drawings.* New York Graphic Society 1967. (o.p.) Classic account of the artist that includes primary source documents, a chronology, a bibliography, and reproductions of Leonardo's work.

*Harris, Nathaniel. *Leonardo and the Renaissance. Life and Times Ser.* Watts 1987 $12.40. ISBN 0-531-18137-5 Basic introduction to the artist and his importance in Renaissance art.

Hart, Ivor B. *World of Leonardo da Vinci.* Kelley (repr of 1962 ed). (o.p.) $35.00. Standard work on Leonardo da Vinci as a scientist and engineer.

*McLanathan, Richard. *Leonardo da Vinci. First Impressions Ser.* Abrams 1990 $17.95. ISBN 0-8109-1256-2 Illustrated account of the life and work of the famous artist.

McMullen, Roy. *Mona Lisa: The Picture and the Myth. Quality Paperback Ser.* Da Capo 1977 $7.95. ISBN 0-306-80067-5 Discusses the artist's most famous work and tries to unravel the myth surrounding it.

LUTHER, MARTIN 1483–1546

Martin Luther was born at Eisleben, Saxony, into a family of free landholders. Although he prepared for a career in law, studying at the University of Erfurt (1501–1505) in Germany, in 1505 he suddenly entered an Augustinian monastery. Ordained a priest in 1507, Luther continued his studies at the University of Wittenberg in Germany, earning a doctorate and a professorship in theology and the scriptures. During this period, he agonized over the state of his soul and feared for his salvation. He eventually resolved his torment by deciding that faith alone, not the performance of good works, was all that was needed for salvation.

In 1517 Luther publicly posted his historic 95 theses, which protested corruption and abuses in Catholicism. This led to his excommunication from the Roman Catholic church in 1521 and to the foundation of the religion of Lutheranism. Beginning in 1520, Luther explained his religious thinking in several important tracts. In his *Address to the Christian Nobility of the German Nation* (1520), he rejected the authority of the pope in secular matters, an idea that appealed to many German princes. In *The Babylonian Captivity of the Church,* he rejected the priesthood and its role as a mediator between God and the faithful and said that the sacraments were only aids to faith. In *The Freedom of a Christian Man* (1520), he explained his reliance on justification by faith alone.

In 1521 the Diet of Worms, the imperial council held at the German city of Worms, called for Luther's seizure as a heretic, and he fled to Saxony and the protection of Elector Frederick III. There, in 1525, he married a former nun named Katharina von Bora. They eventually raised six children. While under Frederick's protection, Luther began a 10-year work of translating the New

Testament into German. Luther's break with Catholicism was also a break from the use of Latin as the language of the church. His many writings, executed in a forceful idiomatic form of German, helped set the standards of the modern German language.

BOOKS BY LUTHER

Basic Luther. Templegate 1984 $14.95. ISBN 0-87243-131-2

Luther's Ninety-Five Theses. C. M. Jacobs (tr). Augsburg Fortress 1957 $1.25. ISBN 0-8006-1265-5

BOOKS ABOUT LUTHER

■Bainton, Roland H. *Here I Stand: A Life of Martin Luther.* Abingdon 1950 $4.95. ISBN 0-687-16894-5 A scholarly interpretation of the contributions of this leader.

Boehmer, Heinrich. *Luther and the Reformation in the Light of Modern Research.* AMS (repr of 1930 ed) $44.50. ISBN 0-404-19823-6 Critical analysis of Martin Luther and his role in the Protestant Reformation.

Erikson, Erik. *Young Man Luther.* Norton $5.95. ISBN 0-393-00170-9 Famous psychobiography that shows the origins of Martin Luther's rebelliousness and his later authoritarianism.

*Fehlauer, Adolph. *Life and Faith of Martin Luther.* Northwest Pub 1981 $5.95. ISBN 0-8100-0125-X Account of the life and theology of the Protestant reformer.

*O'Neill, Judith. *Martin Luther.* Cambridge Topic Bks. Lerner 1979 $8.95. ISBN 0-8225-1215-7 Story of the noted religious leader who established the principles of the Lutheran religion.

*Stepanek, Sally. *Martin Luther.* World Leaders—Past and Present Ser. Chelsea 1986 $17.95. ISBN 0-87754-538-3 Basic introduction to the German religious reformer; especially suitable for younger readers.

Todd, John M. *Luther: A Life.* Crossroad 1982. ISBN 0-8245-0479-8 Personal portrait of Luther that draws from his writings.

MICHELANGELO (BUONARROTI) 1475–1564

Widely regarded as the greatest sculptor of the Renaissance, the Italian artist Michelangelo Buonarroti was also an immensely talented painter, poet, and architect. Michelangelo was born in the town of Caprese near Florence, Italy, on March 6, 1475. Although his father scorned art of any kind, he recognized his son's special talents and sent the young Michelangelo to study art in Florence. There he learned to paint frescoes—paintings executed on plaster— and also the fundamentals of sculpture. While in Florence, he gained the patronage of Lorenzo de' Medici, the ruling prince.

Between 1496 and 1501, Michelangelo worked in Rome, where he created his first major work, the *Pietà,* a statue that shows Mary holding the body of Jesus after the Crucifixion. After returning to Florence in 1501, the young artist began work on the magnificent statue *David,* which amazed the critics and became the city's most popular work of art. Four years later he was called back to Rome by Pope Julius II, a leading patron of the arts, who commissioned Michelangelo to design a vast tomb. Shortly after getting this contract, Michelangelo received another commission from the Pope to paint religious scenes on the ceiling of the Sistine Chapel, the private chapel of the popes in Rome. For four years the artist worked feverishly on the ceiling, stretched out on his back atop a high platform. The difficulty of the work caused cramps in his legs, and his eyesight began to fail. "I have been here a thousand years," he wrote to his father. "I am more exhausted than man ever was." Created under difficult conditions, the Sistine Chapel ceiling is considered by many to the greatest single work of art ever created by one person. Many years later, Michelangelo added a huge dramatic fresco known as the *Last Judgment* to the Sistine Chapel. The fresco was completed in 1541.

Between 1520 and 1534, Michelangelo worked in Florence creating the Medici Chapel in the Church of San Lorenzo. Its sculptures of Giuliano and Lorenzo de' Medici and the allegorical figures of *Day, Night, Dawn,* and *Evening* show a dramatic contrast between action and repose.

A true Renaissance man, Michelangelo was not only an extraordinary sculptor and painter but also a sensitive poet and a talented architect. In 1547, he became chief architect of St. Peter's Church in Rome. Many consider the dome he created for the church to be the crowning achievement of the Renaissance. A prolific artist, Michelangelo worked steadily until his death in 1564 at the age of 89.

BOOKS BY MICHELANGELO

Complete Poems and Selected Letters of Michelangelo. Creighton Gilbert (tr). Vintage 1970. (o.p.)
Life, Letters, and Poetry. The World Classics Ser. George Bull (ed). Oxford Univ Pr 1987 $6.95. ISBN 0-19-281603-9
Michelangelo: A Record of His Life As Told in His Own Letters and Papers. Robert W. Carden (tr). Gordon Pr 1976 $59.95. ISBN 0-8490-2256-8

BOOKS ABOUT MICHELANGELO

The Complete Paintings of Michelangelo. Abrams 1969. (o.p.) Beautifully produced book of the artist's paintings.
De Tolnay, Charles Q. *Michelangelo.* 6 vols. Princeton Univ Pr Vol. 1 *The Youth of Michelangelo.* 1969 $100.00. ISBN 0-691-03858-9. Vol. 2 *The Sistine Ceiling.* 1969 $100.00. ISBN 0-691-03856-2. Vol. 3 *The Medici Chapel.* 1970 $100.00. ISBN 0-691-03854-6. Vol. 4 *The Tomb of Julius Two.* 1970 $100.00. ISBN 0-691-03857-0. Vol. 5 *The Final Period.* 1970 $100.00. ISBN 0-691-03855-4. Vol. 6 *Michelangelo: Sculptor-Painter-Architect.* $65.00. ISBN 0-691-103876-7 Comprehensive look at the life of the artist and analyses of his work.
Grimm, Herman F. *Life of Michelangelo.* Fanny E. Bunnett (tr). 2 vols. Greenwood 1970 repr of 1900 ed $48.00. ISBN 0-8371-2750-5 One of the greatest biographies of the artist.
Hartt, Frederick (ed). *Michelangelo. Masters of Art Ser.* Abrams 1984 $19.95. ISBN 0-8109-1335-6 Attractively illustrated look at the artist's work.
Hibbard, Howard. *Michelangelo.* Harper 1975 $20.00. ISBN 0-06-433323-X Illustrated introduction to all areas of Michelangelo's career.
Seymour, Charles (ed). *Michelangelo: The Sistine Chapel. Critical Studies in Art History.* Norton 1972 $9.95. ISBN 0-393-09889-3 Focuses on the artist's famous paintings in the Vatican's Sistine Chapel.
*Stone, Irving. *The Agony and the Ecstasy.* NAL 1987 $5.95. ISBN 0-451-15947-0 Popular biography of Michelangelo by a well-known American writer and novelist.
Summers, David. *Michelangelo and the Language of Art.* Princeton Univ Pr 1981 $25.50. ISBN 0-691-10097-7 Discusses how the artist's intellectual framework and the concepts of Renaissance thought influenced his art.

PALESTRINA (GIOVANNI PIERLUIGI) *c.* 1525–1594

Born Giovanni Pierluigi, this Italian Renaissance composer took his name from the town of his birth—Palestrina. Palestrina was a master of polyphonic composition, a musical form that combines two or more voices in harmony. His polyphonic compositions include more than 100 masses and 250 motets, or choral compositions based on scriptural texts. Palestrina's use of the polyphonic form led to the decline of traditional Gregorian chant and plainsong, which are based on a single melodic line. Many consider his work to be the culmination of Renaissance music.

While only a child, Palestrina was taken to Rome to study music at the Basilica of Saint Mary Major, where he became a choirboy. At age 19 he was appointed choirmaster of the cathedral in his home town. When the bishop of Palestrina became Pope Julius III, he appointed Palestrina choirmaster of the Julian Chapel Choir in Rome (1551). A few years later, Palestrina became choirmaster of the Cathedral of St. John Lateran (1555–1560) where he composed the *Lamentations of Jeremiah*. After an appointment as choirmaster at Saint Mary Major (1566–1571), followed by a time when he was employed privately (1566–1571), Palestrina resumed leadership of the Julian Chapel Choir. Then in 1578 he was appointed the master of music at the Vatican Basilica.

Besides composing masses and motets, Palestrina also wrote numerous other religious songs, including musical settings of the Biblical Song of Songs. He also composed secular songs called madrigals. Palestrina's best known work is the *Missa Papae Marcelli* (*c.* 1555–1560).

BOOKS ABOUT PALESTRINA

Cametti, Alberto. *Palestrina.* AMS (repr of 1925 ed) $32.00. ISBN 0-404-12878-5 Comprehensive treatment of the Renaissance composer and his work.

Coates, Henry. *Palestrina. Encore Music Editions Ser.* Hyperion 1984 repr of 1938 ed $23.25. ISBN 0-88355-732-0 Study of Palestrina that includes an historical approach, a portrait of the man and the musician, and an examination of the music.

RAPHAEL (RAPHAELLO SANTI) *c.* 1483–1520

The Renaissance painter Raphaello Santi, better known as Raphael, was born in Urbino, Italy. Raphael was taught the basics of art by his father, a court poet and painter to the duke of Urbino. After his father's death, Raphael entered the workshop of the Renaissance artist Perugino, who had a great influence on his early career. Perugino's influence can be seen in such works as Raphael's *The Crucifixion* (1503) and the *Coronation of the Virgin* (1502–1503), both of which are masterful examples of narrative paintings, or paintings that tell a story. Later in his career, Raphael went to Florence and was influenced by the Renaissance artists Leonardo da Vinci and Michelangelo. (*See* da Vinci *and* Michelangelo, Vol. 2, World History: The Renaissance and Reformation.) During this time Raphael's painting matured and his use of anatomy, perspective, and color brought greater clarity and power to his work, especially in the numerous *Florentine Madonnas* that he painted.

In 1508 Raphael moved to Rome where he became involved in remodeling the Vatican. He was completely responsible for the frescoes, the paintings done on wet plaster, on the walls and ceiling of the Stanza della Segnatura, an important meeting room in the Vatican palace. On one wall he painted the *School of Athens,* a portrayal of Aristotle, Plato, and other Greek philosophers in a contemporary architectural setting. On another wall he painted the *Triumph of Religion,* a gathering of prophets, apostles, and other representatives of the Roman Catholic church arranged around God. These two paintings are considered to be among Raphael's greatest works.

In 1514 Raphael was named chief architect of the Vatican and of St. Peter's Basilica. In addition to this responsibility, the artist was given many honors and commissions of work. Although Raphael died at the age of 37, he left a legacy of paintings that are admired for their suppleness of form, the pleasantness of their composition, and their celebration of human grandeur.

BOOKS BY RAPHAEL

Complete Paintings of Raphael. Penguin 1987 $10.95. ISBN 0-14-009273-0

Drawings of Raphael. Master Draughtsman Ser. Stephen Longstreet (ed). Borden $4.95. ISBN 0-87505-181-2

Raphael: Tables of Houses. Wehman $4.95. ISBN 0-685-38474-8

BOOKS ABOUT RAPHAEL

Beck, James. *Raphael.* Abrams 1976 $49.50. ISBN 0-8109-0432-2 Beautifully produced book of the artist's work.

The Complete Paintings of Raphael. Abrams 1969. (o.p.) Comprehensive presentation of the artist's paintings.

The Complete Works of Raphael. Reynal 1969. (o.p.) Contains essays on Raphael's paintings, collaborators, drawings, sonnets, and life.

Joannides, Paul. *The Drawings of Raphael: With a Complete Catalog.* Univ of California Pr 1983 $129.95. ISBN 0-520-05087-8 Excellent collection of commentaries on all of Raphael's drawings.

Jones, Roger, and Nicholas Penny. *Raphael.* Yale Univ Pr 1987 $19.95. ISBN 0-300-04052-0 Scholarly presentation of the life and work of the artist.

Pope-Hennessey, John. *Raphael.* New York Univ Pr $50.00. ISBN 0-8147-0476-X Series of lectures given by the eminent art historian; includes quality reproductions.

See also Vol. 1, British Literature, *and* World Literature.

EXPLORATION AND EXPANSION

*Campbell, Civardi. *Viking Raiders.* EDC 1977 $5.95. ISBN 0-86020-085-X Account of family life during the early Viking era.

Davidson, Basil. *African Slave Trade.* Little 1988 $10.95. ISBN 0-316-17438-6

*Del Castillo, Bernal. *The Discovery and Conquest of Mexico 1517–1521.* A. P. Maudslay (tr). Buccaneer 1986 $31.95. ISBN 0-89966-559-4 Account of the discovery and conquest of Mexico by a foot soldier under the command of the Spanish conquistador Hernán Cortés.

Editors of Time–Life Books. *Voyages of Discovery: 1400–1500. Time Frame Ser.* Time–Life 1989 $22.60. ISBN 0-8094-6445-4

Hoobler, Dorothy, and Thomas Hoobler. *The Voyages of Captain Cook.* Putnam 1983 $10.95. ISBN 0-399-20975-1

*Miquel, Pierre. *Age of Discovery. Silver Burdett Picture Histories Ser.* Silver 1985 $8.95. ISBN 0-382-06922-6 General introduction to the period of European exploration of the Far East and other new lands; especially suitable for younger readers.

*Morison, Samuel E. *The European Discovery of America: The Northern Voyages.* Oxford Univ Pr 1971 $35.00. ISBN 0-19-501377-8 Describes the explorations and discoveries in the northern parts of the Americas.

*Morison, Samuel E. *The European Discovery of America: The Southern Voyages.* Oxford Univ Pr 1974 $35.00. ISBN 0-19-501823-0 Describes the explorations and discoveries in the southern parts of the Americas.

*Morison, Samuel E. *The Great Explorers: The European Discovery of America.* Oxford Univ Pr 1986 $15.95. ISBN 0-19-504222-0 Identifies and discusses the major European explorers credited with the discovery of the Americas.

*Stevens, Paul. *Ferdinand and Isabella. World Leaders—Past and Present Ser.* Chelsea 1988

$17.95. ISBN 0-87754-523-5 Explores the lives and times of the noted Spanish monarchs who reconquered Spain from the Moors and financed the explorations of Christopher Columbus.

COOK, CAPTAIN JAMES   1728–1779

Considered by many to be Britain's greatest explorer, Captain James Cook was born to a poor family in Yorkshire, England, in 1728. After a limited education, he joined the British Navy in 1755 and moved rapidly up the ranks, becoming master of his own ship in 1759. Between 1763 and 1767, Cook spent summers surveying the coast of Newfoundland, and during that time he accurately calculated the longitude of that land. Because of this accomplishment, he was chosen to lead a scientific expedition to the Pacific to observe the movement of the planet Venus between Earth and the sun. Cook was also given secret orders to search for new lands in the South Pacific Ocean that could become British colonies.

In 1768 Cook left England on his ship, the H.M.S. *Endeavour.* A year later, he arrived at the island of Tahiti, where he observed Venus. Cook then sailed west to explore the coasts of New Zealand. From there he sailed west again and reached the uncharted east coast of Australia, which he surveyed and claimed for Great Britain. After exploring a passage between Australia and New Guinea, Cook returned to England in July 1771.

A year later, Cook was sent out on a second voyage to search the southern Pacific for a great continent some scientists believed existed. Sailing west from England, he crisscrossed the Pacific and twice crossed the Antarctic Circle. Although he never saw the Antarctic continent, he concluded that there was a continent there.

Cook's third and last voyage began in July 1776. His goal was to discover the fabled Northwest Passage, a waterway believed to connect the Atlantic and Pacific oceans somewhere in North America. During this voyage Cook discovered the Hawaiian Islands. He then sailed up the northwest coast of North America as far as the Bering Strait and in the Arctic Ocean. Unable to locate a passage through the ice, Cook returned to the Hawaiian Islands for repairs. While there, Cook was killed by the inhabitants during a dispute over a missing boat.

Cook was known as a leader who handled his ships and crews well. Unlike many sea captains of the time, he managed on his voyages to avoid the curse of scurvy, a disease caused by the lack of Vitamin C and common among sailors of the time, by providing a proper diet for his crew.

BOOKS BY COOK

Authentic Narrative of a Voyage Performed by Captain Cook and Captain Clerke in His Majesty's Ships Resolution and Discovery During the Years 1776–1780: In Search of a North-West Passage between the Continents of Asia and America (1782). William Ellis (ed). 2 vols. Da Capo 1969. (o.p.)

Explorations of Captain James Cook in the Pacific, as Told by Selections of His Own Journals, 1768–1779. A. Grenfell Price (ed). Dover $6.95. ISBN 0-486-22766-9

Journal of H.M.S. Endeavour, 1768–1771. Genesis 1977. (o.p.) $460.00.

Voyages of Discovery. John Barrow (ed). Biblio Dist 1976. (o.p.) $10.95.

BOOKS ABOUT COOK

Beaglehole, J. C. *The Life of Captain James Cook.* Stanford Univ Pr 1974 $39.50. ISBN 0-8047-0848-7 Scholarly account of the sea captain and explorer.

Fisher, Robin, and Hugh Johnston (eds). *Captain James Cook and His Times.* Univ of

Washington Pr 1979 $19.95. ISBN 0-295-95654-2 Discusses Cook as a product of his society and of the historical period.

*Harley, Ruth. *Captain James Cook.* Troll 1979 $2.50. ISBN 0-89375-169-3 Introductory account of the noted British sea captain.

*Hoobler, Dorothy, and Thomas Hoobler. *The Voyages of Captain Cook.* Putnam 1983 $10.95. ISBN 0-399-20975-1 Account that covers in detail the three sea journeys Cook made from 1768 to 1779.

Parkinson, Sydney. *Journal of a Voyage to the South Seas in H.M.S. Endeavour.* Christine Holmes (ed). Longwood $20.00. ISBN 0-904573-51-6 Primary authority on the circumnavigation by a young botanical draftsman on Cook's 1768–1771 voyage.

*Sylvester, David W. *Captain Cook and the Pacific.* Then and There Ser. Marjorie Reeves (ed). Longman 1971 $4.75. ISBN 0-582-20462-3 Story of Captain Cook's South Pacific explorations.

Villiers, Alan. *Captain James Cook.* Scribner's 1970 $25.00. ISBN 0-684-15553-2 Comprehensive look at Cook's life and achievements.

CORTES, HERNAN   1485–1547

Hernán Cortés, the Spanish conqueror of Mexico, was born in Medellín, Spain, in 1485. When he was 19 years old he sailed for the West Indies, where he became a planter and later took part in the conquest of Cuba. In 1518 the governor of Cuba chose Cortés to lead an expedition to the Aztec empire in Mexico. Greedy for the reported gold and riches of the Aztecs, Cortés gathered a group of some 600 adventurers and set sail.

In 1519 Cortés's expedition landed on the mainland, founded the town of Vera Cruz, and enlisted the help of local Indians after defeating them. He also burned all his ships to prevent his men from turning back. Cortés learned that various Indian groups ruled by the Aztecs were ready for revolt. He also learned about the Aztec legend of Quetzalcóatl, a white-skinned black-bearded god who had left Mexico centuries before but was supposed to return to fulfill a prophecy. Armed with this knowledge and supported by Indian allies, Cortés marched to Tenochtitlán, the capital of the Aztec empire. Believing the Spanish to be descendants of the god Quetzalcóatl, the emperor Montezuma, and his people did not resist. Cortés took Montezuma hostage and ruled through him.

The following year, Cortés returned to Vera Cruz. While he was gone, his men had massacred several hundred unarmed Aztec nobles during a religious festival. On his return, Cortés found the city in revolt. He tried to use Montezuma to calm the people, but instead the emperor was killed, and Cortés, his soldiers, and his Indian allies were forced to flee. In 1521 Cortés once again marched on Tenochtitlán. The Aztecs held out for several weeks, but finally, weakened by starvation and disease, their city in ruins, they surrendered and their empire fell to the Spaniards.

Over the next few years, Cortés sent out expeditions to conquer other parts of Mexico and Central America. Denied an appointment as royal governor of Mexico, he returned to Spain, where he died in 1547.

BOOKS BY CORTES

The Fifth Letter of Hernando Cortés to the Emperor Charles 5th Containing an Account of His Expedition to Honduras. Hakluyt Society Ser. Pascual De Gayangos (tr). Burt Franklin 1964 $25.50. ISBN 0-8337-0686-1

Five Letters of Cortés. J. Bayard (tr). Norton 1969 $8.95. ISBN 0-393-09877-X

Letters from Mexico. Anthony Pagden (ed and tr). Yale Univ Pr 1986 $16.95. ISBN 0-300-03799-6

BOOKS ABOUT CORTES

Cantu, Caesar C. *Cortés and the Fall of the Aztec Empire.* Modern World 1966 $12.95. ISBN 0-685-16803-4 Discusses the role of the Spanish explorer in the fall of the Aztec empire of Mexico.

*de Castillo, Bernal D. *Cortés and the Conquest of Mexico by the Spaniards in 1521.* Shoe String 1988 repr of 1942 ed $17.50. Tells of the downfall of the capital city and civilization of the Aztecs.

Lopez de Gomara, Francisco. *Cortés: The Life of the Conqueror of Mexico by His Secretary, Francisco Lopez de Gomara.* Lesley B. Simpson (ed and tr). Univ of California Pr 1964 $11.95. ISBN 0-520-00493-0 Portrait of the Spanish explorer and conquistador by his personal secretary.

Prescott, William H. *The Conquest of Mexico.* (bound with *The Conquest of Peru*) Random 1979 $16.95. ISBN 0-394-60471-7 Comprehensive account of the fall of the Aztec empire in Mexico.

Prescott, William H. *History of the Conquest of Mexico.* Harvey C. Gardiner (ed). Univ of Chicago Pr 1985 $18.00. ISBN 0-226-68001-0 Scholarly account of the Spanish conquest of Mexico and the Aztec empire.

*Wepman, Dennis. *Hernan Cortés.* World Leaders—Past and Present Ser. Chelsea 1986 $17.95. ISBN 0-87754-593-6 Introductory biography of Cortés, the Spanish conqueror of Mexico.

*Wilkes, John. *Hernan Cortés: Conquistador in Mexico.* Cambridge Univ Pr 1977 $5.25. ISBN 0-527-20424-0 Well-written story of the Spanish explorer.

DRAKE, SIR FRANCIS   *c.* 1540–1596

Born in Devonshire, England, Francis Drake was apprenticed to a ship captain at an early age and went on to become a slave trader, a pirate, an adventurer, and the first English sea captain to circumnavigate the world (1577–1580). In 1567 Drake commanded a ship on a slave-trading expedition organized by his cousin, the admiral Sir John Hawkins. The small English fleet picked up its cargo of African slaves and then sailed to the West Indies where the slaves were to be sold to the Spaniards who controlled the islands. The Spanish, however, attacked the tiny fleet and all but three of the vessels were destroyed. Thereafter, Drake and Hawkins, who called themselves "sea dogs," began raiding Spanish treasure vessels for the gold, silver, and precious jewels they carried, which earned them the wrath of the Spanish king.

Drake's circumnavigation of the globe resulted from efforts to escape capture after a series of successful raids on Spanish treasure ships and mining towns along the Pacific coast of America. Drake's expedition began the voyage with five ships, but only one—the *Golden Hind* captained by Drake himself—made it around the world. After a three-year voyage, Drake returned to England in 1580 and was knighted by Queen Elizabeth I for his accomplishments. In 1588, as a vice admiral of the English fleet, Drake participated in the defeat of the Spanish Armada, the fleet of warships sent by King Philip II of Spain to invade England. Continuing his raids on Spanish treasure ships and ports, Drake died of dysentery in 1596, while in the West Indies, and was buried at sea.

BOOK BY DRAKE

World Encompassed by Sir Francis Drake. Hakluyt Society, First Ser. W. S. Vaux (ed). Burt Franklin (repr of 1854 ed) $32.00. ISBN 0-8337-0909-7

BOOKS ABOUT DRAKE

*Goodnough, David. *Francis Drake.* Troll 1979 $2.50. ISBN 0-89375-165-0 Introductory account of the English seaman and explorer.

Hampden, John (ed). *Francis Drake Privateer: Contemporary Narratives and Documents.* Univ of Alabama Pr. ISBN 0-8173-5703-3 Begins with Drake's first voyages and ends with the later one; includes many maps and illustrations.

*Lloyd, Christopher. *Sir Francis Drake.* Faber & Faber 1957. Very readable biography covering Drake's major voyages.

*Macdonald, Fiona. *Drake and the Armada.* Hampstead 1988 $12.40. ISBN 0-531-19504-X Biography that centers on the war against Spain.

Thrower, Norman J. (ed). *Sir Francis Drake and the Famous Voyage, 1577–1580: Essays Commemorating the Quadricentennial of Drake's Circumnavigation of the Earth.* Univ of California Pr 1984 $42.50. ISBN 0-520-04876-8 Compilation of essays dealing with Drake's journey around the world and its significance.

HAKLUYT, RICHARD *c.* 1552–1616

Richard Hakluyt was an English geographer and clergyman who devoted much of his life to preserving the records of all English voyages of discovery and promoting the advantages of exploring and settling North America.

While still a schoolboy, Hakluyt visited the law offices of his cousin and saw a large display of geographical materials. He immediately became fascinated with geography. In time he pursued this interest at Oxford University, where later he lectured on geography. Hakluyt was also ordained in the ministry, which enabled him to earn a living while indulging his passion for geography.

In 1582, Hakluyt published the first of his four major works, *Divers Voyages Touching the Discovery of America and the Islands Adjacent.* This work was, in part, propaganda for the English explorer Sir Humphrey Gilbert's doomed voyage to America the following year. Hakluyt next wrote an outline for colonial policy in America, stating some of the advantages of settlement and who should go. Ironically, this work, *The Discourse of Western Planting,* was not published until 1877. Nonetheless, Hakluyt was instrumental in reviving interest in the settlement of Virginia after the disappearance of the ill-fated Roanoke colony. He was one of the petitioners for the Virginia Company's 1606 grant that resulted in the Jamestown settlement. He also helped plan the East India Company, which colonized India.

Hakluyt's best-known work, *Principal Navigations, Voyages, Traffiques, and Discoveries of the English Nation,* first appeared in 1589, with a second edition published in 1599 and 1600. In 1846, the Hakluyt Society was founded, and it still continues today to publish narratives of early explorations.

BOOKS BY HAKLUYT

Divers Voyages Touching the Discovery of America and the Islands Adjacent (1582). (coedited with John W. Jones) Burt Franklin $30.50. ISBN 0-8337-1867-3

Principal Navigations, Voyages, Traffiques and Discoveries of the English Nation (1589). 12 vols. AMS (repr of 1905 ed) $265.00. ISBN 0-404-03030-0

Voyages and Discoveries. Penguin English Library Ser. Jack Beeching (ed). Penguin 1972 $5.95. ISBN 0-14-043073-3

Voyages to the Virginia Colonies. David and Charles 1987 $13.95. ISBN 0-7126-9574-5

BOOKS ABOUT HAKLUYT

David, Richard. *Hakluyt's Voyages.* Houghton 1981 $27.50. ISBN 0-395-31556-5 Study of Hakluyt and his sixteenth-century *Voyages and Discoveries.*

Parks, George B. *Richard Hakluyt and the English Voyages.* Folcroft 1984 repr of 1928 ed $100.00. Discusses Hakluyt's writing and studies; includes maps and illustrations.

VESPUCCI, AMERIGO   1454–1512

The Italian navigator Amerigo Vespucci, who explored the coast of America from Florida to the tip of South America, was the first to declare South America a continent rather than a series of islands as was previously thought. Vespucci also measured the earth's circumference more accurately than anyone before him and devised a system for determining exact longitude.

Born into a noble family in Florence, Italy, Vespucci had an early interest in geography and navigation. However, he trained for a career in business and was sent to Spain in 1492 as a representative of Florence's Medici family. While in Spain, Vespucci may have assisted in providing financing for the voyages of the Italian navigator Christopher Columbus. (*See* Columbus, Vol. 2, United States History: Native Americans and Early Explorers.) His contact with Columbus and other explorers increased his interest in navigation, and he sought to make his own voyages of exploration.

Vespucci made two voyages to the West, the first in 1499–1500 for Spain and the second in 1501–1502 for Portugal, during which he explored over 6,000 miles of coastline. During these voyages he determined that the lands Columbus discovered were not islands off the continent of Asia but were part of a "new world." Using his unique system of celestial navigation, Vespucci also correctly theorized that two oceans, rather than one, lay between the west coast of Europe and the east coast of Asia.

A letter allegedly written by Vespucci in 1504 claimed that he had made four voyages rather than two. However, this matter has been widely disputed, and no positive proof has been found to either prove or disprove the claim. In 1507 the German geographer Martin Waldseemüller published Vespucci's accounts of his voyages and suggested that the new lands to the West be named America in honor of the man who determined that they were new continents. From 1508 until his death in 1512, Vespucci served as the chief navigator of Spain, with responsibility for preparing a chart of the Atlantic Ocean and the new lands that had been explored.

BOOK BY VESPUCCI

Letters of Amerigo Vespucci and Other Documents Illustrative of His Career. Hakluyt Society First Ser. Clements R. Markham (ed). Burt Franklin (repr of 1894 ed) $26.00. ISBN 0-8337-2231-X

BOOKS ABOUT VESPUCCI

Arciniegas, German. *Amerigo and the New World.* Octagon (repr of 1955 ed). (o.p.) $27.50. Study of Vespucci's life and his involvement with the "discovery of the New World."

Pohl, Fredreck J. *Amerigo Vespucci, Pilot Major.* Hippocrene 1966 $21.50. ISBN 0-374-96499-8 Impartial study of the life and voyages that tries to set straight the controversies surrounding Vespucci.

See also Vol. 2, United States History: Native Americans and Early Explorers.

THE SCIENTIFIC REVOLUTION AND THE ENLIGHTENMENT

Artz, Frederick B. *Enlightenment in France.* Kent State Univ Pr 1968 $5.75. ISBN 0-87338-032-0

*Berlin, Isaiah (ed). *Age of Enlightenment: The Eighteenth Century Philosophers.* NAL 1984 $4.95. ISBN 0-452-00904-9 Discusses the thoughts and writings of philosophers and other thinkers during the period of scientific and intellectual advancement known as the Enlightenment, or the Age of Reason.

Commager, Henry S. *The Empire of Reason: How Europe Imagined and America Realized the Enlightenment.* Oxford Univ Pr 1982 $9.95. ISBN 0-19-503062-1

Durant, Will, and Ariel Durant. *Age of Reason Begins.* Simon 1961 $29.95. ISBN 0-671-01320-3

Durant, Will, and Ariel Durant. *Age of Voltaire.* Simon 1965 $29.95. ISBN 0-671-01325-4

Durant, Will, and Ariel Durant. *Rousseau and Revolution.* Simon 1967 $32.95. ISBN 0-671-63058-X

Gay, Peter. *The Enlightenment: An Interpretation—The Science of Freedom.* Vol. 2 Norton 1977 $14.95. ISBN 0-393-00875-4

Gay, Peter. *Voltaire's Politics: The Poet as Realist.* Yale Univ Pr 1988 $15.95. ISBN 0-300-04095-4

*James, Leonard F., *et al. Rivalry, Reason, and Revolution.* Pergamon 1973 $9.00. ISBN 0-08-017201-6 Examines the conflicts of the nation–states, the formation of constitutional governments, and the Age of Reason.

THE AGE OF ABSOLUTISM

Ashley, Maurice. *Louis the Fourteenth and the Greatness of France.* Free Pr 1965 $11.95. ISBN 0-02-901080-2

*Bindoff, S. T. *Tudor England.* Penguin 1950 $5.95. ISBN 0-14-020212-9 Looks at English life and society during the period of the Tudor monarchs.

*Crankshaw, Edward. *The Fall of the House of Hapsburg.* Penguin 1983 $8.95. ISBN 0-14-006459-1 Relates events that caused the decline in influence and power of one of Europe's most powerful royal families.

*Crankshaw, Edward. *Maria Theresa.* Macmillan 1986 $10.95. ISBN 0-689-70708-8 Biographical account of the Hapsburg archduchess of Austria and queen of Bohemia and Hungary.

*Durant, Will, and Ariel Durant. *Age of Louis Fourteenth.* Simon 1963 $29.95. ISBN 0-671-01215-0 Events during the reign of the French monarch King Louis XIV, under whom absolute monarchy in France reached its height.

Editors of Time–Life Books. *Powers of the Crown: 1600–1700. Time Frame Ser.* Time–Life 1990 $22.60. ISBN 0-8094-6454-3

Fraser, Antonia. *Mary Queen of Scots.* Dell 1984 $6.95. ISBN 0-440-35476-5

*Horn, Pierre. *Louis XIV. World Leaders—Past and Present Ser.* Chelsea 1986 $17.95. ISBN 0-87754-591-X Account of the absolute monarch of France who reigned from 1643–1715.

Mattingly, Garrett. *The Armada.* Houghton 1988 $9.95. ISBN 0-395-08366-4

Mattingly, Garrett. *The Invincible Armada and Elizabethan England. Folger Guides to the Age of Shakespeare.* Folger 1979 $4.95. ISBN 0-918016-11-8

*Miller, John. *Bourbon and Stuart: Kings and Kingship in France and England in the 17th Century.* Watts 1987 $19.95. ISBN 0-531-15052-6 Examines the monarchs and governments of France and England during the 1600s.

*Miquel, Pierre. *Eighteenth Century Europe. Silver Burdett Picture Histories Ser.* Silver $14.96. ISBN 0-382-06618-9 Looks at Europe's periods of revolution against absolute monarchy; especially suited for younger readers.

Moote, A. Lloyd. *Louis XIII, The Just.* Univ of California Pr 1989 $29.95. ISBN 0-520-06485-2

Pierson, Peter. *Philip Second of Spain. Men in Office Ser.* Thames Hudson 1977 $16.95. ISBN 0-500-87003-9

Plowden, Alice. *The House of Tudor.* Scarborough Hse 1982 $9.95. ISBN 0-8128-6123-X

Plowden, Alice. *Elizabeth Tudor and Mary Stewart: Two Queens in One Isle.* B & N Imports 1982 $28.50. ISBN 0-389-20518-4

Riasanovsky, Nicholas. *The Image of Peter the Great in Russian History and Thought.* Oxford Univ Pr 1985 $38.00. ISBN 0-19-503456-2

Smith, Lacey B. *Elizabeth Tudor: Biography of a Queen.* Little 1977 $8.95. ISBN 0-316-80153-4

Smith, Lacey B. *Treason in Tudor England: Politics and Paranoia.* Princeton Univ Pr 1986 $26.50. ISBN 0-691-05463-0

Steed, Henry W. *Hapsburg Monarchy.* Fertig 1969 $32.50. ISBN 0-86527-091-0

Trevelyan, George M. *England Under the Stuarts.* Routledge 1966 $19.95. ISBN 0-416-69240-0

See also Vol. 2, United States History: Spanish, French, and Other European Colonies; The English Colonies and Colonial Life.

REVOLUTION AND CHANGE IN ENGLAND AND AMERICA

*Alden, John R. *American Revolution: Seventeen Seventy-Five to Seventeen Eighty-Three. New American Nation Ser.* Harper $9.95. ISBN 0-06-133011-6 Readable account of America's revolution against the authority of the British monarchy.

Alden, John R. *A History of the American Revolution. Quality Paperbacks Ser.* Da Capo 1989 $15.95. ISBN 0-306-80366-6

Ashley, Maurice. *Charles I and Cromwell.* Routledge 1988 $22.50. ISBN 0-317-67336-X

*Bailyn, Bernard. *Voyagers to the West: A Passage in the Peopling of America on the Eve of the Revolution.* Peter Dimock (ed). Random 1988 $14.95. ISBN 0-394-75778-5 Looks at reasons for migration to America just prior to the Revolution.

Bailyn, Bernard, and John B. Hench (eds). *The Press and the American Revolution.* Nebraska Univ Pr 1980 $10.95. ISBN 0-930350-30-8

Fraser, Antonia. *Cromwell: The Lord Protector.* D I Fine 1986 $11.95. ISBN 0-917657-90-X

Fraser, Antonia. *Royal Charles: Charles II and the Restoration.* Knopf 1979 $19.45. ISBN 0-394-49721-X

Fraser, Antonia. *The Weaker Vessel: Woman's Lot in Seventeenth Century England.* Random 1985 $9.95. ISBN 0-394-73251-0

*Hill, Christopher. *The Century of Revolution, 1603–1714.* Norton 1982 $8.95. ISBN 0-393-30016-1 Focuses on England's political and social history during the years 1603–1714.

Hill, Christopher. *Change and Continuity in Seventeenth-Century England.* Harvard Univ Pr 1975 $25.50. ISBN 0-674-10765-9

Hill, Christopher. *God's Englishman: Oliver Cromwell and the English Revolution.* Harper 1972 $8.95. ISBN 0-06-131666-0

Hill, Christopher. *Good Old Cause: English Revolution of 1640–1660.* Edmund Dell (ed). Biblio Dist 1969 $32.50. ISBN 0-7146-1483-1

Hill, Christopher. *Intellectual Origins of the English Revolution.* Oxford Univ Pr 1980 $18.95. ISBN 0-19-822635-7

Miller, John. *The Life and Times of William and Mary. Kings and Queens of England Ser.* Biblio Dist 1974 $17.50. ISBN 0-297-76760-7

Smith, Page. *A New Age Now Begins: A People's History of the American Revolution.* 2 vols. Penguin 1989. ISBN 0-14-095354-X

Smith, Page. *Religious Origins of the American Revolution.* Scholars Pr 1976 $11.95. ISBN 0-89130-121-6

Trevelyan, George M. *England Under Queen Anne.* 3 vols. AMS 1930–1934 $149.50 set. ISBN 0-404-20263-2

Trevelyan, George M. *English Revolution Sixteen Eighty-Eight to Sixteen Eighty-Nine.* Oxford Univ Pr 1938 $6.95. ISBN 0-19-500263-6

BURKE, SIR EDMUND   1729–1797

See also Burke, Vol. 2, American Government/Civics: Surveys and Theories.

A conservative British statesman and political writer, Edmund Burke was born in Ireland of a Catholic mother and an Anglican father. As a youth in British-controlled Ireland, Burke witnessed British mistreatment of its colonial subjects, which influenced his later political thought. After graduating from Trinity College in Dublin, Burke went to England to study law. He soon lost interest in his studies, however, and turned to writing. In 1761, while employed by the British secretary to Ireland, Burke returned to the country of his birth and renewed his interest in the plight of the Irish at the hands of their British rulers.

In 1765 Burke became private secretary to Britain's new prime minister, the marquess of Rockingham. Later that year Burke entered Parliament where, over the next 25 years, he attempted to establish the principles of free government.

Among Burke's most influential writings is *Thoughts on the Present Discontents* (1770), in which he argues the need for political parties to counteract the tendency for quarreling factions to disrupt the operations of government. Burke was the first to argue the value of political parties.

Though strongly opposed to revolution, Burke sided with the American colonists prior to and during the American Revolution. In two historic speeches—*Speech on American Taxation* (1774) and *Speech for Conciliation with America* (1775)—he urged the British Parliament to treat the colonies in a generous and forgiving manner rather than to exercise the right of taxation. Burke also spoke for the rights of British subjects in India, urging the British Crown to end the plunder of that country by taking over its administration from the East India Company.

Throughout his career, Burke argued for administrative reforms that would reduce government corruption. He made himself unpopular with many constituents by insisting that elected representatives had an obligation to consider not only the interests of those they represented, but also the good of the entire country. This political view still resonates today.

In his last years, Burke became the first British politician to speak out against the French Revolution. While others were applauding the Revolution and its talk of freedom from tyranny, Burke accurately predicted the extremes of violence and disruption that would ultimately occur. His treatise on the Revolution, *Reflections on the Revolution in France* (1790), is considered his greatest work.

Throughout his life, Edmund Burke argued for the reform of societal injustices in very practical and moderate ways. He was conservative in the sense of wishing to preserve the values he saw as the cornerstones of civilization, while recognizing the need for constant reform to assure that those values are truly reflected in society.

BOOKS BY BURKE

On the American Revolution. E. R. Barkan (ed). Peter Smith $11.25. ISBN 0-8446-0045-8
Reflections on the Revolution in France (1790). Penguin 1982 $5.95. ISBN 0-14-043204-3
Selected Letters of Edmund Burke. Harvey C. Mansfield, Jr. (ed). Univ of Chicago Pr 1984
    $32.50. ISBN 0-226-08068-4
Selected Works. Walter J. Bate (ed). Greenwood 1975 repr of 1960 ed $25.50. ISBN
    0-8371-8122-4
Selected Writings and Speeches. J. P. Stanlis (ed). Peter Smith $12.75. ISBN 0-8446-1094-1
The Writings and Speeches of Edmund Burke: Party, Parliament and the American Crisis, 1766–1774.
    Paul Langford (ed). Vol. 2 Oxford Univ Pr 1981 $120.00. ISBN 0-19-822416-8

BOOKS ABOUT BURKE

Ayling, Stanley. *Edmund Burke: His Life and Opinions.* St. Martin's 1988 $19.95. ISBN
    0-312-02686-2 Story of Burke that focuses on his political thought and writings.
Kirk, Russell. *Edmund Burke: A Genius Reconsidered.* Sugden 1986 $8.95. ISBN 0-317-
    30086-5 Examines Burke's philosophy and how it revealed itself in concrete
    historical situations in the eighteenth century.
Prior, James. *Memoir of the Life and Character of the Right Honorable Edmund Burke. Research and
    Source Works Ser.* 2 vols. Burt Franklin 1968 repr of 1854 ed $41.00. ISBN 0-8337-
    2864-4 Compares Burke's genius and talents to those of his great contemporaries.

See also Vol. 2, United States History: Protest, Rebellion, and Revolution.

THE FRENCH REVOLUTION AND NAPOLEON

*Brinton, Clarence C. *A Decade of Revolution, 1789–1799. The Rise of Modern Europe Ser.*
    Greenwood 1983 repr of 1934 ed $48.50. ISBN 0-313-24077-9 Interpretive exami-
    nation of the French Revolution.
*Cate, Curtis. *The War of the Two Emperors: The Confrontation Between Napoleon and Tzar
    Alexander.* Random 1985 $24.45. ISBN 0-394-53670-3 Tells of the invasion of
    Russia by the armies of Napoleon.
*Dartford, Gerald P. *The French Revolution.* Wayside 1989 $5.50. Readable account of
    French history in the last decade of the eighteenth century.
*Dickens, Charles. *A Tale of Two Cities.* Bantam 1989 $2.50. ISBN 0-553-21176-5 Story
    of the French Revolution and three young people caught up in its turmoil.
*Durant, Will, and Ariel Durant. *The Age of Napoleon.* Simon 1975 $29.95. ISBN 0-671-
    21988-X Describes life in Europe during the reign of Napoleon.
*Glover, Michael. *Napoleonic Wars: Illustrated History 1792–1815.* Hippocrene 1989 $14.95.
    Illustrated account of the period in which Napoleon conquered and dominated
    much of Europe.
*Herold, J. Christopher. *Age of Napoleon.* American Heritage 1986 $9.95. ISBN 0-8281-
    0491-3 Complete coverage of the Napoleonic era in Europe.
Herold, J. Christopher (ed). *The Mind of Napoleon: A Selection of His Written and Spoken Words.*
    Columbia Univ Pr 1955 $17.50. ISBN 0-231-08523-0
*Hibbert, Christopher. *The Days of the French Revolution: The Day-to-Day Story of the Revolution.*
    Morrow 1981 $10.95. ISBN 0-688-00746-5 Personal accounts of life and events
    during the period of the French Revolution.
*Miquel, Pierre. *Napoleon's Europe. Silver Burdett Picture Histories Ser.* Silver 1985 $14.96. ISBN
    0-382-06622-7 Illustrated account of European life and society during the
    Napoleonic era; especially suited for younger readers.

Palmer, R. R. (ed). *The Two Tocquevilles, Father and Son: Hervé and Alexis de Tocqueville on the Coming of the French Revolution.* Princeton Univ Pr 1987 $28.50. ISBN 0-691-05495-9
Palmer, R. R. *World of the French Revolution.* Harper 1972 $7.95. ISBN 0-06-131620-2

BONAPARTE, NAPOLEON   1769–1821

Sometimes called the "Corsican" because his birthplace was the island of Corsica, or the "Little Corporal," a nickname he acquired in military school because of his small stature, Napoleon Bonaparte was one of the greatest military leaders in history. Trained from an early age in French military schools, Bonaparte rose rapidly in the French military establishment. He received his first commission at age 16 and became a brigadier general at age 24. With his military skill, Bonaparte transformed a ragged and starving French army into a first-class fighting force.

When the French government was overthrown by a coup in 1799, Bonaparte was made First Consul, or dictator. Military successes during the next few years helped him to consolidate his power. Then in 1804, he had himself crowned Napoleon I, Emperor of France. While he was emperor, he expanded French control in Europe and installed his brothers in ruling positions in conquered territories. None, however, proved to be as skillful as Napoleon. In 1796 Bonaparte married Josephine de Beauharnais, the widow of a French nobleman. He ultimately secured an annulment of the marriage, however, on the grounds that she could not bear children. In 1810, he married Marie Louise, the daughter of the Austrian emperor Francis I. She bore him a son, Napoleon II, the "King of Rome," thus ensuring imperial succession to the throne.

Bonaparte's influence on France was profound and enduring. Domestic reforms included a new tax system, establishing the Bank of France, stabilizing the currency, and instituting the Napoleonic Code, a legal code still in use. Bonaparte's influence on Europe was equally profound. Having conquered most of Europe by 1808, Bonaparte altered the continent's balance of power by stimulating movements for national unification in conquered areas and promoting the growth of liberalism through lasting administrative and legal reforms. Bonaparte's decision to invade Russia in 1812 was a fatal mistake. The harsh Russian winter forced a disastrous retreat that led first to his abdication and exile to the island of Elba and ultimately to his downfall in 1815 at the Battle of Waterloo. After that defeat, Bonaparte was exiled to the lonely island of St. Helena, where he died of cancer in 1821.

BOOK BY BONAPARTE

Napoleon's Memoirs. Somerset De Chair (ed and tr). Dufour 1986 $18.95. ISBN 0-948166-10-X

BOOKS ABOUT BONAPARTE

Caulaincourt, Armand. *No Peace with Napoleon.* Jean Hanoteau (ed). George Libaire (tr). Greenwood 1975 repr of 1936 ed $22.50. ISBN 0-8371-7984-X The memoirs of the Duke of Venice, the general who was intimately associated with Napoleon, focusing on the period in Paris after the Russian campaign as Napoleon staved off disaster.
*Harris, Nathaniel. *Napoleon. Reputations Ser.* David and Charles 1989 $19.95. ISBN 0-7134-5730-9 Interesting account of the French emperor and noted soldier.
Herold, J. Christopher. *The Age of Napoleon.* Houghton 1986 $9.95. ISBN 0-317-40584-5 Looks at Napoleon's impact on European politics and society.
Jones, R. Ben. *Napoleon: Man and Myth.* Holmes & Meier 1977 $12.50. ISBN 0-8419-0441-3 Critical discussion of Napoleon's life and accomplishments.

Nafziger, George F. *Napoleon's Invasion of Russia.* Presidio $45.00. ISBN 0-89141-322-7 Study of Napoleon and the crossing of the Russian frontier in 1812; includes 16 maps and appendices with important, hard-to-find documents.

Seward, Desmond. *Napoleon and Hitler: A Comparative Biography.* Penguin 1989 $19.95. ISBN 0-670-81480-6 Compares the lives, rise to power, and conquests of Napoleon and the twentieth-century German dictator Adolf Hitler.

*Shor, Donnali. *Napoleon Bonaparte. Why They Became Famous Ser.* Silver 1987 $6.75. Describes the events that established Napoleon as an outstanding historical figure.

*Weidhorn, Manfred. *Napoleon.* Macmillan 1986 $16.95. ISBN 0-689-31163-X All of the events in Napoleon's life excitingly retold for teenagers.

ROBESPIERRE, MAXIMILIEN   1758–1794

Maximilien Robespierre, a radical leader of the French Revolution, was born at Arras, France, in 1758. The son of a poor family, he managed to get a scholarship to study law in Paris. His studies completed, Robespierre returned to his native city where he became successful in both law and politics. In 1789 he was elected to the new national legislative body, the Constituent Assembly, which was formed in response to growing unrest in France. While in the Assembly, Robespierre became active in the Jacobin Club, a group of mostly middle-class legislators who advocated such ideas as universal suffrage, free primary education, and the separation of church and state.

As the French Revolution proceeded, the Constituent Assembly was replaced by the Legislative Assembly in 1791 and then by the National Convention in 1792. The monarchy abolished, the National Convention voted to behead the king and set up a republic. The new regime soon ran into trouble as several European monarchies invaded France and small armies of French peasants took up arms against the government and the Revolution. In response, the Jacobin members of the National Convention, led by Robespierre, decided to take radical action. In 1793 they created a Committee of Public Safety, which would suppress counterrevolution by purging non-Jacobins from the National Convention and setting up committees in every town to root out suspected opponents of the Revolution. Between September 1793 and July 1794, at least 40,000 men and women were convicted for alleged political crimes, usually without evidence, and were executed. This period became known as the Reign of Terror.

By the spring of 1794, the French government had succeeded in putting down revolts at home and in defeating most of its external enemies. Robespierre, however, continued the Reign of Terror, and even sent long-time Jacobins to the guillotine. Finally, the other members of the National Convention decided that enough was enough. They had Robespierre arrested, tried, and executed on July 28, 1794. With the death of Robespierre, the radical phase of the French Revolution came to an end.

BOOK BY ROBESPIERRE

Oeuvres de Maximilien Robespierre. 3 vols. Burt Franklin 1970 repr of 1840 ed. $88.50. ISBN 0-8337-3028-2

BOOKS ABOUT ROBESPIERRE

*Carson, S. L. *Maximilien Robespierre. World Leaders—Past and Present Ser.* Chelsea 1988 $17.95. ISBN 0-87754-549-9 Introductory biography of the French Jacobin lawyer and leader of the Committee of Public Safety, who led the Reign of Terror following the French Revolution.

Hampson, Norman. *Life and Opinions of Maximilien Robespierre.* Basil Blackwell 1988

$14.95. ISBN 0-631-16226-7 Focuses on the political philosophy of the French revolutionary leader.

Jordan, David P. *The Revolutionary Career of Maximilien Robespierre.* Univ of Chicago Pr 1989 $14.95. ISBN 0-226-41037-4 Scholarly account of Robespierre's role in the French Revolution.

Scott, Otto. *Robespierre: The Reign of Terror.* Found Amer Ed 1989 $10.95. ISBN 0-96238420-8 Examines the Reign of Terror and Robespierre's role in it.

Thompson, J.M. *Robespierre.* Basil Blackwell $34.95. ISBN 0-631-15504-X Classic biography that illustrates Robespierre's impact on Lenin's revolution and the revolutions of the twentieth century.

RESTORATION, REVOLUTION, AND REFORM

Church, Clive. *Europe in Eighteen Thirty.* Unwin 1983 $65.00. ISBN 0-04-940067-3

Church, Clive. *Revolution and Red Tape: The French Ministerial Bureaucracy, 1770–1850.* Oxford Univ Pr 1981 $67.00. ISBN 0-19-822562-8

Collingham, H. A. C. *The July Monarchy: A Political History of France 1830–1848.* Longman 1988 $25.95. ISBN 0-582-01334-8

Gash, Norman. *Aristocracy and People: Britain, Eighteen Fifteen to Eighteen Sixty-Five in Germany. New History of England Ser.* Harvard Univ Pr 1980 $10.95. ISBN 0-674-04491-6

Gash, Norman. *Reaction and Reconstruction in English Politics, 1832 to 1852.* Greenwood 1981 repr of 1965 ed $35.00. ISBN 0-313-22927-9

Hamerow, Theodore S. *Restoration, Revolution, Reaction: Economics and Politics in Germany, 1815–1871.* Princeton Univ Pr 1958 $12.95. ISBN 0-691-00755-1

Hobsbawn, Eric J. *Age of Revolution: Seventeen Eighty-Nine to Eighteen Forty-Eight.* NAL 1964 $5.95. ISBN 0-451-62720-2

Jardin, André, and André-Jean Tudesq. *Restoration and Reaction, 1815–1848. The Cambridge History of Modern France Ser.* Cambridge Univ Pr 1988 $16.95. ISBN 0-521-35855-8

*Nicolson, Harold. *Congress of Vienna: A Study of Allied Unity 1812–1822.* Harcourt 1970 $9.95. ISBN 0-15-622061-X Discusses the Congress of Vienna and its efforts to resolve European problems in the aftermath of Napoleon's defeat.

Price, Roger. *Revolutions of 1848. Studies in European History Ser.* Humanities 1989 $8.50. ISBN 0-391-03595-9

Robertson, Priscilla. *Revolutions of 1848: A Social History.* Princeton Univ Pr 1952 $12.95. ISBN 0-691-00756-X

Stearns, Peter N. *Eighteen Forty-Eight: The Revolutionary Tide in Europe.* Norton 1974 $9.95. ISBN 0-393-09311-5

Thompson, J. L. *Louis Napoleon and the Second Empire.* Columbia Univ Pr 1983 $14.00. ISBN 0-231-05685-0

METTERNICH, PRINCE KLEMENS VON   1773–1859

Prince Klemens von Metternich, Austrian statesman and the leading political figure in Europe from 1815 to 1848, was born at Koblenz, Germany, in 1773. As a law student at the University of Strassburg, Metternich was appalled by the violence he witnessed at political upheavals during the French Revolution, and he determined to support the forces of law and order at all costs. He began a career in Austria's foreign service and in 1809 became foreign minister. As foreign minister, Metternich tried to maintain a balance of power between France to the west and Russia to the east. However, as the French emperor Napoleon's (*see* Bonaparte, Vol. 2, World History: The French Revolution and Napoleon) power continued to spread, Metternich helped organize a coalition of nations, including Austria, Prussia, Russia, and Great Britain, to resist Napoleon's attempt at European domination.

After Napoleon's defeat, Metternich played a leading role in redrawing the political map of Europe, largely through the Congress of Vienna (1814–1815). He was also instrumental in forging the Holy Alliance, an alliance of Austria, Russia, and Prussia, the purpose of which was to suppress revolutionary movements. In general, Metternich's changes maintained peace among the great powers of Europe for some 40 years.

On the domestic scene, Metternich's policies were far less successful. Politically conservative, he strongly opposed many of the ideas of democracy and civil liberties expressed by the French Revolution. He favored government censorship of the press, government control of the universities, political espionage, the suppression of revolutionary and nationalist movements, and other measures designed to prevent political change and to keep Europe's absolute monarchs in power.

Despite Metternich's efforts to maintain the status quo, periodic revolutions erupted in most European nations over the next several decades. One such revolution in Austria in 1848 forced Metternich to flee to Great Britain. Although he returned to Austria three years later, after the revolution had been suppressed, it was clear that the ideas of democracy and nationalism were growing stronger in Europe all the time. Metternich did not return to public office, but he did advise the Austrian government until his death in 1859.

BOOK BY METTERNICH

Memoirs of Prince Metternich, 1773–1835. 5 vols. Fertig 1970 repr of 1881 ed $225.00. ISBN 0-86527-128-3

BOOKS ABOUT METTERNICH

Kraehe, Enno E. *Metternich's German Policy: The Congress of Vienna, 1814–1815.* Vol. 2 Princeton Univ Pr 1983 $19.95. ISBN 0-691-10133-7 Examines Metternich's foreign policy goals toward Germany during the Congress of Vienna.

Reinerman, Alan J. *Austria and the Papacy in the Age of Metternich: Between Conflict and Cooperation, 1809–1830.* Vol. 1 Catholic Univ Pr 1979 $27.95. ISBN 0-8132-0548-4 Uncovers the years between 1809 and 1830—"between conflict and cooperation."

Schroeder, Paul W. *Metternich's Diplomacy at Its Zenith, 1820–1823.* Greenwood 1970 repr of 1962 ed $35.00. ISBN 0-8371-2471-9 Focuses on the foreign policy achievements of the Austrian statesman.

*Von der Heide, John. *Klemens von Metternich. World Leaders—Past and Present Ser.* Chelsea 1988 $17.95. ISBN 0-87754-541-3 Introductory account of the Austrian foreign minister who was the guiding spirit of the Congress of Vienna.

Webster, C. K. *Palmerston, Metternich and the European System: 1830–1841.* Haskell 1972 repr of 1934 ed $39.95. ISBN 0-8383-0135-5 Very slim volume containing a lecture delivered in 1934 that analyzes Europe between 1830 and 1841.

THE ARTS IN EIGHTEENTH-CENTURY EUROPE

Artz, Frederick B. *From the Renaissance to Romanticism: Trends in Style in Art, Literature, and Music.* Univ of Chicago Pr 1965 $23.00. ISBN 0-226-02837-2

Deutsch, Otto E. *Mozart: A Documentary Biography.* Stanford Univ Pr 1966 $49.50. ISBN 0-8047-0233-0

Goya. *Drawings of Goya. Master Draughtsman Ser.* Borden $4.95. ISBN 0-87505-163-4

Hildesheimer, Wolfgang. *Mozart.* Marion Faber (tr). Farquar 1982 $30.00. ISBN 0-374-21483-2

Honour, Hugh. *Neo-Classism.* Penguin 1978 $7.95. ISBN 0-14-020978-6

Huxley, Aldous, *et al. The Complete Etchings of Goya.* Crown 1943. (o.p.)

Ingres, Jean A. *Drawings of Ingres. Master Draughtsman Ser.* Stephen Longstreet (ed). Borden 1964 $4.95. ISBN 0-87505-166-9

Johnson, Lee. *Paintings of Eugene Delacroix.* 2 vols. Oxford Univ Pr 1981 $265.00. ISBN 0-317-68916-9

Solomon, Maynard. *Beethoven.* Schirmer 1977 $19.95. ISBN 0-02-872460-7

Tufts, Eleanor. *Luis Melendez: Eighteenth-Century Master of the Spanish Still Life, with a Catalogue Raisonne.* Univ of Missouri Pr 1985 $49.00. ISBN 0-8262-0429-5

BACH, JOHANN SEBASTIAN   1685–1750

Composer, organist, and the most famous of an illustrious family of German musicians, Johann Sebastian Bach was a master of polyphonic baroque music—a musical form characterized by the use of multiple parts in harmony and an ornate, very exuberant style. Immersed in music almost from the moment of his birth, Bach was taught the violin by his father, Johann Ambrosius. When he was 10, both his parents died, and he went to live with his brother Johann Christoph, an organist, who taught him to play keyboard instruments. Bach's musical genius soon surpassed his brother's skill, which caused a good deal of envy on the part of his brother. During his lifetime, Bach was known more for his skill as an organist than as a composer. His fame as a composer did not come until years after his death when his works were "discovered" by the composers Felix Mendelssohn and Robert Schumann and published in the 1800s.

Bach served as an organist in the German cities of Arnstadt, Muhlhausen, and Weimar between the years 1703 and 1717. During this time his compositions focused on the organ, and he wrote chorales, cantatas, concertos, preludes, and fugues primarily for that instrument. These works fused Italian, French, and German characteristics with a profound mastery of the contrapuntal technique, which is characterized by two or more independent melodies sounded together. While serving as music director at the court of a German prince from 1717 to 1723, Bach's compositions were for the clavier, a stringed keyboard instrument, or for instrumental ensembles. These included preludes, fantasies, toccatas, and dance suites that were useful for music instruction as well as entertainment. Best-known of these works is *The Well-Tempered Clavier,* which is a series of preludes and fugues composed in 1722 and 1740. In his last position as cantor and musical director of St. Thomas's Church in Leipzig, Germany (1724–1750), Bach exerted considerable influence on Lutheran church music. During this period he composed as many as 300 cantatas, 200 of which have been preserved. When Bach died at the age of 65, he had no idea that he would be revered by later generations as one of the world's greatest composers, nor that his compositions would be regarded by some as the most sublime music ever composed.

BOOKS ABOUT BACH

Arnold, Denis. *Bach. Past Masters Ser.* Oxford Univ Pr 1984 $4.95. ISBN 0-19-287554-X Standard presentation of the composer's life and work.

David, Hans T., and Arthur Mendel (eds). *The Bach Reader.* Norton 1966 $12.95. ISBN 0-393-00259-4 Collection of documents dealing with the composer's life and music, including documents up to the late 1820s.

Felix, Warner. *Johann Sebastian Bach.* Norton 1985 $25.00. ISBN 0-393-02232-3 This volume discusses the composer's life, his compositions, and his influence on later periods of music.

Forkel, Johann N. *Johann Sebastian Bach: His Life, Art and Work.* Charles S. Terry (tr). Vienna 1974 $15.00. ISBN 0-8443-0021-7 First biography of Bach, written in 1749, that claims his preeminence.

Geiringer, Karl, and Irene Geiringer. *Johann Sebastian Bach: The Culmination of an Era.* Oxford Univ Pr 1966 $26.00. ISBN 0-19-500554-6 Discusses Bach's significance as a composer and how his music reflected the full flowering of the baroque period.

Schwendowius, Barbara, and Wolfgang Domling (eds). *Johann Sebastian Bach: Life, Times, Influence.* Yale Univ Pr 1984 $40.00. ISBN 0-300-03268-4 Comprehensive account of the composer that considers his role in baroque music and his influence on later composers.

GAINSBOROUGH, THOMAS 1727–1788

Thomas Gainsborough, perhaps the greatest painter of eighteenth-century England, was greatly inspired by the Dutch landscape painters of the seventeenth century, rather than those of the Italian Renaissance preferred by his famous rival, the English painter Sir Joshua Reynolds. (*See* Reynolds, Vol. 2, World History: The Arts in Eighteenth-Century Europe.) A superb portrait painter, Gainsborough's works reflect a highly polished technique and a warm sympathy for his subjects. *The Blue Boy* is his most popular and best-known painting.

Born in Sudbury, Suffolk, in 1727, Gainsborough was sent to London to study art at age 13. On the death of his father in 1748, he returned to Suffolk and stayed there for 11 years, probably making a living as a traveling portrait painter. Around 1750 he painted a portrait of an English couple that broke with tradition by combining landscape painting with portraiture. The portrait, which shows the couple against the background of cornfields on their estate, is remarkable because the landscape is given as much importance as the figures. In 1759 Gainsborough moved to Bath, a fashionable resort where he could be assured of a constant flow of well-to-do patrons. The need to please these patrons forced Gainsborough to go back to using conventional backgrounds and standard poses.

With the spread of his popularity, Gainsborough was soon exhibiting his work in London, and in 1768 he helped to found the Royal Academy. In 1774 the artist moved to London and continued painting up to his death in 1788. Though best known for his portraits, Gainsborough's love of landscapes can be seen in the few landscape paintings and many landscape drawings and sketches he left behind.

BOOK BY GAINSBOROUGH

Letters. Mary Woodall (ed). New York Graphic Society 1963. (o.p.)

BOOKS ABOUT GAINSBOROUGH

Hayes, John. *Drawings of Thomas Gainsborough.* 2 vols. Yale Univ Pr 1971 $125.00. ISBN 0-300-01425-2 Focuses on the artist's drawings; with illustrations and text.

Hayes, John. *Gainsborough's Landscape Paintings: A Critical Text and Catalogue Raisonne.* 2 vols. Cornell Univ Pr 1982 $150.00. ISBN 0-8014-1528-4 Critical look at the artist's landscape paintings; with illustrations and list of works.

Hayes, John. *Thomas Gainsborough.* Salem Hse $8.95. ISBN 0-905005-72-4 General biography of the artist.

Lindsay, Jack. *Gainsborough: His Life and Art.* Academy Chi Pubs 1983 $6.95. ISBN 0-586-05613-0 Complete biography beginning with the childhood of Gainsborough and focusing on the various locations in which he lived and worked.

Rothschild, M. *The Life and Art of Thomas Gainsborough. The Great Art Masters of the World Ser.* Gloucester Art 1983 $117.75. ISBN 0-86650-044-8 Comprehensive, illustrated account of the noted artist and his work.

HANDEL, GEORGE FREDERICK   1685–1759

Born in Halle in the German state of Saxony, George Frederick Handel was trained as an organist and composer. As a young man, he traveled to Italy, where he absorbed the Italian style of music and the operatic form. He eventually settled in Great Britain, where he became famous as one of the greatest masters of baroque music.

As a youth Handel became an accomplished harpischordist and organist, studied violin and oboe, and became familiar with the music of contemporary German and Italian composers. During his stay in Italy from 1706 to 1710, he composed several operas and oratorios, which helped establish his early success. This success led to an appointment in Germany as musical director to the elector of Hanover. After only a brief stay in Hanover, Handel visited Great Britain to stage his opera *Rinaldo*. In 1712 he again returned to Great Britain and decided to make it his permanent residence. Then, in 1714, the elector of Hanover became King George I of England, and Handel enjoyed the patronage of the new royal family of his adopted homeland. He became a naturalized British citizen in 1726.

Handel's musical output was prodigious. He wrote 46 operas, among them *Julius Caesar* (1724) and *Berenice* (1737); 33 oratorios, the most famous being the widely celebrated *Messiah* (1742); 100 Italian solo cantatas; and numerous orchestral works, including twelve *Grand Concertos, Opus 6* (1739). In 1751 Handel suffered an impairment to his sight that led to total blindness by 1753. Nonetheless, Handel continued to conduct performances of his works, which strongly influenced British composers for a century after his death in 1759.

BOOK BY HANDEL

Letters and Writings of George Frideric Handel. Erich H. Muller (ed). *Select Bibliographies Reprint Ser.* Ayer 1935 $16.00. ISBN 0-8369-5286-3

BOOKS ABOUT HANDEL

Deutsch, Otto. *Handel: A Documentary Biography.* Da Capo 1974 repr of 1954 ed $85.00. ISBN 0-306-70624-5 Biography of Handel's life; includes letters, a bibliography, and all important documents.

Flower, Newman. *Handel: His Personality and His Times.* Academy Chi Pubs 1972 $7.95. ISBN 0-586-03778-0 Study of the composer that focuses on his personality and music as reflections of the baroque period.

Hogwood, Christopher. *Handel.* Thames Hudson 1988 $14.95. ISBN 0-500-27498-3 Account of the composer that includes extensive quotations from contemporaneous documents.

Keates, Jonathan. *Handel: The Man and His Music.* St. Martin's 1985 $19.95. ISBN 0-312-35846-6 Story of this German composer, emphasizing his successful stay in England, his final home.

Simon, Jacob (ed). *Handel: A Celebration of His Life and Times, 1685–1759.* Abner Schram 1987 $35.00. ISBN 0-8390-0376-5 Comprehensive account of the life and work of the noted composer.

HAYDN, FRANZ JOSEPH   1732–1809

Franz Joseph Haydn, born in a little Austrian town near the Hungarian border, was one of the great masters of classical music. Haydn's musical training began at about age 6 and came from an uncle with whom he lived. After serving as a choirboy at St. Stephen's Cathedral in Vienna, which dismissed him when his voice changed, Haydn struggled to earn a living as a teacher and accompanist. Largely self-taught, Haydn learned counterpoint—the combining of independent melodic lines—and received some instruction in composition. An important opportunity came in 1761 when he entered the service of the princes Esterhazy, noblemen who were devoted patrons of music and the arts. He remained in their service as a musical director until 1790, at which time he accepted a commission to write and conduct six symphonies in London. After a successful sojourn in London, he returned to Vienna in 1792 and remained there until his death at the age of 77.

Haydn is best known for his symphonies and string quartets, but his sacred works and operas are just as accomplished and important. He had a significant influence on the music of the Austrian composer, Wolfgang Amadeus Mozart, who was his friend, and on the German composer, Ludwig van Beethoven, who was his student. On first hearing, Haydn's music seems clear and direct, but it is filled with instrumental brilliance, subtlety, invention, and emotion, all in classical proportions. During his lifetime, Haydn composed an enormous amount of music. He composed more than 100 symphonies, among them the *Farewell Symphony* (1772), the *Surprise Symphony* (1791), and the *Clock Symphony* (1794). He also composed more than 60 string quartets and 50 piano sonatas as well as numerous operas, songs, and masses.

BOOKS BY HAYDN

Complete London Symphonies. Dover 1985 $12.95. ISBN 0-486-24982-4
Seasons in Full Score. Dover 1986 $10.95. ISBN 0-486-25022-9

BOOKS ABOUT HAYDN

Butterworth, Neil. *Haydn: His Life and Times. Life and Times Ser.* Paganiniana 1980 repr of 1977 ed $14.95. ISBN 0-87666-645-4 Biography of the composer that focuses on his role in the music of the period.
Geiringer, Karl, and Irene Geiringer. *Haydn: A Creative Life in Music.* Univ of California Pr 1982 $11.95. ISBN 0-520-04317-0 Revised biography that draws from present research on Hayden and new letters.
Larsen, Jens P., and Georg Feder. *The New Grove Haydn.* Norton 1983 $12.95. ISBN 0-393-30085-4 Haydn's life and development with a thorough listing of his output by leading scholars.
Robbins-Landon, H. *Haydn: Chronicle and Works.* 5 vols. Indiana Univ Pr Vol. 1 *Haydn: The Early Years, 1732–1765* 1981 $85.00. ISBN 0-253-14630. Vol. 2 *Haydn at Eszterhaza, 1766–1790* 1978 $60.00. ISBN 0-253-37002-7. Vol. 3 *Haydn in England, 1791–1795* 1976 $70.00. ISBN 0-253-37003-5. Vol. 4 *Haydn: The Years of "The Creation," 1796–1800* 1977 $75.00. ISBN 0-253-37004-3. Vol. 5 *Haydn: The Late Years, 1801–1809* 1977 $70.00. ISBN 0-253-37005-1 Comprehensive study of the composer and his music.
Robbins-Landon, H., and David W. Jones. *Haydn: His Life and Music.* Indiana Univ Pr 1988 $45.00. ISBN 0-253-37265-8 General account of the composer's life and work.

PURCELL, HENRY *c.* 1659–1695

Born in Westminster, England, Henry Purcell is considered by many experts to be that country's finest native-born composer. Purcell's musical career began at the age of 10 when he joined the choir of the chapel royal, remaining a member until he was 14 years old. While a choirboy, he was taught to play the organ by his mentor John Blow, the chapel's choirmaster and also the organist at Westminster Abbey. In 1677 Purcell was appointed composer for the king's band, and two years later he was named organist at Westminister Abbey, where he remained as organist until his death.

As a composer, Purcell proved to be a master of lyrical melody and of combining it with harmonic invention and counterpoint. Purcell's *Dido and Aeneas* (1689) is regarded by many to be the finest opera ever written in English. It shows his skill as a dramatist, contrapuntist, and melodist. The opera also highlights the way he was able to incorporate other musical elements, including ones from seventeenth-century English theater, into his own musical style. Among Purcell's many other works are odes for chorus and orchestra, cantatas, songs, anthems, chamber sonatas, and harpsichord suites. Especially notable are *The Fairy Queen* (1692), a masque, or dramatic composition, based on the British playwright William Shakespeare's *Midsummer Night's Dream,* the music for *King Arthur* (1691), a drama written by the English poet and dramatist John Dryden; and *Sound the Trumpets,* a birthday ode for King James II.

BOOKS ABOUT PURCELL

Arundell, Dennis D. *Henry Purcell. Select Bibliographies Reprint Ser.* Ayer (repr of 1927 ed) $12.00. ISBN 0-8369-5223-5 Illustrated biography and study of Purcell's music.

Holst, Imogen. *Henry Purcell. Great Masters Ser.* Boosey & Hawkes 1961 $3.75. ISBN 0-913932-19-1 Collection of essays by various Purcell scholars.

Zimmerman, Franklin B. *Henry Purcell: His Life and Times, 1659–1695.* Univ of Penn Pr 1983 $22.95. ISBN 0-8122-1136-7 Looks at the composer within the context of seventeenth-century England.

REYNOLDS, SIR JOSHUA   1723–1792

Sir Joshua Reynolds, one of England's greatest portrait painters, was born in the town of Plympton Erle in 1923. The son of a schoolmaster and member of a cultured family, he became a learned man in touch with the leading literary men of his time. Reynolds began drawing at an early age and studied portrait painting at age 17. For several years thereafter he worked in London, and then, between 1750 and 1752, he traveled in Italy, where he absorbed the style of such Renaissance masters as the Italian artists Michelangelo Buonarroti, Raphael Santi, and Titian. (*See* Michelangelo *and* Raphael, Vol. 2, World History: The Renaissance and Reformation.) After returning to London, he painted several portraits that brought him into prominence. Besieged with commissions for paintings, he soon established himself as the leading portraitist of his day and became friendly with some of the most influential people in England.

In 1768 Reynolds's prominence made him an obvious choice to become the first president of London's newly founded Royal Academy, a society that exhibited art and provided art instruction. As president, he presented a series of addresses to the students at the academy. Eventually published as a series of essays called *Discourses,* they are a practical explanation of the academic style of art Reynolds espoused. In 1769 Reynolds was granted the honor of knighthood by the English crown.

Reynolds's success continued uninterrupted until failing eyesight in his later years forced him to stop painting about 1789. He died three years later, in 1792, and was buried in St. Paul's Cathedral in London.

BOOK BY REYNOLDS

Letters by Joshua Reynolds. Frederick W. Hilles (ed). AMS (repr of 1929 ed) $23.00. ISBN 0-685-70796-2

BOOKS ABOUT REYNOLDS

Penny, Nicholas (ed). *Reynolds.* Moyer 1987 $23.95. ISBN 0-918825-23-7 Surveys Reynolds's career, milieu, practice, and studio.

Phillips, Claude. *Sir Joshua Reynolds.* Longwood 1980 repr of 1894 ed $45.00. ISBN 0-89341-378-X Focuses on the history of Reynolds's portraits.

Waterhouse, Ellis. *Reynolds.* Praeger 1973. (o.p.) Introduction to Reynolds's life with a collection of his portraits.

See also Vol. 1, British Literature: The Restoration and the Eighteenth Century.

THE INDUSTRIAL REVOLUTION

*Ashton, Thomas S. *The Industrial Revolution, Seventeen-Sixty to Eighteen-Thirty.* Greenwood 1986 repr of 1964 ed $35.00. ISBN 0-313-25041-3 Comprehensive account of the Industrial Revolution in Great Britain.

Bailey, Brian. *The Industrial Heritage of Britain.* State Mutual 1982 $45.00. ISBN 0-85223-228-4

Beard, Charles A. *Industrial Revolution.* Greenwood 1969 repr of 1927 ed $41.50. ISBN 0-8371-2168-X

*Berlin, Isaiah. *Karl Marx: His Life and Environment.* Oxford Univ Pr 1978 $9.95. ISBN 0-19-520052-7 Looks at the life and times of Marx and examines his economic and political thought.

Briggs, Asa. *Age of Improvement, 1783 to 1867. A History of England Ser.* Longman 1979 $17.95. ISBN 0-582-49100-2

Briggs, Asa. *Iron Bridge to Crystal Palace: Impact and Images of the Industrial Revolution.* Thames Hudson 1979 $19.95. ISBN 0-500-01222-9

Cunningham, Hugh. *Leisure in the Industrial Revolution, Seventeen Eighty to Eighteen Eighty.* St. Martin's 1980 $26.00. ISBN 0-312-47894-1

Editors of Time–Life Books. *The Pulse of Enterprise: 1800–1850. Time Frame Ser.* Time–Life 1990 $22.60. ISBN 0-8094-6462-4

Heilbroner, Robert L. *The Worldly Philosophers: The Lives, Times, and Ideas of the Great Economic Thinkers.* Simon 1987 $9.95. ISBN 0-671-63318-X

Henderson, W. O. (ed). *Industrial Revolution on the Continent: Germany, France, Russia 1800–1914.* Biblio Dist 1961 $27.50. ISBN 0-7146-1319-3

*Hobsbawn, Eric. *Age of Empire.* McKay 1989 $12.95. ISBN 0-679-72175-4 Examines the period from 1875 to 1914, during which empires were emerging and societies were industrializing and modernizing.

Hobsbawn, Eric J. *Pelican Economic History of Britain.* Vol. 3 *Industry and Empire.* Penguin 1970 $6.95. ISBN 0-14-020898-4

Jeremy, David J. *Transatlantic Industrial Revolution: The Diffusion of Textile Technologies Between Britain and America, 1790–1830.* MIT Pr 1981 $45.00. ISBN 0-262-10022-3

*Knox, Diana. *Industrial Revolution. World History Ser.* Malcolm Yapp (ed). Greenhaven $2.95. ISBN 0-89908-108-8 Readable account of the Industrial Revolution.

Mantoux, Paul. *Industrial Revolution in the Eighteenth Century: An Outline of the Beginnings of the Modern Factory System in England.* Univ of Chicago Pr 1983 $17.95. ISBN 0-226-50384-4

Rule, John. *The Labouring Classes in Early Industrial England 1750–1850.* Longman 1986 $17.95. ISBN 0-582-49172-X

Shelston, Dorothy, and Alan Shelston. *The Industrial City, 1820–1870. Context and Commentary Ser.* Humanities 1990 $35.00. ISBN 0-333-39494-1

Smith, Adam. *An Inquiry into the Nature and Causes of the Wealth of Nations: Glasgow Edition.* 2 vols. Liberty Fund 1982 $11.00 ISBN 0-86597-008-4

*Smith, Page. *Rise of Industrial America.* McGraw 1984 $29.95. ISBN 0-07-058572-5 Discusses how the United States became a more industrialized nation in the period from 1876 to 1901.

Speed, Peter. *Social Problems of the Industrial Revolution.* Pergamon 1975 $5.90. ISBN 0-08-018883-4

Thompson, Edward P. *Making of the English Working Class.* Random 1966 $14.95. ISBN 0-394-70322-7

Tilly, Louise A., and Joan W. Scott. *Women, Work, and Family.* Routledge 1987 $11.95. ISBN 0-416-01681-2

Trebilcock, Clive. *The Industrialization of the Continental Powers 1780–1914.* Longman 1982 $16.95. ISBN 0-582-49120-7

*Vialls, Christine. *Iron and the Industrial Revolution.* Cambridge Univ Pr 1989 $5.95. ISBN 0-521-36845-6 Examines life in Great Britain prior to and during the Industrial Revolution.

Wrigley, E. Anthony. *Continuity, Chance, and Change: The Character of the Industrial Revolution in England.* Cambridge Univ Pr 1988 $32.50. ISBN 0-521-35648-2

NATIONALISM IN EUROPE

Delzell, Charles F. (ed). *The Unification of Italy, Eighteen Fifty-Nine to Eighteen Sixty-One.* Krieger 1976 $7.50. ISBN 0-88275-658-3

Greenfield, Kent R. *Economics and Liberalism in the Risorgimento: A Study of Nationalism in Lombardy, 1814–1848.* Greenwood 1978 repr of 1965 ed $35.00. ISBN 0-313-20510-8

Griffith, Gwilym O. *Mazzini: Prophet of Modern Europe.* Fertig 1970 $48.50. ISBN 0-86527-124-0

Hamerow, Theodore S. *Social Foundations of German Unification, 1858–1871.* Vol. 1 *Ideas and Institutions.* Princeton Univ Pr 1969 $12.50. ISBN 0-691-00773-X

Hearder, Harry. *Italy in the Age of the Risorgimento 1790–1870. History of Italy Ser.* Dennis Hay (ed). Longman 1983 $18.95. ISBN 0-582-49146-0

Howard, Michael. *The Franco-Prussian War: The German Invasion of France, 1870–71.* Routledge 1981 $16.95. ISBN 0-416-30750-7

Jelavich, Barbara. *History of the Balkans: Eighteenth and Nineteenth Centuries.* Cambridge Univ Pr 1983 $19.95. ISBN 0-521-27458-3

Lincoln, W. Bruce. *In War's Dark Shadow: The Russians Before the Great War.* Simon 1986 $10.95. ISBN 0-671-62821-6

Lucas, James. *Fighting Troops of the Austro-Hungarian Army, 1868–1914.* Hippocrene 1987 $50.00. ISBN 0-87052-362-7

Mosse, George L. *The Nationalization of the Masses: Political Symbolism and Mass Movements in Germany, from the Napoleonic Wars Through the Third Reich.* Fertig 1975 $40.00. ISBN 0-86527-140-2

Palmer, Alan. *The Banner of Battle: The Story of the Crimean War.* St. Martin's 1987 $24.95. ISBN 0-312-00539-3

Plessis, Alain. *The Rise and Fall of the Second Empire, 1852–1871. Cambridge History of Modern France Ser.* Jonathan Mandelbaum (tr). Cambridge Univ Pr 1988 $10.95. ISBN 0-521-35856-6

Ramm, Agatha. *Europe in the Nineteenth Century. Grant and Temperley's Europe in the Nineteenth and Twentieth Centuries Ser.* Longman 1984 $15.95. ISBN 0-582-49029-4

Salisbury, Harrison E. *Black Night, White Snow: Russia's Revolutions 1905–1917. Quality Paperbacks Ser.* Da Capo 1981 $14.95. ISBN 0-306-80154-X

Seton-Watson, Hugh. *Nations and States: An Enquiry into the Origins of Nations and the Politics of Nationalism.* Westview $49.00. ISBN 0-89158-227-4

Seton-Watson, Hugh. *The Russian Empire: Eighteen Hundred One to Nineteen Seventeen. History of Modern Europe Ser.* Oxford Univ Pr 1988 $29.95. ISBN 0-19-822152-5

Smith, Anthony D. *Theories of Nationalism.* Holmes & Meier 1983 $24.95. ISBN 0-8419-0845-1
Smith, Denis Mack. *Cavour: A Biography.* Carol B. Janeway (ed). Knopf 1985 $18.45. ISBN 0-394-53885-4
Sussex, Roland, and J. C. Eade (eds). *Culture and Nationalism in Nineteenth-Century Eastern Europe.* Slavica 1985 $14.95. ISBN 0-89357-146-6
Taylor, A. J. *Germany's First Bid for Colonies, 1884–1885: A Move in Bismarck's European Policy.* Norton 1970 $1.25. ISBN 0-393-00530-5
Tuchman, Barbara. *Proud Tower.* Bantam 1983 $6.95. ISBN 0-553-25602-5

BISMARCK, OTTO VON   1815–1898

Otto von Bismarck, the German statesman and person responsible for the unification of Germany, was born in the German state of Prussia in 1815. A member of the German landowning class, Bismarck studied law at the Universities of Göttingen and Berlin. After graduating, he entered the civil service and served in the army. In 1847 he became a member of the German Parliament, and in 1859 he was made the Prussian ambassador to Russia and later to France. When the king of Prussia, William I, clashed with the Parliament in 1862, he appointed Bismarck prime minister and minister of foreign affairs. Bismarck skillfully gained power over the parliament and began to put his own ideas on domestic and foreign policy into effect.

Bismarck opposed democracy and favored an absolute monarchy. He also considered people incapable of governing themselves and felt that the only basis for government was force and fear. In his words, "The great questions of the day will not be settled by speeches and majority decisions . . . but by blood and iron."

Bismarck began a campaign for German unification by transforming the Prussian army into Europe's most efficient fighting force and then provoking war with neighboring states. The Austro-Prussian War of 1866 resulted in a Prussian victory and in Prussia replacing Austria as the leading German state. With the defeat of Austria, Bismarck set up a Prussian-dominated North German Confederation and became its chancellor. Because of his willingness to settle issues by "blood and iron," he became known as the Iron Chancellor.

Bismarck next turned his attention to France, provoking the Franco-Prussian War of 1870, which resulted in France's defeat. France was forced to cede the provinces of Alsace and Lorraine to Germany, which sowed the seeds of French and German antagonism that resulted in World War I. The climax to Bismarck's campaign for German unification came on January 18, 1871, when all the German states except Austria agreed to come together as the German Empire, or Second Reich. Its capital was to be Berlin, the capital of Prussia, and its kaiser, or emperor, was to be King William I of Prussia. Bismarck became the empire's first chancellor and ruled with almost dictatorial power.

Over the next several years, Bismarck concentrated on building Germany's industrial strength and improving its economy. In an attempt to weaken the appeal of socialism, he adopted revolutionary social reforms, including health insurance, accident insurance, shorter work hours, and old-age pensions for workers. On the diplomatic front, he tried to isolate France by remaining friendly with Russia and by forming the Triple Alliance of Germany, Austria, and Italy.

When Kaiser William I died in 1888, his successor, Kaiser William II, strongly resented Bismarck's power and forced the chancellor to resign in 1890.

In 1891 Bismarck was elected a member of the new German Parliament, the Reichstag, but he never took his seat there. His retirement and death in 1898 marked the end of an era in European history.

BOOK BY BISMARCK

Kaiser vs. Bismarck. Bernard Miall (tr). AMS (repr of 1921 ed) $14.50. ISBN 0-404-00869-0

BOOKS ABOUT BISMARCK

*Booth, Martin, *et al. Bismarck. World History Ser.* Martin Yapp and Margaret Killingray (eds). Greenhaven 1980 $2.95. ISBN 0-89908-023-5 Account of German leader Otto von Bismarck and his place in history.

Busch, Moritz. *Bismarck in the Franco–German War, 1870–1871.* Fertig 1989 $49.50. ISBN 0-86527-010-4 Examines the German leader's role in the Franco–Prussian War.

*Elliot, B. J. *Bismarck: The Kaiser and Germany. Modern Times Ser.* Longman 1972 $4.95. ISBN 0-582-20423-2 Discusses the notable German statesman and his influence on German history.

Eyck, Erich. *Bismarck and the German Empire.* Norton 1964 $9.95. ISBN 0-393-00235-7 Discusses Bismarck's role in the development and expansion of the German Empire, or Second Reich.

Fuller, Joseph V. *Bismarck's Diplomacy at Its Zenith.* Fertig 1922 $48.00. ISBN 0-86527-011-2 Analyzes the diplomacy and foreign policy achievements of the German statesman.

Hamerow, Theodore S. (ed). *Otto Von Bismarck: A Historical Assessment. Problems in European Civilization Ser.* Heath 1990. ISBN 0-669-82008-3 Looks at the accomplishments of the German statesman and leader.

Headlam-Morley, James. *Bismarck and the Foundation of the German Empire. Heroes of the Nations Ser.* AMS (repr of 1899 ed) $30.00. ISBN 0-404-58265-6 Examines Bismarck's role in building the German Empire.

*Rose, Jonathan. *Otto von Bismarck. World Leaders—Past and Present Ser.* Chelsea 1987 $17.95. ISBN 0-87754-510-3 Introductory account of the life and times of the notable nineteenth-century German leader.

Stern, Fritz R. *Gold and Iron: Bismarck, Bleischroder, and the Building of the German Empire.* Random 1979 $14.95. ISBN 0-394-74034-3 Story of Bismarck's actions after unification and an important study of the relations between banking and diplomacy, Jews and Germans, and between economics and politics.

Taylor, Alan J. *Germany's First Bid for Colonies, 1884–1885: A Move in Bismarck's European Policy.* Norton 1970 $1.25. ISBN 0-393-00530-5 Discusses Germany's colonial expansion under the leadership of Bismarck.

Taylor, Alan J. *Bismarck: The Man and the Statesman.* David and Charles 1987 $11.95. ISBN 0-241-11565-5 Standard biography of the German leader.

DISRAELI, BENJAMIN   1804–1881

Benjamin Disraeli, the noted British statesman, novelist, and prime minister, is widely credited with modernizing the Tory party, which came to be called the Conservative party. The eldest son of Italian-Jewish parents, Disraeli was born in London and raised at first in the Jewish religion. In 1813, however, Disraeli was baptized as a Christian after his father quarreled with the local synagogue. Because Jews were excluded from membership in the British Parliament before 1858, this conversion to Christianity later made his political career possible.

Disraeli's first reputation was made as a novelist. His five-volume novel *Vivian Grey* (1826–1827) was followed by other multivolume novels, among them *The Young Duke* (1831) and *Henrietta Temple* (1836). In 1837, after several unsuccessful attempts to be elected to Parliament, his parliamentary career began. In Parliament, Disraeli became an eloquent speaker, and many young Tories, or Conservative Party members, rallied around his views. Particularly successful was his work in passing the Reform Bill (1867), a piece of legislation that added 2 million working-class voters to the electorate. Disraeli's work led to the position of prime minister during a short-lived administration in 1868 and a longer, more successful one from 1874 to 1880. On Great Britain's home front, Disraeli engineered legislation that cleared slums and prevented the exploitation of common laborers and tradespeople. In foreign affairs he bolstered the prestige of the British Empire by annexing territory (the Fiji Islands in 1874 and the Transvaal in 1877) and by strengthening British interests in the Mediterranean through acquisition of controlling shares in the Suez Canal in 1875. A favorite of Queen Victoria, who granted him a peerage as Lord Beaconsfield, Disraeli got the Parliament to name her Empress of India in 1877. One of Disraeli's last triumphs before retiring from public office came in 1878 at the Berlin Congress, at which he played an important role in checking Russian power in the Balkan area and the eastern Mediterranean.

BOOKS BY DISRAELI

Benjamin Disraeli: Letters, 1815–1834. J. A. Gunn, *et al* (eds). Univ of Toronto Pr 1982 $60.00. ISBN 0-8020-5523-0

Benjamin Disraeli: Letters, 1835–1837. J. A. Gunn, *et al* (eds). Univ of Toronto Pr $60.00. ISBN 0-8020-5587-7

Letters of Runnymede. Gregg Intl (repr of 1836 ed) $49.68. ISBN 0-576-02170-9

The Works of Benjamin Disraeli, Earl of Beaconsfield. 20 vols. AMS (repr of 1904 ed) $800.00. ISBN 0-404-08800-7

BOOKS ABOUT DISRAELI

Blake, Robert. *Disraeli.* Carroll & Graf 1987 $14.50. ISBN 0-88184-296-6 Standard biography of the noted statesman.

Bradford, Sarah. *Disraeli.* Scarborough Hse 1986 $12.95. Modern biography that views Disraeli both as a young man and as prime minister.

*McGuirk, Carol. *Disraeli. World Leaders—Past and Present Ser.* Chelsea 1987 $17.95. ISBN 0-87754-565-0 General biography of the nineteenth-century British prime minister, especially suitable for younger readers.

GARIBALDI, GIUSEPPI   1807–1882

Giuseppi Garibaldi, a leader in Italy's struggle for unification, was born in 1807, the son of a poor sailor. As a youth he traveled to Rome, where his imagination was captured by the idea of a union of the various independent Italian states. In 1834, after taking part in an unsuccessful uprising against the king of the Italian state of Sardinia, Garibaldi fled to South America. During a 14-year exile there, he fought in several wars for independence, learning guerrilla tactics and winning fame for his bravery, as well as gaining a romantic reputation because of his battle attire—a red shirt, a white poncho, and a large black ostrich feather on his hat.

In 1848 Garibaldi returned to Italy to join the fights for independence that were erupting in all the Italian states. These revolutions were all unsuccessful, and Garibaldi was once again forced into exile, this time in the United States. In 1854 he returned to Italy and resumed the struggle for unification. Garibaldi had originally favored the formation of a republic, but he gave up that idea and instead supported the idea of a united Italy under the rule of King Victor Emmanuel II of Sardinia.

The Third of May.   Painting by Francisco de Goya (1808).   Courtesy of The
Bettmann Archive.

In the spring of 1860, with the king's support, Garibaldi led a volunteer
force of 1,000 "red shirts" in an invasion of the kingdom of Sicily and Naples.
After outwitting a much larger army and conquering the island of Sicily,
Garibaldi and his troops crossed to the mainland and began a successful march
on Naples. These conquests secured, Garibaldi relinquished control of them to
Victor Emmanuel, who was proclaimed king of Italy in 1861. In 1862 and 1867
Garibaldi led unsuccessful campaigns against Rome, which remained outside
the new kingdom of Italy. Gradually, however, other Italian states were incorporated into the kingdom, and by 1870 the entire Italian peninsula was part
of a single nation. Although he was elected to the Italian Parliament in 1874,
Garibaldi soon resigned and retired to the island of Caprera, near Sardinia,
where he died in 1882.

BOOKS BY GARIBALDI

Autobiography of Guiseppe Garibaldi. J. W. Mario (ed). A. Werner (tr). 3 vols. Fertig 1985
    repr of 1889 ed $95.00. ISBN 0-86527-348-0
Garibaldi's Memoirs from the Manuscript, Personal Notes, and Authentic Sources. (coauthored
    with Elpis Melena) Intl Inst Garibaldian 1981 $12.50. ISBN 92-9013-003-2

BOOKS ABOUT GARIBALDI

Abba, Giuseppe C. *The Diary of One of Garibaldi's Thousand.* E. R. Vincent (tr). Greenwood
    1981 repr of 1962 ed $35.00. ISBN 0-312-22446-3 Diary of one of the thousand
    who accompanied Garibaldi.
Hibbert, Christopher. *Garibaldi and His Enemies: The Clash of Arms and Personalities in the
    Making of Italy.* Penguin 1989 $8.95. ISBN 0-14-007971-8 Focuses on the conflicts
    between Garibaldi and other Italian leaders.
Mack-Smith, Denis. *Cavour and Garibaldi Eighteen Sixty: A Study in Political Conflict.* Cam-

bridge Univ Pr 1985 $21.95. ISBN 0-521-31637-5 Extremely important study of the Risorgimento that focuses on seven essential months in 1860, the events between the Sicilian rebellion in April, and the absorption of the whole south into Victor Emmanuel's Italian kingdom in November.

Trevelyan, George M. *Garibaldi and the Making of Italy.* Greenwood 1982 repr of 1928 ed $48.50. ISBN 0-313-23248-2 Comprehensive account of Garibaldi and the unification of Italy.

Trevelyan, George M. *Garibaldi and the Thousand.* AMS (repr of 1909 ed) $32.50. ISBN 0-404-14729-1 Story of Garibaldi's part in the decisive events of 1859–1860, which "made" Italy.

*Viola, Herman, and Susan Viola. *Giuseppe Garibaldi. World Leaders—Past and Present Ser.* Chelsea 1988 $17.95. ISBN 0-87754-526-X Introductory biography of the notable Italian leader who was instrumental in Italian unification in 1860.

GLADSTONE, WILLIAM EWART   1809–1898

To many people, William Gladstone, the dominant personality of the Liberal party from 1868 to 1894 and four-time prime minister of Great Britain (1868–1874, 1880–1885, 1886, 1892–1894), represented the best qualities of Victorian England. Yet he was disliked by Queen Victoria, his sovereign, and by Benjamin Disraeli, his chief political rival (*See* Disraeli, Vol. 2, Nationalism in Europe.)

Born in Hawarden, Flintshire, Wales, Gladstone was educated at Eton and Oxford University and entered Parliament in 1832. He began his parliamentary career as a member of the Tory party, soon to be called the Conservative party. Gladstone was influenced by Robert Peel, prime minister of Great Britain in 1834 and 1835, and again from 1841 to 1846, in whose cabinets he served. Under that influence, he became more and more liberal in his outlook toward political reform, eventually becoming the leader of the Liberal party. By the time he became prime minister, Gladstone had become known as the "Old Man of Liberalism," clashing often with Disraeli, the leader of the Conservative party.

During his first term as prime minister, Gladstone was primarily concerned with solving problems in Ireland. Under his leadership, the Disestablishment Act of 1869 freed Irish Catholics from supporting the Anglican church. The Irish Land Act of 1870 curtailed the power of absentee landlords to evict their Irish tenants without compensation. Education was another priority, and with the Education Act of 1870 instruction was made free and compulsory throughout Great Britain. Gladstone's efforts on behalf of the Irish led to his defeat as prime minister in 1874. His second term as prime minister, however, saw the passage of the Reform Act of 1884, which nearly doubled the size of the electorate. His third and fourth terms as prime minister both floundered on the issue of home rule for the Irish. Gladstone retired from public life in 1895 and died three years later.

BOOKS BY GLADSTONE

Gleanings of Past Years, 1843–1878: And Later Gleanings. 8 vols. AMS (repr of 1897 ed) $250.00. ISBN 0-404-08850-3

The State in Its Relations with the Church. Gregg Intl (repr of 1841 ed) $62.10. ISBN 0-576-02192-X

BOOKS ABOUT GLADSTONE

*Brand, Eric. *William Gladstone. World Leaders—Past and Present Ser.* Chelsea 1986 $16.95. ISBN 0-87754-528-6 General biography of the British statesman and Liberal party leader; especially suitable for younger readers.

Matthew, H. C. *Gladstone. Eighteen Nine to Eighteen Seventy-Four.* Oxford Univ Pr 1989 $12.95. ISBN 0-19-282122-9 Account of the statesman that focuses on the period from his birth to the end of his first term as prime minister of Great Britain.

Morley, John M. *Life of William Ewart Gladstone.* 3 vols. Greenwood 1971 repr of 1903 ed $64.50. ISBN 0-8371-0576-5 Complete biography of Gladstone beginning with his childhood and focusing on his life in Parliament as a leader.

Stansky, Peter. *Gladstone: A Progress in Politics.* Norton 1981 $5.95. ISBN 0-393-00037-0 Focuses on Gladstone's impact on British politics.

THE ARTS IN NINETEENTH-CENTURY EUROPE

Calvocoressi, Michael D., and Gerald Abraham. *Masters of Russian Music.* Johnson Repr (repr of 1936 ed) $35.00. ISBN 0-384-07218-6

Daumier, Honore. *Drawings of Daumier. Master Draughtsman Ser.* Stephen Longstreet (ed). Borden $4.95. ISBN 0-87505-156-1

DeLeiris, Alain. *Drawings of Edouard Manet.* Univ of California Pr 1969 $125.00. ISBN 0-520-01547-9

Finson, Jon W. *Mendelssohn and Schumann: Essays on Their Music and Its Context.* Larry R. Todd (ed). Duke Univ Pr 1985 $32.50. ISBN 0-8223-0569-0

Layton, Robert. *Sibelius.* Rowman 1984 $7.95. ISBN 0-8226-0387-X

Longstreet, Stephen (ed). *Drawings of Matisse.* Borden $4.95. ISBN 0-87505-174-X

Renoir, Pierre A. *Drawings of Renoir. Master Draughtsman Ser.* Stephen Longstreet (ed). Borden $4.95. ISBN 0-87505-183-9

Rewald, John, and Frances Weitzenhoffer. *Aspects of Monet: A Symposium on the Artist's Life and Times.* Abrams 1984 $45.00. ISBN 0-8109-1314-3

Rewald, John. *The History of Impressionism.* Bulfinch 1980 $29.95. ISBN 0-87070-369-2

Rewald, John. *Post-Impressionism: From Van Gogh to Gauguin.* Bulfinch 1979 $60.00. ISBN 0-87070-532-6

*Rewald, John. *Seurat: A Biography.* Abrams 1990 $75.00. ISBN 0-8109-3814-6 Comprehensive biography of the French artist; with illustrations, color plates, bibliography, and more.

Rosen, Charles, and Henri Zerner. *Romanticism and Realism: The Mythology of Nineteenth-Century Art.* Penguin 1984 $22.50. ISBN 0-670-54817-0

*Taylor, John Russell. *Impressionist Dreams: The Artists and the World They Painted.* Little 1990 $40.00. ISBN 0-8212-1816-6 Examines the artistic intentions of certain French impressionists; includes photographs.

Walker, Robert. *Rachmaninoff: His Life and Times.* Paganiniana 1981 $14.95. ISBN 0-87666-582-2

BERLIOZ, HECTOR 1803–1869

The French composer Hector Berlioz was one of the most influential composers of the romantic period in music. The son of a French physician, Berlioz showed an early aptitude for music and taught himself to perform and compose. For a time his father indulged this pastime, but then, in 1821, Berlioz was sent to Paris to study medicine. Although he attended lectures at the medical school there, he gave most of his attention to music, studying with a private music teacher and composing. Finally, in 1826, Berlioz abandoned his medical studies and enrolled at the Paris Conservatory. To support himself, he gave music lessons and wrote articles on music.

While at the Paris Conservatory Berlioz applied for the Prix de Rome, a prestigious music award. Berlioz entered the contest four times before finally winning the prize in 1830. In that year, Berlioz completed the *Symphonie fantastique,* his most ambitious and well-known work. The symphony is a musical description of the dreams of an artist under the influence of opium. Based on the English writer Thomas De Quincey's *Confessions of an English Opium Eater,* the symphony is an example of program music—music that represents a story or sequence of ideas. Berlioz developed the genre of program music into a highly regarded art, drawing themes from the works of the English writer William Shakespeare and such contemporary writers and poets as the German writer Johann Goethe, the English writer Lord Byron, and the French writer Théophile Gautier.

As part of the Prix de Rome, Berlioz spent two years in Italy. Although he did no composing during this time, he did wander about the Italian countryside making notes of melodies and projects and developed friendships with the composers Felix Mendelssohn and Mikhail Glinka. In 1832 Berlioz returned to Paris.

Because the unusual nature of his compositions failed to win him much recognition, Berlioz was forced to earn a living as a music critic and music librarian. By the time he was 34, a pattern was established in his career. Each new musical composition was greeted by a mixture of wild enthusiasm from younger composers and hostility from the entrenched musical establishment. Although Berlioz did achieve some measure of fame in later life, his genius was largely unrecognized. His last years were lived in bitterness and loneliness after the death of his second wife and his son. He died in Paris in 1869 after a long illness.

Berlioz has been called the greatest composer of melody since the Austrian composer Wolfgang Amadeus Mozart. He is also recognized as a master of the orchestra, having greatly expanded its expressive range through his profound understanding of individual instruments. Finally, his experimentation with new musical structures and meters freed younger composers from the strict requirements of classical musical forms and opened the way to other musical approaches.

BOOKS BY BERLIOZ

Hector Berlioz: Selections from His Letters, and Aesthetic, Humorous and Satirical Writings. (coauthored with William F. Apthorp, tr) Longwood 1976 repr of 1879 ed $40.00. ISBN 0-89341-018-7

The Life, as Written by Himself in His Letters and Memoirs. Katharine F. Boult (tr). AMS (repr of 1803 ed) $18.00. ISBN 0-404-12865-3

Memoirs. Dover 1960 $9.95. ISBN 0-486-21563-6

New Letters of Berlioz, 1830–1868. Jacques Barzun (tr). Greenwood 1974 $22.50. ISBN 0-8371-3251-7

BOOKS ABOUT BERLIOZ

Barzun, Jacques. *Berlioz and His Century: An Introduction to the Age of Romanticism.* Univ of Chicago Pr 1982 $9.95. ISBN 0-226-03861-0 Analyzes the composer's role in the romantic period of music and the arts.

Holoman, D. Kern. *The Creative Process in the Autograph Musical Documents of Hector Berlioz.* George Buelow (ed). UMI 1980. (o.p.) $49.95. Includes documents, the methods of Berlioz's work, and three examples of this method.

MacDonald, Hugh. *Berlioz. The Master Musicians Ser.* Biblio Dist 1983 $17.95. ISBN 0-460-03156-2 Detailed biography of the nineteenth-century composer and his music.

Rushton, Julian. *The Musical Language of Berlioz.* Cambridge Univ Pr 1984 $57.50. ISBN 0-521-24279-7 Analysis of the French composer's musical style, including his use of melody, rhythm, and orchestral features.

BRAHMS, JOHANNES 1833–1897

A composer, pianist, and conductor, Johannes Brahms was born in Hamburg, Germany. Possessing a talent that could have taken him in any musical direction, he chose the piano and composing and made his debut as a pianist at the age of 14. In 1853 Brahms met the German composer Robert Schumann, who regarded Brahms as a genius, and Schumann and his wife Clara, a noted concert pianist, became Brahms's lifelong friends. In 1862 Brahms moved to Vienna where his talents as a composer reached full flower. The music of Brahms shows great respect for the form and structure of eighteenth-century classicism, but it also incorporates the romantic style so typical of the nineteenth century.

Brahms is considered a giant among nineteenth-century composers of chamber music and symphonies. Among his 24 published chamber music works are the Piano Trio in B, Opus 8 (1854), two string quartets, two piano quartets, and the Piano Quintet in F Minor, Opus 34a (1864). He composed four great symphonies. The *Symphony in C Minor* was finished in 1876, after many years of work. His *Symphony in D Minor* appeared in 1877, the *Symphony in F Major* in 1883, and the *Symphony in E Minor* in 1885. While classic in structure and design, the symphonies are romantic in their musical language and sound. Nonetheless, they exhibit feelings of repose that illustrate a return to discipline and a revival of order and form, indicative of changes in music to come in the 1900s. Today many of the works of Brahms are staples of concert repertoire.

BOOK BY BRAHMS

The Herzogenberg Correspondence. Music Reprint Ser. Max Kalbeck (ed). Hannah Bryant (tr). Da Capo 1987 repr of 1909 ed $45.00. ISBN 0-306-76281-1

BOOKS ABOUT BRAHMS

Gal, Hans. *Johannes Brahms: His Work and Personality.* Joseph Stein (tr). Greenwood 1977 $35.00. ISBN 0-8371-9367-2 Brahms's life story, focusing on him as an artist.
Geiringer, Karl. *Brahms: His Life and Work. Music Ser.* Da Capo 1981 $11.95. ISBN 0-306-80223-6 Vivid scholarly and literary portrait of Brahms.
Latham, Peter. *Brahms. Master Musicians Ser.* Littlefield 1975 $7.95. ISBN 0-8226-0707-7 General introduction to the composer's life and work.
May, Florence. *The Life of Johannes Brahms.* 2 vols. Reprint Services 1988 repr of 1976 ed $99.00. Thorough biography that focuses on Brahms's family, music, and concerts.
Schumann, Clara J., and Johannes Brahms. *Letters Eighteen Fifty-Three to Eighteen Ninety-Six. Encore Music Editions Ser.* Berthold Litzmann (ed). Hyperion 1985 repr of 1927 ed $45.00. ISBN 0-88355-761-4 Compilation of letters between the composer and his friend Clara Schumann.

CEZANNE, PAUL 1839–1906

Paul Cézanne was one of the most influential and powerful painters of late nineteenth-century France. His works largely reflect the era of impressionism in which artists were more concerned with color and the effects of light on objects than with the objects themselves. His unique style paved the way for such twentieth-century art movements as cubism, which reduces natural forms to geometric equivalents, and abstract art, which focuses on brushstrokes, texture, and the random placement of images.

Cézanne was born in Aix-en-Provence, France, in 1839, the son of a prosperous banker. At his father's insistence, he began to study law at the University of Aix. Cézanne, however, was interested only in painting, and in 1861 one of his school friends, the French writer Emile Zola (*see* Zola, Vol. 1, World Literature: French Language and Literature), persuaded him to go to Paris to study art. In Paris, Cézanne met Edouard Manet, Camille Pissarro, and other important impressionist painters.

Though Cézanne learned from the impressionists, he was not content to mimic their style. Instead, he wanted to create a style all his own. Whereas the impressionists focused on individual brushstrokes and the play of light on objects, Cézanne experimented with using simplified forms and color to develop geometrical compositions that often portrayed subjects from shifting viewpoints. His subjects include portraits, still lifes, and landscapes. His watercolors are often as masterful as his oil paintings.

When Cézanne exhibited his paintings at impressionist shows in 1874 and 1877, the critics ridiculed and attacked his work. Later in life, however, he won the respect of many young painters. In 1886 Cézanne retired to Provence in the south of France, where he continued to devote all of his energy to his art. By the time of his death from diabetes, his fame was widespread.

BOOKS BY CEZANNE

A Cézanne Sketchbook: Figures, Portraits, Landscapes, and Still Lives. Fine Art Series. Dover 1985 $5.95. ISBN 0-486-24790-2

The Complete Paintings of Cézanne. Classics of World Art Ser. Ian Dunlop and Sandra Orient. Penguin 1986 $10.95. ISBN 0-14-008652-8

Drawings of Cézanne. Master Draughtsman Ser. Stephen Longstreet (ed). Borden $4.95. ISBN 0-87505-154-5

Paul Cézanne, Letters. John Rewald (ed). AMS (repr of 1941 ed) $49.50. ISBN 0-404-20053-2

BOOKS ABOUT CEZANNE

Badt, Kurt. *The Art of Cézanne.* Hacker 1985 repr of 1965 ed $50.00. ISBN 0-87817-302-1 Focuses on Cézanne's watercolor techniques, symbolism, and historical position and significance.

Chappuis, Adrien. *The Drawings of Paul Cézanne: A Catalogue Raisonne.* 2 vols. New York Graphic Society 1973. (o.p) $175.00. Heavily illustrated presentation of the artist's drawings and studies.

Loran, Erle. *Cézanne's Composition: Analysis of His Form with Diagrams and Photographs of His Motifs.* Univ of California Pr 1963 $15.95. ISBN 0-520-05459-8 Gives a deep understanding of Cézanne's art.

*Rewald, John. *Cézanne: A Biography.* Abrams 1986 $75.00. ISBN 0-8109-0775-5 Comprehensive, illustrated look at the artist and his work.

Rewald, John. *Paul Cézanne: The Watercolors—A Catalogue Raisonne.* Bulfinch 1984 $150.00. ISBN 0-8212-1530-2 Richly illustrated presentation of the artist's watercolor paintings.

Rubin, William. *Cézanne: The Late Work.* New York Graphic Society 1977. (o.p.) $45.00. Catalog of Cézanne's major exhibitions with essays by various art historians.

*Schapiro, Meyer. *Paul Cézanne.* Abrams 1988 $19.95. ISBN 0-8109-1043-8 Forty color plates plus a few in black and white follow a biographical sketch of the artist's life.

Wechsler, Judith. *The Interpretation of Cézanne.* UMI 1981. (o.p.) $34.95. Looks at the impressionist style through analyses of the artist's work.

CHOPIN, FREDERIC 1810–1849

Born near Warsaw, Poland, of French and Polish parentage, Frédéric Chopin showed a great talent as a pianist from a very young age. He published his first work—a rondo for two pianos—when he was 14, and continued to compose exclusively for the piano. From 1826 to 1829, he studied composition at the Warsaw Conservatory. At age 19, Chopin left Poland on a concert tour and eventually settled in Paris. In Paris he had a long, stormy, and dependent relationship with the French novelist Amandine Aurore Lucie Dupin, better known as George Sand. The dependency of Chopin's personal life and his poor health contrast dramatically with his musical compositions, which require brilliant technique to master their elaborate melodic and harmonic figurations.

Although he never returned to Poland, Chopin continued to reflect in his compositions his love for his native land and his misery at its political misfortunes. His polonaises, or slow dances, and especially his mazurkas, or lively dances, are filled with rhythms and musical elements found in Polish popular music and are among the earliest and best examples of the inspiration that nationalism had on the music of the romantic period. Chopin's principal works are two concertos—the *Concerto in E Minor* (1833) and the *Concerto in F Minor* (1836); several sonatas—the *Sonata in B Flat Minor* (1840) and the *Sonata in B Minor* (1845); 27 etudes—tone poems based on a single musical motive that concentrate on a specific technical skill; and 24 preludes. Through his piano works, Chopin effectively removed the bonds of symphonic and choral traditions that had restricted the full flowering of the piano as a solo instrument. Interestingly, he disliked playing in public, so he concentrated instead on teaching and composing. Chopin's innovative and brilliant work came to an early end when he died of tuberculosis at the age of 39.

BOOK BY CHOPIN

Chopin's Letters. Henry K. Opienski (ed). E. L. Voynich (tr). Vienna 1972 $15.00. ISBN 0-8443-0090-X

BOOKS ABOUT CHOPIN

Atwood, William G. *Fryderyk Chopin: Pianist from Warsaw.* Columbia Univ Pr 1987 $30.00. ISBN 0-231-06406-3 Focuses on Chopin's concert career, his ardent patriotism, and his noted love affair with French writer George Sand.

Huneker, James G. *Chopin: The Man and His Music.* Herbert Weinstock (ed). Dover 1966 $4.50. ISBN 0-486-21687-X General overview of the composer and his work.

Liszt, Franz. *Frederic Chopin.* Edward N. Waters (tr). Vienna 1973 $10.00. ISBN 0-8443-0066-7 Portrait of Chopin by his friend and fellow composer.

Niecks, Frederick. *Frederic Chopin as a Man and Musician.* 2 vols. Paganiniana 1981 $24.95. ISBN 0-87666-648-9 Comprehensive account of the personal and professional life of the composer.

Walker, Alan (ed). *The Chopin Companion: Profiles of the Man and the Musician.* Norton 1973 $7.95. ISBN 0-393-00668-9 Collection of essays by eminent Chopin scholars with discography, bibliography, and chronological catalog.

CONSTABLE, JOHN 1776–1837

John Constable, the first English artist to focus exclusively on landscapes and to paint them on a large scale, is considered one of England's greatest landscape painters. Constable's love of the English countryside is evident in his work, and his inspiration came from the clouds, trees, rivers, light, and atmosphere found in nature. The fresh and loose technique he used in his work greatly influenced the development of the French impressionist school of painting in the latter part of the nineteenth century.

Born at East Bergholt in Suffolk, Constable left home in 1799 to study art at the Royal Academy schools in London. He lived in or near London for the rest of his life; although he spent many summers in Suffolk gathering ideas and experimenting with techniques for reproducing nature more realistically.

In 1816 Constable married Maria Bicknell. Their happy marriage produced seven children. Constable moved his family to Hampstead in London in 1819 for the sake of his wife's health. There he made a study of cloud formations, which he eventually integrated into many of his later paintings. Another subject he returned to often is Salisbury Cathedral, which he depicted in his paintings many times.

Constable's genius was first recognized in Paris in 1824 when a French art dealer bought one of his paintings for an exhibition. The painting became a sensation and helped launch the romantic movement in art. Recognition in England came in 1829 when Constable was elected a full member of the Royal Academy. Constable's popularity, however, did not reach its peak until around 1890, long after his death, when the public began to view paintings owned by his children.

BOOK BY CONSTABLE

Constable Paintings, Drawings and Watercolours. State Mutual 1975. (o.p.) $50.00.
John Constable's Correspondence. R. B. Beckett (ed). 6 vols. Boydell & Brewer (repr of 1962–1968 ed). (o.p.) $13.50–16.50.

BOOKS ABOUT CONSTABLE

Badt, Kurt. *John Constable's Clouds.* Stanley Godman (tr). Saifer 1971 $15.00. ISBN 0-87556-017-2 Focuses on how the artist rendered clouds in his paintings.
Fleming-Williams, Ian. *Constable Landscape Watercolours and Drawings.* Salem Hse $22.95. ISBN 0-905005-10-4 Looks at Constable's landscapes done in the mediums of watercolor and drawing.
Reynolds, Graham. *Constable: The Natural Painter.* Academy Chi Pubs 1977 $5.95. ISBN 0-586-04401-9 Focuses on the artist's emphasis on the natural landscape and on his direct observation of nature.
Rosenthal, Michael. *Constable.* Thames Hudson $11.95. ISBN 0-500-20107-7 General survey of Constable's artistic projects in the context of a broader cultural milieu; includes reproductions of many paintings, drawings, and watercolors.
Rosenthal, Michael. *Constable: The Painter and His Landscape.* Yale Univ Pr 1983 $25.95. ISBN 0-300-03753-8 Fine color reproductions and historical commentary on East Anglia, where Constable painted and drew throughout his career.
Walker, John. *Constable.* Abrams 1979. (o.p.) $40.00. Comprehensive look at the artist and his work; with illustrations.

DEGAS, EDGAR   1834–1917

Noted impressionist sculptor and painter, Edgar Degas was born in Paris, France. The son of a banker, he prepared for a career as a lawyer but discovered his artistic talent and turned to art. He received his early training at the École des Beaux-Arts in Paris and honed his talents by copying works by fifteenth- and sixteenth-century masters.

Although considered an impressionist because of his concerns for the effects of color and light, Degas had a very individual approach to his art, paying great attention to detail in an attempt to unite the discipline and perfection of classical art with his own impressions of contemporary life. Degas's most famous paintings capture ballet dancers in graceful poses, women fixing their hair and applying makeup in the privacy of their bedrooms, night life in the cafés and restaurants of Paris, and racetrack scenes. His painting *Woman with Chrysanthemums* (1865) shows great balance of design along with an unusual focus of interest, two hallmarks of his art. Another work that exhibits these elements is *Foyer of the Dance* (1872). His works in sculpture also focus on dancers and on horses.

Considered one of the greatest French artists, Degas influenced the work of many others. Among these was his contemporary, Toulouse-Lautrec, who also painted sporting scenes. Degas's paintings show the influence of photography and of Japanese prints in their innovative arrangements and compositions. Unlike other impressionist artists who worked directly from nature, Degas made extensive notes and sketches, which he then used as he perfected his work in his studio. In his last years, Degas suffered from failing eyesight and, although he continued to work at new techniques, producing works of art became more and more difficult for him.

BOOKS BY DEGAS

A Degas Sketchbook: The Halevy Sketchbook, 1877–1883. Dover 1989 $5.95. ISBN 0-486-25926-9
Drawings. Dover 1974 $6.95. ISBN 0-486-21233-5
Drawings of Degas. Master Draughtsman Ser. Stephen Longstreet (ed). Borden $4.95. ISBN 0-87505-158-8

BOOKS ABOUT DEGAS

Boggs, Jean Sutherland, *et al. Degas.* Abrams 1989 $50.00. ISBN 0-8109-1145-0 Includes over 280 excellent color reproductions and 440 black and white illustrations as well as essays by eminent experts.
Gordon, Robert, and Andrew Forge. *Degas.* Abrams 1988 $75.00. ISBN 0-8109-1142-6 Richly illustrated presentation of the artist and his work.
McMullen, Roy. *Degas: His Life, Times, and Work.* Houghton 1985 $29.45. ISBN 0-395-27603-9 Biography that focuses on Degas as a man rather than an artist and views him as a product of his time and social class.
Reff, Theodore. *Degas: The Artist's Mind.* Harvard Univ Pr 1987 $16.95. ISBN 0-674-19543-4 Study of the psychology of creativity by one of the foremost Degas scholars.

GAUGUIN, PAUL   1848–1903

The French artist Paul Gauguin was one of the forerunners of modern art. Born in Paris, France, in 1848, Gauguin spent his youth with his mother's family in Peru and went to sea with the merchant marine at age 17. After six years of traveling around the world, he returned to France and became a stockbroker in Paris in 1871. After marrying and having children, Gauguin settled into a comfortable middle-class life. He admired the work of the impressionist painters with their emphasis on color and light and took up painting in his spare time. During this time he met many of the impressionist painters and began to exhibit his own work with them in 1879. Gauguin's paintings at this time reflected the influence of these impressionist painters.

In 1883 Gauguin gave up his job as a stockbroker to devote all his time to his art. His paintings, however, did not sell, and he was soon without money. Feeling that Gauguin had selfishly sacrificed his family's security, his wife took their children and went to live with her family. Gauguin's existence gradually became one of poverty and desperation. It was during this time that he turned away from impressionism and began to develop his own unique style. He traveled to Brittany, Panama, and Martinique and was influenced by their picturesque and exotic settings. His paintings began to reflect feelings toward the natural and mysterious.

In 1891 Gauguin went to the South Sea islands of Tahiti. Except for one trip to Paris to try to sell some paintings, he lived the rest of his life in Tahiti. Despite poverty, poor health, and periodic struggles with the colonial government of Tahiti, his creativity remained strong. Inspired by the people among whom he was living, he covered his canvases with simple forms, rhythmic patterns, and bold colors. This style was very different from that of the impressionists, who emphasized individual brushstrokes and the play of light on objects. Through his unique style, Gauguin's influence on modern art was very powerful. In addition to his paintings, Gauguin wrote a book, *Noa Noa* (1894–1900), which is a moving account of his thoughts and life. He died in the Marquesas Islands, where he had gone in 1901.

BOOKS BY GAUGUIN

Drawings of Gauguin. Master Draughtsman Ser. Stephen Longstreet (ed). Borden $4.95. ISBN 0-87505-162-6

The Intimate Journals of Paul Gauguin. Routledge 1985 $14.95. ISBN 0-7103-0105-7

Noa Noa: The Tahitian Journal. Fine Arts Ser. Dover 1985 repr of 1919 ed $3.95. ISBN 0-486-24859-3

Paul Gauguin: Letters to His Wife and Friends. Maurice Malingue (ed). Henry J. Stenning (tr). AMS (repr of 1949 ed) $30.00. ISBN 0-404-20106-7

BOOKS ABOUT GAUGUIN

Brettell, Richard, *et al. The Art of Paul Gauguin.* Bulfinch 1988 $85.00. ISBN 0-8212-1723-2 Richly illustrated presentation of the noted French impressionist and his work.

Gray, Christopher. *Sculpture and Ceramics of Paul Gauguin.* Hacker 1980 repr of 1963 ed $75.00. ISBN 0-87817-263-7 Focuses only on the artist's sculptures and ceramic works; heavily illustrated.

Leymarie, Jean. *Gauguin: Watercolors, Pastels, Drawings.* Rizzoli 1989 $25.00. ISBN 0-8478-1050-X Focuses on the artist's sketches, watercolors, and pastels; with illustrations.

Thomson, Belinda. *Gauguin. The World of Art Ser.* Thames Hudson 1987 $11.95. ISBN 0-500-20220-6 General introduction to the artist and his work.

LISZT, FRANZ   1811–1886

A Hungarian composer, conductor, and pianist, Franz Liszt was a child prodigy who began studying piano from his father at age 6. At age 9 he gave his first public performance and a year later went to Vienna, where he studied with the Austrian pianist Karl Czerny and the Italian composer Antonio Salieri. By the end of Liszt's life he was acknowledged as the greatest pianist of his time. One of the foremost musicians of the romantic period, Liszt enthralled audiences with his expressive interpretations and dramatic gestures in a style of playing that greatly influenced the advancement of pianistic techniques.

From about 1822 to 1848, Liszt lived in Paris, France, where he came under the influence of Paganini, the great Italian violin virtuoso. Paganini's virtuosity inspired him to accomplish unheard-of feats in piano technique and expression. Between 1848 and 1861, Liszt was musical director for the court at Weimar in Germany, where he conducted performances of many important works, including those of the German composer Richard Wagner, who later married Liszt's daughter, Cosima. (*See* Wagner, Vol. 2, World History: The Arts in Nineteenth-Century Europe.) After 1861 Liszt spent much time in Rome, where he became a friend of the pope and took minor orders in the Catholic church. The rest of Liszt's life was divided among Rome, Weimar, and Budapest.

Liszt's compositions had an important impact on musical history. Avoiding traditional musical forms, he concentrated on program music—music that told a story, depicted a scene, or elicited a mood and required a program to explain the associations that were meant to arouse mental pictures in the mind of the listener. In this vein, *Liebesträume* (c. 1850) is perhaps one of his most popular works. Also important are his 19 published *Hungarian Rhapsodies* and the *Sonata in B Minor* (1853). Not to be overlooked in historical importance are Liszt's transcriptions of other composers' works. These transcriptions familiarized a wide audience with major musical works and also demonstrated the piano's potential for interpreting orchestral music. Liszt also wrote books and essays on music, in many ways anticipating the music of the twentieth century.

BOOK BY LISZT

Letters of Franz Liszt. 2 vols. Haskell 1969 repr of 1894 ed $79.95. ISBN 0-8383-0307-2

BOOKS ABOUT LISZT

Burger, Ernst. *Franz Liszt: A Chronical of His Life in Pictures and Documents.* Princeton Univ Pr 1989 $75.00. ISBN 0-691-09133-1 Uses primary sources and narrative to recount the composer's life and career.

Rostand, Claude. *Liszt.* John Victor (tr). Vienna 1972 $3.95. ISBN 0-670-43023-4 General introduction to the composer and his work.

Searle, Humphrey. *Music of Liszt.* Dover 1966 $6.95. ISBN 0-486-21700-0 Focuses on the significance of the composer's music.

Sitwell, Sacheverell. *Liszt.* Dover 1967 $7.50. ISBN 0-486-21702-7 Portrait of Liszt beginning with his childhood and ending with the years in Budapest.

Walker, Alan. *Franz Liszt: The Virtuoso Years, 1811–1847.* Knopf 1983 $39.95. ISBN 0-394-52540-X Traces the composer's career from his beginning as a child prodigy to the peak of his success.

Westerby, Herbert. *Liszt, Composer, and His Piano Works.* Greenwood 1971 repr of 1936 ed $25.00. ISBN 0-8371-4365-9 Descriptive and critical analysis of Liszt, written in a popular and concise style.

MAHLER, GUSTAV 1860–1911

The last of the great late romantic composers, Gustav Mahler was born in Austria in 1860. Although born Jewish, he converted to Catholicism in 1897 but held a more expansive philosophy than either religion offered. Mahler began studying piano, harmony, and composition at the Vienna Conservatory at age 15. At age 20 he began conducting and held positions at the Budapest Imperial Opera (1880–1890), the Hamburg Municipal Theater (1891–1897), the Vienna State Opera (1897–1907), the Metropolitan Opera House of New York (1908–1910), and the New York Philharmonic (1909–1911). As a conductor Mahler held his orchestras to very high standards, but it was as a composer of symphonies that he is best remembered and revered.

Mahler completed nine symphonies and at his death left one unfinished, which was later completed by another composer. He also wrote five series of songs for solo voices with orchestra. The last of these—*The Song of the Earth* (1908)—was first performed after Mahler's death and is thought by many music experts to be his finest work. In it, he expresses feelings of pleasure and foreboding, both of which characterized the mood of the late romantic period. Mahler's work often mixed simplicity with sophistication, lofty ideas with strong feelings, and the grotesque or fantastic with the common and ordinary.

While Mahler's symphonies are regarded as the high point of the romantic period, they also include elements that foreshadowed the age to follow, becoming a major influence on such composers as Arnold Schoenberg, Alban Berg, and Anton von Webern.

BOOKS BY MAHLER

Mahler's Unknown Letters. Herta Blaukopf (ed). Richard Stokes (tr). Northeastern Univ Pr 1987 $25.00. ISBN 1-55553-016-8

Selected Letters of Gustav Mahler. Knud Martner and Alma Mahler (eds). Eithne Wilkins, *et al* (tr). Farrar 1979 $30.00. ISBN 0-374-25846-5

BOOKS ABOUT MAHLER

Burnett, James. *The Music of Gustav Mahler.* Fairleigh 1985 $32.50. ISBN 0-8386-3167-3 Challenges the idea that Mahler was predominantly a song symphonist and that his music was morbid.

Cooke, Deryck. *Gustav Mahler: An Introduction to His Music.* Cambridge Univ Pr 1980 $27.95. Scholarly treatment of the composer's music.

Kennedy, Michael. *Mahler.* Schirmer 1991 $13.95. ISBN 0-02-871367-2 A good introduction to the early twentieth-century Austrian musician.

Mitchell, Donald. *Gustav Mahler: The Early Years.* David Mathews and Paul Banks (eds). Univ of California Pr 1980 $42.50. ISBN 0-520-04141-0 Comprehensive account of the composer's early life and career; includes an extensively documented bibliography.

RODIN, AUGUSTE   1840–1917

A celebrated and controversial French sculptor, Auguste Rodin was born in Paris. After failing to gain admission to the École des Beaux Arts, he decided to earn a living as a decorative stonemason while continuing studies in sculpture. After a trip to Italy in 1875, his true genius appeared with his work *The Age of Bronze,* which was inspired by the work of the Italian Renaissance artists Michelangelo (*see* Michelangelo, Vol. 2, World History: The Renaissance and Reformation) and Donatello. The work seemed so lifelike that Rodin was accused of having cast it from a living model. By the age of 40, Rodin had firmly established his personal style and his reputation, and he began receiving important commissions, becoming immensely famous.

One of these commissions was to create a massive bronze door for the Museum of Decorative Arts in Paris. Commissioned for completion in 1884, the door, which Rodin had titled *The Gates of Hell,* remained unfinished at the artist's death. However, many of Rodin's well-known works, including *The Kiss* (1886) and *The Thinker* (1880), were based on figures that had been planned for the panels of the door.

One of Rodin's innovations was casting the torso or the bust of a person as a complete work of art. Orders for portrait busts came from the United States, Germany, Austria, Great Britain, and France. After 1900 Rodin established a workshop at Meudon near Paris, where he became less a sculptor and more of an entrepreneur, employing many assistants to cast sculptures from models that he made in plaster. Many of Rodin's works that are found in museums and private collections around the world are recasts of these models.

BOOKS BY RODIN

Art: Conversations with Paul Gsell. Jacques De Caso and Patricia B. Sanders (trs). Univ of California Pr 1987 $7.95. ISBN 0-520-05887-9

Cathedrals of France. Art of the Middle Ages Ser. Elizabeth C. Geissbuhler (tr). Black Swan Bks 1981 $25.00. ISBN 0-933806-07-8
Drawings of Rodin. Master Draughtsman Ser. Stephen Longstreet (ed). Borden $4.95. ISBN 0-87505-184-7
Rodin on Art and Artists: With Sixty Illustrations of His Work. Fine Art Ser. Dover 1983 $6.95. ISBN 0-486-24487-3
The Sculpture of Auguste Rodin: The Collection of the Rodin Museum, Philadelphia. John L. Tancock Philadelphia Museum of Art 1976. (o.p.) $40.00.

Books about Rodin

Champigneulle, Bernard. *Rodin. World of Art Ser.* Thames Hudson 1986 $11.95. ISBN 0-500-20061-0 General introduction to the life and work of the artist.
Elsen, Albert. *Rodin's Thinker and the Dilemmas of Modern Public Sculpture.* Yale Univ Pr 1986 $11.95. ISBN 0-300-03652-3 History of Rodin's "Thinker," the problems involved with making it public, and its exploitation.
Elsen, Albert E. *The Gates of Hell by Auguste Rodin.* Stanford Univ Pr 1985 $19.95. ISBN 0-8047-1281-6 Illustrated story of the artist's work, *The Gates of Hell,* and of the emergence of Rodin as one of the world's greatest sculptors.
Grunfeld, Frederic V. *Rodin: A Biography.* H. Holt 1987 $35.00. ISBN 0-8050-0279-0 Illustrated account of the artist and his work.
Hale, William H. *World of Rodin. Library of Art Ser.* Wiley 1969. (o.p.) $15.95. Covers the years 1840 through 1917, when Rodin goes from disturber of the peace to the world's foremost sculptor; includes many black and white photos.
Rilke, Rainer Maria. *Rodin.* Haskell 1974 $75.00. ISBN 0-8383-1913-0 Recollection of the artist by the German poet Rilke, who served as Rodin's secretary.

TCHAIKOVSKY, PETER ILYICH   1840–1893

One of Russia's greatest composers, Peter Ilyich Tchaikovsky was born in Votkinsk, Russia, the son of a mining inspector. He received a good early education, his instructors including a French governess and a music teacher. At age 10, the family moved to St. Petersburg and Tchaikovsky continued his studies, although his musical talent did not seem particularly great. Nevertheless, he continued to study music and graduated from the St. Petersburg Conservatory in 1865. From there, he went on to teach theory and composition at the Moscow Conservatory from 1865 to 1878. A generous allowance from a wealthy patroness allowed Tchaikovsky to devote time to his own composition without financial worries. His first successful composition was *Romeo and Juliet* (1869), a fantasy in which Tchaikovsky used the sonata form, adapting it to the demands of the Shakespearean play and its characters. In 1877, Tchaikovsky married, but the marriage only lasted several weeks. Soon after it ended, he quit the Conservatory to devote all his time to composition. In the years that followed he wrote his most popular and well-known works.

In all, Tchaikovsky wrote nine opera, six symphonies, many songs and short piano pieces, three ballets, three string quartets, and other works including suites and symphonic poems. The operas *Eugene Onegin* (1879) and *The Queen of Spades* (1890) were both adapted from stories by the Russian writer, Aleksandr Pushkin. Among Tchaikovsky's best-known works are his last three symphonies—No. 4 in F minor (1877); No. 5 in E minor (1888); No 6 in B minor, also known as the *Symphonie Pathétique* (1893); and his three ballets—*Swan Lake* (1876), *Sleeping Beauty* (1889), and *The Nutcracker* (1892). Tchaikovsky's music is richly orchestrated, of great emotional intensity, and reflects the composer's melancholy nature and fatalism.

Tchaikovsky died of cholera in St. Petersburg.

BOOKS BY TCHAIKOVSKY

The Diaries of Tchaikovsky. Wladimir Lakond (tr). Greenwood 1973 repr of 1945 ed
  $41.50. ISBN 0-8371-5680-7
Letters to His Family: An Autobiography. Percy M. Young (ed). Galina Von Meck (tr).
  Scarborough Hse 1982 $12.95. ISBN 0-8128-6167-1

BOOKS ABOUT TCHAIKOVSKY

Brown, David. *Tchaikovsky: The Crisis Years.* Norton 1983 $24.45. ISBN 0-393-01707-9
  Covers the period from 1874 to 1878 and Tchaikovsky's emotional crisis.
Brown, David. *Tchaikovsky: The Early Years, 1840–1874.* Norton 1979 $24.95. ISBN
  0-393-07535-4 Covers the period of the composer's life when growing fame
  caused serious conflicts in his emotional life.
Brown, David. *Tchaikovsky: The Years of Wandering, 1878–1885.* Norton 1986 $24.45.
  ISBN 0-393-02311-7 Covers the period from 1878–1885 following Tchaikovsky's
  return to Russia.
*Clark, Elizabeth. *Tchaikovsky.* *Great Lives Ser.* Janet Caulkins (ed). Watts 1988 $11.90.
  ISBN 0-531-18245-2 Introductory look at the great Russian composer.
Newmarch, Rosa H. *Tchaikovsky: His Life and Works with Extracts from His Writings and the
  Diary of His Tour Abroad in 1888.* Greenwood 1969 repr of 1900 ed $35.00. ISBN
  0-8371-1116-1 Account of the composer that utilizes primary source documents.
Wiley, Roland J. *Tchaikovsky's Ballets: Swan Lake, Sleeping Beauty, Nutcracker.* Oxford Univ
  Pr 1985 $59.00. ISBN 0-19-315314-9 Detailed look at and analysis of the com-
  poser's three popular ballets.

TURNER, JOSEPH MALLORD WILLIAM   1775–1851

Along with the English artist John Constable (*see* Constable, Vol. 2, World
History: The Arts in Nineteenth-Century Europe), J. M. W. Turner is considered one of England's greatest landscape painters. Turner was also one of the
greatest romantic artists of all time, and his work with nature and the effect
of light on natural scenes made him a forerunner of the impressionist movement of the late nineteenth century with its emphasis on the effects of color
and light.

Born in London, the son of a barber, Turner began drawing as a child and
was accepted into the painting school at the Royal Academy while in his early
teens. His first success came from his picturesque scenes of the English countryside and romantic views of architectural ruins. This success prompted him
to travel extensively throughout his own country and other parts of Europe
collecting material for his paintings and drawings.

From 1800 on, Turner looked to literature for much of his subject matter.
The Bible, mythology, and poetry became the inspiration for imaginary landscapes, which, despite their literary sources, appeared to be real places. Increasingly, Turner's work also became more experimental and abstract, with less
attention on objects and more concern with the portrayal of atmosphere, light,
and the elemental forces of nature. It is this work that resembles that of the
later impressionists.

Between 1807 and 1819 Turner published his *Liber Studiorum,* a book of
engravings modeled on his own landscape drawings and paintings. The engravings were, in a sense, a defense of his art, which had encountered a great deal
of criticism. Turner's latest works are devoted almost exclusively to the effects
of light and color, and the subject matter is not important, if it exists at all.
The Slave Ship (1840) is an example of his mature style.

In addition to his oil paintings, Turner also created numerous drawings and watercolor sketches, which are almost unequaled in their variety, spontaneity, and beauty. In all, he left more than 19,000 works of art for the enjoyment of later generations.

BOOK BY TURNER

Collected Correspondence of J. M. W. Turner with an Early Diary and a Memoir by George Jones. John Gage (ed). Oxford Univ Pr 1980 $55.00. ISBN 0-19-817303-2

BOOKS ABOUT TURNER

Butlin, Martin, and Evelyn Joll. *The Paintings and Drawings of J. M. W. Turner.* Yale Univ Pr 1987 $65.00. ISBN 0-300-03920-4 Detailed look at the artist's drawings and paintings; with numerous illustrations.

Butlin, Martin, and Evelyn Joll. *The Paintings of J. M. W. Turner.* Yale Univ Pr 1984 $250.00. ISBN 0-300-03276-5 Comprehensive, illustrated presentation of the artist's paintings.

Chamot, Mary. *The Early Works of J. M. W. Turner.* Salem Hse $6.95. ISBN 0-905005-91-0 Focuses on the artist's early paintings and drawings.

Finberg, Alexander J. *The Life of J. M. W. Turner.* Oxford Univ Pr 1961. (o.p.) Standard and complete biography with many reproductions of Turner's paintings.

Finberg, Alexander J. *Turner's Sketches and Drawings.* Schocken 1968. (o.p.) Discusses the character of Turner's art in light of his sketches and drawings.

Gage, John. *J. M. W. Turner: A Wonderful Range of Mind.* Yale Univ Pr 1987 $39.95. ISBN 0-300-03779-1 Thematic analysis of the English romantic landscape painter; includes excellent reproductions.

Hermann, Luke. *Turner: Paintings, Watercolors, Prints, and Drawings.* Da Capo 1986 $22.95. 0-306-80270-8 Good visual survey of Turner's career, including a biographical outline and a review of contemporary criticism.

Reynolds, Graham. *Turner, World of Art Ser.* Thames Hudson 1985 $11.95. ISBN 0-500-20083-1 Introductory look at the renowned British landscape painter.

Selz, Jean. *Turner.* Crown 1975 $14.95. ISBN 0-517-52361-2 General biography of the artist and his work.

VAN GOGH, VINCENT   1853–1890

Although he sold only one painting during his lifetime, the Dutch artist Vincent Van Gogh was one of the most important painters of the late nineteenth century. Born in Groot-Zundert, the Netherlands, in 1853, Van Gogh was the son of a Dutch parson. As a young man, he decided to become a minister like his father, but he gave up his studies in 1878 to do missionary work in a Belgian mining district. When his literal interpretation of the teachings of Jesus displeased his superiors, he was removed from his mission and returned to the Netherlands in 1880. Van Gogh had begun to draw in 1873 and was largely self-taught. Upon his return to the Netherlands, he began to devote all his time to art, painting dark, subdued pictures of Dutch peasants and landscapes near his home. *The Potato Eaters* (1885) is an outstanding example of his work during this period.

In 1886 Van Gogh went to Paris to live with his brother Theo, who worked for an art dealer. In Paris, he came under the influence of the Impressionists, whose use of brilliant colors and preoccupation with the effects of light greatly influenced his work. In 1888 the painter moved to sunny Arles in the south of France where, using swirling brushstrokes and pure, bright colors, he began to create the masterpieces of his mature style. Among these works are *The Sunflowers* (1888) and *The Starry Night* (1889), both of which reflect Van Gogh's unique style as well as an inner emotional turmoil. During his time in Arles, Van Gogh

Self-Portrait. Painting by
Vincent van Gogh (1889).
Courtesy of Giraudon/Art
Resource.

wrote frequently to his brother Theo, who helped support him financially.
These letters are a moving and fascinating account of Van Gogh's working
process and also the increasing agony and drama of his daily life.

Van Gogh dreamed of an artists' colony in Arles, and late in 1888 he
convinced the French artist Paul Gauguin (*see* Gauguin, Vol. 2, World History:
The Arts in Nineteenth-Century Europe) to join him there. A short time later,
after an argument with Gauguin, Van Gogh suffered a nervous breakdown
during which he cut off part of his own ear. Afterwards, he painted his *Self-
Portrait with Bandaged Ear* (1889). Increasingly plagued by mental and emotional
disturbances, Van Gogh committed himself to an asylum in May 1889. He
continued to paint, however, during periods of calm. In July 1890, the artist
shot and killed himself while despairing over his mental breakdowns and the
burden he had become to his brother.

BOOKS BY VAN GOGH

The Complete Letters of Vincent Van Gogh. Bulfinch 1979 repr of 1958 ed $85.00. ISBN
0-8212-0735-0
Dear Theo: The Autobiography of Vincent Van Gogh. Irving Stone (ed). NAL 1969 $4.95. ISBN
0-451-14098-2
The Letters of Vincent Van Gogh. Mark Roskill (ed). Macmillan 1963 $8.95. ISBN 0-689-
70167-5
Van Gogh Drawings: Forty Three Plates. Dover 1987 $3.50. ISBN 0-486-25485-2

BOOKS ABOUT VAN GOGH

*Bitossi, Sergio. *Vincent Van Gogh. Why They Became Famous Ser.* Silver 1986 $6.95. Intro-
ductory account of the famous Dutch artist; especially suitable for younger readers.
*Bonafoux, Pascal. *Van Gogh.* H. Holt 1990 $19.95. ISBN 0-8050-1384-9 Traces the
artist's career using many color illustrations and quotations from original sources.

Hagen, Osjkar. *Vincent Van Gogh.* Gordon Pr $59.95. ISBN 0-8490-1261-9

Hammacher, A. M. *Van Gogh: Twenty-Five Masterworks.* Abrams 1984 $14.95. ISBN 0-8109-2277-0 Critical look at twenty-five of the artist's best-known works; with illustrations.

Hammacher, A. M. *Vincent Van Gogh: Genius and Disaster.* Abrams $19.95. ISBN 0-8109-8067-3 Includes Van Gogh's most famous paintings and commentaries on each.

Hammacher, A. M., and Renilde Hammacher. *Van Gogh: A Documentary Biography.* Macmillan 1982. (o.p.) $36.50. Life of the artist through contemporaneous documents and primary source materials.

Pickvance, Ronald. *Van Gogh in Arles.* Abrams 1985 $35.00. ISBN 0-8109-1727-0 Comprehensive exhibition catalog of the period from 1888 to 1889 when Gauguin visited Arles and Van Gogh's mental illness began.

Pickvance, Ronald. *Van Gogh in Saint-Remy and Auvers.* Abrams 1987 $35.00. ISBN 0-8109-1727-0 Focuses on the last years of Van Gogh's life and the work he did in the asylum at Saint-Remy; includes introductory essays and many reproductions.

Nagera, Humberto. *Vincent Van Gogh: A Psychological Study.* Intl Univ Pr 1967 $25.00. ISBN 0-8236-6740-5 Analyzes the psychological conflicts and impulses that motivated the artist in his life and work.

Schapiro, Meyer. *Van Gogh. Masters of Art Ser.* Abrams 1984 $19.95. ISBN 0-8109-1733-5 Classic, informative study of the work and life of Van Gogh, with numerous reproductions.

*Stone, Irving. *Lust for Life.* Doubleday 1959 $17.95. ISBN 0-385-04270-1 Popular biography of the artist by a well-known American writer and novelist.

Sweetman, David. *Van Gogh: His Life and Art.* Crown 1990 $30.00. ISBN 0-517-57406-3 Discusses Van Gogh in the context of art and culture in the late nineteenth century.

VERDI, GIUSEPPE   1813–1901

Giuseppe Verdi, Italy's foremost operatic composer, was born in Le Roncale in northern Italy. The son of an innkeeper, his musical career began with lessons from a local church organist and continued with a teacher in the nearby town of Busseto. Rejected by the Milan Conservatory in 1832 because he did not have enough technical skill as a composer, Verdi nevertheless remained in Milan to study with a private teacher. While in Milan he became interested in opera, which he saw performed at Milan's famous opera house, La Scala. Verdi's first opera was published in 1839, the last in 1893. In between he composed 24 other operas.

Verdi's career as an operatic composer was firmly established with the appearance of *Rigoletto* in 1851. This was quickly followed by *Il Trovatore* and *La Traviata,* both produced in 1853. His reputation as a leading composer of opera was further enhanced with *Aida,* which he was commissioned to compose for the opening of the Suez Canal in 1869, but the opera was not finished until 1871. Instead, they played *Rigoletto.* Nevertheless, *Aida*'s premier was held at the opera house in Cairo in 1871. Except for his *Requiem* (1874), a few other sacred texts, a few songs, and a string quartet, all of Verdi's published works were written for the operatic stage.

In his operas Verdi found a formula that worked and used it consistently. Each opera had four parts—either four acts or three acts with a prologue. The second and third parts ended with important ensemble finales. The third part almost always had a big duet and the fourth almost always opened with a meditative solo, usually sung by the heroine. Constantly striving for refinement of drama and technique, Verdi brought Italian opera to its highest perfection and its greatest renown.

BOOK BY VERDI

Verdi: The Man in His Letters. Reprint Services 1988 repr of 1942 ed $49.00.

BOOKS ABOUT VERDI

Baldini, Gabriele. *The Story of Giuseppe Verdi.* Roger Parker (tr). Cambridge Univ Pr 1980 $14.95. ISBN 0-521-29712-5 Comprehensive biography that also discusses Verdi's music.

Budden, Julian. *The Operas of Verdi.* 3 vols. Oxford Univ Pr. Vol. 1 *From Oberto to Rigoletto* 1978 $17.95. ISBN 0-19-520449-2. Vol. 2 *From Il Trovatore to La Forza Del Destino* 1978 $17.95. ISBN 0-19-520450-6. Vol. 3 *From Don Carlos to Falstaff* 1981 $17.95. ISBN 0-19-520451-4 Comprehensive, scholarly treatment of the composer's operas.

Budden, Julian. *Verdi.* Random 1987 $9.95. ISBN 0-394-75280-5 Traces Verdi's development as an artist from humble beginnings to his discovery of an individual voice.

Busch, Hans (tr). *Verdi's Aida: The History of an Opera in Letters and Documents.* Univ of Minnesota Pr 1978 $15.00. ISBN 0-8166-0800-8 Looks at the development of the opera *Aida* through primary source documents.

Conati, Marcello. *Encounters with Verdi.* Richard Stokes (tr). Cornell Univ Pr 1984 $12.95. ISBN 0-8014-9430-3 Vivid portrait of Verdi based on 50 eye-witness accounts by his contemporaries.

Kimbell, David R. *Verdi in the Age of Italian Romanticism.* Cambridge Univ Pr 1985 $24.95. ISBN 0-521-31678-2 Critical study of the composer and his role in the romantic period of Italian music.

Martin, George. *Aspects of Verdi.* Dodd 1988 $24.95. ISBN 0-396-08843-0 Definitive biography that describes the restless years through which Verdi lived and their impact on his music.

Toye, Francis. *Giuseppe Verdi: His Life and Works.* Vienna 1972 repr of 1946 ed $50.00. ISBN 0-8443-0067-5 Overview of the composer's life and musical works.

Walker, Frank. *The Man Verdi.* Univ of Chicago Pr 1982 $9.95. ISBN 0-226-87132-0 Biography of the personality and life of the great composer.

Weaver, William (ed). *Verdi: A Documentary Study.* Thames Hudson 1977. (o.p.) $37.50. Tells the story of the composer through letters, photographs, and other primary source documents.

Weaver, William, and Martin Chusid (eds). *The Verdi Companion.* Norton 1988 $10.70. ISBN 0-393-30443-4 Examines Verdi's work from various points of views.

WAGNER, RICHARD   1813–1883

Richard Wagner, one of the most influential German composers, was born in Leipzig in 1813. His stepfather, an actor, brought the world of the theater into Wagner's life, and it fascinated him. As a youth he began studying musical composition and wrote a number of pieces. His professional music career began in 1833 with an appointment as chorusmaster of the Würzburg Theater. This was followed by several positions producing operas—his own and those of others. After success with his operas *Rienzi* in 1842 and *The Flying Dutchman* in 1843, Wagner became director of the opera at Dresden. During his stay there, he wrote *Tannhäuser* (1845) and *Lohengrin* (1846–1848). Political troubles in Germany in 1848 forced Wagner to leave Dresden and flee to Switzerland, where he remained for several years. While in exile, Wagner wrote a series of essays about opera and also began work on *The Ring of the Nibelung,* a cycle of four musical dramas based on ancient Germanic folklore. Among the other notable operas Wagner wrote are *Tristan und Isolde* (1857–1859), *Die Meistersinger von Nürnberg* (1862–1867), and *Parsifal* (1882). In 1870, following a series of love affairs, Wagner married Cosina, the daughter of Hungarian composer Franz Liszt (*see* Liszt, Vol. 2, World History: The Arts in Nineteenth-Century Europe). Wagner and Cosina had three children.

Wagner wrote both the music and the libretto for all his operas. Calling these operas "music-dramas," he sought to achieve a complete union between the music and the drama. In doing this, he created a new operatic form and transferred the center of the operatic world from Italy to Germany. Wagner's operatic music is highly dramatic and builds to amazing climaxes. His work symbolizes the synthesis of all the arts in opera—the dramatic content and the scenery, as well as the music—and had a great influence on all operatic composers who came after him. Especially significant was Wagner's view of opera as drama with all components working in harmony. Equally significant was his use of continuous music throughout the opera, with the orchestra maintaining continuity within the divisions of the drama.

BOOKS BY WAGNER

Correspondence of Wagner and Liszt. W. Ashton Ellis (ed). Francis Hueffer (tr). 2 vols. Greenwood 1970 repr of 1897 ed $32.25. ISBN 0-8371-2743-2
Family Letters of Richard Wagner. W. Ashton Ellis (tr). Vienna 1972 repr of 1911 ed $35.00. ISBN 0-8443-0014-4
My Life. Mary Whittall (ed). Andrew Gray (tr). Cambridge Univ Pr 1987 $24.95. ISBN 0-521-35900-7
The Ring of the Nibelung. Andrew Porter (tr). Norton 1977 $9.95. ISBN 0-393-00867-3

BOOKS ABOUT WAGNER

Billington, Barry. *Wagner.* Random 1987 $9.95. ISBN 0-394-75279-1 General introduction to the renowned German composer.
Dahlhaus, John, and Carl Dalhaus. *The New Grove Wagner.* Norton $7.95. ISBN 0-393-30092-7 Wagner's life and development with a thorough listing of his works.
Digaetani, John L. (ed). *Penetrating Wagner's Ring: An Anthology.* Da Capo 1983 repr of 1978 ed $49.50. ISBN 0-306-76205-6 Collection of essays on the theory, background, and interpretation of Wagner's "Ring."
Henderson, William J. *Richard Wagner: His Life and His Dramas.* AMS (repr of 1923 ed) $29.50. ISBN 0-404-03239-7 Colorful biography of Wagner focusing on his works.
Jullien, Adolphe. *Richard Wagner: His Life and Works.* Florence P. Hall (tr). Paganiniana 1981 repr of 1892 ed $19.95. ISBN 0-87666-579-2 Biography of Wagner that includes all of his major works.
Osborne, Charles. *Richard Wagner and His World.* Scribner's 1977. (o.p.) $3.95. Traces Wagner's life through hardship, debt, political exile, long artistic frustration to his eventual success as a composer.
Osborne, Charles. *The World Theater of Wagner: A Celebration of 150 Years of Wagner Productions.* Macmillan 1982. (o.p.) $36.50. Study of a great variety of productions of Wagner's operas in theaters around the world.
Von Westernhagen, Curt. *Wagner: A Biography, 1813–1833.* Mary Whittall (tr). Cambridge Univ Pr 1981 $24.95. ISBN 0-521-28254-3 Focuses on the composer's early life before his professional career began.
Watson, Derek. *Richard Wagner: A Biography.* Schirmer 1981 $19.95. ISBN 0-02-872700-2 Comprehensive portrait of the composer.

See also Vol. 1, British Literature: The Romantic Period *and* The Victorian Age; World Literature.

IMPERIALISM IN AFRICA AND ASIA

Davidson, Basil. *The African Slave Trade.* Little 1988 $10.95. ISBN 0-316-17438-6

Editors of Time–Life Books. *The Colonial Overlords: 1850–1900. Time Frame Ser.* Time–Life 1990 $22.60. ISBN 0-8094-6466-7

*Forster, E. M. *A Passage to India.* Lightyear 1981 $21.95. ISBN 0-89968-223-5 Fictional account of life in India during British rule.

Hibbert, Christopher. *The Dragon Wakes: China and the West, 1793–1911.* Penguin 1989 $8.95. ISBN 0-14-006646-2

Hibbert, Christopher. *The Great Mutiny: India, Eighteen Fifty-Seven.* Penguin 1980 $7.95. ISBN 0-14-004752-2

*Hsu, Immanuel C. *The Rise of Modern China.* Oxford Univ Pr 1989 $35.00. ISBN 0-19-505867-4 Examines nearly four centuries of historical events in China and how they contributed to the development of the modern nation.

Huxley, Elspeth. *Settlers of Kenya.* Greenwood 1975 repr of 1948 ed $22.50. ISBN 0-8371-5457-X

Huxley, Elspeth. *The Sorcerer's Apprentice: A Journey Through East Africa.* Greenwood 1975 repr of 1948 ed $35.00. ISBN 0-8371-7126-1

*Lebra-Chapman, Joyce. *The Rani of Jhansi: A Study of Female Heroism in India.* Univ of Hawaii Pr 1986 $25.00. ISBN 0-8248-0984-X Story of a woman who fought in India's Great Rebellion of 1857.

McEwan, P. J. (ed). *Nineteenth-Century Africa. Readings in African History Ser.* Oxford Univ Pr 1968 $32.00. ISBN 0-19-215662-4

Oliver, Roland, and G. N. Sanderson (eds). *The Cambridge History of Africa: 1870–1905.* Cambridge Univ Pr 1985 $110.00. ISBN 0-521-22803-4

*Pakenham, Thomas. *The Boer War.* Random 1979 $20.00. ISBN 0-394-42742-4 Discusses the origins, actions, and outcomes of the Boer War in South Africa.

Seaman, L. C. *Victorian England: Aspects of English and Imperial History 1837–1901.* Routledge 1973 $15.95. ISBN 0-416-77550-0

Scott, Paul. *The Day of the Scorpion. The Raj Quartet Ser: Vol. II.* Avon 1979 $4.95. ISBN 0-380-40923-2

Scott, Paul. *A Division of the Spoils. The Raj Quartet Ser: Vol. IV.* Avon 1979 $4.50. ISBN 0-380-45054-2

Scott, Paul. *The Jewel in the Crown. The Raj Quartet Ser: Vol. I.* Avon 1979 $4.50. ISBN 0-380-40410-9

Scott, Paul. *The Towers of Silence. The Raj Quartet Ser:Vol. III.* Avon 1979 $4.50. ISBN 0-380-44198-5

Spear, Percival. *The Nabobs: A Study of the Social Life of the English in Eighteenth Century India.* Apt 1982 $20.00. ISBN 0-7007-0142-7

*Spear, Percival, and Margaret Spear. *India Remembered.* Sangam 1981. Examines life in India during British rule.

*Tandon, Prakash. *Punjabi Century, 1857–1947.* Univ of California Pr 1968 $8.95. ISBN 0-520-01253-4 Indian writer's experiences of the independence movement in India.

*Werstein, Irving. *The Boxer Rebellion.* Watts 1971. Account of the Chinese rebellion against foreign influences in China in the early twentieth century.

*Woodford, Peggy. *The Rise of the Raj.* Humanities 1978. Well-illustrated, informative account of India during British rule.

BURTON, SIR RICHARD FRANCIS 1821–1890

A British scholar, explorer, author, adventurer, and remarkable linguist, Richard Burton was born in Torquay in Devonshire, England. Having spent much of his childhood in France and Italy, Burton spoke French and Italian fluently and also learned Latin and Greek by the age of 19. Eventually he spoke fluently in about 40 languages and dialects. Burton loved to travel, and he wrote about his adventures and explorations in more than 40 volumes. He also translated into English 30 volumes of others' works, including a masterful translation of *The Arabian Nights*. Wherever he traveled or lived, Burton took many detailed notes on the customs, traditions, and other behaviors of the people in the lands he visited. Unfortunately, after his death his wife, Isabel Arundell, whom he had secretly married in 1861, destroyed most of these notes.

During his adventurous and controversial life, Burton had a great variety of experiences. From 1842 to 1849 he served as an intelligence officer in India. In 1853 he risked death by entering in disguise the Muslim sacred cities of Mecca and Medina, which were forbidden to non-Muslims. Between 1855 and 1856 he trained Turkish recruits in the Crimean War. Fascinated with finding the source of the White Nile River, Burton explored East Africa in 1855 and again from 1857 to 1858. During these explorations he became the first European to discover Lake Tanganyika, which he mistakenly thought was the source of the Nile. Burton also traveled to the United States where in 1860 and 1861 he spent some time studying the Mormons in Utah. The last years of his life were spent as consul in the British Foreign Service, serving in West Africa, Brazil, Damascus, and Trieste. In 1886 Burton was knighted for his considerable services to the British Crown.

BOOKS BY BURTON

Explorations of the Highlands of Brazil, with a Full Account of the Gold and Diamond Mines (1869). 2 vols. Greenwood 1971 repr of 1869 ed $32.75. ISBN 0-8371-3793-4

The Lake Region of Central Africa: A Picture of Exploration (1860). Scholarly 1972 repr of 1860 ed $69.00.

Nile Basin. Middle East in the Twentieth Century Ser (1864). Da Capo 1967 repr of 1864 ed $25.00. ISBN 0-306-70926-0

Two Trips to Gorilla Land and The Cataracts of the Congo (1876). Johnson Repr (repr of 1876 ed) $45.00. ISBN 0-384-06651-8

Wanderings in West Africa from Liverpool to Fernando Po (1863). 2 vols. Johnson Repr 1971 repr of 1863 ed $42.00.

Zanzibar: City, Island, and Coast (1872). 2 vols. Johnson Repr (repr of 1872 ed) $70.00.

BOOKS ABOUT BURTON

*Brodie, Fawn M. *The Devil Drives: A Life of Sir Richard Burton*. Norton 1984 $9.95. In-depth look at the life and times of one of the nineteenth century's greatest explorers.

Burne, Glenn S. *Richard F. Burton. Twayne English Author Ser*. G. K. Hall 1985 $23.95. ISBN 0-8057-6903-X Comprehensive look at Burton's life and experiences.

Burton, Isabel. *The Life of Captain Sir Richard Burton*. 2 vols. Longwood 1977 repr of 1898 ed $60.00. ISBN 0-89341-468-9 Account of the adventurer's life written by his wife.

Dearden, Seton. *The Arabian Night: A Study of Sir Richard Burton*. Richard West (repr of 1936 ed). (o.p.) $25.00. Study of the preeminent Victorian adventurer and his Arab explorations.

Farwell, Byron. *Burton*. Penguin 1988 $24.95. ISBN 0-670-81333-8 Interesting new portrait of Burton and his travels.

Rice, Edward. *Captain Sir Richard Francis Burton: The Secret Agent Who Made the Pilgrimage to Mecca, Discovered the Kama Sutra, and Brought the Arabian Nights to the West*. Ned Chase (ed). Macmillan 1990 $35.00. ISBN 0-684-19137-7 Portrait of a remarkable man who disguised himself in 1853 to become the first Englishman to visit the sacred cities of Mecca and Medina.

Wright, Thomas. *Life of Sir Richard Burton. Research and Source Works Ser*. 2 vols. Burt Franklin 1968 repr of 1906 ed $35.50. ISBN 0-8337-3893-3 Comprehensive biography in two volumes that covers Burton's exciting life.

GANDHI, MOHANDAS KARAMCHAND 1869–1948

Mohandas Gandhi, also known as the Mahatma ("Great Soul"), was one of India's most important political and spiritual leaders. Born in Porbandar, India, in 1869, he and his family belonged to the Hindu merchant caste. At age 18, Gandhi went to London to study law. In 1893 he moved to South Africa, where he practiced law for 22 years. While in South Africa, Gandhi led the Indian community in its successful struggle against discriminatory laws. He employed the technique of nonviolent civil disobedience, or passive resistance, a technique based partly on Hindu custom and partly on the writings of the American writer and naturalist Henry David Thoreau (*see* Thoreau, Vol. 1, American Literature: Romanticism and the American Renaissance) and the Russian writer Leo Tolstoy (*see* Tolstoy, Vol. 1, World Literature: Russian Literature).

In 1915 Gandhi returned to India and helped the British in World War I. After the war he helped begin his country's struggle for independence from Great Britain. One of the most famous nonviolent protests Gandhi organized was the Salt March of 1930, which protested a tax on salt imposed by the British. Gandhi led thousands of Indians on a 240-mile march to the Indian Ocean, where they evaporated their own salt from seawater. Jailed for this action, as well as many others that followed, Gandhi fasted as a sign of protest. Fearing the wrath of his followers should he die, the British usually released him quickly.

In addition to resisting the British government and pressing for India's independence, Gandhi advocated various economic and social reforms for his country. He favored the development of local, home industries such as spinning and weaving. He struggled to eliminate India's caste system and supported more rights for people in the "untouchable" caste, who were forced to live apart from the rest of society and were allowed to hold only the lowliest jobs. To show his support of the common people, Gandhi gave up most of his possessions, dressed in a white cotton loincloth and a pair of sandals, and led a life of abstinence and spirituality.

In 1947 India was finally granted independence from Great Britain. Because of religious conflicts, however, instead of a single nation, there were two—a predominantly Hindu India and a predominantly Muslim Pakistan. When conflicts broke out between Hindus and Muslims, Gandhi resorted to fasts in an effort to end the violence. Antagonism between Hindus and Muslims continued, however, and during one of Gandhi's vigils in 1948 a fanatic Hindu—angry at Gandhi's toleration of Muslims—fatally shot the Mahatma. The technique of passive resistance used by Gandhi has since been adopted by other political leaders throughout the world, including the American civil-rights leader Dr. Martin Luther King, Jr., (*see* King, Vol. 2, United States History: The Turbulent Sixties) in his struggle to end racial segregation in the United States.

BOOKS BY GANDHI

All Men Are Brothers: Life and Thoughts of Mahatma Gandhi As Told In His Own Words. Continuum $9.95. ISBN 0-8264-0003-5

Autobiography: The Story of My Experiments with Truth. Social Sciences Ser. Dover 1983 $6.95. ISBN 0-486-24593-4

Gandhi Reader: A Source Book of His Life and Writings. Jack Homer (ed). AMS 1970 repr of 1956 ed $34.00. ISBN 0-404-03540-X

The Mind of Mahatma Gandhi. R. K. Prabhu and U. R. Rao (eds). Greenleaf Bks 1988 $30.00. ISBN 0-934676-75-5

The Words of Gandhi. Words Ser. Richard Attenborough (intro by). Newmarket 1982 $12.95. ISBN 0-937858-14-5

BOOKS ABOUT GANDHI

Alexander, Horace. *Gandhi Remembered.* Pendle Hill 1969 $3.00. ISBN 0-87574-165-7 Overview of the life and contributions of the revered Indian statesman.

Alexander, Horace. *Gandhi Through Western Eyes.* New Society 1984 $9.95. ISBN 0-86571-044-9 Useful study showing the Western historical perception of Gandhi.

*Bahree, Patricia. *Gandhi. Reputations Ser.* David and Charles 1989 $19.95. ISBN 0-7134-5663-9 Comprehensive account of the famous leader of the Indian independence movement.

Bakshi, S. R. *Gandhi and Civil Disobedience Movement.* South Asia Bks 1986 $29.00. ISBN 0-8364-1820-4 Analyzes Gandhi's role in the nonviolent civil disobedience movement against oppression.

*Bush, Catherine. *Mohandas K. Gandhi. World Leaders—Past and Present Ser.* Chelsea 1985 $17.95. ISBN 0-87754-555-3 Illustrated story of Mahatma Gandhi, advocate of pacifism and nonviolent civil disobedience.

*Cheney, Glenn A. *Mohandas Gandhi. Impact Biography Ser.* Watts 1983 $12.90. ISBN 0-531-04600-1 Biographical account of the noted Indian pacifist and independence leader.

Easwaran, Eknath. *Gandhi the Man.* Nilgiri 1978 $12.00. ISBN 0-915132-14-1 Focuses on the personal life and philosophy of the noted Indian leader.

*Faber, Doris, and Harold Faber. *Mahatma Gandhi.* Messner 1986 $9.79. ISBN 0-671-60176-8 A good history of the life and philosophy of Gandhi.

*Hunter, Nigel. *Gandhi. Great Lives Ser.* Watts 1987 $11.90. ISBN 0-531-18093-X Introductory look at the revered Indian leader, named Mahatma ("Great Soul") by his people.

Kaur, Harpinder. *Gandhi's Concept of Civil Disobedience: A Study with Special Reference to Thoreau's Influence on Gandhi.* South Asia Bks 1986 $12.75. ISBN 0-8364-2091-8 Examines Gandhi's philosophy of civil disobedience and how he was influenced by the American thinker Henry David Thoreau.

*Yapp, Malcolm. *Gandhi. World History Ser.* Margaret Killingray and Edmund O'Connor (eds). Greenhaven 1980 $2.95. ISBN 0-89908-103-7 Discusses the life, work, and achievements of Gandhi, the noted Indian statesman and spiritual leader.

LIVINGSTONE, DAVID   1813–1873

The Scots missionary David Livingstone was one of the most remarkable explorers of the nineteenth century. As a missionary in Africa, he preached, taught, and tended the sick and also sought to end the slave trade. Much beloved by the Africans who knew him, Livingstone never ceased his efforts in their behalf. As an explorer, he sought the source of the Nile River, and was the first non-African to see Victoria Falls and to cross Africa from west to east.

Livingstone was born in Blantyre, Scotland, in 1813 and went to work in a cotton mill at the age of 10. He was later able to complete his education and became a doctor and an ordained minister. He first went to Africa in 1841 as a medical missionary to Kuruman in South Africa. Bored with the routine of missionary life, Livingstone eventually began to pursue his interest in exploration. In 1849 he led an expedition across the Kalahari Desert to Lake Ngami, where he heard about a great river to the north and about people who had not been reached by missionaries. Driven by the desire to explore and to do his missionary work, Livingstone explored much of central Africa between 1853 and 1856.

Between 1858 and 1863 Livingstone made other expeditions and became the first to describe Lake Nyasa and the area known now as Malawi. Then, in 1866, Livingstone set out to discover the sources of the Nile and Congo rivers and to determine how Africa's great lakes are related to one another and to Africa's great rivers. During this expedition the world lost contact with Livingstone and it was presumed that he was dead. A newspaper reporter, Sir Henry Morton Stanley, was sent to Africa to search for Livingstone. In 1871 Stanley found an ailing Livingstone at an African village on the banks of Lake Tanganyika. The report of Stanley's first remark, "Dr. Livingstone, I presume," amused the world, and the greeting became a humorous byword. Although suffering from malaria, Livingstone continued his explorations and missionary work until his death in Africa on May 1, 1873.

BOOKS BY LIVINGSTONE

Last Journals of David Livingstone in Central Africa from 1865 to His Death (1874). Horace Waller (ed). 2 vols. Greenwood 1971 repr of 1874 ed $35.00. ISBN 0-8371-3899-X

Livingstone's Africa. Black Heritage Library Collection Ser. Ayer (repr of 1872 ed) $25.25. ISBN 0-8369-8732-2

Missionary Travels and Researches in South Africa Select Bibliographies Repr Ser (1857). Ayer 1972 repr of 1857 ed $52.00. ISBN 0-8369-6918-9

Narrative of an Expedition to the Zambesi and Its Tributaries: And of the Discovery of Lakes Shirwa and Nyasa, 1858–1864 (1865). Johnson Repr (repr of 1866 ed) $48.00. ISBN 0-384-32985-3

Some Letters from Livingstone, 1840–1872. Greenwood (repr of 1940 ed) $22.50.

The Zambesi Expedition, 1858–1863. J. P. Wallis (ed). 2 vols. Humanities 1956. (o.p.)

BOOKS ABOUT LIVINGSTONE

Blaikie, William G. *Personal Life of David Livingstone.* Greenwood 1969 $25.00. ISBN 0-8371-0518-8 Focuses on Livingstone as a medical missionary and on his personal and family life.

Latham, Robert O. *Trail Maker. (David Livingstone).* Christian Lit 1973 $3.95. ISBN 0-87508-626-8 Focuses on Livingstone as discoverer and missionary.

Pachai, Bridglal (ed). *Livingstone, Man of Africa: Memorial Essays, 1873–1973.* Longman 1973 $9.00. Collection of essays celebrating Livingstone from a variety of points of view.

Ransford, Oliver. *David Livingstone: The Dark Continent.* St. Martin's 1978 $27.50. Account of the explorer's travels and experiences in Africa.

Stanley, Henry M. *How I Found Livingstone.* Greenwood 1970 repr of 1913 ed $26.00. ISBN 0-8371-1995-2 Account of the African expedition to find the Scots explorer, by the man who found him.

Worchester, J. H., Jr. *David Livingstone. Golden Oldies Ser.* Moody 1980 $3.95. ISBN 0-8024-4782-1 General introduction to the noted Scots missionary and explorer.

PARK, MUNGO 1771–1806

One of the earliest explorers of Africa, the Scots adventurer Mungo Park was born in Selkirk, Scotland, and received training as a surgeon at the University of Edinburgh. While serving as a medical officer with the East India Company, Park studied plant and animal life on the island of Sumatra. His work there brought him to the attention of the African Association, which engaged him to explore and map the Niger River in Africa.

On his first trip to Africa in 1795, Park traveled upstream on the Gambia River for 200 miles to a British trading station in the interior. From there he crossed unknown territory and encountered many hardships, including fever and imprisonment by Arabs, before finally reaching the Niger River, the first

European to look upon its waters. On his return to Great Britain, Park published *Travels in the Interior Districts of Africa* (1799), an account of his adventures that became quite popular. Around this time Park married and practiced medicine for a short time in Peebles, Peeblesshire. Then, in 1803, the government commissioned Park to head a second expedition to trace the Niger to its source. This second expedition proved much more hazardous than the first. About 40 explorers set sail from Portsmouth in January 1805. By August 1805, only 11 survivors remained, the rest having died of fever or dysentery. Further exploration of the Niger resulted in Park's death by drowning when the canoes of his expedition were attacked by natives sometime in the beginning of 1806. Certain news of Park's death and the disaster that befell the remaining explorers did not reach Great Britain until 1812.

BOOKS BY PARK

Journal of a Mission to the Interior of Africa (1815). Scholarly $21.00.
Travels in the Interior Districts of Africa (1799). (coauthored with James Rennell) Ayer $15.00. ISBN 0-405-18974-5

BOOKS ABOUT PARK

Lupton, Kenneth. *Mungo Park: The African Traveler.* Oxford Univ Pr 1979 $32.50. Comprehensive, scholarly account of the British explorer and his expeditions in Africa.
Tames, R. *Mungo Park. Clarendon Biography Ser.* Newbury Bks 1973 $3.50. ISBN 0-912728-69-8 Introductory look at the explorer and his travels.
Thompson, Joseph. *Mungo Park and the Niger.* Argosy 1970 repr of 1890 ed $15.00. Contemporary account of Park's explorations of West Africa and the Niger River.

VICTORIA, QUEEN OF GREAT BRITAIN   1819–1901

Queen of Great Britain and Ireland from 1837 to 1901, Victoria succeeded to the throne at the age of 18. She became the longest-reigning monarch in Great Britain's history. Victoria was the daughter of Edward, the Duke of Kent, and Princess Mary Louise Victoria of Saxe-Coburg-Saalfeld. As the fourth son of King George III, Victoria's father, Edward, was far down the line of succession to the British throne. But Edward died in 1820, and when his older brother George IV died without an heir in 1830, Victoria became the heir apparent and succeeded to the throne on the death of her uncle, William IV, who was also childless.

In 1840 Victoria married her first cousin, Prince Albert of Saxe-Coburg-Gotha, who became the dominant influence in her life. When Albert died in 1861, Victoria went into deep mourning, isolating herself from public view for several years. The marriages of Victoria's nine children and numerous grandchildren allied the British royal family with many other ruling families throughout Europe.

Victoria's 64-year reign saw a great expansion of the British Empire, including control of India where she ruled as empress from 1876 to her death. Her reign also was marked by political reforms at home under the leadership of Prime Ministers Gladstone and Disraeli. (*See* Disraeli *and* Gladstone, Vol. 2, World History: Nationalism in Europe.) Victoria was a conscientious ruler. As a result, the prestige of the British Crown, which had been tarnished by previous rulers, was restored and given a new image as a symbol of public service. Victoria was also noted for her strict personal morality, which carried over into her reign and influenced the society at large.

BOOKS BY QUEEN VICTORIA

Further Letters of Queen Victoria from the Archives of the House of Brandenburg–Prussia. Hector Bolitho (ed). Mrs. J. Pudney and Sudley Pudney (trs). Kraus (repr of 1938 ed) $29.00. ISBN 0-527-93140-3

Leaves from the Journal of Our Life in the Highlands, 1848–1861. Kraus 1969 repr of 1868 ed $23.00. ISBN 0-527-93146-2

Queen and Mister Gladstone. Philip Guedella (ed). Kraus 1969 repr of 1934 ed $36.00. ISBN 0-527-93152-7

BOOKS ABOUT QUEEN VICTORIA

*Glendinning, Sally. *Queen Victoria: English Empress. Century Biographies Ser.* Garrard 1971 $3.98. ISBN 0-8116-4750-1 Biographical account of Victoria, queen of Great Britain.

Marshall, Dorothy. *The Life and Times of Victoria. Kings and Queens of England Ser.* Antonia Fraser (ed). Biblio Dist 1972 $17.50. Illustrated biography focusing on the various stages of Queen Victoria's family life.

Plowden, Alison. *The Young Victoria.* Scarborough Hse 1981 $17.95. ISBN 0-8128-2766-X Focuses on the early years of the British monarch.

*Shearman, Dierdre. *Queen Victoria. World Leaders—Past and Present Ser.* Chelsea 1986 $17.95. ISBN 0-87754-590-1 Story of Great Britain's longest-reigning monarch; especially suitable for younger readers.

Strachey, Lytton. *Lytton Strachey's Queen Victoria.* Weidenfeld 1988 $22.95. ISBN 1-55584-295-X Stunning portrait of the woman who shaped an era.

Weintraub, Stanley. *Victoria: An Intimate Biography.* Dutton 1987 $26.95. ISBN 0-525-24469-7 Account of the British monarch that focuses on her personal life.

Woodham-Smith, Cecil. *Queen Victoria.* D I Fine 1987 $9.95. ISBN 0-917657-95-0 Interesting look at the life and times of the remarkable British queen who had such a great impact on her country and the British Empire.

NATION BUILDING IN LATIN AMERICA

Barman, Roderick J. *Brazil: The Forging of a Nation, 1798–1852.* Stanford Univ Pr 1988 $49.50. ISBN 0-8047-1437-1

Belaunde, Victor A. *Bolivár and the Political Thought of the Spanish–American Revolution.* Hippocrene 1967 $31.50. ISBN 0-374-90532-0

Burns, E. Bradford (ed). *Perspectives on Brazilian History.* Columbia Univ Pr 1967 $27.50. ISBN 0-231-02992-6

Burns, E. Bradford. *The Poverty of Progress: Latin America in the Nineteenth Century.* Univ of California Pr 1980 $10.95. ISBN 0-520-05078-9

Bushnell, David, and Neill Macaulay. *The Emergence of Latin America in the Nineteenth Century.* Oxford Univ Pr 1988 $12.95. ISBN 0-19-504464-0

Cameron, Charlotte. *Mexico in Revolution.* Gordon Pr 1976 $59.95. ISBN 0-8490-0627-9

Godoy, José F. *Porfirio Diaz.* Gordon Pr 1976 $59.95. ISBN 0-8490-0880-8

Graham, Richard. *Independence in Latin America.* McGraw 1972 $8.95. ISBN 0-07-553699-4

*Lynch, John. *Spanish–American Revolutions 1808–1826.* Norton 1986 $11.95. ISBN 0-393-95537-0 Deals with the various independence movements in Latin America during the early nineteenth century.

Macaulay, Neill. *Dom Pedro: The Struggle for Liberty in Brazil and Portugal, 1798–1834.* Duke Univ Pr 1986 $39.95. ISBN 0-8223-0681-6

Metford, J. C. *San Martin the Liberator.* Greenwood 1971 repr of 1950 ed $35.00. ISBN 0-8371-3012-3

Parkinson, Roger. *Zapata: A Biography.* Scarborough Hse 1980 $6.95. ISBN 0-8128-6072-1

Pinchon, Edgcumb. *Viva Villa: A Recovery of the Real Pancho Villa: Peon, Bandit, Soldier, Patriot.* Ayer 1970 repr of 1933 ed $24.50. ISBN 0-405-02045-7

Raat, W. Dirk (ed). *Mexico: From Independence to Revolution, 1810–1910.* Univ of Nebraska Pr 1982 $8.95. ISBN 0-8032-8904-9

*Ragan, John D. *Emiliano Zapata. World Leaders—Past and Present Ser.* Chelsea 1989 $17.95. ISBN 1-55546-823-3 Introductory account of the Mexican rebel who led the peasant rebellion of 1910–1919.

Razuvaev, V. *Bernardo O'Higgins.* Imported 1989 $8.95. ISBN 5-01-001250-2

Redfield, Robert. *The Little Community and Peasant Society and Culture* (1955–1956). Univ of Chicago Pr 1989 $14.95. ISBN 0-226-70670-2

Sater, William F. *Chile and the War of the Pacific.* Univ of Nebraska Pr 1986 $24.95. ISBN 0-8032-4155-0

Tuck, Jim. *Pancho Villa and John Reed: Two Faces of Romantic Revolution.* Univ of Arizona Pr 1984 $5.95. ISBN 0-8165-0867-4

*Wepman, Dennis. *Benito Juárez. World Leaders—Past and Present Ser.* Chelsea 1986 $17.95. ISBN 0-87754-537-5 Readable biography of the noted Mexican statesman, president, and reformer.

*Wepman, Dennis. *Simon Bolívar. World Leaders—Past and Present Ser.* Chelsea 1985 $17.95. ISBN 0-87754-569-3 Introductory biography of the famous South American liberator.

MARTI, JOSE   1853–1895

José Martí was a Cuban poet and patriot who fought for his country's liberation from Spain. He first joined the revolutionary movement in his teens. At age 16, he was arrested for his political views and spent some time on a chain gang before being exiled from Cuba. After several years in Mexico, Guatemala, and Spain, Martí returned to his homeland in 1878. He was soon exiled again, however, because of his support of Cuban independence, and in 1881 he found refuge in New York City. While in New York, Martí wrote newspaper and magazine articles to arouse North American public opinion in favor of Cuban independence and also helped raise money to buy guns and ammunition for the revolutionary cause. In 1895 a series of uprisings broke out in Cuba, and Martí, along with a large number of volunteers, landed on the island to help support the uprisings. Martí was killed shortly after, at the battle of Dos Ríos. Three years later, in 1898, after the United States declared war on Spain and drove Spanish troops from Cuba, the Cuban republic was established.

Martí was a leading figure in literature as well as politics. He was one of the creators of *modernismo,* a movement in Latin American literature that emphasized imagination and fantasy rather than the materialist world. Martí wrote in a simple yet lyrical style that was based largely on folk poetry. Many of his works deal with Cuba's struggle for freedom and with his unhappiness at being exiled from his homeland. His most famous writings include *Ismaelillo* (1882) and *Versos libres,* or *Plain Verses* (1891).

BOOKS BY MARTI

José Martí: Major Poems. Philip S. Foner (ed). Elinor Randall (tr). Holmes & Meier 1982 $14.75. ISBN 0-8419-0834-6

Martí on the U.S.A. Luis A. Baralt (tr). *Contemporary Latin American Classics Ser.* Illinois Univ Pr 1966 $7.95. ISBN 0-8093-0206-3

On Education: Articles on Educational Theory and Pedagogy, and Writings for Children from the Age of Gold. Philip S. Foner (ed). Elinor Randall (tr). Monthly Review 1979 $10.00. ISBN 0-85345-565-1

Our America: Writings on Latin America and the Struggle for Cuban Independence. Philip S. Foner (ed). Elinor Randall (tr). Monthly Review 1979 $10.00. ISBN 0-85345-495-7

Political Parties and Elections in the United States. Philip S. Foner (ed). Elinor Randall (tr). Temple Univ Pr 1989 $24.95. ISBN 0-87722-604-0

BOOKS ABOUT MARTI

Abel, Christopher, and Nissa Torrents (eds). *José Martí: Revolutionary Democrat.* Duke Univ Pr 1986 $32.50. ISBN 0-8223-0679-4 Comprehensive account of the Cuban patriot and revolutionary leader.

Gonzalez, Edward (ed). *José Martí and the Cuban Revolution Retraced.* UCLA Lat Am Ctr 1986 $9.50. ISBN 0-87903-062-3 Examines the role of Martí in the Cuban revolution for independence from Spain.

Kirk, John M. *José Martí: Mentor of the Cuban Nation.* Univ Presses FL 1983 $12.00. ISBN 0-8130-0812-3 Discusses the profound influence Martí had on twentieth-century Cuban politics.

Magdaleno, Mauricio. *José Martí.* Gordon Pr 1976 $59.95. ISBN 0-8490-2108-1 Looks at the life and achievements of the Cuban revolutionary leader.

Manach, Jorge. *Martí: Apostle of Freedom.* Devin-Adair $9.50. ISBN 0-8159-6201-0 Portrait of Martí and the influence of his writings and activism.

Turton, Peter. *José Martí: Architect of Cuba's Freedom.* Humanities 1986 $12.50. ISBN 0-86232-511-0 Focuses on Martí's role in securing Cuban independence from Spain.

WORLD WAR I AND ITS AFTERMATH

Barnett, Correlli. *The Swordbearers: Supreme Command in the First World War.* Indiana Univ Pr 1975 $14.95. ISBN 0-253-20175-6

Editors of Time–Life Books. *The World in Arms 1900–1925. Time Frame Ser.* Time–Life 1989 $22.60. ISBN 0-8094-6470-5

Ellis, John. *Eye-Deep in Hell: Trench Warfare in World War I.* Johns Hopkins Univ Pr 1989 $12.95. ISBN 0-8018-3947-5

Falls, Cyril. *The Great War, 1914–1918.* Capricorn 1961. (o.p.)

Fischer, Fritz. *Germany's Aims in the First World War.* Norton 1968 $8.95.

Gray, Randal, and Christopher Argyle. *Almanac of the Great War: A Chronology of the First World War.* Facts On File 1990 $29.95. ISBN 0-8160-2139-2

Joll, James. *The Origins of the First World War.* Longman 1984 $14.95. ISBN 0-582-49016-2

Kennan, George F. *The Fateful Alliance: France, Russia, and the Coming of the First World War.* Pantheon 1984 $8.95. ISBN 0-394-72231-0

Kennan, George F. *Soviet–American Relations, 1917–1920.* 2 vols. Princeton Univ Pr 1989 Vol. 1 *Russia Leaves the War.* $14.95. ISBN 0-691-00841-8. Vol. 2 *The Decision to Intervene.* $14.95. ISBN 0-691-00842-6

Koch, H. W. (ed). *Origins of the First World War.* Taplinger 1972 $3.95.

Lincoln, W. Bruce. *Passage Through Armageddon: The Russians in War and Revolution 1914–1918.* Simon 1987 $14.95. ISBN 0-671-64560-9

*Marshall, S. L. *American Heritage History of World War I.* Crown 1982 $15.98. ISBN 0-517-38555-4 Pictorial essay of World War I.

*Miquel, Pierre. *World War I. Silver Burdett Picture Histories Ser.* Silver 1986 $14.96. ISBN 0-382-06889-0 Introductory history of the First World War with numerous photographs; especially suited for younger readers.

*Remarque, Erich M. *All Quiet on the Western Front.* Fawcett 1987 $3.95. ISBN 0-449-21394-3 Poignant novel about the experiences of a German soldier during World War I.

Rimell, Raymond L. *World War One in the Air. Vintage Warbirds Ser.* Sterling 1988 $9.95. ISBN 0-85368-798-6

Seton-Watson, R. W. *Sarajevo: A Study in the Origins of the Great War.* Fertig 1988 repr of 1926 ed $35.00. ISBN 0-86527-357-X

Silverman, Dan P. *Reconstructing Europe After the Great War.* Harvard Univ Pr 1982 $30.50. ISBN 0-674-75025-X

Smith, Page. *America Enters the World: A People's History of the Progressive Era and World War I.* McGraw 1985 $29.95. ISBN 0-07-058573-3

Tarrant, V. E. *U-Boat Offensive, Nineteen Fourteen to Nineteen Forty-Five.* Naval Inst Pr 1989 $29.95. ISBN 0-87021-764-X

Taylor, A. J. *First World War: An Illustrated History.* Putnam 1988 $7.95. ISBN 0-399-50260-2

Tuchman, Barbara. *The Guns of August.* Bantam 1982 $5.95. ISBN 0-553-25401-4

Walworth, Arthur. *Wilson and His Peacemakers: The Paris Peace Conference, 1919.* Norton 1986 $35.00. ISBN 0-393-01867-9

Wells, H. G. *Russia in the Shadows.* Hyperion 1973 $18.00. ISBN 0-88355-055-5

*Windrow, Martin. *World War I Tommy. Soldiers Through the Ages Ser.* Watts 1986 $11.90. ISBN 0-531-10083-9 Examines the life and experience of a typical British soldier in World War I; especially suited to younger readers.

LAWRENCE, T. E. (THOMAS EDWARD) 1888–1935

T. E. Lawrence was a soldier, author, archaeologist, traveler, and translator. He is best known as Lawrence of Arabia, the adventurer who led the Arabs to freedom from the Turks during World War I.

Born in North Wales in 1888, Lawrence graduated from Oxford University in 1910. He soon joined an archaeological expedition to excavate an ancient city on the Euphrates River in modern-day Iraq. While there he learned to speak Arabic and dressed and lived as an Arab.

When World War I broke out, Lawrence returned to Great Britain and joined the army. In late 1914 he was sent to Egypt to work in the intelligence section of the Arab Bureau. Eventually, acting as a liaison between the British and the Arabs, Lawrence made two important contributions to the Arab fight against the Turks, who had entered the war against Britain and its allies. First, he was instrumental in getting the Arabs money and supplies from Great Britain. Second, working with Arab leaders, he devised a brilliant guerrilla strategy that more than compensated for the fact that the Turks were more heavily armed than the Arabs.

When the war ended, Lawrence became an increasingly isolated individual who sought anonymity. He enlisted in the Royal Air Force under the name of J. H. Ross, which he later changed to T. E. Shaw. In 1935 Lawrence died in a motorcycle accident while riding on an English country lane.

Lawrence's best-known book, *The Seven Pillars of Wisdom,* was published in 1926. Because the book expressed certain personal and political opinions that Lawrence did not want to publicize, it was offered for sale at an extremely high price. In 1927 Lawrence published an abridgement of the book, called *Revolt in the Desert,* which was made more available to the general public.

Early biographies of Lawrence were enthusiastic and full of praise. In recent years, however, revelations of Lawrence's various quirks, emotional disturbances, and his readiness to embroider the truth have affected popular perceptions of him and have made him a puzzling and enigmatic figure to many.

BOOKS BY LAWRENCE

The Essential T. E. Lawrence: Selections from His Writings (1951). David Garnett (ed). Viking 1963. (o.p.)

The Evolution of a Revolt: Early Postwar Writings of T. E. Lawrence. Stanley Weintraub and Rodelle Weintraub (eds). Penn State Univ Pr 1967 $19.95. ISBN 0-271-73133-8

The Mint. Norton 1963 $4.95.

The Seven Pillars of Wisdom. Reprints Ser. Dorset 1989 $29.95. ISBN 0-88029-258-X

BOOKS ABOUT LAWRENCE

Aldington, Richard. *Lawrence of Arabia: A Biographical Enquiry.* Greenwood 1976 repr of 1955 ed $31.50. ISBN 0-8371-8634-X Famous biography that analyzes Lawrence of Arabia and his legend.

Clements, Frank. *T. E. Lawrence: A Reader's Guide.* Shoe String 1973 $25.00. ISBN 0-208-01313-X Helpful companion to the writings of Lawrence.

Hart, B. H. *Lawrence of Arabia. Quality Paperbacks Ser.* Da Capo 1989 $13.95. ISBN 0-306-80354-2 General account of the British adventurer, soldier, and writer.

Lawrence, A. W. (ed). *T. E. Lawrence by His Friends.* Gordian 1980 repr of 1937 ed $50.00. ISBN 0-87752-196-4 Contemporaneous profiles of Lawrence and his accomplishments.

Liddell Hart, Basil H. *T. E. Lawrence in Arabia and After.* Greenwood 1979 repr of 1936 ed $27.50. ISBN 0-8371-4258-X Focuses on Lawrence's exploits in Arabia.

Richards, Vyvyan. *Portrait of T. E. Lawrence. English Biography Ser.* Haskell 1975 $75.00. ISBN 0-8383-2093-7 Comprehensive look at the noted British adventurer.

Robinson, Edward. *Lawrence: The Story of His Life.* Richard West (repr of 1935 ed) $20.00. (o.p.) Complete biography of Lawrence, his legend, and his career.

Wilson, J. M. *Lawrence of Arabia.* Macmillan 1988 $21.95. ISBN 0-689-11934-8 Examines the life, adventures, and achievements of the famous British adventurer.

LLOYD GEORGE, DAVID   1863–1945

Born in Manchester, England, in 1863, British statesman David Lloyd George was the son of a Welsh schoolteacher. When Lloyd George was 2 years old his father died and he went to live with his mother's brother. His uncle, a master shoemaker and lay preacher, helped shape the political views Lloyd George would hold throughout his life. A brilliant student, Lloyd George began practicing law in 1884 and was also recognized as a rising figure in political circles. He began his political career in 1890 when he was elected to the House of Commons, the lower house of the British Parliament. In 1908 he became chancellor of the exchequer, the equivalent of secretary of the treasury. In Parliament, Lloyd George gained a reputation for his anti-imperialist views and his proposals for social reform, such as national health insurance, unemployment benefits, and old-age pensions. As chancellor of the exchequer, he convinced Parliament to pass a law that deprived the House of Lords, the upper house of Parliament, of its veto power over money bills. This power eventually led to the House of Commons becoming the dominant body of Parliament.

In 1916, halfway through World War I, Lloyd George became prime minister of Great Britain and waged an aggressive war against Germany and its allies. After the war, he played a major role at the 1919 Paris Peace Conference. As one of the so-called "Big Four" heads of state, he helped draft the Treaty of Versailles, which redrew the map of Europe and the Middle East, stripped Germany of its colonial possessions, and established the League of Nations. Unfortunately, several of the treaty's provisions—especially Germany's acceptance of responsibility for causing the war—would eventually help bring about the rise of German dictator Adolf Hitler and World War II.

Lloyd George remained in Parliament as head of the small Liberal party until 1944. Then he was made an earl and left the House of Commons for the House of Lords.

BOOKS BY LLOYD GEORGE

The Truth About Reparations and War Debts. Fertig 1970 $35.00. ISBN 0-86527-197-6

War Memoirs of David Lloyd George. 6 vols. AMS (repr of 1936 ed) $295.00 ISBN 0-404-15040-3

Books about Lloyd George

Gilbert, Bentley B. *David Lloyd George: A Political Life.* Ohio State Univ Pr 1987 $40.00. ISBN 0-8142-0432-5 Focuses on the political achievements of the British statesman and wartime prime minister.

Grigg, John. *Lloyd George: From Peace to War, 1912–1916.* Univ of California Pr 1985 $42.50. ISBN 0-520-03634-4 Looks at the British prime minister in the years prior to and during World War I.

Grigg, John. *Lloyd George: The People's Champion, 1902–1911.* Univ of California Pr 1978 $47.50. ISBN 0-520-03634-4 Comprehensive account of the British statesman during the years when he proposed sweeping social reforms.

Morgan, Kenneth O. *Consensus and Disunity: The Lloyd George Coalition Government, 1918–1922.* Oxford Univ Pr 1979 $27.50. ISBN 0-19-822975-5 Close analysis of the period during World War I when Lloyd George was Prime Minister.

Morgan, Kenneth O. *David Lloyd George: Welsh Radical As World Statesman.* Greenwood 1982 repr of 1964 ed $35.00. ISBN 0-313-23453-1 Biography of the prime minister that draws on his Welsh background and early years.

*Pugh, Martin. *Lloyd George.* Longman 1988 $36.95. ISBN 0-582-02387-4 Interesting portrayal of the controversial British statesman and prime minister.

See also Vol. 2, United States History: World War I.

THE RISE OF TOTALITARIAN STATES

Arendt, Hannah. *The Origin of Totalitarianism.* Harcourt 1973 $12.95. ISBN 0-15-670153-7

Carr, Raymond (ed). *The Spanish Civil War: A History in Pictures.* Norton 1986. (o.p.) $24.95. ISBN 0-393-02337-0

Carsten, F. L. *The Rise of Fascism.* Univ of California Pr 1980 $11.95. ISBN 0-520-04643-9

Fletcher, Miles. *The Search for a New Order: Intellectuals and Fascism in Prewar Japan.* Univ of North Carolina Pr 1982 $27.50. ISBN 0-8078-1514-4

Forman, James D. *Fascism: The Meaning and Experience of Reactionary Revolution.* Studies in Contemporary Politics Ser. Dell 1976 $1.25. ISBN 0-440-94707-3

*Garza, Hedda. *Francisco Franco.* World Leaders—Past and Present Ser. Chelsea 1987 $17.95. ISBN 0-87754-524-3 Introductory biography of the Fascist dictator of Spain.

Gay, Peter. *Weimar Culture: The Outsider As Insider.* Greenwood 1981 repr of 1968 ed $27.50. ISBN 0-313-22972-4

*Hartenian, Larry. *Benito Mussolini.* World Leaders—Past and Present Ser. Chelsea 1988 $17.95. ISBN 0-87754-572-3 Introductory biography of the Italian Fascist leader.

Hemingway, Ernest. *The Fifth Column and Four Stories of the Spanish Civil War.* Scribner's 1969 $7.95. ISBN 0-684-12723-7

Jones, Francis C. *Japan's New Order in East Asia: Its Rise and Fall, 1937–1945.* AMS (repr of 1954 ed) $40.00. ISBN 0-404-59535-9

Kennan, George F. *Russia and the West Under Lenin and Stalin.* NAL 1962 $4.95. ISBN 0-451-62460-2

Kennedy, Malcolm D. *The Military Side of Japanese Life.* Greenwood 1973 repr of 1924 ed $35.00. ISBN 0-8371-6574-1

Kitchen, Martin. *Europe Between the Wars.* Longman 1988 $18.95. ISBN 0-582-49409-5

Kohn, Hans. *Nationalism in the Soviet Union.* AMS (repr of 1933 ed) $15.00. ISBN 0-404-03738-0

Lee, Stephen J. *The European Dictatorships, 1918–1945.* Routledge 1987 $15.95. ISBN 0-416-42280-2

Lory, Hillis. *Japan's Military Masters: The Army in Japanese Life.* Greenwood 1973 repr of 1943 ed $35.00. ISBN 0-8371-6581-4

Lyttle, Richard B. *Il Duce: The Rise and Fall of Benito Mussolini.* Macmillan 1987 $15.95. ISBN 0-689-31213-X

Lyttleton, Adrian. *The Seizure of Power: Fascism in Italy, 1919–1929.* Princeton Univ Pr 1988 $18.50. ISBN 0-691-02278-X

Morris, Warren B. *Weimar Republic and Nazi Germany.* Nelson-Hall 1982 $14.95. ISBN 0-88229-797-X

Mosse, George L. *Nazism: A Historical and Comparative Analysis of National Socialism.* Transaction 1978 $5.95. ISBN 0-87855-236-7

Paley, Allan L. *Benito Mussolini: Fascist Dictator of Italy.* Outstanding Personalities Ser. D. Steve Rahmas (ed). SamHar 1975 $3.95. ISBN 0-87157-581-7

Paley, Allan L. *Spanish Civil War.* Events of Our Times Ser. Sigurd C. Rahmas (ed). SamHar 1982 $2.50. ISBN 0-87157-224-9

Rees, Philip. *Fascism and Pre-Fascism in Europe, Eighteen Ninety to Nineteen Forty-Five: A Bibliography of the Extreme Right.* B & N Imports 1984 $29.95. ISBN 0-389-20472-2

Seton-Watson, Hugh. *Eastern Europe Between the Wars: 1918–1941.* Encore Editions Ser. Westview 1986 $49.50. ISBN 0-8133-7092-2

Shirer, William L. *Berlin Diary: The Journal of a Foreign Correspondent 1934–1941.* Little 1988 $12.95. ISBN 0-316-78704-3

Shirer, William L. *The Rise and Fall of the Third Reich.* Simon 1990 $14.95. ISBN 0-671-72868-7

*Smith, Denis M. *Mussolini: A Biography.* Random 1983 $12.95. ISBN 0-394-71658-2
Biographical account of the Italian dictator and his Fascist regime.

Toland, John. *The Rising Sun: The Decline and Fall of the Japanese Empire, 1936–1945.* Bantam 1971 $5.95. ISBN 0-553-26435-4

Ulam, Adam B. *Bolsheviks.* Macmillan 1968 $11.95. ISBN 0-02-038100-X

Ulam, Adam B. *Stalin: The Man and His Era.* Beacon 1989 $16.95.

Ulam, Adam B. *The Unfinished Revolution: Marxism and Communism in the Modern World.* Westview 1979 $15.95. ISBN 0-89158-496-X

Yoshihashi, Takehiko. *Conspiracy at Mukden: The Rise of the Japanese Military.* Greenwood 1980 repr of 1963 ed $35.00. ISBN 0-313-1514-4

HITLER, ADOLF   1889–1945

German dictator Adolf Hitler—creator of the Third Reich, or German Empire—was born in Austria in 1889. A poor student who barely graduated from high school, he was twice rejected for admission by the Academy of Fine Arts in Vienna and was forced to earn a living as a house painter and a porter at the local railroad station. When World War I broke out in 1914, Hitler joined the German army and won a medal for bravery during the war.

Hitler was embittered by Germany's defeat in 1918 and began to accuse the Jews and the Communists of having betrayed Germany and caused the country's defeat. Settling in Munich, he joined the German Workers' party, an obscure nationalistic, anti-Semitic political party. A spellbinding orator, he soon became the party's chairman. Through the efforts of Hitler and his friends, the party was built up and renamed the National Socialist German Workers' party. Known also as Nazis, party members wore brown uniforms and armbands marked with a swastika, or hooked cross.

In 1923, after a failed Nazi attempt to overthrow the German government, Hitler was sent to jail, where he began writing *Mein Kampf* (My Struggle) (1924). The book sets out Hitler's goals for Germany, which included more living space for Germans (which meant conquest and domination of Europe), extermination of the Jews, and Hitler as *Der Führer,* or absolute leader. After his release from prison, Hitler concentrated on increasing the power of the Nazi party and working toward these goals.

The Great Depression had a devastating effect on Germany, and the Nazi party began to make great strides as it appealed to the dissatisfactions and problems of the German people. In 1933, after much political maneuvering, Hitler was named chancellor of Germany, and he immediately set about establishing a totalitarian state. Granted dictatorial powers by the German Parliament, he crushed all opposition and took control of all aspects of German life. The Gestapo, or secret police, helped enforce his policies through fear, arrest, torture, and execution. Anti-Semitic laws were passed to deprive Jews of their citizenship and take away other rights. In foreign policy, Hitler rebuilt Germany's armed forces and aggressively demanded territorial concessions from smaller nations. At first, other nations such as Great Britain and France did little but question Hitler's actions. In 1939, however, the German invasion of Poland set off World War II.

During the early years of the war, Hitler and his allies succeeded in taking over much of Europe. Especially terrible was the "New Order" that Hitler imposed on the countries he conquered. Almost 8 million Poles, Russians, and other peoples were brought to Germany as slave laborers. Some 6 million Jews were put to death in concentration camps—a mass murder known as the Holocaust. Eventually however, the tide of war began to turn. In April 1945, as his Third Reich collapsed around him, Hitler committed suicide. A little over a week later, on May 8, Germany surrendered. Hitler's legacy was a devastated nation, the deaths of some 50 million people, and the memory of the most horrible period of modern history.

BOOKS BY HITLER

Germany Declares for Peace. Revisionist Pr 1982 $59.95. ISBN 0-87700-330-0
Mein Kampf. Noontide 1986 $6.00. ISBN 0-317-53284-7
The Speeches of Adolf Hitler. 4 vols. Gordon Pr 1975 $800.00. ISBN 0-8490-1107-8
The Testament of Adolf Hitler. Noontide 1978 $3.00. ISBN 0-911038-44-2

BOOKS ABOUT HITLER

Colbert, R. W., and William D. Hyder (eds). *Medallic Portraits of Adolf Hitler.* TAMS 1981 $13.95. ISBN 0-918492-04-1 Collection of different portraits of Hitler.
*Fuchs, Thomas. *The Hitler Fact Book.* Fountain 1990 $14.95. ISBN 0-9623202-9-3 Well–written description of the German dictator that focuses on his character and personal aspects; includes a chronology, bibliography, and photos.
Gordon, Sarah. *Hitler, Germans, and the "Jewish Question."* Princeton Univ Pr 1984 $16.95. ISBN 0-691-10162-0 Examines the German dictator's policies toward the Jewish populations of Europe.
*Harris, Nathaniel. *Hitler. Reputation Ser.* David and Charles 1989 $19.95. ISBN 0-7134-5961-1 Readable account of the German dictator and his leadership.
Hauner, Milan. *Hitler: A Chronology of His Life and Time.* St. Martin's 1983 $29.95. ISBN 0-312-38816-0 Presents significant events during the life of Hitler and Europe of his time.
Herzstein, Robert E. *Roosevelt and Hitler: Prelude to War.* Paragon Hse 1989 $24.95. ISBN 1-55778-021-8 Focuses on the policies of Hitler and U.S. President Franklin D. Roosevelt prior to World War II.
Jackel, Eberhard. *Hitler in History. Tauber Institute Ser.* Univ Pr of New England 1989 $8.95. ISBN 0-87451-502-5 Discusses Hitler's impact on the history of Europe and the world.
Ludwig, Emil. *Three Portraits: Hitler, Mussolini, Stalin. Studies in Fascism: Ideology and Practice.* AMS (repr of 1940 ed) $19.50. ISBN 0-404-16905-8 Compares the Fascist policies of Hitler, Benito Mussolini of Italy, and Joseph Stalin of the Soviet Union.
*Marrin, Albert. *Hitler: A Portrait of a Tyrant.* Penguin 1987 $14.95. ISBN 0-670-81546-2 Describes the personality and temperament of the German fuehrer.
*Pearson, Eileen. *Hitler's Reich. World History Ser.* Malcolm Yapp and Margaret Killingray

(eds). Greenhaven 1980 $2.95. ISBN 0-89908-233-5 Readable history of Germany's Third Reich under Hitler.

Rempel, Gerhard. *Hitler's Children: The Hitler Youth and the SS.* Univ of North Carolina Pr 1989 $39.95. ISBN 0-8078-1841-0 Focuses on the Nazi youth movement in Germany during Hitler's rule.

*Shirer, William L. *The Rise and Fall of Adolf Hitler. Landmark Paperbacks Ser.* Random 1984 $2.95. ISBN 0-394-86270-8 Examines the events that led to Hitler's dictatorship and his eventual loss of power.

*Skipper, G. C. *Death of Hitler. World at War Ser.* Childrens 1980 $14.60. ISBN 0-516-04783-3 Readable description of the events leading up to the death of the German dictator.

Toland, John. *Adolf Hitler.* Ballantine 1986 $5.95. ISBN 0-345-34317-4 Comprehensive biography of the feared and infamous Nazi dictator of Germany.

LENIN, VLADIMIR ILYICH   1870–1924

Lenin, the Russian revolutionary and Communist leader, was born Vladimir Ilyich Ulyanov in Simbirsk, a large trading center on the Volga River in Russia. The son of a civil service official who was loyal to the Russian tzar, Lenin developed more radical political beliefs and ideas. In 1887, when his older brother was killed by the tzarist police for his role in a plot against the tzar, the 17-year-old Lenin started on the road to becoming a revolutionary himself. He began to study the theories of the German philosopher Karl Marx (*see* Marx, Vol. 2, Economics: Comparative Economic Systems), organized and participated in antigovernment demonstrations, and worked to overthrow the tzarist regime. As a result of his activities, Lenin spent several years either in jail or exiled in Siberia. After his release from Siberia in 1900, he went to

Address of Lenin to the Second All-Russian Congress of Soviets.   Copy after Iosef Serebriany (1920s).   Courtesy of SCALA/Art Resource.

Germany and Switzerland and then to London, where he headed the Bolshevik ("majority" in Russian) branch of the Russian Social Democratic Workers' party.

By this time, Lenin had developed the view that force was necessary to end tzarist rule in Russia. He argued that a small, closely knit organization—led by himself—should take control of the revolution and train workers as revolutionaries. These ideas formed the basis of what later became Russian communism.

With the outbreak of World War I, Lenin saw an opportunity for Socialist revolution in Russia. During the war, Russia suffered badly, its people weary, demoralized, and stripped of all faith in their government. After the Russian Revolution broke out in 1917, Lenin returned to Russia and he and his followers, the Bolsheviks, overthrew the provisional government and established a dictatorship of the proletariat, or working class. Lenin became a virtual dictator of the new government.

Under Lenin's rule, Russia was radically transformed. All banks were nationalized, or put under government control or ownership, and the state took control of factory production. Atheism officially replaced all forms of organized religion, and all opposition to the newly formed government was ruthlessly surpressed. Lenin continued to rule Russia and transform the country until his death in 1924, by which time the groundwork for Communist control of the Soviet Union had been firmly established.

BOOKS BY LENIN

The Essentials of Lenin. Russian Studies: Perspectives on the Revolution Ser. 2 vols. Hyperion 1974 repr of 1947 ed $70.00.

Imperialism, the Highest Stage of Capitalism (1916). China Bks (repr of 1975 ed) $2.50.

Lenin on Politics and Revolution: Selected Writings. James E. Connor (ed and tr). Pegasus 1968. (o.p.)

Selected Works. 3 vols. Imported 1977 $18.00. ISBN 0-8285-0169-6

The State and Revolution (1917). China Bks 1965 $2.50. ISBN 0-8351-0372-2

What Is to Be Done? Burning Questions of Our Movement (1902). James S. Allen (ed). Intl Pub Inc 1969 $4.25. ISBN 0-7178-0218-3

BOOKS ABOUT LENIN

*Appignanesi, Richard. *Lenin for Beginners.* Pantheon 1979 $6.95. ISBN 0-394-73715-6 Introductory account of the Russian Communist leader.

Bachma, John E. *Lenin and Trotsky.* I. E. Cadenhead (ed). Barron 1974. (o.p.) Study of the relationship between two of the most important leaders of the Russian Revolution and of Lenin's rise to power.

Clark, Ronald W. *Lenin.* Harper 1988 $27.95. ISBN 0-06-015802-6 A balanced view of the life of the creator of Soviet communism.

Everdale, Carl P. *The Contributions of Lenin and Mao Tse-tung to the Communist Theories Advanced by Marx and Engels.* 2 vols. Inst for Economic and Political World Strategic Studies 1985 $227.45. ISBN 0-86722-111-9 Analyzes Lenin's Communist ideology and how it built on and differed from the ideas of the German writers Karl Marx and Frederick Engels.

Fischer, Louis. *The Life of Lenin.* Harper 1964. (o.p.) General biography of the Russian leader.

Gerson, Leonard D. (ed). *Lenin and the Twentieth Century: A Bertram D. Wolfe Retrospective.* Hoover Inst Pr 1984 $7.95. ISBN 0-8179-7932-8 Examines the influence of Lenin on twentieth-century political thought and world politics.

*Haney, John. *Lenin. World Leaders—Past and Present Ser.* Chelsea 1988 $17.95. ISBN 0-87754-570-7 Story of the powerful Russian Communist leader of the early twentieth century, especially suitable for younger readers.

Hill, Christopher. *Lenin and the Russian Revolution.* Penguin 1978 $5.95. ISBN 0-14-021297-3 Focuses on Lenin's role in the Russian Revolution and the institution of Communist government.

Lewin, Moshe. *Lenin's Last Struggle.* Monthly Review 1978 $10.00. ISBN 0-85345-473-6
Focuses on Lenin's dying days and the problems that he was confronted with.
*Mack, Donald W. *Lenin and the Russian Revolution. Then and There Ser.* Marjorie Reeves
(ed). Longman 1970 $4.75. ISBN 0-582-20457-7 Account of the Communist revo-
lutionary who was a major influence behind the Russian Revolution of 1917.
*Rawcliffe, Michael. *Lenin.* David and Charles 1989 $19.95. ISBN 0-7134-5611-6 Evalu-
ation of Lenin's life and historical significance.
*Resnick, Abraham. *Lenin: Founder of the Soviet Union. People of Distinction Ser.* Childrens 1987
$17.27. ISBN 0-516-03260-7 Biography of Lenin especially suitable for younger
readers.
Rosmer, Alfred. *Moscow Under Lenin.* Ian Birchall (tr). Monthly Review 1973 $8.95.
(o.p.) Examines the early years of Soviet government while under Lenin's leader-
ship.
Trotsky, Leon. *Lenin: Notes for a Biographer.* Tamara Deutscher (tr). Putnam 1971. (o.p.)
Profile of Lenin by his contemporary, Leon Trotsky.

STALIN, JOSEPH   1879–1953

The Soviet dictator Joseph Stalin was born Josif Vissarionovich Dzhugashvili
in the Georgian town of Gori in 1879. The son of a shoemaker, he came from
very humble origins. While studying for the priesthood, Stalin became interested in Marxism and was expelled from the seminary for revolutionary activities aimed at overthrowing the tzarist regime. During the early 1900s, he
became a member of the Bolsheviks, a political group that was the forerunner
of the Russian Communist party. Between 1902 and 1913, he was arrested five
times for his activities, but escaped each time. During that period, he wrote and
published revolutionary literature and also adopted the name Stalin, which
means "man of steel."

In 1917 Stalin took charge of the Bolshevik newspaper *Pravda* and began
to attract the attention of the Bolshevik leader V. I. Lenin. (*See* Lenin, Vol. 2,
World History: The Rise of Totalitarian States.) Five years later Lenin appointed Stalin general secretary of the Communist party. Soon, however, the
two men grew to distrust each other, and Lenin warned on his deathbed in
1922 that Stalin should be removed from power because of his tendency to
tyranny.

Lenin's warning was ignored, and Stalin used his position as general secretary of the Communist party to gain total control of the Soviet Union. Anyone
who opposed his leadership was ruthlessly removed, and in 1929 he was
officially hailed as Lenin's successor. Under Stalin's leadership, the Soviet
Union became a totalitarian dictatorship tightly controlled by Stalin himself.
As dictator, he imposed a policy of rapid industrialization to help the country
catch up to the industrial nations of the West. He also tried to reorganize
agriculture by bringing it forcibly under state control. Through a policy known
as collectivization, small individual farms were brought together under the
control of large state-run operations. In the process, millions of farmers were
either shot or sent to forced labor camps.

During the 1930s Stalin began a number of purges, in which enemies of
the Communist party—enemies of Stalin—were arrested and executed. Between 1935 and 1939 millions of Soviet citizens lost their lives as a result of
these purges.

During World War II, Stalin at first remained out of the war, having signed
a nonaggression pact with Nazi Germany. In 1941, however, Germany invaded
Russia and Stalin joined in the fighting. At the war's end, Stalin ordered
Russian troops to take over the countries of Eastern Europe, a policy that
helped launch the cold war.

At Stalin's death in 1953, he received the funeral of a state hero and was buried next to Lenin in Moscow's Red Square. However, beginning in 1961 Stalin and his policies began to be questioned and later were denounced by the Soviet Union's leaders. Today Stalin is severely criticized both in the Soviet press and by many of the Soviet people.

BOOKS BY STALIN

Dialectical and Historical Materialism. Intl Pub Inc 1940 $.75.
Economic Problems of Socialism in the U.S.S.R. China Bks $1.25.
Foundations of Leninism (1939). China Bks 1965 $2.50.
Great Patriotic War of the Soviet Union. Greenwood 1970 repr 1945 ed $35.00. ISBN 0-8371-2559-6
Marxism and the Problems of Linguistics. China Bks $1.25.
Works. Robert H. McNeal (ed). 3 vols. Hoover Inst Pr 1967. (o.p.)

BOOKS ABOUT STALIN

Alliluyeva, Svetlana. *Twenty Letters to a Friend: A Memoir.* Priscilla MacMillan (tr). Harper 1967 $11.49. Account of the Russian Communist dictator as told through letters by his daughter.

Antonov-Ovseyeneko, Anton. *The Time of Stalin: Portrait of a Tyranny.* Harper 1983 $8.95. ISBN 0-06-039027-1 Examines the dictatorship of the feared Communist leader of Russia.

Bialer, Seweryn (ed). *Stalin and His Generals: Soviet Military Memoirs of World War II.* Encore Ed. Ser. Westview 1984 $55.00. ISBN 0-86531-610-4 Looks at the Communist dictator through his dealings with his wartime military leaders.

*Blassingame, Wyatt. *Joseph Stalin and Communist Russia.* Century Biographies Ser. Garrard 1971 $3.98. ISBN 0-8116-4753-6 Biographical account of the Communist leader who succeeded Lenin as ruler of Russia.

*Caulkins, Janet. *Joseph Stalin.* Watts 1990 $13.90. ISBN 0-531-10945-3 A good summary of the Soviet Union's history in the twentieth century that focuses on the dictator most responsible for its course.

Deutscher, Isaac. *Stalin: A Political Biography.* Oxford Univ Pr $16.95. ISBN 0-19-500273-3 Sympathetic portrait of Stalin.

*Hoobler, Thomas, and Dorothy Hoobler. *Joseph Stalin.* World Leaders—Past and Present Ser. Chelsea $17.95. ISBN 0-87754-576-6 Story of the Soviet dictator, especially suitable for younger readers.

*Killingray, David, *et al.* *Stalin.* World History Ser. Malcolm Yapp, *et al* (eds). Greenhaven 1980 $2.95. ISBN 0-89908-101-0 Historical account of Joseph Stalin and his role as leader of Russia.

*Laqueur, Walter. *Stalin: The Glasnost Revelations.* Macmillan 1990 $24.95. ISBN 0-684-19203-9 An exposé of the horrors during Stalin's reign.

*Marrin, Albert. *Stalin: Russia's Man of Steel.* Penguin 1988 $13.95. ISBN 0-670-82102-0 Examines the life and political career of the Soviet dictator.

Paley, Alan L. *Stalin: The Iron Fisted Dictator of Russia.* Outstanding Personalities Ser. D. Steve Rahmas (ed). SamHar 1972 $2.50. ISBN 0-87157-007-6 General overview of the feared Communist dictator.

Taubman, William. *Stalin's American Policy.* Norton 1983 $9.70. ISBN 0-393-30130-3 Examines Stalin's foreign policy toward the United States.

Trotsky, Leon. *Stalin: An Appraisal of the Man and His Influences.* Scarborough Hse 1970 $7.95. ISBN 0-8128-1262-X Biography of Stalin; includes a chronological guide and an appendix outlining the three concepts of the Russian Revolution.

Tucker, Robert C. *Stalin as Revolutionary, 1879–1929: A Study in History and Personality.* Norton 1974 $11.95. ISBN 0-393-00738-3 Focuses on Stalin's early years, including his development as a revolutionary, his role in the Russian Revolution, and the initial years of Communist rule in Russia.

Urban, George. *Stalinism.* St. Martin's 1982 $25.00. ISBN 0-312-75515-5 Analyzes Stalin's political and economic philosophies and their impact on Russia during his dictatorship.

TROTSKY, LEON 1879–1940

The Russian revolutionary leader Leon Trotsky was an important organizer of the Russian Revolution of 1917 and became one of the founders of the Union of Soviet Socialist Republics. A brilliant thinker, his theoretical writings influenced Socialist movements worldwide.

Born Lev Davidovich Bronstein in the Ukraine, Trotsky was the son of prosperous Jewish farmers. In 1896 he joined the Russian followers of the German philosopher Karl Marx (*see* Marx, Vol. 2, Economics: Comparative Economic Systems) and was imprisoned many times for his revolutionary activities. He escaped from exile in Siberia in 1902 with a forged passport using the name of Trotsky. Assuming that name permanently, he fled to London and worked with other Russian revolutionaries living there. During the Revolution of 1905, Trotsky returned to Russia and became a prominent leader of revolutionary forces in St. Petersburg, later known as Leningrad. When that revolution failed, he was again arrested and exiled to Siberia. Once more he escaped and went to Switzerland, France, and New York City, where he worked as a journalist and edited a Russian-language newspaper.

Trotsky returned to Russia in 1917 and joined V. I. Lenin (*see* Lenin, Vol. 2, World History: The Rise of Totalitarian States) and the Bolsheviks. He became a key organizer of the successful Bolshevik seizure of power in the revolution of November 1917. During the Lenin regime, he served as people's commissar for foreign affairs and later as commissar of war. In the latter position he helped organize the Red Army, which emerged victorious over the White Army during the Civil War of 1918–1920. At Lenin's death in 1924, Trotsky and Joseph Stalin (*see* Stalin, Vol. 2, World History: The Rise of Totalitarian States) were the primary rivals for succession to power. Stalin, a skilled infighter, finally gained control, and Trotsky was expelled from the Communist party in 1927 and exiled from the Soviet Union in 1929. Trotsky sought asylum in Turkey, Norway, France, and finally Mexico, carrying with him material on his experiences in the revolution. After arriving in Mexico in 1936, he began work on a biography of his bitter enemy Stalin. During a series of treason trials held in Moscow between 1936 and 1938, the exiled Trotsky was accused of leading an anti-Soviet plot, and his life was threatened by Soviet agents. Trotsky had only partially completed his biography of Stalin when a member of the Soviet secret police worked his way into the household and killed Trotsky with a pickax at the desk where he was writing. Stalin's biography, spattered with Trotsky's blood, was later completed by a translator working with Trotsky's notes, work sheets, and fragments.

BOOKS BY TROTSKY

Literature and Revolution (c. 1925). Univ of Michigan Pr 1960. (o.p.) $6.95.

Marxism in Our Time. Pathfinder Pr 1972 $1.25.

My Life. Pathfinder Pr 1970 $12.95. ISBN 0-87348-144-5

The Russian Revolution: The Overthrow of Tzarism and the Triumph of the Soviets (1932). Doubleday 1989 $9.95. ISBN 0-385-09398-5

The Third International after Lenin (1930). Pathfinder Pr 1970 $9.95. ISBN 0-87348-185-2

Trotsky's Diary in Exile (1935). Harvard Univ Pr 1976 $18.50. ISBN 0-674-91006-0

Trotsky Papers, 1917–1922. Russian Ser. Jan M. Meijer (ed). 2 vols. Mouton. Vol. 1 1964 $106.75. Vol. 2 1971 $113.00.

Writings of Leon Trotsky. 13 vols. George Breitman, *et al* (eds). Pathfinder Pr 1972–1979 $11.95–$30.00. ISBNs 0-87348-194-1 to 0-87348-565-3

BOOKS ABOUT TROTSKY

Ali, Tariq. *Trotsky for Beginners.* Pantheon 1980 $6.95. ISBN 0-394-73885-3 Introductory look at the Russian revolutionary leader and writer.

Deutscher, Isaac. *The Prophet Armed: Trotsky, 1879–1921.* Oxford Univ Pr 1980 $10.95. ISBN 0-19-281064-2 Examines the early life of Trotsky from his birth to the first years after the Russian Revolution.

Deutscher, Isaac. *The Prophet Unarmed: Trotsky, 1921–1929.* Oxford Univ Pr 1980 $10.95. ISBN 0-19-281065-0 Focuses on the period of Trotsky's life and times during Lenin's leadership of Russia and the early years after Lenin's death.

Deutscher, Isaac. *The Prophet Outcast: Trotsky, 1929–1940.* Oxford Univ Pr 1980 $10.95. ISBN 0-19-281066-9 Looks at the period of Trotsky's life during which he was in exile from Russia.

*Garza, Hedda. *Leon Trotsky. World Leaders—Past and Present Ser.* Chelsea 1986 $17.95. ISBN 0-87754-444-1 Introductory account of the influential Communist party member who helped build up the Red Army; especially suitable for younger readers.

Mandel, Ernest. *Trotsky: A Study in the Dynamic of His Thought.* Schocken 1980 $6.75. Analyzes Trotsky's political and economic philosophy.

Molyneux, John. *Leon Trotsky's Theory of Revolution.* St. Martin's 1981 $25.00. ISBN 0-312-47994-8 Scholarly examination of the political thought and philosophy of the Russian revolutionary leader.

Wolfe, Bertram D. *Three Who Made a Revolution.* Scarborough Hse 1986 $14.95. ISBN 0-8128-6212-0 Biographical history of Trotsky, Lenin, and Stalin.

See also Vol. 2, Economics: Comparative Economic Systems.

WORLD WAR II AND ITS AFTERMATH

American Heritage Illustrated History of the United States. Vol. 15 *World War II.* Choice Pub 1988 repr of 1963 ed $3.49. ISBN 0-945260-15-6 Interesting account of World War II in pictures, illustrations, and informative text.

*Barnett, Correlli (ed). *Hitler's Generals.* Grove-Weidenfeld 1989 $24.95. ISBN 1-55584-161-9 Discussion of Hitler's generals and how they dealt with his leadership; with photos, maps, and more.

Bendersky, Joseph W. *A History of Nazi Germany.* Nelson-Hall 1984 $13.95. ISBN 0-88229-829-1

*Chaikin, Miriam. *A Nightmare in History: The Holocaust 1933–1945.* Clarion 1987 $14.95. ISBN 0-89919-461-3 Traces the step-by-step process devised by the Nazis to free Europe of all Jews and the reactions and results; includes excerpts from diaries and eyewitness accounts.

Donovan, Robert J. *The Second Victory: The Marshall Plan and the Postwar Revival of Europe.* Univ Pr of America 1988 $22.95. ISBN 0-8191-6498-4

Editors of Time-Life Books. *Across the Rhine. Time-Life World War II Ser.* Time-Life 1980 $19.93. ISBN 0-8094-2543-2

*Editors of Time-Life Books. *The Aftermath: Asia. Time-Life World War II Ser.* Time-Life 1983 $19.93. ISBN 0-8094-3435-0 Detailed account of Asia in the years following World War II and the war's effect on that region.

*Editors of Time-Life Books. *The Aftermath: Europe. Time-Life World War II Ser.* Time-Life 1983 $19.93. ISBN 0-8094-3413-X Discusses the situation in Europe after World War II and the war's effect on that region.

Editors of Time-Life Books. *The Air War in Europe. Time-Life World War II Ser.* Time-Life 1979 $19.93. ISBN 0-8094-2496-7

Editors of Time-Life Books. *The Battle of the Atlantic. Time-Life World War II Ser.* Time-Life 1977 $19.93. ISBN 0-8094-2468-1

Editors of Time-Life Books. *The Battle of Britain. Time-Life World War II Ser.* Time-Life 1977 $19.93. ISBN 0-8094-2460-6

Editors of Time-Life Books. *The Battle of the Bulge. Time-Life World War II Ser.* Time-Life 1979 $19.93. ISBN 0-8094-2531-9

Editors of Time-Life Books. *Battles for Scandinavia. Time-Life World War II Ser.* Time-Life 1981 $19.93. ISBN 0-8094-3396-6

Editors of Time-Life Books. *Blitzkrieg. Time-Life World War II Ser.* Time-Life 1976 $19.93. ISBN 0-8094-2456-8

Editors of Time-Life Books. *Bombers Over Japan. Time-Life World War II Ser.* Time-Life 1982 $19.93. ISBN 0-8094-3429-6

Editors of Time-Life Books. *China–Burma–India. Time-Life World War II Ser.* Time-Life 1978 $19.93. ISBN 0-8094-2484-3

Editors of Time-Life Books. *The Commandos. Time-Life World War II Ser.* Time-Life 1981 $19.93. ISBN 0-8094-3401-6

Editors of Time-Life Books. *The Fall of Japan. Time-Life World War II Ser.* Time-Life 1983 $19.93. ISBN 0-8904-3409-1

Editors of Time-Life Books. *The Home Front: Germany. Time-Life World War II Ser.* Time-Life 1982 $19.93. ISBN 0-8094-2508-4

Editors of Time-Life Books. *The Home Front: USA. Time-Life World War II Ser.* Time-Life 1977 $19.93. ISBN 0-8094-2480-0

Editors of Time-Life Books. *Island Fighting. Time-Life World War II Ser.* Time-Life 1978 $19.93. ISBN 0-8094-2487-8

*Editors of Time-Life Books. *The Italian Campaign. Time-Life World War II Ser.* Time-Life 1978 $19.93. ISBN 0-8094-2502-5 Examines the role of Italians in World War II and the struggle to overthrow the Fascist regime.

Editors of Time-Life Books. *Italy at War. Time-Life World War II Ser.* Time-Life 1982 $19.93. ISBN 0-8094-3423-7

Editors of Time-Life Books. *Japan at War. Time-Life World War II Ser.* Time-Life 1980 $19.93. ISBN 0-8094-2528-9

Editors of Time-Life Books. *Liberation. Time-Life World War II Ser.* Time-Life 1978 $19.93. ISBN 0-8094-2510-6

Editors of Time-Life Books. *The Mediterranean. Time-Life World War II Ser.* Time-Life 1981 $19.93. ISBN 0-8094-3384-2

Editors of Time-Life Books. *The Nazis. Time-Life World War II Ser.* Time-Life 1979 $19.93. ISBN 0-8094-2535-1

Editors of Time-Life Books. *The Neutrals. Time-Life World War II Ser.* Time-Life 1982 $19.93. ISBN 0-8094-3431-8

Editors of Time-Life Books. *Partisans. Time-Life World War II Ser.* Time-Life 1978 $19.93. ISBN 0-8094-2491-6

Editors of Time-Life Books. *Prelude to War. Time-Life World War II Ser.* 1976 $19.93. ISBN 0-8094-2452-5

Editors of Time-Life Books. *Prisoners of War. Time-Life World War II Ser.* Time-Life 1982 $19.93. ISBN 0-8094-3393-1

Editors of Time-Life Books. *Red Army Resurgent. Time-Life World War II Ser.* Time-Life 1979 $19.93. ISBN 0-8094-2518-1

Editors of Time-Life Books. *The Resistance. Time-Life World War II Ser.* Time-Life 1979 $19.93. ISBN 0-8094-2522-X

Editors of Time-Life Books. *Return to the Philippines. Time-Life World War II Ser.* Time-Life 1979 $19.93. ISBN 0-8094-2514-9

Editors of Time-Life Books. *The Rising Sun. Time-Life World War II Ser.* Time-Life 1977 $19.93. ISBN 0-8094-2464-9

Editors of Time-Life Books. *Road to Tokyo. Time-Life World War II Ser.* Time-Life 1979 $19.93. ISBN 0-8094-2540-8

Editors of Time-Life Books. *Russia Beseiged. Time-Life World War II Ser.* 1977 $19.93. ISBN 0-8094-2471-1

Editors of Time-Life Books. *The Second Front. Time-Life World War II Ser.* Time-Life 1978 $19.93. ISBN 0-8094-2500-9

Editors of Time-Life Books. *The Secret War. Time-Life World War II Ser.* Time-Life 1980 $19.93. ISBN 0-8094-2546-7

Editors of Time-Life Books. *Shadow of Dictators: 1925–1950. Time Frame Ser.* Time-Life 1989 $22.60. ISBN 0-8094-6483-7

Editors of Time-Life Books. *The Soviet Juggernaut. Time-Life World War II Ser.* Time-Life 1980 $19.93. ISBN 0-8094-3387-7

*Editors of Time-Life Bks. *Time-Life Books History of World War II.* Prentice 1989 $39.95. ISBN 0-13-922022-4 Authentically illustrated; presents a complete picture of the entire war—from the sowing of seeds of international hostility to the rebuilding after the war.

Editors of Time-Life Books. *Victory in Europe. Time-Life World War II Ser.* Time-Life 1983 $19.93. ISBN 0-8094-3405-9

Editors of Time-Life Books. *The War In the Desert. Time-Life World War II Ser.* Time-Life 1977 $19.93. ISBN 0-8094-2474-6

Editors of Time-Life Books. *War in the Outposts. Time-Life World War II Ser.* Time-Life 1980 $19.93. ISBN 0-8094-3381-8

Editors of Time-Life Books. *War Under the Pacific. Time-Life World War II Ser.* Time-Life 1980 $19.93. ISBN 0-8094-3377-X

*Englemann, Bernt. *In Hitler's Germany: Everyday Life in the Third Reich.* Krishna Winston (tr). Pantheon 1986 $21.45. ISBN 0-394-52449-7 Firsthand accounts of life in Germany under the Nazi regime.

Gay, Peter. *Freud, Jews, and Other Germans: Masters and Victims in Modernist Culture.* Oxford Univ Pr 1979 $9.95. ISBN 0-19-50249-3

*Gilbert, Martin. *The Holocaust: The History of the Jews of Europe During the Second World War.* H. Holt 1986 $12.95. ISBN 0-8050-0348-7 Eyewitness accounts of the Holocaust in Europe starting in 1933.

Hastings, Max. *Overlord: D-Day and the Battle of Normandy.* Simon 1985 $8.95. ISBN 0-317-31520-X

Hastings, Max. *Victory over Europe: D-Day to VE Day.* Little 1985 $25.00. ISBN 0-316-81334-6

*Hersch, Giselle, and Peggy Mann. *Giselle, Save the Children.* Dodd 1980 $15.95. ISBN 0-89696-054-4 Story of four sisters who try to survive the Holocaust together.

*Hoobler, Dorothy, and Thomas Hoobler. *An Album of World War II. Picture Albums Ser.* Watts 1977 $13.90. ISBN 0-531-02911-5 The events and people of the period of the war in pictures.

Lucas, James. *Kommando: German Special Forces of World War II.* St. Martin's 1986 $4.95. ISBN 0-312-90497-5

Lucas, James. *Last Days of the Third Reich: Collapse of Nazi Germany.* Morrow 1986 $17.95. ISBN 0-688-06638-0

Lucas, James. *Panzer Army Africa.* Jove 1986 $3.50. ISBN 0-515-08513-8

Lucas, James. *Storming Eagles: German Airborne Forces in World War Two.* Sterling 1989 $24.95. ISBN 0-85368-879-6

Lucas, James. *World War Two Through German Eyes.* Sterling 1988 $24.95. ISBN 0-85368-863-X

Lucas, James S., and James Barker. *The Battle of Normandy: Falaise Gap.* Holmes & Meier 1978 $24.50. ISBN 0-8419-0418-9

Nisbet, Robert. *Roosevelt and Stalin: The Failed Courtship.* Regnery 1988 $14.95. ISBN 0-89526-558-3

Pacific War Research Society Staff (ed). *Japan's Longest Day: Surrender—The Last Twenty-Four Hours Through Japanese Eyes.* Kodansha 1980 $6.95. ISBN 0-87011-423-0

*Pierre, Michel, and Annette Wievorka. *The Second World War. Events of Yesteryear Ser.* Silver 1987 $14.96. ISBN 0-382-09298-8 Easy-to-read, heavily illustrated presentation of the events and people of the war.

*Prager, Arthur, and Emily Prager. *World War II Resistance Stories.* Dell 1980 $2.25. ISBN 0-440-99800-X Tales of the underground fight against the Nazis.

*Resnick, Abraham. *The Holocaust. Lucent Overview Ser.* Lucent 1991 $11.95. ISBN 1-56006-124-3 Discusses the events surrounding the imprisonment and execution of Jews in Nazi prison camps during World War II.

Richardson, Nigel. *How and Why: The Third Reich.* David and Charles 1989 $19.95. ISBN 0-85219-723-3

*Richardson, Nigel. *The July Plot. A Day That Made History Ser.* David and Charles 1987 $17.95. ISBN 0-85219-672-5 Readable account of the attempt to assassinate the Nazi dictator Adolf Hitler.

Salisbury, Harrison E. *The Nine Hundred Days: The Siege of Leningrad. Quality Paperbacks Ser.* Da Capo 1985 $14.95. ISBN 0-306-80253-8

*Saunders, Alan. *Invasion of Poland. Turning Points in World War II.* Watts 1984 $12.90. ISBN 0-531-04864-0 Account of the German invasion of Poland in September 1939, which began World War II.

*Scherman, David E. *Life Goes to War: A Pictorial History of World War II.* Pocket 1979 $14.95. ISBN 0-671-79077-3 Heavily illustrated coverage of the war as pictured in *Life* magazine from 1936–1945.

*Shapiro, William. *Pearl Harbor. Turning Points of World War II Ser.* Watts 1984 $12.90. ISBN 0-531-04865-9 Discusses the Japanese attack on Pearl Harbor in 1941 and the entry of the United States into World War II.

Smith, Bradley F. *The War's Long Shadow: How World War II Shaped the Dynamics of Global Power in the Post-War Era.* Simon 1987 $9.95. ISBN 0-671-64558-7

*Snyder, Louis L. *World War II. First Books Ser.* Watts 1981 $10.40. ISBN 0-531-0433-9 Focuses on the important events and people of World War II; especially suited to younger readers.

Stone, I. F. *The War Years, 1939–1945. A Nonconformist History of Our Times Ser.* Little 1988 $18.95. ISBN 0-316-81771-6

Taylor, A. J. *The Origins of the Second World War.* Macmillan 1983 $9.95. ISBN 0-689-70658-8

Taylor, A. J. *The Second World War: An Illustrated History.* Putnam 1979 $9.95. ISBN 0-399-50434-6

*Toland, John. *Battle: Story of the Bulge.* NAL 1985 $10.95. ISBN 0-452-00993-6 Account of one of the major battles of World War II.

Toland, John. *Infamy: Pearl Harbor and Its Aftermath.* Berkley 1984 $5.50. ISBN 0-425-09040-X

*Toland, John. *The Last One Hundred Days.* Bantam $10.95. ISBN 0-553-34208-8 Account of the final days of World War II.

Toland, John. *Rising Sun: The Decline and Fall of the Japanese Empire: 1936–1945.* Random 1970 $25.00. ISBN 0-394-44311-X

World War, 1939-1943: The Cartoonist's Vision. Routledge 1990 $29.95. ISBN 0-415-0349-8 The war as depicted by illustrations.

Wiesel, Elie, *et al. Dimensions of the Holocaust.* Northwestern Univ Pr 1978 $8.95. ISBN 0-8101-0470-9

*Wiesel, Elie. *Night.* Bantam 198? $2.95. ISBN 0-553-20807-1 Recounts the author's experience in the Auschwitz concentration camp during World War II.

Wright, John M., Jr. *Captured on Corregidor: Diary of an American P.O.W. in World War II.* McFarland 1988 $20.95. ISBN 0-89950-347-0

CHURCHILL, WINSTON S.   1874–1965

Prime minister of Great Britain from 1940 to 1945 and again from 1951 to 1955, Winston Churchill was one of his country's most notable statesmen, as well as a writer of British history. During World War II, he rallied the British people against the Nazis. As a foresighted statesman, he worked with President Franklin Delano Roosevelt of the United States to produce a global strategy that served as a basic framework for peace in the postwar world. As an author, he produced a six-volume series, *The Second World War* (1948–1953), for which he received the Nobel Prize for literature in 1953. In recognition of Churchill's achievements, the British Crown bestowed on him a knighthood in 1953 and the United States Congress made him an honorary United States citizen in 1963.

A graduate of the Royal Military College at Sandhurst, Churchill served with the British army in Cuba, India, and the Sudan. In 1899 he gave up his military career to enter politics. Defeated for a seat in Parliament, he went to South Africa, where he served as a war correspondent in the Boer War and also took part in the fighting there. Returning to Great Britain as a military hero, he became a member of Parliament in 1900 and served thereafter in the cabinet under several prime ministers. As lord of the admiralty, Churchill readied the British navy for both world wars. Prior to World War II, Churchill was one of the few influential voices in England who warned of the Nazi menace. When Prime Minister Neville Chamberlain resigned in 1940, the task of providing Great Britain with wartime leadership fell to Churchill. He also foresaw the cold war and was the first to call the symbolic separation between the Western and Communist countries the "Iron Curtain."

BOOKS BY CHURCHILL

A History of the English-Speaking Peoples (1956–1958). 4 vols. Dodd 1983 $35.00. ISBN 0-396-08275-0
Memories and Adventures. Weidenfeld 1989 $19.95. ISBN 1-55584-168-6
The Second World War (1948–1954). 6 vols. Houghton 1986 $59.95. ISBN 0-395-41685-X
While England Slept: A Survey of World Affairs, 1932–1938 (1938). Irvington 1982 repr of 1938 ed $22.00. ISBN 0-8290-0804-7

BOOKS ABOUT CHURCHILL

Fowler, Michael. *Winston S. Churchill: Philosopher and Statesman. Credibility of Institutions, Policies and Leadership Ser.* Univ Pr of America 1985 $7.75. ISBN 0-8191-4417-7 Scholarly look at the life, thought, and achievements of Great Britain's notable prime minister.
Harbutt, Fraser J. *The Iron Curtain: Churchill, America, and the Origins of the Cold War.* Oxford Univ Pr 1988 $11.95. ISBN 0-19-505422-9 Focuses on British and American foreign policy during the beginning of the cold war era.
*Keller, Mollie. *Winston Churchill. Impact Biography Ser.* Watts 1984 $12.90. ISBN 0-531-04752-0 Introductory account of the respected British prime minister, war leader, statesman, and historian; especially suitable for younger readers.
Kimball, Warren F. (ed). *Churchill and Roosevelt, the Complete Correspondence.* 3 vols. Princeton Univ Pr 1984 $65.00. ISBN 0-691-00817-5 Presents the letters and other correspondence between Churchill and U.S. President Franklin D. Roosevelt.
Manchester, William. *The Last Lion: Winston Spencer Churchill Visions of Glory, 1874–1932.* Little 1983 $25.00. ISBN 0-316-54503-1 Comprehensive account of the early life and achievements of the notable British prime minister.
Pitt, Barrie. *Churchill and the Generals: Their Finest Hours. Battle Standards Ser.* Borgo 1989 $22.95. ISBN 0-8095-7503-5 Examines Churchill and British military strategies during World War II.
*Rodgers, Judith. *Churchill. World Leaders—Past and Present Ser.* Chelsea 1986 $17.95. ISBN 0-87754-563-4 Readable account of the courageous prime minister of Britain who led his country during World War II; especially suitable for younger readers.

DE GAULLE, CHARLES   1890–1970

Born in Lille, France, and trained as a soldier at the Military Academy of Saint-Cyr, Charles de Gaulle always had a sense that he was destined for greatness. De Gaulle joined the French infantry in 1913 and fought in World War I. After the war he served in various military posts and rose steadily in rank and responsibility. He set forth his views on the role of a leader and France's needs in several books. In *The Edge of the Sword* (1932) he urged the creation of a strong executive position for France. In *The Army of the Future* (1940) his proposals for a small professional army, highly trained in tank warfare and able to mobilize quickly, contrasted sharply with the views of his military superiors, who favored a stationary line of defense along France's border with Germany. When the wartime government of France surrendered to German occupation in 1940, de Gaulle fled first to England and then to Algiers where he assumed the leadership of the Free French forces.

After the liberation of Paris in 1944, de Gaulle became deeply involved in France's postwar politics. Frustrated at the weaknesses of the Fourth Republic, de Gaulle retired in 1955 to work on his memoirs, which were published in three volumes—*The Call to Honor* (1955), *Unity* (1959), and *Salvation* (1960). During a political crisis in 1958, created by the Civil War in France's territory of Algeria, de Gaulle returned to the leadership of his country. A new constitution established a new government and provided for a strong president. Under this constitution de Gaulle was elected president of the Fifth Republic in 1959. For 10 years he gave France the leadership it needed, restoring it to a position as a leading European power.

BOOKS BY DE GAULLE

The Army of the Future. (1941). Greenwood 1977 $35.00. ISBN 0-8371-7525-9
The Complete War Memoirs of Charles de Gaulle: 1940–1946. Quality Paperbacks Ser. Richard Howard (tr). Da Capo 1984 $14.95. ISBN 0-306-80227-9
The Edge of the Sword (1960). Greenwood 1975 $35.00. ISBN 0-8371-8366-9

BOOKS ABOUT DE GAULLE

Aglion, Raoul. *Roosevelt and De Gaulle: Allies in Conflict: A Personal Memoir.* Free Pr 1988 $22.50. ISBN 0-02-901540-5 Personalized account of the wartime American and French leaders and the conflicts between them.
*Banfield, Susan. *De Gaulle. World Leaders—Past and Present Ser.* Chelsea 1985 $17.95. ISBN 0-87754-551-0 Introductory account of the staunch defender and leader of wartime and postwar France; especially suitable for younger readers.
Cook, Don. *Charles De Gaulle: A Biography.* Putnam 1984 $22.95. ISBN 0-399-12858-1 Comprehensive look at the life and achievements of the respected French leader.
*Epstein, Sam, and Beryl Epstein. *Charles de Gaulle: Defender of France. Century Biographies Ser.* Garrard 1973 $3.98. ISBN 0-8116-4756-0 Standard biographical account of the former president of France.

See also Vol. 2, United States History: World War II.

THE COLD WAR

Adelman, Jonathan R. *Prelude to the Cold War: The Tsarist, Soviet, and U.S. Armies in the Two World Wars.* Rienner 1988 $30.00. ISBN 1-55587-123-2
American Heritage Illustrated History of the United States. Vol. 16 *Decades of Cold War 1946–1963.* Choice Pub 1988 repr of 1963 ed $3.49. ISBN 0-945260-16-4 Impressive illustrated account of the first years of the cold war era.
Aronsen, Lawrence, and Martin Kitchen. *Origins of the Cold War in Comparative Perspective: American, British, and Canadian Relations with the Soviet Union, 1941–48.* St. Martin's 1988 $39.95. ISBN 0-312-01264-0
Brown, Seyom. *New Forces, Old Forces, and the Future of World Politics.* Scott 1988. ISBN 0-673-39709-2
Calvocoressi, Peter. *World Politics Since Nineteen Forty-Five.* Longman 1988 $21.95.

Challener, Richard D. (ed). *The Cold War: From Iron Curtain to Perestroika.* 15 vols. Meckler 1992 $1,450.00. ISBN 0-88736-573-6

Deighton, Anne. *The Impossible Peace: Britain, the German Problem, and the Origins of the Cold War.* Oxford Univ Pr 1990 $39.95. ISBN 0-19-827332-0

Denitch, Bogdan. *The End of the Cold War: European Unity, Socialism, and the Shift in Global Power.* Univ of Minnesota Pr 1990 $10.95. ISBN 0-8166-1875-5

DePorte, Anton W. *Europe Between the Superpowers: The Enduring Balance.* Yale Univ Pr 1986 $11.95. ISBN 0-300-03758-9

Gaddis, John L. *The Long Peace: Inquiries into the History of the Cold War.* Oxford Univ Pr 1989 $8.95. ISBN 0-19-504335-9

Gelb, Norman. *The Berlin Wall: Kennedy, Krushchev and a Showdown in the Heart of Europe.* Simon 1988 $8.95. ISBN 0-671-65787-9

*Griffiths, John. *Cuban Missile Crisis. Flashpoints Ser.* Rourke 1987 $10.95. ISBN 0-86592-028-1 Illustrated, readable account of the Cuban missile crisis of 1962.

Harbutt, Fraser J. *The Iron Curtain: Churchill, America, and the Origins of the Cold War.* Oxford Univ Pr 1988 $11.95. ISBN 0-19-505422-9

*Hastings, Max. *The Korean War.* Simon 1988 $10.95. ISBN 0-671-66834-X Interesting look at the Korean War in the 1950s and its impact on world relations.

Hyland, William. *The Cold War Is Over.* Random 1990 $18.95. ISBN 0-8129-1871-1

Jessup, John E. *A Chronology of Conflict and Resolution, 1945–1985.* Greenwood 1989 $85.00. ISBN 0-313-24308-5

Kennedy, Robert F. *Thirteen Days: A Memoir of the Cuban Missile Crisis.* Richard Neustadt and Graham T. Allison (eds). Norton 1971 $5.95. ISBN 0-393-09896-6

Medland, William J. *Cuban Missile Crisis of Nineteen Sixty-Two: Needless or Necessary.* Praeger 1988 $35.95. ISBN 0-275-92844-6

Thomas, Hugh. *Armed Truce: The Beginning of the Cold War, 1945–1946.* Macmillan 1987 $27.50. ISBN 0-689-11740-X

Ulam, Adam B. *The Rivals: America and Russia Since World War II.* Penguin 1972 $8.95. ISBN 0-14-004309-8

Waldheim, Kurt. *Building the Future Order: The Search for Peace in an Interdependent World.* Free Pr 1980 $12.95. ISBN 0-02-933670-8

*Weisberger, Bernard A. *Cold War, Cold Peace.* Houghton 1985 $9.95. ISBN 0-8281-1164-2 Illustrated account of various aspects of the cold war.

Wyden, Peter. *Wall: The Berlin Story.* Simon 1989 $27.50. ISBN 0-671-55510-3

BREZHNEV, LEONID   1906–1982

Soviet Communist leader Leonid Brezhnev was born in the Central Ukraine in 1906. During the 1920s he worked as a land surveyor and graduated in 1935 from his home city's metallurgical institute as a technical engineer. Upon joining the Communist party in 1931, Brezhnev became a loyal follower of Soviet leader Joseph Stalin (*see* Stalin, Vol. 2, World History: The Rise of Totalitarian States) and advanced from a regional official of the party in 1939 to a member of the party's Central Committee in 1952. After Stalin's death in 1953, Brezhnev was demoted. However, his transfer to second secretary of the Kazakhstan Communist party in 1954 brought him to the attention of the new Soviet leader, Nikita Khrushchev (*see* Khrushchev, Vol. 2, World History: The Cold War). With Khrushchev's backing, Brezhnev again rose steadily in the party hierarchy, securing reelection to the Central Committee in 1956, full membership in the administrative committee, the Presidium in 1957, and election as chairman of the Presidium of the legislature, the Supreme Soviet, in 1960.

In 1964, only three months after resigning as chairman of the Presidium to become a close assistant to Khrushchev, Brezhnev joined forces with other Communist officials to engineer Khrushchev's ouster. Replacing Khrushchev as general secretary of the Communist party, Brezhnev then became the dominant figure in a period of collective leadership. This collective leadership lasted until 1977 when Brezhnev emerged as both general secretary of the party and chairman of the Presidium. The first Soviet leader to hold these positions concurrently, he held them until his death in 1982.

While Soviet leader, Brezhnev improved relations with the West, especially the United States, and helped initiate a period of eased tensions, or détente. At the same time, he increased and modernized Soviet military power, supported "wars of liberation" in developing nations, and ordered the invasion of Czechoslovakia in 1968 when that nation attempted to liberalize its policies.

BOOKS BY BREZHNEV

How It Was: The War and Post-War Reconstruction in the Soviet Union. Pergamon 1979 $8.00. ISBN 0-08-023578-6
Leonid I. Brezhnev: His Life and Work. Sphinx 1982 $17.95. ISBN 0-943071-03-8
Memoirs. Pergamon 1982 $13.00. ISBN 0-08-028164-8

BOOKS ABOUT BREZHNEV

Academy of Science of the U.S.S.R. *Leonid I. Brezhnev: Pages from His Life.* Pergamon 1981 $13.25. ISBN 0-08-028151-6 Official biography of Brezhnev and his career as Soviet leader.
Breslauer, George W. *Khrushchev and Brezhnev as Leaders: Building Authority in Soviet Politics.* Unwin 1982 $14.95. ISBN 0-04-329041-8 Examines the leadership of Nikita Khrushchev and Leonid Brezhnev.
*Navazelskis, Ina. *Leonid Brezhnev. World Leaders—Past and Present Ser.* Chelsea 1988 $17.95. ISBN 0-87754-513-8 Readable, introductory account of the Soviet leader who controlled the Soviet Union in the latter part of the twentieth century; especially suitable for younger readers.

HAMMARSKJOLD, DAG (HJALMAR AGNE CARL)   1905–1961

Dag Hammarskjold, one of Sweden's leading political economists and diplomats was born in Jönköping, Sweden, in 1905. After receiving a university education, Hammarskjold taught political economy at Stockholm University beginning in 1933. From 1944 to 1948 he served also as chairman of the Bank of Sweden. Then, in 1951, Hammarskjold became Sweden's deputy foreign minister and soon afterward became a member of his country's United Nations delegation. His stature as a UN diplomat grew quickly and in 1953 he replaced the Norwegian diplomat Trygve Lie as Secretary-General of the United Nations.

As Secretary-General, Hammarskjold brought to the office an ideal of international civil service and a passion for the rule of decency and reason. Under his leadership the United Nations Secretariat became a body of much greater importance. Between 1953 and 1961, Hammarskjold worked diligently to free the United Nations from the undue influence of individual governments. He was known for his "quiet diplomacy," which made use of unpublicized meetings with leaders from both sides of a conflict.

During Hammarskjold's term of office, the two major areas of conflict in the world were the Middle East and the Congo, now known as Zaire. For the most part, Hammarskjold was successful in preventing the intervention of major powers in these situations. He played an important role in setting up UN emergency forces in the Middle East in 1956 to deal with the conflicts in that region. While on his way to the Congo in 1961 to discuss a peace settlement for that country, he was killed in a plane crash. After his death, he was awarded the Nobel Peace Prize of 1961 for his peacemaking efforts.

Hammarskjold's book, *Markings,* which was published after his death in

1964, startled the world. Even Hammarskjold's friends were amazed at the revelation of his profoundly religious and mystical inner life. Others felt that the religious aspect of Hammarskjold's life revealed in the diary was only one of many facets of a brilliant and complicated individual.

BOOKS BY HAMMARSKJOLD

Markings. Ballantine 1989 $3.50. ISBN 0-345-32741-1

Public Papers of the Secretaries-General of the United Nations (1953–1961). Andrew W. Cordier and Wilder Foote (eds). Columbia Univ Pr. Vol. 2 1972 $40.00. ISBN 0-231-03633-7. Vol. 3 1973 $45.00. ISBN 0-231-03735-X. Vol. 4 1974 $45.00. ISBN 0-231-03810-0. Vol. 5 1975 $45.00. ISBN 0-231-03897-6

BOOKS ABOUT HAMMARSKJOLD

Jordon, Robert S. (ed). *Dag Hammarskjold Revisited: The United Nations Secretary-General As a Force in World Politics.* Carolina Acad Pr 1983 $16.95. ISBN 0-89089-233-4 Examines Hammarskjold's political philosophy and his influence on world politics and foreign affairs.

Lash, Joseph P. *Dag Hammarskjold: Custodian of the Brushfire Peace.* Greenwood 1974 repr of 1961 ed $22.50. ISBN 0-8371-6995-X Pays special attention to Hammarskjold as Secretary-General of the United Nations; based on research and personal interviews.

*Lichello, Robert. *Dag Hammarskjold: A Giant in Diplomacy. Outstanding Personalities Ser.* D. Steve Rahmas (ed). SamHar 1972 $3.95. ISBN 0-87157-501-9 Interesting account of the Swedish statesman and diplomat who served as Secretary-General of the United Nations.

*Montgomery, Elizabeth R. *Dag Hammarskjold: Peacemaker for the United Nations. Century Biographies Ser.* Garrard 1973 $3.98. ISBN 0-8116-4757-9 Biographical account of the respected U.N. Secretary-General.

*Sheldon, Richard. *Dag Hammarskjold. World Leaders–Past and Present Ser.* Chelsea 1987 $17.95. ISBN 0-87754-529-4 Introductory look at the life, times, and achievements of Dag Hammarskjold, the respected diplomat and U.N. leader; especially suitable for younger readers.

Urquhart, Brian. *Hammarskjold.* Peter Smith 1988 $21.00. ISBN 0-8446-6313-1 Comprehensive look at the life and achievements of the Swedish diplomat and U.N. Secretary-General.

Zacher, Mark W. *Dag Hammarskjold's United Nations. International Organization Ser.* Columbia Univ Pr 1969 $37.50. ISBN 0-231-03275-7 Examines Hammarskjold's leadership of the United Nations and that organization's achievements during his tenure.

KENNAN, GEORGE 1904–

American diplomat and historian George Kennan was born in Milwaukee, Wisconsin, in 1904. After graduating from Princeton University, he entered the foreign service and in 1933 was assigned to the American embassy in Moscow. He later spent time in Vienna, Prague, Berlin, and Lisbon before returning to Moscow during World War II.

Writing anonymously in 1946, Kennan argued against trying to cultivate the trust of the Soviet government. Instead, he recommended that the United States adopt a policy of "containment." According to this policy, threats of Soviet expansion should be resisted by force, political organization, or economic pressure. Kennan believed that the Soviet Union would respond to such resistance by either withdrawing or collapsing.

The United States used Kennan's policy of containment as a basis for much of its foreign policy during the postwar period. The Marshall Plan, for example, provided economic aid to European nations in part to prevent the growth of Communist parties in such countries as France and Italy. The North Atlantic Treaty Organization (NATO) was formed in 1949 to provide a military alliance of western governments that would provide mutual assistance in the event of a Soviet attack.

In the late 1950s Kennan modified his views. Instead of containment, he proposed a policy of disengagement in which both the United States and the Soviet Union would withdraw their military forces from Europe. He advocated the reunification of East Germany and West Germany as a neutral nation. Kennan also opposed arming NATO forces with nuclear weapons and urged a halt to the nuclear arms race between the United States and the Soviet Union. In the 1960s Kennan opposed American participation in the Vietnam War, calling it "an error for which it is hard to find any parallels in our history."

After retiring from the State Department, Kennan became a professor at the Institute for Advanced Study at Princeton. Two of his books, *Russia Leaves the War* (1956) and *Memoirs, 1925–1950* (1967), received Pulitzer Prizes.

BOOKS BY KENNAN

American Diplomacy. WFL Ser. Univ of Chicago Pr 1985 $6.96. ISBN 0-226-43147-9
The Decision to Intervene: Soviet–American Relations, 1971–1972. Vol. 2 Norton 1984 $12.95. ISBN 0-393-30217-2
The Decline of Bismarck's European Order: Franco–Russian Relations, 1875–1890. Princeton Univ Pr 1979 $7.95. ISBN 0-691-00784-5
From Prague After Munich: Diplomatic Papers, 1938–1939. Princeton Univ Pr 1968 $11.50. ISBN 0-691-01063-3
The Nuclear Delusion: Soviet–American Relations in the Atomic Age. Pantheon 1983 $8.95. ISBN 0-394-71318-4
Russia and the West under Lenin and Stalin. NAL 1962 $4.95. ISBN 0-451-62460-2
Russia, the Atom, and the West. Greenwood 1974 repr of 1958 ed $48.50. ISBN 0-8371-7394-9
Sketches from a Life. Pantheon 1990 $12.95. ISBN 0-679-72877-5
Sketches from a Life's Journey. Pantheon 1989 $22.95. ISBN 0-394-57504-0
Soviet–American Relations, 1917–1920. 2 vols. Princeton Univ Pr 1990 $26.95. ISBN 0-691-00847-7
Soviet Foreign Policy: Nineteen Seventeen to Nineteen Forty-One. Anvil Ser. Krieger 1979 $8.50. ISBN 0-88275-749-0

BOOKS ABOUT KENNAN

Hixson, Walter L. *George F. Kennan: Cold War Iconoclast.* Columbia Univ Pr 1989 $32.00. ISBN 0-231-06894-8 Focuses on Kennan's cold war policies and political theories.
Polley, Michael. *A Biography of George F. Kennan: The Education of a Realist.* Mellen 1990 $59.95. ISBN 0-88946-693-9 Comprehensive account of the American statesman and political analyst.

KHRUSHCHEV, NIKITA   1894–1971

Soviet leader Nikita Khrushchev was born in the Ukraine, the son of a miner and the grandson of a former serf. Soon after going to work as a pipe fitter at the age of 15, Khrushchev became attracted to the Russian Communist party and later fought with the Bolsheviks during the Civil War that followed the Russian Revolution of 1917. In 1925, he began working full time for the Communist party. After studying to be a party organizer in Moscow, he moved from position to position, each time rising higher in the Communist party hierarchy. By 1939, he had become a full member of the Central Communist party committee, the Politburo, and a strong supporter of Soviet dictator Joseph Stalin. (*See* Stalin, Vol. 2, World History: The Rise of Totalitarian States.) After Stalin's death in 1953, Khrushchev emerged as the leader of the Soviet Union, as first secretary of the Communist party (1953–1964) and as Soviet premier (1958–1964).

Khrushchev displayed to the world an outgoing personality and an earthy peasant style of humor. During his years as Soviet leader, he attacked the excesses of Stalin's dictatorial rule and overcame political uprisings in the satellite countries of Eastern Europe. While advocating a policy of "peaceful coexistence" with the West, he followed a policy of stockpiling missiles at home and in strategic places in such Communist countries as Cuba. This policy led to the Cuban Missile Crisis of 1962. Forced to back down in this crisis by President John F. Kennedy's strong stand, and faced with an agricultural crisis at home, Khrushchev had no choice but to leave office in 1964. The years preceding his death in 1971 were quiet and uneventful. Historians credit Khrushchev with liberalizing Soviet rule and establishing precedents that his successors were forced to follow.

BOOKS BY KHRUSHCHEV

The Anatomy of Terror. Greenwood 1979 repr of 1956 ed $24.75. ISBN 0-313-21218-X
Khrushchev Remembers. Talbot Strobe (ed and tr). Little 1971 $15.00.
Khrushchev Speaks: Selected Speeches, Articles and Press Conferences, 1949–1961. Thomas P. Whitney (ed). Univ of Michigan Pr 1963. (o.p.)

BOOKS ABOUT KHRUSHCHEV

Breslauer, George W. *Khrushchev and Brezhnev as Leaders: Building Authority in Soviet Politics.* Unwin 1982 $14.95. ISBN 0-04-329041-8 Examines the leadership of Nikita Khrushchev and Leonid Brezhnev.
Crankshaw, Edward. *Khrushchev: A Career.* Penguin 1971. (o.p.) $3.95. Account of the career and political achievements of the Soviet Communist leader.
*Ebon, Martin. *Nikita Khrushchev. World Leaders—Past and Present Ser.* Chelsea 1986 $17.95. ISBN 0-87754-562-6 Introductory look at the Soviet Communist leader who took power in 1955; especially suitable for younger readers.
*Kort, Michael. *Nikita Krushchev.* Watts 1989 $12.90. ISBN 0-531-10776-0 An outline of the life and career of the unpredictable Soviet leader.
Kurland, Gerald. *Nikita Sergeievich Khrushchev: Modern Dictator of the U.S.S.R. Outstanding Personalities Ser.* D. Steve Rahmas (ed). SamHar 1972 $3.95. ISBN 0-87157-512-4 Standard biography of the Soviet Communist leader.
Linden, Carl A. *Khrushchev and the Soviet Leadership, 1957–1964.* Johns Hopkins Univ Pr 1966 $9.95. ISBN 0-8018-0375-6 Scholarly account of Soviet leadership during the Khrushchev years.
Medvedev, Roy A., *et al. Khrushchev: The Years in Power.* Norton 1978 $6.95. ISBN 0-393-00879-7 Focuses on Khrushchev's years as Soviet leader.
Slusser, Robert M. *Berlin Crisis of 1961: Soviet American Relations and the Struggle for Power in the Kremlin, June–November, 1961.* Johns Hopkins Univ Pr 1973 $47.50. ISBN 0-8018-1404-9 Analyzes Soviet policy during the Berlin Crisis of 1961 and internal power struggles within the Soviet leadership structure.

See also Vol. 2, United States History: Postwar Foreign and Domestic Policy.

AFRICA

Aluko, Olajide (ed). *Africa and the Great Powers in the 1980s.* Univ Pr of America 1987 $16.75. ISBN 0-8191-5593-4

Amin, Mohamed, *et al. Kenya: The Magic Land.* Random 1989 $39.95. ISBN 0-370-31225-2

*Bohannan, Paul, and Philip Curtin. *Africa and Africans.* Waveland 1988 $11.95. ISBN 0-88133-347-6 Discusses the land and the people of Africa.

Carter, Gwendolyn M., and Patrick O'Meara (eds). *African Independence: The First Twenty-Five Years.* Indiana Univ Pr 1985 $39.95. ISBN 0-253-30255-2

David, Stephen M. *Apartheid's Rebels: Inside South Africa's Hidden War.* Yale Univ Pr 1987 $9.95. ISBN 0-300-03992-1

Davidson, Basil. *Modern Africa.* Longman 1983 $11.95. ISBN 0-582-65525-0

*Editors of Time–Life Books. *East Africa. Library of Nations Ser.* Time–Life 1987 $14.95. ISBN 0-8094-5194-8 Colorfully illustrated discussion of the lands, people, histories, economics, and governments of the nations of East Africa.

*Fairfield, Sheila. *People and Nations of Africa. People and Nations Ser.* Gareth Stevens 1988 $12.45. ISBN 1-55532-903-9 Provides insight on the people and nations of Africa.

*Hood, Michael (ed). *Tanzania After Nyerere.* Columbia Univ Pr 1988 $35.00. ISBN 0-86187-916-3 Examines the state of the East African nation of Tanzania after the presidency of Julius Nyerere.

Huxley, Elspeth. *Four Guineas: A Journey Through West Africa.* Greenwood 1974 repr of 1954 ed $35.00. ISBN 0-8371-7371-X

Huxley, Elspeth. *Out in the Midday Sun: My Kenya.* Penguin 1988 $6.95. ISBN 0-14-009256-0

*Kurian, George T. *Facts on File National Profile: East Africa.* Facts on File 1989 $35.00. ISBN 0-8160-2030-2 Excellent sourcebook for contemporary information on the nations of East Africa.

*Laure, Jason. *Zimbabwe. Enchantment of the World Ser.* Childrens 1988 $23.93. ISBN 0-516-02704-2 Readable account of the southern African country formerly known as Rhodesia; especially suited to younger readers.

*Laure, Jason, and Ettagale Laure. *South Africa: Coming of Age Under Apartheid.* Farrar 1980 $15.95. ISBN 0-374-37146-6 Accounts of some of the personal experiences of young South Africans.

*Lelyveld, Joseph. *Move Your Shadow: South Africa Black and White.* Times Bks 1986 $7.95. ISBN 0-14-009326-5 Provides an in-depth look at apartheid.

*Lye, Keith. *Africa. Today's World Ser.* Watts 1987 $12.40. ISBN 0-531-17065-9 Introduction to recent history and events in Africa.

McEwan, P. J. (ed). *Twentieth-Century Africa. Readings in African History Ser.* Oxford Univ Pr 1968 $34.00. ISBN 0-19-215663-2

*Maren, Michael. *Land and People of Kenya. Portraits of the World Ser.* Harper 1989 $14.89. ISBN 0-397-32335-2 Basic introduction to contemporary Kenya.

Mathabane, Mark. *Kaffir Boy: The True Story of a Black Youth's Coming of Age in Apartheid South Africa.* NAL 1987 $8.95. ISBN 0-452-25943-6

*Mazrui, Ali A. *The Africans: A Triple Heritage.* Little 1987 $17.95. ISBN 0-316-55201-1 Africa's history based on its native inheritance, Islamic culture, and western traditions.

Meredith, Martin. *The First Dance of Freedom: Black Africa in the Postwar Era.* Harper 1985 $23.45. ISBN 0-06-435658-2

Meredith, Martin. *In the Name of Apartheid: South Africa in the Postwar Era.* Harper 1988 $25.00. ISBN 0-06-430163-X

*Patinkin, Mark. *An African Journey.* Books Demand 1985 $20.00. Firsthand account of famine in Africa.

*Rohr, Janelle (ed). *Problems of Africa. Opposing Viewpoints Ser.* Greenhaven 1986 $7.95. ISBN 0-89908-365-X Examines such issues as poverty, famine, and apartheid.

*Sullivan, Jo (ed). *Global Studies: Africa.* Dushkin 1989 $10.95. ISBN 0-87967-801-1 In-depth introduction to Africa, with current issues highlighted.

*Timberlake, Lloyd. *Famine in Africa.* Watts 1986 $11.90. ISBN 0-531-17017-9 Good introduction to the complex problem of famine in Africa.

*Ungar, Sanford J. *Africa: The People and Politics of an Emerging Continent.* Simon 1989 $14.95. ISBN 0-671-67565-6 Current issues of concern in Africa focusing on African politics and U.S. policies toward Africa.

*Vollmer, Jurgen, and John Devere. *Black Genesis, African Roots.* St. Martin's 1980. Account of the daily life of Mandingo society in West Africa.

*Williams, Oliver F. *The Apartheid Crisis: How We Can Do Justice in a Land of Violence.* Harper 1986 $8.95. ISBN 0-06-250951-9 Discusses apartheid and how some people have reacted to it.

KENYATTA, JOMO   c. 1893–1978

One of the earliest and best-known African nationalist leaders, Jomo Kenyatta was a Kikuyu, the largest ethnic group in Kenya, a British East African colony until 1963. Known as Kamau wa Ngengi as a child, Kenyatta received his early education from English Protestant missionaries and went to England in 1929 to receive an advanced education. By this time he was an ardent black nationalist who campaigned for land reform and political rights for Africans. In England he took to wearing beaded articles of clothing, such as belts and hats, as a sign of pride in his Kikuyu heritage and became known as *Kenyatta,* a Kikuyu term for the beaded articles he always wore. In 1938 Kenyatta changed his first name to *Jomo,* a Kikuyu term meaning "burning spear."

While in England, Kenyatta continued his efforts on behalf of African nationalism. On his return to Kenya in 1947, he assumed the leadership of the Kenya African Union, a nationalist group. By this time, an African group called the Mau Mau were staging brutal attacks on white settlers in Kenya. This rebellion reached a peak between 1952 and 1956. Although Kenyatta publicly disavowed any connection with the terrorist group, he was arrested and imprisoned by the British in 1953 and exiled in 1959. Even in exile, Kenyatta continued his demands for independence. Independence was finally granted to Kenya in 1963. The colony became a republic, and Kenyatta became its first president, serving until his death in 1978.

BOOK BY KENYATTA

Facing Mount Kenya. Random 1962 $4.95. ISBN 0-394-70210-7

BOOKS ABOUT KENYATTA

Delf, George. *Jomo Kenyatta: Towards Truth About "The Light of Kenya."* Greenwood 1975 repr of 1961 ed $35.00. ISBN 0-8371-8307-3 Examines the life and achievements of the African nationalist leader and president of Kenya.

*Wepman, Dennis. *Jomo Kenyatta. World Leaders—Past and Present Ser.* Chelsea 1985 $17.95. ISBN 0-87754-575-8 Account of the first president of Kenya; especially suitable for younger readers.

MANDELA, NELSON   1918–

South African black nationalist leader Nelson Mandela was born in Transkei, South Africa, in 1918. After becoming a lawyer, he joined the African National Congress (ANC), an organization advocating the elimination of the system of apartheid, the separation of the races, in South Africa. In 1956 Mandela and other ANC members were arrested for treason, and in 1960 the ANC was banned by the white South African government. On his release in 1961, Mandela decided to shift from peaceful protest to violence. Over the next three years, he led a group called Umkhonto we Sizwe, or "Spear of the Nation," which participated in bombings and other acts of sabotage aimed at damaging property with no loss of life.

In 1964 Mandela and other ANC leaders were arrested again. This time, Mandela was sentenced to life imprisonment. For the next 26 years he remained a political prisoner. During his imprisonment his wife, Winnie Mandela, acted as his representative to the anti-apartheid movement both in South Africa and abroad. In 1977 her actions led to her being "banned"—forbidden to speak in public and confined to her home town. The South African government repeatedly offered to release Nelson Mandela from prison if he would renounce armed struggle, give up political activities, or go into exile. Each time, Mandela refused. In the meantime, South African blacks carried out strikes against the government and called on foreign businesses and governments not to invest in South Africa's economy.

In the late 1980s South Africa gradually began to dismantle its system of apartheid. In February 1990 it lifted the ban against the African National Congress and released Mandela from prison. A free man, Mandela visited the United States and received great praise from many for his commitment to South African equality. Back in South Africa, Mandela continues discussions with the South African government about the sharing of political power between blacks and whites, the dismantling of apartheid, and other issues of South African governance and policies.

BOOKS BY MANDELA

Nelson Mandela: I Am Prepared to Die. Intl Defense & Aid 1979 $2.00. ISBN 0-904759-29-6
No Easy Walk to Freedom. African Writers Ser. Heinemann 1986 $7.00. ISBN 0-435-90782-4
The Struggle Is My Life. Pathfinder Pr 1986 $10.95. ISBN 0-87348-663-3

BOOKS ABOUT MANDELA

*Benson, Mary. *Nelson Mandela: The Man and His Movement.* Norton 1986 $8.95. ISBN 0-393-30322-5 Account of the notable leader of the African National Congress and his campaign to free South Africa of apartheid.
*Hargrove, J. *Nelson Mandela: South Africa's Silent Voice of Protest.* Childrens 1989 $13.27. ISBN 0-516-03266-6 Readable account of the South African leader who was imprisoned in 1964 for his efforts to eradicate apartheid and gain power for black South Africans.
Mandela, Winnie. *A Part of My Soul Went with Him.* Norton 1985 $16.95. ISBN 0-393-02215-3 Wife of the civil rights leader tells her story in an account written before her husband's release.
Meer, Fatima. *Higher Than Hope: The Biography of Nelson Mandela.* Harper 1989 $19.95. ISBN 0-06-016146-9 Comprehensive account of the South African nationalist leader.
Nelson Mandela: Pictorial History. Imported 1988 $5.95. ISBN 0-904759-85-7
*Vail, John. *Nelson and Winnie Mandela. World Leaders—Past and Present Ser.* Chelsea 1989 $17.95. ISBN 1-55546-841-1 Story of the African National Congress leader and his wife and their struggle against apartheid in South Africa.

NKRUMAH, KWAME 1909–1972

Kwame Nkrumah was the first black African statesman to lead his country to independence after World War II. Educated in Catholic schools in the Gold Coast, now known as Ghana, Nkrumah taught in them after graduating from the Gold Coast's Achimola College in 1930. He also studied for the priesthood for a short time before becoming a nondenominational Christian. For several years, Nkrumah studied in the United States, graduating with masters degrees from Lincoln University in Pennsylvania and the University of Pennsylvania. During this time he became a Marxist Socialist and president of the African Students Association. After further study at the London School of Economics and Political Science, he published *Toward Colonial Freedom* (1947), in which he explained his beliefs in African nationalism, Pan-Africanism, and Marxism.

Nkrumah returned to the British colony of the Gold Coast in 1947, and five years later he became the first prime minister of the newly independent state of Ghana, formed by the union of the Gold Coast and British Togoland. When Ghana became a republic in 1960, Nkrumah became its first president. As president of Ghana, he assumed total control of the government and of the single, ruling Convention People's party. He also made himself supreme commander of the army. In 1964 he was made president for life, but at the same time he began isolating himself from the people and alienated many Ghanaians in the process. While on a trip to Beijing, China, in 1966, his government was overthrown in a military coup. Nkrumah fled to Guinea where he was honored with the title of co-president. Continuing to publish his views, Nkrumah wrote *Handbook of Revolutionary Warfare* (1968) and *Class Struggle in Africa* (1970), a reaffirmation of his Marxist beliefs. In 1972 he died of cancer.

BOOKS BY NKRUMAH

Africa Must Unite. Intl Pubs 1970 $3.95. ISBN 0-7178-0296-5
Class Struggle in Africa. Intl Pubs 1970 $1.95. ISBN 0-7178-0314-7
Consciencism: Philosophy and the Ideology for Decolonization. Monthly Review 1970 $6.00. ISBN 0-85345-136-2
Ghana: Autobiography of Kwame Nkrumah. Intl Pubs 1989 $6.95. ISBN 0-7178-0294-9

BOOKS ABOUT NKRUMAH

Alexander, H. T. *African Tightrope: My Two Years as Nkrumah's Chief of Staff.* Univ Place Bk Shop 1966 $10.00. ISBN 0-685-56706-0 Personal account of Kenyan government by a former presidential chief of staff.
*Kellner, Douglas. *Nkrumah. World Leaders—Past and Present Ser.* Chelsea 1987 $17.95. ISBN 0-87754-546-4 Introductory biography of the president of the West African nation of Ghana; especially suitable for younger readers.
Omari, T. Peter. *Kwame Nkrumah: The Anatomy of an African Dictatorship.* Holmes & Meier 1970 $25.00. ISBN 0-8419-0036-1 Examines the increasingly authoritarian rule of the West African leader.

NYERERE, JULIUS 1921–

Called *Mwalimu,* Swahili for "teacher", by Tanzanians, Julius Nyerere led the African nation of Tanzania for the first 25 years of its independence. Son of the chief of a small tribe, Nyerere was educated at Tabora Secondary School and Makerere College in Uganda. After converting to Catholicism, he taught in several Catholic schools before going to Edinburgh University in Scotland, where he graduated with an advanced degree in history and economics. Returning to the British colony of Tanganyika, Nyerere began working peacefully for independence under United Nations auspices. When the colony received self-government in 1960, Nyerere became its first prime minister. He was also instrumental in the union of Tanganyika and Zanzibar as the republic of Tanzania, of which he became the first president. As president of Tanzania he initiated a program of African socialism, which he called "ujamaa," or pulling together.

During his presidency, Nyerere collectivized peasant villages, nationalized factories and sisal and coffee plantations, established state-run corporations, and discouraged the accumulation of private wealth. He also expanded Tanzania's education system, which helped give the country one of Africa's highest literacy rates. Despite his efforts, Nyerere was unable to develop an industrial base in the Tanzanian economy, and it remains largely an agricultural country with one of the lowest per capita incomes in the world. A prolific writer, Nyerere has translated British playwright William Shakespeare's (*see* Shakespeare, Vol. 1, British Literature: The Renaissance) *Merchant of Venice* and *Julius Caesar* into the African language of Swahili. Among his books are *Freedom and Unity* (1967), *Freedom and Socialism* (1968), and *Freedom and Development* (1973).

BOOKS BY NYERERE

Freedom and Development—Uhuru Na Maendeleo (1973). Oxford Univ Pr 1973 $8.95. ISBN 0-19-519772-0
Ujmaa: Essays on Socialism (1971). Oxford Univ Pr 1971 $6.95. 0-19-501474-X

BOOK ABOUT NYERERE

Killingray, David. *Nyerere and Nkrumah. World History Ser.* Malcolm Yapp and Margaret Killingray (eds). Greenhaven 1980 $2.95. ISBN 0-89908-104-5 Illustrated account of the Tanzanian president and of the president of Ghana, Kwame Nkrumah.

TUTU, DESMOND   1931–

The recipient of the Nobel Peace Prize in 1984 for outspoken opposition to the South African system of apartheid, or separation of the races, Desmond Tutu was born in a goldmining town in the Transvaal, South Africa. Moving with his family to Johannesburg at the age of 12, he earned money by selling peanuts at railroad stations and working as a caddy at a local golf course. His friendship with Anglican bishop Trevor Huddleston, an antiapartheid advocate, led Tutu to study for the Anglican priesthood after graduating from the Bantu Normal College in Pretoria and the University of Johannesburg. Ordained a priest in 1961, Tutu received a Master's degree at King's College in London, England, and was assigned to parishes in England from 1962 to 1966.

After a five-year teaching stint in South Africa, Tutu returned to England where he became a director of the Theological Education Fund, for which he traveled widely. In 1975, Tutu returned to South Africa and became Anglican dean of Johannesburg. He moved up rapidly in the church hierarchy, becoming bishop of Lesotho in 1976, secretary of the South African Council of Churches in 1978, and the first black Anglican bishop of Johannesburg in 1984.

Earning world recognition for his efforts to eradicate apartheid peacefully, Tutu advocated withdrawal of foreign investments from South Africa. In 1981 he began a world tour to gather support for economic sanctions against South Africa. He has written of his views and his struggle against apartheid in his books *Crying in the Wilderness* (1982) and *Hope and Suffering* (1984).

BOOKS BY TUTU

Crying in the Wilderness (1982). Eerdmans 1982 $5.95. ISBN 0-8028-1940-0
Hope and Suffering: Sermons and Speeches (1984). Eerdmans 1984 $6.95. ISBN 0-8028-0085-8
The Words of Desmond Tutu. Naomi Tutu (ed). Newmarket 1989 $12.95. ISBN 1-55704-038-9

BOOKS ABOUT TUTU

du Boulay, Shirley. *Tutu: Voice of the Voiceless.* Eerdmans 1988 $24.95. ISBN 0-8028-3649-6 A stirring biography of the archbishop with emphasis on his struggles against apartheid.

Winner, David. *Desmond Tutu: The Courageous and Eloquent Archbishop Struggling Against Apartheid in South Africa. People Who Have Helped the World Ser.* Rhoda Sherwood (ed). Gareth Stevens 1989 $12.45. ISBN 1-55532-822-9 Close look at the notable South African archbishop and antiapartheid leader.

See also Vol. 2, Geography: Regions: Africa *and* Vol. 1, World Literature: African Literature.

ASIA

Barnett, A. Doak. *China After Mao: With Selected Documents.* Princeton Univ Pr 1967 $12.50. ISBN 0-691-00000-X

*Bartke, Wolfgang (ed). *Who's Who in the People's Republic of China.* K. G. Saur 1987 $200.00. ISBN 3-598-10610-6 Provides an illustrated, alphabetical listing of notable Chinese individuals, particularly government leaders.

Bonner, Raymond. *Waltzing with a Dictator: The Marcoses and the Making of American Policy.* Carolyn Reidy (ed). Random 1988 $11.95. ISBN 0-394-75835-8

Burks, Ardath W. *Japan: A Postindustrial Power. Profiles—Nations of Contemporary Asia Ser.* Westview 1984 $15.95. ISBN 0-86531-714-3

Cady, John F. *The Southeast Asian World. World of Asia Ser.* Forum Pr 1977 $6.95. ISBN 0-88273-502-0

*Caldwell, John C. *India. Let's Visit Places and Peoples of the World Ser.* Chelsea 1990 $14.95. ISBN 0-7910-1371-5 Introductory account of the people and places of India; especially suitable for younger readers.

Chang, David W. *Zhou Enlai and Deng Xiaping in the Chinese Leadership Succession Crisis.* Univ Pr of America 1984 $18.75. ISBN 0-8191-3587-9

Croll, Elisabeth, *et al* (eds). *China's One Child Family Policy.* St. Martin's 1985 $39.95. ISBN 0-312-13356-1

Dutt, Ashok K. *Southeast Asia: Realm of Contrasts.* Westview 1985 $21.95. ISBN 0-86531-562-0

Eames, Andrew. *Crossing the Shadow Line: Travels in Southeast Asia.* David and Charles 1988 $29.95. ISBN 0-340-39862-0

Ehrhart, W. D. *Going Back: An Ex-Marine Returns to Vietnam.* McFarland 1987 $14.95. ISBN 0-89950-278-4

*Fairfield, Sheila. *People and Nations of Asia. People and Nations Ser.* Gareth Stevens 1988 $12.45. ISBN 1-55532-905-5 Provides insight on the people and nations of Asia.

*Fairfield, Sheila. *People and Nations of the Far East and the Pacific. People and Nations Ser.* Gareth Stevens 1988 $12.45. ISBN 1-55532-907-1 Provides insight on the people and nations of the Far East and Pacific region.

Gibney, Frank. *Japan: The Fragile Superpower.* NAL 1986 $12.95. ISBN 0-452-00967-7

Hall, Daniel G. *A History of Southeast Asia.* St. Martin's 1981 $24.95. ISBN 0-312-38641-9

*Hidaka, Rokuro. *The Price of Affluence: Dilemmas of Contemporary Japan.* Gavan McCormick (tr). Kodansha 1984 $14.95. ISBN 0-87011-655-X Looks at Japanese society since World War II and considers various problems the society faces.

*Hoobler, Dorothy, and Thomas Hoobler. *Zhou Enlai. World Leaders—Past and Present Ser.* Chelsea 1986 $17.95. ISBN 0-87754-516-2 Introductory account of the Chinese Communist leader and statesman.

Hsu, Immanuel C. *China.* Oxford Univ Pr 1989 $10.95. ISBN 0-19-506056-3

*Jhabvala, Ruth P. *The Householder.* Norton 1985 $6.70. ISBN 0-393-00851-7 Novel about the life of an Indian school teacher.

*Jhabvala, Ruth P. *Like Birds, Like Fishes, and Other Stories.* Norton 1963. Eleven short stories that show how an Indian family's relationships and home life changed old traditions for newer western ones.

*Kalman, Bobbie. *China—The People.* Crabtree Pub 1989. ISBN 0-86505-208-5 Readable account of the daily life of Chinese people.

*Karnow, Stanley. *Vietnam: A History.* Penguin 1984 $12.95. ISBN 0-14-007324-8 Discusses 2,000 years of Vietnam's history and considers Vietnam's resistance to the interventions of various countries.

*Lawson, Don. *Marcos and the Philippines.* Watts 1984 $12.90. ISBN 0-531-04856-X Introductory account of the Philippines under the leadership of Ferdinand Marcos.

*Lawson, Don. *The New Philippines. Impact Ser.* Watts 1986 $12.90. ISBN 0-531-10269-6 Discusses the overthrow of Ferdinand Marcos and the presidency of Corazon Aquino.

*Lebra, Takie S. *Japanese Women: Constraint and Fulfillment.* Univ of Hawaii Pr 1985 $9.50. ISBN 0-8248-1025-2 Provides insight into the life-style of Japanese women.

*Minear, Richard H. *Through Japanese Eyes.* 2 vols. CITE 1987 Vol. 1 $8.95. ISBN 0-938960-04-0. Vol. 2 $8.95. 0-938960-05-9 Primary reference sources on Japan for secondary students.

Myrdal, Gunnar. *Asian Drama: An Inquiry into the Poverty of Nations.* Random 1972 $4.95. ISBN 0-394-71730-9

*Ogden, Suzanne (ed). *Global Studies: China.* Dushkin 1989 $10.95. ISBN 0-87967-802-X Provides insights on the People's Republic of China, Taiwan, and Hong Kong.

*Ogle, Carol, and John Ogle. *People at Work in India. People at Work Ser.* David and Charles 1988 $19.95. ISBN 0-7134-5157-2 Illustrated account of various types of work in India; especially suitable for younger readers.

Osborne, Milton. *Southeast Asia: An Illustrated Introductory History.* Unwin 1989 $15.95. ISBN 0-04-352238-6

Pye, Lucian W., and Mary W. Pye. *Asian Power and Politics: The Cultural Dimensions of Authority.* Harvard Univ Pr 1988 $12.95. ISBN 0-674-04979-9

*Pye, Lucian W. *China: An Introduction. Little Brown Ser in Comparative Politics.* Scott 1984. ISBN 0-673-39470-0 Introduction to China and its political system.

Raghavan, G. N. *The Making of Modern India: Rammohun Roy to Gandhi and Nehru.* South Asia Bks 1988 $24.00. ISBN 81-212-0112-8

Reischauer, Edwin O. *Japan: The Story of a Nation.* McGraw 1989 $15.00. ISBN 0-07-557074-2

Reischauer, Edwin O. *Japanese Today.* Harvard Univ Pr 1989 $12.50. ISBN 0-674-47182-2

Reischauer, Edwin O. (ed). *Japan. Great Contemporary Issues Ser.* Ayer 1974 $25.00. ISBN 0-405-04168-3

Reischauer, Edwin O., and Albert M. Craig. *Japan: Tradition and Transformation.* Houghton 1989 $33.56. ISBN 0-395-49696-9

*Salisbury, Harrison E. *The Long March.* McGraw 1987 $7.95. ISBN 0-317-56827-2 Account of Chinese Communist Mao Zedong and his followers on their trek across northwestern China in 1934 and 1935 to escape Chiang K'ai-shek and his Nationalist forces.

*Sarin, Amita V. *India: An Ancient Land, A New Nation. Discovering Our Heritage Ser.* Dillon 1984 $12.95. ISBN 0-87518-273-9 Readable account of a modern Indian nation in an ancient land.

Pol Pot: Cambodian Prime Minister. World Leaders—Past and Present Ser. Chelsea 1989 $17.95. ISBN 1-55546-848-9

Scott, Joanna C. *Indochina's Refugees: Oral Histories from Laos, Cambodia and Vietnam.* Mcfarland 1989 $29.95. ISBN 0-89950-415-9

*Seybolt, Peter J. *Through Chinese Eyes: Revolution and Transformation.* Leon Clark (ed). CITE 1988 $19.95. ISBN 0-938960-29-6 Primary sources on China for secondary students.

*Stefoff, Rebecca. *Japan. Places and Peoples of the World Ser.* Chelsea 1988 $13.95. ISBN 1-55546-199-9 Overview of the land and people of Japan.

Steinberg, David J. *In Search of Southeast Asia: A Modern History.* Univ of Hawaii Pr 1987 $18.50. ISBN 0-8248-0987-4

Stone, I. F. *The Hidden History of the Korean War, 1950–1951. A Non-Conformist History of Our Times Ser.* Little 1988 $8.95. ISBN 0-316-81770-8

*Talbot, Phillips. *India in the 1980s. Headline Ser.* Foreign Policy 1983 $4.00. Provides an in-depth study of contemporary India.

Tandon, Prakash. *Beyond Punjab: A Sequel to Punjabi Century.* Univ of California Pr 1971 $40.00. ISBN 0-520-01759-5

Thubron, Colin. *Behind the Wall: A Journey Through China.* Harper 1989 $9.95. ISBN 0-06-097256-4

Tuchman, Barbara. *Stilwell and the American Experience in China 1911–1945.* Bantam 1984 $6.95. ISBN 0-553-25798-6

Ulack, Richard, and Gyuala Pauer. *Atlas of Southeast Asia.* Macmillan 1989 $95.00. ISBN 0-02-933200-1

White, Merry. *The Japanese Educational Challenge: A Commitment to Children.* Free Pr 1988 $9.95. ISBN 0-02-933800-X

Williams, Lea E. *Southeast Asia: A History.* Oxford Univ Pr 1976 $13.95. ISBN 0-19-502000-6

*Wiser, Charlotte V. *Four Families of Karimpur. Foreign and Comparative Studies Program, South Asian Ser.* Syracuse Univ Foreign Comp 1981 $10.00. ISBN 0-915984-78-4 In-depth case study of families in an Indian village.

*Wiser, William, and Charlotte Wiser. *Behind Mud Walls, Nineteen Thirty to Nineteen Sixty; With a Sequel: The Village in 1970.* Univ of California Pr 1972 $10.95. ISBN 0-520-02101-0 Excellent study of life in a traditional Indian village.

Wittington, W.A. (ed). *Southeast Asia. World Cultures Ser.* Gateway Pr 1988 $16.95. ISBN 0-934291-33-0

GANDHI, INDIRA   1917–1984

Few women in the world had the opportunities that were presented to Indira Gandhi. Born in India in 1917, Mrs. Gandhi was the only child of Jawaharlal Nehru, India's first prime minister. (*See* Nehru, Vol. 2, World History: Asia.) Educated in India, Switzerland, and England, she learned her first political lessons while acting as hostess for her widowed father during his tenure as prime minister from 1947 to 1964. Rising through the political ranks, Gandhi soon earned her own place in the government, serving as president of the Indian National Congress in 1959 and 1960 and minister of information from 1964 to 1966. On the death of Shri Lal Bahadur Shastri, who had succeeded her father as prime minister, Gandhi herself became prime minister, an office she held from 1966 to 1977 and again from 1980 to 1984.

As prime minister, Gandhi stressed social programs and government planning, especially in efforts to ease the problems of producing an adequate food supply for India's millions of people. She also supported the nation of Bangladesh in its war with Pakistan and successfully resisted Pakistani efforts to gain control of the disputed province of Jammu and Kashmir, which is located in the northernmost part of India.

When Gandhi's popularity faltered in 1975, she declared a state of national emergency and assumed near-dictatorial powers—a move that led to her defeat at the polls in 1977. However, in 1980 Gandhi returned triumphantly to power as a member of the new Congress party, which had been formed in 1978. After Gandhi's assassination in 1984 by members of her own personal bodyguard who were Sikh separatists—members of an Indian sect that sought to separate from the Indian state of Punjalo and form their own state—her son Rajiv succeeded her as prime minister. In 1991 he too was assassinated.

BOOKS BY GANDHI

Indira Gandhi—Selected Speeches and Writings, 1972–77. Asia Bk Corp 1984 $49.95.
The Task Ahead. Asia Bk Corp 1984 $24.95.
The Years of Challenge: Selected Speeches of Indira Gandhi, 1966–1969. Orient Bk Dist 1973
$7.50. ISBN 0-89684-473-0
The Years of Endeavour. Asia Bk Corp $34.95. ISBN 0-940500-97-3

BOOKS ABOUT GANDHI

Abbas, K. A. *Indira Gandhi: The Last Post.* South Asia Bks 1986 $10.00. ISBN 0-86132-
116-2 Political narrative of the last two to three years Indira Gandhi spent as
prime minister of India.
Abbas, K. A. *That Woman: Indira Gandhi's Seven Years in Power.* Orient Bk Dist 1973 $11.25.
ISBN 0-89684-553-2 Examines the achievements of India's notable prime minister during her terms in office.
Bobb, Dilip, and Ashok Raina. *The Great Betrayal: Assassination of Indira Gandhi.* Advent
1985 $13.95. ISBN 0-89891-008-0 Discusses the situations and events that re-
sulted in the assassination of Prime Minister Indira Gandhi.
Butler, Francelia. *Indira Gandhi. World Leaders—Past and Present Ser.* Chelsea 1986 $17.95.
ISBN 0-87754-596-0 Introductory account of the daughter of India's first prime
minister, who succeeded him in power.
*Currimbhoy, Nayana. *Indira Gandhi. Impact Biography Ser.* Watts 1985 $12.90. ISBN
0-531-10064-2 Introductory biography of India's notable female prime minister.
Fishlock, Trevor. *Indira Gandhi. Profiles Ser.* David and Charles 1986 $9.95. ISBN 0-241-
11772-0 Examines the life and achievements of Prime Minister Indira Gandhi,
whose period in power was clouded by violence.
*Haskins, James. *India under Indira and Rajiv Gandhi.* Enslow 1989 $15.95. ISBN 0-89490-
146-X A readable history of India, with emphasis on Indira Gandhi.

MAO ZEDONG   1893–1976

Even before he became a member of the Communist party in 1921, Mao
Zedong was a revolutionary. Born in the Hunan province of China of peasant
parents, Mao rebelled against his father and left the family farm to pursue
educational studies. Attracted by the cultural and political reforms of the
Chinese revolutionary leader Sun Yat-sen, Mao fought in the revolution that
in 1911 deposed the last dynasty to rule China. Continuing his studies after
the revolution, Mao participated in the student rebellion of May 1919 and
became involved with the organization of political study groups. By 1921, he
had committed himself to the philosophy of Marxism and became one of the
founding members of the Chinese Communist party.

After the Communists split with Chiang Kai-shek, the leader of the Chinese Nationalists, or Kuomintang, in 1927, Mao helped build the Red Army
and developed theories of guerrilla warfare carried out by peasant bands. He
honed these theories during the civil war against the Nationalists, in the inter-
lude of the Long March (1934–1935), and after 1937 while fighting to rid China
of Japanese invaders. By 1949 Mao had enough peasant support to drive
Chiang Kai-shek and the Nationalists from mainland China. By October 1,
1949, the Communists were in control of all of mainland China, and by 1954,
Mao was Chairman of the People's Republic of China, the Communist nation
he had been instrumental in establishing.

As Mao adapted Marxist Communist thought to fit the traditions and
customs of the Chinese people, he forced many changes on the country, some
less successful than others. He organized the peasants into communes; established Five-Year Plans to industrialize the economy; and launched the Cultural

Tea Curing.   Anonymous painting (Nineteenth Century).   Courtesy of SCALA/Art Resource.

Revolution of the late 1960s, a period of widespread agitation. Up until his death in 1976, Mao continued to consolidate his position as the most powerful person in China. Despite the political upheavals and changes in China since his death, many continue to consider him a revolutionary hero and the architect of modern China.

BOOKS BY MAO ZEDONG

China: The March Toward Unity. (coauthored with others) AMS (repr of 1937 ed) $14.50. ISBN 0-404-14475-6

Little Red Book. Hazelden 1946 $4.95. ISBN 0-89486-004-6

Mao Tse-tung on Revolution and War. M. Rejai (ed). Peter Smith $15.25. ISBN 0-8446-5275-X

On the Peoples Democratic Dictatorship. Yale Univ Far Eastern Pubns $2.95. ISBN 0-88710-052-X

Report from Xun wu. Roger R. Thompson (tr). Stanford Univ Pr 1990 $27.50. ISBN 0-8047-1678-1

Selected Readings. China Bks 1971 $9.95.

Selected Works of Mao Tse-tung (1954–1956). 5 vols. China Bks $8.95 ea.

Ten Poems and Lyrics by Mao Tse-tung. Wang Hui-Ming (tr). Univ of Massachusetts Pr 1975 $7.95. ISBN 0-87023-182-0

BOOKS ABOUT MAO ZEDONG

Avakian, Bob. *The Loss in China and the Revolutionary Legacy of Mao Tse-tung.* RCP 1978 $2.00. ISBN 0-89851-017-1 Examines the Chinese Communist leader's effect on Chinese society.

Cohen, Arthur A. *Communism of Mao Tse-tung.* Univ of Chicago Pr 1966 $2.95. ISBN 0-226-11282-9 Analyzes the political philosophy of the Communist leader of China.

*Garza, Hedda. *Mao Zedong. World Leaders—Past and Present Ser.* Chelsea 1988 $17.95. ISBN 0-87754-564-2 Introductory biography of Communist China's noted leader; especially suitable for younger readers.

Karnow, Stanley. *Mao and China: From Revolution to Revolution.* Penguin 1984 $7.95. Examines Mao's influence on China from the Communist takeover to the Cultural Revolution.

Kolpas, Norman. *Mao Zedong. Great Leaders Ser.* McGraw 1981 $7.95. ISBN 0-07-035269-0 Standard account of Mao Zedong and his accomplishments.

Kurland, Gerald. *Mao Tse-Tung: Founder of Communist China. Outstanding Personalities Ser.* D. Steve Rahmas (ed). SamHar 1972 $2.50. ISBN 0-87157-014-9 Describes the Communist Chinese leader whose goal was a strong, modern nation.

Marrin, Albert. *Mao Tse-tung and His China.* Penguin 1989 $14.95. ISBN 0-670-82940-4 Discusses Mao's influence on Chinese government and society.

Painter, Desmond. *Mao Tse-Tung. World History Ser.* Malcolm Yapp and Margaret Killingray (eds). Greenhaven 1980 $2.95. ISBN 0-89908-102-9 Comprehensive look at the Communist Chinese leader whose efforts to renew the revolutionary spirit of the Chinese people led to his Cultural Revolution.

*Poole, Frederick K. *Mao Zedong. Impact Biographies Ser.* Watts 1982 $12.90. ISBN 0-531-04481-5 Introductory biography of one of China's most powerful Communist leaders.

Rice, Edward E. *Mao's Way.* Univ of California Pr 1972 $9.95. ISBN 0-520-02623-3 Summarizes the Communist ideology of Mao Zedong.

Schram, Stuart R. *Mao Zedong: A Preliminary Reassessment.* St. Martin's 1983 $22.50. Analyzes Mao's achievements and legacy to his country.

Terrill, Ross. *Mao: A Biography.* Harper 1987 $9.95. ISBN 0-06-131992-9 Fair assessment and well-researched biography of Mao.

Wilson, Dick. *The People's Emperor: A Biography of Mao Tse-tung.* Doubleday 1980 $17.50. Biography of the Communist leader that focuses on his rapport and support among the Chinese people.

NEHRU, JAWAHARLAL 1889–1964

Architect of India's freedom and its first prime minister, Jawaharlal Nehru was born of Brahmin parents in Allahabad, India, in 1889. After receiving his early education from tutors at home, Nehru was sent to England in 1905 to study at Harrow, an English boys' school, and at Cambridge University. After completing his education and acceptance to the bar as a lawyer, he returned to India in 1912. Four years later he met the Indian nationalist and spiritual leader Mahatma Gandhi (*see* Gandhi, Vol. 2, World History: Imperialism in Africa and Asia) and joined his movement in 1919. By 1929, Nehru had become the second most influential leader, after Gandhi, in the struggle for Indian independence. In that year he became president of the Indian National Congress, a political party devoted to Indian independence. Several times between 1921 and 1934 Nehru was jailed for his actions in protest of British colonial rule. When India gained independence in 1947, Nehru became its first prime minister, a position he held until his death in 1964.

Nehru was much loved but was often criticized for his Socialist views on domestic policy and his neutral stand in foreign affairs. He was as much a revolutionary as he was a philosopher and practical politician. But it was his absorption of Western ways of thinking and his ability to articulate the feelings and goals of Indian nationalists that made him a great leader for India. Able to merge the lessons of the past with the needs of contemporary India, Nehru agreed to Muslim demands for a separate state while he was prime minister. The partition of the Indian subcontinent into Pakistan—a predominantly Muslim state—and India—a predominantly Hindu state—solved a thorny problem that otherwise would have led to years of violence and bloodshed. In many ways, Nehru led his people to an understanding of India's role in South Asia and its place in the world.

BOOKS BY NEHRU

The Discovery of India (1946). Oxford Univ Pr 1989 $8.95. ISBN 0-19-561322-8
Glimpses of World History. Oxford Univ Pr 1989 $9.95. ISBN 0-19-561323-6
Independence and After. Essay Index Repr Ser. Ayer 1950 $26.50. ISBN 0-8369-2003-1
India's Foreign Policy. Asia Bk Corp 1985 repr of 1961 ed $34.95. ISBN 0-940500-94-9
India's Quest: Being Letters on Indian History. Asia Pub Hse 1967. (o.p.)
Jawaharlal Nehru: An Anthology. Sarvepalli Gopal (ed). Oxford Univ Pr 1980 $12.95. ISBN 0-19-561342-2
Mahatma Gandhi. Asia Pub Hse 1966. (o.p.)
Nehru on World History (1942). Saul K. Padover (ed). Indiana Univ Pr 1962 $2.45.

BOOKS ABOUT NEHRU

Akbar, M. J. *Nehru: The Making of India.* Penguin 1989 $24.95. ISBN 0-670-81699-X Examines Nehru's role in the formation of an independent India.

Butler, Lord C. H. *Jawaharlal Nehru.* Cambridge Univ Pr 1967 $1.95. Looks at the life and accomplishments of India's first prime minister.

Chakraborty, A. K. *Jawaharlal Nehru's Writings.* South Asia Bks 1981 $15.00. ISBN 0-685-59378-9 Critical review of Nehru's major writings and of his important themes and issues.

Copeland, Ian. *Jawaharlal Nehru of India, 1889–1964. Leaders of Asia Ser.* Univ of Queensland Pr 1980 $3.00. Comprehensive account of the life and times of the notable Indian prime minister.

Dutt, Vishnu. *Gandhi, Nehru and the Challenge.* South Asia Bks 1979 $14.00. ISBN 0-8364-0322-3 Comparative study of Gandhi's and Nehru's ideas in the context of contemporary political and social problems.

Gopal, Ram. *Trials of Jawaharlal Nehru.* Biblio Dist 1964 $24.00. ISBN 0-7146-1557-9 Examines the challenges Nehru faced in his life and political career.

Gopal, S. *The Mind of Jawaharlal Nehru.* Apt 1980 $3.95. ISBN 0-86131-205-8 Analyzes the thinking and philosophy of the Indian prime minister.

Hayes, John, and Lila Finck. *Jawaharlal Nehru. World Leaders—Past and Present Ser.* Chelsea 1987 $17.95. ISBN 0-87754-543-X Introductory biography of the Indian leader who became the first prime minister after India won independence from Great Britain.

*Rau, M. *Nehru for Children.* Auromere 1979 $5.50. ISBN 0-89744-159-1 Readable account of the noted Indian leader; especially suitable for young readers.

EUROPE AND THE SOVIET UNION

Abel, Elie. *The Shattered Bloc: Behind the Upheaval in Eastern Europe.* Houghton 1990 $20.95. ISBN 0-395-42019-9

Ash, Timothy, G. *The Magic Lantern: The Revolution of 1989 Witnessed in Warsaw, Budapest, Berlin, and Prague.* Random 1990 $17.95. ISBN 0-394-58884-3

Barraclough, Geoffrey. *The Origins of Modern Germany.* Norton 1984 $12.70. ISBN 0-393-30153-2

Black, Cyril E. *Understanding Soviet Politics: The Perspective of Russian History.* Westview 1986 $17.00. ISBN 0-8133-0403-2

*Bradley, John. *The Soviet Union: Will Perestroika Work?* Watts 1989 $11.90. ISBN 0-531-17170-1 Introduction to the challenges faced by Soviet leader Mikhail Gorbachev in restructuring the Soviet economy.

Braun, Aurel, ed. *The Soviet-East European Relationship in the Gorbachev Era: The Prospects for Adaptation.* Westview 1990 $29.00.

Brumberg, Abraham. *Chronicle of a Revolution: A Western-Soviet Inquiry Into Perestroika.* Pantheon 1990 $14.95. ISBN 0-679-72956-9

Budge, Ian, and David McKay. *The Changing British Political System: Into the 1990s.* Longman 1988 $17.95. ISBN 0-582-02041-7

Conquest, Robert. *The Harvest of Sorrow: Soviet Collectivization and the Terror-Famine.* Oxford Univ Pr 1987 $9.95. ISBN 0-19-505180-7

Cook, Don. *Forging the Alliance: NATO, 1945–1950.* Morrow 1990 $9.95. ISBN 0-688-10000-7

Dahrendorf, Ralf. *Reflections on the Revolution in Europe.* Times Bks 1990 $17.95. ISBN 0-8129-1883-5

*DuPlessix Gray, Francine. *Soviet Women: Walking the Tightrope.* Doubleday 1990 $19.95. ISBN 0-385-24757-5 Discusses the rights of Soviet women and the effects of the policies of greater freedom and openness called glasnost.

Echikson, William. *Lighting the Night: Revolution in Eastern Europe.* Morrow 1990 $24.95. ISBN 0-688-09200-4

*Fairfield, Sheila. *People and Nations of Europe.* People and Nations Ser. Gareth Stevens 1988 $12.45. ISBN 1-55532-906-3 Provides insight on the people and nations of Europe.

Golden, James R., *et al* (eds). *NATO at Forty: Change, Continuity, and Prospects for the Future.* Westview 1989 $35.00. ISBN 0-8133-0943-3

*Goldman, Minton F. *Global Studies: Soviet Union and Eastern Europe.* Dushkin 1988 $10.95. ISBN 0-87967-744-9 Geographic, historic, political, and economic information on the Soviet Union and Eastern Europe.

Hoffman, George W. *Geography of Europe: Problems and Prospects.* Wiley 1983 $52.50. ISBN 0-471-89708-6

Kaplan, Lawrence S. *N.A.T.O. and the United States: The Enduring Alliance.* International History Ser. G. K. Hall 1988 $10.95. ISBN 0-8057-9200-7

*Kurland, Gerald. *Czechoslovakian Crisis of 1968.* Events of Our Times Ser. SamHar $3.95. ISBN 0-87157-716-X Account of Soviet repression of the Czechoslovakian reform movement of 1968.

Laqueur, Walter. *Europe Since Hitler: The Rebirth of Europe.* Penguin 1982 $10.95. ISBN 0-14-021411-9

Longford, Elizabeth. *The Queen: The Life of Elizabeth II.* Ballantine 1984 $4.95. ISBN 0-345-32004-2

Longford, Elizabeth. *The Royal House of Windsor.* Crown 1984 $16.95. ISBN 0-517-55586-7

*Lye, Keith. *Europe.* Today's World Ser. Watts 1987 $12.40. ISBN 0-531-17068-3 Readable illustrated introduction to Europe today.

Mayne, Richard (ed). *Western Europe.* Handbooks to the Modern World Ser. Facts on File $45.00. ISBN 0-8160-1251-X

*Popescu, Julian. *Czechoslovakia.* Let's Visit Places and Peoples of the World Ser. Chelsea 1988 $13.95. ISBN 0-222-00923-3 Examines this Eastern European country and its people; especially suited to younger readers.

Ramm, Agatha. *Europe in the Twentieth Century.* Grant and Temperley's Europe in the Nineteenth and Twentieth Centuries Ser. Longman 1984 $15.95. ISBN 0-582-49028-6

*Resnick, Abraham. *Siberia and the Soviet Far East: Unmasking the Myths.* GEM 1985 $10.95. ISBN 0-86596-075-5 Discussion of the region and the people; especially suited to younger readers.

Ripka, Hubert. *Czechoslovakia Enslaved: The Story of the Communist Coup D'Etat.* Hyperion 1979 repr of 1950 ed $27.50. ISBN 0-88355-710-X

*Roberts, Elizabeth. *Europe, 1992.* Watts 1990 $11.95. ISBN 0-531-17204-X Discusses the potential future of Europe in 1992 as a result of greater economic integration within the European Community and Common Market.

Rugg, Dean S. *Eastern Europe.* World's Landscapes Ser. Wiley 1986 $36.95. ISBN 0-470-20715-9

*Sakharov, Andrei. *Memoirs.* Richard Lourie (tr). Knopf 1990 $29.95. ISBN 0-394-53740-8 Account of the harassment and injustice suffered by the notable exiled Soviet nuclear physicist and human rights advocate.

Schopflin, George (ed). *The Soviet Union and Eastern Europe.* Handbooks to the World Ser. Facts on File 1986 $45.00. ISBN 0-8160-1260-1

Shipler, David K. *Broken Idols, Solemn Dreams.* Penguin 1987 $9.95. ISBN 0-14-010376-7

Shoemaker, M. Wesley. *Soviet Union and Eastern Europe.* World Today Ser. Stryker-Post 1988 $6.50. ISBN 0-943448-44-1

Smith, Hedrick. *The Russians.* Ballantine 1984 $5.95. ISBN 0-345-31746-7

Staercke, André De (ed). *NATO's Anxious Birth: The Prophetic Vision of the 1940s.* St. Martin's 1985 $29.95.

Tomas Masaryk: President of Czechoslovakia. World Leaders—Past and Present Ser. Chelsea 1989 $17.95. ISBN 1-55546-816-0

Treadgold, Donald W. *Twentieth Century Russia.* Westview 1988 $24.95. ISBN 0-8133-0507-1

Warmenhoven, Henri J. *Global Studies: Western Europe.* Dushkin 1989 $10.95. ISBN 0-87967-693-0

*Willis, David K. *Klass: How Russians Really Live.* Avon 1987 $4.50. ISBN 0-380-70263-0
Focuses on how the Soviet system affects the daily life of the people.

GORBACHEV, MIKHAIL SERGEYEVICH 1931–

Born into a peasant family in the Stavropol region of southern Russia, Gorbachev witnessed the destruction of parts of his homeland by the Germans in World War II. In 1952, he entered Moscow University, where he studied law and joined the Communist party. After graduating he returned to Stavropol to work as an agricultural specialist. At the same time, he began to rise steadily in the Communist hierarchy, becoming party leader of the Stavropol region in 1970, a member of the Central Committee in 1971, a full member of the Central Communist party committee, the Politburo, in 1980, and, in 1982, the right-hand man of Soviet leader and Communist party secretary Yuri Andropov. In 1985, Gorbachev became Soviet leader and general secretary of the Communist party. His coming to power marked a historic moment in the history of the Soviet Union. No other Soviet leader had displayed the charisma, charm, sophistication, and confident personality that is Gorbachev's.

Since coming to power, Gorbachev, through his programs of "glasnost" and "perestroika," has led the reorganization of the Soviet Union's political and economic structure and has allowed greater freedom and openness in Soviet society. As part of the Soviet Union's political restructuring, Gorbachev assumed the new position of president in 1989. In 1990, he received the Nobel Peace Prize for his efforts in foreign affairs—withdrawing Soviet forces from Afghanistan, permitting political reforms in Eastern Europe, and easing tensions with the United States. In 1991, after a failed coup against him, he abolished the Communist party and resigned as its head. He then freed the Baltic states, after which he set up a power-sharing agreement with the remaining republics. Due in part to his efforts, the cold war was effectively ended and prospects for peace between the world's superpowers seemed greater than any time during the past 50 years.

BOOKS BY GORBACHEV

At the Summit: A New Start in U.S.–Soviet Relations. Eagle Pub Corp 1988 $18.95. ISBN 0-931933-80-3

The Challenges of Our Time: Disarmament and Social Progress. Intl Pubs 1986 $4.95. ISBN 0-7178-0642-1

The Coming Century of Peace. Stewart Richardson (ed). Eagle Pub Corp 1986 $17.95. ISBN 0-931933-22-6

Peace Has No Alternative: Speeches, Articles, Interviews. South Asia Bks 1986 $44.00. ISBN 0-317-61128-3

Perestroika: New Thinking for Our Country and the World. Harper 1988 $8.95. ISBN 0-06-091528-5

Books about Gorbachev

Ashlund, Anders. *Gorbachev's Struggle for Reform.* Cornell Univ Pr 1989 $12.95. ISBN 0-8014-9590-3 Examines the Soviet president's policies and efforts at reforming his nation.

*Butson, Thomas. *Mikhail Gorbachev. World Leaders—Past and Present Ser.* Chelsea 1989 $9.95. ISBN 0-7910-0571-2 Introductory biography of the Soviet president who changed his country during the 1980s and early 1990s; especially suitable for younger readers.

Butson, Thomas G. *Gorbachev: A Biography.* Scarborough Hse 1986 $8.95. ISBN 0-8128-6249-X Standard account of the Soviet leader and architect of political and economic reform.

Morrison, Donald (ed). *Mikhail S. Gorbachev: An Intimate Biography.* NAL 1988 $4.50. ISBN 0-317-70077-4 Focuses on the life and thinking of the reform-minded Soviet president.

*Oleksy, Walter. *Mikhail Gorbachev: A Leader for Soviet Change.* Childrens 1989 $10.95. ISBN 0-516-03265-8 Richly detailed biography that uses many quotations from primary sources.

Sheehy, Gail. *Gorbachev: The Man Who Changed the World.* Harper 1990 $18.95. ISBN 0-06-016547-2 Comprehensive look at Gorbachev's leadership and policies and its effect on world affairs.

THATCHER, MARGARET   1925–

Margaret Thatcher, British Conservative politician and the first woman prime minister in British history, was born in 1925 in Grantham, England. The daughter of a shopkeeper, Thatcher attended Oxford University on a scholarship and received a degree in chemistry. After graduating, she worked as a chemist, but her interests soon led her to law and politics. After two unsuccessful runs for Parliament, Thatcher was finally elected to the House of Commons in 1959 and soon was recognized as a forceful speaker and personality. In 1970 she became a member of the cabinet and in 1975 was chosen as leader of the Conservative party. In 1979, after an energetic campaign that focused on Britain's inflation and other economic problems, Thatcher led the Conservatives to victory and became prime minister.

During her 12 years in office, Thatcher instituted numerous economic changes. She sold off billions of dollars worth of state-owned businesses, as well as tens of thousands of publicly owned housing units. She cut both taxes and government spending and supported a strong military, which she used against Argentina in a war over the Falkland Islands in 1982.

By the late 1980s, Thatcher had antagonized large numbers of British voters. Her opposition to Great Britain's participation in the movement toward greater economic and political cooperation within the European Community was questioned by many British, who feared being left out of a more unified and prosperous European market. Her support of a flat-rate, per-head tax to replace British property taxes was also met with tremendous resistance and public outcry, since it lowered the tax burden on large property owners and raised it on lower- and middle-class homeowners and on poor people who did not own homes.

By December 1990, Thatcher's support had severely eroded. Realizing that she would be defeated as party leader in a general election, Thatcher resigned as prime minister, a post she had held longer than any other person in the last 160 years.

Book by Thatcher

In Defense of Freedom. Prometheus Bks 1987 $17.95. ISBN 0-87975-401-X

Books about Thatcher

Byrd, Peter (ed). *British Foreign Policy Under Thatcher.* St. Martin's 1988 $45.00. ISBN 0-312-02526-2 Analyzes the British prime minister's foreign policy.

Ewing, K. D., and C. A. Gearty. *Freedom Under Thatcher: Civil Liberties in Modern Britain.* Oxford Univ Pr 1990 $11.95. ISBN 0-19-825414-8 Examines Thatcher's views on civil liberties.

*Faber, Doris. *Margaret Thatcher: Britain's Iron Lady. Women of Our Time Ser.* Penguin 1986 $3.95. ISBN 0-14-032160-8 Account of Britain's first female prime minister and her strong leadership.

*Garfinkel, Bernard. *Margaret Thatcher. World Leaders—Past and Present Ser.* Chelsea 1985 $9.95. ISBN 0-7910-0603-4 Introductory biography of Britain's first female prime minister, elected in 1979.

*Hughes, Libby. *Madam Prime Minister: A Biography of Margaret Thatcher. People in Focus Ser.* Dillon 1989 $12.95. ISBN 0-87518-410-3 Biographical sketch of the notable British prime minister.

Kavanagh, Dennis A. *Thatcherism and British Politics: The End of Consensus?* Oxford Univ Pr 1990 $12.95. ISBN 0-19-827755-5 Examines Prime Minister Thatcher's economic and political philosophy and its effects on British government and society.

Kavanagh, Dennis A., and Anthony Seldon (eds). *The Thatcher Effect: A Decade of Change.* Oxford Univ Pr 1989 $12.95. ISBN 0-19-827746-6 Analyzes the changes brought about in Great Britain as a result of Prime Minister Thatcher's policies.

Morrissey, Mike, and Frank Gaffikin. *Northern Ireland: The Thatcher Years.* Humanities 1990 $15.00. ISBN 0-86322-907-8 Focuses on the effects of Thatcher's leadership and policies on Northern Ireland.

Walters, Alan. *Britain's Economic Renaissance: Margaret Thatcher's Reforms, 1979–1984.* Am Enterprise Inst 1986 $28.50. Looks at the effects of Thatcher's economic policies.

LATIN AMERICA

*Aquila, Juan del. *Cuba: Dilemmas of a Revolution. Profiles: Nations of Contemporary Latin America Ser.* Westview 1984 $12.95. ISBN 0-8133-0032-0 Discusses the Cuban Revolution, with an emphasis on the absence of democracy and Cuba's relations with the Soviet Union.

Bello, José M. *History of Modern Brazil, 1889–1964.* James L. Taylor (tr). Stanford Univ Pr 1966 $13.95. ISBN 0-8047-0240-3

Burns, E. Bradford. *At War in Nicaragua: The Reagan Doctrine and the Politics of Nostalgia.* Harper 1987 $14.95. ISBN 0-06-055074-0

*Burns, E. Bradford. *Latin America: A Concise Interpretive History.* Prentice 1986. ISBN 0-13-524356-4 Looks at Latin America and its transition toward a more modern society.

*Cleary, Edward L. *Crisis and Change: The Church in Latin America Today.* Orbis 1985 $12.95. ISBN 0-88344-149-7 Examination by a priest of the position of the Catholic Church in Latin America today.

Dominguez, Jorge I. *Cuba: Order and Revolution.* Harvard Univ Pr 1978 $40.00. ISBN 0-674-17925-0

Dominguez, Jorge I. *U.S. Interests and Policies in the Caribbean and Central America.* Am Enterprise Inst 1982 $6.50. ISBN 0-8447-1097-0

Dominguez, Jorge I., and Raphael Hernandez (eds). *U.S.–Cuban Relations in the 1990s.* Westview 1989 $14.95. ISBN 0-8133-0884-4

*Fairfield, Sheila. *People and Nations of the Americas. People and Nations Ser.* Gareth Stevens 1988 $12.45. ISBN 1-55532-904-7 Provides insight on the people, societies, and nations of Latin America.

Madariaga, Salvador de. *Latin America: Between the Eagle and the Bear.* Greenwood 1976 repr of 1962 ed $35.00. ISBN 0-8371-8423-1

*Mintz, Sidney, and Sally Price (eds). *Caribbean Contours.* Johns Hopkins Univ Pr 1985

$9.95. ISBN 0-8018-3272-1 Describes the ethnic and cultural diversity of the Caribbean region.

*Morner, Magnus. *The Andean Past: Land Societies and Conflicts.* Columbia Univ Pr 1984 $35.00. ISBN 0-231-04726-6 Discusses the processes of change and adaptation in the nations of Bolivia, Peru, and Ecuador.

Morris, Arthur. *Latin America: Economic Development and Regional Differences.* B & N Imports 1981 $27.50. ISBN 0-389-20194-4

*Nash, June, and Helen Safa (eds). *Women and Change in Latin America: New Directions in Sex and Class.* Bergin & Garvey 1985 $18.95. ISBN 0-89789-070-1 Discusses the role of women in Latin American societies.

Nash, June, *et al. Ideology and Social Change in Latin America.* Gordon & Breach 1977 $33.00. ISBN 0-677-04170-5

*Perl, Lila, and Alma F. Ada. *Piñatas and Paper Flowers—Piñatas y Flores de Papel: Holidays of the Americas in English and Spanish.* Ticknor & Fields 1985 $5.95. ISBN 0-89919-155-X Describes holidays and festive customs in Latin America.

Raptis, Michael. *Revolution and Counter Revolution in Chile.* St. Martin's 1975 $29.95. ISBN 0-312-67970-X

*Ribaroff, Margaret Flesher. *Mexico and the United States Today: Issues Between Neighbors.* Watts 1985 $12.90. ISBN 0-531-04757-1 Good introduction to some of the problems and attitudes between Mexico and the United States.

Rojo, Grinor, and John J. Hassett. *Chile: Dictatorship and the Struggle for Democracy.* Edins Hispamerica 1988 $15.00. ISBN 0-935318-14-3

*Rudolph, James (ed). *Honduras: A Country Study.* Area Handbook Ser. USGPO 1984 $13.00. ISBN 0-318-21841-0 Focuses on social, economic, and political developments in contemporary Honduras.

*Rudolph, James D. (ed). *Mexico: A Country Study.* Area Handbook Ser. USGPO 1985 $16.00. ISBN 0-318-19934-3 Focuses on social, economic, and political developments in contemporary Mexico.

*Rudolph, James D. (ed). *Nicaragua: A Country Study.* Area Handbook Ser. USGPO 1987 $12.00. Focuses on social, economic, and political developments in Nicaragua.

*Sexton, James D. *Campesino: The Diary of a Guatemalan Indian.* Univ of Arizona Pr 1985 $29.95. ISBN 0-8165-0814-3 Examines the daily life and troubled times of a Guatemalan Indian.

Thomas, Hugh S., *et al.* (eds). *The Cuban Revolution Twenty-five Years Later.* CSIS Significant Issues Ser. Westview 1984 $23.00. ISBN 0-8133-7007-8

See also Vol. 2, Geography: Regions: Latin America *and* Vol. 1, World Literature: Latin Literature.

CASTRO, FIDEL   1927–

Cuban revolutionary leader Fidel Castro was born in eastern Cuba in 1927. The son of well-to-do farmers, he studied law at the University of Havana, where he read the works of the German Socialist Karl Marx (*see* Marx, Vol. 2, Economics: Comparative Economic Systems) and Russian revolutionary V. I. Lenin (*see* Lenin, Vol. 2, World History: The Rise of Totalitarian States) and became active in student politics. While touring Latin America in 1948, he witnessed a two-day riot in Bogotá, Colombia, which erupted after the assassination of a popular leftist politician. This experience may have encouraged Castro to consider the possibilities of revolution.

In 1952, the brutal and corrupt Cuban dictator Fulgencio Batista, who had run the country directly or indirectly since 1934, seized power again in a military coup. In July of the following year, Castro and a band of followers that included his brother Rául, attacked the military barracks at Santiago in an attempt to launch a revolution. The attempted coup failed, and the Castro brothers were sentenced to prison. His efforts, however, had made Castro a symbol of the opposition to Batista. Granted amnesty in 1954, Castro and his brother Rául went to Mexico, where they organized a group of revolutionaries called the Twenty-sixth of July Movement. Two years later, Castro and his followers landed in Cuba and began waging guerrilla warfare against Batista. Gradually, the revolution gained more fighters, and in January 1959 Batista fled the country. In February of that year Castro became leader of the country, a position he has maintained ever since.

Although Castro came to power as a nationalist, he soon began to move Cuba toward Communism. On the economic front, his government broke up large estates, nationalized most major businesses, guaranteed a job to every citizen, and provided free education and health care for all. This gained Castro the support of Cuba's lower class but caused many members of the upper and middle classes to flee to the United States. On the political front, Castro set up a one-party, Communist dictatorship that controls almost all aspects of life in Cuba. Castro's support of party revolution and revolutionary movements in other countries has made him a controversial political figure.

BOOKS BY CASTRO

Fidel and Religion: Castro Talks on Revolution and Religion with Frei Betto. (coauthored with Frei Betto) Simon 1988 $8.95. ISBN 0-671-66237-6

Fidel by Fidel: A New Interview with Dr. Fidel Castro Ruz, President of the Republic of Cuba. Great Issues of the Day Ser. (coauthored with others) Borgo $12.95. ISBN 0-89370-430-X

Fidel Castro Speeches: Building Socialism in Cuba. Michael Taber (ed). Vol. 2 Pathfinder Pr 1983 $11.95. ISBN 0-87348-650-1

Fidel Castro Speeches, Nineteen Eighty-Four to Nineteen Eighty-Five: War and Crisis in the Americas. *Fidel Castro Speeches Ser.* Michael Taber (ed). Pathfinder Pr 1985 $10.95. ISBN 0-87348-657-9

History Will Absolve Me. Robert Taber (tr). Carol 1984 $3.95. ISBN 0-8065-0852-3

In Defense of Socialism: Four Speeches on the 30th Anniversary of the Cuban Revolution. Pathfinder Pr 1989 $7.95. ISBN 0-87348-539-4

BOOKS ABOUT CASTRO

Bourne, Peter G. *Fidel.* Dodd 1986 $18.95. ISBN 0-396-08518-0 An objective biography of the Cuban leader with details on life inside his country.

Elliot, J. M., and M. M. Dymally. *Fidel Castro: Nothing Can Stop the Course of History.* Pathfinder Pr 1986 $9.95. ISBN 0-87348-661-7 Contains interviews conducted with Castro in 1984 on U.S.–Cuban relations.

Larzelere, Alex. *Castro's Ploy, America's Dilemma: The 1980 Cuba Boatlift.* USGPO 1988 $16.00. Analysis of the events leading up to the Cuban Boatlift and its results.

Llerena, Mario. *The Unsuspected Revolution: The Birth and Rise of Castroism.* Cornell Univ Pr 1978 $32.50. ISBN 0-8014-1094-1 Examines the rise of Castro and his coming to power in Cuba.

Montaner, Carlos A. *Fidel Castro and the Cuban Revolution: Age, Position, Character, Destiny, Personality, and Ambition.* Transaction 1989 $29.95. ISBN 0-88738-235-5 Comprehensive look at Castro and his leadership.

Szulc, Tad. *Fidel: A Critical Portrait.* Avon 1987 $5.95. ISBN 0-380-69956-7 Critical examination of the life and influence of the Cuban Communist leader.

HEYERDAHL, THOR 1914–

A well-known ethnologist and adventurer, Thor Heyerdahl was born in Larvik, Norway, in 1914. While a young man, he did anthropological research in the Marquesas Islands, a part of French Polynesia. While there he conceived a theory that the ancestors of present-day Polynesians originally came from South America. To test his theory, Heyerdahl navigated a primitive raft from Peru to Polynesia in 1947, recounting the details of his voyage in his book, *Kon-Tiki* (1950). Some years later, to test a hypothesis that the pre-Columbian cultures of the Western Hemisphere might have been influenced by ancient Egyptians, Heyerdahl constructed a facsimile of an ancient Egyptian reed boat, which he called the *Ra*. Unsuccessful on his first attempt to cross the Atlantic Ocean in 1969, Heyerdahl tried again in 1971 and succeeded in reaching the east coast of Central America. These journeys were recounted in his book *The Ra Expeditions* (1971) and in a documentary film.

In 1977, in a further effort to show that ancient mariners were agents of cultural diffusion, Heyerdahl and an international crew attempted another voyage. This time they traveled on a reed boat down the Tigris River, through the Persian Gulf, and across the Arabian Sea to Southeast Asia, then made a return voyage to the Red Sea. This expedition demonstrated the possibility that ancient Sumerians could have made contact with distant peoples and cultures, a theory Heyerdahl proposed in his book *The Tigris Expedition* (1979). In *Early Man and the Ocean: A Search for the Beginnings of Navigation and Seaborne Civilizations* (1979), Heyerdahl summarized the main findings from his several expeditions, as well as submitting additional evidence. Despite Heyerdahl's findings, many members of the scientific community have held back acceptance of his theories.

BOOKS BY HEYERDAHL

Easter Island. Random 1989 $24.95. ISBN 0-394-57906-2
Kon-Tiki: Across the Pacific by Raft. Rand 1984 $16.95. ISBN 0-528-81035-9
Ra Expeditions (1971). State Mutual 1971 $100.00.

BOOK ABOUT HEYERDAHL

Blassingame, Wyatt. *Thor Heyerdahl: Viking Scientist.* Lodestar 1979. (o.p.) $7.95. Examines the life, work, and accomplishments of the Norwegian anthropologist and adventurer.

THE MIDDLE EAST

Anderson, Roy R., *et al. Politics and Change in the Middle East: Sources of Conflict and Accommodation.* Prentice 1987. ISBN 0-13-685207-6
Bakhash, Shaul. *Reign of the Ayatollahs: Iran and the Islamic Revolutions.* Basic 1986 $10.95. ISBN 0-465-06889-8
CARDRI Staff. *Saddam's Iraq: Revolution or Reaction?* Humanities 1989 $15.00. ISBN 0-86232-821-7
*Eban, Abba. *My People.* Random 1984 $14.95. ISBN 0-394-72759-2 Illustrated account of the Jewish people.
*Evans, Michael. *The Gulf Crisis.* Watts 1988 $11.90. ISBN 0-531-17110-8 Easy-to-understand explanation of conflicts in the Persian Gulf area of the Middle East.
Fernea, Elizabeth Warock (ed). *Women and Family in the Middle East: New Voices of Change.* Univ of Texas Pr 1985 $11.95. ISBN 0-292-75529-5
*Forbes, William. *Fall of the Peacock Throne: The Story of Iran.* McGraw 1987. Looks at Iran's history for an explanation of the fall of Shah Mohammad Reza Pahlavi in 1979.
Friedman, Thomas L. *From Beirut to Jerusalem.* Doubleday 1990 $12.95. ISBN 0-385-41372-6
Hosni Mubarak: President of Egypt. World Leaders—Past and Present Ser. Chelsea 1989 $17.95. ISBN 1-55546-844-6 Introductory biography of the Egyptian leader who succeeded to his nation's presidency following the assassination of Anwar Sadat.

Khourie, Fred J. *The Arab–Israeli Dilemma. Contemporary Issues in the Middle East Ser.* Syracuse Univ Pr 1985 $15.95. ISBN 0-8156-2340-2

*Lawson, Don. *Libya and Qaddafi. Impact Ser.* Watts 1987 $12.90. ISBN 0-531-10329-3 Introductory account of the North African nation and its stridently anti-Western leader Muammar Qaddafi.

McCuen, Gary E. (ed). *The Iran–Iraq War. Ideas in Conflict Ser.* GEM 1987 $11.95. ISBN 0-86596-060-7

Nugent, Jeffrey B., and Theodore Thomas (eds). *Bahrain and the Gulf: Past Perspectives and Alternative Futures.* St. Martin's 1985 $25.00. ISBN 0-312-06566-3

Oz, Amos. *In the Land of Israel.* Random 1984 $6.95. ISBN 0-394-72728-2

Sadat, Jehan. *A Woman of Egypt.* Pocket 1989 $8.95. ISBN 0-671-67305-X

Said, Edward W. *After the Last Sky: Palestinian Lives.* Pantheon 1986 $17.95. ISBN 0-394-74469-1

*Shapiro, William. *Lebanon.* Watts 1984 $12.90. ISBN 0-531-04854-3 Introductory history of Lebanon and recent conflicts in that nation.

Shipler, David. *Arab and Jew: Wounded Spirits in a Promised Land.* Penguin 1987 $8.95. ISBN 0-14-010376-7

*Spencer, William. *Global Studies: Middle East.* Dushkin 1988 $10.95. ISBN 0-87967-745-7 Provides information on the geography, history, culture, politics, and economics of North Africa and the Middle East.

*Theroux, Peter. *Sandstorms: Days and Nights in Arabia.* Norton 1990 $18.95. ISBN 0-393-02841-0 Conveys the author's experiences traveling and living in Saudi Arabia.

BEN-GURION, DAVID   1886–1973

Born David Green in Poland, Ben-Gurion immigrated to Palestine in 1906, where he worked as a farm laborer and then as editor of a political party magazine. In Palestine he chose the name Ben-Gurion—"son of a lion"—as a sign of devotion to his Jewish heritage. During World War I, Ben-Gurion was arrested and then deported by the Turks. Eventually he made his way to the United States, where he encouraged American Jews to emigrate to Palestine and to become part of the struggle to achieve a Jewish homeland. On returning to Palestine in 1918, he helped organize support for the British, who had promised in the Balfour Declaration of 1917 to assist Jews in establishing a homeland in Palestine. Although Ben-Gurion also supported the British during World War II, he later led the resistance movement against them when they failed to keep their promise of carving a Jewish state out of Palestine.

After Israel's independence was proclaimed in 1948, Ben-Gurion became the new nation's first prime minister and, except for two years (1953–1955), continued serving in that office until 1963. After finally leaving office, Ben-Gurion continued to influence the political life of Israel through his presence and his writings. Among his writings are *Israel: Years of Challenge* (1965), *The Jews in Their Land* (1966), *Memoirs* (1970), *Israel: A Political History* (1971), and *My Talks with the Arabs* (1973). Ben-Gurion died a national hero in 1973.

BOOK BY BEN-GURION

Ben-Gurion Looks at the Bible. Jonathan Kolatch (tr). Jonathan David 1972 $12.50. ISBN 0-8246-0127-0

BOOKS ABOUT BEN-GURION

*Silverstein, Herma. *David Ben-Gurion. Impact Biography Ser.* Watts 1988 $12.90. ISBN 0-531-10509-1 Biography of the Israeli leader; especially suited to younger readers.

*Vail, John. *David Ben-Gurion. World Leaders—Past and Present Ser.* Chelsea 1987 $17.95. ISBN 0-87754-509-X Introductory biography of Ben-Gurion.

MEIR, GOLDA   1898–1978

Born Golda Mabovitch in Kiev, Russia, Golda Meir immigrated with her family to the United States in 1906, settling in Milwaukee. She became a school teacher and, early in her career, became involved in a labor movement that supported the establishment of a Jewish homeland in Palestine. In 1921 Meir and her husband, Morris Meyerson, immigrated to Palestine and joined a kibbutz, or collective settlement community. Once settled in the kibbutz, Meir (the Hebraized form of Meyerson) became the kibbutz's representative to the Histadrut, the General Federation of Jewish Labor. From 1928 to 1932 she was secretary of the Women's Labor Council and, in 1936, became head of the political department of the Histadrut.

After Israel gained its independence in 1948, Meir was appointed minister to Moscow. In 1949 she was elected to the Knesset, the Israeli Parliament, where she served as a member until 1974. From 1949 to 1956 she served as minister of labor, vigorously supporting an unrestricted policy of immigration to Israel. On the death of Prime Minister Levi Eshkol in 1969, she became interim prime minister and retained the post after the 1969 elections. Throughout her years as prime minister (1969–1974), Meir managed to retain the confidence of the coalition that kept her in power. In the Yom Kippur War with Egypt and Syria in 1973, Meir rallied Israeli defense forces to recoup from the surprise attack and force back Arab troops. In the war's aftermath, however, her popularity and that of the Labor party began to decline. Criticism over the country's lack of preparation for the war led to her resignation in 1974. Nevertheless, she continued to have a voice in the Labor party until her death in 1978. Among the books written by Meir is *My Life* (1975), her autobiography.

BOOK BY MEIR

My Life (1975). Dell 1976 $1.95. ISBN 0-440-15656-4

BOOKS ABOUT MEIR

Adler, David A. *Our Golda: The Story of Golda Meir.* Penguin 1984 $11.95. ISBN 0-670-53107-3 Comprehensive account of Israel's female prime minister.

Avallone, Michael. *A Woman Called Golda.* Dorchester 1982 $2.95. ISBN 0-8439-1114-X Examines the life and achievements of the Israeli prime minister.

*Keller, Mollie. *Golda Meir. Impact Biography Ser.* Watts 1983 $12.90. ISBN 0-531-04591-9 Biographical account of the Israeli prime minister that focuses on her role in the development of the nation.

Martin, Ralph G. *Golda Meir: The Romantic Years.* Ivy 1990 $5.95. ISBN 0-8041-0536-7 Biography that focuses on her youth, her love affairs, and her love for Israel.

McAuley, Karen. *Golda Meir. World Leaders—Past and Present Ser.* Chelsea 1985 $17.95. ISBN 0-87754-568-5 Introductory biography of the female prime minister who led Israel from 1969 to 1974.

SADAT, ANWAR   1918–1981

President of Egypt from 1970 until his assassination by terrorists in 1981, Anwar el Sadat was a lifelong proponent of Egyptian nationalism. Born in a small Egyptian village in 1918, Sadat entered a military academy in Cairo in 1936. After graduating from the academy in 1938, Sadat plotted with future

Egyptian president Gamal Abdel Nasser and other army officers to expel the British from Egypt. In 1942, he was dismissed from the army and arrested and imprisoned for participating in antigovernment activities. Reinstated in the army in 1950, Sadat joined forces with Nasser and participated in the coup that ousted Egypt's King Farouk in 1952. Sadat held several positions in the new government, including minister of state, president of the National Assembly, and two terms as Nasser's vice-president (1964–1966, 1969–1970). After Nasser's death in 1970, Sadat was elected president.

As president, Sadat had greater success in foreign relations than in efforts to modernize and diversify the Egyptian economy. In 1973 his popularity and prestige in Egypt and among Arabs everywhere received a tremendous boost when he ordered an attack on Israeli forces and regained Egyptian territory in the Sinai, which had been lost several years before. In 1978 Sadat lost some of this popularity and prestige, especially with other Arab nations, when he negotiated a peace treaty with Israel. Many Arab nations broke off diplomatic relations and Egypt found itself isolated within the Arab world. The rest of the world, however, applauded Sadat for his peacemaking efforts. As a result, Sadat and Prime Minister Menachem Begin of Israel were both awarded the Nobel Peace Prize.

Despite his prestige among Western nations, Sadat's unpopularity among Arabs grew. In 1981, while reviewing a military parade commemorating the Egyptian–Israeli War of 1973, he was assassinated by Muslim extremists.

BOOK BY SADAT

In Search of Identity: An Autobiography. Harper 1979 $9.95. ISBN 0-06-132071-4

BOOKS ABOUT SADAT

*Aufderheide, Patricia. *Anwar Sadat. World Leaders—Past and Present Ser.* Chelsea 1985 $17.95. ISBN 0-87754-560-X Introductory biography of Egyptian president Anwar Sadat; especially suitable for younger readers.

Fernandez-Armesto, Felipe. *Sadat and His Statecraft.* State Mutual 1986 $42.00. ISBN 0-946041-14-8 Examines the leadership and diplomatic achievements of the Egyptian statesman and president.

Finke, Blythe F. *Anwar Sadat, Egyptian Ruler and Peace Maker. Outstanding Personalities Ser.* SamHar 1986 $3.95. ISBN 0-87157-596-5 Focuses on Sadat's role in peacemaking between Israel and the Arab nations of the Middle East.

Friedlander, Melvin A. *Sadat and Begin: The Domestic Politics of Peacemaking.* Westview 1983 $33.00. ISBN 0-86531-949-9 Examines the domestic policies and diplomatic initiatives of Egyptian president Sadat and Israeli prime minister Menachem Begin.

*Sullivan, George. *Sadat: The Man Who Changed Mid-East History.* Walker 1981 $9.85. ISBN 0-8027-6435-5 Takes a close look at the diplomatic achievements of the Egyptian president who negotiated a peace treaty with Israel in 1978.

THE ARTS OF THE TWENTIETH CENTURY

Baker, Kenneth. *Minimalism: Art of Circumstance.* Abbeville 1989 $39.95. ISBN 0-89659-887-X

*Baryshnikov, Mikhail. *Baryshnikov.* Charles E. France (ed). Abrams 1980 $16.95. ISBN 0-8109-2225-8 Autobiographical account of the famous ballet dancer.

*Eisler, Colin. *Paintings in the Hermitage.* Stewart Tabori & Chang 1990 $95.00. ISBN 1-55670-159-4 Discussion of the works found in Leningrad's Hermitage museum.

Fauchereau, Serge. *Braque.* Rizzoli 1987 $19.95. ISBN 0-8478-0794-0

*Fonteyn, Margot. *The Magic of Dance.* Knopf 1982 $22.45. ISBN 0-394-52906-5 Illustrated description of dance by a renowned English ballerina.

Fonteyn, Margot. *Margot Fonteyn: Autobiography.* Knopf 1976 $16.45. ISBN 0-394-48570-X

Fry, Edward F. *Cubism. World of Art Ser.* Thames Hudson 1985 $11.95. ISBN 0-500-20047-5

Gordon, Donald E. *Expressionism: Art and Idea.* Yale Univ Pr $50.00. ISBN 0-300-03310-9

*Greenfield, Howard. *Marc Chagall. First Impressions Ser.* Abrams 1990 $17.95. ISBN 0-8109-3152-4 Well-illustrated biography of the noted modern artist.

Jencks, Charles. *Post-Modernism: The New Classicism in Art and Architecture.* Rizzoli 1987 $75.00. ISBN 0-8478-0835-1

*Keightley, Moy. *Investigating Art: A Practical Guide for Young People.* Facts on File $17.95. ISBN 0-87196-973-4 Easy-to-read illustrated guide to the subject of art.

Klee, Paul. *Drawings of Paul Klee. Master Draughtsman Ser.* Max Huggler (ed). Borden $4.95. ISBN 0-87505-168-5

Lippard, Lucy R. *Pop Art. World of Art Ser.* Thames Hudson 1985 $11.95. ISBN 0-500-20052-1

Munson-Williams-Proctor Institute. *Olympics in Art: An Exhibition of Works Related to Olympic Sports.* Univ of Washington Pr 1980 $12.95. ISBN 0-295-96399-9

Penrose, Roland. *Pablo Picasso Eighteen Eighty-One to Nineteen Seventy-Three.* Crown 1988 $22.95. ISBN 0-517-66846-7

Rubin, William S. *Dada, Surrealism and Their Heritage.* Museum of Modern Art 1968 $14.50. ISBN 0-87070-284-X

Shapiro, David, and Cecile Shapiro. *Abstract Expressionism: A Critical Record.* Cambridge Univ Pr 1989 $17.95. ISBN 0-521-36733-6

Smakov, Gennady. *The Great Russian Dancers.* Knopf 1985 $44.50. ISBN 0-394-51074-7

*Taper, Bernard. *Balanchine: A Biography.* Univ of California Pr 1987 $12.95. ISBN 0-520-06059-8 Biographical account of a world-renowned choreographer and teacher of dance.

BARTOK, BELA   1881–1945

One of the outstanding composers of the twentieth century, Béla Bartók was born in Hungary in 1881. His mother began to teach him piano at the age of five, and by age nine he had begun to compose his own music. Between 1899 and 1903 he attended the Academy of Music in Budapest and was appointed professor of piano there in 1907.

Bartók's early compositions were not well received by the public, and in 1905 he turned his attention to the collection and cataloging of folk music of his native Hungary, as well as other countries. With the help of his friend and fellow Hungarian composer Zoltán Kodály, Bartók produced a series of commentaries, anthologies, and arrangements of the folk music he had collected. Bartók's interest in folk music had a profound effect on his compositions. The influence can be seen in the unadorned power of his music, especially in the rhythmic drive of fast movements, and in his use of folk melodies, rhythms, and harmonic patterns.

Throughout his life, Bartók had to struggle to make a living. Yet he refused to teach musical composition, believing that this would inhibit his own composing. Instead, he earned a living teaching piano and performing. During the 1920s he traveled throughout Europe giving piano recitals, and in 1927 and 1928 he made a concert tour of the United States.

In 1940, after the outbreak of World War II, Bartók left Hungary to settle in the United States, where he continued to perform and compose music. Still plagued by financial problems, he died penniless in 1945 of leukemia. Among his most famous compositions are the *Mikrocosmos* (1926–1927), the *Concerto for Orchestra* (1943), and *Music for Strings, Percussion, and Celeste* (1936).

BOOK BY BARTOK

Béla Bartók: Essays. Benjamin Suchoff (ed). St. Martin's 1976. (o.p.)

BOOKS ABOUT BARTOK

Juhasz, Vilmos. *Bartók's Years in America.* Occidental 1981 $10.00. ISBN 0-911050-51-5
    Discusses American influences on the Hungarian composer's music.
Milne, Hammish. *Bartók: His Life and Times.* Midas 1981 $40.00. Comprehensive account
    of the composer's life and work.
Moreux, Serge. *Béla Bartók.* G. S. Fraser and Erik De Mauny (trs). Vienna 1974 $7.50.
    ISBN 0-8443-0105-1 Focuses on Bartok's interest in folk music and its influence
    on his music.
Stevens, Halsey. *Life and Music of Béla Bartók.* Oxford Univ Pr 1967 repr of 1964 ed $6.95.
    Scholarly examination of Bartók's life and music.

BRITTEN, BENJAMIN 1913–1976

Considered the most significant British composer since the seventeenth-century composer Henry Purcell, (*see* Purcell, Vol. 2, World History: The Arts in Eighteenth-Century Europe), Benjamin Britten excelled in composing series of songs and other types of vocal music, including operas. A conscientious objector in World War II, Britten's *War Requiem* (1962) is a moving tribute to the victims of war everywhere. The composition, which incorporates parts for soloists, choruses, and orchestra, is based on the Latin text of the Mass for the Dead and verses by Wilfred Owen, a young English soldier killed in World War I. (*See* Owen, Vol. 1, British Literature: The Twentieth Century.) Following its first performance at Coventry Cathedral in the city of Coventry, England, it received worldwide acclaim.

Pursuing a youthful interest in the piano, Britten studied at the Royal College of Music in London. His work drew the favorable attention of critics with the premiere of *Fantasy Quartet for Oboe and Strings* in 1934. After World War II, Britten devoted himself principally to composing operas. His first operatic work was *Paul Bunyan* (1941), a choral operetta about a lumberjack who liked to sing ballads. Britten's two most successful operas are *Peter Grimes* (1945) and *The Turn of the Screw* (1954). Other operas by Britten include *The Rape of Lucretia* (1946), *A Midsummer Night's Dream* (1960), and *Death in Venice* (1973). Using a remarkable sensitivity to text, Britten evolved vocal melodic lines followed by orchestral interludes, which punctuate and enhance the dramatic flow of his operas.

BOOKS ABOUT BRITTEN

Brett, Philip (ed). *Benjamin Britten: Peter Grimes.* Cambridge Univ Pr 1983 $10.95. ISBN
    0-521-29716-8 Looks closely at *Peter Grimes,* one of the composer's most successful
    operas.
Evans, Peter. *The Music of Benjamin Britten.* Univ of Minnesota Pr 1979 $29.50. ISBN

0-8166-0836-9 Comprehensive examination of the noted British composer's music.

*Holst, Imogen. *Britten. The Great Composers Ser.* Faber & Faber 1980 $10.95. ISBN 0-571-18000-0 Takes a close look at one of Britain's most celebrated modern composers.

Kennedy, Michael. *Britten. Master Musicians Ser.* Biblio Dist 1981 $17.95. ISBN 0-460-03175-9 Discusses Britten's life and music from childhood through death.

Mitchell, Donald (ed). *Benjamin Britten: A Commentary on His Works from a Group of Specialists.* Greenwood 1972 repr of 1953 and $35.00. ISBN 0-8371-5623-8 Discussion and analysis of the composer's works by musical specialists.

Palmer, Christopher (ed). *The Britten Companion.* Cambridge Univ Pr 1984 $12.95. ISBN 0-521-27844-9 Guide to Britten's life and musical compositions.

White, Eric W. *Benjamin Britten: His Life and Operas.* John Evans (ed). Univ of California Pr 1983 $14.95. ISBN 0-520-04894-6 Critical biography of the British composer and discussion of his operas.

Whittall, Arnold. *The Music of Britten and Tippett: Studies in Themes and Techniques.* Cambridge Univ Pr 1982 $54.50. ISBN 0-521-23523-5 Compares and contrasts Britten and Tippett from the 1930s on.

CHAGALL, MARC 1887–1985

The paintings of the Russian artist Marc Chagall present a colorful fantasy world steeped in images from Russian country life and the heritage of Jewish folklore and religion. Chagall was born Moyshe Shagal in Vitebsk, Russia, of poor Jewish parents. At age 20, Chagall left his native village to study art at the Imperial School of Fine Arts in St. Petersburg, later known as Leningrad. The instruction there failed to inspire his imagination, however, and he began attending the classes of the theater designer Leon Baskt, where the atmosphere was more informal and supportive of Chagall's creative vision.

From 1910 to 1914 Chagall studied in Paris and came in contact with such early modern painters as the Spanish artist Pablo Picasso and the French artist Henri Matisse. Although his studies in Paris broadened his outlook and increased his technical skill, they did not change his fundamental view of the world, which remained true to his Russian Jewish roots. By 1915, Chagall's artistic style was firmly established, and it changed little during the rest of his life.

After the Russian Revolution in 1917, Chagall was made commissar of fine arts in his native Vitebsk, but he resigned his position after differences of opinion with Communist officials. In 1922 he left Russia and went first to Berlin and then to Paris, where he painted and developed a second career as a graphic artist.

In 1941, Chagall left France to escape the Nazi occupation and went to the United States. He remained there until 1948, when he returned to France. In later years, Chagall was commissioned to create several monumental works. They include 12 stained-glass windows for a synagogue in Jerusalem, ceiling decorations for the Paris Opera, and two enormous murals for the Metropolitan Opera House in New York City.

BOOKS BY CHAGALL

My Life (1965). Dorothy Williams (tr). Oxford Univ Pr 1989 $9.95. ISBN 0-19-282621-2

Chagall Lithographs VI (1978–1985). Crown 1986 $85.00. ISBN 0-517-56440-8

Chagall in Chicago. Spertus 1979 $3.00. ISBN 0-935982-15-9

BOOKS ABOUT CHAGALL

Alexander, Sidney. *Marc Chagall: An Intimate Biography.* Paragon Hse 1988 $16.95. ISBN 1-55778-135-4 Comprehensive biography of the notable Russian artist.

Kagan, Andrew. *Marc Chagall. Abbeville Modern Master Ser.* Abbeville 1989 $19.95. ISBN 0-89659-935-3 Interesting presentation of the artist's work.

Voznesensky, Andrei, *et al. Chagall Discovered: From Russia and Private Collections.* H. L. Levin 1988 $50.00. ISBN 0-88363-373-6 Focuses on Chagall's works that are held by private art collectors and by Russian museum collections.

DEBUSSY, ACHILLE CLAUDE 1862–1918

The French composer Claude Debussy is regarded as the chief musical figure in the early twentieth-century impressionist school of music, which was centered in Paris. Debussy showed great musical talent at an early age and began studying music at the Paris Conservatory at age 10. By age 22 he had won the distinguished music award, the Grand Prix de Rome. In Debussy's compositions, his use of the whole-tone scale, common to Oriental music, and other Asian and Russian elements led to expressive harmonies and the achievement of surprising nuances of mood. He also used numerous harsh-sounding harmonies and other new and original compositional techniques and elements. His music, like impressionist painting and poetry, stirs the imagination by its evocation of dreamlike sights and sounds. Because of his revolutionary changes and inventions, Debussy is considered one of the most creative and influential forces in the history of music. A list of composers influenced by his work would include nearly every distinguished composer of the first half of the twentieth century.

Prelude to the Afternoon of a Faun (1894), a tone poem, is a famous Debussy orchestral work, which has been choreographed for ballet. Other outstanding orchestral works are *Nocturnes* (1899) and *La Mer (The Sea)* (1905). Among Debussy's impressive piano works are 24 preludes, 12 études, and the *Suite Bergamesque* (1905), which contains the popular "Clair de Lune." Debussy also wrote many individual songs for voice and an opera *Pelleas et Melisande* (1892–1902), considered by many to be his masterpiece. Debussy died in Paris of cancer in 1918.

BOOKS BY DEBUSSY

Debussy Letters. François Lesure and Roger Nichols (eds). Roger Nichols (tr). Harvard Univ Pr 1987 $27.50. ISBN 0-674-19429-2

The Poetic Debussy: A Collection of His Song Texts and Selected Letters. Margaret G. Cobb (ed). Northeastern Univ Pr 1982 $30.00. ISBN 0-930350-28-6

BOOKS ABOUT DEBUSSY

Agay, Denes. *The Joy of Claude Debussy.* Music Sales 1984 $6.95. ISBN 0-8256-8029-8 Introduction to and appreciation of Debussy's music.

Holloway, Robin. *Debussy and Wagner.* Da Capo 1982 repr of 1979 ed $19.50. ISBN 0-903873-55-9 Comparative look at the work of Debussy and the German composer Richard Wagner.

Vallas, Leon. *Claude Debussy: His Life and Works.* Dover 1973 $7.95. ISBN 0-486-22916-5 Biographical approach to the French composer and his music.

Wenk, Arthur B. *Claude Debussy and the Poets.* Univ of California Pr 1976. (o.p.) $49.50. Examines the influence of contemporary poets such as Baudelaire, Verlaine, and Mallarmé on Debussy and his music.

LE CORBUSIER (PSEUDONYM OF CHARLES EDOUARD JEANNERET-GRIS) 1887–1965

The French architect Le Corbusier was one of the leading figures of modern architecture. His use of new materials—especially reinforced concrete—and mass production techniques simplified architectural design, and his radical ideas for urban design greatly changed the look of cities.

Born near Geneva, Switzerland, Le Corbusier was a lifelong Parisian by choice. After studying architecture, he turned to painting for a while but in 1922 resumed a career in architecture. By 1923 he had published his influential work *Vers une architecture (Towards a New Architecture)* and adopted the name Le Corbusier.

In the 1920s and 1930s, Le Corbusier devoted most of his time to urban planning. His new ideas for cities are laid out in the book *La ville radieuse (The Radiant City)* (1935), in which he rejects the idea of low-rise garden cities proposed by earlier planners and argues instead for high-rise cities. The buildings he designed during this period emphasize geometric forms. They consist of rectangular blocks of concrete, steel, and glass set off the ground on stilts and often topped by roof gardens.

After World War II, Le Corbusier was given an opportunity to put his ideas for urban planning into practice when the French government asked him to plan and build one of his "vertical cities" in Marseilles. The result was the *Unité d'habitation,* built between 1946 and 1952. This complex consists of 340 "superimposed villas" raised off the ground on stilts. The complex also includes elevated arcades of shops and other services and is topped by a roof-garden community center.

Le Corbusier's later work represents a turning away from geometric forms and an emphasis on sculptural and dramatic forms. This phase can be seen in his designs for the city of Chandigarh in the Punjab region of India. These designs, as well as others of Le Corbusier, opened a new chapter in the history of twentieth-century architecture. In 1965 Le Corbusier drowned in a swimming accident in the Mediterranean.

BOOKS BY LE CORBUSIER

Ideas of Le Corbusier: Architecture and Urban Planning. Jacques Guiton and Margaret Guiton (trs). Braziller 1981 $9.95.
Le Corbusier Sketchbooks. 4 vols. MIT Pr 1981–1982 $165.00 ea.
The Modulor and Modulor 2. Harvard Univ Pr 1980 $15.95. ISBN 0-674-58102-4
The Radiant City (La ville radieuse) (1935). Pamela Knight (tr). Viking 1967 $35.00.
Towards a New Architecture (1927). Dover 1986 $8.95. ISBN 0-486-25023-7

BOOKS ABOUT LE CORBUSIER

Besset, Maurice. *Le Corbusier.* Rizzoli 1987 $25.00. ISBN 0-8478-0816-5 Illustrated account of the noted Swiss architect and his work.
Blake, Peter. *The Master Builders: Le Corbusier, Mies van der Rohe, Frank Lloyd Wright.* Norton 1976 $10.95. ISBN 0-393-00796-0 Comparative examination of the designs of three famous architects.
Curtis, William. *Le Corbusier: Ideas and Forms.* Rizzoli $40.00. ISBN 0-8478-0726-6 Draws on new archival material and concentrates on Le Corbusier's formative years, architectural ideals, and social realities.
Gardiner, Stephen. *Le Corbusier. Quality Paperbacks Ser.* Da Capo 1988 $10.95. ISBN 0-306-80337-2 Biographical approach to the architect and his work.

Papadaki, Stamo (ed). *Le Corbusier: Architect, Painter, Writer.* Macmillan 1948. (o.p.) An important early book that examines various facets of Le Corbusier's talent.

Serenyi, Peter. *Le Corbusier in Perspective. Artists in Perspective Ser.* Prentice $3.95. Analyzes the architect's work in relation to other architects and architectural styles.

Van Moos, Stanlislaus. *Le Corbusier: Elements of a Synthesis.* MIT Pr $14.95. ISBN 0-262-72008-6 Standard and comprehensive biography of Le Corbusier.

PICASSO, PABLO (PABLO RUIZ Y PICASSO) 1881–1973

Considered by many the premier artist of this century, Pablo Picasso was not only a painter but a sculptor, engraver, graphic artist, and ceramist as well. As a painter alone, he created more than 6,000 works. As an artist in general, according to the estimates of one critic, he created some 50,000 works in all.

Born into a middle-class family in Málaga, Spain, Picasso displayed artistic ability at an early age. In fact, he could draw before he could talk. His father—a museum curator, art teacher, and artist—encouraged the boy's talent, and by the time the young Picasso was seven years old, his father was giving him serious instruction in art.

In 1895, Picasso's father got a new teaching post in Barcelona. Once the family had settled there, he convinced school officials at the Royal Academy of Fine Arts to allow his 14-year-old son to take the entry test for the advanced class. The two drawings that the young Picasso created for his exam so impressed the judges that they not only admitted him at once but they also classified him as a prodigy.

Two years later, Picasso went to Madrid to attend the most prestigious art school in the country—the Royal Academy of San Fernando. However, he really was not interested in going to school anymore. So, before long, he stopped going to classes and instead visited the Prado Museum, where he sketched the local people and sites.

In 1899, Picasso returned to Barcelona, where he shared a series of studios with other artists. Still restless, however, he and a friend departed for London. On the way they stopped in Paris, and Picasso decided that this was the place for him. During the next few years, he made several trips home to see his family, but he always returned to Paris. In 1904, he settled in Paris, and there he remained for more than 40 years.

In Paris, Picasso absorbed different painting techniques, which he combined with such typically Spanish subjects as the bullfight. Over the years, his personal style evolved and changed. The years 1901 to 1904 constituted his Blue Period, during which he portrayed loneliness, despair, and suffering in moody shades and tones of blue often tinged with green. During this period, he filled his paintings with stooped, angular, imaginatively distorted figures like the old man who is the subject of *The Old Guitarist* (1903). Next, from about 1904 to 1906, he changed to a style that stressed warmer colors and moods. These years were his Rose Period, when a terracotta color, a shade of deep pinkish red, and the world of the circus, of harlequins, and of dancers dominated his canvases. Typical of his Rose Period is *The Family of Saltimbanques* (1905), which depicts the circus family, and which one poet described as "a tapestry lost in the universe."

Then, in 1907, Picasso unveiled a painting that, in one author's words, "did violence to almost every precept of Western painting, recent as well as traditional." Titled *Les Demoiselles d'Avignon,* many hail it as the "first" twentieth-century painting. The focus of the painting is five huge female figures with masks rather than faces that are broken up into geometric shapes. The painting came to represent a major turning point in art because it opened the door to cubism, the school of painting and sculpture that geometrically depicts natural forms. Undaunted by criticism of his new style, Picasso experimented with increasingly analytic and geometric forms. In 1921, his Cubist style reached its highest point in *Three Musicians,* which portrays in dazzling colors a masked clown, harlequin, and monk sitting stiffly in a row. Like everything else in the painting, the three figures are abstracted into geometric forms and arranged in a flat pattern.

Meanwhile, in 1917, Picasso had gone to Rome to design costumes and scenery for the Ballets Russes. His experience in Rome and with the ballet profoundly affected his style. The result was a classic period during which he filled his canvases with massive, gentle figures like the two giantesses running joyfully along the beach in *The Race* (1922). In 1925, that period too came to an end. For the next few years, Picasso ripped apart the human body and made his subjects a mass of distorted and dislocated body parts.

In the 1930s, Picasso became concerned with political and social themes. In this vein, he painted the mural *Guernica* (1937). At the time, the Spanish Civil War was raging, and German bombers who were flying for the eventual dictator of Spain, Francisco Franco, wiped out the small Basque village of Guernica. The huge painting was Picasso's highly emotional response to the brutal bombing in particular and to the horrors of war in general. Painted in severe blacks, dead whites, and deep grays, and strewn with agonized human forms and grotesque beasts, it is considered Picasso's greatest masterpiece.

Through 1939 and the first months of World War II, Picasso's art became more and more agonized. Although he remained in France throughout the war, the Germans condemned modern art and did not allow him to exhibit his work after they occupied the country. In 1944, he joined the French Communist party. After the war, he continued to be productive, producing a stream of paintings, sculpture, drawings, and other art forms. During this period, his works developed a more relaxed and gentle feeling.

In 1955, Picasso moved to the south of France, where he continued to work until he was in his 90s. He died in 1973 in Mougins, France, leaving behind an estate valued at more than $500 million.

BOOKS BY PICASSO

Designs for "The Three-Cornered Hat" (1919). Dover 1979 $6.95. ISBN 0-486-23709-5
Desire Caught by the Tail (1941). Roland Penrose (tr). Riverrun $4.95. ISBN 0-7145-0191-3
Picasso Line Drawings and Prints. Dover 1982 $3.50. ISBN 0-486-24196-3
Picasso Lithographs: Sixty-One Works. Dover 1980 $3.50. ISBN 0-486-23949-7
Late Picasso: Paintings, Sculpture, Drawings, Prints 1953–1972. Univ of Washington Pr $29.95. ISBN 0-295-96785-4
Je Suis Le Cahier: The Sketchbooks of Picasso. (coauthored with others) Atlantic Monthly 1986 $65.00. ISBN 0-87113-072-6

BOOKS ABOUT PICASSO

*Lyttle, Richard B. *Pablo Picasso: The Man and the Image.* Macmillan 1989 $14.95. ISBN 0-689-31393-4 Details the artist's unconventional life, works, and politics.
*Raboff, Ernest. *Pablo Picasso.* Harper Jr Bks 1987 $5.95. ISBN 0-06-44067-3 Brief biography of Picasso, complete with full-color reproductions and interpretations of his works.

*Sommer, Robin L., and Patricia MacDonald. *Pablo Picasso.* Silver 1990 $14.95. ISBN 0-382-24031-6 Easy-to-read exploration of the life, inspiration, and art of Pablo Picasso.

PROKOFIEV, SERGEI 1891–1953

The music of the twentieth-century Russian composer Sergei Prokofiev is a sharp mix of traditional and modern elements. His innovative style is characterized by emotional restraint, strong drum-like rhythms, harsh-sounding harmonies, and humor.

Prokofiev was born in the town of Sontzovka in the Ukraine. His mother, an accomplished pianist, encouraged her young son to play along with her as she practiced. The young Prokofiev showed unusual talent and began composing music at the age of five. At age 13, Prokofiev entered the St. Petersburg Conservatory, where he studied with some of the finest teachers of the day, including the composer Rimsky-Korsakov. By the time he graduated in 1914, Prokofiev had established himself as a musical innovator.

In 1918, Prokofiev left Russia to appear as a pianist and conductor in Europe and the United States. While in the United States, he composed his most popular opera, *The Love of Three Oranges* (1921), a musical satire of traditional operatic plots and conventions. From 1922 to 1933, Prokofiev lived mostly in Paris, where he composed two ballets, three symphonies, and four concertos.

In 1934 Prokofiev returned to the Soviet Union. Back in his native land, Prokofiev's style mellowed and he accepted the idea that a state-supported artist must appeal to a wide audience. During the next few years he composed some of his most popular and best-known pieces, including *Peter and the Wolf* (1936) and *Romeo and Juliet* (1935–1936). In 1948, Prokofiev and other leading Russian composers were denounced by Soviet Communist party leaders for "antidemocratic tendencies alien to the Soviet people." He returned to favor in the early 1950s and enjoyed great success in the Soviet Union. By the time of his death in 1953, Prokofiev's music had become well known throughout the world.

BOOKS BY PROKOFIEV

Peter and the Wolf. Maria Carlson (tr). Penguin 1982 $12.95. ISBN 0-670-54919-3
Prokofiev by Prokofiev: A Composer's Memoir. Doubleday 1979. (o.p.) $14.00.

BOOKS ABOUT PROKOFIEV

Robinson, Harlow. *Sergei Prokofiev: A Biography.* Paragon Hse 1988 $12.95. ISBN 1-55778-009-9 Comprehensive look at the twentieth-century Russian composer.
Samuel, Claude. *Prokofiev.* Miriam John (tr). Vienna 1971 $3.95. ISBN 0-670-57956-4 Examines the life and work of the noted Russian composer.
Seroff, Victor. *Sergei Prokofiev: A Soviet Tragedy.* Taplinger 1979 $14.95. Sympathetic portrait of Prokofiev that traces both his public and private life.
Shostakovich, Dmitri, *et al. Sergei Prokofiev: Materials, Articles, Interviews.* Imported 1978 $9.45. ISBN 0-8285-1618-9 Collection of essays on Prokofiev written by scholars and contemporaries.

RAVEL, MAURICE   1875–1937

The French composer Maurice Ravel was the leading exemplar of musical impressionism, in which music attempts to create a mood or atmosphere rather than express a feeling or tell a story. Ravel entered the Paris Conservatory in 1889, where his teachers included the noted French composer Gabriel Fauré. As composer, Ravel produced highly original, fluid music, much of it within the outlines of musical classicism. He excelled at piano composition and orchestration, and his compositions reveal many of the musical trends active in Paris after the turn of the century. His coloristic effects and occasional use of whole-tone scales and tritones place him with the French composer Claude Debussy (*see* Debussy, Vol. 2, World History: The Arts of the Twentieth Century) and the impressionists. Yet the sense of proportion and the austere aspects of some of his compositions also reflect his interest in and reverence for classic forms of music.

Ravel composed *Pavanne for a Deceased Infant* (1899), the piano work *Jeux d'eau* (1902), his song cycle *Shéhérazade* (1903), and his String Quartet (1904) while still a student at the Conservatory. In subsequent years, Ravel composed ballets, including *Daphne and Chloe* (1912), symphonic poems, such as *La Valse* (1922), two operas, *L'Heure espagnole* and *L'Enfant et les sortileges* (1925), and many pieces for piano, violin, and orchestra. His orchestration of the Russian composer Modest Mussorgsky's *Pictures at an Exhibition* (1921) attracted world-wide attention and inclusion in the repertoire of major orchestras. Another staple of major orchestras is Ravel's *Bolero* (1928), a work performed either as a ballet or a concert piece. Ravel died in Paris following brain surgery in 1937.

BOOKS ABOUT RAVEL

Demuth, Norman. *Ravel. Encore Music Editions Ser.* Hyperion 1979 repr of 1947 ed $22.45. ISBN 0-88355-690-1 Standard account of the noted French impressionist composer and his music.

Myers, Rollo H. *Ravel: His Life and Works.* Greenwood 1973 repr of 1960 ed $41.50. ISBN 0-8371-6841-4 Detailed account of the life and music of Ravel.

Nichols, Roger. *Ravel.* Biblio Dist 1977. (o.p.) $13.50. Narrative that balances both Ravel's work and his personal life.

Nichols, Roger (ed). *Ravel Remembered.* Norton 1988 $24.50. ISBN 0-393-02573-X Comprehensive look at the life and works of the composer.

Orenstein, Arbie. *Ravel: Man and Musician.* Columbia Univ Pr 1975 $29.50. ISBN 0-231-03902-6 Detailed biography of the French composer and his music.

SHOSTAKOVICH, DMITRI   1906–1975

A child of Tsarist Russia and the Russian Revolution, Dmitri Shostakovich was born in the city of Saint Petersburg, later named Leningrad, and suffered his entire life from the effects of a childhood of malnutrition and disease. Despite such deprivation, he became a composer of powerful and advanced music. After studying music at the Leningrad Conservatory between 1919 and 1925, Shostakovich presented his First Symphony in 1925 to critical acclaim. In subsequent years he wrote 14 more symphonies, always attempting to follow the Communist party prescription to portray "Socialist Realism"—an optimistic and realistic look at Socialist society. For his efforts, however, Shostakovich was alternately reviled and hailed by the leadership of the Soviet Union. On his sixtieth birthday, he was finally honored as a Hero of Socialist Labor.

Of his 15 symphonies, only the Fifth (1937) and the Tenth (1953) have gained a prominent place in concert repertoires. The Fifth Symphony is a masterpiece of symphonic composition and follows traditional symphonic construction in its movements. In the Tenth Symphony, Shostakovich introduced musical elements that he also incorporated into other compositions, notably the Fifth and Eighth String Quartets and his concertos for violin and cello. Shostakovich wrote ballets, such as *The Golden Age* (1930), and other people choreographed ballets to his other music as well. He also composed an opera, *Lady Macbeth of the District of Mtsensk* (1934). Although it was roundly condemned by Soviet authorities, who considered it full of "Western decadence," it enjoyed some success outside the Soviet Union. Overall, Shostakovich's music is remarkably consistent in style, technique, and emotional content.

BOOKS BY SHOSTAKOVICH

Sergei Prokofiev: Materials, Articles, Interviews. (coauthored with others) Imported 1978 $9.45. ISBN 0-8285-1618-9
Shostakovich: About Himself and His Times. Imported 1981 $12.00. ISBN 0-8285-2140-9

BOOKS ABOUT SHOSTAKOVICH

Kay, Norman. *Shostakovich.* Oxford Univ Pr 1972 $7.95. Scholarly biography of the notable Russian composer.
Martynov, Ivan I. *Dmitri Shostakovich, the Man and His Work.* T. Guralsky (tr). Greenwood 1969 repr of 1947 ed $35.00. ISBN 0-8371-2100-0 Comprehensive account of the twentieth-century Russian composer and his work.
Norris, Christopher. *Shostakovich: The Man and His Music.* M. Boyars 1983 $25.00. ISBN 0-7145-2778-5 Collection of essays that interpret Shostakovich's string quartets, symphonies, operas, and politics.
Seroff, Victor I. *Dmitri Shostakovich: The Life Background of a Soviet Composer.* Reprint Services 1988 repr of 1943 ed $49.00. Focuses on the life of the composer and how it affected his music.

STRAUSS, RICHARD   1864–1949

The celebrated German conductor and post-Romantic composer Richard Strauss completed his first work, *Polka in C,* at the age of 6. Success as composer came at age 17 with his first major work, *Symphony in D Minor,* closely followed by his Violin Concerto two years later and his Symphony in F Minor a year after that. A turning point in Strauss's life came when he was introduced to the philosophical, literary, and musical depth of the works of the composers Richard Wagner and Franz Liszt. (*See* Liszt *and* Wagner, Vol. 2, World History: The Arts in Nineteenth-Century Europe.) For some time thereafter he devoted himself to producing program music known as symphonic, or tone, poems. These tone poems, especially *Macbeth* (1886), *Till Eulenspiegels lustige Streiche* (1895), *Don Juan* (1889; revised 1891), and *Tod und Verklärung* (1889), are rich tapestries of musical themes and harmonic complexity. Strauss's musical innovations seemed unorthodox and shocking when first introduced, but they now seem commonplace after years of imitation.

Strauss leaped into worldwide fame as a composer of opera with the first performances of *Salomé* (1905). Thereafter, the powers of depiction and characterization that he had used in creating symphonic poems were used almost exclusively in the production of operas. After *Salomé* came *Elektra* (1909) and *Der Rosenkavalier* (1911), the latter considered Strauss's operatic masterpiece. During his lifetime, Strauss composed a total of 15 operas and two ballets, as well as many orchestral works, chamber music, piano pieces, and arrangements of other works. On his death at the age of 85, the world mourned the loss of his multifaceted genius. He is considered one of the last of the German Romantics, influenced by composers Richard Wagner and Franz Liszt.

BOOKS BY STRAUSS

A Confidential Matter: The Letters of Richard Strauss and Stefan Zweig, 1931–1935. Univ of California Pr 1977 $17.95.

The Correspondence Between Richard Strauss and Hugo von Hofmannsthal. Hans Hammelmann and Ewald Osers (trs). Cambridge Univ Pr 1981 $74.50. ISBN 0-521-23476-X

Gustav Mahler and Richard Strauss Correspondence, 1888–1911. Herta Blaukopf (ed). Edmund Jephcott (tr). Univ of Chicago Pr 1985 repr of 1980 ed $22.50. ISBN 0-226-05767-4

Recollections and Reflections. Willi Schuh (ed). L. J. Lawrence (tr). Greenwood 1974 repr of 1953 ed $38.50. ISBN 0-8371-7366-3

BOOKS ABOUT STRAUSS

Hartmann, Rudolf. *Richard Strauss: The Staging of His Operas and Ballets.* Oxford Univ Pr 1981 $75.00. ISBN 0-19-520251-1 Scholarly discussion of the production and staging of the composer's operas and ballets.

Kennedy, Michael. *Richard Strauss.* Rowan 1983 $7.95. ISBN 0-8226-0386-1 Standard biography of the post-romantic German composer and his work.

Schuh, Willi. *Richard Strauss: A Chronicle of the Early Years, 1864–1898.* Mary Whittall (tr). Cambridge Univ Pr 1982 $82.50. ISBN 0-521-24104-9 Focuses on the early life and musical development of the composer.

STRAVINSKY, IGOR   1882–1971

The Russian composer Igor Stravinsky, considered one of the greatest composers of the twentieth century, was born in 1882 near St. Petersburg, later known as Leningrad, Russia. His father was a famous singer at the Imperial Opera, and Stravinsky began piano lessons at the age of nine. He had little interest in a career in music, however, until 1902, when he was introduced to the famous Russian composer Rimsky-Korsakov while studying law at the University of St. Petersburg. For the next three years he studied composition with Rimsky-Korsakov.

In 1909, the ballet impresario Serge Diaghilev heard a performance of one of Stravinsky's symphonic works and commissioned him to compose three ballets for his Ballets Russes in Paris. These three pieces—*Firebird* (1910), *Petrouchka* (1911), and *The Rite of Spring* (1913)—established Stravinsky as the foremost musical innovator of his time. *The Rite of Spring,* in particular, is considered by many scholars to represent the birth of modern music. These and other early works were innovative in their use of syncopated and irregular rhythms and in their harsh-sounding harmonies.

After World War I, Stravinsky settled in France. The Russian Revolution of 1917 and the Communist dictatorships that followed kept him away from his native land until 1962. In France, Stravinsky's association with Diaghilev continued until the impresario's death in 1929. During this time the composer adopted a simpler musical style, inspired by the classical composers of the eighteenth century, which became known as neoclassicism. One of the first indications of this interest in classical music was heard in his ballet *Pulcinella* (1920). Stravinsky's interest in classical forms influenced his music for over 30 years.

Stravinsky moved to the United States in 1939 and became an American citizen in 1945. His continued interest in ballet resulted in an association with the Russian choreographer George Balanchine and his New York City Ballet company, for whom Stravinsky wrote several works. In addition, Stravinsky composed a variety of other works, including several operas, the most famous of which is *The Rake's Progress* (1951). In the mid-1950s, Stravinsky became interested in serialism, a method of writing music based on an ordered arrangement of pitch, rhythm, or dynamics, which is sometimes known as twelve-tone music. The use of serialism in his later works resulted in highly structured and concise compositions, such as his choral composition *Threni* (1958). A unique and unpredictable composer, Stravinsky never founded a specific school of composition. Nevertheless, his work has had a great influence on many modern composers.

BOOKS BY STRAVINSKY

Conversations with Igor Stravinsky. (coauthored with Robert Craft) Univ of California Pr 1980 $8.95. ISBN 0-520-04040-6

Dialogues. (coauthored with Robert Craft) Univ of California Pr 1968 $9.95. ISBN 0-520-04650-1

Expositions and Developments. (coauthored with Robert Craft) Univ of California Pr 1981 $9.95. ISBN 0-520-04403-7

Igor Stravinsky: An Autobiography. Norton 1962 $7.95. ISBN 0-393-00161-X

Memories and Commentaries. (coauthored with Robert Craft) Univ of California Pr 1981 $9.95. ISBN 0-520-04402-9

Poetics of Music in the Form of Six Lessons. Harvard Univ Pr 1970 $6.95. ISBN 0-674-67856-7

Themes and Conclusions. Univ of California Pr 1982 $9.95. ISBN 0-520-04652-8

BOOKS ABOUT STRAVINSKY

Ansermet, Ernest. *Stravinsky. Performing Arts Ser.* Louise Guiney (tr). Black Swan Bks 1989 $20.00. ISBN 0-933806-08-6 Portrait of Stravinsky's life and career as a composer.

Druskin, Mikhail S. *Igor Stravinsky: His Personality, Works, and View.* Martin Cooper (tr). Cambridge Univ Pr 1983 $29.95. ISBN 0-521-24590-7 Scholarly look at the famous twentieth-century Russian composer.

Horgan, Paul. *Encounters with Stravinsky: A Personal Record.* Wesleyan Univ Pr 1989 $14.95. ISBN 0-8195-6215-7 Biography written by Stravinsky's close friend.

Libman, Lillian. *Music at the Close: Stravinsky's Last Years.* Beekman 1972 $22.95. ISBN 0-8464-0659-4 Focuses on the later life and works of the composer.

Siohan, Robert. *Stravinsky.* Eric W. White (tr). Vienna 1970 $7.50. ISBN 0-670-67809-0 General biography of the composer.

Stravinsky, Theodore. *Catherine and Igor Stravinsky.* Boosey & Hawkes 1973 $15.00. ISBN 0-85162-008-6 Personalized account of the life of the composer and his wife.

Stravinsky, Vera, and Robert Craft. *Stravinsky: In Pictures and Documents.* Simon 1979.

(o.p.) Illustrated presentation of the composer that includes primary source documents.

Van den Toorn, Pieter C. *The Music of Igor Stravinsky.* Yale Univ Pr 1987 $17.95. ISBN 0-300-03884-4 Comprehensive discussion and analysis of the composer's music.

See also Vol. 1, British Literature: The Twentieth Century.

**Thomas A. Edison dictating his
morning's correspondence to his
phonograph**

Illustration by C. A. Powell (1890s)

Courtesy of Culver Pictures, Inc.

SCIENCE

AND

HEALTH

The material in Part Two has been assembled to provide readers, teachers, librarians, and others with a selection of resources that offers information on topics and themes and on scientists and health-associated individuals who are normally introduced in the science and health courses offered in upper middle school, in junior high school, and in senior high school. These listings of sources will be useful in a number of ways. Readers can scan them when searching for a book on a particular subject, person, or area of study. The profiles of the scientists and other related individuals and the listings of their major works will be of special help to students gathering sources for a research report.

Teachers can develop or extend supplementary reading lists for units in the sciences and in health by checking to see which works are suitable for their students and what is currently available. Teachers and librarians also will find this part useful for a quick review of a topic or for further developing a collection.

Of course, a reference book must be selective, focusing on some individuals or topics to the exclusion of others. Some people or topics inevitably will be left out or treated more briefly than others.

A reference book also must be a good guide. The books that are marked with an asterisk (*) are especially appropriate for younger readers, ages 12–14, in both reading level and content. Many of these books can be read with enjoyment and profit by older readers as well. Although many of the remaining books listed are within the reading range of senior high school students, some are beyond the range of all but the most able readers. These have been included because they are considered definitive or classic titles in a specific discipline.

The Science and Health portion of *The Young Adult Reader's Adviser* is intended as a tool for students of those disciplines. Like any tool, its effectiveness can be determined only by those who use it.

SCIENCE

The term *science* as it is used here includes general science, biology, earth science, chemistry, and physics. Obviously, there is an overlap among some of these branches of science; for example, general science can include the study of topics from all the branches. Therefore, students and teachers in search of a particular topic are encouraged to begin with the section that seems most applicable and then to skim through other sections, including those devoted to health, to check for related materials.

To make the selections for the science sections, the editors of *The Young Adult Reader's Adviser* began by studying individual state education frameworks to determine the most prevalent trends in and course requirements for each of the science disciplines. The editors also studied a number of texts currently in use in grades 6 through 12 to determine focus and relative depth of concentration on specific topics. Also taken into consideration were relevant publications by such organizations as the National Science Teachers Association, the American Association for the Advancement of Science, and the American Alliance for Health, Physical Education, Recreation, and Dance.

The biographical profiles of each scientist present basic information about the scientist's personal life, education, accomplishments, and theories. The profiles are intended to give students a general idea of the contributions each scientist has made in the ever-changing scientific world. However, the profiles are by no means complete accounts of any scientist's life or career achievements.

For the most part, selected works by a given scientist that are currently in print are included in the Books By category following each profile. The works included in each Books About category have been selected to give additional information about a scientist's life, discoveries, and other achievements. On occasion, more specialized and narrowly focused books also have been included either because they are the only works currently in print or because they have something special to offer. The serious student or researcher will find additional works about many of the scientists listed in Bowker's *Books in Print.* Every effort has been made to list books that are currently in print and easily available from major publishers.

HEALTH

Health is a broad subject, embracing all aspects of living. Among other things, the discipline encompasses the condition of the body, mental and emotional health, social health, community health, and environmental issues. To make the selections for the health sections, the editors of *The Young Adult Reader's Adviser* began by studying individual state education guidelines to determine the most prevalent course requirements for the study of health. The editors also studied a number of texts currently in use in grades 6 through 12 to determine relative depth of concentration on specific topics and themes.

During the course of their research, the editors became increasingly aware of the need to devote special attention to topics that concern modern teenagers. Making the passage from childhood to adulthood is a trying experience, a time of great physical change, and a period during which an adolescent tries out many ways of behaving, coping, and relating to people. The editors, therefore, made a special effort to include titles that address, in a manner appropriate for and interesting to young adults, such issues as living in dysfunctional families, substance abuse, pregnancy, and parenthood.

A major responsibility of the section on health is to enhance the student's ability to make healthy choices. To the best of their ability, the editors, in their selections, have tried to represent the broad spectrum of issues and topics encompassed by the title *health.*

✸ SCIENCE ✸

GENERAL SCIENCE

Works in the General Science section focus on the nature and processes of science and have been divided into three categories, or subsections—General References, Problem Solving and the Scientific Method, and Measurement and Selected Tools of Science.

The books listed under General References apply to all the sciences. Those listed under Problem Solving and the Scientific Method show how scientists work, no matter in which area they chose to concentrate—whether they try to determine how substances react, find the cause of a disease, classify a newly discovered organism, predict when an earthquake will occur, or determine the size of a star. Works that appear under the heading Measurement and Selected Tools of Science contain information about the International System of Units (SI) and some of the instruments scientists use in their research.

The processes of science are of paramount importance in the study of all branches of science. For a comprehensive listing of works relating to specific branches of science, see the readings under Biology, Earth Science, Chemistry, and Physics, found in the science sections immediately following this one. For a comprehensive listing of works relating to the health field, see the readings under Health, immediately following the science sections of *The Young Adult Reader's Adviser.*

GENERAL REFERENCES

*Aaseng, Nathan. *The Inventors: Nobel Prizes in Chemistry, Physics, and Medicine.* Lerner 1988 $11.95. ISBN 0-8225-0651-3 Describes scientists and their achievements, with background on Alfred Nobel and the group teamwork that led to important discoveries by preserving prizewinners.

*Abbott, David (ed). *The Biographical Dictionary of Scientists: Astronomers.* Harper 1984 $28.00. ISBN 0-911745-80-7 Biographical sketches of more than 200 scientists noted for their work in astronomy.

*Abbott, David (ed). *The Biographical Dictionary of Scientists: Biologists.* Harper 1984 $28.00. ISBN 0-911745-82-3 Biographical sketches of more than 200 scientists noted for their work in biology.

*Abbott, David (ed). *The Biographical Dictionary of Scientists: Chemists.* Harper 1984 $28.00. ISBN 0-911745-81-5 Biographical sketches of more than 200 scientists noted for their work in chemistry.

*Abbott, David (ed). *The Biographical Dictionary of Scientists: Physicists.* Harper 1984 $28.00. ISBN 0-911745-79-3 Biographical sketches of more than 200 scientists noted for their work in physics.

*Asimov, Isaac. *Asimov's Biographical Encyclopedia of Science and Technology.* Doubleday 1982 $39.95. ISBN 0-385-17771-2 History of science told through the lives and careers of those who made it.

Asimov, Isaac. *Asimov's New Guide to Science.* Basic 1984 $29.95. ISBN 0-465-00473-3

*Asimov, Isaac. *Far as Human Eye Could See.* Doubleday 1987 $15.95. ISBN 0-385-23514-3 Seven essays on biochemistry, astronomy, physical chemistry, and geochemistry.

*Bunch, Bryan (ed). *The Science Almanac 1985-86.* Doubleday 1984. (o.p.) An extensive fact-filled reference book covering all fields of science, intended for the non-scientist and with good content information as well as trivia.

Burt, McKinley, Jr. *Black Inventors of America.* National Bk 1989 $9.95. ISBN 0-89420-095-X

Dixon, Bernard, *et al. The Encyclopedic Dictionary of Science.* Facts on File 1988 $29.95. ISBN 0-8160-2021-3

Donovan, Richard X. *Black Scientists of America.* National Bk 1990 $8.95. ISBN 0-89420-265-0

Feldman, Anthony, and Peter Ford. *Scientists and Inventors.* Facts on File 1986 $29.95. ISBN 0-87196-410-4

*Franck, Irene M., and David M. Brownstone. *Scientists and Technologists. Work Throughout History Ser.* Facts on File 1988 $17.95. ISBN 0-8160-1450-7 Discussion of the history and significance of careers in science and technology.

Godman, Arthur. *Barnes and Noble Thesaurus of Science.* Harper 1983 $13.45. ISBN 0-06-015176-5

*Goldstein, Martin, and Inge Goldstein. *The Experience of Science: An Interdisciplinary Approach.* Plenum 1984 $27.50. ISBN 0-306-41538-0 Discussion of the nature and process of science using three examples.

*Gornick, Vivian. *Women in Science: 100 Journeys into the Territory.* Simon 1990 $8.95. ISBN 0-671-69592-4 Discussion of women who made pioneering entrances into the male-dominated field of science.

*Gottlieb, William P. *Science Facts You Won't Believe.* Watts 1983 $11.90. ISBN 0-531-02875-5 Examination of some commonly held misconceptions about science.

*Haber, Louis. *Black Pioneers of Science and Invention.* Harcourt 1970 $16.95. ISBN 0-15-208565-3 A look at the lives and contributions to science and industry of 14 African Americans.

*Haber, Louis. *Women Pioneers of Science.* Harcourt 1979. (o.p.) $12.95. ISBN 0-15-299202-2 Presentation of biographies and descriptions of important contributions of 12 outstanding female scientists.

*Haines, Gail Kay. *Test-Tube Mysteries.* Putnam 1982 $11.95. ISBN 0-396-08075-8 Describes the important discoveries in science from Pasteur to Legionnaire's disease.

*Harrison, James (ed). *Science Now.* Arco 1984 $21.95. ISBN 0-668-06209-6 Pictorial study of modern technology and science.

Hawke, David Freeman. *Nuts & Bolts of the Past: A History of American Technology 1776–1860.* Harper 1989 $9.95. ISBN 0-06-091605-2 Technological development in the United States from its independence to the Civil War, with emphasis on the people involved.

*Hayden, Robert C. *Eight Black American Inventors.* Addison 1972. (o.p.) $7.95. ISBN 0-201-02823-9 Stories of eight African Americans who contributed to the industrial, technological, and economic development of America.

*Hayden, Robert C. (ed). *A Salute to Black Scientists and Inventors. Black History Ser.* Vol. 2 Empak 1985 $1.00. ISBN 0-9616156-1-3 Brief biographical sketches of 18 African-American scientists and inventors.

*Hayden, Robert C. *Seven Black American Scientists.* Addison 1970. (o.p.) $4.95. ISBN 0-201-02828-X Biographies of seven scientists in medicine, research, teaching, and astronomy.

*Ingraham, Gloria D., and Leonard W. Ingraham. *An Album of American Women: Their Changing Role.* Watts 1987 $13.90. ISBN 0-531-10317-X Picture album style indicating especially women now in non-traditional women's jobs, especially science.

*Kennedy, DayAnn M., *et al. Science and Technology in Fact and Fiction: A Guide to Young Adult Books.* Bowker 1990 $35.00. ISBN 0-8352-2710-3 "Current bibliography of recommended books on space, cosmology, technological devices, nuclear energy, computers and others; both plot summaries and evaluations for each title listed."

*Klein, Aaron E. *The Hidden Contributors: Black Scientists and Inventors in America.* Doubleday 1971. (o.p.) $4.95. Stories of African Americans who have made significant yet unrecognized contributions to society.

*Martin, Paul D. *Science: It's Changing Your World.* National Geographic 1985 $6.95. ISBN

0-87044-516-2 Explanation of how developments in computers, lasers, industry, food, fuel, transportation, medicine, and space are shaping our lives.

Meadows, Jack. *The Great Scientists.* Oxford Univ Pr 1989 $18.95. ISBN 0-19-520815-3

*Medawar, P. B. *Advice to a Young Scientist.* Harper 1981. ISBN 0-06-013029-6 Nobel Laureate Medawar tells of science literacy; a wit inspires young people who may otherwise not think of a scientific field as a career.

*Mount, Ellis, and Barbara A. List. *Milestones in Science and Technology: The Ready Reference Guide to Discoveries, Inventions, and Facts.* Oryx 1987 $29.50. ISBN 0-89774-260-5 One thousand topics covering basic discoveries, such as relativity and genetics, and practical inventions such as the electric motor and DDT.

*Newton, David E. *Science Ethics.* Watts 1987 $12.90. ISBN 0-531-10419-2 Exploration of the moral and ethical aspects of science and research.

Ogilvie, Marilyn Bailey. *Women in Science: Antiquity Through the Nineteenth Century—A Biographical Dictionary with Annotated Biography.* MIT Pr 1986 $29.95. ISBN 0-262-15031-X

*O'Hern, Elizabeth Moot. *Profiles of Pioneer Women Scientists.* Acropolis 1985 $18.95. ISBN 0-87491-811-1 The lives, contributions, and discoveries of 20 American female scientists.

Parker, Sybil P. (ed). *Dictionary of Science and Engineering.* McGraw 1984 $44.50. ISBN 0-07-045483-3

Parker, Sybil P. (ed). *Encyclopedia of Science and Technology.* 20 vols. McGraw 1987 $1,600.00. ISBN 0-07-079292-5

*Pickering, James S. *Famous Astronomers.* Dodd 1968. (o.p.) A look at the lives and works of the greats of astronomy.

*Siedel, Frank, and James M. Siedel. *Pioneers in Science.* Houghton 1968. (o.p.) $5.00. Brief biographies of 48 scientists; explains how the achievements of each individual built on earlier work and laid the groundwork for future discoveries.

*Stone, Jeanne. *The Julian Messner Illustrated Dictionary of Science.* Messner 1985 $9.79. ISBN 0-671-54548-5 Scientific words, phrases, formulas, people are listed with excellent illustrations in this reference book.

*Sullivan, Navin. *Pioneer Astronomers.* Atheneum 1964. (o.p.) A look at the lives of early astronomers and their explorations of the universe.

*Thomas, Henry, and Dana Lee Thomas. *Living Biographies of Great Scientists. Living Biographies Ser.* Garden City 1959. (o.p.) $3.50. Biographies and achievements of 21 great scientists from Archimedes to Einstein.

Van Sertima, Ivan (ed). *Blacks in Science: Ancient and Modern.* Transaction 1983 $14.95. ISBN 0-87855-941-8

*Wolpert, Lewis, and Alison Richards. *A Passion for Science.* Oxford Univ Pr 1988 $21.95. ISBN 0-19-854213-5 Collection of profiles of important contemporary scientists who explain what science means to them.

ASIMOV, ISAAC 1920–

See also Asimov, Vol. 1, American Literature: The Twentieth Century.

Isaac Asimov is one of the most prolific writers of our time. Born in Petrovichi, Russia, Asimov was brought to the United States at the age of three. After receiving a Ph.D. in biochemistry from Columbia University in 1948, he taught biochemistry at Boston University School of Medicine, a position he held until 1958. During this tenure, he became well known through the many books he wrote and the lectures he delivered to enthusiastic audiences in all parts of the country. Since 1958, he has devoted full time to writing and lecturing, though he is still officially on the Boston University staff.

Asimov makes scientific information easily understandable to lay readers. This talent and his ability to tell an exciting story have made him a popular science writer. He began writing science fiction in 1938. Since then he has produced, alone or with others, more than 400 books.

BOOKS BY ASIMOV

Asimov's Biographical Encyclopedia of Science and Technology (1964). Doubleday 1982 $39.95. ISBN 0-385-17771-2

Asimov's New Guide to Science (1972). Basic 1984 $29.95. ISBN 0-465-00473-3

*Beginnings: The Story of Origins—of Mankind, Life, the Earth, the Universe (1987). Berkeley 1989 $4.50. ISBN 0-425-11586-0 A look at the evolution of the natural world, working from the present to the origin of the universe.

Extraterrestrial Civilizations (1979). Crown 1979. (o.p.). $10.00. ISBN 0-517-53075-9

*How Did We Find Out About Nuclear Power? Walker 1976 $12.85. ISBN 0-8027-6266-2 Asimov explains nuclear reactions and reactors, disclosing the steps in discovery of the elements of atomic energy; well suited for young teens.

In Joy Still Felt: An Autobiography of Isaac Asimov, 1954–1978 (1980). Doubleday 1980. (o.p.) $19.95. ISBN 0-385-15544-1

In Memory Yet Green: An Autobiography of Isaac Asimov, 1920–1954 (1979). Doubleday 1979. (o.p.) $15.95. ISBN 0-385-13679-X

A Short History of Biology (1964). Greenwood 1980 $32.50. ISBN 0-315-22583-4

BOOK ABOUT ASIMOV

**Olander, Joseph D., and Martin H. Greenberg (eds). *Isaac Asimov. Writers of the 21st Century Ser.* Taplinger 1977 $10.95. ISBN 0-8008-4257-X A look at Asimov's science fiction.

See also Vol. 2, Earth Science: Astronomy: The Solar System.

PROBLEM SOLVING AND THE SCIENTIFIC METHOD

*Berman, William. *How to Dissect: Exploring with Probe and Scalpel.* Arco 1984 $5.95. ISBN 0-668-05941-9 Introduction to dissection, with instructions for dissecting 11 common organisms.

*Campbell, Norman R. *What Is Science?* Dover 1953 $4.50. ISBN 0-486-60043-2 Introduction to the nature and methods of scientific thought, with emphasis on experimentation, measurement, and the development of theories and laws.

*Halacy, Daniel S. *Science and Serendipity: Great Discoveries by Accident.* Macrae Smith 1967. (o.p.) Stories of scientists who made significant discoveries through fortunate accidents.

Judson, Horace F. *The Search for Solutions.* Johns Hopkins Univ Pr 1987 $9.95. ISBN 0-8018-3526-7

Killeffer, David H. *How Did You Think of That? An Introduction to the Scientific Method.* Am Chemical 1973 $4.95. ISBN 0-8412-0163-3

*Klein, David, and Marymae Klein. *How Do You Know It's True?* Macmillan 1984 $12.95. ISBN 0-684-18225-4 Discussion of how reality is often distorted by myths and misconceptions, misleading advertising, and misuse of statistics and survey results; presents ways of developing critical thinking skills.

*Morrison, Philip, and Phylis Morrison. *The Ring of Truth: An Inquiry into How We Know What We Know.* Random 1987 $24.95. ISBN 0-394-55663-1 A look at some of the ways scientists have searched for answers.

*Rensberger, Boyce. *How the World Works: A Guide to Science's Greatest Discoveries.* Morrow 1987 $7.95. ISBN 0-688-07293-3 Explanations of the people and discoveries that have contributed to the world view today.

*Wallace, Diane A., and Philip Hershey. *How to Master Science Labs.* Watts 1987 $12.90. ISBN 0-531-10323-4 Explanations of methods and techniques used in a science laboratory.

Watson, James D. *The Double Helix: Being a Personal Account of the Discovery of the Structure of DNA.* Atheneum 1968 $6.95. ISBN 0-689-70602-2

*Wilford, John N. (ed). *Scientists at Work: The Creative Process of Scientific Research.* Dodd 1979 $9.95. ISBN 0-396-07603-3 The story of science through the lives of selected scientists.

BACON, FRANCIS   1561–1626

Born in London, Francis Bacon attended Trinity College, Cambridge University, and then practiced law. He became a member of Parliament in 1584.

Besides being a statesman, Bacon was a philosopher. He advocated the experimental approach to science and problem solving. He believed that the truth could be found by using the inductive method—applying what is known to form generalizations about the unknown—and that the laws of the universe could be discovered by collecting all the facts of nature. Because of Bacon's influence, experimental science became accepted and the Royal Society in London and the Academy of Sciences in Paris were created. Bacon is sometimes called the father of modern science.

BOOKS BY BACON

Advancement of Learning (1605). G.W. Kitchin (ed). Rowman 1973 $7.50. ISBN 0-87471-665-9

Novum Organum and Related Writings (1620). Fulton H. Anderson (ed). Macmillan 1960 $9.63. ISBN 0-672-60289-X

BOOK ABOUT BACON

*Bowen, Catherine D. *Francis Bacon: The Temper of a Man.* Little 1963. (o.p.) $1.95. ISBN 0-316-10382-9 Introduction to the life and thought of Bacon.

MEASUREMENT AND SELECTED TOOLS OF SCIENCE

Bell, Louis. *The Telescope.* Dover 1981 $6.95. ISBN 0-486-24151-3

*Bleifield, Maurice. *Experimenting with a Microscope. Venture Books Ser.* Watts 1988 $11.90. ISBN 0-531-10580-6 Instructions for using a microscope, preparing slides, and observing a variety of objects, substances, and organisms or other biological specimens.

*Blocksma, Mary. *Reading the Numbers: A Survival Guide to the Measurements, Numbers, and Sizes Encountered in Everyday Life.* Viking 1989 $18.95. ISBN 0-670-82682-0 Compelling reference book explaining the numbers reporting the magnitude of an earthquake, the sizes of paper clips, dating of eras, etc; an invaluable guidebook for all ages.

*Branley, Franklyn M. *Space Telescope. Voyage into Space Book Ser.* Harper 1985 $12.89. ISBN 0-690-04434-8 Description of the uses and capabilities of telescopes used in space.

*Chaple, Glen F., Jr. *Exploring with a Telescope. Venture Book Ser.* Watts 1988 $11.90. ISBN 0-531-10581-4 Describes telescopes and shows how to use them.

Cornell, James, and John Carr (eds). *Infinite Vistas: New Tools for Astronomy.* Scribner's 1985 $18.95. ISBN 0-684-18287-4

Feirer, John. *SI Metric Handbook.* Scribner's 1977 $27.50. ISBN 0-87002-908-8

Grave, Eric V. *Discover the Invisible: A Naturalist's Guide to Using the Microscope.* Prentice 1984 $10.95. ISBN 0-13-215336-X

*Grillone, Lisa, and Joseph Gennaro. *Small Worlds Close Up.* Crown 1987 $12.95. ISBN 0-517-53289-1 The electron microscope is explained, with photographs enhancing text.

Hidden Worlds. National Geographic 1981 $6.95. ISBN 0-087044-336-4 Examination of the invisible world as revealed through the use of microscopes, X-rays, and photography.

*Johnson, Gaylord, and Maurice Bleifield. *Hunting with the Microscope.* Arco 1980 $3.95. ISBN 0-668-04783-6 Explanation of how to select and use a microscope for examining several types of plants and animals.

*Metos, Thomas H. *The New Eyes of the Scientist. Impact Ser.* Watts 1988 $12.90. ISBN 0-531-10609-8 A look at instruments being used to expand knowledge—electron microscopes, space probes, and medical imaging machines.

*Muirden, James. *Astronomy with a Small Telescope.* Prentice 1985 $18.95. ISBN 0-13-049941-2 Handbook for the beginning night sky observer.

*Muirden, James. *How to Use an Astronomical Telescope: A Beginner's Guide to Observing the Cosmos.* Simon 1988 $10.95. ISBN 0-671-66404-2 Description of the types of telescopes and how to use them to observe various celestial objects.

Nelson, Robert A. *SI: The International System of Units.* Am Assn Physics 1983 $11.00.

*Riley, Peter. *Looking at Microscopes.* David and Charles 1985 $17.95. ISBN 0-7134-4632-3 History of the microscope and discussion of the many types and uses of microscopes today.

*Stwertka, Eve, and Albert Stwertka. *The Microscope: How to Use It and Enjoy It.* Messner 1988 $4.95. ISBN 0-671-67060-3 Discussion of the development of microscopes, how they work, and techniques for using them.

*Timms, Howard. *Measuring and Computing.* Watts 1989 $12.40. ISBN 0-531-17188-4 Discussion of the history and principles of measurement; includes the development and uses of computers.

*Traister, Robert J., and Susan E. Harris. *Astronomy and Telescopes: A Beginner's Handbook.* TAB 1983 $19.95. ISBN 0-8306-0419-7 History of astronomy and discussion of the types of telescopes; includes information about how to build a telescope.

BIOLOGY

This section is devoted to biology, or life science, the study of living things and the processes that occur within them. Because to study each of the estimated three million types of organisms living today would be impossible, biologists study groups of organisms that are similar in structure and function. The focus of the study of biology, and therefore that of this section, is organized around several major themes, including the unity of living things, the diversity of life, and the continuity of life.

For ease of use, the biology section is divided into subsections, the first of which is a listing of general reference works. The remaining subsections encompass such topics as cells, energy, nucleic acids, the genetic code, organisms, the human body, the evolution of life, human and life origins, animal behavior, ecology and the environment, and conservation of natural resources.

Within a number of the subsections, key biologists associated with the topic are listed alphabetically, their last names appearing first. For each, there is a book or a list of books by that individual. In addition, there is for each a profile that provides personal background and/or information about the individual's role and achievements in the world of science. Further, the profile may refer the reader to other related individuals and their works, which also can be found in *The Young Adult Reader's Adviser.* Such connections between scientists and other thinkers and theorists are usually necessary when doing research in any of the branches of science.

Last, for most profiled individuals, there is a Books About section that, among other types of publications, lists notable biographies for further reading and research. Whenever possible, very recent titles have also been included. In some instances, only a very limited number or no books at all about the individual existed at the time of this compilation.

Obviously, there is an overlap among the various branches of science. For additional works concerning the human body, for example, see the readings under Health, immediately following the science sections of *The Young Adult Reader's Adviser*. For additional works in biochemistry, see the readings under Chemistry.

GENERAL REFERENCES

Arms, Karen, and Pamela S. Camp. *Biology*. Saunders 1987 $48.74. ISBN 0-03-003644-5

*Attenborough, David. *Life on Earth: A Natural History*. Little 1983 $19.95. ISBN 0-316-05747-9 Story of the evolution of life on Earth, with emphasis on vertebrates.

*Attenborough, David. *The Living Planet: A Portrait of the Earth*. Little 1986 $17.95. ISBN 0-316-05749-5 Study of the habitats of Earth.

*Corrick, James A. *Recent Revolutions in Biology*. Watts 1987 $12.90. ISBN 0-531-10341-2 A look at new theories and discoveries in areas such as evolution, gene therapy, and genetic engineering.

Durrell, Gerald, and Lee Durrell. *The Amateur Naturalist*. Knopf 1983 $29.45. ISBN 0-394-53390-9

*Evans, Ifor. *Biology*. Watts 1984 $12.40. ISBN 0-531-04743-1 Introduction to plants and animals, from microscopic organisms to humans; covers topics such as feeding, breathing, reproduction genetics, and ecology.

*Janovy, John. *On Becoming a Biologist*. Harper 1986 $6.95. ISBN 0-06-091363-0 Explanation of what biologists do and discussion of their responsibilities to society.

Keeton, William T., and James L. Gould. *Biological Science*. Norton 1987 $40.00. ISBN 0-393-95392-0

Martin, E. A. *Dictionary of Life Sciences*. Universe 1984 $25.00. ISBN 0-87663-740-3

Medawar, Peter, and J. S. Medawar. *Aristotle to Zoos: A Philosophical Dictionary of Biology*. Harvard Univ Pr 1985 $9.95. ISBN 0-674-04537-8

Purves, William K., and Gordon H. Orians. *Life: The Science of Biology*. Sinauer 1987 $44.95. ISBN 0-87893-733-1

Re, Richard N. *Bioburst: The Impact of Modern Biology on the Affairs of Man*. Louisiana State Univ Pr 1986 $19.95. ISBN 0-8071-1289-5

Stockley, C. *Dictionary of Biology: The Facts You Need to Know—At a Glance*. EDC 1987 $7.95. ISBN 0-86020-819-2

Toothill, Elizabeth (ed). *The Facts on File Dictionary of Biology*. Facts on File 1988 $19.95. ISBN 0-8160-1865-0

CELLS—THE BUILDING BLOCKS OF LIFE

*Adler, Irving. *How Life Began*. Harper 1977 $12.70. ISBN 0-381-99603-4 Exploration and explanation of life at the molecular level, including discussions of biological molecules and biochemical processes.

Becker, Wayne M. *The World of the Cell*. Benjamin-Cummings 1986 $44.95. ISBN 0-8053-0800-8

*Breslow, Ronald. *Enzymes: The Machines of Life*. Carolina Biological 1986 $1.90. ISBN 0-89278-155-6 Introduction to enzymes—what they do and how they do it.

De Duve, Christian. *A Guided Tour of the Living Cell*. Freeman 1985 $33.95. ISBN 0-7167-6002-9

Dyson, Robert D. *Essentials of Cell Biology.* Allyn 1978 $44.00. ISBN 0-205-06117-6
*Fichter, George S. *Cells.* Watts 1986 $10.40. ISBN 0-531-10210-6 Discussion of the discovery of cells and their structure and function; describes experiments in DNA research.
*Moner, John G. *The Animal Cell.* Carolina Biological 1987 $2.40. ISBN 0-89278-347-8 Discussion of the structure and function of the animal cell, including the plasma membrane, organelles, cytoplasmic matrix, and nucleus.
Rees, Anthony R., and Michael J. E. Sternberg. *From Cells to Atoms: An Illustrated Introduction to Molecular Biology.* Basil Blackwell 1984 $14.95. ISBN 0-632-00888-1
*Thomas, Lewis. *The Lives of a Cell: Notes of a Biology Watcher.* Bantam 1984 $5.95. ISBN 0-553-27580-1 Brilliant essays on cells and other topics.

ENERGY FOR LIFE

*Asimov, Isaac. *How Did We Find Out About Photosynthesis?* Walker 1989 $11.85. ISBN 0-8027-6886-5 Stories of the scientific discoveries that led to our understanding of photosynthesis and how this fundamental process relates to other aspects of life.
Baker, Jeffrey W., and Garland E. Allen. *Matter, Energy, and Life: An Introduction to Chemical Concepts.* Addison 1981 $20.50. ISBN 0-201-00169-1
Blaxter, Kenneth. *Energy Metabolism in Animals and Man.* Cambridge Univ Pr 1989 $80.00. ISBN 0-521-36931-2
Danks, Susan M., *et al. Photosynthetic Systems: Structure, Function, and Assembly.* Wiley 1985 $24.95. ISBN 0-471-90178-4
Foyer, Christine H. *Photosynthesis.* Wiley 1984 $37.75. ISBN 0-471-86473-0
Lehninger, Albert L. *Principles of Biochemistry.* Worth 1982 $46.95. ISBN 0-87901-136-X
*Nicholls, Peter. *Cytochromes and Cell Respiration.* Carolina Biological 1984 $1.90 ISBN 0-89278-266-8 Discussion of the structure of cytochromes and how they function in respiration.

KREBS, HANS ADOLF   1900–1981

Born in Hildesheim, Germany, Hans Krebs studied medicine at Göttingen, Freiburg, Munich, and Berlin. In 1925 he received a medical degree from the University of Hamburg and then became a laboratory assistant at the Kaiser Wilhelm Institute of Biology in Berlin. In 1930 he began a private practice and did research. As Adolf Hitler rose to power, Krebs left Germany and went to England, where he received an M.S. in biochemistry from Cambridge University. In 1935 he became a lecturer at the University of Sheffield. There he carried out research in cell metabolism. In 1939, Krebs became an English citizen.

In 1937 Krebs discovered the citric acid cycle, a complex set of reactions that take place continuously in cellular respiration. This cycle, commonly called the Krebs cycle, is thus an essential part of the process in which living bodies obtain energy from food. Krebs received a share of the 1953 Nobel Prize in physiology and medicine for this discovery.

In 1954 Krebs became a professor at Oxford University in England, where he remained until 1967. After his retirement from Oxford, he continued his investigations of cell metabolism.

BOOKS BY KREBS

Otto Warburg: Cell Physiologist, Biochemist, and Eccentric (1981). Oxford Univ Pr 1981 $36.00. ISBN 0-19-858171-8
Reminiscences and Reflections (1981). Oxford Univ Pr 1982 $35.00. ISBN 0-19-854702-1

NUCLEIC ACIDS AND THE GENETIC CODE

*Asimov, Isaac. *How Did We Find Out About DNA?* Walker 1985 $9.95. ISBN 0-8027-6596-3 Story of the investigations leading to an understanding of DNA and its structure.
*Denhardt, David T. *Replication of DNA.* Carolina Biological 1983 $1.90. ISBN 0-89278-320-6 Discussion of DNA and its synthesis, replication, and repair.
Hoagland, Mahlon B. *Discovery: The Search for DNA's Secrets.* Reinhold 1983 $7.95. ISBN 0-442-23620-4

CRICK, FRANCIS HARRY COMPTON   1916–

Francis Crick was born in Northampton, England, and received a B.S. from University College in London in 1937 and a Ph.D. from Cambridge University in 1955. Although Crick began his career as a physicist, in 1949 he began research in molecular biology at Cambridge. In 1951 he and James Watson, a young American biologist, began working intensively to learn the structure of the DNA molecule. With the help of research that British scientists Maurice Wilkins and Rosalind Franklin were carrying out on the structure of nucleic acids, including DNA, in 1953 they succeeded in building a model of the molecule. The Watson–Crick model for DNA was hailed by biologists the world over, and a new era of research and understanding in cell biology and genetics began.

Crick, Watson, and Wilkins were awarded the 1962 Nobel Prize in physiology and medicine in recognition of their great achievement. That same year, Crick became director of Cambridge's Molecular Biology Laboratory. Crick went on to do further work on the genetic code. In 1977, he became a research professor at the Salk Institute in San Diego. (*See* Watson *and* Wilkins, Vol. 2, Biology: Nucleic Acids and the Genetic Code.)

BOOKS BY CRICK

What Mad Pursuit: A Personal View of Scientific Discovery (1988). Basic 1988 $16.95. ISBN 0-465-09137-7 Crick's own account of his life as a scientist and his part in solving the mysteries of DNA.
Life Itself (1981). Simon 1981. (o.p.) $12.95. ISBN 0-671-25562-0 Discussion of the origin of life by directed panspermia, the theory that life came from outer space.

BOOKS ABOUT CRICK

Holton, Gerald (ed). *The Twentieth-Century Scientists: Studies in the Biography of Ideas.* Norton 1972. (o.p.) $15.00. ISBN 0-393-06384-4 Collection of essays on contemporary science topics; includes an essay on Crick.
Judson, Horace F. *The Eighth Day of Creation: Makers of the Revolution in Biology.* Simon 1979 $15.95. ISBN 0-671-22540-5 History of the discoveries in molecular biology and the scientists involved during the period 1930–1970.
Moore, Ruth E. *The Coil of Life: The Story of the Great Discoveries of the Life Sciences.* Knopf 1961. (o.p.) $8.95. ISBN 0-394-41966-9 Discussion of the discoveries pertaining to the chemical basis of heredity; includes information about Crick.
Olby, Robert. *The Path to the Double Helix.* Univ of Washington Pr 1974. (o.p.) $23.50. ISBN 0-295-95359-4 History of molecular biology: the ideas, methods, and people that led to understanding of the structure of DNA.
Watson, James D. *The Double Helix: A Personal Account of the Discovery of the Structure of DNA* (1968). Atheneum 1985 $6.95. ISBN 0-689-70602-2 Watson's own account of the events and people involved in determining the structure of DNA.

Weintraub, Pamela (ed). *The Omni Interviews.* Omni Pr 1984. (o.p.) $17.95. ISBN 0-89919-215-7 Compilation of interviews with leading scientists, including Francis Crick.

WATSON, JAMES DEWEY   1928–

Chicago-born James Watson received a B.S. in zoology from the University of Chicago in 1947 and a Ph.D. from the University of Indiana in 1950. At the University of Indiana, he was a pupil of Hermann Muller, a noted geneticist who won a Nobel Prize for showing that radiation causes mutations. After obtaining his doctorate, Watson spent some time at the University of Copenhagen in Denmark studying bacteriophages—DNA-containing viruses that infect bacteria. There he became interested in the structure of DNA, and in 1951 he moved to the Cavendish Laboratory of Cambridge University in England.

At Cambridge, Watson and British molecular biologist Francis Crick worked together to understand the structure of the DNA molecule. Their rather quick success was due in part to studies of nucleic acids carried out by British scientists Maurice Wilkins and Rosalind Franklin. In 1953 Watson and Crick reported the structure they had worked out for the DNA molecule and displayed the model they had constructed using standard laboratory hardware. The model, the double helix, was immediately applied to understanding chromosomes, which consist of DNA and a protein coat. The model could successfully explain how chromosomes replicate in cell division, and it led to an understanding of many other cell processes. For their outstanding work, Watson, Crick, and Wilkins shared the 1962 Nobel Prize in physiology or medicine.

In 1953 Watson went to the California Institute of Technology and then, in 1956, to Harvard University. In 1968 he became director of the Cold Spring Harbor Laboratory of Quantitative Biology on Long Island, where his research concentrated in the areas of neurology and cancer. Watson is the director of the National Center for Human Genome Research at the National Institutes of Health, which has undertaken the massive project of obtaining a complete map of human genes. (*See* Crick *and* Wilkins, Biology: Nucleic Acids and the Genetic Code.)

BOOKS BY WATSON

* *The Double Helix: A Personal Account of the Discovery of the Structure of DNA* (1968). Atheneum 1968 $6.95. ISBN 0-689-70602-2 Watson's own account of the events and people involved in determining the structure of DNA.

The DNA Story: A Documentary History of Gene Cloning (1981). (coauthored with John Tooze) Freeman 1981 $29.95. ISBN 0-7167-1292-X

The Molecular Biology of the Gene (1965). (coauthored with others) Benjamin-Cummings 1987. Vol. 1 $45.95. ISBN 0-8053-9612-8. Vol. 2 $34.95. ISBN 0-8053-9613-6

Recombinant DNA: A Short Course (1983). (coauthored with John Tooze) Freeman 1983 $17.95. ISBN 0-7167-1484-1

BOOKS ABOUT WATSON

Holton, Gerald (ed). *The Twentieth-Century Scientists: Studies in the Biography of Ideas.* Norton 1972. (o.p.) $15.00. ISBN 0-393-06384-4 Collection of essays on contemporary science topics; includes information about Watson.

Judson, Horace F. *The Eighth Day of Creation: Makers of the Revolution in Biology.* Simon 1979 $15.95. ISBN 0-671-22540-5 History of the discoveries in molecular biology and the scientists involved during the period 1930–1970.

Moore, Ruth E. *The Coil of Life: The Story of the Great Discoveries of the Life Sciences.* Knopf

1961. (o.p.) $8.95. ISBN 0-394-41966-9 Discussion of the discoveries pertaining to the chemical basis of heredity; includes information about Watson.

Olby, Robert. *The Path to the Double Helix.* Univ of Washington Pr 1974. (o.p.) $23.50. ISBN 0-295-95359-4 History of molecular biology: the ideas, methods, and people that led to understanding of the structure of DNA.

WILKINS, MAURICE HUGH FREDERICK   1916–

Born in Pongaroa, New Zealand, Maurice Wilkins received a B.A. in physics from St. John's College, Cambridge University, and a Ph.D. from the University of Birmingham in England in 1940. The research he did for his Ph.D. dissertation led to improvements in radar screens during World War II. During the war, Wilkins worked in the Manhattan District (better known by its unofficial name, the Manhattan Project) at the University of California at Berkeley. This group, a unit of the U.S. Army Corps of Engineers, administered the research team that developed the atomic bomb.

While at Berkeley, Wilkins became interested in biology. In 1945 he became a lecturer in biophysics at St. Andrews University in Scotland and then at King's College, University of London. While at King's College he became an authority on the structure of nucleic acids and began studying DNA. He and British scientist Rosalind Franklin used X-ray diffraction analysis to determine the shape of DNA. These X-ray studies of DNA were the basis for the model of DNA structure developed by American biologist James Watson and British molecular biologist Francis Crick. In 1962, Wilkins shared the Nobel Prize in physiology or medicine with Watson and Crick for his contributions to their findings. Rosalind Franklin had died six years previously, and so could not be awarded a share of the prize. (*See* Crick *and* Watson, Biology: Nucleic Acids and the Genetic Code.)

BOOKS ABOUT WILKINS

Judson, Horace F. *The Eighth Day of Creation: Makers of the Revolution in Biology.* Simon 1979 $15.95. ISBN 0-671-22540-5 History of the discoveries in molecular biology and the scientists involved during the period 1930–1970.

Olby, Robert. *The Path to the Double Helix.* Univ of Washington Pr 1974. (o.p.) $23.50. ISBN 0-295-95359-4 History of molecular biology: the ideas, methods, and people that led to understanding of the structure of DNA.

Watson, James D. *The Double Helix: A Personal Account of the Discovery of the Structure of DNA* (1968). Atheneum 1985 $6.95. ISBN 0-689-70602-2 Watson's own account of the events and people involved in determining the structure of DNA.

CLASSIFICATION OF ORGANISMS

Jeffrey, C. *An Introduction to Plant Taxonomy.* Cambridge Univ Pr 1982 $14.95. ISBN 0-521-28775-8

Margulis, Lynn, and Karlene Schwartz. *Five Kingdoms: An Illustrated Guide to the Phyla of Life on Earth.* Freeman 1987 $24.95. ISBN 0-7167-1912-6

Matthews, R. E. (ed). *Classification and Nomenclature of Viruses.* Karger 1982 $29.00. ISBN 3-8055-3557-0

Porter, Cedric L. *Taxonomy of Flowering Plants.* Freeman 1967 $34.95. ISBN 0-7167-0709-8

*Rose, Kenneth J. *Classification of the Animal Kingdom.* McKay 1980 $8.95. ISBN 0-679-20508-X History of the development of a system for classifying living things; includes classification of protists and animals.

ARISTOTLE 384–322 BC

See also Aristotle, Vol. 2, World History: Ancient Greece.

Born in Stagira, Greece, Aristotle was an able and dedicated student of the Greek philosopher Plato. After Plato's death in 347 BC, Aristotle went to the court of Hermeias, the ruler of two towns in Asia Minor, Assos and Atarneus, and a former student of Plato. Aristotle married Hermeias' adopted daughter, Pythias, and was preparing to settle in Assos, but political events forced him to flee to the island of Lesbos, where he spent some time studying the plants and animals.

In 340 BC Philip, the king of Macedonia, asked Aristotle to undertake the education of his son Alexander, who became Alexander the Great. The result of this assignment was that Alexander became that rare phenomenon—a ruler who, although not a scholar, had a great respect for scholarship. In 334 BC Aristotle returned to Athens and began to teach rhetoric and philosophy in a school he established called the Lyceum.

In a very real way, Aristotle was more of a biologist than a philosopher. He developed a zoological garden and established a museum of natural history in which specimens he gathered himself or were sent to him by his students were displayed.

Aristotle was concerned with reasoning as a process. His writings on logic, collectively called the *Organon,* was the standard text up to modern times. Aristotle was one of the few philosophers of his time and for hundreds of years afterwards who espoused inductive reasoning as well as deductive reasoning and the use of experimentation. Inductive reasoning proceeds from facts to conclusions. Deductive reasoning begins with assumptions, or things that are thought to be true, and proceeds to generalizations, which will be valid if the assumptions are correct. Both types of reasoning are used in the scientific method and both are needed for the advancement of scientific knowledge.

BOOKS BY ARISTOTLE

Aristotle's Physics. H. G. Apostle (tr). Peripatetic 1980 $10.80. ISBN 0-9602870-3-5
The Complete Works of Aristotle: The Revised Oxford Translation. 2 vols. Princeton Univ Pr 1984 $79.00. ISBN 0-691-109950-2
Generation of Animals. Harvard Univ Pr 1943 $14.50. ISBN 0-674-99403-5

BOOKS ABOUT ARISTOTLE

Ackrill, J. L. (ed). *Aristotle the Philosopher.* Oxford Univ Pr 1981 $10.95. ISBN 0-19-289118-9 Guide to the philosophy of Aristotle.
Barnes, Jonathan. *Aristotle.* Oxford Univ Pr 1982 $5.95. ISBN 0-19-287581-7 Introduction to the science and philosophy of Aristotle.
Randall, John A., Jr. *Aristotle.* Columbia Univ Pr 1962 $17.00. ISBN 0-231-08529-X Relates the thinking of Aristotle to the present.

LINNAEUS, CAROLUS 1707–1778

Carolus Linnaeus, also known as Carl von Linne, was born in Rashult, Sweden. He studied at the universities of Lund and Uppsala, and at Harderwyck in the Netherlands, where he received a degree in medicine. At the age of 25, Linnaeus undertook an expedition to Lapland to collect exotic plants. This trip was the most adventurous exploit of his life. It was also the beginning of a project that would involve him for 20 years: naming, describing, and classifying every organism known to the Western world.

While pursuing his botanical and taxonomic research, Linnaeus practiced medicine to earn a living. As his research progressed, he published numerous works. In 1741 he was appointed professor of medicine at Uppsala, and in the following year he became professor of botany at the same institution. By 1758 he had completed his taxonomic project by classifying 4,400 species of animals and 7,700 species of plants. In his middle age, Linnaeus became a university administrator.

Linnaeus was a botanist, physician, teacher, writer, and administrator and the most influential naturalist of his time. Because he developed the biological classification systems for plant and animal life, he is known as the father of biological taxonomy. Linnaeus's enduring contributions were the development of the principles and methods for defining taxonomic groups and the establishment of the need for the use of uniform taxonomic systems. He also established the scientific method of naming plants and animals. With modifications and revisions, Linnaeus's systems have been used until the present.

BOOKS BY LINNAEUS

Hortus Cliffortianus (1737). Lubrecht and Cramer 1968 $144.00. ISBN 3-7682-0543-6
Philosophia Botanica (1751). Lubrecht and Cramer 1966 $90.00. ISBN 3-7682-0350-6
Systema Naturae (1735). Coronet 1964 $44.00. ISBN 0-317-55882-X

BOOK ABOUT LINNAEUS

Blunt, Wilfrid. *The Compleat Naturalist: A Life of Linnaeus.* Viking 1971. (o.p.) $14.95. ISBN 0-670-23396-X Examines the life, work, and accomplishments of the man who developed the modern system of classifying organisms.

VIRUSES AND BACTERIA

*DeKruif, Paul. *Microbe Hunters.* Harcourt 1966 $6.95. ISBN 0-15-659413-7 Stories of scientists who made great discoveries with a microscope.
*Dixon, Bernard. *Magnificent Microbes.* Atheneum 1976. (o.p.) $4.95. ISBN 0-689-70589-1 Exploration of the role of microbes in maintaining life on Earth and human health.
Dube, H. C. *Textbook of Fungi, Bacteria, and Viruses.* Advent 1986 $27.50. ISBN 0-7069-2885-7
*Knight, David E. *Viruses: Life's Smallest Enemies.* Morrow 1981. (o.p.) $11.95. ISBN 0-688-00713-9 Discussion of three types of viruses, their chemical compositions, and links with diseases.
Martin, S. J. *The Biochemistry of Viruses.* Cambridge Univ Pr 1978 $44.50. ISBN 0-521-21678-8
*Nourse, Alan E. *Viruses.* Watts 1983 $10.40. ISBN 0-531-04534-X Story of the discovery of vaccination and discussions of immunity and current research on viruses.
Scott, Andrew. *Pirates of the Cell: The Story of Viruses from Molecule to Microbe.* Basil Blackwell 1987 $12.95. ISBN 0-631-15637-2
Singleton, Paul, and Diana Sainsbury. *Dictionary of Microbiology and Molecular Biology.* Wiley 1988 $155.00. ISBN 0-471-91114-3
Sinha, U., and S. Srivastava. *An Introduction to Bacteria.* Advent 1983 $8.95. ISBN 0-7069-2134-8
*Teasdale, Jim. *Microbes.* Silver 1985 $6.75. ISBN 0-382-09002-0 Introduction to the study of microbes, including viruses, bacteria, algae, fungi, and protozoans.
VanDemark, Paul J., and Barry L. Batzing. *The Microbes: An Introduction to Their Nature and Importance.* Benjamin-Cummings 1987 $44.95. ISBN 0-201-08373-6

KOCH, ROBERT 1843–1910

Robert Koch was born in Clausthal, Germany. He first studied the natural sciences at Göttingen University and then switched to medicine. In 1866 he received a medical degree and went to Berlin, where he worked in charity clinics.

Koch practiced medicine in a rural community for a short time and then joined the army to serve as a field physician. He gained valuable experience serving on the battlefield during the Franco–Prussian War of 1870–1871. Upon leaving the army, he obtained a post as district physician in Wollstein (now Wolsztyn, Poland). There, in 1876, during a severe outbreak of anthrax, a serious disease of cattle and sheep, Koch made his first important discovery. He identified the bacillus that causes anthrax—the first time a specific pathogen was proven to cause a specific disease. This breakthrough earned Koch an appointment to the Imperial Health Service in Berlin.

Berlin was Koch's headquarters for the rest of his lifetime. He became a professor at the University of Berlin in 1885. In 1891 he became director of the Institute for Infectious Diseases, a research center founded for him. Throughout the years he traveled extensively in Europe and Africa to visit the sites of epidemics. He identified the organism that causes cholera, as well as the bacteria that cause many other diseases of humans and animals.

Koch's work established him as the founder of modern bacteriology, tropical medicine, and public health. Among his major contributions are Koch's postulates, the four steps that investigators must take to prove that a specific agent is the cause of a specific disease. He also developed the methods used for culturing and staining bacteria, growing pure bacterial cultures, and using steam as a sterilizer. In addition, he discovered the bacillus that causes tuberculosis and studied this disease extensively. In 1905 he received the Nobel Prize in physiology and medicine for his investigations of tuberculosis.

Koch had enormous impact on the development of the field of public health. He was responsible for much of the early public health legislation in Europe and for developing public awareness of disease control through hygienic and immunologic measures.

BOOK BY KOCH

Founders of Modern Medicine (1939). (coauthored with Ilia Mechnikov, *et al*) D. Berger (tr). Ayer (repr of 1939 ed) $21.00. ISBN 0-8369-2119-9

BOOKS ABOUT KOCH

Brock, Thomas D. *Robert Koch: A Life in Medicine and Bacteriology.* Sci Tech Pubs 1988 $35.00. ISBN 0-910239-19-3 Description of the life and the tremendous accomplishments of Koch.

*DeKruif, Paul. *Microbe Hunters.* Harcourt 1966 $6.95. ISBN 0-15-659413-7 Stories of scientists who made great discoveries with a microscope; includes discussion of Koch.

*Dolan, Edward F., Jr. *Adventure with a Microscope.* Dodd 1964. (o.p.) Story of Koch's achievements, beginning with the gift of a microscope from his wife.

Dubos, René. *The Unseen World.* Rockefeller Institute Pr 1962. (o.p.) $6.00. ISBN 0-874-70002-7 Exploration of the relationship between microbes and other life forms; discusses the scientists who studied these organisms.

Riedman, Sarah R. *Shots Without Guns: The Story of Vaccination.* Rand 1960. (o.p.) Story of the fight against epidemics of diseases from smallpox to polio.

Walker, M. E. *Pioneers of Public Health: The Story of Some Benefactors of the Human Race.* Ayer 1930 $20.00. ISBN 0-8369-0965-8 Sketches of the lives and works of scientists who greatly influenced medicine and public health.

PASTEUR, LOUIS 1822–1895

Louis Pasteur was born in Dole, France. After receiving a B.A. in 1840 and a B.S. in 1842 from the Royal College in Besançon, he studied chemistry at Ecole Normale Supérieure in Paris. He received a Ph.D. in chemistry in 1847.

This many-sided scientific genius spent most of his life teaching at various universities throughout France, including the Sorbonne and the Ecole Normale in Paris. In addition, he was director of the Pasteur Institute in Paris from its creation in 1888 until his death in 1895.

Pasteur had a passion for work and combined his teaching with research of tremendous consequence. In the course of studying microorganisms, he disproved the ancient theory of spontaneous generation. This theory holds that certain living things arise from nonliving matter, such as mud. His studies of fermentation led him to propose that yeast was an organism, not a catalyst, and that its life activities were responsible for the conversion of sugar to alcohol. Pasteur proposed that different organisms acting on different substances produced the different end products of fermentation. Similarly, he said, different diseases were caused by different organisms. Pasteur also discovered anaerobic respiration and found that spoilage of wine and beer is caused by contamination by organisms and that heating destroys these contaminants. The heating process, now called pasteurization, saved the wine and beer industries of France. Pasteur's investigations did not stop there. He investigated diseases of the silkworm, which were threatening the French silk industry, and showed how to prevent these diseases. He confirmed French physician Robert Koch's (*see* Koch, Vol. 2, Biology: Viruses and Bacteria) discovery of a specific bacillus as the cause of anthrax and invented the use of attenuated (weakened) pathogens in vaccines to prevent disease, first applying this technique against anthrax and later against rabies. In studying rabies, he discovered the existence of viruses and developed the only treatment for rabies known until very recent times.

Although Pasteur received many honors, he declined all temptations to wealth. Despite a stroke that left him partially paralyzed at the age of 46, he continued to do research until the end of his life.

BOOKS BY PASTEUR

Founders of Modern Medicine (1939). (coauthored with Ilia Mechnikov, *et al*) D. Berger (tr). Ayer (repr of 1939 ed) $21.00. ISBN 0-8369-2119-9
Studies on Fermentation (1879). James B. Conant (tr and ed). Harvard Univ Pr 1952. (o.p.)

BOOKS ABOUT PASTEUR

*Birch, Beverly. *Louis Pasteur: The Scientist Who Found the Cause of Infectious Disease and Invented Pasteurization.* Gareth Stevens 1990 $12.95. ISBN 1-55532-839-3 An easily read account telling about Pasteur's life, accomplishments, and personality.
Cuny, Hilaire. *Louis Pasteur: The Man and His Theories.* Scribner's 1976. (o.p.) Biography of Pasteur; includes a selection of his writings.
*DeKruif, Paul. *Microbe Hunters.* Harcourt 1966 $6.95. ISBN 0-15-659413-7 Stories of scientists who made great discoveries with a microscope.
Dubos, René. *Louis Pasteur: Free Lance of Science.* Da Capo 1986 $11.95. ISBN 0-306-80262-7 A look at Pasteur's life and contributions to medicine and other fields.
Dubos, René. *Pasteur and Modern Science.* Sci Tech Pubs 1988 $22.00. ISBN 0-910239-18-5 Examination of Pasteur's work as it relates to various aspects of modern scientific research in microbiology and immunology.
Dubos, René. *The Unseen World.* Rockefeller Institute Pr 1962. (o.p.) $6.00. ISBN 0-874-

70002-7 Exploration of the relationship between microbes and other life forms; discusses the scientists who studied these organisms.

Moore, Ruth E. *The Coil of Life: The Story of the Great Discoveries of the Life Sciences.* Knopf 1961. (o.p.) $8.95. ISBN 0-394-41966-9 Discussion of the discoveries pertaining to the chemical basis of heredity; includes information about Pasteur.

Riedman, Sarah R. *Shots Without Guns: The Story of Vaccination.* Rand 1960. (o.p.) Story of the fight against epidemics of diseases from smallpox to polio.

Walker, M. E. *Pioneers of Public Health: The Story of Some Benefactors of the Human Race.* Ayer 1930 $20.00. ISBN 0-8369-0965-8 Sketches of the lives and works of scientists who greatly influenced medicine and public health.

Wood, Laura N. *Louis Pasteur.* Messner 1948. (o.p.) Story of Louis Pasteur's contributions to the progress and welfare of people.

See also Vol. 2, Health: Communicable Diseases.

PROTISTS

*DeKruif, Paul. *Microbe Hunters.* Harcourt 1966 $6.95. ISBN 0-15-659413-7 Stories of scientists who made great discoveries with a microscope.

*Dixon, Bernard. *Magnificent Microbes.* Atheneum 1976. (o.p.) $4.95. ISBN 0-689-70589-1 Exploration of the role of microbes in maintaining life on Earth and human health.

Jahn, Theodore L., *et al. How to Know the Protozoa.* Brown 1978 $12.80. ISBN 0-697-04759-8

Lee, John J., *et al. An Illustrated Guide to the Protozoa.* Allen 1985 $80.00. ISBN 0-914023-25-X

*Teasdale, Jim. *Microbes.* Silver 1985 $6.75. ISBN 0-382-09002-0 Introduction to the study of microbes, including viruses, bacteria, algae, fungi, and protozoans.

FUNGI

Brightman, Frank H. *The Oxford Book of Flowerless Plants.* Oxford Univ Pr 1966. (o.p.) $13.95. ISBN 0-19-217630-7

Dickinson, Colin, and John Lucas. *The Encyclopedia of Mushrooms.* Putnam 1979. (o.p.) $25.00. ISBN 0-399-12104-8

Dube, H. C. *Textbook of Fungi, Bacteria, and Viruses.* Advent 1986 $27.50. ISBN 0-7069-2885-7

*Johnson, Sylvia. *Mushrooms.* Lerner 1982 $12.95. ISBN 0-8225-1473-7 Discussion of mushrooms and other fungi, with explanations of their methods of obtaining food and their growth and reproduction.

Singleton, Paul, and Diana Sainsbury. *Dictionary of Microbiology and Molecular Biology.* Wiley 1988 $155.00. ISBN 0-471-91114-3

*Teasdale, Jim. *Microbes.* Silver 1985 $6.75. ISBN 0-382-09002-0 Introduction to the study of microbes, including viruses, bacteria, algae, fungi, and protozoans.

PLANTS

*Asimov, Isaac. *How Did We Find Out About Photosynthesis?* Walker 1989 $11.95. ISBN 0-8027-6899-7 Scientists are still trying to understand the phenomenon of turning sunlight into food.

Beck, Charles B. (ed). *Origin and Evolution of Gymnosperms.* Columbia Univ Pr 1988 $45.00. ISBN 0-231-06358-X

*Beller, Joel. *Experimenting with Plants.* Prentice 1985 $7.95. ISBN 0-668-05991-5 Guide for conducting experiments with plants.

Bold, Harold C., and Michael J. Wynne. *Introduction to the Algae.* Prentice 1985 $56.00. ISBN 0-13-477746-8

Brightman, Frank H. *The Oxford Book of Flowerless Plants.* Oxford Univ Pr 1967. (o.p.) $35.00. ISBN 0-19-910004-7

Buvet, R. *Ontogeny, Cell Differentiation, and Structure of Vascular Plants.* Springer-Verlag 1989 $175.00. ISBN 0-387-19213-1

*Collingwood, G. H., and Warren D. Brush. *Knowing Your Trees.* American Forestry 1978 $9.50. ISBN 0-686-26731-1 Pictorial guide to 182 species of trees.

Conard, Henry S., and Paul L. Redfearn, Jr. *How to Know the Mosses and Liverworts.* Brown 1979 $12.80. ISBN 0-697-04768-7

Cronquist, Arthur. *How to Know the Seed Plants.* Brown 1979 $12.80. ISBN 0-697-04761-X

Dahlgren, R. M., *et al. The Families of the Monocotyledons.* Springer-Verlag 1985 $135.00. ISBN 0-387-13655-X

*Dowden, Anne O. *From Flower to Fruit.* Crowell 1984 $14.70. ISBN 0-690-04402-X Pictorial guide to the anatomy of the flowers of some temperate-zone plants.

Esau, Katherine. *Anatomy of Seed Plants.* Wiley 1977 $45.95. ISBN 0-471-24520-8

*Eshleman, Alan. *Poison Plants.* Houghton 1970 $12.95. ISBN 0-395-25298-9 A description of all kinds of poisonous plants, including fungi, and how to identify them.

Foged, Niels. *Diatoms in Alaska.* Lubrecht and Cramer 1981 $48.00. ISBN 3-7682-1303-X

Fryxell, Greta A. (ed). *Survival Strategies of the Algae.* Cambridge Univ Pr 1983 $42.50. ISBN 0-521-25067-6

Gelderen, Dick van, and Richard van Hoey Smith. *Conifers.* Timber 1986 $65.00. ISBN 0-88192-056-8

Guedes, M. *Morphology of Seed Plants.* Lubrecht and Cramer 1979 $30.00. ISBN 3-7682-1195-9

Hall, John, *et al. Plant Cell Structure and Metabolism.* Wiley 1986 $34.95. 0-470-20487-7

Heywood, Vernon H. (ed). *Flowering Plants of the World.* Prentice 1985 $39.95. ISBN 0-13-322405-8

Hora, Bayard (ed). *The Oxford Encyclopedia of Trees of the World.* Oxford Univ Pr 1981 $24.95. ISBN 0-19-217712-5

*Johnson, Sylvia A. *Mosses.* Lerner 1983 $12.95. ISBN 0-8225-1482-6 Descriptions of the mosses and liverworts, including life cycles and ecological relationships.

*Kavaler, Lucy. *Green Magic: Algae Rediscovered.* Crowell 1983 $12.70. ISBN 0-690-04221-3 Discussion of one-celled algae, their characteristics, where they are found, and their uses.

Little, R. John, and C. Eugene Jones. *A Dictionary of Botany.* Van Nostrand 1980 $18.50. ISBN 0-442-24169-0

McFarlane, Ruth B. *Collecting and Preserving Plants for Science and Pleasure.* Arco 1985 $8.95. ISBN 0-668-06013-1

Northington, David K., and J. R. Goodin. *The Botanical World.* Mosby 1984 $36.95. ISBN 0-8016-1893-2

Parsons, Frances T. *How to Know the Ferns.* Peter Smith $12.75. ISBN 0-8446-2707-0

*Pickett-Heaps, Jeremy. *New Light on the Green Algae.* Carolina Biological 1982 $1.90. ISBN 0-89278-315-X A look at the evolution of green algae based on their structural details as revealed by the electron microscope.

*Pringle, Laurence. *Being a Plant.* Crowell 1983. (o.p.) $12.89. ISBN 0-690-04347-3

Thorough discussion of the structure and functions of plants and their complex relationships with other living things.

Rushforth, Keith D. *Conifers.* Facts on File 1987 $24.95. ISBN 0-8160-1735-2

Schofield, Wilfred B. *Introduction to Bryology.* Macmillan 1985 $45.00. ISBN 0-02-949660-8

Slack, Adrian. *Insect-Eating Plants and How to Grow Them.* Univ of Washington Pr 1988 $19.95. ISBN 0-295-96637-8

*Stone, Doris M. *The Lives of Plants: Exploring the Wonders of Botany.* Scribner's 1983 $15.95. ISBN 0-684-17907-5 Discussion of seed plants, including structure, reproduction, seed germination, making and using food, and cloning.

Street, H., and H. Opik. *The Physiology of Flowering Plants.* Elsevier 1976 $18.50. ISBN 0-444-19505-X

Toothill, Elizabeth, and Stephen Blackmore (eds). *The Facts on File Dictionary of Botany.* Facts on File 1984 $21.95. ISBN 0-87196-861-4

*Wexler, Jerome. *From Spore to Spore: Ferns and How They Grow.* Dodd 1985 $9.95. ISBN 0-396-08317-X Explanation of ferns and how they reproduce and grow.

*Woods, Sylvia. *Plant Facts and Fancies.* Faber & Faber 1985 $10.95. ISBN 0-571-13436-X A survey of plant life that covers such topics as their history and uses, and unusual facts about them.

ANIMALS

Alexander, R. McNeill. *The Encyclopedia of Animal Biology.* Facts on File 1987 $24.95. ISBN 0-8160-1817-0

Buchsbaum, Ralph, *et al. The Audubon Society Encyclopedia of Animal Life.* Portland House 1986 $24.95. ISBN 0-517-54657-4

*Loeper, John J. *Crusade for Kindness: Henry Bergh and the ASPCA.* Atheneum 1991 $12.95. ISBN 0-689-31560-0 Establishment of the ASPCA in 1866 by Bergh is described and its growth to 400,000 members today.

*Rowland-Entwistle, Theodore. *Illustrated Facts and Records Book of Animals.* Arco 1983 $9.95. ISBN 0-688-05730-0 Collection of facts and records covering the entire animal kingdom.

*Rahn, Joan Elma. *Ears, Hearing, and Balance.* Macmillan 1984 $12.95. ISBN 0-689-31055-2 Discussion of how humans and animals hear and of how animal hearing differs in usage from human hearing.

*Simon, Hilda. *Sight and Seeing: A World of Light and Color.* Putnam 1983 $12.95. ISBN 0-399-20929-8 Comparison of the sense of sight in animals, from insects to humans; includes discussion of eye structure, binocular vision, and color vision.

Villee, Claude A., *et al. General Zoology.* Saunders 1984 $48.00. ISBN 0-03-062451-7

INVERTEBRATES

Audubon Society Staff *et al. The Audubon Society Field Guide to North American Insects and Spiders.* Knopf 1980 $14.45. ISBN 0-394-50763-0

Bland, Roger G., and H. E. Jaques. *How to Know the Insects.* Brown 1978 $5.95. ISBN 0-697-04752-0

*Buchsbaum, Ralph. *Animals Without Backbones: An Introduction to the Invertebrates.* Univ of Chicago Pr 1972 $15.00. ISBN 0-226-07870-1 A classic book, detailing the basic structure and habits of the main groups of invertebrates.

Buchsbaum, Ralph. *Butterflies of the World.* Facts on File 1988 $22.95. ISBN 0-8160-1601-1

*Cottam, Clarence, and Herbert S. Zim. *Insects.* Western Pub 1987 $3.95. ISBN 0-307-24055-X A field guide identifying and describing over 200 common insects, for young readers.

*Evans, Howard E. *Life on a Little-Known Planet.* Univ of Chicago Pr 1984 $11.95. ISBN 0-226-22258-6 Introduction to the enormous, diverse class of insects, with an exposition of the interrelatedness of all life.

Foelix, Rainer F. *Biology of Spiders.* Harvard Univ Pr 1987 $14.95. ISBN 0-674-07432-7

*Jacobson, Morris K., and Rosemary K. Pang. *Wonders of Sponges.* Dodd 1976. (o.p.) Discussion of sponges, their classification, characteristics, and uses; includes information about the sponge-fishing industry and sponge collecting.

O'Toole, Christopher (ed). *The Encyclopedia of Insects.* Facts on File 1986 $24.95. ISBN 0-8160-1358-6

*Patent, Dorothy H. *The Lives of Spiders.* Holiday 1980 $12.95. ISBN 0-8234-0418-8 Introduction to the world of spiders.

*Patent, Dorothy H., and Paul C. Schroeder. *Beetles and How They Live.* Holiday 1978 $7.95. ISBN 0-8234-0332-7 Story of beetles, with descriptions of their habits and habitats, discussion of their usefulness and harmfulness to humans, and instructions for collecting them.

Preston-Mofham, Rod, and Ken Preston-Mofham. *Spiders of the World.* Facts on File 1984 $22.95. ISBN 0-87196-996-3

*Whalley, Paul. *Butterfly Moth.* Knopf 1988 $13.99. ISBN 0-394-99618-6 Characteristics of moths and butterflies; various species and their life cycles are described in short chapters.

Wooten, Anthony. *Insects of the World.* Facts on File 1985 $22.95. ISBN 0-87196-991-2

VERTEBRATES

Audubon Society Staff, *et al. The Audubon Society Field Guide to North American Fishes, Whales, and Dolphins.* Knopf 1983 $14.45. ISBN 0-394-53405-0

Audubon Society Staff, *et al. The Audubon Society Field Guide to North American Reptiles and Amphibians.* Knopf 1979 $14.45. ISBN 0-394-50824-6

Baker, Mary L. *Whales, Dolphins, and Porpoises of the World.* Doubleday 1987 $35.00. ISBN 0-385-15366-X

Burton, Maurice. *The World of Birds.* Facts on File 1985 $9.95. ISBN 0-8160-1063-3

Cloudsley-Thompson, John. *Crocodiles and Alligators.* Raintree 1980 $10.65. ISBN 0-8172-1084-9

Duellman, William E., and Linda Trueb. *Biology of Amphibians.* McGraw 1986 $44.95. ISBN 0-07-017977-8

*Ellis, Richard. *The Book of Whales.* Knopf 1985 $24.95. ISBN 0-394-73371-1 Description of the evolution, anatomy, and behavior of whales.

*Ellis, Richard. *Dolphins and Porpoises.* Knopf 1989 $24.95. ISBN 0-679-72286-6 Discussion of dolphins and porpoises, including classification, behavior, reproduction, and intelligence.

Grzimek, Bernhard (ed). *Grzimek's Encyclopedia of Mammals.* 5 vols. McGraw 1990 $500.00. ISBN 0-07-909508-9

Halliday, Tim R., and Kraig Adler. *The Encyclopedia of Reptiles and Amphibians.* Facts on File 1986 $24.95. ISBN 0-8160-1359-4

Harrison, Richard, *et al. Whales, Dolphins, and Porpoises.* Facts on File 1988 $35.00. ISBN 0-8160-1977-0

*Jenkins, Marie M. *Kangaroos, Opossums, and Other Marsupials.* Holiday 1975. (o.p.) $6.95. ISBN 0-8234-0264-9 History and characteristics of marsupials and monotremes.

Kavanagh, Michael. *A Complete Guide to Monkeys, Apes, and Other Primates.* Viking 1984 $19.95. ISBN 0-670-43543-0

Lanham, Url N. *The Fishes.* Columbia Univ Pr 1967 $12.00. ISBN 0-231-08581-8

MacDonald, David W. (ed). *The Encyclopedia of Mammals.* Facts on File 1984 $65.00. ISBN 0-87196-871-1

*Minelli, Giuseppe. *Amphibians.* Facts on File 1987 $12.95. ISBN 0-8160-1557-0 Description of amphibians, their characteristics and evolutionary history.

*Napier, John R. *Primates and Their Adaptations.* Carolina Biological 1987 $1.90. ISBN

0-89278-228-5 Discussion of the primates, with emphasis on characteristics of their hands, skull, posture, movement, brain, and behavior.

Napier, John R., and P. H. Napier. *The Natural History of the Primates.* MIT Pr 1985 $19.95. ISBN 0-262-14039-X

Nelson, Joseph S. *Fishes of the World.* Wiley 1984 $52.50. ISBN 0-471-86475-7

Perrins, Christopher, and Alex L. Middleton (eds). *The Encyclopedia of Birds.* Facts on File 1985 $45.00. ISBN 0-8160-1150-8

*Poole, Robert M. (ed). *The Wonder of Birds.* National Geographic 1983 $39.95. ISBN 0-87044-471-9 Collection of information about birds, including their evolution, diversity, behavior, and life cycles, the relationship of humans to birds, and endangered species of birds.

Richard, Alison F. *Primates in Nature.* Freeman 1985 $17.95. ISBN 0-7167-1647-X

*Scott, Shirley L. (ed). *Field Guide to the Birds of North America.* National Geographic 1983 $14.95. ISBN 0-87044-472-7 Identification guide that includes scientific names, plumages, field marks, measurements, voices, behaviors, and habitats.

*Smith, Hobart, and Edmund Brodie, Jr. *Reptiles of North America.* Western Pub 1982 $9.95. ISBN 0-307-13666-3 Field identification guide to reptiles and interesting facts about them.

THE HUMAN BODY

*Asimov, Isaac. *How Did We Find Out About Blood?* Walker 1986 $10.95. ISBN 0-8027-6647-1 Story of how our knowledge of the function of blood and the circulatory system developed.

*Asimov, Isaac. *How Did We Find Out About the Brain?* Walker 1987 $10.95. ISBN 0-8027-6736-2 Account of how scientists have learned about the brain and how it works.

*Avraham, Regina. *The Circulatory System.* Chelsea 1989 $18.95. ISBN 0-7910-0013-3 In addition to describing the heart and circulatory systems, various heart ailments and their treatments are discussed.

*Avraham, Regina. *The Digestive System.* Chelsea 1989 $18.95. ISBN 0-7910-0015-X With text, photographs, and diagrams the human digestive system is explained.

*Blake, Charles A. *The Pituitary Gland.* Carolina Biological 1984 $1.90. ISBN 0-89278-318-4 Discussion of the structure and function of the pituitary gland and the hormones it secretes.

Brody, Jane. *Jane Brody's Good Food Book.* Bantam 1987 $12.95. ISBN 0-553-34346-7

*Bruun, Ruth D., and Bertel Bruun. *The Human Body.* Random 1982 $9.95. ISBN 0-394-84424-6 Regional and systemic approach to the structure and physiology of the human body.

Clemente, Carmine D. (ed). *Gray's Anatomy of the Human Body.* Lea & Febiger 1984 $79.50. ISBN 0-8121-0644-X

Cunningham, John D. *Human Biology.* Harper 1983 $34.50. ISBN 0-06-041451-0

*Dunbar, Robert E. *The Heart and Circulatory System.* Watts 1984 $12.40. ISBN 0-531-04766-0 Discussion of the structure and function of the heart and circulatory system; includes projects students can carry out to further or to apply learnings.

*Facklam, Margery, and Howard Facklam. *The Brain: Magnificent Mind Machine.* Harcourt 1982 $12.95. ISBN 0-15-211388-6 Discussion of the human brain; includes such topics as the history of brain research, evolution of brain structures, how the brain works, and current research on the brain.

*Gray, Henry. *Gray's Anatomy.* Running Pr 1987 $12.98. ISBN 0-89471-135-0 Unabridged reprint of the 1901 classic edition; heavily illustrated, thorough descriptions of human anatomy.

*Kittredge, Mary. *The Human Body: An Overview.* Chelsea 1990 $18.95. ISBN 0-7910-0019-2 A history of the human body and the scientists who made discoveries about it; each system explained, with illustrations.

*Lewis, Paul, and David Rubenstein. *The Human Body.* Bantam 1972 $3.95. ISBN 0-553-23608-3 Color guide to the basic systems of the human body; includes information about how the body systems work and interrelate.

*Moffat, D. B. *The Control of Water Balance by the Kidney.* Carolina Biological 1978 $1.90. ISBN 0-89278-214-5 Structure of the kidney and the process of urine production.

*Montagna, William. *Human Skin.* Carolina Biological 1986 $1.90. ISBN 0-89278-159-9 Discussion of the skin, its layers, glands, and other structures, with an explanation of the sense of touch.

*Nourse, Alan. *Your Immune System.* Watts 1982 $10.40. ISBN 0-531-04462-9 Discussion of the workings of the body's immune defense system; includes what happens when the system functions imperfectly, too vigorously, or not at all and describes current research in immunology.

*Peavy, Linda S., and Ursula Smith. *Food, Nutrition, and You.* Scribner's 1982 $13.95. ISBN 0-684-17461-8 Discussion of nutrients—carbohydrates, proteins, fats, minerals, and vitamins—and how the body uses them.

Vander, Arthur J., and Dorothy S. Luciano. *Human Physiology: The Mechanisms of Body Function.* McGraw 1989 $48.95. ISBN 0-07-066969-4

*Ward, Brian. *Body Maintenance.* Watts 1983 $12.40. ISBN 0-531-04457-2 Descriptions of the control systems that work to keep the body healthy.

*Ward, Brian. *The Brain and Nervous System.* Watts 1981 $12.40. ISBN 0-531-04288-X Study of the structure and function of the brain and nervous system; includes consideration of learning and memory.

*Ward, Brian. *Food and Digestion.* Watts 1982 $12.40. ISBN 0-531-04458-0 Discussion of the digestive system, its structure and function.

*Ward, Brian. *The Lungs and Breathing.* Watts 1982 $12.40. ISBN 0-531-04358-4 Discussion of the human respiratory system and how it works.

Woodburne, Russell T., and William E. Burkel. *Essential Human Anatomy.* Oxford Univ Pr 1988 $41.95. ISBN 0-19-504502-5

See also Vol. 2, Health: Body Systems *and* Personal Care.

REPRODUCTION AND DEVELOPMENT

*Edwards, R. G. *Beginnings of Human Life.* Carolina Biological 1981 $1.90. ISBN 0-89278-217-X A look at the formation of an egg in the ovary, fertilization of the egg, and implantation of the egg in the uterus.

*Edwards, R. G. *Test-Tube Babies.* Carolina Biological 1981 $1.90. ISBN 0-89278-289-7 A look at the methods of fertilizing eggs outside the body.

Gilbert, Scott. *Developmental Biology.* Sinauer 1988 $42.95. ISBN 0-87893-248-8

*Goran, Morris, and Marjorie Goran. *Lure of Longevity: The Art and Science of Living Longer.* R & E Pubs 1984 $12.95. ISBN 0-88247-709-9 A review of aging—life style, diet, behavior, and the biology of older people.

*John, Bernard, and Kenneth Lewis. *The Meiotic Mechanism.* Carolina Biological 1984 $2.40. ISBN 0-89278-265-X Examination of the process of meiosis.

*John, Bernard, and Kenneth Lewis. *Somatic Cell Division.* Carolina Biological 1980 $2.40. ISBN 0-89278-226-9 Discussion of mitosis and cytokinesis in prokaryotic and eukaryotic cells.

*Johnson, Sylvia. *Inside an Egg.* Lerner 1982 $12.95. ISBN 0-8225-1472-9 Illustrated development of a chicken egg, from fertilization to hatching.

Katchadourian, Herant. *The Biology of Adolescence.* Freeman 1977 $13.95. ISBN 0-7167-0375-0

*McKinnell, Robert G. *Cloning of Frogs, Mice, and Other Animals.* Univ of Minnesota Pr 1985 $15.95. ISBN 0-8166-1360-5 Explanation of the cloning process and its importance in studies of cancer and aging.

*Meeuse, B. J. D. *Pollination.* Carolina Biological 1984 $1.90. ISBN 0-89278-333-8 Discussion of pollination carried out by bees, moths, birds, and mammals; also covers fertilization in seed plants.

*Miller, Jonathan, and David Pelham. *The Facts of Life.* Penguin 1984 $18.95. ISBN 0-670-30465-4 Presentation of three-dimensional models showing reproductive organs, conception, development of the fetus, and birth.

*Rankin, Chrissy. *How Life Begins.* Putnam 1984 $11.95. ISBN 0-399-21199-3 A look at birth and prenatal care in single-celled organisms, insects, reptiles, birds, and mammals; also considers prenatal care and protection after birth.

*Ward, Brian. *Birth and Growth.* Watts 1983 $12.40. ISBN 0-531-04459-9 Presentation of basic facts about human reproduction and development.

See also Vol. 2, Health: Growth and Development; Psychology: Human Development.

GENETICS AND HEREDITY

*Asimov, Isaac. *How Did We Find Out About Our Genes?* Walker 1983 $10.85. ISBN 0-8027-6500-9 History of the development of our knowledge of genes and heredity, beginning with Mendel.

*Bornstein, Sandy, and Jerry Bornstein. *New Frontiers in Genetics.* Messner 1984 $10.79. ISBN 0-671-45245-2 Discussion of recent advances in genetics, including the benefits and risks and problems that might arise through manipulation of genes.

*Gutnik, Martin J. *Genetics Projects for Young Scientists.* Watts 1985 $12.90. ISBN 0-531-04936-1 Suggestions for science projects relating to cell theory, cellular reproduction, and modern genetic theory.

*John, Bernard, and Kenneth Lewis. *The Meiotic Mechanism.* Carolina Biological 1984 $2.40. ISBN 0-89278-265-X An examination of the process of meiosis.

King, Robert C., and William D. Stansfield. *A Dictionary of Genetics.* Oxford Univ Pr 1985 $18.95. ISBN 0-19-503495-3

*Rosenfield, Israel, *et al.* *DNA for Beginners.* Writers & Readers 1983 $7.95. ISBN 0-86316-023-9 Comic-book presentation of the history of genetics, the discoveries leading to the determination of the structure of DNA, and problems created by genetic engineering.

*Silverstein, Alvin, and Virginia B. Silverstein. *The Genetics Explosion.* Four Winds 1980 $12.95. ISBN 0-02-782740-2 History of genetics; considers the implications of genetic research.

Wingerson, Lois. *Mapping Our Genes: The Genome Project and the Future of Medicine.* Dutton 1990 $19.95. ISBN 0-525-24877-3

McCLINTOCK, BARBARA   1902–

Born in Hartford, Connecticut, Barbara McClintock received a Ph.D. in 1927 from Cornell University. She has spent her life conducting research on the genetics of maize at Cornell, the California Institute of Technology, the University of Missouri, the Kaiser Wilhelm Institute in Berlin, and, since 1941, at the Carnegie Institute of Washington in Cold Spring Harbor, New York.

McClintock discovered anomalies in pigmentation and in other features of maize *(Zea mays)* that led her to question the prevailing picture of the chromosome as a linear arrangement of fixed genes. Her proposed picture of the chromosome involved a process of "transposition," in which the chromosome releases chromosomal elements (genes and groups of genes) from their original positions in a subprocess called dissociation and reinserts them into new positions. Though her original work was published in the 1940s and 1950s, she did not receive professional recognition until the advent of molecular biology in the 1950s. As knowledge of DNA grew, her theories were confirmed. She was awarded the Nobel Prize in physiology and medicine in 1983.

BOOKS ABOUT MCCLINTOCK

Hammond, Allen L. (ed). *A Passion to Know.* Scribner's 1984 $15.95. ISBN 0-684-18209-2 A collection of profiles of 20 scientists, including McClintock, who possess a drive to discover the unknown.

Keller, Evelyn F. *A Feeling for the Organism: The Life and Work of Barbara McClintock.* Freeman 1983 $8.95. ISBN 0-7167-1504-X Story of the relationship between the scientist and her field of science, genetics.

MENDEL, GREGOR JOHANN   1822–1884

Gregor Mendel was a Roman Catholic priest and a biologist. Born in Heinzendorf, Austria (now part of Czechoslovakia), he entered the monastery of St. Thomas in Brunn, Austria (now Brno, Czechoslovakia) in 1843 and later studied science and mathematics at the University of Vienna. After his return to the monastery in 1854, Mendel taught at the local high school and conducted research on heredity. His scientific studies were limited when he became abbot of the monastery in 1868.

In 1866 Mendel published in an obscure journal his classic article on the breeding of peas. Ignored in his lifetime, it was rediscovered in 1900, 16 years after his death. The article described Mendel's crucial findings about inheritance in pea plants. Mendel showed by intensive experimentation and mathematical analysis of his observations the incidence of dominant and recessive characteristics in the offspring of the pea plants and offered an explanation for the results he found. His findings, now known as Mendel's laws, apply to inheritance of many characteristics in plants, animals, and humans. Mendel's work is especially striking because chromosomes and genes were unknown in his time. His findings were of importance not only for the understanding of inheritance but also for the great practical assistance they provided in the breeding of animals and plants.

BOOK BY MENDEL

Experiments in Plant-Hybridisation (1866). Harvard Univ Pr 1965 $4.50. ISBN 0-674-27800-3

BOOKS ABOUT MENDEL

Moore, Ruth E. *The Coil of Life: The Story of the Great Discoveries of the Life Sciences.* Knopf 1961. (o.p.) $8.95. ISBN 0-394-41966-9 Discussion of discoveries pertaining to the chemical basis of heredity; includes information about Mendel.

Olby, Robert C. *Origins of Mendelism.* Univ of Chicago Pr 1985 $14.95. ISBN 0-226-62592-3 A look at Mendel and those who preceded him in work related to Mendelism.

Sootin, Harry. *Gregor Mendel: Father of the Science of Genetics.* Vanguard 1959 $12.95. ISBN 0-8149-0409-2 Biography of Mendel with explanations of his experiments.

Webb, Robert N. *Gregor Mendel and Heredity.* Watts 1963. (o.p.) Biography of Gregor Mendel with emphasis on his experiments with pea plants.

MORGAN, THOMAS HUNT 1866–1945

Thomas Morgan was born in Lexington, Kentucky. He receive a Ph.D. from Johns Hopkins University in 1890 and then taught at Bryn Mawr College from 1891 to 1904. He was professor of biology at Columbia University from 1904 to 1928 and director of the William G. Kirckhoff Biology Laboratory at the California Institute of Technology from 1928 to 1941.

Morgan's early research focused on embryology and regeneration. However, his growing interest in genetics put him at the center of genetics research in the first half of the twentieth century. In 1933, Morgan received the Nobel Prize in physiology and medicine for work that he had begun in 1910, involving heredity in the fruit fly. The results of the experiments, conducted in Morgan's laboratory at Columbia University, showed that two apparently different approaches to heredity—the chromosome theory (which identified the chromosomes of the cell nuclei as the agents of heredity) and the laws of inheritance formulated by the Austrian monk and biologist Gregor Mendel—were one. (*See* Mendel, Vol. 2, Biology: Genetics and Heredity.) Morgan's contributions to genetics included the ideas that what Mendel called factors or determinants of characteristics (currently called genes) are grouped together on chromosomes, that some characteristics are sex linked, and that the position of genes on chromosomes can be mapped.

BOOK BY MORGAN

The Mechanism of Mendelian Heredity (1915). (coauthored with Hermann Muller) Johnson Repr 1972 repr of 1915 ed $35.00. ISBN 0-384-40136-8

BOOKS ABOUT MORGAN

Moore, Ruth E. *The Coil of Life: The Story of the Great Discoveries of the Life Sciences.* Knopf 1961. (o.p.) $8.95. ISBN 0-394-41966-9 Discussion of discoveries pertaining to the chemical basis of heredity; includes information about Morgan.

Shine, Ian B., and Sylvia Wrobel. *Thomas Hunt Morgan: Pioneer of Genetics.* Univ Pr of Kentucky 1976 $15.00. ISBN 0-8131-0095-X Biography of Morgan, as well as a history of genetics.

MULLER, HERMANN JOSEPH 1890–1967

Born in New York City, Hermann Muller received his undergraduate and master's degrees from Columbia University, where he was a student of American geneticist Thomas Hunt Morgan. After graduation, he taught at Cornell University and later at Columbia. He also taught at the Rice Institute in Houston and the University of Texas at Austin. In 1945 he became professor of zoology at Indiana University.

Muller was the coauthor with Thomas Morgan of *The Mechanism of Mendelian Heredity* (1915). In this book, Muller and Morgan codified their view that chromosomes contained the factors or determinants of heredity proposed by Gregor Mendel, the Austrian monk and biologist who formulated the laws of heredity. (*See* Mendel, Vol. 2, Biology: Genetics and Heredity.) Muller received the 1946 Nobel Prize in physiology or medicine for work that grew out of Morgan's laboratory. Muller's work demonstrated that radiation causes mutations in genes.

BOOKS BY MULLER

Man's Future Birthright: Essays on Science and Humanity (1973). Elof A. Carlson (ed). SUNY 1973 $39.50. ISBN 0-87395-097-6

The Mechanism of Mendelian Heredity (1915). (coauthored with Thomas Hunt Morgan) Johnson Repr 1972 repr of 1915 ed $35.00. ISBN 0-384-40136-8

The Modern Concept of Nature (1973). Elof A. Carson (ed). SUNY 1973 $39.50. ISBN 0-87395-096-8

Out of the Night: A Biologist's View of the Future (1937). Garland 1984 $22.00. ISBN 0-8240-5821-6

BOOK ABOUT MULLER

Moore, Ruth E. *The Coil of Life: The Story of the Great Discoveries of the Life Sciences.* Knopf 1961. (o.p.) $8.95. ISBN 0-394-41966 Discussion of discoveries pertaining to the chemical basis of heredity; includes information about Muller.

See also Vol. 2, Psychology: Heredity and Environment; Biology: Genetic Engineering; *and* Health: Noncommunicable Diseases.

GENETIC ENGINEERING

*Dudley, William (ed). *Genetic Engineering: Opposing Viewpoints.* Greenhaven 1990 $15.95. ISBN 0-89908-477-X Discusses how far science should go in changing humans.

*Facklam, Howard, and Margery Facklam. *From Cell to Clone: The Story of Genetic Engineering.* Harcourt 1979 $9.95. ISBN 0-15-230262-X Discussion of genetic engineering, especially its history and the techniques of cloning; also includes the topics of recombinant DNA research and test-tube babies.

*Hyde, Margaret O., and Lawrence E. Hyde. *Cloning and the New Genetics.* Enslow 1984 $15.95. ISBN 0-89490-084-6 Explanations of clones, genes, DNA, and recombinant DNA; discussion of the risks and controversies associated with research involving genetic material.

*Lampton, Christopher. *DNA and the Creation of New Life.* Arco 1985 $12.95. ISBN 0-668-05396-8 Presentation of background information about research in molecular biology and genetic engineering; discusses the development and goals of the biotechnology industry.

*McKinnell, Robert G. *Cloning of Frogs, Mice, and Other Animals.* Univ of Minnesota Pr 1985 $15.95. ISBN 0-8166-1360-5 Explanation of the cloning process and its importance in studies of cancer and aging.

*Stwertka, Eve, and Albert Stwertka. *Genetic Engineering.* Watts 1989 $12.90. ISBN 0-531-10775-2 Discussion of recombinant DNA techniques and the applications of the technology, including amniocentesis, genetic counseling, and test-tube parenthood; also considers the ethical and moral questions raised by genetic engineering.

*Watson, James D., and John Tooze. *The DNA Story: A Documentary History of Gene Cloning.* Freeman 1981 $29.95. ISBN 0-7167-1292-X History of the discovery of DNA and its application in genetic engineering.

THE EVOLUTION OF LIFE

*Adler, Irving. *How Life Began.* Harper Jr Bks 1977 $12.95. ISBN 0-381-99603-4 Discusses molecular structure and compares various theories on how life began.

*Asimov, Isaac. *Beginnings: The Story of Origins—of Mankind, Life, the Earth, the Universe.* Walker 1987 $19.95. ISBN 0-8027-1003-4 Account of the beginnings of the universe and the evolution of life on Earth.

Atchley, W. R., and David S. Woodruff. *Evolution and Speciation.* Cambridge Univ Pr 1981 $75.00. ISBN 0-521-23823-4

*Attenborough, David. *Life on Earth: A Natural History.* Little 1983 $19.95. ISBN 0-316-05747-9 Story of the evolution of life, especially the vertebrates.

*Ayala, Francisco J. *The Origin of Species.* Carolina Biological 1983 $1.90. ISBN 0-89278-269-2 A look at the meaning of species and the factors that influence speciation.

*Benton, Michael. *The Story of Life on Earth.* Watts 1986 $13.90. ISBN 0-531-19019-6 Discussion of fossils, evolution, and the future; examination of life throughout geologic time.

Darwin, Charles. *The Origin of Species.* Penguin 1982 $3.95. ISBN 0-14-043205-1

Dobzhansky, Theodosius. *Genetics and the Origin of Species.* Columbia Univ Pr 1982 $19.00. ISBN 0-231-05475-0

*Edey, Maitland A. *Blueprints: Solving the Mystery of Evolution.* Little 1989 $19.95. ISBN 0-316-21076-5 History of evolutionary theory from the eighteenth century to the unraveling of the genetic code.

Eldredge, Niles. *Time Frames: The Rethinking of Darwinian Evolution and the Theory of Punctuated Equilibrium.* Simon 1985 $16.95. ISBN 0-671-49555-0

*Fox, Sidney W. *The Emergence of Life: Darwinian Evolution from the Inside.* Basic 1988 $19.95. ISBN 0-465-01925-0 Account of the process used by the author and others to develop a model for how amino acids combine to form proteins.

*Gallant, Roy A. *Before the Sun Dies: The Story of Evolution.* Macmillan 1989 $15.95. ISBN 0-02-735771-6 Examination of modern evolutionary thinking from the Big Bang through human evolution.

*Jastrow, Robert. *Until the Sun Dies.* Warner Bks 1977 $12.95. ISBN 0-393-06415-8 A look at the creation of the universe and life on Earth, using Biblical accounts and evolutionary theory.

Margulis, Lynn. *Early Life.* Jones & Bartlett 1982 $12.50. ISBN 0-86720-005-7

Mayr, Ernst. *Systematics and the Origin of Species.* Columbia Univ Pr 1982 $18.00. ISBN 0-231-05449-1

*Miller, Jonathan, and Brian Van Loon. *Darwin for Beginners.* Pantheon 1982 $5.95. ISBN 0-394-74847-6 History and explanation of British naturalist Charles Darwin's theory of natural selection.

*Taylor, Ron. *Story of Evolution.* Warwick 1981 $12.90. ISBN 0-531-09180-5 Discussion of evolution and related topics, including heredity, survivors and specialists, and people vs. nature.

DARWIN, CHARLES ROBERT   1809–1882

Born in Shrewsbury, England, Charles Darwin attended the University of Edinburgh and graduated from Christ's College, Cambridge University, in 1831. Although obviously intelligent, he was a poor student and showed little promise of success.

Darwin became the official naturalist on the H.M.S. *Beagle,* which sailed around the world from 1831 to 1836. During the voyage, Darwin was amazed by the great number and variety of life forms he encountered. He was intrigued and puzzled by the similar but different species he saw in widely separated lands. After his return to England, he spent nearly 30 years developing a theory to account for what he had seen and for further observations he made in domesticated plants and animals. He concluded that "selection [is] the key to man's success." He theorized that species with variations which were beneficial in an environment survived, while species whose variations were not beneficial were eliminated. Darwin's theory was published in 1859 in the book *The Origin of Species by Means of Natural Selection.* Although the theory has been modified by more recent learnings, Darwin's discoveries were corroborated by Mendelian genetics and became the basis of most contemporary biological studies.

Darwin had the faculty of writing simply on difficult topics. His use of reminiscence and discursive anecdote lends great color to his scientific expositions.

BOOKS BY DARWIN

The Descent of Man and Selection in Relation to Sex (1871). Princeton Univ Pr 1981 $14.50. ISBN 0-691-02369-7

The Life and Letters of Charles Darwin (1899). Francis Darwin (ed). 2 vols. AMS 1972 $85.00. ISBNs 0-404-08417-6, 0-404-08418-4

The Origin of Species by Means of Natural Selection (1859). 2 vols. AMS 1972 $85.00. ISBNs 0-404-08404-4, 0-404-08405-2

The Voyage of the Beagle (1831). NAL 1988 $4.95. ISBN 0-451-62620-6

BOOKS ABOUT DARWIN

Allan, Mea. *Darwin and His Flowers: The Key to Natural Selection.* Taplinger 1977 $14.50. ISBN 0-8008-2113-0 Biography of Darwin centered on his interest in plants.

Brent, Peter. *Charles Darwin: A Man of Enlarged Curiosity.* Harper 1981 $20.75. ISBN 0-06-014880-2 Biography of Darwin that stresses the extent of his accomplishments.

Clark, Ronald W. *The Survival of Charles Darwin: A Biography of a Man and an Idea.* Random 1984 $19.45. ISBN 0-394-52134-X Story of Darwin and discussion of the theory of evolution as it has changed since the time of Darwin.

DeBeer, Gavin. *Charles Darwin: Evolution by Natural Selection.* Greenwood 1976 $45.00. ISBN 0-8371-7378-7 Biography of Darwin with emphasis on his scientific contributions.

GOULD, STEPHEN JAY   1941–

Born in New York City, Stephen Jay Gould received his B.A. from Antioch College in New York in 1963. He received a Ph.D. in paleontology from Columbia University in 1967 and has been a professor at Harvard University since then. He is also curator of invertebrate paleontology at Harvard's Museum of Comparative Zoology. His research has been mainly in the evolution and speciation of land snails.

Gould is a leading proponent of the theory of punctuated equilibrium. This theory holds that few evolutionary changes occur among organisms over long periods of time, and then a brief period of rapid changes occurs before another long, stable period of equilibrium sets in.

An outspoken advocate of the scientific outlook, Gould has been a vigorous defender of evolution against its creation-science opponents in popular magazines focusing on science. He writes a column for *Natural History* and has produced a remarkable series of books that display the excitement of science for the layperson.

BOOKS BY GOULD

Ever Since Darwin: Reflections on Natural History (1977). Norton 1979 $5.95. ISBN 0-393-00917-3

The Flamingo's Smile: Reflections on Natural History (1985). Norton 1987 $8.70. ISBN 0-393-30375-6
Hen's Teeth and Horse's Toes: Further Reflections on Natural History (1983). Norton 1984 $6.70. ISBN 0-393-30200-8
The Mismeasure of Man (1981). Norton 1983 $7.95. ISBN 0-393-30056-0
Ontogeny and Phylogeny (1977). Harvard Univ Pr 1985 $12.50. ISBN 0-674-63941-3
The Panda's Thumb: More Reflections in Natural History (1980). Norton 1982 $5.95. ISBN 0-393-30023-4
An Urchin in the Storm: Essays About Books and Ideas (1987). Norton 1988 $7.70. ISBN 0-393-30537-6

LAMARCK, JEAN BAPTISTE DE MONET DE   1744–1829

Lamarck made significant contributions to the disciplines of botany, zoology, meteorology, and paleontology. Born in Picardy, France, he studied at a Jesuit seminary, but he never completed his training for the priesthood. Lamarck joined the army and fought in the Seven Years' War, which began in 1756 with a territorial dispute between Austria and Prussia and later involved other European countries, America, and India before ending in 1763. During this time Lamarck developed an interest in botany and began to do botanical research. The first recognition Lamarck received as a scientist was for his design of a new classification scheme for plants. He also developed a system for classifying invertebrate animals. Lamarck was the first person to try to predict the weather. He gave the cloud types names still in use today.

Lamarck believed that over long periods of time, life forms evolved and grew increasingly complex due to the inheritability of acquired traits. This

Ivory-Billed Woodpeckers. Painting by John James Audubon (early 1820s). Courtesy of The Metropolitan Museum of Art, Rogers Fund, 1941. (41.18)

theory was widely publicized and had great impact on the future of biology. Although his theories were eventually proven to be incorrect by the work of other evolutionists, Lamarck paved the way for British naturalists Charles Darwin and Alfred Wallace, who introduced the theory of selection of the most fit as the basis for evolution. (*See* Darwin *and* Wallace, Vol. 2 Biology: The Evolution of Life.)

In 1788 Lamarck became conservator of the royal herbarium. In 1793 he became professor of zoology at the Museum of Natural History in Paris. Ten years before his death, Lamarck went blind but continued to work.

BOOK BY LAMARCK

Zoological Philosophy: An Exposition with Regard to the Natural History of Animals (1809). Elliot Hugh (tr). Univ of Chicago Pr 1984 $15.00. ISBN 0-226-46810-0

BOOK ABOUT LAMARCK

Barthelemy-Madaule, Madeline. *Lamarck, the Mythical Precursor: A Study of the Relations Between Science and Ideology.* M. H. Shank (tr). MIT Pr 1982 $25.00. ISBN 0-262-02179-X Interpretation of Lamarck's importance in history.

WALLACE, ALFRED RUSSEL   1823–1913

Alfred Wallace, born in Usk, Wales, had a very limited education, yet he became a noted naturalist and independently developed the theory of evolution, which is most commonly associated with the name of Charles Darwin, the English naturalist. (*See* Darwin, Vol. 2, Biology: The Evolution of Life.) Wallace's formal education was completed with his graduation from grammar school at the age of 14. Having developed an interest in natural history, he avidly pursued this study during his years as a teacher in Leicester, England.

In 1848 he went to Brazil to study animals of the Amazon. Returning to England in 1853, he departed a year later on an expedition to the East Indies, where he remained for nine years. It was during this time that he developed his theory of evolution, essentially the same theory of natural selection and survival of the fittest that Darwin had developed and had been painstakingly perfecting before making his views known. Wallace sent his paper setting forth his theory to Darwin, who recognized that his and Wallace's theories were the same. The theory was presented in a joint paper before the Linnaean Society, an organization of scientists, in London in 1858. With Wallace's agreement, Darwin was given the major credit for developing the theory because of the wide-ranging body of evidence he amassed in support of it.

BOOKS BY WALLACE

The Action of Natural Selection on Man (1871). AMS (repr of 1871 ed).
Contribution to the Theory of Natural Selection (1870). AMS 1978 $33.00. ISBN 0-404-08181-9
Darwinism: An Exposition of the Theory of Natural Selection with Some of Its Applications (1891). AMS 1975 $39.50. ISBN 0-404-08182-7
The Malay Archipelago (1869). Dover 1978 $9.95. ISBN 0-486-20187-2
My Life, a Record of Events and Opinions (1905). Gregg Intl (repr of 1905 ed) $82.80. ISBN 0-576-29128-5
A Narrative of Travels on the Amazon and Rio Negro (1853). Greenwood 1969 $35.00. ISBN 0-8371-1641-4

BOOK ABOUT WALLACE

Fichman, Martin. *Alfred Russel Wallace.* Twayne 1981. (o.p.) $16.50. ISBN 0-8057-6797-5 A biography of Wallace that emphasizes his biogeographical system.

See also Vol. 2, Anthropology: Evolution.

THE ORIGIN OF HUMANS

*Day, Michael H. *The Fossil History of Man.* Carolina Biological 1984 $1.90. ISBN 0-89278-232-3 Examination of the fossil record of early hominids and early *Homo sapiens.*

Lambert, David, *et al. The Field Guide to Early Man.* Facts on File 1987 $21.95. ISBN 0-8160-1517-1

*Leakey, Richard E., and Roger Lewin. *Origins: What New Discoveries Reveal About the Emergence of Our Species and Its Possible Future.* Dutton 1982 $8.95. ISBN 0-525-48246-6 Discussion of the evolution of humans; includes the predecessors of modern humans and survival and future development of our species.

Lewin, Roger. *Human Evolution: An Illustrated Introduction.* Freeman 1984 $14.95. ISBN 0-7167-1636-4

*Lewin, Roger. *In the Age of Mankind: A Smithsonian Book of Human Evolution.* Smithsonian Bks 1988 $37.50. ISBN 0-89599-022-9 Examination of the background and significance of discoveries related to human evolution.

*Tanner, Nancy M. *On Becoming Human.* Cambridge Univ Pr 1981 $15.95. ISBN 0-521-28028-1 Study of the predecessors of humans using the chimpanzee as a model.

JOHANSON, DONALD CARL   1943–

Chicago-born Donald Johanson received a B.A. in anthropology from the University of Illinois in 1966, followed by an M.A. in 1970 and a Ph.D. in 1974 from the University of Chicago. In 1972 he became assistant professor at Case Western Reserve University and associate curator of anthropology at the Cleveland Museum of Natural History. In 1981 he moved to California, where he became director of the Institute of Human Origins in Berkeley.

Johanson led expedition teams in Africa, searching for the origins of humans. In 1974, "Lucy," the skeleton of a 2- to 3-million-year-old *Australopithecus afarensis* was discovered as well as many bones of *Homo habilis.* Johanson's findings have made him an authority on the origins of humans.

BOOKS BY JOHANSON

Lucy: The Beginnings of Human Kind (1981). (coauthored with Maitland A. Edey) Warner Bks 1982 $13.95. ISBN 0-446-38625-1

Lucy's Child: The Search for Our Origins (1989). (coauthored with James Shreeve) Morrow 1989 $22.95. ISBN 0-688-06492-2

BOOK ABOUT JOHANSON

Reader, John. *Missing Links: The Hunt for Earliest Man.* Penguin 1989 $7.95. ISBN 0-14-022808-X Account of the search for the ancestors of humans and the scientists doing the searching.

THE ORIGIN OF LIFE

*Adler, Irving. *How Life Began.* Harper 1977 $12.70. ISBN 0-381-99603-4 An introduction to the nature of life and its origin.

Cairns-Smith, A. G. *Seven Clues to the Origin of Life: A Scientific Detective Story.* Cambridge Univ Pr 1986 $9.50. ISBN 0-521-33793-3

Day, William. *Genesis on Planet Earth: The Search for Life's Beginnings.* Yale Univ Pr 1984 $13.95. ISBN 0-300-03202-1

*Gamlin, Linda. *Origins of Life.* Watts 1988 $12.40. ISBN 0-531-17119-1 A look at the origin of life and the evolution of organisms; discusses genetics and heredity.

*Woese, Carl R. *The Origin of Life.* Carolina Biological 1984 $2.40. ISBN 0-89278-213-7 A look at the theories of the origin of life on Earth.

OPARIN, ALEXANDER IVANOVICH   1894–1980

Alexander Oparin was born near Moscow and graduated from Moscow State University in 1917. He then conducted research at the university and in 1929 became a professor there. He helped found and worked at the Bakh Institute of Biochemistry in Moscow, becoming its director in 1946.

Oparin is most well known for developing a theory to explain the origin of life from chemical substances. He also conducted research on the biochemistry of agricultural crops.

BOOK BY OPARIN

The Origin of Life (1936). Dover 1953 $5.95. ISBN 0-486-60213-3

ANIMAL BEHAVIOR

*Adamson, Joy. *Born Free: A Lioness of Two Worlds.* Pantheon 1987 $11.95. ISBN 0-679-56141-2 Story of Elsa, a lion cub, and the humans who raised her and trained her to return to the wild.

Barnett, S. A. *Modern Ethology: The Science of Animal Behavior.* Oxford Univ Pr 1981 $32.50. ISBN 0-19-502780-9

Bright, Michael. *Animal Language.* Cornell Univ Pr 1985 $12.95. ISBN 0-8014-9340-4

Caras, Roger. *The Private Lives of Animals.* McGraw 1987 $12.95. ISBN 0-07-009794-1

*Crump, Donald J. *How Animals Behave.* National Geographic 1984 $6.95. ISBN 0-87044-500-6 Discussion of how animals get food, protect themselves, court, mate, care for eggs and young, and live together; includes profiles of animal behaviorists and discussion of research methods.

*Desmond, Morris. *The Illustrated Naked Ape: A Zoologist's Study of the Human Animal.* Crown 1986 $19.95. ISBN 0-517-56320-7 A look at humans as animals.

Downer, John. *Supersense: Perception in the Animal World.* H. Holt 1989 $24.95. ISBN 0-8050-1087-4

*Evans, Peter, and Gerald Durrell. *Ourselves and Other Animals.* Pantheon 1987 $24.95. ISBN 0-394-55962-2 Discussion of how animals communicate with parallels drawn with human methods of communication.

*Fossey, Diane. *Gorillas in the Mist.* Houghton 1984 $11.95. ISBN 0-395-36638-0 Account of the author's 13 years in the natural habitat of mountain gorillas in Africa.

*Goodenough, Judith E. *Animal Communication.* Carolina Biological 1984 $1.90. ISBN 0-89278-343-5 Discussion of the reasons for and nature of animal communication; describes signals used by animals, and methods of animal communication.

*Griffin, Donald R. *Animal Thinking.* Harvard Univ Pr 1985 $9.95. ISBN 0-674-03713-8 Descriptions and analysis of developments in ethology, psychology, and neurobiology.

*Hinde, R. A., and J. S. Hinde. *Instinct and Intelligence.* Carolina Biological 1987 $1.90. ISBN 0-89278-063-0 A look at behavior, with discussions of instinct, learning, and intelligence.

*Kohl, Judith, and Herbert Kohl. *Pack, Band, and Colony: The World of Social Animals.* Farrar 1983 $13.95. ISBN 0-374-35694-7 Study of the social lives of wolves, lemurs, and termites.

Mackintosh, N. J. *Conditioning and Associative Learning.* Oxford Univ Pr 1983 $19.95. ISBN 0-19-852126-X

*Milne, Lorus, and Margery Milne. *A Time to Be Born: An Almanac of Animal Courtship and Parenting.* Sierra 1982 $15.95. ISBN 0-87156-317-7 Descriptions of the reproductive cycles of several animal species.

*Palmer, John D. *Human Biological Rhythms.* Carolina Biological 1983 $1.90. ISBN 0-89278-304-4 A look at cyclic changes that occur in humans, including changes in body temperature and heart rate.

*Palmer, John D. *Biological Rhythms and Living Clocks.* Carolina Biological 1984 $1.90. ISBN 0-89278-192-0 A look at the factors that influence daily rhythms in animals and the living clocks of animals.

*Patent, Dorothy H. *Where the Bald Eagles Gather.* Houghton 1984 $12.95. ISBN 0-89919-230-0 Story of the hundreds of bald eagles that arrive in Glacier National Park during salmon spawning.

Pavlov, Ivan P. *Conditioned Reflexes: An Investigation of the Physiological Activity of the Cerebral Cortex.* Dover 1927 $9.95. ISBN 0-486-60614-7

*Richard, Alison F. *Primate Ecology and Social Organization.* Carolina Biological 1982 $1.90. ISBN 0-89278-308-7 A look at the ecological variations and the five social organizations among the species of primates.

Seeley, Thomas. *Honeybee Ecology: A Study of Adaptation in Social Life.* Princeton Univ Pr 1985 $14.95. ISBN 0-691-08392-4

*Slater, Peter J. *Encyclopedia of Animal Behavior.* Facts on File 1987 $24.95. ISBN 0-8160-1816-2 Discussion of behavior and of individual animal behaviors, animal relationships, and social organizations.

*Winfree, Arthur T. *The Timing of Biological Clocks.* Freeman 1987 $32.95. ISBN 0-7167-5018-X Intriguing discussion of the human biological clock and its relationship to insomnia, jet lag, and pacemakers, among other topics of interest.

FRISCH, KARL VON   1886–1982

Karl von Frisch was born in Vienna, Austria. He attended medical school at the University of Vienna and studied animal behavior at the Zoological Institute of the University of Munich. In 1910 he received a Ph.D. in animal behavior from the University of Munich.

In 1912 Frisch joined the faculty of the University of Munich and was associated with it intermittently until his retirement as professor of zoology in 1958. He also spent many years as the director of the Zoological Institutes in Rostock, Breslau, and Munich and was active in the international scientific community, lecturing in the United States and Europe.

Frisch achieved international recognition for his pioneer work in animal behavior. His research on sense functions in fish showed that fish can see colors. He also discovered the "language" of bees. In 1973 he shared the Nobel Prize in physiology or medicine with Austrian naturalist Konrad Lorenz and Dutch-born zoologist Nikolaas Tinbergen for his contributions in sociobiology. (*See* Lorenz *and* Tinbergen, Vol. 2, Biology: Animal Behavior.)

BOOKS BY FRISCH

Animal Architecture (1974). (coauthored with Otto von Frisch) Lisbeth Gombrich (tr). Harcourt 1974. (o.p.) $12.95. ISBN 0-15-107251-5

Bees: Their Vision, Chemical Senses, and Language (1950). Cornell Univ Pr 1971 $10.95. ISBN 0-8014-9126-6

The Dance Language and Orientation of Bees (1967). Leigh E. Chadwick (tr). Harvard Univ Pr 1967 $43.00. ISBN 0-674-19050-5

GOODALL, JANE 1934–

Jane Goodall was born in London. A childhood interest in animals prompted her to go to Africa, where she became secretary to Louis Leakey (*see* Leakey, Vol. 2, Anthropology: Evolution), paleoanthropologist at the National Museum of Natural History in Nairobi, Kenya. She acted on Leakey's suggestion that a field study of some of the higher primates would be a major contribution to the understanding of animal behavior. She went to the Gombe Stream Reserve in Tanzania in 1960 and lived for years with chimpanzees to study their behavior. While in the field and after making trips to England, Goodall received her Ph.D. in ethology from Cambridge University.

Goodall discovered much about the lives and behavior of chimpanzees. Two of her findings were that chimpanzees eat animals in addition to fruits and vegetables and that they use tools. She also studied African hyenas, jackals, and wild dogs.

BOOKS BY GOODALL

The Chimpanzees of Gombe (1986). Harvard Univ Pr 1986 $37.95. ISBN 0-674-11649-6

**In the Shadow of Man* (1971). Houghton 1983 $9.95. ISBN 0-395-33145-5 The author's account of her years of observing chimpanzees in Tanzania.

**My Friends, the Wild Chimpanzees* (1967). National Geographic 1967. (o.p.) $5.75. Pictorial and narrative account of the lives of chimpanzees in the wild.

**Through a Window: My Thirty Years with the Chimpanzees of Gombe* (1990). Houghton 1990 $21.95. ISBN 0-395-50081-8 Continuation of *In the Shadow of Man*; author goes on with her story of the study of chimpanzees.

LORENZ, KONRAD ZACHARIAS 1903–1989

Born in Vienna, Austria, Lorenz as a child developed a deep interest in animals and animal behavior. Although he preferred the study of animal behavior, he studied medicine at Columbia University and the University of Vienna. He received a medical degree from the University of Vienna in 1928 and a Ph.D. in zoology from the University of Vienna in 1933. In 1954 he became codirector of the Max Planck Institute for Physiology of Behavior in West Germany. He served in various academic and research positions and was involved in the study of animal behavior for most of his life. He studied animals in their natural environments and raised wild animals. His studies led to the discovery of imprinting, an early and centrally important learning process for many animal species. His works benefit from his rare talent of being able to write for both general and technical audiences.

In 1973 Lorenz shared the Nobel Prize in physiology or medicine with Karl von Frisch and Nikolaas Tinbergen for his work on animal behavior. (*See* Frisch *and* Tinbergen, Vol. 2, Biology: Animal Behavior.)

BOOKS BY LORENZ

Behind the Mirror: A Search for a Natural History of Human Knowledge (1977). Ronald Taylor (tr). Harcourt 1978 $3.95. ISBN 0-15-611776-2

Civilized Man's Eight Deadly Sins (1974). Marjorie Kerr-Wilson (tr). Harcourt 1978 $150.00. ISBN 0-15-118061-X

The Evolution and Modification of Behavior (1965). Univ of Chicago Pr 1986 $9.95. ISBN 0-226-49334-2

The Foundations of Ethology (1981). Springer-Verlag 1981 $38.50. ISBN 0-387-81623-2

King Solomon's Ring (1952). Peter Smith 1988 $18.00. ISBN 0-8446-6309-3 Lorenz describes his life in animal research.

Man Meets Dog (1954). Penguin 1988 $6.95. ISBN 0-14-002214-7

On Aggression (1963). Harcourt 1974 $9.95. ISBN 0-15-668741-0

On Life and Living: Konrad Lorenz in Conversation with Kurt Mundl (1988). Richard D. Bosley (tr). St. Martin's 1990 $17.95. ISBN 0-312-03901-8 Compilation of conversations with Lorenz giving a portrait of him and a look at his beliefs.

Studies in Animal and Human Behavior (1970–1971). 2 vols. Harvard Univ Pr Vol. 1 1970 $18.95. ISBN 0-674-84630-3. Vol. 2 1971 $28.00. ISBN 0-674-84631-1

The Waning of Humaneness (1983). Little 1987 $17.95. ISBN 0-316-53291-6

BOOKS ABOUT LORENZ

Evans, Richard I. (ed). *Konrad Lorenz: The Man and His Ideas.* Harcourt 1975. (o.p.) $10.00. ISBN 0-15-147285-8 Compilation of information about Lorenz and his thinking; includes some of his essays.

Nisbett, Alec. *Konrad Lorenz.* Harcourt 1976. (o.p.) $10.00. ISBN 0-15-147286-6 Biography of Lorenz that reviews his life, science, ideas, and influence.

PAVLOV, IVAN PETROVICH   1849–1936

Born in Ryazan, Russia, Ivan Pavlov was educated in Russia and Germany. He received a medical degree in 1879 and a Ph.D. in 1883.

Pavlov conducted physiological research on digestion and circulation. In 1890 he established a department of physiology at the Institute of Experimental Medicine at Leningrad. In 1904 he received the Nobel Prize in physiology and medicine for his work on the physiology of digestion, particularly the role of the vagus nerve. His research during the 1900s centered on the conditioned reflex, which he developed in studies of dogs. His conditioned reflex research is the work for which he is most well known and has had enormous effects on the study of behavior.

BOOK BY PAVLOV

Conditioned Reflexes: An Investigation of the Physiological Activity of the Cerebral Cortex (1927). G.V. Anrep (ed). Dover 1960 $9.95. ISBN 0-486-60614-7

BOOKS ABOUT PAVLOV

Babkin, Boris P. *Pavlov: A Biography.* Univ of Chicago Pr 1974 $4.25. ISBN 0-226-03373-2 Biography of Pavlov with emphasis on his investigations of the cardiovascular, digestive, and nervous systems.

Gray, Jeffrey A. *Ivan Pavlov.* Viking 1980. (o.p.) $12.95. ISBN 0-670-40457-8 Account of Pavlov's work on conditioning—brain function, behavior, and personality.

TINBERGEN, NIKOLAAS   1907–1988

Born in The Hague, a city in the Netherlands, Tinbergen developed a love of nature as a child. After studying animal behavior and receiving a Ph.D. from Leiden University in 1932, he remained there to teach, becoming professor of zoology in 1947. Two years later he moved to Oxford University. He retired from Oxford in 1974.

BIOLOGY 465

Tinbergen spent his life studying the behavior of animals. Some of his reports on the behavior of sea gulls are exceptionally interesting. Tinbergen's work concentrated on how behavior is adapted and the evolution of behavior. Besides gulls, he worked with other birds and with butterflies, fish, and wasps. He shared the 1973 Nobel Prize in physiology and medicine with Austrian scientists Konrad Lorenz and Karl von Frisch for his work in animal behavior. (*See* Lorenz *and* Frisch, Vol. 2, Biology: Animal Behavior.)

BOOKS BY TINBERGEN

The Animal in Its World, Explorations of an Ethologist, 1932–1972 (1973). 2 vols. Harvard Univ Pr 1973. Vol. 1 *Field Studies.* $9.95. ISBN 0-674-03724-3. Vol. 2 *Laboratory Experiments and General Papers.* $8.95. ISBN 0-674-03728-6
Curious Naturalist (1958). Univ of Massachusetts Pr 1984 $12.95. ISBN 0-87023-456-0
Social Behavior in Animals: With Special Reference to Vertebrates (1953). Routledge 1965 $10.95. ISBN 0-412-20000-7
The Study of Instinct (1951). Oxford Univ Pr 1989 $22.50. ISBN 0-19-857740-0
Tracks (1967). (coauthored with Eric Ennion) Oxford Univ Pr 1967. (o.p.) Analyses of animal tracks with interpretations of the activities that caused them.

See also Vol. 2, Psychology: Behavior.

ECOLOGY AND THE ENVIRONMENT

*Attenborough, David. *The Living Planet: A Portrait of the Earth.* Little 1985 $25.00. ISBN 0-316-05748-7 Study of the habitats of Earth.
Barnes, R. S. K., and R. N. Hughes. *Introduction to Marine Ecology.* Basil Blackwell 1988 $29.95. ISBN 0-632-02047-4
Bowen, Ezra. *Grasslands and Tundra.* Time-Life 1985 $13.99. ISBN 0-8094-4520-4
*Brown, Lauren. *Grasslands.* Knopf 1985 $14.95. ISBN 0-394-73121-2 Discussion of the grassland habitat of North America.
Campbell, Andrew. *The Encyclopedia of Aquatic Life.* Facts on File 1985 $45.00. ISBN 0-8160-1257-1
Campbell, R. *Microbial Ecology.* Basil Blackwell 1983 $22.00. ISBN 0-632-00988-8
*Fain, Theodore C. *Ecological Energetics.* Carolina Biological 1984 $1.90. ISBN 0-89278-291-9 Examination of how energy passes through individual organisms, communities, and ecosystems.
*Gerrard, Jonathan, and Gary R. Bortolotti. *The Bald Eagle: Haunts and Habits of a Wilderness Monarch.* Smithsonian 1988 $12.95. ISBN 0-87474-451-2 Examination of the morphology, behavior, flight patterns, hunting, migration, nesting, development, and growth of bald eagles.
*Gutnik, Martin J. *Ecology Projects for Young Scientists.* Watts 1984 $12.90. ISBN 0-531-04765-2 Suggestions for experiments students can carry out to investigate the balance of ecosystems and how this balance can be destroyed.
*Hughey, Pat. *Scavengers and Decomposers: The Clean-Up Crew.* Macmillan 1984 $13.95. ISBN 0-689-31032-3 Descriptions of the characteristics and habits of organisms that clean up the environment.
McConnaughey, Bayard H., and Robert Zottoli. *Introduction to Marine Biology.* Waveland 1989 $29.95. ISBN 0-88133-446-4
*McMahon, James A. *Deserts.* Knopf 1985 $15.95. ISBN 0-394-73139-5 Discussion of the desert habitats of North America.
Miller, G. Tyler, Jr. *Living in the Environment: An Introduction to Environmental Science.* Wadsworth 1990 $36.50. ISBN 0-543-08052-9

*Milne, Lorus, and Margery Milne. *The Mystery of the Bog Forest.* Dodd 1984 $8.95. ISBN 0-396-08318-8 Description of bogs including conditions needed for the existence of a bog and the plants and animals that inhabit bogs.

*Milne, Lorus, and Margery Milne. *Nature's Great Carbon Cycle.* Atheneum 1983. (o.p.) $9.95. ISBN 0-689-31003-X Discussion of the cycling of carbon in living things, addition of new carbon to the cycle, and radiocarbon dating.

*Niering, William A. *Wetlands.* Knopf 1985 $15.95. ISBN 0-394-73147-6 Descriptions of the flora, fauna, and natural wonders of the rivers, lakes, swamps, and marshes of North America.

Owen, Denis. *Camouflage and Mimicry.* Univ of Chicago Pr 1982 $12.50. ISBN 0-226-64188-0

*Perry, Donald R. *Life Above the Jungle Floor: A Biologist Explores a Strange and Hidden Treetop World.* Simon 1988 $8.95. ISBN 0-671-64426-2 A look at the multitude of life forms in a rain-forest canopy.

*Perry, Nicolette. *Symbiosis: Close Encounters of the Natural Kind.* Sterling 1983 $16.95. ISBN 0-7137-1229-5 Examination of some of the beneficial relationships between organisms.

Putnam, R. J., and S. D. Wratten. *Principles of Ecology.* Univ of California Pr 1984 $18.95. ISBN 0-520-05254-4

Sackett, Russel. *The Edge of the Sea.* Time-Life 1983 $13.99. ISBN 0-8094-4332-5

*Silver, Donald M. *Life on Earth: Biology Today.* Random 1983 $7.99. ISBN 0-394-95971-X Basic explanations of how plants and animals function and relate to each other.

*Stevens, Laurence. *Ecology Basics.* Prentice 1986 $10.95. ISBN 0-13-223215-4 Introduction to ecology: how organisms interact with each other, energy use and misuse, pollution.

CARSON, RACHEL LOUISE   1907–1964

See also Carson, Vol. 2, United States History: The Turbulent Sixties.

Rachel Carson was born in Springdale, Pennsylvania. She received a B.A. from Pennsylvania College in 1929 and an M.A. from Johns Hopkins University in 1932. She began working for the U.S. Fish and Wildlife Service as a marine biologist in 1936 and in 1947 became editor-in-chief of their publications.

In her work and writings, Carson stresses the interrelationships of all living things and our dependence on natural processes. Her book, *Silent Spring* (1962), was a best-seller and awakened the ordinary citizen to the dangers of pesticides. This book was instrumental in the eventual ban of the use of DDT.

BOOKS BY CARSON

The Edge of the Sea (1954). Houghton 1979 $9.95. ISBN 0-395-28519-4
The Sea Around Us (1951). Oxford Univ Pr 1989 $18.95. ISBN 0-19-506186-1
The Sense of Wonder (1965). Harper 1987 $10.95. ISBN 0-06-091450-5
Silent Spring (1962). Houghton 1987 $7.95. ISBN 0-395-45390-9

BOOKS ABOUT CARSON

Gartner, Carol B. *Rachel Carson.* Ungar 1983 $16.95. ISBN 0-8044-5425-6 Look at the life of Carson and analyses of her works.

Harlan, Judith. *Sounding the Alarm: A Biography of Rachel Carson.* Dillon 1989 $11.95. ISBN 0-87518-407-3 Focuses on the life and achievements of the scientist/environmentalist.

Jezer, Marty. *Rachel Carson.* Chelsea 1988 $17.95. ISBN 1-55546-646-X Biography of a marine biologist who stressed the relationship between humans and natural processes.

*Kudlinski, Kathleen V. *Rachel Carson: Pioneer of Ecology. Women of Our Time Ser.* Penguin

1989 $3.95. ISBN 0-14-032242-6 Brief, illustrated biography of the famous environmentalist.

See also Vol. 2, Geography: Environmental Issues.

CONSERVATION OF NATURAL RESOURCES

Bloyd, Sunni. *Endangered Species: Our Endangered Planet.* Lucent 1989 $10.95. ISBN 1-56006-106-5

*Carr, Terry. *Spill! The Story of the Exxon Valdez.* Watts 1991 $18.95. ISBN 0-531-15217-0 In repertorial fashion, the events leading up to this ecological disaster are presented; includes numerous photos.

Chiras, Daniel D. *Environmental Science.* Benjamin-Cummings 1988 $37.95. ISBN 0-8053-2257-4

*Cochrane, Jennifer. *Water Ecology.* Watts 1987 $12.40. ISBN 0-531-18152-9 Seventeen chapters cover the many aspects of water; within each section author presents an activity, with instructions and diagrams, thereby presenting an informative reference book for teenagers.

*Davidson, Art. *In the Wake of the Exxon Valdez: The Devastating Impact of the Alaska Oil Spill.* Sierra 1990 $19.95. ISBN 0-87156-614-1 Story of our most destructive oil spill.

*Gay, Kathlyn. *Acid Rain.* Watts 1983 $12.90. ISBN 0-531-04682-6 Discussion of the direct and indirect effects of acid rain: how it is formed, how it is studied, and what can be done to alleviate it.

*Gay, Kathlyn. *The Greenhouse Effect.* Watts 1986 $12.90. ISBN 0-531-10154-1 A look at how rising levels of carbon dioxide in the atmosphere may be changing Earth's climate and how scientists are studying the problem.

*Goldin, Augusta. *Water: Too Much, Too Little, Too Polluted.* Harcourt 1983 $12.95. ISBN 0-15-294819-8 Description of the quest for water all over the world, the hydrologic cycle, and how fresh water is obtained from saline water and from other sources.

*Johnson, Rebecca. *Greenhouse Effect: Life on a Warmer Planet.* Lerner 1990 $15.95. ISBN 0-8225-1591-1 Photos, charts, maps, and diagrams present a dramatic picture of our changing climate.

*Lampton, Christopher. *Endangered Species.* Watts 1988 $12.90. ISBN 0-531-10510-5 Explanation of species, extinction, and the effects of extinction on ecology.

*Nations, James D. *Tropical Rainforests: Endangered Environments.* Watts 1988 $12.90. ISBN 0-531-10604-7 Introduction to the wonders, importance, and people of tropical rain forests; discusses threats against these forests.

Pringle, Laurence. *Rain of Troubles: The Science and Politics of Acid Rain.* Macmillan 1988 $13.95. ISBN 0-02-775370-0

*Pringle, Laurence. *Water: The Next Great Resource Battle.* Macmillan 1982 $12.95. ISBN 0-02-775400-6 Good photos, clear text, and logical explanations make book ideal for younger readers.

*Sigford, Ann E. *Tall Grass and Trouble.* Dillon 1978 $9.95. ISBN 0-87518-153-8 Story of the destruction of the prairie and the efforts of citizens' groups to preserve the remaining prairie; discusses the delicate ecosystem the prairie supports.

*Weiss, Malcolm E. *The Nuclear Question.* Harcourt 1981. (o.p.) $10.95. ISBN 0-15-257596-0 Examination of the development of nuclear power, the benefits and dangers of nuclear power, the outlook for future nuclear power production, and controversy surrounding nuclear power production.

*Weiss, Malcolm E. *Toxic Waste: Cleanup or Coverup?* Watts 1984 $12.90. ISBN 0-531-

04755-5 Examination of the increasing problem of hazardous waste disposal in our society.

*Woods, Geraldine, and Harold Woods. *Pollution.* Watts 1985 $10.40. ISBN 0-531-04916-7 Discussion of various types of pollution and the need to conserve resources.

See also Vol. 2, Earth Science: Geology *and* Oceanography.

EARTH SCIENCE

The term *earth science* as it is used here includes four separate disciplines—astronomy, the study of the universe; meteorology, the study of the composition and characteristics of the atmosphere and the processes that occur in the atmosphere; oceanography, the study of the oceans; and geology, the study of the earth itself and the history of the earth. All of these disciplines are especially important in today's world. In the not-too-distant past, there were great voids in the existing knowledge about Earth and the universe. However, due in great part to new and improved technology, knowledge of Earth and the universe has greatly expanded in the last half of this century. Recent findings have helped provide a better understanding of Earth and its place in the universe.

For ease of use, the earth science section is divided into four subsections. Each encompasses one of the four separate disciplines that fall under the umbrella of earth science.

Within the subsections, key scientists associated with the discipline are listed alphabetically, their last names appearing first. For each, there is a book or a list of books by that individual. In addition, there is for each a profile that provides personal background and/or information about his or her role and achievements in the world of science. Further, the profile may refer the reader to other related individuals and their works, which also can be found in *The Young Adult Reader's Adviser.* Such connections between scientists and other thinkers and theorists are usually necessary when doing research in any of the branches of science.

Last, for most profiled individuals, there is a Books About section that, among other types of publications, lists notable biographies for further reading and research. Whenever possible, very recent titles have also been included. In some instances, only a very limited number or no books at all about the individual existed at the time of this compilation.

ASTRONOMY

*Adler, David A. *Hyperspace! Facts and Fun from All Over the Universe.* Penguin 1982 $4.95. ISBN 0-670-05117-9 Introduction to outer space, the solar system, and space exploration.

*Alter, Dinsmore, *et al. Pictorial Astronomy.* Harper 1983 $19.95. ISBN 0-06-181019-3 General guide to astronomy.

Angelo, Joseph A., Jr. *Dictionary of Space Technology.* Facts on File 1982 $24.95. ISBN 0-87196-583-6

*Apfel, Necia H. *Astronomy and Planetology: Projects for Young Scientists.* Watts 1983 $12.90. ISBN 0-531-04668-0 Hands-on approach to the study of astronomy, with ideas for projects young people can successfully carry out.

Asimov, Isaac. *Asimov on Astronomy.* Doubleday 1974 $5.50. ISBN 0-385-06881-6

*Asimov, Isaac. *How Did We Find Out About the Universe?* Walker 1983 $10.85. ISBN 0-8027-6477-0 Discussion of the telescope and the discoveries of astronomers.

*Audouze, Jean, and Guy Israel (eds). *The Cambridge Atlas of Astronomy.* Cambridge Univ Pr 1988 $90.00. ISBN 0-521-36360-8 Collection of photos and accompanying articles explaining what is known about the universe.

*Berger, Melvin. *Space Talk.* Messner 1985 $9.29. ISBN 0-671-54290-7 Dictionary of space terms.

*Berger, Melvin. *Star Gazing, Comet Tracking, and Sky Mapping.* Putnam 1985 $7.99. ISBN 0-399-61211-4 Guide to observing the night sky without binoculars or a telescope.

*Branley, Franklyn M. *Star Guide.* Crowell 1987 $11.95. ISBN 0-690-04350-3 Basic information pertaining to the sun, light-years, and facts about the stars; authored by prominent writer and geared for younger readers.

*Branley, Franklyn M. *Sun Dogs and Shooting Stars: A Skywatcher's Calendar.* Houghton 1980 $13.95. ISBN 0-395-29520-3 Guide to observing the sky; includes facts, suggestions for activities, and calendars.

*Brecher, Kenneth, and Michael Feirtag (eds). *Astronomy of the Ancients.* MIT Pr 1987 $8.95. ISBN 0-262-52070-2 A look at the role of astronomy in ancient cultures.

*Brown, Peter Lancaster. *Astronomy.* World of Science Ser. Facts on File 1984 $12.95. ISBN 0-87196-985-8 Encyclopedia of astronomy topics, with outstanding photos and diagrams.

Calder, Nigel. *Timescale: An Atlas of the Fourth Dimension.* Viking 1983 $19.95. ISBN 0-670-71571-9

*Chartrand, Mark R., III. *Skyguide: A Field Guide for Amateur Astronomers.* Western Pub 1982 $9.95. ISBN 0-307-13667-1 Guide to observing stars with binoculars or a small telescope.

Christianson, Gale E. *The Wild Abyss: The Story of the Men Who Made Modern Astronomy.* Free Pr 1979 $9.95. ISBN 0-317-30517-4

Cornell, James. *The First Stargazers: An Introduction to the Origins of Astronomy.* Scribner's 1981. (o.p.) $15.95. ISBN 0-684-16799-9

*Dunlop, Storm. *Macmillan Practical Guides: Astronomy.* Macmillan 1985 $8.95. ISBN 0-02-079650-1 Beginner's guide to viewing the night sky.

Ebbighausen, Edwin B. *Astronomy.* Merrill 1985 $15.95. ISBN 0-675-20413-5

*Editors of Time–Life Books. *The Cosmos.* Voyage Through the Universe Ser. Time–Life 1989 $17.27. ISBN 0-8094-6862-X Exploration of the cosmos and discussion of research in astronomy; beautiful illustrations.

*Feldman, Anthony. *Space.* Facts on File 1980 $24.95. ISBN 0-87196-416-3 Overview and history of astronomy.

*Ford, Adam. *Spaceship Earth.* Lothrop 1981. (o.p.) $11.95. ISBN 0-688-00259-5 Pictorial introduction to astronomy.

Friedlander, Michael W. *Astronomy: From Stonehenge to Quasars.* Prentice 1985 $32.95. ISBN 0-13-049867-X

*Gallant, Roy A. *The Macmillan Book of Astronomy.* Macmillan 1986 $8.95. ISBN 0-02-043230-5 Source book of information about the solar system, including the big bang theory.

*Gallant, Roy A. *Once Around the Galaxy.* Watts 1983 $12.90. ISBN 0-531-04681-8 History of astronomy and a discussion of current knowledge and unanswered questions in the field.

Graham-Smith, Francis, and Bernard Lovell. *Pathways to the Universe.* Cambridge Univ Pr 1989 $24.95. ISBN 0-521-32004-6

Hawking, Stephen M. *A Brief History of Time from the Big Bang to Black Holes.* Bantam 1988 $18.95. ISBN 0-553-05340-X

*Heidmann, Jean. *Extragalactic Adventure: Our Strange Universe.* Cambridge Univ Pr 1982 $8.95. ISBN 0-521-28045-1 Introduction to astronomy.

Henbest, Nigel, and Michael Marten. *The New Astronomy.* Cambridge Univ Pr 1983. (o.p.) $24.95. ISBN 0-521-25683-6

Howard, Neale E. *Standard Handbook for Telescope Making.* Harper 1984 $15.45. ISBN 0-06-181394-X

*Illingworth, Valerie (ed). *The Facts on File Dictionary of Astronomy.* Facts on File 1988 $12.95. ISBN 0-8160-1892-8 Encyclopedic dictionary of astronomy terms and instruments; includes tables.

*Jastrow, Robert. *God and the Astronomers.* Warner Bks 1980 $4.95. ISBN 0-446-32197-4 Discussion of the big bang and its theological implications.

Jefferys, William H., and R. Robert Robbins. *Discovering Astronomy.* Wiley 1988 $41.50. ISBN 0-471-83211-1

*Jones, Brian. *The Beginner's Guide to Astronomy.* Smith 1987 $7.98. ISBN 0-8317-0745-3 Presents for teenagers in text and illustration information on telescopes, the solar system, etc.

Kaufman, William J., III. *Universe.* Freeman 1987 $36.95. ISBN 0-7167-1927-4

*Kelsey, Larry, and Darrel Hoff. *Recent Revolutions in Astronomy.* Watts 1987 $12.90. ISBN 0-531-10340-4 Informative discussion of the recent discoveries and innovations in the field of astronomy.

*Kerrod, Robin. *Stars and Planets.* Arco 1984 $6.95. ISBN 0-668-06263-0 Introduction to astronomy.

*Lampton, Christopher. *Astronomy: From Copernicus to the Space Telescope. First Books Ser.* Watts 1987 $10.40. ISBN 0-531-10300-5 Brief history of astronomy and the place of Earth in the universe; intended for younger readers.

*Lampton, Christopher. *Space Sciences.* Watts 1983 $10.40. ISBN 0-531-04539-0 Dictionary of space-science terms.

Levitt, I. M., and Roy K. Marshall. *Star Maps for Beginners.* Simon 1987 $7.95. ISBN 0-671-63676-6

McGraw-Hill Encyclopedia of Astronomy. McGraw 1983 $79.50. ISBN 0-07-045251-2

*Moche, Dinal L. *Astronomy Today: Planets, Stars, Space Exploration.* Random 1982 $11.99. ISBN 0-394-84423-8 A look at our understanding of the universe.

*Moore, Patrick. *The New Atlas of the Universe.* Crown 1984 $24.95. ISBN 0-517-55500-X Discussion of the history of astronomy; explores the development of astronomical instruments and presents a tour of the universe.

*Moore, Patrick. *Stargazing: Astronomy Without a Telescope.* Barron 1985 $21.95. ISBN 0-8120-5644-2 Star charts and guides for observing stars and constellations.

Moore, Patrick. *The Unfolding Universe.* Crown 1982 $17.95. ISBN 0-517-54836-4

Muirden, James. *The Amateur Astronomer's Handbook: A Guide to Exploring the Heavens.* Harper 1987 $10.95. ISBN 0-06-091426-2

*Muirden, James. *The Astronomy Handbook.* Arco 1984 $8.95. ISBN 0-668-06235-5 Information about the origin and structure of the universe; includes stargazing maps and charts and instructions for building a planetarium.

Muirden, James. *Astronomy with Binoculars.* Arco 1983 $7.95. ISBN 0-668-05832-3

*Muirden, James. *How to Use an Astronomical Telescope: A Beginner's Guide to Observing the Cosmos.* Simon 1988 $10.95. ISBN 0-671-66404-2 Information about types of telescopes and how to use them to observe various celestial objects.

*Pasachoff, Jay M. *Peterson First Guide to Astronomy.* Houghton 1988 $3.95. ISBN 0-395-46790-X Guide to the stars, constellations, and other celestial bodies for the beginning observer.

Pasachoff, Jay M., and Donald H. Menzel. *A Field Guide to the Stars and Planets. Peterson Field Guide Ser.* Houghton 1983 $12.95. ISBN 0-395-34835-8

*Poynter, Margaret, and Michael J. Klein. *Cosmic Quest: Searching for Intelligent Life Among the Stars.* Atheneum 1984 $11.95. ISBN 0-689-31068-4 Argument for the need to search for extraterrestrial life.

Protheroe, W. M., *et al. Exploring the Universe.* Merrill 1989 $29.95. ISBN 0-675-20898-X

*Ridpath, Ian. *The Concise Handbook of Astronomy.* Smith 1986 $7.98. ISBN 0-8317-1766-1 Introduction to the history of astronomy and the tools and equipment of astronomers.

*Ridpath, Ian, and Wil Tirion. *Universe Guide to Stars and Planets.* Universe 1984 $11.95. ISBN 0-87663-859-0 Guide to observing the stars and planets; provides information about these heavenly bodies.

*Ronan, Colin A. (ed). *The Sky Watcher's Handbook.* Crown 1985 $13.95. ISBN 0-517-55703-7 Guide to observing stars, rainbows, clouds, and other atmospheric and celestial phenomena.

*Schaaf, Fred. *The Starry Room: Naked Eye Astronomy in the Intimate Universe.* Wiley 1988 $19.95. ISBN 0-471-62088-2 Essays about what can be observed in the night skies without the aid of a telescope.

*Silk, Joseph. *The Big Bang.* Freeman 1989 $24.95. ISBN 0-7167-1997-5 History of the universe and its study; discusses the big bang theory and alternative explanations of the origin of the universe.

*Simon, Seymour. *Look to the Night Sky: An Introduction to Star Watching.* Penguin 1979 $5.95. ISBN 0-14-049185-6 Introduction to observing the night sky with the naked eye.

*Snowden, Sheila. *The Young Astronomer.* EDC 1983 $5.95. ISBN 0-86020-651-3 Overview of astronomy and discussion of observing the night sky.

*Traister, Robert J., and Susan E. Harris. *Astronomy and Telescopes: A Beginner's Handbook.* TAB 1983 $19.95. ISBN 0-8306-0419-7 History of astronomy and discussion of types of telescopes; includes instructions for building a telescope.

Tyson, Neil De Grasse. *Merlin's Tour of the Universe.* Columbia Univ Pr 1989 $29.95. ISBN 0-231-06924-3

Zeilik, Michael, and John Gaustad. *Astronomy: The Cosmic Perspective.* Wiley 1983 $54.50. ISBN 0-471-60394-5

BRAHE, TYCHO 1546–1601

Tycho Brahe was born in Knudstrup, Denmark (now Sweden). Despite the wishes of an uncle who wanted him to study law, Brahe developed a keen interest in astronomy while he was a student at the University of Copenhagen. His observations of an eclipse in 1560 (which occurred at the predicted time) and a planetary conjunction in 1563 (which occurred at a time quite different from the one predicted) were the beginning of a career in astronomy. In 1577 he established a magnificent observatory on the island of Ven, where he and his assistants measured planetary positions. In 1599 he moved to Prague.

Brahe never accepted Copernicus's (*see* Copernicus, Vol. 2, Physics: Mechanics: Forces and Motion) suggestion that the sun rather than Earth was the center of the solar system. He believed that the planets revolved around the sun and the sun revolved around Earth. Nonetheless, his records became a key contribution to the Copernican revolution. His comprehensive and precise observations of planetary positions were used by his successor, Johannes Kepler, as additional evidence for the Copernican model of the solar system. (*See* Kepler, Vol. 2, Earth Science: Astronomy.)

BOOK ABOUT BRAHE

Dreyer, John L. *Tycho Brahe: A Picture of Scientific Life and Work in the Sixteenth Century.* Peter Smith 1977 $13.25. ISBN 0-8446-1996-5 Biography of the life and work of Tycho Brahe.

GALILEO 1564–1642

Born Galileo Galilei in Pisa, Italy, this early physicist and astronomer is universally known by his first name alone. As a young man, Galileo exhibited talents in many areas, including art, music, and mathematics. At his father's encouragement, he entered the University of Pisa to pursue an education in medicine. However, while at school, he attended a lecture on geometry, which so excited him that he persuaded his father to allow him to study mathematics and science.

Galileo made his first important scientific discovery while attending services at the cathedral of Pisa. Watching the motion of a swaying chandelier, Galileo timed the swings with his pulse beat and thus discovered the law of pendulums. He later suggested that a simple pendulum be used to time the pulse beat of medical patients. Some years after Galileo's death, Dutch mathematician and scientist Christiaan Huygens was to use the principle of the law of pendulums to regulate the movements of a clock.

In 1586 Galileo invented a hydrostatic balance. With this device, the specific gravity (a physical property of matter) of an object can be found by weighing the object submerged in water. This invention brought Galileo to the attention of the scholars of his time.

Galileo next turned his attention to studying the behavior of falling bodies. At the time of his investigations, it was universally accepted that the rate of fall of any body was proportional to the mass of the body—a belief that had been suggested by Aristotle. Galileo's demonstrations showed that there was no relationship between mass and rate of fall. Galileo showed that, instead, all bodies of matter fall at the same rate.

Legend has it that Galileo demonstrated the behavior of falling bodies by dropping two cannonballs of different masses from the Leaning Tower of Pisa. It is said that both balls reached the ground at approximately the same instant. Whether or not the demonstration actually took place in this way, Galileo did, in fact, provide evidence to support his hypothesis. He explained that air resistance accounted for any differences in the rates of fall of objects with different masses, and conjectured that in a vacuum all objects would fall at the same rate. Galileo's studies of the pendulum and falling bodies helped to form the foundations of modern physics.

Galileo also demonstrated that a body constantly accelerates as it moves down an inclined plane. This demonstration disproved another Aristotlean belief, namely, that in order to keep a body moving, a force had to be applied continually to the body.

Galileo's successful demonstrations of the mechanics of moving bodies were not universally accepted with enthusiasm. In fact, followers of Aristotlean physics bitterly opposed Galileo's views, and he was forced to leave the University of Pisa.

Galileo moved to Padua, from which city he carried on a correspondence with the German scientist Johannes Kepler (*see* Kepler, Vol. 2, Earth Science: Astronomy), the outstanding astronomer of the time. Galileo came to embrace the view of a sun-centered solar system and a universe in which all heavenly bodies were in motion. These ideas had been set forth by Danish mathematician and astronomer Nicolaus Copernicus in a book published in 1543 (*see* Copernicus, Vol. 2, Physics: Mechanics: Forces and Motion), but the prevailing view and the only one allowed by the all-powerful Church was the earth-centered solar system described in the the second century by the Alexandrian astronomer Ptolemy.

In 1609 Galileo learned of a magnifying tube that had been invented in Holland. Within the year, Galileo designed and built a powerful telescope, which he then turned toward the heavens. He discovered that the moon has mountains and observed spots on the surface of the sun. By keeping track of the positions of the sunspots, he found that the sun revolves about an axis, much as the planets do.

Galileo went on to make many important astronomical discoveries and observations about the motions of heavenly bodies. His championing of Copernican views eventually brought him into conflict with the Church. In 1616 Pope Pius V declared Copernicanism to be a heresy, and Galileo was forced into silence.

In 1632 Galileo was persuaded that the new prelate, Pope Urban VIII, held a friendlier attitude toward his beliefs, and he published his masterpiece, *A Dialogue Concerning the Two Principal Systems of the World*. In this work, Galileo presented opposing views in the words of two people—one who argued for the position of Ptolmey and the other who argued for the Copernican view. The book was written in Italian so that ordinary people could read it. This widespread promotion of the Copernican model brought immediate condemnation from the Pope, who was not persuaded that Galileo had presented the two arguments fairly. Brought before the Inquisition in 1633 on charges of heresy, Galileo was forced to renounce all views that were not in agreement with those of Ptolmey.

With the silencing of the voice of Galileo, the scientific revolution that had begun with Copernicus received a setback. The battle was lost, but the revolution would continue and would be won.

However, Galileo was not completely stifled, although he could no longer speak of planetary systems. While under house arrest, he continued his investigations in physics, and in 1638 he published another, less controversial book, *Dialogues Concerning Two New Sciences*.

BOOKS BY GALILEO

Dialogue Concerning the Two Chief World Systems, Ptolemaic and Copernican (1632). Stillman Drake (tr). Univ of California Pr 1967 $12.95. ISBN 0-520-00450-7
Dialogues Concerning Two New Sciences (1638). Dover 1914 $6.95. ISBN 0-486-60099-8
Sidereus Nuncius (The Sidereal Messenger) (1610). Albert Van Helden (tr). Univ of Chicago Pr 1989 $7.95. ISBN 0-226-27903-0

BOOKS ABOUT GALILEO

Bernkopf, Michael. *Science of Galileo,* Level 3. *Regents Readers Ser.* J. McConochie (ed). Prentice 1983 $2.50. ISBN 0-88345-457-2 Readable biography focusing on Galileo's scientific experiments.
Butts, Robert E., and Joseph C. Potts (eds). *New Perspectives on Galileo.* Kluwer Academic 1978 $15.80. ISBN 90-277-0891-6 Succeeds in reflecting and integrating many of the dimensions of this great thinker in the development of modern sciences.
Campanella, Thomas. *The Defense of Galileo. History, Philosophy, and Sociology of Science Ser.* Ayer 1975 $14.00. ISBN 0-405-06582-5 Trial of Galileo as seen through the eyes of his contemporary.
*Cobb, Vicki. *Truth on Trial: The Story of Galileo Galilei. Science Discovery Book Ser.* Coward 1979. (o.p.) Personalized account of Galileo's life and accomplishments, with emphasis on his innovative scientific thought and the personal effects of his enforced life imprisonment.
Drake, Stillman. *Galileo at Work: His Scientific Biography.* Univ of Chicago Pr 1981. (o.p.) $9.95. ISBN 0-226-16227-3 Includes Galileo's autobiography and commentary on his accomplishments.
Hummel, Charles. *The Galileo Connection.* Inter-Varsity 1986 $10.95. ISBN 0-87784-500-X New perspective on the relationship between science and theology; traces the rise of modern science and looks at its goals and limitations.
Langford, Jerome J. *Galileo, Science, and the Church.* Univ of Michigan Pr 1971 $8.95. ISBN 0-472-06173-9 Balanced review of the circumstances surrounding Galileo's confrontation with the Catholic church.
McMullin, Einan (ed). *Galileo: Man of Science.* Scholars Bookshelf 1988 $14.95. ISBN 0-945626-03-1 Large collection of essays by various authors covering Galileo's life and contribution to science.
Redondi, Pietro. *Galileo: Heretic.* R. Rosenthal (tr). Princeton Univ Pr 1989 $9.95. Drawing on newly discovered documents, a new interpretation of Galileo's trial for heresy.
Santillana, Giorgio de. *The Crime of Galileo.* Univ of Chicago Pr 1978 $14.00. ISBN 0-226-73481-1 Details of the confrontation between Galileo and the Catholic church.

KEPLER, JOHANNES 1571–1630

Born in Weil der Stadt, Germany, Johannes Kepler earned an undergraduate degree in 1584 and an M.S. in 1591 from the University of Tübingen. In 1594 he began teaching science at the University of Graz in Austria.

While in Graz, Kepler began to think about astronomy and planetary motion. His first work, *Mysterium cosmographicum,* was published in 1596. In 1598 he moved to Prague and became an apprentice to the Danish astronomer Tycho Brahe. (*See* Brahe, Vol. 2, Earth Science: Astronomy.) When Brahe died, he left his collection of astronomical observations to Kepler. Using Brahe's observations, Kepler determined the orbit of Mars and concluded that planets move in elliptical, rather than circular, orbits. Kepler's approach of seeking a broad sense of order and harmony in the universe led him to discover three laws of planetary motion. Ultimately these laws led to Newton's Laws of Motion. (*See* Newton, Vol. 2, Physics: Mechanics: Forces and Motion.)

An interesting aspect of Kepler's personality and accomplishments is revealed by his book *Somnium,* translated as *The Dream.* This book, which has been called the first work of science fiction in the modern sense, describes a dream about a trip to the moon. Kepler first set down the story and then added notes to it over a period of 20 years. Eventually the additions outgrew the length of the original story. Kepler began printing the story on a press that had been set up in his home to enable him to print astronomical tables. At the time of his death, printing of *Somnium* was still incomplete, but the book was published posthumously in 1634.

BOOKS BY KEPLER

Concerning the Most Certain Fundamentals of Astrology (1602). Holmes Pub 1987 $4.95. ISBN 0-916411-68-0

Mysterium cosmographicum (1596). A. M. Duncan (tr). Abaris 1981. (o.p.) $20.00. ISBN 0-913-87064-1

Kepler's Dream (1634). John Lear (ed). Patricia Kirkwood (tr). Univ of California Pr 1965. (o.p.) $25.00. ISBN 0-520-00716-6

Somnium: The Dream, or Posthumous Work on Lunar Astronomy (1634). Edward Rosen (tr). Books Demand $72.30. ISBN 0-317-07803-8

BOOKS ABOUT KEPLER

Armitage, Angus. *John Kepler.* Roy 1967. (o.p.) Short introduction to the life and work of Kepler.

Koestler, Arthur. *The Watershed: A Biography of Johannes Kepler.* Univ Pr of America 1985 $13.75. ISBN 0-8191-4339-1 A look at the life and accomplishments of Kepler and the nature of creativity in science.

ASTRONOMY: THE SOLAR SYSTEM

*Apfel, Necia H. *The Moon and Its Exploration.* Watts 1982. (o.p.) $8.90. ISBN 0-531-04385-1 Discussion of the moon: its geology, movements, eclipses, and exploration by humans.

*Asimov, Isaac. *Asimov's Guide to Halley's Comet: The Awesome Story of Comets.* Walker 1985 $12.95. ISBN 0-8027-0836-6 A wealth of information about comets, including their composition and place in our solar system.

*Asimov, Isaac. *How Did We Find Out About Comets?* Walker 1975 $8.95. ISBN 0-8027-6204-2 Introduction to comets.

*Asimov, Isaac. *Mars, the Red Planet.* Lothrop 1977. (o.p.) $12.88. ISBN 0-688-51812-5
    Discussion of the planet Mars and its place among the other inner planets.
*Asimov, Isaac. *Venus, Near Neighbor of the Sun.* Lothrop 1981 $12.95. ISBN 0-688-41976-3
    A look at Venus and its neighbor, Mercury, as well as at comets and asteroids.
*Berger, Melvin. *Comets, Meteors, and Asteroids.* Putnam 1981 $6.99. ISBN 0-399-61148-7
    A discussion of the composition, movements, and relationships among comets,
    meteors, and asteroids.
*Branley, Franklyn M. *Jupiter: King of the Gods, Giant of the Planets.* Elsevier 1981 $12.95.
    ISBN 0-525-66739-3 Introduction to Jupiter and its moons.
*Branley, Franklyn M. *Mysteries of the Satellites. Mysteries of the Universe Ser.* Lodestar 1986
    $11.95. ISBN 0-525-67176-5 Introduction to natural satellites, their origins, and
    their features.
*Branley, Franklyn M. *Saturn: The Spectacular Planet.* Harcourt 1987 $4.95. ISBN 0-06-
    446056-8 Introduction to Saturn and its moons and rings.
 Briggs, Geoffrey, and Fredric Taylor. *A Photographic Atlas of the Planets.* Cambridge Univ
    Pr 1986 $17.95. ISBN 0-521-31058-X
*Burgess, Eric. *Venus: An Errant Twin.* Columbia Univ Pr 1985 $29.95. ISBN 0-231-
    05856-X Discussion of what is known about Venus and controversies relating to
    knowledge about this planet.
 Cadogan, Peter H. *The Moon: Our Sister Planet.* Cambridge Univ Pr 1981 $34.50. ISBN
    0-521-28152-0
*Calder, Nigel. *The Comet Is Coming! The Feverish Legacy of Mr. Halley.* Penguin 1982 $7.95.
    ISBN 0-14-006069-3 Presents many superstitions and legends about comets, as
    well as historical and scientific views about cometology; a very entertaining and
    well-written commentary.
*Couper, Heather. *Comets and Meteors.* Watts 1985 $11.90. ISBN 0-531-10000-6 Introduc-
    tion to comets and meteors, their origins, and their cycles.
*Couper, Heather, and Nigel Henbest. *The Sun.* Watts 1987 $11.90. ISBN 0-531-10055-3
    Introduction to the characteristics of the sun and phenomena associated with the
    sun; explains day/night and the seasons.
*Dodd, Robert T. *Thunderstones and Shooting Stars: The Meaning of Meteorites.* Harvard Univ
    Pr 1988 $24.95. ISBN 0-674-89138-4 Examination of meteorites, their origins, and
    their role in the evolution of the solar system and of Earth.
*Editors of Time–Life Books. *The Far Planets. Voyage Through the Universe Ser.* Time–Life
    1988 $17.27. ISBN 0-8094-6854-9 Explores the universe from the time of the big
    bang with emphasis on the outer planets; beautiful illustrations.
 Elliot, James, and Richard Kerr. *Rings: Discoveries from Galileo to Voyager.* MIT Pr 1984
    $8.95. ISBN 0-262-55013-X
**The Far Planets. Voyage Through the Universe Ser.* Time-Life 1989 $14.95. ISBN 0-8094-
    6855-7 Pictorial look at the outer planets.
**Fire of Life: The Smithsonian Book of the Sun.* Smithsonian Bks 1981 $24.95. ISBN 0-89599-
    006-7 Pictorial presentation of the genealogy, birth, and lifespan of the sun and
    its effects on Earth.
*Fisher, David E. *The Third Experiment: Is There Life on Mars?* Atheneum 1985 $12.95. ISBN
    0-689-31080-3 A look at the possibility of life on Mars and ways of investigating
    the question.
*Frazier, Kendrick. *Solar System. Planet Earth Ser.* Time-Life 1985 $13.99. ISBN 0-8094-
    4529-8 History of the sun and planets; discusses current knowledge of the solar
    system.
*Gallant, Roy A. *National Geographic Picture Atlas of Our Universe.* National Geographic 1986
    $16.95. ISBN 0-87044-644-4 Pictorial introduction to the solar system.
*Gallant, Roy A. *The Planets: Exploring the Solar System.* Macmillan 1985 $15.95. ISBN
    0-02-736930-7 History of the sun, planets, moon, asteroids, and comets; discusses
    present knowledge of the solar system.
*Gallant, Roy A. *Rainbows, Mirages, and Sundogs: The Sky As a Source of Wonder.* Macmillan
    1987 $12.95. ISBN 0-02-737010-0 Explanations of phenomena seen in the sky.
 Giovanelli, Ronald G. *Secrets of the Sun.* Cambridge Univ Pr 1984 $27.95. ISBN 0-521-
    25521-X
*Harpur, Brian. *The Official Halley's Comet Book.* David and Charles 1985 $20.95. ISBN

0-340-36511-0 Discussion of Halley's comet, especially its 1910 appearance; explores comets in general.

*Hockey, Thomas A. *The Book of the Moon: A Lunar Introduction to Astronomy, Geology, Space Physics, and Space Travel.* Prentice 1986 $9.95. ISBN 0-13-079963-7 A look at astronomy from the perspective of the moon; considers space exploration, laws of the universe, and studies of the moon itself.

*Jabor, William. *Exploring the Sun.* Messner 1980 $8.97. ISBN 0-671-32997-9 Discussion of the sun and its importance.

Jackson, Joseph H., and John H. Baumert. *Pictorial Guide to the Planets.* Harper 1981 $22.50. ISBN 0-06-014869-1

*Lampton, Christopher. *The Sun.* Watts 1982 $10.40. ISBN 0-531-04390-8 A look at our understanding of the sun, past and present; includes discussion of the sun's formation, composition, and activities.

*Miller, Ron, and William K. Hartman. *The Grand Tour: A Traveler's Guide to the Solar System.* Workman 1980 $12.95. ISBN 0-89480-146-5 Visits to the bodies of of our solar system, through illustrations and narrative.

*Moore, Patrick. *Guide to Mars.* Norton 1977. (o.p.) $14.95. ISBN 0-393-06432-8 Comparison of our knowledge of Mars before and after spacecraft visited the planet.

Moore, Patrick. *New Guide to the Moon.* Norton 1976. (o.p.) $12.95. ISBN 0-393-06414-X

*Moore, Patrick, and John Mason. *The Return of Halley's Comet.* Warner Bks 1985 $6.95. ISBN 0-446-38303-1 Discussion of comets in general and detailed information on Halley's comet.

*Moskin, Marietta D. *Sky Dragons and Flaming Swords: The Story of Eclipses, Comets, and Other Strange Happenings in the Skies.* Walker 1985 $12.85. ISBN 0-8027-6575-0 A look at folklore and myths relating to eclipses, meteors, and comets; discusses modern understanding of these phenomena.

*Nourse, Alan E. *The Giant Planets.* Watts 1982 $10.40. ISBN 0-531-00816-9 Discussion of present knowledge about and current research involving the outer planets.

*Powers, Robert M. *Mars: Our Future on the Red Planet.* Houghton 1986 $17.95. ISBN 0-395-35371-8 Detailed study of what an Earth-to-Mars mission would involve.

*Roop, Peter, and Connie Roop. *The Solar System: Opposing Viewpoints.* Greenhaven 1987 $12.95. ISBN 0-89908-053-7 Presentation of different opinions about the origin of the solar system and the possibility of life on Mars.

Sagan, Carl, and Ann Druyan. *Comet.* Random 1985 $27.50. ISBN 0-394-54908-2

Seargent, David A. *Comets: Vagabonds of Space.* Doubleday 1982. (o.p.) $15.95. ISBN 0-385-17869-7

*Smithsonian Institution. *Fire of Life: The Smithsonian Book of the Sun.* Norton 1981 $24.95. ISBN 0-89599-006-7 Spectacularly illustrated essays about the sun, its place in the cosmos, and its relationship to life on Earth.

*Taylor, G. Jeffrey. *Volcanoes in Our Solar System.* Dodd 1983 $10.95. ISBN 0-396-08118-5 A look at volcanoes on Earth and other planets, moons, and asteroids.

*Vogt, Gregory. *Mars and the Inner Planets.* Watts 1982 $10.40. ISBN 0-531-04384-3 Examination of the planets Mars, Venus, and Mercury.

Washburn, Mark. *Distant Encounters: The Exploration of Jupiter and Saturn.* Harcourt 1983 $12.95. ISBN 0-15-626108-1

*Whipple, Fred L. *Orbiting the Sun: Planets and Satellites of the Solar System.* Harvard Univ Pr 1981 $9.95. ISBN 0-674-64126-4 Introduction to the solar system.

*Wilford, John Noble. *Mars Beckons.* Knopf 1990 $24.95. ISBN 0-394-58359-0 Story of what we know about Mars and what we are learning from data collected by *Viking.*

Zirker, Jack B. *Total Eclipses of the Sun.* Van Nostrand 1984. (o.p.) $23.00. ISBN 0-442-29455-7

HALLEY, EDMOND   1656–1742

Edmond Halley was born near London, in Haggerston, England. Even as a child he was interested in astronomy. Halley set up the first observatory in the Southern Hemisphere on the island of St. Helena and in 1678 published a catalog of southern stars. This brought him almost immediate recognition.

Halley is most famous for his study of comets. In 1682 he recognized that the comets seen in 1456, 1531, and 1607 were actually earlier appearances of the same comet he currently observed, the one now known as Halley's comet. Halley predicted that the comet would reappear in 1758. It was a prediction that proved true.

Halley made many important contributions to science. He played a key role in the publication of Isaac Newton's major work, the *Principia*, in 1687. (*See* Newton, Vol. 2, Physics: Mechanics: Forces and Motion.) He established the distance between Earth and the sun through measurements of a transit of Venus. Halley was the first to observe stellar motion across the sky. In addition, by his studies of terrestrial magnetism and his demonstration that solar heating causes the trade winds and monsoons, Halley founded the science of geophysics.

BOOK BY HALLEY

Correspondence and Papers of Edmond Halley. History, Philosophy, and Sociology of Science Ser. Ayer 1975 $30.00. ISBN 0-405-06596-5

BOOK ABOUT HALLEY

Baldwin, Louis. *Edmond Halley and His Comet.* Maverick 1985 $7.95. ISBN 0-89288-107-0 Biography of Halley; includes a discussion of comets in general and information on Halley's comet in particular.

HERSCHEL, WILLIAM   1738–1822

William Herschel was born in Hannover, Germany. His first profession was music. He began by playing in his father's regimental band. Then, in 1757, he moved to England, where several years later he became the organist at a chapel in Bath. His interest gradually shifted from music to astronomy. He began to grind his own lenses and to build large telescopes. A reflecting telescope he built was better than any existing refracting telescope.

With his telescopes, Herschel made extensive, systematic observations of stars. This work led him to discover the planet Uranus in 1781, making him the first person to discover a planet with a telescope. Herschel's most important achievement in astronomy, however, was to establish that the Milky Way is a flat galaxy. He drew this conclusion from his studies of the distribution of stars in space and his comprehensive mapping and cataloging of the sky observable from England.

Among his major accomplishments, Herschel showed the existence of binary stars and discovered two satellites of Uranus, two additional satellites of Saturn, and infrared radiation.

BOOK ABOUT HERSCHEL

Whitney, C. A. *The Discovery of Our Galaxy.* Knopf 1971. (o.p.) $10.00. ISBN 0-394-46068-5 A look at Herschel's key role in the discovery of the shape of the Milky Way.

HUBBLE, EDWIN POWELL   1889–1953

Born in Marshfield, Missouri, Edwin Hubble attended the University of Chicago and, later, as a Rhodes Scholar, Oxford University in England. After receiving a law degree in 1910, he practiced law for a short time. In 1914 he found his niche in astronomy and went to the Yerkes Observatory, operated by the University of Chicago on Lake Geneva in Wisconsin, to do graduate work. In 1917 he received a Ph.D. from the University of Chicago. Two years later he went to the Mount Wilson Observatory in California, where he remained for the rest of his career.

Hubble conducted research on galaxies. He was the first person to determine that there are swarms of hundreds of billions of stars outside our galaxy. These swarms also became known as galaxies. Hubble classified galaxies by size and shape. His discovery of a particular type of variable star in the Andromeda Galaxy allowed him to determine its distance from Earth. In 1929 Hubble established that there is a uniform relationship between the distance of light-emitting objects from Earth and the red shift of the objects—the shift of the wavelengths of the light given off toward longer wavelengths, which are toward the red end of the spectrum. These findings are interpreted as proof that the galaxies are moving away from our solar system—an important part of the evidence for an expanding universe. Hubble's name was given to the orbiting space telescope that was launched in 1990.

BOOKS BY HUBBLE

The Hubble Atlas of Galaxies. Allan Sandage (ed). Carnegie Institution of Washington 1984. (o.p.) $29.00. ISBN 0-872-79-629-9

The Realm of the Nebulae (1936). *Silliman Milestones in Science Ser.* Yale Univ Pr 1982 $12.95. ISBN 0-300-02500-9

ASTRONOMY: DEEP SPACE ASTRONOMY

*Adler, Irving. *The Stars: Decoding Their Messages.* Crowell 1980 $9.57. ISBN 0-690-03993-X A look at the composition, brightness, distance, motion, mass, and density of stars.

*Asimov, Isaac. *The Collapsing Universe: The Story of Black Holes.* Walker 1977 $14.95. ISBN 0-8027-0486-7 A look at forces at work in the universe and a collapsing universe resulting from the effects of these forces.

Asimov, Isaac. *The Exploding Suns: The Secrets of the Supernovas.* NAL 1985 $4.50. ISBN 0-451-62481-5

*Asimov, Isaac. *How Did We Find Out About Black Holes?* Walker 1978 $9.85. ISBN 0-8027-6337-5 Introduction to our understanding of black holes.

*Asimov, Isaac. *Universe.* Walker 1980 $15.95. ISBN 0-8027-0655-X History of our study of the universe.

*Berger, Melvin. *Bright Stars, Red Giants, and White Dwarfs.* Putnam 1983 $6.99. ISBN 0-399-61209-2 Description of the life cycle of stars.

Bok, Bart J., and Priscilla F. Bok. *The Milky Way.* Harvard Univ Pr 1981 $29.95. ISBN 0-674-57503-2

*Branley, Franklyn M. *Mysteries of Life on Earth and Beyond. Mysteries of the Universe Ser.* Lodestar 1987 $11.95. ISBN 0-525-67195-1 Introduction to the possibility of extraterrestrial life.

*Editors of Time–Life Books. *Stars. Voyage Through Space Ser.* Time–Life 1988 $17.27. ISBN 0-8094-6858-1 Discusses stars, their study, and life history; presents information about research using radio and X-ray astronomy.

*Friedman, Herbert. *The Amazing Universe.* National Geographic 1975 $7.95. ISBN 0-87044-179-5 Discussion of the stars and changing theories about them.

*Galaxies. *Voyage Through the Universe Ser.* Time-Life 1989 $14.95. ISBN 0-8094-6850-6 Discussion of the history of the study of galaxies and the latest information about galaxies.

*Gallant, Roy A. *The Constellations: How They Came to Be.* Four Winds 1979. (o.p.) $12.95. ISBN 0-590-7552-7 Introduction to 44 constellations visible in the Northern Hemisphere.

*Gallant, Roy A. *Private Lives of the Stars.* Macmillan 1986 $12.95. ISBN 0-02-737350-9 Introduction to the big bang and the life cycles of stars.

*Jastrow, Robert. *Red Giants and White Dwarfs.* Warner Bks 1980 $3.95. ISBN 0-446-32193-1 Discussion of the life cycles of stars and planets and the evolution of life on Earth; considers the possibility of extraterrestrial life.

*Jesperson, James, and Jane Fitz-Randolf. *From Quarks to Quasars: A Tour of the Universe.* Atheneum 1987 $16.95. ISBN 0-689-31270-9 A look at the theories, past and present, of the nature of the universe.

*Lampton, Christopher. *Black Holes and Other Secrets of the Universe.* Watts 1980. (o.p.) $9.90. ISBN 0-531-02284-6 Examination of black holes—their origin and an explanation of them.

*Lampton, Christopher. *Supernova!* Watts 1988 $12.90. ISBN 0-531-10602-0 Discussion of the history of astronomy and supernovae.

*Marschall, Laurence A. *The Supernova Story.* Plenum 1988 $22.95. ISBN 0-306-42955-1 Thorough discussion of stars and the life cycle of stars; includes the history of research in astronomy.

Murdin, Paul, and Leslie Murdin. *Supernovae.* Cambridge Univ Pr 1985 $24.95. ISBN 0-521-30038-X

*Poynter, Margaret, and J. Michael Klein. *Cosmic Quest: Searching for Intelligent Life Among the Stars.* Macmillan 1984 $11.95. ISBN 0-689-31068-4 Explores the possibility of the existence of life in outer space.

*Ridpath, Ian. *Space.* Silver 1983 $14.96. ISBN 0-382-06726-6 Pictorial introduction to space.

Silk, Joseph. *The Big Bang.* Freeman 1989 $24.95. ISBN 0-7167-1997-X

Sullivan, Walter. *Black Holes: The Edge of Space, The End of Time.* Warner Bks 1987 $4.50. ISBN 0-446-32288-1

*Trefil, James S. *Space, Time, Infinity: The Smithsonian Views the Universe.* Pantheon 1985 $16.95. ISBN 0-394-54843-4 Introduction to astronomy, beginning with the big bang.

SAGAN, CARL 1934–

A respected planetary scientist best known outside the field for his popularizations of astronomy, Carl Sagan was born in New York City and educated at the University of Chicago. He received his Ph.D. in 1960 and had several early scholarly achievements. One was the experimental demonstration of the synthesis of the energy-carrying molecule ATP (adenosine triphosphate) in primitive-earth experiments. Another was the proposal that the greenhouse effect explained the high temperature of the surface of Venus. More recently, Sagan was one of the driving forces behind the mission of the U.S. satellite Viking to the surface of Mars. He also has been part of a team that investigated the effects of nuclear war on the earth's climate—the "nuclear winter" scenario.

Sagan's role in developing the "Cosmos" series, one of the most successful series of any kind to be broadcast on the Public Broadcasting System, and his many popular books have established his career as a science popularizer. His book *The Dragons of Eden* (1977) won the Pulitzer Prize in 1978.

BOOKS BY SAGAN

Broca's Brain: Reflections on the Romance of Science (1979). Ballantine 1986 $4.95. ISBN 0-345-33689-5

Comet (1985). (coauthored with Ann Druyan) Random 1985 $27.50. ISBN 0-394-54908-2 The definitive book about comets, written to commemorate the return of Halley's comet in 1985–1986.

The Cosmic Connection: An Extraterrestrial Perspective (1973). Doubleday 1980 $10.95. ISBN 0-385-17365-2

Cosmos (1980). Random 1983 $21.95. ISBN 0-394-71596-9 Exploration of the universe, developed concurrently with the "Cosmos" television series.

The Dragons of Eden (1977). Ballantine 1986 $4.95. ISBN 0-345-34629-7

Intelligent Life in the Universe (1966). (coauthored with I.S. Shlovskii) Holden-Day 1978. (o.p.) $17.95. ISBN 0-8162-7913-0

UFO's: A Scientific Debate (1972). (coauthored with Thornton Page) Norton 1974 $8.95. ISBN 0-393-00739-1

BOOK ABOUT SAGAN

Cohen, Daniel. *Carl Sagan: Superstar Scientist.* Putnam 1987 $13.95. ISBN 0-399-21702-9 Examines Sagan the scientist and Sagan the explicator who deciphers the heavens for the lay person.

ASTRONOMY: SPACE EXPLORATION

*Asimov, Isaac. *How Did We Find Out About Outer Space?* Walker 1977. (o.p.) $11.85. ISBN 0-8027-6284-0 History of space flight.

*Baker, David. *The History of Manned Space Flight.* Crown 1982. (o.p.) $35.00. ISBN 0-517-54377-X History of piloted space flight; describes unpiloted rocket launches and the technology that made piloted flight possible.

*Bendick, Jeanne. *Artificial Satellites.* Watts 1982. (o.p.) $8.90. ISBN 0-531-04381-9 Discussion of satellites, including orbits, and how we communicate with these objects we have launched.

*Bendick, Jeanne. *Space Travel.* Watts 1982. (o.p.) $8.90. ISBN 0-531-04388-6 Description of the solar system and a possible explanation of the planets.

*Berger, Melvin. *Space Shots, Shuttles, and Satellites.* Putnam 1983 $7.99. ISBN 0-399-61210-6 Introduction to space flight; discusses astronauts, the history of space exploration, and the space shuttle and its uses.

*Branley, Franklyn M. *Mysteries of Outer Space.* Dutton 1985 $11.95. ISBN 0-525-67149-8 Discussion of the prospects and difficulties of living in space.

*Branley, Franklyn M. *Space Colony: Frontier of the 21st Century.* Lodestar 1982 $10.95. ISBN 0-525-66741-5 Discussion of the reasons for the establishment of space colonies.

*Briggs, Carole S. *Women in Space: Reaching the Last Frontier.* Lerner 1988 $5.95. ISBN 0-8225-9547-8 Reference book featuring lives and achievements of women in space programs; mostly American women are discussed.

*Collins, Michael. *Flying to the Moon and Other Strange Places.* Farrar 1976 $3.45. ISBN 0-374-42355-5 Description of the training of the Apollo astronauts and their flights.

*Collins, Michael. *Liftoff: The Story of America's Adventure in Space.* Grove 1989 $10.95. ISBN 0-8021-3188-3 History of space exploration by the United States through the 1980s, told by astronaut Michael Collins.

Cornell, James, and Paul Gorenstein (eds). *Astronomy from Space: Sputnik to Space Telescope.* MIT Pr 1985 $9.95. ISBN 0-262-53061-9

*Couper, Heather, and Nigel Henbest. *Space Probes and Satellites.* Watts 1987 $11.90. ISBN 0-531-10360-9 A look at space exploration by unpiloted and piloted spacecraft.

Darling, David J. *The Planets: The Next Frontier.* Dillon 1984 $10.95. ISBN 0-87518-263-1 Introduction to the planets—history and facts about them.

Davies, Owen (ed). *The Omni Book of Space.* Zebra 1983 $3.95. ISBN 0-8217-1275-6

*Dwiggins, Don. *Flying the Frontiers of Space.* Putnam 1982 $10.95. ISBN 0-396-08041-3 Account of the development of the technology that led to the space shuttle flights.

*Editors of Time-Life Books. *Life in Space.* Little 1985 $19.95. ISBN 0-316-85063-2 Pictorial and narrative look at the first 25 years of space exploration.

*Elwood, Ann, and Linda C. Wood. *Windows in Space.* Walker 1982. (o.p.) $10.95. ISBN 0-8027-6431-2 Introduction to the solar system, space flight, and the space shuttle program.

*Fichter, George S. *The Space Shuttle.* Watts 1981 $10.40. ISBN 0-531-04354-1 History of the space shuttle program.

*Fox, Mary Virginia. *Women Astronauts: Aboard the Shuttle.* Messner 1987 $5.95. ISBN 0-671-64841-1 Description of a shuttle flight and biographies of women astronauts.

*Gardner, Robert. *Space: Frontier of the Future.* Doubleday 1980. (o.p.) $8.95. ISBN 0-385-14500-4 Discussion of space travel, both unpiloted and piloted.

*Gatland, Kenneth. *The Illustrated Encyclopedia of Space Technology.* Crown 1989 $24.95. ISBN 0-517-57427-6 Excellent resource for information on the history of major events in space exploration.

*Hawkes, Nigel. *Space Shuttle.* Watts 1982 $12.40. ISBN 0-531-04583-8 History of the space shuttle; describes the interior of a space shuttle.

*Hohler, Robert T. *"I Touch the Future": The Story of Christa McAuliffe.* Random 1986 $16.45. ISBN 0-394-55721-2 Much of McAuliffe's own words are recollected here and, though she saw herself as an ordinary woman on an extraordinary mission, it is apparent she was an extraordinary person.

*Jastrow, Robert. *Journey to the Stars: Space Exploration—Tomorrow and Beyond.* Bantam 1989 $18.95. ISBN 0-553-05386-8 Discusses accomplishments of the space age and what might still be done; speculates about the existence of intelligent life in space.

*Lampton, Christopher. *The Space Telescope.* Watts 1987 $10.40. ISBN 0-531-10221-1 Introduction to the Hubble Space Telescope.

*Lewis, Richard S. *Challenger: The Final Voyage.* Columbia Univ Pr 1988 $29.95. ISBN 0-231-06490-X Examination of the *Challenger*—the explosion, recovery of its wreckage, the inquiry into the causes of the explosion, and recommendations for avoiding future disasters.

*Lewis, Richard S. *The Voyages of Columbia: The First True Spaceship.* Columbia Univ Pr 1984. (o.p.) $24.95. ISBN 0-231-05924-8 History of the space shuttle program from the initial plans to the first flight.

*McKay, David W., and Bruce G. Smith. *Space Science Projects for Young Scientists.* Watts 1986 $12.90. ISBN 0-531-10244-0 Collection of projects young people can carry out that simulate what happens to animals, plants, people, materials, and processes in space.

Needell, Allan A. (ed). *The First 25 Years in Space: A Symposium.* Smithsonian 1983 $17.50. ISBN 0-87474-668-X

*Newton, David E. *U.S. and Soviet Space Programs: A Comparison.* Watts 1988 $12.40. ISBN 0-531-10515-6 Comparison of the space programs of the United States and the Soviet Union.

*O'Connor, Karen. *Sally Ride and the New Astronauts.* Watts 1983 $11.90. ISBN 0-531-04602-8 Discussion of how astronauts are selected and trained, featuring female astronauts.

*Oberg, James E. *The New Race for Space: The U.S. and Russia Leap to the Challenge for Unlimited Rewards.* Stackpole 1984 $14.95. ISBN 0-8117-2177-9 A look at the space race since *Sputnik* and the future of space exploration.

*Osman, Tony. *Space History.* St. Martin's 1983 $16.95. ISBN 0-312-74945-7 Highlights of space history beginning with people who only imagined traveling in space.

*Poynter, Margaret, and Arthur L. Lane. *Voyager: The Story of a Space Mission.* Atheneum 1981 $12.95. ISBN 0-689-30827-2 Discussion of the Voyager space mission from the planning stages through the encounter with Saturn.

*Ride, Sally K., and Susan Okie. *To Space and Back.* Lothrop 1989 $9.95. ISBN 0-688-09112-1 Description of a space shuttle flight from blast-off to landing.

*Schulke, Flip, *et al. Your Future in Space: The U.S. Space Camp Training Program.* Crown 1986 $14.95. ISBN 0-517-56418-1 Description of a U.S. space camp.

*Shapland, David, and Michael Rycroft. *Spacelab: Research in Earth Orbit.* Cambridge Univ Pr 1984 $32.50. ISBN 0-521-26077-9 Discussion of the Spacelab program from planning to the launch in 1983.

*Smith, Howard E. *Daring the Unknown: A History of NASA.* Harcourt 1987 $16.95. ISBN 0-15-200435-1 A look at the U.S. space program—past, present, and future.
*Spangenberg, Ray, and Diane Moser. *Opening the Space Frontier.* Facts on File 1989 $22.95. ISBN 0-8160-1848-0 Space exploration from Jules Verne to the realities of today.
 Stine, G. Harry. *Handbook for Space Colonists.* Holt 1985. (o.p.) $11.95. ISBN 0-03-070741-2
*Stine, G. Harry. *Handbook of Model Rocketry.* Arco 1983 $10.95. ISBN 0-668-05360-7 Introduction to model rocketry.
*Trefil, James S. *Living in Space.* Scribner's 1981 $10.95. ISBN 0-684-17171-6 Discussion of the design, construction, and uses of space colonies.
*Vogt, Gregory. *Model Rockets.* Watts 1982. (o.p.) $8.90. ISBN 0-531-04467-X History, principles, and practical aspects of model rocketry; includes experiments.
*Vogt, Gregory. *Space Satellites.* Watts 1987 $11.90. ISBN 0-531-10141-X Introduction to satellites used for communication, weather observations, defense, and space exploration.
*Vogt, Gregory. *Space Shuttles: Projects for Young Scientists.* Watts 1983 $12.90. ISBN 0-531-04669-9 Guide to the space shuttle with emphasis on past and future experiments carried out on board.
*Vogt, Gregory. *A Twenty-fifth Anniversary Picture Album of NASA.* Watts 1983 $12.90. ISBN 0-531-04655-9 Story of the National Aeronautic and Space Administration (NASA), including accounts of piloted and unpiloted flights.
 Von Braun, Wernher, *et al. Space Travel: A History.* Harper 1985 $29.45. ISBN 0-06-181898-4
*White, Jack R. *Satellites of Today and Tomorrow.* Dodd 1985. (o.p.) $10.95. ISBN 0-396-08514-8 Introduction to the kinds of satellites, their uses, and how they are built.
*Wold, Allen L. *Computers in Space.* Watts 1984. (o.p.) $9.90. ISBN 0-531-04847-0 Discussion of how space exploration affected the development of computers and how computers are used in space exploration.
*Wolfe, Tom. *The Right Stuff.* Bantam 1984 $4.95. ISBN 0-553-25596-7 Lively and colorful discussion of the U.S. space program and the early astronauts.

VON BRAUN, WERNHER   1912–1977

Wernher von Braun was born in Wirsitz, Germany (now Wyrzysk, Poland). As a child, he became interested in rockets and eventually made them his life's work. He studied in Zurich, Switzerland, and in Berlin, Germany. In 1934 he received a Ph.D. from the University of Berlin.

In 1937 von Braun became technical director of the Nazi rocket program at Peenemunde, on the shore of the Baltic Sea. His group was responsible for the development and production of German V-2 rockets. A total of 4,300 V-2s were used during World War II; 1,230 of them were directed against England in the closing days of the war. As the war ended, von Braun and most of his group chose to surrender and were sent to the United States. Von Braun became a United States citizen in 1955.

In the years following the war, von Braun and his team first worked on guided missile systems. Then, responding to congressional concern following the launch of the satellite *Sputnik* by the Soviet Union in October 1957, the team hastily put together the rocket for the *Explorer 1* satellite. Launched by the National Aeronatics and Space Administration (NASA) in January 1958, it was the first satellite successfully put into orbit by the United States. Von Braun also directed the teams responsible for the rockets that sent American astronauts into space and to the moon.

In 1970, von Braun became a deputy assistant administrator for NASA. In 1972 he joined the aerospace company Fairchild Industries, and from 1975 until his death in 1977 he was president of the National Space Institute, the purpose of which is to aid the public in understanding the space program of the United States.

BOOKS BY VON BRAUN

First Men to the Moon (1960). Holt 1960. (o.p.) $3.95. ISBN 0-03-030295-1
The Mars Project (1962). Univ of Illinois Pr 1962. (o.p.) $5.95. ISBN 0-252-72544-1
New Worlds: Discoveries from Our Solar System. (coauthored with Frederick I. Ordway III) Doubleday 1979. (o.p.) $24.95. ISBN 0-385-14065-7
The Rocket's Red Glare: An Illustrated History of Rocketry Through the Ages (1976). (coauthored with Frederick I. Ordway III) Doubleday 1976. (o.p.) $9.95. ISBN 0-385-07847-1
Space Frontier (1971). Holt 1971. (o.p.) $4.95. ISBN 0-03-063705-8
Space Travel: A History. (coauthored with Frederick I. Ordway III, *et al*) Harper 1985 $29.95. ISBN 0-06-181898-4

BOOKS ABOUT VON BRAUN

David, Heather M. *Wernher von Braun.* Putnam 1967. (o.p.) A biography of von Braun and the development of the U.S. space program.
Lampton, Christopher. *Wernher von Braun. Impact Biography Ser.* Watts 1988 $12.90. ISBN 0-531-10606-3 Life and achievements of Wernher von Braun.
Ordway, Frederick I., III, and Mitchell R. Sharpe. *The Rocket Team.* Crowell 1979. (o.p.) ISBN 0-690-01656-5 Story of von Braun's involvement in the history of space flight, beginning in Germany.

METEOROLOGY

Barry, Roger, and Richard J. Charley. *Atmosphere, Weather, and Climate.* Routledge 1988 $27.50. ISBN 0-416-07152-X
Fairbridge, Rhodes W., and John E. Oliver. *The Encyclopedia of Climatology. Encyclopedia of Earth Sciences Ser.: Vol. XI.* Van Nostrand 1986 $97.95. ISBN 0-87933-009-0
McGraw-Hill Encyclopedia of Ocean and Atmospheric Sciences. McGraw 1979 $76.00. ISBN 0-07-045267-9

HENRY, JOSEPH   1797–1878

Joseph Henry was born in Albany, New York, and was educated at Albany Academy, where he later taught for several years. In 1832 he began teaching at New Jersey College (known today as Princeton University). He stayed there until 1846 when he became the first director of the Smithsonian Institution. The following year he served as president of the National Academy of Sciences.

As director of the Smithsonian, Henry was involved in many areas of science, including electromagnetism and meteorology. In his work in meteorology, Henry investigated sun spots and solar radiation. His studies in meteorology became the basis for the founding of the U.S. Weather Bureau.

BOOK ABOUT HENRY

Crowther, James G. *Famous American Men of Science.* Ayer 1937 $27.50. ISBN 0-8369-0040-5 Biographies of four American scientists, including Henry.

SHAW, WILLIAM NAPIER   1854–1945

Born in Birmingham, England, William Shaw attended King Edward VI School there before going on to Emmanuel College, Cambridge. He then taught at Emmanuel as well as at the Cavendish Laboratory of Cambridge University. In addition to his teaching responsibilities, Shaw held several positions involving meteorology. He became secretary of the Meteorological Council in 1900 and director of the British Meteorological Office in 1905.

Shaw conducted research on the atmosphere, including work on hygrometry, evaporation, and ventilation. He pioneered the use of kites and balloons to transport weather instruments to the upper atmosphere and wrote several books on weather.

BOOKS BY SHAW

Life History of Surface Air Currents (1906). (coauthored with R. Lempfert) Darling & Son Ltd. 1906. (o.p.)

Manual of Meteorology (1926–1931). 4 vols. Cambridge Univ Pr 1936 $130.00. ISBN 0-404-16230-4

The Smoke Problem of Our Great Cities (1925). (coauthored with J. S. Owens) Constable 1925. (o.p.)

Weather Forecasting (1911). (coauthored with R. Lempfert) Constable 1940. (o.p.)

METEOROLOGY: THE ATMOSPHERE

*Allen, Oliver E. *Atmosphere. Planet Earth Ser.* Time-Life 1983 $13.99. ISBN 0-8094-4336-8 Introduction to the atmosphere—its composition and structure, winds, and clouds; discusses pollution of the atmosphere.

*Asimov, Isaac. *How Did We Find Out About the Atmosphere?* Walker 1985 $9.95. ISBN 0-8027-6588-2 Discussion of the history of our knowledge of the atmosphere.

*Heuer, Kenneth. *Rainbows, Halos, and Other Wonders: Light and Color in the Atmosphere.* Dodd 1978. (o.p.) $8.95. ISBN 0-396-07557-6 A look at phenomena visible in the sky.

Johnson, Gary L. *Wind Energy Systems.* Prentice 1985 $51.00. ISBN 0-13-957754-8

Schaefer, Vincent J., and John A. Day. *A Field Guide to the Atmosphere. Peterson Field Guide Ser.* Houghton 1983 $12.95. ISBN 0-395-33033-5

METEOROLOGY: WEATHER AND CLIMATE

*Alth, Max, and Charlotte Alth. *Disastrous Hurricanes and Tornadoes.* Watts 1981. (o.p.) $8.90. ISBN 0-531-04327-4 Examination of weather dynamics and weather patterns; major storms; weather proverbs; scientific weather forecasting.

*Boesen, Victor. *Doing Something About the Weather.* Putnam 1975. (o.p.) $6.95. ISBN 0-399-20465-2 A look at possible ways of controlling the weather.

*Branley, Franklyn M. *It's Raining Cats and Dogs: All Kinds of Weather and Why We Have It.* Houghton 1987 $12.95. ISBN 0-395-33070—X Fascinating and some unusual facts, with experiments, folklore, and specific events, all guaranteed to hold teenagers' interest.

*Compton, Grant. *What Does a Meteorologist Do?* Dodd 1981. (o.p.) $5.95. ISBN 0-396-07931-8 Description of the many aspects of weather forecasting.

*Cosgrove, Margaret. *It's Snowing.* Dodd 1980. (o.p.) $5.95. ISBN 0-396-07851-6 Discussion of snow—how it forms, its effects, and how it can cause damage.

Critchfield, Howard J. *General Climatology.* Prentice 1983 $51.00. ISBN 0-13-349217-6

Dunlop, Storm, and Francis Wilson. *The Larousse Guide to Weather Forecasting.* Larousse 1982. (o.p.) $8.95. ISBN 0-88332-280-3

*Dunlop, Storm, and Francis Wilson. *Weather and Forecasting. Field Guides Ser.* Macmillan 1987 $9.95. ISBN 0-02-013700-1 Pocket field guide to weather and forecasting, with emphasis on the middle latitudes.
*Gallant, Roy A. *Earth's Changing Climate.* Macmillan 1979 $13.95. ISBN 0-02-736840-8 Discussion of what climate is and the causes of changes in climate.
*Gribbin, John (ed). *The Breathing Planet.* Basil Blackwell 1986 $12.95. ISBN 0-631-14289-4 Collection of essays and articles about the world's changing climate.
Hardy, Ralph, *et al. The Weather Book.* Little 1982. (o.p.) $24.95. ISBN 0-316-34623-3
*Lambert, David. *Weather.* Watts 1983 $10.90. ISBN 0-531-04621-4 Introduction to weather phenomena.
*Lambert, David. *The Work of the Wind.* Bookwright 1984. (o.p.) $9.40. ISBN 0-531-04789-X Discussion of wind formation and the effects of wind on living things.
*Lambert, David, and Ralph Hardy. *Weather and Its Work. World of Science Ser.* Facts on File 1985 $12.95. ISBN 0-87196-987-4 Encyclopedia of weather topics.
Ludlum, David M. *The American Weather Book.* Houghton 1982. (o.p.) $14.95. ISBN 0-395-32049-6
*Ludlum, David M. *The Weather Factor.* Houghton 1984. (o.p.) $17.95. ISBN 0-395-27604-7 Collection of little-known facts about how the weather has influenced the American scene from colonial to modern times.
*Purvis, George, and Ann Purvis. *Weather and Climate.* Bookwright 1983. (o.p.) $9.40. ISBN 0-531-04788-1 Introduction to the atmosphere, weather, and climate.
*Ramsey, Dan. *How to Forecast Weather.* TAB 1987 $11.50. ISBN 0-8306-0168-6 Discussion of weather, weather folklore, weather instruments, and weather forecasting.
*Sattler, Helen R. *Nature's Weather Forecasters.* Nelson 1978. (o.p.) ISBN 0-8407-6594-0 A fascinating look at natural phenomena used to predict weather.
*Stommel, Henry, and Elizabeth Stommel. *Volcano Weather: The Story of 1816, the Year Without a Summer.* Seven Seas 1983. (o.p.) $15.95. ISBN 0-915160-71-4 Discussion of geologic and weather events that occurred in 1815–1817.
*Tordjman, Nathalie. *Climates Past, Present and Future.* Barron 1988. ISBN 0-8120-3838-X Information on climatology; its past, present, and future with warnings of a global warming, the greenhouse effect, and another ice age.
*Whipple, A. B. *Storm. Planet Earth Ser.* Time-Life 1982 $13.95. ISBN 0-8094-4312-0 Discussion of the causes and effects of several types of storms.
*Zim, Herbert S., *et al. Weather.* Western Pub 1987 $3.95. Illustrated, handy guide to all kinds of weather.

See also Vol. 2, Geography: Climate and Weather.

METEOROLOGY: THE ATMOSPHERE AND SOLAR RADIATION

*Asimov, Isaac. *How Did We Find Out About Solar Power?* Walker 1981 $10.95. ISBN 0-8027-6423-1 Discussion of the development of solar power, the solar origins of most energy, and the future of solar power.
Greenwald, Martin L., and Thomas K. McHugh. *Practical Solar Energy Technology.* Prentice 1985 $34.00. ISBN 0-13-693979-1
Mazria, Edward. *The Passive Solar Energy Book.* Rodale $29.95. ISBN 0-87857-238-4
*McPhillips, Martin (ed). *The Solar Energy Almanac.* Facts on File 1983 $17.95. ISBN 0-87196-727-8 Discussion of the practical applications of solar energy with emphasis on passive solar technology.
*Spooner, Maggie. *Sunpower Experiments: Solar Energy Explained.* Sterling 1980. (o.p.) $9.95. ISBN 0-8069-3110-8 Presentation of projects to carry out to investigate the uses of solar power.

METEOROLOGY: ATMOSPHERIC POLLUTION

Fisher, David. E. *Fire and Ice: The Greenhouse Effect, Ozone Depletion, and Nuclear Winter.* Harper 1990 $19.95. ISBN 0-06-016214-7

*Gay, Kathlyn. *Acid Rain.* Watts 1983 $12.90. ISBN 0-531-04682-6 Discussion of the direct and indirect effects of acid rain: how it is formed, how it is studied, culprits in its creation, and what can be done to alleviate it.

*Gay, Kathlyn. *The Greenhouse Effect.* Watts 1986 $12.90. ISBN 0-531-10154-1 A look at the effects of increasing amounts of carbon dioxide in the atmosphere.

Gribbin, John. *The Hole in the Sky: Man's Threat to the Ozone Layer.* Bantam 1988 $4.95. ISBN 0-553-27537-2

Roan, Sharon L. *Ozone Crisis: The Fifteen Year Evolution of a Sudden Global Emergency.* Wiley 1990 $9.95. ISBN 0-471-52823-4

Schneider, Stephen. *Global Warming: Are We Entering the Greenhouse Century?* Sierra 1989 $18.95. ISBN 0-87156-693-1

OCEANOGRAPHY

*Bascom, Willard. *The Crest of the Wave: Adventures in Oceanography.* Doubleday 1990 $9.95. ISBN 0-385-26633-2 Personal account of oceanic research projects; recommended for aspiring oceanographers.

Bascom, Willard. *Waves and Beaches: The Dynamics of the Ocean Surface.* Doubleday 1980 $9.95. ISBN 0-385-14844-5

Charlier, Roger Henri. *Tidal Energy.* Van Nostrand 1982. (o.p.) $28.00. ISBN 0-442-24425-8

*Davies, Eryl. *Ocean Frontiers. How It Works Ser.* Penguin 1979 $11.50. ISBN 0-670-52026-8 Discussion of the devices used in undersea explorations.

*Dudley, Walter C., and Min Lee. *Tsunami!* Univ of Hawaii Pr 1988 $10.95. ISBN 0-8248-1125-9 Discussion of tsunamis and their effect on people.

Duxbury, Alison, and Alyn C. Duxbury. *An Introduction to the World's Oceans.* Brown 1988. ISBN 0-679-04272-3

*Earle, Sylvia A., and Al Giddings. *Exploring the Deep Frontier: The Adventure of Man in the Sea.* National Geographic 1980 $14.95. ISBN 0-87044-343-7 Pictorial look at humans and their need to explore the oceans.

*Goldin, Augusta. *Water: Too Much, Too Little, Too Polluted.* Harcourt 1983 $12.95. ISBN 0-15-294819-8 Introduction to the uses and abuses of water.

Hendrickson, Robert. *The Ocean Almanac.* Doubleday 1984 $15.95. ISBN 0-385-14077-0

*Johnson, Sylvia A. *Coral Reefs.* Lerner 1989 $4.95. ISBN 0-8225-9545-1 A look at the structure of coral reefs and coral reef ecosystems.

*Lambert, David, and Anita McConnell. *Seas and Oceans. World of Science Ser.* Facts on File 1985 $12.95. ISBN 0-8160-1064-1 A look at features of the oceans, including tides, waves, coral reefs, and the plant and animal life of the ocean; includes information on ocean exploration.

McGraw-Hill Encyclopedia of Ocean and Atmospheric Sciences. McGraw 1979 $76.00. ISBN 0-07-045267-9

*Meyerson, A. Lee. *Seawater: A Delicate Balance.* Enslow 1988 $13.95. ISBN 0-89490-157-5 Introduction to the composition of sea water.

*Padget, Sheila. *Coastlines.* Bookwright 1983. (o.p.) $9.40. ISBN 0-531-04729-X A look at the features of coastlines and the forces that are changing them.

Parker, Henry S. *Exploring the Oceans: An Introduction for the Traveler and Amateur Naturalist.* Prentice 1985 $15.95. ISBN 0-13-297706-0

Poynter, Margaret, and Donald Collins. *Under the High Seas: New Frontiers in Oceanography.* Atheneum 1983 $11.95. ISBN 0-689-30977-5

Ross, David A. *Introduction to Oceanography.* Prentice 1988 $36.00. ISBN 0-13-491408-2

*Settle, Mary Lee. *Water World.* Lodestar 1984. (o.p.) $11.95. ISBN 0-525-66777-6

Discussion of the early understanding of the oceans, instruments used in exploring oceans, and a description of knowledge of the oceans today.

Thurman, Harold V. *Essentials of Oceanography.* Merrill 1987 $28.95. ISBN 0-675-20716-9
*Whipple, A. B. *Restless Oceans. Planet Earth Ser.* Time-Life 1983 $13.99. ISBN 0-8094-4340-6 Discussion of ocean currents, marine life, and ocean pollution.

COUSTEAU, JACQUES–YVES   1910–

Jacques Cousteau is known the world over for his explorations under the sea, which he has recorded in documentary films and many books. Cousteau was born near Bordeaux, in St.-André-de-Cubzac, France. In 1930, after graduating from the naval academy in Brest, he joined the navy and entered the naval flying school. An automobile accident that cut short these plans could be credited as the event that sent Cousteau to the underseas world, for it was during his daily swimming sessions, designed to help him recover from his injuries, that he became interested in diving and began to experiment with diving equipment. In 1943 he and Emile Gagnan, another French diver, invented the Aqua-Lung, a *self-c*ontained *u*nderwater *b*reathing *a*pparatus, or scuba. With this portable device, a person could stay underwater at depths up to 300 feet for an hour.

During World War II, Cousteau worked with his fellow divers in the French underground, and after the war this group formed an underseas research team in the navy. Their mission was to study the physiology of diving—and to rid French harbors of mines.

In 1951 Cousteau outfitted an old minesweeper, *Calypso,* as a research laboratory and diving platform and began his underseas explorations. In that year he began conducting yearly expeditions under the sea, which he documented in films and books, including *The Silent World* (1953), written with Frédéric Dumas. The film version of this book won an Oscar and the French equivalent of this award.

In 1957 Cousteau was appointed director of the oceanographic museum of Monaco. In 1959 he produced the first small submersible for research underwater, and in 1963 he began a series of underwater explorations called Conshelf, in which crews spent long periods of time on the ocean floor. His film about these expeditions, *World Without Sun,* won him his second Oscar in 1965.

Cousteau developed much of the equipment that enabled him to film the underseas world. He devised waterproof cameras and lights and the first underwater television system. With the sponsorship of The National Geographic Society, he has produced since 1967 many spectacular specials for television.

In 1973 Cousteau founded the Cousteau Society, a nonprofit organization for the protection of the marine environment. The expeditions of *Calypso* continue and have included explorations of the Antarctic and the Amazon River. Cousteau the inventor is also still at work. In 1985 he developed with French engineers the Turbosail, a wind-powered propulsion system for ships.

BOOKS BY COUSTEAU

Jacques Cousteau's Calypso (1983). (coauthored with Alexis Sivirine) Abrams 1983 $39.95. ISBN 0-8109-0788-7 Discusses Cousteau's ship and his sailing techniques used to explore the world's oceans.

The Living Sea (1963). (coauthored with Frédéric Dumas) Lyons 1988 $12.95. ISBN 0-941130-73-8

The Silent World (1953). (coauthored with Frédéric Dumas) Lyons 1987 $12.95. ISBN 0-941130-45-2 A description of development of the aqualung.

BOOK ABOUT COUSTEAU

Madsen, Axel. *Cousteau: An Unauthorized Biography.* Beaufort 1987 $17.95. ISBN 0-8253-0386-9 Public and private lives of Cousteau.

OCEANOGRAPHY: MARINE BIOLOGY

*Blumberg, Rhoda. *The First Travel Guide to the Bottom of the Sea.* Lothrop 1983. (o.p.) $10.00. ISBN 0-688-01692-8 Description of an imaginary voyage to the bottom of the sea to observe sea creatures.
*Carson, Rachel L. *The Sea Around Us.* Oxford Univ Pr 1989 $18.95. ISBN 0-19-506186-1 History of oceans and ocean life; discusses present knowledge of the oceans.
*Cook, Jan Leslie. *The Mysterious Undersea World.* Books for World Explorers Ser. National Geographic 1980 $6.95. ISBN 0-87044-317-8 Pictorial introduction to the sea and life in the sea.
*Crump, Donald J. (ed). *The Ocean Realm.* Special Publication Ser. National Geographic 1978 $7.95. ISBN 0-87044-251-1 Pictorial look at ocean life.
Niesen, Thomas. *The Marine Biology Coloring Book.* Harper 1982 $10.95. ISBN 0-06-460303-2
Seibold, E., and W. Berger. *The Sea Floor: An Introduction to Marine Biology.* Springer-Verlag 1982 $36.00. ISBN 0-387-11256-1

OCEANOGRAPHY: OCEAN RESOURCES AND CONSERVATION

*Bright, Michael. *The Dying Sea.* Watts 1988 $8.99. ISBN 0-531-17126-4 Portrayal of the threats to Earth's waters: pollution, coastline erosion, and nearly extinct animal and plant life are discussed.
*Fine, John Christopher. *Oceans in Peril.* Atheneum 1987 $15.95. ISBN 0-689-31328-4 Discussion of resources in the oceans and the pollution that threatens these resources.
*Goldin, Augusta. *Oceans of Energy: Reservoir of Power for the Future.* Harcourt 1980 $9.95. ISBN 0-15-257688-6 A look at the possible energy sources in the oceans—tides, waves, currents, and geothermal energy.
*Miller, Christine G., and Louise A. Berry. *Coastal Rescue: Preserving Our Seashores.* Atheneum 1989 $13.95. ISBN 0-689-31288-1 Introduction to coastal erosion and pollution and what can be done to preserve the coasts.
*Polking, Kirk. *Oceans of the World: Our Essential Resource.* Philomel 1983 $14.95. ISBN 0-399-20919-0 Introduction to oceanography—formation of the oceans, features and uses of the oceans, and the future of the oceans.

See also Vol. 2, Biology: Conservation of Natural Resources *and* Ecology and the Environment; Earth Science: Geology; Geography: Environmental Issues.

GEOLOGY

Bates, Robert L., and Julia A. Jackson (eds). *Dictionary of Geologic Terms.* Doubleday 1984. (o.p.) $10.95. ISBN 0-385-18100-0
Campbell, John. *Introductory Cartography.* Prentice 1984. (o.p.) $41.33. ISBN 0-13-501304-6

Earth, Sea, and Sky. Science Universe Ser. Arco 1984. (o.p.) $9.95. ISBN 0-668-06181-2 Illustrated encyclopedia of geology.

Foster, Robert J. *General Geology.* Merrill 1988 $30.95. ISBN 0-675-20886-6

*Francis, Peter. *Images of Earth.* Prentice 1984 $24.95. ISBN 0-13-451394-0 Descriptions of aerial photographs of Earth, showing many of its characteristics and processes of geology.

Hay, Edward A., and A. Lee McAlester. *Physical Geology: Principles and Perspectives.* Prentice 1984 $25.95. ISBN 0-13-669549-3

Lambert, David. *Field Guide to Geology.* Facts on File 1989 $14.95. ISBN 0-8160-2032-9

Lutgens, Frederick K., and Edward J. Tarbuck. *Essentials of Geology.* Merrill 1988 $24.95. ISBN 0-675-20749-5

*Lye, Keith. *The Earth.* Silver 1983 $14.96. ISBN 0-382-06727-4 Pictorial introduction to earth science.

*McConnell, Anita. *The World Beneath Us. The World of Science Ser.* Facts on File 1985 $12.95. ISBN 0-8160-1068-4 Introduction to geology.

McGraw-Hill Dictionary of Earth Sciences. McGraw 1984 $44.50. ISBN 0-07-045252-0

McGraw-Hill Encyclopedia of Geological Sciences. McGraw 1988 $85.00. ISBN 0-07-045500-7

Press, Frank, and Raymond Sevier. *Earth.* Freeman 1986 $34.95. ISBN 0-7167-1743-3

*Rhodes, Frank H. T. *Geology.* Golden Pr 1972 $3.95. ISBN 0-307-24349-4 Introduction to the physical geology of Earth.

*Rossbocher, Lisa A. *Recent Revolutions in Geology.* Watts 1986 $12.90. ISBN 0-531-10242-4 Examination of the latest information on geological topics.

Sanders, John E., and R. Carola. *Principles of Physical Geology.* Wiley 1981 $22.95. ISBN 0-471-08424-7

Spencer, Edgar W. *Physical Geology.* Addison 1983 $46.25. ISBN 0-201-06423-5

Strahler, Arthur N., and Alan H. Strahler. *Elements of Physical Geography.* Wiley 1989 $45.95. ISBN 0-471-61647-8

Tarbuck, Edward J., and Frederick K. Lutgens. *The Earth: An Introduction to Physical Geology.* Merrill 1987 $36.95. ISBN 0-675-20698-7

Tarbuck, Edward J., and Frederick K. Lutgens. *Earth Science.* Merrill 1988 $35.95. ISBN 0-675-20748-7

*Wiener, Jonathan. *Planet Earth.* Bantam 1986 $14.95. ISBN 0-553-34358-0 Discussion of Earth's origin, its geology, climate, and life forms, and its dependence on the sun.

*Zim, Herbert S. *Caves and Life.* Morrow 1978. (o.p.) $5.95. ISBN 0-688-22112-2 Introduction to the structure and formation of caves and the organisms in them.

HUTTON, JAMES   1726–1797

James Hutton was born in Edinburgh, Scotland. He originally studied law and began an apprenticeship, but at the urging of his father, he gave up law to study medicine. After attending medical schools in Edinburgh and Paris, he received an M.D. degree from Leiden University, the Netherlands, in 1749. Hutton, however, chose not to go into medical practice. Instead, he became a farmer, which allowed him time for pursuing his interests in chemistry and geology. In 1768, he turned his farm and business over to others in order to devote full time to the study of geology.

Based on his many observations, Hutton disagreed with the prevailing theory of rock formation, which held that all rocks were formed at one time from sediments at the bottom of an ocean that once covered the earth. Hutton believed that the surface of the earth constantly undergoes gradual changes and that the forces at work on Earth have been occurring throughout Earth's history. In his view, rocks are formed by a variety of means, including deposition and the cooling of molten material. He presented his ideas, known as the theory of uniformitarianism, in his two-volume work, *Theory of the Earth.* Ultimately uniformitarianism became the prevailing theory. Because Hutton published the theory, he is often referred to as the father of modern geology.

BOOK BY HUTTON

Theory of the Earth (1795). 2 vols. Lubrecht and Cramer 1960 repr of 1795 ed $87.00. ISBN
3-7682-0025-6

LYELL, CHARLES 1797–1875

Charles Lyell was born in Kinnordy, Forfarshire, Scotland. Although his interest was in geology, he studied mathematics and law at Oxford University. He
graduated in 1819 and passed the bar in 1825, after which he practiced law. In
1827 he abandoned these endeavors to devote his time to work in the area that
had always been his primary interest—geology.

Lyell took every opportunity he could to study geology. He traveled extensively in Europe studying rocks, land formations, and fossils, and everything
he saw convinced him that Scots geologist James Hutton's theory of uniformitarianism was correct (*see* Hutton, Vol. 2, Earth Science: Geology). Lyell
himself made no discoveries in geology. He did, however, write a three-volume
discourse on geology—*Principles of Geology*—in which he reviews the history of
geology and presents evidence for uniformitarianism. The volumes, which
proved very popular and were revised several times during Lyell's lifetime,
succeeded in winning support for the theory of uniformitarianism.

With the publication of Charles Darwin's *Origin of Species* (*see* Darwin, Vol.
2, Biology: Evolution of Life), Lyell accepted Darwin's theory and incorporated
it into *Principles of Geology.* In 1863 Lyell published a book on the evolution of
humans, *Geological Evidence of the Antiquity of Man.*

BOOKS BY LYELL

Geological Evidence of the Antiquity of Man (1863). AMS 1985 repr of 1873 ed $47.50. ISBN
0-404-08138-X
Life, Letters, and Journals (1881). Katharine M. Lyell (ed). 2 vols. AMS 1983 $94.50. ISBN
0-404-08156-8
Principles of Geology (1830–1833). 3 vols. Lubrecht and Cramer 1970 repr of 1833 ed
$117.00. ISBN 3-7682-0685-8

WEGENER, ALFRED LOTHAR 1880–1930

Alfred Wegener, a geologist, meteorologist, and explorer, was born in Berlin,
Germany, the son of a theologist who was the director of an orphanage.
Wegener studied at the universities of Heidelberg and Innsbruck and in 1905
received a Ph.D. in astronomy from the University of Berlin. From 1908 to 1912
he taught meteorology at the Physical Institute in Marburg, Germany, and
from 1924 until the end of his life he was professor of meteorology at the
University of Graz.

In 1924 Wegener went on the first of four expeditions to Greenland. His
original interest in this frozen land was in studying polar air masses and the
geology of Greenland. In 1912–1913 he led the second expedition with the
Danish explorer J. P. Koch, this time to study the glaciers and climate of the
island. After interruptions brought about by military service during World War
I and work at a meterological experimental station at Gross Borstel, near Hamburg, Germany, Wegener led another expedition to Greenland, in 1929–1930.
Then, in 1930 he led a relief expedition to bring supplies to scientists spending
the winter at a research station halfway across Greenland. He died of exhaustion in his attempt to return to the coast. He was buried by his Greenlander
guide, Rosmus, who then himself died before reaching the coast.

Wegener is best known for his explication of the theory of continental drift. He said that he formulated the theory because of his observation that the east coast of South America and the west coast of Africa looked as though they might fit together (like pieces of a puzzle). Although he was not actually the first to propose this theory, he is considered to be its father because he made the most complete formulation of the theory and presented a large body of evidence for it. According to the theory, all the land of the world was once one supercontinent called Pangaea. About 200 million years ago, Pangaea broke apart and the fragments of the supercontinent became the continents that now exist and migrated to the positions they now occupy. Wegener first became interested in this theory in 1911, and in 1912 he published two papers setting forth the theory. He offered evidence from climate, plant life, glaciers, and the shape of the continents in support of the theory. The theory was not well received during his lifetime, mainly because he could offer no satisfactory explanation for the energy that would be required for the breakup and movement of these enormous land masses. As more has been learned about the forces that exist within the earth, however, the theory of continental drift, modified as the theory of plate tectonics, has been widely accepted. Scientists now believe that heat-driven convection currents in the mantle, the thick layer of hot solid rock between Earth's core and crust that extends below Earth's surface, are responsible for the movement of the continents and the ocean floor.

BOOK BY WEGENER

Origin of Continents and Oceans (1915). Gordon Pr 1977. (o.p.) $69.95. ISBN 0-8490-2384-X

BOOKS ABOUT WEGENER

Hallam, Anthony. *Great Geological Controversies.* Oxford Univ Pr 1983. (o.p.) $21.95. ISBN 0-19-854430-8 Includes discussion of Wegener and the controversy that raged about the theory of continental drift.

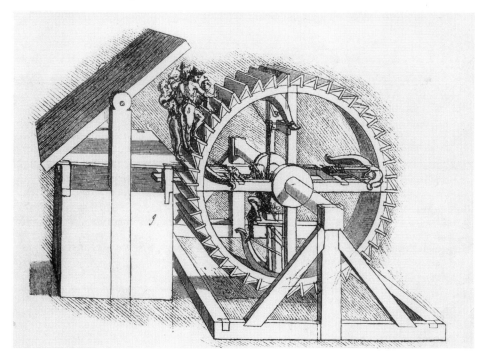

Men on treadmill device charge giant crossbow. Military engine designed and drawn by Leonardo da Vinci (late 1400s). Courtesy of The Bettmann Archive.

Schwarzbach, Martin. *Alfred Wegener: The Father of Continental Drift. Scientific Revolutionaries—A Biographical Ser.* Sci Tech Pubs 1986 $35.00. ISBN 0-910239-03-7 Story of Wegner and his controversial theory.

See also Vol. 2, Biology: Conservation of Natural Resources *and* Ecology and the Environment; Earth Science: Geology; Geography: Environmental Issues.

GEOLOGY: MINERALS AND ROCKS

Barker, Daniel. *Igneous Rocks.* Prentice 1983 $48.67. ISBN 0-13-450692-8
*Chesterman, Charles W., and Kurt E. Lowe. *The Audubon Society Field Guide to North American Rocks and Minerals.* Knopf 1978 $14.45. ISBN 0-394-50269-8 Pictorial identification guide and resource book.
Crowson, Philip. *Minerals Handbook: 1984–1985.* Gulf Pub 1985 $55.00. ISBN 0-87201-566-1
*Dietrich, R.V. *Stones: Their Collection, Identification, and Uses.* Freeman 1980 $11.95. ISBN 0-7167-1139-7 Introduction to geology through collecting and identifying stones.
Dietrich, R.V., and E. Reed Wicander. *Minerals, Rocks, and Fossils.* Wiley 1983. (o.p.) $9.95. ISBN 0-471-89883-X
Ehlers, Ernest G., and Harry Blatt. *Petrology: Igneous, Sedimentary, and Metamorphic.* Freeman 1982 $42.95. ISBN 0-7167-1279-2
Fry, Norman. *The Field Description of Metamorphic Rocks.* Halsted 1984 $15.95. ISBN 0-470-27485-9
*Keen, Martin L. *The World Beneath Our Feet: The Story of Soil.* Messner 1974. (o.p.) ISBN 0-671-32673-2 Description of soil—formation, kinds, organisms in it, and conservation.
*Pellant, Chris, and Roger Phillips. *Rocks, Minerals, and Fossils of the World.* Little 1990 $17.95. ISBN 0-316-69796-6 Photographs and data for identification of the three subjects.
*Pough, Frederick H. *A Field Guide to Rocks and Minerals.* Houghton 1976 $12.95. ISBN 0-395-24049-2 Handbook for identifying rocks and minerals.
Thorpe, Richard, and Geoffrey Brown. *The Field Description of Igneous Rocks.* Wiley 1985 $16.95. ISBN 0-470-20111-8

GEOLOGY: WEATHERING, EROSION, AND DEPOSITION

*Bailey, Ronald H. *Glacier. Planet Earth Ser.* Time-Life 1982 $13.99. ISBN 0-8094-4318-X Discussion of our present understanding of glaciers and theories about the ice ages.
*Bramwell, Martyn. *Glaciers and Ice Caps.* Watts 1986 $11.40. ISBN 0-531-10178-9 Discussion of glaciers and the polar regions.
*Branley, Franklyn M. *Water for the World.* Crowell 1982. (o.p.) $9.50. ISBN 0-690-04172-1 Discussion of water and its sources, water pollution, and the water cycle.
*Fodor, Ronald V. *Angry Waters: Floods and Their Control.* Dodd 1980. (o.p.) $4.95. ISBN 0-396-07799-4 Discussion of why floods occur, the effects of floods, and how people react to floods.
*Fodor, Ronald V. *Chiseling the Earth: How Erosion Shapes the Land.* Enslow 1989 $14.95. ISBN 0-89490-282-2 A look at how erosion changes the surface of the earth and how erosion can be prevented.

*Fodor, Ronald V. *Frozen Earth: Explaining the Ice Ages.* Enslow 1989 $13.95. ISBN 0-89490-281-4 Discussion of past and present theories for the causes of the ice ages.

*Gallant, Roy A. *The Ice Ages.* Watts 1985 $10.40. ISBN 0-531-04912-4 Explanation of how and why ice ages occur.

*Gardner, Robert. *Water: The Life-Sustaining Resource.* Messner 1982. (o.p.) $9.29. ISBN 0-671-43655-4 Discussion of water resources and how to conserve and protect them.

Imbrie, John, and Katherine P. Imbrie. *Ice Ages: Solving the Mystery.* Harvard Univ Pr 1986 $8.95. ISBN 0-674-44075-7

*Laycock, George. *Caves.* Four Winds 1976. (o.p.) $8.95. ISBN 0-590-07392-3 Discussion of cave formation, animals that live in caves, and uses of caves.

Morgan, R. P. *Soil Erosion and Its Control.* Van Nostrand 1985 $50.95. ISBN 0-442-26441-0

*Pringle, Laurence, *et al.* *Rivers and Lakes.* *Planet Earth Ser.* Time-Life 1985 $19.94. ISBN 0-8094-4509-3 Natural history of lakes and rivers in the United States and the ecology of the organisms living in them.

*Radlauer, Ruth, and Lisa S. Gitkin. *The Power of Ice.* Childrens 1985 $14.60. ISBN 0-516-07839-9 Introduction to glaciers.

*Robin, Gordon de Q. *Glaciers and Ice Sheets.* Bookwright 1984 $11.40. ISBN 0-531-03801-7 Introduction to glaciers, ice caps, and the ice ages.

*Rowland-Entwhistle, Theodore. *Rivers and Lakes.* *Our World Ser.* Silver 1987 $12.96. ISBN 0-382-09499-9 A look at fresh water, including where it occurs, freshwater organisms, uses of fresh water, and water pollution.

GEOLOGY: CRUSTAL MOVEMENTS

*Asimov, Isaac. *How Did We Find Out About Earthquakes?* Walker 1978 $10.85. ISBN 0-8027-6306-5 Discussion of the history of theories about why earthquakes occur and how these lines of questioning led to the theory of plate tectonics.

*Asimov, Isaac. *How Did We Find Out About Volcanoes?* Walker 1981 $10.85. ISBN 0-8027-6412-6 Discussion of past and current explanations of volcanoes and consideration of the possibility of preventing eruptions.

*Aylesworth, Thomas G. *Geological Disasters: Earthquakes and Volcanoes.* Watts 1979 $9.90. ISBN 0-531-02288-9 A look at earthquakes and volcanoes as results of the stresses caused by continental drift.

*Aylesworth, Thomas G., and Virginia Aylesworth. *The Mount St. Helens Disaster: What We've Learned.* Watts 1983. (o.p.) $9.90. ISBN 0-531-04488-2 Description of the eruption of Mount St. Helens and the effects of this dramatic event.

*Berger, Melvin. *Disastrous Volcanoes.* Watts 1981. (o.p.) $7.40. ISBN 0-531-04329-0 Discussion of the various types of volcanoes, including their causes and effects.

*Carson, James. *Volcanoes.* Bookwright 1983. (o.p.) $9.40. ISBN 0-531-04793-8 Discussion of the causes and types of volcanoes.

*Carson, Rob. *Mount St. Helens: The Eruption and Recovery of a Volcano.* Sasquatch 1990 $19.95. ISBN 0-912365-32-3 With excellent photos, this is the story of the Mount St. Helens eruption.

*Crump, Donald J. (ed). *Powers of Nature.* National Geographic 1978 $7.95. ISBN 0-87044-234-1 Discussion of the natural forces that cause volcanoes, earthquakes, floods, windstorms, and droughts.

*Decker, Robert, and Barbara Decker. *Volcanoes.* Freeman 1989 $14.95. ISBN 0-7167-1851-0 Introduction to volcanoes; discusses causes and effects, locations, and geothermal power.

*Fodor, Ronald V. *Earth Afire! Volcanoes and Their Activity.* Morrow 1981. (o.p.) $9.95. ISBN 0-688-00706-6 Discussion of the theories of volcano activity and earth movements.

*Gallant, Roy A. *Our Restless Earth.* Watts 1986 $10.40. ISBN 0-531-10205-X Introduction to the forces acting on Earth today and in the past.

*Golden, Frederic. *The Trembling Earth: Probing and Predicting Quakes.* Scribner's 1983 $13.95. ISBN 0-684-17884-2 Discussion of earthquakes, including theory and facts, research, and the history of seismology.

*Heppenheimer, T. A. *The Coming Quake: Science and Trembling on the California Earthquake Frontier.* Times Bks 1988 $17.45. ISBN 0-8129-1616-6 Discussion of earthquakes and seismology.

*Kohler, Pierre. *Volcanoes, Earthquakes, and the Formation of Continents.* Barron 1987 $4.95. ISBN 0-8120-3832-0 Brief, illustrated general information on volcanic eruptions, drifting of continents, the Richter scale, etc.

*Lauber, Patricia. *Volcano. The Eruption and Healing of Mount St. Helens.* Bradbury Pr 1986 $14.95. ISBN 0-02-754500-8 Describes the catastrophic eruption of Mount St. Helens, the devastation it caused, and the eventual revitalization of the damaged areas; for younger readers.

Morris, Charles. *The San Francisco Calamity by Earthquake and Fire.* Citadel 1986 $9.95. ISBN 0-8065-0984-8

*Place, Marian T. *Mount St. Helens.* Putnam 1981 $10.95. ISBN 0-396-07976-8 Eruption of Mount St. Helens and the devastation that resulted.

* *Volcano. Planet Earth Ser.* Time-Life 1982 $13.99. ISBN 0-8094-4304-X Pictorial account of volcanic eruptions and the attempts by scientists to understand and predict them.

* *Volcano: The Eruption of Mount St. Helens.* Madrona 1980 $7.95. ISBN 0-914842-54-4 Pictorial account of the eruption of Mount St. Helens and its aftermath.

*Walker, Bryce. *Earthquake. Planet Earth Ser.* Time-Life 1982 $18.60. ISBN 0-8094-4302-3 Presentation of the history of earthquakes, our present understanding of them, and how to predict and prepare for them.

*Watson, Nancy, *et al. Our Violent Earth. Books for World Explorers Ser.* National Geographic 1982 $6.95. ISBN 0-87044-383-6 Pictorial introduction to natural disasters.

GEOLOGY: PLATE TECTONICS AND CONTINENTAL DRIFT

*Berger, Melvin. *The New Earth Book: Our Changing Planet.* Crowell 1980. (o.p.) ISBN 0-690-04074-1 Introduction to continental drift, mountain building, and earthquakes.

Condie, Kent C. (ed). *Plate Tectonics and Crustal Evolution.* Pergamon 1982 $49.50. ISBN 0-08-028075-7

Cox, Allan, and Brian R. Hart. *Plate Tectonics: How It Works.* Basil Blackwell 1986 $29.95. ISBN 0-86542-313-X

*Fodor, Ronald V. *Earth in Motion: The Concept of Plate Tectonics.* Morrow 1978. (o.p.) $9.95. ISBN 0-688-22135-1 Introduction to the theory of continental drift including historical background and evidence to support it.

*Harrington, John W. *Dance of the Continents: Adventures with Rocks and Time.* Tarcher 1983 $9.95. ISBN 0-87477-247-8 Introduction to rocks, fossils, and plate tectonics.

*Kiefer, Irene. *A Global Jigsaw Puzzle: The Story of Continental Drift.* Atheneum 1978 $8.95. ISBN 0-689-30621-0 A look at the evidence that supports continental drift and the movement of plates as the processes that shaped the present continents.

*Lampton, Christopher. *Planet Earth.* Watts 1982. (o.p.) $8.90. ISBN 0-531-04387-8 A look at the history of Earth and the forces that are at work in and on it today.

*Miller, Russell. *Continents in Collision. Planet Earth Ser.* Time-Life 1983 $18.60. ISBN 0-8094-4326-0 Discussion of plate tectonics and continental drift; beautifully illustrated.

*Redfern, Ron. *The Making of a Continent.* Times Bks 1986 $19.95. ISBN 0-8129-1617-4 Discussion of the geologic history of Earth and plate tectonics.

Young, Louise B. *The Blue Planet.* Little 1983 $18.95. ISBN 0-316-97707-1

GEOLOGY: HISTORY OF EARTH AND PREHISTORIC LIFE FORMS

*Ballard, Robert D. *Exploring Our Living Planet.* National Geographic 1983 $19.95. ISBN 0-87044-459-X Discussion of the origin of Earth and the changes presently occurring on Earth—continental drift, seafloor spreading, and building of mountains, volcanoes, earthquakes.

Colbert, Edwin H. *Great Dinosaur Hunters and Their Discoveries.* Dover 1984 $6.95. ISBN 0-486-24701-5

Cooper, John D., *et al. A Trip Through Time: Principles of Historical Geology.* Merrill 1986 $39.95. ISBN 0-675-20140-3

*Crump, Donald J. (ed). *Giants from the Past: The Age of Mammals. Books for World Explorers Ser.* National Geographic 1983 $6.95. ISBN 0-87044-424-7 Introduction to the first mammals.

Dixon, Dougal, *et al. The Macmillan Illustrated Encyclopedia of Dinosaurs and Prehistoric Animals: A Visual Who's Who of Prehistoric Life.* Macmillan 1988 $39.95. ISBN 0-02-580191-0

Dott, Robert H., Jr., and Roger L. Batten. *Evolution of the Earth.* McGraw 1988 $42.95. ISBN 0-07-017677-9

Eicher, Don L., *et al. The History of the Earth's Crust.* Prentice 1984. ISBN 0-13-389982-9

Fortey, Richard. *Fossils: The Key to the Past.* Sabbot 1983 $15.00. ISBN 0-565-00884-6

*Gallant, Roy A. *The Rise of Mammals.* Watts 1986 $10.40. ISBN 0-531-10206-8 A look at the evolution of mammals, including humans.

Halstead, L. B. *The Search for the Past: Fossils, Rocks, Tracks, and Trails, the Search for the Origin of Life.* Doubleday 1982. (o.p.) $19.95. ISBN 0-385-18212-0

*Hoyle, Fred. *The Intelligent Universe.* Holt 1983. (o.p.) $18.95. ISBN 0-03-070083-3 Argument against the origin of life on Earth and evolution and for the theory that life came from outer space.

Lane, N. Gary. *Life of the Past.* Merrill 1985 $19.95. ISBN 0-675-20508-5

*Lambert, Mark. *Fossils.* Arco 1978. (o.p.) ISBN 0-668-04805-0 Introduction and guide to fossils.

Stanley, Steven M. *Earth and Life Through Time.* Freeman 1985 $35.95. ISBN 0-7167-1677-1

Thompson, Ida. *The Audubon Society Field Guide to North American Fossils.* Knopf 1982 $14.45. ISBN 0-394-52412-8

GEOLOGY: EARTH RESOURCES AND CONSERVATION

Adelman, M. A., *et al. Energy Resources in an Uncertain Future: Coal, Gas, Oil, and Uranium Supply Forecasting.* Ballinger 1983 $45.00. ISBN 0-88410-644-6

Allaby, Michael. *Dictionary of the Environment.* New York Univ Pr 1984 $60.00. ISBN 0-8147-0582-0

*Asimov, Isaac. *How Did We Find Out About Coal?* Walker 1980 $7.85. ISBN 0-8027-6400-2 Discussion of heat, light, and fire and the use of coal in the past, present, and future.

*Asimov, Isaac. *How Did We Find Out About Oil?* Walker 1980 $10.85. ISBN 0-8027-6381-2 Discussion of the formation of oil, drilling for oil, and the dwindling of oil reserves.

*Brown, A. S. *Fuel Resources.* Watts 1985 $10.40. ISBN 0-531-04911-6 A look at the use and rapid depletion of fossil fuels.

*Burt, Olive W. *Rescued! America's Endangered Wildlife on the Comeback Trail.* Messner 1980. (o.p.) $7.79. ISBN 0-671-32984-7 Discussion of programs to save endangered animals.

Cahn, Robert. *Footprints on the Planet: A Search for an Environmental Ethic.* Universe 1978 $12.50. ISBN 0-87663-324-6

*Cheney, Glenn Alan. *Mineral Resources.* Watts 1985 $9.40. ISBN 0-531-04915-9 A look at the use and rapid depletion of minerals.

Cohen, Bernard L. *Before It's Too Late: A Scientist's Case for Nuclear Energy.* Plenum 1983 $18.95. ISBN 0-306-41425-2

*Cook, Brian. *Gas.* Watts 1981. (o.p.) $8.90. ISBN 0-531-04198-0 Introduction to finding, refining, and using natural gas.

*Deudney, Daniel, and Christopher Flavin. *Renewable Energy: The Power to Choose.* Norton 1985 $8.70. ISBN 0-393-30201-6 Discussion of residential and small-scale use of alternative energy sources, such as the sun, wind, geothermal energy, tides, and water.

*Douglas, John H., *et al. The Future World of Energy. Epcot Center Book.* Watts 1984 $11.90. ISBN 0-531-04881-0 Discussion of the problems of achieving a stable supply of energy.

*Dubos, René. *The Wooing of Earth.* Scribner's 1980 $8.95. ISBN 0-684-16951-7 Discussion of how Earth's ecosystems have been shaped by humans.

*Epstein, Samuel, *et al. Hazardous Waste in America: Our Number One Environmental Crisis.* Sierra 1983 $12.95. ISBN 0-87156-807-1 Introduction to the sources, problems, and handling of hazardous wastes.

Gibbons, John H., and William Chandler. *Energy: The Conservation Revolution.* Plenum 1981 $35.00. ISBN 0-306-40670-5

*Goldin, Augusta. *Geothermal Energy: A Hot Prospect.* Harcourt 1981. (o.p.) $11.95. ISBN 0-15-230662-5 Introduction to historical and present uses of geothermal energy.

*Goode, Stephen. *The Nuclear Energy Controversy.* Watts 1980. (o.p.) $9.90. ISBN 0-531-04165-4 A look at the pros and cons of nuclear energy.

Greenland, David. *Guidelines for Modern Resource Management.* Merrill 1983 $19.95. ISBN 0-675-20004-0

*Haines, Gail Kay. *The Great Nuclear Power Debate.* Dodd 1985. (o.p.) $11.95. ISBN 0-396-08486-9 Pros and cons of using nuclear energy as a power source.

*Halacy, Dan. *Nuclear Energy.* Watts 1984 $10.40. ISBN 0-531-04829-2 Discussion of the atom, nuclear energy plants, the dangers of nuclear energy, and radioactive wastes.

Hayes, Harold T. *The Last Place on Earth.* Scarborough Hse 1982 $9.95. ISBN 0-8128-6087-X

Heppenheimer, T. A. *The Man-Made Sun: The Quest for Fusion Power.* Little 1984. (o.p.) $19.95. ISBN 0-316-35793-6

Hinckley, A. D. *Renewable Resources in Our Future.* Pergamon 1980 $13.75. ISBN 0-08-023433-X

*Hyde, Margaret O., and Bruce G. Hyde. *Everyone's Trash Problem: Nuclear Wastes.* McGraw 1979. (o.p.) $9.95. ISBN 0-07-031551-5 Discussion of the problems of nuclear wastes.

Johansson, Thomas B., and Peter Stern. *Radioactive Wastes from Nuclear Power Plants.* Univ of California Pr 1981 $25.00. ISBN 0-520-04199-2

Keller, Edward A. *Environmental Geology.* Merrill 1988 $34.95. ISBN 0-675-20889-0

*Kraft, Betsy Harvey. *Oil and Natural Gas.* Watts 1982. (o.p.) $8.90. ISBN 0-531-01411-8 Discussion of the formation, refining, and uses of oil and natural gas.

Law, Dennis L. *Mine-Land Rehabilitation.* Van Nostrand 1984 $34.95. ISBN 0-442-25987-5

*Lyttle, Richard B. *Shale Oil and Tar Sands: The Promises and Pitfalls.* Watts 1982 $12.90. ISBN 0-531-04489-0 A look at the possible use of oil locked in shale and tar pools.

*Milne, Lorus, and Margery Milne. *Dreams of a Perfect Earth.* Atheneum 1982. (o.p.) $9.95. ISBN 0-689-30871-X A look at the condition of Earth, how humans are affecting it, and the future.

*Pampe, William R. *Petroleum: How It Is Found and Used.* Enslow 1984 $13.95. ISBN 0-89490-100-1 Introduction to the geology, engineering, and use of oil and natural gas.

*Poynter, Margaret. *Wildland Fire Fighting.* Atheneum 1982. (o.p.) $9.95. ISBN 0-689-30939-2 Examination of the dangers and strategies of fighting fires in natural areas and at the destruction fires cause.

*Pringle, Laurence. *Lives at Stake: The Science and Politics of Environmental Health.* Macmillan 1980. (o.p.) $9.95. ISBN 0-02-775410-3 Overview of the environmental factors that affect human health; includes discussion of the scientific and political complexities involved in providing a healthful environment.

*Pringle, Laurence. *What Shall We Do with the Land? Choices for America.* Crowell 1981 $9.50. ISBN 0-690-04108-X Discussion of the conflicts involved in making decisions about the possible uses of land.

*Simon, Noel. *Vanishing Habitats.* Gloucester 1987 $11.90. ISBN 0-531-17062-4 Examination of the effects of damaging and destroying habitats and ecosystems.

Tver, David F. *Dictionary of Dangerous Pollutants, Ecology, and Environment.* Industrial Pr 1981 $24.50. ISBN 0-8311-1060-0

*Woods, Geraldine and Harold Woods. *Pollution.* Watts 1985 $10.40. ISBN 0-531-04916-7 Examination of many types of pollution.

CHEMISTRY

This section is devoted to chemistry, which is perhaps best defined as the study of living and nonliving substances. When considered together with physics, chemistry falls under the broad field of science frequently classified under the umbrella title of physical science. Chemists want to know what a substance is made of and how that substance responds to a given set of circumstances and conditions. They also try to learn why chemical changes take place, what those changes constitute, and how the changes can be controlled.

For ease of use, the chemistry section is divided into 12 subsections. The first eight subsections are concerned with the major topics universally covered in a study of chemistry—matter; the structure of the atom; chemical reactions; chemical bonds; the periodic table; solutions and colloids; acids, bases, and salts; and rates of reaction. The final four subsections encompass specific types of chemistry—electrochemistry, nuclear chemistry, organic chemistry, and biochemistry.

Within a number of the subsections, key scientists associated with the topic or theme are listed alphabetically. For each, there is a book or a list of books by that individual. In addition, there is for each a profile that provides personal background and/or information about the individual's role and contributions to the world of science. Further, the profile may refer the reader to other related individuals and their works, which also can be found in *The Young Adult Reader's Adviser.* Such connections between chemists and other scientists and theorists are usually necessary when doing research in any of the branches of science.

Last, for most profiled individuals, there is a Books About section that, among other types of publications, lists notable biographies for further reading and research. Whenever possible, very recent titles have been included. In some instances, only a very limited number or no books at all about the individual existed at the time of this compilation.

MATTER

Apfel, Necia. *It's All Elementary.* Lothrop 1985 $7.25. ISBN 0-688-04092-6

*Asimov, Isaac. *Asimov on Chemistry.* Doubleday 1975. (o.p.) $5.50. ISBN 0-385-04005-9 Essays about the various areas of study in the field of chemistry: inorganic, organic, and nuclear chemistry, biochemistry, and geochemistry.

Cobb, Vicki. *Chemically Active!* Lippincott 1985 $12.70. ISBN 0-397-32079-5

Goodstein, David L. *States of Matter.* Dover 1985 $9.95. ISBN 0-486-64927-X

*Harré, Rom (ed). *A History of the Physical Sciences Since Antiquity.* St. Martin's 1986 $29.95. ISBN 0-312-38174-3 All nine essays (by six writers) discuss our understanding of the behavior of matter.

*Ley, Willy. *The Discovery of the Elements.* Delacorte 1968. (o.p.) $4.95. ISBN 0-440-01952-4 Interesting descriptions of the circumstances surrounding the discovery of the different elements.

Maxwell, James C. *Maxwell on Molecules and Gases.* MIT Pr 1986 $55.00. ISBN 0-262-07094-4

Mulvey, J. M. (ed). *The Nature of Matter: Wolfson College Lectures, 1980.* Oxford Univ Pr 1981 $18.95. ISBN 0-19-851151-5

Pais, Abraham. *Inward Bound: Of Matter and Forces in the Physical World.* Oxford Univ Pr 1986 $17.95. ISBN 0-19-851997-4

Walter, Alan J. *Three Phases of Matter.* Oxford Univ Pr 1983 $26.95. ISBN 0-19-851953-2

BOYLE, ROBERT   1627–1691

Robert Boyle was born of wealthy parents in Lismore Castle, Ireland. A child prodigy, he attended Eton College at the age of eight, and at 11 years of age, he began a period of extensive travel, studying the works of the great thinkers and scientists of his day—such august figures as the English philosopher Francis Bacon (*see* Bacon, Vol. 2, General Science: Problem Solving and the Scientific Method) and the Italian physicist and astronomer Galileo Galilei. (*See* Galileo, Vol. 2, Earth Science: Astronomy.)

Boyle was captivated by the idea of experimentation in scientific investigation, a practice that was in its infancy early in the fifteenth century. His earliest area of investigation dealt with the study of air. With the help of another young scientist, Robert Hooke, Boyle devised an air pump that could remove all the air from a container, thereby producing a vacuum in the container. Using the pump, Boyle studied the compressibility of air. He discovered that the volume of an enclosed quantity of air is inversely related to the amount of pressure exerted on the air. This relationship, which was later found to hold for all gases, is still referred to as Boyle's law in many countries of the world, including the United States and Great Britain. (In France, the discovery of this relationship is credited to Edme Mariotte, a French physicist. Mariotte conducted similar investigations of air at the same time as Boyle and reached many of the same conclusions.)

The results of the investigations of the compressibility of air led to the conclusion that air must consist of individual particles separated by "empty" space. The idea that all matter is made up of tiny, discrete particles, called atoms, had been suggested by Democritus, a Greek philosopher, some 2,000 years earlier. This idea came to be called atomism, and its followers were known as atomists. Boyle's investigations with air led him to become a firm atomist.

Early in his career, Boyle was also something of an alchemist. He believed that baser metals could be transmuted, or changed, to gold. In his book *The Sceptical Chemist* (1661) Boyle changed the pseudoscience of alchemy into the science of chemistry. In this work, he abandoned the Greek practice of imbuing elements with mystical properties and powers. Rather, Boyle insisted, each element is an individual substance that can be identified only by experimentation. With his book, Boyle established chemistry as a separate science from medicine.

One of Boyle's most important contributions was his insistence that all experimental work be clearly recorded and the results reported as quickly as possible, thereby making it possible for others to repeat experiments and confirm or refute the observations and conclusions. As a result, the practice of sharing information became an integral and invaluable part of scientific research.

BOOK BY BOYLE

The Works of the Honourable Robert Boyle. Thomas Birch (ed). 6 vols. George Olms Hildesheim 1966 repr of 1772 ed.

LAVOISIER, ANTOINE LAURENT   1743–1794

Antoine Lavoisier was born in Paris, France. His father was a lawyer of considerable means, which made it possible for Antoine to receive an excellent education. Although his father hoped Antoine would study law, the young man showed an early interest in science, an interest he would hold throughout his life. After completing his studies, Lavoisier chose chemistry as his field of endeavor. That he chose wisely is attested to by the fact that Lavoisier is often called the father of modern chemistry.

From his earliest investigations, Lavoisier recognized the importance of accuracy and precision in all measurements. Although he was not the first chemist devoted to measurement, he was its most outspoken and persistent spokesperson. Eventually this persistence, aided in no small part by Lavoisier's successes in experimentation, convinced the majority of chemists of the importance of accurate measurement in their work.

Lavoisier is best known for his investigations of the chemical and physical properties of air. As a result of one investigation, a century-old theory was discredited and new information was gained. The theory held that all combustible materials contained a substance called phlogiston that was released during burning. Lavoisier's investigation not only disproved the existence of phlogiston, but eventually led to the discovery and identification of the gases oxygen and nitrogen.

Another of Lavoisier's major accomplishments was the development of a language that could be understood and used by all chemists. In collaboration with other chemists, Lavoisier published *Methods of Chemical Nomenclature* in 1787. This book presented a system whereby every known substance was assigned a definite name based on the elements that made up the substance. The system still forms the basis of chemical nomenclature today. Lavoisier also published the first modern chemistry textbook, *Elementary Treatise on Chemistry* (1789).

Lavoisier met an untimely death, a victim of the fervors unleashed during the French Revolution. He was accused of crimes relating to certain tax practices and arrested by revolutionists in 1792. At his trial a man who had reason to hate him gave false testimony, and Lavoisier was found guilty. He was executed on May 8, 1794, a brilliant scientific mind stilled forever at the age of 50. Lavoisier's death has been characterized as the most deplorable single casualty of the French Revolution.

BOOKS BY LAVOISIER

Elements of Chemistry. Dover 1984 $11.95. ISBN 0-486-64624-6

Essays, Physical and Chemical (1776). H. Thomas (tr). Biblio Dist 1970 $45.00. ISBN 0-7146-1604-4

Memoir on Heat. (coauthored with P. S. Laplace) H. Gueriac (ed). Watson Pub Intl 1981 $14.95. ISBN 0-88202-195-8

BOOKS ABOUT LAVOISIER

*Grey, Vivian. *The Chemist Who Lost His Head: The Story of Antoine Lavoisier.* Putnam 1982 $9.95. ISBN 0-698-20559-6 An intriguing account of the personal and professional life and tragic death of one of history's most important scientists.

Grimaux, Edouard. *Lavoisier: Seventeen Forty-three to Seventeen Ninety-four. Development of Science Ser.* Ayer 1981 $35.00. ISBN 0-405-13963-2 Account of Lavoisier's life and accomplishments.

Guerlac, Henry. *Antoine Lavoisier: Chemist and Revolutionary.* Scribner's 1975 $2.95. ISBN 0-684-14222-8 Story of Lavoisier, his work, and his tribulations and death during the turbulence of the French Revolution.

Holmes, Frederic. *Lavoisier and the Chemistry of Life: An Exploration of Scientific Creativity.* Univ of Wisconsin Pr 1985 $15.75. ISBN 0-299-09980-6 Study of Lavoisier and his important contributions to chemistry and scientific procedures.

See also Vol. 2, Physics: States of Matter.

STRUCTURE OF THE ATOM

*Asimov, Isaac. *How Did We Find out About Atoms?* Walker 1976 $10.85. ISBN 0-8027-6248-4 Story of the atom: how knowledge of the structure of the atom grew and changed over time and through the efforts of many investigators.

Asimov, Isaac. *Inside the Atom.* Abelard-Schuman 1974. (o.p.)

Condon, E. U., and H. Odabasi. *Atomic Structure.* Cambridge Univ Pr 1980 $34.50. ISBN 0-521-29893-8

Dorin, Henry. *Chemistry: The Study of Matter.* Allyn 1987 $27.80. ISBN 0-205-09620-4

*Ellis, R. Robard, Jr. *Knowing the Atomic Nucleus.* Lothrop 1973. (o.p.) ISBN 0-688-41295-5 An interesting history of atomic exploration, with biographical sketches of those who participated in the search for understanding.

Gallant, Roy A. *Explorers of the Atom.* Doubleday 1974. (o.p.) $6.95. ISBN 0-385-06459-4

*Mebane, Robert. *Adventures with Atoms and Molecules: Chemistry Experiments for Young People.* Enslow. Bk 1 1985 $14.95. ISBN 0-89490-120-6. Bk 2 1987 $16.95. ISBN 0-89490-164-8. Bk 3 1991 $16.95. ISBN 0-894-90-254-7 Thirty enjoyable activities in each book illustrate simple chemistry principles using easy-to-find materials.

BOHR, NIELS HENRIK DAVID   1885–1962

Niels Bohr, the son of a physiology professor, studied physics at the University of Copenhagen. On receipt of his doctorate in 1911, Bohr obtained a grant to travel abroad to further his education. He went at once to Cambridge, England, where he worked under New Zealand chemist Ernest Rutherford. (*See* Rutherford, Vol. 2, Chemistry: Structure of the Atom.) He remained at Cambridge until 1916, at which time he returned to the University of Copenhagen as professor of physics.

While at Cambridge, Bohr set out to investigate the mechanisms responsible for the radiant energy emitted and absorbed by substances when they are treated in a way that excites their atoms. Toward this end, he combined the concept of the nuclear atom, set forth by Rutherford only three years earlier, with German physicist Max Planck's quantum theory of energy. (*See* Planck, Vol. 2, Physics: Electromagnetic Waves: Light and the Quantum Theory.)

As a result of his research, Bohr developed a model of the atom in which electrons moved around the nucleus at discrete distances from it. These distances were known as energy levels, or orbitals. As it turned out, Bohr's model of the atom was flawed, and subsequently it underwent many modifications. However, his model proved to be the first reasonably acceptable attempt at using the internal structure of the atom to explain external phenomena. In 1922, Bohr was awarded the Nobel Prize in physics in recognition of his contribution.

BOOKS BY BOHR

Atomic Theory and the Description of Nature (1934). The Philosophical Writings of Niels Bohr Ser. Vol. 1 Ox Bow 1987 $12.00. ISBN 0-918024-50-1

Essays on Atomic Physics and Human Knowledge, Nineteen Fifty-eight to Nineteen Sixty-two (1963). Ox Bow 1987 $12.00. ISBN 0-918024-54-4

Essays on Atomic Physics and Human Knowledge, Nineteen Thirty-three to Nineteen Fifty-seven (1958). Ox Bow 1987 $12.00. ISBN 0-918024-52-8

BOOKS ABOUT BOHR

Blaedel, Niels. *Harmony and Unity: The Life of Niels Bohr.* Sci Tech Pubs 1988 $35.00. ISBN 0-910239-14-2 History of physics and physicists as well as a biography of Bohr.

Folse, Henry, Jr. *The Philosophy of Niels Bohr: Framework of Complementarity.* Elsevier 1985 $19.50. ISBN 0-444-86938-7 Development of the most widely accepted approach to quantum mechanics by Bohr and his colleagues at the institute for Theoretical Physics in Copenhagen.

French, A. P., and P. J. Kennedy (eds). *Niels Bohr: A Centenary Volume.* Harvard Univ Pr 1987 $14.95. ISBN 0-674-62416-5 Life, ideals, and creative work of Bohr, as recalled by his students.

Pauli, Wolfgang. *Niels Bohr and the Development of Physics: Essays Dedicated to Bohr on the Occasion of his Seventieth Birthday.* McGraw 1955. An interesting account by a close colleague of Bohr.

Rozental, S. (ed). *Niels Bohr: His Life and Work as Seen by His Friends and Family.* Elsevier 1985 $27.95. ISBN 0-444-86977-8 Essays about Bohr starting with his childhood and including his years as a thinker and scientist in the 1930s, 1940s, and 1950s.

DALTON, JOHN   1766–1844

John Dalton, was a "born scientist." Born in Eaglesfield, England, and a lifelong Quaker, Dalton started teaching in a Quaker school at the tender age of 12. There he developed an interest in science that was to remain with him all his life.

Although best known for his contributions relating to the atomic structure of matter, Dalton's first love was meteorology. Using homemade instruments, he studied weather conditions and recorded all his observations. When he was 27 years old, he wrote a book on the subject, *Meteorological Observations and Essays* (1793). Even after he moved on to the study of chemistry later in life, Dalton kept detailed weather records until he died.

Starting in about 1800, Dalton began experimenting with gases. The behavior of gases under varying conditions led him to conclude that gases were made up of tiny particles. This conclusion agreed with the findings of earlier scientists, such as the English scientist Robert Boyle and the English physicist and mathematician Isaac Newton. (*See* Boyle, Vol. 2, Chemistry: Matter *and* Newton, Vol. 2, Physics: Mechanics: Forces and Motion.) In 1803 Dalton advanced the first definitive law of multiple proportions, which explained how various elements combine to produce different compounds.

When Dalton first expressed his ideas about the atomic nature of matter in 1803, he recognized that this concept had been advanced 21 centuries earlier by the Greek philosopher Democritus. There was a critical difference between the proposals of these two men, however. Democritus' ideas were not based on scientific fact. Rather, they were deductions based on supposition and speculation. Dalton's ideas were based on evidence obtained through observations of the behavior of matter under controlled conditions during carefully designed experiments. Further, in his experiments, Dalton had considered the masses of the particles taking part in chemical reactions. Thus Dalton was the first to advance a *quantitative* atomic theory. He was also the first scientist to organize the elements according to their atomic weights.

The first published account of Dalton's atomic theory was included in his book *New System of Chemical Philosophy* (1808). Because the ideas presented in his theory were so logical and well supported, they were widely accepted by most chemists with little opposition. In the nearly 200 years that have passed since Dalton's theory was first advanced, new evidence has made it necessary for the concept of the "solid, indivisible, indestructible particle" known as the atom to undergo many changes and revisions. However, Dalton's incalculable contributions to chemistry, in particular, and to humanity, in general, are universally recognized and appreciated.

BOOKS ABOUT DALTON

Greenaway, Frank. *John Dalton and the Atom.* Cornell Univ Pr 1966. Complete biography with illustrations that focuses on Dalton's theories and their reception.

Patterson, Elizabeth C. *John Dalton and the Atomic Theory.* Doubleday 1970. Readable biography that looks at the revolution Dalton effected in physical science.

Thackray, Arnold. *John Dalton: Critical Assessments of His Life and Science. Monographs in the History of Science.* Harvard Univ Pr 1972 $17.00. ISBN 0-674-47525-9 Analysis of Dalton's ideas that illuminates the cognitive aspects of science and science as an empirical and conceptual undertaking.

PAULI, WOLFGANG   1900–1958

Wolfgang Pauli, born in Vienna, Austria, showed an early interest in physics. He studied under physics professor Arnold Sommerfeld at the University of Munich and obtained his doctorate in physics from that institution in 1921. From Munich he went to Copenhagen, where he did post-doctorate work with Danish physicist Niels Bohr. (*See* Bohr, Vol. 2, Chemistry: Structure of the Atom.)

In 1923 he joined the faculty of the University of Hamburg. Two years later he announced his exclusion principle, which helped to explain some puzzling aspects of the model of the atom proposed by Bohr. Bohr and Sommerfeld had worked out energy levels for the atom. These energy levels could be expressed with three quantum numbers. Although this model could be used to explain many characteristics of the atom, many unanswered questions still remained.

Pauli completed the structure of the atom by adding a fourth quantum number. This led to the idea that two, and only two, electrons could possibly be present in any given energy level (hence the name "exclusion principle"). In addition, Pauli stated that the electrons in each electron pair were spinning in different directions—one clockwise and the other counterclockwise.

This deceivingly simple concept and interpretation led to the arrangement of electrons in shells and subshells and helped to explain why certain groups of elements exhibit similar properties. For his important discovery, Pauli received the 1945 Nobel Prize in physics, some 20 years after he had announced the exclusion principle.

During this 20-year period, Pauli did not rest on his laurels. He joined other physicists in seeking an explanation for a puzzling problem. It had been known for some time that certain atoms emit beta particles. However, the particles—high-speed electrons—have less energy than they should. Some physicists went so far as to suggest that some energy was being destroyed. If these scientists were correct, the law of conservation of energy would have to be revised or abandoned.

In 1931 Pauli suggested that a second particle was emitted along with each beta particle that was emitted. This second particle, without charge and per-haps without mass, carried off the "missing" energy. In 1932, Italian-born American physicist Enrico Fermi named Pauli's suggested particle the neutrino. (*See* Fermi, Vol. 2, Physics: Nuclear Physics.)

Because such a chargeless, massless particle is virtually impossible to de-tect, many physicists refused to accept the possibility of its existence. Some suggested that the neutrino was a gimmick invented for the sole purpose of preserving the sacrosanct law of conservation of energy. However, in 1956 the neutrino was finally detected and its existence firmly established.

In the 1930s, Pauli spent a good deal of time in the United States. With the coming of World War II, he took up permanent residence. He became an American citizen in 1946.

BOOKS BY PAULI

Collected Scientific Papers. 2 vols. Krieger 1964 $125.00. ISBN 0-470-67254-4

General Principles of Quantum Mechanics. Springer-Verlag 1983 $25.00. ISBN 0-387-09842-9

Theory of Relativity (1958). Dover 1981 $6.00. ISBN 0-486-64152-X

Pauli Lectures on Physics. C. P. Enz (ed). S. Marguilles and H. R. Lewis (trs). 6 vols. MIT Pr 1973. Vol. 1 *Electrodynamics.* $8.95. ISBN 0-262-66033-4. Vol. 2 *Optics and the Theory of Electrons.* $8.95. ISBN 0-262-66034-2. Vol. 3 *Thermodynamics and the Kinetic Theory of Gases.* $8.95. ISBN 0-262-66035-0. Vol. 4 *Statistical Mechanics.* $8.95. ISBN 0-262-66036-9. Vol. 5 *Wave Mechanics.* $8.95. ISBN 0-262-66037-7. Vol. 6 *Selected Topics in Field Quantization.* $8.95. ISBN 0-262-66032-6

RUTHERFORD, ERNEST 1871–1937

Ernest Rutherford was born in New Zealand. His father was a wheelwright and a farmer. If the son had not shown great promise and glimpses of brilliance in school, he might have followed in his father's footsteps. However, in his teens he earned a scholarship to New Zealand University. Because of his academic ability, he received a scholarship to Cambridge University in England, where he remained for most of his life.

Rutherford arrived at Cambridge during a period of unprecedented scien-tific activity and research. Publication of John Dalton's atomic theory in 1808 had generated an enormous amount of interest in the elemental building blocks of matter. (*See* Dalton, Vol. 2, Chemistry: Structure of the Atom.) In the ensuing years the electrical nature of the atom had been determined, and electrons had been discovered by British physicist J. J. Thompson in 1897.

Although Rutherford's greatest accomplishments were to come in the area of atomic structure, his interest at the time he arrived at Cambridge was in another area of intense scientific interest: radioactivity. Rutherford was one of the scientists, along with Marie and Pierre Curie, who decided that different kinds of rays were given off by radioactive substances. (*See* Curie, Vol. 2, Chemistry: Types of Study: Nuclear Chemistry.) Rutherford named the positively charged rays alpha rays and the negatively charged ones beta rays. These names are still used today to refer to the high-energy particles that make up the "rays."

Rutherford was particularly fascinated by the positively charged alpha rays. It was while studying the effects of alpha rays on metal foils that he made his most important discovery. The behavior of alpha rays when they struck a piece of thin gold foil led Rutherford to conclude that the atoms of gold that made up the foil consisted mainly of empty space. Each atom contained a very dense, positively charged core made up of protons. This core, which Rutherford called a nucleus, was surrounded by negatively charged electrons, situated at the outer regions of the atom.

The model atom based on Rutherford's discoveries resembles a miniature solar system, with a dense central nucleus (the "sun") surrounded by much smaller bodies ("planets") orbiting the nucleus at some distance from it. While the model itself has undergone many revisions since it was introduced in 1908, the concept of the nuclear atom is still accepted today.

BOOK BY RUTHERFORD

Rutherford and Boltwood: Letters on Radioactivity. Yale Studies in the History of Science and Medicine Ser. No. 4. (coauthored with Bertram B. Boltwood) Lawrence Badash (ed). Books Demand $100.50. ISBN 0-8357-9490-3

BOOKS ABOUT RUTHERFORD

Andrade, E. N. *Rutherford and the Nature of the Atom.* Peter Smith 1978 $11.25. ISBN 0-8446-2953-X A study of Rutherford, investigator of the atom.

Shea, William R., and M. A. Bunge (eds). *Rutherford and Physics at the Turn of the Century.* Watson Pub Intl 1979 $20.00. ISBN 0-88202-184-2 Consideration of Rutherford and his work in the setting of his time.

Wilson, David. *Rutherford: Simple Genius.* MIT Pr 1983 $37.50. ISBN 0-262-23115-8 Biography of Rutherford.

CHEMICAL REACTIONS

Baer, Michael. *Theory of Chemical Reaction Dynamics,* Vols. 2, 3, 4. CRC Pr 1985 $620.00. ISBN 0-8493-6113-3

*Cherrier, François. *Fascinating Experiments in Chemistry.* Sterling 1973. (o.p.) $12.95. ISBN 0-999-93102-7 The instructions for carrying out a few easy, well-planned experiments, using readily available materials; good illustrations.

*Cobb, Vicki. *Chemically Active! Experiments You Can Do at Home.* Harper 1985 $12.89. ISBN 0-397-32080-9 Simple experiments designed for learning about crystallization, distillation, electrical solutions, and other chemical actions and techniques; introduces symbols, formulas, and equations.

Hess, Fred C. *Chemistry Made Simple.* Doubleday 1984 $6.95. ISBN 0-385-18850-1

*Mcbane, Robert C., and Thomas R. Rybolt. *Adventures with Atoms and Molecules, Bk 1: Chemistry Experiments for Young People.* Enslow 1985 $14.95. ISBN 0-89490-120-6 Experiments that can be done using easily obtainable household materials; suitable for middle and junior high school students (adult supervision recommended).

*Mcbane, Robert C., and Thomas R. Rybolt. *Adventures with Atoms and Molecules, Bk 2: More Chemistry Experiments for Young People.* Enslow 1987 $14.95. ISBN 0-89490-164-8 Another collection of experiments that can be done at home under the supervision of an adult.

*Neubauer, Alfred. *Chemistry Today: The Portrait of a Science.* Arco 1983. (o.p.) Interesting, readable treatments of the highlights of modern research in chemistry.

Sherman, Alan, and Sharon J. Sherman. *Chemistry and Our Changing World.* Prentice 1983 $10.95. ISBN 0-13-129361-3

Walters, Derek. *Chemistry. Science World Ser.* Watts 1983 $11.90. ISBN 0-531-0458-1 Presents the principles of chemistry for the young reader and explains the chemistry of many common actions and events.

See also Vol. 2, Chemistry: Types of Study: Nuclear Chemistry *and* Physics: Nuclear Physics.

CHEMICAL BONDS

Boschke, F. L. (ed). *Bonding and Structure.* Springer-Verlag 1976. (o.p.) $42.00. ISBN 0-387-07605-0

*Dorin, Henry. *Chemistry: The Study of Matter* Allyn 1987 $27.82. ISBN 0-205-09620-4 A high school textbook with discussion of chemical bonds in Chapters 14 and 15.

Gray, Harry B. *Chemical Bonds: An Introduction to Atomic and Molecular Structure.* Benjamin-Cummings 1973 $21.95. ISBN 0-8053-3402-5

Murrell, John N. *The Chemical Bond.* Wiley 1985 $59.95. ISBN 0-471-90759-6

PAULING, LINUS CARL   1901–

Born in Portland, Oregon, Linus Pauling graduated from Oregon State College in 1922. He obtained his Ph.D. at the California Institute of Technology in 1925 and taught there until 1963. He then joined the faculty of the University of California in San Diego, leaving to head the Linus Pauling Institute, a privately funded research institute set up in the 1960s.

Pauling's major contributions to chemistry have been in the areas of chemical bonding and the structure of molecules. By the age of 30, Pauling had revolutionized thinking concerning the structure of molecules. Pauling used quantum mechanics to develop a theory whereby electrons interacted in pairs, forming a more stable system in combination than when operating separately. This interaction could only occur when the atoms to which the electrons belonged remained in close proximity. Separating such atoms required the addition of energy.

Pauling's theory accounted for the chemical bonds that were known to exist among atoms in a molecule. The theory also provided a system of depicting molecules. Pauling published his ideas in *The Nature of the Chemical Bond and the Structure of Molecules and Crystals* (1939). This book proved to be one of the most influential chemistry textbooks of the twentieth century.

Pauling went on to apply his concepts of molecular structure to the complex molecules of living tissue. His suggestion that protein molecules were arranged in helical, or spiral, form preceded the work of American biologist James Watson and English molecular biologist Francis Crick, who proposed a helical structure for nucleic acids. The Watson–Crick model for DNA was an extraordinary breakthrough in the field of genetics. (*See* Crick, Watson, *and* Wilkins, Vol. 2, Biology: Nucleic Acids and the Genetic Code.)

Starting in the mid-1940s, Pauling moved to the forefront of those members of the scientific community who were fearful of the dangers inherent in the use, and particularly the misuse, of nuclear energy. He vigorously fought against nuclear testing and campaigned for nuclear disarmament.

In 1954 Pauling was awarded the Nobel Prize in chemistry for his work on molecular structure. In 1963 he was awarded the Nobel Prize in peace for his efforts to bring about nuclear disarmament. Thus he became only the second person, joining Polish-born French physicist Marie Curie (*see* Curie, Vol. 2, Chemistry: Types of Study: Nuclear Chemistry), to receive two Nobel Prizes.

BOOKS BY PAULING

General Chemistry (1947). Dover 1988 $18.95. ISBN 0-486-65622-5
The Nature of the Chemical Bond and the Structure of Molecules and Crystals (1939). Cornell Univ Pr 1960 $49.95. ISBN 0-8014-0333-2
No More War! (1958). Dodd 1983 $7.95. ISBN 0-396-08157-6
Vitamin C, the Common Cold, and the Flu (1970). Freeman 1976 $10.95. ISBN 0-7167-0361-0

BOOK ABOUT PAULING

Serafini, Anthony. *Linus Pauling: A Man and His Science.* Paragon Hse 1989 $22.95. ISBN 0-913729-88-4 The life and work of Pauling.

THE PERIODIC TABLE

Asimov, Isaac. *Building Blocks of the Universe.* Harper 1973. (o.p.)
Boudreau, Edward A. *Elementary Aspects of Chemical Periodicity.* Paladin Hse 1976 $4.00. ISBN 0-88252-061-X
Matsubara, T. (ed). *The Structure and Properties of Matter.* Springer-Verlag 1982 $67.00. ISBN 0-387-11098-4
Pode, J. S. *The Periodic Table: Experiments and Theory.* Halsted 1985. (o.p.) $4.95. ISBN 0-470-69144-1
Relationships and Mechanisms in the Periodic Table. Topics in Current Chemistry Ser. Springer-Verlag 1989 $89.50. ISBN 0-387-50045-6
Ruben, Samuel. *Handbook of the Elements.* Open Court 1985 $5.95. ISBN 0-87548-399-2
Sisler, Harry H. *Electronic Structures and Properties and the Periodic Law.* Books Demand $32.00. ISBN 0-317-08782-7

MENDELEEV, DIMITRI IVANOVICH   1834–1907

Although the records are not precise, it is known that Dimitri Mendeleev was born in Siberia, Russia, the youngest of at least 14 children. He received his first lessons in science from a political prisoner who had been exiled to Siberia.

Mendeleev attended college in St. Petersburg. After graduating at the top of his class, he traveled to France and Germany for postgraduate training. He returned to St. Petersburg and became a highly successful and respected professor of chemistry. Many still consider Mendeleev's *The Principles of Chemistry* (1870), the best chemistry textbook written in Russian.

Mendeleev gained worldwide renown for his organization of the elements into a meaningful format. He started by arranging all the known elements according to their atomic weights, from lowest to highest. Keeping this order, he then organized the elements in a chart consisting of vertical columns and horizontal rows. He arranged the elements in such a way that all the elements in a given column and all those in a given row had similarities in several of their chemical properties. When this arrangement was complete (for the elements then known), an interesting fact became clear. The elements in each row showed periodic rises and falls of valence and periodic repetitions of properties. This feature of Mendeleev's chart led to its eventual name: the periodic table of the elements.

Mendeleev's table was successful for what it did not contain as well as for what it did include. While Mendeleev was working on his organizational scheme for the elements, other scientists were working toward the same goal, using many of the same techniques. One of these scientists, British chemist John Newlands, failed in his attempts because he tried to force the known elements to fit into the organization schemes he developed. In contrast, Mendeleev left gaps in his table. He explained that the gaps would be filled, in time, as new elements were discovered.

Mendeleev's first periodic table, published in 1869, was met with a great deal of skepticism. However, Mendeleev's confidence in his scheme eventually paid dividends. He explained that as-yet-undiscovered elements would fill the gaps and even predicted the properties that three of these missing elements would exhibit, once the elements were discovered. And he was right! Over the next several years, all three of these elements were found and each had precisely the properties Mendeleev had predicted. Mendeleev and his periodic table were vindicated, and he became the best-known chemist of his time. In 1955 a newly discovered element was named mendeleevium in recognition of Mendeleev's achievements.

BOOK BY MENDELEEV

Principles of Chemistry (1868–1871). 2 vols. Thomas H. Pope (ed). G. Kamensky (tr). Kraus 1969 $66.00. ISBN 0-527-63100-0

SOLUTIONS AND COLLOIDS

Cohen, I. Bernard. *Theory of Solutions and Stereo Chemistry.* Ayer 1981 $35.00. ISBN 0-405-13868-7

Dickinson, E., and G. Stainsby. *Colloids in Food.* Elsevier 1982 $129.50. ISBN 0-85334-153-2

Fialkov, Yu. *Extraordinary Properties of Ordinary Solutions.* Imported 1985 $2.95. ISBN 0-8285-3073-4

Murrell, J. N., and E. A. Boucher. *Properties of Liquids and Solutions.* Wiley 1982 $81.95. ISBN 0-471-10201-6

Nielson, Lawrence. *Predicting the Properties of Mixtures.* Dekker 1978. (o.p.) $39.75. ISBN 0-824-76690-3

Walton, Alan G. *The Formation and Properties of Precipitates.* Krieger 1979 $20.50. ISBN 0-88275-990-6

ACIDS, BASES, AND SALTS

*Dorin, Henry. *Chemistry: The Study of Matter.* Allyn 1987 $28.70. ISBN 0-205-09620-4 High school textbook with a full discussion of acids, bases, and salts in Chapters 23–25.

Imelik, B. *Catalysis by Acids and Bases.* Elsevier 1985 $137.00. ISBN 0-444-42449-0

Jensen, William B. *The Lewis Acid–Base Concepts: An Overview.* Wiley 1980. (o.p.) $59.95. ISBN 0-471-03902-0

Pearson, R. G. (ed). *Hard and Soft Acids and Bases.* Van Nostrand 1973 $65.95. ISBN 0-87933-021-X
Perrin, D. D. (ed). *Ionization Constants of Inorganic Acids and Bases in Aqueous Solutions.* Pergamon 1982 $62.00. ISBN 0-08-029214-3
Tunabe, Kozo. *Solid Acids and Bases: Their Catalytic Properties.* Academic Pr 1971 $66.00. ISBN 0-12-683250-1
Tocci, Salvatore. *Chemistry Around You.* Arco 1985. (o.p.)

RATES OF REACTIONS

Benson, Philip G., *et al.* (eds). *The Foundations of Chemical Kinetics.* Krieger 1982 $52.50. ISBN 0-89874-194-7
Crynes, B. L., and H. S. Folger (eds). *Rate of Reaction, Sensitivity, and Chemical Equilibrium.* Am Inst Chem Eng 1981 $30.00. ISBN 0-8169-0174-0
*Dorin, Henry. *Chemistry: The Study of Matter.* Allyn 1987 $27.80. ISBN 0-205-09620-4
A high school textbook that treats rates of reaction in Chapter 19.
Espenson, James H. *Chemical Kinetics and Reaction Mechanisms.* McGraw 1981 $44.95. ISBN 0-07-019667-2
Hague, David N. *Fast Reactions.* Books Demand 1985 $41.80. ISBN 0-317-09314-2
Skinner, Gordon B. *Introduction to Chemical Kinetics.* Academic Pr 1974 $58.00. ISBN 0-12-647850-3

TYPES OF STUDY: ELECTROCHEMISTRY

Bard, Allen J. and Henning Lund (eds). *Encyclopedia of Electrochemistry of the Elements*, Vol. 9A Dekker 1982 $119.50. ISBN 0-8247-2509-3
Bard, Allen J. and Henning Lund (eds). *Encyclopedia of Electrochemistry of the Elements*, Vol. 9B Dekker 1986 $119.50. ISBN 0-8247-2519-0
Bockris, J. O. *An Introduction to Electrochemical Science.* Taylor & Francis 1974 $18.00. ISBN 0-85109-410-4
*Dorin, Henry. *Chemistry: The Study of Matter.* Allyn 1987 $27.80. ISBN 0-205-09620-4
A high school textbook that treats electrochemistry in Chapters 27 and 28.
Gutman, Felix, and Harry Bloom (eds). *Electrochemistry: The Past Thirty and the Next Thirty Years.* Plenum 1977 $85.00. ISBN 0-306-30921-1
Walters, Derek. *Chemistry.* Watts 1983 $11.90. ISBN 0-531-04581-1

See also Vol. 2, Physics: Electricity and Magnetism.

TYPES OF STUDY: NUCLEAR CHEMISTRY

Berger, Melvin. *Atoms, Molecules, and Quarks.* Putnam 1986 $10.00.
*Caufield, Catherine. *Multiple Exposures: Chronicles of the Radiation Age.* Univ of Chicago Pr 1990 $13.95. ISBN 0-226-09785-4 Discussion of high-energy radiation—X rays, neutrons, and alpha, beta, and gamma rays; discovery and early experiments with radiation described in part one.
Jenkins, E. N., and I. Lewis. *Radioactivity: A Science in Its Historical and Social Context.* Taylor & Francis 1979 $18.00. ISBN 0-8848-1371-0

*McGowen, Tom. *Radioactivity: From the Curies to the Atomic Age.* Watts 1986 $10.40. ISBN 0-531-10132-0 An easy-to-read discussion of radioactivity and its discovery, emphasizing the work of the Curies; for younger readers.

*Milne, Lorus J., and Margery Milne. *Understanding Radioactivity.* Macmillan 1989 $12.95. ISBN 0-689-31362-4 Discusses radioactivity, its uses, and sources of possibly harmful radiation.

*Pringle, Laurence. *Radiation: Waves and Particles.* Enslow 1983 $13.95. ISBN 0-89490-054-4 Examines the forms of radiation and how they affect humans.

Roginskii, S. Z., and S. E. Shnol'. *Isotopes in Biochemistry.* Coronet 1965 $72.50. ISBN 0-7065-0555-7

Trenn, T. J. *Radioactivity and Atomic Theory.* Krieger 1975 $40.50. ISBN 0-470-88520-3

Trenn, T. J. *Transmutation: Natural and Artificial. Nobel Prize Topics in Chemistry Ser.* Wiley 1982 $47.00. ISBN 0-471-26105-X

CURIE, MARIE   1867–1934

Marie Curie was born Marja Sklodowska in Warsaw, Poland, then under Russian domination. In the repressed society, it was impossible for her to continue her education beyond high school. For several years after graduating, she worked to help meet the expenses of a brother and sister, both of whom had immigrated to Paris in search of education.

By 1891 Marie had managed to save enough money to move to Paris and enter the Sorbonne. In 1894 she met Pierre Curie, a French chemist who had discovered piezoelectricity—the production of a small electric potential across certain crystals under pressure. This discovery was to play a significant role in Marie's future work.

Marie and Pierre Curie were married in 1895, the same year that German physicist Wilhelm Konrad Roentgen announced his discovery of X rays. This discovery was quickly followed in 1896 by the discovery of radiant emanations from uranium by French physicist Henri Becquerel. These discoveries were to galvanize Marie Curie into action and to dictate the course of her scientific career.

She launched into the study of the radiations emitted by uranium, giving the name radioactivity to the process whereby these radiations are given off. The results of her studies confirmed the findings of British physicist Ernest Rutherford (*see* Rutherford, Vol. 2, Chemistry: Structure of the Atom) and French physicist Henri Becquerel that the radiations consist of three kinds of rays—alpha, beta, and gamma.

Curie's next step was to apply her husband's discovery of piezoelectricity to the measurement of radioactivity. In the course of her measurements, she discovered other radioactive elements, some considerably more radioactive than uranium. In time, her work led to the discovery of radium, an intensely radioactive element so scarce that it is found only as a trace impurity in certain ores.

During the course of Marie Curie's investigations, Pierre Curie abandoned his own research and joined his wife, serving as her assistant. After the discovery of radium, the Curie team set out to obtain pure radium in a quantity large enough to enable them to study the element. Working with waste ore from a silver mine, the Curies succeeded in isolating 0.1 gram of radium over a four-year period.

In 1903, Marie and Pierre Curie shared the Nobel Prize in physics with Henri Becquerel. In 1906, Pierre was run over and killed by a horse-drawn cart. Marie took over his professorship at the Sorbonne, the first woman to teach there. Despite her success and the attendant prestige, however, she was denied membership in the French Academy by one vote, cast against her because she was a woman.

Marie Curie's published works include *Radioactive Substances* (1902), *Traité de radioactivité* (1910), and *Radioactivité* (1935). Her biography of her husband, *Pierre Curie,* was published in 1923.

In 1911 Marie Curie was awarded the Nobel Prize in chemistry for her discovery of two new elements, polonium and radium. She is the only person to win two Nobel Prizes in science. Marie died in 1934 of leukemia caused by overexposure to radioactive radium.

BOOKS BY CURIE

Pierre Curie (1923). Charlotte Kellogg and Vernon Kellogg (trs). Dover 1963. (o.p.) $1.25. ISBN 0-486-20199-6

Radioactive Substances. Philosophical Paperbook Ser. (1902). Philosophical Lib 1983 $4.95. ISBN 0-8022-2433-4

BOOKS ABOUT CURIE

Curie, Eve. *Madame Curie.* Vincent Sheean (tr). Da Capo 1986 $11.95. ISBN 0-306-80281-3 The story of Marie Curie's life and accomplishments, written by her daughter.

Giroud, François. *Marie Curie: A Life.* Lydia Davis (tr). Holmes & Meier 1986 $34.50. ISBN 0-8419-0977-6 Biography focusing on the entire life as a family member and scientist.

*Keller, Mollie. *Marie Curie. Impact Biographies Ser.* Watts 1982 $12.50. ISBN 0-531-04476-9 Story of Marie Curie and her accomplishments; includes photographs and bibliography.

Pflaum, Rosalynd. *Grand Obsession: Madame Curie and Her World.* Doubleday 1990 $22.50. ISBN 0-385-26135-7 Life of Marie Curie inside and outside the laboratory as well as a re-creation of the times in which she lived.

See also Vol. 2, Chemistry: Structure of the Atom *and* Physics: Nuclear Physics.

TYPES OF STUDY: ORGANIC CHEMISTRY

Buscall, R., *et al.* (eds). *Science and Technology of Polymer Colloids.* Elsevier 1985 $83.00. ISBN 0-85334-312-8

Gallant, Robert, and Jay M. Railey. *Physical Properties of Hydrocarbons.* Vol. 2 Gulf Pub 1984 $48.00. ISBN 0-87201-690-0

Jenkens, Gwyn M., and K. Kawamura. *Polymeric Carbons—Carbon Fibre, Glass, and Charcoal.* Books Demand 1976 $46.50. ISBN 0-317-29379-6

Kahn, M. A., and R. H. Stanton (eds). *Toxicology of Halogenated Hydrocarbons: Health and Ecological Effects.* Pergamon 1981 $100.00. ISBN 0-08-027530-3

Salmen, L., *et al. Composite Systems from Natural and Synthetic Polymers.* Elsevier 1986 $100.00. ISBN 0-444-42-650-7

Walker, Philip L. (ed). *Chemistry and Physics of Carbon.* Vol. 4 Books Demand 1968 $102.80. ISBN 0-317-08348-1

*Whyman, Kathryn. *Plastics. Resources Today Ser.* Watts 1988 $8.90. ISBN 0-531-17084-5 Discusses types of plastics and how they are made and used.

Zubrick, James W. *The Organic Chemistry Laboratory Survival Manual.* Wiley 1988 $17.50. ISBN 0-471-85519-7

TYPES OF STUDY: BIOCHEMISTRY

Asimov, Isaac. *Chemicals of Life.* NAL 1962 $3.95. ISBN 0-451-62418-1

Binkley. *Modern Carbohydrate Chemistry.* Dekker 1987 $90.00. ISBN 0-8247-7789-1

Bohinski. *Modern Concepts in Biochemistry.* Allyn $56.00. ISBN 0-205-08852-X

Boyer, Rodney F. *Modern Experimental Biochemistry.* Benjamin-Cummings 1985 $40.95. ISBN 0-201-10131-9

Collins, P. M. *Carbohydrates.* Routledge 1986 $195.00. ISBN 0-412-25440-9

Fasman, Gerald D. (ed). *CRC Practical Handbook of Biochemistry and Molecular Biology.* CRC Pr 1989 $45.00. ISBN 0-8493-3705-4

Gutman, Felix, and Hendrik Keyzer (eds). *Modern Bioelectrochemistry.* Plenum 1986 $115.00. ISBN 0-306-41981-5

Harborne, J. B. *Introduction to Ecological Biochemistry.* Academic Pr 1988 $29.95. ISBN 0-12-324684-9

Hockachka, P. W. (ed). *Biochemistry at Depth.* Pergamon 1976 $53.00. ISBN 0-08-019960-7

Holum, John R. *Elements of General and Biological Chemistry.* Wiley 1987. ISBN 0-471-09935-X

Hughes, M. N. *The Inorganic Chemistry of Biological Processes.* Wiley 1981 $59.95. ISBN 0-471-27815-7

Kleinkauf, Horst, *et al* (eds). *The Roots of Modern Biochemistry: Fritz Lipmann's Squiggle and Its Consequences.* de Gruyter 1988 $250.00. ISBN 3-11-011585-9

Lehninger, Albert L. *Biochemistry: The Molecular Basis of Cell Structure and Function.* Worth 1975 $47.95. ISBN 0-87901-047-9

McGilvery, Robert W. *Biochemistry: A Functional Approach.* Saunders 1983 $45.95. ISBN 0-7216-5913-6

Neurath, Hans. *Perspectives in Biochemistry.* Vol. 1 Am Chemical 1989 $14.95. ISBN 0-8412-1621-5

O'Connor, R. F. *Chemical Principles and Their Biological Implications.* Wiley 1974 $31.95. ISBN 0-471-65246-6

Peacocke, A. R. *An Introduction to the Physical Chemistry of Biological Organization.* Oxford Univ Pr 1983 $92.00. ISBN 0-19-855359-5

Werner, Rudolph. *Essentials of Modern Biochemistry.* Jones & Bartlett 1983 $22.50. ISBN 0-86720-019-7

Wood, E. J. (ed). *Practical Biochemistry for Colleges.* Pergamon 1986 $195.00. ISBN 0-08-036140-4

PHYSICS

This section is devoted to physics, the science that deals with the effects of energy, force, and time on matter. When considered together with chemistry, physics falls under the broad field of science frequently classified under the umbrella title of physical science. Physics explains such disparate occurrences as why water boils and how the heavenly bodies move. Every aspect of people's lives is influenced by physics. The electricity that lights homes, the machines that carry people about, and the systems that heat buildings are all the products of the minds of physicists. Further, it is an understanding of the physical laws that has enabled scientists to split the atomic nucleus and to send spacecraft to the far reaches of the solar system and beyond.

For ease of use, the physics section is divided into eight subsections, the first of which consists of a listing of general reference works. The six subsections that follow focus on topics universally covered in a study of physics—

mechanics: forces and motion; mechanics: work, energy, and power; states of matter; electromagnetic waves: light and the quantum theory; sound; and electricity and magnetism. The final subsection deals with works on nuclear physics.

Within a number of the subsections, key scientists associated with the topic or theme are listed alphabetically. For each, there is a book or a list of books by that individual. In addition, there is for each a profile that provides personal background and/or information about the individual's role and contributions to the world of science. Further, the profile may refer the reader to other related individuals and their works, which also can be found in *The Young Adult Reader's Adviser.* Such connections between physicists and other scientists and theorists are usually necessary when doing research in any of the branches of science.

Last, for most profiled individuals, there is a Books About section that, among other types of publications, lists notable biographies for further reading and research. Whenever possible, very recent titles have also been included. In some instances, only a very limited number or no books at all about the individual existed at the time of this compilation.

GENERAL REFERENCES

Abro, A. *The Rise of the New Physics.* 2 vols. Dover 1950 $17.95. ISBNs 0-486-20003-5, 0-486-20004-3

*Asimov, Isaac. *Asimov on Physics.* Avon 1979 $4.95. ISBN 0-380-41848-7 Collection of essays on various branches of physics.

Concise Dictionary of Physics. Oxford Univ Pr 1986 $17.95. ISBN 0-19-866142-8

CRC Handbook of Chemistry and Physics. CRC Pr 1989 (annual) $97.50. ISBN 0-8493-0470-9

Daintith, John (ed). *The Facts on File Dictionary of Physics.* Facts on File 1988 $19.95. ISBN 0-8160-1868-5

The Dictionary of Physics. Warner Bks 1986 $7.95. ISBN 0-446-38126-8

*McGrath, Susan. *Fun with Physics. Books for World Explorers Ser.* National Geographic 1986 $6.95. ISBN 0-87044-576-6 Explores the physics of fun and sports and physics in nature and in the home; suggests experiments that clarify principles.

McGraw-Hill Editors. *Dictionary of Physics.* McGraw 1986 $21.95. ISBN 0-07-045418-3

McGraw-Hill Editors. *Encyclopedia of Physics.* McGraw 1983 $82.50. ISBN 0-07-045253-9

Rothwell, William S. *The Vocabulary of Physics.* National Bk 1988 $13.95. ISBN 0-89420-250-2

MECHANICS: FORCES AND MOTION

*Bergmann, Peter G. *The Riddle of Gravitation.* Scribner's 1987 $2.65. ISBN 0-684-18460-5 Past and present theories of relativity and gravitation explained in readily understandable language by one of the world's leading experts in this field.

Casper, Barry M., and Richard Noer. *Revolutions in Physics.* Norton 1972 $21.95. ISBN 0-393-09405-7

Desloge, Edward A. *Classical Mechanics.* 2 vols. Krieger 1989. Vol. 1 $54.50. ISBN 0-89464-321-5. Vol. 2 $63.50. ISBN 0-89464-322-3

Dugas, René. *A History of Mechanics.* Dover 1988 $14.95. ISBN 0-486-65632-2

French, Anthony P. *Newtonian Mechanics.* Norton 1971 $14.95. ISBN 0-393-09970-9

Gallavotti, G. *The Elements of Mechanics.* Springer-Verlag 1983 $65.50. ISBN 0-387-11753-9

*Hancock, Ralph. *Understanding Movement. Understanding Science Ser.* Silver 1985. (o.p.) $15.66. ISBN 0-382-09084-5 Part of a series that demonstrates scientific content as it relates to different areas of life.

*Laithwarte, Eric. *Force: The Power Behind Movement. Science at Work Ser.* Watts 1986. (o.p.) $11.90. ISBN 0-531-10181-9 Investigates the art of using natural forces such as gravity and friction to make our lives better.

Lightman, Alan P., *et al. Problem Book in Relativity and Gravitation.* Princeton Univ Pr 1975 $19.95. ISBN 0-691-08162-X

MacKinnon, L. *Mechanics and Motion.* Oxford Univ Pr 1978 $10.95. ISBN 0-19-851843-9

McMullin, Ernan. *Newton on Matter and Activity.* Univ of Notre Dame Pr 1979 $5.95. ISBN 0-268-01343-8

Morecki, A. (ed). *Biomechanics of Motion.* Springer-Verlag 1981 $39.00. ISBN 0-387-81611-9

Pick, M., *et al. Theory of the Earth's Gravity Field.* Elsevier 1973. (o.p.) $147.50. ISBN 0-444-04939-4

Sears, Francis W. *Mechanics, Heat, and Sound.* Addison 1950 $35.50. ISBN 0-201-06905-9

*Taylor, Barbara. *Force and Movement. Science Starters Ser.* Watts 1990 $11.40. ISBN 0-531-14082-2 An investigative approach to demonstrate to younger readers how things start, stop, or change direction as a result of forces acting on them.

Watson, Philip. *Super Motion.* Lothrop 1982. (o.p.) $7.95. ISBN 0-688-00976-X

COPERNICUS, NICOLAUS   1473–1543

Nicolaus Copernicus's father died when his son was quite young, and the boy was raised by a wealthy and prestigious uncle. Thus young Copernicus had the advantage of a good education. He studied math and painting in his native Poland, and in 1496 he traveled to Italy to expand his studies. During the 10 years he remained in Italy, Copernicus studied medicine and law and dabbled in astronomy.

The time of Copernicus's youth, the latter part of the fifteenth century, was a time of intellectual ferment in Italy during which established ways were questioned and tested in all areas of society. Even the concept of a geocentric universe, propounded by the ancient Greek astronomers Hipparchus and Ptolemy, was open to debate. This universe was a system in which all heavenly bodies rotated about the earth. It might better have been called an egocentric universe. Scientists and astronomers placed human emotion before logic and scientific objectivity in concluding that our planet was the central body around which all other bodies in the universe rotated. The Church was in complete agreement with this concept.

The geocentric system was incredibly complex. Despite all the careful mathematics involved, however, the system was not very useful for predicting the positions of the planets over long periods of time. It occurred to Copernicus that tables of planetary motions could more easily be calculated for a heliocentric universe—one in which the sun was at the center. In such a system, the earth and all the other planets would move through space and revolve around the sun.

Copernicus set about working out the mathematical details that would demonstrate how planetary motions and positions could be calculated for a sun-centered universe. This new system explained some of the puzzling motions of the planets for which the old system could not account. In particular, the retrograde, or apparently backward, movement of several planets at different times was simply explained.

Copernicus's new system worked so well that he was tempted to consider it more than just a device for calculating planetary motions and positions. He began to think that perhaps this was the way things really were. Perhaps the earth, along with all the other heavenly bodies, really did move around the sun. The one significant error Copernicus made was to consider planetary orbits to be perfectly circular. His assumption required a number of mathematical adjustments to explain certain motions of some heavenly bodies. This error was corrected by the German astronomer Johannes Kepler some 50 years later. (*See* Kepler, Vol. 2, Earth Science: Astronomy.)

Copernicus described his system in a book, but he was reluctant to publish it, fearing that he would be labeled a heretic for suggesting that the earth was not the center of the universe, but instead moved around the sun. He returned to Poland in 1505. A few years later he circulated his manuscript among scholars, who received it with considerable enthusiasm.

Finally Copernicus agreed to have his book published. Prior to publication, the manuscript fell into the hands of a Lutheran minister who added an unauthorized preface to the effect that the Copernican theory was not advanced as a description of the actual facts. Because the preface was mistakenly attributed to Copernicus, the qualification weakened the book and compromised his reputation.

The book, *De Revolutionibus Orbium Coelestium,* was published in 1543, shortly before Copernicus's death, and began to win new adherents immediately. Within a few years of its publication, the book was used to create new tables of planetary motion. Thus began the Scientific Revolution.

BOOKS ABOUT COPERNICUS

Cohen, I. Bernard. *The Birth of a New Physics.* Norton 1985 $7.95. ISBN 0-393-30045-5 Survey of astronomy from Copernicus to Newton.

Hoyle, Fred. *Nicolas Copernicus: An Essay on His Life and Work.* Harper 1973. (o.p.) ISBN 0-06-011971-3 Reassessment of the work of the father of modern astronomy by another great astronomer.

Kuhn, Thomas S. *The Copernican Revolution: Planetary Astronomy in the Development of Western Thought.* Harvard Univ Pr 1957 $9.95. ISBN 0-674-17103-9 Exceptional account of Copernicus's thought, background, and impact.

NEWTON, ISAAC   1642–1727

The life of English physicist and mathematician Isaac Newton, whom many consider the greatest intellect of all time, got off to a rather inauspicious beginning. Born prematurely on Christmas day, 1642, Newton barely survived infanthood. At school he displayed no signs of unusual brightness. In fact, he was an ordinary student until well into his teens.

When he was in his teens, Newton was taken out of school to work on his mother's farm. Fortunately, his uncle urged that the young man be sent to Cambridge University. In 1660, Newton entered Trinity College of the university and graduated in 1665.

In 1666 Newton returned to his mother's farm to escape the plague epidemic that was ravaging London. He was already displaying some of the mathematical genius that the world would come to know. He had worked out a binomial theorem, and was working on the beginnings of what would later become the calculus.

Newton stayed on his mother's farm for about two years, and during this brief period he laid the foundations for the work that would make him famous. An apocryphal story is told that seeing an apple fall from a tree to the ground, Newton wondered if the same force which attracted the apple to the earth also attracted the moon to the earth. This bit of whimsy is said to have inspired

Newton to formulate the basis for the law of universal gravitation. His early attempts at calculating the value of this attractive force were unsuccessful, and he set the problem of gravitation aside for some 15 years.

During his stay at the farm, Newton conducted some revolutionary optical experiments. He observed the behavior of light as it passed through a prism. Not only was the light bent, or refracted, but it was separated into a band of colors similar to that seen in a rainbow. To prove that these colors were not produced within the prism, Newton directed the colored band of light into a second prism. This prism recombined the colors, and a beam of white light emerged from the prism. Thus Newton proved that visible white light consists of a spectrum of colors.

Newton's experiments with light made him famous. They also convinced him that spectra would be produced by light passing through the lenses of a refracting telescope and that the spectra would blur the details of the image produced (a phenomen called chromatic aberration). So in 1668 Newton invented a reflecting telescope, which concentrated light by means of a parabolic mirror.

Returning to Cambridge, Newton quickly became noted for his brilliance in mathematics. Three years later, in 1669, he was made a professor, when the head of the department resigned in his favor. He remained at Cambridge for the next 28 years.

In 1684 Newton successfully completed his calculations to prove the law of universal gravitation. In so doing, he calculated that planetary orbits are elliptical rather than circular. In that same year Newton began working on what is generally considered the greatest scientific book ever written. Newton wrote this work, *Philosophiae Naturalis Principia Mathematica,* entirely in Latin and completed it in 18 months. In it he codified the findings of Italian astronomer Galileo Galilei (*see* Galileo, Vol. 2, Earth Science: Astronomy) into three laws of motion. Included, of course, was the equation by which Newton was able to calculate the gravitational force between the earth and the moon. Newton maintained that this law of attraction applied to any two bodies in the universe, and thus it became the law of universal gravitation. The *Principia* was published in 1687, but no English version appeared until 1729, two years after Newton's death.

After the publication of his book, Newton's activities were diverted from science. He was elected a member of Parliament in 1689. Although he held his seat for more than two years, his only "speech" during that time was a simple request that a window be closed.

In 1696 Newton was appointed warden of the mint. He resigned his professorship at Cambridge to devote his full-time energies to improving the workings of the mint. His efforts thwarted the activities of the many counterfeiters who had flourished up to that time.

In 1704 Newton wrote *Opticks,* a book in which he summarized his work on light. Nine years later he wrote a second edition to his *Principia.* However, these works pale in significance when compared with his first book. With the first edition of *Principia,* Newton showed that the universe runs according to natural laws that are readily understood and without exception. He thus ushered in the Age of Reason—the intellectual movement of the 1600s and 1700s also known as the Enlightenment.

BOOKS ABOUT NEWTON

Boss, Valentin. *Newton and Russia: The Early Influence 1698–1796.* Harvard Univ Pr 1972 $28.00. ISBN 0-674-62275-8 Traces the influence of Newton during the reign of Peter the Great up through the Catherinian era and how his revolutionary theories altered the development of natural philosophy in Russia and laid the foundations for modern science.

Brewster, Sir David. *Memoirs of the Life, Writings, and Discoveries of Sir Isaac Newton. The Sources of Science Series.* 2 vols. Johnson Repr 1966 $60.00. ISBN 0-384-05703-9 Classic and complete account of all the important aspects of Newton's life.

Christianson, Gale E. *In the Presence of the Creator: Isaac Newton and His Times.* Free Pr 1984 $19.95. ISBN 0-02-905190-8 Portrait of Newton in the context of the world and science before the Enlightenment.

Hall, Rupert. *From Galileo to Newton.* Dover 1981 $7.95. ISBN 0-486-24227-7 Ends with Newton's major contributions to science.

Hawking, Stephen, and W. Israel (eds). *Three Hundred Years of Gravitation.* Cambridge Univ Pr 1989 $34.50. ISBN 0-521-37976-8 Eleven papers presented by world-class cosmologists and physicists to commemorate the three hundredth anniversary of the publication of Newton's *Principia.*

Mandrou, Robert. *From Humanism to Science, 1480–1700.* Penguin 1979 $6.95. ISBN 0-14-022079-8 Intellectual developments and their social context, from Erasmus to Newton.

*McTavish, Douglas. *Isaac Newton. Pioneers of Science Ser.* Watts 1990 $12.40. ISBN 0-531-18351-3 Story of Newton and his great achievements, written for younger readers; includes diagrams, glossary, and bibliography.

Palter, Robert (ed). *The Annus Mirabilis of Sir Isaac Newton.* MIT Pr 1970 $18.00. ISBN 0-262-16035-8 Wide variety of essays by specialists and general historians of ideas, science, art, philosophy, and religions covering all aspects of Newton's life and thought.

Westfall, Richard. *Never at Rest: A Biography of Isaac Newton.* Cambridge Univ Pr 1983 $24.95. ISBN 0-521-27435-4 Portrait of Newton's many-faceted personality.

MECHANICS: WORK, ENERGY, AND POWER

Adkins, Robert K. *An Introduction to Thermal Physics.* Cambridge Univ Pr 1987 $12.95. ISBN 0-521-33715-1

Bulliet, R. W. *The Camel and the Wheel.* Harvard Univ Pr 1975. (o.p.) $27.00. ISBN 0-674-09130-2

Fenn, John B. *Engines, Energy and Entropy: A Thermodynamics Primer.* Freeman 1982 $13.95. ISBN 0-7167-1282-2

*Gardner, Robert. *Energy Projects for Young Scientists.* Watts 1987 $12.90. ISBN 0-531-10338-2 Suggests more than 60 projects students can carry out to investigate energy, work, and power.

Gattegno, Caleb. *Forms of Energy.* Ed Solutions 1963 $3.85. ISBN 0-85225-682-5

Gordon, Douglas. *Energy.* David and Charles 1984 $19.95. ISBN 0-7134-4484-3

Grannis, Gary E. *Modern Power Mechanics.* Macmillan 1979 $26.56. ISBN 0-672-97130-5

Hesse, Mary. *Forces and Fields.* Greenwood 1970 $27.50. ISBN 0-8371-3366-1

*McKie, Robin. *Energy. Science Frontiers Ser.* Watts 1989 $12.90. ISBN 0-531-19509-0 Presents the latest research and developments in energy and discusses alternative energy sources, including the sun, wind, and tides; for younger readers.

*Taylor, Barbara. *Energy and Power. Science Starters Ser.* Watts 1990 $11.40. ISBN 0-531-14080-6 Discusses for young readers the nature of energy, energy sources, and uses of energy.

ARCHIMEDES *c.* 287 BC–212 BC

See also Archimedes, Vol. 1, Geometry: Solid Geometry and Space.

Archimedes was perhaps the greatest scientist and mathematician of ancient times. His equal did not appear on the scene until English mathematician and physicist Isaac Newton (*see* Newton, Vol. 2, Physics: Mechanics: Forces and Motion) was born some 1,800 years after Archimedes' death.

Archimedes was born in Syracuse, Sicily, and studied in Alexandria under the tutelage of a former student of Greek mathematician, Euclid. (*See* Euclid, Vol. 1, Geometry: Euclidean Geometry.) After completing his studies, Archimedes returned to Syracuse and resumed his friendship with the Syracusan king, Hieron II.

Archimedes is credited with a great number of scientific and mathematical discoveries and inventions, and the stories about this Greek genius are legion. One of the best-known stories is that of Archimedes' response to Hieron's request to test the king's new crown to determine whether it was pure gold or, as the king suspected, a mixture of silver and gold. Hieron instructed that the test be conducted without damaging the crown in any way.

As the story goes, Archimedes used the volume of water displaced by the crown to make his determination. He discovered that the crown was not pure gold, and the goldsmith who created the crown was summarily executed for trying to cheat the king.

Archimedes also worked out the principle of the lever in full mathematical detail. He demonstrated that a large weight placed near the fulcrum of the lever would be balanced by a smaller weight placed at some distance from the fulcrum. He went on to determine the quantitative relationships between the weights and their respective distances from the fulcrum.

In explaining how a lever worked, Archimedes proclaimed, "Give me a place to stand and I can move the world" (with a lever, of course). On hearing this boast, Hieron challenged Archimedes to move something remarkably large. As the story goes, Archimedes constructed a system of compound levers and singlehandedly raised a fully loaded ship from the water and carried it to shore.

Archimedes is also credited with other achievements, such as the invention of a hollow, screw-shaped cylinder that could be used as a water pump. Such a device is still known as the Archimedes screw.

However impressive his accomplishments in the field of physics, Archimedes was not impressed with his own mechanical achievements. He was much happier with his mathematical works, which he was more than willing to publish.

He calculated the value for *pi*—the ratio of the circumference of any circle to its diameter—to a greater degree of precision than anyone had theretofore obtained. He did so by calculating the dimensions of polygons described inside and outside a circle. His method was similar to methods used in the calculus hundreds of years later. Many scholars agree that Archimedes would have discovered the calculus hundreds of years before Newton if he had had a reliable system of mathematical symbols to work with.

Archimedes' fame was not limited to his achievements in the fields of science and mathematics. Among his contemporaries, in fact, his greatest fame was as a warrior. When he was in his nineties, Archimedes served Syracuse in its defense against a Roman invasion. For three years, Archimedes almost singlehandedly kept an entire Roman fleet at bay. According to the stories, Archimedes constructed giant lenses that were used to set the Roman ships on fire, large cranes that overturned the ships, and other ingenious devices designed to prevent the fleet from invading. Eventually, however, the Romans were victorious, and during the looting and pillaging of Syracuse, Archimedes was killed. Out of respect for Archimedes' reputation and accomplishments, the Roman general Marcellus mourned his death and directed that he be given an honorable burial.

BOOKS ABOUT ARCHIMEDES

Clagett, Marshall. *Archimedes in the Middle Ages.* Vol. 2 *The Translation from the Greek by William Moerbeke. Memoir Ser.* Vol. 117 Am Philos 1976 $40.00. ISBN 0-87169-117-5 Volumes I through V (see below) explore and document Archimedes' influence on thought in the Middle Ages.

Clagett, Marshall. *Archimedes in the Middle Ages.* Vol. 3 *Fate of the Medieval Architect. Memoir Ser.* Vol. 125 Am Philos 1978 $90.00. ISBN 0-87169-125-6

Clagett, Marshall. *Archimedes in the Middle Ages.* Vol. 4 *Medieval Traditions of Conic Sections. Memoir Ser.* Vol. 137 Am Philos 1980 $80.00. ISBN 0-87169-137-X

Clagett, Marshall. *Archimedes in the Middle Ages.* Vol. 5 *Quasi-Archimedean Geometry in the Thirteenth Century. Memoir Ser.* Vol. 157 Am Philos 1984 $90.00. ISBN 0-87169-157-4

STATES OF MATTER

Frisch, Otto R. *The Nature of Matter.* Dutton 1972. (o.p.) $7.95.

Goodstein, David L. *States of Matter.* Dover 1985 $9.95. ISBN 0-486-64927-X

*Gottleib, Milton, *et al. Seven States of Matter. Westinghouse Search Books.* Walker 1966. (o.p.) $7.95. ISBN 0-8027-0258-9 Excellent discussion of the nature of matter; an easily accessible, nonmathematical treatment.

Mathias, Marilynne, and Robert Johnson. *Matter and Energy.* New Readers 1983 $10.00. ISBN 0-88336-850-1

Maxwell, James C. *Maxwell on Molecules and Gases.* MIT Pr 1986. (o.p.) $55.00. ISBN 0-262-07094-4

Mulvey, J. H. (ed.). *The Nature of Matter: Wolfson College Lectures, 1980.* Oxford Univ Pr 1981 $18.95. ISBN 0-19-851151-5

See also Vol. 2, Chemistry: Matter.

ELECTROMAGNETIC WAVES: LIGHT AND THE QUANTUM THEORY

*Calder, Nigel. *Einstein's Universe.* Penguin 1980 $7.95. ISBN 0-14-005499-5 Using no mathematics, the theory of relativity is explained.

Davies, P. C., and J. Brown (eds). *The Ghost in the Atom: A Discussion of the Mysteries of Quantum Physics.* Cambridge Univ Pr 1986 $14.95. ISBN 0-521-31316-3

DeBoer, J., and E. Dal (eds). *The Lesson of Quantum Theory.* Elsevier 1986 $48.75. ISBN 0-444-87012-1

DeBroglie, Louis. *Revolution in Physics: A Non-Mathematical Survey of Quanta.* Ralph Niemeyer (tr). Greenwood 1970 $35.00. ISBN 0-8371-2582-0

Fine, Arthur. *The Shaky Game: Einstein, Realism, and the Quantum Theory.* Univ of Chicago Pr 1986 $25.00. ISBN 0-226-24946-8

Fluegge, S. *Practical Quantum Mechanics.* Springer-Verlag 1987 $38.00. ISBN 0-387-07050-8

Gamow, George. *Thirty Years That Shook Physics: The Story of Quantum Mechanics.* Dover 1984 $4.95. ISBN 0-486-24895-X

*Gribbin, John. *In Search of the Big Bang: Quantum Physics and Cosmology.* Bantam 1986 $9.95. ISBN 0-553-34258-4 A clear explanation of quantum physics and theories devised to explain creation of the universe.
*Hecht, Jeff. *Understanding Lasers.* Sams 1988 $17.95. ISBN 0-672-27274-1 Introduction to lasers, what they are, how they work, and how they are used.
Jackson, Daphne F. *Atoms and Quanta.* Academic Pr 1989 $29.95. ISBN 0-12-379075-1
Jauch, Josef M. *Are Quanta Real? A Galilean Dialogue.* Indiania Univ Pr $7.95. ISBN 0-253-20545-X
Shankar, R. *Principles of Quantum Mechanics.* Plenum 1980 $37.50. ISBN 0-306-40397-8

EINSTEIN, ALBERT 1879–1955

Whenever scientific giants are discussed, German-born physicist Albert Einstein is often placed in the same category as English physicist and mathematician Isaac Newton—head and shoulders above all others. (*See* Newton, Vol. 2, Physics: Mechanics: Forces and Motion.) It seems fitting, then, that Einstein, like Newton, was a "late bloomer." As a child, Einstein showed no intellectual promise. In fact, he was so slow in learning to speak that his parents feared he might be learning-impaired.

As it turned out, Einstein was not incapable of learning; he was simply uninterested in all subjects except mathematics. He also felt that the strict discipline and exercise drills at school interfered with intellectual curiosity and growth. He dropped out of school at the age of 15, but later returned for a year to make up the courses he needed to graduate.

Einstein gained admittance to a college in Switzerland and managed to graduate. After graduation, the only job he was able to find was as a junior official at the patent office in Berne, Switzerland. The job left him with plenty of free time to work on problems in physics.

In 1905, with virtually no academic connections, he earned his Ph.D. in physics and had three important papers published. One paper dealt with the photoelectric effect. Einstein applied the quantum theory to solve a problem that had proved impossible to solve using classical physics. This was the first practical application of German physicist Max Planck's revolutionary theory. (*See* Planck, Vol. 2, Physics: Electromagnetic Waves: Light and the Quantum Theory.) Sixteen years later Einstein would receive the Nobel Prize in physics for this feat. It is now claimed that Einstein's wife was an unacknowledged contributor to this work and the resulting paper.

As improbable as it may seem, Einstein's work with the photoelectric effect was not his most important accomplishment of the year. A second paper dealt with statistical aspects of molecular motion and Brownian movement. This paper provided a proof for the existence of atoms. His third, and most important, paper introduced his special theory of relativity.

Ten years later, Einstein published his theory of general relativity, a new theory of gravitation that included Newton's theory as a special case. The work accomplished by Einstein over this 10-year period was to make him the most famous and highly respected scientist since Isaac Newton.

In 1933 Einstein was visiting the United States when Adolf Hitler came to power in Germany. Einstein spoke out against Hitler's racial and political policies and resigned his position at the University of Berlin. He accepted a position at the Institute for Advanced Study in Princeton, New Jersey, and became a U.S. citizen in 1940. To the end of his life, Einstein fought for nonproliferation of nuclear weapons and for some accord among world powers to end the threat of nuclear warfare.

BOOKS BY EINSTEIN

Essays in Physics. Philosophical Lib 1985 $3.95. ISBN 0-8022-2482-2
Ideas and Opinions (1954). Crown 1985 $6.95. ISBN 0-517-55601-X
Investigations on the Theory of the Brownian Movement (1905). R. Furch (ed). Dover 1926 $3.50. ISBN 0-486-60304-0
The Principles of Relativity (1923). Dover 1950 $4.50. ISBN 0-486-60081-5
Relativity: The Special and General Theory (1918). Robert W. Lawson (tr). Crown 1961 $3.95. ISBN 0-517-02530-2
Sidelights on Relativity. Dover 1983 $2.95. ISBN 0-486-24511-X
Out of My Later Years (1950). Carol 1973 $6.95. ISBN 0-8065-0357-2

BOOKS ABOUT EINSTEIN

*Apfel, Necia H. *It's All Relative: Einstein's Theory of Relativity.* Lothrop 1985 $7.25. ISBN 0-688-04301-1 By using simple examples, a very difficult theory is explained; a complex subject in an understandable treatment.
*Bernstein, Jeremy. *Einstein.* Penguin 1976 $6.95. ISBN 0-14-004317-9 Biography and scientific theories of Einstein.
Clark, Ronald W. *Einstein: The Life and Times.* Avon 1979 $5.95. ISBN 0-380-01159-X Complete biography using new material to present a moving portrait of Einstein as a tragic figure of our time and a man of great contradictions.
*Cwiklik, Robert. *Albert Einstein and the Theory of Relativity.* Barron 1987 $4.95. ISBN 0-8120-3921-1 Traces the life and work of the physicist; a highly readable account that keeps the young reader spellbound.
French, A. P. (ed). *Einstein: A Centenary Volume.* Harvard Univ Pr 1979. (o.p.) $26.00. ISBN 0-674-24230-0 Total assessment of the life and works of Einstein with main chapters by famous scientists.
Friedman, Alan J., and Carol Donley. *Einstein as Myth and Muse.* Cambridge Univ Pr 1989. (o.p.) $22.95. ISBN 0-521-26720-X A scientist and a literary critic assess the impact of the revolution in physical theory on literature.
Goldsmith, Maurice, *et al* (eds). *Einstein: The First Hundred Years.* Pergamon 1980 $34.00. ISBN 0-08-025019-X Collection of articles on the impact of Einstein by various thinkers, including Roland Barthes and Arthur C. Clarke.
Hoffmann, Banesh. *Albert Einstein, Creator and Rebel.* NAL 1973 $8.95. ISBN 0-452-26193-7 Illustrated memoir by a collaborating physicist showing the growth of ideas that led Einstein to his most important theories.
Holton, Gerald, and Yehuda Elkana (eds). *Albert Einstein: Historical and Cultural Perspectives: The Centennial Symposium in Jerusalem.* Princeton Univ Pr 1982 $13.95. ISBN 0-691-02383-2 Impact of Einstein's work on science to humanistic studies by various contributors.
*Sayen, Jamie. *Einstein in America.* Crown 1985 $17.95. ISBN 0-517-55604-9 An emphasis on the scientist's personal life and the many causes he supported, including Zionism and pacifism.

PLANCK, MAX KARL ERNST LUDWIG   1858–1947

German-born Max Planck attended college at the University of Berlin, where he studied under such highly regarded contemporary scientists as Hermann Helmholtz and Gustav Kirchoff. In 1880, at the age of 22, he joined the faculty at Munich, and five years later he received a professorship at Kiel University. In 1889 he replaced Kirchoff, who had died two years earlier, at the University of Berlin. He remained there until he retired in 1926.

Planck was particularly interested in a problem, first raised by Kirchoff, concerning a black body. Simply stated, the problem was that if the black body absorbs all frequencies of light, then it should, when heated, radiate all frequencies. Scientists had been unable to work out mathematical equations to describe how the radiation of the black body was distributed.

In 1900 Planck worked out an equation that solved the problem. The equation was based on the radical assumption that energy, like matter, existed in particles, or bundles. Planck called these bundles *quanta,* plural of the Latin *quantum,* which means "how much?" Planck further theorized that the size of the quantum for any particular electromagnetic radiation was in direct proportion to the frequency of the radiation. Thus, a quantum of high-frequency violet light would contain twice as much energy as a quantum of low-frequency red light.

Planck made one final assumption, that energy can be absorbed or emitted only in whole quanta. Using these assumptions, he was able to explain the distribution of radiation from a black body.

Planck's quantum theory was so revolutionary that it was not readily accepted by physicists. In fact, Planck had some difficulty believing it himself. He half suspected that it might be a mathematical anomaly, with no correspondence to anything real.

In 1905, German-born physicist Albert Einstein applied the quantum theory to the photoelectric effect. (*See* Einstein, Vol. 2, Physics: Electromagnetic Waves: Light and the Quantum Theory.) Eight years later, Danish physicist Niels Bohr incorporated the theory into the structure of the atom. (*See* Bohr, Vol. 2, Chemistry: Matter.) In both cases, phenomena were explained that could not be explained by nineteenth-century physics. The quantum theory thus introduced a new age of physics. The classical physics of the period before 1900 had to make room for the era of modern physics. In 1918 Planck was awarded the Nobel Prize in physics for his notable contribution.

BOOKS BY PLANCK

Scientific Autobiography and Other Papers (1949). Frank Gaynor (tr). Greenwood 1968 $22.50. ISBN 0-8371-0194-8

Where Is Science Going? (1933). James Murphy (tr). Ox Bow 1981 $10.00. ISBN 0-918024-21-8

Between Elite and Mass Education: Education in the Federal Republic of Germany. State Univ of New York Pr 1983 $19.95. ISBN 0-87395-708-3

BOOKS ABOUT PLANCK

Heilbron, J. L. *The Dilemmas of an Upright Man: Max Planck as Spokesman for German Science.* Univ of California Pr 1986 $25.00. ISBN 0-520-05710-4 Concentrates on Planck's courageous efforts to oppose Nazi policies on behalf of German science.

Rosenthal-Schneider, Ilse. *Reality and Scientific Truth: Discussions with Einstein, von Laue, and Planck.* Books Demand 1980 $38.80. Includes selections of correspondences between the author and Planck and well as connecting text concerning the nature of scientific truth and physical reality, in addition to lighter topics.

SOUND

Berg, Richard E., and David G. Stork. *The Physics of Sound.* Prentice 1982. ISBN 0-13-674283-1

Burrows, David. *Sound, Speech, and Music.* Univ of Massachusetts Pr 1990 $20.00. ISBN 0-87023-685-7

Dowling, Ann, and John E. Williams. *Sound and Sources of Sound.* Prentice 1983 $36.95. ISBN 0-470-27388-7

Hunt, Frederick V. *Origins in Acoustics: The Science of Sound from Antiquity to the Age of Newton.* Yale Univ Pr 1978 $25.00. ISBN 0-300-02220-4

*Knight, David C. *Silent Sound: The World of Ultrasonics.* Morrow 1980. (o.p.) $10.00. ISBN

0-688-2244-7 Clear, easy-to-read introduction to the subject and the applications of ultrasonics.

Rayleigh, Strutt. *Theory of Sound.* Dover Vol. 1 $9.95. ISBN 0-486-60292-3. Vol. 2 $9.95. ISBN 0-486-60293-1

Rossing, Thomas D. *The Science of Sound: Musical, Electronic, Environmental.* Addison 1981 $34.36. ISBN 0-201-06505-3

Schafer, R. Murray. *The Tuning of the World.* Knopf 1977. (o.p.) $12.95. ISBN 0-394-40966-3

White, Frederick. *Our Acoustic Environment.* Krieger 1975 $39.50. ISBN 0-471-93920-X

ELECTRICITY AND MAGNETISM

Bleaney, B. I., and B. Bleaney. *Electricity and Magnetism.* Oxford Univ Pr 1976 $29.95. ISBN 0-19-851141-8

Chikazumi, Sushin, and Stanley H. Charap. *Physics of Magnetism.* Krieger 1978 $45.50. ISBN 0-88275-662-1

Dobles, E. R. *Electricity and Magnetism.* Good Apple 1985. (o.p.) $4.95. ISBN 0-86653-269-2

Duffin, W. J. *Electricity and Magnetism.* McGraw 1989 $21.00. ISBN 0-07-084111-X

Edminster, Joseph. *Schaum's Outline of Electromagnets.* McGraw 1983 $9.95. ISBN 0-07-018984-6

Foner, S. *Magnetism: Selected Topics.* Gordon & Breach 1976 $233.00. ISBN 0-677-15390-2

Fowler, Richard J. *Electricity: Principles and Applications.* McGraw 1984 $35.40. ISBN 0-07-021708-4

*Goldberg, Joel. *Fundamentals of Electricity.* Prentice 1981 $40.00. ISBN 0-13-337006-2 An introduction to electricity, with topics ranging from batteries to electronics.

*Gutnik, Martin J. *Electricity: From Faraday to Solar Generators.* First Books Ser. Watts 1986 $10.40. ISBN 0-531-10222-X Discusses discoveries and inventions involving electricity, with emphasis on Faraday's electric motor; for younger readers.

Kaganov, M. T., and V. M. Tsukernik. *The Nature of Magnetism.* Imported 1985 $4.95. ISBN 0-8285-2948-5

*Math, Irwin. *Wires and Watts: Understanding and Using Electricity.* Macmillan 1988 $14.95. ISBN 0-689-71298-7 Excellent introduction to electricity; provides clear working models and simple experiments.

McCaig, M. *Permanent Magnets in Theory and Practice.* Halsted 1987. (o.p.) $94.95. ISBN 0-470-21003-6

*Vogt, Gregory. *Electricity and Magnetism.* First Books Ser. Watts 1985 $10.40. ISBN 0-531-10038-3 A history, written for a young audience, of our understanding of electricity and magnetism; includes discussion of recent developments and simple experiments with magnets, batteries, and electrical circuits.

*White, Jack R. *The Hidden World of Forces.* Putnam 1987 $11.95. ISBN 0-396-08947-X Renowned author shows how forces are working around us all the time.

Wood, Robert. *Understanding Magnetism: Magnets, Electromagnets, and Superconducting Magnets.* TAB 1988 $10.60. ISBN 0-8306-2772-3

EDISON, THOMAS ALVA   1847–1931

Thomas Edison was one of the greatest inventors in history. Although he received virtually no formal training in science, he made up for this lack with intelligence, ingenuity, and an insatiable curiosity. These traits, combined with a boundless energy, meant that Edison was virtually unstoppable as an inventive genius. (He, modestly perhaps, defined genius as "one percent inspiration and ninety-nine percent perspiration.")

In his early years Edison's great curiosity was both an asset and a liability.

He constantly bombarded his mother, a former schoolteacher, with questions she could not answer. When Edison entered school at age 7, he soon irritated his teacher with his unending barrage of questions. The teacher said that the young Edison was "addled," so infuriating Edison's mother that she took him out of school. Thus Edison's formal education lasted a grand total of three months.

Edison's mother took over her son's education, but he learned so fast that by age 9, she could no longer teach him. She bought him a chemistry book, and young Thomas set out to test every experiment described in the book. He explained that he could not trust the statements in the book until he had seen the results for himself.

At age 12 Edison took a job selling newspapers on a train that ran between Port Huron and Detroit, Michigan. Having set up a makeshift laboratory and a printing press in the baggage car of the train, he published a weekly newspaper and conducted experiments in his spare time. Unfortunately a chemical fire led to his being thrown off the train—printing press, chemicals, and all.

An accident Edison suffered as a young man led to his becoming increasingly deaf as he grew older. In his later years, Edison could barely hear a shout. Rather than considering his deafness to be a handicap, he claimed that the condition made it easier for him to concentrate.

Edison's career advanced from selling newspapers to working as a telegrapher. In 1868, while working in Boston, Edison patented his first invention—a device designed to speed up the recording of votes in Congress. Dismayed to learn that congressmen had no desire to streamline their time-honored system, Edison vowed never to produce another unneeded or unwanted invention.

In 1869, Edison drifted to New York. Sleeping at night in the office of a stock-ticker firm, Edison became well acquainted with the stock ticker and, when this device broke down, repaired it when no one else was able to do so. He was immediately offered a supervisory job, which he quickly accepted. In the course of these labors, he made improvements in the stock ticker, which he patented. He sold these patents for the then unheard-of sum of $40,000, and his career as a full-time inventor was launched.

In 1876 Edison set up a laboratory in Menlo Park, New Jersey. That same year he improved the telephone by adding a carbon transmitter, which made it possible to talk over the telephone without having to shout. He also invented the phonograph, which he always claimed was his favorite invention.

In 1878 Edison set about the task of producing light by electricity. He determined that this feat could be accomplished by means of a glowing filament sealed in an evacuated glass bulb. However, the search for a suitable material for the filament almost proved to be Edison's undoing. Eventually he discovered that a simple piece of scorched thread would do the job.

On New Year's Eve 1879, Edison's electric light bulbs were used to illuminate the main street of Menlo Park, an event that was reported in newspapers all over the world. However, Edison realized that in order to make electric lighting practical, a system for generating electricity and delivering it on demand was needed. By 1881 Edison had built a generating station to serve part of Manhattan in New York City with direct current. This was a major achievement.

Edison's later inventions included important improvements to the motion picture camera, invented earlier by American inventor and industrialist George Eastman, and initial efforts at producing talking pictures. He also invented or improved upon the storage battery, a cement mixer, the dictaphone, and a duplicating machine. Edison was active until his death in 1931. In 1960 he was elected a member of the Hall of Fame for Great Americans.

BOOK BY EDISON

Diary and Sundry Observations of Thomas Alva Edison. D. D. Runes (ed). Greenwood 1968 $35.00. ISBN 0-8371-0067-4

BOOKS ABOUT EDISON

Buranelli, Vincent. *Thomas Alva Edison. Pioneers in Change Ser.* Silver 1989 $11.98. ISBN 0-382-09522-7 Explores the life, work, and legacy of this outstanding contributor to world progress.

Clark, Ronald W. *Edison: The Man Who Made the Future.* Putnam 1977. (o.p.) $12.95. ISBN 0-399-11952-3 Illustrated biography that describes Edison's early untutored upbringing, his first inventions, and his struggle with the industrial jungle after the Civil War and up through World War I.

*Greene, Carol. *Thomas Alva Edison: Bringer of Light. People of Distinction Ser.* Childrens 1985 $15.93. ISBN 0-516-03213-5 In-depth biography on the work Edison performed and the ideas he projected.

Jenkins, Reese V., *et al* (eds). *The Papers of Thomas Alva Edison.* Vol. 1 *The Making of an Inventor, February 1847–June 1873.* Johns Hopkins Univ Pr 1989 $65.00. ISBN 0-8018-3100-8 Documents Edison's inventions; includes journal entries, sketches, and drawings; first volume in a series to be published.

Josephson, Matthew. *Edison.* McGraw 1959 $10.95. ISBN 0-07-033046-8 Complete biography focusing on Edison's life and individuality as an inventor.

FARADAY, MICHAEL   1791–1867

Michael Faraday was one of 10 children born to an English blacksmith and his wife. Faraday's father had neither the background to recognize the importance of an education nor the means to pay for one. Young Michael was apprenticed to a bookbinder. While a formal education was not possible, Faraday's exposure to books was fortunate indeed. His employer permitted him to attend scientific lectures and to read the books he was helping to bind.

In 1812 Faraday attended a lecture given by Humphrey Davy, a noted specialist in electrochemistry. Captivated by Davy's lecture, Faraday contacted the famous scientist, requesting a position as his assistant. At first Faraday's request was denied, but he persisted and eventually Davy hired him.

Faraday proved himself more than worthy of Davy's consideration. He spent every waking hour working in the laboratory. In 1825 Faraday became director of the laboratory. Eight years later this self-educated son of a blacksmith became a professor of chemistry at the Royal Institution.

Faraday's career as a chemist and physicist is marked by a number of milestones. His earliest accomplishment was to devise methods for liquefying gases under pressure. During the course of this activity, he became the first person to produce temperatures colder than 0 degrees on the Fahrenheit scale. In 1825 Faraday discovered benzene, a compound that was to have significant importance in the field of organic chemistry.

While pursuing his own investigations, Faraday continued to carry out Davy's work in electrochemistry. He named the process of electrolysis and also named many of the components used in the process. Many terms, such as *electrolyte, electrode, anode,* and *cathode,* still in use today, were coined by Faraday.

In 1832 Faraday identified certain physical regularities, known today as Faraday's laws of electrolysis. These laws, which reduced electrolysis to quantitative terms, concerned the masses of substances liberated during electrolysis reactions. These laws established the modern basis for electrochemistry.

As if Faraday had not been busy enough with his activities in electrochemistry, he also found time to indulge his fascination with the relationship between electricity and magnetism. In 1821 he constructed a device that converted electric current to mechanical movement—a simple electric motor. But this was merely a diversion for Faraday. Over the next 10 years, his investigations led to the discovery of electrical induction and the invention of the electric generator. This former bookbinder's apprentice had set the stage for the future electrification on planet Earth.

BOOK BY FARADAY

The Chemical History of a Candle: Six Illustrated Lectures with Notes and Experiments. Chicago Review 1988 $19.95. ISBN 0-89783-047-4

BOOKS ABOUT FARADAY

Agassi, Joseph. *Faraday as a Natural Philosopher.* Univ of Chicago Pr 1971. ISBN 0-226-01046-5 Integrates two portraits—the private, personal, and psychological with the public, scientific man, demonstrating that Faraday saw himself as a natural philosopher.

*Epstein, Sam, and Beryl Epstein. *Michael Faraday: Apprentice to Science.* Garrard 1971. (o.p.) ISBN 0-8116-4511-8   An interesting, well-written account of Faraday's rise from apprentice bookbinder to scientist and inventor.

Williams, L. Pearce. *Faraday: A Biography.* Basic 1964. (o.p.) Definitive biography using unpublished and published papers and Faraday's diaries to trace the metamorphosis of Faraday's ideas from speculation to orthodox scientific theory.

FRANKLIN, BENJAMIN   1706–1790

See also Franklin, Vol. 2, United States History: The United States Constitution.

Benjamin Franklin, who was selected as a charter member of the Hall of Fame for Great Americans in 1900, was a man of many talents and accomplishments. He was a scientist, an inventor, a printer, a writer, a politician, a diplomat, and a philosopher. And he filled all these roles with flair and a style that made him one of the best-known persons of his time. He was the only American of colonial times to achieve a reputation in Europe.

Franklin invented many useful and diverse devices, among the most notable being bifocal glasses and a stove that was a vast improvement over previous models in its capacity to heat a room efficiently. He seemed almost to accomplish these things in his spare time.

Perhaps Franklin's most famous scientific investigations dealt with static electricity. Franklin was fascinated with the Leyden jar, a metal-lined jar that could store large quantities of static electric charge. The jar could be discharged by bringing a hand near a metal rod inserted in the jar. The discharge consisted of a discernable and sometimes quite powerful electric spark.

Franklin thought that the spark was similar to lightning, and he set out to test this observation. During a thunderstorm, Franklin flew a kite to which a pointed wire and a silk thread were attached. He reckoned that these items would be charged by the electricity associated with the storm. At the height of the storm, Franklin placed his hand near a key that had been tied to the silk thread, and a spark leaped between his hand and the key. He had proved that lightning was, indeed, an electric discharge.

News of the results of Franklin's kite experiment quickly spread throughout the scientific community. He was made a member of the prestigious Royal Society. At the same time, the dangerous nature of the experiment became tragically apparent when the next two people to repeat the experiment were killed.

A practical outcome of the kite experiment was Franklin's invention of the lightning rod. These pointed metal rods were attached to roofs of buildings, with wire conductors leading to the ground. By discharging electricity from clouds safely, these devices protected the buildings.

Even while he was serving his nation as a statesman, Franklin's scientific mind continued to work. It had been known for some time that there are two kinds of electric charge. Items charged with similar types of charge repel one another, and items charged with different types of charge are attracted to one another. Franklin suggested that the terms *positive* and *negative* be given to the two types of charge. This convention is still in use today.

Throughout his life, Franklin was constantly making observations and seeking answers to scientific phenomena. He plotted the courses of storms over the North American continent. He was the first person to study the northward flow of ocean water along the east coast of the United States. This huge stream of warm ocean water is now called the Gulf Stream. And he accomplished all these things while deeply involved in many unrelated but very demanding activities. He was a writer, printer, and publisher. He was Postmaster of Philadelphia, and he organized that city's first fire department. He served as a diplomat in England during the difficult years before the American Revolution, and he helped draft the Declaration of Independence when his diplomatic efforts were unsuccessful. He was appointed minister to France. And he was a delegate to the Constitutional Convention. The question is—when did he find time for his scientific endeavors?

BOOKS BY FRANKLIN

Autobiography (1789). Random 1990 $8.50. ISBN 0-679-72613-6

The Autobiography and Other Writings Peter Shaw (ed). Bantam 1982 $2.50. ISBN 0-553-21075-0

Benjamin Franklin: An Autobiographical Portrait. Alfred Tamarin (ed). Macmillan 1969. (o.p.) Collection of excerpts from Franklin's writings, which form an autobiography; includes the years after Franklin's *Autobiography.*

Poor Richard: The Almanack for the Years 1733–1758. Richard Saunders (ed). Heritage 1964. (o.p.) Each issue includes wise and witty sayings including, "Early to bed and early to rise, makes a man healthy, wealthy, and wise."

BOOKS ABOUT FRANKLIN

Bowen, Catherine D. *The Most Dangerous Man in America: Scenes From the Life of Benjamin Franklin.* Little 1986 $8.95. ISBN 0-313-10379-9 Selective narrative beginning with Franklin's boyhood in Boston and ending just before the Revolution.

Burlingame, Roger. *Benjamin Franklin, Envoy Extraordinary: The Secret Missions and Open Pleasures of Benjamin Franklin in London and Paris.* Coward 1967. (o.p.) Biography spanning Franklin's remarkable 30-year career as a diplomat and politician abroad, focusing on his secret missions.

Buxbaum, Melvin H. *Critical Essays on Benjamin Franklin. Critical Essays on American Literature Ser.* G. K. Hall 1987 $35.00. ISBN 0-8161-8699-5 Collection of essays on Franklin by various critics focusing on literary, political, economic, scientific, and religious concerns; includes D. H. Lawrence's attack on Franklin.

Clark, Ronald W. *Benjamin Franklin: A Biography. Quality Paperbacks Ser.* Da Capo 1989 $15.95. ISBN 0-306-80368-2 Biography that evaluates Franklin's many facets as a scientist, businessman, writer, and diplomat.

Lopez, Claude-Anne, and Eugenia W. Herbert. *The Private Franklin: The Man and His Family.* Norton 1985 $7.70. ISBN 0-303-30227-X A portrait of Franklin as family member—son, brother, husband, father, uncle, and grandfather—not as politician or scientist.

*Meltzer, Milton. *Benjamin Franklin: The New American.* Watts 1988 $14.95. ISBN 0-531-10582-2 Biography of Franklin the printer, publisher, businessman, author, inventor, scientist, politician, and diplomat.

Wright, Esmond. *Franklin of Philadelphia.* Harvard Univ Pr 1988 $12.95. ISBN 0-674-31809-9 Biography that presents Franklin as "an Old English man" and a reluctant revolutionary.

MAXWELL, JAMES CLERK   1831–1879

Scots physicist James Maxwell showed early signs of mathematical talent. He graduated second in his class in mathematics at Cambridge University and was appointed to his first professorship at Marischal College in Aberdeen, Scotland, in 1856.

In 1860 Maxwell applied his mathematical genius to understanding the behavior of the particles that make up gases. Maxwell treated the random, rapid motion of gas molecules statistically. In this work, he considered the molecules to be moving in all directions and at all velocities. He also considered collisions between molecules and collisions of molecules with the walls of the container. In association with Austrian physicist Ludwig Boltzmann, he worked out the Maxwell–Boltzmann kinetic theory of gases.

Maxwell's most significant work dealt with magnetic lines of force. He put forth the theory that electricity and magnetism could not exist in isolation. Where one was found, so, too, would the other. For this reason, Maxwell's work is often referred to as the electromagnetic theory.

Maxwell showed that the oscillation of an electric charge produces a magnetic field that radiates out from its source at the speed of light. This finding led him to suggest that light was a form of electromagnetic radiation. He also suggested that, since charges can oscillate at any velocity, an entire family of electromagnetic radiations should exist.

Maxwell died before his fiftieth birthday. A few years later, German physicist Heinrich Rudolf Hertz verified Maxwell's predictions for a broad spectrum of electromagnetic radiation.

BOOKS BY MAXWELL

Dynamical Theory of the Electromagnetic Field. Thomas F. Torrence (ed). Longwood 1983 $19.95. ISBN 0-7073-0324-9
Electricity and Magnetism (1891). 2 vols. Dover (repr of 1891 ed). Vol. 1 $9.50. ISBN 0-486-60637-6. Vol. 2 $9.50. ISBN 0-486-60637-6
Theory of Heat (1872). Greenwood 1970 $35.00. ISBN 0-8371-40497-8

BOOKS ABOUT MAXWELL

Buchwald, Jed Z. *From Maxwell to Microphysics: Aspects of the Electromagnetic Theory in the Last Quarter of the Nineteenth Century.* Univ of Chicago Pr 1988 $17.95. ISBN 0-226-07883-3 Study of one of the great transitions in the history of physics showing the importance of Maxwell.
Campbell, Lewis, and William Garnett. *Life of James C. Maxwell.* Johnson Repr 1970 $50.00. ISBN 0-384-07295-X Official biography written by an old school friend together with Maxwell's laboratory assistant.
Tricker, R. A. R. *The Contributions of Faraday and Maxwell to Electrical Science. Selected Readings in Physics Series.* Pergamon 1966. (o.p.) $25.00. Life story and important discoveries of Maxwell and Faraday, including papers written by each.

See also Vol. 2, Chemistry: Types of Study: Electrochemistry.

NUCLEAR PHYSICS

*Asimov, Isaac. *How Did We Find Out About Nuclear Power?* Walker 1976 $10.85. ISBN 0-8027-6266-2 Tells the story of how we learned to split the atom and harness the energy released.

*Halacy, Dan. *Nuclear Energy. First Book Ser.* Watts 1984 $10.40. ISBN 0-531-04829-2 Describes the production of nuclear energy and the development of nuclear science.

Waltar and Reynolds. *Fast Breeder Reactors.* Pergamon 1983 $37.50. ISBN 0-08-025982-0

FERMI, ENRICO 1901–1954

Enrico Fermi received his Ph.D. in physics at the University of Pisa in 1922, the same year that Benito Mussolini seized power in Italy. By 1926 Fermi was a professor of physics at the University of Rome.

Fermi developed a special interest in the neutron as soon as it was discovered by English physicist James Chadwick in 1932. Because the neutron carried no charge, it was not repelled by the positively charged nuclei of other atoms. This characteristic of the neutron made it possible for many new types of nuclear reactions to be initiated.

Fermi experimented with the bombardment of atomic nuclei by slow-moving neutrons. He hoped that the neutrons would be absorbed by the nuclei of the atoms, resulting in the creation of atoms of another, heavier element.

In 1934 Fermi bombarded the element uranium with neutrons in an attempt to produce an artificial element above uranium in the periodic table. He soon learned that he was flirting with the fission of uranium nuclei.

Fermi's anti-Fascist loyalties, along with his wife's Jewish ancestry, made it necessary for him and his wife to leave Italy. They immigrated to the United States in 1938, remaining there for the rest of their lives.

Knowledgeable about the tremendous amounts of energy that could be unleashed in a chain reaction during the fission of uranium nuclei, Fermi was placed in charge of building the structure needed to contain such a reaction. On December 2, 1942, the first successful controlled chain fission reaction was carried out. A little more than two years later, the first atomic bomb was exploded over Japan.

In the ensuing years, Fermi witnessed the development of a far deadlier nuclear weapon—the H-bomb, which used the fusion reaction of hydrogen nuclei. Fermi joined with the American physicist Robert Oppenheimer and other scientists in opposing the more deadly nuclear devices. He did not live to see the application of the fission reaction to more peaceful endeavors—the production of power by nuclear plants.

BOOKS BY FERMI

Collected Papers of Enrico Fermi (1962). Emilio Segre (ed). 2 vols. Univ of Chicago Pr 1962 $60.00. ISBN 0-226-24359-1

Elementary Particles (1951). Elliots 1951 $49.50.

Nuclear Physics. Midway Reprints Ser. Univ of Chicago Pr 1974 $17.95. ISBN 0-226-24365-6

BOOKS ABOUT FERMI

Fermi, Laura. *Atoms in the Family: My Life with Enrico Fermi.* Univ of New Mexico Pr $10.95. ISBN 0-8263-1060-5 Biography of Fermi, written by his wife.

Lichello, Robert. *Fermi: Father of the Atomic Bomb. Outstanding Personalities Ser.* SamHar 1972 $3.95. ISBN 0-87157-511-6 Biography of Fermi, focusing on his personal life and his major contributions to the creation of the atomic bomb.

See also Vol. 2, Chemistry: Types of Study: Nuclear Chemistry *and* Structure of the Atom.

⁂ HEALTH ⁂

GENERAL REFERENCES

American Medical Association Staff. *The American Medical Association Family Medical Guide.* Random 1987 $24.95. ISBN 0-394-55582-1

American Medical Association Staff. *The American Medical Association Encyclopedia of Medicine.* Random 1989 $39.95. ISBN 0-394-56528-2

Bennett, William I., and G. Timothy Johnson. *Your Good Health: How to Stay Well and What to Do When You're Not.* Harvard Univ Pr 1987 $24.95. ISBN 0-674-96631-7

Blus, S. (ed). *The New Holistic Health Handbook.* Stephen Greene 1985. (o.p.)

Borysenko, Joan. *Minding the Body, Mending the Mind.* Addison 1987 $14.95. ISBN 0-201-10707-4

*Bourdillon, Hilary. *Women as Healers: A History of Women and Medicine.* Cambridge Univ Pr 1989 $5.95. ISBN 0-521-31090-3 Account of roles played by women in the history of western medicine.

Brody, Jane. *Jane Brody's The New York Times Guide to Personal Health.* Avon 1983 $12.95. ISBN 0-380-64121-6

* *The Complete Manual of Fitness and Well-Being.* Reader's Digest 1988 $26.95. ISBN 0-89577-270-1 Discusses human growth, body parts, exercise, diet, and health.

Dawood, Richard. *How to Stay Healthy Abroad.* Penguin 1988 $8.95. ISBN 0-14-010692-8

*Diagram Group Staff. *The Healthy Body: A Maintenance Manual.* NAL 1981 $8.95. ISBN

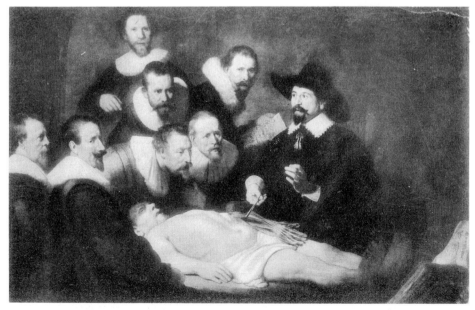

The Anatomy Lecture of Dr. Nicolaes Tulp. Painting by Rembrandt Harmensz van Rijn (1632). Courtesy of Culver Pictures, Inc.

0-452-25352-7 Through diagrams, illustrations, and text, presents information on nutrition, hygiene, safety, body systems, and other health subjects.

Dixon, Bernard (ed). *Health, Medicine, and the Human Body.* Macmillan 1986 $50.00. ISBN 0-02-908040-1

Edlin, Gordon, and Eric Golanty. *Health and Wellness: A Holistic Approach.* Jones & Bartlett 1988 $22.50. ISBN 0-86720-055-3

Hafen, Brent Q. *Acupuncture to Yoga: Alternative Methods of Healing.* Prentice 1983 $12.95. ISBN 0-13-330845-6

Insel, Paul, and Walton Roth. *Core Concepts in Health.* Mayfield 1988 $33.95. ISBN 0-87484-795-8

Johnson, G. Timothy, and Stephen E. Goldfinger (eds). *The Harvard Medical School Health Letter Book.* Harvard Univ Pr 1981 $21.00. ISBN 0-674-37725-7

Justice, Blair. *Who Gets Sick: Thinking and Health.* Peak 1987 $17.95. ISBN 0-9605376-1-9

*Klass, Perri. *A Not Entirely Benign Procedure: Four Years as a Medical Student.* NAL 1988 $4.50. ISBN 0-451-15358-8 A woman describes the process of becoming a doctor through four years of Harvard Medical School.

Lowe, Carl, and Jim Nechas. *Whole Body Healing.* Rodale 1983 $21.95. ISBN 0-87857-441-7

*McCuen, Gary E. (ed). *Poor and Minority Health Care.* GEM 1988 $12.95. ISBN 0-86596-065-8 Various views on private vs. government health care and world health problems are offered.

*Orlandi, Mario, *et al. Maintaining Good Health. Encyclopedia of Good Health Ser.* Facts on File 1989 $18.95. ISBN 0-8160-1667-4 Brief discussion of the various body parts and how to keep them functioning well.

Ornstein, Robert, and David Sobel. *The Healing Brain: Breakthrough Medical Discoveries About How the Brain Manages Health.* Simon 1987 $19.45. ISBN 0-671-61945-4

*Ranahan, Demerris C. *Contributions of Women: Medicine.* Dillon 1981. (o.p.) $8.95. ISBN 0-87518-213-5 Biographies of five female doctors who made significant contributions to our quality of life.

Reader's Digest Staff. *ABC's of the Human Body.* Reader's Digest 1987 $26.95. ISBN 0-89577-220-5

Roberts, Scott W. *Health–Wellness: An Introductory Approach.* E. Bowers 1989 $17.95. ISBN 0-912855-90-8

Simons, Richard C., and Herbert Pardes. *Understanding Human Behavior in Health and Disease.* Williams and Wilkins 1985 $31.50. ISBN 0-683-07741-4

*Stiller, Richard. *Your Body Is Trying to Tell You Something.* Harcourt 1979 $7.95. ISBN 0-15-299894-2 Discusses the diseases and conditions that affect young people particularly and considers the relationship between the health of the mind and the health of the body.

Vogt, Thomas M. *Making Health Decisions: An Epidemiologic Perspective on Staying Well.* Nelson-Hall 1983 $22.95. ISBN 0-8304-1001-5

*Ward, Brian R. *Body Maintenance.* Watts 1983 $12.40. ISBN 0-531-04457-2 The body's support systems, including immune and repair systems, and how they work.

Ways, Peter. *Take Charge of Your Health: The Guide to Personal Health Competence.* Stephen Greene 1985 $12.95. ISBN 0-8289-0548-7

Weil, Andrew. *Health and Healing: Understanding Conventional and Alternative Medicine.* Houghton 1984 $8.95. ISBN 0-395-37764-1

Wilkinson, Doris Y., and Marvin B. Sussman. *Alternative Health Maintenance and Healing Systems for Families.* Haworth 1988 $32.95. ISBN 0-86656-701-1

Young, Bob. *How to Stay Healthy While Traveling: A Guide for Today's World Traveler.* Ross-Erikson 1980 $4.95. ISBN 0-915520-31-1

CUSHING, HARVEY 1869–1939

A renowned brain surgeon and winner of a Pulitzer Prize, Harvey Cushing was born in Cleveland, Ohio, and received a B.A. degree from Yale University and an M.D. degree from Harvard Medical School. In 1896, after interning at

Massachusetts General Hospital, Cushing went to Johns Hopkins Hospital in Baltimore, Maryland, where he was a surgical resident. In 1912 he became professor of surgery at Harvard Medical School and chief of surgery at Peter Bent Brigham Hospital in Boston. From 1933 to 1937, he was professor of neurology at Yale University in New Haven, Connecticut.

While at Johns Hopkins, Cushing began to specialize in neurosurgery, particularly in surgery of the brain. At that time, brain surgery carried an extremely high risk, with as many as one-half of all patients dying. Cushing drove himself and others who worked with him to reduce these terribly high numbers. He introduced and perfected techniques that eventually resulted in a mortality rate of less than 10 percent. Cushing also did research, investigating brain tumors and tumors of other kinds, growth disorders, and eye problems.

The author of many books and papers, Cushing won the Pulitzer Prize in 1925 for his work *Life of Sir William Osler,* a biography of a Canadian physician associated with Johns Hopkins Hospital soon after it was established and an influential teacher of Cushing. (*See* Osler, Vol. 2, Health: General References.)

BOOKS BY CUSHING

From a Surgeon's Journal, 1915–1918 (1936).
Life of Sir William Osler (1925). 2 vols. Oxford Univ Pr 1940 repr of 1925 ed.

BOOKS ABOUT CUSHING

*Denzel, Justin F. *Harvey Cushing.* Messner 1971. (o.p.) $3.95. ISBN 671-32367-9 Life story of a great doctor, suitable for young readers.

Fulton, John F. *Harvey Cushing: A Biography. Three Centuries of Science Ser.* Ayer 1980 repr of 1946 ed $71.50. ISBN 0-405-12542-9 Life of Cushing taken largely from his diaries and other writings.

Thomson, Elizabeth H. *Harvey Cushing: Surgeon, Author, Artist.* Neale Watson 1981 repr of 1951 ed. (o.p.). ISBN 0-88202-194-X Story of Cushing and his many accomplishments.

HIPPOCRATES   *c.* 460–377 BC

Hippocrates was an ancient Greek physician, writer, and teacher who is called the father of medicine. His name is known to all physicians today, who swear to conduct their professional lives according to the moral standards delineated in the Oath of Hippocrates. When they take this oath, they promise to use their art and skills to heal and to save lives, not to cause harm or to take lives; to keep secret the confidences of their patients; and to uphold the honor and traditions of the medical profession. Although Hippocrates may not have been the author of the oath, medical historians believe that it reflects his character, ideals, and principles and the school of medicine that formed around him.

Little is known for certain about the life of Hippocrates. It is believed that he was born on Cos (Kos), an island in the south Aegean Sea, that his earliest studies of medicine were under his physician father, and that he might also have studied in Athens. It is also believed that he traveled and practiced medicine on various Greek islands and in places on the mainland.

Although a large body of writings bears Hippocrates' name, the works were undoubtedly written not only by Hippocrates but also by many other physicians of the Hippocratic, or Coan, school of medicine. This school is notable for having separated the practice of medicine from religion, superstition, and spiritual healing. At the time of Hippocrates, disease was widely believed to be caused by the gods, and miraculous cures took place at temples with the help of the temple priests. Hippocrates and his followers, however, believed that disease resulted from an imbalance of bodily humors and that these imbalances were caused by forces outside the body. In the book *Airs, Waters and Places,* Hippocrates connected three environmental factors with health: the weather, local climatic conditions such as the prevailing wind, and the nature of the water supply. These physicians believed that a patient should be treated as an individual and that treatment should be tailored to the individual and his or her circumstances. This philosophy was in direct contrast to a rival school of medicine, the Cnidian school, which practically ignored the patient and, instead, emphasized classification of diseases and detailed diagnoses and provided specific treatments for specific diseases.

Hippocrates and others of his school observed and recorded the signs of diseases and were aware that symptoms could appear throughout a family and over many generations. They also observed that diseases could affect many people of a community. Many of these observations appear in two volumes of a work titled *Epidemics* (five other volumes of this work are thought to have been written later). In these books of case histories, facts about individual patients and their diseases are recorded along with statistics about diseases. Carefully observing many patients and compiling the facts about their diseases enabled the physicians to perceive patterns in illnesses and thus for the first time to give prognoses, that is, to forecast the course a disease would take and its eventual outcome.

Prognosis of disease was the subject of several Hippocratic books. The most famous of these is *Aphorisms,* a compilation of observations about disease and advice to physicians. The advice includes many sayings that are well known today, including "Life is short, art is long. . . ."

The Hippocratic books were translated into many languages and influenced the teaching of medicine for centuries. Even today the influence of Hippocrates and his fellow physicians is felt, for they were responsible for putting medicine on a sound scientific basis.

BOOKS BY HIPPOCRATES

Hippocrates. Vol. 5. *Loeb Classical Library: No. 472.* Paul Potter (tr). Harvard Univ Pr 1988 $14.95. ISBN 0-674-99520-1

Hippocrates. Vol. 6. *Loeb Classical Library: No. 473.* Harvard Univ Pr 1988 $14.95. ISBN 0-674-99522-8

Hippocrates Latinum: Repertorium of Hippocratic Writings in the Latin Middle Ages. Fordham Univ Pr 1985 $50.00. ISBN 0-8232-1120-7

Hippocratic Writings. G. E. Floyd (ed). J. Chadwick and W. N. Nann (trs). Penguin 1984 $6.95. ISBN 0-14-04451-3

The Writings of Hippocrates on the Human Body, Its Diseases and Their Cure. Francis Adams (tr). 2 vols. American Classical Coll Pr 1988 $237.45. ISBN 0-89266-612-9

BOOKS ABOUT HIPPOCRATES

Heidel, William A. *Hippocratic Medicine. Development of Science Ser.* Ayer 1981 $15.00. ISBN 0-405-13878-4 Discussion of the school of medicine that formed around Hippocrates.

Moon, Robert O. *Hippocrates and His Successors in Relation to the Philosophy of Their Time.* AMS (repr of 1923 ed) $20.00. ISBN 0-404-13351-7 Discusses the work of Hippocrates and the Hippocratic school of medicine.

OSLER, WILLIAM   1849–1919

One of the best-known physicians and medical teachers of modern times, William Osler was born in Ontario, Canada. The son of a minister, Osler first studied theology but soon turned to medicine instead. After receiving his M.D. degree in 1872 from McGill University in Montreal, Canada, he taught there and in 1875 became chief of medicine at the medical school. In 1884 he began teaching at the University of Pennsylvania, and in 1889 he joined the staff of Johns Hopkins Hospital in Baltimore, Maryland. At Johns Hopkins, he introduced the clinical system of teaching medical students and the practice of using recent medical school graduates as resident physicians. In 1905 he became professor of medicine at Oxford University in England.

A prolific writer, Osler was the author of a famous textbook, *The Principles and Practice of Medicine* (1891). He was a collector of rare books and at Oxford University was the curator of the Bodleian Library.

Osler carried out research on the blood, malaria, stomach cancer, the liver, and the spleen. A proponent of preventive medicine, he fought for improvements in sanitary conditions as a way of combatting tuberculosis and other infectious diseases. He also helped to organize the National Tuberculosis Foundation (now the American Lung Association).

BOOK BY OSLER

Aphorisms from His Bedside Teachings and Writings. W. B. Bean (ed). 1950.

BOOK ABOUT OSLER

Cushing, Harvey W. *Life of Sir William Osler.* 2 vols. Oxford Univ Pr 1940 repr of 1925 ed. Pulitzer Prize-winning biography of one great doctor by another.

SCHWEITZER, ALBERT   1875–1965

World-famous as a philosopher, theologian, musician, and medical missionary, Albert Schweitzer was the son of a Lutheran minister. Born in Kaysersberg in Alsace, then part of Germany, in 1899 Schweitzer received a doctor of philosophy degree from the University of Strasbourg and in 1900 a more advanced degree in theology from the same university. In 1903, after serving as a curate and deacon in Strasbourg, Schweitzer became head of the Theological College at the university.

A man of great intellect, Schweitzer was also a gifted musician who was noted as an organist and for his interpretations of the works of German composer Johann Sebastian Bach. His study of Bach, *J. S. Bach,* was published in 1905. A year later a theological study called *The Quest of the Historical Jesus* was published. Schweitzer the musician, theologian, and philosopher became famous with these publications.

At about this time, at the age of 30, Schweitzer returned to school as a medical student. He received his M.D. degree from the University of Strasbourg in 1913 and left for Africa as a medical missionary. Arriving at Lambaréné in Gabon, then a province of French Equatorial Africa, he set up a hospital for the treatment of African patients. Schweitzer spent the rest of his life at Lambaréné. At first, he supported the hospital with the proceeds of organ recitals and lectures he gave. Later, as Schweitzer and his humanitarian work at the hospital became known throughout the world, gifts from individuals and foundations poured in to meet the expenses of the hospital and staff.

Schweitzer continued to write, particularly during a 10-year absence from Lambaréné, when he was interned in a French prisoner-of-war camp during World War I. His writings included autobiographical, theological, and philosophical works. In two of his books, both published in 1923, he analyzed the reasons for what he perceived as the collapse of civilization and discussed how civilization could be reconstructed. These books included his personal philosophy, which he called "Reverence for Life." In 1949 the books were revised and published as one volume titled *Philosophy of Civilization.*

Schweitzer received many honors, including the 1952 Nobel Peace Prize. With the money accompanying the Nobel medal, Schweitzer added a hospital for lepers to the settlement at Lambaréné.

During the 1960s, Schweitzer was often criticized, mainly for failing to modernize his hospital and for treating patients in a paternalistic manner that many found condescending. Whatever the merits of these charges, Schweitzer remained for most people an outstanding, selfless person who devoted his life to the care of others.

BOOKS BY SCHWEITZER

Albert Schweitzer: Living Philosophies Ser. Ann Repath (ed). Richard Winston and Clara Winston (trs). Creative Ed 1985 $9.95. ISBN 0-88682-013-8 Philosophy of Albert Schweitzer edited and translated for high school readers.

J. S. Bach (1905). Ernest Newman (tr). 2 vols. Dover 1966. Vol. 1 $7.50. ISBN 0-486-21631-4. Vol. 2 $7.50. ISBN 0-486-21632-2 Schweitzer's famous study of Bach and his music translated for young readers.

On Nuclear War and Peace. Homer A. Jack (ed). Brethren 1987 $9.95. ISBN 0-87178-536-6 One of Schweitzer's books dealing with the need for people to find peace in our time.

Philosophy of Civilization (1923). Prometheus Bks 1988 $14.95. ISBN 0-87975-403-6 Schweitzer's thoughts on the loss of civilization and how to restore it, written while he was interned in a prisoner-of-war camp during World War I.

BOOKS ABOUT SCHWEITZER

Frank, Frederick. *Days with Albert Schweitzer: A Lambaréné Landscape.* H. Holt 1959. Account of an American dentist who lived and worked at Schweitzer's African settlement for three months.

Hagedorn, Hermann. *Prophet in the Wilderness: The Story of Albert Schweitzer.* Macmillan 1954. Classic biography of Schweitzer that draws on letters the author received from Schweitzer answering specific questions.

Joy, Charles R. *Music in the Life of Albert Schweitzer.* Harper 1951. Many of Schweitzer's writings on music arranged chronologically, providing a biography of his life in music.

McKnight, Gerald. *Verdict on Schweitzer: The Man Behind the Legend of Lambaréné.* John Jay 1964 $4.95. Discusses the criticisms that were leveled against Schweitzer and Lambaréné in the 1960s.

Ostergaard-Christensen, L. *At Work with Albert Schweitzer.* F. H. Lyon (tr). Beacon 1962. Description of daily life at Lambaréné and a warm, candid portrait of Schweitzer by a Danish surgeon who spent a few months at the hospital.

MENTAL AND EMOTIONAL HEALTH

*Adderholdt-Elliott, Miriam. *Perfectionism: What's Bad About Being Too Good.* Free Spirit 1987 $8.95. ISBN 0-915793-07-5 Discussion of the problems that can arise when people aspire to the impossible level of absolute perfection; suggests how to set more reasonable goals.

Benson, Herbert, and Miriam Z. Klipper. *The Relaxation Response.* Avon 1976 $3.95. ISBN 0-380-00676-6

Benson, Herbert, and William Proctor. *Beyond the Relaxation Response.* Berkley 1985 $3.50. ISBN 0-425-08183-4

Buscaglia, Leo F. *Love.* Fawcett 1985 $4.95. ISBN 0-449-20846-X

*Carter, Sharon, and Penny Van Dyne. *Coping with Your Image.* Coping with Ser. Rosen 1985 $12.95. ISBN 0-8239-0634-5 Explains how self-image develops and the desirability of having a realistic view of self.

Charlesworth, Edward A., and Ronald G. Nathan. *Stress Management: A Comprehensive Guide to Wellness.* Ballantine 1989 $4.95. ISBN 0-345-32734-9

*Cohen, Susan, and Daniel Cohen. *Teenage Stress.* M. Evans 1983. (o.p.) $10.95. ISBN 0-87131-423-1 Offers sample stress-producing situations and techniques for dealing with them; discusses stresses of adolescence, including school performance, interactions with parents, and sex.

Cooper, Cary L., *et al. Living with Stress.* Penguin 1988 $7.95. ISBN 0-14-009866-6

Faulkner, P. *Making Things Right When Things Go Wrong: Ten Proven Ways to Put Your Life in Order.* Sweet 1986 (o.p.)

*Filson, Brent. *There's a Monster in Your Closet! Understanding Phobias.* Messner 1986 $9.29. ISBN 0-671-55496-4 Describes a variety of phobias, their causes, and some current treatments for these problems.

Gaylin, Willard. *Feelings: Our Vital Signs.* Harper 1988 $6.95. ISBN 0-06-091480-7

*Gilbert, Sara. *Get Help: Solving the Problems in Your Life.* Morrow 1989 $7.95. ISBN 0-688-08010-3 Discusses the stressful situations teenagers have to cope with and gives advice about getting help for problems that seem overwhelming.

*Gilbert, Sara. *What Happens in Therapy.* Lothrop 1982. (o.p.) $6.50. ISBN 0-688-01459-3 Describes different types of psychotherapy, what treatment involves, and when it might be wise to seek such help.

*Gilman, Sander L. *Seeing the Insane.* Wiley 1985 $21.00. ISBN 0-471-82457-7 History of the treatment of mental illness in this and other cultures; for more advanced students.

Goleman, Daniel. *Vital Lies, Simple Truths: The Psychology of Self-Deception.* Simon 1986 $9.95. ISBN 0-671-62815-1

*Gordon, James S. *Stress Management.* Chelsea 1990 $18.95. ISBN 0-7910-0042-7 A book addressed to teenagers that discusses stress and how to reduce it.

*Greenberg, Harvey Roy. *Emotional Illness in Your Family: Helping Your Relatives, Helping Yourself.* Macmillan 1989 $16.95. ISBN 0-02-736921-8 Advice about what to do, what to avoid doing, and how to get help when someone in the family or a friend has an emotional illness.

Greenberg, Jerrold S. *Coping with Stress: A Practical Guide.* Brown 1989 $16.95. ISBN 0-697-11013-3

Hunt, Douglas. *No More Fears.* Warner Bks 1988 $4.95. ISBN 0-446-35344-2

Jacobson, Edmund. *You Must Relax.* McGraw 1978 $5.95. ISBN 0-07-032184-1

Kagan, Jerome, and Howard A. Moss. *Birth to Maturity: A Study in Psychological Development.* Yale Univ Pr 1983 $11.95. ISBN 0-300-03029-0

*Lee, Essie E., and Richard Wortman. *Down Is Not Out: Teenagers and Depression.* Messner 1986 $11.29. ISBN 0-671-52613-8 Discussion of depression and the difference between to-be-expected "down" days and serious depression; explains when to seek help.

*McFarland, Rhoda. *Coping Through Assertiveness.* Coping with Ser. Rosen 1986 $12.95. ISBN 0-8239-0680-9 Advice about how to become more assertive and when it is appropriate to be assertive.

*McLellan, Tom, *et al. Escape from Anxiety and Stress. The Encyclopedia of Psychoactive Drugs Ser.* Chelsea 1986 $18.95. ISBN 0-87754-772-6 Discusses the causes of stress and how stress affects the body; explores the use and abuse of alcohol and drugs in relation to stress.

*Mill, James W. *Coping with Stress: A Guide to Living.* Wiley 1982 $14.95. ISBN 0-471-87678-X Discusses the skills for coping with stress; for more advanced students.

*Myers, Irma, and Arthur Myers. *Why You Feel Down and What You Can Do About It.* Macmillan 1982 $12.95. ISBN 0-684-17442-1 Discussion of the "blues" and of depression and how to deal with both.

*Orlandi, Mario. *Stress and Mental Health. Encyclopedia of Good Health Ser.* Facts on File 1988 $18.95. ISBN 0-8160-1668-2 Describes the stresses of growing up and explains how to deal with them in ways that ensure good health.

*Osborne, Cecil G. *The Art of Understanding Yourself.* Zondervan 1987 $7.95. ISBN 0-310-30591-8 Explores how to develop and nurture self-esteem and to learn to love yourself.

*Shedd, C. W. *You Are Somebody Special.* McGraw 1982 $12.95. ISBN 0-07-056511-2 Encourages the reader to learn about himself or herself: to consider feelings, attitudes, relationships with friends and family, the person he or she might marry, and what he or she wants to do in the future.

Tart, Charles T. *Waking Up: Overcoming the Obstacles to Human Potential.* Shambhala 1987 $14.95. ISBN 0-87773-426-7

SUICIDE

*Davis, Patricia. *Suicidal Adolescents.* Thomas 1983 $22.75. ISBN 0-398-04866-5 Thorough examination of teenage suicide; causes and prevention.

*Francis, Dorothy B. *Suicide, a Preventable Tragedy.* Lodestar 1989 $13.95. ISBN 0-525-67279-6 Excellent book that discusses the causes of suicide and the methods of its prevention.

*Giffen, Mary, and Carol Felsenthal. *A Cry for Help.* Doubleday 1983. (o.p.) Explores the topic of suicide and describes many of the signs that warn of an attempt.

Hafen, Brent Q., and Kathryn J. Frandsen. *Youth Suicide: Depression and Loneliness.* Cordillera 1986 $9.95. ISBN 0-917895-11-8

*Hermes, Patricia. *A Time to Listen: Preventing Youth Suicide.* Harcourt 1987 $12.95. ISBN 0-15-288196-4 Discussion of suicide; suitable reading for high-school students and adults.

*Hyde, Margaret O., and Elizabeth Held Forsyth. *Suicide: The Hidden Epidemic.* Watts 1986 $12.90. ISBN 0-531-10251-3 Discussion of suicide: why some people, including teenagers, end their lives; includes list of suicide prevention centers.

*Langone, John. *Dead End: A Book About Suicide.* Little 1986 $12.95. ISBN 0-316-51432-2 Explores what is known about suicide and answers questions often asked about suicide.

*Leder, Jane M. *Dead Serious: A Book for Teenagers About Teenage Suicide.* Avon 1989 $2.95. ISBN 0-380-70661-X Discussion of suicide; suitable reading for young teenagers.

Maulitz, Russell C. (ed). *Unnatural Causes: The Three Leading Killer Diseases in America.* Rutgers Univ Pr 1989 $15.95. ISBN 0-8135-1406-1

Pfeffer, Cynthia R. *The Suicidal Child.* Guilford 1986 $29.95. ISBN 0-89862-664-1

DEATH

*Gravelle, Karen, and Charles Haskins. *Teenagers Face to Face with Bereavement.* Messner 1989 $5.95. ISBN 0-671-65975-8 Using case studies of 17 teenagers who grappled with the death of a parent, sibling, or close friend, discusses how adolescents deal with grief.

Morgan, Ernest. *Dealing Creatively with Death: A Manual of Death Education and Simple Burial.* Celo 1988 $9.00. ISBN 0-914064-26-6

*Richter, Elizabeth. *Losing Someone You Love: When a Brother or Sister Dies.* Putnam 1986 $12.95. ISBN 0-399-21243-4 Addresses grief and other emotions that a young person experiences with the death of a sibling.
Rohr, Janelle (ed). *Death and Dying: Opposing Viewpoints. Opposing Viewpoints Ser.* Greenhaven 1987 $7.95. ISBN 0-89908-368-4
*Williams, Guinevere, and Julia Ross. *A Matter of Life and Death: A Discussion About Death for Young People.* State Mutual 1982 $20.00. ISBN 0-904265-99-4

RELATIONSHIPS: IN AND OUT OF THE FAMILY

Arnstein, Helene S. *Brother and Sister/Sisters and Brothers.* Dutton 1987 $2.95. ISBN 0-451-161963
*Carter, Sharon. *Coping Through Friendship. Coping with Ser.* Rosen 1987 $12.95. ISBN 0-8239-0789-9 Discusses the benefits of friendships and how to form and keep those relationships.
*Barbeau, Clayton C. *How to Raise Parents: Questions and Answers for Teens and Parents.* Harper Jr Bks 1987 $13.95. ISBN 0-06-250044-9 Provides advice for teenagers and their parents on getting through the teenage years; includes discussion of divorce, the blues, sexuality, and schoolwork.
*Cohen, Susan, and Daniel Cohen. *Teenage Competition: A Survival Guide.* M. Evans 1988 $11.95. ISBN 0-87131-487-8 Discusses relationships among teenage siblings and peers.
*Craven, Linda. *Stepfamilies: New Patterns of Harmony. Teen Survival Library Ser.* Messner 1983 $4.95. ISBN 0-671-49486-4 Considers the special circumstances of stepfamilies and discusses in a positive way the conflicts that are likely to arise.
*Dinner, Sherry H. *Nothing to Be Ashamed of: Growing up with Mental Illness in Your Family.* Lothrop 1989 $7.95. ISBN 0-688-08493-1 A psychologist's advice to those who must live with a mentally ill person.
*Fast, Julius, and Barbara Fast. *Talking Between the Lines: How We Mean More Than We Say.* Pocket 1980 $2.50. ISBN 0-671-83244-1 Examines the effects of words and how words interact with actions; suggests different ways of using words; explores the negative and positive results of talking.
*Gay, Kathlyn. *The Changing Families: Meeting Today's Challenges.* Enslow 1988 $15.95. ISBN 0-89490-139-7 Explores nontraditional families that are common today and discusses ways of coping with the special circumstances and issues that may arise within them.
*Gay, Kathlyn. *The Rainbow Effect: Interracial Families.* Watts 1987 $12.90. ISBN 0-531-10343-9 Focuses on the joys and the problems of children in interracial families; includes discussion of topics such as dating, friendships, and divorce.
*Getzoff, Ann, and Carolyn McClenahan. *Stepkids: A Survival Guide for Teenagers in Stepfamilies.* Walker 1984 $13.95. ISBN 0-8027-0757-2 Explores the sometimes complicated relationships in blended families and ways of improving them; stresses that bonding in new families takes time, effort, and communication.
*Gilbert, Sara. *How to Live with a Single Parent.* Lothrop 1982 $12.88. ISBN 0-688-00633-7 Advice to teenagers on relationships with a single parent; suggests ways of dealing with issues that arise in a single-parent family.
Hafen, Brent Q., and Kathryn J. Frandsen. *People Need People: The Importance of Relationships to Health and Wellness.* Cordillera $9.95. ISBN 0-917895-14-2
*Hellmuth, Jerome. *Coping with Parents. Coping with Ser.* Rosen 1985 $12.95. ISBN 0-8239-0640-X Discusses adolescents' relationships with their parents; includes sections dealing with infidelity and divorce; provides an appendix that suggests where and how to get help with problems.
*Johnson, Eric W. *How to Live with Parents and Teachers.* Westminster John Knox 1986 $12.95. ISBN 0-664-21273-5 Advice to teenagers about their relationships with the important adults in their lives.
*Kaplan, Leslie S. *Coping with Peer Pressure. Coping with Ser.* Rosen 1987 $12.95. ISBN

0-8239-0768-6 Discusses the well-known phenomenon of peer pressure and explores ways of keeping one's own integrity without damaging meaningful friendships.

*Klein, David, and Marymae E. Klein. *Your Parents and Your Self: Alike-Unlike, Agreeing-Disagreeing.* Macmillan 1986 $12.95. ISBN 0-684-18684-5 Discusses the joys and the problems of relationships with parents during teenage years.

Lamb, Michael E. *Nontraditional Families: Parenting and Child Development.* Erlbaum 1982 $29.95. ISBN 0-89859-178-3

*Mazzenga, Isabel Burk. *Compromise or Confrontation: Dealing with the Adults in Your Life.* Venture Books Ser. Watts 1989 $12.40. ISBN 0-531-10805-8 Guide to understanding adults' expectations and motivations, building good communications skills, and learning when and how to compromise with parents, teachers, and other adults.

*McGuire, Paula. *Putting It Together: Teenagers Talk About Family Breakups.* Delacorte 1987 $15.95. ISBN 0-385-29564-2 Through teenagers' own words, explores the problems that occur when a family breaks up.

Murphy, Kevin J. *Effective Listening: Hearing What People Say and Making It Work for You.* Bantam 1989 $3.95. ISBN 0-553-27030-3

*Rashkis, Harold A., and Levon D. Tashjian. *Understanding Your Parents.* Stickley 1978 $6.95. ISBN 0-89313-009-5 Discusses family relationships with the view that mutual understanding is needed; includes material on separation and divorce, infidelity, and alcoholism.

Rosin, Mark B. *Stepfathering: Stepfathers' Advice on Creating a New Family.* Ballantine 1988 $6.95. ISBN 0-345-35408-7

*Ryan, Elizabeth A. *Straight Talk About Parents.* Straight Talk for Teens Ser. Facts on File 1989 $14.95. ISBN 0-8160-1526-0 Discusses ways to negotiate areas of disagreement in families; considers one-parent and foster families as well as dysfunctional families in which alcoholism or abuse is a problem.

*Vedral, Joyce L. *My Parents Are Driving Me Crazy.* Ballantine 1986 $2.95. ISBN 0-345-33011-0 Discussion of the difficulties often experienced in families as teenagers work toward independence.

Yablonski, Lewis. *Fathers and Sons.* Simon 1982. (o.p.) $13.95. ISBN 0-671-25461-8

Yogman, Michael W., and T. Berry Brazelton (eds). *In Support of Families.* Harvard Univ Pr 1986 $12.95. ISBN 0-674-44736-0

DYSFUNCTIONAL FAMILIES

*Berger, Gilda. *Violence and the Family.* Watts 1990 $12.90. ISBN 0-531-10906-2 Discussion of severe family problems including child abuse, abuse of the elderly, and sexual abuse.

*Greenberg, Harvey R. *Emotional Illness in Your Family: Helping Your Relatives, Helping Yourself.* Macmillan 1989 $16.95. ISBN 0-02-736921-8 A guide to coping with mental illness.

*Jorgensen, Donald G., Jr., and June A. Jorgensen. *Secrets Told By Children of Alcoholics.* TAB 1990 $12.95. ISBN 0-8306-5008-3 Interviews with young people who tell how alcoholism affected their families.

Mains, Karen B. *Abuse in the Family.* Helping Others in Crisis Ser. Cook 1987 $6.95. ISBN 1-55513-796-2

*Martin, Jo. *Drugs and the Family.* Encyclopedia of Psychoactive Drugs Ser: No. 2. Chelsea 1988 $18.95. ISBN 1-55546-220-0 Discusses the ramifications of drug abuse in the family and what can be done about the problem.

Oates, K. *Child Abuse and Neglect: What Happens Eventually?* Brunner-Mazel 1985 $27.50. ISBN 0-87630-405-6

Orford, Jim, and Judith Harwin (eds). *Alcohol and the Family.* St. Martin's 1982 $39.95. ISBN 0-312-01706-5

*Porterfield, Kay Marie. *Coping with an Alcoholic Parent.* Coping with Ser. Rosen 1985 $12.95.

ISBN 0-8239-0662-0 Explores the problems that occur in a family with an alcoholic parent; suggests ways of dealing with the afflicted parent so that the child's feelings and life are not controlled by the parent's drinking; includes an appendix that suggests where to get help.

*Seixas, Judith S. *Living with a Parent Who Takes Drugs.* Greenwillow 1989 $11.95. ISBN 0-688-08627-6 Excellent book allowing the reader to identify with a teenager whose father is a "pothead"; good factual information including prospects for recovery.

Siegel, Mark A., *et al. Domestic Violence: No Longer Behind the Curtains. Information Plus Ser.* Info Plus 1989 $21.95. ISBN 0-936474-87-4

Steinglass, Peter, *et al. Alcoholic Family.* Basic 1987 $27.95. ISBN 0-465-00097-5

See also Vol. 2, Psychology: Emotions.

GROWTH AND DEVELOPMENT

Berger, Kathleen S. *The Developing Person Through the Life Span.* Worth 1988 $35.95. ISBN 0-87901-381-8

Kagan, Jerome, and Howard Moss. *Birth to Maturity.* Yale Univ Pr 1983 $11.95. ISBN 0-300-03029-0

CHILDHOOD

Berger, Kathleen S. *Developing Person Through Childhood and Adolescence.* Worth 1986 $35.95. ISBN 0-87901-241-2

Caplan, Theresa, and Frank Caplan. *Early Childhood Years: The Two to Six Year Old.* Bantam 1984 $4.50. ISBN 0-553-26310-2

Gesell, A. Ames, *et al. Child from Five to Ten.* Harper 1977 $29.95. ISBN 0-06-011501-7

Humphrey, Joy N., and James H. Humphrey. *Child Development During the Elementary School Years.* Thomas 1989 $29.75. ISBN 0-398-05622-6

Max, M. (ed). *Child Development and Child Health.* Year Bk Med 1990 $39.95. ISBN 0-632-02048-2

National Research Council. *Development During Middle Childhood.* National Academy 1984 $28.50. ISBN 0-309-03478-7

O'Shea, M.V. (ed). *The Child: His Nature and His Needs. Classics in Child Development Ser.* Ayer 1975 $51.00. ISBN 0-405-06473-X

SPOCK, BENJAMIN McLANE 1903–

A pediatrician and peace activist, Benjamin Spock is known the world over for helping generations of parents raise their children through the advice he gave them in a best-selling guidebook. Born in New Haven, Connecticut, the oldest of six children, Spock's early schooling began with classes taught by a governess in a private home and then progressed to attendance at a "fresh air" school. This school, the inspiration of his mother, consisted of one outdoor classroom, which was a platform partially covered by a tent. The desks were beneath the tent; the uncovered portion of the platform served as a stage. Throughout the cold, snowy winters typical of Connecticut, Spock and about 20 other children snuggled in felt bags, pursuing their third-grade studies whatever the weather.

The rest of Spock's schooling was more conventional. He attended a country day school and then a prep school and graduated from Yale University with a B.A. degree in 1925. As an undergraduate, he was a member of the Yale rowing crew that won a gold medal in the Olympic Games of 1924. After graduation, Spock went to medical school at Yale and in 1929 obtained his M.D. degree from the College of Physicians and Surgeons of Columbia University in New York City. After completing his internship, he served residencies in pediatrics and in psychiatry at New York hospitals and trained as a psychoanalyst. He was the first doctor to train in both pediatrics and psychoanalysis.

Spock began his practice in pediatrics in New York City in 1933. At the suggestion of an editor, he began writing advice for parents during these years. He completed his manuscript during his spare time while he served as a psychiatrist in the U.S. Naval Reserve from 1944 to 1946. Published as *The Common Sense Book of Baby and Child Care* in 1946, the book was later retitled simply *Baby and Child Care.* From its publication, it became the "bible" of parents and has been revised many times.

Spock's book, written in warm, informal language, became a best seller because of its common-sense approach and the reassurance it gave anxious parents. Spock said that he wanted to inform parents about the normal development of infants and children—to tell parents what children are like and what they can do at different stages—so that parents could know what to expect in their offspring and could act on their own knowledge. With his book in hand, parents often felt they had a resident pediatrician at their side. Beginning in 1954, parents could also obtain Spock's advice from columns he wrote for magazines.

After his service at naval hospitals, Spock went to the University of Minnesota in Minneapolis, where he was professor of psychiatry and consultant at the Mayo Clinic in Rochester, Minnesota. In 1951 he went to Western Reserve University in Cleveland, Ohio, to become professor of child development.

In 1967, with the war in Vietnam raging, Spock resigned from Western Reserve to devote full time to the cause of peace. Concerned about the resumption of atmospheric testing of nuclear bombs in 1962, Spock had become a member of the board of the National Committee for a Sane Nuclear Policy (SANE) and in 1963 cochairperson of the organization. With other groups protesting the war in Vietnam, Spock engaged in demonstrations and was twice arrested for his activities, many of which were connected with the antidraft movement. In 1968 Spock and four other men were put on trial by the federal government for conspiring to aid and abet violation of the Selective Service Act. All but one of the defendants were found guilty. Each was fined $5,000 and sentenced to two years in jail. Spock and another defendant were acquitted by an appeals court; the others were to be retried but were later exonerated.

BOOKS BY SPOCK

Baby and Child Care (1946). Pocket 1981 $3.95. ISBN 0-671-43671-6
Dr. Spock on Parenting. Pocket 1989 $4.95. ISBN 0-671-68386-1
Spock on Spock: A Memoir of Growing Up with the Century (1985). (coauthored with Mary Morgan) Pantheon 1989 $19.95. ISBN 0-394-57813-9

BOOK ABOUT SPOCK

Bloom, Lynn Z. *Doctor Spock: Biography of a Conservative Radical.* Bobbs 1972 $10.00. Story of Spock's life, ending with his trial and eventual acquittal.

ADOLESCENCE

*Bell, Ruth, *et al.* *Changing Bodies, Changing Lives. A Book for Teens on Sex and Relationships.* Random 1988 $12.95. ISBN 0-394-75541-3 Addresses changes that occur in the body during the teen years, relationships with the opposite sex, care of emotional and physical health, and other major concerns of adolescents.

*Blume, Judy. *Letters to Judy: What Kids Wish They Could Tell You.* Pocket 1987. (o.p.) $4.50. ISBN 0-671-62695-5 Letters to an author who is popular with adolescents reveal the issues that most concern teenagers; addressed to adults but interesting reading for teenagers.

*Boston Women's Health Book Collective Staff. *Our Bodies, Ourselves.* Simon 1976 $14.95. ISBN 0-671-22145-0 Addresses the health of women and women's understanding of their own bodies; suitable for older students.

Dusek, Jerome B. *Adolescent Development and Behavior.* Prentice 1991 $29.00. ISBN 0-13-009119-7

*Gordon, Sol. *The Teenage Survival Book: The Complete, Revised, Up-dated Edition of You.* Times Bks 1981 $12.95. ISBN 0-8129-0972-0 Discusses the ups and downs of growing up: relationships with self, family, and friends, sexuality, sex, and related topics.

*Gordon, Sol. *Ten Heavy Facts about Sex.* Ed-U Pr 1983 $1.95. ISBN 0-934978-32-8 Discussion of sex and sexuality for teenagers.

Hawley, Richard A. *The Big Issues in the Passage to Adulthood.* Walker 1988 $17.95. ISBN 0-8027-1033-6

*Johnson, Sue. *Talk Sex.* Penguin 1989 $4.50. ISBN 0-14-010377-5 In question-and-answer format, provides information on sex and human sexuality; addresses dating, love, pregnancy, homosexuality, and sexual abuse.

Jones, Elise F., *et al.* *Teenage Pregnancy in Industrialized Countries.* Yale Univ Pr 1988 $12.95. ISBN 0-300-04325-2

*Kelly, Gary F. *Learning About Sex: A Contemporary Guide for Young Adults.* Barron 1986 $6.95. ISBN 0-8120-2432-X Discussion of human sexuality and responsible, loving relationships.

*Levine, Saul, and Kathleen Wilcox. *Dear Doctor.* Lothrop 1987 $6.95. ISBN 0-688-07095-7 Sensible answers to teenagers' most troubling questions.

*Lindsay, Jeanne Warren. *Teenage Marriage: Coping with Reality.* Morning Glory 1988 $9.95. ISBN 0-930934-30-X Discusses teenage marriages, the problems that can arise in them, and the need for both partners to work at the success of their marriage.

*Madaras, Lynda, and Area Madaras. *What's Happening to My Body? Book for Girls: A Growing Up Guide for Parents and Daughters.* Newmarket 1987 $9.95. ISBN 0-937858-98-6 Discusses the changes that take place in the body as a girl matures.

*Madaras, Lynda, and Dane Saavedra. *What's Happening to My Body? Book for Boys: A Growing Up Guide for Parents and Sons.* Newmarket 1987 $9.95. ISBN 0-937858-99-4 Discusses the changes that take place in the body as a boy matures.

*Mahoney, Ellen Voelckers. *Now You've Got Your Period. Coping with Ser.* Rosen 1988 $12.95. ISBN 0-8239-0792-9 Discusses reproduction and menstruation; explains what happens during a pelvic examination.

*Mucciolo, Gary. *Everything You Need to Know About Birth Control.* Rosen 1990 $12.95. ISBN 0-8239-1014-8 Discusses all possible forms of birth control and each one's effectiveness, as well as abstinence.

*Nourse, Alan E. *Menstruation. First Books Ser.* Watts 1987 $10.40. ISBN 0-531-10308-0 Discussion of menstruation with information about premenstrual syndrome and toxic shock syndrome.
*Orlandi, Mario, *et al. Human Sexuality. Encyclopedia of Good Health Ser.* Facts on File 1989 $16.95. ISBN 0-8160-1666-6 Explores what it means to be a female and what it means to be a male.
*Packer, Kenneth L. *Puberty: The Story of Growth and Change. Venture Books Ser.* Watts 1989 $12.40. ISBN 0-531-10810-4 Discusses the physical and emotional changes of adolescence; includes information on pregnancy and birth.
*Pomeroy, Wardell B. *Boys and Sex.* Dell 1981 $2.95. ISBN 0-440-90753-3 Discussion of sexual development in boys and relationships between boys and girls.
*Pomeroy, Wardell B. *Girls and Sex.* Dell 1981 $3.25. ISBN 0-440-92904-0 Discussion of sexual development in girls and how girls and boys relate.
Rinzler, Jane. *Teens Speak Out: A Report from Today's Teens on Their Most Intimate Thoughts, Feelings, and Hopes for the Future.* D I Fine 1986 $7.95. ISBN 0-917657-50-0
*Simon, Nissa. *Don't Worry, You're Normal: A Teenager's Guide to Self-Health.* Harper 1982 $12.89. ISBN 0-690-04139-X Guide to health in adolescence covering topics such as growth, nutrition, skin care, drugs, and sex.
Steinberg, Laurence. *Adolescence.* Knopf 1989 $34.95. ISBN 0-394-38623-X
Steinberg, Laurence. *Adolescent Development.* McGraw 1984 $34.95. ISBN 0-07-554388-5
Ulene, Art. *Safe Sex in a Dangerous World.* Random 1987 $3.95. ISBN 0-394-75625-8
*Vedral, Joyce L. *The Opposite Sex Is Driving Me Crazy: What Boys Think About Girls.* Ballantine 1988 $3.50. ISBN 0-345-35221-1 Discussion of sexuality and relationships between the sexes.

PREGNANCY AND PARENTHOOD

Ashford, Janet I. (ed). *The Whole Birth Catalog: A Sourcebook for Choices in Childbirth.* Crossing Pr 1983. (o.p.) $12.95. ISBN 0-025-36250-X
Boston Children's Hospital Staff. *What Teenagers Want to Know About Sex.* Little 1988 $16.95. ISBN 0-316-25063-5
Cherry, Sheldon H. *Planning Ahead for Pregnancy.* Penguin 1987 $18.95. ISBN 0-670-80890-3
Cassell, Carol. *Straight From the Heart: How to Talk to Your Teenagers About Love and Sex.* Simon 1988 $6.95. ISBN 0-671-66198-1
Galinsky, Ellen. *The Six Stages of Parenthood.* Addison 1987 $10.95. ISBN 0-201-10529-2
Guttmacher, Alan F. *Pregnancy, Birth, and Family Planning.* NAL 1986 $9.95. ISBN 0-452-25827-8
Hales, Dianne, and Robert K. Creasy. *New Hope for Problem Pregnancies: Helping Babies BEFORE They're Born.* Berkley 1984 $3.95. ISBN 0-425-06847-1
*Kuklin, Susan. *What Do I Do Now? Talking About Teenage Pregnancy.* Putnam 1991 $15.95. ISBN 0-399-21843-2 Invaluable source for teenagers based on two years of interviews with pregnant teens.
Lindsay, Jeanne Warren. *Teens Parenting: The Challenge of Babies and Toddlers.* Morning Glory 1981 $9.95. ISBN 0-930934-06-7
*McGuire, Paula. *It Won't Happen to Me: Teenagers Talk About Pregnancy.* Dell 1983 $6.95. ISBN 0-385-29201-5 Fifteen teenagers talk about their experiences with pregnancy and the responsibilities of motherhood.
Milunsky, Aubrey. *How to Have the Healthiest Baby You Can.* Simon 1987 $17.45. ISBN 0-671-52459-3
Overvold, Amy Z. *Surrogate Parenting: Personal, Medical, and Legal Aspects of One of the Most Dramatic Biomedical Developments of Our Time.* Pharos 1988 $16.95. ISBN 0-88687-328-2
*Poirier-Brode, Karen. *Adolescent Pregnancy and Prenatal Care.* Carolina Biological 1987 $1.90. ISBN 0-89278-348-6 Discussion of pregnancy and proper prenatal care, including doctor visits, drugs, diet, and exercise.

AGING

*Buckman, Robert. *I Don't Know What to Say . . . How to Help and Support Someone Who Is Dying.* Dutton 1990 $13.95. ISBN 0-525-44559-5 The dying process and how to cope with it.

Burdman, Geri Marr. *Healthful Aging.* Prentice 1986 $23.95. ISBN 0-13-385543-0

Crichton, Jean. *The Age Care Sourcebook: A Resource Guide for the Aging and Their Families.* Simon 1987. (o.p.)

*Edelson, Edward. *Aging. The Life Cycle Ser.* Chelsea 1989 $18.95. ISBN 0-7910-0035-4 Explores what it means to grow old and the special problems of aging people.

Gillies, John. *Caregiving: When Someone You Love Grows Old. Heart and Hand Ser.* Shaw 1988 $9.95. ISBN 0-87788-104-9

Horne, Jo. *Caregiving: Helping an Aged Loved One.* American Assn of Retired Persons 1987 $13.95. ISBN 0-673-24822-4

Kart, Cary S., *et al. Aging, Health, and Society.* Jones & Bartlett 1988 $30.00. ISBN 0-86720-406-0

*Landau, Elaine. *Growing Old in America.* Messner 1985. (o.p.) $9.79. ISBN 0-671-42409-2 Discusses how older people feel about aging, how they spend their time, and some of their financial, legal, and medical concerns.

Pauling, Linus. *How to Live Longer and Feel Better.* Avon 1987 $4.95. ISBN 0-380-70289-4

*Swisher, Karen, and Tara Deal (eds). *The Elderly: Opposing Viewpoints Ser.* Greenhaven 1990 $7.95. ISBN 0-89908-450-8 Describes the needs and problems of the elderly.

*Worth, Richard. *You'll Be Old Someday, Too.* Watts 1986 $11.90. ISBN 0-531-10158-4 An exploration of what it is like to be old, with examples of how some ordinary and famous elderly people live.

See also Vol. 2, Biology: Reproduction and Development; Psychology: Human Development; Sociology: Age and Aging *and* Family, Marriage, Life-Course Events.

BODY SYSTEMS

*Allen, Oliver E., and the Editors of Time-Life Books. *Building Sound Bones and Muscles.* Time-Life 1981. (o.p.) Well-illustrated guide to muscles and bones, good for reference work and browsing.

*Arnold, Caroline. *Sex Hormones.* Morrow 1981. (o.p.) $12.95. ISBN 0-688-00696-5 Discusses sex hormones and their effects on the body.

*August, Paul. *Brain Function. Encyclopedia of Psychoactive Drugs.* Chelsea 1987 $18.95. ISBN 1-55546-204-9 Explanation of how the brain works in controlling the body.

*Avraham, Regina. *The Circulatory System. The Healthy Body Ser.* Chelsea 1989 $18.95. ISBN 0-7910-0013-3 Explains the circulatory system, its functioning, and disorders that affect it.

*Avraham, Regina. *The Digestive System. The Healthy Body Ser.* Chelsea 1989 $9.95. ISBN 0-7910-0455-4 Explains the functioning of the digestive system; discusses disorders affecting the digestive organs and the treatment of these disorders.

*Avraham, Regina. *The Reproductive System. The Healthy Body Ser.* Chelsea 1989 $18.95. ISBN 0-7910-0025-7 Discusses the reproductive system, its structure and function; includes information about pregnancy and birth.

*Berger, Melvin. *Exploring the Mind and Brain. Scientists at Work Ser.* Harper 1983 $12.89. ISBN 0-690-04252-3 Reports on research into how the mind and brain work and on treatment for mental dysfunctions.

*Bergland, Richard. *The Fabric of Mind.* Penguin 1989 $9.95. ISBN 0-14-007460-0 A neurosurgeon explains how the brain functions and the unsolved mysteries about it.

Brunn, Ruth Dowling, and Bertal Brunn. *The Human Body.* Random 1982 $9.95. ISBN 0-394-84424-6

*Corrick, James. *The Human Brain: Mind and Matter.* Arco How-It-Works Ser. Arco 1983 $12.95. ISBN 0-668-05519-7 Discusses the structure, functioning, and chemical makeup of the brain, brain disorders, and sense perception.

*Desowitz, Robert S. *The Thorn in the Starfish: How the Human Immune System Works.* Norton 1988 $7.70. ISBN 0-393-30556-2 Very readable book for older students about the mysterious, intricate workings of the immune system.

*Diagram Group. *The Human Body on File.* Facts on File 1983 $145.00. ISBN 0-87196-706-5 Information about how the body functions, presented through more than 2,000 illustrations and highly informative descriptive text.

*Edelson, Edward. *Genetics and Heredity.* The Healthy Body Ser. Chelsea 1989 $18.95. ISBN 0-7910-0018-4 Explains the mechanisms of heredity.

*Edelson, Edward. *The Immune System.* The Healthy Body Ser. Chelsea 1989 $18.75. ISBN 0-7910-0021-4 Discusses the functions of the immune system.

*Facklam, Margery, and Howard Facklam. *The Brain: Magnificent Mind Machine.* Harcourt 1982 $12.95. ISBN 0-15-211388-6 History of research into brain functioning and current research in this area, including such topics as hypnosis, memory, dreams, and biofeedback.

Gilling, Dick, and Robin Brightwell. *The Human Brain.* Facts on File 1982. (o.p.)

Jovanovic, Lois, and Genell J. Subak-Sharpe. *Hormones: The Woman's Answer Book.* Macmillan 1987 $21.95. ISBN 0-689-11647-0

*Kittredge, Mary. *The Respiratory System.* The Healthy Body Ser. Chelsea 1989 $18.95. ISBN 0-7910-0026-5 Explains the structure and functioning of the respiratory system and some common disorders of these organs.

Lewin, Roger. *In Defense of the Body: An Introduction to the New Immunology.* Doubleday 1974 $2.50. ISBN 0-385-03790-X

*Meltzer, Milton. *The Landscape of Memory.* Viking 1987 $12.95. ISBN 0-670-80821-0 Explores the nature of memory and describes ways we remember and causes of memory loss.

*Miller, Jonathan. *The Body in Question.* Random 1981 $10.95. ISBN 0-394-74746-1 Beautifully illustrated discussion of the body and how it functions in good health and poor, based on a 13-part television series broadcast by the British Broadcasting Company (BBC).

*Montagna, William. *Human Skin.* Carolina Biological 1986 $1.90. ISBN 0-89278-150-9 Discussion of the structure and function of the skin, its layers, glands, and other structures; explains the sense of touch.

*Nilsson, Lennart, and Jan Lindberg. *Behold Man: A Photographic Journey of Discovery Inside the Body.* Little 1978 $19.95. ISBN 0-316-60752-5 Macroscopic and microscopic views of anatomical structures and processes that occur in the human body.

Nilsson, Lennart, and Jan Lindberg. *The Body Victorious: The Illustrated Story of Our Immune System and Other Defences of the Human Body.* James Clare (tr). Delacorte 1987 $25.00. ISBN 0-385-29507-3

*Nourse, Alan E. *Your Immune System.* Venture Books Ser. Watts 1989 $12.40. ISBN 0-531-10817-1 Explains how the immune system functions and presents new findings in cancer and immunology research; discusses experimental immunotherapy.

*Parker, Steve. *The Heart and Blood.* The Human Body Ser. Watts 1989 $12.90. ISBN 0-531-10711-6 Discusses the circulatory system, including information on heart disease, heart surgery, drugs, and how the blood helps fight infections.

*Parker, Steve. *The Lungs and Breathing.* The Human Body Ser. Watts 1989 $12.90. ISBN 0-531-10710-8 Explains respiration and discusses smoking-related diseases and the effects of air pollution and exercise on the respiratory system.

Potts, Eva, and Marion Morra. *Understanding Your Immune System.* Avon 1986 $3.95. ISBN 0-380-89728-8

*Silverstein, Alvin, and Virginia B. Silverstein. *World of the Brain.* Morrow 1986 $12.95. ISBN 0-688-05777-2 Discussion of the brain and its functions.

*Silverstein, Alvin, and Virginia B. Silverstein. *Genes, Medicine, and You.* Enslow 1989 $16.95. ISBN 0-89490-154-0 Explains heredity and DNA, gene manipulation, and genetic screening and discusses genetic factors that influence diseases and behavior; raises provocative questions about gene manipulation.

Silverstein, Arthur M. *A History of Immunology.* Academic Pr 1989 $39.95. ISBN 0-12-643770-X

GALEN c. AD 129–200

A Greek physician, Galen wrote hundreds of treatises and books on anatomy and physiology, works that for hundreds of years were considered the authoritative source of knowledge about the structure and function of the human body. Galen used scientific methods to learn about the body, conducting dissections and performing experiments to learn facts such as that blood, not air, flows through blood vessels. At the time, however, dissections of the human body were not allowed, so Galen's learnings were based on dissections of animals, a fact usually not made clear in his published works. Thus his findings as applied to the human body were often erroneous. Nonetheless, he provided important understandings of muscles, bones, blood vessels, nerves, and the brain.

Born in Pergamum, a center of Greek culture in Asia Minor and now part of Turkey, Galen studied in Pergamum, Smyrna, and Alexandria, returning in AD 157 to Pergamum. There he served as physician to gladiators and athletes and began his investigations of physiology. From AD 162 to AD 166 he lived in Rome, where he practiced medicine. Among his patients was Emperor Marcus Aurelius. Although Galen went back to Pergamum in AD 166, Marcus Aurelius persuaded him to return to Rome in AD 168. While acting as court physician to Marcus Aurelius's son, Galen also saw other patients, lectured, wrote, and continued to carry out dissections and experiments. In AD 192 he once again returned to Pergamum and remained there for the rest of his life.

Much of Galen's work survived either in the original Greek or in Arabic translations and was translated into Latin in the sixteenth century. *De methodo medendi (Method of Healing)* became the "bible" of medieval medicine. Galen's greatest work, *On Anatomical Procedure,* was published in 16 volumes. Not until the sixteenth century were the errors in his teachings recognized by Andreas Vesalius, a Belgian physician working at the University of Padua in Italy, one of the centers of medical teaching in Europe. (*See* Vesalius, Vol. 2, Health: Body Systems.)

BOOKS BY GALEN

Galen on Bloodletting. Peter Brain (ed). Cambridge Univ Pr 1986 $44.50. ISBN 0-521-32085-2

Galen on Respiration and the Arteries. David J. Furley and J. S. Wilkie (eds). Princeton Univ Pr 1983 $33.50. ISBN 0-691-08286-3

Galen on the Affected Parts: Translation from the Greek Text with Explanatory Footnotes. R. E. Siegel (ed). Karger 1976 $60.00. ISBN 3-8055-2201-0

Galen on the Usefulness of the Parts of the Body. Margaret Tallmadge May (tr). Cornell Univ Pr 1968.

Greek Medicine: Being Extracts Illustrative of Medical Writing from Hippocrates to Galen. AMS 1977 $16.00. ISBN 0-404-07806-0

BOOK ABOUT GALEN

Persaud, T. V. N. *Early History of Human Anatomy: From Antiquity to the Beginning of the Modern Era.* Thomas 1984 $27.25. ISBN 0-398-05038-4 Brief survey of investigations of anatomy from earliest times through the work of Belgian anatomist Andreas Vesalius; includes information on Galen.

HARVEY, WILLIAM   1578–1657

William Harvey, an English physician, is remembered for having discovered how blood circulates in the human body. Born in the county of Kent, England, Harvey graduated from Caius College of the University of Cambridge in 1597. He then attended medical school at the University of Padua, receiving his M.D. degree in 1602. The Padua medical school was famous as the place where Belgian anatomist Andreas Vesalius had carried out his studies of the structure of the human body. (*See* Vesalius, Vol. 2, Health: Body Systems.) After Vesalius's departure from Padua, studies of the human body had continued, first under Italian anatomist Gabriel Fallopius, who discovered the fallopian tubes leading from the ovaries to the uterus, and then Italian anatomist and embryologist Hieronymus Fabricus, who became Harvey's teacher. Fabricus had discovered the valves of the veins and had observed that their openings were always directed toward the heart. He did not grasp the significance of this discovery, however.

Having completed his studies, Harvey returned to England, where he became a member of the College of Physicians and began to practice medicine in London. In 1607 he became a fellow of the College of Physicians, and in 1609 he was appointed physician to the Hospital of St. Bartholomew, a position he held for 20 years. In 1615 he became lecturer of the College of Physicians, a prestigious position he held for 41 years. During this time he continued his private medical practice and carried out research. In 1631 he was named a physician in the court of King Charles I, who became Harvey's friend and supported his experimental work in many ways.

From Hippocrates, who was born about 460 BC, through the anatomists of the sixteenth century (*see* Hippocrates, Vol. 2, Health: General References *and* Galen *and* Vesalius, Vol. 2, Health: Body Systems), physicians had learned much about the structure of the blood vessels, but the function of these tubes had remained elusive. In 1628, Harvey set forth in his book *Exercitatio anatomica de motu cordis et sanguinis in animalibus (An Anatomical Treatise on the Movement of the Heart and Blood in Animals)* the revolutionary theory together with supporting evidence that the blood circulates continuously through the body, pumped by the heart through the blood vessels. Although Harvey believed that blood flowed away from the heart in arteries and returned to the heart in veins, he was not able to show that the arteries and veins are connected. After the microscope was perfected, the connecting blood vessels—the capillaries—were discovered by Italian anatomist Marcello Malpighi, who published his findings in 1661. With this work, Harvey's theory was proved.

Harvey's fascination with animals of all kinds was recorded in his book *Exercitationes de generatione animalium (On the Generation of Living Things)*, published in 1651. This work contains all that Harvey observed and learned through the experiments he carried out during most of his life.

BOOK BY HARVEY

De Motu Cordis: Anatomical Studies on the Motion of the Heart and Blood (1628). Chauncey D. Leake (tr). Thomas 1978 $23.00. ISBN 0-398-00793-4

BOOKS ABOUT HARVEY

Bylebyl, Jerome J. *William Harvey and His Age: The Professional and Social Context of the Discovery of the Circulation.* Johns Hopkins Univ Pr 1979. ISBN 0-8018-2213-0 Discussion of Harvey's work in the context of his times.

Chauvois, Louis. *William Harvey: His Life and Times, His Discoveries, His Methods.* Philosophical Lib 1957. (o.p.) ISBN 0-8022-0235-7 Discusses Harvey's life as an investigator.

Frank, Robert G., Jr. *Harvey and the Oxford Physiologists: A Study of Scientific Ideas.* Univ of California Pr 1980 $45.00. ISBN 0-520-03906-8 Study of Harvey and the "English School" of physiology.

Franklin, Kenneth J. *William Harvey, Englishman.* MacGibbon and Kee 1961. (o.p.) Biography of Harvey covering his major accomplishments.

Keynes, George. *The Life of William Harvey.* Oxford Univ Pr 1966. (o.p.) Biography of Harvey focusing on his major discoveries in physiology.

Lehrer, Steven. *Explorers of the Body.* Doubleday 1979. Biographies of famous scientists including Harvey.

Singer, Charles. *Short History of Anatomy and Physiology: From the Greeks to Harvey.* Dover 1957. (o.p.) $4.95. ISBN 0-486-20389-1 Classic work on the history of science; includes a discussion of Harvey and his work.

VESALIUS, ANDREAS 1514–1546

A Belgian physician and anatomist, Andreas Vesalius was the first to conduct scientific studies of the human body. His work was revolutionary, for until this time all knowledge of the human body was based on animal dissections that the Greek physician Galen (*see* Galen, Vol. 2, Health: Body Systems) had carried out in the second century AD. For 13 centuries Galen's findings had been considered infallible. Vesalius was the first to challenge his authority.

Vesalius was born in Brussels, Belgium. He studied in Brussels, Louvain, and Paris and obtained his M.D. degree in 1537 at the University of Padua in Italy. He then headed the department of surgery and anatomy at that institution. Becoming convinced that Galen's work had been based on animal studies, Vesalius concentrated on learning about the human body by carrying out dissections of cadavers. In 1543 his findings were published in *De humani corporis fabrica (On the Structure of the Human Body).* The remarkable woodcut illustrations that form the body of this work have been admired ever since. While it is believed that some of the illustrations were the work of Vesalius, most of them probably were executed by artists in the workshop of the Italian painter Titian. In time, the book was expanded, and a revised edition was published in 1555. But, because the book overthrew the teachings of Galen, it inspired a storm of criticism. Vesalius defended his findings in one of two essays published in *Letter on the China Root* (1546).

In 1543 Vesalius left Padua to become a court physician to Holy Roman Emperor Charles V and later, in 1556, to Charles V's son, Philip II of Spain. During this time he became famous as a physician. Wishing to have more time for research, however, he returned to Padua in 1564 to resume his work as head of surgery and anatomy at the university. He never took up the position, though. Before beginning work, he made a pilgramage to Jerusalem and died on the return trip.

BOOKS ABOUT VESALIUS

O'Malley, C. D. *Andreas Vesalius of Brussels, 1514–1564.* Univ of California Pr 1964. (o.p.) Definitive biography of the great anatomist drawing on new information from the last 70 years and reevaluating his contributions to anatomy and medical science.

Persaud, T. V. N. *Early History of Human Anatomy: From Antiquity to the Beginning of the Modern Era.* Thomas 1984 $30.00. ISBN 0-398-05038-4 Brief survey of investigations of anatomy from earliest times to Vesalius in the sixteenth century.

Saunders, J. B. de C. M., and C. D. O'Malley. *The Illustrations from the Works of Andreas Vesalius of Brussels.* Dover 1973 repr of 1950 ed $10.95. ISBN 0-486-20968-7 Woodcuts from works of Vesalius, with discussion of the plates and a biographical sketch of Vesalius.

Singer, Charles. *Short History of Anatomy and Physiology: From the Greeks to Harvey.* Dover

1957. (o.p.) $4.95. Classic work on the history of science; includes a discussion of Vesalius's findings.

See also Vol. 2, Biology: The Human Body.

NUTRITION, DIET, AND WEIGHT CONTROL

Anderson, Kenneth, and Lois Harmo. *The Prentice-Hall Dictionary of Nutrition and Health.* Prentice 1985 $9.95. ISBN 0-13-695602-5

Boston Children's Hospital Staff with S. Baker and R. R. Henry. *Parent's Guide to Nutrition: Eating from Birth Through Adolescence.* Addison 1987 $9.57. ISBN 0-201-05739-5

Brody, Jane. *Jane Brody's Nutrition Book.* Bantam 1982 $12.95. ISBN 0-553-34421-8

*Carper, Jean. *The Food Pharmacy: Dramatic New Evidence That Food Is Your Best Medicine.* Bantam 1989 $9.95. ISBN 0-553-34524-9 Discusses how common foods fight disease and promote good health.

Carper, Jean. *Jean Carper's Total Nutrition Guide: The Complete Official Report on Healthful Eating.* Bantam 1987 $12.95. ISBN 0-553-34350-5

Chilnick, Larry, *et al. The Food Book: The Complete Guide to the Most Popular Brand-name Foods in the United States.* Dell 1987 $9.95. ISBN 0-440-52570-5

Cooper, Kenneth H. *Controlling Cholesterol: Dr. Kenneth H. Cooper's Preventive Medicine Program.* Bantam 1988 $17.95. ISBN 0-553-05254-3

*Eagles, Douglas A. *Nutritional Diseases. First Book Ser.* Watts 1987 $10.40. ISBN 0-531-10391-9 Discussion of nutrition-related diseases, including arteriosclerosis, anorexia, and osteoporosis; for younger readers.

*Eagles, Douglas A. *Your Weight.* Watts 1982 $10.40. ISBN 0-531-04395-9 A guide to weight control for preteenagers and teenagers; contains reference tables giving the energy equivalents of certain foods and activities.

*Edelson, Edward. *Nutrition and the Brain. Encyclopedia of Psychoactive Drugs Ser: No 2.* Chelsea 1988 $18.95. ISBN 1-55546-209-X Explains how a proper diet is essential to normal development and maximal functioning of the brain.

Ensminger, Audrey H., *et al. Food for Health.* Pegus 1986 $49.95. ISBN 0-941218-07-4

Ensminger, Audrey H., *et al. Foods and Nutrition Encyclopedia.* 2 vols. Pegus 1983 $99.00. ISBN 0-941218-05-8

Gussow, Joan D., and Paul R. Thomas. *The Nutrition Debate: Sorting Out Some Answers.* Bull 1986 $10.95. ISBN 0-91590-677-7

Hamilton, Eva M., and Eleanor N. Whitney. *Nutrition Concepts and Controversies.* West Pub 1985 $37.25. ISBN 0-314-85243-3

Igoe, Robert S. *Dictionary of Food Ingredients.* Van Nostrand 1982 $26.95. ISBN 0-442-24002-3

Jacobson, Michael F. *The Complete Eater's Digest and Nutritional Scoreboard.* Doubleday 1986 $11.95. ISBN 0-385-18245-7

Jacobson, Michael F., and Sarah Fritschner. *The Fast Food Nutrition Guide: What's Good, What's Bad and How to Tell the Difference.* Workman 1986 $4.95. ISBN 0-89480-351-4

Kirschmann, John D., and Lavon J. Dunne (eds). *Nutrition Almanac.* McGraw 1985 $12.95. ISBN 0-07-034905-3

Koop, C. Everett. *The Surgeon General's Report on Nutrition and Health: Summary and Recommendations.* USGPO 1988 $2.75.

Kratzner, Brice L., *et al. Nutrition: Where Have All These Labels Been? The "Secret" Nutrition Labels for Over 1200 Common Foods.* Dallas Sandt 1987 $16.95. ISBN 0-936263-78-4

*Lee, Sally. *New Theories on Diet and Nutrition.* Watts 1990 $13.40. ISBN 0-531-10930-5

Introduces the latest information on diet and health, including material on cholesterol, exercise, artificial sweeteners, and pesticides used in food production.

*Lukes, Bonnie L. *How to Be a Reasonably Thin Teenage Girl (Without Starving, Losing Your Friends, or Running Away from Home).* Macmillan 1986 $12.95. ISBN 0-689-31269-5 Discusses nutrition and sensible weight control for preteenage and teenage girls.

Mayer, Jean, and Jeanne P. Goldberg. *Dr. Jean Mayer's Diet and Nutrition Guide.* Pharos 1990 $19.95. ISBN 0-88687-568-4

Natow, Annette B., and Jo-Ann Heslin. *No-Nonsense Nutrition for Kids.* Pocket 1986 $3.95. ISBN 0-671-60779-0

Natow, Annette B., and Jo-Ann Heslin. *Nutrition for the Prime of Your Life.* McGraw 1984 $8.95. ISBN 0-07-028418-0

Nieman, David C., *et al. Nutrition.* Brown 1989 $30.40. ISBN 0-697-05214-1

Null, Gary. *The Complete Guide to Health and Nutrition.* Dell 1986 $13.95. ISBN 0-385-29510-3

*Orlandi, Mario, *et al. Nutrition. Encyclopedia of Good Health Ser.* Facts on File 1988 $18.95. ISBN 0-8160-1670-4 Discusses the nutrients and their effects on the body and how to achieve healthful eating habits.

Osborn, S. *The Great American Guide to Diet and Health.* McGraw 1982 $12.95. ISBN 0-07-069072-3

*Peavy, Linda, and Ursula Smith. *Food, Nutrition, and You.* Macmillan 1982 $13.95. ISBN 0-684-17461-8 Sensible approach to achieving a well-balanced diet; allows some inclusion of fast food and so-called junk foods.

Rinzler, Carol A. *The Complete Book of Food: A Nutritional, Medical, and Culinary Guide.* Pharos 1989 $14.95. ISBN 0-88687-463-7

Smith, Lendon. *Foods for Healthy Kids.* Berkley 1987 $3.95. ISBN 0-425-09276-3

Smith, Lendon. *Lendon Smith's Diet Plan for Teenagers.* McGraw 1987 $4.95. ISBN 0-07-058706-X

Tver, David F. *Nutrition and Health Encyclopedia.* Van Nostrand 1989 $39.95. ISBN 0-442-23397-3

U. S. Public Health Service, Department of Health, Office of the Surgeon General. *The Surgeon General's Report on Nutrition and Health.* Prima 1989 $18.95. ISBN 0-914629-96-4

*Ward, Brian R. *Diet and Nutrition. Life Guides Ser.* Watts 1987 $12.40. ISBN 0-531-10259-9 Guide to what constitutes a healthy diet and ways of improving eating habits; discusses topics such as heart disease and anorexia; includes table of food content and a height–weight chart developed for young people.

Whelan, Elizabeth M., and Frederick J. Stare. *The One-Hundred-Percent Natural, Purely Organic, Cholesterol-Free, Megavitamin, Low-Carbohydrate Nutrition Hoax.* Atheneum 1983. (o.p.) $7.95. ISBN 0-689-70680-4

*Yudkin, John. *The Penguin Encyclopedia of Nutrition.* Penguin 1986 $7.95. ISBN 0-14-008563-7 In dictionary format, contains entries on food, diseases, digestion, and nutrition.

EATING DISORDERS

*Boskind-White, Marlene, and William C. White, Jr. *Bulimarexia: The Binge–Purge Cycle.* Norton 1987 $18.45. ISBN 0-393-02368-0 Discussion of the eating disorders bulimia and anorexia nervosa, the causes and treatment of these disorders, and how to get help.

Bowen-Woodward, Kathy. *Coping with a Negative Body Image. Coping with Ser.* Rosen 1989 $12.95. ISBN 0-8239-0978-6 Advice to teenage girls about viewing their bodies in a positive way so that they do not embark on possibly harmful programs of diet and exercise.

Byrne, Katherine. *Parent's Guide to Anorexia and Bulimia. Understanding and Helping Self-Starvers and Binge-Purgers.* H. Holt 1989 $7.95. ISBN 0-8050-1037-8

Elisabeth L. *Listen to the Hunger: Why We Overeat.* Harper Jr Bks 1988 $6.95. ISBN 0-06-255469-7

Elisabeth L. *Twelve Steps for Overeaters: An Interpretation of the Twelve Steps of Overeaters Anonymous.* Harper Jr Bks 1988 $7.95. ISBN 0-06-255478-6

Hall, Lindsey, and Leigh Cohn. *Eating Without Fear: A Guide to Understanding and Overcoming Bulimia.* Bantam 1990 $3.95.

Hasken, Paul, and Cynthia H. Adams. *Eating Disorders: Managing Problems with Food.* Glencoe 1989.

*Landau, Elaine. *Why Are They Starving Themselves? Understanding Anorexia Nervosa and Bulimia.* Messner 1983 $4.95. ISBN 0-671-49492-9 Presents the facts about the eating disorders anorexia nervosa and bulimia.

*O'Neill, Cherry Boone. *Dear Cherry: Questions and Answers on Eating Disorders.* Continuum 1987 $8.95. ISBN 0-8264-0387-5 Collection of letters received after publication of author's *Starving for Attention* (1982); account of bout with anorexia nervosa.

*Rumney, Avis. *Dying to Please: Anorexia Nervosa and Its Cure.* McFarland 1983 $13.95. ISBN 0-89950-083-8 Discussion of anorexia nervosa and its treatment.

EXERCISE AND FITNESS

*Alter, Judy. *Surviving Exercise: Judy Alter's Safe and Sane Exercise Program.* Houghton 1989 $6.95. ISBN 0-395-50073-7 Well-illustrated guide to exercise for everyone from beginners to athletes.

*Bachman, David C., and Marilynn Preston. *The People's Guide to Sports and Fitness.* Dutton 1980. (o.p.) Comprehensive, informative guide to exercise of various types including running, swimming, bicycling, golf, skiing, and ball and racket sports.

Benyo, Richard. *The Exercise Fix.* Leisure Pr 1989 $10.95. ISBN 0-88011-341-3

Cooper, Kenneth H., and Mildred Cooper. *The New Aerobics for Women.* Bantam 1988 $12.95. ISBN 0-553-34513-3

Diagram Group. *Enjoying Racket Sports.* Stoeger 1972 $4.95. ISBN 0-88317-100-7

Diagram Group. *Enjoying Skating.* Stoeger 1972 $3.95. ISBN 0-88317-101-5

Diagram Group. *Enjoying Swimming and Diving.* Stoeger 1972 $3.95. ISBN 0-88317-102-3

Diagram Group. *Enjoying Track and Field Sports.* Stoeger 1972 $3.95. ISBN 0-88317-104-X

Dominguez, Richard H. *The Complete Book of Sports Medicine.* Warner Bks 1980 $7.95. ISBN 0-446-38181-0

*Fixx, James F. *The Complete Book of Running.* Random 1977 $16.45. ISBN 0-394-41139-5 The classic book on running, with a special chapter for younger runners.

Fixx, James F. *Jim Fixx's Second Book of Running.* Random 1980 $11.95. ISBN 0-394-50898-X

Greenberg, Jerrold S. *Physical Fitness.* Prentice 1988 $21.00. ISBN 0-13-668872-1

Hatfield, Frederick C. *Ultimate Sports Nutrition: A Scientific Approach to Peak Athletic Performance.* Contemporary Bks 1987 $11.95. ISBN 0-8092-4887-5

Jerome, John. *Staying Supple.* New Age Ser. Bantam 1987 $8.95. ISBN 0-553-34429-3

Jokl, Peter, *et al. Sports Fitness and Training.* Pantheon 1987 $27.95. ISBN 0-394-54972-4

*Kettelkamp, Larry. *Modern Sports Science.* Morrow 1986 $12.95. ISBN 0-688-0549-3 Explains how the body functions in athletic performances and discusses advances in understanding of muscle mechanics, metabolism, stress, peak performance, and related topics.

*Kostrubala, Thaddeus. *The Joy of Running.* Pocket 1986 $3.50. ISBN 0-671-54340-7 Introduction to running, an exercise that anyone can practice with little expenditure of money.

Melby, Christopher L., and Gerald C. Hyner. *Exercise and Physical Fitness: A Personalized Approach.* E. Bowers 1988 $10.95. ISBN 0-912855-83-5

Nieman, David C. *The Sports Medicine Fitness Course.* Bull 1986 $22.95. ISBN 0-915950-76-6

*Orlandi, Mario, *et al. Exercise.* Encyclopedia of Good Health Ser. Facts on File 1988 $18.95. ISBN 0-8160-1671-2 Discusses exercise and the beneficial effects of exercise.

Pearl, Bill, and Gary T. Moran. *Getting Stronger: Weight Training for Men and Women.* Shelter 1988 $12.95. ISBN 0-679-73948-3

Polunin, Miriam (ed). *The Health and Fitness Handbook.* Van Nostrand 1981. (o.p.) ISBN 0-442-28785-2

*Prudden, Bonnie. *Teenage Fitness.* Ballantine 1988 $10.95. ISBN 0-345-33303-9 Guide to fitness; provides a test to assess physical strengths and weaknesses, an exercise program that makes use of the school gym, and shape-up activities for various sports.

Smith, Ann. *Stretch! The Total Fitness Program.* Acropolis 1982 $6.95. ISBN 0-87491-239-3

Smith, Anthony. *The Body.* Penguin 1987 $7.95. ISBN 0-14-022614-1

Vedral, Joyce L. *The Twelve-Minute Total-Body Workout.* Warner Bks 1989 $12.95. ISBN 0-446-38961-7

*Ward, Brian R. *Exercise and Fitness. Life Guides Ser.* Watts 1988 $12.40. ISBN 0-531-10562-8 Discusses strength, stamina, and suppleness and explains the benefits of exercise, stressing that fitness can be fun; includes guidelines for exercising and some exercises the reader can try.

PERSONAL CARE

Bark, Joseph. *Skin Secrets: A Dermatologist's Prescription for Beautiful Skin at Any Age.* McGraw 1988 $8.95. ISBN 0-07-003672-1

*Bettancourt, Jeanne. *Smile! How to Cope with Braces.* Knopf 1982. (o.p.) $4.95. ISBN 0-394-84732-6 Explores how wearing braces affects one's life and discusses how to get along with the orthodontist.

Cranin, A. Norman. *The Modern Family Guide to Dental Health.* Scarborough Hse 1973 $4.95. ISBN 0-936437-00-6

De Haas, Cherie. *Natural Skin Care: All You Need to Know for Healthy Skin.* Avery 1987 $8.95. ISBN 0-89529-400-1

Ehrlich, Ann. *Nutrition and Dental Health.* Delmar 1987 $17.95. ISBN 0-8273-2536-3

*Fields, Mike. *Getting It Together: The Black Man's Guide to Good Grooming and Fashion.* Dodd 1983 $12.95. ISBN 0-396-08177-0 A model's suggestions for care of the hair and skin, diet, and nutrition; addressed to the black male.

Flandermeyer, Kenneth, L. *Clear Skin: A Step-by-Step Program to Stop Pimples, Blackheads, Acne.* Little 1979 $8.95. ISBN 0-316-28546-3

Freese, Arthur S. *You and Your Hearing: How to Protect It, Preserve It, and Restore It.* Scribner's 1980 $3.95. ISBN 0-684-16240-7

Fulton, James E., and Elizabeth Black. *Clearing Acne.* Harper 1983. (o.p.)

Kelman, Charles D. *Cataracts: What You Must Know About Them.* Crown 1982 $12.95. ISBN 0-517-54850-X

*Lamberg, Lynn. *Skin Disorders.* Chelsea 1990 $18.95. ISBN 0-7910-0076-1 How the skin functions and malfunctions (acne, skin cancer, and herpes).

Moss, Stephen J. *Your Child's Teeth. A Parent's Guide to Making and Keeping Them Perfect.* Houghton 1979 $7.95. ISBN 0-395-27592-X

*Novick, Nelson Lee. *Skin Care for Teens.* Watts 1988 $12.90. ISBN 0-531-10521-0 A dermatologist's guide to care of the skin and dealing with skin problems; discusses effects of the sun on the skin and cosmetic surgery.

*Parker, Steve. *The Ear and Hearing. Human Body Ser.* Watts 1989 $12.90. ISBN 0-531-10712-4 Explains the structure and functioning of the ear and how to protect hearing; gives information on hearing aids and ear surgery.

*Parker, Steve. *The Eye and Seeing. Human Body Ser.* Watts 1989 $12.90. ISBN 0-531-10654-3 Describes and illustrates the structure of the eye and discusses common vision problems, corrective surgery, and care of the eyes.

*Saunders, Rubie. *Good Grooming for Boys.* Watts 1989 $12.90. ISBN 0-531-10768-X Advice on cleanliness, exercise, and manners; care of the skin, hair, and teeth; selecting and caring for clothes; for preteenage and young teenage boys.

*Saunders, Rubie. *Good Grooming for Girls.* Watts 1989 $12.90. ISBN 0-531-10769-8 Advice for preteenage and early teenage girls about nutrition, exercise, clothes, makeup, and cleanliness.

*Silverstein, Alvin, and Virginia B. Silverstein. *Glasses and Contact Lenses: Your Guide to Eyes, Eyewear, and Eye Care.* Harper 1989 $11.89. ISBN 0-397-32185-6 Explains how the eye functions, problems of eyesight that can be corrected by lenses, and the pros and cons of wearing eyeglasses and contact lenses.

*Silverstein, Alvin, and Virginia B. Silverstein. *So You're Getting Braces.* Harper 1978 $3.95. ISBN 0-397-31787-5 Discusses types of braces and how they work; includes photographs of patients at various stages of their orthodontic procedures.

*Sims, Naomi. *All About Health and Beauty for the Black Woman.* Doubleday 1986 $9.95. ISBN 0-385-18333-X Advice about caring for the hair, skin, hands, and nails and on fashion, beauty, and behavior; discusses mental health and provides information about hospitals and health agencies.

*Sydney, Sheldon B. *Ignore Your Teeth . . . & They'll Go Away: The Patient's Complete Guide to Prevention and Treatment of Periodontal (Gum) Disease.* Davida 1982. (o.p.) Describes the causes and treatment of periodontal disease and provides a nontechnical, step-by-step guide to the prevention of gum disease.

*Ward, Brian R. *Dental Care.* Watts 1986 $12.40. ISBN 0-531-10179-7 Guide to caring for the teeth with discussions of physiology, orthodontics, and nutrition.

*Ward, Brian R. *Touch, Taste and Smell.* Watts 1982 $12.40. ISBN 0-531-04460-2 Describes touch, taste, and smell, as well as the organs involved.

*Zacarian, Setrag A. *Your Skin: Its Problems and Care.* Chilton 1978. (o.p.) $8.95. ISBN 0-80196-669-8 Discussion of topics related to the skin and its care: birthmarks, acne, psoriasis, skin cancer, use of cosmetics, and warts; includes information on the hair.

*Zeldis, Yona. *Coping with Beauty, Fitness and Fashion: A Girl's Guide. Coping with Ser.* Rosen 1987 $12.95. ISBN 0-8239-0731-7 Guide to good grooming and personal care for teenage girls.

*Zimor, Jonathan, and Diane English. *Doctor Zimor's Guide to Clearer Skin.* Lippincott 1980. (o.p.) Discusses acne and gives advice about diet, cosmetics, scar treatment, and seeing a dermatologist.

DRUGS

Cawson, Roderick, and Roy Spector. *Drugs and Medicines: A Consumers' Guide.* Oxford Univ Pr 1990 $14.95. ISBN 0-19-261655-2

*Consumer Guide. *Prescription Drugs.* NAL 1989 $6.95. ISBN 0-451-16287-0 Resource book about prescription drugs.

Hatterer, Lawrence J. *The Pleasure Addicts: The Addictive Process—Food, Sex, Drugs, Alcohol, Work, and More.* Barnes 1980. (o.p.)

Julien, Robert M. *Drugs and the Body in Health and Disease. Psychology Ser.* Freeman 1987 $14.95. ISBN 0-7167-1842-1

*Kittredge, Mary. *Prescription and OTC Drugs. Medical Disorders and Their Treatment Ser.* Chelsea 1989 $18.95. ISBN 0-7910-0062-1 Guide to drugs that can be obtained by prescription and to those available over-the-counter.

*Meer, Jeff. *Drugs and Sports. Encyclopedia of Psychoactive Drugs Ser: No. 2.* Chelsea 1988 $9.95. ISBN 0-7910-0794-4 A look at amateur and professional athletes and the drugs they take either for therapeutic reasons or illegally to enhance performance; discusses the pressures placed on athletes by fans and society.

Melville, Arabella, and Colin Johnson. *Cured to Death: The Effects of Prescription Drugs.* Stein 1983. (o.p.)

Strauss, Richard H. *Drugs and Performance in Sports.* Saunders 1987 $22.00. ISBN 0-7216-1865-0

*Zimmerman, David R. *The Essential Guide to Nonprescription Drugs.* Harper Jr Bks 1983 $12.95. ISBN 0-06-091023-2 Resource book about over-the-counter drugs.

DRUG ABUSE

*Avraham, Regina. *The Downside of Drugs. The Encyclopedia of Psychoactive Drugs Ser: No. 2.* Chelsea 1988 $18.95. ISBN 1-55546-232-4 Exploration of drugs, including nicotine, alcohol, narcotics, stimulants, depressives, halluncinogens, crack, and "designer drugs."

*Avraham, Regina. *Substance Abuse: Prevention and Treatment.* Chelsea 1988 $9.95. ISBN 0-7910-0807-X Discusses the problems of drug and alcohol abuse, effects of these substances on the body, and ways of treating addictions to these substances.

*Berger, Gilda. *Addiction: Its Causes, Problems, and Treatments.* Watts 1982 $12.90. ISBN 0-531-04427-0 Discussion of compulsive dependence on pleasure-giving substances; considers the causes of, treatments for, and attitudes of society toward addiction; includes illegal substances such as narcotics, heroin, depressants, stimulants, and marijuana and legal substances such as inhalants, alcohol, tobacco, and caffeine.

*Berger, Gilda. *Crack—The New Drug Epidemic.* Watts 1987 $12.90. ISBN 0-531-10410-9 Discussion of the manufacture, sale, and dangers of crack, treatment of addiction, and efforts to end the crack trade; lists resources for information or help.

*Berger, Gilda. *Drug Abuse: The Impact on Society.* Watts 1988 $12.90. ISBN 0-531-10579-2 Discussion of how drug abuse is affecting our society, including transmission of AIDS, street crime, drug dealing and trafficking, disruptions of home and workplace; also covers ethical issues, such as testing for drugs.

*Berger, Gilda, and Melvin Berger. *Drug Abuse A–Z. A–Z Reference Ser.* Enslow 1990 $15.95. ISBN 0-89490-193-1 Dictionary of drugs; includes references and lists of agencies that provide information; reviews federal legislation regulating drugs.

Bodenhammer, Gregory. *Drug Free: The Back in Control Program for Keeping Your Kids Off Drugs.* Prentice 1988 $7.95. ISBN 0-13-055336-0

*Browne, David. *Crack and Cocaine.* Watts 1989 $8.90. ISBN 0-531-17047-0 Specific information on origins and effects of crack and cocaine and the operation of the drug trade, as well as forceful warnings about lethality of drug use; a serious and concerned tone for teenagers.

*Gilbert, Richard. *Caffeine: The Most Popular Stimulant.* Chelsea 1986 $18.95. ISBN 0-87754-756-4 Discussion of caffeine, its effects, use, and abuse.

Girdano, Daniel A., and Dorothy Dusek. *Drug Education.* McGraw 1987 $16.95. ISBN 0-07-554988-3

*Hughes, Barbara. *Drug-Related Diseases. First Book Ser.* Watts 1987 $10.40. ISBN 0-531-10381-1 Explains how drugs weaken and put stress on body systems, promoting disease, especially in young people; discusses alcohol, cocaine, heroin, and amphetamines and the health problems associated with these drugs.

*Hughes, Barbara. *Drug Use and Drug Abuse. First Book Ser.* Watts 1986 $10.40. ISBN 0-531-10114-2 Discussion of prescription and over-the-counter drugs, their medical uses and ways they are abused; includes a list of agencies to contact for further information or help.

*Hyde, Margaret Oldroyd. *Mind Drugs.* Putnam 1986 $10.95. ISBN 0-396-08813-9 Discusses the difficulties of treating those who abuse "street" drugs, including hallucinogens and heroin; for older students and adults who counsel them.

LaLoge, Bob. *Drugs and Your Child: What Can a Parent Do?* Namaste 1987 $8.95. ISBN 0-938147-03-X

*Lee, Essie. *Breaking the Connection: How Young People Achieve Drug-free Lives.* Messner 1988 $5.95. ISBN 0-671-67059-X Discusses effective treatment for substance addiction in young people.

*Lindblad, Richard A., and Jerri Lindblad. *Drug Abuse.* Carolina Biological 1984 $1.90. ISBN 0-89278-329-X Considers various types of drugs, their sources, effects, and the risks of taking them.

*Newman, Susan. *You Can Say No to a Drink or a Drug: What Every Kid Should Know.* Putnam 1986 $8.95. ISBN 0-399-51228-4 Discussion of the problems and dangers of alcohol and drug use, with suggestions for ways of resisting pressures to participate.

*Newman, Susan. *It Won't Happen to Me: True Stories of Teen Alcohol and Drug Abuse.* Putnam 1987 $8.95. ISBN 0-399-51342-6 How abuse of chemical substances affected nine young people, including problems they experienced in their home and school lives and in their relationships with family and friends; includes information on alcohol and drugs.

*Orlandi, Mario, and Donald Prue (eds). *Substance Abuse. Encyclopedia of Good Health Ser.* Facts on File 1989 $16.95. ISBN 0-8160-1669-0 Comprehensive overview of drugs in a question-and-answer format; includes information on crack, alcohol, tobacco, and marijuana and gives suggestions for how to get help.

*Seixas, Judith S. *Living with a Parent Who Takes Drugs.* Greenwillow 1989 $11.95. ISBN 0-688-08627-6 Discusses the problems of a fictional boy, Jason, whose family is disrupted by his father's use of drugs; provides information about drugs, addiction, side effects, and treatment.

*Ward, Brian R. *Drugs and Drug Abuse. Life Guides Ser.* Watts 1988 $12.40. ISBN 0-531-10358-7 Discussion of drugs and their effects, with emphasis on the "hard" drugs; covers heroin, cocaine, marijuana, solvents, and "designer" drugs.

*Weil, Andrew, and Winifred Rosen. *From Chocolate to Morphine: Understanding Mind-active Drugs.* Houghton 1983 $16.95. ISBN 0-395-33108-0 Discussion of mind-active drugs, the history of their use, and their effects on individuals and, sometimes, on society.

*Woods, Geraldine. *Drug Use and Drug Abuse.* Watts 1986 $10.40. ISBN 0-531-10114-2 Discussion of several drugs and their recreational uses.

*Young, Patrick. *Drugs and Pregnancy. Encyclopedia of Psychoactive Drugs Ser.: No. 2.* Chelsea 1987 $18.95. ISBN 1-55546-203-0 Explains the dangers of a mother's use of drugs and smoking on her unborn child.

ALCOHOL ABUSE

*Abbey, Nancy, and Ellen Wagman. *Say No to Alcohol.* Network 1987 $11.95. ISBN 0-941816-38-9 Discussion of the problems of alcohol abuse, with suggestions for avoiding addiction and resisting pressure to drink too much, too often.

Black, Claudia. *It Will Never Happen to Me.* Ballantine 1987 $3.95. ISBN 0-345-34594-0

Cahalan, Donn. *Understanding America's Drinking Problem: How to Combat the Hazards of Alcohol. Social and Behavioral Science Ser.* Jossey-Bass 1987 $24.95. ISBN 1-55542-057-5

*Coffey, Wayne. *Straight Talk About Drinking: Teenagers Speak Out About Alcohol.* NAL 1988 $7.95. ISBN 0-452-26061-2 Discussion of alcohol and the problems associated with its abuse, in the words of teenagers.

Forrest, Gary G. *How to Cope with a Teenage Drinker: New Alternatives and Hope for Parents and Families.* Fawcett 1984 $10.95. ISBN 0-449-20535-5

Johnson, Vernon E. *Intervention: How to Help Someone Who Doesn't Want Help.* Johnson Inst 1986 $8.95. ISBN 0-935908-31-5

Leite, Evelyn, and Pamela Espeland. *Different Like Me: A Book for Teens Who Worry About Their Parents' Use of Alcohol/Drugs.* Johnson Inst 1987 $6.95. ISBN 0-935908-34-X

Ludwig, Arnold M. *Understanding the Alcoholic's Mind: The Nature of Craving and How to Control It.* Oxford Univ Pr 1987 $16.95. ISBN 0-19-504873-4

Marlin, Emily. *Hope: New Choices and Recovery Strategies for Adult Children of Alcoholics.* Harper Jr Bks 1987 $15.95. ISBN 0-06-015769-0

Martin, Joseph C. *No Laughing Matter: Chalk Talks About Alcohol.* Harper Jr Bks 1982 $14.95. ISBN 0-06-065440-6

*Newman, Susan. *It Won't Happen to Me: True Stories of Teen Alcohol & Drug Abuse.* Putnam 1987 $8.95. ISBN 0-399-51342-6 How substance use grows into substance abuse, as revealed in the stories of teenagers.

Porterfield, Kay M. *Keeping Promises: The Challenge of a Sober Parent.* Hazelden 1984 $4.95. ISBN 0-89486-245-6

Robertson, Nan. *Getting Better All the Time: Inside Alcoholics Anonymous.* Fawcett 1989 $3.95. ISBN 0-449-21711-6

Schaefer, Dick. *Choices and Consequences: What to Do When a Teenager Uses Alcohol–Drugs: A Step-by-Step System That Really Works.* Johnson Inst 1987 $9.95. ISBN 0-935908-42-0

*Scott, Sharon. *How to Say No and Keep Your Friends: Peer Pressure Reversal.* Human Resource Development Pr 1986 $5.95. ISBN 0-87425-039-0 Explores successful techniques for refusing to join friends in taking alcohol or drugs.

*Silverstein, Herma. *Alcoholism. Venture Book Ser.* Watts 1990 $12.40. ISBN 0-531-10879-1 Describes the different types of alcoholism, the addictive personality, warning signs of alcoholism, and treatments for alcoholism; includes a list of support groups for those who live with an alcoholic.

Smith, Ann. *Grandchildren of Alcoholics.* Health Commications 1988 $8.95. ISBN 0-932194-55-9

*Ward, Brian R. *Alcohol Abuse. Life Guides Ser.* Watts 1988 $12.40. ISBN 0-531-10359-5 Thorough presentation of alcohol, including information on its production, effects on the body, danger signs of abusive use of alcohol, and treatments for alcoholism; includes sources to contact for more information or help.

SMOKING

American Cancer Society. *Facts and Figures on Smoking, 1976–1986.* American Cancer Society 1986. (o.p.)

Benner, J. *Smoking Cigarettes: The Unfiltered Truth: Understanding Why and How to Quit.* Joelle 1987 $10.95. ISBN 0-942723-12-0

*Berger, Gilda. *Smoking Not Allowed.* Watts 1987 $12.90. ISBN 0-531-10420-6 Examines the controversies involved in bans on smoking in the workplace and in public places, as well as proposals to make smoking illegal and to ban tobacco advertising.

Casewit, Curtis W. *Quit Smoking: Forty Major Techniques to Help You Stop Smoking.* Research 1983. (o.p.) $7.95. ISBN 0-914981-44-3

*Condon, Judith. *Smoking. Issues Ser.* Watts 1989 $8.90. ISBN 0-531-17174-4 Examines all sides of the smoking issue: the dangers of smoking, including smoking as a cause of fires, the actions of antismoking activists, the tobacco industry's efforts to grow, and government efforts to educate people about smoking.

Gahagan, D. D., and F. G. Gahagan. *Switch Down and Quit: What the Cigarette Companies Don't Want You to Know About Smoking.* Ten Speed 1988 $5.95. ISBN 0-89815-204-6

*Hyde, Margaret O. *Know About Smoking.* McGraw 1983 $10.95. ISBN 0-07-031671-6 Easy-to-read discussion of smoking and its effects on the body.

*Keigley, Peggy. *Quit and Win: The War of Cigarette Withdrawal Once and for All.* PBK 1987 $9.95. ISBN 0-942285-00-X A personal account of a plan to quit smoking.

Morgan, Cynthia. *If You Love Somebody Who Smokes: Confessions of a Nicotine Addict.* City Miner 1987 $5.95. ISBN 0-933944-14-4

Rogers, Jacquelyn. *You Can Stop: The Smokenders Guide on How to Give Up Cigarettes.* Pocket 1983 $3.95. ISBN 0-671-62691-4

*Sonnett, Sherry. *Smoking. First Books Ser.* Watts 1988 $10.40. ISBN 0-531-10489-3 Reports how the custom of smoking started and spread, the effects of smoking on the body, and the risks of addiction; suggests techniques for quitting.

Sussman, Les, and Sally Bordwell. *An Ex-smoker's Survival Guide: Positive Steps to a Slim, Tranquil, Smoke-free Life.* McGraw 1986 $12.95. ISBN 0-07-062344-9

*Ward, Brian R. *Smoking and Health. Life Guides Ser.* Watts 1986 $12.40. ISBN 0-531-10180-0 Discusses the dangers of smoking, both for the individual and for society, and the benefits of quitting the habit.

COMMUNICABLE DISEASES

*Archer, Jules. *Epidemic! The Story of the Disease Detective.* Harcourt 1977. (o.p.) $5.95. ISBN 0-15-225980-5 Presents a variety of case studies about the epidemic spread of disease.

Bennett, L. Claire, and Sarah Searl. *Communicable Disease Handbook.* Wiley 1982. (o.p.) $20.00. ISBN 0-471-09271-1

*Defoe, Daniel. *A Journal of the Plague Year.* NAL 1984 $4.95. ISBN 0-452-00689-9 Account by the author of *Robinson Crusoe* of the plague oₓ 1665 and how it affected London; one of the earliest documentations of a major epidemic.

*Eron, Carol. *The Virus That Ate Cannibals: Six Great Medical Detective Stories.* Macmillan 1981. (o.p.) $12.95. ISBN 0-02-536250-X Describes the search for the causes of yellow fever, polio, and other virus infections, the scientists involved, and the research they carried out.

*Gregg, Charles T. *A Virus of Love and Other Tales of Medical Detection.* Scribner's 1983. (o.p.) $16.95. ISBN 0-684-17766-8 Describes the detective work involved in discovering the causes of 10 mysterious illnesses, including toxic shock syndrome, herpes, and Legionnaire's Disease.

*Imperato, Pascal James. *What to Do About the Flu.* Dutton 1976. (o.p.) Provides answers to many questions about the flu, including how to avoid infection, how the flu affects the body, treatment, and vaccines.

*Kittredge, Mary. *The Common Cold. Medical Disorders and Their Treatment Ser.* Chelsea 1989 $18.95. ISBN 0-7910-0060-5 Discusses the common cold: what it is and how to cope with it.

*Landau, Elaine. *Lyme Disease.* Watts 1990 $10.90. ISBN 0-531-10931-3 Account of a "new" disease, its causes, how it affects people, and the treatment known currently.

*Metos, Thomas H. *Communicable Diseases. First Books Ser.* Watts 1987 $10.40. ISBN 0-531-10380-3 Discusses the causes and diagnoses of some communicable diseases including sexually transmitted diseases, the common cold, and plagues; for younger readers.

*Scott, Andrew. *Pirates of the Cell: The Story of Viruses from Molecule to Microbe.* Basil Blackwell 1985 $34.95. ISBN 0-631-14046-8 Explores the biology of viruses and how they cause diseases.

*Shader, Laurel, and Jon Zonderman. *Mononucleosis and Other Infectious Diseases.* Chelsea 1989 $18.95. ISBN 0-7910-0069-9 Emphasis on a disease that often attacks teens.

*Silverstein, Alvin, *et al.* *Lyme Disease: The Great Imitator.* Avstar 1990 $4.95. ISBN 0-9623653-9-4 Clear discussion of how the disease was discovered, how it is transmitted, and how to avoid it.

*Stedman, Nancy. *The Common Cold and Influenza. Understanding Disease Ser.* Messner 1986 $11.98. ISBN 0-671-60022-2 Discusses the causes of colds and influenza, the treatment of these diseases, and methods of prevention.

Thomas, Gordon, and Max Morgan-Watts. *Anatomy of an Epidemic.* Doubleday 1982. (o.p.)

Wickett, William H., Jr. *Herpes: Cause and Control.* Pinnacle Bks 1982. (o.p.)

FLEMING, ALEXANDER   1881–1955

Alexander Fleming, a British bacteriologist and the discoverer of penicillin, was born on a farm in Scotland. Although he began working in London when he was only 13 years old, he eventually inherited some money that enabled him to go to medical school. He obtained his license to practice medicine in 1906 from St. Mary's Hospital in London and began work as a bacteriologist at the University of London.

World War I interrupted Fleming's laboratory work but strengthened his determination to find a way of combatting bacterial infections. Serving with the Royal Medical Corps in France, he tended wounded soldiers, many of whom died of infected wounds. Fleming realized both that the antiseptics used to clean wounds were inadequate and that these same chemicals harmed the tissues to which they were applied.

Back in his laboratory, Fleming had two experiences that are often cited to illustrate the meaning of the word *serendipity*. The first instance occurred in 1922. Fleming was working with bacteria that were growing on culture plates. The bacteria colony on one plate was accidentally contaminated by drops that fell from Fleming's runny nose. Fleming kept the plate, and in a few days he noticed that the bacteria on it had died. He realized that something in the material from his nose had killed the bacteria. This antibacterial "something," which was given the name lysozyme, proved to be a chemical that is present in tears, saliva, and mucus and is one of the body's defenses against bacterial infections.

The second instance occurred in 1928. Again Fleming was working with bacteria growing on culture plates. Again some plates became contaminated, this time with a green mold, *Penicillium.* Fleming noticed a clear area near the mold, where bacteria should have been growing. Obviously, something in or produced by the mold had killed the bacteria. This "something" was the antibacterial agent penicillin. Recognizing the importance of his discovery, Fleming investigated penicillin's ability to kill different types of bacteria, but he was not able to isolate the substance in sufficient quantity to use in the treatment of human diseases. In 1941 a group of investigators at Oxford University, including Australian pathologist Howard Florey and German-born British biochemist Ernst Chain, purified penicillin and proved that it was not

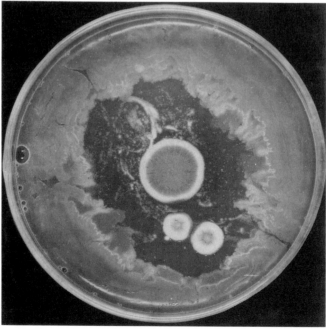

Colonies of penicillium notatus.   Phenomenon noted by Alexander Fleming (1929) who later discovered penicillin. Courtesy of The Bettmann Archive.

toxic. Penicillin came into use in the military during World War II and into civilian use after the war. It was the first of many powerful antibiotics that eventually were obtained from molds or soil and that brought bacterial diseases under control.

Although Fleming's discoveries started with accidents, it was his training as a scientist, his curiosity, and his powers of observation that led from these accidents to the development of new, life-saving drugs. Fleming was knighted in 1944 and shared the 1945 Nobel Prize in physiology and medicine with Florey and Chain.

BOOKS ABOUT FLEMING

Bolton, Sarah K. *Famous Men of Science* Crowell 1960. (o.p.) Biographies of famous scientists including Fleming.

Jacobs, Francine. *Breakthrough: The True Story of Penicillin.* Putnam 1985 $10.95. ISBN 0-396-08579-2 History of penicillin from its discovery by Fleming through its testing and synthesis to its eventual widespread use.

MacFarlane, Gwyn. *Alexander Fleming: The Man and the Myth.* Harvard Univ Pr 1984 $23.95. ISBN 0-674-01490-1 Biography of Fleming that reassesses the man and traces the development of antibiotics.

Maurois, André. *The Life of Sir Alexander Fleming, Discoverer of Penicillin.* Gerard Manley Hopkins (tr). Dutton 1959. (o.p.) Complete biography with photographs of Fleming, his original experiments, and his notes.

*Tames, Richard. *Alexander Fleming. Lifetime Ser.* Watts 1990 $11.90. ISBN 0-531-14005-9 Short biography of Fleming for young readers.

SEXUALLY TRANSMITTED DISEASES

*Landau, Elaine. *Sexually Transmitted Diseases.* Enslow 1986 $14.95. ISBN 0-89490-115-X Discussion of the characteristics, symptoms, diagnosis, and treatment of sexually transmitted diseases.

*Nourse, Alan E. *Teen Guide to Safe Sex.* Watts 1988 $12.40. ISBN 0-531-10592-X Discusses sexually transmitted diseases including gonorrhea, syphilis, genital herpes, and AIDS, the causes and treatment of these diseases, and how to avoid infection.

Rinear, Charles E. *The Sexually Transmitted Diseases.* McFarland 1986 $19.95. ISBN 0-89950-185-0

*Woods, Samuel G. *Everything You Need to Know About Sexually Transmitted Disease.* Rosen 1990 $12.95. ISBN 0-8239-1010-5 Various diseases, with their symptoms and treatments.

*Zinner, Stephen H. *How to Protect Yourself from STD's.* Summit Bks 1986 $6.95. ISBN 0-671-62876-3 Thorough discussion of the causes and effects of sexually transmitted diseases, including gonorrhea, genital herpes, chlamydia, nonspecific urinary tract infection, syphilis, and AIDS.

AIDS

*Ambati, Balamurali, and Jayakrishna K. Ambati. *AIDS—The True Story: A Comprehensive Guide.* BJ Pubns 1988 $12.95. ISBN 0-924385-00-6 Discussion of AIDS, written by the 11-year-old and 17-year-old authors for their peers; foreword by John G. Bartlett, M.D., of Johns Hopkins University.

*Armstrong, Donald. *AIDS.* Carolina Biological 1986 $1.90. ISBN 0-89278-354-0 Discussion of the causes, risk factors, treatment, and prevention of AIDS.

Brighthope, Ian, and Peter Fitzgerald. *The AIDS Fighters.* Keats 1988 $9.95. ISBN 0-87983-482-X

Cahill, Kevin M. (ed). *The AIDS Epidemic.* St. Martin's 1983 $7.95. ISBN 0-312-01499-6

*Consumer Reports Books Editors, *et al.* *AIDS: Trading Fears for Facts: A Guide for Teens.* Consumer Reports 1989 $3.95. ISBN 0-89043-269-4 Discussion of the sensitive issues surrounding AIDS and the impact of the disease on youths; reports current research findings; includes a resource guide that provides AIDS information hotlines for every state.

Dalton, Harlon, and Scott Burris (eds). *AIDS and the Law: A Guide for the Public.* Yale Univ Pr 1987 $9.95. ISBN 0-300-04078-4

*Eagles, Douglas. *The Menace of AIDS.* First Books Ser. Watts 1988 $10.40. ISBN 0-531-10567-9 Discusses the origins and characteristics of AIDS, methods of infection, possible cures, and ways to prevent infection.

Fettner, Ann Giudici, and William A. Check. *The Truth About AIDS: Evolution of an Epidemic.* H. Holt 1984 $8.95. ISBN 0-8050-0199-9

Freudenberg, Nicholas. *Preventing AIDS: A Guide to Effective Education for the Prevention of HIV Infection.* American Public Health Assn 1989 $28.50.

*Gallo, Robert C., and Luc Montagnier. *The Science of AIDS: Readings from Scientific American Magazine.* Freeman 1989 $9.95. ISBN 0-7167-2036-1 Articles about AIDS, its causes, and research efforts; originally published in *Scientific American Magazine,* October 1988.

Hay, Louise L. *The AIDS Book: Creating a Positive Approach.* Hay 1988 $10.00. ISBN 0-317-58538-X

*Hyde, Margaret O., and Elizabeth H. Forsyth. *AIDS: What Does It Mean to You?* Walker 1986 $11.85. ISBN 0-8027-6633-1 Discussion of AIDS geared to preteenagers and teenagers.

Imperato, Pascual J. (ed). *Acquired Immunodeficiency Syndrome: Current Issues and Scientific Studies.* Plenum 1989 $39.50. ISBN 0-306-43188-2

*Le Vert, Suzanne. *AIDS: In Search of a Killer.* Messner 1987 $5.95. ISBN 0-671-65662-7 Describes the on-going search for the causes of AIDS and ways to cure it.

*Jacobs, George, and Joseph Kerrins. *The AIDS File: What We Need to Know About AIDS Now!* Cromlech 1987 $7.95. ISBN 0-9618059-0-0 Discusses AIDS, its transmission, and research into its cause and cure.

Kaplan, Helen S. *The Real Truth About Women and AIDS.* Simon 1987 $5.95. ISBN 0-671-65743-7

*Kurland, Morton L. *Coping with AIDS: Facts and Fears.* Coping with Ser. Rosen 1987 $10.97. ISBN 0-8239-0687-6 Discussion of AIDS, its causes and prevention; explores the myths and fears associated with the epidemic.

Langone, John. *AIDS: The Facts.* Little 1988 $8.95. ISBN 0-316-51412-8

*Madaras, Lynda. *Lynda Madaras Talks to Teens About AIDS: An Essential Guide for Parents, Teachers, and Young People.* Newmarket 1988 $5.95. ISBN 1-55704-009-5 Information about AIDS for adolescents and those who guide them.

Malinowsky, H. Robert, and Gerald J. Perry. *AIDS: Information Sourcebook.* Oryx 1990 $24.50. ISBN 0-89774-598-1

McKusick, Leon (ed). *What to Do About AIDS: Physicians and Mental Health Professionals Discuss the Issues.* Univ of California Pr 1986 $10.95. ISBN 0-520-05936-0

*Nourse, Alan E. *AIDS.* Watts 1989 $12.90. ISBN 0-531-10662-4 Discusses viruses and the immune system, outlines preventive measures to stop the spread of AIDS, describes research efforts and findings.

*Silverstein, Alvin, and Virginia B. Silverstein. *AIDS: Deadly Threat.* Enslow 1986 $14.95. ISBN 0-89490-128-1 Discussion of AIDS, its causes, prevention, and available treatments.

World Health Organization. *AIDS. Prevention and Control.* Pergamon 1988 $36.00. ISBN 0-08-036142-0

NONCOMMUNICABLE DISEASES

American Medical Association Staff. *The American Medical Association Straight Talk No Nonsense Guide to Back Care.* Random 1984 $8.95. ISBN 0-679-73864-0

*Anderson, Madelyn Klein. *Arthritis. Venture Books Ser.* Watts 1989 $12.40. ISBN 0-531-10801-5 Explains the various forms of arthritis, their effects, and the treatments available.

*Arnold, Caroline. *Heart Disease. Venture Book Ser.* Watts 1990 $12.40. ISBN 0-531-10884-8 Discusses diseases of the circulatory system, including strokes, and the treatment and prevention of these diseases.

Berland, Theodore, and Lucia Fischer-Pap. *Living with Your Allergies and Asthma.* St. Martin's 1983 $5.95. ISBN 0-312-49249-9

*Biermann, June, and Barbara Toohey. *The Diabetic's Total Health Book.* Tarcher 1988 $9.95. ISBN 0-87477-473-X Explores how to live a healthy life despite diabetes.

Bracken, Jeanne M. *Children with Cancer: A Comprehensive Reference Guide for Parents.* Oxford Univ Pr 1986 $24.95. ISBN 0-19-503482-1

*Bliss, Michael. *The Discovery of Insulin.* Univ of Chicago Pr 1984 $10.95. ISBN 0-226-05898-0 Account of the medical detective work, competition, and politics involved in the discovery of insulin and the awarding of the Nobel Prize for that work.

*Brown, Fern G. *Hereditary Diseases.* Watts 1987 $10.40. ISBN 0-531-10386-2 Discusses four diseases: diabetes, Tay-Sachs, cystic fibrosis, and sickle-cell anemia.

*Bruce, Shelley. *Tomorrow Is Today.* Macmillan 1983 $15.95. ISBN 0-672-52756-1 Story of the author's theatrical career, particularly her role of Annie in the musical of the same name, and her battle against leukemia.

Cohen, D., and C. Eisdorfer. *The Loss of Self: A Family Resource for the Care of Alzheimer's Disease and Related Disorders.* NAL 1989. (o.p.) $9.95. ISBN 0-452-25946-0

Cooper, Kenneth H. *Dr. Kenneth H. Cooper's Preventive Medicine Program: Preventing Osteoporosis.* Bantam 1989 $18.95. ISBN 0-553-05335-3

Cox, Barbara G., *et al. Living with Lung Cancer: A Guide for Patients and Their Families.* Triad 1987 $7.95. ISBN 0-937404-19-5

*Dolger, Henry, and Bernard Seeman. *How to Live with Diabetes.* Norton 1986 $6.70. ISBN 0-393-30308-X Discusses diabetes, its management, and hope for future improvements in methods of combating the disease.

*Edelson, Edward. *Allergies. Medical Disorders and Their Treatment Ser.* Chelsea 1989 $18.95. ISBN 0-7910-0055-9 Comprehensive treatment of allergies with practical advice for living with them.

*Editors of Time-Life. *Fighting Cancer.* Little 1981. (o.p.) $12.95. ISBN 0-809-43762-7 Explores the types of cancer, causes, prevention, and treatment.

Fine, Judylaine. *Conquering Back Pain: A Comprehensive Guide.* Prentice 1987 $10.95. ISBN 0-13-167826-4

Gelb, Harold, and Paula M. Siegel. *Killing Pain Without Prescription: A New and Simple Way to Free Yourself from Headache, Backache, and Other Sources of Chronic Pain.* Harper Jr Bks 1982 $7.95. ISBN 0-06-463562-7

Goldberg, Myron D., and Julie Rubin. *The Inside Tract: The Complete Guide to Digestive Disorders.* Beaufort 1982 $13.95. ISBN 0-8253-0102-5

*Goodheart, Barbara. *Diabetes. Venture Books Ser.* Watts 1990 $12.40. ISBN 0-531-10882-1 Describes the differences between juvenile- and adult-onset diabetes; discusses causes, complications, and treatment.

*Gravelle, Karen, and John Bertram. *Teenagers Face-to-Face with Cancer.* Messner 1986 $11.29. ISBN 0-671-54549-3 Teenagers discuss hair loss, amputation, and male/female relationships.

Glucksberg, Harold, and Jack W. Singer. *Cancer Care: A Personal Guide.* Johns Hopkins Univ Pr 1980 $39.50. ISBN 0-8018-2255-6

*Hart, Dudley. *Overcoming Arthritis.* Arco 1981. (o.p.) Explains how different forms of arthritis develop, the symptoms of arthritis, and treatments.

*Herda, D. J. *Cancer. Venture Books Ser.* Watts 1989 $12.40. ISBN 0-531-10803-1 Discusses types of cancers, causes, and treatments including surgery, radiation, and chemotherapy; describes cancer research; explores diet and cancer; offers suggestions for coping with cancer.

Keim, Hugo A. *How to Care for Your Back.* Prentice 1981. (o.p.) $5.95. ISBN 0-13-403162-8

*Kerby, Mona. *Asthma. Venture Books Ser.* Watts 1989 $12.40. ISBN 0-531-10697-7 Explores the causes of and treatments for asthma, which is on the increase; offers advice for preventing flare-ups; lists organizations, hospitals, clinics, and summer camps that specialize in the treatment of asthma.

Knight, Allan. *Asthma and Hay Fever: How to Relieve Wheezing and Sneezing.* Arco 1981. (o.p.)

*Landau, Elaine. *Alzheimer's Disease.* Watts 1987 $10.40. ISBN 0-531-10376-5 Explains this degenerative disease of the nervous system and discusses how it affects the family of a person with the disease; gives suggestions for coping with and caring for the patient.

*McGowen, Tom. *Epilepsy. Venture Books Ser.* Watts 1989 $12.40. ISBN 0-531-10807-4 Explanation of this brain dysfunction, the causes of seizures, diagnosis, and treatment; tells what to do for someone who is having an epileptic seizure.

McKhann, Charles F. *The Facts About Cancer.* Prentice 1981 $8.95. ISBN 0-13-299495-X

O'Brien, Eoin, and Kevin O'Malley. *High Blood Pressure: What It Means for You and How to Control It.* Arco 1982. (o.p.)

*Pardee, Arthur B., and G. P. veer Reddy. *Cancer, Fundamental Ideas.* Carolina Biological 1986 $2.40. ISBN 0-89278-128-9 Presents the biology of cancer, including types, causes, and biochemical aspects.

Prescott, David M., and Abraham S. Flexer. *Cancer: The Misguided Cell.* Sinauer 1986 $24.95. ISBN 0-87893-708-0

Scientific American Editors, and Errol C. Friedberg. *An Introduction to Cancer Biology: Readings from Scientific American. Scientific American Reader Ser.* Freeman 1985 $12.95. ISBN 0-7167-1751-4

Shulman, Neil B., and Elijah Saunders. *High Blood Pressure.* Macmillan 1987 $14.95. ISBN 0-02-547440-5

*Silverstein, Alvin, and Virginia B. Silverstein. *Cancer: Can It Be Stopped?* Harper 1987 $12.89. ISBN 0-397-32203-8 Consideration of the symptoms, possible causes, and treatments for several types of cancers; discusses cancer research.

*Silverstein, Alvin, and Virginia B. Silverstein. *Epilepsy.* Harper 1975 $12.70. ISBN 0-397-31615-1 Discussion of epilepsy, its causes and treatment.

*Silverstein, Alvin, and Virginia B. Silverstein. *Headaches: All About Them.* Lippincott 1984 $12.70. ISBN 0-397-32077-9 Discussion of the types and causes of headaches and methods for recognizing, preventing, and treating different types of headaches.

*Silverstein, Alvin, and Virginia B. Silverstein. *Itch, Sniffle, and Sneeze.* Four Winds 1978. (o.p.) Discusses asthma, hay fever, and other allergies.

*Simonides, Carol, and Diane Gage. *I'll Never Walk Alone: The Inspiring Story of a Teenager's Struggle Against Cancer.* Jove 1984 $2.95. ISBN 0-515-08067-5 The author's story about her experiences as a high school student who was active and involved despite having an artificial leg and undergoing chemotherapy and surgery.

*Stockton, William. *Altered Destinies.* Doubleday 1979. (o.p.) Stories of several families affected by hereditary disorders, such as Tay-Sachs disease and Down syndrome.

Williams, Gordon F. *Children with Chronic Arthritis: A Primer for Patients and Parents.* Year Bk Med 1981 $32.00. ISBN 0-88416-273-7

WHITE, PAUL DUDLEY   1886–1973

A world-recognized authority on diseases of the heart and circulatory system, Paul Dudley White was born near Boston, Massachusetts. The son of a general practitioner, he often accompanied his father as he made house calls, driving a horse and buggy. White received an A.B. degree from Harvard College in

1908 and an M.D. degree from Harvard Medical School in 1911. After interning at Massachusetts General Hospital in Boston, he became a resident physician there and maintained his association with the hospital for the rest of his life, eventually heading its cardiac clinic and laboratory. From 1914 until 1956, he also taught at Harvard Medical School.

White's interest in heart disease was stimulated by the death of a sister from rheumatic fever. In 1913, he spent a year in England studying under the heart specialists Sir Thomas Lewis and Sir James Mackenzie. He returned to Massachusetts General Hospital with the first electrocardiograph the hospital had ever owned. Although White was one of the pioneers in the use of this instrument to detect and diagnose heart diseases, he is best known for advocating diet, weight control, and exercise in the prevention and treatment of heart disorders. Summoned to help in the care of President Dwight David Eisenhower after the President suffered a coronary thrombosis in 1955, he became chief medical consultant to the President.

White was a founder of the American Heart Association in 1922 and served as the organization's president from 1942 to 1944. In 1954 he served as president of the International Society of Cardiology. His book *Heart Disease,* first published in 1931 and subsequently revised many times, became a standard in the field of cardiology.

White believed that the cause of world peace could be advanced through the sharing of medical knowledge. From the days of his service overseas in World War I through a visit to the People's Republic of China in 1971 for the purpose of studying medical practices in that country, White acted on this belief. He headed foreign teaching missions, fought a typhus epidemic in Macedonia in 1919, and consulted on the health and care of leaders of many countries. In recognition of his work, he received many honors from foreign countries.

BOOK BY WHITE

My Life and Medicine: An Autobiographical Memoir. Gambit 1971.

BOOK ABOUT WHITE

Paul, Oglesby. *Take Heart: The Life and Prescription for Living of Dr. Paul Dudley White.* Harvard Univ Pr 1986. (o.p.) $19.95. ISBN 0-674-86745-9 Story of the life of the world's most famous heart doctor.

PHYSICAL DISABILITIES

*Gordon, Jacquie. *Give Me One Wish: A True Story of Courage and Love.* Norton 1988 $18.45. ISBN 0-393-02518-7 How one person lives a full, productive life despite disability.

*Hayman, LeRoy. *Triumph! Conquering Your Physical Disability.* Messner. (o.p.) ISBN 0-671-423118-0 The author's story about coping with his disability; information on travel, education, and working.

*Massie, Robert, and Suzanne Massie. *Journey.* Ballantine $3.95. ISBN 0-345-31629-0 Parents tell the story of raising a son with hemophilia; discusses research on blood.

Neal, H. K. *Low Vision: What You Can Do to Preserve—And Even Enhance—Your Usable Sight.* Simon 1987 $16.45. ISBN 0-671-52379-1

Simons, Robin. *After the Tears: Parents Talk About Raising a Child with a Disability.* Harcourt $5.95. ISBN 0-15-602900-6

*Ward, Brian R. *Overcoming Disability. Life Guides Ser.* Watts 1989 $12.40. ISBN 0-531-10645-4 Discusses the disabilities associated with such conditions as Down syndrome, deafness, spinal bifida, and muscular dystrophy; includes addresses of societies and associations that offer support and information.

RUSK, HOWARD ARCHIBALD   1901–

Howard Rusk is renowned for his work in rehabilitation of disabled persons. Born in Brookfield, Missouri, Rusk was educated in the public schools of Brookfield. When his father, a businessman, lost his money, Rusk found work as an orderly and laboratory aid in a hospital, earning enough money to enable him to pursue his goal of becoming a doctor. He graduated from the University of Missouri with a B.A. degree in 1923 and obtained his M.D. degree from the School of Medicine of the University of Pennsylvania in 1925. After interning at St. Luke's Hospital in St. Louis, Missouri, he opened a practice in internal medicine in St. Louis in 1926. He maintained this practice until 1942, when he was called into military service. From 1929, he also taught at the medical school of Washington University in St. Louis, and in 1935, he became assistant chief of staff at St. Luke's Hospital.

Rusk's intense interest in rehabilitating disabled persons became focused during his military service. For Rusk, this interest was a natural outgrowth of his philosophy that a physician must treat the whole person, not just the disease. At the time, rehabilitation was an aspect of medical treatment that was not widely addressed. As a major in the Army Air Forces Medical Corps, Rusk was first assigned to an air forces hospital in Missouri, where he was chief of medical services and responsible for the care of patients recovering from wounds. Observing that morale among the patients was low and that little was being done to help them regain or maintain skills, Rusk instituted corrective measures. Soon patients had the equipment necessary to practice what they had been trained to do in the service, and when they rejoined their units they were fully functioning.

Rusk's work gained the attention of the Commanding General of the Air Forces, General Henry Harley ("Hap") Arnold, who in 1943 appointed Rusk as chief of the convalescent training division in the office of the Air Surgeon. In this position, Rusk introduced training courses in rehabilitation at all air forces hospitals. Under his direction, each patient was given individually prescribed physical therapy that helped to restore him to peak functioning. In time, Rusk's methods were applied to helping the most severely wounded—those who were paraplegics, blind, or lacking one or more limbs. Appalled by the poor quality of prostheses (artificial limbs) available to patients who had suffered amputations, Rusk remedied this problem also, setting up workshops in which new and improved prostheses were developed. Through physical therapy, each patient learned how to do the most possible with whatever parts of the body remained functioning. The result was that many patients who would otherwise have faced a life of dependence on others attained a self-sufficient life; all patients benefited from Rusk's programs.

When Rusk was discharged from the service in 1945, he organized a department of physical medicine and rehabilitation at New York University medical school in New York City. In 1948, he became director of the university's newly constructed Institute of Physical Medicine and Rehabilitation, now called the Institute of Rehabilitation Medicine. There Rusk continued to refine and improve methods of rehabilitating the disabled and to seek better prostheses and equipment to aid those in need. He also enlarged the scope of the institute, accepting those disabled by heart and circulatory problems, victims of stroke, cancer patients, and mentally ill persons. Today the institute is known the world over for its work in restoring disabled persons to functioning, contributing roles in society.

Rusk became familiar to readers of *The New York Times* through a weekly column he wrote for the newspaper. The column, in which he discussed rehabilitation and other health-related topics, appeared for more than 20 years, beginning in 1945.

In addition to his newspaper articles and articles he wrote for professional journals, Rusk was the author or coauthor of a number of medical books, including *New Hope for the Handicapped* (1949) and *Living with a Disability* (1953). In 1972 he published his autobiography, *A World to Care For.*

BOOK BY RUSK

*A World to Care for: The Autobiography of Howard A. Rusk, M.D. (1972). Random 1978. (o.p.) $10.00. ISBN 0-394-48198-4 Rusk tells in delightful detail the story of his life and how rehabilitation came to be regarded as a vital part of patient care.

TRANSPLANTS, ARTIFICIAL PARTS, AND HEART SURGERY

*Berger, Melvin. *The Artificial Heart. Impact Ser.* Watts 1987 $12.90. ISBN 0-531-10409-5 Explores the ethical, legal, psychological, and economic issues involved in the use of artificial hearts.

*Facklam, Margery, and Howard Facklam. *Spare Parts for People.* Harcourt 1987 $14.95. ISBN 0-15-277410-6 Discussion of organ transplants, implants, and grafts and the medical and ethical problems involved in modern medical technology.

*Kittredge, Mary. *Organ Transplants. Medical Disorders and Their Treatment Ser.* Chelsea 1989 $18.95. ISBN 0-7910-0071-0 Discusses organ transplants and some ethical issues involved in these procedures.

*Lee, Sally. *Donor Banks: Saving Lives with Organ and Tissue Transplants. First Book Ser.* Watts 1988 $10.40. ISBN 0-531-10475-3 Overview of transplantation, including problems in finding suitable donors and a list of organizations to contact for more information.

Reinfeld, Nyles V. *Open Heart Surgery: A Second Chance.* Prentice 1983 $14.95. ISBN 0-13-637512-X

Richards, N. V., et al. *Heart to Heart: A Cleveland Clinic Guide to Understanding Heart Disease and Open Heart Surgery.* Antheneum 1987. (o.p.) $14.95. ISBN 0-689-11854-6

Shaw, Margery W. (ed). *After Barney Clark: Reflections on the Artificial Heart Program.* Univ of Texas Pr 1984 $22.00. ISBN 0-292-70376-7

CONSUMER HEALTH

*Anderson, Madelyn Klein. *Environmental Diseases. First Book Ser.* Watts 1987 $10.40. ISBN 0-531-10382-X Discusses pollution and other environmental factors that affect human health, including radon emissions, radioactive fallout, mercury pollution, asbestos, air inversions, and drought.

Belsky, Marvin S., and Leonard Gross. *How to Choose and Use Your Doctor.* Arbor Hse 1975. (o.p.) $4.95. ISBN 0-87795-242-6

*Carter, Sharon, and Judith Monnig. *Coping with a Hospital Stay. Coping with Ser.* Rosen 1987

$12.95. ISBN 0-8239-0682-5 Explains what to expect when you have to go to the hospital and how to help yourself while you are there.

Fein, Rashi. *Medical Care, Medical Costs: The Search for a Health Insurance Policy.* Harvard Univ Pr 1989 $10.95. ISBN 0-674-56053-1

Freese, Arthur S. *Managing Your Doctor: How to Get the Best Possible Medical Care.* Scarborough Hse 1977 $2.95. ISBN 0-8128-2342-7

Goldstein, Sue. *The Underground Shopper's Guide to Health and Fitness.* Fawcett 1987. (o.p.)

*Greenberg, Harvey R. *Hanging In: What You Should Know About Psychotherapy.* Scholastic 1982. (o.p.) $2.95. ISBN 0-590-36351-4 Explains for the teenager what psychotherapy is and how to find a therapist; discusses the stresses and special problems of adolescence.

Jones, J. Alfred. *Communicating with Your Doctor: Rx for Good Medical Care.* Southern Illinois Univ Pr 1988 $19.95. ISBN 0-8093-1367-7

*Kenyon, Carl. *How to Avoid Ripoffs at the Dentist.* Sovereign 1979. (o.p.) Information on choosing a dentist, dental fees, dental disease, and related topics.

*Laws, Priscilla W., and the Public Citizen Health Research Group. *X-Ray Information Book: A Consumer's Guide to Avoiding Unnecessary Medical and Dental X-Rays.* Farrar 1983. (o.p.) $14.00. ISBN 0-374-29342-X Discusses the benefits and problems of X-rays and the physical effects of X-rays.

*Levine, Saul, and Kathleen Wilcox. *Dear Doctor.* Lothrop 1987 $6.95. ISBN 0-688-07095-7 Offers advice and information on choosing a doctor and making other decisions about health self-care.

Mayer, Thomas R., and Gloria G. Mayer. *Health Insurance Alternative: A Guide to Health Maintenance Organizations.* Putnam 1984 $9.95. ISBN 0-399-50979-8

Napoli, Maryann. *Health Facts. A Critical Evaluation of the Major Problems, Treatments, and Alternatives Facing Medical Consumers.* Overlook Pr 1984 $8.95. ISBN 0-87951-196-6

Nash, David T. *Medical Mayhem: How to Avoid It and Get the Best Possible Care from Your Doctor and Hospital.* Walker 1985 $14.95. ISBN 0-8027-0868-4

Plessner, Donna R., and Mark A. Siegel. *Health, a Concern for Every American.* Information Plus 1987. (o.p.) $16.95. ISBN 0-936474-29-7

*Vickery, Donald M., and James F. Fries. *Take Care of Yourself: The Consumer's Guide to Medical Care.* Addison 1988 $14.95. ISBN 0-201-08292-6 Resource book with advice on preventing and self-treating common conditions, when to seek help from a physician, and how to choose a hospital.

Williams, Greg H. *A Consumer's Guide to Emergency Medical Services.* Star Valley 1983 $6.95. ISBN 0-911223-00-2

PERSONAL SAFETY AND FIRST AID

Airhihenbuwa, Collins O. *First Aid and Emergency Care: Procedure and Practice.* Kendall-Hunt 1986 $18.95. ISBN 0-8403-3973-9

American Medical Association Staff. *The American Medical Association Handbook of First Aid and Emergency Care.* Random 1980 $6.95. ISBN 0-394-73668-0

*American Red Cross. *Standard First Aid and Personal Safety.* Am Red Cross 1979. (o.p.) Detailed, easy-to-follow instructions for giving first aid in a wide range of emergency situations.

*Arnold, Peter. *Emergency Handbook: A First-aid Manual for Home and Travel.* Doubleday 1980. (o.p.). ISBN 0-385-42637-2 Tells what to do about accidents that happen in the home and away from home; includes information on preventive measures.

*Auerbach, Paul S. *Medicine for the Outdoors: A Guide to Emergency Medical Procedures and First Aid for Wilderness Travelers.* Little 1986 $24.95. ISBN 0-316-05928-5 How to cope with emergency medical situations when professional help may be far away.

*Benedict, Helen. *Safe, Strong, Streetwise: The Teenager's Guide to Preventing Sexual Assaults.* Little 1987 $5.95. ISBN 0-87113-100-5 Explores ways of preventing and protecting oneself against assault.

*Carter, Sharon, *et al. Coping with Medical Emergencies. Coping with Ser.* Rosen 1988 $12.95. ISBN 0-8239-0782-1 Instructions for dealing with a variety of medical emergencies.

Curtis, Lindsay R. *How to Save a Life Using CPR: Cardiopulmonary Resuscitation.* HP 1981. (o.p.)

Deltakron Institute Staff. *Emergency Medical Procedures for the Home, Auto, and Workplace.* Prentice 1987 $7.95. ISBN 0-13-274408-2

Green, Martin I. *A Sigh of Relief: First Aid Handbook for Childhood Emergencies.* Bantam 1984 $14.95. ISBN 0-553-34364-5

Hafen, Brent Q. *First Aid for Health Emergencies.* West Pub 1988 $30.00. ISBN 0-314-65674-X

Heimlich, Henry J. and Lawrence Galton. *Dr. Heimlich's Home Guide to Emergency Medical Situations.* Simon 1980. (o.p.) $10.95. ISBN 0-671-24447-9

Rosenberg, Stephen N. *The Johnson & Johnson First Aid Book.* Warner Bks 1985 $16.95. ISBN 0-446-38252-3

*Tegner, Bruce, and Alice McGrath. *Self-defense and Assault Prevention for Girls and Women.* Thor 1977 $5.95. ISBN 0-87407-026-0 Discusses how to protect yourself against and prevent assault; common-sense advice for women.

*Tegner, Bruce, and Alice McGrath. *The Survival Book.* Bantam 1983. (o.p.) Manual on coping with and surviving many kinds of emergency situations.

Waisbren, Burton, and Charles J. Waisbren. *The Family First-aid Handbook.* Grosset 1978. (o.p.)

Weiss, Jeffrey. *The People's Emergency Guide.* Bell 1980. (o.p.)

COMMUNITY HEALTH

Brickner, Philip, *et al. Health Care of Homeless People.* Springer-Verlag 1985 $29.95. ISBN 0-8261-4990-1

Caldwell, Mark. *The Last Crusade: The War on Consumption, Eighteen Seventy-two to Nineteen Fifty-four.* Macmillan 1988 $22.50. ISBN 0-689-11810-4

Califano, Joseph A., Jr. *America's Health Care Revolution: Who Lives? Who Dies? Who Pays?* Simon 1989 $9.95. ISBN 0-671-68371-3

Callahan, Daniel. *Setting Limits: Medical Goals in an Aging Society.* Simon 1988 $8.95. ISBN 0-671-66831-5

Haber, David. *Health Care for an Aging Society. Death Education, Aging, and Health Care Ser.* Hemisphere 1989 $29.50. ISBN 0-89116-683-1

*Landau, Elaine. *The Homeless.* Messner 1987 $11.29. ISBN 0-317-61794-X Explores the growing problem of homelessness in society, the causes of homelessness, and attempts to aid homeless people.

Leavitt, Judith W., and Ronald L. Numbers (eds). *Sickness and Health in America: Readings in the History of Medicine and Public Health.* Univ of Wisconsin Pr 1985 $14.95. ISBN 0-299-10274-2

*Leinwand, Gerald. *Hunger and Malnutrition in America. Impact Ser.* Watts 1985 $12.90. ISBN 0-531-10063-4 Discussion of the issues surrounding the fact that many people in this country get too little to eat and others get too little of the proper foods.

Pearman, William A., and Philip Starr (eds). *Medicare: A Handbook in the History and Issues of Health Care Services for the Elderly.* Garland 1988 $22.00. ISBN 0-8240-8391-1

Rosenberg, Charles E. *The Care of Strangers: The Rise of America's Hospital System.* Basic 1989 $12.95. ISBN 0-465-00878-X

Rosenberg, Charles E. *The Cholera Years: The United States in 1832, 1849, and 1866.* Univ of Chicago Pr 1987 $12.95. ISBN 0-226-72677-0

Sagan, Leonard A. *The Health of Nations: The True Causes of Sickness and Well-Being.* Basic 1989 $9.95. ISBN 0-465-02894-2

Shorter, Edward. *The Health Century.* Doubleday 1987 $21.95. ISBN 0-385-24236-0

Whorton, James C. *Crusaders for Fitness: The History of American Health Reformers.* Princeton Univ Pr 1984 $11.50. ISBN 0-691-00594-X

Williams, Guy. *The Age of Miracles: Medicine and Surgery in the Nineteenth Century.* Academy Chi Pubs 1987 $8.95. ISBN 0-89733-285-7

BARTON, CLARA HARLOWE 1821–1912

See also Barton, Vol. 2, United States History: The Civil War.

Clara Barton, the founder of the American Red Cross, was born Clarissa Harlowe Barton in North Oxford, a rural community in Massachusetts. After teaching school in Massachusetts and New Jersey, in 1854 she became a clerk in the patent office in Washington, D.C. With the outbreak of the Civil War in 1861, she independently organized the collection and distribution of supplies for the army and mobilized civilians to send "care" packages to soldiers. Later, she assisted army surgeons, cared for the wounded, and cooked for the troops. Wounded twice, she was known as the Angel of the Battlefield and was beloved by soldiers. When the war ended in 1865, Barton was appointed by President Abraham Lincoln (*see* Lincoln, Vol. 2, United States History: The Civil War) to track down missing prisoners of war. Through her records, many thousands of Union soldiers who died at the Confederate prison at Andersonville, Georgia, were identified.

In 1868 Barton went to Europe. There she met officials of the International Red Cross, who asked her to introduce the organization's work to the United States. She stayed on in Europe and worked with the Red Cross behind the German lines during the Franco–Prussian War, which began in 1870. Returning to the United States in 1873, she began a long campaign to persuade the United States to become a part of the Red Cross and to ratify the Geneva Treaty, which established international guidelines for the treatment of prisoners of war, the sick, and the wounded. Finally, the first chapter of the American Red Cross was established in 1881. The U.S. Senate ratified the Geneva Treaty in 1882.

As head of the American Red Cross, Barton broadened its purpose, and the organization began to provide aid in nonwar-related disasters, such as floods, fires, hurricanes, and epidemics of disease. Barton also directed relief efforts for victims of famines in Europe.

In 1904 Barton resigned from the Red Cross. She died eight years later.

BOOKS BY BARTON

*The Story of My Childhood. Signal Lives Ser (1907). Annette K. Baxter (ed). Ayer 1980 repr of 1907 ed $16.00. ISBN 0-405-12823-1 Barton's story of her youth.

*A Story of the Red Cross (1904). Airmont 1968 $1.50. ISBN 0-8049-0170-8 History of the Red Cross suitable for younger readers.

BOOKS ABOUT BARTON

*Bains, Rae. *Clara Barton: Angel of the Battlefield.* Troll 1982 $2.50. ISBN 0-89375-753-5 Barton's story during the Civil War, told for very young readers.

Barton, William E. *Life of Clara Barton.* 2 vols. AMS (repr of 1922 ed) $44.50. ISBN 0-404-00730-9 Complete biography covering Barton's early life and later years, written by her brother.

Pryor, Elizabeth B. *Clara Barton: Professional Angel.* Univ of Penn Pr 1987 $18.95. ISBN 0-8122-1273-8 In-depth portrait of Barton that confronts the paradoxes of her life.

Stevenson, Augusta. *Clara Barton: Founder of the American Red Cross. Childhood of Famous Americans Ser.* Macmillan 1983 $3.95. ISBN 0-672-52736-7 Biography of Clara Barton emphasizing the early years.

NIGHTINGALE, FLORENCE   1820–1910

Considered the founder of modern nursing, Florence Nightingale was born in Florence, Italy, grew up in England, and traveled widely with her wealthy English parents. She became interested in nursing as a young woman, and in 1844 she began to visit hospitals whenever she could. In 1850 she visited the nursing sisters of St. Vincent de Paul in Alexandria, Egypt. Although she received little training as a nurse—three months of study at the Institute for Protestant Deaconesses in Kaiserswerth, Germany, and two weeks of study in Paris, France—in 1853 she became superintendent of a small hospital in London. Her administrative capabilities were so admired that she was asked to supervise army hospital nurses during the Crimean War between England and Russia. She served in Turkey and the Crimea from 1854 until the end of the war in 1856. During this time she became known as the Angel of the Crimea and the Lady with the Lamp because of her belief that a nurse's care never ceased, day or night.

During her service at army hospitals, Nightingale began a lifelong crusade for hospital and nursing reform. Recognizing that unsanitary conditions and inadequate care of patients were responsible for high death rates in army hospitals (42 percent of patients died), she instituted changes that brought mortality down to 2.2 percent in only six months. Still in the Crimea, she badgered government officials with long reports, filled with statistics, demanding government cooperation and aid in effecting the improvements in army medical services she deemed necessary. She finally achieved her goal in 1857 when a commission to carry out her recommendations was established. The reforms included provision for proper ventilation and drainage systems in hospitals, institution of training courses for orderlies, and establishment of an army medical school.

In 1860 Nightingale founded the Nightingale School and Home for Training Nurses at St. Thomas's Hospital in London. The concept and reality of nurses' training spread as graduates of her school established schools of nursing at other hospitals.

Nightingale remained committed to nurses' training, hospital reform, and public health matters for the rest of her life. In 1907 she was awarded the British Order of Merit, the first woman to be given this honor. In 1915, after her death, the Crimean Monument, Waterloo Place, was erected in London in her honor. In 1934 the Florence Nightingale Foundation was inaugurated, also in her honor.

Among the many books Nightingale wrote are *Notes on Matters Affecting the Health, Efficiency and Hospital Administration of the British Army* (1857), *Notes on Nursing: What It Is and What It Is Not* (1859), and *Notes on Hospitals* (1859). Much of the correspondence she carried on over the years has also been published under various titles.

BOOKS BY NIGHTINGALE

I Have Done My Duty: Florence Nightingale in the Crimean War, 1854–56. Sue M. Goldie (ed). Univ of Iowa Pr 1988 $32.00. ISBN 0-87745-185-0

Letters from Egypt: A Journey on the Nile, 1849–1850. Connie Sayre (ed). Weidenfeld 1988 $24.95. ISBN 1-55584-204-6

Notes on Nursing: What It Is and What It Is Not (1859). Dover 1969 $3.50. ISBN 0-486-22340-X

BOOKS ABOUT NIGHTINGALE

Boyd, Nancy. *Three Victorian Women Who Changed Their World.* Oxford Univ Pr 1982 $29.95. ISBN 0-19-520271-6 Examination of the theological views of Nightingale, Josephine Butler, and Octavia Hill that attributes their social vision to their deep religious faith.

Huxley, Elspeth. *Florence Nightingale.* Putnam 1975. ISBN 0-399-91480-7 Illustrated, accessible biography that presents Nightingale's contradictions as nurse, administrator, and invalid.

Strachey, Lytton. *Eminent Victorians.* Penguin 1987 repr of 1918 ed $6.95. ISBN 0-14-00649-4 Classic book that includes the story of Florence Nightingale.

Rosenberg, Charles E. (ed). *Florence Nightingale on Hospital Reform. Medical Care in the United States Ser.* Garland 1989 $60.00. ISBN 0-8240-8340-7 A look at the modernization of hospitals through the efforts of Nightingale and others who worked for reform.

*Tames, Richard. *Florence Nightingale. Lifetimes Ser.* Watts 1990 $11.90. ISBN 0-531-14005-9 Short biography of Nightingale for young readers.

Woodham-Smith, Cecil Blanche. *Florence Nightingale, 1820–1910.* Atheneum 1983. Classic biography of the founder of the nursing profession.

THE ENVIRONMENT AND HEALTH

*Anderson, Modelyn Klein. *Environmental Diseases.* Watts 1987 $10.40. ISBN 0-531-10382-X Discussion of different kinds of environments that can cause health problems and serious diseases caused by toxic wastes.

*Bach, Julie S., and Lynn Hall (eds). *The Environmental Crisis: Opposing Viewpoints. Opposing Viewpoint Ser.* Greenhaven 1986 $7.95. ISBN 0-89908-366-8 Balanced discussions of environmental issues.

*Berger, Melvin. *Hazardous Substances: A Reference.* Enslow 1986 $15.95. ISBN 0-89490-116-8 Informative book dealing with hazardous substances in the home, workplace, and environment.

Dadd, Debra L. *The Nontoxic Home: Protecting Yourself and Your Family from Everyday Toxics and Health Hazards.* Tarcher 1986 $9.95. ISBN 0-87477-401-2

Epstein, Samuel S., *et al. Hazardous Waste in America: Our Number One Environmental Crisis.* Sierra Club 1983 $12.95. ISBN 0-87156-807-1

*Gay, Kathlyn. *Silent Killers: Radon and Other Hazards. Impact Books Ser.* Watts 1988 $12.90. ISBN 0-531-10598-9 Addresses the problem of radiation, substances, and objects in the home and workplace that may be harmful to health; includes radon radiation, asbestos, and dioxin, benzene, formaldehyde, and many other common chemicals.

Gershey, Edward L. *Low-Level Radioactive Waste: From Cradle to Grave.* Van Nostrand 1990 $32.95. ISBN 0-442-23958-0

Liroff, Richard A. *Reforming Air Pollution Regulation: The Toil and Trouble of EPA's Bubble.* Conservation Foundation 1986 $16.50. ISBN 0-89164-072-X

Lillyquist, Michael J. *Sunlight and Health: The Positive and Negative Effects of the Sun on You.* Dodd 1987 $7.95. ISBN 0-396-08957-7

*Miller, Christina G., and Louise A. Berry. *Acid Rain: A Sourcebook for Young People.* Messner 1986 $9.79. ISBN 0-671-60177-6 Discusses acid rain, what causes it, its effects, and what is being done to decrease its occurrence.

*Panati, Charles, and Michael Hudson. *The Silent Intruder: Surviving the Radiation Age.* Houghton 1981 $9.95. ISBN 0-395-29478-9 Discussion of radiation in the environment and its effects on health.

Regenstein, Lewis. *How to Survive in America the Poisoned.* Acropolis 1986 $9.95. ISBN 0-87491-838-3

Schuck, Peter H. *Agent Orange on Trial: Mass Toxic Disasters in the Courts.* Harvard Univ Pr 1988 $12.95. ISBN 0-674-01026-4

*Ward, Brian R. *The Environment and Health.* Watts 1989 $12.40. ISBN 0-531-10644-6 Discusses the effects of air pollution, food additives, and chemicals in water on health; includes addresses of agencies concerned with protecting the environment.

Weir, David. *The Bhopal Syndrome: Pesticides, Environment, and Health.* Sierra Club 1988 $8.95. ISBN 0-87156-797-0

See also Vol. 2, Biology: Ecology and the Environment; Geography: Environmental Issues.

APPENDIX:
LIST OF PUBLISHERS

The following list includes the abbreviations and full names of publishers whose titles appear in *The Young Adult Reader's Adviser.* The abbreviated form of a publisher's name as it appears throughout the two volumes is shown in boldface. The abbreviation is followed by the complete form of the name. The alphabetization method is word-by-word. Those university presses with standard abbreviations that need no further explanation have been omitted. For full information, addresses, and telephone and fax numbers, see the latest edition of *Books in Print.*

A

A & M   A & M Books
AAHPERD   American Alliance for Health, Physical Education, Recreation & Dance
Abaca   Abaca Books
Abacus Pr   Abacus Press
Abacus Pub   Abacus Publishing Co.
Abacus Soft   Abacus Software, Inc.
Abaris   Abaris Books, Inc.
ABBE   ABBE Publishers, Association of Washington, D.C.
Abbeville   Abbeville Press, Inc.
ABC-Clio   ABC-CLIO, Inc.
Aberdeen   Aberdeen Group
Abingdon   Abingdon Press
Ablex   Ablex Publishing Corp.
Abner Schram   Abner Schram, Ltd.
Abrams   Harry N. Abrams, Inc.
Academia   Academia Press
Academic Intl   Academic International Press
Academic Pr   Academic Press, Inc.
Academic Pubns   Academic Publications
Academy Bks   Academy Books
Academy Chi Pubs   Academy Chicago Publishers, Ltd.
Acadia   Acadia Publishing Co.
Ace   Ace Books

Acropolis   Acropolis Books
Activity Resources   Activity Resources Co., Inc.
Adama   Adama Publishers, Inc.
Adams Inc MA   Bob Adams, Inc.
Adams Pr   Adams Press
Addison   Addison-Wesley Publishing Co., Inc.
Adlers   Adlers Foreign Books, Inc.
Advent   Advent Books, Inc.
Airmont   Airmont Publishing Co., Inc.
ALA   American Library Association
Alba   Alba House
Aldine   Aldine de Gruyter
Algonquin   Algonquin Books of Chapel Hill
Allen   Allen Press, Inc.
Allyn   Allyn & Bacon, Inc.
Am Acad Pol Soc Sci   American Academy of Politics and Social Science
Am Assn Physics   American Association of Physics Teachers
Am Chemical   American Chemical Society
Am Christian Pr   American Christian Press
Am Enterprise Inst   American Enterprise Institute for Public Policy Research

Am Inst Chem Eng American Institute of Chemical Engineers

Am Inst Psych The American Institute for Psychological Research

Am Jewish Comm American Jewish Committee

Am Philos American Philosophical Society

Am Red Cross American Red Cross, Allen-Wells Chapter

Am Soc Pub Admin American Society for Public Administration

Amer Mus of Nat Hist American Museum of Natural History

Amereon Amereon, Ltd.

American Assn of Retired Persons American Association of Retired Persons

American Cancer Society American Cancer Society, Inc.

American Classical Coll Pr American Classical College Press

American Forestry American Forestry Association

American Heritage American Heritage

American Poetry American Poetry & Literature Press

American Psychological Assn American Psychological Association

American Public Health Assn American Public Health Association Publications

American-Scandinavian American-Scandinavian Foundation

AMS AMS Press, Inc.

AMSCO AMSCO School Publications, Inc.

Anchor Anchor Press, *imprint of* Doubleday & Co., Inc.

Andrew Mountain Andrew Mountain Press

Andrews Andrews & McMeel

Andrews Univ Pr Andrews University Press

Annual Reviews Annual Reviews, Inc.

Antelope Island Antelope Island Press

Anthroposophic Anthroposophic Press, Inc.

Aperture Aperture Foundation, Inc.

Aperture NW Aperture Northwest, Inc.

APL Pr APL Press

Applause Theatre Bk Applause Theatre Book Publishers

Apt Apt Books, Inc.

Arbor Hse Arbor House, *imprint of* William Morrow & Co., Inc.

Arcade Arcade Publishers

Archway Archway Paperbacks, *imprint of* Pocket Books, Inc.

Arco Arco Publishing, Inc.

Ardis Ardis Publishers

Ardsley Ardsley House Publishers, Inc.

Ares Ares Publishers, Inc.

Argosy Argosy

Aronson Jason Aronson, Inc.

ARS ARS Enterprises

Arte Publico Arte Publico Press

Asia Bk Corp Asia Book Corp. of America

Assn Amer Geographers Association of American Geographers

Assn Inform & Image Association for Information & Image Management

Assn Supervision Association for Supervision & Curriculum Development

Assoc Faculty Pr Associated Faculty Press, Inc.

Assoc Univ Pr Associated University Presses

Athelstan Athelstan Publications

Athenaeum Athenaeum of Philadelphia

Atheneum Atheneum, *imprint of* Macmillan Publishing Co., Inc.

Atlantic Monthly Atlantic Monthly Press

Auburn Auburn House Publishing Co., Inc., *imprint of* Greenwood Publishing Group, Inc.

Augsburg Fortress Augsburg Fortress Publishers

Augustinian Augustinian Press

Augustinian Coll Pr Augustinian College Press

Auromere Auromere, Inc.

Avery   Avery Publishing Group, Inc.
Avon   Avon Books
Avstar   Avstar Publishing Corp.
Ayer   Ayer Co. Publishers, Inc.

B

B & N Imports   Barnes & Noble Books—Imports
B. C. Scribe   B. C. Scribe Publications
Baen   Baen Books
Baker Bk   Baker Book House
Baker Pub   Baker Publishing
Ballantine   Ballantine Books, Inc.
Ballinger   Ballinger Publishing Co.
Banner of Truth   The Banner of Truth
Bantam   Bantam Books, Inc.
Barnes   Barnes & Noble Books
Barron   Barron's Educational Series, Inc.
Basic   Basic Books, Inc.
Basil Blackwell   Basil Blackwell, Inc.
Battery Pk   Battery Park Book Co.
Battery Pr   Battery Press
Battle Rd   Battle Road Press
Beacon   Beacon Press, Inc.
Bearly   Bearly, Ltd.
Beatty   R. W. Beatty
Beau Lac   Beau Lac Publishers
Beaufort   Beaufort Books, Publishers
Bedrick   Peter Bedrick Books
Beekman   Beekman Publishers, Inc.
Beil   Frederic C. Beil Publisher, Inc.
Bellerophon   Bellerophon Books
Benjamin Co.   Benjamin Co., Inc.
Benjamin-Cummings   Benjamin-Cummings Co. Publishing
Benjamin Pr   Benjamin Press
Benjamin Pub   Benjamin Publishing Co.
Benjamins   John Benjamins North America, Inc.
Bentley   Robert Bentley, Inc. Publishers
Bergin & Garvey   Bergin & Garvey Publishers, Inc., *imprint of* Greenwood Publishing Group, Inc.

Berkley   Berkley Publishing Group
Berkley West   Berkley West Publishing
Berkshire Traveller   Berkshire Traveller Press
Berle   Berle Books
Bess Pr   Bess Press, Inc.
Betterway Pubns   Betterway Publications
Biblio Dist   Biblio Distribution Center
Biblio Pub   Biblio Publishing
Biblio Pr   Biblio Press, the Jewish Women's Publisher
Biblio Siglo   Biblioteca Siglo de Oro
Bibliotheca   Bibliotecha Islamica, Inc.
Biblo   Biblo & Tannen Booksellers & Publishers, Inc.
Bilicki   Bilicki Publications
Birch Lane   Birch Lane Press, *imprint of* Carol Publishing Group
Birkhauser   Birkhauser Boston, Inc.
BJ Pubns   BJ Publications
Black Classic   Black Classic Press
Black Rose   Black Rose Books
Black Swan Bks   Black Swan Books, Ltd.
Black Swan Pr   Black Swan Press
BMDP Stat   BMDP Statistical Software
Bobbs   Bobbs-Merrill Co., *imprint of* Macmillan Publishing Co., Inc.
Bolchazy-Carducci   Bolchazy-Carducci Publishers
Bonus   Bonus Books, Inc.
Book-Lab   Book-Lab
Book Sales   Book Sales, Inc.
Books Demand   Books on Demand
Bookwrights   Bookwrights
Boone & Crockett   Boone & Crockett Club
Boone-Thomas   Boone-Thomas Enterprises
Boosey & Hawkes   Boosey & Hawkes, Inc.
Borden   Borden Publishing Co.
Borgo   Borgo Press
Boston Coll Math   Boston College Mathematics Institute
Boulevard   Boulevard Books
Bowker   R. R. Bowker
Boxwood   Boxwood Press

Boy Scouts   Boy Scouts of America
Boyd & Fraser   Boyd & Fraser
Publishing Co.
Boyd Co   Boyd Co.
Boyd Deep Canyon   University of
California at Riverside, Boyd
Deep Canyon Desert Research
Center
Boyd Griffin   Boyd Griffin, Inc.
Boydell & Brewer   Boydell &
Brewer, *imprint of* Longwood
Publishing Group, Inc.
Boynton   Boynton Cook
Publishers, Inc.
Bradbury Pr   Bradbury Press
Brady Bks   Brady Books
Branden   Branden Publishing Co.
Braziller   George Braziller, Inc.
Brethren   Brethren Press
Broadside   Broadside Press
Brookings   Brookings Institution
Brookline   Brookline Books
Brooklyn Coll Pr   Brooklyn
College Press
Brooks   Brooks Publishing Co.
Brooks-Cole   Brooks/Cole
Publishing Co.
Brooks Ent   Brooks Enterprises
Brown   William C. Brown
Publishers
Brunner-Mazel   Brunner/Mazel
Publishers
Buccaneer   Buccaneer Books
Bulfinch   Bulfinch Press, *imprint of*
Little, Brown & Co.
Bull   Bull Publishing Co.
Burt Franklin   Burt Franklin
Publisher
Butterworth   Butterworth
Publishers

C

C. Coolidge Memorial   Calvin
Coolidge Memorial Foundation,
Inc.
C. H. Kerr   Charles H. Kerr
Publishing Co.
Cambridge   Cambridge Book
Co.
Cambridge Univ Pr   Cambridge
University Press
Camelot   Camelot Books, *imprint of*
Avon Books

Camelot Consult   Camelot
Consultants
Camelot Pr   Camelot Press, Ltd
Camelot Pub   Camelot Publishing
Camelot Pub Co   Camelot
Publishing Co.
Camelot Pubs   Camelot Publishers
Camelot Self   Camelot Self
Subsidy Publishers
Cameron   Cameron & Co., Inc.
Capitalist   Capitalist Press
Capra   Capra Press
Capricorn Bks   Capricorn Books
Capricorn Corp   Capricorn
Corp.
Caravan   Caravan Books
Carcanet   Carcanet Press
Carlson   Carlson Publishing, Inc.
Carnegie Institution of Washington
Carnegie Institution of
Washington
Carol   Carol Publishing Group
Carolina Acad Pr   Carolina
Academic Press
Carolina Biological   Carolina
Biological Supply Co.,
Publications Department
Carroll & Graf   Carroll & Graf
Publishers
Carroll Coll   Carroll College Press
Carroll Pr   Carroll Press
Carroll Pub   Carroll Publishing Co.
Catbird   Catbird Press
Catholic Bk Pub   Catholic Book
Publishing Co.
Caxton   Caxton Printers, Ltd.
Cayucos   Cayucos Books
Celo   Celo Press
Chandler & Sharp   Chandler &
Sharp Publishers
Charles   Charles Press Publishers
Charles Pub   Charles Publishing
Co.
Charles River   Charles River
Books
Chelsea   Chelsea House Publishers
Chicago Review   Chicago Review
Press, Inc.
Childrens   Children's Press
Chilton   Chilton Book Co.
China Bks   China Books &
Periodicals, Inc.
China Hse Arts   China House of
Arts
China Res   China Research

China West China West Books
Choice Pub Choice Publishing, Inc.
Christian Classics Christian Classics, Inc.
Christian Lit Christian Literature Crusade, Inc.
Christopher Christopher Publishing House
Chronicle Chronicle Books
Citadel Citadel Press, *imprint of* Carol Publishing Group
CITE Center for International Training & Education
City Lights City Lights Books
City Miner City Miner Books
Clarendon Clarendon Group, Inc.
Clarity Pr Clarity Press
Clarity Pub Clarity Publishing
Clark Clark Publishing, Inc.
Clark City Pr Clark City Press
Clark Davis Clark Davis Publishing Co.
Clark Univ Pr Clark University Press
Cleckley-Thigpen Cleckley-Thigpen Psychiatric Associates
College-Hill College-Hill Press, Inc.
Collins Collins Publishers
Colton Colton Book Imports
Columbia Scholastic Columbia Scholastic Press Association
Comptr Pub Computer Publishing Enterprises
Compute Pubns Compute! Publications, Inc.
Computer Based Pubns Computer Based Publications
Computer Direct Computer Directions for Schools
Computer-Prop Computer-Propaganda Press
Computer Science Pr Computer Science Press, Inc., *imprint of* W. H. Freeman & Co.
Computing Computing!
Computing Trends Computing Trends
Concord Grove Concord Grove Press
Congressional Quarterly Congressional Quarterly, Inc.

Connecticut Historical Soc The Connecticut Historical Society Press
Conservation Foundation Conservation Foundation
Consumer Reports Consumer Reports Books
Contact Contact/II Publications
Contemporary Bks Contemporary Books, Inc.
Continuum Continuum Publishing Co.
Cook David C. Cook Publishing Co.
Cooper Square Cooper Square Publishers, Inc.
Cordillera Cordillera Press, Inc.
Corner Corner House Publishers
Coronet Coronet, The Multimedia Co.
Coronet Bks Coronet Books
Coun Exc Child Council for Exceptional Children
Council Oak Council Oak Books
Council of State Governments Council of State Governments
Counter Prop The Counter-Propaganda Press
Coward Coward, McCann & Geoghegan, *imprint of* The Putnam Publishing Group
Crabtree Crabtree Publishing
Crabtree Pub Crabtree Publishing Co.
Create Learn Creative Learning Press, Inc.
Creative Ed Creative Education, Inc.
Creative Pubns Creative Publications
CRC Pr CRC Press, Inc.
CRC Pubns CRC Publications
Cromlech Cromlech Books, Inc.
Cross Cultural Cross-Cultural Communications
Crossing Pr The Crossing Press
Crossroad Crossroad Publishing Co.
Crowell Thomas Y. Crowell Co.
Crown Crown Publishers, Inc.
Crown Bks Crown Books
Crown Intle Crown Internationale
Crown Pub Crown Publishing Co., Inc.

Crown Pubns Crown Publications, Inc.
Ctr for Creative Photography Center for Creative Photography
Curbstone Curbstone Press

Dufour Dufour Editions, Inc.
Durbin Assoc Durbin Associates
Dushkin Dushkin Publishing Group, Inc.
Dutton E. P. Dutton

D

D I Fine Donald I. Fine, Inc.
Da Capo Da Capo Press, Inc.
Dallas Sandt Dallas Sandt Co.
Dante Univ Dante University of America Press, Inc.
Darien Darien House Books
Daring Daring Books
Daughters St. Paul Daughters of Saint Paul
David and Charles David & Charles, Inc.
Davida Davida Publications
Davis Pubns Davis Publications, Inc.
de Gruyter Walter de Gruyter, Inc.
Dekker Marcel Dekker, Inc.
Del Rey Del Rey Books, *imprint of* Ballantine Books, Inc.
Delacorte Delacorte Press
Dell Dell Publishing Co., Inc.
Delmar Delmar Publishers, Inc.
Dembner Dembner Books
Devin-Adair Devin-Adair Publishers, Inc.
Dial Dial Press, *imprint of* Doubleday & Co., Inc.
Dillon Dillon Press, Inc.
Documentary Pubns Documentary Publications
Dodd Dodd, Mead & Co.
Dodd-Blair Dodd-Blair & Associates
Donald Cohen Donald Cohen
Dorchester Dorchester Publishing Co., Inc.
Dorset Dorset Press
Dorset Hse Dorset House Publishing Co., Inc.
Dorset Pub Dorset Publishing Co., Inc.
Dorsett Dorsett
Doubleday Doubleday & Co., Inc.
Dover Dover Publications, Inc.
Dow Jones Dow Jones-Irwin
Dryden Dryden Press

E

E. Bowers Eddie Bowers Publishing Co.
E. J. Brill E. J. Brill (U.S.A.), Inc.
Eagle Bks Eagle Books
Eagle Cliff Eagle Cliff Publications
Eagle Comm Eagle Communications
Eagle North Eagle North Communications
Eagle Peak Pub Eagle Peak Publishing Co.
Eagle Pr Eagle Press
Eagle Pr Inc Eagle Press, Inc.
Eagle Pub Eagle Publishing Co.
Eagle Pub Corp Eagle Publishing Corp.
Eagle Pubn Co Eagle Publication Co.
Eagle Wing Bks Eagle Wing Books
Eakin Eakin Press
Eakins Eakins Press Foundation
Ecco Ecco Press
Ed Research Education Research Associates
Ed Solutions Educational Solutions, Inc.
Ed-U Pr Ed-U Press, Inc.
EDC EDC Publishing
Edins Hispamerica Ediciones Hispamerica
Editions Publisol Editions Publisol
Educ Tech Pubns Educational Technology Publications, Inc.
Eerdmans William B. Eerdmans Publishing Co.
Eisenbrauns Eisenbrauns
Elliots Elliot's Books
Elsevier Elsevier Science Publishing Co, Inc.
EMC EMC Publishing
Empak Empak Publishing Co.
Enslow Enslow Publishers, Inc.
Environmental Design Environmental Design & Research Center

Ergosyst   Ergosyst Associates, Inc.
Eridanos   Eridanos Press
Erlbaum   Lawrence Erlbaum Associates, Inc.
Ethnology Monographs   Ethnology Monographs
Eurasia   Eurasia Press

F

Faber & Faber   Faber & Faber, Inc.
Facts on File   Facts on File, Inc.
Fairleigh   Fairleigh Dickinson University Press
Fairmont   Fairmont Press, Inc.
Farrar   Farrar, Straus & Giroux, Inc.
Fawcett   Fawcett Book Group
Feminist Pr   Feminist Press at the City University of New York
Fertig   Howard Fertig, Inc.
Finnish American   Finnish American Literary Heritage Foundation
Fireside   Fireside Paperbacks, *imprint of* Simon & Schuster, Inc.
Fjord   Fjord Press
Flare   Avon Flare Books, *imprint of* Avon Books
Fleet   Fleet Press Corp.
Flint Inst of Arts   Flint Institute of Arts
FlipTrack   FlipTrack Learning Systems
Focal   Focal Press
Focal Point   Focal Point Press
Focus Information   Focus Information Group, Inc.
Folger   Folger Books
Folkcroft   Folkcroft
Follett   Follett Press
Foreign Language   Foreign Language for Young Children
Foreign Policy Assn   Foreign Policy Association
Forum Pr   Forum Press, Inc.
Found Amer Ed   The Foundation for American Education
Found Class Repr   The Foundation for Classical Reprints
Foundation   Foundation Books, *imprint of* Doubleday & Co., Inc.
Foundation Bks   Foundation Books

Foundation Hse   Foundation House Publications, Inc.
Foundation Pr   Foundation Press, Inc.
Four Winds   Four Winds Press, *imprint of* Macmillan Publishing Co., Inc.
Free Pr   Free Press
Free Spirit   Free Spirit Publishing, Inc.
Freeland   Freeland Press
Freeland Pubns   Freeland Publications
Freeman   W. H. Freeman & Co.
French and European   French & European Publications, Inc.
Friends Univ of Toledo   Friends of the University of Toledo Library
Freundlich   Freundlich Books
Fromm Intl   Fromm International Publishing Corp.
Fulcrum   Fulcrum, Inc.

G

G. K. Hall   G. K. Hall & Co.
Gale   Gale Research, Inc.
Garber   Garber Communications, Inc.
Garden City   Garden City Historical Society
Gardner   Gardner Press, Inc.
Gareth Stevens   Gareth Stevens, Inc.
Garland   Garland Publishing, Inc.
Garrard   Garrard Publishing Co.
Garrett   Garrett Park Press
Garrett Ed   Garrett Educational Corp.
Gateway   Gateway Press, Inc.
Gateway Pr   Gateway Press
Gaus   Theo Gaus, Ltd.
General Hall   General Hall, Inc.
Genesis   Genesis Publishing, Inc.
Genesis Pr   Genesis Press
Genesis Pub   Genesis Publishing Co.
Gibbs Smith   Gibbs Smith Publisher
Gifted Educ   Gifted Education Press
Glenhurst   Glenhurst Publications, Inc.

Glenmary Research Center
Glenmary Research Center
Globe Pequot Globe Pequot Press
Gloucester Gloucester Press, *imprint of* Franklin Watts, Inc.
Gloucester Art Gloucester Art Press
Godine David R. Godine Publisher, Inc.
Golden Hind Golden Hind Press
Goldstein & Blair Goldstein & Blair
Goldstein Soft Goldstein Software, Inc.
Good Apple Good Apple, Inc.
Good Bks Good Books
Gordian Gordian Press, Inc.
Gordon & Breach Gordon & Breach Science Publishers, Inc.
Gordon Pr Gordon Press Publishers
Gorsuch Gorsuch Scarisbrick Publishers
Gower Gower Publishing Co.
Graylock Graylock Press
Graywolf Graywolf Press
Great Quotations Great Quotations, Inc.
Greene Stephen Greene Press
Greenhaven Greenhaven Press
Greenleaf Bks Greenleaf Books
Greenleaf Classics Greenleaf Classics, Inc.
Greenleaf Co Greenleaf Co.
Greenleaf Pub Greenleaf Publishing Co.
Greenwillow Greenwillow Books
Greenwood Greenwood Press, Inc., *imprint of* Greenwood Publishing Group, Inc.
Greenwood Hse Greenwood House
Greenwood Pub Greenwood Publishing
Gregg Gregg, Inc.
Gregg Intl Gregg International
Grey Fox Grey Fox Press
Grosset Grosset & Dunlap Inc., *imprint of* The Putnam Publishing Group
Grove Grove Press
Groves Dict Music Groves Dictionaries of Music, Inc.

Guilford Guilford Press
Gulf Pub Gulf Publishing Co.

H

H. Holt Henry Holt & Co.
Hacker Hacker Art Books
Hackett Hackett Publishing Co., Inc.
Halsted Halsted Press
Hammond Hammond, Inc.
Hampstead Hampstead Press, *imprint of* Franklin Watts, Inc.
Harcourt Harcourt Brace Jovanovich, Inc.
Harlan Davidson Harlan Davidson, Inc.
Harper Harper & Row Publishers, Inc.
Harper Jr Bks Harper & Row Junior Books Group
Harper Pr Harper Press
Harper Sq Pr Harper Square Press
Harris H. E. Harris & Co., Inc.
Harris Acad Harris Academy
Harris Learn Syst Harris Learning Systems, Inc.
Harris Pub Harris Publishing Co.
Harris Stonehouse Harris Stonehouse Press
Harvard Common Pr Harvard Common Press
Haskell Haskell Booksellers, Inc.
Hastings Hastings House Publishers
Hastings Bks Hastings Books
Hastings Ctr Hastings Center
Hastings Pr Hastings Press
Haworth The Haworth Press, Inc.
Hay Hay House, Inc.
Haynes Haynes Publications, Inc.
Hazelden Hazelden Foundation
Health Communications Health Communications, Inc.
Heath D. C. Heath & Co.
Heineman James H. Heineman, Inc., Publisher
Heinemann Heinemann Educational Books, Inc.
Heisler Suzanne Heisler
Helene Obolensky Helene Obolensky Enterprises, Inc.

Hemisphere   Hemisphere Publishing Corp.
Hendricks   Hendricks House, Inc.
Herald   Herald Press
Here's Life   Here's Life Publishers, Inc.
Heridonius   Heridonius Foundation
Hermon   Sepher-Hermon Press, Inc.
Heyeck   The Heyeck Press
Higginson   Higginson Book Co.
High Plains   High Plains Publishing Co., Inc.
High Plains Pub   High Plains Publishing Co.
Hill & Wang   Hill & Wang, Inc.
Hippocrene   Hippocrene Books, Inc.
Holden-Day   Holden-Day, Inc.
Holiday   Holiday House, Inc.
Holmes   Holmes Book Co.
Holmes & Meier   Holmes & Meier Publishers, Inc.
Holmes Pub   Holmes Publishing Group
Holt   Holt, Rinehart & Winston, Inc.
Hoover Inst Pr   Hoover Institution Press
Hoover Lib   Herbert Hoover Presidential Library & Association Inc.
Horton   Thomas Horton & Daughters
Houghton   Houghton Mifflin Co.
House Fire Pr   House of Fire Press
HP   HP Books, *imprint of* Price Stern Sloan, Inc.
Hudson Hills   Hudson Hills Press, Inc.
Human Kinetics   Human Kinetics Publishers
Human Relations   Human Relations Area Files Press, Inc.
Human Resource   Human Resource Development Press
Humanities   Humanities Press International, Inc.
Humanities Art   Humanities & Arts Press
Huntington Lib   Huntington Library Publications
Huntington Pr   Huntington Press
Hyperion   Hyperion Press, Inc.

I

ICS Bk   ICS Books, Inc.
ICS Pr   ICS Press
ICS Pubns   ICS Publications, Institute of Carmelite Studies
Ideals   Ideals Publishing Corp.
IEEE   IEEE Computer Society Press
ILR Pr   ILR Press
Imported   Imported Publications, Inc.
Ind-US   Ind-US, Inc.
Indian Historian Pr   Indian Historian Press, Inc.
Indochina Curriculum Gp   Indochina Curriculum Group
Industrial Pr   Industrial Press, Inc.
Info Plus   Information Plus
Inst Economic Pol   Institute for Economic & Political World Strategic Studies
Inst for Economics and Finance   Institute for Economic & Financial Research
Inst for Social Research   University of Michigan, Institute for Social Research
Inst for Studies in Am Music   Institute for Studies in American Music
Integrity   Integrity Press
Inter Print Pubs   Interstate Printers & Publishers, Inc.
Inter-Varsity   Inter-Varsity Press
Interbook   Interbook, Inc.
Intersystems   Intersystems Publications
Intl Advertising Assn   International Advertising Association
Intl Book   International Book Co.
Intl Book Ctr   International Book Center
Intl City Management   International City Management Association
Intl Defense & Aid   International Defense and Aid Fund for Southern Africa
Intl Inst Garibaldian   International Institute of Garibaldian Studies, Inc.

Intl Pub International Publishing Corp.

Intl Pub Inc International Publishing, Inc.

Intl Pubns International Publications Service

Intl Pubs International Publishers, Co.

Intl Specialized Bk International Specialized Book Services

Intl Univ Pr International University Press

Invisible Invisible City/Red Hill Press

Irvington Irvington Publishers

Irwin Richard D. Irwin, Inc.

ISGS International Society for General Semantics

ISI Pr ISI Press

Island Island Press

Ism Pr Ism Press, Inc.

Ivy Ivy Books

J

JAI JAI Press, Inc.

James River James River Press

Jamestown Jamestown Publishers, Inc.

Janson Janson Publications

Janssen Janssen Education Enterprise, Inc.

Janus Bks Janus Book Publishers, Inc.

Janus Lib Janus Library, *imprint of* Abaris Books, Inc.

Janus Pr Janus Press

JCEE Joint Council on Economic Education

Jenkins Jenkins Publishing Co.

Joelle Joelle Publishing, Inc.

John Jay John Jay Press

John Knox John Knox Press, *imprint of* Westminster/John Knox Press

Johnson Inst Johnson Institute

Johnson Repr Johnson Reprint Corp.

Jonathan David Jonathan David Publishers, Inc.

Jones & Bartlett Jones & Bartlett Publishers, Inc.

Jossey-Bass Jossey-Bass, Inc., Publishers

Jove Jove Publications, Inc.

JPS Jewish Publication Society

Judson Judson Press

K

K. G. Saur K. G. Saur

Karger S. Karger, AG

Karz-Cohl Karz-Cohl Publishers, Inc.

Katonah Gallery Katonah Gallery

Kazi Kazi Publications

Keats Keats Publishing, Inc.

Kelley Augustus M. Kelley Publishers

Kelley Comm Dev Kelley Communication Development

Kelley Pubns Kelley Publications

Kendall Kendall Publishing Co.

Kendall Enterp Kendall Enterprises, Inc.

Kendall-Hunt Kendall/Hunt Publishing Co.

Kent Kent Popular Press

Kern Intl Kern International, Inc.

Kimbell Art Kimbell Art Museum

Kingston Kingston Ellis Press

Kipling Kipling Press

Kluwer Academic Kluwer Academic Publishers

Knopf Alfred A. Knopf, Inc.

Kodansha Kodansha International U.S.A., Ltd.

Kraus Kraus Reprint & Periodicals

Kregel Kregel Publications

Krieger Robert E. Krieger Publishing Co., Inc.

Krishna Krishna Press

Ktav Ktav Publishing House, Inc.

L

L Hill Bks Lawrence Hill Books

Landfall Landfall Press, Inc.

Larlin Larlin Corp.

LBJ Sch Pub Aff Lyndon B. Johnson School of Public Affairs

Lea & Febiger Lea & Febiger

League of Women Voters NYS League of Women Voters of the City of New York

Learning Works The Learning Works, Inc.

Leisure Pr   Leisure Press
Lerner   Lerner Publications, Co.
Lexikon   Lexikon Services
Lexikos   Lexikos Publishing
Lexington   Lexington Center, Inc.
Lexington Bks   Lexington Books
Lexington Data   Lexington Data, Inc.
Lexington-Fayette   Lexington-Fayette County Historic Commission
Lib of America   The Library of America
Liberty Fund   Liberty Fund, Inc.
Libraries Unlimited   Libraries Unlimited, Inc.
Lightyear   Lightyear Press, Inc.
Limelight   Limelight, Ltd.
Limelight Edns   Limelight Editions
LinguiSystems   LinguiSystems, Inc.
Lion   Lion Books
Lippincott   J. B. Lippincott Co.
Little   Little, Brown & Co.
Little Bks   Little Books & Co.
Littlefield   Littlefield Adams Quality Paperbacks
Liveright   Liveright Publishing Corp.
Lodestar   Lodestar Books
Longman   Longman, Inc.
Longwood   Longwood Publishing Group, Inc.
Longwood Cottage   Longwood Cottage Publishing
Lord John   Lord John Press
Lothrop   Lothrop, Lee & Shepard Books
Lubrecht and Cramer   Lubrecht & Cramer, Ltd.
Lucent   Lucent Books
Lyceum   Lyceum, *imprint of* Carlton Press, Inc.
Lyceum Bks   Lyceum Books, Inc.
Lyceum Pr   Lyceum Press
Lyon Pr   Lyon Press
Lyon Prods   Lyon Productions
Lyons & Burford   Lyons & Burford Publishers, Inc.

M

M and T   M & T Publishing, Inc.
M. Boyars   Marion Boyars Publishers, Inc.
M. Evans   M. Evans & Co., Inc.

McDougal   McDougal, Littell & Co.
McFarland   McFarland & Co., Inc., Publishers
McGraw   McGraw-Hill Publishing Co.
McKay   David McKay Co., Inc.
McKay Busn Systs   McKay Business Systems
Macmillan   Macmillan Publishing Co., Inc.
Madrona   Madrona Publishers, Inc.
Main Street   The Main Street Press
Manusoft   Manusoft Corp.
Marine Corp   Marine Corps Association
Marine Educ   Marine Education Textbooks
Math Sci Pr   Math-Sci Press
Mathematical Assn   Mathematical Association of America
Maverick   Maverick Publications
Mayfield   Mayfield Publishing Co.
MECC   Minnesota Educational Computing Corp.
Meckler   Meckler Corp.
Meghan-Kiffer   Meghan-Kiffer Press
Melior   Melior Publications
Mellen   The Edwin Mellen Press
Mentor   Mentor Books, *imprint of* New American Library
Meredith Pr   The Meredith Press, *imprint of* New Amsterdam Books
Meridian   Meridian Books, *imprint of* New American Library
Merriam Webster   Merriam-Webster, Inc.
Merrill   Merrill Publishing Co.
Messner   Julian Messner
Methuen   Methuen, *imprint of* Heinemann Educational Books, Inc.
Metropolitan Mus of Art   Metropolitan Museum of Art
Microsoft   Microsoft
Mid Atlantic   Middle Atlantic Press
Midwest   Midwest Publications Co., Inc.
Military Affairs/Aerospace Historian   Military Affairs/ Aerospace Historian Publishing

Minnesota Hist Soc   Minnesota Historical Society Press
Mirage   Mirage Press, Ltd.
MIS Pr   MIS Press
MIT Pr   Massachusetts Institute of Technology Press
MLA   Modern Language Association of America
Modern Lib   Modern Library, Inc.
Modern World   Modern World Publishing Co.
Monarch Pr   Monarch Press
Monthly Review   Monthly Review Press
Moody   Moody Press
Moon   Moon Publications, Inc.
Moosehead   Moosehead Products
Morgan   Morgan & Morgan, Inc.
Morgan Kaufmann   Morgan Kaufmann Publishers, Inc.
Morgan Pr   Morgan Press
Morgan-Rand   Morgan-Rand Publications, Inc.
Morgan State   Morgan State University Press, English Department
Morning Glory   Morning Glory Press, Inc.
Morrow   William Morrow & Co., Inc.
Mosby   Mosby/Multi-Media
Mott Media   Mott Media
Mouton   Mouton de Gruyter
Moyer   Moyer Bell, Ltd.
MTL   Materials for Today's Learning, Inc./JV Corp.
MUMPS   MUMPS Users Group
Music Sales   Music Sales Corp.
Mutual   Mutual Publishing Co.
Mysterious   Mysterious Press

N

N Ross   Norman Ross Publishing Inc.
NAL   New American Library
Namaste   Namaste Publications
National Academy   National Academy Press

National Assn of Social Workers   National Association of Social Workers
National Bk   National Book Co.
National Bureau of Economic Research   Nation Bureau of Economic Research, Inc.
National Gallery of Art   National Gallery of Art
National Geographic   National Geographic Society
National Journal   National Journal
National Pr   National Press, Inc.
National Textbook   National Textbook Co.
Natl Ctr Constitutional   National Center for Constitutional Studies
Naval Inst Pr   Naval Institute Press
NCTE   National Council of Teachers of English
NCTM   National Council of Teachers of Mathematics
Neale Watson   Neale Watson Academic Publications, *imprint of* Watson Publishing International
Nelson-Hall   Nelson-Hall, Inc.
Network   Network Publications
New Amsterdam   New Amsterdam Books
New College & Univ Pr   The New College & University Press
New Directions   New Directions Publishing Corp.
New Jersey State Museum   New Jersey State Museum
New Politics   New Politics Publishing
New Readers   New Readers Press
New Riders   New Riders Publishing
New Society   New Society Publishers
New York Zoetrope   New York Zoetrope
Newbury Bks   Newbury Books
Newbury Hse   Newbury House Publishers
Newmarket   Newmarket Press
Newspaper Ent   Newspaper Enterprise Association, Inc.
Nightingale   Nightingale-Conant Corp.
Nilgiri   Nilgiri Press
Noontide   The Noontide Press

North Atlantic   North Atlantic Books
North Carolina Archives   North Carolina Division of Archives & History
North Point   North Point Press
North Point Hist Soc   North Point Historical Society
North River   North River Press, Inc.
Northland   Northland Press
Northland Bks   Northland Books
Northland Pub Co   Northland Publishing Co.
Northland Pubns   Northland Publications
Northland Winona   Northland Press of Winona
Northwest Pub   Northwest Publishing House
Norton   W. W. Norton & Co., Inc.
Nova Pub   Nova Publishing Co.
NY Acad Sci   New York Academy of Sciences

O

Oak Tree   Oak Tree Publications, Inc.
OAS   Organization of American States
Obelisk   Obelisk, *imprint of* E. P. Dutton
Occidental   Occidental Press
Oceana   Oceana Publications, Inc.
Octagon   Octagon Press
October   October House
Odyssey   Odyssey Publications, Inc.
Odyssey Pr   Odyssey Press
OECD   Organization for Economic Cooperation & Development
Ohio Hist Soc   Ohio Historical Society
Omnigraphics   Omnigraphics, Inc.
Onyx   Onyx, *imprint of* New American Library
Open Court   Open Court Publishing Co.
Open Hand   Open Hand Publishing, Inc.
Orbis   Orbis Books

Orbis Pubns   Orbis Publications, Inc.
Oregon Hist   Oregon Historical Society Press
Orient Bk Dist   Orient Book Distributors
Oriental   The Oriental Book Store
Oryx   Oryx Press
Outlet   Outlet Book Co.
Overlook Pr   Overlook Press
Ox Bow   Ox Bow Press
Oxford Univ Pr   Oxford University Press, Inc.
Oyster River   Oyster River Press
Ozer   Jerome S. Ozer Publisher, Inc.

P

P. H. Fejer   Paul Haralyi Fejer
Pacific   Pacific Press
Pacific Bk Supply   Pacific Book Supply, Co.
Pacific Bks   Pacific Books, Publishers
Pacific Edns   Pacific Editions
Pacific Gallery   Pacific Gallery Publishers
Pacific Hse   Pacific Publishing House
Pacific Info   Pacific Information, Inc.
Pacific Inst   Pacific Institute
Pacific Intl   Pacific International Publishing Co.
Pacific Pr   Pacific Press
Pacific Pr Pub Assn   Pacific Press Publishing Association
Pacific Pub   Pacific Publishing
Pagan   Pagan Press
Paganiniana   Paganiniana Publications, Inc.
Paideia   Paideia House, Publishers
PAJ   PAJ Publications
Paladin   Paladin Software Corp.
Paladin Hse   Paladin House Publishers
Paladin Pr   Paladin Press
Pantheon   Pantheon Books
Paperbacks   Paperbacks Plus Press
Paragon Benson   Paragon Associates/Benson Co., Inc.

Paragon Bk Paragon Book Gallery, Ltd.
Paragon Group The Paragon Group, Inc.
Paragon Hse Paragon House Publishers
Paragon Pr Paragon Press
Paragon Prodns Paragon Productions
Paragon Pub Paragon Publishing Co.
Paragon-Reiss Paragon-Reiss
Park Row Park Row Software
Parkwest Parkwest Publications, Inc.
Pathfinder Fund Pathfinder Fund
Pathfinder Pr Pathfinder Press
Pathfinder Pub Pathfinder Publishing
Pathfinder Pubns Pathfinder Publications
Pathfinder Pubns Inc Pathfinder Publications, Inc.
Patterson Smith Patterson Smith Publishing Corp.
Paulist Paulist Press
PBK PBK Publications
PC-SIG PC Software Interest Group
Peachpit Peachpit Press
Peachtree Peachtree Publishers, Ltd.
Peacock F. E. Peacock Publishers, Inc.
Peak Peak Press
Pegasus Pegasus
Pegasus Bks Pegasus Books, Ltd.
Pegasus Co Pegasus Co.
Pegasus Pr Pegasus Press
Pegasus Pub Pegasus Publishing
Pegasus Pubns Pegasus Publications
Pegus Pegus Press
Pelican Pelican Publishing Co., Inc.
Pendle Hill Pendle Hill Publications
Pendulum Pendulum Books
Penguin Penguin Books
Penguin Comm Penguin Communications Group
Performance Enhancement The Performance Enhancements Products Press

Pergamon Pergamon Press, Inc.
Perigee Bks Perigee Books, *imprint of* The Putnam Publishing Group
Perigee Pr The Perigee Press
Peripatetic The Peripatetic Press
Perivale Perivale Press
Persea Persea Books, Inc.
Peter Lang Peter Lang Publishing, Inc.
Peter Pauper Peter Pauper, Inc.
Peter Smith Peter Smith Publisher, Inc.
Petersons Guide Peterson's Guides, Inc.
Petrocelli Petrocelli Books
Phanes Phanes Press
Pharos Pharos Books
Phi Delta Kappa Phi Delta Kappa Educational Foundation
Philadelphia Museum of Art Philadelphia Museum of Art
Philomel Philomel Books, *imprint of* The Putnam Publishing Group
Philos Res Philosophical Research Society, Inc.
Philosophical Lib Philosophical Library, Inc.
Pinnacle Bks Pinnacle Books
Piper Piper Publishing, Inc.
Plenum Plenum Publishing Corp.
Plenum Pr Plenum Press, *imprint of* Plenum Publishing Corporation
Plume Plume Books, *imprint of* New American Library
Pocket Pocket Books, Inc.
Polish Inst Art & Sci Polish Institute of Arts & Sciences of America, Inc.
Pomegranate Artbooks Pomegranate Artbooks, Inc.
Population Reference Bureau Population Reference Bureau
Porcupine Porcupine Press, Inc.
Portland House Portland House, *imprint of* Outlet Book Co.
Poseidon Poseidon Press, *imprint of* Pocket Books, Inc.
Poynster Poynster Institute
Praeger Praeger Publishers
Prentice Prentice Hall
Presidential Acct Presidential Accountability Group
Presidio Presidio Press
Price Prodns Price Productions

Price Pub Price Publishing Co.
Price Stern Price Stern Sloan, Inc.
Prima Prima Publishing & Communication
Pro Ed Pro-Ed
Prog Peripherals Prog Peripherals & Software, Inc.
Prog Studies Programmed Studies, Inc.
Prometheus Bks Prometheus Books
Proscenium Proscenium Press
PSL PSL Computer Products
Pub Horizons Publishing Horizons, Inc.
Public Affairs Public Affairs Press
Puckerbrush Puckerbrush Press
Putnam The Putnam Publishing Group
Pythagorean Pr Pythagorean Press

Q

QED Info Sci QED Information Sciences, Inc.
QED Pr Q. E. D. Press of Ann Arbor, Inc.
QED Pubns Q. E. D. Publications
QED Research QED Research, Inc.
Quality Soft Quality Software, Inc.
Que Que Corp.

R

R & E Pubs R & E Publishers
RK Edns RK Editions
Rada Rada Press
Raintree Raintree Publishers, Inc.
Rand Rand McNally & Co.
Random Random House, Inc.
Raven Raven Press, Publishers
RCP RCP Publications
Reader's Digest Reader's Digest Press
Redgrave Redgrave Publishing Co.
Redpath Redpath Press
Reed Reed & Cannon Co.
Regina Bks Regina Books
Regina Pr Regina Press, Malhame & Co.

Regnery Regnery Gateway, Inc.
Reinhold Reinhold Publishing Corp., *imprint of* Van Nostrand Reinhold
Reprint Services Reprint Services Corp.
Research Research Publications
Research & Education Research & Education Association
Revisionist Pr Revisionist Press
Reynal Reynal, *imprint of* William Morrow & Co., Inc.
Richard West Richard West
Ridgeview Ridgeview Publishing Co.
Rienner Lynne Rienner Publishers, Inc.
Rinehart Roberts Rinehart, Inc., Pubs.
Riverdale The Riverdale Co., Inc.
Riverrun Riverrun Press, Inc.
Rizzoli Rizzoli International Publications, Inc.
Rodale Rodale Press, Inc.
Rosen Rosen Publishing Group
Ross-Erikson Ross-Erikson
Roth Roth Publishing, Inc.
Rothman Fred B. Rothman & Co.
Rourke Rourke Corp.
Routledge Routledge, Chapman & Hall, Inc.
Rowman Rowman & Littlefield Publishers, Inc.
Running Pr Running Press Book Publishers
Russell Sage Russell Sage Foundation

S

Sabbot Sabbot-Natural History Books
Sage Sage Publications, Inc.
Sage Creek Pr Sage Creek Press
Sage Pr Sage Press
Sage Pub Sage Publishing Co.
Sage Pubns Sage Publications
Saifer Albert Saifer Publisher
St. Martin's St. Martin's Press, Inc.
Salem Hse Salem House Publishers
Salem Pr Salem Press, Inc.
Salem Pub Salem Publishing Co.

SamHar   SamHar Press
Sams   Howard W. Sams & Co.
Saphrograph   Saphrograph
   Corp.
SAS Inst   SAS Institute, Inc.
Saunders   Saunders College
   Publishing
Saybrook Pr   The Saybrook Press
Saybrook Pub Co   Saybrook
   Publishing Co., Inc.
Scarborough Faire   Scarborough
   Faire, Inc.
Scarborough Hse   Scarborough
   House
Scarecrow   Scarecrow Press, Inc.
Schenkman   Schenkman Books,
   Inc.
Schirmer   Schirmer Books
Schocken   Schocken Books, Inc.
Schoenhof   Schoenhof's Foreign
   Books, Inc.
Schol Am Res   School of American
   Research Press
Schol Facsimiles   Scholars'
   Facsimiles & Reprints
Scholarly   Scholarly Press, Inc.
Scholarly Res   Scholarly Resources,
   Inc.
Scholars Bk   Scholars Book Co.
Scholars Bks   Scholars Books
Scholars Bookshelf   Scholar's
   Bookshelf
Scholars Ref Lib   Scholar's
   Reference Library
Scholars Pr   Scholars Press
Scholars Pr Ltd.   Scholars' Press,
   Ltd.
Scholastic   Scholastic, Inc.
Scholium   Scholium International,
   Inc.
Sci-Tech Pubns   Sci Tech
   Publications
Sci Tech Pubs   Science Tech
   Publishers
Scott   Scott, Foresman & Co.
Scribner's   Charles Scribner's Sons
Seaver   Seaver Books
Seven Hills   Seven Hills Book
   Distributors
Seven Locks   Seven Locks Press
Seymour   Dale Seymour
   Publications
Shambhala   Shambhala
   Publications, Inc.

Shapolsky   Shapolsky Publishers,
   Inc.
Sharon   Sharon Publications, Inc.
Sharpe   M. E. Sharpe, Inc.
Shaw   Harold Shaw Publishers
Sheed & Ward   Sheed & Ward
Shelter   Shelter Publications, Inc.
Sheridan Med Bks   Sheridan
   Medical Books
Shoe String   Shoe String Press, Inc.
Sierra   Sierra Club Books
Signet   Signet Books, *imprint of*
   New American Library
Silicon   Silicon Press
Silver   Silver, Burdett & Ginn, Inc.
Simon   Simon & Schuster, Inc.
Sinauer   Sinauer Associates, Inc.
Slavica   Slavica Publishers, Inc.
Smith   W. H. Smith Publishers,
   Inc.
Smith & Smith   Smith & Smith
   Publishing Co.
Smith & Varina   Smith & Varina
   Publishers
Smith Coll   Smith College
   Publications
Smith Coll Mus Art   Smith
   College Museum of Art
Smith Collins   Smith Collins Co.
Smith Lib   Warren Hunting Smith
   Library
Smith Prod   Smith Productions
Smithsonian   Smithsonian
   Institution Press
Smithsonian Bks   Smithsonian
   Books
Soc Computer Sim   Society for
   Computer Simulation
Society Tech Comm   Society for
   Technical Communication
Solaris   Solaris Press, Inc.
Somerset   Somerset Publishers, Inc.
Sophia   Sophia Press
Sophia Inst Pr   Sophia Institute
   Press
Sound Mgmt   Sound Management
   Productions
South Asia Bks   South Asia Books
South End   South End Press
South-Western   South-Western
   Publishing Co.
Sovereign   Sovereign Press
Spertus   The Spertus College of
   Judaica Press

Sphinx Sphinx Press
SPIE SPIE—International Society for Optical Engineering
Springer-Verlag Springer-Verlag New York, Inc.
SPSS SPSS, Inc.
SRA Science Research Associates
Stackpole Stackpole Books
Star Valley Star Valley Publications
Starmont Starmont House, Inc.
State Mutual State Mutual Book & Periodical Service, Ltd.
Station Hill Station Hill Press
Steck-Vaughn Steck-Vaughn Co.
Steiner Rudolf Steiner Institute
Stephen Greene Stephen Greene Press
Sterling Sterling Publishing Co., Inc.
Sterling & Selesnick Sterling & Selesnick
Stewart Tabori & Chang Stewart, Tabori, & Chang, Inc.
Stickley George F. Stickley Co.
Stipes Stipes Publishing Co.
Stoeger Stoeger Publishing Co.
Stokes Stokes Publishing Co.
Storm King Storm King Press
Stryker-Post Stryker-Post Publications
Sugden Sherwood Sugden & Co.
Summa Summa Publications
Summit Bks Summit Books
Sunrise Bks Sunrise Books
Sunrise Pr Sunrise Press
Swedenborg Swedenborg Foundation, Inc.
Swedenborg Sci Assn Swedenborg Science Association
Sybex Sybex, Inc.
Syracuse Univ Foreign Comp Syracuse University, Foreign & Comparative Studies Program

T

TAB TAB Books, Inc.
TAMS Token & Medal Society, Inc.
Taplinger Taplinger Publishing Co., Inc.
Tarcher Jeremy P. Tarcher, Inc.

Tavistock Tavistock Poetry Press
Taylor Taylor Publishing Co.
Taylor & Francis Taylor & Francis, Inc.
Taylor and Ng Taylor and Ng
Taylor-James Taylor-James, Ltd.
Taylor Taylor Taylor, Taylor & Taylor
Taylor Winnstead Pubs Taylor Winnstead Publishers
Teachers and Writers Coll Teachers & Writers Collaborative
Teachers College Teachers College Press
Templegate Templegate Publishers
Ten Speed Ten Speed Press
TeNeues TeNeues Publishing Co.
Territ Pr Territorial Press
Thames Hudson Thames & Hudson
Theatre Arts Theatre Arts Books
Third World Third World Book Shop
Thomas Charles C. Thomas Publisher
Thomasson-Grant Thomasson-Grant, Inc.
Thor Thor Publishing Co.
Thorndike Thorndike Press
Three Continents Three Continents Press
Thunder's Mouth Thunder's Mouth Press
Ticknor Ticknor & Fields
Timber Timber Press
Time-Life Time-Life Books
Times Bks Times Books
Timken Timken Publishers, Inc.
Torres Eliseo Torres & Sons
Touchstone Touchstone Books, *imprint of* Simon & Schuster, Inc.
Transaction Transaction Publications
Tree Bks Tree Books
Tree City Tree City Press
Tree Communications Tree Communications, Inc.
Tree Hse Tree House Press
Tree Life Tree of Life Publications
Triad Triad Press
Trillium Trillium Press
Troll Troll Associates
Tundra Tundra Books of Northern New York

Turtle Island Turtle Island
Foundation, Netzahaulcoyotl
Historical Society
Tuttle Charles E. Tuttle Co., Inc.
Twayne Twayne Publishers, *imprint
of* G. K. Hall, & Co.
Twenty-First Pr Twenty-First
Century Press

U

UCLA Lat Am Ctr University of
California, Latin American Center
UMI UMI Research Press
UN United Nations
Underwood Barry Underwood
Underwood-Miller Underwood/
Miller
Ungar Ungar Publishing Co.
Unicorn Unicorn Press
Unicorn Bkshop Unicorn
Bookshop
Unicorn Comm Unicorn
Communications
Unicorn Ent Unicorn Enterprises
Unicorn Pub The Unicorn
Publishing House, Inc.
**Univ of California Inst of East
Asian Studies** University of
California, Institute of East Asian
Studies
Univ Place Bk Shop University
Place Book Shop
Univ Pr of America University
Press of America
Univ Presses FL University
Presses of Florida
Universe Universe Books, Inc.
Universe Pub Universe Publishing
Co.
Unwin Unwin Hyman, Inc.
Urban Inst Urban Institute Press
USGPO U. S. Government
Printing Office

V

Valley Hill Valley Hill Publishing
Company
Van Nostrand Van Nostrand
Reinhold

Vance Biblios Vance
Bibliographies
Vanguard Vanguard Press, Inc.
Vanguard Inst Vanguard
Institutional Publishers
Vanni S. F. Vanni
Vantage Vantage Press, Inc.
Vantage Info Vantage Information
Vantage Printing Vantage Printing
Co.
VCH Pubs VCH Publishers, Inc.
Ventana Ventana Press
Vienna Vienna House, Inc.
Viking Viking Penguin
Vintage Vintage Publications
Vintage America Vintage America
Publishing Co.

W

Wadsworth Wadsworth
Publishing Co.
Wadsworth Atheneum
Wadsworth Atheneum
Walck Henry Z. Walck, Inc.
Walker Walker & Co.
Walker Ed Walker Educational
Book Corp.
Walker, Evans, & Cogswell
Walker, Evans, & Cogswell Co.
Walker Pub Walker Publishing
Co., Inc.
Walker Pubns Walker
Publications
Walter J. Johnson Walter J.
Johnson, Inc.
Warner Bks Warner Books, Inc.
Warthog Warthog Press
Warwick Warwick Press, *imprint of*
Franklin Watts, Inc.
Washington Square Pr
Washington Square Press, Inc.
Watson Watson Publishing House
Watson-Guptill Watson-Guptill
Publications, Inc.
Watson Pub Intl Watson
Publishing International
Watts Franklin Watts, Inc.
Waveland Waveland Press, Inc.
Waverly Waverly Publishers
Waverly Comm Hse Waverly
Community House, Inc.
Wayside Wayside Publishing

Weber Systems   Weber Systems, Inc.
Wehman   Wehman Brothers, Inc.
Weidenfeld   Weidenfeld & Nicolson
Welstar   Welstar Publications
West Pr   West Press
West Pub   West Publishing Co., College & School Division
Western Pub   Western Publishing Co., Inc.
Westminster John Knox   Westminster/John Knox Press
Westview   Westview Press
White House Hist   White House Historical Association
Whitston   Whitston Publishing Co., Inc.
Wiener   Markus Wiener Publishing, Inc.
Wieser   Wieser & Wieser, Inc.
Wilderness   Wilderness Press
Wiley   John Wiley & Sons, Inc.
Williams and Wilkins   Williams & Wilkins
Wilson   H. W. Wilson
Wittenborn   George Wittenborn, Inc.
Wizards Bookshelf   Wizards Bookshelf
Wizards Pr   Wizard's Press
Woodbridge   Woodbridge Press Publishing Co.
Wordware   Wordware Publishing, Inc.
Workman   Workman Publishing Co., Inc.

World Book   World Book, Inc.
World Eagle   World Eagle, Inc.
World Future   World Future Society
World Info Inst   World Information Institute
World Scientific   World Scientific Publishing Co., Inc.
World Without War   World Without War Council
Worth   Worth Publishers, Inc.
Writer   Writer, Inc.
Writers and Readers   Writers & Readers Publishing, Inc.
Writers Digest   Writer's Digest Books
WWAI   Who's Who in Artificial Intelligence

Y

Yale Univ Far Eastern Pubns   Yale University, Far Eastern Publications
Year Bk Med   Year Book Medical Publishers, Inc.
Youth Education   Youth Education Systems, Inc.

Z

Zebra   Zebra Books
Zenger   Zenger Publishing Co., Inc.
Zondervan   Zondervan Publishing House

PROFILE INDEX

This index appears in each of the two volumes of *The Young Adult Reader's Adviser.* It presents in alphabetical sequence the authors who are profiled in each volume. The number of the volume in which a profiled author appears is given with a colon followed by the page number on which the profile begins. For example, the entry **2:169** indicates that the profile of Abigail Adams can be found on page 169 of Volume 2.

The volume number and page number that immediately follow the author's name appear in boldface type. This always indicates the location of the profile, or biographical sketch. Some individuals are profiled twice (for example, Archimedes) and are followed by two boldface volume and page numbers. Sometimes more numbers in lightface may follow. These lightface numbers indicate additional secondary references to profiled authors, references that may occur in general introductions or in other biographical narratives.

M

Muir, John, **2:220**
Muller, Hermann Joseph, **2:454**
Munro, Alice, **1:145**
Murdoch, Dame Iris, **1:107**
Murdock, George Peter, **2:51**
Murrow, Edward R., **1:467**
Myers, Walter Dean, **1:269**
Myrdal, Gunnar, **2:134**, 2:128

N

Naipaul, V. S., **1:406**
Nast, Thomas, **1:460**
Nehru, Jawaharlal, **2:403**, 2:400
Neruda, Pablo, **1:406**
Newman, Edwin, **1:443**
Newton, Isaac, **2:514**, 1:526; 2:474, 2:477, 2:519
Ngugi Wa Thiong'o, **1:415**
Nightingale, Florence, **2:569**
Nixon, Richard Milhous, **2:253**, 2:23, 2:247, 2:251, 2:252
Nkrumah, Kwame, **2:395**, 2:210
Noether, Emmy, **1:509**, 1:517
Norris, Frank, **1:180**
Nyerere, Julius, **2:396**

O

O'Casey, Sean, **1:108**
O'Connor, Flannery, **1:270**
O'Connor, Frank, **1:109**
O'Connor, Sandra Day, **2:31**
O'Dell, Scott, **1:271**
Odets, Clifford, **1:272**
O'Faolain, Sean, **1:110**
O'Keeffe, Georgia, **2:268**
O'Neill, Eugene, **1:273**
Oparin, Alexander Ivanovich, **2:461**
Orwell, George, **1:110**, 1:441
Osborne, John, **1:112**
Osler, William, **2:534**, 2:532
Ovid, **1:321**
Owen, Wilfred, **1:112**, 1:70, 1:116; 2:416

P

Paine, Thomas, **2:165**
Palestrina, **2:318**
Park, Mungo, **2:367**
Parker, Dorothy, **1:274**
Parsons, Talcott, **2:127**
Pascal, Blaise, **1:532**
Pasternak, Boris, **1:393**
Pasteur, Louis, **2:445**
Paterson, Katherine, **1:484**

Paton, Alan, **1:416**
Pauli, Wolfgang, **2:502**
Pauling, Linus Carl, **2:505**
Pavlov, Ivan Petrovich, **2:100**, **2:464**, 2:101
Paz, Octavio, **1:407**
The Pearl Poet, **1:7**
Pearson, Drew, **1:458**
Peck, Richard, **1:275**
Pepys, Samuel, **1:27**
Perkins, Frances, **2:24**
Petrarch, **1:18**, **1:350**, 1:9, 1:18, 1:348
Piaget, Jean, **2:110**
Picasso, Pablo, **2:420**
Pinter, Harold, **1:113**
Pirandello, Luigi, **1:351**
Planck, Max Karl Ernst Ludwig, **2:520**, 2:500, 2:519
Plath, Sylvia, **1:276**, 1:94
Plautus, Titus Maccius, **1:321**
Pliny the Younger, **2:295**, 2:296
Plutarch, **2:288**
Poe, Edgar Allan, **1:163**, 1:330
Pohl, Frederik, **1:278**
Poincaré, Henri, **1:500**
Polo, Marco, **2:308**
Pope, Alexander, **1:27**
Porter, Katherine Ann, **1:279**
Potok, Chaim, **1:280**
Priestley, J. B., **1:114**
Prokofiev, Sergei, **2:422**
Puig, Manuel, **1:408**
Purcell, Henry, **2:337**, 2:416
Pushkin, Aleksandr, **1:394**
Pythagoras, **1:500**

R

Racine, Jean, **1:339**
Radcliffe, Anne, **1:28**
Radcliffe-Brown, A. R., **2:53**, 2:45
Ramanujan, Srinivara, **1:502**
Rank, Hugh, **1:441**
Raphael, **2:319**
Ravel, Maurice, **2:423**
Rayburn, Sam, **2:34**
Reagan, Ronald Wilson, **2:259**, 2:31, 2:68, 2:256, 2:259
Redfield, Robert, **2:54**
Reynolds, Sir Joshua, **2:338**, 2:335
Ricardo, David, **2:73**, 2:7, 2:59
Rich, Adrienne, **1:281**
Richardson, Samuel, **1:28**
Richler, Mordecai, **1:145**
Riesman, David, **2:132**
Riis, Jacob August, **2:211**
Rilke, Rainer Maria, **1:370**
Rivlin, Alice Mitchell, **2:67**
Robespierre, Maximilien, **2:331**

AUTHOR INDEX

This index appears in both volumes of *The Young Adult Reader's Adviser.* It presents in alphabetical sequence the authors (both personal and corporate) of all books listed in the bibliographies. Names of the editors, compilers, and translators are also indexed.

The number of the volume in which a person's name appears is given with a colon followed by the page number on which the book title connected to that person can be found. For example, the entry 2:184 indicates that the book written by Thomas P. Abernethy can be found on page 184 of Volume 2.

A

AAHPERD Research Consortium
   Computer Network Committee, 1:568
AAHPERD Staff, 1:568
Aarons, Victoria, 1:384
Aaseng, Nathan, 2:431
Abba, Giuseppe C., 2:344
Abbas, K. A., 2:401
Abbey, Nancy, 2:555
Abbott, David (ed), 2:431
Abbott, Edwin A., 1:519
Abdelnoor, R. E., 1:496
Abel, Christopher (ed), 2:371
Abel, Elie, 2:404
Abelson, Harold, 1:511, 1:565
Aberle, David F., 2:52
Abernethy, Thomas P., 2:184
Aboulafia, Mitchell, 2:139
Abraham, Gerald, 2:346
Abraham, Henry J., 2:12
Abrahams, Israel, 2:303
Abrahams, Roger D., 1:411
Abrams, Philip, 2:124
Abramson, Edward A., 1:280
Abramson, Paul R., 2:39, 2:255
Abro, A., 2:512
Aburdene, Patricia, 2:51
Academy of Science of the U.S.S.R, 2:389
Acerson, Karen L., 1:575

Achebe, Chinua, 1:411
Ackerman, Bruce, 2:26
Ackrill, J. L. (ed), 2:442
Ada, Alma F., 2:409
Adair, Gene, 2:206
Adams, Abigail, 2:170
Adams, Ansel, 2:263
Adams, Cynthia H., 2:551
Adams, Douglas, 1:64–65
Adams, George, 1:519
Adams, Henry, 2:214
Adams, J. Alan, 1:578
Adams, John (ed), 2:71
Adams, John, 2:171
Adams, John Quincy, 2:173
Adams, Lee, 1:577
Adams, Samuel Hopkins, 2:225
Adams, Steve, 1:572
Adams, W., 1:504
Adams, Walter, 2:57
Adamson, Joy, 2:461
Addams, Jane, 2:208
Adelman, Gary, 1:77
Adelman, Jonathan R., 2:387
Adelman, M. A., 2:495
Adelson-Velsky, G. M., 1:585
Adderholdt-Elliott, Miriam, 2:536
Adkins, Robert K., 2:516
Adler, David A., 2:413, 2:468
Adler, Irving, 1:534

H

Lope de Vega Carpio, Félix, 1:358
Lopez, Claude-Anne, 2:526
Lopez, Enrique Hank, 1:280
Lopez, George A., 2:36
Lopez, George A. (ed), 2:7
Lopez de Gomara, Francisco, 2:323
Loran, Erle, 2:349
Lorber, Judith, 2:148
Lorch, Robert S., 2:41
Lord, Louis E., 1:313
Lord, Walter, 2:218
Lorenz, Hans-Walter, 2:57
Lorenz, Konrad, 2:100, 2:103, 2:104, 2:464
Lory, Hillis, 2:375
Loss, Archie, 1:106
Loth, David G., 2:30
Lothrop, Gloria Ricci, 2:184
Lottman, Herbert, 1:335
Louchheim, Katie (ed), 2:229
Lounsbury, John F., 2:92
Lovallo, Len, 1:74
Love, John F., 2:63
Loveless, Richard L. (ed), 1:577
Lovell, Bernard, 2:469
Lovett, Gabriel H., 2:275
Lowder, Stella, 2:94
Lowe, Carl, 2:531
Lowe, John C., 2:84
Lowe, Kurt E., 2:492
Lowe, W. D., 2:288
Lowell, Amy, 1:258
Lowell, James Russell, 1:161
Lowell, Robert, 1:259
Lowi, Theodore J., 2:21
Lowrie, Robert H., 2:201, 2:251
Lowth, Robert, 1:429
Luard, Evan, 2:238
Lubetkin, Wendy, 2:240
Lucas, James, 2:340, 2:384
Lucas, John, 2:446
Luchetti, Cathy, 2:201
Luciano, Dorothy S., 2:451
Luckiesh, M., 1:515
Ludlum, David M., 2:485
Ludwig, Arnold M., 2:555
Ludwig, Emil, 2:376
Luehrmann, Arthur, 1:557
Lukas, J. Anthony, 2:238
Lukes, Bonnie L., 2:550
Lund, Henning (ed), 2:508
Lundberg, Ferdinand, 2:218
Lundell, Allan, 1:554
Lundquist, James, 1:217, 1:256, 1:257, 1:283, 1:296
Lundstrom, David E., 1:538
Lunt, Paul S., 2:51, 2:144
Lunt, Steven D., 2:58
Lupoff, Richard A., 1:208
Lupson, Peter, 1:326

Lupton, Kenneth, 2:368
LURNIX, 1:562
Lutgens, Frederick K., 2:489
Luther, Martin, 2:317
Luttbeg, Norman R., 2:39
Lutz, Alma, 2:185, 2:207
Lutz, William, 1:437, 1:440
Lydolph, Paul E., 2:80
Lye, Keith, 2:83, 2:85, 2:88, 2:90, 2:91, 2:275, 2:393, 2:405, 2:489
Lyell, Charles, 2:490
Lyman, Elizabeth, 2:226
Lynch, Dudley, 2:246
Lynch, Gerald, 1:141
Lynch, John, 2:369
Lynch, Kevin, 2:94
Lynd, Helen Merrell, 2:131–32
Lynd, Robert Staughton, 2:131–32
Lyons, David, 2:8
Lyons, John, 1:435
Lyons, Malcolm C., 2:301
Lyons, Thomas T. (ed), 2:21
Lyttle, Clifford, 2:135
Lyttle, Richard B., 1:568; 2:375, 2:421, 2:496
Lyttleton, Adrian, 2:375

M

Maalouf, Amin, 2:306
Mabbutt, J. A., 2:83
Mabery, D. L., 1:470
McAfee, J., 1:554
McAlester, A. Lee, 2:489
Macaulay, David, 2:280, 2:291, 2:306
Macaulay, Neill, 2:369
McAuley, Karen, 2:413
Mcbane, Robert C., 2:500, 2:504
McBurney, Donald H., 2:113
McCabe, John, 2:224
McCabe, Joseph, 1:120
McCaig, M., 2:522
McCall, Samuel W., 2:15
McCarthy, David J., Jr, 2:41
McClelland, D. C., 2:113
McClenahan, Carolyn, 2:538
McClintock, Jack, 2:76
McCloskey, Herbert, 2:12
McClure, Rhyder, 1:573
McConnaughey, Bayard H., 2:465
McConnell, Anita, 2:486, 2:489
McConnell, Campbell R., 2:56
McConnell, John, 2:56
McCord, A., 2:278
McCorduck, Pamela, 1:581, 1:582
McCormick, John, 2:82, 2:255
McCormick, Mona, 1:490
McCormick, Richard L., 2:218

Meier, Matt S., 2:155
Meinig, D. W., 2:90
Meinig, D. W. (ed), 2:93
Meir, Golda, 2:413
Melby, Christopher L., 2:551
Mele, Jim, 1:194
Melhem, D. H., 1:205
Mellers, Wilfrid, 2:155
Mellor, Anne K., 1:37
Mellow, James R., 1:178
Meltzer, Milton, 1:182; 2:14, 2:70, 2:133,
　2:155, 2:164, 2:179, 2:229, 2:232, 2:244,
　2:275, 2:526, 2:545
Melville, Arabella, 2:553
Melville, Herman, 1:162–63
Melville, Keith, 2:138
Mencken, H. L., 1:436
Mendal, Geoff O., 1:565
Mendel, Arthur, 2:334
Mendel, Gregor Johann, 2:453
Mendeleev, Dimitri Ivanovich, 2:507
Menshikov, Stanislav, 2:274
Menzel, Donald H., 2:470
Meredith, Martin, 2:85, 2:393
Meredith, Robert C., 1:490
Meredith, Roy, 2:193
Mergener, Robert J., 1:524
Meritt, H. D., 1:429
Meriwether, Louise, 2:238
Merk, Frederick, 2:185, 2:218
Merk, Lois B., 2:185, 2:218
Merril, Thomas F., 1:225
Merrill, John, 1:458
Merrill, Robert, 1:234
Merriman, Nick, 2:278
Merton, Robert, 2:98
Merton, Robert E., 2:144
Merton, Robert K., 2:145
Merton, Robert K. (ed), 2:129, 2:141
Merzbach, Uta C. (ed), 1:532
Metford, J. C., 2:369
Metos, Thomas H., 2:436, 2:557
Metropolis, N., 1:559
Metropolis, N. (ed), 1:540
Metternich, Prince Klemens von, 2:333
Metz, William, 1:487
Metzger, Larry, 2:198
Meyer, Herbert E., 1:477
Meyer, Jill M., 1:477
Meyer, Michael, 1:378
Meyer, Samuel (ed), 1:503
Meyers, Jeffrey, 1:142
Meyerson, A. Lee, 2:486
Michalopoulos, Andre, 1:316
Michel, Stephen L., 1:580
Michelangelo, 2:318
Michelini, Ann Noris, 1:315
Michener, James, 1:264
Middlemiss, Ross G., 1:514

Middleton, Alex L. (ed), 2:450
Middleton, Harry, 2:246
Miers, Earl S., 2:200
Mihailovich, Vasa D., 1:383
Mikami, Y., 1:497
Mikasinovich, Branko, 1:383
Mikhail, E. H., 1:68
Miklosko, J., 1:559
Milavsky, J. Ronald, 2:98, 2:130
Milford, Nancy, 1:223
Milgate, Jane, 1:36
Milgram, Stanley, 2:98, 2:104
Milgrom, Harry, 1:512
Milheim, William (ed), 1:570
Mill, James W., 2:537
Mill, John Stuart, 2:72
Millar, Fergus, 2:291
Millard, A., 2:278, 2:284, 2:285
Millay, Edna St. Vincent, 1:265
Miller, Arthur, 1:266
Miller, Casey, 1:479
Miller, Christina G., 2:488, 2:570
Miller, Chuck (ed), 1:249
Miller, David L., 2:140
Miller, David M., 1:14
Miller, Douglas T., 2:190
Miller, E. Willard, 2:93
Miller, G. Tyler, Jr, 2:465
Miller, Gabriel, 1:273
Miller, J. Hillis, 1:47
Miller, James, 2:11
Miller, John, 2:326, 2:327
Miller, John C., 2:164
Miller, Jonathan, 2:452, 2:456, 2:545
Miller, Mark Crispin, 1:465
Miller, Mary Ellen, 2:300
Miller, Merle, 2:237, 2:246
Miller, Neal E., 2:112
Miller, P. L., 1:583
Miller, Perry, 1:154
Miller, Perry (ed), 2:162
Miller, Philip, 1:470
Miller, Richard K. (ed), 1:555
Miller, Roger Leroy, 2:65
Miller, Ron, 2:476
Miller, Russell, 2:494
Miller, Stuart, 1:440
Millgate, Michael, 1:52
Millichap, Joseph R., 2:188
Millington, T. Alaric, 1:497
Millington, William, 1:497
Mills, C. Wright, 2:145
Mills, Dorothy, 2:306
Mills, Judie, 2:248
Mills, Theodore M., 2:104
Millward, C. M., 1:429
Milne, Hammish, 2:416
Milne, Lorus, 2:462, 2:466, 2:496, 2:509
Milne, Margery, 2:462, 2:466, 2:496, 2:509

Thomas, Hugh S., 2:388
Thomas, Hugh S. (ed), 2:409
Thomas, Lewis, 2:438
Thomas, Lowell, 1:463
Thomas, Paul R., 2:549
Thomas, Terry, 1:572
Thomas, Theodore (ed), 2:89, 2:412
Thomas, William L. (ed), 2:82
Thompson, Chris, 2:121
Thompson, D'Arcy Wentworth, 1:516
Thompson, Dennis (ed), 2:19
Thompson, E. A., 2:306
Thompson, Edward P., 2:340
Thompson, Ida, 2:495
Thompson, J. E., 1:524
Thompson, J. L., 2:332
Thompson, J.M, 2:332
Thompson, Joseph, 2:368
Thompson, Kenneth, 2:126
Thompson, Kristin, 1:469
Thompson, Lawrence, 1:223
Thompson, Silvanus P., 1:523
Thompson, Virgil, 2:262
Thompson, Wayne C., 2:91
Thomson, Belinda, 2:353
Thomson, Elizabeth H., 2:532
Thoreau, Henry David, 1:165; 2:13
Thorell, Lisa G., 1:578
Thornburg, D., 1:565
Thorndike, Edward L., 2:110
Thorner, J. Lincoln, 1:234
Thornton, Richard C., 2:37
Thornton, Robert, 1:577
Thorpe, James, 1:14
Thorpe, Richard, 2:492
Thorson, Esther, 1:441
Thorton, Richard C., 2:252
Thrower, Norman J. (ed), 2:324
Thubron, Colin, 2:87, 2:90, 2:285, 2:400
Thucydides, 2:289
Thurber, James, 1:290
Thurman, Harold V., 2:487
Thurow, Lester, 2:56, 2:144
Thwaite, Anthony, 1:425
Tienda, Marta, 2:141
Tietze, Heinrich, 1:535
Tiley, W. Edward, 1:572
Tilly, Louise A., 2:340
Tilton, Eleanor M., 1:158
Timberlake, Lloyd, 2:86, 2:394
Timberlake, Michael, 2:94, 2:147
Timms, Howard, 2:436
Tinbergen, Elizabeth A., 2:122
Tinbergen, Niko, 2:122
Tinbergen, Nikolaas, 2:98, 2:465
Tindall, William Y., 1:124
Tingay, Graham I. F., 2:291
Tirion, Wil, 2:470
Tischer, M., 1:585

Tocci, Salvatore, 2:508
Tocqueville, Alexis de, 2:16, 2:180
Tod, M. N., 1:498
Todaro, Michael P., 2:72
Todd, John M., 2:317
Todhunter, Isaac, 1:533
Toffler, Alvin, 1:453; 2:62
Tofte, M., 1:586
Toland, John, 2:236, 2:375, 2:377, 2:385
Tolbert-Rouchaleau, Jane, 1:245
Tolegian, Aram (tr), 1:420
Tolkien, J. R. R., 1:125–26, 1:482
Toll, Robert, 1:454
Tollison, Robert D., 2:71
Tolstoy, Leo, 1:397
Tonnen, Deborah, 1:445
Toohey, Barbara, 2:561
Toor, Rachel, 2:233
Toothill, Elizabeth (ed), 2:437, 2:448
Tooze, John, 2:455
Topham, Douglas, 1:562
Topsfield, Valerie, 1:331
Tordjman, Nathalie, 2:485
Torrance, S., 1:582
Torrence, Bruce, 1:469
Torrents, Nissa (ed), 2:371
Torres, Angelo, 1:467
Toth, Emily, 1:173
Toth, Marian, 1:427
Toupence, William F., 1:203, 1:239
Touretsky, 1:566
Tourlakis, George J., 1:585
Tourtellot, Jonathan B. (ed), 2:76
Towns, Saundra, 1:235
Townsend, Carl, 1:562
Townsend, Kim, 1:190
Toye, Francis, 2:361
Tracton, Ken, 1:564
Tracy, Martin, 1:566
Trager, Oliver (ed), 2:37
Traister, Robert J., 1:565, 1:578; 2:436, 2:471
Trape, Augustine, 2:304
Trappi, R. (ed), 1:582
Trask, David F., 2:219
Traub, J. F., 1:538
Traubner, Richard, 2:263
Travers, K., 1:530
Traynor, John, 2:277
Treadgold, Donald W., 2:92, 2:277, 2:406
Treadgold, Warren, 2:301, 2:311
Trebilcock, Clive, 2:340
Trefil, James S., 2:479, 2:482
Trefousse, Hans L., 2:198
Tremblay, Jean-Paul, 1:538, 1:586
Trench, Richard, 2:90
Trenn, T. J., 2:509
Trevelyan, George M., 2:311, 2:327, 2:328, 2:345

TITLE INDEX

This index appears in each of two volumes of *The Young Adult Reader's Adviser.* It presents in alphabetical sequence the titles of all books listed in the bibliographies. It also includes notable books, poems, ballads, and essays that may be mentioned in general introductions and biographical narratives.

The number of the volume in which a title is cited is given with a colon followed by the page number on which the title can be found. For example, the entry 1:219 indicates that the title *Absalom, Absalom!* can be found on page 219 of Volume 1. Some titles refer to more than one page number. For example, the entry 1:284, 2:197 indicates that the title *Abe Lincoln Grows Up* can be found both on page 284 of Volume 1 (in American Literature) and on page 197 of Volume 2 (in United States History). When two or more identical titles by different authors appear, the last name of each author is given in parentheses following the title.

A

A. E. Housman: A Collection of Critical Essays, 1:54
A. J. Cronin, 1:78
Aaron Burr: A Biography, 2:169
Aaron Copland, 2:261
Aaron's Rod, 1:101
The Abbess of Crewe, 1:121
The ABC Murders, 1:73
ABC's of the Human Body, 2:531
Abe Lincoln Grows Up, 1:284; 2:198
Abigail Adams, 2:170
Abigail Adams: A Biography, 2:170
Abigail Adams: Advisor to a President, 2:170
Abigail Adams: First Lady of Faith and Courage, 2:170
Aboriginal Population of Northwestern Mexico, 2:80
The Abortion: An Historical Romance 1966, 1:203
About Thinking, 1:477
Above Hawaii, 2:90

Above London, 2:87
Above Paris, 2:87
Above San Francisco, 2:90
Abraham Lincoln, 2:198
Abraham Lincoln: Citizen of New Salem, 2:198
Abraham Lincoln: His Speeches and Writings, 2:197
Abraham Lincoln: The Prairie Years and the War Years, 1:284; 2:198
Abraham Lincoln and the Union, 2:198
Absalom, Absalom!, 1:219
The Absolute at Large, 1:384
Abstract Expressionism: A Critical Record, 2:415
Abstraction for Programmers, 1:563
Abundance for What? And Other Essays, 2:132
Abuse in the Family, 2:539
The Academic Mind: Social Scientists in Time of Crises, 2:125
The Academic Revolution, 2:132
The Academic Scribblers: Economists in Collision, 2:55

F

G

I

K

L

M

N

R

T

V

W

Z